Lecture Notes in Computer Science

Vol. 142: Problems and Methodologies in Mathematical Software Production. Proceedings, 1980. Edited by P.C. Messina and A. Murli. VII, 271 pages. 1982.

Vol. 143: Operating Systems Engineering. Proceedings, 1980. Edited by M. Maekawa and L.A. Belady. VII, 465 pages. 1982.

Vol. 144: Computer Algebra. Proceedings, 1982. Edited by J. Calmet. XIV, 301 pages. 1982.

Vol. 145: Theoretical Computer Science. Proceedings, 1983. Edited by A.B. Cremers and H.P. Kriegel. X, 367 pages. 1982.

Vol. 146: Research and Development in Information Retrieval. Proceedings, 1982. Edited by G. Salton and H.-J. Schneider. IX, 311 pages. 1983.

Vol. 147: RIMS Symposia on Software Science and Engineering. Proceedings, 1982. Edited by E. Goto, I. Nakata, K. Furukawa, R. Nakajima, and A. Yonezawa. V. 232 pages. 1983.

Vol. 148: Logics of Programs and Their Applications. Proceedings, 1980. Edited by A. Salwicki. VI, 324 pages. 1983.

Vol. 149: Cryptography. Proceedings, 1982. Edited by T. Beth. VIII, 402 pages. 1983.

Vol. 150: Enduser Systems and Their Human Factors. Proceedings, 1983. Edited by A. Blaser and M. Zoeppritz. III, 138 pages. 1983.

Vol. 151: R. Piloty, M. Barbacci, D. Borrione, D. Dietmeyer, F. Hill, and P. Skelly, CONLAN Report. XII, 174 pages. 1983.

Vol. 152: Specification and Design of Software Systems. Proceedings, 1982. Edited by E. Knuth and E. J. Neuhold. V, 152 pages. 1983.

Vol. 153: Graph-Grammars and Their Application to Computer Science. Proceedings, 1982. Edited by H. Ehrig, M. Nagl, and G. Rozenberg. VII, 452 pages. 1983.

Vol. 154: Automata, Languages and Programming. Proceedings, 1983. Edited by J. Díaz. VIII, 734 pages. 1983.

Vol. 155: The Programming Language Ada. Reference Manual. Approved 17 February 1983. American National Standards Institute, Inc. ANSI/MIL-STD-1815A-1983. IX, 331 pages. 1983.

Vol. 156: M.H. Overmars, The Design of Dynamic Data Structures. VII, 181 pages. 1983.

Vol. 157: O. Østerby, Z. Zlatev, Direct Methods for Sparse Matrices. VIII, 127 pages. 1983.

Vol. 158: Foundations of Computation Theory. Proceedings, 1983. Edited by M. Karpinski, XI, 517 pages. 1983.

Vol. 159: CAAP'83. Proceedings, 1983. Edited by G. Ausiello and M. Protasi. VI, 416 pages. 1983.

Vol. 160: The IOTA Programming System. Edited by R. Nakajima and T. Yuasa. VII, 217 pages. 1983.

Vol. 161: DIANA, An Intermediate Language for Ada. Edited by G. Goos, W.A. Wulf, A. Evans, Jr. and K.J. Butler. VII, 201 pages. 1983.

Vol. 162: Computer Algebra. Proceedings, 1983. Edited by J.A. van Hulzen. XIII, 305 pages. 1983.

Vol. 163: VLSI Engineering. Proceedings. Edited by T.L. Kunii. VIII, 308 pages. 1984.

Vol. 164: Logics of Programs. Proceedings, 1983. Edited by E. Clarke and D. Kozen. VI, 528 pages. 1984.

Vol. 165: T.F. Coleman, Large Sparse Numerical Optimization. V, 105 pages. 1984.

Vol. 166: STACS 84. Symposium of Theoretical Aspects of Computer Science. Proceedings, 1984. Edited by M. Fontet and K. Mehlhorn. VI, 338 pages. 1984.

Vol. 167: International Symposium on Programming. Proceedings, 1984. Edited by C. Girault and M. Paul. VI, 262 pages. 1984.

Vol. 168: Methods and Tools for Computer Integrated Manufacturing. Edited by R. Dillmann and U. Rembold. XVI, 528 pages. 1984.

Vol. 169: Ch. Ronse, Feedback Shift Registers. II, 1–2, 145 pages. 1984.

Vol. 170: Seventh International Conference on Automated Deduction. Edited by R.E. Shostak. IV, 508 pages. 1984.

Vol. 171: Logic and Machines: Decision Problems and Complexity. Proceedings, 1983. Edited by E. Börger, G. Hasenjaeger and D. Rödding. VI, 456 pages. 1984.

Vol. 172: Automata, Languages and Programming. Proceedings, 1984. Edited by J. Paredaens. VIII, 527 pages. 1984.

Vol. 173: Semantics of Data Types. Proceedings, 1984. Edited by G. Kahn, D.B. MacQueen and G. Plotkin. VI, 391 pages. 1984.

Vol. 174: EUROSAM 84. Proceedings, 1984. Edited by J. Fitch. XI, 396 pages. 1984.

Vol. 175: A. Thayse, P-Functions and Boolean Matrix Factorization, VII, 248 pages. 1984.

Vol. 176: Mathematical Foundations of Computer Science 1984. Proceedings, 1984. Edited by M.P. Chytil and V. Koubek. XI, 581 pages. 1984.

Vol. 177: Programming Languages and Their Definition. Edited by C.B. Jones. XXXII, 254 pages. 1984.

Vol. 178: Readings on Cognitive Ergonomics – Mind and Computers. Proceedings, 1984. Edited by G.C. van der Veer, M.J. Tauber, T.R.G. Green and P. Gorny. VI, 269 pages. 1984.

Vol. 179: V. Pan, How to Multiply Matrices Faster. XI, 212 pages. 1984.

Vol. 180: Ada Software Tools Interfaces. Proceedings, 1983. Edited by P.J.L. Wallis. III, 164 pages. 1984.

Vol. 181: Foundations of Software Technology and Theoretical Computer Science. Proceedings, 1984. Edited by M. Joseph and R. Shyamasundar. VIII, 468 pages. 1984.

Vol. 182: STACS 85. 2nd Annual Symposium on Theoretical Aspects of Computer Science. Proceedings, 1985. Edited by K. Mehlhorn. VII, 374 pages. 1985.

Vol. 183: The Munich Project CIP. Volume I: The Wide Spectrum Language CIP-L. By the CIP Language Group. XI, 275 pages. 1985.

Vol. 184: Local Area Networks: An Advanced Course. Proceedings, 1983. Edited by D. Hutchison, J. Mariani and D. Shepherd. VIII, 497 pages. 1985.

Vol. 185: Mathematical Foundations of Software Development. Proceedings, 1985. Volume 1: Colloquium on Trees in Algebra and Programming (CAAP'85). Edited by H. Ehrig, C. Floyd, M. Nivat and J. Thatcher. XIV, 418 pages. 1985.

Vol. 186: Formal Methods and Software Development. Proceedings, 1985. Volume 2: Colloquium on Software Engineering (CSE). Edited by H. Ehrig, C. Floyd, M. Nivat and J. Thatcher. XIV, 455 pages. 1985.

Vol. 187: F.S. Chaghaghi, Time Series Package (TSPACK). III, 305 pages. 1985.

Vol. 188: Advances in Petri Nets 1984. Edited by G. Rozenberg with the cooperation of H. Genrich and G. Roucairol. VII, 467 pages. 1985.

Vol. 189: M.S. Sherman, Paragon. XI, 376 pages. 1985.

Vol. 190: M.W. Alford, J.P. Ansart, G. Hommel, L. Lamport, B. Liskov, G.P. Mullery and F.B. Schneider, Distributed Systems. Edited by M. Paul and H.J. Siegert. VI, 573 pages. 1985.

Vol. 191: H. Barringer, A Survey of Verification Techniques for Parallel Programs. VI, 115 pages. 1985.

Lecture Notes in Computer Science

Edited by G. Goos and J. Hartmanis

225

Third International Conference on Logic Programming

Imperial College of Science and Technology,
London, United Kingdom, July 14–18, 1986
Proceedings

Edited by Ehud Shapiro

Springer-Verlag
Berlin Heidelberg New York London Paris Tokyo

Editor

Ehud Shapiro
Department of Computer Science
The Weizmann Institute of Science
Rehovot 76100, Israel

CR Subject Classifications (1985): D.1, D.3, F.1, F.3, I.2

ISBN 3-540-16492-8 Springer-Verlag Berlin Heidelberg New York
ISBN 0-387-16492-8 Springer-Verlag New York Heidelberg Berlin

Library of Congress Cataloging-in-Publication Data. International Conference on Logic Programming (3rd: 1986: Imperial College of Science and Technology, London, England). Third International Conference on Logic Programming, Imperial College of Science and Technology, London, United Kingdom. (Lecture notes in computer science; 225) Includes bibliographies. 1. Logic programming–Congresses. I. Shapiro, Ehud Y. II. Title. III. Series.
QA76.6.I5466 1986 005.1 86-13477
ISBN 0-387-16492-8 (U.S.)

Printed in Germany

Printing and binding: Beltz Offsetdruck, Hemsbach/Bergstr.
2145/3140-543210

Foreword

This is the report on the proceedings of the Third International Conference on Logic Programming, held on July 14-18, 1986, at Imperial College of Science and Technology. The two previous conferences took place in Uppsala, Sweden, in 1984, and in Marseille, France, in 1982.

Around 140 papers were submitted to the conference. They were refereed by the members of the program committee and by external referees, who are listed below. It is a pleasure to thank the authors who responded to the call for papers. Unfortunately, only 56 could be accepted, out of which 54 are included in this volume. In addition, seven speakers have responded to our invitation to lecture at the conference: K. Fuchi (keynote speaker), J. McCarthy (banquet speaker), and T. Chikayama, J.L. Lassez, M. McCord, A. Takeuchi, and J.D. Ullman. Papers by the invited speakers (except for the banquet speaker) are also included.

I would like to thank the program committee members, who deliberated in an attempt to provide a high-quality and balanced program, the referees who reviewed several papers each under a short schedule, and to Sarah Fliegelmann, Michael Codish, Michael Hirsch, and Steve Taylor for helping with the management of the refereeing procedure. Thanks to John Conery for the Prolog programs for maintaining the submissions database.

Rehovot, April 1986 Ehud Shapiro

General Chairman

Keith Clark, Imperial College, U.K.

Program Committee

Michel van Caneghem, University of Marseille-Aix, France
Keith Clark, Imperial College, U.K.
Veronica Dahl, Simon Fraser University, Canada
Maarten van Emden, University of Waterloo, Canada
Kazuhiro Fuchi, ICOT, Japan
Koichi Furukawa, ICOT, Japan
Åke Hansson, Uppsala University, Sweden
Kenneth M. Kahn, Xerox PARC, U.S.A.
Peter Koves, Logicware Inc., Canada
Giorgio Levi, University of Pisa, Italy
John Lloyd, University of Melbourne, Australia
Frank G. McCabe, Imperial College, U.K.
Jack Minker, Maryland University, U.S.A.
David H.D. Warren, Manchester University, U.K.
Antonio Porto, University of Lisbon, Portugal
Ehud Shapiro, Weizmann Institute, Israel; Chairman

List of Referees

Abramson, Harvey
Angluin, Dana
Barbuti, R.
Ben-Ari, Mordechai
Berkling, Klaus
Bowen, Ken
Bruynooghe, Maurice
Byrd, Lawrence
Carlsson, Mats
Chikayama, Takashi
Clocksin, William F.
Codish, Michael
Cohen, Jacques
Cohen, Shimon
Colmerauer, Alain
Conery, John
Crammond, Jim
Darlington, John
Davis, Al
DeGroot, Doug
Dershowitz, Nachum
Eggert, P.
Francez, Nissim
Futo, Ivan
Gallaire, Herve
Gaugin, J.A.
Gostelow, Kim P.
Goto, Atsuhiro
Gregory, Steve
Hammond, Peter
Harel, David
Haridi, Seif
Harrison, P.G.
Jchiyoshi, Nobuyuki
Jaffar, J.
Kaplan, Stephane
Kasif, Simon
Keller, Robert M.
Kibler, Dennis
Kitakami, H.
Kodratoff, Yves
Komorowski, Jan
Kowalski, Robert
Kusalik, Tony
Lassez, J.L.
Levy, Jacob
Lieberman, Henry
Lindstrom, Gary
Lowry, Andy
Lusk, Ewing
Maher, Michael
Malachi, Yonni
Maler, Oded
Martelli, Maurizio
Matsumoto, Yuji
McCord, Michael C.
McDermott, Drew V.
Mellish, Christopher S.
Miranker, Dan
Miyazaki, T.
Mizugochi, F.
Naish, Lee
Nakushima, H.
O'Keefe, Richard A.
Onai, Rikio
Overbeek, Ross
Pereira, Fernando
Pereira, Luis M.
Pinter, Ron
Plaisted, David
Pnueli, Amir
Reddy, Uday
Reeve, Mike
Robinson, Alan
Roussel, Phillipe
Rudolph, Larry
Safra, Shmuel
Sammut, Claude
Saraswat, Vijay
Sato, Masahiko
Sato, Taisuke
Sergut, M.
Shamir, Adi
Shertz, Zahava
Shmueli, Oded
Snir, Mark
Spacek, Libor
Sridharan, N.S.
Sterling, Leon
Stickel, Mark E.
Takeuchi, Akikazu
Tamaki, Hisao
Tarnlund, Sten Ake
Taylor, Steve
Tick, Evan
Ueda, Kazunori
Veinbaum, David
Waldinger, R.
Walker, Adrian
Warren, David S.
Weiner, Jim
Wilson, Walter
Wise, Michael
Yokota, M.
Yoshida, Hiroyuki

Contents

Session 2b: Inductive inference and debugging

Wednesday, July 16

Session 3a: Concurrent logic languages

Session 3b: Theory and semantics

Thursday, July 17

Friday, July 18

Session 6a: Implementations and databases

Session 6b: Theory and negation

Session 7a: Compilation

Session 7b: Models of computation and implementation

The Role of Logic Programming in the Fifth Generation Computer Project

Kazuhiro Fuchi and Koichi Furukawa
ICOT Research Center
Institute for New Generation Computer Technology
1-4-28, Mita, Minato-ku, Tokyo 108 Japan

Abstract. This paper describes the role of logic programming in the Fifth Generation Computer Project. We started the project with the conjecture that logic programming is the "bridge" connecting knowledge information processing and parallel computer architecture. Four years have passed since we started the project, and now we can say that this conjecture has been substantially confirmed. The paper gives an overview of the developments which have reinforced this foundational conjecture and how our "bridge" is being realized.

1. INTRODUCTION

The FGCS project started four years ago, but its roots go back three years before that. More than a hundred representative researchers in Japan participated in the discussions during those three years. A clear consensus emerged that logic programming should be placed at the center of the project.

We announced this idea at FGCS '81 in the fall of 1981. It was the most controversial issue at the conference, criticized as a reckless proposal without scientific justification.

Why did we persist in our commitment to logic programming? Because we were inspired by the insight that logic programming could become the newly unified principle in computer science. At the conference, one of the authors pointed out that logic programming covers computer architecture, new programming style, semantics of program language and database semantics. It was also pointed out that logic programming is playing an important role in linguistics and artificial intelligence.

Looking at the situation now, we can say that our conjecture has taken more concrete shape. It is not too much to say that the successes of the project so far are in large measure due to our adoption of logic programming. We would like to emphasize that the key feature of our project is not knowledge information science or non von Neumann architecture, but logic programming.

The results we have achieved seem to be quite natural. Therefore, it may be more appropriate to say that what we have here is a case of "discovery" rather than "invention."

Our approach may be compared to the process of solving a jigsaw puzzle. The process of putting each piece of a jigsaw puzzle in the right place may correspond to the process of discovering truth in our research. Also, the completed form of the jigsaw puzzle corresponds to the highly parallel computer for knowledge information processing realized in VLSI. Logic programming is the centerpiece of the jigsaw puzzle. To use Kowalski's expression [Kowalski 82], logic programming is the "missing link" connecting knowledge information processing and highly parallel architecture. Once we realized this, the puzzle started falling into place rapidly.

We often hear people say that our project ought to be more software-oriented rather than hardware-oriented. But our perspective is the whole jigsaw puzzle, of which software and hardware are certainly inseparable aspects, but neither takes priority as such. We proceed step by step, with our vision of the new computer guiding our approach to solution of each problem as it arises.

How much of this giant jigsaw puzzle have we solved in these four years? To answer this question, we would like to describe the achievements of the FGCS Project in Section 2. Section 3 is an attempt to summarize trends in research around the world and noteworthy results. We will give the conclusion in Section 4. As a part the conclusion, we discuss what research topics remain for the future, emphasizing the importance of international cooperation.

2. MAIN RESULTS OF FGCS PROJECT SO FAR

The work of the FGCS project extends over four research areas: software research, hardware research, development of software tools for R & D, and applications researches as feasibility studies.

In this section, we survey the main results in each of the first three areas. With regard to the fourth areas, we omit the description because of space limitation.

2.1. Software Research

2.1.1. Kernel Language

The most important issue in a programming language is its expressive power. The reason we put logic programming languages at the heart of the project is because we realized that logic programming is potentially very rich in expressive power.

When we started the project, we selected Prolog as a tentative target language and proceeded with research. The fact was that for practical purposes, Prolog was the only logic programming language available at that time. It was well known that Prolog possessed superior database and solution-searching capabilities. For us, its suitability for algorithm description, list processing and meta programming was actually more important. The importance of these functions became even clearer over the four years research of the project.

By the way, when the project started, we had already recognized that what was lacking in Prolog was the object-oriented programming facility. Object-oriented programming mechanisms cannot be realized by simple call-return control structures. Interrupt/resume computation facilities are necessary for handling exchange of messages. What this means is that we need the functions of parallel programming. Various studies have been carried out to realize parallel programming in logic programming. The following three approaches predominate in these studies: (1) Addition of parallel control primitives such as "wait" and "resume" to Prolog. (2) Delay of evaluation of goals until the specific data arrives. (3)

```
oneDigitCounter([],Os,State) :- true | Os=[].
oneDigitCounter([up|Is],Os,State) :-State=<8 |
   NewState := State+1, oneDigitCounter(Is,Os,NewState).
oneDigitCounter([up|Is],Os,State) :- State=9 |
   Os=[up|NewOs], oneDigitCounter(Is,NewOs,0).
oneDigitCounter([clear|Is],Os,State) :- true |
   Os=[clear|O1s], oneDigitCounter(Is,O1s,0).
oneDigitCounter([show(X)|Is],Os,State) :- true |
   X=[State|X1], Os=[show(X1)|O1s], oneDigitCounter(Is,O1s,State).

interface([],Ms) :- true | Ms=[].
interface([up|Is],Ms) :- true |
   Ms=[up|M1s], interface(Is,M1s).
interface([clear|Is],Ms) :- true |
   Ms=[clear|M1s], interface(Is,M1s).
interface([show(X)|Is],Ms) :- true |
   Ms=[show([Y,Z|])|M1s], X:=Y+Z*10, interface(Is,M1s).

twoDigitCounter(Is,Os) :- true |
   interface(Is,Ms),
   oneDigitCounter(Ms,O1s,0), oneDigitCounter(O1s,Os,0).
```

Fig. 1. A composition of a two-digit counter from two one-digit counters and an interface. **oneDigitCounter** is a recursive program defining an object that counts up numbers from 0 to 9 and causes overflow at the next increment.

Imposition of guards on Horn clauses and restriction of nondeterminism where the clause which has passed the guard first is used for subsequent computation.

We chose the third approach. Relational Language [Clark 81], Concurrent Prolog [Shapiro 83a] and PARLOG [Clark 84] are the pioneering works of this approach. Guarded Horn Clauses (GHC) [Ueda 85] was developed from these sources.

All of these languages are very similar and their common feature is that each clause has a guard part and a body part, separated by a so-called commit operator (denoted by '|'). The guard part is reserved for nondeterministic choice. If one of the guards has succeeded, then the clause is selected for the successive computation and others are killed. Another common feature is that all conjunctive goals can be executed in parallel if they can run. A goal can run if all necessary input data have arrived. The differences between these four languages lie in the way they detect the data arrival and how programmers give information to aid the detection.

In these languages, "objects" can be represented very naturally by recursive processes as shown in Fig. 1. This program, written in GHC, represents a two-digit counter built by combining three parts, an "interface" part and two one-digit counters. All of these three parts are tail recursive programs representing prototype objects.

Let us take a look at the **oneDigitCounter** program. The first argument of the predicate is an input command sequence whose elements are either up, `clear` or `show(X)` for some variable X, where the command up means increment the counter, `clear` means clear the counter value to zero and show(X) means give the state of the one-digit counter. The second argument is an output command sequence which will be connected to another one-digit counter for the next higher order position. The third argument is a state of the counter holding the number of up commands modulo 10 since the last clear command. An object instance is created by executing a oneDigitCounter goal. The program is defined by five clauses: the first clause says that the object will disappear when the input command sequence becomes empty. The second clause defines the behavior of a one-digit counter object when it accepts an up command while the state is less than or equal to eight. The third clause is for the same command while the state is equal to nine. Note that it will assign an output command up to the output variable Os. The fourth clause defines the behavior of clearing the counter. It will assign an output command clear to Os to propagate the command to the next counter. The last clause defines how to respond to the command show(X). It will unify X to the list [State|X1], where State is the current value of the counter, and X1 is a response for the command show(X1) to the next counter.

The goal twoDigitCounter(Is,Os) means that given a sequence of commands Is, the twoDigitCounter will output a sequence of outputs Os. The interface part is used to provide an interface between users and the two-digit counter. When a user requests the current state of the counter by giving the command show(X), it will forward the show message to the first one-digit counter changing its parameter from X to [Y,Z|_], where Y is a variable for the state of the first one-digit counter and Z for the state of the second one-digit counter.

The origin of the expressive power of concurrent programming in GHC-like languages is the ability of a goal to observe the values of any argument of any goal to which it stands in AND-relation at any time. This does not hold for ordinary Prolog because the execution of a goal only starts after the completion of the previous goal, that is, at any given time there is only one active goal.

We are designing the parallel logic language KL1 based on FGHC. FGHC is a subset of GHC that does not permit the use of user-defined predicates in the guard part. Codish [Codish 85] has implemented a system that transforms Safe Concurrent Prolog, a subset of Concurrent Prolog, into Flat Concurrent Prolog. This shows that FGHC has sufficient functional capability as a machine language.

Extracting a subset of a language that efficiently simplifies it is a very important issue from the hardware point of view. Such a relation exists between GHC and FGHC. We are now extending this relation upwards. This is an effort to obtain all-solution-search capability based on don't-know nondeterminism, which GHC does not possess. Ueda has developed a system to translate a certain class of all-solution-search programs to FGHC [Ueda 86]. Continuing with this kind of work, our aim is to achieve a more expressive programming language.

Although we had already developed the object-oriented language MANDALA for knowledge programming, we could not proceed further because of execution inefficiency. The experience was a good lesson for us. Expressive power is only effective if it is efficiently implemented. We have succeeded in developing the optimization technique which MANDALA lacked. This topic is discussed in the next section.

2.1.2. Meta Programming and Partial Evaluation

Although Prolog is known as a programming language with deductive capability, it has been regarded as being unsuitable for constructing flexible inference engines. This is because it treats only Horn logic, not the full first order logic, and has only one proof strategy, which indeed seems to have been the main criticism from A.I. researchers.

However, after the extensive evolution of meta programming techniques, it has become clear that more flexible and powerful inference engines can be written in Prolog.

Meta programming can be characterized informally in the following way:

(1) To handle a program as data.
(2) To handle data as programs and to evaluate them.
(3) To handle a result (success or fail) of computation as data.

The meta programming approach has the following advantages.

1) Clear separation of object-level control and meta-level control can be achieved.
2) 1) makes it easy to understand the system and easy to modify it.

Now, meta programming is widely used in logic programming applications such as problem solving systems, programming systems and database management systems.

Since a meta program usually takes the form of a meta interpreter, interpretive execution of an object program by the meta interpreter runs slower than direct execution of the object program by around one order of magnitude. Thus, meta programming achieves flexibility at the expense of efficiency.

We have succeeded in transforming a pair of a meta program and an object program to an efficient program by applying the well-established technique of partial evaluation.

Generally speaking, partial evaluation transforms a program into another specialized program using information about the run-time environment, including partial input data. In the case of an inference system consisting of an inference engine and inference rules, a set of rules is regarded as partial input data to the inference system. The result of partial evaluation of the inference engine with respect to the inference rules is a specialized inference engine just for those given rules. Partial evaluation can be considered as a compilation process, that is, a given set of rules are "compiled" into a more efficient program incorporating the inference engine.

For a small logic-based inference system and a bottom-up parsing system, we succeeded in speeding up the original interpretive program about three times [Takeuchi 85]. We also increased the speed of an algebraic manipulation system five times [Takewaki 85]. These numbers show that the optimization of meta programs based on partial evaluation is very promising.

Goebel *et al.* [Goebel 86] described a MYCIN-like diagnosis system in terms of the combination of a meta interpreter and a set of logical formulas connecting malfunctions and symptoms. In their system, the connection is represented in such a way that "*If X has a malfunction A, then it has a set of symptoms B,*" instead of "*If X has a set of symptoms B, then you can conclude that X has a malfunction A,*" which is the representation style in

MYCIN. The behavior of a meta interpreter is described by something like "*If you want to identify that X has some malfunction A, then you need to show that X has all symptoms that A causes.*" By partially executing the meta interpreter together with logical formulas describing the relationship between malfunctions and symptoms, we succeeded in obtaining a set of "compiled" rules similar to those in MYCIN.

These experiences suggest a new programming methodology wherein a system is constructed of layers of meta programs, utilizing the expressive power of meta programming, and is executed after transformation into a one layer program by partial evaluation. In this approach, the semantic clarity of the system is achieved by clear separation of levels of programs so that the system is easy to understand and easy to modify. Partial evaluation simultaneously guarantees the efficiency of the system.

2.1.3. Knowledge Base Management

A knowledge based system consists of an inference engine and a knowledge base. It has been clarified that the inference engine can easily be developed by meta programming techniques mentioned in the preceding section. On the other hand, there still remain several problems to be solved, constructing a knowledge base. Among these problems, we have focused especially on integrity constraint of knowledge base in the process of knowledge acquisition and clarified its general framework. Knowledge base management was formulated as a problem of knowledge assimilation and knowledge accommodation. Its prototype was developed by meta programming techniques. In particular, knowledge accommodation can be considered as a kind of inductive inference. A knowledge accommodation system was developed by utilizing Shapiro's MIS [Shapiro 83b]. A new approach was proposed where integrity constraints are used in place of negative facts (oracle).

As an extension of the research of knowledge acquisition, we started basic researches for the logic of diagnosis. Namely, we regarded observations of a diagnosis-target as knowledge acquisition, and formulated the hypotheses-formation as knowledge accommodation. In this framework, we clarified the hypotheses selection criteria in the case where hypotheses are hierarchically structured. Furthermore, we developed an algorithm for selecting a hypothesis among several possible hypotheses modifying Shapiro's algorithmic debugging technique.

2.1.4. Natural Language Applications

We attach the greatest significance in our project to the natural language processing application area. Since natural language processing includes a variety of aspects, it is indispensable to set up a framework in which we are able to handle these aspects in a uniform manner. The FGCS project considers logic or logic languages as the basic conceptual framework and seeks to construct a total environment for describing every component of natural language processing in terms of it. Certainly, this field is the best suited to exhibiting the enormous power of logic programming languages.

It is well-known that Definite Clause Grammars (DCGs) [Pereira 80] have a very close correspondence with Horn logic and can be translated into Prolog clauses one-to-one. This means that syntactic and semantic description of natural language grammars can be expressed in logic.

Colmerauer's Q-system [Colmerauer 70] and Metamorphosis Grammars [Colmerauer 78] are the origin of the grammar formalisms in the field. A series of grammar systems have been proposed to augment their descriptive power. In parallel with them, a number of recent grammar theories in computational linguistics focus on context-free grammars as their syntactic basis.

We first took DCGs as our description language for natural language applications and tried to build an efficient parsing system. The top-down parser, used as the direct translation of a DCG to a Prolog program, is a simple backtracking parser that cannot handle left recursive rules. We developed a translation method to produce a bottom-up based parser [Matsumoto 83] incorporating the so-called tableau method. This system was equipped with various facilities and is now called GALOP (Grammar As LOgic Programming). We then proposed a grammar description language called GDL0 [Morishita 84] enabling users to make clear his intention in using arguments in grammar rules.

Although these systems cover the important part of analyzing natural language sentences, we needed a richer framework to cope with the problems of context processing and knowledge representation, which surely are the essential parts of practical natural language systems. We devoted two years of our natural language research to developing an experimental discourse understanding system called DUALS [Yasukawa 84] based on Situational Semantics [Barwise 83]. The first version of DUALS analyzes a short story taken from a textbook for elementary school students, and answers some questions. The experience motivated us to design the augmented logic programming language CIL [Mukai 85], a reinforced Prolog system with a freeze mechanism and association lists. CIL is implemented both in DEC-10 Prolog and in ESP on our personal logic programming machine PSI. The latest version of DUALS will be fully implemented in CIL.

2.2. Hardware Research

2.2.1. Parallel Inference Machine

The architecture research on the Parallel Inference Machine (PIM) started with the assumption that the target language would be so-called OR-Parallel Prolog. We worked on the construction of three kinds of experimental systems based on data flow architecture, graph reduction architecture and an architecture called "Kabu-wake," respectively.

After the new target language GHC was developed in software research, we shifted the research direction to cope with AND-parallelism as well as OR-parallelism. The new direction also includes the practical aspect of supporting the development of such basic software systems as an operating system and a programming system including various debuggers.

To achieve an efficient implementation of such activities as goal allocation among processors, dynamic load balancing, synchronization, and communication accompanied with distributed unification, we need to design the machine to achieve the proper balance between hardware and software. We are now designing a machine language and hardware architecture for PIM with these criteria in mind.

The machine language for PIM is being designed primarily for parallel execution of GHC, utilizing results obtained from the research on data flow and reduction machine architecture. It should be suitable for achieving high performance in both single and multiprocessors.

The tentative idea of the experimental PIM's hardware configuration is the connection of around ten clusters, each of which is a combination of about ten processing elements (PE). Each PE is supposed to be a sequential machine dedicated to execution of GHC programs. The experimental PIM will be completed by the end of the intermediate stage and is expected to have a performance of several MLIPS.

2.2.2. Multi-PSI System

The research on the operating system for PIM (PIMOS) is also crucial because it is the only way to clarify the requirements for the hardware system to achieve its desired performance.

In application areas like knowledge information processing, it is rather difficult to determine at compile time the dynamic behavior and therefore we need to take account of dynamic load balancing. For this, we need not only a language feature to allow users to specify goal allocation strategies explicitly, but also a mechanism for detecting unbalance and resolving it.

We are now developing a multi-PSI system comprising several PSI's connected by a high speed network in a mesh as a tool for PIMOS research. The hardware of this system, called multi-PSI/V1, has just been completed and a distributed language processor for FGHC including an operating system will be developed on it. Since GHC has the ability to describe concurrent phenomena, it is also possible to write the language processor in GHC itself. This is another reason why we prefer GHC to OR-Parallel Prolog.

We are also planning to build an extended version called multi-PSI/V2 based on PSI-II's expected to be more than three times faster than the current PSI. It will comprise around 20 PSI-II's and the language processor will be heavily supported by firmware. As a result, we can expect a rather high performance experimental machine for developing the PIMOS and other application programs.

2.2.3. Knowledge Base Machine

The main feature of knowledge based systems, the main application systems of the Fifth Generation computers, is the dual structure of the inference engine and the knowledge base. Although the central part of the Fifth Generation computer is supposed to be the PIM, we are also planning to build dedicated hardware to support high-speed operations on the knowledge base.

We have begun construction of a relational database machine (RDBM) the contents of which are limited only to ground instances, utilizing the database machine technology. We developed an RDBM called Delta in the initial stage, which executes relational algebra operations on large relational databases at high speed by applying stream parallelism.

The evaluation of the system revealed that there are two serious problems in the interface between the inference machine and Delta. One is a physical interface problem and the other is a logical one. It takes too much time to transfer data from Delta to the host due to the insufficient power of the interface processor (a minicomputer) and I/O overhead of its operating system. To resolve the problem, we need to upgrade the interface processor and to improve the operating system.

The logical problem is the mismatch of predicate logic and relational algebra. In order to solve a recursive query, we need to find a least fixed point of a relational algebraic equation associated with the query. We recently found an algorithm to terminate the iteration cycles in calculating the least fixed point [Yokota 86].

The fundamental problem of the above approach based on the RDBM is its lack of expressive power because of the fact that it can only represent ground instances. To resolve the problem, we recently proposed a knowledge base machine capable of storing general Horn clauses. The machine will perform dynamic optimization of retrieval processes using meta knowledge about the physical structure, sizes of relations, and so on, of its own database. It will be equipped with a built-in inference engine for these functions. As far as the management of the object knowledge is concerned, we are working on two separate methods:

(1) Facts and rules are stored and managed separately.

(2) Facts and rules are stored and managed altogether.

The former is adequate for realizing deductive databases where the number of rules is small compared with the number of the facts. On the other hand, the latter is quite adequate for realizing a large knowledge base with very many rules.

To retrieve knowledge in the latter machine, we need to expand relational algebra operators to cope with unification between terms. We introduced a set of extended relational algebra operators such as unification-join and unification-selection. A retrieval based on the extended relational algebra is called *Retrieval by Unification.* We are currently designing dedicated hardware for efficiently executing these operations.

2.3. Sequential Inference Machine

We first planned to build a sequential inference machine to provide researchers with a rich programming environment, and to get experience on the development of dedicated hardware for logic programming. We designed the kernel language KL0, a Prolog derivative adjusted for firmware implementation. We also designed the dedicated computer named PSI for direct execution of KL0 [Taki 84] [Yokota 84]. In parallel with the development of the hardware, we also started to develop a software system for PSI called SIMPOS (Sequential Inference Machine Programming and Operating System) [Takagi 84]. Since the software system was expected to grow quite large, we first developed a system description language ESP (Extended Self-contained Prolog) [Chikayama 84a], [Chikayama 84b]. In the following, we will explain the key features of PSI, KL0, ESP and SIMPOS.

Table 1. Two Versions of PSI Machines

	PSI	PSI-II
Size	Big refrigerator	Desk side
Device	TTL (fast)	CMOS Gate Array LSI
Cycle time	200 nsec.	200 nsec.
Cache memory	4 KW × 2	4 KW × 1
Main memory	16 MW (Max.)	64 MW (Max.)
Max. num. of processes	64	No limit
Machine code type	Table type	Instruction type
Structure rep.	Sharing	Copying
Performance (ave.)	30 KLIPS	Around 100 KLIPS

2.3.1. PSI and KL0

PSI is a sequential inference machine designed to be used as a single-user, multi-process machine. Its machine language called KL0 (Kernel Language version-0) is a logic programming language with various extensions to meet the requirements for building up a practical system by itself. The current PSI can have up to 16 MW (80 MB) of memory and supports up to 64 hardware-supported processes running KL0 in 30 KLIPS (in average).

As a logic programming language, KL0 has all the essential features of Prolog. For handling exceptional cases such as errors, KL0 provides multiple level cut which can be used to implement non-local control transfer mechanism, like `CATCH` and `THROW` of Lisp. To describe everything required in system description, KL0 also has quite low-level features such as control register manipulation or I/O device manipulation.

$$
\begin{aligned}
\text{KL0} \;=\; & \text{Logic Programming Mechanism} \\
& + \text{ Extended Control Structure} \\
& + \text{ Hardware Oriented Operation.}
\end{aligned}
$$

We are now developing a new version of the PSI machine, called PSI-II, targeted for completion in the spring of 1987. This new machine will be much smaller than the current machine as well as much faster in its execution speed. Table 1 shows the main features of PSI and PSI-II.

2.3.2. ESP

ESP is the language used both for the system implementation of SIMPOS, and for various application programs on PSI/SIMPOS system.

ESP is a logic programming language based on Prolog adopting the concept of object orientation. The object-oriented feature realizes the mechanism of modularization and hierarchy, which are necessary to develop large-scale programs like operating systems. ESP also has a very flexible macro expansion mechanism.

ESP is translated into KL0 and executed. KL0 has several simple built-in predicates for speeding up the execution of ESP programs. Various features of KL0 are also directly available in ESP.

ESP = Logic Programming Mechanism
+ Object Oriented Mechanism
+ Macro Expansion Mechanism
+ KL0 Builtin Predicates.

2.3.3. SIMPOS

SIMPOS is a programming and operating system for PSI machines. It has been developed as a system software prototype whose objective is to provide a good programming environment on PSI. It is constructed in an object-oriented approach, which has drastically reduced the specification and development efforts of the system. This feature of SIMPOS also makes it easier to change and extend the system. In the following, we briefly explain its design principles, its organization, and its implementation.

2.3.3.1. Principles

SIMPOS has been developed under the following principles.

- To provide a good programming environment for logic programming.
- To provide a good man-machine interface through a multi-window system.
- To provide the necessary computer network facilities.
- To provide a unique language system based on a logic programming language: ESP.
- To develop an object-oriented paradigm which would realize a simple, consistent and flexible system.

2.3.3.2. Organization

SIMPOS consists of a programming system (PS) and an operating system (OS). The OS is made up of a kernel, a supervisor and I/O media for single user, multi-process and interactive processing. The PS consists of subsystems called experts, which form the easy-to-use user interface.

(1) Kernel—The kernel manages the hardware resources; for example, processor, memory, I/O devices and so on.

- *Processor management:* manages the execution environment on the physical level.
- *Memory management:* manages the memory space and performs garbage collection.
- *Device management:* manages and controls several I/O devices.
- *IPL(Initial Program Loader):* loads the main part of SIMPOS and initializes the execution environment.

(2) Supervisor—The supervisor provides various kinds of basic facilities necessary to execute a program.

- *Process management:* manages the process, the execution environment on the logical level.
- *Pool management:* provides classes to use as various kinds of abstract containers (which are also objects) of objects of any class. For example, there are list, array, stack, index and so on.
- *Stream management:* provides classes to communicate among and to synchronize processes.
- *World management:* manages the directory tree, a kind of pool of named objects.
- *User management:* manages users and analyzes their login files.
- *Timer management:* handles the real time clock and the interval timer in the system.
- *Japanese language processing:* supports Japanese language I/O.
- *Situation subsystem:* supports error processing flexibly according to the situation.

(3) I/O Media system—The I/O media system provides the communication channel between PSI and the outside world.

- *Window subsystem:* manages multi-windows and the mouse.
- *File subsystem:* manages access to the external storage.
- *Network subsystem:* provides facilities for communication with other PSI's and different kinds of machine like the VAX.

(4) Programming system—The programming system consists of the support tools for developing programs, allowing users to manipulate them directly.

- *Coordinator:* coordinates the interactive interface between the user and the system.
- *Editor:* used to create and edit a program or text.
- *Transducer:* converts between the character representation and the internal structure of program and data. It is used with I/O media like windows and files.
- *Library:* compiles programs and manages the code and the objects.
- *Librarian:* an user interface with the library subsystem.
- *Debugger/Interpreter:* used to execute and to debug ESP programs.

(5) Manipulator—The manipulator provides an interactive tool to enable utilization of SIMPOS through menu selection.

- *Window manipulator:* a user interface enabling alteration of attributes of a window, such as position and size.
- *File manipulator:* a user interface for displaying listing of file names, copying and deleting files.
- *Network manipulator:* a user interface for file transfer, electric mail, and so on.
- *Whiteboard manipulator:* a user interface for referring, deleting and copying objects on the whiteboard which the coordinator provides.

2.3.3.3. Implementation

All of the SIMPOS program is written in ESP, from the device handlers, memory manager and process manager at the lowest level, to the programming system at the highest. ESP was crucial in enabling development of such a large operating system. To be practical, an operating system has to provide sufficient processing speed at the lower levels and sufficient descriptive power at the higher levels. ESP satisfies both of the requirements.

The size of SIMPOS version 1.5 is as follows.

Source program:	approximately 145,000 lines
The number of classes:	960
The number of predicates:	approximately 15,000
(local predicates:	approximately 5,300)

3. RELATED ACTIVITIES AROUND THE WORLD

We would like to point out that the successful progress of our project to date owes very much to the pioneers in this field. The work of the founding fathers of logic programming, Colmerauer and Kowalski, is much appreciated [Roussel 75], [Kowalski 74], not to mention the work on mechanized theorem proving that goes back to Robinson [Robinson 65]. The next landmark is Warren's work that made logic programming truly practical [Warren 77]. We also acknowledge Clark and Gregory's work on the Relational Language [Clark 81] as the origin of parallel logic programming languages.

In the following, we survey current trends in several research areas listing recent important results from around the world they may influence our project.

3.1. Parallelism

One of the unique features of the logic programming paradigm is that we can consider logic separately from control, and this is the reason why parallel execution of logic programs has been one of the most important goals from the very beginning of the history of logic programming.

IC-Prolog by Clark, McCabe and Gregory [Clark 82] is noteworthy as one of the first works introducing the concept of coroutines into Prolog. Its successor, Relational Language by Clark and Gregory, focused on parallel execution and had a great influence as the first well-organized parallel logic programming language. Shapiro [Shapiro 83a] proposed Concurrent Prolog as a more powerful alternative using read-only annotation for the control of bindings to variables. On the other hand, the successor of Relational Language, PARLOG [Clark 84], succeeded in augmenting the expressive power of Relational Language, while keeping the direction of bindings analyzable at compile time. Flat Concurrent Prolog [Mierowsky 85] was proposed to get around the difficulties of multiple environments. One may suspect that the restriction reduces expressive power. However, Codish defined the "safe" class of Concurrent Prolog programs and showed that a program in that class can be transformed into Flat Concurrent Prolog under a certain condition [Codish 85]. Guarded Horn Clauses proposed in the FGCS project is closely related both to Concurrent Prolog and to PARLOG.

3.2. More Logical Languages

Another characteristic of logic programming is that a program is described in some form of logic. Prolog is based on Horn logic, a subset of first-order logic, and employs SLD-resolution for control. Although the descriptive power of Horn logic has been shown to be equivalent to first-order logic [Tärnlund 77] in the sense of computability, various extensions of Prolog have been proposed to enhance performance and rectify illogical aspects of Prolog.

Coroutining is the major extension to the control structure of Prolog (IC-Prolog [Clark 82], Prolog II [Colmerauer 82], Epilog [Porto 82], LM-Prolog [Carlsson 83], MU-Prolog [Naish 85a], NU-Prolog [Naish 85b]). All of these languages provide control governed by instantiation of a variable. LM-Prolog allows attachment of conditions to a variable activated at the instantiation time. Although freeze mechanism of Prolog II provides a similar mechanism, it works as a coroutine. MU- and NU-Prolog give some methodologies to automate control information.

Another promising approach to more sophisticated control structures is describing control in meta programs and deriving a final program by transformation, which will be described elsewhere.

Horn logic does not allow explicit description of negative information. Clark's "negation as failure" [Clark 78] is well known as a framework for handling negation. The essential issue in implementing negation as failure is to avoid the problems pointed out in [Dahl 80] and [Naish 85c] to assure soundness. IC-Prolog, Epilog, MU-Prolog and NU-Prolog take account of this issue; and MU- and NU-Prolog address performance problems as well.

Several logic programming languages have been proposed that go beyond Horn logic [Bowen 85] [Lloyd 84] [Naish 85b]. Lloyd's language allows arbitrary first-order formulas in the body of a Prolog clause, which are transformable into ordinary Horn clauses with negation as long as a sound implementation of negation is available. This language has good expressive power and efficiency characteristics.

3.3. Program Transformation

Program transformation is also a very important research topic. It is one of the fundamental techniques supporting the multi-level language system. Techniques like partial evaluation or fold/unfold are already well-known. In particular, partial evaluation is especially important since it makes possible automatic generation of a compiler when it is applied to a language processor. These results were established by Futamura [Futamura 71]. The works of Komorowski [Komorowski 81], Kahn [Kahn 82], etc. applied techniques of partial evaluation to logic programs. Quite recently, by applying partial evaluation to the unification algorithm, Kursawe [Kursawe 86] presented a method for generating Warren's code [Warren 83] "logically." This very significant result, which provides a theoretical basis for the multi-level language system, will be reported on at this conference.

Program transformation based on fold/unfold has its origin in Burstall and Darlington [Burstall 77]. Their results were applied to logic programming field by Clark and Sickel [Clark 77], Hogger [Hogger 81]. They *"naturally formulated the unfold and fold transformations as just special cases of logical deduction. Thus each clause in the synthesized program is a theorem deduced from the specification axioms. This ensures the partial correctness of the synthesized program"* (cited form Tamaki and Sato [Tamaki 84]). Tamaki and Sato [Tamaki 84] proposed another approach holding the equivalence of fold/unfold transformation under certain conditions. It need hardly be said that all of these basic researches are very important in supporting the multi-level language system.

3.4. Meta Programming

It is rather difficult to pinpoint the origin of meta programming. There were no noticeable results—apart from control abstraction in programming languages—among attempts to make the control structures of programs more declarative, before Davis's work [Davis 77]. Davis's work may be regarded as the origin since it clarified the importance of meta knowledge in practical application. While constructing the consultation system for stock investment, he introduced meta-level descriptions for data representations and forms of rules. When new rules were acquired by the system, these meta descriptions were used to check their validity.

In logic programming, the work by Bundy *et al.* [Bundy 79] is noteworthy. They represented domain specific know-how to control inference by rules in their QA system on mechanics problems.

Another significant innovation was invention of the demo predicate by Bowen and Kowalski [Bowen 82]. Combined with a Prolog interpreter written in Prolog [Pereira 78], it can be regarded as forming the basis of meta programming.

It has already been mentioned that, combined with the technique of partial evaluation, meta programming has evolved into a practical and efficient technique.

3.5. Declarative Debugging

The debugging environment is extremely important for programming languages. Debugging systems for logic programs have to be developed to make logic programming still more practical.

The most remarkable feature of debugging logic programs is the evidence that logic programming enables declarative debugging methods with theoretical foundation other than conventional trace and spy methods.

We have to note again two aspects of logic programming, logic and control. Conventional debugging methods utilize the control aspects of programs. A user takes a look at an execution trace and tries to find a bug by detecting a mismatch between the intended and actual program behavior. Thus, users are required to have complete knowledge on the control aspects of programs, a serious imposition.

With the declarative method, it is enough for a user to know the logic aspect of a program, that is, its declarative meaning. Users do not need to consider program behavior. A bug is found by checking the validity of solved literals with respect to their intended declarative semantics. In the case of extending or transforming logic programs, it is impossible to require users to have full knowledge of program behavior. Declarative debugging is a very powerful method that is highly effective for languages with declarative semantics.

Shapiro has done pioneering work on declarative debugging of logic programs [Shapiro 83b]. He formulated possible bugs in logic programs by analyzing types of errors, such as termination with incorrect answer and finite failure with missing solution. An incorrect clause instance and an uncovered atom were defined to be the causes of these errors. He also implemented the declarative debugger using the "divide and query" strategy. These concepts form the basis of subsequent research on declarative debugging.

Pereira [Pereira 85] applied a modified unification algorithm to the implementation of the declarative debugger, called the rational debugger. The algorithm, which was originally introduced for intelligent backtracking, preserves dependencies among terms. Owing to this, the rational debugger can reduce the search space of a bug and perform discourse at a finer level, that is, at the term-level.

Refinements of declarative debugging on a firmer theoretical foundation were done by [Lloyd 86a], [Ferrand 85]. Lloyd applied it to declarative debugging of his extended Prolog, which allows an arbitrary first order formula in the body of Horn clauses.

Declarative debuggers for parallel logic programming languages are now being developed. Since it is clear that there are serious limitations to debugging parallel programs by conventional methods, the declarative method is very promising. Takeuchi [Takeuchi 86] developed an algorithmic debugger for GHC, that considers both declarative and procedural aspects of programs. Lloyd *et al.* [Lloyd 86b] refined the possibilities and difficulties of declarative debugging of parallel logic programming languages.

3.6. Natural Language Processing

The most prominent and congenial application area of logic programming languages is natural language processing. It is well-known that Prolog itself was born from Colmerauer's work on the development of a language for natural language processing [Colmerauer 70, 78]. Pereira and Warren proposed a language formalism called Definite Clause Grammars (DCGs) [Pereira 80] as a successor to Colmerauer's Metamorphosis Grammars, and implemented the system in their DECsystem-10 Prolog. A DCG is an augmented context-free grammar that translates into a Prolog program. The descriptive power of DCG formalism is equivalent to ATNG [Woods 70], in that both of them are as powerful as the type-0 language. What is better for DCGs is that the description can be independent of the procedural semantics of the interpreter. Since grammar rules are logical clauses in DCGs, parsing can be regarded as proof procedure [Pereira 83].

Recent research in linguistics and computational linguistics focuses growing attention on context-free syntactic structure. Most current representative grammar theories, such as LFG [Kaplan 82], GPSG [Gazdar 82, 85], Unification Grammars [Kay 84], and Head Grammars [Pollard 84] employ a context-free grammar framework augmented with various features or meta rules. Logic based grammar formalism is probably the most suitable environment for describing and implementing these linguistic theories.

Quite a few successors of DCGs have been devised and proposed. Pereira's Extrapositional Grammars (XG) [Pereira 81] extends DCGs so that they can express left extraposition more directly and naturally. Dahl and Abramson's Gapping Grammars [Dahl 84a, 84b] gave a still more powerful formalism, allowing a direct description of production rules of type-0 languages. Other well-known grammar formalisms designed to extend the descriptive power of DCGs are Slot Grammars [McCord 82], Definite Clause Translation Grammars [Abramson 84], Puzzle Grammars [Sabatier 84], PATR-II [Shieber 83, 85], and Modular Logic Grammars [McCord 85].

These activities have clearly demonstrated the suitability of logic programming languages for natural language applications. Several efforts utilizing Prolog for natural language analysis show that logic programming can cover most of the aspects of natural language phenomenon uniformly and clearly. Warren and Pereira's Chat-80 [Warren 81] and Dahl's work [Dahl 81, 82] are noteworthy since they demonstrated how Prolog makes it easy to develop natural language systems.

3.7. Logic Databases

Logic is a powerful language for database systems. Basic research on the relation between logic and databases can be found in [Gallaire 78, 81, 84a, 84b]. We all owe a debt to Robert Kowalski for his breakthroughs in the use of logic and logic programming languages for databases [Kowalski 78, 79, 81]. As Nicolas and Gallaire showed in [Nicolas 78], there are two different ways to look at a database from the logical point of view. They are an interpretation viewpoint (i.e. a model-theoretic view) and a theory viewpoint (i.e. a proof-theoretic view). [Kowalski 81] and [Reiter 84] investigated these two approaches in greater detail. Conventional relational databases are understood from the model-theoretic view. These two views coincide if assumptions such as the closed world assumption, the domain closure assumption and the unique name assumption normally employed by conventional databases are formulated as axioms in a logic database. [Reiter 78, 84] and [Clark 78] give the theoretical foundations for this topic.

Regarding a database system as a logical system gives a firm theoretical foundation, and hence imports a number of desirable properties to the system. Logic can be a uniform language to represent data, to formulate queries, and to express views and integrity constraints. Implementation of database systems using logic programming languages has tremendous potential.

More uniform approaches to the use of logic programming languages not only for representing databases, but for implementing natural language user interfaces are attempted in Warren and Pereira [Warren 81] and Dahl [Dahl 82]. Another approach to make use of the powerful feature of logic for formulating various aspects in database systems is the meta programming approach taken by Bowen and Kowalski [Bowen 82]. Meta language and object language are amalgamated in a single logic programming language. This approach proves to be the basis for formulating updating and deletion of data to and from a database, as well as for realizing the aspects discussed above (e.g. see [Miyachi 84]).

Efforts to extend the descriptive power of Prolog and to apply it to logic databases are pursued by Lloyd [Lloyd 85a, 85b] and Naish [Naish 83]. Lloyd proposed an extension of Prolog that allows any formulas of first order predicate logic in clause bodies and showed that they are transformable to Horn clauses with negation.

The logical approach to databases is undoubtedly promising and much more general than conventional approaches. Progress in logic programming languages has had a great influence on the development of logic databases and it will undoubtedly go on from strength to strength.

4. CONCLUSION

We set out in the Fifth Generation Computer project to develop a highly parallel computer with logic programming as the centerpiece. We have already designed several language levels, starting from the high level programming language which handles large applications, down to the machine language that can be executed in a highly parallel manner. We also aim to develop unified program transformation techniques to fill the gaps between these language levels.

We are confident that we have produced the first approximations to solutions of most parts of this giant jigsaw puzzle. Fig. 2 is the picture of the levels of programming languages we have obtained through our activities so far.

We can now see the basic outline of the path from applications to parallel execution, although the path has not taken concrete shape yet. Application programs are written in a powerful knowledge programming language equipped with meta programming facilities. These are transformed to more efficient programs written in a general purpose user language. Then these programs are further translated into the more primitive parallel logic programming language FGHC, which can be executed by Multi-PSI and/or PIM.

What remains is to give this path concrete shape. Our approach is to isolate the component problems and solve them one by one and put the results in the right places piece by piece to complete the jigsaw puzzle.

The important problems which remain to be solved can be enumerated as follows:

(1) How to add meta language features to GHC?

(2) How to realize constraint programming in GHC?

(3) Implementation of the programming environment supporting GHC programming. Especially, an efficient debugging system.

(4) Design and implementation of the operating system of the parallel inference machine.

(5) Decreasing the communication overhead in the parallel inference machine.

(6) Design of the logical/physical interface between PIM and KBM.

These problems may be further divided into sub-problems.

Finally, we would like to return to the theme of international cooperation. The proliferation of research in logic programming around the world in recent years implicitly confirms the tremendous potential of this still new outlook. More active international cooperation can

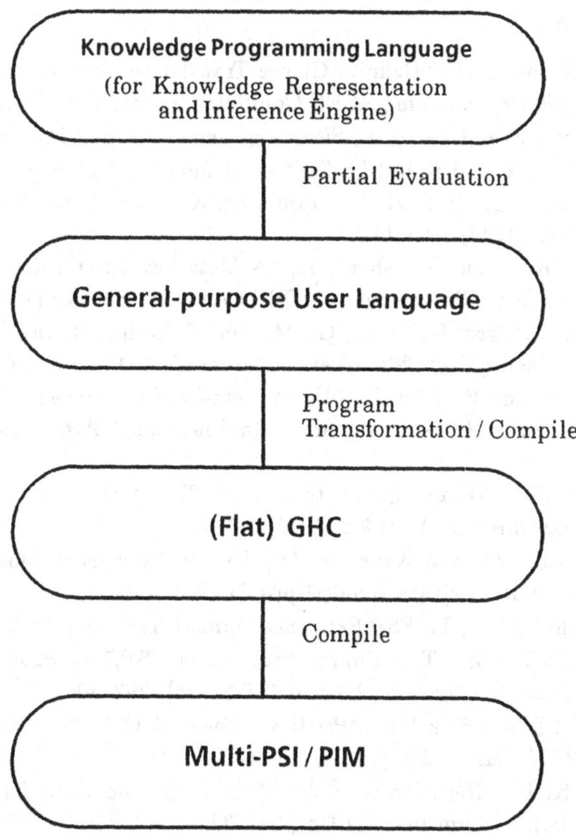

Fig. 2. Levels of Programming Languages

make a valuable contribution to realizing this potential to the benefit of computer science and the advanced information society of the next decade.

ACKNOWLEDGMENT

The authors are grateful to their young colleagues in ICOT, who are earnest to argue over various aspects of our project. Special thanks are due to Shunichi Uchida, Hidenori Ito, Takashi Chikayama, Yuji Matsumoto, Akikazu Takeuchi, Toshihiko Miyazaki, Kazunori Ueda, Jiro Tanaka, Toshiaki Takewaki and Hirohisa Seki, who helped them in preparing this paper and producing the printed output.

REFERENCES

[Abramson 84] Abramson, H., "Definite Clause Translation Grammars," In *Proc. 1984 Int. Symp. on Logic Programming*, IEEE Computer Society (1984), 233–240.

[Barwise 83] Barwise, J. and Perry, J., *Situations and Attitudes*, MIT Press (1983).

[Bowen 82] Bowen, K. A. and Kowalski, R., "Amalgamating Language and Metalanguage in Logic Programming," In *Logic Programming*, K. L. Clark and S. -Å. Tärnlund (eds.), Academic Press (1982), 153–172.

[Bowen 85] Bowen, K. A. and Weinberg, T., "A Meta-Level Extension of Prolog," In *Proc. 1985 Symp. on Logic Programming*, IEEE Computer Society (1985), 48–53.

[Bundy 79] Bundy, A., Byrd, L., Luger, G., Mellish, C., Milne, R. and Palmer, M., "Solving Mechanics Problems Using Meta-Level Inference," In *Proc. 6th IJCAI*, Tokyo (1979).

[Bundy 81] Bundy, A. and Welham, B., "Using Meta-level Inference for Selective Application of Multiple Rewrite Rules in Algebraic Manipulation," *Artif. Intell.* **16** (1981), 189–212.

[Burstall 77] Burstall, R. M. and Darlington, J., "A Transformation System for Developing Recursive Programs," *J. ACM* **24** (1977), 46–67.

[Carlsson 83] Carlsson, M. and Kahn, K. M., *LM-Prolog User Manual*, Tech. Report 24, UPMAIL, Computer Science Dept., Uppsala Univ. (1983).

[Chikayama 84a] Chikayama, T., *ESP Reference Manual*, Tech. Report TR-044, ICOT (1984).

[Chikayama 84b] Chikayama, T., "Unique Features of ESP," In *Proc. Int. Conf. on Fifth Generation Computer Systems 1984*, ICOT (1984), 292–306.

[Clark 77] Clark, K. L. and Sickel, S., "Predicate Logic: A Calculus for Deriving Programs," *Proc. 5th IJCAI*, Cambridge (1977), 419–420.

[Clark 78] Clark, K. L., "Negation as Failure," In *Logic and Data Bases*, H. Gallaire and J. Minker (eds.), Plenum Press (1978), 293–322.

[Clark 81] Clark, K. L. and Gregory, S., "A Relational Language for Parallel Programming," In *Proc. 1981 Conf. on Functional Programming Languages and Computer Architecture*, ACM (1981), 171–178.

[Clark 82] Clark, K. L., McCabe, F. and Gregory, S., "IC-Prolog Language Features," In *Logic Programming*, K. L. Clark and S. -Å. Tärnlund (eds.), Academic Press (1982), 253–266.

[Clark 84] Clark, K. L. and Gregory, S., *PARLOG: Parallel Programming in Logic*, Research Report DOC 84/4, Dept. of Computing, Imperial College of Science and Technology, London (1984).

[Codish 85] Codish, M., *Compiling OR-parallelism into AND-parallelism*, Master Thesis, Computer Science, Feinberg Graduate School of the Weizmann Institute of Science, Rehovot (1985).

[Colmerauer 70] Colmerauer, A., *Les Systèmes-Q ou un Formalisme pour Analyser er Synthétiser des Phrase sur Ordinateur*, Internal Publication 43, Départment d'Informatique, Université de Montreal (1970).

[Colmerauer 78] Colmerauer, A., "Metamorphosis Grammars," In *Natural Language Communication with Computers*, L. Bolc (ed.), Springer-Verlag (1978).

[Colmerauer 82] Colmerauer, A., *Prolog II: Reference Manual and Theoretical Model*, Internal Report, Groupe Intelligence Artificielle, Université d'Aix-Marseille II (1982).

[Dahl 80] Dahl, V., "Two Solutions for the Negation Problem," In *Logic Programming Workshop*, S. -Å. Tärnlund (ed.), Debrecen, Hungary (1980).

[Dahl 81] Dahl, V., "Translating Spanish into Logic through Logic," *Am. J. Comput. Linguist.* **7** (1981), 149–164.

[Dahl 82] Dahl, V., "On Database Systems Development through Logic," *ACM Trans. on Database Syst.* **7** (1982), 102–123.

[Dahl 84a] Dahl, V. and Abramson, H., "On Gapping Grammars," In *Proc. Second Int. Logic Programming Conf.*, Uppsala Univ. (1984), 77–88.

[Dahl 84b] Dahl, V., "More on Gapping Grammars," In *Proc. Int. Conf. on Fifth Generation Computer Systems 1984*, ICOT (1984), 669–677.

[Davis 77] Davis, R. and Buchanan, B. G., "Meta-Level Knowledge: Overview and Applications," In *Proc. 5th IJCAI*, Cambridge (1977), 920–927.

[Ferrand 85] Ferrand, G., *Error Diagnosis in Logic Programming: An Adaptation of E. Y. Shapiro's Method*, Rapport de Recherche 375, INRIA (1985).

[Futamura 71] Futamura, Y., "Partial Evaluation of Computation Process: An Approach to a Compiler-Compiler", *Systems, Computers, Controls* **2** (1971), 721–728.

[Gallaire 78] Gallaire, H. and Minker, J. (eds.), *Logic and Data Bases*, Plenum Press (1978).

[Gallaire 81] Gallaire, H., Minker, J. and Nicolas, J. -M. (eds.), *Advances in Data Base Theory*, Vol. 1, Plenum Press (1981).

[Gallaire 84a] Gallaire, H., Minker, J. and Nicolas, J. -M. (eds.), *Advances in Data Base Theory*, Vol. 2, Plenum Press (1984).

[Gallaire 84b] Gallaire, H., Minker, J. and Nicolas, J. -M., "Logic and Databases: A Deductive Approach," *Computing Surveys* **16** (1984), 153–185.

[Gazdar 82] Gazdar, G., "Phrase Structure Grammar," In *The Nature of Syntactic Representation*, P. Jacobson and G. K. Pullum (eds.), D. Reidel (1982), 131–186.

[Gazdar 85] Gazdar, G., Klein, E., Pullum, G. and Sag, I., *Generalized Phrase Structure Grammar*, Basil Blackwell (1985).

[Goebel 86] Goebel, R. and Furukawa, K., "Using Definite Clauses and Integrity Constraints as the Basis for a Theory Formation Approach to Diagnostic Reasoning," In *Proc. Third Int. Conf. on Logic Programming*, Springer-Verlag (1986).

[Hogger 81] Hogger, C. J., "Derivation of Logic Programs," *J. ACM* **28** (1981), 372–422.

[Kahn 82] Kahn, K., *A Partial Evaluator of Lisp Written in a Prolog Written in Lisp Intended to be Applied to the Prolog and Itself which in Turn is Intended to be Given to Itself Together with the Prolog to Produce a Prolog Compiler*, UPMAIL, Dept. of Computing Science, Uppsala Univ. (1982).

[Kaplan 82] Kaplan, R. and Bresnan, J., "Lexical-Functional Grammar: A Formal System for Grammatical Representation," Chapter 4 of *The Mental Representation of Grammatical Relations*, J. Bresnan (ed.), MIT Press (1982), 173–281.

[Kay 84] Kay, M., "Unification in Grammar," In *Proc. First Workshop on Natural Language Understanding and Logic Programming*, V. Dahl and P. Saint-Dizier (eds.), Rennes, France (1984).

[Komolowski 81] Komolowski, H. J., *A Specification of Abstract Prolog Machine and Its Application to Partial Evaluation*, Linköping Studies in Science and Technology Dissertations, No. 69, Linköping Univ. (1981).

[Kowalski 74] Kowalski, R., "Predicate Logic as Programming Language," In *Proc. IFIP '74*, North-Holland (1977), 569–574.

[Kowalski 78] Kowalski, R. A., "Logic for Data Description," In *Logic and Data Bases*, H. Gallaire and J. Minker (eds.) Plenum Press, New York (1978), 77–103.

[Kowalski 79] Kowalski, R. A., *Logic for Problem Solving*, Elsevier Science Publishers B. V. (1979).

[Kowalski 81] Kowalski, R. A., "Logic as a Data Base Language," In *Proc. Advanced Seminar on Theoretical Issues in Data Bases*, Cetraro, Italy (1981).

[Kowalski 82] Kowalski, R., "Logic Programming in the Fifth Generation," In *Proc. Fifth Generation Conf.*, SPL International, London (1982).

[Kursawe 86] Kursawe, P., "How to Invent a Prolog Machine," In *Proc. Third Int. Conf. on Logic Programming*, Springer-Verlag (1986).

[Lloyd 84] Lloyd, J. L. and Topor, R. W., "Making PROLOG More Expressive," *J. Logic Programming* **1** (1984), 225–240.

[Lloyd 85a] Lloyd, J. L. and Topor, R. W., "A Basis for Deductive Database Systems," *J. Logic Programming* **2** (1985), 93–109.

[Lloyd 85b] Lloyd, J. L. and Topor, R. W., *A Basis for Deductive Database Systems II*, Tech. Report 85/6, Dept. of Computer Science, Univ. of Melbourne (1985).

[Lloyd 86a] Lloyd, J. W., *Declarative Error Diagnosis*, Tech. Report 86/3, Dept. of Computer Science, Univ. of Melbourne (1986).

[Lloyd 86b] Lloyd, J. and Takeuchi, A., *A Framework for Debugging GHC*, to appear as ICOT Tech. Report (1986).

[Matsumoto 83] Matsumoto, Y., Tanaka, H., Hirakawa, H., Miyoshi H. and Yasukawa, H., "BUP: A Bottom-Up Parser Embedded in Prolog," *New Generation Computing* **1** (1983), 145–158.

[McCord 82] McCord, M. C., "Using Slots and Modifiers in Logic Grammars for Natural Language," *Artif. Intell.* **18** (1982), 327–367.

[McCord 85] McCord, M. C., "Modular Logic Grammars," In *Proc. 23rd Annual Meeting of ACL* (1985), 104–117.

[Mierowsky 85] Mierowsky, C., Taylor, S., Shapiro, E., Levy, J. and Safra, M., *The Design and Implementation of Flat Concurrent Prolog*, Tech. Report CS85-09, The Weizmann Institute of Science, Rehovot (1985).

[Miyachi 84] Miyachi, T., Kunifuji, S., Kitakami, H., Furukawa, K., Takeuchi, A. and Yokota, H., "A Knowledge Assimilation Method for Logic Databases," In *Proc. 1984 Int. Symp. on Logic Programming*, IEEE Computer Society (1984), 118–130.

[Morishita 84] Morishita, T. and Hirakawa H., *GDL0: A Grammar Description Language Based on DCG*, Tech. Memorandum TM-0084, ICOT (1984).

[Mukai 85] Mukai, K. and Yasukawa, H., "Complex Indeterminates in Prolog and Its Application to Discourse Models," *New Generation Computing* **3** (1985), 441–466.

[Naish 83] Naish, L. and Thom, J. A., *The MU-PROLOG Deductive Database*, Tech. Report 83/10, Dept. of Computer Science, Univ. of Melbourne (1985).

[Naish 85a] Naish, L., *MU-PROLOG 3.2 Reference Manual*, Tech. Report 85/11, Dept. of Computer Science, Univ. of Melbourne (1985).

[Naish 85b] Naish, L., *Negation and Quantifiers in NU-PROLOG*, Tech. Report 85/13, Dept. of Computer Science, Univ. of Melbourne (1985).

[Naish 85c] Naish, L., *Negation and Control in Prolog*, Tech. Report 85/12, Dept. of Computer Science, Univ. of Melbourne (1985).

[Nicolas 78] Nicolas, J. -M., and Gallaire, H., "Database: Theory vs. Interpretation," In *Logic and Data Bases*, H. Gallaire and J. Minker (eds.) Plenum Press (1978), 33–54.

[Pereira 78] Pereira, L. M., Pereira, F. C. N. and Warren, D. H. D., *User's Guide to Decsystem-10 Prolog*, Occasional Paper No. 15, Dept. of Artificial Intelligence, Univ. of Edinburgh (1978).

[Pereira 80] Pereira, F. C. N. and Warren, D. H. D., "Definite Clause Grammars—A Survey of the Formalism and a Comparison with Augmented Transition Networks," *Artif. Intell.* **13** (1980), 231–278.

[Pereira 81] Pereira, F., "Extraposition Grammars," *Am. J. Comput. Linguist.* **7** (1981), 243–256.

[Pereira 83] Pereira, F. and Warren, D. H. D., *Parsing as Deduction*, SRI Tech. Note 295 (1983). Also in *Proc. 21st Annual Meeting of ACL* (1983), 137–144.

[Pereira 86] Pereira, L. M., "Rational Debugging in Logic Programming," In *Proc. Third Int. Conf. on Logic Programming*, Springer-Verlag (1986).

[Pollard 84] Pollard, C. J., *Generalized Phrase Structure Grammars, Head Grammars, and Natural Languages*, Ph. D. Dissertation, Stanford Univ. (1984).

[Porto 82] Porto, A., "EPILOG: A Language for Extended Programming in Logic" In *Proc. First Int. Logic Programming Conf.* (1982), 31–37.

[Reiter 78] Reiter, R., "On Closed World Database," In *Logic and Data Bases*, H. Gallaire and J. Minker (eds.) Plenum Press (1978), 56–76.

[Reiter 84] Reiter, R., "Towards a Logical Representation of Relational Database Theory," In *On Conceptual Modeling*, M. Brodie, J. Mylopoulos and J. W. Schmidt (eds.) Springer-Verlag (1985).

[Robinson 65] Robinson, J. A., "A Machine-Oriented Logic Based on Resolution Principle," *J. ACM* **12** (1965), 23–41.

[Roussel 75] Roussel, P., *Prolog: Manual de Reference et d'Utilisation*, Groupe d'Intelligence Artificielle, Marseille-Luminy.

[Sabatier 84] Sabatier, P., "Puzzle Grammars," In *Proc. First Workshop on Natural Language Understanding and Logic Programming*, V. Dahl and P. Saint-Dizier (eds.), Rennes, France (1984).

[Shapiro 83a] Shapiro, E. Y., *A Subset of Concurrent Prolog and Its Interpreter*. Tech. Report TR-003, ICOT (1983).

[Shapiro 83b] Shapiro, E. Y., *Algorithmic Program Debugging*, MIT Press (1983).

[Shieber 83] Shieber, S. M., Uszkoreit, H., Pereira, F. C. N., Robinson, J. J. and Tyson, M., "The Formalism and Implementation of PATR-II", In *Research on Interactive Acquisition and Use of Knowledge*, Artificial Intelligence Center, SRI International, California (1983).

[Shieber 85] Shieber, S. M., "An Introduction to Unification-Based Approaches to Grammar," In *Proc. 23rd Annual Meeting of the Association for Computational Linguistics* (1985).

[Takagi 84] Takagi, S., Yokoi, T., Uchida, S., Kurokawa, T., Hattori, T., Chikayama, T., Sakai, K. and Tsuji, J., "Overall Design of SIMPOS," In *Proc. Second Int. Logic Programming Conf.*, Uppsala Univ. (1984), 1–12.

[Takeuchi 85] Takeuchi, A. and Furukawa, K., *Partial Evaluation of Prolog Programs and Its Application to Meta Programming*, ICOT Tech. Report TR-126 (1985). Also to appear in *Proc. IFIP '86* (1986).

[Takeuchi 86] Takeuchi, A., *Algorithmic Debugging of GHC programs*, to appear as ICOT Tech. Report (1986).

[Takewaki 85] Takewaki, T., Takeuchi, A., Kunifuji, S. and Furukawa, K., *Application of Partial Evaluation to the Algebraic Manipulation System and its Evaluation*, Tech. Report TR-148, ICOT (1985).

[Taki 84] Taki, K., Yokota, M., Yamamoto, A., Nishikawa, H., Uchida, S., Nakashima, H. and Mitsuishi, A., "Hardware Design and Implementation of the Personal Sequential Inference Machine (PSI)," In *Proc. Int. Conf. on Fifth Generation Computer Systems 1984*, ICOT (1984), 398–409.

[Taki 86] Taki, K., Kimura, Y., Yokota, M., Chikayama, T. and Uchida, S., "The Overview of Multi-PSI System," In *Proc. 32nd Annual Convention IPS Japan* (1986), 5Q-8 (in Japanese).

[Tamaki 84] Tamaki, H. and Sato, T., "Unfold/Fold Transformation of Logic Programs," In *Second Int. Logic Programming Conf.*, Uppsala Univ. (1984), 127–138.

[Tärnlund 77] Tärnlund, S.-Å., "Horn Clause Computability," *BIT* **17** (1977), 215–226.

[Uchida 84] Uchida, S. and Yokoi, T., "Sequential Inference Machine: SIM–Progress Report," In *Proc. Int. Conf. on Fifth Generation Computer Systems 1984*, ICOT (1984), 58–69.

[Ueda 85] Ueda, K., *Guarded Horn Clauses*, Tech. Report TR-103, ICOT (1985). Also to appear in *Logic Programming '85*, E. Wada (ed.), Lecture Notes in Computer Science 221, Springer-Verlag (1986).

[Ueda 86] Ueda, K., "Making Exhaustive Search Programs Deterministic," In *Proc. Third Int. Conf. on Logic Programming*, Springer-Verlag (1986).

[Warren 77] Warren, D. H., *Implementing PROLOG—Compiling Predicate Logic Programs, Vol. 1–2*, D. A. I. Research Report No. 39, Dept. of Artificial Intelligence, Univ. of Edinburgh (1977).

[Warren 81] Warren, D. H. D. and Pereira, F. C. N., *An Efficient Easily Adaptable System for Interpreting Natural Language Queries*, D. A. I. Research Paper No. 155, Dept. of Artificial Intelligence, Univ. of Edinburgh (1981).

[Warren 83] Warren D. H. D., *An Abstract Prolog Instruction Set*, Tech. Note 309, Artificial Intelligence Center, SRI International (1983).

[Woods 70] Woods, W. A., "Transition Network Grammars for Natural Language Analysis," *Comm. ACM* **13** (1970), 591–606.

[Yasukawa 85] Yasukawa, H., Hirakawa, H., Mukai, K., Miyoshi, H. and Tanaka, Y., *The Outline of Discourse Understanding System DUALS*, Tech. Memorandum TM-0118, ICOT (1985) (in Japanese).

[Yokoi 84] Yokoi, T., Uchida, S. and ICOT Third Lab., "Sequential Inference Machine: SIM—Its Programming and Operating System," In *Proc. Int. Conf. on Fifth Generation Computer Systems 1984*, ICOT (1984), 70–81.

[Yokota 84] Yokota, M., Yamamoto, A., Taki, K., Nishikawa, H., Uchida, S., Nakajima, K. and Mitsui, M., "A Microprogrammed Interpreter for the Personal Sequential Inference Machine," In *Proc. Int. Conf. on Fifth Generation Computer Systems 1984*, ICOT (1984), 410–418.

[Yokota 86] Yokota, H., Sakai, K. and Itoh, H., "Deductive Database System Based on Unit Resolution," In *Proc. Int. Conf. on Data Engineering*, IEEE Computer Society (1986), 228–235.

An Abstract Machine for Restricted AND-Parallel Execution of Logic Programs

M. V. Hermenegildo
Department of Electrical and Computer Engineering
The University of Texas at Austin; Austin, TX 78712

Abstract

Although the sequential execution speed of logic programs has been greatly improved by the concepts introduced in the Warren Abstract Machine (**WAM**), parallel execution represents the only way to increase this speed beyond the natural limits of sequential systems. However, most proposed parallel logic programming execution models lack the performance optimizations and storage efficiency of sequential systems. This paper presents a parallel abstract machine which is an extension of the **WAM** and is thus capable of supporting AND-Parallelism without giving up the optimizations present in sequential implementations. A suitable instruction set, which can be used as a target by a variety of logic programming languages, is also included. Special instructions are provided to support a generalized version of "Restricted AND-Parallelism" (**RAP**), a technique which reduces the overhead traditionally associated with the run-time management of variable binding conflicts to a series of simple run-time checks, which select one out of a series of compiled execution graphs.

KEYWORDS: LOGIC PROGRAMMING, PARALLEL PROCESSING, WARREN ABSTRACT MACHINE, RESTRICTED AND-PARALLELISM, PROLOG.

1 Introduction[1]

The execution speed of sequential logic programming systems has been constantly improving since Warren's Prolog interpreter/compiler for the DECsystem-10 [14] proved the usefulness of logic as a practical programming tool [11]. Pipelined architectures [16] and microprogrammed Prolog machines [7] seem to be approaching the 1Mlips (Logic Inferences per Second) line. Most of these implementations are based on the Abstract Machine recently proposed by Warren [17] (the "**WAM**") which has made very fast and space efficient systems possible. Yet, in order to meet the requirements of applications as ambitious as those contemplated in next generation computer systems, vast improvements in performance are still needed. The source for performance improvement beyond the natural limits of sequential systems is *executing logic programs in parallel.*

Of the different sources of parallelism present in logic programs [4], in this paper we will study **AND-Parallelism** because, among other reasons, it offers promising results even for highly deterministic programs. Although the management of AND-Parallelism has traditionally involved excessive run-time overhead, we hope to show throughout this paper that it can in fact be implemented very efficiently by applying similar techniques to those brought by the **WAM** to the sequential logic programming implementation arena. We will present an abstract machine capable of AND-Parallel

[1]This research was partially supported by the Microelectronics and Computer Technology Corporation (MCC).

execution while still supporting most of the optimizations present in current sequential systems. Its data areas, registers, operation, and instruction set will be described. The high overhead previously associated with the resolution of variable binding conflicts [5] will be greatly reduced in this model by providing special instructions to support a generalized version of Restricted AND-Parallelism (**RAP**) [6] [10]. However, other approaches can also be supported with the same basic instruction set.

Organization of the paper is as follows: in the next section we will explain the problems associated with variable binding conflicts and **RAP** will be presented as an efficient technique for detecting and dealing with them. In the following section we will review some of the concepts introduced by the **WAM**. We will then describe the extended AND-Parallel abstract machine, specifying data areas, instructions, and operation. An example of compiled parallel code will be fully commented on in order to further clarify the function of each instruction. Finally we will present some conclusions and suggestions for future work.

2 Towards AND-Parallelism: resolving binding conflicts

Consider the following clause:

```
child(X,Y,Z):- father(Y,X), mother(Z,X).
```

During the resolution of a query of the form "`?:- child(X, peter, mary).`" we cannot go ahead and evaluate "`father(peter,X)`" and "`mother(mary,X)`" in parallel (AND-Parallelism) because they will independently find a value for X but both values may not be the same, as needed by the semantics of the clause: a "binding conflict". The simplest course of action in this case is simply to evaluate the goals involved sequentially, with conventional backtracking.

Many approaches have been proposed in order to detect and deal with these variable conflicts either at compile-time or at run-time. In some of them the user is required to annotate some variables or goals in the program in order to identify goals as "readers" or "writers" for each variable. This and other techniques are used in Concurrent Prolog [15], Parlog [2], IC-Prolog [3], Delta-Prolog [13] etc. Other approaches attempt to solve binding conflicts without variable annotations and with minimal (or no) information from the user, using either a complex run-time system (such as Conery's [5]) or an extensive compile-time analysis (such as Chang's **SDDA** [1]).

Restricted And-Parallelism ("**RAP**") [6] is a technique which deals with these conflicts by *combining a compile-time analysis of the clauses involved, with simple checks on variables at run-time.* While analyzing the example above, a **RAP** compiler would find that "`father(Y,X)`" and "`mother(Z,X)`" cannot in general run in parallel, but that it is possible to execute them concurrently if the clause happens to be called with the first argument (X) being "ground" (i.e. fully instantiated), and the other two (Y and Z) being independent (i.e. they do not "share"). This information can be encoded in the form of a "Conditional Graph Expression" (**CGE**), and the clause rewritten as shown below. This "rewritten" clause can represent a clause which was annotated by the user and/or an intermediate step of the compiler if it is capable of performing the analysis described above[2]:

```
child(X,Y,Z):-( ground(X), indep(Y,Z) | father(Y,X) & mother(Z,X)).
```

The declarative semantics of the clause above remains identical to that of the original clause, but the procedural semantics is now:

- Try to unify "`child(X,Y,Z)`" with the calling goal. If successful,
- Check if "X" is ground and if "Y" and "Z" are independent. In that case, start execution of "`father(Y,X)`" and "`mother(Z,X)`" in parallel.
- If the checks fail, execute "`father(Y,X)`" and "`mother(Z,X)`" sequentially.

---

[2]Note that the definition and syntax of **RAP** and **CGEs** are slightly different than DeGroot's. **CGEs** are shown here *embedded* within the original clause. See [10] for more details.

Thus, the **CGE** embedded within the clause above can generate (depending on the result of the "checks" *at run-time*) two execution graphs: a sequential and a parallel one. Nesting of Conditional Graph Expressions can generate more complicated execution graphs, and the run-time system, while executing the **CGE**, will select different branches of the graphs depending on the results of the checks.

It is interesting to compare **RAP** to other related solutions: Conery's approach would perform all the binding conflict analysis at run-time, with very high execution overhead, while Chang's would perform a data dependency analysis at compile-time but it would only select the worst of all possible cases due to the lack of run-time checks. The **RAP** compromise between run-time and compile-time analysis thus appears as a good choice for implementation and some instructions in the parallel abstract machine will be tailored to support it. However, we believe that the design of the machine and its instruction set is general enough that it can be used as a target by other approaches with only minor modifications.

Backtracking in AND-Parallel Execution

In DeGroot's model, only the forward execution semantics was specified. However, a backward execution semantics is clearly also needed for any implementation. The subject of backtracking in AND-Parallel systems is discussed in [10]. For the sake of completeness we include the following algorithm, taken from [10]. It turns out to be very simple to implement at the abstract machine level, and it offers *restricted intelligent backtracking* with very little overhead:

- *Forward Execution: During forward execution, leave a choice point marker (***CPM***) at each choice point (traditional sequential mode) and a parallel call marker (***PCM***) at each* **CGE** *which evaluates to true (i.e. each* **CGE** *which can actually be executed in parallel). Mark each* **PCM** *as* **"inside"** *when it is created, trigger the parallel resolution of the* **CGE** *goals, and change the* **PCM** *mode to* **"outside"** *when all those goals report success.*

- *Backward Execution: When failure occurs, find the most recently created marker (***PCM** *or* **CPM***). Then:*

  - *If the marker is a* **CPM**, *backtrack normally (i.e. as in sequential execution) to that point.*

  - *If the marker is a* **PCM** *and its value is* **"inside"**, *cancel ("kill") all goals inside the* **CGE**, *fail (i.e. recursively perform the Backward execution).*

  - *If it is a* **PCM** *and its value is* **"outside"**, *find the first goal, going right to left in the* **CGE**[3], *with pending alternatives which succeeds after a "redo", and then "restart" all goals in the* **CGE** *"to its right" in parallel. If no* **CGE** *goal is found to succeed in this manner, fail (i.e. recursively perform the Backward execution).*

3 An Abstract Machine for AND-Parallelism

Although logic programs can present considerable opportunities for AND-Parallelism, there are always code segments requiring sequential execution. A system which can support parallelism while still incorporating the performance optimizations and storage efficiency of current sequential systems is thus highly desirable. This is the approach taken in our design: to support forward and backward execution of AND-Parallel programs through mechanisms which are extensions to the ones used in a high performance Prolog implementation: the **WAM**. This has several advantages: first, sequential

---

[3]This is obviously an arbitrary choice, but it is a simple way of keeping track of which goals have been "redone", in order to make sure that all "tuples" are generated. Also note that only goals which have alternatives (i.e. had a *choice point* available after return) need to be sent a redo.

execution is still as fast and space efficient as in the high performance Prolog implementation (modulo some minimal run-time checks). Second, the model is offered in the form of *extensions*, which are fairly independent, in spirit, of the peculiarities of that implementation. Therefore, the approach described here is applicable to a variety of compilation/stack based sequential models. Finally, the upward compatibility with **WAM** code makes it possible for a sequential program to run without modification on a single processor, and to make use of existing compiler technology.

3.1 Implementing Sequential Logic: the Warren Abstract Machine

The Warren Abstract Machine (**WAM**) [17] is a remarkably efficient execution model coupled with a host of compilation techniques leading to one of the highest performance implementations of Prolog today. The ideas it incorporates are believed to be a major breakthrough in the design of computational logic systems [12]. Lack of space prevents us from fully describing the **WAM** here. Instead we will only point out those basic concepts which are necessary for the understanding of our extensions. For a complete description of the **WAM** the reader is referred to Warren's original SRI report [17] or to the tutorial on the **WAM** available from Argonne Labs [8].

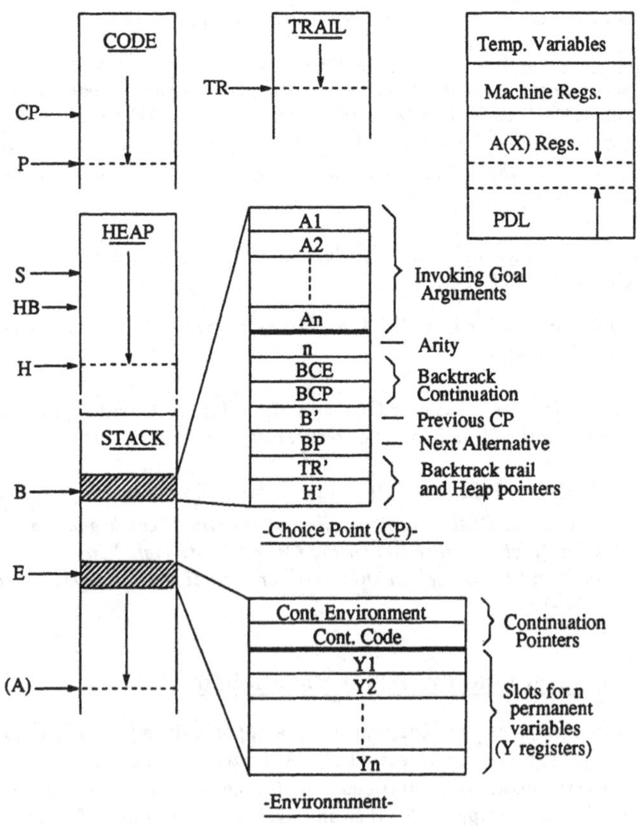

Figure 1: Data areas and registers for the **WAM**

Figure 1 shows a general view of the data areas of the **WAM**. They include the *Code* area, which contains the program *in compiled form,* and three areas operated as stacks:

- The *Heap*: where data structures and long-lived global variables are created, updated, and discarded (upon backtracking). Structure copying (rather than structure sharing) is used in the *Heap*: new structures are pushed on to the *Heap* explicitly, as modified copies of old ones.

- The *Stack*: which contains two types of objects: *environments* and *choice points*.

  - An *environment* is pushed on to the *Stack* every time a clause is entered[4]. It contains a number of value cells which are used to store variables which can be accessed by the goals within the body of the clause or by children clauses called by these goals. It also contains some continuation information which is equivalent to the return address in a subroutine call: it points to the instruction in the body of the calling clause where execution will continue after the called clause finally succeeds. Environments which are no longer needed (for example before the last call in a clause) can be discarded ("last call optimization").

  - A *choice point* is pushed on to the *Stack* when the first clause of a set of alternative clauses is entered. It contains all necessary information to restore the state of the machine and a pointer to the next alternative clause. Upon failure, backtracking is accomplished by simply finding the last *choice point* in the *Stack* (pointed to by register **B**), reloading all machine registers from its contents, and restarting execution at the alternative clause. Resetting the registers takes care of discarding the top of the *Heap* and *Stack* (i.e. discarding variables and structures created since the *choice point*), but there will still be one detail left: we might have done some *variable instantiations* deeper in the data areas which need to be undone upon backtracking. This is taken care of by

- The *Trail*: where variable instantiations which need to be undone are recorded. These entries are used on backtracking to restore the corresponding variables to "uninstantiated". This is called "detrailing" or "unwinding" the *Trail*.

In addition to the data areas (*Code/Stack/Heap/Trail*) there are other elements in the design of the **WAM**: a number of argument registers (called A or X registers) are used for passing arguments when a procedure (i.e. a collection of clauses with the same head functor and number of arguments) is called. There is also a small "Push-Down List" (*PDL*) which is used by the recursive general purpose unification routine.

Prolog programs are compiled into a series of instructions which perform different operations on the above mentioned areas. In order to broadly describe the function of some of these instructions, we will follow a normal procedure call ("goal invocation") sequence: the first step involves loading the argument registers (A1 through An, where n is the number of arguments in the call -the Arity of the procedure) with the appropriate values; *"put"* instructions are used for this purpose. The procedure is then called (*"call/execute"* instructions). Upon entry into a procedure, a *choice point* is created if it has more than one alternative (*"try"* instructions) and then each of the terms in the head of the clause is unified (*"get/unify"* instructions) with the corresponding argument loaded in (or pointed to by) the argument register. If unification does not succeed, failure occurs and backtracking to the last *choice point* will occur as described above. *"Get"* instructions are basically used to encode at compile-time cases where unification defaults to a simple assignment or a set of very simple determinate steps. Because the main activity of a Prolog program is centered around unification of goals with candidate clauses, the simplification of this step results in important performance improvements.

The **WAM** offers many other features designed towards improving speed and space economy, such as

[4]This is really only true if the clause has "permanent variables".

retrieval of all used space upon backtracking, last call optimization, "*environment trimming*" etc. Instructions are also provided for supporting the technique of indexing the clauses based on the first argument. This reduces the number of alternatives to be tried and has an important role in improving execution speed and detecting determinate cases.

3.2 Extending the WAM for Parallel Execution

Several issues have to be taken care of in order to extend the sequential **WAM** for AND-Parallel execution. Support has to be provided for the forward execution semantics described in section 2: upon arrival at a parallel call, some scheduling mechanism has to assign available work (i.e. the parallel goals) to the available processors. Also, some data structure has to be provided to keep track of the state of execution of parallel siblings. Of course, this has to be done in an as efficient and unobtrusive as possible way, so that all the performance advantages of the **WAM** are retained. Figure 2 shows one processor of the Restricted AND-Parallel Abstract Machine[5] . Clearly, each "processor" is equivalent to a standard **WAM** except for the addition of a "*Goal Stack*" and the inclusion of "*Parcall Frames*" in the local *Stack*, together with *environments* and *choice points*. These additions will be described in the rest of this section.

Support also has to be provided for the backward execution algorithm being used. Because of space limitations, in this paper we will be mainly concerned with forward execution. However, the basic elements for *local goals first* backtracking [10] are also included in the description for reference.

3.2.1 The Goal Stack

As seen in figure 2, each processor has a private *Goal Stack* (pointed to by **GS**) where goals which are ready to be executed in parallel can be pushed on to. Each entry in the *Goal Stack* is called a *Goal Frame*. A *Goal Frame* contains all necessary information for remote execution of the goal. In particular, it contains the following items:

- **Procedure_name**: points to the first instruction of the procedure to be executed.
- **P(1),...,P(n) registers**: Parameter Registers. They are a copy of the n argument registers for the procedure.
- **#of parameters**: this cell contains "n", the *Arity* of the procedure.
- *Parcall Frame* **Pointer (EPF)**: identifies which *Parcall Frame* this goal corresponds to.
- **Slot #**: identifies which slot in the *Parcall Frame* this goal corresponds to.

When a *parallel call* (a **CGE** whose "checks" succeed) is arrived at, all goals can be pushed on to the *Goal Stack*. Then a goal can be "stolen" from this stack by a "remote" processor, which will copy the parameter registers into its argument registers, load **P** with the address of "Procedure_name", and start execution from there. A goal can also be picked up from its own *Goal Stack* by the **local** processor (the one which just pushed it there), using the same technique.

3.2.2 The Parcall Frame

Entries in the *Goal Stack* completely disappear after they are "picked up" by remote processors. An additional data structure is thus needed in the local processor in order to:

1. keep track during forward execution of the parallel activities of the children processors which "picked up" the goals inside a parallel call,

---

[5] In this paper we will assume one process per processor for simplicity.

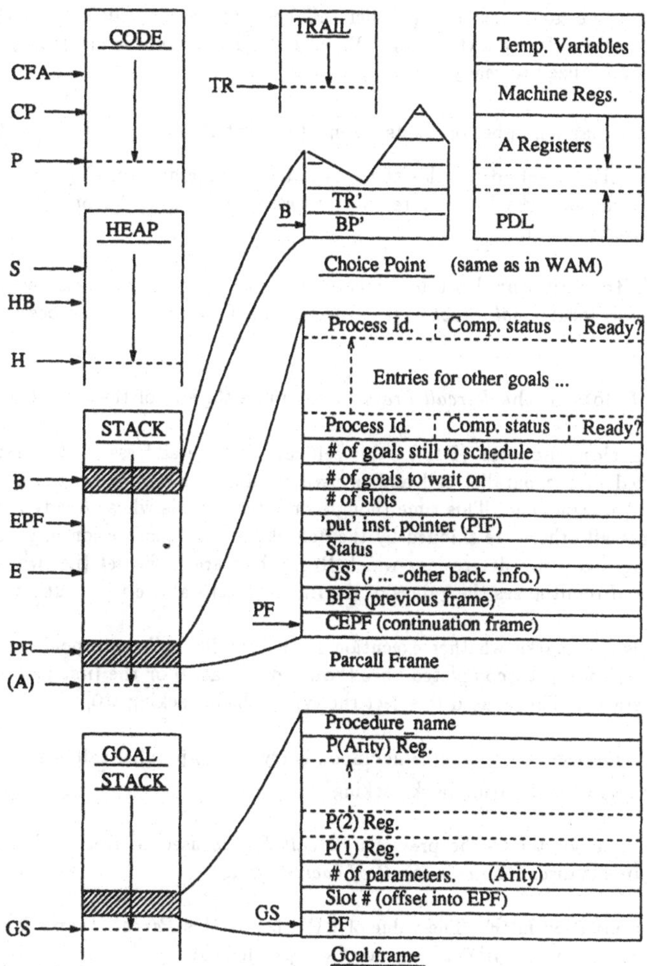

Figure 2: Data areas and registers for one processor of the Extended **RAP-WAM**

2. select the appropriate actions during backtracking.

We will call this structure a "*Parcall Frame*". One *Parcall Frame* is created for each parallel call. For each goal available for execution in parallel (i.e. for each goal pushed on to the *Goal Stack*) within this parallel call, there is one *slot* in the *Parcall Frame*. Each one of these slots has the following fields:

- **Process Id.**: this field contains the id. of the processor which picked up the corresponding goal. If it was the local processor, this field is marked accordingly ("*")[6].
- **Completion Status**: this is a one bit field, set by the corresponding processor when it returns, marking whether it still has alternatives or not.
- **Ready/NotReady**: this is also a one bit field, used (by the "check_ready" instruction) to select the goals that are actually going to be pushed on to the *Goal Stack*. It is used when

[6] If "local goals first" backtracking is used, the order in which the goals are picked up also has to be stored. A simple way of doing this is by recording the current value of the outgoing goals counter described below.

only *some* of the goals inside a parallel call need to be scheduled, as is the case during forward execution after backtracking. When a *Parcall Frame* is created, all Ready bits in all slots are initialized to ready.

In addition to a variable number of "slots", some fixed entries are needed in the *Parcall Frame*:

- **# of goals still to schedule**: this cell is initialized to the number of goals to be executed in parallel. Each time the local or remote processors take a goal from the *Goal Stack* this number is decremented.

- **# of goals to wait on**: this cell is incremented by a remote processor when it "steals" a goal from the local *Goal Stack*. It is decremented every time a processor returns with success.

- **Total # of slots in the** ***Parcall Frame***: determines the size of the *Parcall Frame*.

- **Put instructions pointer (PIP)**: this cell contains the address of the first instruction of the first goal in the parallel call and is used to start pushing goals again on to the *Goal Stack* after backtracking. This time though, only those goals whose Ready field is set will be pushed, since all others are skipped by the "check_ready" instruction in front of them. The backtracking algorithm determines which Ready bits are to be set (i.e. which goals will be restarted) and reinitializes the values of the first two cells above to the appropriate value.

- **Status**: this cell marks whether execution of the parallel call corresponding to this *Parcall Frame* has already been completed once (**"outside"** status) or the first pass is still going on (**"inside"** status). This is used to select the type of backtracking [10].

- **GS' (, ...)**: the top of the *Goal Stack* upon entry to the parallel call is saved in this cell so that it can be restored during backtracking[7].

- **BPF**: this is a pointer to the previous *Parcall Frame* used to reset **PF** when the current *Parcall Frame* is discarded *as a result of backtracking.*

- **CEPF**: continuation **EPF**. The value of **EPF** before this *Parcall Frame* is created is saved here. It is used to reset **EPF** after exiting the parallel call.

Parcall Frames are just one more type of object which resides in the local *Stack*, together with *environments* and *choice points*. **PF** is an extra machine register which always points to the last *Parcall Frame*, i.e. the one which will be used for backtracking in the event of failure [10] (much in the same manner as **B** always points to the last *choice point*). **EPF** in turn, always points to the *current Parcall Frame*, i.e. the one being used for the management of scheduled goals.

3.3 General Operation of the Extended RAP-WAM

As stated before, each "processor" (figure 2) is equivalent to a standard **WAM** with a complete set of registers and stacks. This includes the new "*Goal Stack*" and the addition of "*Parcall Frames*" to *environments* and *choice points* in the local *Stack*. Note that there is also a new pointer into the *Code* area (**CFA** --"Check fail address") which points to the code which should be executed if the conditions in the **CGE** fail, i.e. the sequential code.

---

[7] Depending on the particular type of backtracking strategy being used, other backtracking information may also be saved (see [10]).

As soon as processor "steals" a goal (a *Goal Frame*) from another processor's *Goal Stack*, it will start working on it by loading its argument registers from the parameter registers in the *Goal Frame* and fetching instructions starting at the location (procedure address) received. The local stacks will then grow (and shrink) as indicated by the semantics of the standard **WAM** instructions it is executing. It will be the "local" processor for this instruction stream and its data areas will be the "local *Stack*", "local *Heap*", and "local *Trail*", etc. Note though, that the *environments* in its local *Stack* and the data structures in its local *Heap will contain references to the data areas of ancestor processors.* The character of these references will vary depending on the memory organization used in the underlying architecture (i.e. from absolute addresses for uniform addressing space, shared memory architectures to, for example, Pid./remote-address pairs for non-shared memories). Also note that although there might be reading conflicts (two or more processors trying to read the same memory location), there can be no writing conflicts if the **CGE**'s have been generated correctly! The ill-effects of reading conflicts on performance are much easier to avoid than those of writing conflicts, for example by using multiported memories and/or data caching. Also all synchronization is guaranteed by the wait instructions marking parallel call boundaries. This will become more clear after the instruction set has been introduced and an example commented on, but it shows how all program or data dependent control and synchronization issues are concealed within the semantics of the **CGE**'s.

Execution obviously differs from normal **WAM** execution when a parallel call is reached. In this case, a *Parcall Frame* is created in the local *Stack* and its goals are pushed on to the *Goal Stack*, ready to be picked up by the local processor or other remote processors. These remote processors will in turn work on their assigned goals growing their own stacks with references to ancestor stacks. Eventually all dependents of the processor we are looking at will terminate and, if no failures occur, success will be reported to the parent. However, there may be some entries (i.e. *choice points*, if the goal still has alternatives) left in the local *Stack*, some data structures in the local *Heap* that ancestors need to access (the "output" of the procedure), and also some entries in the *Trail*. This is left this way, and when the next goal is received its data structures can be grown above these[8]. This space is only retrieved upon local failure, or if a kill message is received from the parent processor (because of a failure there or in some other related processor), much in the same way as in the sequential **WAM**.

Note that if an appropriate ordering of events is chosen (for example, if processors which still have underlying *Stack* or *Heap* segments only take goals from siblings of their last goal or their dependents) then a kill message necessarily always refers to the last goal executed (i.e. to the last set of structures on the *Stack*) and space is always retrieved from the top of the *Stack* or *Heap* as in the sequential model. Local unwinding of the *Trail* will undo any bindings done outside the local data areas. This unwinding of the distributed *Trail* is done completely in parallel by all the AND-siblings which receive "kill" messages. Also note that with the above mentioned ordering of events, a "redo" message, when received, always refers to the last *choice point* in the local *Stack* and it can be executed just as if a local failure had occurred!

3.4 The Extended RAP-WAM Instruction Set

In the current version, all **WAM** instructions are supported in addition to the new instructions implementing AND-Parallelism, but we will not list the **WAM** instruction set here since it is widely available. Note how, although "check" instructions are somewhat particular to the implementation of **RAP**, all other instructions could be used in any AND-Parallel system.

---

[8]Note that the current pointers into the data areas should be saved at this point (see section 3.6), in order to detect, for example, goal failure (i.e. $\mathbf{B} <$ top of the stack when the goal was "picked up")

3.4.1 Check Instructions

Check instructions are used to encode the "conditions" in a **CGE**. Two types of checks[9] ("ground" and "independent") and a branch instruction are provided. Note that by combining these, any kind of disjunctions or conjunctions of checks on any number of variables can be expressed:

check_me_else Label

- load check failure address with Label (**CFA**=Label).

check_ground Vn

- dereference register Vn and check to see if its contents are ground. If so, continue with next instruction; otherwise **P**=**CFA** (i.e. branch to Check Failure Address).

check_independent Vn,Vm

- dereference Vn and Vm. If they are independent, next instruction; otherwise **P**=**CFA**.

3.4.2 Goal Scheduling Instructions

These are the instructions used for pushing goals with their arguments on to the *Goal Stack* and for picking up these goals in the local processor:

push_call Procedure_name/Arity,Slot#

- request exclusive access to *Goal Stack*; push on to the *Goal Stack*: "Procedure_name", registers A_{Arity}, $A_{Arity-1}$, ...A_1, "Arity" ("n"), Slot# (i.e. offset from **EPF** for the slot corresponding to this goal), and current **EPF** pointer; release access to *Goal Stack*.

The arguments should be first loaded into the argument (A) registers using normal "put" instructions (as for a conventional "call"). Then, they will be transferred in one block to the *Goal Stack* with the push_call instruction. This eliminates the need for new "put" instructions and minimizes the time the *Goal Stack* is locked.

pop_pending_goal

- if no goals are pending to be scheduled ("# of goals to schedule" in *Parcall Frame* = 0), continue with next instruction; else pop a goal from the local *Goal Stack*.

This instruction is used by the local processor to pop a goal from its own *Goal Stack* for local execution. The corresponding slot in the *Parcall Frame* (as indicated by "Slot #" in the *Goal Frame*) is marked as "local" and the arguments are popped back from the *Goal Stack* to the local argument registers. Then **P** is loaded with the address of "Procedure_name" and execution continues from there. The continuation for forward execution is set to return to this instruction, so that when this goal finally succeeds, the next one can also be popped from the *Goal Stack*. This process continues until there are no more goals left (# of goals to schedule = 0). The next instruction is then executed.

3.4.3 Control Instructions

These instructions take care of the control issues involved in a parallel call: creating and deleting *Parcall Frames*, selecting the goals to schedule and waiting for children to report results.

---

[9]DeGroot's algorithms can be used to efficiently perform the checks. Note that any "conservative" algorithm can be used, i.e. one that never declares two dependent variables as independent although it may give up on complicated terms or long dereferencing chains.

allocate_pcall_frame **#_of_slots,M**

This instruction creates a properly initialized *Parcall Frame* in the local *Stack* with the correct number of slots. M, the number of "permanent variables" still needed in the *environment* is used to extend the concept of *environment trimming.* **EPF** and **PF** now point to the top of the stack.

check_ready **Slot_#,Label**

- Check that slot in **EPF**. If not ready, jump to Label; else, continue with next instruction.

Check_ready instructions are used to skip those goals whose slots are marked as "NotReady" in the *Parcall Frame* so that they are not pushed on to the *Goal Stack*. This is useful during backtracking, as only some of the goals inside a parallel call may need to be restarted after failure.

wait_on_siblings

- wait until "# of goals to wait on" in current *Parcall Frame* is 0; then, restore **EPF** from the *Parcall Frame* (**EPF**=**CEPF**), change status to "**outside**" (if it is "**inside**"), and go on to next instruction.

An extension of last call optimization can be implemented in the wait_on_siblings instruction by discarding the current *Parcall Frame* (**PF**=**BPF**) if all slots in it are either "local" or they have no alternatives: the frame is not needed in these cases because there are no goals to backtrack into inside it. However, the Pid's of the processors involved should be "trailed" so that the necessary "unwind" messages are sent to them during backtracking.

3.5 An Example

This example illustrates the code generated by the compiler for a simple clause. The comments provided explain the operation of the instructions involved. Suppose this is the original "Prolog" clause as written by the user in the source program[10] :

```
f(X,Y,Z):- a(X,Y), b(X,Y), c(X,Y), d(X,Y,Z), e(X,Y,Z).
```

The Graph Expression generated by the compiler after its analysis might be:

```
f(X,Y,Z):- a(X,Y), (ground(X,Y) | b(X,Y) & c(X,Y) & d(X,Y,Z)), e(X,Y,Z).
```

Obviously, in this graph expression it is expected that **a** will ground `X` and `Y`. In this case, "`ground(X,Y)`" will succeed and then **b**, **c**, and **d** can run in parallel. Otherwise they will run sequentially and the annotated clause will execute the same instructions as the original one would have in a conventional system. The code that the compiler would generate for the clause above follows. Since there is in general no point in pushing *all* goals in the parallel call on to the *Goal Stack* (the local processor is going to pick one up immediately) one of them (**d**) is called locally without going through the *Goal Stack*. In order to understand the first part of the example, note that at the point of entering this code the calling procedure has already loaded registers A_1, A_2, and A_3 with the arguments for **f**:

```
f/3:                                | (Entry point for procedure f)
     allocate                       | Push an environment on to the stack. It will
                                    | have space for "X"(Y3), "Y"(Y2) and "Z"(Y1)
     -----------------------------------------------------------------------------
                                    | HEAD INSTRUCTIONS: f(X,Y,Z):- ...
     get_variable   "X",A1          | X <- (A1)  Unify (just "get" in this case) the
     get_variable   "Y",A2          | Y <- (A2)  arguments (X,Y,Z) from the parameter
     get_variable   "Z",A3          | Z <- (A3)  registers into the environment.
```

---

10 This clause is purposedly chosen so that the code generated is as simple as possible (no "unsafe variables", no special unification instructions) in attention to the reader with no previous exposure to **WAM** code. Also some of the instructions are obviously unnecessary but leaving them there makes it easier to visualize the structure of the code.

```
                                | BODY INSTRUCTIONS: ... :- a(X,Y), ...
     put_value "X",A1           | (X) -> A1  Load argument registers from the
     put_value "Y",A2           | (Y) -> A2  environment for a.
     call  a/2,3                |            Call a.
-----------------------------------------------------------------------------
                                | ... ( ground(X,Y) | ...
     check_me_else SEQ_CODE     | Set the address to branch to in
                                | case the conditions fail (CFA).
     check_ground  "X"          | X ground?  if not go to SEQ_CODE
     check_ground  "Y"          | Y ground?  if not go to SEQ_CODE
-----------------------------------------------------------------------------
                                | The checks succeeded: parallel execution.
     allocate_pcall_frame 2,3   | First, create a Parcall Frame in the stack with
                                | 2 slots (slot 1 for c, slot 2 for b)
                                | (3 is # of perm. vars. -used for env. trimming)
-----------------------------------------------------------------------------
P_I_P:                          | ... | b(X,Y) & ...
     check_ready 2,PUSH_C       | See if slot 2 in Parcall Frame (i.e. "b") is
                                | ready (always true except when backtracking);
                                | else, jump to PUSH_C (skip this goal)
     put_value "X",A1           | (X) -> A1   Load argument registers from the
     put_value "Y",A2           | (Y) -> A2   environment for b.
     push_call b/2,2            | Push call to "b" with its arguments on to Goal
                                | Stack (it can now be "stolen" by another proc.)
PUSH_C:                         |
     check_ready 1,CALL_D       | ... & c(X,Y) & ...
     put_value "X",A1           | (same as b above)
     put_value "Y",A2           |
     push_call c/2,1            |
-----------------------------------------------------------------------------
CALL_D:                         | ... & d(X,Y,Z) ) ...
     put_value "X",A1           | (X) -> A1   Load argument registers from the
     put_value "Y",A2           | (Y) -> A2   environment for d.
     put_value "Z",A3           | (Z) -> A3
     call d/3,0                 | "d" is executed locally (normal call)
-----------------------------------------------------------------------------
     pop_pending_goal           | If no goals are pending, next instruction;
                                | else execute remaining goals locally.
     wait_on_siblings           | Wait until all "remote" goals in the
                                | Parcall Frame have returned.
     execute  CALL_E            | Go on to execute "e" (CALL_E).
-----------------------------------------------------------------------------
SEQ_CODE:                       | Checks failed: sequential execution.
     put_value  "X",A1          | (X) -> A1   Normal WAM code for executing b,
     put_value  "Y",A2          | (Y) -> A2   c, and d sequentially.
     call  b/2,3                | call "b".
                                |
     put_value  "X",A1          | (X) -> A1
     put_value  "Y",A2          | (Y) -> A2
     call  c/2,3                | call "c".
                                |
     put_value  "X",A1          | (X) -> A1
     put_value  "Y",A2          | (Y) -> A2
     put_value  "Z",A3          | (Z) -> A3
     call  d/3,3                | call "d".
-----------------------------------------------------------------------------
CALL_E:                         | "Normal" WAM call to "e".
     put_value  Y3,A1           | (X) -> A1
     put_value  Y2,A2           | (Y) -> A2
     put_value  Y1,A3           | (Z) -> A3
     deallocate                 | Discard environment: last call optimization.
     execute  e/3               | Execute "e".
```

3.6 Other Non-Instruction Related Actions: fail/ kill/ redo ...

In addition to the operations associated with particular instructions, each processor has to support other actions resulting from exceptions such as messages arriving from other processors or failure. These actions obviously differ somewhat from the corresponding ones in a sequential implementation. Due to space limitations we will only sketch some of them in this section:

- **failure**: in the Restricted AND-Parallel Abstract Machine, there are several cases of backtracking depending on the origin of the failure (the local processor or one of the remote processors) and also on the state of the computation ("**inside**" vs. "**outside**" backtracking) [10]. However, thanks to the existence of *Parcall Frames*, the operations involved remain similar to those in the sequential implementation: *local failure* is treated in the same way as in the **WAM** unless the "last" *choice entry* on the *Stack* is a *Parcall Frame* (**PF** > **B**) in which case the backtracking algorithm is applied to it, in order to select the goals to be "killed" or "restarted". *Remote failure*, i.e. failure coming from a different processor, basically involves undoing all local work done since the *Parcall Frame* associated with the failed goal was pushed on to the *Stack* (sending "kill" or "unwind" messages to all remote slots in *Parcall Frames* above it), and applying the backtracking algorithm to that *Parcall Frame*. These actions are explained in more detail in [9] and [10].

- **kill**: kill is a message which can arrive from the parent processor indicating that the goal being solved in the local processor is not useful any more and should be discarded: reset all registers to goal invocation point (i.e. throw away everything since execution of the goal was started), unwind the *Trail* until the last goal invocation point (i.e. undo all bindings in ancestors), reinitialize, go to idle. If there are any *Parcall Frames* in the *Stack*, all Pid.'s in non-local slots in them have to be sent kill messages also. Note how the values of all pointers before a goal is received (entries can still remain in the *Stack* or *Heap* from previous goals) have to be saved in order to do this. This remains an implementation issue but it can be solved using a small independent push-down list or "input goal markers" in the *Stack*.

- **redo**: redo is also received from the parent processor after reporting a solution which had a *choice point* available (i.e. after reporting "success with alternatives"). It is executed just as if local failure had occurred: go to the first *choice point* (or **PF**) on the *Stack*, continue with next alternative.

- **unwind**: this message is sent by the parent when backtracking, to a processor without alternatives but with a segment of the *Trail* pending. The *Trail* is unwound and the *Heap* is flushed to the point before the goal was received.

4 Conclusions

In the previous sections we have presented an AND-Parallel Abstract Machine level execution model for logic programs, based on combining the techniques used in the **WAM** with the advantages of **RAP** in dealing with variable binding conflicts. The same abstract machine and basic instruction set could also support with minor modifications many other AND-Parallel models and serve as a target for compilation of a variety of logic programming languages.

We feel that other solutions previously proposed lack the potential for storage efficiency and performance improvement that the Warren Abstract Machine has brought to the sequential logic programming arena. Conversely, we argue that this model is an attractive vehicle for the implementation of AND-Parallelism: the compatibility with conventional **WAM** code makes sequential speed almost identical to that of the **WAM** and permits the use of current **WAM** compiler technology. Simultaneously, most **WAM** optimizations are still supported, even during parallel execution. Also, a form of restricted intelligent backtracking is provided with virtually no additional overhead. "Soft" degradation of performance with resource exhaustion and user-transparent distributed control are attained as well.

The description in this paper has dealt mainly with *forward execution* at the abstract machine level. We have also covered other areas of the design, such as the backtracking algorithm [10], goal scheduling and memory management issues, and a more detailed system architecture. These results will be reported elsewhere. The reader can find more specific information regarding some of these subjects in [9]. Still, there are many areas in which work remains to be done, both in depth (i.e. further specification and implementation of the design) and breath (i.e. inclusion of other types of parallelism, support for a more sophisticated database interface etc.). Issues of interest which we are currently investigating are: a backtracking scheme which preserves the conventional ordering of alternatives, optimizations for determinate execution, development of better heuristics for the automatic generation of **CGE**'s, and treatment of cut and other side effects, etc.

5 Acknowledgements

The parallel abstract machine is built by extending the Warren Abstract Machine to support Restricted AND-Parallelism and therefore owes much to the work of David Warren and Doug DeGroot. The author would like to thank Roger Nasr for his interesting suggestions and for explaining many of the intricacies of the **WAM**. Also thanks to Chua-Huang Huang, Richard Warren, and David Warren for their valuable comments and observations. Finally, the author is indebted to all the members of the MCC ACA/Parallel Processing group for their encouragement, and to MCC for its support.

References

[1] J.-H. Chang, A. M. Despain, and D. DeGroot.
AND-parallelism of Logic Programs Based on Static Data Dependency Analysis.
In *Digest of Papers of COMPCON Spring '85*, pages 218-225. 1985.

[2] K. Clark and S. Gregory.
PARLOG: A Parallel Logic Programming Language.
Research Report DOC 83/5, Dept. of Computing, Imperial College of Science and Technology, May, 1983.
University of London.

[3] Clark, K.L. and G. McCabe.
The Control Facilities of IC-Prolog.
Expert Systems in the Micro Electronic Age.
Edinburgh University Press, 1979.

[4] J.S. Conery and D.F. Kibler.
Parallel Interpretation of Logic Programs.
In *Proc. of the ACM Conference on Functional Programming Languages and Computer Architecture.*, pages 163-170. October, 1981.

[5] J.S. Conery.
The AND/OR Process Model for Parallel Interpretation of Logic Programs.
PhD thesis, The University of California at Irvine, 1983.
Technical Report 204.

[6] Doug DeGroot.
Restricted And-Parallelism.
Int'l Conf. on Fifth Generation Computer Systems , November, 1984.

[7] T. P. Dobry, A. M. Despain, and Y. N. Patt.
Performance Studies of a Prolog Machine Architecture.
In *Proceedings of the 12 Int'l. Symp. on Computer Architecture*, pages 180-191. IEEE Computer Society Press, 1985.

[8] John Gabriel, Tim Lindholm, E. L. Lusk, and R. A. Overbeek.
A Tutorial on the Warren Abstract Machine.
Technical Report, Argonne National Laboratory, Argonne, Ill. 60439, 1985.

[9] Manuel V. Hermenegildo.
A Restricted AND-parallel Execution Model and Abstract Machine for Prolog Programs.
Technical Report PP-104-85, Microelectronics and Computer Technology Corporation (MCC), Austin, TX 78759, 1985.

[10] Manuel V. Hermenegildo and Roger I. Nasr.
Efficient Implementation of Backtracking in AND-parallelism.
In *Proceedings of the 3rd. Int'l. Conf. on Logic Programming.* Springer-Verlag, 1986.

[11] Kowalski, R.A.
Predicate Logic as a Programming Language.
Proc. IFIPS 74 , 1974.

[12] R. A. Overbeek, J. Gabriel, T. Lindholm, and E. L. Lusk.
Prolog on Multiprocessors.
Technical Report, Argonne National Laboratory, Argonne, Ill. 60439, 1985.

[13] Luis M. Pereira and Roger I. Nasr.
Delta-Prolog: A Distributed Logic Programming Language.
In *Proceedings of the Intl. Conf. on 5th. Gen. Computer Systems.* 1984.
Japan.

[14] Pereira, L.M., F. C. N. Pereira, and D. H. D. Warren.
User's Guide to DECsystem-10 Prolog
Dept. of Artificial Intelligence, Univ. of Edinburgh, 1978.

[15] E. Y. Shapiro.
A subset of Concurrent Prolog and its interpreter.
Technical Report TR-003, ICOT, January, 1983.
Tokyo.

[16] E. Tick and D.H.D. Warren.
Towards a Pipelined Prolog Processor.
In *1984 International Symposium on Logic Programming, Atlantic City*, pages 29-42. IEEE Computer Society Press, Silver Spring, MD, February, 1984.

[17] David H. D. Warren.
An Abstract Prolog Instruction Set.
Technical Note 309, SRI International, AI Center, Computer Science and Technology Division, 1983.

Efficient Management of Backtracking in AND-Parallelism

M. V. Hermenegildo[1]

R. I. Nasr[2]

Abstract

A backtracking algorithm for AND-Parallelism and its implementation at the Abstract Machine level are presented: first, a class of AND-Parallelism models based on goal independence is defined, and a generalized version of Restricted AND-Parallelism (**RAP**) introduced as characteristic of this class. A simple and efficient backtracking algorithm for **RAP** is then discussed. An implementation scheme is presented for this algorithm which offers minimum overhead, while retaining the performance and storage economy of sequential implementations and taking advantage of goal independence to avoid unnecessary backtracking ("restricted intelligent backtracking"). Finally, the implementation of backtracking in sequential and AND-Parallel systems is explained through a number of examples.

KEYWORDS: LOGIC PROGRAMMING, PARALLEL PROCESSING, INTELLIGENT BACKTRACKING, AND-PARALLELISM, PROLOG.

1 Introduction[3]

The execution of logic programs [9] in parallel is a subject of great interest because of the dual relationship between logic and parallelism: parallel execution seems to be a promising way of increasing the execution speed of logic programs; logic programs in turn offer multiple sources of parallelism [4] so that concurrency can (ideally) be uncovered automatically (or expressed cleanly) and mapped onto parallel architectures.

Of the several types of parallelism present in logic programs, we are specially interested in **AND-Parallelism**, because it offers the advantage that, in general, all work done by a collection of AND-Parallel processes is "useful" for finding a particular solution to a query. If OR-Parallelism is supported in addition to AND-Parallelism, backtracking is not needed; a set of "solutions" is maintained instead for each goal invocation. While the relative simplicity of this solution and the additional source of parallelism make it attractive in principle, keeping multiple solutions around simultaneously obviously tends to complicate data storage management and use up excessive amounts of it. Moreover, the additional parallelism often leads to combinatorial explosion of the search space.

---

[1]Department of Electrical and Computer Engineering, The University of Texas at Austin; Austin, TX 78712.

[2]Digital Equipment Corporation, Assigned Representative, Microelectronics and Computer Technology Corporation, Artificial Intelligence Program; 9430 Research Boulevard, Austin, TX 78759.

[3]This research was partially supported by the Microelectronics and Computer Technology Corporation (MCC).

As an alternative, we have presented a parallel abstract machine [7] [8] capable of implementing AND-Parallelism with very similar storage efficiencies and sequential-mode speed to that of the best sequential implementations. This is achieved in part by using backtracking rather than OR-Parallelism in the management of alternative paths in the search tree, and by implementing a stacking strategy with full space recovery on backtracking, as in sequential systems. In this paper we will deal with the problem of finding a suitable backtracking algorithm for this very general model of AND-Parallel execution, which can be implemented with minimum overhead, is compatible with the storage management strategy, and still takes advantage of the information available at run-time regarding goal independence in order to avoid unnecessary backtracking.

The organization of the paper is as follows: first, we will introduce "goal independence" models of AND-Parallelism and present a generalized version of Restricted AND-Parallelism (**RAP**) as a typical representative of this class. An efficient backtracking algorithm will then be elaborated for **RAP**. We will also study a suitable implementation strategy for this scheme capable of retaining most of the efficiency of sequential systems. Finally, some conclusions will be presented.

2 A General Model for AND-Parallelism: Goal Independence

Conery [5] showed how "brute force" exploitation of AND-Parallelism (i.e. the automatic scheduling of a process for every goal in the body of a clause) leads to binding conflicts if the goals involved have variables in common. This can occur even in cases where the goals appear not to share variables at all. Consider the following clause:

```
crew(X,Y):- pilot(X), radio_operator(Y).
```

During the resolution of a query of the form "`?- crew(X,X).`" (looking for a person who is a pilot and can also operate a radio) X and Y in the clause above are coerced to be the same through unification. Thus, we cannot go ahead and evaluate "`pilot(X)`" and "`radio_operator(Y)`" in parallel (AND-Parallelism) because of the potential of conflicting instantiations for the identical variables X and Y.

Many approaches have been proposed in order to detect and deal with these variable binding conflicts either at compile-time or at run-time. Some of them, attempt to solve these conflicts without variable annotations and with minimal (or no) information from the user [5] [1] [6]. In other approaches, the user is required to annotate some variables or goals in the program in order to identify goals as "readers" or "writers" for each variable. This and other techniques are used in Concurrent Prolog [11], Parlog [2], IC-Prolog [3], Delta-Prolog [10] etc.

Although an interesting issue, we will not be concerned in this paper with the origin of these annotations. Instead, we will concentrate on dealing with how execution proceeds once a set of goals has been determined as being (variable-wise) independent, (i.e. after determining that they can be run in parallel with no conflicts) and, in particular, on how backtracking can still be efficiently supported in such an environment[4] . Consequently, rather than analyzing a particular source-level language, we will focus on an *intermediate code level* useful for a variety of programming languages, and we will pursue development of an efficient execution model for it. This level, which will be discussed in the next section, can be best described as *horn clauses augmented with literal-level conditional control expressions*. Such control expressions can, for example, be generated when a static analysis uncovers parallel execution potential. Alternatively, the source language could provide the user with the syntactic tools to explicitly trigger their generation.

[4] This is in contrast with other approaches [11] [2] where "don't know" non-determinism has been given up in order to improve efficiency or simplify the implementation.

Concerning the character of these expressions, note that in logic programs, the same clause can be used in various ways, depending on the run-time polarity (instantiation state) of interceding variables. Ideally, these expressions should be capable of dealing with the different cases involved, with a minimum of run-time overhead. *Restricted AND-Parallelism* (**RAP**) [6] is a technique which provides this capability by making it possible to choose at run-time between parallel and sequential execution (i.e. to generate several possible execution graphs) based on variable dependency checks. Such run-time determinations are embodied in what has been referred to as *Conditional Graph Expressions* (**CGE**'s). In the next section we will present a generalized version of such a computation model which subsumes DeGroot's original definition of **RAP** and **CGE**'s. It will be the backtracking behavior of this generalized model that we will study in the subsequent sections.

3 Forward Execution

As explained above, **CGE**'s can be used for reducing run-time data dependency analysis overhead for AND-Parallel logic programming systems to a number of simple checks. Herein, a **CGE** is (informally) defined as a series of conditions followed by a conjunction of goals, i.e.:

```
( <CONDITIONS> | goal1 & goal2 & ... & goalN )
```

where "<CONDITIONS>" represents *any number of conjunctions or disjunctions of checks on a* **<variable_list>**. A **<variable_list>** is a collection of variable names which have their first occurrence before (i.e. "to the left of", in Prolog) the <CONDITIONS> field of the current graph expression[5]. In this definition **CGE**'s can appear in the body of a clause in any place a conventional goal may be placed. Therefore they can also appear in a goal position *inside* a **CGE** (nested **CGE**'s). Types of checks which can appear inside <CONDITIONS> are:

- **ground(<variable_list>**): evaluates to ***true*** if and only if all variables in **<variable_list>** are ground, i.e. they are instantiated to a term with no uninstantiated variables.

- **independent(<variable_list>**): We associate with each variable its "set of contained variables" (**SCV**), defined as follows: If the variable is instantiated to a fully ground term, the **SCV** is ***empty***. If the variable is uninstantiated, the **SCV** is the singleton containing the variable itself. If the variable is instantiated to a term, and some of its arguments are variables, the **SCV** is recursively defined as the union of the **SCV**'s for each of those variables. The **independent(<variable_list>**) check succeeds if and only if the intersection of all the **SCV**'s associated with each variable in **< variable_list >** is ***empty***[6].

- The logical values **true** and **false**.

Since each of the checks inside **<CONDITIONS>** will evaluate to **true** or **false**, **<CONDITIONS>**, being constructed as conjunctions and/or disjunctions of these checks, will also eventually evaluate to **true** or **false**. The forward semantics of **CGE**'s dictates that:

> *if <CONDITIONS> evaluates to true, then all expressions inside the **CGE** **can** execute in parallel. Otherwise, they **must** be executed sequentially and in the order in which they appear within the expression.*

---

[5]i.e. only those variables in the head or in goals to the left of the current **CGE** (including those in a **CGE** the current expression may be nested in) can be checked.

[6]Much more economical independence algorithms (such as DeGroot's [6]) can be used in practice, as long as they are conservative, i.e. they never declare a set of dependent variables as independent (although they may "give up" and declare some variables as dependent rather than traversing very complex terms).

An example will clarify this further. Suppose we have the following clause:

```
f(X,Y) :- g(X,Y), h(X), k(Y).
```

In general, the three goals in the body of **f** (**g**, **h** and **k**) cannot run in parallel because they have variables in common. Nevertheless, if both X and Y are ground when **f** is called, all goals can then run in parallel. This fact can be expressed by using the following **CGE**:

```
f(X,Y) :- ( ground(X,Y) | g(X,Y) & h(X) & k(Y) )
```

According to the forward execution semantics above, this means that X and Y should be checked and, if they are both ground, then **g**, **h**, and **k** can be executed in parallel and execution will proceed to the right of the expression only after all goals inside succeed. Note that this also means that if X and Y are ground but for some reason (for example, lack of free processors) **g**, **h**, and **k** are executed sequentially, this can be done in any order. Otherwise, if X and Y are not both ground, **g**, **h**, and **k** will run sequentially and in the order in which they appear inside the **CGE**. Selection between one mode of execution and the other is done by a simple run-time check. Of course the expression above only takes care of a rather trivial case. A more interesting execution behavior can be extracted from the following expression:

```
f(X,Y) :- ( ground(X,Y) | g(X,Y) & ( indep(X,Y) | h(X) & k(Y) ) ).
```

Now, if X and Y are not ground upon entry to the graph expression, **g** will be executed first. As soon as **g** succeeds, indep(X,Y) is checked in the hope that X and Y will be independent (either because one of them was ground by **g** or because they are still uninstantiated and do not "share" --as they would if **g** had matched against "**g**(X,X)."). If they are still independent then **h** and **k** can run in parallel. Note that if X and Y are ground upon entry of **f** then *all* goals will run in parallel as in the previous expression.

Sometimes it is necessary to express the fact that a number of goals can run in parallel, independently of any other consideration (perhaps because the programmer knows how a procedure is going to be used). This can be easily accomplished by writing **true** in place of **<conditions>** or eliminating the **<conditions>** field altogether. Thus, in the following expressions, g, h, and k can always run in parallel:

```
f(X,Y) :- ( true | g(X) & h(Y) & k(Z) ).

f(X,Y) :- ( g(X) & h(Y) & k(Z) ).
```

This illustrates how **CGE**'s are a superset of other control annotation schemes such as the parallel connective of Delta-Prolog ("/") [10].

4 Backward Execution

We refer to backward execution as the series of actions that follow failure in the head or body of a clause. In normal (i.e. sequential) Prolog execution this involves going back to the most recent point at which alternatives were still unexplored (most recent choice point). This definition is not directly applicable any more if some of the goals in the body of a clause have been executed in parallel: since execution of these goals was concurrent, there is no chronological notion of "most recent" to apply to the different choice points available. Although several sophisticated approaches have been proposed in order to solve this problem [5] [1] they are either not applicable to the semantics of **CGE**'s (and other Goal Independence models) or they involve too much bookkeeping overhead at run-time. In this section we will analyze the different cases involved in the backtracking of **CGE**'s and we will propose a general backtracking algorithm that will handle these cases efficiently, while taking advantage in some cases of goal independence in order to achieve limited intelligent backtracking.

Throughout this analysis we will consider the following annotated clause:

f(..):- a(..), b(..), (**<conditions>**| **c(..) & d(..) & e(..)**), g(..), h(..).

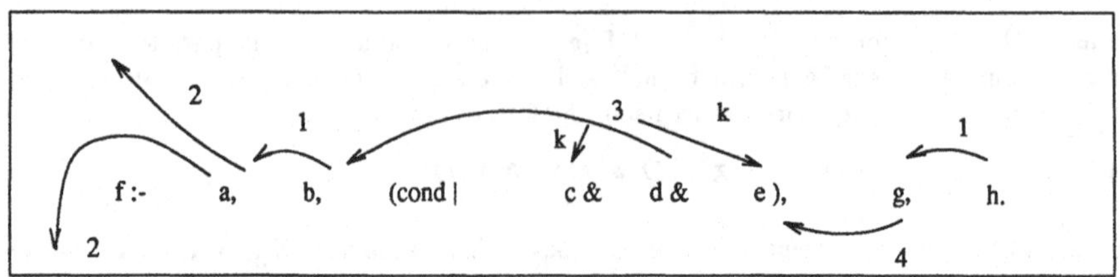

Figure 1: Backtracking cases for a **CGE**

In the trivial case when **<conditions>** is evaluated to false, execution defaults to sequential, and normal (Prolog) backtracking semantics can obviously be applied. We will therefore shift our attention to the cases where **<conditions>** evaluates to **true**. We illustrate in figure 1 the different backtracking situations through back arrows annotated by case numbers, where the cases are the subject of the following text.

Conventional Backtracking:

- **Case 1-** This is the trivial case in which backtracking still remains the same as for sequential execution. For example, if **b** fails and **a** still has alternatives, or if **h** fails and **g** still has alternatives.

- **Case 2-** This is also a trivial case: if **a** fails, the next alternative of **f** will be executed next. If there are no more alternatives for **f**, then **f** will fail in its parent and we recursively deal with the failure at that level.

Conjunctive failure; "inside" backtracking:

- **Case 3-** This is the case if **c**, **d**, or **e** fail while the body of the **CGE** is being executed the first time through (i.e. we are still **"inside"** the **CGE**).

  Suppose **d** fails. Since we are running in parallel, we know that **<conditions>** evaluated to true. This means that **c**, **d**, and **e** do not share any uninstantiated variables. Thus, the variable binding that caused the failure of **d** could not have been generated by **c** or **e**. Therefore it would be useless to ask **c** and/or **e** for alternatives and it is safe to kill the processes running **c**, **d**, and **e**, and to backtrack to the most recent choice point before the **CGE** (for example, **b** here). In this way this scheme very simply incorporates a restricted version of intelligent backtracking with only the overhead of remembering that we are **"inside"** the **CGE** when failure occurs.

"Outside" backtracking:

- **Case 4-** This is the most interesting case: we have already finished executing all goals inside the **CGE** -we are **"outside"** the **CGE**- and we fail, having to backtrack into the expression. This is the case if **g** fails.

  First, since this information will prove very useful, we will assume that processors not only report eventual goal resolution success, but also whether unexplored alternatives still remain for this goal. It will be shown how such information can be used in our context to simply extend the conventional backtracking algorithm to one that deals with **CGE**'s:

  - If **g** fails and none of the **CGE** goals has unexplored alternatives, we will backtrack to **b** just as we would in the sequential execution model.

- If **g** fails and one or more **CGE** goals still has unexplored alternatives, our object will be to establish a methodology whereby all the combinations of those alternatives will have a chance to be explored, if needed, before we give up on the whole **CGE** and backtrack to alternatives prior to it. The methodology we chose is one that will generate those alternatives *in the same order as that produced by naive sequential backtracking.* The idea is then to reinvoke the process which corresponds to the first goal with alternatives found when scanning the **CGE** *in reverse order* (i.e. reinvoking the "rightmost" goal with alternatives). This process will then, in turn, report either **success** (with or without pending alternatives) or **failure**.

  - If **failure** is reported, we simply perform the next invocation in the order described above. Of course when a **failure** is reported by the leftmost goal with alternatives in the **CGE**, we give up on the whole expression and backtrack as in **Case 1** above.

  - If **success** is reported, then we shift into forward AND-Parallel execution mode and *trigger the parallel evaluation of all the goals, if any exist, to the right of the succeeding one in the* **CGE**. Note that, if such goals do exist, they will be started from scratch since the last thing they would have reported would have been a **failure**, which we will assume here would have caused the termination of the corresponding process.

Note how the approach described above extends the "most recent choice point" backtracking model to a parallel execution model, preserving the generation of all "tuples" and offering parallel forward execution after backtracking. Also, goal ordering information provided by the user or by the compiler is preserved, and used in tuple generation. Alternatively, sometimes we might not be interested in generating all possible tuples for a conjunction of independent goals. Instead we might be interested in generating only one and "committing" to it. This can be easily annotated by including a "cut" after the **CGE** or by substituting the "|" in the **CGE** by "!".

In the above, we presented the AND-Parallel model backtracking algorithm through the use of a specific example. The general algorithm can be described as follows:

- <u>*Forward Execution:*</u> *During forward execution leave a choice point marker (***CPM***) at each choice point (traditional sequential mode) and a parallel call marker (***PCM***) at each* **CGE** *which evaluates to true (i.e. each* **CGE** *which can actually be executed in parallel). Mark each* **PCM** *as* **"inside"** *when it is created, trigger the parallel resolution of the* **CGE** *goals, and change the* **PCM** *mode to* **"outside"** *when all those goals report success.*

- <u>*Backward Execution:*</u> *When failure occurs, find the most recently created marker (***PCM** *or* **CPM***). Then:*

  - *If the marker is a* **CPM**, *backtrack normally (i.e. as in sequential execution) to that point.*

  - *If the marker is a* **PCM** *and its value is "inside", cancel ("kill") all goals inside the* **CGE**, *fail (i.e. recursively perform the Backward execution).*

  - *If it is a* **PCM** *and its value is "outside", find the first goal, going right to left in the* **CGE**, *with pending alternatives which succeeds after a "redo", and then "restart" all goals in the* **CGE** *"to its right" in parallel. If no* **CGE** *goal is found to succeed in this manner, fail (i.e. recursively perform the Backward execution).*

We have not mentioned nested **CGE**'s until now in order to make the discussion clearer. However, the algorithm works just as nicely with nested **CGE**'s, if it is applied recursively. A simple way of proving this intuitively is to "unravel" the recursive treatment of a nested **CGE** into treatment of a "dummy" goal whose corresponding clause simply embodies the nested **CGE**. The algorithm also turns out to be very simple to implement at the abstract machine level. This will be clear when we present the implementation scheme in the following section. Other special cases will be covered then. In particular we will see how backtracking in the case where some of the goals which could have been executed in parallel are executed locally in a sequential way (e.g. due to a lack of resources) fits trivially within the same scheme[7].

5 Efficient Implementation of the Algorithm

Although logic programs can present considerable opportunities for AND-Parallelism, there are always (determinate) code segments requiring sequential execution. A system which can support parallelism while still incorporating the performance optimizations and storage efficiency of current sequential systems is thus highly desirable. This is the approach taken in our design: to provide the mechanism for supporting forward and backward execution models for AND-Parallelism as extensions to the ones used in a high performance Prolog implementation. This has two clear advantages: first, sequential execution is still as fast and space efficient as in the high performance Prolog implementation (modulo some minimal run-time checks); second, the model is offered in the form of *extensions*, which are fairly independent, in spirit, of the peculiarities of that implementation. Therefore, the approach described here is applicable to a variety of compilation/stack based sequential models.

5.1 Implementing Backtracking in Sequential Systems

The Warren Abstract Machine (WAM) [12] is an execution model coupled with a host of compilation techniques leading to one of the most efficient implementations of Prolog today. Before we present our strategies for implementing **CGE** based AND-Parallelism with the associated backward execution mechanism, we will review here summarily the backtracking mechanism of the WAM since that will constitute our starting point.

In the WAM, backtracking is accomplished through the use of *choice point* frames. A *choice point* is created when the first of a sequence of alternative clauses is entered. It contains all the necessary information needed to restore the state of the machine and pick up the next alternative clause when it becomes necessary to do so. This is the case when we have a failure (e.g. when an invoking goal does not find a matching clause head). Backtracking at that point is accomplished by simply locating the most recent *choice point* (pointed to by register B), restoring the machine state from its content, and restarting from there with the next alternative. This can be seen in figure 2 where the following data areas are shown:

- The *Stack*: where *choice points* and *environments* are created, updated and discarded as needed. Only *choice points* will be shown and discussed here since we want to concentrate on the backward execution model.
- The *Heap*: where data structures and long-lived global variables are created, updated, and discarded (upon backtracking).
- The *Trail*: where variables getting instantiated, but potentially needing undoing such instantiations, are remembered (one entry per such variable).

---

[7] We call the approach described in this section "*point backtracking*". In "*streak backtracking*" literals to the right of the one being reinvoked are restarted in parallel with this reinvocation. Due to space limitation we will have to avoid discussing here *streak backtracking* or possible optimizations for these approaches.

Figure 2 corresponds to the execution of the clauses in the following example (labels have been given to the different clauses involved):

```
procedure a:                  procedure b:
a1:   a :- b, c, d, e.        b1:   b :- ..., ..., ... .
a2:   a :- b, c, d, e.        b2:   b :- ..., ..., ... .
a3:   a :- b, c, d, e.        b3:   b :- ..., ..., ... .

procedure c:                  procedure e:
c:    c :- ..., ..., ... .    e1:   e :- ..., ..., ... .
                              e2:   e :- ..., ..., ... .
procedure d:                  e3:   e :- ..., ..., ... .
d:    d :- ..., ..., ... .
```

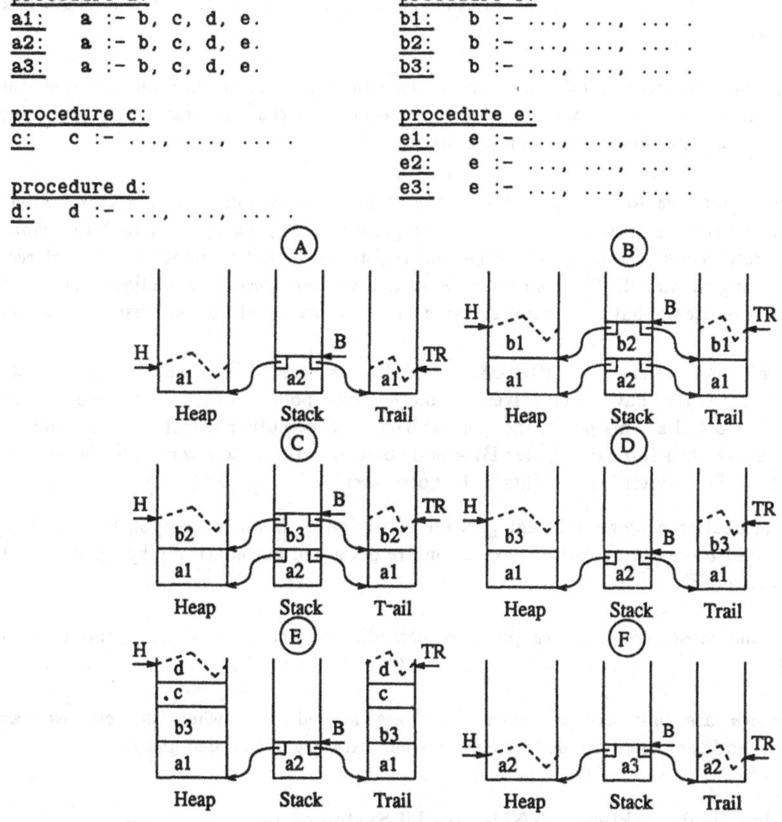

Figure 2: Choice Point Based Backtracking in Sequential Systems

Upon entering *procedure a:*, since **a** has alternatives, we create the corresponding *choice point* needed in the event of backtracking back to this point. Execution of **a** then starts with the first alternative *a1:*. This situation is depicted in figure 2-A. We show here only the following information included in the *choice point* (other information will be skipped for the sake of brevity):

- A pointer to the next unexplored alternative clause *a2:*.
- The value of the *Heap* pointer in register **H** at the time this *choice point* was created.
- The value of the *Trail* pointer in register **TR** at the time this *choice point* was created.

When the head of *a1:* unifies successfully with the invoking goal, *procedure b:* is entered. Again a *choice point* is created, since **b** also has alternatives (figure 2-B). Suppose now that some goal fails in the body of *b1:*, and that no more choice points have been created. The following sequence of actions takes place resulting in *backward execution* (this is illustrated in figure 2-C):

- The most recent *choice point* is fetched through register **B**'s content.
- The top of the *Heap* pointer (register **H**) is reset to the value saved in the fetched *choice point*. This will discard all the data just made obsolete by the failure that caused the backtracking.

- The variables remembered through entries located between the current top of the *Trail* stack and the *Trail* pointer saved in the fetched *choice point* are reset to uninstantiated. This is done because the instantiations being reset were made obsolete by the failure that caused the backtracking. Of course the top of the *Trail* pointer (register **TR**) is also reset appropriately.

- Finally, the next alternative *b2:* indicated in the *choice point* is picked up and execution proceeds from there. We also want at this point to indicate that the next alternative clause is *b3:* by updating the *choice point* appropriately.

If **b** should fail again, we would repeat the above sequence of actions, and start execution of *b3:*. However this time there are no more alternatives for *procedure b:*. This means that the *choice point* associated with *procedure b:* should be discarded and register **B** should be reset to the most recent one prior to the one being discarded. This is only possible if the *choice points* are chained together (This is one of the information items that we are not showing in the *choice point* frames illustrated in figure 2).

In figure 2-E we depict the situation after *b3:* and *c:* have succeeded, and we are executing *d:*. Note that since neither *c:* nor *d:* have alternatives, no more choice points have been created on the *Stack*. Therefore, if *d:* should fail at this point, the general backward execution model using the current most recent *choice point* (fetched through register **B**) would correctly take us to alternative clause *a3:*. This is shown in figure 2-F. Some interesting points to be noted are:

- This implementation achieves efficient garbage collection of *Heap* space upon backtracking: all data created there during forward execution are discarded automatically by appropriately resetting register **H**.

- Identifying the most recent *choice point* is immediate, since it is always pointed to by register **B**.

- *Choice points* are only created when they are needed (i.e., when the clauses have alternatives) and they are discarded efficiently when they are not needed any more.

5.2 Implementing Backtracking in AND-Parallel Systems

As stated before, our objective is to implement an AND-Parallel system with the associated backward execution mechanism presented earlier in section 4, while still preserving the efficiency present in sequential implementations similar to the WAM reviewed above. Our conceptual starting point is that a parallel execution of AND-siblings is going to correspond to a parent process controlling children processes handling independently the execution of the parallel siblings. Also processes have their own execution environments (*Stack*, *Heap*, *Trail*, as well as a machine state). The allocation of processes to processors is of course subject to the availability of such parallel system resources. One of the natural extensions to such a general model is that the parent process could execute one or more children processes instead of just idling while waiting for other children processes' responses: this will be discussed in more detail in section 5.3 on local execution of parallel goals, showing how the existing data areas (*Stack*, *Heap*, and *Trail*, etc.) can be shared for this purpose.

The control structure that the parent uses for its supervisory task will be referred to as a "parallel call" frame (*Parcall frame* in short) and will be located in the parent process's *Stack* (therefore three types of frames can now be found there: *Environments*, *Choice Points*, and now, *Parcall Frames*). The most recent *Parcall Frame* is pointed to by register **PF**. *Parcall Frames* are created when a **CGE** evaluates to **true**, hence clearing the way for the parallel execution of the **CGE**'s sibling literals. The Parcall frame, among other information, contains the following items important for our discussion here[8]:

[8] See [8] or [7] for other details on this subject.

- One slot for each of the sibling literals inside the **CGE**, consisting of the following fields:
  - o the Id of the child process corresponding to this literal
  - o completion status of the process (i.e. *processing, succeeded with pending alternatives, succeeded with no alternatives*, or *failed*).
- A flag indicating whether we have just entered the **CGE** or whether we are backtracking into it after the initial entry and at least one successful exit. This is a materialization of the "inside"/"outside" indication discussed in the backtracking algorithm in section 4.

In addition to these slots, a *Parcall Frame* contains other information needed for process synchronization, as well as in the event of backtracking out of a **CGE** to a preceding literal.

We will now show how the introduction of *Parcall Frames*, their relationship to *Choice Points*, and the manipulation of both types of frames will materialize the algorithms introduced in section 4 and make it possible to manage both forward and backward execution as a natural extension to the WAM model. First we will define two types of failure:

- *Local Failure*: the local processor fails while executing a goal, and
- *Remote Failure*: a "Failure" message is received from a child process.

Now our extended backward execution mechanism is based on recognizing, when either type of failure occurs, whether a *Choice Point* or a *Parcall Frame* is more recent (comparing registers **B** and **PF**). The algorithm then follows:

- If *Local Failure*, then:
  - o If $\mathbf{B} > \mathbf{PF}$ then perform the normal *Choice Point* backtracking.
  - o If $\mathbf{PF} > \mathbf{B}$ then find the first[9] *Parcall Frame* child process slot with pending alternatives to respond successfully to a "redo" message. When such a process is found, invoke the parallel execution of all the literals that correspond to the following slots, getting us back in (parallel) forward execution again. If none succeeds, fail by recursively performing this backward execution algorithm in a "local failure" mode.
- If *Remote Failure*, then, knowing definitely that $\mathbf{PF} > \mathbf{B}$ and that we are in the "inside backtracking" case (that is until we introduce next section's optimization):
  - o "Kill" all goals in the *Parcall Frame*, fail by recursively performing this backward execution algorithm in a "local failure" mode.

The following example will illustrate the above algorithm. Suppose the clauses for "a" in the example in the previous section were annotated in the following way (with embedded **CGE**'s):

[9] Slots should always be scanned in the same order, e.g. from the higher addressed ones (hopefully corresponding to rightmost ones in the **CGE**) to the lower addressed ones. If parallel goals are allowed to execute locally (next section's optimization), then the order of scanning has to be from most recently executed goals (by remote processors) to less recent ones (see section 5.3).

```
procedure a:
a1:    a :- ( cond1 | b & c & d ), e.

a2:    a :- ( cond2 | b & c & d ), e.

a3:    a :- ( cond3 | b & c & d ), e.
```

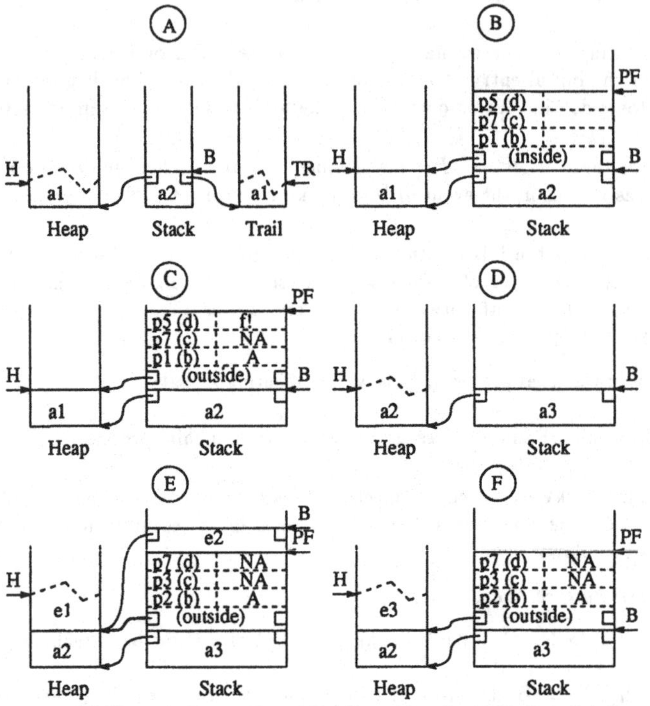

Figure 3: CP/Parcall Frame Based Backtracking in AND-Parallel Systems

Figure 3 illustrates the execution of this example in parallel. Execution of **a** in the "parent" process starts exactly as in the sequential case (figure 2-A vs. figure 3-A). If **cond1** failed, execution would proceed just as in figure 2. On the other hand, if **cond1** succeeds, a *Parcall Frame*, initialized to "inside" is created, with slots for **b**, **c**, and **d**. This is illustrated in figure 3-B where these goals have been "picked up"[10] by **p1**, **p7**, and **p5** respectively (the *Trail* is omitted in both the diagrams and the discussions for the sake of clarity). At this point the parent process simply waits for all goals to update their slot's *completion status* field . With the *Parcall Frame* still flagged as "inside", if one of the goals returns failure (*Remote* Failure)) we can backtrack "intelligently" to the last *Choice Point* before the *Parcall Frame*. In figure 3-C, **p5** returned failure for **d** (**p1** and **p7** returned with success, with **p1**'s success qualified as with pending alternatives, i.e. there is a *Choice Point* in **p1**'s *Stack*). Since the corresponding *Parcall Frame* is still flagged as "inside", an "unwind" message is sent to **p7** and **p1** (thus disregarding the alternatives in **b**), and execution is continued with the next alternative of **a** (figure 3-D).

The next two parts of figure 3 illustrate "outside" backtracking. In figure 3-E we have a situation similar to that in figure 3-B. Processors **p2**, **p3**, and **p7** "picked up" the goals but this time they all returned successfully (b still having alternatives). At this point we succeed the whole **CGE** by changing

[10] All goals in the parallel call are pushed on to a special stack as soon as the parallel call is entered (the checks succeed). From there they can be picked up by other processors or, as we will consider in the next section, by the local one.

the status of the *Parcall Frame* to "outside", and move on to goal **e**, pushing a choice point (since **e** has alternatives), and finally entering clause *e1:*. If *e1:* fails, we will then use the available choice point to try *e2:* (*Local Failure*; **B** > **PF**). Figure 3-F illustrates the situation if *e2:* also fails: the *Choice Point* has been deallocated and we are executing *e3:*.

Note that in the event of a *local* failure now, the last *Parcall Frame* is more recent than the last *Choice Point* (PF > B) and, since its status is "outside", the corresponding backtracking algorithm will be run on it: select the first goal with alternatives (**b**), send a "redo" to it (to **p2**, which will execute it by making use of the *Choice Point* on top of its local *Stack*, just as if a local failure had occurred). If **p2** now returns failure, since there are no more slots with alternatives in the *Parcall Frame*, we will deallocate it (after sending "unwind" messages to the child processes corresponding to all the slots, so that their *Heaps* will be deallocated and their *Trails* unwound) and use the next entry on the *Stack* (**a**'s choice point) to backtrack to *a3:*. If, on the other hand, **p2** had returned success, we would invoke the parallel execution of all the goals corresponding to the following slots, hence "shifting gears" to "Forward Execution". Note that we can safely assume that the **CGE** will be successfully exited at this point since those goals are being redone from scratch and we know that they have succeeded in the past!

5.3 Local Execution of Parallel Goals

One obvious optimization to the scheme above is to let the local processor pick up some of the goals in the *Parcall Frame* and work on them itself, instead of just idling while waiting for children processes responses. This is very important in that it allows the generalization of the architecture to any number of processors (including a single one). Such scalable systems could then run parallel code with "graceful" performance improvement or degradation depending on the available resources. Also, a single processor would run the parallel code at comparable speed to equivalent sequential code, while still taking advantage of the opportunity for "intelligent backtracking" present in "inside" backtracking.

In a multiprocessing system, local execution of parallel goals can be accomplished by creating a new process which will pick up the goal. Figure 4 shows a more efficient way of handling the execution of parallel goals locally, by stacking them on the local stack much in the same way as they would be in a sequential implementation. In figure 4-A, *b1:* has been immediately "picked up" by the local processor (and the corresponding slot has been marked accordingly -- "=*=") while **c** and **d** have been "picked up" by **p7** and **p5**, as in figure 3-B. Execution of the goal taken locally proceeds as normal (figure 4-B), but note that the *Parcall Frame* is still marked as "inside". In this figure **p5** has returned (with *no alternatives*) and **p7** is still working on its goal. In the event of either a local or a remote failure now, "inside" (i.e. "intelligent") backtracking would occur (as in figure 3-D). However, this would only be triggered locally if **b** runs out of alternatives. A first failure in *b1:* in figure 4-B would use the *Choice Point* and continue with *b2:*, just as if it were being executed remotely.

If all goals succeed, we will continue with **e**, data structures and *Choice Points* being again simply pushed on top of their respective areas (*Heap* and *Stack*, figure 4-C). "Outside" backtracking will work in a similar way as before, but with the difference that *goals executed locally will always be backtracked first*: in figure 4-C, if **e** runs out of alternatives, we will try all the alternatives of **b** before using the *Parcall Frame*. This is perfectly valid, as long as it is used consistently, since the order of execution is immaterial inside a parallel call. The *Stack* status of figure 4-C is therefore equivalent to the one found while executing the following clause using the scheme described in the previous section:

```
a :- ( c & d ), b, e.
```

Figure 4-D depicts "outside" backtracking after all goals executed locally have run out of alternatives. We are executing *e3:* after *b3:* (both choice points have been discarded). If failure occurs in *e3:*, we will find the *Parcall Frame* above any choice points, and execute the "outside" algorithm. In this case, since no goals in the *Parcall Frame* have alternatives, we will simply discard the *Parcall Frame* itself (sending "unwind" messages to **p5** and **p7**) and try the next alternative of **a** (*a2:*) as in figure 3-D.

An interesting situation occurs if external failure arrives while the local processor is executing a goal

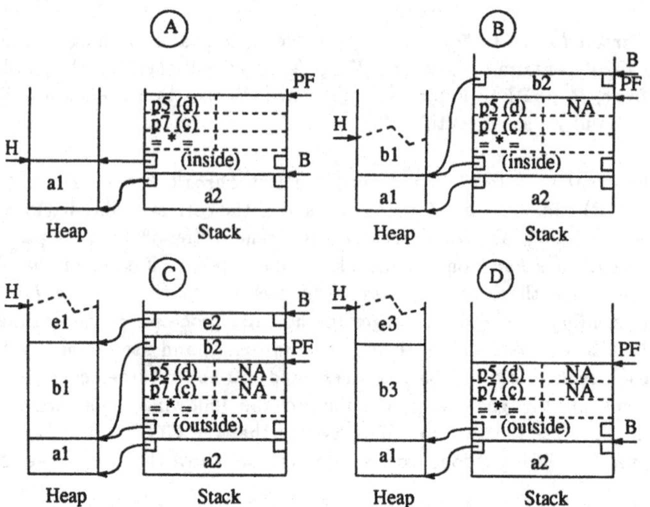

Figure 4: CP/Parcall Frame Based Backtracking With "Local Goals"

from the parallel call, and this goal in turn has generated other *Parcall Frames*. Suppose that in figure 4-B execution of *b1:* has pushed other *choice points* and *Parcall Frames* on the *Stack*. If **p7 (c)** returns at this point with failure, all those entries, and their corresponding data structures (in the *Heap*) have to be deallocated. This turns out to be simple if **p7** provides the value of the PF pointer for the *Parcall Frame* containing the goal failing (it can be "picked up" with the goal). Then we only need to use the backtracking information in that Frame to recover all space (i.e. just above *a1:* for the *Heap* in figure 4-B). Of course, all processes started by the execution of **b** need to be cancelled. This is also easily accomplished by following the chain of *Parcall Frames*, from the one on top to the one given by **p7**, sending "kill", "unwind" etc. messages to all slots that are not marked local ("=*="). This is very similar to what a processor has to do when it *receives* a "kill" message.

In summary, an algorithm along the same lines as the one presented in the previous section can be used when **CGE** goals are executed locally, provided it is adapted to handle the extra special cases involved:

- If *Local Failure*, then:
  - If **B** > **PF** then perform the normal *Choice Point* backtracking.
  - If **PF** > **B** and the status of the *Parcall Frame* is "inside", "kill" all goals in the *Parcall Frame* (by sending "kill"/"unwind" messages to all non-local slots in this *Frame*; local goals will be deallocated automatically by the local trimming of the stacks) and fail by recursively executing this algorithm in a *Local Failure* mode.
  - If **PF** > **B** and the status of the *Parcall Frame* is "outside", then find the first[11] parcall frame child process slot with pending alternatives to respond successfully to a "redo" message. When such a process is found, invoke the parallel execution of all the literals that correspond to the following slots, and of all those literals which were executed locally[12] . If none succeeds, fail by recursively executing this algorithm in a *Local Failure* mode.

---

[11]The correct scanning order now is *opposite to that in which the goals were picked up by remote processors*. A simple way of following this order by making use of an extra field in the child process slot is shown in [8].

[12]Note that all local goals have been completely backtracked before we arrive at this point.

- If there are no choice points or *Parcall Frames* available, report failure to parent.

- If ~*emote failure*, then:
  - If the **PF** value received is the same as the current one: we are in a similar case to the second one above.
  - If the **PF** value received is lower than the current one: follow chain of *Parcall Frames* "killing" dependent processes up to and including referred Frame; fail by recursively executing this algorithm in a *Local Failure* mode.

Note that although the description is lengthy because of the many cases involved, the abstract machine can select the appropriate case using extremely simple arithmetic checks ($\mathbf{B} > \mathbf{PF}$ or $\mathbf{B} < \mathbf{PF}$; Status= 1 or 0) and the actions are in any case very simple and determinate. Backward execution can be performed in parallel (i.e. unwinding of *Trails*, killing of descendants etc.) with very little overhead. Then forward execution is resumed also in parallel. Also note that, since in this model local goals are backtracked first, and there is no a priory knowledge of which goals will be executed locally, the order in which solutions are produced depends on run-time factors, even though *all* solutions will still be produced. We are also considering a slightly different model where any compile-time established order can be preserved. A description of such a model will be reported elsewhere.

6 Conclusions

In the previous sections we have presented an approach to AND-Parallel execution of logic programs, goal independence, which characterizes models such as our generalized version of restricted AND-Parallelism. We have then proposed a series of algorithms for management of backtracking in this class of AND-Parallel execution models, offering an efficient implementation scheme and some examples to illustrate its operation. We argue that this solution cleanly integrates one form of AND-Parallelism with the implementation technologies of high performance Prolog systems with efficient data storage management similar to the Warren Abstract Machine. Also, a form of restricted intelligent backtracking is provided with virtually no additional overhead. "Soft" degradation of performance with resource exhaustion is attained: even a single processor will run any parallel program while still supporting restricted intelligent backtracking when goals are independent.

The discussions in this paper concentrated on the backtracking algorithms. We have also covered other areas of the design of an AND-Parallel implementation, such as an instruction set and Abstract Machine [8], goal scheduling and memory management issues, and a more detailed system architecture. The reader can find more detailed information regarding some of these subjects in [7].

7 Acknowledgements

The execution model presented here is an extension of the Warren Abstract Machine and therefore owes much to the work of David Warren. The backtracking strategy presented in the first part of this paper is the result of a series of very interesting discussions between Chua-Huang Huang, David Warren, Richard Warren and the authors. We are also indebted to the MCC ACA/Parallel Processing and ACA/AI groups for their encouragement, and to MCC for its support.

References

[1] J.-H. Chang, A. M. Despain, and D. DeGroot.
AND-parallelism of Logic Programs Based on Static Data Dependency Analysis.
In *Digest of Papers of COMPCON Spring '85*, pages 218-225. 1985.

[2] K. Clark and S. Gregory.
PARLOG: A Parallel Logic Programming Language.
Research Report DOC 83/5, Dept. of Computing, Imperial College of Science and Technology, May, 1983.
University of London.

[3] Clark, K.L. and G. McCabe.
The Control Facilities of IC-Prolog.
Expert Systems in the Micro Electronic Age.
Edinburgh University Press, 1979.

[4] J.S. Conery and D.F. Kibler.
Parallel Interpretation of Logic Programs.
In *Proc. of the ACM Conference on Functional Programming Languages and Computer Architecture.*, pages 163-170. October, 1981.

[5] J.S. Conery.
The AND/OR Process Model for Parallel Interpretation of Logic Programs.
PhD thesis, The University of California at Irvine, 1983.
Technical Report 204.

[6] Doug DeGroot.
Restricted And-Parallelism.
Int'l Conf. on Fifth Generation Computer Systems , November, 1984.

[7] Manuel V. Hermenegildo.
A Restricted AND-parallel Execution Model and Abstract Machine for Prolog Programs.
Technical Report PP-104-85, Microelectronics and Computer Technology Corporation (MCC), Austin, TX 78759, 1985.

[8] Manuel V. Hermenegildo.
An Abstract Machine for Restricted AND-parallel Execution of Logic Programs.
In *Proceedings of the 3rd. Int'l. Conf. on Logic Programming.* Springer-Verlag, 1986.

[9] Kowalski, R.A.
Predicate Logic as a Programming Language.
Proc. IFIPS 74 , 1974.

[10] Luis M. Pereira and Roger I. Nasr.
Delta-Prolog: A Distributed Logic Programming Language.
In *Proceedings of the Intl. Conf. on 5th. Gen. Computer Systems.* 1984.
Japan.

[11] E. Y. Shapiro.
A subset of Concurrent Prolog and its interpreter.
Technical Report TR-003, ICOT, January, 1983.
Tokyo.

[12] David H. D. Warren.
An Abstract Prolog Instruction Set.
Technical Note 309, SRI International, AI Center, Computer Science and Technology Division, 1983.

An Intelligent Backtracking Algorithm for Parallel Execution of Logic Programs

Yow-Jian Lin, Vipin Kumar, Clement Leung
Artificial Intelligence Laboratory
Department of Computer Sciences
The University of Texas at Austin
Austin, Texas 78712

ABSTRACT

In this paper we present a simple but efficient backtracking scheme which works when AND-parallelism is exploited in a logic program. The scheme is well suited for implementation on a parallel hardware. We show that the backtracking scheme presented by Conery and Kibler in the context of AND/OR process model is incorrect, i.e., in some cases it may miss solutions while performing backtracking. Even if no AND-parallelism is exploited (i.e., all literals are solved sequentially), our scheme is more efficient than the "naive" depth-first backtracking strategy used by Prolog because our scheme makes use of the dependencies between literals in a clause. Chang and Despain have recently presented a backtracking scheme which also makes use of the dependencies between literals. We show that our scheme is more efficient than their scheme in the sense that our scheme does less backtracking.

1. Introduction

AND-parallelism in logic programs refers to executing more than one literal of a clause at the same time. When the literals in a clause don't share any uninstantiated variable, the literals can be solved independently. But if more than one literal share uninstantiated variables, then solving these literals independently could lead to excessive computation. Various techniques have been developed to exploit AND-parallelism when literals in a clause are dependent (i.e., they share uninstantiated variables) [2], [5], [7], [8]. One technique, introduced by Conery and Kibler in the context of AND/OR process model, is to execute only one of the dependent literals to find a binding for the shared variable, and then execute the remaining literals in parallel if they do not share any other variable [3], [5]. Due to the non-deterministic nature of logic programs, a literal may fail because the variable bindings it has received from other literals are not satisfactory. In this case, we have to re-solve some literals and generate new bindings. For example, in solving a goal statement such as

← p(X), q(Y), r(X,Y).

if r(X,Y) does not satisfy the bindings received from both p(X) and q(Y), then either p(X) or q(Y) will have to generate a new binding. Conery and Kibler have presented a backtracking scheme, called

This work was supported by Army Research Office grant #DAAG29-84-K-0060 to the Artificial Intelligence Laboratory at the University of Texas at Austin.

"backward execution algorithm" in [5], for deciding which literals to re-solve in case some literals fail. We found that their backward execution algorithm is incorrect, i.e., in some cases it may miss solutions while performing backtracking. In this paper we present a simple but efficient backtracking scheme, and prove that it is correct. Even if no AND-parallelism is exploited (i.e., all literals are solved sequentially), our scheme is more efficient than the "naive" depth-first backtracking strategy used by Prolog because our scheme makes use of the dependencies between literals in a clause. Chang and Despain have recently presented a backtracking scheme which also makes use of the dependencies between literals [2]. Compared to their scheme, our scheme is more efficient in the sense that our scheme does less backtracking.

2. Background and Definitions

The discussion in this paper is based upon an abstract model similar to the AND/OR process model of Conery and Kibler [3], [5]. We assume that we are given a clause body (with some variables instantiated because of unification on the head). If more than one literal in the clause body share an uninstantiated variable V, then we designate one of these literals as the *generator* of V, and designate the remaining literals as the *consumers* of V. A literal can be the generator of some variables, and at the same time, it can be a consumer of some other variables. The generator-consumer relationship between the literals of a clause can then be depicted via a data dependency graph D. D is a directed graph in which a literal L is a *parent* of a literal M (and M is a *child* of L) if for some variable V, M is the generator of V and L is a consumer of V. The meanings of "L is an *ancestor* of M in D" and "M is a *descendant* of L in D" simply follow. To simplify our discussion in this paper, we assume that generators and consumers for various literals are carefully chosen such that D remains acyclic. Furthermore, we assume that the designated generator M of a variable V always generates a ground binding for V. Note that if the execution of M does not bind V to a ground term, then the subgraph of D below M will have to be reconstructed such that one of the children of M is the generator of variables in the new binding, and the remaining ones are consumers.

We also assume that the literals in the clause body have been linearly ordered. The reason for this will become clear in Section 5. The ordering between the literals should be such that a generator must come before all the literals that consume the variable bindings it generates. One way to construct this linear ordering is to traverse the data-dependency graph D in the breadth-first manner. From now on P_i is used to refer to the i-th literal in the linear ordering.

To exploit AND-parallelism, each literal is executed by a different process. The process executing a literal can be in one of the three modes: GATHER, EXECUTION and FINISHED. While in the EXECUTION mode, a process can be in one of the two states: SOLVED and UNSOLVED. For brevity, we will often use "a literal P_i" to mean "the corresponding process which is executing P_i". Literals (i.e., the corresponding processes) can communicate with each other via exchanging messages.

When a literal P_i is in the GATHER mode, it is waiting to receive bindings for the variables it is consuming. After P_i has advanced to the EXECUTION mode, P_i is in the UNSOLVED state if it is trying to find a satisfactory binding. P_i is in the SOLVED state if it has produced a satisfactory binding but some of its descendants are still in the EXECUTION mode. P_i is in the FINISHED mode if all of its descendants (i.e., literals which are consumers of some of the bindings generated by P_i) and itself have succeeded.

Each literal P_i also maintains a list of literals denoted as B-list(P_i). B-list(P_i) consists of those literals which may be able to cure the failure of P_i (if P_i fails) by producing new bindings. The literals P_k on each B-list are sorted according to the descending order of k.

The following "forward execution" algorithm determines the state, mode and message pattern of the processes.

3. The Forward Execution Algorithm

For all literals P_i such that P_i has no ancestors in the data-dependency graph D, start P_i in the UNSOLVED state of the EXECUTION mode. Start the remaining literals in the GATHER mode. Literals in the UNSOLVED state of the EXECUTION mode can start executing.

When a literal P_i, running in the UNSOLVED state of the EXECUTION mode, finds a combination of bindings for the variables it is generating, it then goes from the UNSOLVED state to the SOLVED state, and sends the bindings of the generated variables to its children. If P_i has no child in D, then it goes to the FINISHED mode. In either case, P_i suspends its execution[1].

If a literal P_i is in GATHER mode and receives bindings for all the variables it is consuming, then it goes to the UNSOLVED state of the EXECUTION mode and its B-list is initialized to the list of its parents. At this point we can start executing P_i.

If a literal has descendants in D and all of its children are in the FINISHED mode, then it goes to the FINISHED mode. If all the literals of the clause are in the FINISHED mode, then the execution of the clause terminates. Figure 1 shows the forward execution algorithm in a graphical form.

If a literal P_i fails (i.e., when P_i can find no more solutions while executing in the UNSOLVED state of the EXECUTION mode), then the "backward execution" algorithm is executed. Our backward execution algorithm lets each literal P_i collect its backtracking candidates in B-list(P_i) dynamically during the execution. When P_i fails, it backtracks to a literal P_j = head(B-list(P_i)). If P_j fails to cure the failure of P_i, literals in tail(B-list(P_i)) may still be able to cure the failure of P_i. Therefore, when P_i backtracks to P_j, tail(B-list(P_i)) is merged into the B-list of P_j. In the next section we present our backward execution algorithm in detail. In Section 5 we prove that at the time a literal P_i fails, B-list(P_i) indeed contains enough backtracking candidates so that no solution to the clause is missed.

4. The Backward Execution Algorithm

If the B-list of P_i is a null list, then the execution of the clause fails. If the B-list of P_i is a nonempty list [P_j|Y], then backtracking is done to P_j by performing the following steps.

---

[1] Note that P_i could have continued to execute to find its next solution. This is called OR-parallelism by Conery [3], [4], [5]. To simplify discussion in this paper we assume that no OR-parallelism is being exploited. Our backward execution scheme works even when OR-parallelism is exploited (see Lin's dissertation [10] for details).

1. Cancel all the descendants of P_j in the data dependency graph D.
2. Reset every generator P_k, where $k > j$, and P_k has not been canceled in Step 1.
3. Merge [Y] to the B-list of P_j. Remove duplicate literals from the new B-list of P_j.
4. Perform a redo operation on P_j.
5. If a literal M is in the FINISHED mode and any of its descendants is no longer in the FINISHED mode (due to steps 1 and 2), then M is moved to the SOLVED state of the EXECUTION mode.

The three operations, *reset, cancel* and *redo* are explained in the following.

Reset P_i

1. Set the B-list of P_i to a list containing only its parents in D.
2. Cancel all the descendants of P_i in the data-dependency graph D (if they have not already been canceled).
3. Start the execution of P_i from the beginning, i.e., as if it has just made the transition from the GATHER mode to the UNSOLVED state of the EXECUTION mode.

Cancel P_i

1. Switch P_i to the GATHER mode. Previous B-list and bindings of P_i are discarded.

Redo P_i

1. Change the state of P_i to "UNSOLVED", so that P_i can resume execution to find a new set of bindings for the variables it generates.

See Appendix B for an illustration of the algorithm. Note that while presenting the forward and backward execution algorithms, we have not specified the actual mechanism for transferring information between various literals (i.e., processes representing the literals). This has to be done carefully to ensure that messages do not get out of synchronization. The actual mechanism for message transfer is described in detail in [9]. To simplify the discussion in this paper, we assume that the message passing and processing take zero time.

The forward and backward execution algorithms presented so far would only find one solution for a given clause. In practice, we may need more than one solution for a clause. To find the next solution of a given clause, we simply send a fail message from a dummy literal to the rightmost generator of the clause in the linear order (i.e., P_m such that $m = \max\{k \mid P_k \text{ is a generator}\}$). This would restart the execution of the clause. If there are no more solutions, then the execution will terminate with failure. Otherwise, a new solution will be found when all the literals of the clause are in the FINISHED mode. Note that the dummy literal remains invisible at all times except when a new solution to the clause is needed.

5. The Correctness Proof of our Backward Execution Algorithm

By correctness we mean that if there are solutions for a given clause body, the backward execution algorithm should guarantee that every solution can be generated eventually. The order in which these solutions are generated is unimportant.

At the time a literal P_i fails, let X_i = {L| L is an ancestor of P_i} ∪ {L| L is an ancestor of M and the failure of M has directly or indirectly[2] caused a redo operation on P_i since P_i was most recently changed from the GATHER mode to the EXECUTION mode}. Clearly, the only way to correct the current failure of P_i is to re-solve some literals in X_i. But it is not clear beforehand as to which literals in X_i should be re-solved to make P_i succeed again. To ensure that all possible combinations of the bindings generated by the literals in X_i can be tried, we make use of the linear ordering on the literals defined in section 2. If P_i fails, then we always backtrack to a literal P_m such that m = $\max\{k \mid P_k$ can possibly cure the failure of $P_i\}$. This is reminiscent of the nested-loop model discussed in [5]. The following lemma says that $\{P_m \mid P_m \in X_i \text{ and } m<i\}$ is precisely the set of literals which can possibly cure the failure of P_i.

Lemma 1. If P_i fails, then P_m can possibly cure the failure of P_i if and only if $P_m \in X_i$ and $m<i$.
Proof: See Appendix A.

Let $bi = \max\{k \mid P_k \in X_i \text{ and } k<i\}$. From Lemma 1 and the preceding discussion, it is clear that the failure of P_i should result in backtracking to P_{bi}. The following lemmas help us prove that our algorithm does precisely that.

Let S_i = {L| L is a parent of P_i} ∪ {L| L is a parent of M and the failure of M has directly or indirectly caused a redo operation on P_i since P_i was most recently changed from the GATHER mode to the EXECUTION mode}. Lemma 2 says that bi is equal to $\max\{k \mid P_k \in S_i \text{ and } k<i\}$.

Lemma 2. $bi = \max\{k \mid P_k \in S_i \text{ and } k<i\}$.
Proof: See Appendix A.

Lemma 3. At the time P_i fails, $\{P_j \mid P_j \in$ B-list$(P_i)\} = \{P_j \mid P_j \in S_i \text{ and } j<i\}$.
Proof: See Appendix A.

Note that the B-list of each literal is always ordered such that if B-list(P_i) = [P_j|Y], then j = $\max\{k \mid P_k \in$ B-list$(P_i)\}$. Hence, from Lemma 2 and Lemma 3 it follows that in our algorithm, the failure of P_i causes backtracking to P_{bi}.

6. Intelligent Backtracking without AND parallelism

Even in the absence of parallel hardware, our backtrack algorithm is useful because it is potentially much more efficient than the "naive" backtracking strategy used by Prolog. If only one processor is available, then we can execute P_i such that $i = \min\{j \mid P_j$ is in the UNSOLVED state of the EXECUTION mode$\}$. In this case, the work done by our algorithm (except for the communication overhead) is a subset of the work done by the backtracking strategy of Prolog. This happens because, if a literal P_i fails, then our algorithm causes backtracking to P_{bi}, whereas Prolog backtracks to all the literals P_j such

[2] Failure of M indirectly causes a redo operation on P_i if failure of L directly causes a redo operation on P_i, and the failure of M directly or indirectly causes a redo operation on L.

that $bi<j<i$ before backtracking to P_{bi}. The discussion in section 5 makes it clear that backtracking to any literal P_j such that $bi<j<i$ is guaranteed to be wasteful.

7. Related Work

7.1. Conery and Kibler's Backward Execution Algorithm

The backward execution algorithm presented by Conery and Kibler [3], [5] is incorrect because, in some cases, it may miss solutions while performing backtracking. The problem with their algorithm is that it uses only one failure context list to record the history of failure. When a new process is created for a failed literal, that literal is removed from the failure context, and the history of the failure is lost. We run Conery's algorithm on the example given in Appendix B.1 to illustrate out point.

Assume that we are solving P_0(A,B,C) with the following set of clauses.

P_0(A,B,C) ← P_1(A), P_2(A,B), P_3(A,C), P_4(C), P_5(B,C).
P_1(a1).
P_2(a1, b1).
P_2(a1, b2).
P_3(a1, c1).
P_3(a1, c2).
P_4(c1).
P_5(b1, c2).
P_5(b2, c1).

The data-dependency graph for solving P_0(A,B,C) is in Figure 2. In this example we use the same notation as Conery used in [5]. #N denotes the literal P_N and ↑N denotes the OR process created to solve P_N.

Suppose that #1, #2, and #3 have succeeded. After the success messages arrived, the status of the AND process is: subgoals #1, #2, and #3 solved; subgoals #4 and #5 pending; failure context empty. The current bindings are a1/A, b1/B, c1/C.

After AND process received fail message from ↑5. The failure context is set to [#5], which is the prefix of the redo list [#5, #3, #2, #1, head]. A redo message is sent to ↑3, and the actions taken for each subgoals to the right of #3 in the linear ordering are:

#4: canceled.

#5: already terminated.

The current bindings are a1/A, b1/B.

The success from ↑3 arrived again. New processes for #4 and #5 are created. Since there is a new process for #5, it is removed from the failure context. The state of the AND process: subgoals #1, #2, and #3 solved; subgoals #4 and #5 pending; failure context empty. The current bindings are a1/A, b1/B, c2/C.

This time AND process receives fail message from ↑4. The failure context is set to [#4], which is the prefix of the redo list [#4, #3, #1, head]. A redo message is sent to ↑3 again, and the remaining subgoals in the linear ordering are handled as follows:

#4: already terminated.

#5: canceled.

The current bindings are a1/A, b1/B.

#3 fails this time. It sends back a fail message. After receiving fail message from ↑3, AND process sets the failure context to [#4, #3], which is the prefix of the redo list [#4, #3, #1, head]. This time a redo message is sent to ↑1, and the actions taken for each remaining subgoals are:

#2: canceled.

#3: already terminated.

#4: already terminated.

#5: already terminated.

The current binding is none.

Since there is only one solution for P_1, AND process will receive fail message from ↑1. It then sets the failure context to [#4, #3, #1], which is the prefix of the redo list [#4, #3, #1, head]. The suffix is [head], and the AND process fails. However a solution a1/A, b2/B, and c1/C does exist for P_0. The reason Conery's algorithm cannot find this is because part of the history of failure for #3 (i.e., the failure of #5) was removed from the failure context and lost.

7.2. Semi-intelligent Backtracking of Chang and Despain

Chang and Despain have recently presented a semi-intelligent backtracking scheme [2]. Their scheme is similar to our scheme except that the backtrack point at each literal is statically determined. In their scheme, each literal is involved in either type-I backtracking or type-II backtracking. Type-I backtracking occurs when a literal has a failure level of 0 (failure level is defined in the proof of Lemma 3 in Appendix A). In this case, the two schemes backtrack exactly to the same literal.

When a literal is involved in type-II backtracking, then it backtracks to P_j such that $j = \max\{m \mid P_m$ is an ancestor of any literal P_k which may cause the failure of P_i and $m<i<k\}$. Since the analysis is done for the worst case, the set they use to choose P_j is a superset of X_i defined in the section 5. Therefore $bi \leq j<i$. If $bi<j$, then P_i would keep failing for all the new values generated by P_j for exactly the same reasons for which it failed before. And hence backtracking to P_j is guaranteed to be wasteful. Appendix B.2 presents an example to show the superiority of our approach.

7.3. The Intelligent Backtracking Scheme of Bruynooghe, Pereira, and Porto

Bruynooghe, Pereira, and Porto proposed an Intelligent Backtracking scheme which involves complicated run-time data structures [1], [11]. (Cox proposed a similar scheme in [6].) In order to achieve intelligent backtracking in their scheme, it is necessary to keep track of a set of candidate goals for backtracking upon failure of a goal G. This set consists of the ancestor (parent is sufficient) of G, the modifying goals for G, and the legacy set of G.

Since their method is based on a "deduction tree", backtracking to parent simply means re-solving the failed goal with different alternatives, which is taken care of implicitly in our algorithm when we try to solve a literal. The legacy set is also passed around in our algorithm when backtrack operation is performed. From these two view-points, the complexity of their schemes and our algorithm is about the same. The major difference between our algorithm and theirs is the method of deciding the set of modifying goals. In our algorithm, when a goal fails, each of its parents in the data dependency graph D is a modifying goal. But in their scheme, deciding a modifying goal involves a lot of run-time analysis on things such as where the unification conflicts happened, which literal is strongly deterministic, etc. It also needs a lot of run-time bookkeeping for information such as which literal binds which variable. Although the run-time analysis and bookkeeping may help their scheme to reduce the number of modifying goals, the overhead in terms of both time and space can be excessive as compared to our algorithm.

8. Concluding Remarks

We have presented a backtracking scheme which works when AND-parallelism is exploited in a logic program. Since, the scheme makes use of the dependencies between the literals in a clause, it is potentially useful (as a replacement for the naive backtracking strategy of Prolog) even if no parallel hardware is available to exploit AND-parallelism. In the sequential case, our scheme avoids unnecessary backtracking at the expense of the overhead associated with the transfer of messages between literals. This overhead is potentially smaller than the overhead associated with the intelligent backtracking scheme of Porto, Pereira, and Bruynooghe. If the linear ordering chosen in Section 2 corresponds to the left-to-right ordering of the literals in the clause, and if no OR parallelism is exploited, then our scheme generates solutions in exactly the same order as Prolog does.

Our scheme is based on the following assumptions:

i) generators and consumers of different variables can all be designated at compile time;
ii) the data-dependency graph is acyclic; and
iii) the message passing and processing take zero time.

In [9] we present a more general version of our backward execution (as well as forward execution) algorithm which works even if generators and consumers are chosen at run time. This generalized version also works when the message passing and processing take non-zero time. If the data-dependency graph is cyclic (because, for example, of two literals each is a generator and a consumer for the other), then it would not be possible to find a linear ordering of the literals in the clause such that the generator of a variable always comes before its consumers. We are currently working on a scheme in which the cycles of the graph are resolved (and the linear ordering is constructed) dynamically as the execution of the clause proceeds [10].

References

1. Bruynooghe, M. and L. M. Pereira, "Deduction Revision by Intelligent Backtracking," in *Implementations of Prolog*, ed. J. A. Campbell, pp. 194-215, Ellis Horwood Limited, 1984.
2. Chang, J.-H. and A.M. Despain, "Semi-Intelligent Backtracking of Prolog Based on a Static Data Dependency Analysis," *Proceedings of IEEE Symposium on Logic Programming*, pp. 10-21, August, 1985.
3. Conery, J. S., "The AND/OR Process Model for Parallel Interpretation of Logic Programs," Ph.D. Thesis, (Technical Report 204), University of California, Irvine, California, June, 1983.
4. Conery, J. S. and D. F. Kibler, "Parallel Interpretation of Logic Programs," *Proceedings of the Conference on Functional Programming Languages and Computer Architecture*, pp. 163-170, ACM, October, 1981.
5. Conery, J.S. and D.F. Kibler, "AND Parallelism and Nondeterminism in Logic Programs," *New Generation Computing*, vol. 3(1985), pp. 43-70, OHMSHA,LTD. and Springer-Verlag, 1985.
6. Cox, P. T., "Finding Backtrack Points for Intelligent Backtracking," in *Implementations of Prolog*, ed. J. A. Campbell, pp. 216-233, Ellis Horwood Limited, 1984.
7. Kale, L.V. and D.S. Warren, "A Class of Architectures for a Prolog Machine," *Proceeding of the Second International Logic Programming Conference*, pp. 171-182, Uppsala, Sweden, July, 1984.
8. Kasif, S. and J. Minker, "The Intelligent Channel: A Scheme for Result Sharing in Logic Programs," *Proceedings of the 9th IJCAI*, pp. 29-31, Los Angeles, August, 1985.
9. Lin, Y.J. and V. Kumar, "A Decentralized Model for Executing Logic Programs in Parallel," AI Lab TR, The University of Texas at Austin, Austin, Texas, April, 1986.
10. Lin, Y.J., "A Parallel Implementation of Logic Programs," *Ph.D. dissertation*, The University of Texas at Austin, Austin, Texas, in preparation.
11. Pereira, L. M. and A. Porto, "Selective Backtracking," in *Logic Programming*, ed. K. L. Clark and S.-A. Tarnlund, pp. 107-114, Academic Press, 1982.

Appendix A

Lemma 1. If P_i fails, then P_m can possibly cure the failure of P_i if and only if $P_m \in X_i$ and $m<i$.

Proof: The if part is trivial. Let us focus on the other direction. Assume that literals are divided into two sets. Set S_1 consists of every literal which has directly or indirectly caused the failure of P_i; and set S_2 consists of the rest of the literals. If P_m is not a member of X_i, then re-solving P_m will not affect the success or failure of any literal in S_1. Therefore P_i would keep failing for exactly the same reasons for which literals in S_1 have caused its failure before. Hence P_m must be a member of X_i.

Assume that $m>i$. Then P_m is not an ancestor of P_i. Let P_m be an ancestor of P_j, where the failure of P_j has directly or indirectly caused the failure of P_i. In order to possibly cure the failure of P_i, P_m should be able to prevent P_j from causing the failure of P_i. However P_m should have failed to do so, otherwise P_j would not have caused the failure of P_i.

□

Lemma 2. $bi = \max\{k|P_k \in S_i \text{ and } k<i\}$.

Proof: First we prove that $P_{bi} \in S_i$. By definition, the set S_i is the union of the parents of P_i and those literals which are parents of some P_j such P_j has directly or indirectly caused the failure of P_i. Suppose P_{bi} is not a parent of any such P_j, and P_{bi} is not a parent of P_i. Then since $P_{bi} \in X_i$, P_{bi} must be an ancestor of some P_m which is either a parent of a certain P_j, or a parent of P_i. Therefore P_m can possibly cure the failure of P_i. Hence by lemma 1, $P_m \in X_i$ and $m<i$. However, $bi<m$ because P_{bi} is an ancestor of P_m. Thus, there is a $P_m \in X_i$ such that $bi<m<i$, which is contrary to the definition of bi.

Now we prove that $bi = \max\{k|P_k \in S_i \text{ and } k<i\}$. From the definition of X_i and S_i, it follows that $\{P_k|P_k \in S_i \text{ and } k<i\} \subseteq \{P_k|P_k \in X_i \text{ and } k<i\}$. Hence $bi = \max\{k|\, P_k \in X_i \text{ and } k<i\} \geq \max\{k|\, P_k \in S_i \text{ and } k<i\}$. But $P_{bi} \in S_i$ and $bi<i$; therefore $bi \leq \max\{k|\, P_k \in S_i \text{ and } k<i\}$. It follows that $bi = \max\{k|P_k \in S_i \text{ and } k<i\}$.

□

Lemma 3. At the time P_i fails, $\{P_j|\, P_j \in \text{B-list}(P_i)\} = \{P_j|\, P_j \in S_i \text{ and } j<i\}$.

Proof: By induction on the failure level of the failed literal. The failure level of a literal L is defined as follows.

1. If no redo operations have been done on L since the most recent instant when L was changed from the GATHER mode to the EXECUTION mode, then the failure level of L=0.
2. Otherwise, the failure level of L = n+1, where n = max{f(Q)| failure of Q has directly invoked a redo operation on L since L started executing most recently, and f(Q) was the failure level of Q at the time Q failed}.

Base Case: Failure level of $P_i = 0$.

Since no redo operation has been done on P_i, $\{P_j|\, P_j \in \text{B-list}(P_i)\} = S_i = \{P_j|\, P_j \text{ is a parent of } P_i\}$. Furthermore, each j is smaller than i, as P_j is an ancestor of P_i.

Induction Step: Suppose the theorem holds for every failed literal whose failure level is less than or equal to r, and let P_i is a failed literal whose failure level is r+1.

From the time P_i was most recently transferred to the EXECUTION mode, assume that the failure of $P_{i1},\ldots,P_{ik},\ldots,P_{in}$ have directly invoked redo operations on P_i. Note that each P_{ik} $(1 \leq k \leq n)$ is either a child of P_i or an ancestor of a descendant of P_i such that $ik > i$. By definition S_i is the union of S_{ik}, $ik = i1$ to in, and the set of ancestors of P_i. Therefore, any literal P_j in $\{P_j|\, P_j \in S_i \text{ and } j<i\}$ should be either a parent of P_i or in S_{ik} for some $1 \leq k \leq n$. If P_j is a parent of P_i, then P_j is surely in B-list(P_i). If P_j is not a parent of P_i, then (because $j<i<ik$) P_j should appear in B-list(P_{ik}) by the induction hypothesis. Hence, it would have been merged into B-list(P_i) by our backward execution algorithm while handling the failure of P_{ik}. Therefore B-list(P_i) contains every literal in $\{P_j|\, P_j \in S_i \text{ and } j<i\}$.

If P_m is in B-list(P_i), then either P_m is a parent of P_i or P_m is in B-list(P_{ik}) for some ik (and was merged into B-list(P_i) after the failure of P_{ik}). If P_m is a parent of P_i, then clearly $P_m \in S_i$ and $m<i$. Otherwise, P_m is in B-list(P_{ik}), and is also in S_{ik} (and therefore in S_i) by the induction hypothesis. Furthermore, it must be true that $m<i$, as otherwise in our backward execution algorithm the failure of P_{ik} would have caused a redo operation on P_m instead of P_i. This proves that $\{P_j|\, P_j \in S_i \text{ and } j<i\}$ contains every literal in B-list(P_i).

□

Appendix B

B.1

The following is an example of how our backward execution algorithm works. Assume that we are solving P_0(A,B,C) with the following set of clauses.

P_0(A,B,C) ← P_1(A), P_2(A,B), P_3(A,C), P_4(C), P_5(B,C).
P_1(a1).
P_2(a1, b1).
P_2(a1, b2).
P_3(a1, c1).
P_3(a1, c2).
P_4(c1).
P_5(b1, c2).
P_5(b2, c1).

The data dependency graph for solving P_0(A,B,C) is in Figure 2.

Unfinished-successors of P_i represents the set of its children which are not in the FINISHED mode. It becomes non-empty only when P_i sends out generated values. #N denotes subgoal P_N and $\uparrow$N denotes the process created to solve P_N.

<1> #1, #2, #3, and #4 have succeeded. Process for #5 is still executing.
Current bindings are a1/A, b1/B, c1/C.

Literal	Mode	Status	Unfinished-successors	B-list
#1	execution	solved	(#2, #3)	()
#2	execution	solved	(#5)	(#1)
#3	execution	solved	(#5)	(#1)
#4	finished	-	()	(#3)
#5	execution	unsolved	()	(#3, #2)

<2> #5 fails. $\uparrow$3 is sent a redo message. $\uparrow$4 and $\uparrow$5 are canceled.
Current bindings are a1/A, b1/B.

Literal	Mode	Status	Unfinished-successors	B-list
#1	execution	solved	(#2, #3)	()
#2	execution	solved	(#5)	(#1)
#3	execution	unsolved	()	(#2, #1)
#4	gather	-	()	()
#5	gather	-	()	()

<3> #3 succeeds again. Both P_4 and P_5 start executing.
Current bindings are a1/A, b1/B, c2/C.

Literal	Mode	Status	Unfinished-successors	B-list
#1	execution	solved	(#2, #3)	()
#2	execution	solved	(#5)	(#1)
#3	execution	solved	(#4, #5)	(#2, #1)
#4	execution	unsolved	()	(#3)
#5	execution	unsolved	()	(#3, #2)

<4> #4 fails. ↑3 is sent another redo. ↑4 and ↑5 are canceled.
Current bindings are a1/A, b1/B.

Literal	Mode	Status	Unfinished-successors	B-list
#1	execution	solved	(#2, #3)	()
#2	execution	solved	(#5)	(#1)
#3	execution	unsolved	()	(#2, #1)
#4	gather	-	()	()
#5	gather	-	()	()

<5> #3 can not generate any new binding and therefore it fails. ↑2 is sent a redo message. ↑3 is reset. ↑4 and ↑5 are already canceled.

Conery's backward execution algorithm will incorrectly decide to send ↑1 a redo message in this case, as we have shown in section 7.1.

Current bindings are a1/A.

Literal	Mode	Status	Unfinished-successors	B-list
#1	execution	solved	(#2, #3)	()
#2	execution	unsolved	()	(#1)
#3	execution	unsolved	()	(#1)
#4	gather	-	()	()
#5	gather	-	()	()

<6> #2 succeeds and generates a new value for variable B. #3 also succeeds and generates a value for variable C which is the first value it generated before. Both ↑4 and ↑5 can start executing.

Current bindings are a1/A, b2/B, c1/C.

Literal	Mode	Status	Unfinished-successors	B-list
#1	execution	solved	(#2, #3)	()
#2	execution	solved	(#5)	(#1)
#3	execution	solved	(#4, #5)	(#1)
#4	execution	unsolved	()	(#3)
#5	execution	unsolved	()	(#3, #2)

<7> This time both #4 and #5 succeed.
The final bindings are a1/A, b2/B, c1/C.

Literal	Mode	Status	Unfinished-successors	B-list
#1	finished	-	()	()
#2	finished	-	()	(#1)
#3	finished	-	()	(#1)
#4	finished	-	()	(#3)
#5	finished	-	()	(#3, #2)

B.2

Now suppose that we are solving P_0(A,B,C) with the following set of clauses.

P_0(A,B,C) ← P_1(A), P_2(A,B), P_3(A,C), P_4(C), P_5(B,C).
P_1(a1).
P_1(a2).
P_2(a1, b1).
P_2(a2, b2).
P_3(a2, c1).
P_3(a1, c2).
P_4(c1).
P_5(b1, c2).
P_5(b2, c1).

<1> #1, #2, and #3 have succeeded. Processes for #4 and #5 are still executing.
Current bindings are a1/A, b1/B, c2/C.

Literal	Mode	Status	Unfinished-successors	B-list
#1	execution	solved	(#2, #3)	()
#2	execution	solved	(#5)	(#1)
#3	execution	solved	(#5)	(#1)
#4	execution	unsolved	()	(#3)
#5	execution	unsolved	()	(#3, #2)

It is easy to see that P_4 will fail and cause the failure of P_3. Since B-list(P_3) in this case is (#1) instead of (#2, #1), P_3 will backtrack directly to P_1. In Chang and Despain's approach, P_3 always backtracks to P_2, as P_2 is the type-II backtracking literal of P_3.

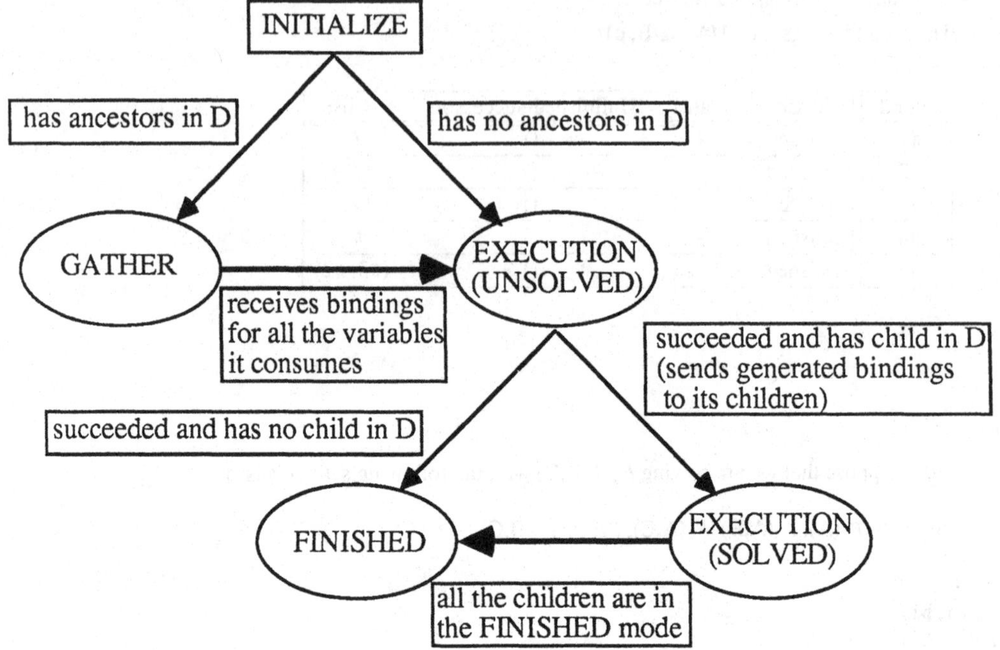

Figure 1: Graphical form of the Forward Execution Algorithm

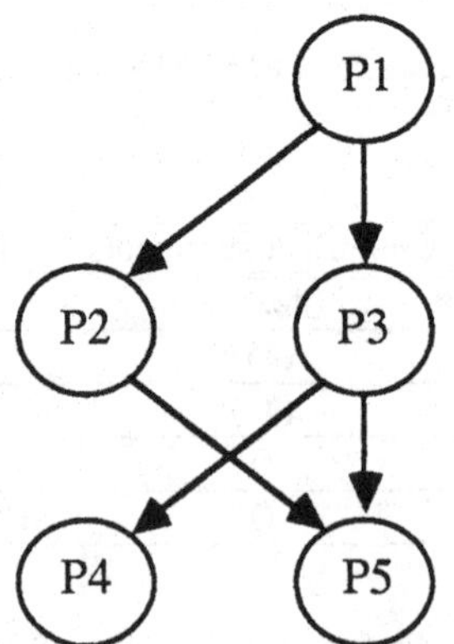

Figure 2: Data-dependency graph of the example

DELTA PROLOG:
A DISTRIBUTED BACKTRACKING EXTENSION WITH EVENTS

Luís Moniz Pereira, Luís Monteiro, José Cunha, Joaquim N. Aparício
Universidade Nova de Lisboa, Portugal

Abstract

We present Delta Prolog, a distributed logic programming language that extends Prolog to include AND-parallelism (in a single processor or across a network of processors), interprocess communication via message passing with two-way pattern matching, interprocess synchronization with simultaneous message passing, and distributed backtracking among a family of processes. The extension is achieved, at the language level, by just two additional types of goals — events and splits. The implementation is written part in Prolog and part in C, with a small number of core primitives, to help portability. It is still experimental and expected to evolve. In this work we present the language's distinguishing features, describe its semantics, exhibit programs and analyse their behaviour, examine the implementation, and mention conclusions, advantages of the approach and the next developments.

1 Summary of language concepts

Delta Prolog extends Prolog, with the following concepts [cf. LM83, LMP84] :

1- Families of processes are defined using the operators "," and "//", for sequential and parallel composition of goals. "//" is defined as a right associative operator, `a//b//c` meaning `a//(b//c)`, and executed as a binary Prolog goal — the split.

2- Process comunication and synchronization is supported through event goals, a construct based on the Distributed Logic notion of event.

3- The computation rule uses the following mechanisms :

3.1- explicit AND-parallelism "//" and the sequentially constraint for goal activation, with `a,b//c,d` meaning `a,(b//c),d` and left to right goal selection within a clause body.
3.2- interprocess synchronization and communication achieved by executing event goals.
3.3- the search rule, at present, is based on sequential search and backtracking within each process computation, using a global control strategy with distributed backtracking when a "family of processes" is involved.

4- a program without event or split goals is a Prolog program.

2 Programming model defined by the language

2.1 Parallelism

A distributed Delta Prolog program is a set of clauses with usual Prolog syntax, plus the parallel execution of goals that may communicate through events.

The programming model assumes the user is responsible for exploiting the potential parallelism that may exist in each specific problem. When using G1//G2, goals G1 and G2 are activated in parallel, still meaning a conjunction, the parallel composition succeeding only if both G1 and G2 succeed, with compatible bindings. If the bindings are not compatible the following procedure takes place: G2 initiates backtracking and G1 awaits for the next solution. If no more solutions for G2 are found, G1 backtracks and G2 is relaunched. If no compatible solutions are found the split goal G1//G2 fails. When there occurs backtracking into a split goal after it has solved, the same above procedure applies.

If a program uses no event goals, it reduces to an ordinary Prolog program plus "//" meaning a conjunction, although implying parallel execution of goals. No distributed backtracking occurs then, paralleled processes behaving as if serialized when backtracking reaches a split goal.

2.2 Process communication through events

2.2.1 Synchronous event goals

Events are introduced in Prolog by the use of "event goals". Synchronous "event goals" [LMP84] have the form `Term1 ! Name : Cond1` or `Term2 ? Name : Cond2` with "!" and "?" meaning complementary parts of the event `Name` and being binary predicate symbols. When no condition is needed they can reduce to `Term1 ! Name` and `Term2 ? Name`.

Synchronous communication is binary and each process contributes with its complementary part to the event. Two processes communicating via some event EV must have the goals :

Process 1	Process 2
`Term1 ! EV : Cond1`	`Term2 ? EV : Cond2`

and they both solve iff Term1 and Term2 match, and conditions Cond1 and Cond2 are satisfied locally to each process, with event EV succeeding. For a sucessfull synchronous event, the following must hold:

1- in the family of processes a pair of processes must try the event ;
2- the two "complementary" parts of the event (i.e. "!" and "?") must be present ;
3- the terms presented by the pair must unify ;
4- in case the terms unify, the conditions must solve (local to each process).

The absence of conditions means they are true. When one process first attempts the event, it waits until its partner is ready to engage in the event. Distributed backtracking can start for one of two reasons, be discussed later:

1- two complementary event goals are reached, but the event may not occur (because unification failed or some of the conditions are not satisfied)
2- one process backtracks to an event that has already succeeded in the past

2.2.2 Asynchronous event goals

If synchronicity is not required, Delta Prolog provides additional complementary events, T^^E and T??E, where T^^E does not wait for T??E, but not vice-versa. The semantics of these asynchronous events is defined in a way comparable, respectively, to the one for "write" and "read" in i/o streams. No special backtracking applies to event goals of this type. Using this event type, the user may impose synchronicity without distributed backtracking simply by defining other event type clauses such as (E' and E'' are name variants of E):

```
T !* E :- T ^^ E', T ?? E''.
T ?* E :- T ?? E', T ^^ E''.
```

2.3 Operational semantics of Delta Prolog

We examine now the forward and backward components of the operational semantics. Like the declarative semantics, the operational semantics extends that of Prolog to account for the two new types of goals, events and splits. The basic principles that govern it are:

1- There is defined a total order among each family tree of Delta Prolog processes descendants from an initial root Delta Prolog process, as follows: (a) the root process is the first in the order (b) in a split goal a//b, the left argument goal execution will continue the process where the split goal is activated, and the right argument goal will execute in a new spawned Delta Prolog process, inserted immediately to the right of the spawning one in the total order (c) a process is removed from the total order when its spawning split goal fails. Within each process forward execution is as in Prolog.

2- For each root top goal, we want an exhaustive search for solutions to take place. In Delta Prolog, backtracking follows Prolog's within each process. When backtracking reaches a split goal or a synchronous event between processes in the same family, distributed backtracking is sparked off, disciplined by the rules in a subsequent section, which require the total order defined above.

3- Each process may communicate through synchronous events with any other process in the same family, save itself; the distributed backtracking discipline (cf.below) within a family ensures completeness of search except for loops and deadlocks.

4- A synchronous event name may not be used by more then two processes of the same family, otherwise completeness is not guaranteed by the search strategy. (If multiple consumers or producers for some term are desired, asynchronous events or a communications manager can be used.)

5- Each process may communicate with processes from different families through synchronous events; no distributed backtracking discipline is imposed then because no interpretation of logical conjunction is assumed regarding families of different roots. Such event names must not then be used in the same family, for the sake of completeness.

6- Each process may communicate through asynchronous events with any other process, including itself; again, no distributed backtracking discipline applies in that case.

7- Events are atomic and instantaneous. No synchronous events may appear in the conditions of an event. Conditions are seen as an extension to the unification between the two event terms, and thus allow expression of additional constraints on those terms. Consequently conditions are allowed to solve once only or not at all.

3 Quick sort example

This is an example of dynamic spawning of goals (where no events are used). Difference lists are used common to both goals in the split (partition is defined as usual):

```
quicksort(Unsorted,Sorted) :- qsort(Unsorted,Sorted-[]).
qsort([A|Unsorted],Sorted-L) :-
                partition(Unsorted,A,Smaller,Larger),
                qsort(Smaller,Sorted-[A|Sortedlarger])//
                qsort(Larger,Sortedlarger-L).
qsort([],L-L).
```

4 Distributed backtracking

When introducing the parallel composition of goals in Delta Prolog, and further requiring that it read like a conjuntive goal, an option must be made about the following point : should `G1//G2` be able to perform an exhaustive search of the solutions space of goals `G1` and `G2`, the same way Prolog does for `G1,G2` ? (we defer this discussion till later).

When both processes participating in an event move forward in their (sequential) computations, and later on one of them backtracks to its event goal, what should happen ? The process simply backtracks past that point without warning its partner ; or a well-defined strategy controls the global evolution of the concurrent processes, through distributed backtracking. The first option was taken in the first version as described in [LMP84]. It is the easiest to implement, and gives the user full responsability for the control of the concurrent evolution of the processes. Before seeing the general control strategy for multiple processes used in the current version, let us see a simple example:

```
a(X) :- aa(X) , t(X) ! ev.        and        aa(1).     bb(1).
b(X) :- bb(X) , t(X) ? ev.                   aa(2).     bb(2).
```

Let the top goal be `a(X)//b(Y)` and let us follow its step by step execution.

1) Root process `P1` at the split goal launches `P2` to solve `b(Y)` and itself solves `a(X)`
2) `P1` solves `aa(1)`, then tries `t(1) ! ev` and `P2` solves `bb(1)`, then tries `t(1) ? ev`
3 and 3') event `ev` succeeds with `P1` solving `t(1) ! ev` and `P2` solving `t(1) ? ev`
4) the top goal solves with `a(1)//b(1)`
5) If another solution is sought the backtracking starts; as `P2` is on the right, it's its responsability to find an alternative to the previous event; so `P2` backtracks to `bb(Y)` and `P1` retries `t(1) ! ev`
6') `P2` solves `bb(2)` and proceeds to the event goal `t(2) ? ev`
7 and 7') The event can not succeed since the terms do not unify
8) As `P1` is on the left, it waits on the event for an alternative and `P2` backtracks again
9') `P2` fails its top goal `b(Y)`. As `P1` is waiting for an event, `P1` backtracks from `t(1) ! ev` and `P2` restarts its top goal anew.
10 and 10') `P1` backtracks, solves `aa(2)`, tries `t(2) ! ev`. `P2` solves `bb(1)`, tries `t(1) ? ev`
11 and 11') The event cannot succeed since the terms do not unify

12) Again, P1 waits at t(2) ! ev and P2 backtracks
13') P2 solves bb(2) in backtracking, then tries t(2) ? ev
14 and 14') Event ev succeeds with P1 solving t(2) ! ev and P2 solving t(2) ? ev
15) The top goal solves with a(2)//b(2).
16) If yet another solution is required P2 backtracks to bb(Y) and P1 retries t(2) ! ev
17') P2 fails top goal b(Y); as before, it restarts anew and P1 backtracks from t(2) ! ev
18) P1 fails a(X), then fails the top goal.

4.1 The rules of distributed backtracking

When a process fails in the course of a normal computation, it starts backtracking. If it reaches a synchronous event in backtracking, the event must be undone, and for this reason the other process participating in the event must jump back to that event while undoing all the subsequent computation. The problem of distributed backtracking is that of guaranteeing the completeness of the search space of all processes, so that possible solutions are not passed over unnoticed. The main decision to be taken, then, concerns the strategy of recovering from an undone event (any other goal being local to a single process, its backtracking is governed by the underlying Prolog interpreter). This only applies to synchronous events between two processes in the same family, i.e. with the same root ancestor. When events are asynchronous, or synchronous between events in different families, no distributed backtracking discipline is imposed (i.e. such goals in a process are backtracked over, just like any other goal). The reason we make the distinction is that we interpret a family of processes as solving a logical conjunction of goals. Processes not in the same family are not necessarily interpreted as participating in a logical conjunction. One immediate possible extension is to allow for syntactically distinguished synchronous events to which no distributed backtracking discipline is applied, whether or not the participating processes are in the same family. This will allow for more efficiency when so desired, as there will be no distributed backtracking overheads in that case, nor the need to use the "cut" to curtail it.

A synchronous event is the joint resolution of two complementary event goals in distinct processes. To undo the event, one of the event goals must be retried (i.e. launched in the same conditions as in the last time), and the other one must fail, giving rise to backtracking in the corresponding process. The problem is then which goal is retried and which one fails. There is a subsidiary problem, related to the fact that, when a process jumps back to a past event and undoes the computation thencefrom, it may in particular jump over (undo) some other events, with consequences to the intervening processes. In the sequel we establish an overall distributed backtracking strategy that retains completeness of search, except for deadlocks and non-terminating computations. We distinguish three execution modes of Delta Prolog programs: forward execution, backtracking and jumping back. Forward execution has been explained before at some length. We concentrate now on the description of backtracking and jumping back. We recall here some basic principles:

1- All processes existing at any one time have a unique root ancestor process.
2- There is defined a total order among all processes with the same root which are active at any moment. We refer to this order as the left-right order.
3- Any synchronous event name is shared by only two distinct processes (i.e. events are

necessarily binary and with the same partner; subsequent research will delve into the problem of allowing other event types).

The general rule for undoing an event, to be explained in more detail below, is that the event goal in the left process is retried and the event goal in the right process fails. A similar left/right-based rule will be used for jumping back. To simplify the presentation, we assume there are no "cuts" in the program. The effect of the "cut" on distributed backtracking will be discussed at the end of the section on jumping back.

4.1.1 Backtracking

What happens if process P attempts goal g and fails (we consider only synchronous events in one family):

1- If g is a non-event goal, P backtrackings controlled by the underlying interpreter.
2- If g is an event goal, let Q be the other process trying to participate in the event. Of P and Q, the left process retries its event goal and becomes a waiting process, while the right process backtracks in search of communication alternatives (both must solve for the AND to succeed).

We now describe the backtracking procedure. Suppose a process P starts backtracking, either because some ordinary goal in P has failed, or because P is searching for communication alternatives with a waiting process Q. It is important to differentiate between the two reasons, since the first concerns the process P alone, while the second involves another process Q waiting to communicate with P. We shall say respectively that P backtracks freely or backtracks to satisfy a request from Q.

While backtracking is governed by the underlying Prolog interpreter, two cases may arise which need added control: backtracking eventually reaches an event, or process P fails. Let us analyse the two cases in turn. We start with the first one, viz. when backtracking of P reaches an event. Let R be the other process participating in that event. We distinguish two subcases, depending on whether P is backtracking freely or to satisfy a request from Q. (The reader may find it useful to sketch on paper the situations that follow. On a first reading he may assume there are only two processes, and read items 1 and 2.2 below, skipping the other subcases of 2 and the section on jumping back.)

1- If P is backtracking freely, R jumps back to the corresponding event goal. (The jump back procedure will be described in the next section; if P and R are the only processes, however, R's jumping back consists simply in undoing all the computation from the P-R event onwards.) Of P and R, the left process retries its event goal, and the right process backtracks beyond the event goal and tries to satisfy the request from the left process.

2- If P is trying to satisfy a request from Q, however, then Q must be to the left of P. Four cases may arise, depending on the relative left/right position of R with respect to Q and P:

2.1- If R is to the left of Q then Q fails the waiting event goal and starts to backtrack freely, while P restarts anew at the goal immediately after the P-R event. The reason for this choice is the following. P is not able to satisfy Q's request unless the P-R event is undone. However, since R is to the left of Q, the P-R event should not be undone before all search possibilities to its right have been exhausted. Therefore, the only possibility left is for Q to bactrack freely from the P-Q event and to relaunch P anew after the P-R event, so that for other Q alternatives all P alternatives after P-R are available.

2.2- If R=Q we conclude that P has not been able to satisfy Q's request in the context established by the previous communication between P and Q. Rather than undoing the new event backtracked to by P, it is Q's turn to try and make another request. Thus Q fails from the event goal and starts backtracking freely, while P starts anew immediately after the new event it backtracked to.

2.3- If R is between Q and P we have two possibilities: either to undo the event between P and R, or to force the backtracking of Q. The undoing of the P-R event depends on the possible consequences of R's jumping back to that event. If R's jumping back is not possible (see the section on jumping back) then Q has to backtrack freely while P restarts anew immediately after the P-R event. Otherwise the P-R event will be undone, R retries the corresponding event goal and P backtracks from the event to satisfy R's request.

2.4- The case in which R is to the right of P is similar to the previous one, except that, when the event P-R has to be undone, P retries the corresponding event goal and R backtracks from it.

We now describe the consequences of a top goal failure of process P:

1- Assume first P was bactracking freely. If P is the only process in existence then it must be the root process, and the execution as a whole fails. If not, P is one of the processes associated with the execution of a split goal g//h (it does not matter which), and the immediate effect of P's failure is to fail the aforementioned goal.
2- If P was trying to satisfy a request of another process Q, then Q fails the corresponding event goal and backtracks freely, and P restarts anew its top goal.

4.1.2 Jumping back

We have seen that backtracking of one process may force another process to jump back to a given event, undoing all the computation thencefrom. The computation that must be undone may comprise a number of events with still other processes, which accordingly have to undo the corresponding computations, and so on. This jumping back procedure is not always possible, as we shall see below. A process R first jumps back in response to a demand originated in another process P. The process P originating the demand may have been backtracking freely or to satisfy a request from another process Q. In any case, the immediate reason for the demand is that, in its backtracking, P has reached an event with R, which consequently must jump back to the corresponding event goal whenever possible. The undoing of all the computation of R from the event P-R onwards may possibly result in the undoing of other events, with the corresponding jumping back of the processes participating in those events, and so on.

To analyse the situation we construct a jump back tree with the jumping back processes as follows. The root of the tree is labeled with the P-R event. For each process S which communicated with R after the P-R event (if any), there is a son of the root labeled by the earliest R-S event which occurred after the P-R event. The procedure iterates for the sons of the root, and so on. A node labelled by X-Y will be called a jump back node for process Y. The meaning of such a node is that process X forces process Y to jump back to the X-Y event. The purpose of the jump back tree is to centralize all the information concerning the processes which have to jump back. (This is needed only to simplify the presentation; the implementation of the jumping back procedure needs not construct the tree explicitly.) What if some process Z has two jump back nodes X-Z, Y-Z ? (Note that, by the construction of the jump back tree, X and Y are distinct processes). As Z participated in both events, one was executed before the other in Z's computation, say X-Z was executed before Y-Z. This fact has two consequences. First, X-Z does not occur in the sub-tree rooted at Y-Z (the reason is that, as each event in the tree was executed before its sons, by transitivity it was executed before all its successors). Second, the jump back information contained in the sub-tree rooted at Y-Z (viz. the processes which have to jump back due to the fact that Z jumps back at least to the event Y-Z) is already contained in the subtree rooted at X-Z. Since anyway Z has to jump back at least to the event X-Z, the information recorded by the sub-tree rooted at Y-Z is redundant, and so this sub-tree may be deleted from the jump back tree. Thus, given all jump back nodes for a process, the sub-trees rooted at all but the one corresponding to the earliest event may be discarded, since no relevant information is lost. Thus each process is left with a unique jump back node. We still call jump back tree to this modified tree.

If P has been backtracking freely, the jumping back is always possible, while if P has been backtracking to satisfy a request from Q it is not possible if Q or some process to the left of Q has a jump back node. The reason for the latter case is that if P is not able to satisfy a request from Q without interfering with Q itself or the processes to the left of Q, then Q's request can not be satisfied at all — otherwise some events would be undone prior to the exhaustion of all search possibilities to their right. The appropriate measures to be taken in this situation have been described in the previous backtracking section. When the second case is possible, a single procedure applies to both cases, to be described now. What happens to R has been spelled out in the backtracking section. We now proceed to the sons of the root, to the sons of the sons, and so on. Consider an arbitrary jump back node S-T for process T in the jump back tree. We distinguish two cases, depending on whether S is to the left or to the right of T.

1- If S is to the left of T, T restarts anew immediately after the first event preceeding the S-T event, or, in case such an event does not exist, T restarts anew at its top goal. The reason for this choice is to make available all T alternatives for communication when S tries later to communicate with T (remember that a right process has, by convention, the responsability of supplying a left process with communication alternatives).
2- If S is to the right of T, T retries the S-T event. (This time, T waits for S to supply it with the communication alternatives.)

The effect of the "cut" on backtracking is as follows. Suppose in the course of backtracking process P reaches a "cut". The desired behaviour is exactly as if an imaginary leftmost process had backtracked to an imaginary event just before the "cut", therefore provoking a jumping back of P to that event.

4.2 Ordered permutation sort example of distributed backtracking

Two processes cooperate to sort a list using distributed backtracking. One process (perm) makes successive permutations of the list sending each element, as they became available, to the other process (ord), which tests them with regard to order. As soon as the order is violated backtracking starts, so that a permutation does not have to be completed before it is rejected.

```
sort(L,S) :- perm(L,S) // ord(S).                                    (s1)

perm([],[])  :- [] ! ev.                                             (p1)
perm([H|T],[E|S]) :- choose(E,[H|T],R), E ! ev, perm(R,S).           (p2)

choose(H,[H|T],T).                                                   (p3)
choose(X,[H|T],[H|L]) :- choose(X,T,L).                              (p4)
```

The ord process will receive element by element, admiting them only if they are ordered.

```
ord(S)    :- Y ? ev : ( number(Y) ), ord([Y],S).                     (o1)
ord([])   :- Y ? ev : ( Y == [] ).                                   (o2)

ord(L,S)  :- Y ? ev : ( number(Y), admit(Y,L,NL) ), ord(NL,S).       (o3)
ord(S,S)  :- Y ? ev : ( Y == [] ).                                   (o4)

admit(Y,[H|T],[H|R]) :- admit(Y,T,R).
admit(Y,[E],[E,Y])   :- Y >= E.
```

Note that we could just as well have `sort(L,S) :- ord(S) // perm(L,S).`

Consider the top goal for `s1`: `sort([3,1,2],S)`, where `S` will be come `[1,2,3]`.

0) The `sort([3,1,2],S)` matches `s1` ; next the split goal is activated.

1) `perm([3,1,2],S)` matches p2 and 3 is chosen as the first element to send.
1') `ord(S)` matches o1 and waits at the event goal.

2) `perm` solves event `3 ! ev`, then recurses with `perm([1,2],S)`.
2') `ord` solves event `3 ? ev : number(3)` then recurses with `ord([3],S)`.

The event has succeeded with the exchange of the number 3.

3) `perm([1,2],S)` matches p2, chooses 1, then tries the event `1 ! ev`.
3') `ord([3],S)` matches o3 and tries `Y ? ev : number(Y), admit(Y,[3],NL)`.

4 and 4') The event fails as 1 is not admited to the list `[3]`.

5) `perm` is the left process so it waits trying the event goal `1 ! ev`.
5') As `ord` is the process on the right, it starts backtracking, trying to find an alternative to the event.

6') `ord([3],S)` matches now o4, trying event goal `Y ? ev : Y==[]`.

7 and 7') The event fails again in the ord's side because `1==[]` fails.

8) `perm` stays trying `1 ! ev` in clause p2.
8') `ord` has no alternatives for `ord([3],S)`, and fails to the event goal where it received the number 3, in clause `o1`.

9 and 9') `ord` has no way to solve the event goal, so it's `perm`'s turn to find an alternative.

10) **perm** starts backtracking from 1 ! ev.
10') ord starts anew after the event 3 ? ev : number(3).

11) **perm** chooses 2 and tries 2 ! ev.
11') again ord([3],S) matches o3 and tries Y ? ev : number(Y), admit(Y,[3],NL).

12 and 12') the event fails as 2 is not admited in the list [3].

13) **perm** is on the left and stays trying 2 ! ev.
13') ord starts backtracking from the event and matches o4, then tries Y ? ev.

14 and 14') the event fails in the ord's side because 2 == [] fails.

15) **perm** is on the left and stays trying 2 ! ev.
15') ord starts backtracking and as it has no more alternatives to ord([3],S), it backtracks to the event 3 ? ev : number(3).

16 and 16') ord has no way to solve the event goal, so it's **perm**'s turn to find an alternative.

17) **perm** starts bcktracking from the event goal is trying 2 ! ev.
17') ord starts anew after the "exchange" of the 3.

18) **perm** has no alternatives to choose and fails perm([3],S).

19 and 19') As **perm** has no alternatives, the "exchange" of the 3 must be undone.

20) **perm** retries 3 ! ev.
20') ord starts backtracking past 3 ? ev : number(3).

21') ord(S) matches o2 and tries Y ? ev : Y == [].

22 and 22') event fails as 3 == [] fails in the ord's side.

23) as ord has no alternatives for the first event, is **perm**'s turn to start backtracking.
23') ord(S) starts anew, matches o1, then tries Y ? ev : number(Y).

24) **perm** chooses 1 and tries 1 ! ev.

25) **perm** solves 1 ! ev, then recurses with perm([3,2],S).
25') ord solves 1 ? ev : number(1), then recurses with ord([1],S).

26) perm([3,2],S) matches p2 chooses 3 then tries 3 ! ev.
26') ord([1],S) matches o3 and tries event goal Y ? ev : number(Y), admit(Y,[1],NL).

27) **perm** solves event goal 3 ! ev, then recurses with perm([2],S).
27') ord solves event goal 3 ? ev : number(3), admit(3,[1],[1,3]), then recurses with ord([1,3],S).

28) perm([2],S) matches p2, chooses 2, then tries 2 ! ev.
28') ord([1,3],S) matches o3, then tries Y ? ev : number(Y), admit(Y,[1,3],NL).

29 and 29') The event fails because the condition admit(2,[1,3],NL) fails, in ord's side.

30) **perm** is on the left and stays trying 2 ! ev.
30') ord starts backtracking from the event and matches clause o4.

31') ord tries Y ? ev : Y==[].

32 and 32') Event fails.

33) **perm** is on the left and stays trying 2 ! ev.
33') ord initiates backtracking from the failed event.

34 and 34') As ord has no alternatives after the "exchange" of the 3 perm must try to find an alternative after the "exchange" of the number 3.

35) perm starts backtracking past 2 ! ev.
35') ord starts anew after receiving 3, matches o3 and waits at the event.

36) perm has no further numbers to choose, fails perm([2],S) reaching 3 ! ev.

37) perm is on the left and tries again 3 ! ev.
37') ord must undo the reception of the number 3, backtracking past the event 3 ? ev.

38) perm waits at 3 ! ev.
38') ord([1],S) matches o4 and tries event Y ? ev : Y==[].

39 and 39') Event fails.

40') ord backtracks past the event, fails ord([1],S), reaching 1 ? ev.

41) As ord has no more alternatives after the reception of 1, perm must start backtracking past 3 ! ev.
41') ord waits for alternatives from perm.
The "exchange" of number 3 has been undone.

42) perm backtracks from 3 ! ev, and chooses 2, then tries 2 ! ev.
42') ord is waiting at Y ? ev : number(Y), admit(Y,[1],NL).

43) perm solves 2 ! ev, then recurses with perm([3],S).
43') ord solves 2 ? ev : number(2), admit(2,[1],[1,2]), then recurses with ord([1,2],S

44) perm([3],S) matches p2, chooses 3, then tries 3 ! ev.
44') ord([1,2],S) matches o3 and tries Y ? ev : number(Y), admit(Y,[1,2],NL).

45) perm solves 3 ! ev and recurses with perm([],S).
45') ord solves 3 ? ev : number(3), admit(3,[1,2],[1,2,3]), then recurses with ord([1,2,3],S).

46) perm([],S) matches p1, then tries [] ! ev.
46') ord([1,2,3],S) matches o3 then tries Y ? ev : number(Y), admit(Y,[1,2,3],NL).

47 and 47') Event fails because condition number([]) fails.

48) perm is on the left and stays trying [] ! ev.
48') ord fails the event goal and starts backtracking, matching now o4.

49) perm solves [] ! ev, succeeding perm([],[]).
49') ord solves [] ? ev : []==[], succeeding ord([1,2,3],[1,2,3]).

50) the call perm([3],S) succeeds with perm([3],[3]).
the call perm([3,2],S) succeeds with perm([3,2],[2,3]).
the call perm([3,1,2],S) succeeds with perm([3,1,2],[1,2,3]).
50') the call ord([1,2],S) succeeds with ord([1,2],[1,2,3]).
the call ord([1],S) succeeds with ord([1],[1,2,3]).
the call ord(S) succeeds with ord([1,2,3]).

perm([3,1,2],S)//ord(S) succeeds with perm([3,1,2],[1,2,3])//ord([1,2,3]), then sort([3,1,2],S) succeeds with sort([3,1,2],[1,2,3]).

The same example could be written without executing the conditions in the events but after them. There would be more interaction between processes because of more backtracking into events. Conditions on events allow decreasing the amount of interaction.

5 Implementation issues

5.1 Language environment.

Delta Prolog relies on the development of a prototype that runs on top of an existing Prolog interpreter and operating system, and is easily integrated into different Prolog systems. The environment provides other tools (like debuggers, editors, and graphics all interfacing with Prolog), with the purpose of having an integrated logic programming environment. The event based communication appears to be adequate to build interfaces between heterogeneous systems, allowing for instance, for distributed database access. Since the beginning we have decided that the prototypes should have most of their code written in Prolog, so that it is easy to modify them, experimenting with alternative solutions, and at the same time supporting their incremental extension; this was a high priority goal, to be achieved even at the expense of a decreased efficiency in the implementation. The current implementation of Delta Prolog is based upon the Edinburgh C Prolog interpreter, and consists of the following levels: a Delta Prolog layer (event goals and process distribution), a C Prolog layer (C Prolog extended with predicates for process control and interprocess communication on one machine or across network), and an operating system layer (any multiprocessed operating system also supporting network operation (currently running under VAX/VMS+DECnet and easily ported to BSD UNIX 4.2).

5.2 Binary events implementation

Events provide for bidirectional synchronous interprocess communication, using the unification mechanism. In order to implement it we must have a system facility that allows establishment of a two-way communication channel between two unrelated processes. In our implementation there are a few "built-in" predicates, extending Prolog so that the high level protocol supporting "!" and "?" is currently written in Prolog. Further requirements are assumed for binary event implementation, namely that the above specified channel must be a "point-to-point" connection between two processes only, i.e. an exclusion mechanism must guarantee no third process interferes during a currently active event protocol. Actually, for the current Delta Prolog implementations, we use mailboxes under VAX/VMS and sockets under UNIX 4.2. In Delta Prolog there is no need for shared memory to support the communication model. The only requirement is a communication medium allowing message passing between processes, on the same machine or network.

5.3 Control strategy

5.3.1 Parallelism

At system level a "process" corresponds to the execution of an instance of a C Prolog interpreter, suitably extended to support interprocess communication and process control. This is an expensive way to obtain parallelism but, besides the reduction in implementation effort, it eases the experimenting with distinct mechanisms for parallel goal execution. At the language level we have parallel execution of goals, through an explicit parallel AND "//". Currently Delta Prolog uses the approach of having a goal G1 solved "locally" by the process invoking G1//G2, while goal G2 is solved by a child process. In any case, the execution of G2 is performed under the control of a small manager (written in Delta Prolog), which is activated from the spawned process' input channel (where its creator writes a top goal), and receives and solves goals, sending solutions back, or advising that no more are available.

5.3.2 Distributed backtracking

The algorithm is based on the establishment of a linear order among processes, such that the search made by one process is dependent on the choices made by "earlier" processes in the order. To record the order among processes, we have a global structure, accessible to all in mutual exclusion, which is updated on launching a new parallel "//" composition of goals, and consulted in cases of communication failure or backtracking to a previous communication point, so that each process knows what to do without the need for an overall manager. Additionally, each process keeps local information on the event goal invocation numbers and process identifications for all its communications that proviously took place. The following system facilities must be provided :

1- a mechanism for asynchronously interrupting a Prolog process, including the support for interrupt handling, inside each Prolog process.
2- mechanisms for backtracking control, local to each Prolog process.

Point 1 is dealt with a built-in predicate `sendinterrupt(process,term)`, which interrupts a Prolog process, and additionally sends it a Prolog term, that the destination process may read on receiving the interrupt. The coherence of the Prolog computation is preserved by having the interrupt being handled at well defined points within the Prolog interpreter. On catching an interrupt the C code activates a predefined goal that is responsible for the actual interrupt handling, the handler being written in Prolog. In our system, a process reads a term from a communication channel dedicated to interrupt control, and proceeds depending on the term received. Currently this term usually makes the process consider backtracking, but other possibilities are open. Point 2 is supported by the built-in predicates : `goalno(N)` returns the invocation number for the current goal (i.e. itself) ; `retry(N)` recommences the execution at the goal whose invocation number is `N`, undoing all until that point.

6 Current work

We are experimenting with a choice operator "::" [HOARE85], providing for non-determinis in the selection of a goal expression among several alternatives. The first goal in each alternative is an event goal. A process executing this construct waits until one of these events succeeds . For all purposes the alternative thus selected replaces the choice construct text in the program; e.g. a buffer process is:

```
buffer([])     :-    X ? put, buffer([X]).
buffer([H|T]) :-    H ? get, buffer(T)
                  :: X ? put, append([H|T],[X],NB), buffer(NB).
```

Other current work relates to the following topics:

1- Porting Delta Prolog to Unix, installing it in heterogeneous computer networks and augmenting its efficiency at bottlenecks, as well as defining a Delta Prolog abstract machine and portability conditions to other Prologs.
2- Experience with large programs, different application areas and programming styles (such as object oriented) and also coupling it to logic programming environments and tools.
3- Compare it extensively with other concurrent logic programming languages.

7 Conclusions and future research

7.1 Advantages of Delta Prolog

Delta Prolog subsumes full Prolog augmenting its expressiveness, not limiting it. Its declarative semantics has a sound theoretical foundation and its operational semantics is well-defined. It already provides AND-parallelism on a single machine or across a network of processors and it allows interprocess communication via message passing, including two-way pattern matching, and thus interprocess synchronization. It includes automatic distributed backtracking among processes communicating through synchronous events. Note that in the case of communication via asynchronous events there is no distributed backtracking, and thus none of its overheads.

It can be ported without much effort, and is amenable to heterogeneous network implementation. Common memory is not a requirement but it can be made good use of if available (allowing unification of free variables in events, and thus streams shared through events). Note that slot-filling is possible, as when difference lists are shared by different processes, even if common memory is not available (cf. quicksort example above).

7.2 Efficiency and the language model

A suitable compromise must be found by the programmer between the complete search posited by synchronous events usage, and efficiency. As far as distributed backtracking is concerned, one must be aware that the amount of interactions between processes may become a limiting factor in system performance. If completeness is not a requirement, asynchronous events can be used, even to the extent of imposing synchronism, but without backtracking overheads (cf. section 2.2.2). However, distributed backtracking can be further improved upon using the techniques of [LMP 82, BRU84]. In order to get an efficient implementation one must have a dedicated run time environment, which integrates the described mechanisms for inter-process communication and process control. As most of the other Delta Prolog requirements are the same as for Prolog, a possible direction is to suitable extend the Warren abstract machine with the required features for Delta Prolog support. Another implementation issue is to get an efficient network implementation, which is not so difficult if one uses the strategy for handling clusters of processes on each node (sharing memory) and communicating through message-passing between separate machines. Of course, the ultimate performance factor depends on the nature of the problem being solved, more or less amenable to distributed processing. But that issue is left to the programmer's responsability.

Acknowledgements

To JNICT and MIE in Portugal, as well as DEC for their support.

References

[BRU84] Bruynooghe, M. ; Pereira L. M., "Deduction revision through intelligent backtracking" in "Implementations of Prolog" (Campbell ed.) Ellis Horwood 1984

[HOARE85] Hoare, C.A.R. "Communicating sequential processes" Prentice-Hall, 1985

[JC,JNA84] Cunha, J. C. ; Aparício, J. N., "Delta Prolog implementation: progress report no.1", Universidade Nova de Lisboa, December 1984

[JC,JNA85] Cunha, J. C. ; Aparício, J. N., "Delta Prolog implementation: progress report no.2", Universidade Nova de Lisboa, July 1985

[LM83] Monteiro, L. "A proposal for distributed programming in logic", in "Implementations of Prolog" (Campbell ed.) Ellis Horwood 1984

[LMP82] Pereira M. L. ; Porto, A. "Selective Backtracking" in "Logic Programming" (Clark, Tarnlund eds.) Academic Press 1982

[LMP84] Pereira, L. M.; Nasr, R. "Delta Prolog: a distributed logic programming language", in "Proceedings of FCGS", Tokyo, November 1984.

OLD Resolution with Tabulation

Hisao TAMAKI
Ibaraki University
Nakanarusawa 4-12-1
Hitachi, 316, JAPAN

Taisuke SATO
Electrotechnical Laboratory
Umezono 1-1-4
Sakuramura, 305, JAPAN

ABSTRACT

To resolve the search-incompleteness of depth-first logic program interpreters, a new interpretation method based on the tabulation technique is developed and modeled as a refinement to SLD resolution. Its search space completeness is proved, and a complete search strategy consisting of iterated stages of depth-first search is presented. It is also proved that for programs defining finite relations only, the method under an arbitrary search strategy is terminating and complete.

1. Introduction

The most fundamental principle of logic programming is the equivalence of the declarative and the procedural semantics[1], which has led many researchers to believe logic programming to be a suitable framework for various program manipulation tasks such as verification, synthesis, transformation, and formal debugging. The unfortunate fact is that this equivalence is always sacrificed in real implementations like Prolog, for the sake of execution efficiency. As a result, logically correct logic programs do not necessarily run correctly on Prolog.

One may argue that Prolog is just a programming language with its own procedural semantics, of which programmers should have sufficient knoledge. But the abandonment of the equivalence is so deeply concerned with the philosophy and the potential of logic programming that it could not be approved easily.

There are several causes of this dis-equivalence: the absence of occur check, the depth-first search strategy, and inclusion of many extra-logical feartures. We atack the second problem in this paper: we develope an interpretation method which is complete even under essentially depth-first search strategies.

The completeness of SLD refutation [2,3,4] ensures that given a conjunction of atomic formulas as a query, every instance of it implied by the program can be obtained as a result of some computation path. Though a typical Prolog interpreters are essentially SLD refutation procedures, they are not complete in the sense that they can, with their depth-first search strategy, be trapped by an infinite computation path in the search tree, and fail to find an actually existing successful computation path.

The breadth-first strategy might seem a sufficient theoretical answer to this problem, since it will eventually find any successful computation path in the search tree. But apart from the practical problem of its storage requirement, it also suffers from infinite paths of the search tree. In this case, though it is not trapped from succesful computation paths, it can be trapped from termination if all solutions are requested, even when the set of solutions is finite.

Several authors, including Brough and Walker [5], proposed tecniques to prune the infinite paths in the search tree by detecting identical or matching goals on a path. However, all of such tecniques are incomplete in two ways (as was studied in [5]) : some infinite paths can escape the pruning, and some pruned infinite paths can have side branches which constitute successfull computaion paths.

The interpretation method we develope here can be considered as a remedy to such pruning tecniques, as well as a generalization of the tabulation tecniques [6] for functional programs, where the result of evaluating a function call is stored in a table to eliminate repeated evaluation of the function calls for the same arguments. Though the same effect of avoiding the redundant evaluation of a goal is achieved as a side bennefit, the principal purpose of applying the technique here is to prevent the interpreter from repeatedly entering the evaluation of the same goal in a single computation path and thus from being trapped by an infinite path. The suspended computation node in the path is later fed, through the table, with the solutions of the other computation paths for the goal in question. In this way, the completeness of the SLD refutation is preserved.

The next Section presents an example to illustrate the above discussion and to informally explain our interpretation method. Section 3 and Section 4 contain more detailed description and some completeness results. Finally in Section 5, we conclude by summarizing the advantage of our method.

2. Examples

2.1 Infinite paths in search trees

Consider the following program to define the reachability relation in a directed graph. (We follow the DEC10 Prolog convention of designating variables by upper case letters.)

PROGRAM 2.1 (graph reachability)

```
(C1)    reach(X,Y) ← reach(X,Z), edge(Z,Y).
(C2)    reach(X,X).
(C3)    edge(a,b).
(C4)    edge(a,c).
(C5)    edge(b,a).
(C6)    edge(b,d).
```

Fig.2.1 shows the search tree, which we call an *OLD tree*, for a query $\leftarrow reach(a,X)$ given to this program. Each node is (labeled with) a ***goal statement*** or ***negetive clause***, and each child node of a node is the result of applying a clause in the program to the *leftmost* goal (atom) of the parent goal statement. The symbol □ denotes the ***emtpy goal statement*** or ***null clause***. Each edge is labeled with the substitution for the variables of the parent goal statement necessary to make this clause application possible. An OLD tree is a special case of an SLD tree[3,4].

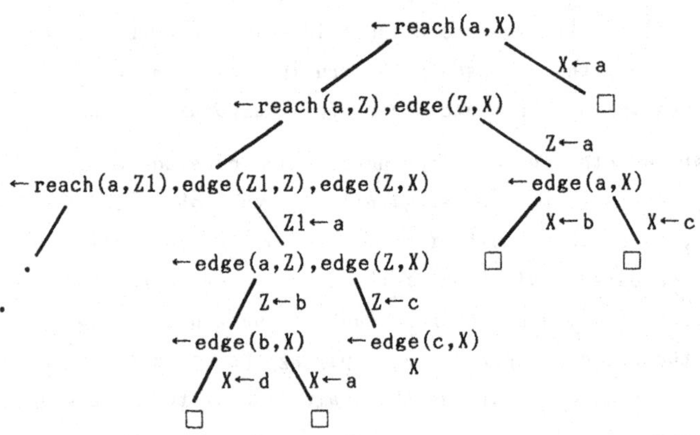

Fig.2.1 an OLD tree

We can learn several things from this example.

(1) The depth-first interpreter is trapped by the leftmost infinite path giving no solution, provided the two clauses for *reach* is ordered as in the program.

(2) If the order of the clauses for *reach* is reversed, the interpreter runs infinitely repeating the solutions.

(3) The behavior of (2) is related to the nature of the graph in question. If it is acyclic, the interpreter gives the finite set of solutions and then goes into the infinite path without giving any further solutions.

(4) The infiniteness of the search tree is partly due to the left-recursive style of the definition of the predicate *reach*. Though the right-recursive reformulation of the program succeeds in eliminating the infiniteness if the object graph is acyclic, it does not work for graphs with cycles like this example.

In this simple example, an experienced programmer could immediately modify the program, adopting right-recursion and an explicit data structure for the set of already reached nodes, to run it correctly on Prolog. But there are cases where such programming solutions are neither trivial nor preferable, just as the conversion from left-recursive grammars to right-recursive ones is not always preferable. In fact, this work is motivated by a desire to run directly a dataflow analyzer of logic programs, which is concisely formulated by definite clause logic but loops on ordinary prolog interpreters. The programming effort to avoid such looping is certainly what we would like to dispense with, at least in the early stage of the developement.

2.2. Illustration of the method

Now we return to the first example to show how our interpretation method works. We start with the root of the search tree, labeled with the goal $\leftarrow$*reach(a,X)*, which is stored in a table called the *solution table*, to be associated with the list of its solutions. Expansion by the clause (C1) gives the new goal statement $\leftarrow$*reach(a,Z),edge(Z,X)*, and expansion by the unit clause (C2) gives the null statement with the solution *reach(a,a)*, which is stored into the solution list of *reach(a,X)* (Fig.2.2).

Since the subgoal *reach(a,Z)* is an instance of the goal *reach(a,X)* in the solution table, expansion of the node 2 is suspended and the reference to the solution list is established via another table called the *lookup table*.

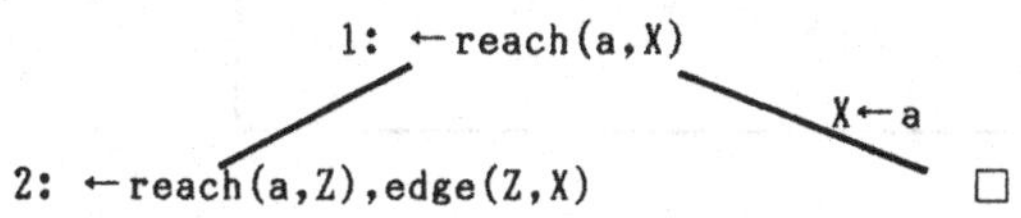

Solution table

reach(a,X): [reach(a,a)]

Lookup table

2:

Fig.2.2

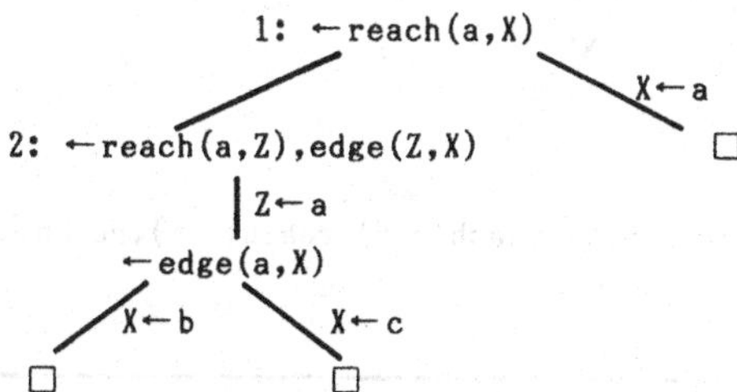

Solution table

reach(a,X): [reach(a,a),reach(a,b),reach(a,c)]

Lookup table

2:

Fig.2.3

Unlike the pruning techniques mentioned in Section 1, we do not stop here but use the solution in the solution list to expand the goal statement of the node 2, obtaining two more solutions to the goal on the root (Fig.2.3). The pointer in the lookup table makes this *solution lookup* possible, and is now advanced to point to the list of new solutions.

Application of the second and the third solutions gives only one more solution (Fig.2.4). Then finally the application of the fourth solution adds nothing to the solution list, and the whole process terminates (Fig.2.5).

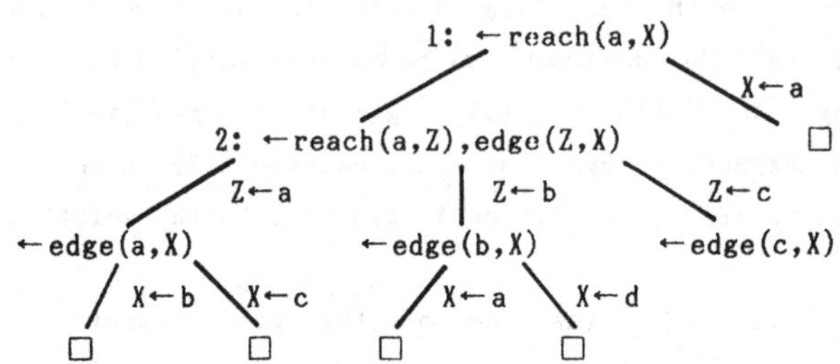

Solution table

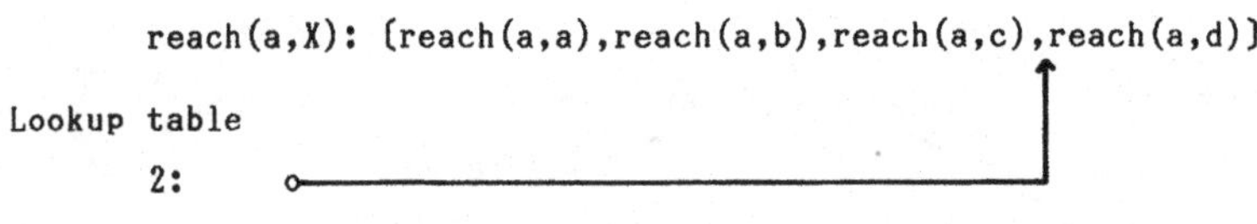

Fig.2.4

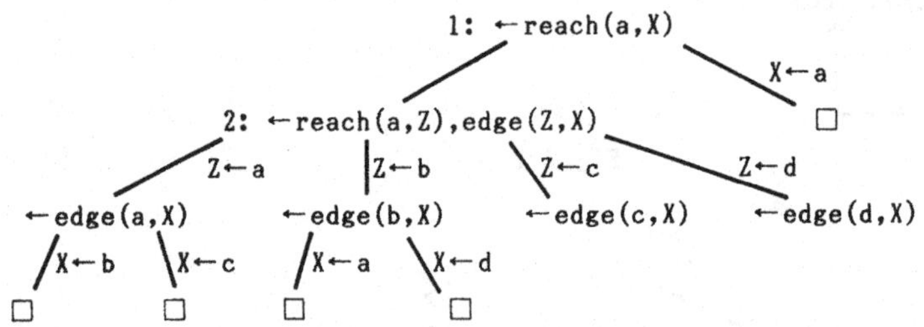

Solution table

reach(a,X): [reach(a,a),reach(a,b),reach(a,c),reach(a,d)]

Lookup table

2:

Fig.2.5

This example might be too simple to illuminate the inportant fact that the top down process (ordinary expansion) and the bottom up process (table lookup) can arbitrarily be intermingled with each other. For example, it is possible that some goal statement resulted from a table lookup is executed further in top down manner, and then suspended again as another entry in the lookup table. The detailed description and the completeness proof in the succeeding sections are thus motivated.

It should also be noted that the entire process is controlled by the top down search, and only those solutions required by the top goal are generated. For example, if we add arbitrary number of nodes and edges not reachable form 'a' to the graph in this example, the interpretation process described above remains completely unchanged.

3. OLDT refutation and its completeness

In this section, we formulate the interpretation method as OLDT refutation and prove its completeness. Mostly we follow the standard terminology and conventions in the basic theory of logic programming [3,4], and omit definitions of basic terms and notions, such as *term, atom, definite clause, negative clause, null clause, unification*, and so on.

First we model the conventional Prolog interpreter by means of *OLD refutation*, which is a special case of SLD refutation[3].

DEFINITION 3.1 (OLD resolution)

Let C be a negative clause $\leftarrow A_1,..,A_n$ $(n>0)$ and D be a definite clause. Let D', of the form $A \leftarrow B_1,..,B_m$ $(m \geq 0)$, be D with all variables renamed so that there is no conflict with those in C. C and D are said to be *OLD resolvable* if A_1 and A are unifiable, and the negative clause (or null clause when n = 1 and m = 0) $\leftarrow (B_1,..,B_m,A_2,...,A_n)\theta$ is the *OLD resolvent* of C and D where θ is the mgu of A_1 and A. The restriction of the substitution θ to the variables of A_1 is called *the substitution of the OLD resolution.*

The OLD resolvent and the substitution of the resolution are unique up to renaming of variables.

DEFINITION 3.2 (OLD tree)

Let P be a program and C_0 be a negative clause. Then the *OLD tree* for the pair (P, C_0) is a possibly infinite tree with its nodes labeled with negative or null clauses so that the following condition is satisfied.

1. The root is labeled with C_0.
2. Assume a node v is labeled with C.

 2.1 If C is a null clause then v is a terminal node.

 2.2 Otherwise, let $D_1,..,D_n$ $(n\geq 0)$ be all the clauses in P which are OLD resolvable with C, and $C_1,..,C_n$ the respective OLD resolvents. Then v has n child nodes, labeled with $C_1,..,C_n$. The edge from v to the node labeled with C_i is labeled with θ_i, where θ_i is the substitution of the OLD resolution of C and Di.

DEFINITION 3.3 (OLD refutation)

Given a program P and a negative clause C, an *OLD refutation* of C by P is a path in the OLD tree of (P, C), from the root to a node labeled with the null clause. Let $\theta_1,..,\theta_k$ be the labeles of the edges on the path. The *substitution of the refutation* is the composition $\theta = \theta_1 \circ \theta_2 \circ \ldots \circ \theta_k$, and the *solution of the refutation* is $C\theta$.

DEFINITION 3.4 (Counterexample of a negative clause)

Given a program P, an instance $\leftarrow A_1,..,A_n$ of a negative clause C is said to be a *counterexample* of C in P if the universal closure of $A_1 \& .. \& A_n$ is a logical consequence of P.

The soundness and completeness of OLD refutation is just an instance of those of general SLD refutation [2,3,4].

THEOREM 3.5 (Soundness of OLD refutation)

If C' is the solution of an OLD refutation of a negative clause C by P, C' is a counterexample of C in P.

THEOREM 3.6 (Completeness of OLD refutation)

If C' is a counterexample of a negative clause C in P, there is an OLD refutation of C by P such that C' is an instance of the solution of the refutation.

The following notion of subrefutation is specific to the OLD refutation and will be frequently used in the sequel.

DEFINITION 3.7 (Subrefutation)

For a node v in an OLD tree, we denote the number of atoms in the negative clause labeling v by $leng(v)$.

Consider a path from a node v_1 in an OLD tree to one of its descendants v_2 such that for every node v on the path other than v_2 $leng(v) > leng(v_2)$ holds. Let $\leftarrow A_1,..,A_n$ be the label of v_1, where $n = leng(v_1)$, and let $k = n - leng(v_2)$. Since this path can be viewed as a refutation of $\leftarrow A_1,..,A_k$ by neglecting last $leng(v_2)$ atoms in the label of every node on the path, we call it a *subrefutation* of $\leftarrow A_1,..,A_k$. We call it a *unit subrefutation* if $k = 1$. The substitution and the solution of a subrefutation is defined as for a refutation.

We need a few more definitions before describing the OLDT refutation.

DEFINITION 3.8 (Partial OLD tree)

A partial OLD tree is a finite top segment of an OLD tree. That is, any finite tree obtained by deleting arbitrary number of subtrees from an OLD tree is a partial OLD tree.

DEFINITION 3.9 (Table predicates and their term-depth)

We assume that among the predicate symbols used in the program, some are designated by the programmer as *table predicates*. Moreover, we assume that each table predicate p is assigned a non-negative integer called the *term-depth* of p.

The intention of the first assumption is to give flexibility to our method by limiting the tabulation only to the designated table predicates. As an extreme, the OLD refutation will be a special case of OLDT refutation, where no predicates are designated as table predicates. The second assumption is related to the abstraction operation defined below, which is used to bound the number of distinct subgoals (atoms) to be solved.

DEFINITION 3.10 (Term-depth abstraction)

Let *A* be an atom of a table predicate *p*, and *k* be the term-depth of the *p*. Then the term-depth abstraction of *A*, denoted by *abs*(*A*) is *A*, with every subterm of depth more than *k* replaced by distinct new variables.

For example, if the term-depth of p is 1, *abs*(p(f(g(X),h(Y)),a)) is p(f(U,V),a).

DEFINITION 3.11 (OLDT structure)

An *OLDT structure* is a forest of partial OLD trees with two tables, the *solution table* and the *lookup table*.

A node is called a *table node* if the leftmost atom of its label is of a table predicate. A table node is either a *lookup node* or a *solution node*. The solution table associates the leftmost atom of the label of each solution node with a list of instances of that atom, called the *solution list*. The lookup table associates each lookup node with a pointer pointing *into* some solution list in the solution table.

We now describe the valid construction process of OLDT structures for a given pair of a program and a negative clause.

DEFINITION 3.12 (Table node registration)

Given an OLDT structure and a table node *v* in it, the *table node registration procedure* classifies it as a solution node or a lookup node, and does necessary table manipulation, resulting in a new OLDT structure.

According to the leftmost atom *A* of *v*'s label, we distinguish among the following cases. (Note that by definition the predicate of *A* is a table predicate.)

(1) (Lookup node)
A is an instance of some key entry *A'* in the solution table.
Put *v* into the lookup table with the pointer to the entire solution list of *A'*.

(2) (Abstraction)
Otherwise, and the nesting depth of *A* is greater than the term-depth of the predicate of *A*.
Create a new root v0 in the forest, label it with *abs*(*A*),
put *abs*(*A*) in the solution table with an empty solution list, and
put *v* in the lookup table with a pointer to this empty solution list.

(3) (Solution node) Otherwise, put *A* in the solution table with an empty solution list.

DEFINITION 3.13 (Initial OLDT structure)

Given a program P and a negative clause C0, the *initial OLDT structure* for the pair (P, C_0) is the result of the following operation.

(1) Let T_0 be an OLDT structure consisting of a forest with a single node v_0, labeled with C_0, an empty solution table, and an empty lookup table.

(2) Apply the table node registration procedure to the node v_0 in T_0.

DEFINITION 3.14 (Extension of an OLDT structure)

Given a program P and an OLD structure T, an *immediate extension of T by P* is the result of either of the following operations.

(1) (OLD extension) Select a terminal node v, which is not a lookup node, such that its label C is not a null clause and at least one clause in P is OLD resolvable with C.

(1.1) Let $D_1,..,D_n$ $(n \geq 1)$ be all the clauses in P which are OLD resolvable with C, and $C_1,..,C_n$ the respective OLD resolvents. Then add n child nodes, labeled with $C_1,..,C_n$, to v. The edge from v to the node labeled with each C_i is labeled with θ_i, where θ_i is the substitution of the resolution of C and D_i.

(1.2) For each new node, register it if it is a table node.

(1.3) For each unit subrefutation (if any) starting from a solution node and ending with some of the new nodes, assume that the subrefutation is of $\leftarrow A$, and let $\leftarrow A'$ be its solution. Add A' to the last of the solution list of A, if A' is not an instance of any entry in the solution list.

(2) (Lookup extension) Select a lookup node v, such that the pointer associated with it points to a nonempty sublist of a solution list. Let A be the head element of this sublist. Advance the pointer by one to skip A. Let C be the label of v. If C and $A\leftarrow$ are OLD resolvable, then create a child node of v, labeled with the resolvent, and label the new edge with the substitution of the resolution. Do the same thing as in (1.3).

An OLDT structure T' is an *extension* of another OLDT structure T, if T' is obtained from T through succesive application of immediate extensions.

DEFINITION 3.15 (OLDT refutation)

Given a program P and a negative clause C, an *OLDT refutation* of C by P is a path in some extension of the initial OLDT structure for (P, C), from the *initial root* to a node labeled with the null clause. Here, by initial root we mean the root inherited from the initial OLDT structure.

The notions such as the substitution and the solution of refutation or subrefutation are defined similarly as for OLD refutation.

Note that an OLDT refutation by P is an OLD refutation by P plus some set of unit clause theorems of P for table predicates. Thus the soundness of OLDT refutation is an immediate consequence of the soundness of OLD refutation. For the completeness proof we need the following lemma.

DEFINITION 3.16 (subsumption of subrefutation)

A (sub)refutaion r is said to ***subsume*** a (sub)refutation r' if the solution of r' is an instance of the solution of r.

LEMMA 3.17 (OLDT simulation of OLD subrefutation)

Assume r is an OLD subrefutation of a negative (or null) clause $\leftarrow A_1,..,A_n$ $(n \geq 0)$ by a program P, T is an OLDT structure for the clause and the program, and v is a node in T. Assume further that v is labeled with $\leftarrow B_1,..,B_m$, $m \geq n$, and the sequence $A_1,..,A_n$ is an instance of $B_1,..,B_n$.

Then there exists an extension of T such that T contains an OLDT subrefutation of $\leftarrow B_1,..,B_n$ which starts from v and subsumes r.

Proof. The proof is by induction on the triple (r,T,v), ordered by the following well-founded ordering.

(r,T,v) precedes (r',T',v')

iff $|r| < |r'|$, or

$|r| = |r'|$ and v' is a lookup node but v is not,

where $|r|$ means the length of the refutation.

Induction basis: $|r| = 1$. Trivial since r is a subrefutation of a null clause.

Induction step: We consider two cases depending on whether the node v is a lookup node or not.

(*Case* 1): v is a lookup node. Then there is a corresponding solution node v' in T. Let r be divided as concatenation of two subrefutations r_1 and r_2 so that r_1 is a subrefutation of $\leftarrow A_1$. Since $|r_1| \leq |r|$, and A_1 is an instance of the leftmost atom B_1 of the label of v, hence of the leftmost atom B_1' of the label of v', by the induction hypothesis we have an extension T' of T such that T' contains a subrefutation of $\leftarrow B_1'$ which starts from v' and subsumes r_1. That is, if we let $\leftarrow A_1'$ be the solution of the subrefutation r_1, and $\leftarrow B_1''$ be the solution of the above OLDT subrefutation, $\leftarrow A_1'$ is an instance of $\leftarrow B_1''$. By the operation (1.3) of the definition of the OLDT structure extension, the solution list of B_1' in T' includes B_1''.

Now consider the negative clause $\leftarrow B_1,..,B_n$ and the unit clause $B_1'' \leftarrow$. Since their instances $\leftarrow A_1,..,A_n$ and $A_1' \leftarrow$ have an OLD resolvent $\leftarrow A_2',..,A_n'$, they also have an OLD resolvent $\leftarrow B_2',..,B_n'$ such that $\leftarrow A_2',..,A_n'$ is an instance of $\leftarrow B_2',..,B_n'$. This means that T' can be extended (if necessary) to T'' by lookup extension, so that the node v has a child node v'' with the first $n-1$ atoms of its label being $B_2',..,B_n'$.

Since r_2 is a subrefutation of $\leftarrow A_2',..,A_n'$ and $|r_2| < |r|$, again by the induction hypothesis we have an extension T''' of T'' which contains an OLDT subrefutation s of $\leftarrow B_2',..,B_n'$, starting from v'' and subsuming r_2. The path in T''' starting from v and followed by the subrefutation s constitutes the required subrefutation of $\leftarrow B_1,B_2,..,B_n$.

(*Case* 2): v is not a lookup node. Let u and r' be the first node and the remaining path of the subrefutation r, and D be the definite clause in P used in the first step of the subrefutation r. Then r' is a subrefutation of $\leftarrow L_1,..,L_k,A_2',...,A_n'$, the OLD resolvent of $\leftarrow A_1,..,A_n$ and D. By the assumption, the label $\leftarrow B_1,..,B_m$ of v and D are also OLD resolvable, and the resolvent $\leftarrow L_1',...,L_k',B_2',...,B_m'$ is such that the sequence $L_1,..,L_k,A_2',..,A_n'$ is an instance of the sequence $L_1',..,L_k',B_2',...,B_n'$. Extending T (if necessary) by the OLD resolution on the node v, we can get an OLDT structure T' in which v has a child node v' labeled with $\leftarrow L_1',..,L_k',B_2',...,B_m'$. Then by the induction hypothesis we have an extention T'' of T' which contains a subrefutation s of $\leftarrow L_1',..,L_k',B_2',...,B_n'$, starting from v' and subsuming r'. The path in T'' starting from v and followed by s constitutes the required subrefutation of $\leftarrow B_1,B_2,..,B_n$. □

THEOREM 3.18 (Completeness of OLDT refutation)

Let P be a program, C_0 a negative clause. Assume that an instance C_0' of C_0 is a counterexample of C_0 in P. Then any extension of the initial OLDT structure for (P, C_0) can be further extended to contain an OLDT refutation of C_0, such that C_0' is an instance of the solution of the refutation.

Proof. By the completeness of OLD refutation, there exists an OLD refutation satisfying the above condition. Lemma 3.17, applied to this OLD (sub)refutation, the given OLDT structure, and the initial root of the OLDT structure, provides the required extension. □

Before concluding this section, it should be stressed that OLDT structures are conceptual structures like SLD trees for formal treatment, and need not be fully maintained in real implementations. What portion of the structure is to be maintained depends on the search strategy employed, just as in the case of the SLD tree.

4. Search strategies

Search strategies for OLDT refutation determine, at each step of OLDT structure construction, which of the extension operations is to be applied to which node, when there are several possibilities. Unfortunately, not all search strategies are complete. For example, consider the following program.

PROGRAM 4.1

```
(C1) p(X) ← q(X), r.
(C2) q(s(X)) ← q(X).
(C3) q(0).
(C4) r.
```

Fig.4.1 is a possible snap shot of an OLDT structure for the query $\leftarrow p(X)$.

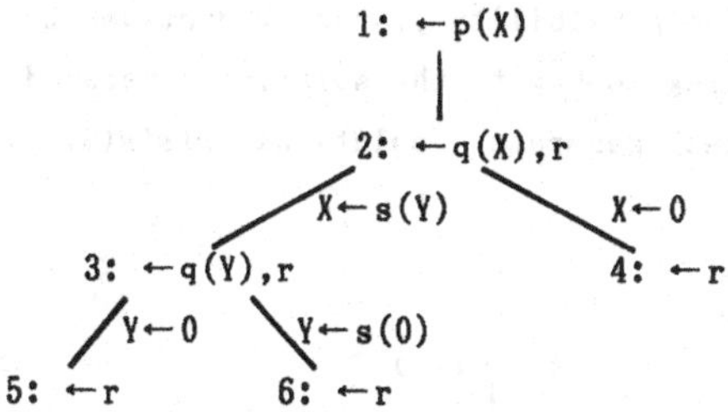

solution table

p(X) : []

q(X) : [q(0),q(s(0)),q(s(s(0)))]

lookup table

3: o

Fig.4.1

If the extension by lookup continues to be preferred, the refutations of the initial goal $\leftarrow p(X)$ will never be found.

It is not difficult to avoid this situation: we have only to prevent sticking to some (group of) lookup node(s). The following strategy is a candidate suitable for sequential implementations.

DEFINITION 4.1 (Multistage depth-first strategy)

We assume here that the forest in an OLDT structure is an *ordered forest*: the roots are ordered by the order of creation, the child nodes of a non-lookup node are ordered by the textual order of clauses used, and the child nodes of a lookup node are again ordered by the order of creation. We say a node u is *to the left of* a node v, if u precede v in the left-to-right post order traversal of the ordered forest.

The search process in the ***multistage depth-first strategy*** consists of multiple stages. At each step in the i-th stage, one of the following extension operation is applied to the node of the current OLDT structure which is leftmost among the possible.

(1) OLD extension.

(2) Lookup extension, with the solutions to be looked up limited to those *which are generated in the (i-1)th or earlier stages*.

When there are no nodes to which they are applicable, one stage is finished and the next stage begins. When a stage adds no solutions to the solution lists, the entire process terminates.

For example, consider Program 4.1 executed under the multistage depth-first strategy. The first stage ends with the OLDT structure shown in Fig.4.2, successfully generating a solution $p(0)$ to the top goal. The lookup extension of the node 3 is suppressed since the only solution $q(0)$ in the corresponding solution list is generated in this stage. The second stage generates another solution $p(s(0))$ to the top goal (Fig.4.3). The possibility of non-productive iteration suggested in Fig.4.1 is avoided by prohibiting lookup to the solution generated within the current stage. The succeeding stages generate solutions *p(s(s*(0))), ..., giving the complete set.

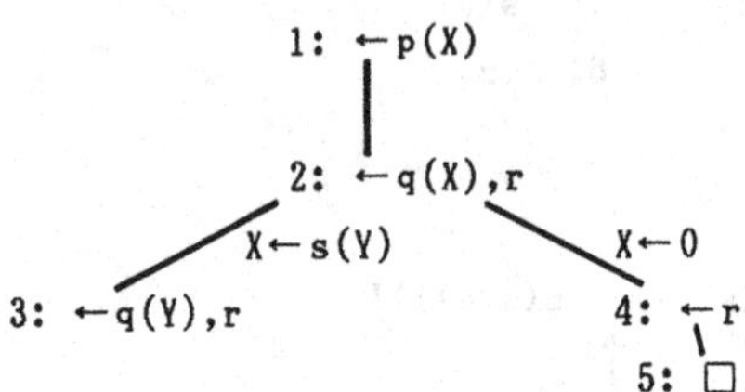

solution table

p(X) : [p(0)]

q(X) : [q(0)]

lookup table

3: ○

Fig.4.2

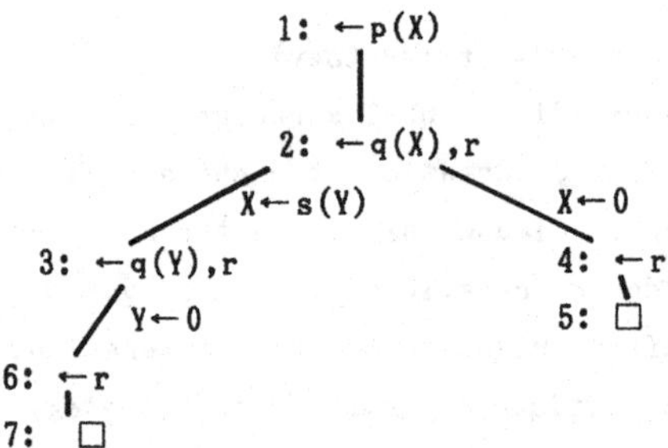

solution table

p(X) : [p(0),q(s(0))]

q(X) : [q(0),q(s(0))]

lookup table

3: ○

Fig.4.3

Note that the mode of search within a stage is exactly depth-first, with the solution lists treated as additional data bases of assertions. Lookup nodes alone can be resumed for further search in succeeding stages.

THEOREM 4.2 (Completeness of the multistage depth-first strategy)

Assume that all predicates in a program P is designated as table predicates. Then for any negative clause C_0 and its counterexample C_0' in P, the search process for OLDT refutation of (P, C_0) under the multistage depth-first strategy finds a refutation such that C_0' is an instance of its solution.

Proof. Noting that the number of solution nodes in any OLDT structure for the program P is bounded by a constant owing to the abstraction operation in the table node registration procedure, this is an easy consequence of the completeness of OLDT refutation. The details are omitted. □

In the special case where all the relations defined by the program is finite, OLDT refutation has a nice property which OLD refutation lacks. (See the example in Section 2.)

THEOREM 4.3 (Completeness and termination for finite-model programs)

Assume that the minimum Herbrand model of a program P is finite, and all predicates in P is designated as table predicates. Then for any negative clause C_0, the search process for the OLDT refutation for (P,C_0) under *any* search strategy terminates, and gives a complete set of solutions.

Proof. Since the length of a solution list in any OLDT structure for (P,C_0) is bounded by a constant, the branching factor of lookup nodes is bounded by a constant. The length of a path is also bounded by a constant, since the number of solution nodes is bounded by a constant and every lookup node in a path decrease the number of atoms in the label by one. Thus the size of the OLDT structures is bounded by a constant. Therefore the completeness of the search directly follows the completeness of the OLDT refutation. □

REMARK (Comparison with the bottom up interpretation method)

Since this termination property is also possessed by the usual bottom up interpretation method, it should be compared with our method.

The bottom up interpretation also consists of succesive stages. In each stage, every positive unit theorem directly derivable from a definite clause in the program and positive unit theorems obtained in previous stages is calculated. The process terminates when a stage does not produce any new theorems. When the minimum model is finite, it obviously terminates giving the complete set of positive unit theorems.

The advantage of our method over the bottom up interpretation is that it is essentially top down, and only those theorems required by the top goal is derived, in principle. We say 'in principle', because the abstraction operation generalizes a goal and may require solutions which is not required by the original goal. In fact, if we set the term-depth of every predicate to be 0, then the multistage search for the OLDT refutation becomes nothing but an implementation of the bottom up interpretation method.

The abstraction operation is, however, a kind of theoretical safety valve, and it seems that in most applications we can set appropriate term-depth for each predicate so that the abstraction operation never actually occurs, as in the example of Section 2, preserving the top-down nature of our interpretation method.

5. Conclusion

We do not claim that the interpretation method described above should be a single, ultimate solution to the problem of the search-incompleteness of Prolog: the storage requirement can be too demanding in some cases, and the overhead of table manipulation can be too large.

Rather, the advantage of the method exists in providing a spectrum of procedural approximations to the declarative semantics: as two extremes, if we designate all predicates as table predicates, then the multistage strategy gives the complete interpretation procedure; if we choose no predicates as table predicates, then the multistage search for OLDT refutation is exactly the same as the depth-first search for OLD refutation. For some programs the latter extreme is still an exact approximation, but for others we must choose some appropriate intermediate approximations. The common techniques for proving termination could be used for this purpose, to ensure that some predicates need not be designated as table predicates.

The ideal logic programming system which we envision will consist of a variety of approximating implementation methods, tools to determine which approximation is exact or sufficient, and a powerful set of optimization tecniques, rather than of a complete and efficient universal interpreter.

References

〔1〕 Van Emden, M.H. and Kowalski, R.A. "The semantics of predicate logic as a programming languages", *Journal of the ACM* 23, No.4, 1976.

〔2〕 Clark, K.L. "Predicate logic as a computational formalism", Imperial College research monograph 79/59 TOC, December 1979.

〔3〕 Apt, K.R. and Van Emden, M.H. "Contributions to the theory of logic programming", *Journal of the ACM* 29, NO.3, 1982.

〔4〕 Lloyd, J.W. *Foundations of logic programming*, Springer-Verlag, 1984.

〔5〕 Brough, D.R. and Walker, A. "Some practical properties of logic programming interpreters", *Proc. International Conference on FGCS 1984*, Tokyo, Nov. 1984.

〔6〕 Bird, R.S. "Tabulation techniques for recursive programs", *Computing Surveys* 12, No.4, 1980.

LOGIC PROGRAMS AND ALTERNATION

Petr Štěpánek
Department of Computer Science and Op. Res.
Charles University, Malostranské nám. 25
118 00 Praha 1, Czechoslovakia

Olga Štěpánková
Institute of Computational Techniques
ČVUT, Horská 3, 128 00 Praha 2
Czechoslovakia

Shapiro (1984) showed that there is a close relationship between logic programs and Alternating Turing Machines (ATM) introduced by Chandra and Stockmeyer (1977). Shapiro showed that the computations of an arbitrary ATM M are described by a logic program P_M (Simulation 1) and that for each logic program P, there is an ATM M_P which accepts just those variable-free atoms that are provable by P (Simulation 2). Since all information is stored on work tapes, the space complexity of M_P is at least linear. To cope with sublinear space complexity, it is necessary to use ATM which distinguish between input and work tapes.

We shall extend Shapiro's method to the case of ATM with one additional read-only input tape. The corresponding logic programs are called programs with input. The complexity of derivations of logic programs with input is related to the complexity of computations of the corresponding ATM. This makes it possible e.g. to characterize the complexity class PTIME of languages accepted in polynomial time by deterministic Turing machines in terms of the goal-size complexity of related logic programs. This result was obtained by Y. Gurevich and one of the authors during his stay at the University of Michigan. The authors thank for his permission to include the result in this paper.

The class EXPTIME of languages accepted by deterministic Turing machines in exponential time is characterized by logic programs of polynomial goal-size complexity.

ATM with read-only input tape

Let us suppose that a word w of length n is written on the input tape on the positions enumerated by 1,2,...,n. Denote by Σ the input alphabet and by Γ the work-tape alphabet. Given the contents of the input tape, the configuration of ATM is completely specified by the quadruple q - the state of ATM

i - a natural number denoting the position of the head on the input tape ($i \leq$ length)

L - the contents of the left part (with respect to the head) of the work tape

R - the contents of the right-hand part of the work tape including the symbol read by the head.

Each transition of ATM is described by a quintuple

$$\langle q , \langle a,\sigma\rangle , q', \tau , \langle d_{inp}, d_w\rangle\rangle ,$$

which is interpreted as follows: if ATM M is in the state q and the head reads the symbol a on the input tape and the symbol σ on the work tape, then M

- enters the state q'
- rewrites the symbol σ on the work tape to τ
- moves to the next cell on the input tape in the direction d_{inp} and moves on the work tape in the direction d_w.

The definitions of a step, a configuration and of a computation tree for an ATM with one input tape are straightforward generalization of these concepts for ATM using work tapes only. Let us recall that the space complexity of an ATM with one input tape is defined by the maximal space used on its work tape only.

<u>Simulation 2 - i of an ATM M with one input tape and one work tape by a logic program P</u>

Following the original Simulation 2 of Shapiro, the logic program simulating the computation of an ATM with one read-only input tape will use the predicate 'accept' with arguments characterizing the configuration of the machine, i.e. 'accept(Q,I,L,R)' is proved by a logic program iff the configuration $\langle Q,I,L,R\rangle$ leads to acceptance of the input word.

The actions on the work tape can be described uniformly by a predicate 'move' for both existential and universal states. The atom

$$\text{move}(L, [\sigma | R] , \tau ; d_w , L_1 , R_1)$$

has the following meaning: if the head is reading the symbol σ on the work tape and L is written to the left and R to the right of the machine's head, then the situation of the work tape is changed as follows

- the symbol σ is rewritten to τ
- the head is moved to the next cell in the direction d_w, L_1 being

written to the left and R_1 to the right of the new position of the head (including the symbol read by the head).

The actions on the input tape are described by predicates 'increment' and 'decrement'. We suppose that the cells on the input tape are enumerated 1,2,...,n where n is the length of the input word. The head on the input tape can move inside these bound only. The atom 'increment(x,y,length)' holds iff y is the resulting position of the head after moving one step to the right from the position x if possible. Similarly, 'decrement(u,v)' binds the new position v with the previous position u after moving one cell to the left whenever possible.

The contents of the input tape can be coded by a set of facts about the symbols written on the input tape. Let Σ be a finite input alphabet. Each symbol of Σ can be identified with a unary predicate of the same name. If $a \in \Sigma$, then the atomic formula a(i) is interpreted as "the i-th symbol of the input word w is a ".

For instance, if the word written on the input tape is "input", then the corresponding set of facts is

```
i (1).
n (2).
p (3).
u (4).
t (5).
```

Let us denote the set of axioms describing the input word w by Input(w).

<u>Schema 2 - i describing the construction of a logic program P simulating an ATM M with one input tape (a modification of Figure 3 of Shapiro 1984)</u>

Careful analysis of all configurations on the work tape shows that the predicat 'move' can be described by unconditional statements depending on the position of the head. For instance, the center of the tape is characterized by the following axioms

move($[\rho \mid L]$, $[\sigma, R]$, τ, left, L, $[\rho, \tau \mid R]$).
move($[\rho \mid L]$, $[\sigma, R]$, τ, right,$[\tau, \rho \mid L]$, R) .

where ρ , σ are non-blank symbols of the work tape alphabet Γ . The left and the right end of the work tape are described similarly.

The transitions of M are described by two types of clauses in P corresponding to the existential and universal states of M .

- Existential states. For every existential state q and symbols $a \in \Sigma$, $\sigma \in \Gamma$, we define

  Left move. The transition $\langle q, \langle a,\sigma\rangle, q', \tau, \langle left, D_w\rangle\rangle$ of M is described by the clause

  accept(q,I,L,[σ | R]): -a(I),decrement(I,J),move(L,[σ | R], τ, D_w, L_1,R_1),accept(q′,J,L_1,R_1).

  Right move. The transition $\langle q, \langle a,\sigma\rangle, q', \tau, \langle right, D_w\rangle\rangle$ of M is described by the clause

  accept(q,I,L,[σ | R]): -a(I), increment(I,J,length), move(L,[σ | R], τ, D_w,L_1,R_1), accept(q′,J,L_1,R_1) .

- Universal states. For every universal state q and the symbol a read actually on the input tape, the program P contains a clause

  accept(q,I,L,[σ | R]): -a(I),A_1,...,A_k ,

  where $k \geq 0$ is the number of all the transitions the machine M has for this configuration. Let us consider the i-th transition $\langle q, \langle a,\sigma\rangle, q', \tau, \langle left, d_w\rangle\rangle$, then A_i is the conjunctive goal

  decrement(I,J),move(L,[σ | R] ,d_w,L_1,R_1), accept(q′,J,L_1,R_1) .

  If the i-th transition moves on the input to the right, then A_i is again conjunctive goal as in the upper case - the only difference is that increment is used instead of decrement.

As in Shapiro (1984), it might be verified throught a detailed case analysis of clauses in P and axioms Input(w) describing the contents of the read-only input tape, that

- P ∪ Input(w) ⊢ accept(q_0,1, [] , []) iff the ATM M accepts the word w starting the work from the initial state q_0 of M .
- The goal-size complexity of the proof of accept(q_0,1, [] , []) by P ∪ Input(w) is proportional to the length of the maximal used space on the work tapes of M , i.e. to the number denoted as the space of M′s computation for the input w .

  More precisely, there is a constant k uniform in the machine M such that if the space complexity of M is bounded by the function S(n) for any input word of length n , then the length of any goal in the proof P ∪ Input(w) ⊢ accept (q_0,1,[] ,[]) is bounded by

  $$k \cdot (S(n) + \log(n)) .$$

The occurence of log in this formula is caused by the use of natural numbers for coding the actual position of the head on the read-only input tape.

- The length and depth complexity of the proof $P \cup \text{Input}(w) \vdash \text{accept}(q_0, 1, [\,], [\,])$ are proportional to the tree-size and time complexity of the computation accepting w written on the input tape. The multiplicative constant is again k as in the former case.

All the above observations materialize in the following theorem.

Theorem 1. Let M be an ATM with one work tape, and one read-only input tape that accepts a language L in time T(n), space S(n), and tree-size Z(n). Then there exists a logic program P , a variable-free goal $\text{accept}(q_0, 1, [\,], [\,])$ and a set of axioms Input(w) such that

$$L(M) = \{ w : P \cup \text{Input}(w) \vdash \text{accept}(q_0, 1, [\,], [\,]) \}$$

The following holds for the complexity of the proof of $\text{accept}(q_0, 1, [\,], [\,])$ from $P \cup \text{Input}(w)$:

- goal-size complexity is smaller than $k.[\, S(n) + \log(n) \,]$
- length complexity is less than $k.Z(n)$ and depth is less than $k.\ T(n)$,

where k is a constant uniform in M and n is the length of the input word w .

Simulation of a logic program accepting a word.

Let P be a logic program and S a distinguished variable-free atom of the language of P . Let Σ be a finite alphabet and $w \in \Sigma^*$. Let Input(w) be the set of variable-free axioms defined in Simulation 2 - i for the description of w . We say that P confirms the word w with the starting predicate S iff $P \cup \text{Input}(w) \vdash S$.

Obviously, any logic program resulting from Simulation 2-i confirms the word w with the starting predicate $\text{accept}(q_0, 1, [\,], [\,])$. Now, the complexity measures of derivations of logic programs can be modified as follows.

We say that P confirms words of Σ with the starting predicate S in <u>length complexity L(n)</u> iff for any $w \in \Sigma^*$ which is confirmed by P , there is a proof R of S from P $\cup$ Input(w) such that the number of nodes in R is at most L(n) .

The definitions of depth and goal-size complexity are modified similarly.

<u>P confirms in depth complexity</u> D(n) iff for each confirmed $w \in \Sigma^*$ of length n , there exists a proof R of S from P $\cup$ Input(w) such that the maximal depth of R is less than D(n) .

<u>P confirms in goal-size complexity</u> G(n) iff for any confirmed word w of length n there is a proof R of P $\cup$ Input(w) $\vdash$ S such that the maximum size of any goal occuring in the proof tree of R is less than G(n).

The confirmation of the word w by a program P $\cup$ Input(w) be simulated by the Simulation 1 of Shapiro, i.e. there can be defined on ATM M_w such that M_w accepts a word w iff P $\cup$ Input(w) $\vdash$ S . The main drawback of this method is that the corresponding ATM differ for different inputs - they have different sets of states. The ATM with an input tape offer a very natural solution of this problem - the axioms Input(w) of the logic program could be coded by the input tape, thus the control strategy of the machine might be the same for all inputs. Let us describe this method by the following simulation.

<u>Simulation 1-i. A construction of ATM M with input tape simulating the confirmations of words of Σ by a logic program P.</u>

Let M_P be an ATM obtained by simulation 1 (Shapiro 1984) of the program P . The ATM M is an extension of M_P in the following sense:

- M differs from M_P by its use of the input tape for denoting and verifying the facts expressed by Input(w). It is natural to write the input word w on an initial segment of the input tape, w being the only content of the tape.
- If M has to satisfy a goal on the work tape, it either follows the computation of M_P , or if the goal is of the form a(i) where $a \in \Sigma$, then it scans the input tape to verify that a is the content of the i-th cell. It is obvious that the scanning and return to the initial position of the head takes at most 2.length(w) steps. Thus if each iteration of M_P is performed in time at most t , then the time for one iteration of M is at most

max(t,2.length(w)).

- The space needed for one iteration of M is the same as that of M_P .

These observations lead us to the following statements:

Lemma 1 : Let P be a logic program, S a variable-free starting predicate of P and w a word of length n . Let M be the ATM computing P obtained by Simulation 1-i.

Then there is a constant c uniform in P that bounds the complexity of iterations of M as follows:

If P confirms w by a computation in which the size of any goal is bounded by some $g > 0$, then M accepts the word w . Moreover, M performs the same selection of clauses, operates in space c.g and performs each iteration in time c.max(g,2.n).

Theorem 2. Let P be a logic program with input and starting predicate S which confirms in depth-complexity D(n), goal-size complexity G(n) and length complexity L(n) for any word of length n . Then there is a constant c uniform in P such that the ATM M constructed by Simulation 1-i operates in space c.G(n), time D(n).c.(G(n)+2n) and $L(M) = \{w : P \cup \mathrm{Input}(w) \vdash S\}$.

The next theorem, motivated the above results

Theorem 3. (Y.Gurevich, P.Štěpánek). Let P be a decision problem. The following conditions are equivalent

a) P is polynomial-time decidable
b) There is a logic program A with input that decides P in goal-size complexity O(log n).

Proof: (a) $\rightarrow$ (b) By Chandra et al.(1981), there is an ATM M with read-only input tape that decides P and has the space-complexity proportional to log of the input size. By Theorem 1, Simulation 2-i produces a logic program A which confirms just words $w \in P$. The goal-size complexity of confirmations of A is less than 2.k.log(n) for some constant k .

(b) $\rightarrow$ (a) According to Theorem 2, Simulation 1-i of the program A gives an ATM with input tape accepting just the elements of P in space O(log(n)), where n is the length of the input word. Then (a) follows from corollary 3.6 of the above cited paper that states the equality PTIME = ALOGSPACE.

On the other hand, the class EXPTIME can be characterized by ordinary logic programs.

Theorem 4. Let R be a decision problem. The following statements are equivalent.

a) R is exponential time decidable

b) There is a logic program B of polynomial goal-size complexity such that

$$R = \{w : B \vdash accept(q_0, [\,], w)\}$$

Proof. Chandra et al. (1981) have shown in Corollary 3.6 that the class EXPTIME of languages accepted by deterministic Turing machines in exponential time is characterized by alternating Turing machines which accept in polynomial space. Hence, if R is exponential time decidable, then there is an alternating Turing machine M_R accepting R in polynomial space S(n). According to Theorem 4.5 of Shapiro (1984), there is a logic program B of goal-size complexity c.S(n) accepting R.

On the other hand, if a logic program B accepts R with polynomial goal-size complexity G(n), it follows from Theorem 4.4 of Shapiro (1984) that R is accepted by an alternating Turing machine M that operates in space c.G(n). Consequently, R is exponential time decidable.

References

Chandra, A.K., Stockmeyer, L.J., 1977 Alternation, Proc. IEEE Symp. on Foundations of Comp. Sci., Providence, R.I. 1977, pp. 95-99

Chandra, A.K., Kozen, D.C., Stockmeyer, L.J., 1981 Alternation, JACM 28 (1981), pp. 114-133

Shapiro, E., 1984 Alternation and the Computational Complexity of Logic Programs, J. Logic Programming 1 (1984), pp. 19-33

INTRACTABLE UNIFIABILITY PROBLEMS AND BACKTRACKING

David A. Wolfram

School of Computer and Information Science,
Syracuse University,
Syracuse, NY 13244-1240, USA.

ARPANET: wolfram%syr@csnet-relay
BITNET: wolfram@sutcase
CSNET: wolfram%syr

ABSTRACT

Intelligent backtracking in logic programs analyses unification failure to avoid thrashing, which is an inefficient behaviour of ordinary backtracking. We show that the computation of all maximal unifiable subsets of constraints, as a means to avoid thrashing, is intractable in the sense that the solution length can be non-polynomially related to the input length. We also give a corresponding result for minimal nonunifiability. Restrictions of the problem of finding all maximal unifiable (minimal nonunifiable) subsets to those of certain sizes, for use with heuristics, are shown to be NP-hard. The results apply not only to standard unification but for unification without the occur-check as in many versions of Prolog. This now justifies the necessity for approximate or heuristic approaches in general.

1. Introduction

Implementations of logic programming such as the various versions of Prolog, use backtracking to perform a depth-first search on a tree formed by matching a selected atom with the conclusions of an input clause [5, 13]. It is well known that backtracking can be inefficient because of thrashing [14], which arises when backtracking does not detect that certain earlier decisions will never lead to a solution, so that subtrees of a search space which predictably have no solution branches will be searched. The number of nodes in these subtrees can exponentially increase with the height of the subtree, so that substantial speed-ups in backtracking could occur if thrashing is reduced [14].

In logic programming, there have been two main approaches to find a refinement of backtracking which could reduce thrashing and speed up the search for all solutions to a goal. One is the Cox-Matwin-Pietrzykowski approach, which was developed from [7], where there is characterization of nonunifiability in some linear resolution theorem provers. Algorithms based on this work were discussed in [4, 8, 9, 10, 16, 20] and applications to backtracking in linear resolution theorem proving were presented in [11, 16, 17, 20]. The other is the Bruynooghe-Pereira-Porto approach which was summarised in [2], and it has been closely developed with Prolog implementations.

A common feature of these approaches is that an analysis of unification failure is used in pruning a tree-like search space to reduce thrashing. They differ in the extent to which unification failure is analysed. In [4, 8, 10], methods are given for finding all maximal unifiable subsets of constraints and in [7] the heuristic of minimal pruning of the search space is proposed. However in [2], the issue of the computational complexity of such an approach is questioned, and only one of the corresponding sets of minimal nonunifiable constraints seems to be utilised.

Although no intelligent backtrack algorithm is provided in [2], their method seems to locate where to backtrack to at a failed goal, by using one minimal nonunifiable constraint set corresponding to each attempted unification of the conclusion of an input clause with the last selected atom.

This paper investigates the computational complexity question for intelligent backtracking, based on finding either all or particular maximal unifiable or minimal nonunifiable subsets of constraints.

This is a basic question in determining the viability of such approaches since in intelligent backtracking, as in most search methods, there is a trade-off between the execution time that a refinement of the search method takes, and the execution time that would have been required to search failed branches had the refinement not been used [18].

In the first section of this paper, some definitions and preliminary results are given. The second and third sections address some complexity questions for maximal unifiability and minimal nonunifiability. Finally, there is a summary of results, and a discussion of their relevance to practice.

2. Definitions and Preliminary Results

Let an *atom* be a positive literal. We call a pair of atoms $<p = q>$ a *constraint*, and a finite set of constraints a *constraint set* [7].

A constraint set $C=\{<p_1 = q_1>, ..., <p_n = q_n>\}$ is unifiable if and only if there is a substitution θ, which is called a *unifier* of C, such that $p_i\theta$ is identical to $q_i\theta$,$(1 \leq i \leq n)$ [7, 21].

A *maximal unifiable subset* of a constraint set C is a subset $C' \subseteq C$ such that C' is unifiable and no proper superset of C' with respect to C is unifiable.

Similarly, a *minimal nonunifiable subset* of a constraint set C is a subset $C' \subseteq C$ such that C' is not unifiable and every proper subset of C' is unifiable.

Some approaches to intelligent backtracking rely on determining maximal unifiable subsets or minimal nonunifiable subsets of a constraint set [2, 11, 16, 17, 20], where each constraint $<p = q>$ of the set represents the attempted unification, during a proof, of a selected atom p with an atom q.

One of these is the Cox-Pietrzykowski-Matwin approach which determines all maximal unifiable subsets of a constraint set [11, 16, 17, 20] formed from proofs with general clauses, but there is no investigation of the computational complexity of finding these subsets.

To do this, it suffices to consider a constraint set formed from a proof using a Horn clause logic program [26] rather than that from a set of general clauses, because we will see that the complexity of finding these subsets is already too great even in the Horn clause case. Each constraint <p = q> from such a constraint set, represents the attempted unification of a selected atom p with the conclusion q of an input clause with renamed variables from the program. The Cox-Pietrzykowski-Matwin approach allows a Horn clause program as a special case.

Let C be a constraint set. Consider the following four properties:

(i) C is nonunifiable and there is a constraint s in C such that C – {s} is unifiable. (We call s a *failure constraint*).

(ii) If <p = q> ∈ C then the variables occurring in q are distinct from those occurring in p.

(iii) If <p = q> and <p′ = q′> are distinct constraints occurring in C, then the variables occurring in q are distinct from those occurring in q′.

(iv) If <p = q> is a constraint occurring in C, then there is at most one other constraint <p′ = q′> occurring in C such that p and q′ have a variable in common.

If C satisfies properties (ii), (iii) and (iv), it is called a *resolution constraint set.* Properties (iii) and (iv) characterize strict renaming of variables in input clauses during a proof. If, in addition, C satisfies property (i), it is called a *failed resolution constraint set.*

A failed resolution constraint set could be obtained from a SLD-resolution deduction [13] at a unification failure. It could also be formed for and-parallel GLD-resolution strategies discussed in [26], which uses a Church-Rosser like property of unification to prove soundness and completeness results for these strategies.

It will also be sufficient to use a restriction of failed resolution constraint sets; the *0-X-1 constraint set* is a failed resolution constraint set in which the arguments of atoms are only the constant symbols 0 and 1, or variables.

The *length* of a 0-X-1 constraint set is defined as the sum of the lengths of each constraint in the set. The length of an atom is the number of arguments plus one and the length of a constraint <p = q> is the sum of the lengths of p and q. It seems unlikely that the input length of a reasonable encoding [12] for a 0-X-1 constraint set would not be polynomially related to this length measure.

The following NP-complete problem will be used to prove further NP-completeness results.

ONE-IN-THREE SATISFIABILITY [23]

INSTANCE: Set U of Boolean variables, collection B of clauses over U such that each clause has exactly 3 positive literals.

QUESTION: Is there a truth assignment for U such that each clause in B has exactly one true literal?

3. Intractability of Maximal Unifiability and Minimal Nonunifiability

It is now possible to to show the intractability of finding all maximal unifiable subsets since the 0-X-1 constraint set:

$$\{<T(y_k, 0) = T(x_{2k-1}, x_{2k-1})>, <T(y_k, z) = T(x_{2k}, x_{2k})> \mid 1 \leq k \leq n\} \cup \{<R(z) = R(1)>\}. \quad (1)$$

has length 12n + 4 and $2^n + 1$ maximal unifiable subsets; 2^n of which have length 6n + 4, and one has length 12n. The exponential growth arises because for each maximal unifiable subset which includes $<R(z) = R(1)>$ and for each k: $(1 \leq k \leq n)$ either $<T(y_k, 0)= T(x_{2k-1}, x_{2k-1})>$ or $<T(y_k, z) = T(x_{2k}, x_{2k})>$ can be included in the subset, but not both of them.

Similarly, finding all minimal nonunifiable subsets is intractable since the 0-X-1 constraint set:

$$\{<P(x_1) = P(0)>\}$$
$$\cup\{<T(x_k, x_{k+1}) = T(y_{2k-1}, y_{2k-1})>,<T(x_k, x_{k+1}) = T(y_{2k}, y_{2k})> \mid 1 \leq k \leq n\}$$
$$\cup \{<R(x_{n+1}) = R(1)>\} \quad (2)$$

has length 12n + 8, and 2^n minimal nonunifiable subsets; each of which has length 6n + 8. The exponential growth in the number of minimal nonunifiable subsets arises because for each k: $(1 \leq k \leq n)$ either

$<T(x_k, x_{k+1}) = T(y_{2k-1}, y_{2k-1})>$ or $<T(x_k, x_{k+1}) = T(y_{2k}, y_{2k})>$ can be included in a minimal nonunifiable subset, but not both of them.

These examples show that there are problems for which the overhead of finding the maximal unifiable or minimal nonunifiable subsets would far outweigh any benefit of improved backtracking behaviour. The algorithms in [4, 8, 9, 10, 11, 16, 17] for determining these subsets are thus limited in practice by the difficulty of the problems they solve. Considerable memory overheads have been observed in the system described in [11, 17].

The choice to use only one minimal nonunifiable subset in the Bruynooghe-Pereira-Porto approach in fact can now be justified on grounds of computational complexity.

4. Maximal Unifiability

Although the problems of finding all maximal unifiable subsets or all minimal nonunifiable subsets of a set of constraints can be intractable, it may seem reasonable to determine only a particular subset in the hope that this can be more efficiently computed.

Suppose that attention is restricted to the problem of finding the largest maximal unifiable subset so that more of the constructed proof can be retained. This leads to the following NP-complete problem:

0-X-1 UNIFIABLE SUBSET

INSTANCE: 0-X-1 constraint set C with a failure constraint s, and a positive integer $k \leq |C|$.

QUESTION: Is there a unifiable subset C' of C such that $s \in C'$ and $|C'| \geq k$?

Theorem 1 **0-X-1 UNIFIABLE SUBSET** is NP-Complete.

Proof

The problem is in NP, since a nondeterministic algorithm can guess a subset of C of size at least k and verify in polynomial time that it is a unifiable subset [1, 15, 19].

The NP-complete problem **ONE-IN-THREE SATISFIABILITY** will be polynomially transformed to **0-X-1 UNIFIABLE SUBSET.**

Let $U = \{x_1, ..., x_n\}$, $B = \{c_1, ..., c_m\}$ be any instance of **ONE-IN-THREE SATISFIABILITY.** A 0-X-1 constraint set C and a positive integer $k \leq |C|$ must be constructed so that C has a unifiable subset of size at least k iff B is satisfiable with exactly one true literal per clause.

The 0-X-1 constraint set C is produced by applying the following steps:

(1) Initially, $C = \{<R(y) = R(1)>\}$

(2) For each clause $c_l = \{x_i, x_j, x_k\} \in B$ where $1 \leq l \leq m$, add the following constraints to C:

$$<T(x_i, x_j, x_k, y) = T(0, 0, y_{l.1}, y_{l.1})>$$
$$<T(x_i, x_j, x_k, y) = T(0, y_{l.2}, 0, y_{l.2})>$$
$$<T(x_i, x_j, x_k, y) = T(y_{l.3}, 0, 0, y_{l.3})>$$

This procedure results in $3m + 1$ constraints in C with a total length of $30m + 4$. Clearly C is a 0-X-1 constraint set with failure constraint $s \equiv <R(y) = R(1)>$.

Let θ be a unifier of s. It is a direct consequence of the construction that $(C - \{s\})\theta$ has a unifiable subset of size at least m iff B is satisfiable with at most one true literal per clause.

Therefore set $k = m$. It is easy to see that C and k can be constructed in polynomial time. □

Let C be a constraint set and C_2 be a failed resolution constraint set with a failure constraint s. The largest maximal unifiable subset method can also incur unacceptable overheads because it is easy to derive the following NP-hardness results from this result:

LARGEST MAXIMAL UNIFIABLE SUBSET

INSTANCE: Given C.

PROBLEMS:

(i) Find a largest maximal unifiable subset of C.

(ii) Find the size of a largest maximal unifiable subset of C.

INSTANCE: Given C_2, and s.

PROBLEMS:

(i) Find a largest maximal unifiable subset of C_2 which includes s.

(ii) Find the size of a largest maximal unifiable subset of C_2 which includes s.

The second group of problems are similar to those encountered in intelligent backtracking. The condition that the subset must include s is because $C_2 - \{s\}$ is always the largest maximal unifiable subset of C_2. These problems are NP-hard.

We can also derive from theorem 1 that problems of determining whether there are unifiable subsets of certain sizes are NP-complete. In the problems, C is a constraint set and k is a positive integer not exceeding $|C|$; C_2 is a failed resolution constraint set with a failure constraint s, and k_2 is a positive integer not exceeding $|C_2| - 1$. The following problems are generalizations and extensions of theorem 1 for constraint sets and resolution constraint sets, and they are also NP-complete.

BOUNDED UNIFIABILITY

INSTANCE: Given C and k.

QUESTIONS:

Is there a unifiable subset of C

(i) of size at least k?

(ii) of size k?

Is there a maximal unifiable subset of C

(iii) of size at least k?

(iv) of size k?

BOUNDED RESOLUTION UNIFIABILITY

INSTANCE: Given C_2, s, and k_2.

QUESTIONS:

Is there a unifiable subset of C_2 which includes s

(i) of size at least k_2?

(ii) of size k_2?

Is there a maximal unifiable subset of C_2 which includes s

(iii) of size at least k_2?

(iv) of size k_2?

5. Minimal Nonunifiability

An interesting and important open problem is whether there are corresponding results for minimal nonunifiability to those for maximal unifiability. It is possible to envisage a backtracking system which might find the smallest minimal nonunifiable subsets, or those within a certain size range, for example.

However, by looking instead at the problem of finding the largest minimal nonunifiable subset, some complementary results to those for maximal unifiability can be found:

0-X-1 MINIMAL NONUNIFIABLE SUBSET

INSTANCE: 0-X-1 constraint set C with a failure constraint s and a positive integer $k \leq |C|$.

QUESTION: Is there a minimal nonunifiable subset C' of C such that $s \in C'$ and $|C'| \geq k$?

Theorem 2 **0-X-1 MINIMAL NONUNIFIABLE SUBSET** is NP-Complete.

Proof

The problem is in NP, since a nondeterministic algorithm can guess a subset of C of size at least k and verify in polynomial time that it is a minimal nonunifiable subset [1, 15, 19].

The NP-complete problem **ONE-IN-THREE SATISFIABILITY** will be polynomially transformed to **0-X-1 MINIMAL NONUNIFIABLE SUBSET.**

Let $U = \{x_1, ..., x_n\}$, $B = \{c_1, ..., c_m\}$ be any instance of **ONE-IN-THREE SATISFIABILITY.** A 0-X-1 constraint set C and a positive integer $k \leq |C|$ must be constructed so that C has a minimal nonunifiable subset of size at least k iff B is satisfiable with exactly one true literal per clause.

A 0-X-1 constraint set C is produced by applying the following steps:

(1) Initially,

$$C = \{<S(0) = S(z_1)>, <S(z_{m+1}) = S(w)>, <R(y, w) = R(1, 1)>\}$$

(2) For each clause $c_l = \{x_i, x_j, x_k\} \in B$ where $1 \leq l \leq m$, add the following constraints to C:

$$<T(x_i, x_j, x_k, y, z_l, z_{l+1}) = T(0, 0, y_{l.1}, y_{l.1}, z_{l.1}, z_{l.1})>$$

$$<T(x_i, x_j, x_k, y, z_l, z_{l+1}) = T(0, y_{l.2}, 0, y_{l.2}, z_{l.2}, z_{l.2})>$$

$$<T(x_i, x_j, x_k, y, z_l, z_{l+1}) = T(y_{l.3}, 0, 0, y_{l.3}, z_{l.3}, z_{l.3})>$$

This procedure results in $3m + 3$ constraints in C with a total length of $42m + 14$. Clearly C is a 0-X-1 constraint set with failure constraint $s \equiv <R(y, w) = R(1, 1)>$.

Let θ be a unifier of s. It is a direct consequence of the construction that $(C - \{s\})\theta$ has a minimal nonunifiable subset of size at least $m + 2$ iff B is satisfiable with one true literal per clause.

Therefore set $k = m + 2$. It is easy to see that C and k can be constructed in polynomial time. □

Some further NP-hardness results are easily derived from the theorem. These problems could also conceivably have relevance to the design of improved back-tracking in theorem-provers. As in the preceding section, C is a constraint set and k is a positive integer not exceeding $|C|$; C_2 is a failed resolution constraint set with a failure constraint s, and k_2 is a positive integer not exceeding $|C_2| - 1$.

LARGEST MINIMAL NONUNIFIABLE SUBSET

INSTANCE: Given C.

PROBLEMS:

(i) Find a largest minimal nonunifiable subset of C.

(ii) Find the size of a largest minimal nonunifiable subset of C.

INSTANCE: Given C_2, s.

PROBLEMS:

(i) Find a largest minimal nonunifiable subset of C_2 which includes s.

(ii) Find the size of a largest minimal nonunifiable subset of C_2 which includes s.

The following problems are generalizations and extensions of theorem 2 for constraint sets and resolution constraint sets, and they are also NP-complete.

BOUNDED NONUNIFIABILITY

INSTANCE: Given C, k.

QUESTIONS:

is there a minimal nonunifiable subset of C

(i) of size at least k?

(ii) of size k?

BOUNDED RESOLUTION NONUNIFIABILITY

INSTANCE: Given C_2, s, and k_2.

QUESTIONS:

Is there a minimal nonunifiable subset of C_2 which includes s

(i) of size at least k_2?

(ii) of size k_2?

6. Discussion

The results give limitations for methods of intelligent backtracking based on finding all maximal unifiable subsets or minimal nonunifiable subsets as they show that the problems are intractable in the worst case because of the possible non-polynomial growth in output length. This indicates that the methods proposed should be restricted to heuristic use because there is more information than we could ever hope to use [12].

If heuristics such as minimal pruning of the search space is used instead [7, 16, 17, 20], a largest maximal unifiable or smallest minimal nonunifiable constraints, or those exceeding or not exceeding a given bound, must be determined. Unfortunately, there are further limitations as the problems, except for the open problem of the complexity of finding a smallest minimal nonunifiable subset, are NP-hard and so it is most improbable that an efficient algorithm to solve them in general, can be found [12].

These observations apply not only where standard unification [21] is used, but also where the occur-check is omitted as in many Prolog implementations [6] and in fact to any form of unification which will give the same results as standard unification does for the 0-X-1 constraint sets.

For NP-completeness results using polynomial transformations to 0-X-1 constraint sets, it may seem appropriate to further restrict failed resolution constraint sets, by not only disallowing non-constant function symbols in subterms, but by putting some bound on the number of arguments, for example. In this way, the weakest restrictions for which the problems could be solved in polynomial time might be found. However, logic programs with 0-X-1 constraint sets are already a highly restricted form, and any further restrictions on constraints would be objectionably prohibitive in practice.

It should be noted that algorithms for NP-complete problems may have very reasonable average time complexity [25], and that the results in the preceding sections are worst case ones for sufficiently large problem instances. An interesting problem would be to analyse the average time complexity for **0-X-1 UNIFIABLE SUBSET** and **0-X-1 MINIMAL NONUNIFIABLE SUBSET**. Even so, it is undesirable to unwittingly use a search method which has the potential for producing huge overheads with currently known algorithms.

We can now justify the use of one minimal nonunifiable subset in the Bruynooghe-Pereira-Porto approach [2], and the necessity for the approximations in [22, 24] and semi-intelligent backtracking [3], in general.

7. Acknowledgements

This paper is based on part of a thesis which was submitted for the Degree of Master of Science to the Department of Computer Science of the University of Melbourne on 13 August, 1985. I should like to thank my supervisor Rodney Topor, and Howard Blair at Syracuse University, and also the referees, for their comments. This research was supported by an Australian Government Postgraduate Research Award 1984 - 1985, and a University of Melbourne Faculty of Science Postgraduate Writing-Up Award 1985.

8. References

[1] Baxter, L.D. The Complexity of Unification, Ph.D. thesis, Department of Computer Science, University of Waterloo, Ontario, Canada, 1976.

[2] Bruynooghe, M. and Pereira, L.M. Deduction Revision by Intelligent Backtracking, in: J.A. Campbell (ed.), *Implementations of Prolog*, Ellis Horwood, Chichester, 1984.

[3] Chang, J.-H. and Despain, A.M, Semi-Intelligent Backtracking of Prolog based on a Static Data Dependency Analysis, 1985 Symposium on Logic Programming, IEEE, Boston, 10-21.

[4] Chen, T.Y., Lassez, J-L. and Port, G.S. Maximal Unifiable Subsets and Minimal Non-unifiable Subsets, Technical Report 84/16, May, 1985, Department of Computer Science, The University of Melbourne, Australia.

[5] Clocksin, W.F. and Mellish, C.S. *Programming in Prolog*, Springer, Berlin, 1984.

[6] Colmerauer, A. Prolog and Infinite Trees, in: K.L. Clark and S-A. Tärnlund (eds.), *Logic Programming*, Academic, New York, 1982.

[7] Cox, P.T. Deduction Plans: a graphical proof procedure for the first-order predicate calculus, Research Report CS-77-28, Ph.D. thesis, Department of Computer Science, University of Waterloo, Ontario, Canada, 1977.

[8] Cox, P.T. Finding Backtrack Points for Intelligent Backtracking, in: J.A. Campbell (ed.), *Implementations of Prolog*, Ellis Horwood, Chichester, 1984.

[9] Dilger, W. and Janson, A. Unifikationsgraphen für Intelligentes Backtracking in Deduktionssystemen, Proceedings of GWAI-83, Dassel, Federal Republic of Germany, 1983.

[10] Forster, D.R. GTP: A Graph Based Theorem Prover, M.S. thesis, University of Waterloo, Waterloo, Ontario, Canada, 1982.

[11] Forsythe, K. and Matwin, S. Implementation Strategies for Plan-Based Deduction, Proceedings of the Seventh International Conference on Automated Deduction, (R.E. Shostak, ed.), Napa, California, USA, Lecture Notes in Computer Science, Springer, **170** (1984).

[12] Garey, M.R. and Johnson, D.S. *Computers and Intractability: A Guide to the Theory of NP-Completeness*, Freeman, San Francisco, 1979.

[13] Kowalski, R.A. *Logic for Problem Solving*, North-Holland, New York, 1979.

[14] Mackworth, A.K. Consistency in Networks of Relations, Artificial Intelligence **8** (1977), 99-118.

[15] Martelli, A. and Montanari, U. Unification in Linear Time and Space: A Structured Presentation, Internal Report B76-16, Istituto di Elaborazione della Informazione, Pisa, 1976.

[16] Matwin, S. and Pietrzykowski, T. Exponential Improvement of Exhaustive Backtracking: Data Structure and Implementation, Proceedings of the Sixth Conference on Automated Deduction, Lecture Notes in Computer Science, Springer, New York, **138** (1982), 240-259.

[17] Matwin, S. and Pietrzykowski, T. Intelligent Backtracking in Plan-Based Deduction, IEEE Transactions on Pattern Analysis and Machine Intelligence, **7**, 6 (1985), 682-692.

[18] Nilsson, N.J. *Principles of Artificial Intelligence*, Springer, 1982.

[19] Paterson, M.S. and Wegman, M.N. Linear Unification, JCSS **16** 158-167 (1978).

[20] Pietrzykowski, T. and Matwin, S. Exponential Improvement of Efficient Backtracking: A Strategy for Plan-Based Deduction, Proceedings of the Sixth Conference on Automated Deduction, Lecture Notes in Computer Science, Springer, New York, **138** (1982), 223-239.

[21] Robinson, J.A. A Machine-Oriented Logic Based on the Resolution Principle, Journal of the ACM, **12**, 1 (January, 1965), 23-41.

[22] Sato, T. An Algorithm for Intelligent Backtracking, Proceedings of the RIMS Symposia on Software Science, and Engineering, (S. Goto et alia, eds.), Lecture Notes in Computer Science, **147**, Springer, 1983.

[23] Schaefer, T.J. The Complexity of Satisfiability Problems, Conference Record of the Tenth Annual ACM Symposium on Theory of Computing, ACM, New York, 216-226, (1978).

[24] Vasey, P.E. A Logic-in-Logic Interpreter, M.Sc. Thesis, 1980, Imperial College of Science and Technology, University of London.

[25] Wilf, H.S. Backtrack: An O(1) Expected Time Algorithm for the Graph Coloring Problem, Information Processing Letters, **18** (1984), 119-121.

[26] Wolfram, D.A., Maher, M.J. and Lassez, J.-L. A Unified Treatment of Resolution Strategies for Logic Programs, *Proceedings of the Second International Logic Programming Conference*, Uppsala, Sweden, 1984, 263-276.

ON THE COMPLEXITY OF UNIFICATION SEQUENCES

Extended abstract

Heikki Mannila and Esko Ukkonen
Department of Computer Science, University of Helsinki
Tukholmankatu 2, SF-00250 Helsinki, Finland

ABSTRACT

The execution of a Prolog program can be viewed as a sequence of unifications and backtracks over unifications. We study the time requirement of executing a sequence of such operations (the unify-deunify problem). It is shown that the well-known set union problem is reducible to this problem. As the set union problem requires nonlinear time on large class of algorithms, the same holds for the unify-deunify problem. Thus the linearity of single unifications does not give a complete picture of the time complexity of Prolog primitives. We discuss the methods for executing sequences of unifications used in Prolog interpreters and show that many of them require even quadratic time in the worst case. We also outline some theoretically better methods.

1. Introduction

The execution of a Prolog program creates the runtime data structures by means of unifications, and by backtracks of unifications. Advanced Prolog interpreters, like the structure sharing and copying methods (see e.g. [Ho84]), do all their data structure manipulations via unifications. Implementing these operations is by no means as simple as implementing e.g. the assignment statement, which in procedural languages performs the corresponding task of forming the desired results.

One can abstractly view the execution of a Prolog program as a sequence

o(1),o(2),...,o(n)

of operations, where

o(i) = UNIFY(t(i),s(i)) or

o(i) = DEUNIFY

for all i = 1,...,n. Here t(i) and s(i) are terms (or term lists), which either occur in the program or have been obtained as the result of a previous operation. The operation UNIFY(t,s) tries to unify terms t and s. If the unification succeeds, this operation forms the common instance of these terms. The operation DEUNIFY cancels the last successful unify operation which has not yet been cancelled.

For example, the program

```
:- p(X),q(X).

p(a).

p(b).

q(c).

q(b).
```

creates the following sequence of operations:

UNIFY(X,a),UNIFY(X,c),UNIFY(X,b),DEUNIFY,

UNIFY(X,b),UNIFY(X,c),UNIFY(X,b).

We call the problem of executing a sequence o(1),...,o(n) of UNIFY(t,s) and DEUNIFY operations the unify-deunify problem. A natural question is finding the time complexity of this problem, as a function of the sizes of the terms occurring in the operations.

The results about the linearity of unification ([PW78], [VS84]) suggest that the unify-deunify problem, too, would be solvable in linear time. In this paper we give strong indications that this is not the case. Namely, we show that the set union problem ([AHU74], [Ta75]) is reducible to the unify-deunify problem. On a large class of algorithms, the set union problem cannot be solved in linear time; hence the same holds for the unify-deunify problem.

Our result is in a sense still stronger: we show that the set union problem is reducible to the restricted unify-deunify problem. By this we mean the problem of executing a sequence of unify and deunify operations where the terms contain only variables and constants, no functions. From the point of view of Prolog interpreters, this is, of course, a very simple case.

We also show that some naive methods for solving the restricted unify-deunify problem always take quadratic time, and outline two methods using O(n log n) and O(n log log n) time, respectively. Finally, we address briefly the general unify-deunify problem.

The rest of this paper is organized as follows. In Section 2 we introduce the set union problem and show how it can be reduced to the restricted unify-deunify problem. We also discuss the result from the point of view of Prolog interpreters.

Section 3 shows how certain simple methods for the restricted unify-deunify problem always take quadratic time. It also gives some methods for solving that problem. Section 4 is a short conclusion.

2. Reducing the set union problem to the unify-deunify problem

The set union problem is the problem of manipulating a partition of $U = \{1,2,...,n\}$ on-line under the operations

FIND(x) - output the name of the block currently containing element $x \in U$;

UNION(x,y,C) - take blocks containing elements x and y and combine them to a block named C.

The manipulating process starts with the partition of U consisting of n singleton sets. Initially, the name of set {i} is i.

Applications of the set union problem include the compilation of FORTRAN EQUIVALENCE and COMMON statements, finding minimum spanning trees and various graph algorithms (see [TvL84] and [GT83] for references).

The set union problem has been studied extensively. Tarjan [Ta75] showed that a simple path-compression algorithm for the problem has the surprising running time $O(m \cdot \alpha(m,n))$, where m is the number of find operations, n is the number of elements and α is an extremely slowly growing function, an inverse of Ackermann's function. In [Ta79] Tarjan showed that this lower bound is the best possible in a rather large class of algorithms (so called separable algorithms). A very general analysis of various algorithms for the set union problem is presented in [TvL84], while [GT83] presents a linear time algorithm for a special case.

We show that the restricted unify-deunify problem is at least as difficult as the set union problem. This is done by showing how one can modify an algorithm for the unify-deunify problem to solve also the set union problem without loosing more than a constant factor in time.

We have to make some assumptions about the algorithm used for the unify-deunify problem. All algorithms are on-line, i.e., they process each operation request before the next one arrives. We consider the class of <u>separable</u> algorithms, which use only linked structures and do not utilize the power of random access memory (see [TvL84] for a more precise definition). In particular, at the start of an operation UNIFY(X,Y) a separable algorithm has access only to the nodes corresponding to X and Y; other nodes have to be found by searching from these nodes. We also have to require that the algorithm has <u>outdegree</u>

<u>one</u>, i.e. from each node starts at most one link, and that the data structures are <u>acyclic</u>. We will call algorithms satisfying these requirements <u>tree algorithms</u>, since the data structures are basically trees. The classical methods for Prolog implementation (see [Ho84]) satisfy these requirements.

Let A be a tree algorithm which solves the restricted unify-deunify problem. We change A to an algorithm for the set union problem as follows. We first add to A a preprocessing stage, which maps a sequence of union and find operations to a sequence of unify and deunify operations. This is done by transforming a UNION(x,y,C) to

UNIFY(X,Y); UNIFY(X,b); DEUNIFY

and a FIND(x) to

UNIFY(X,b); DEUNIFY.

Here x,y are element names, X and Y are corresponding variable names, C is a block name and b is a new constant (one which has not appeared in the operation sequence). Thus unifications between variables correspond to unions, and unification of a variable with a constant corresponds to a find. The preprocessing takes linear time.

We next augment A so that when given a set union sequence transformed as above, it will produce the answer to FIND(x) as a by-product of the execution of the operation UNIFY(X,b). The augmentation increases the running time of A by at most a constant factor.

Assume for the moment that A satisfies the following condition. A <u>block</u> in the execution of a unify-deunify algorithm is a collection of variables which have been unified together. The algorithm A has the <u>common representative property</u>, if for each block E there is a node p such that for each operation UNIFY(X,b), where $X \in E$, A traverses p. That is, there is a node representing the whole block in the sense that all operations on the block traverse that node. Note that the mapping of the set union operations created one such UNIFY(X,b) operation for each union and find.

If A has the common representative property, then the block names can be stored in these nodes. They can be retrieved during the operations UNIFY(X,b) corresponding to FIND(x) and they can be updated during the operations UNIFY(X,Y); UNIFY(X,b) corresponding to UNION(x,y,C). Thus this property makes it possible to simulate the set union problem. In more detail, we associate a name field to each node in the data structures. Suppose an operation UNIFY(X,b) arising from UNION(x,y,C) is to be executed. Then we change to C the name fields of all nodes reachable from X which are traversed by the algorithm. The answer to FIND(x) is given by the name field of the last node traversed by the operation UNIFY(X,b) corresponding to that find.

The augmentation of A is now complete. We still have to show that algorithms satisfying our restrictions have the common representative property.

Theorem 1. Let A be a tree algorithm for the unify-deunify problem. Then A has the common representative property.

Proof. Let E be a nonempty block and X a variable in E. Define root(E) to be the first node p in the path starting from X such that for all variables Y in E, p is reachable from Y. If root(E) exists, it is independent of the choice of the variable X.

We first show that root(E) exists for all E. If there is no such node for a block E, then for some variables X and Z in E there in no node q which is reachable both from X and Z. But then an operation UNIFY(X,b) does not affect Z in any way, by separability; thus a subsequent UNIFY(Z,a) will succeed, although it should not. Thus root(E) exists. (Note that the on-line property was used.)

Consider now an operation UNIFY(X,b), where X belongs to E. We show that this operation traverses root(E). Assume it does not. By separability, UNIFY(X,b) starts from X and b. By the definition of root(E) there is a variable Z in E such that the operation UNIFY(X,b) does not traverse the nodes reachable from Z. Thus we have again by separability the following: if after UNIFY(X,b) we perform the operation UNIFY(Z,a), this operation succeeds, although it should not.

Thus UNIFY(X,b) must traverse root(E). Hence root(E) is a common representative for block E and the theorem is proved.

Theorem 1 and the preceding discussion now give the next results.

Theorem 2. In the class of tree algorithms the restricted unify-deunify problem is at least as difficult as the set union problem.

Corollary 3. The (restricted) unify-deunify problem cannot be solved in linear time by tree algorithms.

It is interesting to note that in the linear time unification algorithms of [PW78] and [VS84] special care is taken to avoid the use of union and find operations, as they require nonlinear time. Our result shows that in the wider setting of the whole execution of a Prolog program one cannot avoid the equivalents of these operations.

3. Algorithms for the unify-deunify problem

In existing Prolog implementations it is customary to solve the restricted unify-deunify problem by using tree algorithms. A natural method is to represent the unified blocks of variables as trees with the common representative as the root. UNIFY(X,Y) means traversing the paths from X and Y to the corresponding roots and linking them together in either direction. The direction of the link does not depend on the sizes (or heights) of the two trees linked together. In fact, this is the classical set union data structure where the unions are implemented without balancing (see e.g. [AHU74]). The DEUNIFY operation simply cancels the last link which is still valid.

Then it can happen that the i'th UNIFY(X,Y) creates a tree of height i; this takes O(i) steps, since the algorithm has to traverse paths of length i. A simple example of such a situation is solving the query

```
?- p(X,X1), p(X,X2), ... , p(X,Xn).
```

using the program

p(Z,Z).

This gives the following sequence of UNIFY operations

UNIFY(X,Z),UNIFY(X1,Z),UNIFY(X,Z),UNIFY(X2,Z),...,
UNIFY(X,Z),UNIFY(Xi,Z),...,UNIFY(X,Z),UNIFY(Xn,Z).

The first UNIFY(X,Z) creates a link, say, from Z to X. Then UNIFY(X1,Z) creates a link from the root of Z (that is, from X) to X1. In general, the i'th UNIFY(X,Z) first traverses the path from X to the corresponding root. The path is (X,X1,...,X(i-1)), hence the traversal takes time $\Theta(i)$. Then a link is created from Z to X(i-1). The next operation, UNIFY(Xi,Z), then adds a link from X(i-1) to Xi which again continues the path from X to its new root with one link. The total time for executing the operation sequence is proportional to n^2.

On the other hand, after i UNIFY operations the data structures can contain paths of length at most i. This is because each UNIFY adds at most one new link at the end of some existing paths. Hence the i'th UNIFY always needs at most time $O(i)$.

Each DEUNIFY operation takes constant time, if the well-known trail-stack technique is used for implementing it: as a side-effect of each UNIFY, push into the stack a pointer to the new link. The DEUNIFY operation pops a pointer to the link to be cancelled from the stack.

We have the following.

Theorem 4. A sequence of n restricted unify-deunify operations can be implemented in $\Theta(n^2)$ steps by a tree algorithm.

Balancing improves the upper bound of Theorem 4. Then the direction of the link created by UNIFY(X,Y) is chosen from the smaller block of variables to the larger one. To implement this we have to store the size of the tree at the root; this is normally not done in Prolog implementations. The maximum path length in a tree representing n variables is now bounded by log n. Thus we get the next theorem.

Theorem 5. A sequence of n restricted unify-deunify operations can be implemented in $\Theta(n \log n)$ steps by a balancing tree algorithm.

We still have a wide gap between the upper bound of Theorem 5 and the almost linear lower bound of Corollary 3. The algorithm of Theorem 5 can be made asymptotically faster by using so-called path compression to make the paths in the tree shorter as a side effect of traversing a path. By modifying a special form of path compression, the splitting method of [TvL84, vLvW77], an improved algorithm (whose overhead seems rather large) can be developed (details are given in [MU86]) with running time $O(n \log \log n)$.

Theorem 4, which analyzes actual Prolog implementations, suggests that the implementations are very slow in the worst case: n unification steps of a Prolog program without functions can take $\Theta(n^2)$ time. Fortunately, this is not true in general. It turns out that the direction of the links created by UNIFY operations is crucial in obtaining a better upper bound. In the framework of the usual Prolog implementations, with a stack of activation records, we can define the <u>age</u> of a variable in a natural way. Variable X is younger than variable Y, if the field in an activation record corresponding to X is closer to the top of the stack than the field corresponding to Y. This gives an ordering by age for all variables occurring in our unify-deunify problem.

Lemma 6. If the link created by UNIFY(X,Y) is always directed from the root with younger variable to the root with older variable, then the length of paths traversed by any UNIFY operation is at most M, where M is the maximum number of variables occurring in one clause of the Prolog program.

Proof. Let X be a variable which occurs in a clause C and let the total number of variables in C be m. Consider some activation of C during an execution of the program. Take a sequence of operations from the corresponding unify-deunify sequence, starting from the first UNIFY that has X as a parameter, and ending at the last such UNIFY. Let the sequence be u1, ..., uk. To prove the lemma, it suffices to show that the length of the path starting from X is at most m during these operations.

Consider first u1. Since this is the first operation referring to X, the path starting from X before the operation is of length 0 and after it of length 1. We account the only link on the path to X itself. The idea in the rest of the proof is to account all links on the path starting from X to some of the variables of C. Each variable will get at most one link, which proves the claim. Whenever a link is cancelled by a DEUNIFY, also the corresponding account is made zero.

Assume that a UNIFY operation uj creates a new link at the end of the path starting from X. Let the link be from variable V to variable W. If W is a variable of C then this link is accounted for W. Otherwise W is a variable of an older activation. However, W must be unified with some variable U of C by this moment; account link (V,W) to U. Such a U must exist since operation uj, where j is at most k, can access variables which are older than C's variables only by unifying them with some variable U of C. (Recall that uk was the last operation that has X as a parameter; hence uj occurs before the activation of C is completed.) The blocks of variables unified together always constitute a partition of all variables. Then, the number of links accounted to the same variable of C is at any moment at most 1.

By Lemma 6, each UNIFY takes time O(M). Since DEUNIFY still takes constant time, our final result follows.

Theorem 7. Let M be as in Lemma 6. A sequence of n restricted unify-deunify operations can be implemented in O(Mn) steps by a tree algorithm.

Finally, consider the general case where the terms can also contain function symbols. It seems that this does not add very much to the complexity of the unify-deunify problem, nor do we have any essentially stronger results for this case. The main difficulty in globally handling the unifications in a Prolog implementation comes from the set union problem behind Prolog.

4. Conclusions

We exhibited a close relationship between Prolog program executions and the set union problem. This led to some computational complexity results which locate some inherent difficulty in Prolog and partially explain why Prolog implementations have to be rather complicated.

Acknowledgements
This research was supported by the Academy of Finland and by TEKES.

References

[AHU74]

A.V. Aho, J.E. Hopcroft and J.D. Ullman: The Design and Analysis of Computer Algorithms. Addison-Wesley, 1974.

[GT83]

H.N. Gabow and R.E. Tarjan: A linear-time algorithm for a special case of disjoint set union. STOC '83, 246-251.

[Ho84]

C.J. Hogger: Introduction to Logic Programming. Academic Press, 1984.

[MU86]

H. Mannila and E. Ukkonen: The set union problem with backtracking. Thirteenth International Colloquium on Automata, Languages, and Programming, Rennes, France, July 15-19, 1986 (ICALP 86), to appear.

[PW78]

M.S. Paterson and M.N. Wegman: Linear unification. Journal of Computer and System Sciences 16, 158-167.

[Ta75]

R.E. Tarjan: Efficiency of a good but not linear disjoint set union algorithm. J. ACM 22, 2 (April 1975), 215-225.

[Ta79]

R.E. Tarjan: A class of algorithms which require nonlinear time to maintain disjoint sets. J. Computer and System Sciences 18 (1979), 110-127.

[TvL84]

R.E. Tarjan and J. van Leeuwen: Worst-case analysis of set union algorithms. J. ACM 31, 2 (April 1984), 245-281.

[vLvW77]

J. van Leeuwen and T. van der Weide: Alternative path compression techniques. Technical Report RUU-CS-77-3, Rijksuniversiteit Utrecht, Utrecht, The Netherlands.

[VS84]

J.S. Vitter and R.A. Simons: New classes for parallel complexity: a study of unification and other complete problems in P. Technical Report CS-84-Ø6, Department of Computer Science, Brown University, 1984.

How to Invent a Prolog Machine*

Peter Kursawe

Gesellschaft für Mathematik und Datenverarbeitung mbH
Forschungsstelle an der Universität Karlsruhe
Haid-und-Neu-Str.7, D-7500 Karlsruhe 1, Germany (West)
CSNET: kursawe@germany

Abstract

In this paper we study the compilation of Prolog by making visible hidden operations (especially unification), and then optimizing them using well-known partial evaluation techniques. Inspection of straight forward partially evaluated unification algorithms gives an idea how to design special abstract machine instructions which later form the target language of our compilation. We handle typical compiler problems like representation of terms explicitely. This work gives a logical reconstruction of abstract Prolog machine code, and represents an approach of constructing a correct compiler from Prolog to such a code. As an example, we are explaining the unification principles of Warren's New Prolog Engine within our framework.

1. Introduction

Recently, a lot of proposals for the design of instructions for a Prolog machine have been made (e.g. [Bowe83], [TiWa84], [Cloc85]). All of them state a set of instructions explaining how they work, but none even asks the question "why do they work?" and "how can we get them?". We will give an answer to this question which is an outcome of a project concerned with optimizing Prolog programs.

To have a basic Prolog system this project we implemented an abstract machine well-suited for compiling Prolog to the instructions of that machine [Neid86]. Concerning the question of a correct (= semantic preserving) compiler we have got a deeper insight in the process of inventing and describing an instruction set for abstract Prolog machines: instead of defining an instruction set and giving some suggestions, how to compile Prolog to these instructions, we start with a description of the compilation process of Prolog (based on partial evaluation), and then, in a very natural manner, we develop the instructions out of the compilation process.

1.1 Partial Evaluation and Compiling

The partial evaluation principle (also called *mixed computation* [Ersh77]. A partial evaluator for Prolog is described in [Venk84]) is based on executing statements of a program the inputs of which are (partially) known at compile time. It is well-known that an interpreter for a (source) language

* This work has been done within a joint project of the GMD and the SFB 314 (artificial intelligence) at the University of Karlsruhe

together with a partial evaluator for the interpreter language can be used as a compiler from the source language to the interpreter language ([Futa71], [Ersh82], [Jone85]). But a practical realization of this principle suffers from two problems: (1) usually an entire interpreter is very complex (resulting in very long partial evaluation times), (2) in most interpreters the change of source language data structures to interpreter language data structures, does not take place (especially in the very interesting case of an interpreter language equalling source language, this step is left out; but often "more efficient" data structures are desired).

To overcome these problems, we conceptually distinguish three aspects of a source language with respect to compilation:

1. *hidden operations*: e.g. parameter passing (by value, by reference, by unification,...), variable binding mechanism (especially a dynamic one as in LISP), built-in predicates and functions (e.g. **functor/3** in Prolog, **CAR** in LISP, arithmetical operations in most languages), ...
2. *data representation*: how to represent source language data objects in the target language?
3. *control flow*: how to map source language control structures to target language control structures?

Partial evaluation presents a solution to these three problems: 1. and 3. are compiled by partially evaluating algorithms which implement the operations and the control, whereas 2. is compiled by partial evaluation of an algorithm which maps source language data structures to target language constructs. In the following we call these algorithms *key algorithms*. Compiling a program is done by first inserting calls of the key algorithms into the program (*enrichment* of the program) and then partially evaluating them.

The advantages of using partial evaluation for compilation are the following: (1) only one partial evaluator is necessary to compile different source languages (provided the language in which the interpreter (the key algorithms, respectively) is written, always is the same), (2) correctness of the partial evaluator and of the interpreter ensures correctness of compilation, (3) writing the necessary interpreter is much more easier than writing a compiler.

1.2 Defining Instructions

For first experiments we used Prolog itself as implementation language for the key algorithms and applied a very simple partial evaluator which only performs unfolding, and a special kind of controlled backward unification (necessary for calls of predicates like **var(X)**). The results of partially evaluating calls of a unification algorithm (as key algorithm) were very disappointing: the "code" became very long and complex, a lot of disjunctions appeared very often in a similar manner. We tried to introduce new predicates generalizing similar pieces of code, but this approach failed (because the "similar" pieces of code were not similar enough!). So we changed the unification algorithm, and after some iterations of (1) implementing the key algorithm, (2) partial evaluation, (3) defining instructions (if possible), we found a set of instructions realizing unification on an abstract Prolog machine. The Prolog implementation of an instruction can be taken as an operational specification to implement this instruction as efficiently as possible in any language. The combination of key algorithms for unification and term representation results in instructions very similar to those of Warren's New Prolog Engine [TiWa84]. The described iteration process can be performed with any other key algorithm, two examples are given below.

After a final definition of the instructions, the compilation of a program comprises two steps: (1) to enrich the program by calls of the key algorithms, (2) to partially evaluate the enriched program (especially with respect to the key algorithms). The program runs on an abstract machine with the defined instructions. Correctness of the compilation is guaranteed provided the enrichment process can be justified.

Our approach is applicable to the compilation of any language. However, the results are better if very complex implicit operations exist in the language (e.g. the unification in Prolog), so Prolog is a very good example to verify this approach.

1.3 Relation to Other Work

The literature on partial evaluation is growing, cf. [Jone85] and the references there. Compiling Prolog by partial evalution is described by Kahn and Carlsson [KaCa84]. They partially evaluate a Prolog interpreter written in LISP (= target language). The data representation problem does not appear, because clauses are transformed a priori to LISP structures, on which the interpreter is working. Kahn and Carlsson mention the problem of code size (without solution): our answer is the definition of instructions and modifications of the key algorithms.

Recently, a lot of meta-interpreters written in Prolog became a matter of interest: as an example, an interpreter for Concurrent Prolog written in Flat Concurrent Prolog. Given a Concurrent Prolog program, the interpreter can be partially evaluated away. In this case, data representation is not a problem because terms are the same in both languages. The interpreter only realizes the translation of control flow.

Partial evaluation of Prolog programs for changing data structures is used in [HeAv84] and [HsSr85] in order to implement an abstract data type by another one. Systems as proposed by these authors may be useful in implementing a complete environment for the development of abstract machines.

1.4 Overview

The paper is organized as follows: in chapter 2 we give some necessary definitions and relate certain key algorithms to abstract Prolog machines. In chapter 3 we enrich programs with calls of a unification algorithm to show the process of inventing instructions for a Prolog machine without implicit unification. In 4 we talk about problems related to the change of data representations during compilation. In 5 we give a key algorithm which results in machine instructions similar to those used in Warren's Prolog machine. Chapter 6 offers ideas for further research and some conclusions.

2. Abstract Prolog Machines

We use the term ***abstract Prolog machine*** (*apm* for short) for any abstract machines designed for running (possibly compiled) Prolog programs[1]. Different machines realize different instruction sets with different meanings. A machine hides some key algorithms, others are explicitly usable by the instruction set. We classify ***apms*** according to the following basic principles: (1) Parameter passing, (2) term representation and (3) control structure. As prototypes we describe four abstract Prolog machines *apm-i* (*i*=0...3) which differ from each other in the treatment of these features:

---

1 Exactly spoken, there is only *one* abstract Prolog machine: the one which runs Prolog programs. We follow common use in extending the meaning of abstract Prolog machine to "lower level" machines, too.

apm-0 is the well-known Prolog machine implemented by any Prolog interpreter (hopefully). It entails implicit unification during calls, usage of Prolog terms and automatic backtracking.

apm-1 is the same machine but parameter passing is always carried out by unifying a term (actual parmeter) with a variable (formal parameter; implementable by a simple assignment). It follows that all clauses must only have distinct variables in their head. An explicit (call of a) unification algorithm is necessary.

apm-2 is the same as *apm-1*, but the representation of terms is made visible. In our examples, we use a representation on a heap. The primitive data structures are constants, functors (name and arity) and heap addresses. Only heap addresses are allowed to be parameters in calls.

apm-3 is the same as *apm-2*, but backtracking is no longer implicit.

The order of the four machines is not significant: one might also define a machine with Prolog terms and explicit backtracking. It is obvious that *implementing apm-i* is a much easier task than implementing *apm-(i-1)* where one has to cope with more implicit operations. In this paper we only deal with *apm-1* and *apm-2*. *apm-3* is mentioned as logical next step following *apm-2*.

For these machines, we do not define special machine instructions a priori; this paper points out how such instructions can be invented starting with key algorithms necessary to realize some of the above mentioned features. The implementation of the key algorithms and of the instructions can be carried out in any language. Here we implement the key algorithms in Prolog.

Programs for the abstract machines are sets of clauses and a query, where a *clause* `Head :- Body` consists of a single Literal `Head` and a conjunction of Literals `Body`. A *query* is also a conjunction of literals. *Literals* comprise a *m*-ary predicate symbol and *m* terms as arguments. As usual a *term* (or *Prolog term*) is either a constant or a variable, or a compound term having a functor *f* with arity *n* and *n* terms as arguments.

We introduce a *classification* of variables in the following way: in a clause the first occurrence (reading the clause from left to right) of a variable is called a *free* occurrence; any other occurrence of the variable is called *unknown.*

The Prolog notation used in this paper is CProlog syntax with some system predicates surely incorporated in any other Prolog system (cf. [ClMe84]).

3. Instructions for Unification

In this chapter we are showing the definition of instructions for a machine like *apm-1.* Explicit handling of unification simplifies the parameter passing mechanism.

3.1 Explicit Unification

We emphasize the procedural semantic of Prolog, so that the body of a clause is interpreted as a series of procedure calls. A call like `p(t1,...,tn)` means: "search for a clause `Head :- Body`, so that `p(t1,...,tn)` is unifyable with `Head` with unifier θ". Then follows the execution of θ`Body` (or backtracking if there is no unifier θ, respectively).

Now we make the unification explicit by *enriching* a clause `p(t1,...,tn) :- Body.` with calls of a unification algorithm getting the procedurally equivalent clause `p(V1,...,Vn) :- unipp(t1,V1),...,unipp(tn,Vn), Body.` `Vi` are new distinct variables. `unipp` *uni*fies a *P*rolog term with a *P*rolog term.

Clauses transformed this way are clauses for a machine like *apm-1* with a special instruction **unipp(T1,T2)** which unifies two Prolog terms. So we have simplified the parameter passing, but the whole problem of unification still is hidden in the machine.

3.2 Compiling by Partial Evaluation

To overcome this disadvantage we give an implementation of **unipp** in Prolog as follows[1]:

```
unipp(S,T) :- atomic(S), ( var(T), T:=S  ;  S==T).
unipp(S,T) :- var(S), S:=T.
unipp(S,T) :- struct(S), functor(S,F,N),
                         ( var(T),    functor(T,F,N)
                          ; struct(T), functor(T,G,M), F==G, N==M ),
                         T =.. [_|TL],
                         unipp_args(SL,TL).
   unipp_args([],[]).
   unipp_args([S|SL],[T|TL]) :- unipp(S,T), unipp_args(SL,TL).
```

:=/2 is executed as normal unification, but the first argument must be a variable. **struct(S)** holds when **S** is instantiated to a compound term. Note that this is not the most obvious version of a unification algorithm: it is a refined version of a simple unification algorithm shown in Appendix I. The reasons for the refinement are explained (cf. also 3.3).

To see the advantage of inserting the explicit calls of **unipp**, we transform the clauses for **append/3**

```
append([],L,L).
append([X|L1],L2,[X|L3]) :- append(L1,L2,L3).
```

into

```
    append(A1,A2,A3) :- unipp([],A1), unipp(L,A2), unipp(L,A3).
(*) append(A1,A2,A3) :- unipp([X|L1],A1), unipp(L2,A2), unipp([X|L3],A3),
                        append(L1,L2,L3).
```

In this program, heads of clauses do not contain compound terms or a variable twice. Several optimizations are possible: most calls of **unipp** have a known first argument, so we open all these calls with respect to the first argument using a partial evaluator for Prolog. This leads to (**'.'** is the binary function symbol for composing lists)

```
append(A1,A2,A3) :-  (var(A1), A1:=[] ; []==A1),
                     unipp(A2,A3).
append(A1,A2,A3) :-  ( var(A1), functor(A1,'.',2)              % I
                      ; functor(A1,F,N), F=='.', N==2 ),       % I
                     A1 =.. [_,A11,A12],                       % I
                     ( var(A3), functor(A3,'.',2)              % II
                      ; functor(A3,G,M), G=='.', M==2 ),       % II
                     A3 =.. [_,A31,A32],                       % II
                     unipp(A11,A31),
                     append(A12,A2,A32).
```

---

1 For simplicity **unipp** does not realize the occurcheck, but one can also implement correct unification.

So we have unfolded the **unipp** predicate as far as possible. The two remaining calls of **unipp** cannot be removed because there is nothing known about the arguments at compile time (*unknown* variable occurrences). All other calls are *compiled* into series of system calls like tests and assignments. None of the remaining tests can be evaluated at compile time, so this is the best we can achieve.

The partial evaluation process uses several facts such as

- A call in an or-branch cannot be evaluated if it might affect the binding of variables also occuring in the other branch.
- Backward unification across metalogical predicates is forbidden (e.g. in **var(A1), A1:=[]**).
- **var(X)** evaluates to true iff **X** here occurs *free*, otherwise **var(X)** is not evaluable.

3.3 Defining Machine Instructions

Of course, there is a problem with the code size: a simple call as **unipp([X|L1],A1)** compiles into six statements (above marked with **I**). Comparing the **I**-part with the **II**-part above gives the idea to create machine instructions for unifications of basic elements of terms (constants, functors). So we get the two instructions:

```
unipp_constant(C,T) :- var(T), T:=C ; T==C.
unipp_struct(F,N,T,ArgList) :- (   var(T),       functor(T,F,N)
                                 ; struct(T), functor(T,G,M), F==G, N==M ),
                               T =.. [_|ArgList] .
```

After successful execution of **unipp_struct(F,N,T,ArgList)** T is always bound to a term **F(T1,...,TN)**!

Redefinition of **unipp** with these instructions yields:

```
unipp(S,T) :- atomic(S), unipp_constant(S,T).
unipp(S,T) :- var(S), S:=T.
unipp(S,T) :- struct(S), functor(S,F,N),
                         unipp_struct(F,N,T,TL),
                         unipp_args(SL,TL).
```

with **unipp_args** as above. Partial evaluation of **(*)** with respect to this definition yields:

```
     append(A1,A2,A3) :- unipp_constant([],A1), unipp(A2,A3).
     append(A1,A2,A3) :- unipp_struct('.',2,A1,[A11,A12]),
(**)                     unipp_struct('.',2,A3,[A31,A32]),
                           unipp(A11,A31),
                         append(A12,A2,A32).
```

The code becomes less complex if there is an implicit mechanism for getting the next argument of a term (deleting the fourth argument of **unipp_struct**).

So, all cases which cannot be decided at compile time, are hidden in machine instructions and executed at run time. Of course, the set of instructions for a machine like *apm-1* must also contain a full unification algorithm for Prolog terms, because some unifications cannot be simplified at compile time (when both arguments are *unknown* variable occurrences). With the modified **unipp** predicate the clauses **(**)** are the result of opening all calls of **unipp** in **(*)** using the heuristic "if the first argument is not enough instantiated then stop opening".

As an interesting application of this method, we studied a matching algorithm (as it is used to interpret rewrite rule systems). The resulting match instructions are incorporated in the KAP-machine (*KA*arlsruhe *P*rolog machine) [Neid86].

4. Term Representation

One of the most important tasks of a compiler is to create suitable (target language) representations of (source language) data objects. This chapter first describes one way to represent Prolog terms using a heap, then shows a Prolog predicate for changing representations, and discusses *when* a term has to be represented on the heap.

4.1 Heap Representation

We organize the heap as a stack of addressable cells. Each cell has a unique address and contains a tag field and a value. Table I shows possible tags and values.

tag	value
CONST	*constant*
FREE	*address* of cell
REF	*address*
FUNCT	*functionsymbol/arity*

Table I. Possible tags and values in heap cells.

constant and *functionsymbol* are arbitrary Prolog atoms, *arity* is always a positive integer and *address* is any non-negative integer. The value of a cell tagged with **FREE** is the address of the cell itself. There is a heap pointer to the next free cell of the heap.

Access to the heap is possible by three predicates[1]:

heap(Addr,Tag,Value)
: **Addr** must be instantiated to a non-negative integer smaller than the heap pointer. The heap cell with address **Addr** has tag **Tag** and value **Value**.

heap_entry(Addr,Tag,Value)
: the next free heap cell gets tag **Tag** and value **Value**. If **Addr** is a variable it becomes instantiated to the heap pointer. The heap pointer is incremented by 1.

heap_change(Addr,Tag,Value)
: **Addr** must be instantiated to a non-negative integer smaller than the heap pointer. The heap cell with address **Addr** gets the new contents **Tag** and **Value**.

The heap predicates are given as an interface to an abstract data type "heap". We do not discuss the question of implementing the heap in Prolog. In this work, we are not interested in this but in having an interface to the heap which we can use in Prolog programs.

Terms are represented on the heap by first storing the function symbol and the arity of the main

1 These are the three predicates necessary for our programs. For a complete implementation of a heap further predicates have to be added e.g. for creating a new heap and deleting heap cells.

functor, and then recursively storing the arguments in a consecutive manner. An argument can be replaced by a **REF** tagged cell which points to an other part of the heap where the term is stored. Figure 1. gives two examples.

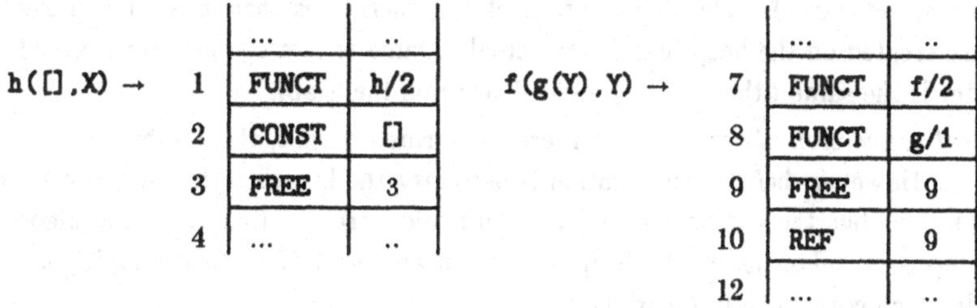

Figure 1. Examples of term representation in *apm-2*

Note that this representation is unique, that is, given an address **A**, there is exactly one term whose representation starts at **A**. Of course, this representation is only one possibility, but following procedure is also applicable for other methods. Later on we will discuss the influence of certain design decisions on the resulting compiler and machine.

We are giving a Prolog program which turns a Prolog term into heap representation. For this purpose, we represent a heap address **A** in the Prolog program as the term **($h,A)** and extend the definition of terms (given in chapter 2) to *mixed terms*: these are terms built in the mentioned way on constants, variables *and* heap addresses. So Prolog terms are a subset of mixed terms. A genuine mixed term (containing at least one heap address) is a term partially represented on the heap. The predicate **rep(MT,Addr)** represents a mixed term on the heap starting at address **Addr**:

```
rep(MT,Addr) :- atomic(MT), heap_entry(Addr,'CONST',MT).
rep(MT,Addr) :- var(MT), heap_entry(Addr,'FREE',Addr), MT=($h,Addr).
rep(MT,Addr) :- heap_address(MT,P), heap_entry(Addr,'REF',P).
rep(MT,Addr) :- struct(MT), functor(MT,F,N), heap_entry(Addr,'FUNCT',F/N),
                MT=..[_|TL],
                rep_args(TL).
    rep_args([]).
    rep_args([MT|TL]) :- rep(MT,_), rep_args(TL).
```

Unification of a variable with its heap address (in the second clause) ensures that the same variable is represented only once on the heap. **heap_address(MT,P)** holds iff **MT** is a heap address **($h,P)**.

As an example for dealing with heap terms, Appendix II gives an implementation of a predicate **arg_adresses(Addr,AddrList)**. Given the address **Addr** of the function symbol of a heap term *t*, this predicate computes the list **AddrList** of addresses of the direct subterms of *t*.

4.2 Conversion Process

A compiler compiling Prolog to something intended to run on *apm-2* has to represent terms on the heap or has to create code for doing so, respectively. There are several ways to achieve this goal:

1. *Conversion at compile time.* Each known term (e.g. the terms in the head of a clause) is changed to heap representation and then replaced by the address in the heap. The main problem is the creation of variants of terms either by copying at run time or by using the technique of structure sharing, and creating new environments when needed.

2. *Conversion at runtime.* Every time a term is needed, the compiler creates code for writing this term on the heap. Usually, this is the case before a unification or before a call of another predicate in the body of a clause takes place (because the parameter passing is carried out by passing heap addresses). The disadvantage of this method is that in a lot of cases, too much terms are created on the heap (e.g. if the actual parameter is a complex term *t*, and the formal parameter is the same *t* then *t* is represented twice on the heap).
3. *Optimized conversion at runtime.* To represent terms for calls, this method works exactly like method 2. However, before a unification is necessary the known term is not converted to heap representation, but the conversion and the unification are "melted" into one algorithm which creates terms or subterms on the heap only when necessary (i.e. when unifying a term with a heap cell which contains a free variable).

The most interesting case is version 3 which we will elaborate in the next chapter. For version 1 *apm-2* has to realize a "representation pass" and an interpretation pass which uses the results of the representation pass. In our framework, parts of the representation pass and all accesses to terms in the interpretation pass are good candidates for serving as key algorithms.

In version 2 a program gets enriched by calls of **rep** and of a unification algorithm for heap terms. The resulting instruction set mainly writes elements on the heap.

5. Combining Term Unification with Heap Representation

In this chapter we concentrate on version 3 as to changing term representation (cf. 4.2). As key algorithm, we use **uniph** which *uni*fies a *P*rolog term with a *h*eap term and, if necessary creates heap representations of subterms (of the Prolog term). A working version of **uniph** is

```
uniph(T,Addr) :- atomic(T), ( var(Addr), heap_entry(Addr,'CONST',T)
                             ; ( heap(Addr,Tag,Value),
                                 ( Tag=='FREE', heap_change(Addr,'CONST',T)
                                  ;Tag=='CONST', T==Value))).
uniph(T,Addr) :- var(T), ( var(Addr), heap_entry(Addr,'FREE',Addr)
                          ; true),
                          T=($h,Addr).
uniph(T,Addr) :- heap_address(T,P), ( var(Addr), heap_entry(Addr,'REF',P)
                                      ; unihh(P,Addr)).
uniph(T,Addr) :- struct(T), functor(T,F,N),
                 ( var(Addr), heap_entry(Addr,'FUNCT',F/N),
                              get_var_list(N,AddrList)
                  ; heap(Addr,Tag,Value),
                          ( Tag=='FREE' ,heap_entry(A,'FUNCT',F/N),
                                         heap_change(Addr,'REF',A),
                                         get_var_list(N,AddrList),
                          ; Tag=='FUNCT',Value==F/N,
                                         arg_addresses(Addr,AddrList))),
                 T=..[_|TL],
                 uniph_args(TL,AddrList).

   uniph_args([],[]).
   uniph_args([T|TL],[Addr|AddrList]) :- uniph(T,Addr), uniph_args(TL,AddrList).
```

There must be an adequate definition for **unihh** which *uni*fies a *h*eap term with a *h*eap term. **get_var_list(N,VL)** computes a list **VL** of **N** distinct Prolog variables. For **arg_addresses** see Appendix II. The key to understanding **uniph** is distinguishing two cases: either (1) **Addr** is given: then there is a term on the heap and **T** has to be compared with this term; or (2) **Addr** is a variable: then **T** has to be constructed on the heap.

In *apm-2* only heap addresses are allowed as parameters. To get these addresses, we replace each call **p(t1,...,tn)** in the body of a clause by **put(t1,B1),...,put(tn,Bn),p(B1,...,Bn)** where the **Bi** are new distinct variables. **put(T,B)** delivers a heap address **B** where a representation of the mixed term **T** starts. One possible implementation of **put** is

```
put(T,B)  :- heap_address(T,B), !.
put(T,B)  :- rep(T,B).
```

As an example we show the enrichment and compilation (by opening) of **append**. The two clauses of **(*)** (see chapter 3) are transformed into

```
append(A1,A2,A3)  :- uniph([],A1), uniph(L,A2), uniph(L,A3).
append(A1,A2,A3)  :- uniph([X|L1],A1), uniph(L2,A2), uniph([X|L3],A3),
                     put(L1,B1), put(L2,B2), put(L3,B3).
```

Straight forward opening of the calls of **uniph** results in

```
append(A1,A2,A3)  :-  heap(A1,Tag,Value),
                               ( Tag=='FREE', heap_change(A1,'CONST',[])
                               ; Tag=='CONST', []==Value),
                      unihh(A2,A3).
append(A1,A2,A3)  :-  heap(A1,Tag1,Value1),
                         ( Tag1=='FREE' , rep([X|L1],A), heap_change(A1,'REF',A)
                         ; Tag1=='FUNCT', Value1='.'/2,
                                          arg_addresses(A1,AddrList),
                                          uniph_args([X,L1],ArgList) ),
                      heap(A3,Tag3,Value3),
                         ( Tag3=='FREE' , rep([X|L3],A), heap_change(A3,'REF',A)
                         ; Tag3=='FUNCT', Value3='.'/2,
                                          arg_addresses(A3,AddrList),
                                          uniph_args([X,L3],ArgList) ),
                      put(L1,B1), put(($h,A2),B2), put(L3,B3),
                      append(B1,B2,B3).
```

The idea of using **uniph** is the same as in chapter 3 with **unipp**: the calls of **uniph** should (and could) be opened with respect to their first argument.

5.1 Machine Instructions

A look at the definition for **uniph** shows that decisions like **var(Addr)** and decisions depending on the content of the heap must be dealt with at run time. So we define the following four instructions according to the four types of a mixed term:

```
uniph_const(C,Addr) :- (  var(Addr), heap_entry(Addr,'CONST',C)
                       ; ( heap(Addr,Tag,Value),
```

```
                          ( Tag=='FREE', heap_change(Addr,'CONST',C)
                          ;Tag=='CONST', C==Value))).
uniph_var(V,Addr) :- ( var(Addr), heap_entry(Addr,'FREE',Addr)
                     ; true).
uniph_value(P,Addr) :- ( var(Addr), heap_entry(Addr,'REF',P)
                       ; unihh(P,Addr)).
uniph_struct(F/N,Addr,S) :- ( var(Addr), heap_entry(Addr,'FUNCT',F/N),
                                     get_var_list(N,S)
                            ; heap(Addr,Tag,Value),
                                     ( Tag=='FREE' ,heap_entry(A,'FUNCT',F/N),
                                                  heap_change(Addr,'REF',A),
                                                  get_var_list(N,S),
                                     ; Tag=='FUNCT',Value==F/N,
                                                  arg_addresses(Addr,S))).
```

With these instructions the **uniph** predicate reduces to

```
uniph(T,Addr) :- atomic(T), uniph_constant(T,Addr).
uniph(T,Addr) :- var(T), uniph_var(T,Addr), T=($h,Addr).
uniph(T,Addr) :- heap_address(T,P), uniph_value(P,Addr).
uniph(T,Addr) :- struct(T), functor(T,F,N),
                            uniph_struct(F/N,Addr,S),
                            uniph_args(TL,S).
  uniph_args([],[]).
  uniph_args([T|TL],[Addr|AddrList]) :- uniph(T,Addr), uniph_args(TL,AddrList).
```

The compilation by opening (also opening the **put** calls) with this definition of **uniph** delivers in the case of **append**:

```
append(A1,A2,A3) :- uniph_const([],A1),
                    uniph_value(A2,A3).
append(A1,A2,A3) :- uniph_struct('.'/2,A1,[A11,A12]),
                      uniph_var(X,A11),
                      uniph_var(L1,A12),
                    uniph_var(L2,A2),
                    uniph_struct('.'/2,A3,[A31,A32]),
                      uniph_value(A11,A31),
                      uniph_var(L3,A32),
                    append(A12,A2,A32).
```

Applying special heuristics for using a partial evaluator for compiling, it is possible to reduce the code for the second clause of append to

```
append(A1,A2,A3) :- uniph_struct('.'/2,A1,[A11,A12]),
                      uniph_var(X,A11),
                      uniph_var(L1,A12),
                    uniph_struct('.'/2,A3,[A31,A32]),
                      uniph_value(A11,A31),
                      uniph_var(L3,A32),
                    append(A12,A2,A32).
```

The necessary heuristics include opening of calls of **uniph_var(X,A)** if **X** is guarenteed to be *free* and **A** is bound to an address. Other heuristics deal with defined instructions in special cases which depend on the classification of variables occuring as arguments.

Of course, the instruction set of the machine has to include a complete unification algorithm for two heap terms (**unihh** necessary in **uniph_value**). However, this algorithm is only called when none of the arguments can be decomposed at compile time.

5.2 Relation to Warren's machine

Obviously, there is a close relation to Warren's New Prolog Engine [TiWa84]. Warren's result of compiling **append** is[1]

```
append/3: switch_on_term(C1a,C1,C2,fail)        % 1
C1a:      try_me_else C2a                       % 2
C1:       get_constant([],A1)                   % 3
          get_value(A2,A3)                      % 4
          proceed.                              % 5
C2a:      trust_me_else fail                    % 6
C2:       get_structure('.'/2,A1)               % 7
            unify_variable(X4)                  % 8
            unify_variable(A1)                  % 9
          get_structure('.'/2,A3)               % 10
            unify_value(X4)                     % 11
            unify_variable(A3)                  % 12
          execute append/3                      % 13
```

Besides the features dealing with the control (line 1,2,5,6,(13)) and the optimizations having special instructions for lists (not shown here[2]), the main difference seems to be the distinction of **get**, **unify** and **put** instructions (**put** instructions do not appear in this example). But all instructions are basically **unify** instructions which differ in a *mode* indicating if the term must be written on the heap (*writing*), or if there is a term on the heap which can be read (*reading*). Warren's **unify** instructions are used when at compile time nothing is known about the mode. This difference is indicated in **uniph** by looking at the second argument: if it is a variable the mode is *writing*, otherwise it is *reading*.

A second difference is the representation of terms: Warren represents terms on the heap by first storing the function symbol with its arity n, and in the next n heap cells are (references to) the n arguments (instead of storing whole subterms as in our example). An implicit *structure pointer s* points to the argument under consideration. Proceeding to the next argument is done by just incrementing s by one. So the **unify** instructions have only one argument (the other one is pointed to by the s pointer).

In our algorithms, s is made explicit (by a list of addresses; the computation of this list is rather complicated, cf. Appendix II). This kind of representation is chosen because it extremely simplifies the presentation of the basic ideas. It is also possible to use Warren's representation but this involves to very complicated **rep** and **uniph** algorithms not suited for a presentation in a paper.

---

1 cf. [TiWa84] p.330. There it is called **concatenate**. We do not use the special list instructions and adopt our notation.

2 To get special list instructions only a clause has to be defined for **uniph** dealing with lists.

6. Conclusion

We are distinguishing three aspects of a source language, namely hidden operations, data representation and control flow. For all aspects, the technique of partial evaluation can be used to get a compiler for the source language. To overcome the problem of code size, we define instructions which comprise actions not executable at partial evaluation time. This approach leads to compact code, to a correct compiler (according to the partial evaluation technique), and to a theoretically well-founded explanation of the instruction set. Starting with key algorithms which represent terms on a heap and unify Prolog terms with heap terms, we derived unify instructions very similar to the instructions of Warren's New Prolog Engine.

Some problems remain open: a formal justification of the process of enrichment should exist. In our opinion this can be realized by regarding a concrete interpreter (in our case written in Prolog) in connection with a program to be compiled. Further problems are a formal derivation of algorithms like `uniph`, and optimizations which are based on an elaborate classification of variables (e.g. temporal or global) or of predicates (e.g. functional). The main question is: can all optimizations be described by means of partial evaluation? Our working hypothesis is "yes". However, especially with optimizations based on global analyses (cf. [Mell85]) the verification of this hypothesis is very difficult.

Anyway, an elaborate and theoretically well-founded partial evaluator (at which we are working) will help to solve (or at least clarify) these problems. This partial evaluator will also incorporate source to source transformations before or during the compilation process.

Acknowledgement

I would like to thank my colleagues I.Varsek and especially R.Dietrich whose encouragements made this paper possible. The KAP-group at Karlsruhe (*KA*rlsruhe *P*rolog compiler, machine, environment) provided a very stimulating atmosphere for this research.

Literature

[Bowe83] D.L.Bowen, L.M.Byrd, *A Portable Prolog Compiler*, Proc. of the Logic Programming Workshop (1983) Portugal 74-83.

[ClMe84] W.F.Clocksin, C.S.Mellish, *Programming in Prolog*, 2nd Ed. Springer (1984).

[Cloc85] W.F.Clocksin, *Design and Simulation of a Sequential Prolog Machine*, New Generation Computing 3 (1985) 101-120.

[Ersh77] A.P.Ershov, *On the Partial Evaluation Principle*, Information Processing Letters Vol.6 No.2 (1977) 38-41.

[Ersh82] A.P.Ershov, *Mixed Computation: Potential Applications and Problems for Study*, Theor. Comp. Sci. 18 (1982) 41-67.

[Futa71] Y.Futamura, *Partial Evaluation of Computation Process - an Approach to a Compiler-Compiler*, Systems, Computers, Controls Vol.2, 5 (1971) 45-50.

[HeAv84] N.Heck, J.Avenhaus, *Automatic Implementation of Abstract Data Types Specified by the Logic Programming Language*, Proc. of the International Conference on Fifth Generation Computer Systems 1984, ed. ICOT (1984) 210-219.

[HsSr85] J.Hsiang, M.K.Srivas, *A Prolog Environment for Developing and Reasoning about Data Types*, in : Formal Methods and Software Development (Vol.2) (ed. by H.Ehrig et al.) LNCS 186 (1985) 276-293.

[Jone85] N.D.Jones, P.Sestoft, H.Søndergaard, *An Experiment in Partial Evaluation: The Generation of a Compiler Generator*, 1st Int.Conf. on Rewriting Techniques and Applications, Dijon LNCS 202 (1985) 124-140.

[KaCa84] K.M.Kahn, M.Carlsson, *The Compilation of Prolog Programs without the Use of a Prolog Compiler*, Proc. of the International Conference on Fifth Generation Computer Systems 1984, ed. ICOT (1984) 348-355.

[Mell85] C.S.Mellish, *Some Global Optimizations for a Prolog Compiler*, Journal of Logic Programming 1 (1985) 43-66.

[Neid86] B.Neidecker, *KAP-Maschine: Maschinenmodell Version 0.5*, forthcoming internal report, University of Karlsruhe 1986 (in German).

[TiWa84] E.Tick, D.H.D.Warren, *Towards a Pipelined Prolog Processor*, New Generation Computing 2 (1984) 323-345.

[Venk84] R.Venken, *A Prolog Meta-Interpreter for Partial Evaluation and its Application to Source to Source Transformation and Query-Optimisation*, ECAI 84, Elsevier Sc. Publ., North-Holland (1984) 91-104.

Appendix I: Motivation for unipp

A simple unification algorithm in Prolog is:

```
unipp(S,T) :- atomic(S), ( var(T), T:= S ; S==T ).
unipp(S,T) :- var(S), S:=T.
unipp(S,T) :- struct(S), S=..[F|SL],
                         ( var(T), T:=S
                         ; struct(T), T=..[F|TL], unipp_args(SL,TL) ).
```

unipp_args is defined in chapter 3. Partial evaluation of the call **unipp([X|L],A)** with **A** classified *unknown* yields:

```
( var(A), A:=[X|L]
; struct(A), A=..['.'|AL],
  unipp_args([X,L],AL) )
```

Besides the problem of what to do with **AL**, the main drawback is here that the two cases **var(A)** and **struct(A)** cannot be hidden in a machine instruction, because such an instruction has to recurse internally on the argument list at runtime: so further optimizations are not possible.

The version of **unipp** in chapter 3 solves this problem by instantiating **A** (in the case **var(A)**) only partially to a. list with two variables which are further instantiated later in the recursion **unipp_args**:

```
( var(A), functor(A,'.',2)
```

```
 ; struct(A), functor(A,G,M), G=='.', M==2 ),
A=..[_,A1,A2],
unipp_args([X,L],[A1,A2])
```

Now both is possible: further partial evaluation on the arguments, and the definition of a **unipp_struct** instruction, as shown in chapter 3.

Similar considerations lead to the use of **get_var_list** and **arg_addresses** in **uniph** (chapter 5). The idea of breaking down both the decomposition and the construction of a term, into corresponding actions is very essential for Warrens New Prolog Engine. We claim that our framework is well-suited to communicate such ideas.

Appendix II: arg_addresses

Given a heap address **Addr** (the **Value** of which is a *n*-ary function symbol) **arg_addresses(Addr,AddrList)** computes the list of addresses where the *n* arguments start in the heap.

```
arg_addresses(Addr,AddrList) :- heap(Addr,'FUNCT',F/N),
                                Addr1 is Addr+1,
                                address_list(0,Addr1,AddrList,N).
   address_list(N,_,[],N).
   address_list(M,Addr,[Addr|AddrList],N) :- M<N, next_address(Addr,Addr1),
                                             M1 is M+1,
                                             address_list(M1,Addr1,AddrList,N).
```

If **Addr** is an address in the heap (smaller than the heap pointer), there is a term *t* the representation of which starts at **Addr**. **next_address(Addr,Addr1)** computes the next address **Addr1** not belonging to the representation of *t*.

```
next_address(Addr,Addr1) :- heap(Addr,Tag,Value),
                            next_address_case(Addr,Tag,Value,Addr1).
   next_address_case(Addr,'CONST',_,Addr1) :- Addr1 is Addr+1.
   next_address_case(Addr,'FREE',_,Addr1) :- Addr1 is Addr+1.
   next_address_case(Addr,'REF',_,Addr1) :- Addr1 is Addr+1.
   next_address_case(Addr,'FUNCT',F/N,Addr1) :- arg_addresses(Addr,AddrList),
                                                last_element(AddrList,A),
                                                next_address(A,Addr1).
last_element([X],X).
last_element([X,Y|L],Z) :- last_element([Y|L],Z).
```

Examples (cf. figure 1.):

```
arg_addresses(1,L)     =>    L=[2,3]
next_address(8,A)      =>    A=10
arg_addresses(7,L)     =>    L=[8,10]
```

A SEQUENTIAL IMPLEMENTATION OF PARLOG

Ian Foster[+] Steve Gregory[+] Graem Ringwood[+] Ken Satoh[*]

[+] Department of Computing
Imperial College
180 Queen's Gate
London SW7 2BZ
England

[*] AI Laboratory
Fujitsu Laboratories Ltd.
1015 Kamikodanaka
Nakahara-ku, Kawasaki 211
Japan

ABSTRACT

The Sequential PARLOG Machine (SPM) is an abstract instruction set designed specifically for the efficient implementation of the parallel logic programming language PARLOG on sequential computers. This paper introduces a simple computational model for supporting PARLOG. The SPM embodies several refinements of this model that improve its performance in a sequential context; these are described, along with other key issues of the SPM system.

1. INTRODUCTION

PARLOG [Clark and Gregory 1986, Gregory 1985] is one of a family of parallel logic programming languages which are descendants of the Relational Language [Clark and Gregory 1981]. These languages are characterized by guarded clauses and committed choice non-determinism, and can be distinguished primarily by the way in which communication is controlled. In PARLOG each procedure has a fixed mode of use: mode declarations state whether each argument is input or output. Processes suspend on input arguments which are not sufficiently instantiated.

For Concurrent Prolog [Shapiro 1983], the "mode" is determined by the call and not by the procedure so the use of a relation is not as restrictive as in PARLOG. Read-only annotations on the variables constrain the communication. Or-parallel clause guards are allowed to perform arbitrary computation, even binding a variable in the call to several different (alternative) values. In general, this requires a complex "multiple environment" mechanism: a variable may have a binding in the environment of several clauses.

Guarded Horn Clauses [Ueda 1985a], like PARLOG, maintains a single binding environment by preventing guard evaluations from binding variables in the invoking call. In GHC, this prohibition is enforced by a run-time check performed at each attempt to bind a variable: in general, a guard evaluation must be able to determine whether a variable belongs to its own environment or to the environment of the invoking call [Ito et al. 1985]. In contrast, PARLOG features a compile-time check that guards are "safe" [Clark and Gregory 1985]. This minimizes the run-time overhead and means that variables need not be tagged with environment information. A discussion of these matters is to be found in [Gregory 1985].

In order to make PARLOG available to a wide audience, an efficient portable implementation of PARLOG, for sequential machines, has been constructed at Imperial College. This is based on an abstract machine, the Sequential Parlog Machine (SPM) [Gregory 1986]. The SPM system comprises a compiler (written in PARLOG) and an emulator, written in the C language to run on Unix machines. The SPM compiler is described in detail in [Foster 1986].

PARLOG can be compiled into a kernel language, Kernel PARLOG [Clark and Gregory 1985]. This is described briefly in Section 2. A computational model for the implementation of Kernel PARLOG is described in Section 3. Refinements of the computational model which improve its performance on sequential machines are embodied in the instruction set of the SPM. These refinements are described in Section 4. Other aspects of the SPM are briefly discussed in Section 5.

2. KERNEL PARLOG

The principal difference between the languages noted in the introduction is the mechanism used to constrain the eagerness of processes to communicate. In PARLOG, mode declarations for each relation state which of its arguments are input and which are output. An example is the following procedure for the **amerge** relation. **amerge(x,y,z)** can be read logically as: if **x** and **y** are lists of items ordered by the '<' relation, with no duplicates, then so is **z**, which contains each of the elements of **x** and **y** and no others.

```
mode amerge(?,?,^).
amerge([u|x],[u|y],[u|z]) <- amerge(x,y,z).
amerge([u|x],[v|y],[u|z]) <- u < v : amerge(x,[v|y],z).
amerge([u|x],[v|y],[v|z]) <- v < u : amerge([u|x],y,z).
amerge([],y,y).
amerge(x,[],x).
```

(Lower-case identifiers are variables. The ':' symbol is used to separate the guard of a clause from its body.)

The mode declaration for **amerge** states that the first and second arguments are input ('**?**') and the third argument is output ('^'). This means, for example, that the **amerge** call in the parallel conjunction:

```
producer1(x), producer2(y), amerge(x,y,z), consumer(z)
```

acts as a consumer of lists **x** and **y** and the producer of **z**, all of which may be generated incrementally, as streams.

The first stage of compilation of PARLOG is the translation into Kernel PARLOG [Clark and Gregory 1985, 1986]. Kernel PARLOG differs from (source) PARLOG in that there are no mode declarations and each clause is in a "standard form". The PARLOG mode declarations are used to control the translation into Kernel PARLOG. In the standard form of a clause, the head arguments are all distinct variables and the unification is performed by explicit primitive calls in the guard and body. The Kernel PARLOG form of the above **amerge** procedure is:

```
amerge(p1,p2,p3) <- [u|x] <= p1, [v|y] <= p2, u = v :
     p3 <= [u|z], amerge(x,y,z).
amerge(p1,p2,p3) <- [u|x] <= p1, [v|y] <= p2, u < v :
     p3 <= [u|z], amerge(x,[v|y],z).
amerge(p1,p2,p3) <- [u|x] <= p1, [v|y] <= p2, v < u :
     p3 <= [v|z], amerge([u|x],y,z).
amerge(p1,p2,p3) <- [] <= p1 : p3 <= p2.
amerge(p1,p2,p3) <- [] <= p2 : p3 <= p1.
```

Here, the input matching is performed by calls to the '**<=**' primitive that have been added to the guards, one for each input argument. The call **[u|x] <= p1** suspends until **p1** is instantiated: if **p1** is bound to a list, the call binds the local variable **u** to the head of the list and **x** to its tail; the call fails if **p1** is not a list. A similar call is added to the guard for the second argument. In the first clause, an explicit call to the '=' primitive is added to the guard to check the equality of the head items of each list, because the variable **u** appears twice in input arguments in the source PARLOG clause. In each clause, the output matching (on the third argument) is achieved by a call such as **p3 <= [u|z]**, which simply binds the left argument variable to the right argument term. A run-time error occurs if **p3** is already instantiated.

In evaluating a call **amerge(x,y,z)**, the guards of all five clauses are evaluated concurrently to search for a "candidate". All calls in each guard are also evaluated concurrently because of the use of the parallel conjunction operator ',' in the standard form. The latter has the consequence that unification in PARLOG is order-independent. That is, the calls **amerge(2,y,z)** and **amerge(x,2,z)** will both fail; if arguments were matched sequentially, the first call would fail while the second would remain suspended. This example shows that a PARLOG evaluation may generate a large number of very simple processes; these are optimized by the SPM.

As well as the default parallel conjunction and clause search, Kernel PARLOG (and PARLOG) allow sequential evaluation to be specified by the conjunction operator '&' (instead of ',') and the sequential clause search operator ';' (in place of the '.' between clauses).

3. THE AND-OR TREE MODEL

The most natural computational model for PARLOG is the "and-or tree" model [Gregory 1985]: an abstract architecture which corresponds directly to the structure of a Kernel PARLOG program. PARLOG relations can be defined either explicitly, by PARLOG programs, or implicitly, by primitives. The granularity of the and-or tree model can be defined (approximately) by stating that each processor has the ability to execute a sequential conjunction of primitive calls.

In the and-or tree model, the state of a PARLOG evaluation is recorded by a <u>process tree</u>. The <u>code pointer</u> of each process indicates the code still to be evaluated. At any point in the computation, each leaf node in the tree represents either a <u>runnable</u> process or a <u>suspended</u> process (one that is waiting for some variable to be bound). Non-leaf nodes are neither runnable nor suspended: they have an associated <u>process type</u> (AND or OR) which determines their course of action when their offspring processes terminate.

3.1 Conjunction

If a sequential conjunction (one using '&') begins with a call to a relation defined by a PARLOG program, a new offspring process is created to evaluate the call. The process type of the current process is set to AND and its code pointer is updated to the code that follows the call: this is the code that will be executed (by the parent process) if and when the call (the offspring process) eventually succeeds. Suppose that the code pointer of a process addresses the conjunction **(P & B)**. The process tree changes as shown below -- the process evaluating **(P & B)** becomes an "AND process", and its code pointer is set to the remainder of the conjunction, **B**:

```
        P & B            -->            AND: B                (3.1.1)
                                           |
                                           |
                                           P
```

A parallel conjunction is handled by the same mechanism. In general, any number of offspring processes may be created: one for each call in the parallel conjunction. For example, if the process's code pointer addresses **((P, P2) & B)**, new processes are created to solve both **P** and **P2**, as shown:

```
        (P, P2) & B      -->          AND: B                  (3.1.2)
                                       / \
                                      /   \
                                     P     P2
```

A special case of parallel conjunction arises when a parallel conjunction occurs at the end of a clause body. An optimization, <u>tail forking</u>, is adopted to prevent the process tree from increasing in depth. If, in (3.1.2), **P** is defined by the clause:

P <- P11, P12. the process tree changes as follows:

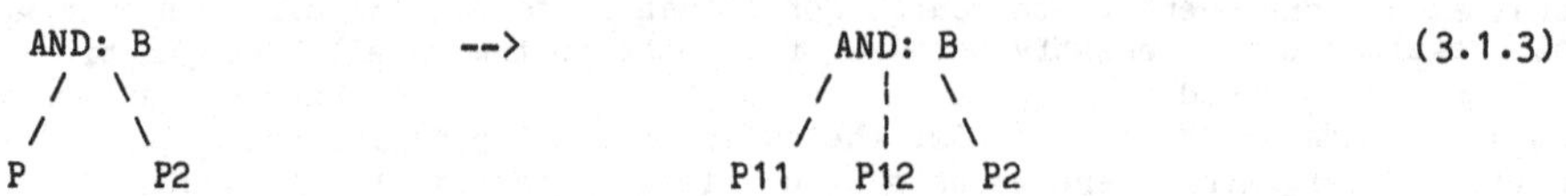

The processes created to solve the members of a conjunction will ultimately <u>succeed</u> or <u>fail</u>. A succeeding process is removed from the process tree. Additionally, if the parent has no remaining offspring processes, the parent is reactivated to continue evaluation at its stored code pointer. Failure of any process causes its parent process to fail.

3.2 Clause search

The search for a candidate clause is handled analogously to conjunction. In evaluating a call to a PARLOG relation defined by several clauses, the process type of the current process is set to OR, its code pointer is updated, and a process is created to evaluate the guard of each clause.

Suppose that **P** is defined by a procedure that contains a parallel clause group (';' is the sequential clause search operator in PARLOG, so **G1** and **G2** are to be evaluated in parallel, and the third clause selected only if both fail):

```
P <- G1 : B1.                                                    (3.2.1)
P <- G2 : B2;
P <- B3.
```

An offspring process is created to evaluate the guard of each clause. The parent becomes an "OR process" and its code pointer is set to the next clause (the code to be executed if **G1** and **G2** fail):

```
          P                  -->              OR: B3
                                               / \
                                              /   \
                                          G1:B1   G2:B2
```

Unless all guard processes fail, one of them will ultimately succeed and <u>commit</u>. When this occurs, any sibling guard processes are killed and the committed process is promoted in the tree to the level of the parent process, overwriting it. The following figure depicts the situation before and after commitment to the first clause of a parallel clause group (**G1** has just succeeded):

3.3 Failure

The action to be taken upon the failure of a process depends upon the process type of its parent. If this is OR, the failing process (a guard process) is removed from the process tree. Additionally, if the parent has no remaining offspring processes, the parent is reactivated at its current code pointer. This is analogous to the <u>success</u> of a process whose parent's type is AND.

The failure of a process whose parent has type AND represents the failure of a call in a conjunction, and therefore the entire conjunction. In this case, all sibling processes are killed and the parent process is explicitly failed:

4. THE SEQUENTIAL PARLOG MACHINE

The and-or tree model represents an ideal situation in which an unlimited number of processors are available. In implementing Kernel PARLOG on any architecture, sequential or parallel, some form of <u>scheduling</u> is necessary to map the possibly unbounded number of runnable processes in the and-or tree onto the finite number of processors available. In the limiting case -- a uniprocessor machine -- only one of the runnable processes can be active at any time: the <u>current process</u>.

The SPM uses a depth-first scheduling strategy which gives two benefits. First, processes can be spawned "lazily". That is, process descriptors are created only when needed, not immediately a process forks (c.f. Section 3.5). Second, a process buffering optimization can be introduced, which further reduces the overhead in process creation for parallel, as well as sequential, evaluation.

4.1 Scheduling

A scheduler might select a current process by walking over the and-or tree structure in order to locate a runnable leaf process. This would be a <u>busy-waiting</u> scheme: leaf processes must be repeatedly tested to determine whether they are suspended or runnable. The overhead of busy-waiting is unlikely to be acceptable.

The SPM employs a <u>non-busy-waiting</u> scheme, using a <u>scheduling structure</u> in addition to the process tree. This comprises a variable number of process lists: one <u>runnable list</u> and various <u>suspension lists</u>. Each process which is a leaf in the process tree is necessarily a member of <u>one</u> of these lists: either the runnable list (if a runnable process), or the suspension list of variable **v** (if the process is suspended on **v**). (Note that it is not possible for a process to be on two suspension lists.) In this "non-busy-waiting" scheme, the scheduler can, when necessary, obtain a new current process from the head of the runnable list. When a process suspends on an (unbound) variable **v**, it is put onto **v**'s suspension list. When **v** is subsequently instantiated, all processes on its suspension list are moved into the runnable list.

4.2 Birth control

In the SPM, process creation is minimized by a depth-first scheduling strategy: parallel conjunction (and clause search) are handled almost as if they were sequential. Consider the evaluation of the parallel conjunction (3.1.2) by the SPM:

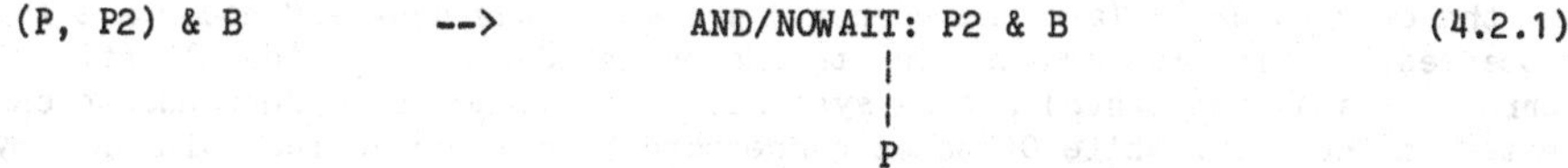

The process for **P** becomes active and the parent process is added to the runnable list. In the SPM, a non-leaf process may be runnable; this is indicated by the status NOWAIT. On a single processor machine the parent will become active only after the child succeeds <u>or</u> suspends.

If the process **P** suspends on variable **v**, it is added to the suspension list for variable **v**. Because the parent remained runnable, it <u>may</u> now become the current process. If so, the parent will spawn a process for **P2**, which becomes current. Because of the sequential conjunction the parent is not now added to the runnable list, but must await the result of its offspring before continuing.

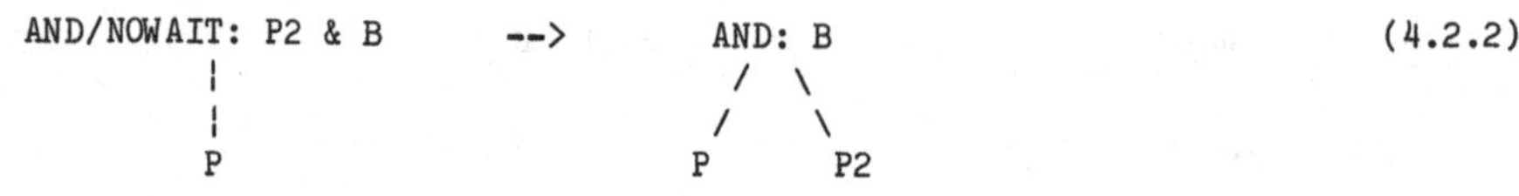

4.3 Process buffering

In the SPM, a further optimization is applied: a new process is not immediately inserted in the process tree structure or the scheduling structure (the runnable list). Instead, a newly-created process is kept only in the process buffer; it will be added to the normal data structures at a later time only if necessary. For example, the situation depicted in (4.2.1) is as shown below in the SPM: the new process created to solve **P** is placed only in the process buffer (marked NEW):

```
(P, P2) & B          -->          AND/NOWAIT: P2 & B

                                         NEW: P
```

This scheme permits very efficient treatment of simple processes. If **P** succeeds without suspension or forking, the parent continues and evaluates **P2** by creating another new process in the process buffer:

If, instead, process **P** suspends, it will be added to the process tree structure in the normal place; **P2** is then created in the process buffer:

```
AND/NOWAIT: P2 & B          -->          AND:  B
                                           |
     NEW: P                                |
                                           P

                                         NEW: P2
```

A process that forks will be added to the process tree if it is not already there; its offspring is then created in the process buffer.

4.4 Discussion

The buffering optimizations incorporated in the SPM design were inspired by those of Warren's [1983] abstract Prolog instruction set, but are more general.

If only sequential operators ('**&**' and '**;**') are used in a PARLOG program, its behaviour is very similar to Prolog. The and-or process tree of the PARLOG evaluation is then linear: each node has just one offspring except the leaf, which is the only runnable (and the current) process; the non-leaf nodes are AND and OR processes. This linear and-or tree corresponds to the (local) stack used in Warren's (and some other) Prolog systems: the AND nodes corresponds to environment frames on the stack while OR nodes correspond to stacked choice points. By keeping the leaf node in a process buffer, calls to relations defined by assertions (unit clauses) are executed cheaply, an effect which is achieved by a similar buffering of the stack in Warren's system.

The run-time data structure in PARLOG has to be a tree, rather than a stack, because of the use of parallel operators ('**,**' and '**.**') combined with the possible suspension of processes. However, because of the depth-first scheduling, parallel processes that do not suspend can be evaluated almost as inexpensively as if they were evaluated in sequence; only processes that fork or suspend are added to the SPM run-time data structures. This optimization greatly improves the efficiency of typical PARLOG programs, which comprise many simple (non-forking) processes.

5. OTHER KEY ISSUES

5.1 The evaluation space

In addition to the process type and code pointer (following the Warren Machine [Warren 1983]) each SPM process is equipped with a set of a-registers which store terms needed by the process. Scalar terms are stored directly in these a-registers, while structured terms and unbound variables are stored in a heap and accessed by processes via pointers from their a-registers. The data stored in a process's a-registers varies: the a-registers of a process created to solve a relation call are loaded with the arguments of the call; those of a process created to solve a clause guard are loaded with a copy of the arguments of the invoking call. Certain simple processes, usually the input matching primitive ('<='), directly access the a-registers of their parent, to avoid the overhead of copying.

The size of each set of a-registers in memory is the same as the size of a process descriptor, so a common area of memory is used for both types of object and a free list employed for memory allocation. This area grows towards the heap, which is managed by a compacting garbage collector. Process descriptors contain fields for pointers to link the process into the process tree and into a suspension list, as explained in Section 4.1. Each unbound variable in the heap includes a list (possibly empty) of the processes suspended on it.

5.2 Process switching

The depth-first scheduling employed by the SPM is essential for efficiency on uniprocessor machines. However, if no precautions are taken, a non-terminating (recursive) process will monopolize the processor. To prevent this, the SPM features a time-slicing mechanism: at regular intervals, the current process is moved to the end of the runnable list and the process at the head of the runnable list is made current. This happens so infrequently that the degradation to performance is negligible.

The time-slicing mechanism cannot terminate a badly-written "user process", but can ensure it does not prevent other user processes running. By utilizing the powerful control metacall primitive of PARLOG [Clark and Gregory 1984], an operating system program (written in PARLOG) can manage the execution of many user processes. When a non-terminating user process exceeds its time-slice, an operating system process can be invoked to kill the offending user process.

5.3 Discussion

At the time of writing, the untuned performance of the SPM running on a VAX 750 is 1K LIPS on favourable (deterministic) benchmarks. We expect substantial improvements to the speed to result from optimization of the emulator, which will be performed for future releases. Copies of the SPM system are available from the authors.

The similarity between GHC and Kernel PARLOG will allow the SPM to support GHC on a sequential machine with relatively few modifications. However, the run-time guard safety check, generally necessary in GHC, is likely to degrade the performance appreciably. The main area of future research is to extend the SPM for coarse-grained parallel implementation, where the same techniques will be applicable. This will enable PARLOG to exploit the multiprocessor Unix machines that are becoming increasingly widely available.

6. ACKNOWLEDGEMENTS

Research on the design of PARLOG and the SPM has been supported by the Science and Engineering Research Council. Implementation of the SPM was funded by the SERC, International Computers Ltd., and Fujitsu Ltd. We are grateful to Alastair Burt and Tony Kusalik for their contributions to the SPM implementation, and their comments on drafts of this paper. Martyn Cutcher of ICL (Reading) has provided invaluable feedback as the first user of the system.

REFERENCES

Clark, K.L., and Gregory, S. [1981]. A relational language for parallel programming. In _Proceedings of the ACM Conference on Functional Programming Languages and Computer Architecture_ (Portsmouth, NH, October), Arvind and J. Dennis (Eds.), pp 171-178.

Clark, K.L., and Gregory, S. [1984]. Notes on systems programming in PARLOG. In _Proceedings of the International Conference on Fifth Generation Computer Systems_ (Tokyo, November), H. Aiso (Ed.), Elsevier North-Holland, Amsterdam, pp 299-306.

Clark, K.L., and Gregory, S. [1985]. Notes on the implementation of PARLOG. In _Journal of Logic Programming 2_, 1 (April), pp 17-42.

Clark, K.L., and Gregory, S. [1986]. PARLOG: parallel programming in logic. In _ACM Transactions on Programming Languages and Systems 8_, 1 (January).

Foster, I.T. [1986]. Compiling PARLOG for the SPM. Research report, Department of Computing, Imperial College, London.

Furukawa, K., Kunifuji, S., Takeuchi, A., and Ueda, K. [1984]. The conceptual specification of Kernel Language version 1. Technical report TR-054, ICOT, Tokyo.

Gregory, S. [1985]. _Design, application and implementation of a parallel logic programming language_. PhD thesis, Department of Computing, Imperial College, London, September. To be published by Addison-Wesley.

Gregory, S. [1986]. The Sequential PARLOG Machine. Research report (in preparation), Department of Computing, Imperial College, London.

Ito, N., Kishi, M., Kuno, E., and Rokusawa, K. [1985]. The dataflow-based parallel inference machine to support two basic languages in KL1. Technical report, ICOT, Tokyo.

Kusalik, A.J. [1985]. Semantic issues with Concurrent Prolog. Presentation at Imperial College, London, May.

Mierowsky, C., Taylor, S., Shapiro, E., Levy, J., and Safra, M. [1985]. The Design and implementation of Flat Concurrent Prolog. Technical report CS85-09, Department of Applied Mathematics, Weizmann Institute of Science, Rehovot, July.

Miyazaki, T., Takeuchi, A., and Chikayama, T. [1985]. A sequential implementation of Concurrent Prolog based on the shallow binding scheme. In _Proceedings of the IEEE Symposium on Logic Programming_ (Boston, MA, July), pp 110-118.

Saraswat, V.A. [1985]. Problems with Concurrent Prolog. Technical report, Department of Computer Science, Carnegie-Mellon University, June.

Shapiro, E.Y. [1983]. A subset of Concurrent Prolog and its interpreter. Technical report TR-003, ICOT, Tokyo, February.

Ueda, K. [1985a]. Guarded Horn Clauses. Technical report TR-103, ICOT, Tokyo, September.

Ueda, K. [1985b]. Concurrent Prolog re-examined. Technical report TR-102, ICOT, Tokyo, November.

Warren, D.H.D. [1983]. An abstract Prolog instruction set. Technical note 309, SRI International, Menlo Park, CA, October.

A GHC Abstract Machine and Instruction Set

Jacob Levy

Department of Computer Science
The Weizmann Institute of Science
Rehovot 76100, Israel

Abstract

A description of a GHC abstract machine and its implementation are given.

1. Introduction

Guarded Horn Clauses (GHC) was recently proposed by Ueda [1]. It provides an alternative to Concurrent Prolog [2] and PARLOG [3]. The current paper describes an implementation of GHC, and presents a design of a GHC abstract machine. The design of the Prolog and Flat Concurrent Prolog (FCP) abstract machines [4,5] strongly influenced this work.

The GHC abstract machine is more complex than the FCP abstract machine. Or-parallelism requires more complicated control structures. The instruction set of the GHC abstract machine is simpler than that of the FCP abstract machine. The GHC abstract machine does not have unify instructions.

Many of the ideas included in this paper originated in [5]. Section 2 describes an extension to the syntax and semantics introduced in the current implementation. Section 3 shows an overview of the abstract machine. It explains the basic execution cycle. Section 4 discusses the data structures and memory areas needed by the implementation. Section 5 summarises the instructions.

2. Guarded Horn Clauses

Ueda [1] described the syntax and semantics of GHC. For another discussion of these subjects see [8].

2.1 Test-commit-and-set

It is impossible to describe unification, as the '=' predicate, in the language as defined by Ueda [1]. In order to facilitate this definition an earlier version of Ueda's paper [K. Ueda, personal communication] proposed a new primitive call *test-commit-and-set*.

A clause in which the new primitive appears has, instead of the normal commit operator, a test-commit-and-set operator. Its syntax is as follows.

$$H \leftarrow G1 \,..\, Gn \mid V \leftarrow T \mid B1 \,..\, Bm \;(n,m \geq 0).$$

V is a variable contained in the head and T can be any term. The part between the two '|' signs is called the *test-commit-and-set* part.

The semantics of commitment for a clause containing a test-commit-and-set operator is as follows ([8] gives the full description of the rules of GHC semantics).

{3} (*Commitment*) When a guard is solved successfully, the clause activation attempts to commit for its calling goal. If some other clause activation in the procedure already committed for this goal, the clause activation is discarded. Otherwise, if no test-commit-and-set operator appears in this clause, the clause activation commits for its calling goal. Otherwise, if V is a variable and instantiating it to a non-variable should not suspend, V is instantiated to T and the clause activation commits for its calling goal. Otherwise this clause activation is discarded.

If V is a variable, an attempt to instantiate it should suspend only if it is bound to a variable which is a global ('goal') variable in the guard system containing the calling goal. Otherwise, it is permissible to instantiate it as part of, or after, commitment.

2.2 Definition of Unification

This section shows how unification, as the '=' predicate, can be defined in GHC itself, using the new test-commit-and-set primitive. Clearly a clause of the form

$$A = A \leftarrow \text{true} \mid \text{true}$$

is insufficient. If it is called with the goal

$$X = 15$$

it will suspend instead of succeeding. The full definition of unification is given below.

```
X = X ← true | true.
X = Y ← true | X ← Y | true.
X = Y ← true | Y ← X | true.
X = Y ← functor(X,F,N), functor(Y,F,N) | unify_args(X,Y,N).

unify_args(X,Y,0) ← true | true.
unify_args(X,Y,N) ←
    N > 0 |
        arg(N,X,Xn),
        arg(N,Y,Yn),
        N1 := N - 1,
        Xn = Yn,
        unify_args(X,Y,N1).
```

The first clause will be used if the two arguments can be unified without making any bindings. The second clause will be used if the first argument is a variable, instantiating it to the second argument. The third clause will be used if the second argument is a variable, instantiating it to the first argument. The fourth clause will be used when both arguments are non-variables. It checks that both have the same main functor and arity, and recursively unifies each pair of arguments.

The current implementation does not restrict the use of test-commit-and-set to the definition of unification. It allows its use in user origrams, instead of requiring explicit calls to unification through the '=' predicate, in the body of the clause.

3. Overview of the Implementation

This section provides an overview of the implementation. The following sections describe its different aspects in greater depth.

The abstract machine proposed here is adapted from the FCP abstract machine [5]. It also uses some concepts from Warren's Prolog abstract machine [4]. The instructions were adapted to be especially suited for execution of GHC programs.

The same representation of the computation tree as used in FCP is used here also. A single goal record is created to represent the attempted reduction of a goal with all clause activations of potentially unifiable clauses. This representation was extended in several ways to allow modeling of the restricted Or-parallelism required for GHC. This is explained in the next section.

The set of all goals ready for reduction is represented by a queue, called the *active queue*. At the start of the computation, the active queue contains one or more goals to be reduced. At all times, the goal at the head of the active queue is selected to be reduced first. A form of bounded-depth-first scheduling was implemented, by allowing a selected goal to reduce several times, until its allotted time-slice runs out. At that time, the next goal to be reduced is scheduled.

The following is a description of a computation cycle of the abstract machine. The abstract machine repeatedly exectues these steps –

(1) A goal is dequeued from the active queue for reduction.

(2) The goal is selected for computation and startup actions are performed for this goal. The startup actions are described in a subsection of Section 5.

(3) All clauses are tried in sequence.

For each clause whose head is not unifiable with the goal, the failure of this unification is noted and the next clause is tried.

For each clause whose head is unifiable with the goal, the abstract machine attempts to solve the guard.

If the guard system is empty, it is assumed to succeed immediately. Otherwise, if the guard system contains only kernel predicates, these are solved directly. If some kernel predicate suspended or failed, this clause activation is discarded, the failure of this clause noted and the next clause is tried. Otherwise, if the guard system contains at least one user-defined goal, the guard goals are created and enqueued, the existence of an active guard system for this clause is noted, and the next clause is tried.

If the guard computation ends successfully, the clause commits, and execution proceeds from the next step.

If the unification of the head with the goal suspended, the variable causing the suspension is noted and the next clause is tried.

(4) If some clause activation commits, the rest of the clauses are not tried. The commitment of this clause activation is noted. The body of the committing clause is created and replaces the current goal in its guard system All goals except the last one are enqueued on the active queue.

If the time-slice for this goal has not yet ended, tail-recursion optimization is done. The abstract machine directly executes the last goal in the body and execution proceeds from step 2 above. Otherwise, execution proceeds from step 1.

(5) If, after all clauses have been tried and no clause activation committed, if the suspension table contains some variables, the process record is suspended on all of these variables.

If, after all clauses have been tried and none committed or suspended, if some clause activations are suspended because of attempts to instantiate goal variables, the goal is suspended on all the noted variables and execution proceeds from step 1.

Otherwise, if there is at least one active guard system computing for a clause activation of this goal, execution proceeds from step 1.

Otherwise, a goal failure has occurred, and failure handling is done. After failure handling, if the failure was not propagated to the root of the computation tree, execution proceeds from step 1.

4. Data Objects

GHC data objects are represented as a sequence of memory words. A memory location consists of two fields, a *tag* field and a *value* field. Objects can be compound or atomic. The first memory word of an object contains a *tag* field and a *value* field holding additional data. If the object is compound, the tags of the following memory words identify the type of the component objects. If a component object can be represented directly, the value field contains its representation. Otherwise the value field contains the address of the component object, and the tag field indicates that this is a indirect reference.

4.1 Description of the Tags and Values

The different tags and corresponding value fields are as follows.

(1) *VAR* – Uninstantiated variable. The value is either NULL or a pointer to a queue of suspended computations.

(2) *REF* – A reference to some other term. The value is the address of the referenced term.

(3) *CER* – A cross-environment reference to some other term. The value is the address of the referenced term. This is exactly like a *REF* except that if the referenced term is a variable or contains variables, it (they) cannot be instantiated through this reference.

(4) *INT* – An integer. The value is the integer's value.

(5) *STRING* – A packed string of characters. The internal structure of strings is left unspecified at this time.

(6) *TUPLE* – A tuple. The value field contains the arity of this tuple. The next *arity* words are the tuple's arguments. If an argument does not fit into a single word, the corresponding slot

will be a reference to the actual structure of the argument. The first argument is commonly referred to as the tuple's *functor*. It may be, but need not be, a string object.

4.2 Data Areas and Runtime Structures

The main data area is the ***heap***. The heap is logically divided into two areas – tuple and constant space, and variable space. All runtime objects, created before and during the running of the abstract machine, are allocated on the heap.

(1) The modules containing the programs executed by processes. These are allocated in tuple space.

(2) The representation of goals to be solved. These representations are called *process records*. The fields of a process record are discussed in detail below.

(3) Data constructed by execution of the program.

(4) The active processes queue. This queue contains all process records currently ready for execution.

(5) Environments of variable cells. These are allocated in variable space.

A process record has the following six fields –

(1) The *GT* field – contains a reference to a tuple called the *guard tuple*. The purpose of this tuple is explained below.

(2) The *PR* field – contains a reference to the procedure to use in the computation of this goal. This is a reference into the code, probably in the middle of some module.

(3) The *AB* field – contains a reference to the arguments block for this goal. The arguments block is a legal GHC tuple, holding the arguments of the goal.

(4) The *EV* field – contains a reference to a vector of environments, one for each clause computing for this goal. Each environment is a legal GHC tuple, containing as many slots as there are local variables in the clause.

(5) The *SW* field – contains a reference to a vector of status words, one for each clause computing for this goal.

(6) The *ME* field – contain a reference to a mutual exclusion ring. The purpose of this ring will be explained below.

A single process record is created for each goal to be solved. It keeps the state of all guards computing for this goal. For each such guard, a *guard tuple* exists. A guard tuple has the following three fields –

(1) A reference to the status word for this guard.

(2) The number of goals currently computing in this guard.

(3) A reference to the process record for which this guard is computing.

A process record can be in one of three states –

(1) It can be the current process. This is called the *running* state.

(2) It can be in the active queue, ready for computation. This is called the *ready* state.

(3) It can be suspended on one or more variables, and/or waiting for the completion of one of the guards computing for it. This state is called the *suspended* state.

When a process record is in the *running* state, ME is NULL. Otherwise ME points to a mutual exclusion ring, of three-argument tuples [7]. Each tuple contains a reference to the process record, to the next tuple in the ring and to the next element in the suspension queue in which it appears. A process record can be suspended on more than one variable. A process record may also be waiting for guards computing for it to succeed. A mutual exclusion ring contains one tuple for each variable this process record is suspended on. The suspension queue of a variable contains one tuple for each process record that is suspended on it. The mutual exclusion ring ensures that the process will be reactivated only once. A process can be restarted when some variable it was suspended on is instantiated, or when some guard computing for it reaches commitment. When the process is restarted, the mutual exclusion ring is traversed, and all references to the process record are set to NULL. The ME field in the process record is also set to NULL, and the process record is enqueued in the active queue. After this, the process record is not accessible any more from any suspension queue.

The environment vector of a process record contains an environment for each guard computing for this goal. At the start of the computation of this goal, all fields of this vector are set to NULL. When the computation of a certain clause is started, an environment is allocated and stored in the correct slot in this vector. Each environment is an n-ary tuple, where n is one more than the number of variables needed to define the environment. The first $n-1$ slots are used to store the variable bindings, and the last slot is used to chain environments. The use of this slot will be explained in a following subsection.

The status word vector is a vector of words, one for each guard computing for this goal. A status word can have one of four values –

(1) *PRE* – this clause has not yet started to compute.

(2) *RUN* – this clause is currently waiting for its guard to complete computation.

(3) *FAIL* – the computation of the head or guard of this clause failed.

(4) *COMMIT* – the computation of the head and guard of this clause completed and this clause is ready to commit for the goal.

Another working area is the *suspension table*. This area is not allocated on the heap, but instead is contained in static storage. If, when a clause is computing, a suspension occurs, the variable causing the suspension is entered into the suspension table. When all clauses for a goal have been tried, if none committed, the goal is suspended on all variables in the suspension table. A new mutual exclusion tuple is allocated, initialized and stored in ME of the current process record. The mutual exclusion tuple is entered into the suspension queues of all variables in the suspension table.

4.3 Registers

The state of the abstract machine is defined by a number of registers which contain pointers into the data area.

HP	Heap Top Pointer
STI	Suspension Table Index

CP Current Process
PC Program Counter

SW Status Word Pointer
EV Environment Vector Pointer
GT Guard Tuple Pointer

QF Queue Front – Head of active queue
QB Queue Back – Tail of active queue

FL Failure Label

TS Time Slice

A Argument Pointer
SP Tuple Pointer
X1,X2.. Variable Registers.
T1,T2.. Temporary Registers.

The purpose of the registers is as follows –

HP Points at the top of the heap, i.e. at the next free heap location. It is advanced as data is allocated on the heap. When a certain point on the heap is passed, a garbage collection should be performed. This is (should be) done automatically by the implementation.

STI This indicates the next free slot in the suspension table. When a suspension occurs, the address of the variable causing the suspension is entered in the suspension table at the location indicated by STI, and STI is incremented.

CP Current Process. This points to the process record whose procedure the abstract machine is currently executing.

PC This points at the next instruction to be executed.

SW A pointer into the status word vector of CP. As the computation of each clause is done, SW is advanced to the status word of the current clause.

EV A pointer into the environment vector of CP. As the computation of each clause is done, EV is advanced to the environment slot of the current clause.

GT A pointer to the guard tuple for this process record. When a guard is created, this points to the newly allocated guard tuple for this guard.

QF, QB The head and tail of the active queue.

FL Contains an address in the code to jump to when the computation for this clause should be aborted because of failure, suspension or because the guard has not yet finished computing.

TS The time left for this process to run. This register is used to implement time-limited tail recursion optimization. If it is non-zero, the last goal in the body of the committing clause is selected for computation immediately when created, and the value of this register is decremented by one. If it is zero, another process record is dequeued and selected for computation.

A Used for reading the structure of an argument to a clause or for writing the structure of an argument of a goal. When writing a sequence of arguments, A contains the starting location of the arguments block of the goal.

SP Used for reading a substructure of an argument to a clause or for writing a substructure of an argument of a goal.

Xi Variable registers, holding the variables defining this clause's environment. There is one register per named variable and all anonymous variables use a single X register.

Ti Temporary registers, holding temporary quantities needed during the computation. These are used for example when a place in a tuple must be remembered in order to write a reference into it at a later time.

4.4 Handling of Cross-environment References

When a clause commits, the cross-environment references created for it must be set to normal references. However, some care must be exercised in this action, since otherwise a variable may become writeable too early. An example showing this problem is shown below.

Goal - $p(X),\ X = f(A)$
Clause 1 - $p(Y) \leftarrow q(Y), r(Y) \mid \ldots$
Clause 2 - $q(Z) \leftarrow Z = f(B) \mid \ldots$

Suppose the following sequence of events takes place.

(1) The goal $p(X)$ is unified with the head of clause 1. A cross-environment reference from Y to X is created.

(2) The goal $q(Y)$ is unified with the head of clause 2. A cross-environment reference from Z to Y is created.

(3) The unification $X = f(A)$ is done.

(4) The unification $Z = f(B)$ is done. This creates a cross-environment reference from B to A.

(5) Clause 2 commits. The cross-environment references from Z to Y and from B to A are set to normal references.

Now the goal $r(Y)$ can instantiate A through the reference to B. Thus, A is writeable in the guard of clause 1, which is incorrect.

The solution to this problem is to change cross-environment references to normal references only if they refer to variables in the environment of the committing goal. Cross-environment references to variables not in the environment of the committing goal cannot be modified at this time. Cross-environment references to locations in tuple space can always be safely modified, since they refer only to arguments of the committing goal.

To determine whether a cross-environment reference can be changed or not, the address of the referenced object is examined. If it is in tuple space the reference can be modified. Otherwise, if it is in variable space, we must check whether the object is contained in the environment of the committing goal. If it is, the reference can be modified. Otherwise, we cannot modify the cross-environment reference at this time.

Environments which contain cross-environment references which are not modified to normal references must be saved. Then, when it becomes possible to modify the references, this will be done. When such an environment is found, it is chained to the environment of the committing goal. Each environment is allocated with an additional slot, reserved for this purpose. When the guard system of the clause activation containing the committing goal itself reaches commitment, all environments chained to its own one are scanned. All cross-environment references which can be modified at this time are set to normal references. When a chained environment no longer contains cross-environment references it can be discarded. Environments which still contain cross-environment references are saved in the chain of the committing goal, recursively.

In this way, an environment containing cross-environment references migrates to the point where all such references can be modified. Then the environment is discarded.

Ueda and Miazaki [K. Ueda, personal communication] propose a different solution to this problem. A discussion of the relative merits of the two schemes is beyond the scope of this paper.

5. Instruction Set

5.1 The Instructions

There are five types of instructions – *read* instructions, *write* instructions, *sequencing* instructions, *temporary register* instructions and *control* instructions.

The *read* instructions correspond to the arguments of the head of the clause, and are responsible for matching the head of the clause against the structure of the goal. The *read* instructions are divided into two subclasses, differing in whether they advance the A register or the SP register. At the start of this matching, the A register is set to the first argument of the structure of the corresponding goal. The *toplevel* read instructions advance the A to point at the next argument. The *substructure* read instructions do not modify A but modify SP instead. The *toplevel* read instructions are named *read*-X while the *substructure* read instructions are named *subread*-X. The instructions are

```
read_var Xn                  read_value Xn
read_string Offset           read_integer Value
read_tuple Arity

subread_var Xn               subread_value Xn
subread_string Offset        subread_integer Value
subread_tuple Arity,Tn       subread_tuple_direct Arity
```

Here and below, in the description of all following instructions, Xn denotes a variable register, Ti denotes a temporary register, $Offset$ represents the address of a string and $Arity$ and $Value$ are integer values.

The *write* instructions are responsible for creating the structure of a goal, and to initialize the correct slot in the goal record with a reference to the argument. The *write* instructions are divided into two subclasses, according to their handling of the HP register. At the beginning of a sequence of *write* instructions, the A registers is set to the location of the first free location on the heap. The *toplevel* write instructions advance the HP register to the location of the next argument. The *substructure* write instructions do not modify HP but modify SP instead. The *toplevel* write instructions are named *write*-X while the *substructure* write instructions are named *subwrite*-X. The instructions are

write_var Xn	write_string Offset
write_integer Value	write_tuple Arity
subwrite_var Xn	subwrite_string Offset
subwrite_integer Value	subwrite_tuple Arity,Tn

subwrite_tuple_direct Arity

It seems possible to use a stack for *read* and *write* instructions. This would do away with the need for two sub-classes of instructions, one for top level and one for sub-structure reading or writing. This is currently being investigated.

The read and write instructions are described in detail in [8].

The only sequencing instruction provided is *try_me_else.*

try_me_else Fl

Fl is the address of the failure label. The instruction sets the value of FL to the correct location in the code for use when a failure or suspension occurs.

The *temporary register* instructions save a location into a specified temporary register. There are two instructions, for saving HP and SP.

save_hp Tn   save_sp Tn.

The *save_hp* instruction is used to save the starting address of the structure to be assigned in a test-commit-and-set operation. The *save_sp* instruction serves to store an address of a substructure which will be read or written by subsequent instructions. It is used when an argument of a tuple does not fit in a single heap location.

The *control* instructions are responsible for controlling the execution of the code. The instructions are

allocate N,Cl	guard	commit
test_commit_set Xn,Tn	spawn P	execute P
halt	suspend	

The control instructions, except for *allocate* and *test-commit-and-set* are inherited from [5].

5.2 Skeleton Encoding of Clauses

Below is the general skeleton for encoding of clauses.

```
    Unit clause         Iterative Clause      General Clause

    P.                  P :- Q.               P :- Q1,Q2,..,Qn
    allocate K,Cl       allocate K,Cl         allocate K,Cl
    read args of P      read args of P        read args of P
Cl:commit           Cl:commit             Cl:commit
    halt                write args of Q       write args of Q1
                        execute Q             spawn Q1
                                              write args of Q2
                                              spawn Q2
                                              ..
                                              write args of Qn
                                              execute Qn
```

```
Clause with guard                 Clause with test-set-and-commit

   P :- G1,..Gn | B1,..Bm            P :- ..| V ← T |..
   allocate K,Cl                     allocate K,Cl
   read args of P                    read args of P
   guard                             <sequence for guard>
   write args of G1               Cl:save_hp Ti
   spawn G1                          write T
   ..                                test_set_commit V,Ti
   write args of Gn                  commit
   spawn Gn                          <sequence for body>
Cl:commit
   <sequence for body>
```

```
Encoding of a Procedure

P1 :- ... | ...
P2 :- ... | ...

P  : n clauses
L1 : try_me_else L2
     <code for P1>
L2 : try_me_else L3
     ..
Ln : try_me_else Lm
     <code for last clause>
Lm : suspend
```

5.3 Semantic Conventions

In the code and text below, a few semantic conventions are used throughout. The construct $[V1, V2]$ represents a heap word with tag $V1$ and data field $V2$. The construct $*X := V$ denotes the assignment of V to the location addressed by X. When $*X$ is used as in 'the instruction unifies *X and ..', $*X$ denotes the value of the location referenced by X. The construct $\&X$ denotes the address of the location addressed by X.

There are two modes of dereferencing. One mode, called *full dereferencing* or simply dereferencing, follows references until a non-reference is reached. The second mode, called *partial dereferencing*, stops when a non-reference or a cross-environment reference is seen. When used without qualification, dereferencing denotes *full dereferencing* in the following text.

5.4 Startup Actions

At the start of computation of a process record, the following startup actions are done –

(1) *GT* is set to the value of the *GT* field in *CP*.

(2) The status of the guard in which this process record is computing is checked, and if the status is *FAIL* then the status of all slots in the status word vector is set to *FAIL* and another process record is dequeued.

(3) *PC* is restored from the *PR* field of *CP*, *STI* is set to zero, *EV* is restored from the *V* field in *CP*, *A* is restored from the *AB* field in *CP* and *SW* is restored from the *SW* field of *CP*.

These actions require about thirty operations. Nearly all of this overhead is avoided when tail recursion optimization is used.

5.5 Control Instructions

The control instructions are responsible for managing the flow of control through the code and to ensure that computation proceeds according to the semantic meaning of the program.

allocate N,Cl

If the status word of this clause is PRE, a tuple of N variables is allocated on the heap and stored in the appropriate slot in the environment vector. X1 is set to the first slot of the tuple. If the status word of this clause is COMMIT control is transferred to Cl.

guard

This instruction appears at the beginning of a guard which contains recursive calls (i.e. not only test predicates). The instruction sets the status word for this clause to RUN, allocates a new guard tuple, sets GT to it and sets A to HP in preparation for writing the arguments of the first guard goal.

commit

This instruction commits the GHC computation to choose this clause for the current goal. If the status word for this clause is RUN, control is transferred to *FL. Otherwise, the guard count field of the tuple referenced by the GT register is decremented, the status words of all clauses computing for this goal are set to FAIL, X1 is set to the first slot of the tuple referenced by EV, A is set to HP in preparation for writing the arguments of the first goal, the environments accessible through the tuple referenced by EV are scanned and all cross-environment references which can be modified now are set to normal references. If, after the scan, some environment accessible through EV still contains cross-environment references, the environment is spliced into the chain of environments accessible from the environment of the committing goal.

test_commit_set Xn,Tn

If the status word for this clause is RUN, control is transferred to *FL. X1 is set to the first slot of the tuple in the appropriate slot of the environment vector. Xn is set to a normal reference to its referenced object. Xn is partially dereferenced and the dereferenced result is stored back in Xn. If the result is not a variable control is transferred to *FL. Otherwise if Xn has a suspension queue, the process records suspended on it are enqueued in the active queue. Xn is initialized to [REF,*Tn].

spawn P

This instruction creates a new process record that will execute the procedure *P*. The instruction allocates a new process record, inserts *P* in the PR slot, sets the GT field to [REF,GT], increments the guard count field of the tuple referenced by the GT register, initializes ME to [VAR,NULL], allocates a new status word tuple of the appropriate size and initializes SW to [REF,This tuple], allocates a new environment tuple of the appropriate size and initializes EV to [REF,This tuple], initializes AB to [REF,*A], enqueues the new process record in the active queue and sets A to HP.

execute P

This instruction starts computation of a process record. The instruction reuses the current process record. It inserts *P* in the PR slot, sets the GT field to [REF,GT], increments the guard count field of the tuple referenced by the GT register, initializes ME to [VAR,NULL], allocates a new status word tuple of the appropriate size and initializes SW to [REF,This tuple], allocates a new environment tuple of the appropriate size and initializes EV to [REF,This tuple], and initializes AB to [REF,*A]. If the time slice for this procedure has ended, the process record is enqueued and another process record is selected for computation. Otherwise, the process record is selected for computation and the time slice is decremented.

halt

The instruction checks the guard count field of the tuple referenced by the GT register. If it is not zero, the instruction resets the time slice, dequeues another process and selects it for computation. If it is zero, the instruction sets CP to the process referenced in the process reference field of the guard tuple referenced by GT, sets the status word of the committing clause in the status word vector of CP to COMMIT, sets the status words for all other clauses of CP to FAIL, enqueues CP in the active queue and selects another process for computation.

suspend

If the suspension table is non-empty, the instruction allocates a new mutual exclusion tuple, sets ME to [REF,This tuple], sets the argument of the tuple to [REF,CP] and inserts the mutual exclusion tuple in the suspension queues of all the variables in the suspension table. Otherwise, if some of the status words in the status word vector of CP are RUN, the time slice is reset, another process record is dequeued and selected for computation. Otherwise a process failure has occurred. The following sequence of actions is done repeatedly, until the failure cannot be propagated further.

(1) The status word referenced through GT is set to FAIL, CP is set to the process record retrieved through GT and GT is set to the value of the GT field of the new CP.

(2) If CP is the root of the computation tree, the abstract machine halts with an error. If all slots of the status word vector of CP are FAIL, execution proceeds at step 1.

After the failure is propagated as far as possible another process is selected for computation and the time slice is reset.

5.6 Temporary Register Instructions

There are two such instructions, for saving addresses into temporary registers. The first instruction, *save_hp*, is used to store the address of the structure to be written in a *test_commit_set* instruction in a *T* register. The second instruction, *save_sp*, is used to store the address of sub-structures to be read or written later into a *T* register.

save_hp Tn

The value of HP is saved into Tn.

save_sp Tn

The value of SP is saved into Tn and SP is incremented by one location.

5.7 Sequencing Instructions

There is now only one sequencing instruction, but certainly others could be added in the future. Sequencing instructions are responsible for clause selection and management of control flow within the body of a procedure.

try_me_else Fl

This is the first instruction in the body of a clause. SW and EV are advanced to the next slot in their respective vectors. If the status word for the current clause is FAIL or RUN, control is transferred to Fl. Otherwise, the FL register is set to Fl.

6. Results and Conclusions

The abstract machine described in this paper was implemented in *C* on a VAX. The speeds achieved compare favourably with those achieved by the FCP emulator [A. Houri, personal communication]. For naive reverse, the GHC emulator achieved ~1200 LIPS as opposed to ~2100 LIPS for the FCP emulator. For Or-parallel code, e.g. a program to determine tree isomorphism, the abstract machine runs at ~950 LIPS. Some significant optimizations such as cdr-coding of lists have not yet been incorporated. Cdr-coding alone should improve the performance of the GHC emulator by about thirty percent [M. Safra, personal communication]. It is expected that the GHC abstract machine will achieve eighty percent of the performance of FCP.

Some of the overhead of GHC as opposed to FCP or Flat GHC is unavoidable. We must keep enough information to manage the separate Or-parallel environments correctly. The addition of EV and SW slots to the structure of process records is thus necessary. The reason for the addition of the ME field requires more explanation – a process record in FCP could be reactivated only by instantiation of some variables on which it was suspended. In GHC it is also possible that some guard has completed its computation and is now ready to commit. In order to avoid a situation where the process record is reactivated many times, e.g. when some guard completes and when a variable is instantiated, the connection between the mutual exclusion ring must be broken; therefore it must be accessible from the process record.

Related work in our group [7] makes the translation of Or-parallel programs written in GHC to And-parallel programs in Flat GHC a close reality. The performance of programs translated in this way may approach that of programs directly written in the And-parallel language [M. Codish, personal communication]. However, it can be shown that the subset of programs for which this translation is possible is smaller than the set of programs expressible in GHC. Thus, the direct emulation of Or-parallel languages such as GHC is justifiable in its own right.

A GHC abstract machine is also useful in other ways – it can serve as as a starting point for exploring different possible Or-parallel languages such as Safe GHC [7], CP [2] and PARLOG[3].

Acknowledgements

I wish to thank Dr. S. Cohen for encouraging me to work on this subject and for many useful discussions. Many thanks are also extended to my advisor, Dr. E. Shapiro, to our guests Mats Carlsson of Uppsala University and Tony Kusalik of the University of British Columbia, and to S. Taylor, M. Hirsch, M. Safra, A. Houri and M. Codish for many helpful suggestions and insights. This work was supported by IBM Poughkeepsie, Data System Division.

References

[1] K. Ueda, Guarded Horn Clauses. ICOT Technical Report TR-103, June 1985.

[2] E. Shapiro, A Subset of Concurrent Prolog and Its Interpreter. ICOT Technical Report TR-003, February 1983.

[3] K.L. Clark and F.G. McCabe, PARLOG: a Parallel Logic Programming Language. Research Report DOC 84/15, Dept. of Computing, Imperial College, London, 1984.

[4] D. H. D. Warren, An Abstract Prolog Instruction Set. Technical Note 309, SRI International, Stanford, October 1983.

[5] A. Houri and E. Shapiro, Tailoring The Warren Abstract Machine for FCP. To appear as Weizmann Institute Technical Report.

[6] C. Mierowsky, Design and Implementation of Flat Concurrent Prolog. Weizmann Institute Technical Report CS84-21, 1984.

[7] M. Codish, Compiling Or-parallelism into And-parallelism. Weizmann Institute Technical Report CS85-18, 1985.

[8] J. Levy, A GHC Abstract Machine and Instruction Set. Weizmann Institute Technical Report CS85-11, 1985.

A PROLOG PROCESSOR BASED ON A PATTERN MATCHING MEMORY DEVICE

Ian Robinson

Schlumberger Palo Alto Research
Computer Aided Systems Laboratory
3340 Hillview Ave.
Palo Alto, CA 94304

ABSTRACT

A Prolog processing system using a parallel pattern matching component is outlined. The component, called a Pattern Addressable Memory (PAM), is used to store the clause heads from a Prolog database, and match them against an input goal/subgoal. It is shown that using this device has advantages not only for clause selection, but also for the unification function itself. Such a system, it is argued, demonstrates superior performance compared to serial approaches.

INTRODUCTION

This work arose as part of the research effort connected with the FAIM-1 symbolic multiprocessing system under development at Schlumberger [DaR85a,b,c]. This machine is a homogenous ensemble of processing sites, each communicating with its neighbours over a topologically regular wiring network. Each processing site is characterised by a number of specialised hardware functional units, allowing some degree of concurrent processing internally. The 'granularity' of the system is at the 'task' level, i.e. each site is capable of performing some useful part of the overall program with minimal communication with its neighbours.

The use of custom hardware allows the parallelism inherent in certain application areas to be exploited. In the context of support for logic programming this paper concentrates on exploiting what opportunities there are for parallelism in the unification function itself. Previous work has shown that unification in general requires polynomial size circuitry for a solution [Yas84, Dwo84]. However the important sub-task of pattern matching *is* amenable to solution in parallel hardware at reasonable cost.

This leaves the problem of binding resolution, i.e. the 'logical variable' in D.H.D.Warren's dictum:

unification = pattern matching + the logical variable [War77]

This part is considered best left to serial hardware. There it takes the form of pointer manipulations and stack operations, functions that can readily be handled by an attached processor of more conventional design.

This paper describes the operation of this pattern matching co-processor, called a 'pattern addressable memory' (PAM), and outlines a processing system that uses it. In order to consider the advantages of this approach separately from other FAIM-1 project issues the language domain is chosen to be that of Prolog. Also to this end, and for the purposes of comparison, the PAM is considered connected to a 'processor' characterised by the abstract instruction set developed by Warren [War77,83]. This is used as the exemplar of the serial approach to unification. Indeed it forms the basis for many contemporary attempts at high performance Prolog machines [TiW83, Dob85, Nak85]. It will be argued that the parallel operations of the PAM can significantly increase the performance of the system as a whole.

THE PAM

The PAM can be thought of as an extension to the conventional content addressable memory (CAM). Whereas single words are stored and matched upon in the latter, in the PAM arbitrary length strings of symbols are dealt with. These strings are structured in the form of LISP-style s-expressions. Consequently the Prolog syntax is modified to place the functor inside its parentheses. The PAM uses the following symbol types (identified by tag bits):

constants

variables - indicated by a '?' prefix

CDR-variables - variables used to represent the CDR-part of a list structure.

structure markers - parentheses with an associated nesting depth.

It is necessary for the matching function that the symbol strings be represented linearly, i.e. with substructure expanded in place, hence the parentheses and the absence of symbols corresponding to internal pointers.

The pattern matching rules are correspondingly simple. Constants only match constants of the same name, parentheses only match other parentheses of the same polarity and nesting depth, variables match any other constant, variable or sub-structure, and CDR-variables match any sequence of the latter. In the implementation CAM-style comparators are used on the names and indices, together with simple logical operations on the symbols' associated tag bits. Note that no account is taken of variable names. The PAM treats all variables as anonymous, thereby leaving the issues of bindings and contexts to resolved externally.

A brief overview of the PAM's operation is as follows: a goal is entered symbol by symbol into the chip. As this is done the pattern match is computed for all the clause heads stored. The result, at the end of goal input, is that each matching structure is marked. This marking is then used to guide output of the matching clause heads.

In more detail the PAM can be thought of as several words-worth of logic-enhanced storage. This includes match-detection circuitry for each word and an associated slot for a 'match token'. This match token is 'set' whenever its associated word matches the goal symbol, according to the above rules, AND the previous word's token was still present; otherwise it is 'reset'. The effect is of a match token being passed down each structure as it matches against the goal (as illustrated in Figure 1.). Hence, at the end of the goal, only those clause heads with a match token at their ends constitute a matching structure. Initially all match tokens are set so that a match can start anywhere. Note that only one cycle is required per goal symbol entered, and so matching occurs 'on the fly'.

In order to reduce the hardware complexity inherent in this scheme the comparators and match logic are actually shared, each set between ten (in the present implementation) words of memory. This effectively splits the storage into ten 'pages', as illustrated in figure 2. These pages are tried in sequence for each goal symbol. Consequently each 'cycle' consists, in the worst case, of ten 'micro-cycles'. This is worst case because circuitry is included that removes from further consideration any pages on which no matches exist. Thus processing time benefits from putting similar clause heads on the same page(s). In this way the other pages

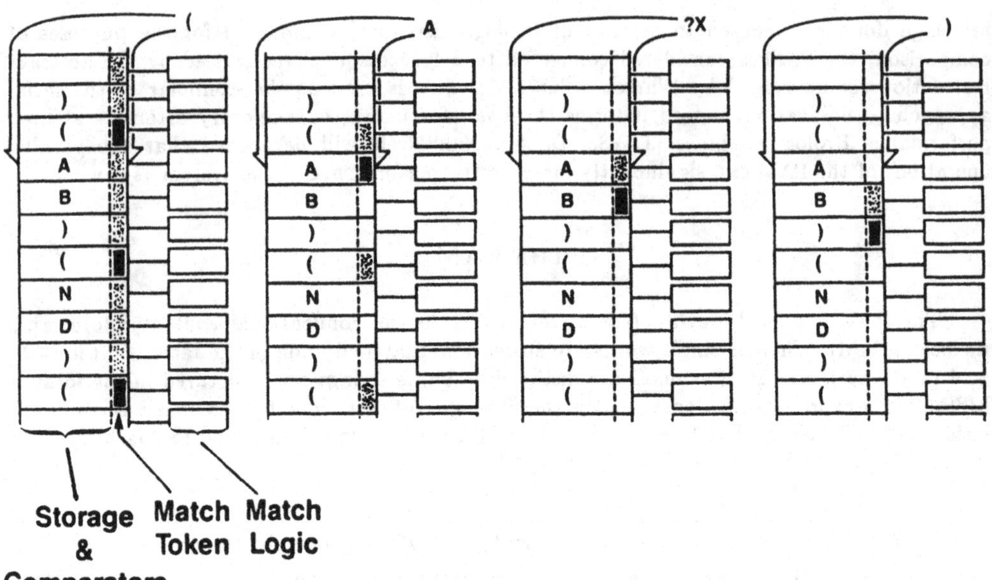

FIGURE 1 : PAM with input goal (A ?X). *Match tokens are shown solid, previous token positions are shown dotted.*

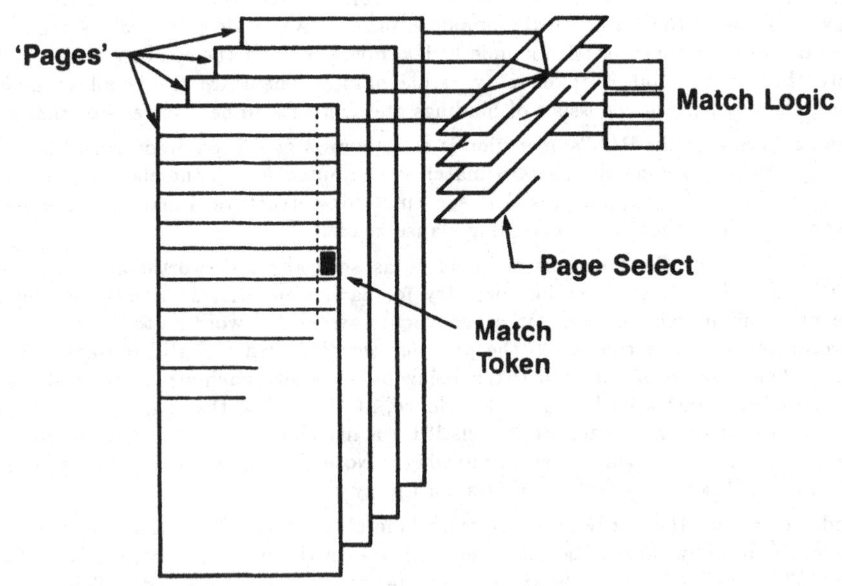

FIGURE 2 : Multiplexing pages (only four shown) into the match logic.

will be discounted early on, and pattern matching proceeds at the ideal rate of one micro-cycle per goal symbol.

Output is directed by a 'read pointer' which can be moved (in one cycle) to the first/next match token and used to direct output from there. In the application considered here the PAM is used to provide a pointer to the code area for that clause in main memory. By storing this pointer as the last word in each structure only those words actually marked by a match token need be read out, rather than the whole expression.

There is a corresponding 'write pointer' which always indicates the first empty word in the memory. The PAM is written/loaded/appended to as one long array, it is not randomly addressable for write (or read) operations. Other functions built into the PAM include deletion and garbage collection of unwanted structures, and miscellaneous setting and clearing operations.

A prototype PAM chip has been laid out and the floor-plan is shown in Figure 3. It contains 560 words, 56 to a page, of 16-bit symbols (excluding tag-bits). Positing an average clause head size of seven PAM words then one chip can store eighty such structures. The chips are designed so that an arbitrary number of them can be used in parallel to implement a larger PAM with no performance penalty for the pattern matching operation. Hence it is a simple matter to support hundreds of facts/rules per processing site in the FAIM-1 application. This should be more than adequate bearing in mind that each site need store only the clause heads pertaining to a certain task, and not the whole database.

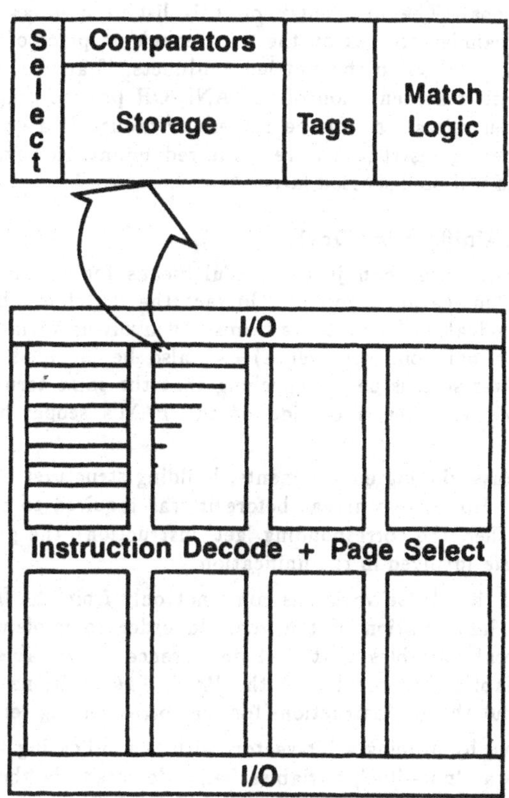

FIGURE 3 : PAM chip floor-plan.

THE PAM AND THE PROLOG PROCESSOR

The interaction of the PAM and its host processor will now be considered. For the purposes of this exposition Warren's abstract processor model is used (this includes the memory organisation, register descriptions and the high level instruction set), as explained in the introduction. For the sake of this discussion it does not really matter how this processor is implemented; for comparison purposes however it is only fair to assume that it takes the form of a tagged and pipelined custom architecture [TiW83, Dob85, Nak85].

The PAM as a Clause Indexing Device

Perhaps the more obvious function of the PAM is to serve as a clause indexing device. Goal/subgoal arguments are input to the PAM at the same time as they are entered into the processor registers, i.e. by the 'put' instructions. Note that instructions such as 'put_structure' will need to then send that structure to the PAM in order to format the goal in the required linear fashion.

Each clause head ends in a pointer to the code area for that clause. When matching is complete, all of the 'successful' pointers are read out to the processor. This constitutes a list that includes all the possible continuations from that juncture, i.e. a list of candidate clauses to be tried on backtracking. This is termed the OR-list, after the AND-OR process model of Conery [Con83]. It is important to note that this list is ordered in the same way as the entries in the PAM. This order is used by the processor to control the sequence in which they are tried against the goal. The first entry on this list is used as the current 'program counter', whilst the remainder are put on the 'local stack' in place of the usual choice-point information. By adding pointers to the untried conjuncts, if any, of active goals, the local stack becomes an explicit representation of the AND-OR process graph. This graph can be walked by simple pointer operations on the success or failure of a goal. In this way all the conventional clause indexing instructions are made redundant. However there are occaisions when they are useful, as will be discussed later.

The PAM as a 'Mock Unification' Device

Pattern matching is more than just a useful means for clause selection, it is also a significant part of the unification algorithm. In fact the matching that takes place in the PAM amounts to full unification for all those terms not involving variables. Functionally, void variables (ie. ones with only one occurrence) can also be included as their bindings will always 'succeed'. However such issues as checking that the same term gets bound to all the instances of a repeated variable is outside of the PAM's scope; hence the term 'mock unification'.

Taking care of clause binding environments, building structures etc. remains the job of the attached processor. However, whereas before it was required to process each symbol in the clause head (or, rather, the corresponding 'get' instruction), the processor now only need bother with each *variable* involved in the unification.

It should be noted that these variables come not only from the (compiled) clause head, but also the run-time instantiation of the goal. In order to implement this some way is needed of detecting goal variables that still dereference to variables at the time of the unification, ie. all variables that are fed to the PAM. The positions of these variables can then be used to index out the get instructions for the corresponding terms in the clause head.

This is implemented by forming a bit-vector, with '1's indicating variable positions, from the argument registers at 'put-time'; variables being detected via their tag. Deriving these indices need only be done the once for each invocation of the procedure, and the vector is stored along with the OR-list. This information is then used to 'edit' the code for the candidate clause heads. Such editing is well suited to an instruction pre-fetch pipeline stage.

No-op's are performed unless the instruction refers to a clause head variable or is indexed via a '1' in the bit vector, in which case the instruction is executed.

PERFORMANCE

The PAM-enhanced Prolog processor outlined above has the following performance advantages.

Compared to Hashing

Pattern matching will, in general, return fewer failing candidates than will a hash function. This is particularly so when that hashing is only on the first argument as with Warren's indexing instructions. In fact the only matches that could fail in unification will be those on clause heads containing repeated variables. Since these are not common in typical Prolog programs the number of non-unifiable returns should be minimal. The PAM's advantage in this respect will increase with the number of clauses in a procedure. This is well suited to the usual case in Prolog where its depth-first search tends to bottom out in a large database of facts.

The net result of having fewer false candidates is that less processing time is wasted detecting them. Unfortunately, making the hashing function better in order to return fewer spurious collisions also makes it slower; dividing by a prime number is not a fast operation.

A second, and perhaps more important, advantage appears in the case of there being *no* matching clause heads for a particular goal/subgoal. This is a common occurrence in Prolog, leading to backtracking. In the case of hashing the function is designed to optimally map the domain of database clauses onto a set of addresses, with the ideal being one per hash bucket and none left over. In these circumstances, however, *any* input to the hash unit will give rise to a valid address, which will therefore probably return some clause - or worse still a collision list-full of clauses - for processing. Thus the costs of attempting unification with hashing into the database are roughly the same whether or not they are successful.

The PAM, on the other hand, is equipped with hardware to detect the absence of match tokens. In this way the case of no clauses being present in the database that will unify with the goal can be detected as soon as the 'offending' element in the goal is entered. The ability to 'give an answer before the question is finished' represents the fastest possible response in this common case.

When, however, clause indexing is a trivial matter (eg. the *concatenate* benchmark) the PAM can be at a disadvantage. In such cases an indexing instruction can save the PAM look-up routine. Hence these instructions are retained, although in a very simplified form.

Lastly the PAM is to some extent self-managing. Setting it up and performing asserts and retracts are reasonably simple propositions. The same cannot be said for hash-based schemes.

The above comments also apply to other encoding schemes, for example the superimposed codeword technique proposed in [WiP84]. Again the encoding is an imperfect representation of the clause head leading to spurious matches, and time must be spent encoding the query/goal.

Compared to Pattern Matching in the Processor

A particular advantage of this approach to pattern matching is that it is only performed once on each procedure invocation. Different candidate clause heads will then only vary in their variable bindings, a new pattern match need not be computed on backtracking. Typically for each procedure invocation only one or two variables actually get bound and/or serve to communicate bindings between goals. Hence variable binding resolution takes a second place to pattern matching, which predominates. This again favours the performance of the PAM-enhanced processor.

Lastly this one-time process takes place in the PAM on the fly. Its processing time is masked to a large extent by the put instructions loading the processor registers.

CONCLUSION

In general the success of DEC10 Prolog has proven the performance of this overall approach to compiling Prolog clauses. The PAM is essentially a 'mock unification' co-processor/accelerator; in the FAIM-1 application its operation is independent of the 'CPU'. The PAM-based processor, through the advantages discussed above, constitutes a significant performance improvement over the conventional serial approach. Furthermore the cost of this improvement in terms of hardware complexity is quite acceptable.

The PAM is still at a fairly experimental stage. Such matters as the number of pages, the complexity of the match logic etc., are still under consideration. The design is very modular and so can take full advantage of technology scaling. Hence it is reasonable to assume a 1k word PAM in the next instantiation. Such a chip would hold in the order of 150 clause heads. 16 PAM's in parallel would hold 2400 clause heads - a reasonable size database. Thus the PAM could also serve as a valuable component in a high performance uni-processor system.

ACKNOWLEDGEMENTS

Thanks to Al Davis, Shimon Cohen and Gary Lindstrom for significant contributions to the ideas behind this paper.

REFERENCES

[Con83] J.S. Conery 'The AND/OR Process Model for Parallel Interpretation of Logic Programs' PhD. thesis, Univ. of California at Irvine, June '83.

[DaR85a] A.L. Davis S.V. Robison 'The FAIM-1 Symbolic Multiprocessing System' Proc. Compcon, Feb '85.

[DaR85b] A.L. Davis S.V. Robison 'An Overview of the FAIM-1 Multiprocessing System' Proc. 1st AI & Adv. Computer Tech. Conf., April '85.

[DaR85c] A.L. Davis S.V. Robison 'The Architecture of the FAIM-1 Symbolic Multiprocessing System' Proc. IJCAI, August '85.

[Dob85] T.P. Dobry A.M. Despain Y.N. Patt 'Performance Studies of a Prolog Machine Architecture' 8th Annual Int'l Symp. on Comp. Arch., June '85.

[Dwo84] C. Dwork P.C. Kanellakis J.C. Mitchell 'On the Sequential Nature of Unification' J. Logic Programming, Vol 1, '84.

[Nak85] R. Nakazaki et al. 'Design of a High-Speed Prolog Machine' 8th Annual Int'l Symp. on Comp. Arch., June '85.

[Rob84] I. Robinson 'The Pattern Addressable Memory' SPAR internal publication, Nov '84.

[TiW83] E. Tick D. Warren 'Towards a Pipelined Prolog Processor' Tech. report, SRI AI Centre, Aug '83.

[War77] D. Warren 'Implementing Prolog' Tech. report 39, Edinburgh University, May '77.

[War83] D. Warren 'An Abstract Prolog Instruction Set' Tech. Report 309, AI Centre, SRI International, October '83.

[WiP84] M.J.Wise D.M.W.Powers 'Indexing Prolog Clauses via Superimposed Code Words and Field Encoded Words' Proc. Int. Symp. on Logic Programming, Feb '84.

[Yas84] H. Yasuura 'On Parallel Computational Complexity of Unification' Proc. Int. Conf. on FGCS '84.

AN IMPROVED VERSION OF SHAPIRO'S MODEL INFERENCE SYSTEM

Matthew M. Huntbach
Cognitive Studies Programme
University of Sussex
Brighton, England.

Abstract

We discuss the Model Inference System of E.Y.Shapiro, giving particular attention to the refinement operator which is used during the synthesis of new Prolog clauses. An improved refinement operator which has been found in practice to reduce synthesis times by up to a factor of five is introduced.

1. ALGORITHMIC PROGRAM DEBUGGING

This report is based on work done with E.Y.Shapiro's Algorithmic Program Debugging system [5], which is able to debug existing Prolog programs and synthesise new ones. We review the system and describe a new implementation which improves on the efficiency of the original in several ways.

A major part of Shapiro's work is concerned with algorithms and a theoretical framework for diagnosing bugs in Prolog programs. Since these have been widely implemented and we have left them essentially unchanged, we describe them only briefly here. A more detailed description is given in [1].

The program diagnosis system consists of three algorithms to deal with different categories of bug. During their execution, the user is asked simple queries such as whether a particular goal is required to terminate true or false, or to which values a particular variable should be set for a given goal to succeed.

The first algorithm deals with a program which succeeds on some goal where it is required to fail. It locates a particular clause where there is a substitution such that the head is a fact that should be false according to the user, but all the subgoals should be true.

The second diagnostic algorithm deals with a program which fails on some goal where the user wants it to succeed. It finds a goal, identified as true by the user, which is not covered by any existing clause. A clause is said to cover a goal if there is some substitution such that the head of the clause is unified with the goal and all the subgoals are unified with facts identified as true by the user.

The third algorithm deals with non-terminating programs. It locates a clause which leads to divergence, that is a clause where there is some substitution such that there is a subgoal which is not less than the head in some well-founded ordering.

2. THE MODEL INFERENCE SYSTEM

2.1 The basic algorithm

The diagnostic algorithms can be used in the inference of a program which behaves correctly on a set of examples, that is facts identified as either true or false, given to it by the user. The system works by starting with an incomplete program, which may be the empty set of clauses. It attempts to execute the program with each of the example facts as goal. Should the program succeed on a false example, the first algorithm is used to locate the faulty clause which is then retracted. Should the program fail on a true example, the second algorithm is used to find an uncovered goal. A new clause is synthesised to cover this goal and added to the program. If during the checking of an example, a depth bound on the computation is exceeded, the program is assumed to be looping or diverging and the third algorithm is used to find the clause at fault which is then retracted.

The user interaction will identify more facts which are added to the library of facts. The asserting and retracting of clauses will lead to changes in the set of examples covered by the program. So the system repeats the process of checking all the facts until it has a set of clauses which executes correctly with each fact as a goal.

2.1 Clause synthesis

The clause synthesis system simply searches the set of possible clauses until it finds one which covers the goal in question. The root of the search tree is the predicate of the goal with each argument set to a simple variable and no subgoals. Its descendants are clauses produced by applying simple refinements, their descendants being produced by further refinements and so on. When the system is used for debugging rather than synthesis, the root of the search tree is a clause taken from the program and altered slightly by a 'derefinement operator'.

An additional restriction is that the system is incremental, that is no clause that has been previously removed is added again. Instead, search continues among its descendants and other clauses.

The refinement operator is such that if a clause in the search tree does not cover a goal then none of its descendants will. So the subtree rooted in that clause can be pruned.

3. THE SHAPIRO REFINEMENT OPERATOR

3.1 Declaration of input and output

The refinement operator given in [5] depends on the fact that for many Prolog programs it is possible to declare arguments in a predicate as used for either input or output. A similar use of mode declarations is used by Warren [6] to optimise his Prolog compiler. It is also necessary to name all further predicates that the program being synthesised may call. As an example, the predicate 'insert' which inserts an integer into a list of integers is declared as having mode: insert(+n,+[n],-[n]) (n being used to indicate integer type, [n] type list of integer). It may call 'insert' itself, and '<'.

Besides each clause in the refinement search tree is stored a list of its variables with their types, divided into input and output variables. So, for example, a clause consisting of just the head insert(N,[X|L1],[Y,Z|L2]) has input variables (with associated types):

<N,integer>, <X,integer>, <L1,list(integer)>

and output variables

<Y,integer>, <Z,integer>, <L2,list(integer)>.

3.2 Refinements: instantiations

The refinement operator to produce descendants of nodes in the search tree is based on two types of operations: (i) instantiate a variable (ii) add a subgoal to the body of the clause. Operations of type (i) are in general applied only to clauses consisting of just a head.

Instantiation operations instantiate a variable either to a constant, in which case the variable is removed from the variable list, or a function of further new variables in which case the old variable is replaced by the new ones.

Another type of instantiation unifies two variables. They must both be input variables and both of the same type. The two are replaced by one in the variable list.

Output variables are only unified with input variables by means of the 'close clause' operation. This sets each of the output variables in a clause to one of the input variables. Clauses produced by this operation are the only ones in which output values will be set. Because of this, only clauses produced by the 'close clause' operation may be added to the program to cover any goal for a predicate with output arguments. For any other clause, the descendants are produced, and search is continued.

3.3 Refinements: adding subgoals

When a subgoal is added to a clause, each of its input arguments are set to one of the existing input variables. The new variables for the output of the subgoal are added to the list of input variables since they may be used as input for further subgoals. They are also used to form a new list of 'free variables' - variables which would be set values, but are not used in any way. If a free variable is subsequently used as input for a further subgoal, it is removed from this list.

The close clause operation may be applied to clauses with subgoals. If an output variable is unified with a free variable, then that variable is removed from the free variable list. In fact the close clause operation is only applied when it would lead to the free variable list becoming empty.

Figure 1 gives an example of a path in the search tree leading to the recursive clause in insert sort.

```
sort(X,Y).
input variables = <X,list(integer)>
output variables = <Y,list(integer)>
                  |
                  ↓  instantiate X to [H|T]
sort([H|T],Y).
input variables = <H,integer>, <T,list(integer)>
output variables = <Y,list(integer)>
                  |
                  ↓  add subgoal sort(T,S)
sort([H|T],Y) :- sort(T,S).
input variables = <H,integer>, <T,list(integer)>, <S,list(integer)>
output variables = <Y,list(integer)>
free variables = <S,list(integer)>
                  |
                  ↓  add subgoal insert(H,S,I)
sort([H|T],Y) :- sort(T,S),insert(H,S,I)
input variables = <H,integer>, <T,list(integer)>, <S,list(integer)>,
                                                   <I,list(integer)>
output variables = <Y,list(integer)>
free variables = <I,list(integer)>
                  |
                  ↓  close clause, unifying I with Y
sort([H|T],I) :- sort(T,S),insert(H,S,I).
```

Figure 1. Steps in the synthesis of the recursive clause for insertion sort.

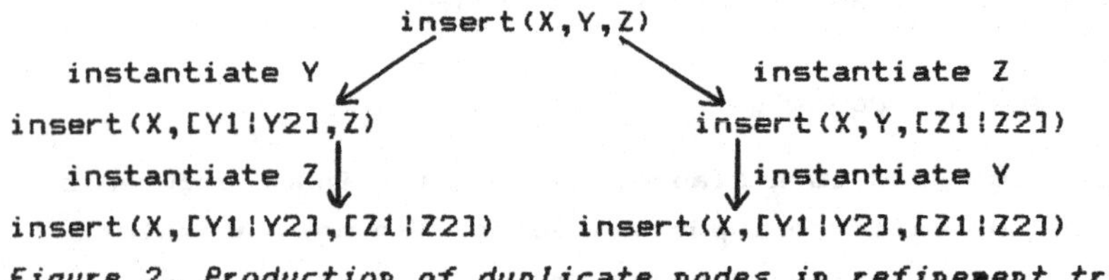

Figure 2. Production of duplicate nodes in refinement tree.

4. IMPROVING THE REFINEMENT OPERATOR

Having implemented the program diagnosis system as developed in [5], we decided that as the refinement operator is not directly dependent on facilities provided by Prolog, we would implement it in the procedural language Pop-11. This gave us the opportunity to give close consideration to the refinement operator which is not described in detail in [5] and on which little work has been done by others. It also enabled us to make a number of modifications, detailed below.

4.1 Removing duplicate nodes

One of the problems with Shapiro's system, noted in [1], is that duplicate nodes appear in the refinement tree. The problem is that the refinement operator as given allows refinements to be made in any order. This means that given a set of operations needed to produce a head from the most general term, each permutation of the operations is treated as a separate path leading to a separate node. Figure 2 shows an example.

The solution is to insist that operations are carried out in a fixed order. Since instantiations of input variables are entirely independent of instantiations of output variables, none of the latter need be carried out before the former. Unification of inputs can always take place after any instantiation of inputs, since any head produced by unifying two input variables and then instantiating the result, can also be produced by first instantiating then unifying.

We associate a value, the 'stage' with each clause. The root clause is assigned stage 1. No operation may be carried out which would result in a clause having a lower stage than its parent.

A clause produced by instantiating inputs is assigned stage 1.
A clause produced by unifying inputs is assigned stage 2.
A clause produced by instantiating outputs is assigned stage 3.
A clause produced by adding subgoals is assigned stage 4.
A clause produced by the close clause operation is assigned stage 5.

In addition, for each clause at stages 1 to 3, a list of instantiable variables is kept. At stages 1 and 2 this is initially the input variables, at stage 3 the output variables. When a variable is instantiated or unified with another, only those following it, and the new ones introduced are given as instantiable variables to the clause produced. Since the instantiation of one variable does not affect any other, this ordering of instantiations does not affect the clauses able to be produced.

4.2 Adding heuristics

Another problem with Shapiro's system is that it performs breadth first search on the refinement tree. This can lead to it considering clauses which are unlikely to lead to a covering clause before more obvious candidates. It can be overcome by generating a value for each clause representing the likelihood that this clause will lead to a solution. The clauses waiting consideration are stored in order of this value.

The necessity for heuristics in the search of the refinement tree lies in the fact that nodes in this tree can have a large number of descendants (20 or more are not uncommon). So the search tree soon becomes unmanageablely large if it is necessary to search every clause at a given depth before considering any deeper clauses.

The heuristic we have used assigns values to clauses depending on the complexity of the head. This leads to the system considering clauses that can be produced by adding subgoals to a simple head before going back and considering more complex heads. Additional factors considered include using the length of the list of free variables, and counting the number of subgoals. The former heuristic leads to the system prefering to use free variables as inputs to subgoals rather than variables which have already been used as inputs to others. The latter should be used in addition to the heuristic of using the complexity of the head, preventing the system from searching too deeply a subtree rooted in one particular head when the solution clause lies in the subtree rooted in a slightly more complex head.

5. FURTHER MODIFICATIONS

In [1] it is noted that unless the user gives the Model Inference System some facts which are required to be false, the system will just keep adding clauses and the program will grow large.

If an output producing program is known to be determinate though, it is possible to generate false facts automatically. Consider the predicate 'sort' declared as sort(+[n],-[n]). Since it is determinate we know that for any given value of the input argument there will be only one value for the output argument to give a true fact. But in the sample run given in [5], at one stage the fact <sort([2,3,1],[1,2,3]),true> is entered while later on it is necessary to specifically enter the fact <sort([2,3,1],[2,3,1]), false>. The system ought to know that if sort([2,3,1],[1,2,3]) is true then sort([2,3,1],X) is false for any X ≠ [1,2,3].

A simple modification to the system overcomes this. When the current program is found to cover a true fact in the database, it is made to backtrack to see if it produces any other solutions for the same input. If so, these other solutions are asserted as false facts, and the clauses which led to them are removed as they would be had the user specifically noted them as false facts.

This mechanism may also be used to reduce the number of queries made to the user during program diagnosis. If a fact is known to be true then any fact with the same input but a different output will always be false. So it is not necessary to query the user about it, or specifically store it as a false fact.

6. CONCLUSIONS AND FUTURE WORK

The work presented here indicates there is considerable scope for improvement in the Model Inference System. The new version has been tested against an implementation closer to the original and found to be up to five times faster in C.P.U. time.

Further research has been directed towards providing a refinement operator to produce Prolog clauses which may be easily translated to more standard programming languages, or to a generalised plan notation such as that of the Programmer's Apprentice [3]. This may lead to a system which could be incorporated as an element in a Knowledge Based Programmer's Assistant [2].

We are also working towards incorporating some of the ideas found in Lisp synthesis from examples systems, such as [4] into our program inference system. We describe some of the results in [7].

__Acknowledgements__

Financial support for this work was given by the G.E.C. Marconi Research Centre at Chelmsford. I thank members of the Artificial Intelligence Group there for assistance in preparing this paper. paper. I also thank my supervisor at Sussex, Rudi Lutz, and other people in the Cognitive Studies Programme for helpful comments.

REFERENCES

[1] M.R.Kennett. Towards Program Synthesis and Debugging. MTR 84/109. 1984. G.E.C. Marconi Research Centre, Chelmsford, U.K.
[2] R.C. Waters. The Programmer's Apprentice: knowledge based program editing. IEEE Trans. Soft. Eng. SE-8,1 pp.1-13. 1982.
[3] C.Rich. Inspection in Programming. TR-604, Artificial Intelligence Laboratory, M.I.T. 1981.
[4] D.Shaw, W.Swartout C.Green. Inferring Lisp programs from example problems. In Proceedings of the fourth International Joint Conference on Artificial Intelligence. IJCAI 1975.
[5] E.Y.Shapiro. Algorithmic Program Debugging. M.I.T. Press 1982.
[6] D.H.D.Warren. Implementing Prolog - Compiling Predicate Logic Programs. D.A.I. Research reports Nos.39,40. University of Edinburgh 1977.
[7] M.M.Huntbach. Program synthesis by inductive inference. European Conference on Artificial Intelligence ECAI 1986.

A Framework for ICAI Systems Based on Inductive Inference and Logic Programming

Kazuhisa KAWAI*, Riichiro MIZOGUCHI**,
Osamu KAKUSHO** and Jun'ichi TOYODA**

*TOYOHASHI University of Technology
Department of Information and Computer Science
1-1, Hibarigaoka, Tenpaku-cho, Toyohashi, Aichi 440 JAPAN

**OSAKA University
The Institute of Scientific and Industrial Research
8-1, Mihogaoka, Ibaraki, Osaka 567 JAPAN

abstract The main components of an Intelligent Computer-Assisted Instruction (ICAI) system are the expertise, the student model and tutoring strategies. The student model manages what the student does and does not understand, and the performance of an ICAI system depends largely on how well the student model approximates the human student. We propose a new framework for ICAI systems which uses the inductive inference for constructing the student model from the student's behavior. In the framework, both the expertise and the student model are represented as Prolog programs, which enables to express the meta-knowledge that is the knowledge of how to use the knowledge. Since the construction of the student model is performed independently of the expertise, the framework is domain-independent. Therefore, an ICAI system for any subject area can be built with the framework. As an example, the ICAI system teaching chemical reaction is presented together with a sample performance. The authors believe that the new framework for ICAI systems based on logic programming and inductive inference could be a breakthrough of the future ICAI systems.

1. Introduction

Since a success of SCHOLAR project [1], AI techniques have been applied in Computer-Assisted Instruction (CAI) systems [2]. These CAI systems are called Intelligent CAI (ICAI) systems. In ICAI systems, the course material and the teaching procedure are implemented separately so that the system can offer the instruction suitable for each student. This paper describes a general framework for ICAI systems based on logic programming [3] and inductive inference [4]. After giving the observation on the disadvantages of the modelling schemes used in the traditional ICAI systems, we propose the model representation which can cope with meta-knowledge and the modelling scheme using the inductive inference. Since the construction of the student model is performed independently of the expertise, the framework is domain-independent. Therefore, an ICAI system for any subject area can be built with the framework. We then present an ICAI system teaching chemical reaction which is built on the framework.

2. Traditional Student Modelling Schemes and their Disadvantages

The main components of an ICAI system are following three modules [2]:

1) Expertise module; this module has the knowledge of the subject matter, and uses it to generate problems, to evaluate student's replies and to reply to questions from the student.

2) Student model module; this module generates the student model which manages what each student does or does not understand, and how he obtains the solution.

3) Tutoring module; according to the student model, this module chooses the next problem or the remedial comment, and instructs them to the expertise module. Also, this module controls overall system behavior.

Figure.1 illustrates the three components and the mutual relations. Since the system performance depends on how closely the student model approximates the student's status, the student model module is considered to be the most important one. In particular, what kind of student's misconceptions the student model can manage determines the educational effect. The student's misconceptions are divided into three categories:

1) A lack of knowledge; a student does not have the specific knowledge of the course material. He, for example, does not know the capital of Brazil.

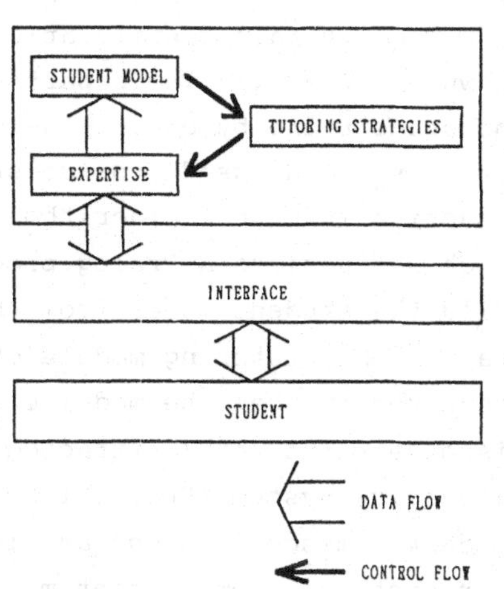

Fig.1 Block diagram of general ICAI systems.

2) The incorrect knowledge; a student has the incorrect knowledge. For example, he believes that the capital of Brazil is Rio de Janeiro.
3) The incorrect use of knowledge; a student has the specific knowledge, nevertheless, he cannot use it or uses it incorrectly.

Most traditional ICAI systems have employed either the overlay or bug approach to modelling. In the overlay approach [5], the student's understanding is represented as a subset of the expertise. In this approach, only one category of misconceptions, a lack of knowledge, can be modelled, and the others, the incorrect knowledge and the incorrect use of knowledge, cannot be done. In the bug approach [6], the student's knowledge is represented as a perturbation of or derivation from the expertise. The bug model has a good representablity and can manage all of three categories of misconceptions. The modelling, however, depends so heavily on the expertise contents that it is difficult to make the modelling process independent of the course material.

We develop a new framework for ICAI systems based on logic programming and inductive inference. In the framework, both the expertise and the student model are represented as Prolog programs so as to represent the knowledge of how to use the knowledge. Furthermore, the student model is constructed by a general inductive inference to model all of three categories of student's misconceptions.

3. The Framework and its Implementation

The overall configuration of the framework for ICAI systems is shown in Fig.2. The expertise module gives problems and comments to the student one by one. The student's responses are evaluated by the expertise and used to construct the student model. Shapiro's inductive inference algorithm called Model Inference System (MIS) [7], which synthesizes a Prolog program from the given facts, is applied to build the student model from the student's behavior. In a modelling stage, the tutoring module chooses the next problem or comment to be presented. When the model construction is completed, the student's misconceptions are extracted from the student model using Program Diagnosis System (PDS) which is also developed by Shapiro [7]. The student's misconceptions are identified as bugs in the Prolog program representing the student model. The identified misconceptions are sent to the tutoring module. The tutoring module chooses the next problem or remedial comment suited for the misconceptions and indicates it to the expertise module.

The framework is quite independent of the subject area. Any specific ICAI system can be built based on the framework with the specific expertise, tutoring strategies and the knowledge for interface.

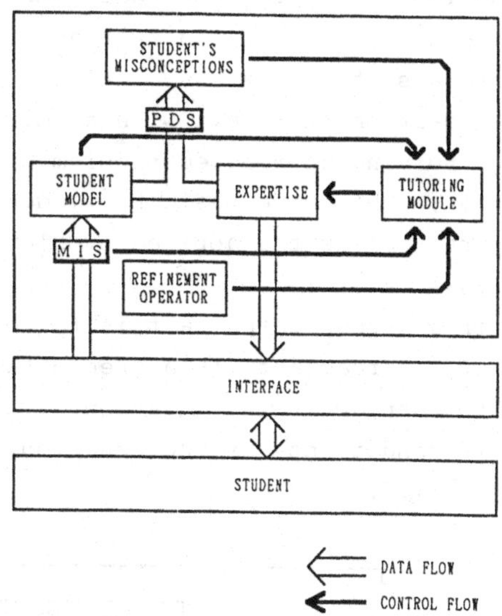

Fig.2 Diagram of the framework for ICAI systems.

3.1 Knowledge Representation Based on Logic Programming

3.1.1 Prolog: A Logic Programming Language

Both the expertise and the student model are not simple data-bases of the course material, but include the procedural knowledge concerning causal or relational reasoning, deduction and problem-solving. A logic-based programming language Prolog has capability to represent both data and procedure as a program. Prolog is also suitable for the inductive inference. Therefore, we employ Prolog for representing the expertise and the student model.

3.1.2 The Use of Meta-Knowledge

Some students can solve the basic problems but cannot solve the applied problems. They have the specific knowledge but cannot use it correctly, i.e. they have the third category of misconceptions, incorrect use of knowledge. In order to model this category of misconceptions, the model (knowledge) representation must be possible to manage the meta-knowledge which is the knowledge of how to use the knowledge. For example, we consider a chemical reaction of an acid and a salt.

(1) soluble salt + acid
    -> precipitated salt + acid

(2) salt with volatile acid + unvolatile acid
    -> salt with unvolatile acid + volatile acid

Each of the above equations represents the basic knowledge.

Equation(1) represents that when a soluble salt reacts with an acid, it forms a precipitated salt and an acid. Equation(2) also represents that a salt with an unvolatile acid and a volatile acid are formed by the reaction of a salt with a volatile acid and an unvolatile acid.

Solving an applied problem of a chemical reaction of an acid and a salt, the above basic knowledge must be used in correct manner. An expert solves the applied problem using the above basic knowledge as follows:

1) if a precipitated salt is formed, then apply the equation(1).

2) if a reactant is a precipitated salt and a product is a soluble salt, then apply the equation(1) in the opposite direction.

3) if conditions of the equation(2) are satisfied, then equation(2) is applied.

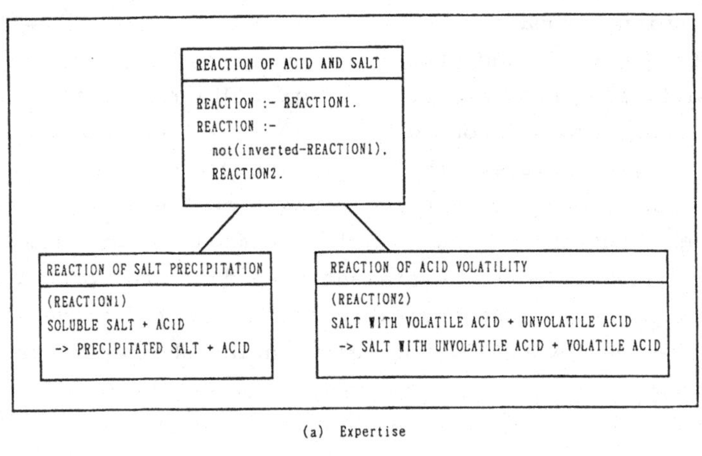

(a) Expertise

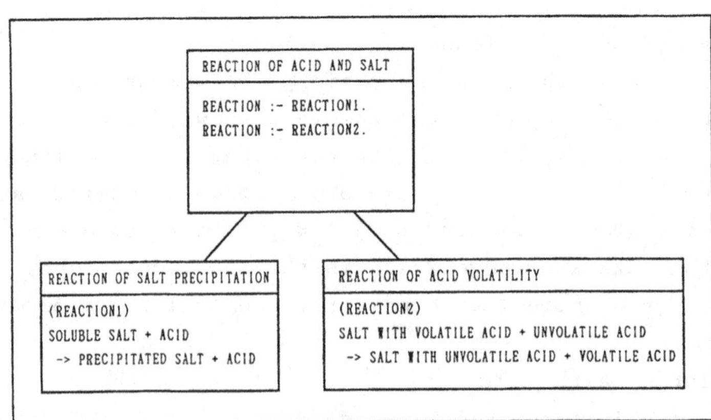

(b) Student model

Fig.3 Schematic representation of knowledge for reaction of acid and salt.

This expertise is the meta-knowledge of the knowledge for chemical reactions of the salt precipitation (equation(1)) and for chemical reactions of the acid volatility (equation(2)).

The framework incorporates a hierarchical structure in the model representation, so that the meta-knowledge is represented in the meta-level world. Figure.3 illustrates the hierarchy of the above example. A meta-level world named reaction of acid and salt represents the meta-knowledge of the basic knowledge that is represented as two worlds named reaction of salt precipitation and reaction of acid volatility. Figure.3-(b) shows the model of a student who cannot solve applied problems. The student's misconception categorized in the incorrect use of knowledge is modelled as the bug in the meta-level world.

The hierarchical structure of the expertise contributes to forming the hierarchy of the expertise that is usually represented as chapters and sections. This hierarchical structure gives the formalism of the expertise a modularity. Moreover, restricting the range of student modelling within one world makes the modelling efficient. The hierarchical structure is implemented by giving each predicate an extra argument indicating the world which includes the predicate.

A teacher can organize course material according to its hierarchical structure, since no restriction on the identification of the hierarchical structure is imposed in the framework. The important point is that the framework has a facility of representing hierarchical material and that a teacher can use it very easily.

3.2 Student Modelling Based on Inductive Inference

The student modelling can be considered as a process of inducing the whole understandings from the student's behavior. Hence, it is possible to model any kind of the student's understandings using a general inductive inference on the model representation language. In this modelling, it is no matter that the student has any kind of misconceptions.

3.2.1 Modelling using MIS

Since the model representation language of the framework is Prolog, a model inference algorithm called MIS can be used as model-constructor. MIS induces the Prolog program which satisfies all of the given facts. In modelling of the framework, facts are obtained from problems and student's replies. The induction process is a repetition of making a hypothesis and verifying it until obtaining a complete program. When MIS generates a clause, MIS gives the oracle, who knows everything on the target program [7], the following three kinds of queries concerned with the clause.

(1) What predicates are used in the body of the clause.

(2) The argument structure of each predicate.

(3) The validity of each predicate.

The refinement operator [7] of MIS generates a new clause as a hypothesis using the oracle replies to these queries. In the framework, the most general refinement operator is employed so as to synthesize all of the program that is indicated by the oracle. A hypothesis for the target program is set up, and then it is verified whether all of the given facts are satisfied by the hypothesized program. If there is an unsatisfied fact, the bug of the hypothesized program is identified by PDS. PDS also gives the oracle a type of queries as follow:

(4) The validity of each goal that is executed.

A clause identified as a bug is removed, and a new hypothesis is set up. In the student modelling the oracle is the student, because he is the one who knows everything about himself. Thus, the oracle queries are raised to the student.

3.2.2 Pedagogical Validity of Student Modelling by MIS

In this section, we describe the modelling using MIS in detail, and show the pedagogical validity of the modelling.

First, we consider the range of the model that can be constructed. The range of the program MIS can synthesize is determined by a refinement operator. Since the most general refinement operator is employed in the framework, every clause indicated by the oracle can be synthesized. Nevertheless, the predicate that is not provided in the system is not useful as the oracle reply for the query(1) described in previous section. For example, let us consider that the system provides only a predicate "precipitated" and that the student use the predicate "deposited" as a reply for the oracle query(1). In this case, MIS constructs the student model that use the predicate "deposited". However, the system does not identify "deposited" with "precipitated". Thus, the clause that has the predicate "deposited" is identified as a bug i.e. a misconception. As this example, MIS can synthesize any clause that is indicated by the oracle, nevertheless, the clause with the predicate not provided in the system is not effective pedagogically. Therefore, MIS synthesizes the program that uses only predicates provided in advance. Although the oracle query(1) does not have to be raised in this synthesizing manner, the system raises it to a student for the modelling efficiency and for the pedagogical effectiveness of the query as described below. This modelling approach has a same representability as the bug approach. Furthermore, this approach can synthesize any clause (a piece of knowledge) that can be obtained the combination of provided predicates, although the bug approach must provide all pieces of knowledge that is used in modelling.

Second, let us consider the efficiency of the modelling. The efficiency of the program synthesis by MIS depends on both the given facts and the refinement operator. The most effective fact is that of the difference between the synthesizing program and the target program. In the student modelling, the target program is the human student understandings. Since the human student understandings are almost same as the expertise, the most effective fact is that of the difference between the constructing student model and the expertise. Therefore, in order to model efficiently, we give the priority to the problem that is answered contrary when it is solved with the expertise and the student model. Although the framework has a general refinement operator, the student modelling can be performed more efficiently using the specific refinement operator. When the domain-specific ICAI system is built with the framework, it is useful to employ the domain-specific refinement operator.

The third problem is the termination of the modelling. Usually it is impossible to determine the exact termination of the student modelling. It is also impossible for a human teacher to do so. In the framework, it is regarded as the termination that the student model is not changed during a certain number of problems. The number is decided by a teacher.

The fourth problem is the pedagogical validity of the oracle queries. Since the query(2) described in previous section must be needed to the transformation of the external form and the internal form, the reply to the query is provided in the system and the query need not be raised to the student. The query(4) is inherently same as the query(3). Thus, we consider the remaining two queries i.e. query(1) and query(3). We demonstrate that they are pedagogically valid using the chemical reaction teaching.

query(1): queried predicates represent the inference process or reason for the concept that is represented as the head predicate of the hypothesized clause. Hence, the query can be transformed to the question about the reason as Fig.4-(A). The query is raised when the predicates are needed, that is, a student uses a new concept and the system models it. Thus, the query is raised exactly after the student uses the new concept.

```
(1) Pb(NH(3))(2) + H(2)CO(3) -> PbCO(3) + 2HNH(3)
!: no.
Tell the reason why you answered 'no'?
!: Pb(NH(3))(2) is not a salt.                      ----- (A)
!: ***

Is PbCO(3) precipitated?
!: yes.                                             ----- (B)
```

Fig.4 Examples of queries set to student.

query(3): this query is about the subconcept of currently teaching concept. Thus, it is a simple basic problem as illustrated in Fig.4-(B).

Finally, we consider the change of student's understandings. In order to synthesize the complete program by MIS, all of the given facts and the oracle replies must be consistent. This means that the student may not change his understandings during modelling. However, it often happens that the student finds his misconceptions and he changes his replies. Therefore, the modelling facility of the framework makes the student indicate his change of understandings. When a student finds his misconceptions, he indicates his change of understandings to the system and then replies the changed answer. The framework removes all of the student's replies related to the indicated change and resumes the modelling with new replies.

3.2.3 Meta-Knowledge Modelling

The student model forms the hierarchy as well as the expertise. Since the construction of the student model is done in bottom up way and the modelling in the worlds which are lower than the current world is already completed, the student model for the lower knowledge can be assumed to have almost the same contents as the expertise. Therefore, we can restrict the range of modelling within one specific world so as to improve the efficiency. If the student has a misconception categorized in incorrect use of knowledge, Prolog program that has a bug corresponding to the misconception is synthesized by MIS.

3.3 Extraction of Misconception by PDS

PDS is an interactive system that can identify bugs in a Prolog program that behaves incorrectly. In extracting misconceptions, the program given to PDS is the student model and the bug identified by PDS is the student's misconception. The oracle is the expertise, so the oracle queries are never raised to the student. The identified bug is either a missing clause or a false clause. These correspond to a lack of knowledge and the incorrect knowledge, respectively. The bug in a program of the meta-level world corresponds to the incorrect use of knowledge. Hence, all of three categories of student's misconceptions described in chap.2 can be extracted using PDS.

3.4 Expertise Module Functions

The expertise module uses the expertise to generate problems, to evaluate student's replies and to reply to questions from the student. Figure.5 illustrates these functions. A part enclosed with bold lines is the domain-specific knowledge.

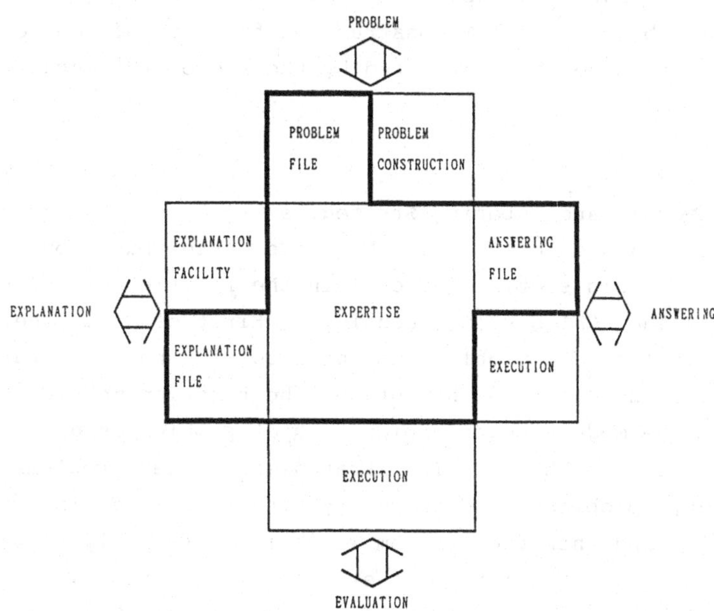

Fig.5 Illustration of expertise module.

The evaluation of a student's reply is performed by executing the Prolog goal that represents the pair of the problem and the student's reply.

There are two types of questions from students, called "yes/no" and "what/how". "Is AgCl a precipitated salt?" is an example of the "yes/no" question. This type of questions is transformed into a Prolog goal and the goal is executed. If the execution succeeds, the module answers "Yes, it is". If not, the module answers "No, it isn't". "What is the precipitation?" is an example of the "what/how" question. This type of questions is answered by displaying the contents of the file for answering.

The expertise of the framework is articulate, that is, the expertise can solve the problem in the same manner as the expert does [2]. Hence, the simple explanation by the expertise is useful and understandable to students. In addition to this explanation facility, the expertise module can display the contents of the file for explanation. The file is provided for each Prolog clause of the expertise.

The problems for students are classified into two categories. First of them is the problem that is provided by the teacher as the file. This category of problems is displayed as well as the explanation and answering. Second one of problems is of the problems that are made by the problem-construction facility of the expertise module. The problem is constructed by the Prolog retrieval in the expertise.

3.5 Tutoring Module and Tutoring Strategies

The tutoring module controls the whole system based on tutoring strategies. In this section, we explain the function of the tutoring module along the ICAI system execution. First of all, the system gives explanations and problems to the student and constructs the student model using MIS. In this stage, the tutoring module instructs to the expertise module which explanation or problem is given to the student according to the tutoring strategies. When problems are set to a student, problems are solved by both the expertise and the student model, and then the problem which is differently answered is given to the student prior to other problems. This is aimed at efficient modelling and at finding misconceptions by the student himself. When the student modelling reaches a certain extent and the model is not changed during a certain number of problems, the student modelling is regarded to terminate and then the student's misconceptions are extracted by PDS. The tutoring module receives the extracted misconceptions and instructs to the expertise module that the remedial problems are given to the student. In the current framework, the only one tutoring strategy for retraining is incorporated. The strategy is that the problems which expect to be answered incorrectly because of the student's misconception are given to the student in order to find his misconception by himself. The more general tutoring strategies for retraining require further investigation.

3.6 Man-Machine Interface

The interface module mutually transforms an internal form and an external form that is suitable to the students. Although the natural language interface is the most favourite one and has been studied by many researchers [2,5,8], many complicated problems still remain unsolved. In the framework, the interface module only performs the transformation between a Prolog form and a simple sentence (natural language). For example,

precipitated(Ag,Cl) <=> AgCl is precipitated.
precipitated(Ag,Cl) <=> AgCl is deposited.
precipitated(Ag,Cl) <=> AgCl is settled.

The dictionary for these transformations is provided as Prolog clauses and it is changeable for each ICAI system.

4. Chemical Reaction Tutor: A Specific System Built on The Framework

We build a chemical reaction tutor on the framework with the domain-specific knowledge. The tutor teaches a chemical reaction of an acid and a salt. The expertise of the tutor is formalized with eight worlds as illustrated in Fig.6. The most top level world named reaction of acid and salt consists of the meta-knowledge for the two lower level worlds as described in section 3.1.2. The rest five worlds are constructed based on the course material hierarchy. Figure.7 is an example of teaching the meta-knowledge in the world named reaction of acid and salt. A part of the expertise is shown in Fig.8. The sequence of problems from (1) to (6) is for the modelling. After replying to the problem (6), the constructed model that is a correponding part of Fig.8 is shown in Fig.9. The first, second and third arguments of a predicate in the expertise and the student model represent, respectively, the flag for the distinction of the expertise and the student model, the name of the world where the predicate is

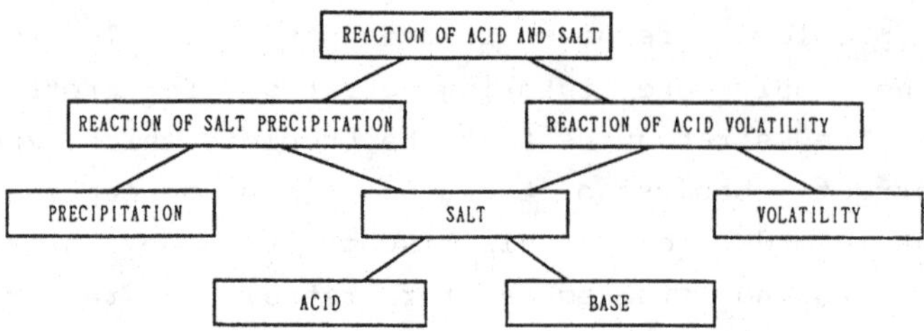

Fig.6 Diagram of knowledge hierarchy.

```
Are the following chemical reaction equations correct or not?
If correct, answer 'yes.' If not, answer 'no.'
(1) K(2)CO(3) + H(2)SO(4) -> K(2)SO(4) + H(2)CO(3)
|: yes.
Tell the reason why you answered 'yes'?
|: K(2)SO(4) is not precipitated.
|: H(2)CO(3) is a volatile acid.
|: ***
(2) Na(2)SO(4) + 2HCl -> 2NaCl + H(2)SO(4)
|: no.
(3) Pb(NO(3))(2) + 2HCl -> PbCl(2) + 2HNO(3)
|: yes.
(4) BaCO(3) + 2HCl -> BaCl(2) + H(2)CO(3)
|: no.
(5) Ag(2)SO(4) + 2HCl -> 2AgCl + H(2)SO(4)
|: yes.
(6) 2AgCl + H(2)SO(4) -> Ag(2)SO(4) + 2HCl
|: yes.
(7) PbCl(2) + H(2)SO(4) -> PbSO(4) + 2HCl
|: yes.
(8) CuCl(2) + H(2)SO(4) -> CuSO(4) + 2HCl
|: '**'.
|: no.
Tell the reason why you answered 'no'?
|: CuCl(2) is precipitated.
|: Inverted reaction takes place.
|: ***
(9) Ag(2)CO(3) + H(2)SO(4) -> Ag(2)SO(4) + H(2)CO(3)
|: no.
```

Fig.7 Example of a training.

```
rule(i_model,'ROAS',1,X,Y,Z) :-
        rule1(i_model,'ROSP',_,X,Y,Z).
rule(i_model,'ROAS',2,X,Y,Z) :-
        not_rule1(i_model,'ROAS',_,X,Z,Y),
        rule2(i_model,'ROAV',_,X,Y,Z).
not_rule1(i_model,'ROAS',3,X,Y,Z) :-
        not(rule1(i_model,'ROSP',_,X,Y,Z)).

rule1(i_model,'ROSP',1,X,Y,Z) :-
        salt(i_model,'SALT',_,X,Y),
        precipitated(i_model,'PRECIPITATION',_,X,Z).

rule2(i_model,'ROAV',1,X,Y,Z) :-
        salt(i_model,'SALT',_,X,Y),
        volatiled(i_model,'VOLATILITY',_,Y),
        unvolatiled(i_model,'VOLATILITY',_,Z).
```

Fig.8 Contents of expertise.

```
rule(s_model,'ROAS',1,X,Y,Z) :-
        rule1(s_model,'ROSP',_,X,Y,Z).
rule(s_model,'ROAS',2,X,Y,Z) :-
        rule2(s_model,'ROAV',_,X,Y,Z).

rule1(s_model,'ROSP',1,X,Y,Z) :-
        salt(s_model,'SALT',_,X,Y),
        precipitated(s_model,'PRECIPITATION',_,X,Z).

rule2(s_model,'ROAV',1,X,Y,Z) :-
        salt(s_model,'SALT',_,X,Y),
        volatiled(s_model,'VOLATILITY',_,Y),
        unvolatiled(s_model,'VOLATILITY',_,Z).
```

Fig.9 Constructed student model.

included and the index to the file for explanation. Predicates "rule", "rule1" and "rule2" represent the knowledge in the top three level worlds. The forth, fifth and sixth arguments of them characterized as "X", "Y" and "Z" mean the following chemical reaction.

$$XY + H_nZ \rightarrow XZ + H_nY$$

In the above equation, "XY" is the reactant salt, "H_nZ" is the reactant acid, "XZ" is the product salt and "H_nY" is the product acid. The student does not consider the use of the inverted reaction as described in section 3.1.2, and then he makes a wrong answer to the problem (6). The tutor constructs the student model which has an incorrect meta-knowledge as shown in Fig.9. Based on this misconception, the tutor gives the remedial problems from (7) to (9) that must use the correct meta-knowledge concerned to the inverted reaction. The student finds his misconception, indicates the change of his understanding to the tutor (replying '**' to problem (8)), and then he makes the correct answer. The tutor removes the answers to the problem (6) and (7), and reconstructs the student model with the answers to the problem from (1) to (5) and (8) and (9). The constructed model is equivalent to the expertise.

5. Conclusions

We have presented a new framework for ICAI systems with a powerful student modelling scheme. The framework is implemented on the super mini-computer MV/8000II. The implementation language is MV-Prolog. The framework is summarized as follows:

1) Model representation in logic program.
2) Student modelling based on inductive inference.
3) Domain-independence.

The effectiveness of modelling the student's misconceptions in the domain-independent way is demonstrated by the teaching example of the chemical tutor in chap.4. Further, the Prolog tutor with the framework has been implemented [9] so that the domain-independence of the framework is confirmed. The framework will be extended as a general tool for ICAI system building. The problems for this extension are generalizing the tutoring strategies mentioned in section 3.5, fulfilling the interface facilities and developing the utilities for the teachers.

References

[1] Carbonell,J.R.: AI in CAI: An artificial intelligence approach to computer-aided instruction, IEEE Trans. Man-Mach. Syst., Vol.MMS-11, No.4, pp.190-202 (1970).

[2] Barr,A. and Feigenbaum,E.A.: The Handbook of Artificial Intelligence, Vol.II, PITMAN, London, pp.225-235 (1983).

[3] Clocksin,W.F. and Mellish,C.S.: Programming in Prolog, Springer-Verlag, New York (1981).

[4] Angluin,D. and Smith,C.H: Inductive Inference: Theory and Methods, ACM Comput. Surv., Vol.15, No.3, pp.237-269 (1983).

[5] Clancey,W.J.: Tutoring rules for guiding a case method dialogue, in Sleeman,D. et al. (ed.), Intelligent Tutoring Systems, Academic Press, London, pp.201-225 (1982).

[6] Brown,J.S. and Burton,R.R.: Diagnostic models for procedural bugs in basic mathematical skills, Cognitive Science 2, pp.155-192 (1978).

[7] Shapiro,E.Y.: Algorithmic Program Debugging, MIT Press, London (1982).

[8] Sleeman,D. and Hendley,R.J.: ACE: A system which Analyses Complex Explanations, in Sleeman,D. et al. (ed.), Intelligent Tutoring Systems, Academic Press, London, pp.99-118 (1982).

[9] Ganke,M. et al.: An ICAI System for Prolog Programming Based on Inductive Inference, Proc. of 28th National Conference of Information Processing Society of Japan, 1G-1, Tokyo, [in Japanese] (1984).

RATIONAL DEBUGGING IN LOGIC PROGRAMMING

Luís Moniz Pereira
Universidade Nova de Lisboa, Portugal

Abstract

A debugger for Prolog has been developed which automates the reasoning ability required to pinpoint errors, resorting to the user only to ask about the intended program semantics, and making cooperative use of the declarative and the operational semantics. The algorithm is expressed in detail, a session protocol exhibited, comparison to other work made, but the implementation is not examined, nor the treatment of Prolog's extra-logical features. This is an abridged version of [Pereira 86].

Introduction

The debugging of logic programs is amenable to a general content independent approach. It can be envisaged as a precise rational activity, whose purpose is to identify inconsistent or incomplete logic program statements, by systematically contrasting actual with intended program behaviour. A program can be thought of as a theory whose logical consequences engender its actual input/output behaviour, whereas the program's intended input/output behaviour is postulated by the theory's purported models, i.e. the truths the theory supposedly accounts for. The object of the debugging exercise is to pinpoint erroneous or missing axioms, from erroneous or missing derived truths, so as to account for each discrepancy between a theory and its models.

I have developed a Prolog debugger, which relies on information about each term's dependency on the set of previous derivation steps. The approach could be adopted for logic programming, theorem proving, and distributed systems in general. It contrasts theory and model, questioning the user about the intended program model. The types of question are if goals are admissible (have correct argument types), solvable or unsolvable (have some true instance or not), if solved goals are true or false, and whether a set of solutions to a goal is complete. The user is not required to produce solutions to goals nor to know the operational semantics of Prolog. All answers are stored and repetition of same or subsumed questions avoided.

Rationality requires that the debugging steps should not only be sufficient but necessary as well. The present approach contends that the dynamic information regarding term dependency on derivation nodes, provides a basis for a practical method of automated rational debugging. It uses such information to track down wrong solutions, and to delimit the search to identify goals with missing solutions. The information is generated by a modified unification algorithm It is also used to provoke direct backtracking to a specific node in a derivation with the purpose of examining it for bugs. The ability to jump back over subderivations irrelevant to failures avoids unnecessary questioning. Predicates may be stated correct, but those incorrectly stated so can be detected.

The Modified Unification Algorithm that Keeps Track of Dependencies

For a full treatment consult [Bruynooghe Pereira 84, Pereira Porto 82]. A deduction tree is a skeletal proof tree, i.e. a proof tree with all the substitutions completely ignored. Each deduction tree is an extension of a previous one, provided by a modified unification algorithm. To obtain the wanted behaviour we associate a deduction tree with each term involved in unification. With a call, which is a term, we associate the nodes necessary for the existence of that call, i.e. those on the path from the root to the call (including the call). With the head of an applied clause, also a term, we associate the empty deduction tree (the clause is given). As a result of the unification algorithm below, each substitution has an associated deduction tree, which is the minimal one necessary for obtaining that substitution. When the unification algorithm consults a substitution component, it requires the existence of the associated deduction tree. The formal presentation of the algorithm follows, where t-T denotes a term t with associated deduction tree T.

1. matching t-T1 with t-T2 generate 'empty' (the empty substitution) with deduction tree $T1 \cup T2$(information important to the debugger; a bug could be the t's should differ).
2. matching f(t1,...,tm)-T1 with g(t1,...,tn)-T2 generate 'failure' with $T1 \cup T2$ as an inconsistent deduction tree (information important to guide backtracking).
3. matching f(t1,...,tn)-T1 with f(r1,...,rn)-T2 (with n>0 and some $ti \neq ri$) match, for each i, ti-T1 with ri-T2.
4. matching x1-T1 with t2-T2 where t2 is not a free variable, and a substitution component x1<-t exists with associated deduction tree T, match t-$T1 \cup T$ with t2-T2.
5. matching x1-T1 with t2-T2 with x1 a free variable, generate the substitution component x1<-t2 with $T1 \cup T2$ as deduction tree.

The Rational Debugging Algorithm and Its Rationale

Two basic algorithm modes are used: one for tracking down wrong solutions, the other to account for missing solutions to derivations that terminate. For the failure to terminate case, we have no improvement over depth-bound checking.

(A) Wrong Solution Mode: The basic idea is to thread back through a derivation tree, by successively following a wrong term's dependencies, until at some node a clause instance is found whose premises are all true but whose conclusion is false, and produces or passes back the wrong term.

A1. A goal known to have a wrong solution is presented to the debugger. It solves it and asks you whether the solution found is wrong. If not wrong,it then produces the next solution and queries you again, until a wrong solution is obtained.

A2. A wrong solution has been found and you point, with the cursor, at some wrong term.

A3. The debugger then uses the set of dependencies of the wrong term to thread back through the execution tree to the most recent one.

A4. At the (next) most recent dependency node, the debugger queries you whether the goal at that node is admissible.

A5=A4.no. If the goal is not admissible, the debugger asks you to point at some wrong term within it and continues at A3 with the new term, unless the term is textual in the goal, in which case a bug has been found.

A6=A4.yes. If the goal is admissible, the debugger then matches the goal with the head of the clause used at that node in the derivation, and queries whether the resulting literal is solvable. If the clause body is empty it asks instead whether the literal is true.

A7=A6.no. You answer "no" to the matched head literal being solvable or true. (cf. A9 for the A6.yes case). First note that the goal did solve. So at least one of the following holds: the clause head is wrong because it produced a wrong binding, or because it should not have matched the goal; some body goal should have failed but didn't, or some goal that would fail is missing.

The debugger first inquires about the clause head by asking you to point at a wrong term in the literal, so it can detect whether it was passed by the goal on to and accepted by the clause, or is textually present in the clause head. Next, it inquires about the clause body.

A8.1. If the body is empty, then a wrong unit clause has been found, and an error according to your previous answer (i.e. whether the term was textually present).

A8.2. If the body is not empty, the debugger next asks you whether each of the solved subgoal instances (except for the built-in's) is i) inadmissible t) true or f) false. Note that the t) and f) questions assume universal quantification over any variables.
case i) It requests you point at a wrong term. If it's textual a bug is found, otherwise it reverts to wrong solution mode at step A3, with the new term.
case t) If all solved clause body goals are true, then the clause is wrong because it has produced a false conclusion from true premises. The debugger reports an error according to what term you pointed at in the matched clause head literal, at step A7.
case f) As the goal has solved, it starts debugging it at step A1.

A9=A6.yes. You answer "yes" to the matched head literal being solvable or true. If you were asked whether the matched clause head was true, continue at A4 (note the question implies universal quantification). Otherwise, if the body is not empty, you were asked if the matched clause head was solvable (note the question implies existencial quantification).

The wrong term being tracked down might not be a variable, or alternatively, it is a variable, and then an overgeneral solution is being produced. In either case, the clause invocation and execution are not blameable for producing the wrong term. Note that it cannot have been produced by the clause body. If it were so, any node producing it would have already been examined and detected before, since the wrong term's dependencies are visited in reverse time order.

Though the matched head literal is solvable, a wrong solution may be being produced by the clause. So you are asked if the solved clause head is true. If yes goto A4. If no, then to detect whether any of the body goals should have failed so that the wrong conclusion would not follow, you are queried about each of them in turn, as in A8.2.

(B) Missing Solution Mode: The basic idea is that for a goal to have a missing solution, i.e. to finitely fail to produce it, it is necessary that in the attempt at least one goal that failed should not done so. The problem is to find one such "uncovered" failing goal for which there is no "uncovered" subgoal beneath (which could be making it fail).

The user knows if a goal should fail, but we don't want to prompt him about each failing goal. i.e. we need to distinguish relevant from irrelevant failures. A failure is irrelevant if there is some ancestor of the goal that solves when enough backtracking is allowed. Too low an ancestor may not give backtracking enough chances. It is also irrelevant if some ancestor is unsolvable. Furthermore, if we find some solvable ancestor that doesn't solve, we can lower the ceiling on the bug, for we have found a goal with a missing solution lower than the original one. Thus, from that point of view, the lower the ancestor the better.

Given a failing goal, what the algorithm does, basically, is to identify an appropriate ancestor (using an heuristic below) about which it tries to obtain an answer to the above cases. Only if the failing goal is not found to be irrelevant is the user queried about it. Whilst looking for a missing solution, a wrong solution may be found You can then revert to wrong mode on that goal.

B1. A solution is missing for a finitely failed goal presented to the debugger. It then attempts to find solutions to the goal until you state the missing solution would be next.

B2. The debbuger attempts to find the next solution, aware that one failed goal should not have failed. The top goal is the current lowest unsolving ancestor.

B3. When a failed goal is detected, the failure may be legitimate or unjustified.

B4=B3.legitimate. (B3.unjustified is dealt with in case "s" of B8.2)
If legitimate, it cannot be the cause of a missing solution. Rather than asking you immediately which is the case, the debugger attempts to find some ancestor of the failed goal that solves. Which is appropriate ? It picks the most recent ancestor, below the currently known lowest unsolving ancestor goal, that is above all the non-ancestor dependency nodes of the failed goal, so as to give opportunity for backtracking to take place to those nodes and eventually solve the failed goal. Another possibility is that, on backtracking, some alternative is found that makes the goal failure irrelevant (if the chosen ancestor does solve), by avoiding it altogether. If there is no such ancestor continue at B8.

B5. The appropriate ancestor may be known unsolving though it should solve. If so, goto B8. If not, it considers if it has backtracked over it to the failing goal or not.

B6=B5.no. If not, it tries solving the ancestor (calling an interpreter) and goes to B7.

B6=B5.yes. If so, it finds out whether the ancestor has a next solution. It calls on the interpreter to find if there are N+1 solutions to the ancestor,where N is the number of times backtracking to it tooks place. Goto B7.

B7.1. If the ancestor solves, debugger is switched off and it backtracks from the failed goal until the ancestor solves, whence it returns to missing mode at B3.

B7.2. If the ancestor does not solve, then it queries you whether this failure is legitimate or not. It asks if the ancestor goal is i) inadmissible u) unsolvable or s) solvable.

case i) Point at a wrong term and it reverts to wrong mode at A3, with the new term.
case u) Failure of the ancestor was expected ; it switches off debugging and backtracks from the failed goal until the ancestor is reached, where it returns to missing mode at B4.
case s) The ancestor becomes the currently known lowest unsolving one; goto B8.

B8. The failed goal is reconsidered, and a failure analysis takes place :

B8.1. There are no matching clauses for the goal. A bug is found.

B8.2. There are matching clauses, but the goal fails without ever producing a solution. (cf. B8.3 otherwise.) It inquires if the goal is i) inadmissible u) unsolvable or s) solvable.

case i) You point at a wrong term and it reverts to wrong mode at A3.
case u) Failure is justified ; it continues execution backtracking from the goal.
case s) The bug is that no matching clause solves its body. All the failures in the execution of any matching clause are legitimate, for otherwise they would have been detected previously, since they must have occured and been considered before the present one. The goal is reported having a missing solution.

B8.3. The goal had solved before, and fails after backtracking to where it was activated. The debugger inquires whether the goal is i) inadmissible u) unsolvable or s) solvable.

case i) Same as in B8.2.
case u) It solved before, so the solution is wrong ; debugging of goal begins.
case s) Though it solved before, not all intended solutions may have been produced; the debugger calls an interpreter to compute all produceable ones and asks if it is a correct and complete set. You indicate if some solution is m) missing w) wrong or n) neither.
case m)A goal was detected with a solution missing whose descendents have no missing solutions, otherwise they would have unjustifiedly failed before and been reported.
case w) Wrong mode can be entered to debug the goal.
case n) The failure is legitimate and backtracking ensues ; debugging proceeds at step B4.

Comparison to Other Work

Similar work is algorithmic debugging [Shapiro 82,83, Fernand 85, Av-Ron 84]. [Lloyd 86] adapts it to MU-Prolog. The following contrast rational (R) and algorithmic (A) debugging :

(A1) The discourse level is that of literals (R1) The level is finer, that of terms (A2) Asks unnecessary questions not ignoring irrelevant subderivations (R2) Follows term dependencies to jump over irrelevant subderivations (A3) Requires user to supply correct and complete sets of argument instances (R3) Requires user to recognise a wrong term, or incomplete sets of solutions, but not to produce them (A4) It cannot switch from missing mode for a goal to wrong mode for another (Incidently, that's why the user must input all correct ground instances in its missing solution algorithm, so as to guarantee satisfiable goals are correctly solved) (R4) Switches from one mode to another (Cf. B7.2, B8.2, B8.3 above) (A5) Does not use knowledge about Prolog's operational semantics, except that it's top-down (R5) Uses both semantics, as the rationale above shows.

In short, (R) converges faster on bugs than (A) with less user effort. The difference becomes bigger with larger programs.

Rational Debugger Protocols

Now we show the quicksort example with 6 bugs of [Shapiro 82]. Comments on the right refer to the the steps in the algorithm, or regard questions unasked, subsumed by a previous answer.

```
qsort([X|L],LO) :- partition(L,X,L1,L2)              % qsort([],[]).
                   qsort(L1,L3), qsort(L2,L4),       % is missing
```

```
                      append([X|L3],L4,L0).          % should be
                                                     % append(L3,[X|L4],L0
    partition([X|L],Y,L1,[X|L2]) :- partition(L,Y,L1,L2)   % X>Y is missing
    partition([X|L],Y,[X|L1],L2) :- Y=<X,                  % should be X=<Y
                                    partition(L,Y,L1,L2)
    partition([],X,[],[]).

    append([X|L1],L2,[X|L3]) :- append(L1,L2,L2).   % should be
                                                    % append(L1,L2,L3)
    append([],L,[]).                                % should be
                                                    % append([],L,L)
?- fails qsort([2,1],P).                          % steps B1, B2, B3
missing solution next ? y                         % qsort([],L3) failed
                                  % steps B4, B8: no appropriate ancestor
qsort([],X)                                       % step B8.1
This goal is  i) inadmissible  u) unsolvable  s) solvable, choose one: s

No matching clause causes a missing solution to qsort([],L3) called in
        qsort([X|L],L0) :- partition(L,X,L1,L2),
                           qsort(L1,L3), qsort(L2,L4), append([X|L3],L4,L0)
        % here  qsort([],[]).  is added to the program

?- fails qsort([2,1],P).            % debugging continues; steps B1, B2, B3
missing solution next ? y           % append([],[1|X],[1|X]) failed
                                    % steps B4, B5, B6, B7, B7.2
append([2],[1|X1],X2)               % this is the ancestor
This goal is:  i) inadmissible  u) unsolvable  s) solvable, choose one: s

append([],[1|X],[1|X])              % steps B8, B8.1
This goal is:  i) inadmissible  u) unsolvable  s) solvable, choose one: s

No matching clause causes a missing solution to append([],[1|X1],[1|X1])
called in append([X|L1],L2,[X|L3]) :- append(L1,L2,L2).
        % here the second clause of append is changed to  append([],L,L).

?- wrong qsort([2,1],P).                          % debugging continues

qsort([2,1],[2|X])  top goal solution ok ? n                 %  steps A1, A2
                 ^  use arrow to point at a wrong term.
 % append([2],[1|X1],X2)  admissible goal? y  subsumed above; steps A3, A4

append([2],[1|X1],[2|X2])  solvable goal ? y                 % step
append([2],[1|X1],[2|X2])  true ? n                          % step A9
                        ^  use arrow to point at a wrong term.
append([],[1|X],[1|X])  i) t) or f) ? t                      % step A8.2
```

```
Error in clause   append([X|L1],L2,[X|L3]) :- append(L1,L2,L2).
in unsufficiently constrained variable present in the head.
        % here the first clause for append is replaced by
        % append([X|L1],L2,[X|L3]) :- append(L1,L2,L3).

?- wrong qsort([2,1],P).                              % debugging continues

qsort([2,1],[2,1])  top goal solution ok ? n                 % steps A1, A2
              ^     use arrow to point at a wrong term.
append([2],[1],X)   admissible goal ? y                      % steps A3, A4
append([2],[1],[2|X])  solvable goal ? y                     % step A6
append([2],[1],[2,1])  true ? y                              % step A9
partition([],2,X1,X2)  admissible goal ? y                   % step A4
partition([],2,[],[])  true ? y                              % steps A6, A9
partition([1],2,X1,X2)  admissible goal ? y                  % step A4
partition([1],2,X1,[1|X2])  solvable goal ? n                % steps A6, A7
                    ^      use arrow to point at a wrong term.

 % partition([],2,[],[])  i) t) or f) ? t  subsumed above; steps A8, A8.2

Error in clause partition([X|L],Y,L1,[X|L2]) :- partition(L,Y,L1,L2). in
misused variable occurring in the head; or goal missing in body.
        % here the first clause for partition is replaced by
        % partition([X|L],Y,L1,[X|L2]) :- X>Y, partition(L,Y,L1,L2).

?- fails qsort([2,1],P).               % debugging continues; steps B1, B2, B3
missing solution next ? y              % partition([1],2,L1,L2) failed
                                       % steps B4, B8: no appropriate ancestor
partition([1],2,X1,X2)                 % step B8.2
This goal is  i) inadmissible  u) unsolvable  s) solvable, choose one: s

The clauses for it legitimately fail, so there is a missing solution to the
goal partition([1],2,L1,L2)   activated in clause
        qsort([X|L],L0) :- partition(L,X,L1,L2), qsort(L1,L3), qsort(L2,L4)
                           append([X|L3],L4,L0).
        % here the second clause for partition is replaced by
        % partition([X|L],Y,[X|L1],L2) :- X=<Y, partition(L,Y,L1,L2).

?- wrong qsort([2,1],P).                  % debugging continues

 % qsort([2,1],[2,1])  top goal solution ok ? n        % steps A1, A2
 %                ^     use arrow to point at a wrong term; subsumed above

append([2,1],[],X)  admissible goal ? y                      % steps A3, A4
append([2,1],[],[2|X])  solvable goal ? y                    % step A6
append([2,1],[],[2,1])  true ? y                             % steps A9, A4
```

```
 % partition([],2,X1,X2)  admissible goal? y  subsumed above; step A6
 % partition([],2,[],[])  true? y             subsumed above; steps A9, A4
 % partition([1],2,X1,X2) admissible goal? y  subsumed above; step A6

partition([1],2,[1|X1],X2) solvable goal? y                % steps A3, A4
partition([1],2,[1],[])  true ? y                          % steps A9, A4

qsort([2,1],X)  admissible goal ? y                        % step A6
qsort([2,1],X)  solvable goal? y                           % step A9
 % partition([1],2,[1],[])  true ? y  subsumed above; step A8.2

qsort([1],[1])  true ? y                                   % step A8.2
qsort([],[])  true ? y                                     % step A8.2

append([1],[],[1])  true ? y                               % step A8.2

Error in clause   qsort([X|L],LO) :- partition(L,X,L1,L2), qsort(L1,L3),
                                     qsort(L2,L4), append([X|L3],L4,LO).
in wrongly constrained variable present in the head.

    % here the first clause for qsort is changed to
    % qsort([X|L],LO) :- partition(L,X,L1,L2),  qsort(L1,L3), qsort(L2,L4),
    %                    append(L3,[X|L4],LO).

?- qsort([2,1],P).
P = [1,2] ;
no              % debugging of this goal is complete; truth at last!
```

Acknowledgements

Thanks are due to S. Abreu, I. Bratko, P. Cox, L. Monteiro, R. Nasr, M. Poe and K. Puder. To JNICT, INIC, MIE in Portugal, DEC, APPLE, ESPRIT and other contracts.

References

[Lloyd 86] Lloyd, J. Declarative error diagnosis, Research report, Melbourne Univ.

[Bruynooghe Pereira 84] Bruynooghe, M.; Pereira, L.M. Deduction revision through intelligent backtracking in "Issues in Prolog Implementation" (J.Campbell ed.), Ellis Horwood

[Ferrand 85] Ferrand, G. Error diagnosis in logic programming, an adaptation of E.Y.Shapiro method, Rapport de Recherche 375, INRIA, Rocquencourt, 78153 Le Chesnay, France

[Av-Ron 84] Av-Ron, E. Top-down diagnosis of Prolog programs, Weizmanm Institute

[Pereira Porto 82] Pereira, L.M. ; Porto, A. Selective backtracking in "Logic Programming" (K.Clark, S.Tarnlund eds.), Academic Press 1982

[Pereira 86] Pereira, L.M., Rational debugging in logic programming, Research report, Univ. Nova de Lisboa

[Shapiro 82] Shapiro, E. Algorithmic program debugging in "Proc. of 9th annual ACM Symp. on Principles of Programming Languages"

[Shapiro 83] Shapiro, E. "Algorithmic Debugging" M.I.T. Press 1983

Using definite clauses and integrity constraints as the basis for a theory formation approach to diagnostic reasoning

Randy Goebel†
Koichi Furukawa‡
David Poole†

†Logic Programming and AI Group
Department of Computer Science
University of Waterloo
Waterloo, CANADA N2L 3G1

‡First Research Laboratory
Inst. for New Generation Computer Technology
21F, Mita Kokusai Bldg, Minato-ku
Tokyo, 108 JAPAN

Abstract

If one desires that an automatic theory formation program detect inconsistency in a set of hypotheses, the Horn clause logic of Prolog is unsuitable as no contradiction is derivable. Full first order logic provides a suitably expressive alternative, but then requires a full first order theorem-prover as the basic theory construction mechanism. Here we present an alternative for augmenting definite clauses with the power to express potentially inconsistent scientific theories. The alternative is based on a partitioning of definite clauses into two categories: ordinary assertions, and integrity constraints. This classification provides the basis for a simple theory formation program. We here describe such a theory formation system based on Prolog, and show how it provides an interesting reformulation of rule-based diagnosis systems like MYCIN.

1. Introduction

In general, the automatic formation of scientific theories seems to require formalization in a language in which it is possible to derive the negation of a formula [Poole86b]. This is because we are interested in systems that deduce contradictions to reject inconsistent theories, rather than those that reject theories by being told of an inconsistency with respect to a complete description of the intended interpretation. The latter view of theory formation is appropriate when considering the problem of synthesising logic programs from example facts [Shapiro82]. The former, however, requires that the system detect inconsistent theories syntactically, if possible, and maintain a consistent theory of a partial description of the intended interpretation.

Horn clause logic, in particular the definite clause subset comprising Prolog assertions, is not capable of expressing that some formula f is not true. Furthermore, Prolog's proof procedure is incapable of deriving that negation of a formula, except by negation-as-failure [Clark78].

As a representation language for expressing formulas from which theories can be formed, Prolog's definite clauses are unsuitable, as every set of definite clauses is consistent. Poole et al. [Poole86b] have demonstrated a program called Theorist that shows how first order logic can provide the foundation for defining a system for automated theory formation. That program uses full first order logic, and requires a full first order theorem-prover as the basic reasoning mechanism (cf. [Umrigar85]).

Here we present an alternative for augmenting definite clauses with the power to express potentially inconsistent scientific theories. Our motivation is to investigate the problem solving power of a system that is simpler than Theorist, but that uses the same idea of deduction-based theory formation. The alternative is an extension to the definite clause assertion language of Prolog, and is based on a partitioning of definite clauses into two categories: ordinary assertions, and integrity constraints. This classification provides the basis for the development of a simple theory formation program based on Prolog.

In section 2 we summarize the method for defining a theory formation program in terms of a representation and reasoning system based on first order logic. Section 3 describes a partitioning of definite clause knowledge bases that creates a distinction between tacit and necessary assertions. The concept of necessary assertion is based on the integrity constraints used in logic data bases (e.g., [Kohli83, Miyachi84, Goebel85a, Goebel85b) These necessary assertions provide the basis for accepting some collections of formulas as consistent and rejecting others as inconsistent. This, in turn, provides the necessary expressive power to specify a theory formation program like Theorist, but based on a simpler deductive mechanism. This version of Theorist is called *Theorist-S*. In section 4, Theorist-S is used to specify a simple rule-based diagnosis system. A comparison with MYCIN shows how MYCIN's rules can be viewed as Theorist-S assertions. While other versions of Prolog in MYCIN have already been described (e.g., [Hammond82]), our explanation differs in that we demonstrate how the rules of MYCIN incorporate both object and meta level logical assertions, and that the separation of these kinds of information is useful in developing new diagnosis systems based on theory formation. In addition, we show how the separated object and meta level MYCIN rule knowledge can be automatically reconstructed by using the partial evaluation technique of Takeuchi et al. [Takeuchi85]

Finally, we suggest a method for dealing with a limited form of "certainty factor," based on an objective measure that records the numbers of tacit and necessary facts used to explain the observations. We conclude with a list of ways in which this work should be further pursued.

2. Using deduction to build scientific theories

Our definition of "scientific theory" derives from Poole et al. [Poole86b], which is based on Popper's logic of scientific discovery [Popper58]. Like Theorist, the framework of Theorist-S consists of the basic components shown in fig. 1.

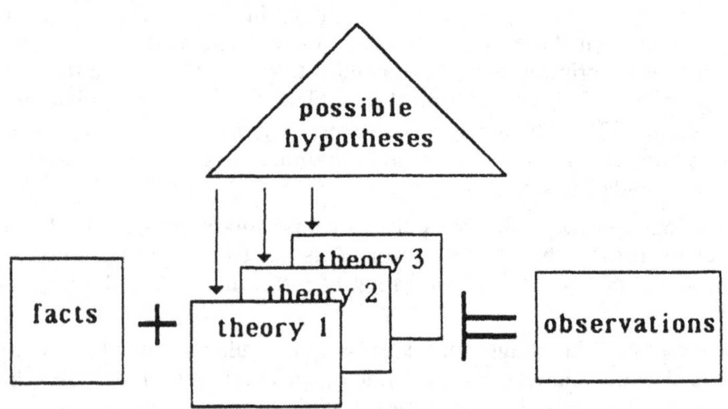

Figure 1 Framework of Theorist and Theorist-S

The knowledge of the system is represented as a set of formulas of a logical language, say L, which is divided into four categories. The *facts* are a set of formulas of L that have the user's intended problem domain as a model. The *possible hypotheses* are a set of formulas of L, instances of which may be required to augment the facts in order to explain the *observations* — another set of formulas of L representing domain observations for which an explanation is desired. The relation $\vdash$ denotes the provability relation for the logic of language L. A *scientific theory* T (e.g., $T1$, $T2$, $T3$ in fig. 1) is an *explanation* for a set of observations O if and only if $\forall t \in T$, t is an instance of h, where $h \in$ possible hypotheses, and

$$T \bigcup Facts \vdash O \tag{1}$$

$$\forall t \in T, T \bigcup Facts \nvdash \neg t. \tag{2}$$

Intuitively, T is a set of consistent hypotheses that, together with the facts, support the deduction of the observations.

As has been elsewhere suggested (e.g., [Meltzer73]), Theorist uses deduction to *attempt* to show the consistency of a set of formulas augmented with unverified hypotheses. If this consistency is established and the set of formulas can be shown to derive the observations, that set of consistent hypotheses is called a theory that explains the observations.

The word "attempt" is most important here, for if the language L has as least the expressive power of first order predicate language with dyadic predicate symbols then the relationship described by formula (2) cannot, in general, be effectively determined. Furthermore, the proof procedure denoted by the symbol E must be complete so that, in cases when the relationship is determined, one can conclude the consistency of the hypothesis in question. Note that appealing to an oracle with complete knowledge of the intended interpretation does not make theory formation decidable. For example, without heuristic control, Shapiro's *model inference system* is undecidable because it has a step requiring the proof of an arbitrary formula [Shapiro81, Shapiro82].

These theoretical difficulties not withstanding, Poole et al. argue that the Theorist framework should be considered as a unifying framework for various reasoning paradigms used in artificial intelligence research. For example, default reasoning and diagnostic reasoning can be simply reformulated in the Theorist framework [Poole86a]. The potential value of Theorist is based on identifying classes of theories which can be effectively formed, and which can be applied to interesting problem domains. For example, Reiter speculates that most diagnosis problems are propositional hence the consistency computation is effective.†

Note that Theorist does not suggest any particular method for selecting hypotheses to augment the current facts or suggest any method for dynamically inducing relevant hypotheses. However, is does provide a logic programming system in which various strategies for automatic theory formation can be investigated and developed.

3. Falsifiability and the expressive power of L

A final qualification on the expressive power of L must be made, in order that theories being formed are *falsifiable*. This requirement is based on Popper's thesis that a scientific theory must not only be consistent, but must be potentially falsifiable, in order to be able to distinguish between all subsequent observations that might be made (e.g., see [Popper58], pps. 91-92). In the Theorist program of Poole et al., the property of falsifiability is viewed as the ability to deduce the negation of observed facts, e.g., an observation o will falsify a theory $T \bigcup Facts$ if $T \bigcup Facts \vdash \neg o$. The necessary expressive power is obtained by choosing L as a full first order predicate language, in which case the proof procedure named as $\vdash$ is a complete first order predicate calculus theorem-prover.

† personal communication

The prototype implementation of Theorist reported in [Poole86b] chose L to be the full clausal form of the first order predicate calculus language, and implements $\vdash$ in Prolog, according to Loveland's MESON procedure [Umrigar85, Loveland78] Our simplified version of Theorist, called Theorist-S, is strictly weaker than Theorist, but does not require the implementation of a full clausal theorem-prover for $\vdash$. In addition, the representation language L of Theorist-S is based on a simple extension of definite clauses, rather than the full clausal form of first order predicate calculus.

4. Definite clauses as integrity constraints

If we select the definite clause subset of the first order predicate logic as our representation language L of Theorist-S, we face an immediate problem. Every set of definite clauses is consistent, and therefore any hypothesis in the form of a new definite clause can be added to an existing clause set without affecting that set's consistency. In fact, with L chosen as the set of definite clauses, the initial facts F can be merely augmented with the observations O to create a consistent theory $F \bigcup O$ that explains those observations.

Required here is some method for denying "theory membership" to certain hypotheses. In other words we require some extension to L, together with the related semantic and proof theoretic extensions, that allows one to express a fact that may be inconsistent with a number of potential hypotheses. Here the notion of *integrity constraint* is appropriate, especially as used by Miyachi et al [Miyachi84]. and Goebel [Goebel85a, Goebel85b]. These authors extend the usual definition of a definite clause database by classifying certain clauses as integrity constraints, and then using those constraints to verify the consistency of new assertions at database update time. This use of constraints is similar to that of Kohli and Minker who show how integrity constraints can be dynamically used to prune the search space of an SLD proof procedure [Kohli83].

This notion of integrity constraint is particularly attractive because it is so simple. First, a subset of database clauses is syntactically distinguished as integrity constraints. For example, since it is common to write definite clauses in the form

$$\langle consequent \rangle \subset \langle antecedent \rangle \tag{3}$$

we might distinguish constraints by writing them as

$$\langle antecedent \rangle \supset \langle consequent \rangle . \tag{4}$$

Though the logical semantics of schemata (3) and (4) are identical we can use the syntactic distinction to identify formulas of the form (4) as assertability conditions as new assertions. In other words, given a database KB and a new assertion α, all consequents of formulas of the form (4) whose antecedents unify with α define a conjunction whose derivability determines α's assertability. For example, one could not assert "$has(Ohki, cold)$" if the constraint "$\forall x \ has(x, cold) \supset has(x, sneezing)$" was asserted and "$has(Ohki, sneezing)$" was not derivable in the current KB.

In the theory formation framework, integrity constraints such as these provide a simple method for denying theory membership to a hypothesis. The consistency of a theory will be constrained by the user's specification of integrity constraints.

5. Diagnosis as theory formation

The problem of diagnosing malfunctions in a complex system can be viewed as a special case of automatic theory formation (e.g., [Pople77, Brown82, Genesereth85]). For example, the medical diagnosis problem can be formulated as the problem of determining which of a number of possible diseases "best" account for a set of observed symptoms. In terms of theory formation, the facts comprise statements that represent relationships between diseases and their symptoms, and possible hypotheses include all those diseases that are acceptable as explanations for a given set of symptoms.

5.1. A simple diagnosis system based on Theorist-S

The facts of Theorist-S are specified as a collection of simple formulas of the form

<disease>$\supset$*<symptoms>*.

In the diagnosis system described here, relationships between diseases and symptoms are further classified as "tacit" or "necessary" in order to distinguish symptoms which may appear and those which must appear. These necessary relationships are treated as the integrity constraints which constrain the admissible hypotheses. For example, the formulas of fig. 2 represent naive knowledge about the symptoms of several common afflictions.

---

1. ∀x has(x, cold) ⊃ has(x, sneezing)
2. ∀x has(x, cold) ⊃ has(x, coughing)
3. ∀x has(x, cold) ⊃ has(x, runny-nose)*

4. ∀x has(x, hayfever) ⊃ has(x, runny-nose)
5. ∀x has(x, hayfever) ⊃ has(x, sneezing)
6. ∀x has(x, hayfever) ⊃ has(x, watery-eyes)*

7. ∀x has(x, influenza) ⊃ has(x, diarrheoa)
8. ∀x has(x, influenza) ⊃ has(x, headache)
9. ∀x has(x, influenza) ⊃ has(x, fever)*

10. ∀x has(x, cold)
11. ∀x has(x, hayfever)
12. ∀x has(x, influenza)

Figure 2 Theorist-S naive diagnosis knowledge base

The asterisks distinguish integrity constraints, which are facts that describe "necessary" symptoms of the disease. Note that necessary symptoms are *not* pathognomonic (cf. [Pople77]) because they are not sufficient conditions for diagnosing the affliction in question. Intuitively, the facts of fig. 2 assert that you *may* cough if you have a cold, but that you will certainly have a runny-nose.

Note that tacit and necessary assertions are distinguished in that assertions with an asterisk *always* imply their consequences while the tacit assertions do not. One possible interpretation is that the meaning of "⊃" is modified by "*"; intuitively, the computational interpretation is that "*" assertions must be verified while others need not be. This distinction can be used, for example, as a heuristic to distinguish preferred theories. Another view is that only the "*" assertions are facts, and that all others are default assumptions. This view, which combines defaults and diagnosis, is elaborated elsewhere [Poole86a].

Hypotheses are written as universally quantified statements, for example as in formulas 10, 11 and 12 of fig. 2. Instances of the these hypotheses will be used to form an explanation of some observed symptoms, for example with $x = Fred$, the hypothesis instance *has*(*Fred*,*hayfever*) might explain Fred's watery-eyes and runny-nose.

The algorithm for computing an explanation of the observed symptoms is based on Prolog's depth-first backtracking algorithm for SLD resolution [Lloyd84]. In general, one views the facts and hypotheses as a pure Prolog program and the list of observed symptoms as the query to be derived. For example, Theorist-S will explain Ohki's runny nose and sneezing if the facts and possible hypotheses in fig. 2 are viewed as a pure Prolog program and we pose the query

$$?has(Ohki, runny-nose) \wedge has(Ohki, sneezing) \quad (5)$$

When an instance of a possible hypothesis is used in a branch of the SLD proof tree for the goal (5), that instance is recorded as part of the explanation for the observed symptoms. An explanation for a set of symptoms is the union of the instances of possible hypotheses that where used in an SLD derivation of the symptoms. This strategy is the same one suggested by Shapiro [Shapiro82, p. 160], and used by Finger and Genesereth's RESIDUE system [Finger85] For example, fig. 3 is a diagram of the SLD proof tree for the goal (5), using the facts and possible hypotheses given in fig. 2.

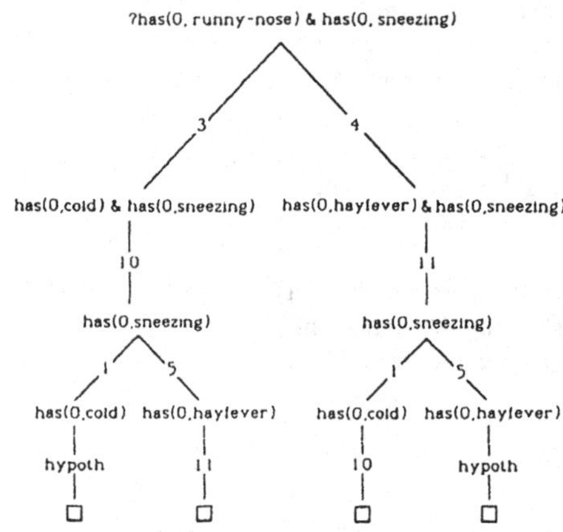

Figure 3 SLD proof tree for Theorist-S diagnosis

We can extract the four possible theories or explanations from the complete SLD tree; there is one for each successful SLD branch:

I: {has(Ohki, cold)}
II: {has(Ohki, cold), has(Ohki, hay-fever)}
III: {has(Ohki, hay-fever), has(Ohki, cold)}
IV: {has(Ohki, hay-fever)}

Each of the above explanations, together with the facts, support the derivation of the observed symptoms. However, we have not yet tested the consistency of the explanations. In Theorist-S the constraints (indicated by * in fig. 2) specify those symptoms that must be present in order to consistently assume the possible hypothesis. For example, the assertion

$$\forall x \; has(x, cold) \supset has(x, runny-nose)^*$$

declares that $has(\alpha, cold)$ and $\neg has(\alpha, runny-nose)$ are incompatible for any individual α. In other words, the possible hypothesis $has(\alpha, cold)$ is acceptable only if it can be verified that $has(\alpha, runny-nose)$.

In the current Theorist-S prototype, new instances of possible hypotheses are verified as consistent as they arise in the SLD proof tree. For example, when the possible hypothesis instance $has(Ohki, hay-fever)$ is first considered at the point labeled (*) in fig. 3, all relevant constraints are accumulated using the algorithm specified by Miyachi et al. and Goebel. The only relevant constraint here is given by assertion (6) in fig. 2, which requires that the observation $has(Ohki, water-eyes)$ be verified. If the needed observation is not contained in the original list of observations, Theorist-S consults the user by interactively asking the question "Does Ohki have watery eyes?" If the response is "yes," the hypothesis instance is verified, and the SLD derivation continues. If the response is anything other than "yes," Theorist-S assumes the answer is "no" and rejects the hypothesis instance as inconsistent with the observations. Note that the answer "unknown" is not possible – Theorist-S assumes that the user can either answer the question or perform some experiment that will decide what the answer is. As noted by others (e.g., [Shapiro81), this interaction corresponds to conducting an experiment.

For the example query (5) above, this hypothesis verification technique would reject explanations I, II, and IV, assuming that the user answered "no" to the question about Ohki's watery eyes. Therefore the explanation that Ohki has a cold is the only explanation.

It is important to realize that this incremental verification of hypothesis consistency is, in general, inadequate. As the incremental approach is inherently sequential, it is sensitive to the order in which observations are explained. For example, consider the following example knowledge base:

1. A^*
2. B^*
3. $A \supset \neg B$

If we attempt to explain $A \wedge B$, we first assume A using 1, and since there are no axioms to disprove A, we conclude it is consistent. Then, while assuming A, we are further to required to assume B using 2. However, in this case, the previous assumption A allows the consistency test $? \neg B$ to succeed, which contradicts our assumption of B and prevents us from constructing a consistent explanation. However, an explanation of $B \wedge A$ is possible: the initial assumption of B using 2 is consistent and there is no clause whose head matches A, so we conclude the second necessary assumption is consistent as well. This gives the theory A, B as explanation, which is inconsistent. In Theorist proper [Poole86b], the first order clausal theorem prover has avaliable the contrapositive forms of all clauses. Its proof procedure can use the contrapositive of 3 in order to verify the inconsistency at the first opportunity, i.e., when A is first assumed.

5.2. Expert rules versus medical knowledge

On the surface, the knowledge encoded in rule-based expert systems like MYCIN appear to be wrong way around, i.e., they have the form

$$symptoms \supset disease \tag{6}$$

while Theorist and Theorist-S rules have the form

$$disease \supset symptoms \tag{7}$$

However, the knowledge *embedded* in MYCIN rules have the form of schema (7), as can be seen by viewing schema (6) as a *meta rule* that says "if you observe *symptoms*, then you should consider the hypothesis *disease*." This meta language expression embeds rules of the form (7) into a control framework that simplifies the description and implementation of the MYCIN production rule interpreter, at the expense of complicating the expression of knowledge about the relationship between diseases and symptoms.

The view that MYCIN combines meta and object level knowledge in its rules is further supported by noting that MYCIN is claimed to be a backward reasoning system [Buchanan84, p. 71ff.] — in fact the rule interpreter for MYCIN does *backward reasoning* on rules of the form given in schema (6), which amounts to forward reasoning on rules of the form given in schema (7).

The advantage of expressing rules in the form suggested by schema (7), is that there is *no a priori* requirement for any "expert" level control knowledge to be combined with the basic statement of relationships amongst symptoms and diseases. The theory formation procedure works on the object level knowledge expressed in the natural way (i.e., diseases causes symptoms). This has the following consequences. First, this rule form completely decouples expert experience about how to use rules, and the rules themselves. Expert knowledge like "if symptom A is observed then disease B is likely" is now viewed as a meta language assertion about the usefulness (or, in some cases, statistical appropriateness) of the object level rule (cf. [Bowen85]).

This detachment of meta and object level knowledge provides for the expression of general as well as specific meta level reasoning strategies. As Sterling suggests [Sterling84], the meta level is the appropriate level for specifying problem solving strategies. In fact, the rules of MYCIN are really *ground facts* of the logical meta language; the general predicates of the meta level axiomatization of Theorist provide an example of the concepts that should be used to express meta level knowledge or problem-solving strategies, e.g., the concepts of *fact*, *hypothesis*, *explanation*, *constraint*, and *consistent*.

Second, the meta and object decoupling means that general purpose interpreters like Theorist-S are potentially less efficient than an equivalent MYCIN-like interpreter and rule knowledge base combination. In fact the Theorist-S system uses Prolog to interpret the definition of Theorist-S, which then interprets the object level assertions of a Theorist-S application. This disadvantage, however, obviates the need for different kinds of rules (cf. MYCIN's antecedent rule [Buchanan84]). For example, Theorist-S's facts and constraints are syntactically identical — they are distinguished by the problem-solving strategy specified at the meta level.

5.3. Using partial evaluation to combine methods and knowledge

The potential inefficiency of the multi-level interpretation of Theorist-S (and all systems with similar structure) can be addressed in at least two ways. One is to construct an efficient meta level interpreter directly in a procedural language. This amounts to compilation of the meta level problem-solving strategy, which makes that strategy more efficient but more difficult to understand and modify. Since this alternative negates one of the claimed advantages of the decoupling of meta and object level knowledge, an attractive alternative for improving efficiency is partial compilation, or *partial evaluation* [Kahn84, Takeuchi85]. This technique retains most of the advantages of the meta/object decoupling, while increasing efficiency for instances of meta interpreter and object knowledge base pairs.

Returning to the claimed difference between rules of the form (6) and (7), given above, partial evaluation shows the difference to be negligible. For example, consider the MYCIN rule of fig. 4.

```
PREMISE: ($AND
      (SAME CNTXT GRAM GRAMNEG)
      (SAME CNTXT MORPH ROD)
      (SAME CNTXT AIR ANAEROBIC))
ACTION: (CONCLUDE CNTXT IDENTITY BACTEROIDES TALLY .6)
```

Figure 4 An example MYCIN rule

This rule asserts that if you have the observations about gramstain, morphology and metabolism, then you can conclude that the identity of the organism is bacteriodes. Ignoring the certainty facts for the moment, we can express the information in the MYCIN rule of fig. 4 as

$$\forall x \; identity(x, bacteriodes) \supset gramstain(x, negative) \wedge morphology(x, rod) \wedge metabolism(x, anaerobic) \tag{8}$$

which asserts the relationship between the malfunction and symptoms in the form suggested by the schema (6) above. The enclosing "premise/action" directive can be viewed as a more general problem-solving strategy at the meta level, e.g.,

$$\forall identity, symptoms \;\; establish(identity) \subset fact(identity \supset symptoms) \; verify(symptoms). \tag{9}$$

In fact, Takeuchi and Furukawa's partial evaluation algorithm will take an appropriate form of (8) and (9) and use a program transformation technique to produce the rule

$$establish(identity(x, bacteriodes)) \subset verify(gramstain(x, negative) \wedge morphology(x, rod) \wedge metabolism(x, anaerobic))$$

which has the same form as the original MYCIN rule of fig. 4.

5.4. Preferring one diagnosis over another

We earlier noted that the '*' annotation on formulas of fig. 2 have at least two possible interpretations, both of which alter their interpretation as formulas of the first order predicate calculus. One possible interpretation retains the view of all rules as Theorist-S *facts*, and interprets unmarked formulas as those having a lower probability than those carrying the '*' annotation. The apparent discrepancy between generalizations which are always true and those which are sometimes true is then explained by associating a probability value less than one to unmarked formulas. This results in a logic programming system whose formal properties can be specified in a way similar to Shapiro's logic programming with uncertainties [Shapiro83]. Furthermore, the choice of a function or functions for determining probabilistic entailment can be based on Nilsson's description of probabilistic logic [Nilsson84].

Another possible interpretation of the '*' annotation treats only the marked formulas as *facts* and the unmarked formulas as default assumptions. The assumptions are viewed as default assertions, any instance of which may be used as an axiom so long as it is consistent with the current set of observations. For example, under this interpretation rule (1) of fig. 2 asserts that "one who has a cold can be assumed to have sneezing, as long as that is consistent with the facts and observations." In other words, by treating unmarked formulas as defaults, the universal generalization normally entailed by a classical first order interpretation is not required. The formal foundation of this default interpretation is already exploited in Theorist proper [Poole86b], and is similar to the interpretation of defaults described in the Residue system of Finger and Genesereth [Finger85].

Both of these interpretations provide the rudiments of a procedure for preferring one diagnosis over another. For example, consider the possible diagnoses of the observations

$$has(O, fever) \wedge has(O, runny-nose) \wedge has(O, cold)$$

All of the necessary symptoms are observed for the known afflictions so that all of $has(O, influenza)$, $has(O, hayfever)$ and $has(O, cold)$ are possible diagnoses. If we confirm the absence of the sneezing, coughing, headache and diarrheoa we would intuitively prefer the hayfever diagnosis over the others on the basis of volume of evidence. In probabilistic terms, we want the negative affect of the confirmed absence of relevant symptoms to make the probability of runny-nose and watery-eyes to exceed that of the other two entailed symptoms. Similarly for the default interpretation, where the number of inconsistent default symptoms negatively impacts the "quality" of the hypothesized diagnoses of cold and influenza.

6. Conclusions

In general, automatic theory formation of the form suggested by the Theorist system requires that the representation language be able to express potential contradictions. The SLD proof procedure of Prolog is defined only for a language in which no contradiction is expressible, but a suitable interpretation of integrity constraints provides a simple notion of potential contradiction. Theorist-S is a very simple theory formation system that distinguishes from tacit symptoms to provide a way of denying theory membership to some possible hypotheses.

Diagnosis systems based on Theorist-S offer a potential advantage in that the relationship between diseases and symptoms can be expressed in a natural way independent of any qualifications that indicate how that information should be used. The simple annotation that provides a binary classification of symptoms can be exploited with a very simple proof mechanism based on SLD resolution. Furthermore, at least two possible interpretations of the classification both provide the necessary semantics for preferring one theory over another in an intuitively plausible way.

There are many problems that remain to be investigated, however. There are know difficulties with any system that uses a resolution proof procedure on clausal form, e.g., the problem of reverse Skolemization when attempting to establish consistency, and consistency verification requires a complete proof procedure whose inefficiencies have been explicitly avoided in the standard Prolog implementation of SLD resolution. Furthermore, it is not yet clear how to generalize either the probabilistic or default interpretation in a way that provides an effective and efficient method of preferring one diagnosis over another.

Despite these major difficulties, the simplicity of the theory formation procedure warrants further investigation as it so easily captures the intuition behind the diagnostic process.

Acknowledgements

Romas Aleliunas and Maarten van Emden suggested numerous improvements to an earlier draft of this paper. We are grateful to the referees for pointing us to some relevent work we had overlooked. This research was supported by National Sciences and Engineering Research Council of Canada grant A0894.

References

[Bowen85] K.A Bowen and T. Weinberg (1985), A meta-level extension of Prolog, *IEEE 1985 Symposium on Logic Programming*, July 15-18, Boston, Massachusetts, 48-53.

[Brown82] J.S. Brown, R.R. Burton, and J. de Kleer (1982), Pedagogical, natural language and knowledge engineering techniques in SOPHIE I, II and III, *Intelligent Tutoring Systems*, J.S. Brown (eds.), Academic Press, New York,

227-282.

[Buchanan84] B.G. Buchanan and E.H. Shortliffe (1984, eds.), *Rule-Based Expert Systems The MYCIN Experiments of the Stanford Heuristic Programming Project*, Addison-Wesley, Reading, Massachusetts.

[Clark78] K.L. Clark (1978), Negation as failure, *Logic and Data Bases*, H. Gallaire and J. Minker (eds.), Plenum Press, New York, 293-322.

[Finger85] J.J. Finger and M.R. Genesereth (1985), Residue: a deductive approach to design synthesis, STAN-CS-85-1035, Computer Science Department, Stanford University, Stanford, California, January.

[Genesereth85] M.R. Genesereth (1985), The use of design descriptions in automated diagnosis, *Qualitative Reasoning about Physical Systems*, D.G. Bobrow (eds.), MIT Press, Cambridge, Massachusetts, 411-436.

[Goebel85a] R.G. Goebel (1985), DLOG: an experimental PROLOG-based database management system, *Proceedings of the IFIP Working Conference on Data Bases in the Humanities and Social Sciences*, R.F. Allen (ed.), Paradigm Press, New York, 293-306.

[Goebel85b] R.G. Goebel (1985), A logic-based data model for the machine representation of knowledge, Ph.D. dissertation, Computer Science Department, The University of British Columbia, Vancouver, British Columbia, October, 253 pages.

[Hammond82] P. Hammond (1982), Logic programming for expert systems, DOC 82/4, Department of Computing, Imperial College of Science and Technology, University of London, March.

[Kahn84] K.M. Kahn and M. Carlsson (1984), The compilation of Prolog programs without the use of a Prolog compiler, *Proceedings of the International Conference on Fifth Generation Computer Systems*, November 6-9, Tokyo, Japan, 348-355.

[Kohli83] M. Kohli and J. Minker (1983), Intelligent control using integrity constraints, *Proceedings of the National Conference on Artificial Intelligence (AAAI-83)*, August 22-26, University of Maryland/George Washington University, Washinton, D.C., 202-205.

[Lloyd84] J.W. Lloyd (1984), *Foundations of logic programming*, Springer-Verlag, New York.

[Loveland78] D.W. Loveland (1978), *Automated theorem proving: a logical basis*, North-Holland, Amsterdam, The Netherlands.

[Meltzer73] B. Meltzer (1973), The programming of deduction and induction, *Artificial and Human Thinking*, A. Elithorn and D. Jones (eds.), Jossey-Bass, London, England, 19-33.

[Miyachi84] T. Miyachi, S. Kunifuji, H. Kitakami, K. Furukawa, A. Takeuchi, and H. Yokota (1984), A knowledge assimiliation method for logic databases, *Proceedings of the IEEE International Symposium on Logic Programming*, February 6-9, Atlantic City, New Jersey, 118-125.

[Nilsson84] N.J. Nilsson (1984), Probabilistic logic, Technical Note 321, Artificial Intelligence Center, SRI International, Menlo Park, California, February.

[Poole86a] D.L. Poole (1986), Default reasoning and diagnosis as theory formation, Technical Report CS-86-08, Department of Computer Science, University of Waterloo, Waterloo, Ontario, March.

[Poole86b] D.L. Poole, R.G. Goebel, and R. Aleliunas (1986), Theorist: a logical reasoning system for defaults and diagnosis, *Knowledge Representation*, N.J. Cercone and G. McCalla (eds.), Springer-Verlag, New York [invited chapter, submitted September 10, 1985].

[Pople77] H.E. Pople (1977), The formation of composite hypotheses in diagnostic problem solving: an exercise in synthetic reasoning, *Proceedings of the Fifth International Joint Conference on Artificial Intelligence*, August 22-25, Cambridge, Massachusetts, 1030-1037.

[Popper58] K.R. Popper (1958), *The Logic of Scientific Discovery*, Harper & Row, New York.

[Shapiro83] E. Shapiro (1983), Logic programs with uncertainties: a tool for implementing rule-based systems, *Proceedings of IJCAI-83*, August 8-12, Karlsruhe, Germany, 529-532.

[Shapiro81] E.Y. Shapiro (1981), An algorithm that infers theories from facts, *Proceedings of the Seventh International Joint Conference on Artificial Intelligence*, August 24-28, The University of British Columbia, Vancouver, British Columbia, 446-451.

[Shapiro82] E. Y. Shapiro (1982), *Algorithmic program debugging*, MIT Press, Cambridge, Massachusetts.

[Sterling84] L. Sterling (1984), Logical levels of problem solving, *Proceedings of the Second International Logic Programming Conference*, July 2-6, Uppsala University, Uppsala, Sweden, 231-242.

[Takeuchi85] A. Takeuchi and Koichi Furukawa (1985), Partial evaluation of Prolog programs and its application to meta programming, Technical report TR-126, Institute for New Generation Computer Technology, Tokyo, Japan, September [to appear in *Lecture Notes in Computer Science*, Springer].

[Umrigar85] Z.D. Umrigar and V. Pitchumani (1985), An experiment in programming with full first-order logic, *IEEE 1985 Symposium on Logic Programming*, July 15-18, Boston, Massachusetts, 40-47.

Some Issues and Trends in the Semantics of Logic Programming

J. Jaffar, J-L. Lassez, M.J. Maher

IBM T.J. Watson Research Center,
Yorktown Heights,
NY 10598,
USA

A major problem facing the designers of programming languages is the conflict between expressive power (or "high-levelness") and efficiency of execution. In the conventional approach expressive power has been consistently sacrificed in an ad hoc manner to efficiency and often has been confused with the accumulation of "useful" features. This has resulted in the design of intricate languages such as ADA. Both Backus and Hoare in their Turing award addresses have been highly critical of this approach. The hope that the complexity of such languages could be mastered by using the sophisticated theoretical tools of denotational semantics has not been fulfilled.

Logic-based programming languages, on the other hand, have the great advantage that formal tools such as models and resolution used to capture their semantic properties do so in a simple and natural manner.

In the first part we will review the main semantic properties of definite clauses, which form a theoretical basis for the study of PROLOG. These are model theoretic semantics, least fixedpoint semantics, finite failure and negation as failure. We will mention forthcoming results and discuss some remaining open problems. We assume some familiarity with the literature, and refer the reader to Lloyd's account [25] for the basic results and terminology. In a second part we consider extensions to definite clause logic programs. Our concern is to characterize extensions which still possess the unique semantic properties that are discussed in the first part. These properties do not depend on the Herbrand universe and standard unification, but on their abstract relationship. Any domain and unification theory which satisfy this relationship can be used without incurring any loss in semantic properties. This approach is then substantially extended by allowing constraints over user-oriented domains. This results in a formalism which brings the theory of logic programming closer to standard programming practice.

Definite clause logic programs.

In 1879 Frege invented a system of symbolic representation, manipulation and computation of "pure thought" which he called BEGRIFFSSCHRIFT. This system is better known in English under the name of Predicate Calculus. The two relevant aspects of Predicate logic are model theory and proof theory: model theory corresponds to specification and declarative notions, proof theory corresponds to operational semantics and implementations. In other words model theory is used to formalize "what" we want to be computed and proof theory is used to formalize "how" to compute it.

The meaning we give to a program, *as a logic formula*, is the set of logical consequences, that is the set of formulas which are true in every model of the program. The meaning we give to a program, *as a program*, (rather than as as a logic formula) is the set of formulas which are true in all models of the program which use an intended domain and an intended interpretation of the predicate and function symbols. The fact that logical consequence does not depend on the interpretation given to the various symbols allows the intended interpretation to be factored out and the computation can be safely performed in a purely symbolic context.

The best known example is within clausal form predicate logic, and devised by Robinson. Using unification and resolution to manipulate the symbols of the Herbrand universe and the Herbrand base, the logical consequences of a program can be symbolically computed in a sound and complete manner. When the computation finds that A is true in all Herbrand (that is symbolic) models it follows that A is true in all models and a fortiori in the model intended by the person who wrote the program. It should be noted here that this very strong property might be more than what we require. The Skolem-Lowenheim theorem shows that we can find an arbitrary number of arbitrarily complex models for our program. To know that A will also be true in models which are artificial, arbitrary and altogether irrelevant to our problem, is neither required nor useful. This prompts the idea of the algebraic approach, which we will mention later, in which a single domain is considered, in contrast with the logic approach which allows a multiplicity of domains.

However speeds of execution that are expected of programming languages have not been achieved in the general framework of clausal form. The restriction to definite clauses, which leads to a drastic loss in expressive power, has nevertheless distinct advantages: computationally, the combination of definite clauses and the specialization of Kowalski and Kuehner's SL resolution [18] to definite clauses (called LUSH resolution by Hill [11] and SLD resolution by Apt and van Emden [1]), is sufficiently efficient to form a basis for the implementation of a programming language; logically, SLD resolution is sound and complete for atomic logical consequences; and definite clauses retain the ability to represent all computable functions as shown by Tarnlund [40], Sebelik and Stepanek [37]. We will review now some key semantic properties of definite clause logic programs.

Model theoretic semantics

As we observed above, we can restrict our attention to Herbrand models. For brevity, throughout this section we will simply say "model" when referring to Herbrand models and we will assume that A is a ground atom. For A to be a logical consequence means that A belongs to all models. In general the intersection of models is not a model so no model can be selected as fully representative of the notion of logical consequence. However, in the case of definite clauses, the intersection of all models is a model, as pointed out by Van Emden and Kowalski [7]. Consequently the notion of ground atomic logical consequence can be captured by a single model, namely the intersection of all models, which is the least one.

However one must be careful when using this least model approach: although the assignment of true to an atom A corresponds to A being a logical consequence, the assignment of false never corresponds to ¬A being a logical consequence. The approach makes sense only in conjunction with the closed world assumption, where all ground atoms not in the least model are assumed to be false. But this implies incompleteness: some atoms will lead to infinite computations and the interpreter will not be able to determine their truth value.

An alternative approach, has been proposed by Lassez and Maher [23] whereby an atom is assigned true (false) if and only if it is true (false) in all models. Otherwise there is not enough information in the program to assign a truth value to an atom, it will be true in some models and false in others. This ambiguity is reflected by the assignment of an undefined truth value to the atom. Consequently we can have completeness, as atoms which lead to infinite computations are assigned the value undefined. This approach has been pursued recently by Fitting [9] and is based on work of Manna and Shamir [28, 29, 30], Kripke [20] and old ideas of Herbrand, Godel and Buchi [2]. Together with Mycroft [31] we believe that the notion of undefined should be part of any declarative or operational semantics of programming languages, whether based on logic or not.

Fixedpoint semantics

As narrated by Lassez, Nguyen and Sonenberg [24] there is a fair amount of confusion concerning fixedpoint semantics in the literature. Fortunately in the case of logic programs the situation is very clear and simple. Consider the informal semantics of a program, "You have facts and you have rules. Apply the rules to the facts to generate new facts. Repeat this operation until you cannot generate new facts." This amounts to define a set inductively. If a function represents the application of the rules to transform a old set of facts into a new set of facts, we have a fixedpoint when the new set of facts is equal to the preceding set of facts. The fixedpoint constructed that way happens to be the least.

This is a very general phenomenon, but the choice of the least fixedpoint is, from a declarative point of view, somewhat arbitrary or inadequate, as argued in previously mentioned references [28, 29, 30]. The fact that we have a least fixedpoint simply means that we have abstracted a computational process, by itself it does not provide a strongly motivated declarative semantics. The fixedpoint which, according to Manna and Shamir, is the most "natural" is called the optimal fixedpoint and is, in general, not equal to the least one. One advantage of logic programs over conventional programs is that the least fixedpoint is equal to the least model, as shown by Van Emden and Kowalski [7], therefore it is associated to logical consequence and has a meaningful declarative interpretation.

In the context of three valued logic, that is when undefined is assigned to literals which are not logical consequences, the situation is even more striking. Lassez and Maher [23] have shown that the notions of models and fixedpoints coincide. Models are used to give semantics to logic formulas, fixedpoints are used to give semantics to recursive definitions. As a program can be viewed both as a logic formula and as a recursive definition, it is more satisfactory to have the two notions of model and fixedpoint coincide, rather than having the equality only in the case of least elements. Now we still have that the least model captures the notion of logical consequence and is the right choice to give a declarative semantics based on logic. Furthermore it is equal to the optimal fixedpoint which is the right choice to give a declarative semantics to a recursive definition. As models and fixedpoints coincide, the optimal fixedpoint is equal to the least fixedpoint. There is no need to argue over which fixedpoint semantics is more desirable.

Further fixedpoint semantics have been given by Lassez and Maher [21, 22] where definite clauses are viewed as a production system. Here again the notions of fixedpoint and model coincide. This view also allows the establishment of a relationship between the semantics of the rules and the semantics of the program, in other words it provides an elementary denotational semantics. This semantics was used to study the decomposition of a program into an equivalent collection of subprograms which can be run independently. It is also suitable for the study of the dual problem of composition of modules to form whole programs. This was shown by O'Keefe [34] who essentially used this semantics to formalize a notion of modularity.

Finite Failure

By definition, when we compute partial recursive functions, there are inputs which lead to infinite computations. As Kowalski pointed out [19], in the context of logic programming there is no limit to the amount of infinite branches that can be pruned from the search space (by loop-checking methods etc.), and no algorithm can exist to eliminate all of them. Consequently we can further and further approximate the closed world assumption but never, in general, reach it.

If we cannot eliminate all infinite computations which are due to the nature of the problem, we should at least do our best not to introduce new ones via our interpreter. In that respect resolution behaves badly - a large number of infinite computations that have nothing to do with the problem to be solved are nevertheless introduced.

Apt and Van Emden [1] introduced fixedpoint techniques to establish in a more elegant way various results, for instance Hill's soundness and completeness of SLD resolution [11]. Their methods have become standard since. They met, however, with difficulties when characterizing the finite failure of SLD resolution to prove an atom to be a logical consequence. This led to long and involved proofs and a weak result, difficult to interpret semantically: the SLD finite failure set is equal to the complement of $T{\downarrow}\omega$. The result is difficult to interpret semantically, as the complement of $T{\downarrow}\omega$ is an abstract mathematical object implicitly defined; we just have a purely mathematical characterization of the SLD finite failure set. It is weak in the sense that $A \notin T{\downarrow}\omega$ only implies that there exits a finitely failed SLD tree for A while infinite SLD trees for A may also be present. If we wish to make use of this result, we must build an interpreter which generates all SLD trees, a fairly daunting prospect.

Lassez and Maher [22] made the remark that the standard concept of fairness should be introduced in SLD resolution in order to remove a class of infinite computations due to the interpreter's design. The result was startling; most difficulties in the treatment of SLD finite failure were due to the presence of these unnecessary loops. With this modification, all trees (for a given goal) behave the same way: either all fail or none fail. Furthermore, if some SLD tree for A is finitely failed then all fair SLD trees for A are finitely failed. Consequently, if we have a fair implementation of SLD resolution, testing for SLD finite failure simply requires the generation of a single tree, as is the case for success.

Moreover, a general definition of the finite failure set FF was provided, independent of any implementation (SLD or otherwise), which was clearly needed and simple to derive. It turned out that $A \in FF$ can be easily reformulated into $A \notin T{\downarrow}\omega$, so this abstract mathematical formula has, in fact, a meaning: it defines the general notion of finite failure! Consequently one could derive the soundness and strong completeness of fair SLD resolution with respect to finite failure and the soundness and weak completeness of SLD resolution with respect to finite failure. These results provided an appropriate setting in which to address the problem of negation as failure.

We conclude this section on finite failure with a brief presentation of a topic of current research.

An approach to increasing the finite failure set, while preserving the success set has been proposed by Naish and Lassez [33]. For any program P, the set of instances of P (that is programs more specific than P) which have the same set of successful ground derivations has a least element, called a most specific logic program. This most specific logic program has not only a larger finite failure set than P but its SLD trees are shorter than those of P. There is no known algorithm to transform a program into its most specific version and we strongly suspect that there is none. However some heuristics are developed, which show that this most specific version of a program can be obtained in a significant number of cases.

Negation as Failure

Clark provided a formal framework to study negation as failure [3], via the notion of complete logic programs, and proved the soundness of this rule. This was quite important as it provided a better understanding of the negation as failure rule and opened an active area of research. But also it was very nice technically as, complete programs not being in clausal form, it was not evident that resolution could still be meaningful.

Apt and Van Emden [1] used their fixedpoint techniques to formalize negation as failure. However, they worked in the restricted case of the Herbrand Universe and syntactic identity as an equality theory, so their result of soundness was weaker than Clark's. The time was ripe to put together Clark's formalism, Apt and Van Emden's fixedpoint techniques, Lassez and Maher's results on the soundness and completeness of finite failure. This is what Jaffar, Lassez and Lloyd did in [13] where they established the completeness of the negation as failure rule with a fairly involved proof, which has since been presented in many different ways.

We present now a different point of view for the negation as failure rule, which relates it to standard theorem proving techniques. This will be done in the propositional case and illustrated by the following simple example

$$
\left.\begin{array}{l}
A \leftrightarrow (B \wedge C) \vee D \\
B \leftrightarrow E \vee F \\
C \\
\neg D \\
\neg E \\
\neg F
\end{array}\right.
$$

IFF

We can rewrite this complete program in clausal form by considering separately the if and only-if parts of IFF. It is well-known that a complete program has an if part which is made up of definite clauses IF and that an atom is made true by IFF exactly when it is made true by IF. In this case the only-if part can also take a form similar to definite clauses FI where *negated* atoms appear in the head and the body.

IF	FI
A ← B, C	¬A ← ¬B, ¬D
A ← D	¬A ← ¬C, ¬D
B ← E	¬B ← ¬E, ¬F
B ← F	¬D
C	¬E
	¬F

The duality between IF and FI enables us to characterize the atoms made false by IFF using the previous result: an atom is made false by IFF exactly when it is made false by FI.

Clearly this result enables us to optimize a resolution theorem-prover by using SLD resolution on just the IF part of IFF, if we have an atom to prove, and using SLD resolution on just the FI part if we have a negated atom to prove. The optimization comes from the fact that SLD resolution can be used, useless interactions between the IF and FI parts are automatically avoided. More surprising is the fact that this is, essentially, what is done when the negation-as-failure rule is used with SLD resolution on IF. To make this point clearer, consider the following finitely failed SLD tree for A using IF as the program and the successful SLD derivation for ¬A using FI as the program.

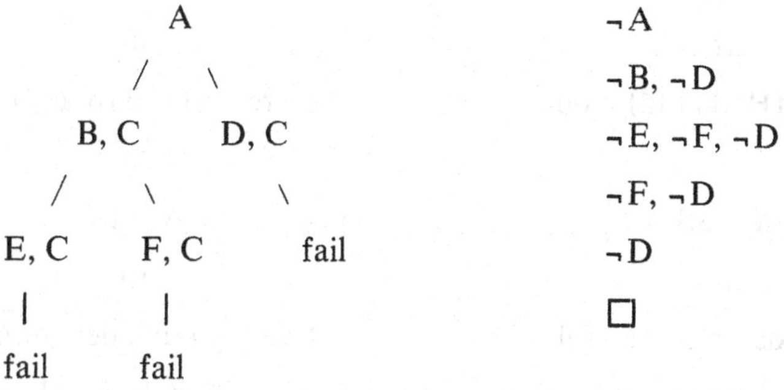

Here we can see that the goals in the derivation correspond to cross-sections of the branches of the failed SLD tree, each atom in a goal corresponding to a single failed subtree. SLD resolution on an atom in the derivation corresponds to considering all the immediate subtrees of the goal containing that atom in the failed SLD tree. Atoms, such as C, which do not contribute to failure in the SLD tree are ignored in the derivation.

In general the relation between a finitely failed tree for the IF part and a successful SLD derivation for the FI part is not so obvious. In particular, it is necessary to Skolemize the existential variables in the FI part of IFF and to include some form of Clark's equality axioms. A demonstration that every false atom has a proof from IFF, in a conventional proof system, that corresponds to a finitely failed tree of the IF part, would constitute a more direct proof of the completeness of the negation as failure rule. If the proof system were similar to SLD resolution then the demonstration would be a step towards an incremental implementation of negation in a manner similar to the work of Sato and Tamaki [35], Schultz [36] and Naish [32].

The Asymmetric Theory

The formal semantics of complete logic programs are not well balanced. We would like a duality between True and False, success and failure, least fixedpoint and greatest fixedpoint, least model and greatest model such that:

A is True	A is False
iff	iff
A $\in$ least (Herbrand) model	A $\notin$ greatest (Herbrand) model
A $\in$ SS	A $\in$ FF
iff	iff
There exists a successful ground derivation	Every ground derivation is finitely failed

$T\uparrow\omega = \mathrm{lfp}(T)$ $\qquad\qquad$ $T\downarrow\omega = \mathrm{gfp}(T)$

As we pointed out earlier A True implies that A is true in all models, not just the models over an intended domain of interpretation, here the Herbrand Universe. So we would also like to have the duality:

A is true in all models	A is false in all models
iff	iff
A is true in all Herbrand models	A is false in all Herbrand models

This duality would imply that the logic approach and the algebraic approach coincide. Unfortunately, if all the statements on the left hand side hold, none of the statements on the right hand side hold. The reason lies in the discrepancy between two notions of finite failure:

The first notion is the one introduced by Lassez and Maher [22] which can be worded in the following way

A $\in$ FF iff there exists n such that all ground derivations for A are failed with length $\leq$ n

This set FF is computable via fair SLD resolution.

The second notion was introduced in Jaffar, Lassez and Maher [15]. It is called ground finite failure:

A $\in$ GFF iff all ground derivations for A are failed finitely.

The difference with FF is that even though all derivations are finitely failed, their length is not bounded, and most importantly the set GFF is not computable.

We compute FF, but it is the non computable GFF which is characterized via the greatest fixedpoint

$$FF \subset GFF = \overline{\mathrm{gfp}(T)}$$

If A $\in$ GFF and A is not in FF, then there exists an infinite SLD derivation for A which cannot be grounded. So the interpreter is manipulating symbols that cannot be bound to elements of the intended domain, leading to the discrepancy between the logic and algebraic approaches. This also implies that in the algebraic approach the negation as failure rule is not complete.

However all the right hand side results hold, and we have a symmetric theory, if we restrict ourselves to programs such that FF = GFF or, equivalently, $T\downarrow\omega$ is equal to the greatest fixedpoint. From a purely mathematical point of view this is a rather exceptional case. However, it appeared that even though it is easy to construct programs such that $T\downarrow\omega$ is not equal to the greatest fixedpoint they are all very contrived and do not correspond to any program arising from standard practice. Thus we were led to conjecture that all "decent" programs satisfy $T\downarrow\omega$ =gfp(T). If this informal conjecture holds then we have a much simpler and elegant theory for logic programs.

An important step in that direction was achieved by Jaffar and Stuckey [17]. Calling "canonical" the programs such that $T\downarrow\omega$=gfp(T), they show that every logic program is equivalent to a canonical program. Therefore the class of canonical programs is representative of the class of all programs.

In a similar attempt to define a class of programs with good semantic properties, Fitting [9] recently proposed that the only acceptable programs were those satisfying a condition which, for definite clauses, is equivalent to requiring T to be down-continuous. Down-continuity implies that $T\downarrow\omega$=gfp(T), so the "acceptable" programs form a subclass of the "decent" programs. However Maher's characterization of down-continuous programs [26, 27] shows that the "acceptable" program class is too small - "acceptable" programs cannot express transitive closure, for example.

Conservative Extensions

Much of the present research in Logic Programming concentrates on extensions to Prolog. An important issue is the integration of the essential concepts of functional and logic programming. Another issue is the use of equations to define data types. Recent work along these lines, from Goguen and Meseguer, Kahn, Komorowski,

Kornfeld, Reddy, Sato and Sakurai, Subrahmanyam and You will be found in the text edited by DeGroot and Lindstrom [6].

There is some concern that these extensions have little connection left with logic. In fact, the very nature of the concepts in these extensions is such that it is not difficult to accommodate them in standard logic or some variant thereof. The crucial point we want to address is not the issue of formalization within or without logic, but whether the unique semantic properties of logic programs are preserved in the extensions.

For instance, Hansson and Haridi [10] and, independently, van Emden and Lloyd [8] re-interpreted PROLOG II in standard logic but did not address the key semantic issues: establish the existence of least model and least fixedpoint semantics and the corresponding soundness and completeness results for successful derivations, establish also the soundness and completeness results for finite failure and for the negation as failure rule. In fact what we require is that all the basic theory for definite clauses be rewritten for PROLOG II. This could represent a major undertaking, which should be repeated for any extension or modification to PROLOG. We will describe now a comparatively simple method to solve that problem.

The Scheme

In Jaffar, Lassez and Maher [15] we proposed a "logic programming language scheme" that is now briefly explained. Consider the language of definite clauses as being defined with the following components: The syntax of definite clauses, the Herbrand universe as the domain of symbolic computation together with syntactic identity as underlying equality theory, an interpreter based on fair SLD resolution, a unification algorithm, and negation as failure.

Many extensions can be viewed or formalized by replacing the domain of symbolic computation by another which is obtained by replacing syntactic identity by another equality theory. We would like to preserve the key property of the Herbrand universe, namely that we have a single domain in which logical consequence can be determined. This property will hold if and only if the equality theory has a finest congruence. In such a case one can easily derive least model and least fixedpoint semantics similar to those of definite clauses. This is not a contrived case as Horn equality theories admit finest congruences, and represent a large and useful class of equality theories, they include in particular equational theories. It then appears that the declarative properties of Definite Clauses over the Herbrand Universe are shared by Definite Clauses over a large class of domains which naturally generalize the Herbrand Universe. The operational aspects of success and failure can be adapted by considering generalized unification and preserving SLD resolution. The corresponding results of soundness and completeness follow naturally.

As for the standard case negation as failure requires more attention. For an equality theory E, terms s and t are unifiable iff $E \models \exists x(s = t)$. With the negation issue at hand we need a dual property; that is we need to establish a relationship between non existence of E unifiers and falsity in E. Informally we say that E is unification complete if every possible solution of a given equation can be represented by an E unifier of the equation. In particular when there are no E unifiers there can be no solution. The soundness and completeness of the negation as failure rule holds for unification complete equality theories.

Consequently we have established the existence of a Logic Programming language scheme. Its syntax is the syntax of Definite Clauses, its domain of computation is left unspecified but it is assumed to be definable by a unification complete equality theory, its interpreter is based on SLD resolution and an appropriate generalized unification algorithm. The semantic properties of definite clauses hold for the scheme and all its instances. Now instead of establishing one by one the various semantic results for a given extension to PROLOG, one can use the scheme to obtain them all in one move. This is exemplified in Jaffar, Lassez and Maher [16] in the case of Colmerauer's PROLOG II [4], defined over the domain of rational trees. Essentially we proceed in two steps, first give an equality theory whose standard model is the intended domain of rational trees, then show that this equality theory is unification complete. PROLOG II can be viewed as an instance of the scheme and possesses its semantics properties. We therefore have a logical interpretation of Colmerauer's rewriting system.

This treatment does not address the problem of inequalities in PROLOG II [5]. It is done in the next section which considers constraints in Definite Clauses.

Constraints

The idea of the scheme defining a class of languages which share the same abstract semantic properties is repeated here. Instead of mapping the intended domain on the Herbrand Universe and using specialized unification, programming is done directly in the intended domain using its natural constraints. We thus use an algebraic framework as well as a logic programming one. This revision of the scheme is called CLP which stands for Constraint Logic Programming.

A CLP program consists of constrained rules which are of the form

$$A \leftarrow c_1, c_2, \ldots, c_k \,[]\, B_1, B_2, \ldots, B_n$$

where $A, B_1, B_2, \ldots, B_n$ are atoms and $c_1, c_2, \ldots, c_k$ form a set of constraints. A goal is of the form

$$\leftarrow c_1, c_2, \ldots, c_k \,[]\, B_1, B_2, \ldots, B_n$$

The interpreter of an instance of CLP consists of the standard goal reduction technique of logic programming and a constraint solver. Implementations of this model of computation can benefit from the wide literature on the problem of constraint solving.

Allowing constraints in the goals and bodies considerably raises the expressive power. A comparison can be made with the introduction of negated atoms in the body of clauses of definite clause programs. It is well known (Clark [3], Shepherdson [38, 39]) that the implementation of negation via variants of SLD resolution and negation as failure works only in restricted cases. Furthermore, the semantic properties of definite clauses that we have described no longer hold. It is therefore quite significant to note that CLP programs have least fixedpoint and least model semantics, and results of soundness and completeness that are similar to those of definite clause logic programs, despite the introduction of constraints. Furthermore, the algebraic and logical approaches also coincide for canonical programs. A formal presentation of these results is to be found in Jaffar and Lassez[12].

Colmerauer is now working on Prolog III and it seems that, as in the case of Prolog II and the scheme, we will be able to show that Prolog III can be viewed as an instance of CLP given the formal definition of Prolog III.

Conclusion

The simplicity and elegance of definite clauses makes this formalism attractive from a theoretical point of view. The objects in this formalism are the uninterpreted terms over the Herbrand universe. Programming however is not done exclusively in the Herbrand universe, but uses higher level concepts such as arithmetic. In that sense we can view definite clauses as the Turing machines of Logic Programming. This gap between theory and programming practice can be reduced by introducing user-oriented domains into the formalism. We have seen that this can be achieved without losing the important properties of definite clauses.

Acknowledgements: The support from IBM Australia is gratefully acknowledged and we thank the text consultants at Yorktown Heights for their advice.

References

[1] K.R. Apt and M.H. van Emden, Contributions to the Theory of Logic Programming, Journal of the ACM 29, 3 (1982), 841-862.

[2] R. Buchi, Private communication.

[3] K.L. Clark, Negation as Failure, in: Logic and Databases, H. Gallaire, J. Minker (eds.), Plenum Press, 1978.

[4] A. Colmerauer, Prolog and Infinite Trees, in: Logic Programming, K.L. Clark and S.A. Tarnlund (eds.), Academic Press, New York, 1982.

[5] A. Colmerauer, Solving Equations and Inequations on Finite and Infinite Trees, Proc. Conference on Fifth Generation Computer Systems, Tokyo, November 1984.

[6] D. DeGroot and G. Lindstrom (eds.), Logic Programming: Relations, Functions and Equations, Prentice Hall, 1986.

[7] M.H. van Emden and R.A. Kowalski, The Semantics of Predicate Logic as a Programming Language, Journal of the ACM 23, 4 (1976), 733-742.

[8] M.H. van Emden and J.W. Lloyd, A Logical Reconstruction of Prolog II, Proc. 2nd. Conference on Logic Programming, Uppsala, Sweden, 1984, 35-40.

[9] M. Fitting, A Kripke-Kleene Semantics for Logic Programs, Journal of Logic Programming 2, 4 (1985), 295-312.

[10] A. Hansson and S. Haridi, Programming in a Natural Deduction Framework, Proc. Conference on Functional Languages and their Implications for Computer Architecture, Goteborg, Sweden, 1981.

[11] D. Hill, LUSH-resolution and its Completeness, DCS Memo 78, Dept. of Artificial Intelligence, University of Edinburgh, 1974.

[12] J. Jaffar and J-L. Lassez, Constraint Logic Programming, forthcoming.

[13] J. Jaffar, J-L. Lassez and J.W. Lloyd, Completeness of the Negation-as-Failure Rule, Proc. 8th. IJCAI, Karlsruhe, 1983, 500-506.

[14] J. Jaffar, J-L. Lassez and M.J. Maher, A Theory of Complete Logic Programs With Equality, Proc. Conference on Fifth Generation Computer Systems, Tokyo, November 1984, 175-184.

[15] J. Jaffar, J-L. Lassez and M.J. Maher, A Logic Programming Language Scheme, in: Logic Programming: Relations, Functions and Equations, D. DeGroot, G. Lindstrom (eds.), Prentice Hall, 1986. Also Technical Report TR 84/15, University of Melbourne, 1984.

[16] J. Jaffar, J-L. Lassez and M.J. Maher, Prolog II as an Instance of the Logic Programming Language Scheme, Technical Report, Monash University, 1984.

[17] J. Jaffar and P.J. Stuckey, Canonical Logic Programs, Journal of Logic Programming, to appear.

[18] R.A. Kowalski and D. Kuehner, Linear Resolution with Selector Function, Artificial Intelligence 2, (1971), 227-260.

[19] R.A. Kowalski, Logic for Problem Solving, North Holland, New York, 1979.

[20] S. Kripke, Outline of a Theory of Truth, Journal of Philosophy 72 (1975), 690-716.

[21] J-L. Lassez and M.J. Maher, The Denotational Semantics of Horn Clauses as a Production System, Proc. National Conference on Artificial Intelligence (AAAI-83), Washington D.C., August 1983, 229-231.

[22] J-L. Lassez and M.J. Maher, Closures and Fairness in the Semantics of Programming Logic, Theoretical Computer Science 29, (1984), 167-184.

[23] J-L. Lassez and M.J. Maher, Optimal Fixedpoints of Logic Programs, Theoretical Computer Science 39, (1985), 15-25.

[24] J-L. Lassez, V. Nguyen and E.A. Sonenberg, Fixed Point Theorems and Semantics: A Folk Tale, Information Processing Letters 14, 3 91982), 112-116.

[25] J.W. Lloyd, Foundations Of Logic Programming, Springer-Verlag, 1984.

[26] M.J. Maher, Semantics of Logic Programs, Ph.D. dissertation, University of Melbourne, 1985.

[27] M.J. Maher, Equivalences of Logic Programs, Proc. 3rd. Logic Programming Conference, London, 1986.

[28] Z. Manna and A. Shamir, The Theoretical Aspect of the Optimal Fixed Point, SIAM Journal on Computing 5 (1976), 414-426.

[29] Z. Manna and A. Shamir, The Optimal Approach to Recursive Programs, Communications of the ACM 20 (1977), 824-831.

[30] Z. Manna and A. Shamir, A New Approach to Recursive Programs, in: Perspectives on Computer Science, A.K. Jones (ed.), Academic Press, New York, 1977.

[31] A. Mycroft, Logic Programs and Many-valued Logic, Proc. 1984 Symposium on Theoretical Aspects of Computer Science, M. Fontet and K. Mehlhorn (eds.), Springer Lecture Notes in Computer Science 166, 274-286.

[32] L. Naish, Negation and Control in PROLOG, Ph.D. dissertation, University of Melbourne, 1985.

[33] L. Naish and J-L. Lassez, Most Specific Logic Programs, Technical Report, Dept. of Computer Science, University of Melbourne, 1984.

[34] R.A. O'Keefe, Towards an Algebra for Constructing Logic Programs, Proc. Symposium on Logic Programming, Boston, 1985.

[35] T. Sato and H. Tamaki, Transformational Logic Program Synthesis, Proc. Conference on Fifth Generation Computer Systems, Tokyo, 1984.

[36] J.W. Schultz, The Use of First-Order Predicate Calculus as a Logic Programming System, M.Sc. dissertation, University of Melbourne, 1984.

[37] J. Sebelik and P. Stepanek, Horn Clause Programs Suggested by Recursive Function, Logic Programming, K.L. Clark and S.A. Tarnlund (eds.), Academic Press, New York, 1982.

[38] J.C. Shepherdson, Negation as Failure: A Comparison of Clark's Completed Data Base and Reiter's Closed World Assumption, Journal of Logic Programming 1, 1 (1984), 51-79.

[39] J.C. Shepherdson, Negation as Failure II, Journal of Logic Programming 2, 3 (1985), 185-202.

[40] S.A. Tarnlund, Horn Clause Computability, BIT 17, 2 (1977), 215-226.

Parallel Logic Programming Languages

Akikazu Takeuchi and Koichi Furukawa
ICOT Research Center
Institute for New Generation Computer Technology
1-4-28, Mita, Minato-ku, Tokyo 108 Japan

1. Introduction

Any programming language which can be treated mathematically has its own logic in its semantic model. Logic programming languages are examples of such languages. They are based on predicate logic and characterized by the fact that logical inference corresponds to computation. Owing to this, a program can be written declaratively and can be executed procedurally by computer. Many logic programming languages can be imagined. The one based on Horn logic is the most successful and has been extensively studied.

A logic program is represented by a finite set of universally quantified Horn clauses. A program can be read procedurally and declaratively [Kowalski, 1974]. A goal statement is used to invoke computation that can be regarded as refutation of the goal statement under the given set of clauses. Prolog is the first language which realized the idea [Roussel, 1975]. Its computation rule corresponds to left-to-right and depth-first traversal of an AND-OR tree.

Given a set of Horn clauses, there are many strategies for refutation other than the one adopted in Prolog. Among these, parallel strategies are of great interest. These correspond to the parallel interpretation of logic programs. Conery *et al.* classified them into four models, OR-parallelism, AND-parallelism, Stream-parallelism and Search-parallelism [Conery and Kibler, 1981]. Stream-parallelism has received much attention recently, because of its expressive power suitable for systems programming and other applications. Several parallel logic programming languages based on stream-parallelism have been proposed. They include Relational Language [Clark and Gregory, 1981], Concurrent Prolog [Shapiro, 1983], Parlog [Clark and Gregory, 1984a], Guarded Horn Clauses [Ueda, 1985a], [Ueda, 1986] and Oc [Hirata, 1986].

The following ideas and requirements seem to be what motivated these languages. The first was to create a parallel execution model for logic programs to fully utilize new parallel computer architecture. As hardware technology evolves, highly parallel computers become realizable using VLSI technology. However, to write a program for a parallel computer is a complicated task and involves new problems quite different from those in programming on a sequential computer. The gap between hardware and software seems to increase. It is believed that the success of the parallel computer depends on the software technology. Choosing languages for parallel programming is the most important decision in parallel software technology. In order for a programmer to avoid various problems and extract parallelism easily, languages should have clear semantics and be inherently parallel themselves. Because of their semantic clarity and high level constructs useful for programming and debugging, logic programs are being regarded as a candidate to fully utilize the power of parallel architectures.

The second issue is the extension of control of logic programming languages. Control facilities of Prolog are similar to conventional procedural languages, although the model for logic programming languages includes no specific control mechanism. There have been several proposals for more flexible computation. They augment Prolog by introducing new control primitives such as coroutines [Clark, McCabe and Gregory, 1982], [Colmerauer, 1982], [Naish, 1984]. Languages based on stream-parallelism can be regarded as an alternative attempt to extend control. These languages abandoned the rules of sequential execution, and thus first introduced parallelism. A great deal of effort was devoted to finding reasonable set of control primitives managing the parallelism obtained as a result.

The third point is to exploit new programming styles in logic programming and thus to exploit new applications of logic programming. Logic programming languages such as Prolog are suitable for database applications and natural language processing, but were suspected of being inadequate for applications such as operating systems. Parallel logic programming languages with control primitives managing parallelism aims at covering such applications as systems programming, object oriented programming and simulation and thus enlarging the applications of logic programming.

The parallel logic programming languages have a relatively short history, just six years or so. In this short time researches have been intensive around the world and many fruitful results have been obtained. A general view to these languages will be presented in this paper. The purpose of this paper is to present common features of the languages, to delineate the differences between them at the abstract level and to address the problems they present.

The paper is organized as follows. The stream-parallel computation model will be informally introduced in section 2. Section 3 provides definitions of several parallel logic programming languages. Common features shared among them and their difference are discussed. In final section, unsolved problems of semantics of parallel logic programming languages will be discussed briefly.

2. Stream-parallel Computation Model

Stream-parallel computation models were studied by [Clark, McCabe and Gregory, 1982] and [van Emden and de Lucena, 1982] independently as extended interpretation models of logic programs. Without introducing specific languages, we review the stream-parallel computation models informally. Consider the following logic program (syntax similar to Edinburgh Prolog [Bowen *et al.* , 1983] is used throughout).

```
quicksort(List,Sorted) :- qsort(List,Sorted,[]).                    (1)

qsort([],H,H).                                                        (2)
qsort([A|B],H,T) :-
      partition(B,A,S,L),
      qsort(S,H,[A|T1]),
      qsort(L,T1,T).                                                  (3)

partition([],X,[],[]).                                                (4)
partition([A|B],X,[A|S],L) :- A < X, partition(B,X,S,L).             (5)
partition([A|B],X,S,[A|L]) :- A >= X, partition(B,X,S,L).            (6)
```

The predicate, **quicksort(List,Sorted)**, expresses the relation that **Sorted** is the sorted list of the list **List**. **qsort(List,H,T)** represents the fact that the difference list **H-T** is the sorted list of the list **List**. **partition(List,E,S,L)** says that **S** is a sublist of **List** each element of which is less than **E**, and **L** is a sublist each element of which is greater than or equal to **E**. Given the above program and the following goal statement,

```
?- quicksort([2,1,3],X),
```

the Prolog interpreter will return the following answer substitution,

```
X = [1,2,3].
```

The algorithm used in the above logic program is "divide and conquer". Given a list, the CDR is divided into two lists, one consisting of elements less than CAR, and the other of elements greater than or equal to CAR. Both lists are sorted independently and they are combined to construct the sorted list of the original list. The algorithm is typically embodied in the clause (3). The clause can be read procedurally in the following way: To sort a list **[A|B]**, partition **B** into **S** and **L** with respect to **A**, and sort **S** and **L**. According to the sequential computation rule of Prolog, these subgoals are executed from left to right, that is, first the list **B** is partitioned, then **S** is sorted and finally **L** is sorted.

There are two possibilities for exploiting parallelism in the above program, especially in clause (3). One is cooperative parallelism. Since the lists **S** and **L** can be sorted independently, execution of two qsorts can be done in parallel. Although they share a variable, **T1**, they can cooperate in the construction of a list **H-T** by constructing non-overlapping sublists, **H-T1** and **T1-T**, of **H-T** in parallel. The other is pipelining parallelism. Note that both lists, **S** and **L**, are constructed incrementally from the heads by partition and that these two lists are consumed from their heads by two separate qsorts. Therefore, it is possible to start execution of the two qsorts with available parts of the lists before partition completes the lists. The parallelism of the partition and the two separate qsorts resembles so-called pipelining parallelism. Both parallelisms, processed by a parallel computer, are expected to be effective in reducing computation time.

Cooperative parallelism and pipelining parallelism are typical kinds of parallelism which stream-parallel interpretation can extract from logic programs. Generally speaking, there are two kinds of parallelism in stream-parallel interpretation. One for parallel interpretation of conjunctive goals and the other for parallel search for clauses. Cooperative and pipelining parallelism are special cases of the former parallelism. The latter is not discussed in this section; it will be introduced in the next section.

In the former parallelism, goals sharing variables are not independent and can interact with each other. Stream-parallelism involves cooperation of goals executed in parallel through shared variables. This is in clear contrast with AND parallelism, where no collaboration among goals is considered. In AND-parallel interpretation, conjunctive goals are solved independently and consistent solutions are extracted from their solutions. AND-parallel interpretation is in danger of generating a lot of irrelevant computation, since unnecessary computation is only proved to be irrelevant when it terminates.

Stream-parallel interpretation avoids this problem in the following way. First, bindings created in the course of computation are transported to other computations as soon as possible. This helps parallel computations to exchange bindings of shared variables in order to maintain consistency. Secondly, it provides new control primitives which can restrict access modes to shared variables. There can be two modes in access to a variable, although the mode is implicit and multiple in logic programming. These modes are "input (read)" and "output (write)". New primitives can be used to restrict the access mode to a shared variable to either input or output. Appropriate restriction of access modes to a shared variable enables the variable to be used as an asynchronous communication channel between parallel computations. Using such asynchronous communication channels programmers can coordinate parallel goals and suppress irrelevant computation. In sum, the parallelism explored in stream-parallelism is controlled parallelism and the languages based on stream-parallelism can extract maximum parallelism while reducing irrelevant parallel computation.

3. Languages

Several parallel logic programming languages have been proposed. They are Relational Language, Concurrent Prolog, Parlog, Guarded Horn Clauses (hereafter called GHC), Oc. We start by defining the common features of these languages. These common features were first proposed in Relational Language.

3.1 Common Features

(1) *Syntax*:

For notational convenience, we define the common syntax. A program is a finite set of guarded clauses. A guarded clause is a universally quantified Horn clause of the form:

$$H :- G1,\ \ldots,\ Gn \mid B1,\ \ldots,\ Bm. \qquad n, m \geq 0$$

"|" is called a "*commitment*" operator or "*commit*". "$G1, ..., Gn$" is called the guard part and "$B1, ..., Bm$" the body part. H is called the head of the clause. A set of clauses sharing the same predicate symbol with the same arity is defined to be the definition of that predicate. A goal statement is a conjunction of goals of the form:

$$:-\ P1, \ldots, Pn. \qquad n > 0.$$

(2) *Declarative semantics*:

The declarative meaning of "," is "*and*" ("$\wedge$"). The clause can be read declaratively as follows:

For all term values of the variables in the clause,
H is true if both $G1, ..., Gn$ and $B1, ..., Bm$ are true.

(3) *Sketch of operational semantics*:

Roughly speaking, "," procedurally means fork. Namely a conjunction, "p, q", indicates that goals, p and q, are to be solved in different processes. The procedural meaning of a commitment operator is to cut off alternative clauses. We give a sketch of operational semantics using two kinds of processes, an AND-process and an OR-process [Miyazaki, Takeuchi and Chikayama, 1985].

The goal statement is fed to a root-process, a special case of an OR-process. Given a conjunction of goals, a root-process creates one AND-process for each goal. When all these AND-processes succeed, the root-process succeeds. When one of these fails, it fails.

Given a goal G with the predicate symbol P, an AND-process creates one OR-process for each clause defining the predicate P and passes the goal to each process. When at least one of these OR-processes succeeds, the AND-process commits itself to the clause sent to that OR-process, and aborts all the other OR-processes. Then it creates an AND-process for each goal in the body part of the clause and replaces itself by these AND-processes. It fails, when all of these OR-processes fail.

Given a goal and a clause, an OR-process unifies the goal with the head of the clause and solves the guard part of the clause by creating an AND-process for each goal in the guard. When all these AND-processes succeed, then it succeeds. When one of these fails, it fails.

(3) *Remarks*:

Conjunctive goals are solved in parallel by AND-processes. A clause such that the head can be unified with the goal and the guard can successfully terminate is searched for in parallel by OR-processes, but only one is selected by commitment. Parallel search is similar to OR-parallelism, but not the same because it is bounded in the evaluation of guard parts. A commitment operator selects one clause, cuts off the rest and terminates OR-parallelism.

Computation is organized hierarchically as an AND- and OR-process tree. Each OR process may be associated with a local environment storing bindings that would influence other competing OR processes if they were revealed to them. This will be discussed later.

In general, if access to a variable is restricted to input mode, then no unification which instantiates the variable to a non-variable term is allowed and such unification is forced to suspend until the variable is instantiated. This kind of synchronization mechanism is useful for delaying commitment until enough information is obtained. Languages proposed so far have different syntactic primitives for specification of restriction of access mode. We review them in the next section.

3.2 Restriction of Access Mode

• *Mode Declaration*

Parlog and its predecessor, Relational Language, take this approach. Restriction of access mode is specified by mode declaration. In Parlog, each predicate definition must be associated with one mode declaration. It has the form

$$mode\ \ R(m_1,\ \ldots,\ m_k).$$

where R is a predicate symbol with arity k. Each m_i is "?" or "^". "?" indicates that access to a variable at this position in a goal is restricted to *"input"* mode. "^" indicates *"output"* mode. Note that there is no neutral (multiple) mode. During head unification, any attempt to instantiate a variable appearing in an argument specified as input in a goal to a non-variable term is forced to suspend. Output mode indicates that a term pattern at the corresponding argument position in the head will be issued from the clause. Unification between such output patterns and corresponding variables in the goal could be performed after the clause is selected. Implementation of Parlog is presented in [Clark and Gregory, 1984b]. The approach is to translate a general Parlog program to a program (called standard form) in a simple subset of the language, called Kernel Parlog. Kernel Parlog has only AND-parallelism and has no mode declaration. Input-mode unification and output-mode unification are achieved by special one-way unification primitives. For example, if the relation "p" has a mode declaration stating that the first argument is input and the second is output, the clause

```
p(question(P), answer(A)) :- good_question(P) | solve(P,A).
```

has the standard form

```
p(X,Y) :- question(P) <= X, good_question(P) |
          Y:= answer(A), solve(P,A).
```

T <= X is one-way unification which can bind variables in T, but suspends on an attempt to bind variables in X. Y := T is assignment unification. Note that mode declaration only restricts head unification. In general, there may be a case in which a variable appearing in an input argument in a goal is instantiated to a non-variable term during computation of a guard part. In Parlog, a program indicating this possibility is regarded as a dangerous program and excluded at compile-time by mode analysis. A merge operator merging two lists into one in arbitrary order can be defined in Parlog as follows:

```
mode merge(?,?,^).

merge([A|X],Y,[A|Z]) :- true | merge(X,Y,Z).
merge(X,[A|Y],[A|Z]) :- true | merge(X,Y,Z).
merge([],Y,Y) :- true | true.
merge(X,[],X) :- true | true.
```

- *Read-only annotation*

Concurrent Prolog adopts this primitive. Read-only annotation is denoted by "?". It can be attached to any variable. A variable with read-only annotation is called a read-only variable. Read-only annotation restricts access to the variable to read mode only. Any attempt to instantiate an unbound variable with read-only annotation to a non-variable term is forced to suspend until the variable is instantiated. Read-only annotation must be handled in the general unification procedure, since read-only variables can appear anywhere in a term. Using this annotation, the merge operator can be defined as follows:

```
merge([A|X],Y,[A|Z]) :- true | merge(X?,Y,Z).
merge(X,[A|Y],[A|Z]) :- true | merge(X,Y?,Z).
merge([],Y,Y) :- true | true.
merge(X,[],X) :- true | true.
```

Invocation of the goal takes the form:

```
merge(X?,Y?,Z).
```

• *Input guard*

This is adopted in GHC and Oc. Restriction of access mode to variables in a goal is subsumed in the definition of a guard part. In GHC, given a goal G and a clause C, during head unification and computation of the guard part of C, any attempt to instantiate a variable appearing in the goal to a non-variable term is forced to suspend. Oc has no guard condition, in other words, a guard part is always "*true*". Hence, specification of synchronization in Oc is simpler than in GHC. In Oc, any attempt to instantiate a variable in the goal to a non-variable term in head unification is forced to suspend. Intuitively, a head and a guard part of GHC and Oc specify conditions to be satisfied by input data received from a goal. The definition of merge is:

```
merge([A|X],Y,Oz) :- true | Oz=[A|Z], merge(X,Y,Z).
merge(X,[A|Y],Oz) :- true | Oz=[A|Z], merge(X,Y,Z).
merge([],Y,Oz) :- true | Oz=Y.
merge(X,[],Oz) :- true | Oz=X.
```

Note that output unification must be put in the body part of each clause. Otherwise it will cause suspension, since the output pattern will be regarded as the input pattern.

• *Comparison*

Different primitives for restricting access mode are adopted by different languages. In fact, the way to represent this restriction characterizes each language. They are basically separated into two classes. One in *procedure level* representation and the other in *data level*. Relational language, Parlog, GHC and Oc belong to the first class. Concurrent Prolog belongs to the second class. The fact that procedures and data are complementary objects in a programming language indicates the clear contrast between these two approaches.

Procedure level representation of input and output: Relational language and Parlog adopt mode declaration for specification of input and output. GHC and Oc utilize a guard part for the specification of input. One mode is given for each predicate definition. On the other hand, an input guard can include input specifications for each clause. Although they put input specifications at different levels, a predicate definition and a clause, both approaches associate input specification with a procedure.

Data level representation of input and output: Concurrent Prolog adopted read-only annotation to restrict access mode. A variable with read-only annotation cannot be instantiated (written), but can be read. In general, a variable with read-only annotation can be regarded as a "*protected term*" [Hellerstein and Shapiro, 1984], [Takeuchi and Furukawa, 1985], since it is protected from instantiation. Only a process which has access to the variable without read-only annotation can instantiate it. Since input synchronization is embedded in a data object, it becomes difficult to predict where and when synchronization will occur. This may impair transparency of control flow of the program. On the other hand, embedding control in a data object will enable novel control abstraction. Authors investigated this in the implementation of bounded buffer communication using protected terms [Takeuchi and Furukawa, 1985].

3.3 OR-parallel Multiple Environments and Guard Safety

Given a goal and a clause, an OR process evaluates head unification and the guard part. Since there are competing OR processes, bindings made for variables in the goal must be hidden from processes other than descendants of the OR-process. Therefore, conceptually, each OR-process has a local environment where these bindings are stored. Local environments associated with OR-processes form a tree, since AND-processes and OR-processes are hierarchically organized. The tree can dynamically expand and contract as computation proceeds. There is no need to manage this dynamic tree if no local binding is made, but otherwise it is an unavoidable task.

A clause is defined to be safe if and only if, for any goal, evaluation of head unification and the guard part never instantiates a variable appearing in the goal to a non-variable term. The definition is due to Clark and Gregory [Clark and Gregory, 1984b]. We add a few definitions. A program is defined to be safe, if and only if each clause in the program is safe. A language is defined to be safe if and only if any program written in it is safe. If a languages is safe, then it does not need to manage local environments. The concept of safety clarifies the difference between the languages.

Parlog, GHC and Oc are safe languages. The design philosophy of Parlog excludes any program which requires multiple environments. In Parlog, a program which may be unsafe is excluded as a dangerous program at compile-time mode analysis. GHC and Oc also do not need multiple environments. In fact, the rule of suspension in GHC and Oc can be paraphrased so that any attempt to make bindings which should be stored in the local environment is forced to suspend. Thus, safety is guaranteed at run-time by the suspension mechanism.

Concurrent Prolog is not safe. Thus, the tree of local environments has to be managed. Several attempts to implement Concurrent Prolog have been reported [Levy, 1984], [Miyazaki, Takeuchi and Chikayama, 1985]. Levi proposed a lazy copying scheme for implementation of multiple environments. Miyazaki *et al.* proposed a shallow binding scheme for this purpose. Implementation of Concurrent Prolog must solve two complicated problems associated with multiple environments. One is value access control. The other is detection of inconsistency between local environments.

Local environments are organized as a tree structure. An environment in a node must be accessible from nodes under the node, but must be hidden from others until the OR process associated with the environment succeeds in being selected. Once the OR process successfully terminates and it is selected, its local environment is merged with the local environment of the parent AND process (the local environment associated with the parent OR process of the AND process). Controlling the scope of variable access in this way is called value access control. On commitment, however, it may happen that these two environments contains inconsistent bindings. When should the inconsistency be detected ? This is called the problem of detection of inconsistency of local bindings. Ueda [Ueda, 1985b] presents two possible solutions. One is called *early detection*, which seeks to detect inconsistency as soon as possible. If there exists inconsistency, the clause fails before commitment and the clause is never selected. The other solution is called *late detection* and seeks to detect inconsistency immediately after commitment. In this case, the clause succeeds in being selected, but immediately fails after commitment. Programmers may prefer early detection, but it requires a complicated locking mechanism for variables when implemented on a distributed memory machine. Ueda examined the semantics of Concurrent Prolog from the point of view of parallel execution and highlighted several subtle issues which become crucial problems in distributed implementation of the languages [Ueda, 1985b].

Codish defines a concept of safety in Concurrent Prolog which is different from the one stated here [Codish, 1985]. He introduced output annotation into Concurrent Prolog. Output annotation is used to declare which terms will be issued to a goal in head unification. In his model, a clause is defined to be safe if, for any goal, no binding for variables in the goal is made except those declared by output annotation during head unification and guard computation. Management of local binding becomes simple in execution of a program ensured to be safe, since such bindings are syntactically predictable. Codish tries to define a subset of Concurrent Prolog with output annotation such that the safety of any program written in it can be verified syntactically.

3.4 Hierarchical Computation Structure and Flatness

As already mentioned, computation is organized as an AND- and OR-process tree. The depth of the tree corresponds to the depth of nesting of guard computations. Some parallel logic programming languages have a flat computation structure.

[Flat Concurrent Prolog] Flat Concurrent Prolog is a subset of Concurrent Prolog in which guard parts are restricted to specify system predicates [Mierowsky *et al.* , 1985]. Since no general computation is allowed in a guard, computation structure is always flat. No tree-structured multiple local environments exist. This greatly reduces the complexity of implementation of the language, but it does not eliminate the problem of detecting inconsistency. Flat Concurrent Prolog seems to adopt late detection, but it is not clear how it is realized in a distributed memory environment.

[Parlog] Owing to the safe property of a clause, OR-parallel search for a clause can be translated into AND-parallel goals. In the course of translation from a legal Parlog program to a Kernel Parlog program, clauses defining a predicate are collected into one clause. In this clause, OR-parallel evaluation of guards is expressed by AND-parallel evaluation of conjunction of meta-calls, each of which calls the guard of each clause. The commitment operator is also expressed by a goal, which receives results from meta-calls, selects one and aborts the other meta-calls. Thus, there exists simple hierarchy of AND-processes in Parlog.

[GHC] AND- and OR-process tree is essential. In GHC, unification suspends if and only if binding made by the unification has to be stored in a local environment. In order to know whether a binding of a variable has to be stored in a local environment or not, the birth place of the variable in the hierarchy has to be identified. If it is the location where the binding is about to be made, then the binding can be made. Otherwise the attempt to bind is forced to suspend. This is why the hierarchical computation structure has to be managed with appropriate information on variables.

[Oc and Flat GHC] Flat GHC is a subset of GHC. In Flat GHC, as well as Flat Concurrent Prolog, a guard part is restricted to being a set of system predicates. Both Oc and Flat GHC have no computation hierarchy, since no general computation is allowed in a guard and this makes implementation of suspension simpler than in GHC. In fact, it can be implemented by one-way unification primitives similar to those of Parlog.

3.5 Summary of Comparison

We have reviewed parallel logic programming languages from the following three viewpoints.

(1) Suspension mechanism

(2) Multiple OR-parallel environments

(3) Hierarchically organized computation

Safety and flatness contribute to reduce the complexity of implementation. Safety make the management of multiple local environments quite simple. Flatness excludes the hierarchical structure of computation.

The suspension mechanism is independent of the other mechanisms in Concurrent Prolog. However, management of hierarchy of computation and multiple environments is complicated. Safe Concurrent Prolog is an attempt to revise the language to reduce the complexity of managing multiple environments. Flat Concurrent Prolog has neither hierarchy of computation nor multiple environments.

Owing to compile-time mode analysis, at run-time a Parlog program has a simple computation model, where suspension is realized by one-way unification primitives, computation hierarchy management is simple and no multiple environments exist. What Parlog compiler does at compile-time can be regarded as detection of multiple environments over the hierarchical structure inferred from a program with mode declaration for possible data flow. One flaw of Parlog is that one cannot write a meta-interpreter for the language in itself, while in other languages this is possible. The ability to write a meta-interpreter for the language in itself is an important property of a language for the self-contained development of its programming system.

In GHC, the suspension mechanism and computation hierarchy are closely coupled, though GHC needs no multiple environments. Oc and Flat GHC are similar to Kernel Parlog. In fact, any program written in Oc and Flat GHC can be translated into a Kernel Parlog program. If we can imagine Flat Kernel Parlog which prohibits general goals and meta-calls in a guard, then Oc, Flat GHC and Flat Kernel Parlog are equivalent to each other and constitute the simplest parallel logic programming language.

4. Semantics of Parallel Logic Programming Languages

In this final section, we present an open problem on semantics of parallel logic programs.

The semantics of logic programs has been extensively investigated [van Emden and Kowalski, 1976], [Apt and van Emden, 1982], [Lloyd, 1984]. These provide a rigid basis for various mathematical manipulations of logic programs such as program verification, equivalent program transformation and declarative debugging. Logical foundations for parallel logic programming languages are also indispensable for the development of the theory of parallel logic programming including verification, transformation and debugging. However, the results for pure logic programs are not directly applicable to parallel logic programming languages because of the new control primitives.

Given a program P (a set of Horn clause), the success set of the program is defined to be the set of all A in the Herbrand base of P such that $P \cup \{\leftarrow A\}$ has an SLD-refutation. The finite-failure set is defined to be the set of all A in the Herbrand base of P such that there exists a finitely-failed SLD-tree with $\leftarrow A$ as root. It is well known that the success set, the minimum model and the least fixpoint of the function associated with the program are equivalent. The finite-failure set is characterized by the greatest fixpoint under a certain condition. If a goal succeeds under sound computation rules, the result is assumed of being included in the success set. If a goal finitely fails, then the result is ensured to be included in the finite-failure set.

The declarative semantics of parallel logic programming languages recommends reading a guarded clause as just a Horn clause. This is sufficient as long as a goal succeeds, but this does not happen sufficient in many cases. Suppose that a goal failed. This implies neither that the result is not in the success set, nor that the result is in the finite-failure set, since the goal may fail even if there is a possibility of success because of commitment to an incorrect clause. The declarative semantics becomes insufficient also if two programs with different input/output behavior need to be distinguished.

Parallel logic programming languages have two control primitives not appearing in pure logic programs. These are a commitment operator and a synchronization primitive. Parallel logic programming relies heavily on these control primitives. However, a commitment operator changes the semantics of failure and a synchronization primitive introduces procedural flavor. It is now obvious that declarative semantics for pure logic programs cannot characterize such aspects of parallel logic programs as failure and input/output behavior.

Let us consider the algorithmic debugging for parallel logic programming languages, where the intended interpretation of a program plays an important role in guiding debugging. Declarative semantics such as success set is no longer sufficient. Intended interpretations should be abstract semantics characterizing all aspects which programmers intend to express. One of the authors developed an algorithmic debugger for GHC, where the intended interpretation with procedural flavor of a GHC program was defined [Takeuchi, 1986]. Lloyd *et al.* refined the framework for the above algorithmic debugging and discussed some difficult cases to handle [Lloyd and Takeuchi, 1986]. These are just starting points.

Semantics of parallel logic programming languages discussed in this paper have been defined only operationally. None of them provides a method to modelling abstract meaning of a program. What is required is semantics of parallel logic programs that can characterize what a programmer intends to express in a program. Meanings of programs should be abstract and independent from concrete implementation since the detail of implementation is not of interest. Furthermore semantics should be mathematically manipulatable so that important properties of programs can be derived from their meanings. Such semantics is strongly desired for the theory of parallel logic programming.

References

Apt, K. R. and van Emden, M. H. [1982] Contributions to the Theory of Logic Programming. *J. ACM*, Vol. 29, No. 3 (1982), pp. 841-862.

Bowen, D. L. (ed.), Byrd, L., Pereira, F. C. N., Pereira, L. M. and Warren, D. H. D. [1983] *DECsystem-10 Prolog User's Manual.* Dept. of Artificial Intelligence, Univ. of

Edinburgh.

Clark, K. L. and Gregory, S. [1981] A Relational Language for Parallel Programming. In *Proc. 1981 Conf. on Functional Programming Languages and Computer Architecture*, ACM, pp. 171-178.

Clark, K. L. McCabe, F. and Gregory, S. [1982] IC-Prolog language features. In *Logic Programming*, Clark, K. L. and Tarnlund, S. A. (ed.), Academic Press, pp. 253-266.

Clark, K. L. and Gregory, S. [1984a] *PARLOG: Parallel Programming in Logic*. Research Report DOC 84/4, Dept. of Computing, Imperial College of Science and Technology, London.

Clark, K. L. and Gregory, S. [1984b] *Notes on the Implementation of PARLOG*. Research Report DOC 84/16, Dept. of Computing, Imperial College of Science and Technology, London, 1984. Also in *J. of Logic Programming*, Vol. 2, No. 1 (1985), pp. 17-42.

Codish, M. [1985] *Compiling OR-parallelism into AND-parallelism*. Master Thesis, Computer Science, Feinberg Graduate School of the Weizmann Institute of Science, Rehovot.

Colmerauer, A. et al. [1982] *PROLOG II Reference Manual and Theoretical Model*. Groupe Intelligence Artificielle, Faculte des Sciences de Luminy, Marseille.

Conery, J. S. and Kibler, D. F. [1981] Parallel Interpretation of Logic Programs. In *Proc. 1981 Conf. on Functional Programming Languages and Computer Architecture*, ACM, pp. 163-170.

Hellerstein, L. and Shapiro, E. [1984] Implementing Parallel Algorithms in Concurrent Prolog: The MAXFLOW Experience. In *Proc. 1984 Symp. on Logic Programming*, IEEE Computer Society, pp. 99-117.

Hirata, M. [1985] Self-Description of Oc and Its Applications. In *Proc. Second National Conf. of Japan Society of Software Science and Technology*, pp. 153-156. (in Japanese)

Kowalski, R. [1974] Predicate Logic as Programming Language. In *Proc. IFIP-74 Congress*, North-Holland, pp. 569-574.

Levy, J. [1984] A Unification Algorithm for Concurrent Prolog. In *Proc. Second Int. Logic Programming Conf.*, Uppsala Univ., Sweden, pp. 331-342.

Lloyd, J. W. [1984] *Foundations of Logic Programming*. Springer-Verlag, Berlin Heidelberg New York Tokyo.

Lloyd, J. W. and Takeuchi, A. [1986] *A Framework of Debugging GHC*. to appear Tech. Report, Institute for New Generation Computer Technology, Tokyo.

Mierowsky, C. , Taylor, S. , Shapiro, E. , Levy, J. and Safra, M. [1985] *The Design and Implementation of Flat Concurrent Prolog*. Tech. Report CS85-09, The Weizmann Institute of Science, Rehovot.

Miyazaki, T. , Takeuchi, A. and Chikayama, T. [1985] A Sequential Implementation of Concurrent Prolog Based on the Shallow Binding Scheme. In *Proc. 1985 Symp. on Logic Programming*, IEEE Computer Society, pp. 110-118.

Naish, L. [1984] *MU-Prolog 3.1db Reference Manual*. Internal Memorandum, Department of Computer Science, Univ. Melbourne.

Roussel, P. [1975] *Prolog: Manuel reference et d'utilisation*. Tech. Report, Groupe d'Intelligence Artificielle, Marseille-Luminy.

Shapiro, E. Y. [1983] *A Subset of Concurrent Prolog and Its Interpreter*. Tech. Report TR-003, Institute for New Generation Computer Technology, Tokyo.

Takeuchi, A. and Furukawa, K. [1985] Bounded Buffer Communication in Concurrent Prolog. *New Generation Computing*, Vol. 3, No. 2 (1985), pp. 145-155.

Takeuchi, A. [1986] *Algorithmic Debugging of GHC programs*. to appear Tech. Report, Institute for New Generation Computer Technology, Tokyo.

Ueda, K. [1985a] *Guarded Horn Clauses*. ICOT Tech. Report TR-103, Institute for New Generation Computer Technology. Also to appear in *Lecture Notes in Computer Science*, Springer-Verlag, Berlin Heidelberg (1986).

Ueda, K. [1985b] *Concurrent Prolog Re-examined*. ICOT Tech. Report TR-102, Institute for New Generation Computer Technology, Tokyo.

Ueda, K. [1986] *Guarded Horn Clauses*. Doctoral Thesis, Information Engineering Course, Faculty of Engineering, Univ. of Tokyo.

van Emden, M. H. and Kowalski, R. [1976] The Semantics of Predicate Logic as a Programming Language, *J. ACM*, Vol. 23, No. 4 (1976), pp. 733-742.

van Emden, M. H. and de Lucena Filho, G. J. [1982] Predicate logic as a programming language for parallel programming. In *Logic Programming*, Clark, K. L. and Tarnlund, S. A. (ed.), Academic Press, pp. 189-198.

P-Prolog: A Parallel Logic Language Based on Exclusive Relation

Rong Yang and Hideo Aiso
Department of Electrical Engeneering
Keio University
Yokohama 223
Japan

ABSTRACT

This paper presents a parallel logic programming language named P-Prolog which is being developed as a logic programming language featuring both and- and or-parallelism. Compared with the other parallel logic programming languages, syntactic constructs such as read-only annotation [Shapiro 83], mode declaration [Clark and Gregory 84] and communication constraints [Ueda 85] are not used in P-Prolog. A new concept introduced in P-Prolog is the exclusive relation of guarded horn clauses. Advances included in P-Prolog are:

(1) The synchronization mechanism can determine the direction of data flow dynamically.

(2) Guarded horn clauses can be interpreted as either *don't care* non-determinism or *don't know* non-determinism.

A prototype interpreter of P-Prolog has been implemented in C-prolog. We are now implementing a P-Prolog interpreter in the C language.

1. Introduction

Algorithms are composed of the logic of the information to be used in solving problems and the control over the manner in which the information is put to use. This has been generalized as the symbolic equation:

Algorithm = Logic + Control

by R.Kowalski [Kowalski 79]. He argues that functional programming languages combine logic with control, but logic programming languages separate logic from control. The difference between logic programming languages and conventional functional languages is that the former only expresses the logic of problem-solving methods and leaves the control to the program executor. This means that the user need only consider the logic without anxiety over the control. Instead, methods of supporting a powerful efficient program executor are very important for a designer of logic languages. In fact, it is difficult to design a control strategy for a pure logic programming language that can work efficiently in most cases. For the sake of efficiency, most logic programming systems introduce some specifications for control in the practical language, that is to say, sacrificing some logical completeness for efficiency. For instance, the 'cut' operator was developed for telling the program executor where backtracking is unnecessary in the sequential logic programming language PROLOG [Clocksin and Mellish,81]. For parallel programming languages, the 'commit' operator was developed for making parallel processing more efficient, and some syntactic constructs were introduced for synchronization. Obviously, logical completeness and efficiency are somewhat conflicting for logic programming languages. The aim of designing a logic programming system should be to get as high an efficiency as possible but with a minimum loss of logical completeness.

In this paper, a parallel logic language named P-Prolog is presented. There have been three representative parallel logic programming languages developed so far: Concurrent Prolog [Shapiro 83], PARLOG [Clark and Gregory 84] and GHC [Ueda 85]. All of them are based on the guarded horn clause, but they use different synchronization mechanisms. When we started to design P-Prolog, we directed our attention to the following two problems:

(1) In existing parallel logic languages, the syntactic construction for synchronization lose some degree of logical completeness. For instance, in Concurrent Prolog, read-only variables stand for input. In PARLOG, a mode declaration is used to state whether each argument is input or output. And in GHC, an output argument must be represented as a variable at the head of a clause, and unified after becoming committed. As a result, the pattern of input/output (I/O for short) must be fixed when the user writes a program. But, in fact, the ability to execute the same procedure with various I/O patterns is an important feature of a logic language. In other words, to use a single relationship in more than one direction is a distinguishing characteristic of logic programming. Therefore we want to find a synchronization mechanism in which the I/O pattern need not be fixed.

(2) The non-determinism of logic programming language is divided into two types: *don't care* and *don't know* by [Kowalski 79]. *Don't care* non-determinism is used to make the program executors "don't care" whether there will be other solutions to be found after obtaining one solution. *Don't know* non-determinism is used to find the other solutions. Since guarded horn clauses incorporate *don't care* non-determinism, but not *don't-know* non-determinism, only one solution can be found. In Concurrent Prolog and GHC, an or-parallel search for all solutions is executed in an and-parallel mechanism, that means programs must be rewritten. In PARLOG, **all_solutions relations** have been developed. But we must use **setof** or **bagof** for getting a list of all solutions, and the clauses which are defined by **all-solutions relations** are evaluated only by or-parallelism but not and-parallelism. Therefore we want to present a parallel logic language which can express or-parallel more naturally.

Taking these two problems into consideration, P-Prolog has been developed based on the exclusive guarded horn clause (defined in next section). The aim of designing P-Prolog is to give the user a simple logical interface while minimizing efficiency loss. In the next section, we discuss the concept of P-Prolog. Then we describe its syntax and semantics in section 3. In section 4, P-Prolog is compared with the other parallel logic languages. Finally, we discuss some problems about programming.

2. Basic Concept of P-Prolog

In this paper, the clauses defined for the same relationship are called *alternative clauses*. When a guarded horn clause succeeds in unifying with a goal P and successfully executes its guard, we say this clause is *committable* for P.

2.1. Exclusive Guarded Horn Clause -- Synchronization Mechanism

In a parallel logic programming system, shared variables are used to communicate between processes, and a synchronization mechanism must determine which process is able to bind a shared variable. Without pointing out which argument is input or output, how can the system distinguish whether a binding to a shared variable is profitable or not? In other words, how can the system distinguish whether or not data has arrived? For solving this problem, we introduce the exclusive relation of guarded horn clauses into P-Prolog.

First, we present a definition of the exclusive relation:

Definition 1: Exclusive relation EXC(F1,...,Fn) is a n_ary relation (n >= 2) between atomic formula (Ref. [Kowalski 79] for definition of atomic formula).

$$\mathbf{EXC(F1,F2,\ldots,Fn)} =_{def} (F1 \,\&\, \neg F2,\ldots,\& \,\neg Fn) V$$
$$(\neg F1 \,\&\, F2,\ldots,\& \,\neg Fn) V$$
$$\ldots$$
$$(\neg F1 \,\&\, \neg F2,\ldots,\& \,Fn)$$

namely, if any Fi is true, the others must be false.
(here, notation &, V, and ¬ are propositional logical operators interpreted as *and*, *or*, and *not* respectively.)

When n = 2, it is the same as the conventional definition of exclusive-or relation, that is

$$\mathbf{EXC(\,F1,F2\,)} =_{def} (\,F1\&\neg F2 \;V\; \neg F1\&F2\,).$$

If alternative guarded horn clauses are exclusively committable for a goal P, we can say they are exclusive for P. A precise definition of an exclusive relation of guarded horn clauses is as follows:

Definition 2:
(1) Let C1, ..., and Cn be alternative guarded horn clauses:

(C1). $H_1 \leftarrow G_1 \colon B_1.$

...

(Cn). $H_n \leftarrow G_n \colon B_n.$

(2) Let **unifiable**(H,P) stand for whether H can unified with a goal P.
For goal P, clause C1, ..., and clause Cn are exclusive if and only if

$$\mathbf{EXC(\;unifiable(}H_1,P)\&\{G1\}s_1 , \ldots , \mathbf{unifiable(}H_n,P)\&\{Gn\}s_n\;)$$

Here, s_i is the **mgu** of unification of P with H_i (i = 1,2, ... n).

We can explain definition 2 simply as follows: a set of alternative guarded horn clauses is exclusive for P, if and only if there is only one committable clause for P.

The exclusive relation of guarded horn clauses defined above is used as a synchronization mechanism in P-Prolog. Suppose that of a set of clauses

$$P \leftarrow G_1: B_1.$$

$$P \leftarrow G_2: B_2.$$

$$P \leftarrow G_3: B_3.$$

it is pointed out that they should be exclusive in reducing. When a program executor tries to reduce the goal **P**, it will check whether they are exclusive for goal **P** first. If only one clause is committable, it can be reduced. The other case in which there is more than one committable clause is not consistent with the exclusive relation. It means that reducing the goal **P** is not profitable at this time. Therefore the program executor suspends goal **P** and waits for data input.

For example, a program for summing the elements of a stream is defined as follows:

Program 1 summing the elements of a stream

(0). **summing(S,Total):− sum(S,0,Total).**
(1). **sum([X|Xs],N,Total):− N1 is N + X, sum(Xs,N1,Total).**
(2). **sum([], N, N).**

If the user tells the system that a goal **sum**(S,N,T) can be reduced only when (1) and (2) are exclusive for this goal, then **sum**(S,N,T) will be reduced provided that S has been bound to a list. If S is a non-bounded variable, **sum**(S,N,T) will be suspended, because both (1) and (2) are committable for it in this case.

2.2. Non-exclusive Guarded Horn Clause -- Or-parallel Mechanism

Along with the exclusive relation of guarded horn clauses, we also use a non-exclusive relation in P-Prolog.

Definition 3: A set of alternative guarded horn clauses is non-exclusive for a goal P, if and only if at least one pair of clauses in this set can be found which are not exclusive.

The non-exclusive clauses are used for the or-parallelism. In the conventional guarded horn clause, after one clause is committed, the other alternative clauses are omitted. But, in P-Prolog, if some alternative clauses are treated as non-exclusive relation clauses, after one is committed, the other ones that are not exclusive to C (if it exists) are not omitted. They will be evaluated in parallel in order to search for all the solutions.

2.3. Parallelism in Execution

P-Prolog has been developed for featuring both *and_* and *or_* parallelism.

For *and* parallelism, the *and* goals in the guard and body are evaluated in parallel, and the guard part and body part are evaluated sequentially.

For *or* parallelism,

(1) the alternative clauses are committed in parallel, and
(2) more than one candidate clauses which is needlessly exclusive can be reduced in parallel for searching multi-solutions.

3. Syntax and Semantics

Like most parallel logic programming languages, P-Prolog program is a finite set of guarded horn clauses with the following form:

$$H \leftarrow G_1, \ldots, G_m: B_1, \ldots, B_n \quad (m \geq 0, n \geq 0).$$

where *H* is the head clause, the *Gi* are guards of the clauses, *Bi* are the bodies of the clauses, and ':' is the commit operator. It is read as

H is implied by G_1, . . . ,and $G_m$and B_1, . . . ,and B_n.

When m = 0, it can be expressed as

$$H \leftarrow B_1, \ldots, B_n \qquad (n \geq 0).$$

and it is interpreted as

$$H \leftarrow true : B_1, \ldots, B_n \qquad (n \geq 0).$$

by the program executor.

3.1. Expected Exclusive Clauses

As mentioned in section 2, the exclusive relation of guarded horn clauses is introduced into P-Prolog. Some alternative clauses are checked as to whether they are exclusive for the sake of synchronization. On the other hand, some alternative clauses which are used to search for multi-solutions in parallel need not be checked. For this reason, the system needs information about which group of clauses is expected to be checked, namely, is *expected exclusive clauses*. Therefore, a set of alternative clauses is divided into several subsets in P-Prolog. The semantics of divided subsets is as follows:

(1) Clauses in the different subsets should be exclusive for a goal **P**, when they are called by **P**. It means these clauses must be checked as to whether they are exclusive for **P**.

(2) Clauses in a same subset need not satisfy the exclusive relation when they are called.

In contrast to existing logic programming languages, the implying operator ' ← ' is defined in the following way:

$$< \leftarrow > ::= :-\{-\}_0^P \qquad (P \geq 0).$$

Though all use ':–', ':– –', ':– – –', etc. read as implying, they play a role in separating alternative clauses into several subsets:

(1) A subset in which there is only one clause is indicated by ':–'.

(2) A subset having more than one clauses is indicated by ':– –', ':– – –' , and etc.

In the current implementation of P-Prolog, we only use ':–'(single neck) and ':– –'(double neck) in our practical version, because it seems sufficient for defining a relationship (this is easily extended if necessary). Let's call a clause with ':–' a *single neck clause*, and a *double neck clause* with ':– –'. Then we can give a brief explanation about exclusive check: An exclusive check does not occur between *double neck clauses*. Otherwise, a check occurs between *single neck clauses*, and also occurs between a *single neck clause* and a *double neck clause*.

We will call the clauses which need to be checked *expected exclusive clauses*.

For instance, if a relationship is defined by the set of clauses

H_1 :- G_1: B_1.

H_2 :- G_2: B_2.

H_3 :-- G_3: B_3.

H_4 :-- G_4: B_4.

H_5. (The unit clause H are regarded as H :- true.)

it will be theoretically divided into

{H_1 :- G_1: B_1.} ,

{H_2 :- G_2: B_2.} ,

{H_3 :-- G_3: B_3. , H_4 :-- G_4: B_4.} ,

{H_5.} .

In this case, only the pair of clauses (H_3 and H_4) need not to be checked.

In summary, there three kinds of results in trying to reduce a goal:

(1) FALSE: when all of its alternative clauses are not committable.

(2) SUSPEND: when there is more than one committable clause which is *expected exclusive clauses*.

(3) SUCCESS: when *expected exclusive clauses* are really exclusive.

3.2. Built-in Predicates

P-Prolog supports a set of built-in predicates similar to conventional sequential logic languages. Some difference are explained as below.

(1). Built-in Predicates with a Return Value 'suspend'

In a sequential Prolog system, the predicates such as "is", ">", etc. return an answer *false* when their arguments are unbound. In P-Prolog, an answer *suspend* will be returned in this case. And we also support some built-in predicates which are suspended for variables. For example, we introduced '**@write**' and '@==' which are the same as '**write**' and '==' when their arguments are bound to instances. But, when their arguments are unbound, the former will be suspended while the later will be executed.

(2). **other**

In P-Prolog, the search for a candidate clause can be controlled by the built-in predicate 'other' which is used in PARLOG(named ';' operator). 'other' must appear on the left of a guard. A clause marked by 'other' and the clauses below it will not be candidated for execution until the previous clauses have been found to be suspended or false.

(3). **seq**

Because there are some problems which must be evaluated sequentially, a built-in predicate **seq(X)** is supported(**X** is a series of goals). **seq(X)** will evaluate

X with a depth first scheduler.

4. Programming Example and Comparison with Other Languages

This section compares the capabilities of P-Prolog with three representative parallel logic programming languages - Concurrent Prolog, PARLOG and GHC by programming examples. All of the examples in this paper have been tested using a prototype interpreter of P-Prolog.

(the differences with P-Prolog are marked by under line)

* *quick sort by Concurrent Prolog*

```
quicksort( Unsorted,Sorted ):-
    qsort( Unsorted,Sorted,[] ).

qsort( [X|Unsorted], Sorted, Rest ):-
    partition( Unsorted?, X,Smaller,Larger ),
    qsort( Smaller?, Sorted,[X|Sorted1] ),
    qsort( Larger?, Sorted1,Rest ).
qsort( [],Rest,Rest ).

partition([X|Xs],A,Smaller,[X|Larger]):-
    A < X : partition( Xs?, A,Smaller,Larger )
partition([X|Xs],A,[X|Smaller],Larger):-
    A >= X : partition( Xs?, A,Smaller,Larger
partition([],_,[],[]).
```

* *quick sort by PARLOG*

```
mode quicksort( ?, ^ ).
mode qsort( ?, ^, ^ ).
mode partition( ?, ?, ^, ^ ).

quicksort( Unsorted,Sorted ):-
    qsort( Unsorted,Sorted,[] ).

qsort( [X|Unsorted], Sorted, Rest ):-
    partition( Unsorted,X,Smaller,Larger ),
    qsort( Smaller,Sorted,[X|Sorted1]),
    qsort(Larger,Sorted1,Rest).
qsort( [],Rest,Rest ).

partition([X|Xs],A,Smaller,[X|Larger]):-
    A < X : partition(Xs,A,Smaller,Larger).
partition([X|Xs],A,[X|Smaller],Larger):-
    A >= X : partition(Xs,A,Smaller,Larger).
partition([],_,[],[]).
```

* *quick sort by GHC*

```
quicksort( Unsorted,Sorted ):-
    true : qsort( Unsorted,Sorted,[] ).

qsort( [X|Unsorted], Sorted, Rest ):-
    true :
    partition( Unsorted,X,Smaller,Larger ),
    qsort( Smaller,Sorted,[X|Sorted1]),
    qsort(Larger,Sorted1,Rest).
qsort( [], Rest0,Rest1 ):- true : Rest0 = Rest1.

partition([X|Xs],A,Smaller, Larger):-
    A < X : Larger=[X|L1],
    partition(Xs,A,Smaller,L1).
partition([X|Xs],A, Smaller, Larger):-
    A >= X : Smaller=[X|L1],
    partition(Xs,A,S1,Larger).
partition([],_, Smaller,Larger):- true :
    Smaller=[], Larger=[].
```

Figure 1 Quick Sort Programs

4.1. Simplicity

An efficient sort algorithm [Hoare 61] can be expressed in P-Prolog as follows.

Program 2 quick sort

```
(1)   quicksort( Unsorted,Sorted ):-
              qsort( Unsorted,Sorted,[] ).

(2)   qsort( [X|Unsorted], Sorted, Rest ):-
              partition( Unsorted,X,Smaller,Larger ),
              qsort( Smaller,Sorted,[X|Sorted1]),
              qsort(Larger,Sorted1,Rest).
(3)   qsort( [],Rest,Rest ).

(4)   partition([X|Xs],A,Smaller,[X|Larger]):-
              A < X : partition(Xs,A,Smaller,Larger).
(5)   partition([X|Xs],A,[X|Smaller],Larger):-
              A >= X : partition(Xs,A,Smaller,Larger).
(6)   partition([],_,[],[]).
```

Three *quick sort* programs written by the other languages are listed in Fig. 1, because the direct way for comparing the simplicity is to list a program which describes the same algorithm for each language. Comparing program 2 with the programs in Fig. 1, it is obvious that P-Prolog is the simplest. In Concurrent Prolog, users must think about which variables are read-only. In PARLOG, users must add a mode declaration for every predicate. And in GHC, users must avoid allowing a variable in a goal unify with any instances before the clause to be committed. But, in P-Prolog, except for substituting the commit operator ':' for the cut operator '!', program 2 is exactly the same as a quicksort program written by the sequential logic programming language PROLOG. (It may be hard to believe that this program can be executed in parallel.) A simple example ?- **quicksort([2,1,3],X)** described below, demonstrates how it works and how processes are synchronized with each other by exclusive relation checking. A flow diagram for the execution is shown in Fig. 2. For saving space, we substitute **p** and **qs** for **partition** and **qsort**, respectively. At step 0, we have an initial goal **quicksort([2,1,3],X)**. Every step **i** is the result from the reduction of the goals of step **i−1**. The numbered arrow(marked by **n**) between the two blocks A and B means that a unification between A and the **n**_th clause defined in program 2 produces **B**. The line arrow indicates a suspension from reducing. For instance, at step 2, **p([1,3],2,S,L)**, **qs(S,X,[2|W])** and **qs(L,W,[])** try to reduce. Obviously, **p([1,3],2,S,L)** can be reduced to **p([3],2,S1,L1)** by unifying it with clause 5. But **qs(S,X,[2|W])** and **qs(L,W,[])** are suspended because they successfully unify with two clauses(2 and 3 in program 2) which are *expected exclusive clauses*. After step 3, **S** is bound to **[1|S1]**, so there is only one clause is committable. Therefore **qs(S,X,[2|W])** can be reduced immediately. Last, at step 7 all clauses have been reduced to true, then the execution is stopped and a sorted list **[1,2,3]** is obtained.

Another example is shown below. Like other parallel logic programming languages, streams are used to communicate with each of the distributed processes

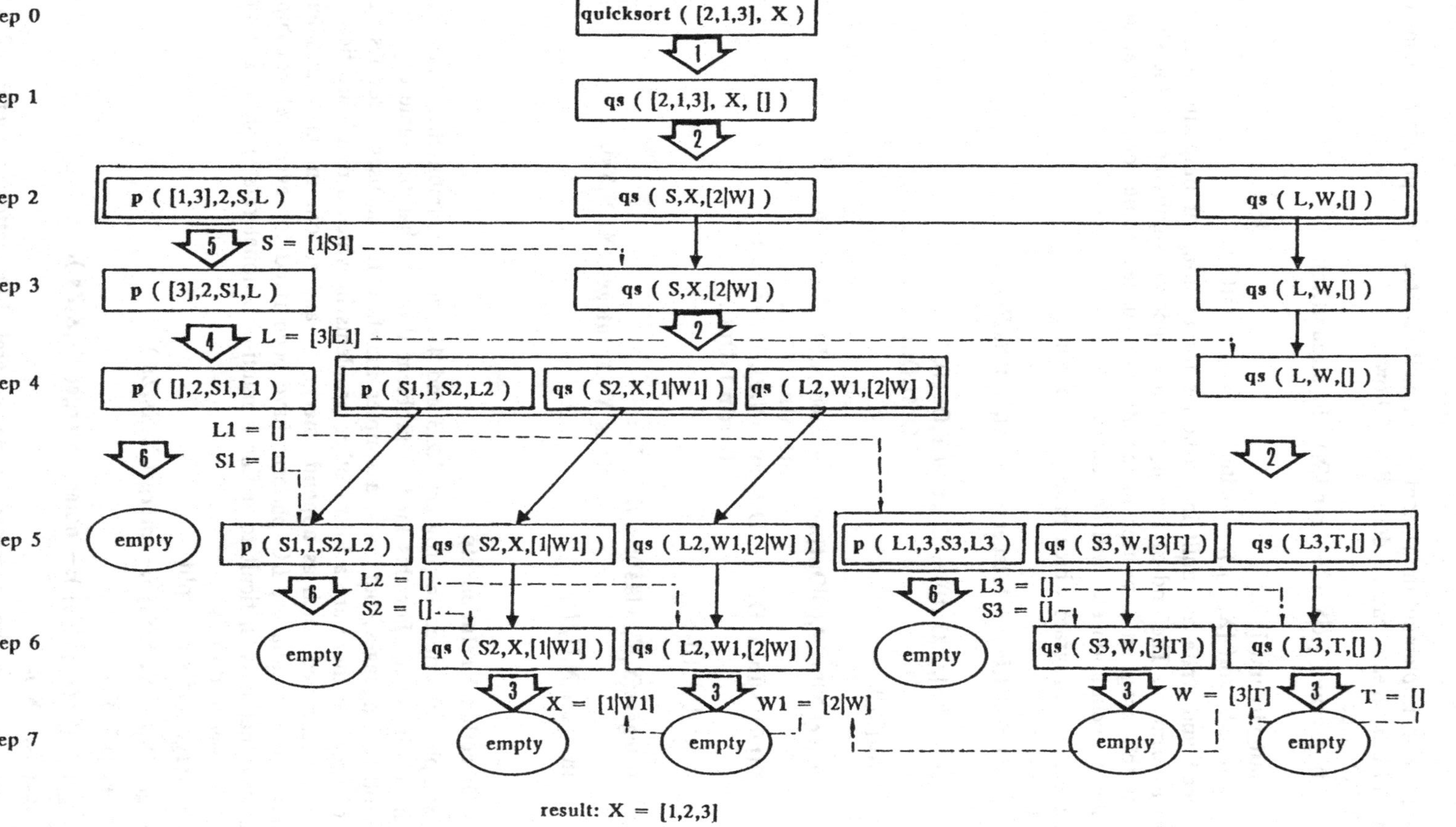

Figure 2 The Execution of ?-quicksort([2,1,3],X)

in P-Prolog. For implementing stream I/O functions, the two programs named **in_stream** and **out_stream** can be defined as follows:

Program 3 I/O stream

```
in_stream( [X|Xs] ):- read(X) : in_stream(Xs).

out_stream( [] ).
out_stream( [X|Xs] ):- write(X) , outstream(Xs).
```

Here, **read** and **write** are built_in predicates for inputing or outputing a term from or to a terminal. The end of the in_stream is ignored signifying for the simplification. If this program is written in the other languages, some read-only annotation, or mode declaration etc. will be added.

Next, there is a program which produces the primes.

Program 4 primes

```
primes(N,Ps):- integers(2,N,Ns), sift(Ns,Ps).

sift([P|In],[P|Out]):- filter(In,P,Out1),
                       sift(Out1,Out).
sift([],[]).

filter([N|In],P,[N|Out]):- D is mod(N,P), D \== 0 :
                           filter(In,P,Out).
filter([N|In],P,Out):- D is mod(N,P), D == 0 :
                           filter(In,P,Out).
filter([],P,[]).

integers(X,N,[X|Xs]):- X < N :
                           X1 is X+1, integers(X1,N,Xs).
integers(N,N,[N]).
```

4.2. Multi-directional relationship

The examples described in program 1,2,3 and 4 have a common characteristic, namely, single direction. For this kind of problem P-Prolog has the same capability as the other languages, but gives a simpler interface to the user. Besides of this kind of problem there are a lot of other problems in which a multi-directional relationship is described, such as **append**, **merge** ... and so on. In most parallel logic programming languages, I/O patterns have been fixed for every relationship in such a way that it is difficult to define a multi-directional relationship. But in P-Prolog it is easy to do this.

Program 5 merge and strict split

```
(1)  merge( [X|Xs],Y,[X|Zs] ):- merge( Y,Xs,Zs ).
(2)  merge( [],Y,Y ).
(3)  merge( X,[Y|Ys],[Y|Zs] ):- other : merge( Ys,X,Zs ).
(4)  merge( X,[],X ).
```

This program can be executed using several I/O patterns: merge(?,?,^),

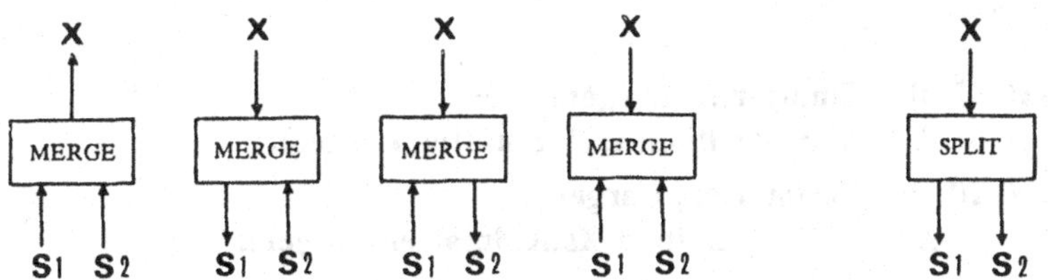

Figure 3 Multi-directional of Merge

Figure 4 A Split

merge(?,^,?), merge(^,?,?), and merge(?,?,?). Here, '?' denotes input and '^' denotes output. Clause (1) and clause (2) will be candidated for execution before clause (3) and clause (4). For merging two input streams, it works as follows. If the first argument of the caller is a substitution instance of a non-empty list, then only clause (1) can be committed so that clause (1) will be reduced. If the first argument is an unbound variable, then clause (1) and clause (2) are committed at same time, so that they fail to become candidacies. Therefore, clause (3) and clause (4) will be executed continuously. Now, if the second argument is also an unbound variable, it will be suspended and wait for input, otherwise clause (3) or clause (4) will be reduced. Besides this I/O pattern, this program can also be used to accept two input streams **X, S1**, and produce an output stream **S2** which is a split stream created by separating **S1** from **X**. For instance, if the first argument and the third argument are the substitution of a non-empty list, either clause (1) or clause (3) will succeed to candidacy depending on whether or not the first elements of two lists are the same.

The behavior of program 5 is shown in Fig. 3. The synchronization mechanism initiates its process only if more than one stream is accepted at any port (the position of argument), or one stream is accepted at the first or the second port. If we want to expand its I/O pattern so that it can accept a stream at the third port, and output two split streams (Fig. 4), we can rewrite program 5 as follows:

Program 6 merge and split

```
(1)   merge( [X|Xs],Y,[X|Zs] ):- merge( Y,Xs,Zs ).
(2)   merge( [],Y,Y ).
(3)   merge( X,[Y|Ys],[Y|Zs] ):- other : merge( Ys,X,Zs ).
(4)   merge( X,[],X ):- var(X) : true.
(5)   merge( [],[],[] ).
```

Another interesting example is rewriting a sort program which can also be regarded as a permutation program.

Program 7 sort and permutation

```
(1)   qsort( [X|Unsorted], Sorted ):- Sorted \== [] :
                          partition( Unsorted,X,Smaller,Larger ),
                          qsort( Smaller,Sorted1 ),
                          qsort(Larger,Sorted2 ),
                          append( Sorted1,[X|Sorted2],Sorted ).
```

(2) **qsort([],[]).**

(3) **partition([X|Xs],A,Smaller,[X|Larger]):--**
A < X : partition(Xs,A,Smaller,Larger).

(4) **partition([X|Xs],A,[X|Smaller],Larger):--**
A >= X : partition(Xs,A,Smaller,Larger).

(5) **partition([],_,[],[]).**

(**append** is defined in program 9)

Program 7 can be used to execute a goal such as ?- qsort(X,[1,2,3]), and it will give six solutions of X, namely [1,2,3], [1,3,2], [2,3,1], [2,1,3], [3,1,2] and [3,2,1].

Because P-Prolog uses exclusive relations to synchronize, one relationship can be defined multi-directionally, and the streams can change their directions dynamically.

4.3. Not Only *Don't care* Non-determinism but also *Don't know* Non-determinism

Compared with the other parallel logic programming languages, the semantics of the guarded horn clause in P-Prolog incorporates an extended meaning of *don't know* non-determinism. In P-Prolog, the guarded horn clauses defined by *expected exclusive relation* are evaluated in the conventional way called 'committed the choice non-determinism' in which only one clause is reduced, and the others are omitted. This is also called '*don't care* non-determinism'. An other type of non-determinism called '*don't know* non-determinism', which is executed in a sequential Prolog system by backtracking, is ignored in guarded horn clause style programs. Therefore, only one solution can be solved in those guarded horn clause programs. In P-Prolog we can use the non-exclusive relation to express the or-parallelism for all solution searching. The guarded horn clauses defined by *expected non-exclusive relation*(double neck clauses) are executed in parallel. And their committed operator has lost the original meaning of committed choice; they just play the role of a sequential-and operator. This syntax style is very convenient. For instance, a program for finding an element in the intersection of two lists can be written in P-Prolog as follows:

Program 8 intersect

(1) **intersect(X,L1,L2):- member(X,L1), member(X,L2).**

(2) **member(X,[X|_]):-- true.**

(3) **member(X,[_|Y]):-- member(X,Y).**

Because clause (2) and (3) are *double neck clauses*, success in committing one of them does not exclude the others. As a result, clause **member(X,L)** can be evaluated in parallel, and more than one solution of **X** will be returned from different search paths. If the second argument of **member** is sent from another process dynamically, it is necessary to synchronize it. In this case, the relationship of **member** can be defined as follows:

(1) **member(X,[X|Y]):-- Y \== [] : true.**

(2) **member(X, [_|Y]):-- Y \== [] : member(X,Y).**

(3) **member(X, [X]).**

Compared with the other parallel logic programming languages, the synchronization mechanism of P-Prolog seems less efficient in terms of implementation, because it must try to execute the guards of all alternative clauses. But, in fact, the guards of candidates are evaluated in parallel. Therefore, we can say that it does not decrease efficiency very much.

5. Programming in P-Prolog

When a program is written in P-Prolog, the important point is how to decide which clause is *single neck* or *double neck*.

First, we give a definition of the relationship's *universe*.

Definition 4: Let S be a set of clauses by which our program is composed, and H be a Herbrand universe [Chang and Lee 1973] of S. For any relationship defined in S, its *universe* **U** is an infinite set defined as

$$\mathbf{U} =_{def} \bigcup_{i=0}^{\infty} (P(x_{i1}, \cdots, x_{in}))$$

here, n is an arity of P, $x_{ij} \in$ H or x_{ij} is unbound.

Definition 5: Let U be a universe of P in a set of S. A *subuniverse* of P named U_s is a subset of U. that is

$$U_s \subseteq U.$$

It is known that, for defining a relationship P, a subuniverse U_s of P is usually considered (U_s = U , if not to be considered). Therefore, one of the basic rules may be summarized as: *expected exclusive clauses* (single neck clauses) should be exclusive for U_s.

For example, a program appending two lists can be written as

(1) **append([],X,X).**

(2) **append([X|Y],Z,[X|W]):– append(Y,Z,W).**

for a U_s which is composed by all of the goals whose first argument is a list.

If U_s = U, the **append** program will be rewritten as:

(1) **append([],X,X):-- true.**

(2) **append([X|Y],Z,[X|W]):-- append(Y,Z,W).**

If we want to restrict U_s to a special set which does not include the goals all of whose arguments are unbound, the **append** program can be written as follows:

program 9 append

(1) **append([],X,X):-- X \== [] : true.**

(2) **append([X|Y],Z,[X|W]):-- append(Y,Z,W).**

(3) **append([],[],[]).**

There is another **append** whose U_s is composed by all of the goals which at least have two list arguments.

program 10 append

(1) **append([],X,X).**

(2) **append([X|Y],Z,[X|W]):− Z\==[X|W] : append(Y,Z,W).**

In contrast to the other parallel logic languages, in P-Prolog, users pay attention to the exclusive relation of clauses rather than the declaration of I/O pattern. It seems to us, the syntactic construct of *expected exclusive clauses* has more logicality than the declaration of I/O pattern.

One may doubt whether the synchronization mechanism based on the exclusive check is effective in given case, or not. The answer is 'yes', because the two OR-conditions can be rewritten as EXC- conditions easily. Another suspicion is about a relationship defined by only one clause, which is not eligible to be checked for exclusive relation. In fact, since there is no alternative choice for it, synchronization is not necessary unless this clause is a specially built-in predicate which has a side effect, such as **write** and so on. As mentioned in section 3, some special built-in predicates which can return a 'suspend' signal are supported in P-Prolog. Therefore, it is not a problem from this point of view.

For making write programs easier, an auxiliary system named Semantics Checker has been implemented. It can analyze the P-Prolog programs, and warn users of what kinds of goals may be suspended in reducing.

Finally, two interesting cases are discussed below:

(1) a subset of P-Prolog using only *single neck clauses*, and

(2) a subset of P-Prolog using only *double neck clauses*.

The former is an and-parallel logic language, and cannot search for multi-solutions in parallel. It is similar to Concurrent Prolog, GHC etc. from this point of view. As for the latter, it can be regarded as a parallel logic language without a synchronization mechanism. A translator for compiling the former subset of P-Prolog into the other parallel logic languages may be implemented easily.

6. Conclusions and Future Work

A new parallel logic programming language named P-Prolog was presented. Two characteristics of P-Prolog are

(1) We need not designate the 'input' and 'output' for an argument. And we can use a single relationship in more than one direction.

(2) Guarded horn clause is extended to process or-parallelism. The system can find all solutions without using special syntactic constructs like all-solutions.

A interpreter of P-Prolog has been implemented in C-prolog. We are starting to write a interpreter of P-Prolog in the C language. The main problem is how to combine and- parallelism with or-parallel search for multi-solutions efficiently. We are investigating the implementation of P-Prolog based on a shared environment scheme. The detail of P-Prolog's implementation will be discussed in another paper.

7. Acknowledgements

The authors gratefully acknowledge the advice and guidance of Dr. Mario Tokoro, the Dept. of E.E., Keio Univ. Also the authors would like to thank Yasuro Shobatake, Jun Miyazaki, Hideharu Amano, Michio Isoda, Takaichi Yoshida, Yutaka Ishikawa and Yutaka Akiyama, who are students of Aiso Lab. and Tokoro Lab. in the Dept. of E.E., Keio Univ., for many interesting hours of discussion.

Last but not least, the authors are especially grateful to Toshiki Kikuchi and Hideo Tamura who joined this project in Sept. 1985. Toshiki Kikuchi is designing and implementing the kernal of the P-Prolog system with us. And Hideo Tamura is designing and implementing P-Prolog's debug system.

References

[1] Chang C. and Lee R. C.,
"Symbolic Logic and Mechanical Theorom Proving",
Academic Press, New York San Francisco London, 1973.

[2] Clark K. and Gregory S.,
"PARLOG: Parallel Programming in Logic",
Research Report DOC, April,1984.

[3] Clocksin W.F. and Mellish C.S.,
"Programming in Prolog",
Springer-Verlag Berlin Heidelbery New York, 1981.

[4] Hoare C.A.R.,
"Algorithm 64",
CACM, Vol. 4, pp 321, 1961.

[5] Kowalski R.,
"Logic for promlem solving",
NORTH-HOLLAND, 1979.

[6] Shapiro E.Y.,
"A Subset of Concurrent Prolog and Its Interpreter",
Technical Report TR-003 ICOT, Tokyo, Feb.,1983.

[7] Ueda K.,
"Guarded Horn Clauses",
Technical Report TR-103 ICOT, Tokyo, June, 1985.

Making Exhaustive Search Programs Deterministic

Kazunori Ueda
ICOT Research Center
Institute for New Generation Computer Technology
1-4-28, Mita, Minato-ku, Tokyo 108 Japan

Abstract. This paper presents a technique for compiling a Horn-clause program intended for exhaustive search into a GHC (Guarded Horn Clauses) program. The technique can be viewed also as a transformation technique for Prolog programs which compiles away the '**bagof**' primitive and non-determinate bindings. The class of programs to which our technique is applicable is shown with a static checking algorithm; it is nontrivial and could be extended. An experiment on a compiler-based Prolog system showed that our technique improved the efficiency of exhaustive search by 6 times for a permutation generator program. This compilation technique is important also in that it exploits the AND-parallelism of GHC for parallel search.

1. Introduction

We often use Horn-clause logic, or more specifically the language Prolog, to obtain all solutions of some problem, that is, to obtain all answer substitutions for the variables in a goal to be solved. In this framework, however, it is difficult to *collect* the obtained solutions into a single environment to make further processing such as counting the number of the solutions, comparing them, classifying them, and so on. This is because these solutions correspond to different, independent paths of a search tree. For this reason, many of Prolog implementations support system predicates for creating a list of solutions of a goal given as an argument; examples are '**setof**' and '**bagof**' of DEC-10 Prolog (Bowen et al. [1983]). Naish [1985] made a survey of all-solutions predicates in various Prolog systems. These system predicates, however, internally use some extralogical features to record the obtained solutions. So it should be an interesting question whether it is possible to do exhaustive search without such primitives.

Another motivation is that we may sometimes wish to do exhaustive search in GHC (Ueda [1985]; Ueda [1986]) or other parallel logic programming languages which do not directly support exhaustive search. In this case, parallelism inherent in GHC should be effectively used for the search.

One possible way to achieve the above requirements is to write down a first-order relation directly which states, for example, that *"S is a list of all solutions of the N-queens problem"*. It is almost evident that such a relation can be described within the framework of Horn-clause logic. However, in practice, it is much harder to write it manually than to write a program which finds only one solution at a time. A programming tool which automatically generates an exhaustive search program could resolve this situation, and this is the way which we will pursue in this paper.

2. Outlines of the Method

Our method is to compile a Horn-clause program intended for exhaustive search by means of backtracking or OR-parallelism into a GHC program or a deterministic Prolog program which returns the same (multi-)set of solutions in the form of a single list. The word 'deterministic' means that all bindings given to variables are determinate and never undone. Prolog programs in this subclass are interesting from the viewpoint of implementation, since they never call for a trail stack. Furthermore, determinism in this sense has a similarity with the semantical restriction which GHC imposed to a proof procedure for Horn-clause logic in order to make all activities done in a single environment. This similarity is reflected by the fact that a transformed program can be interpreted both as a GHC program and as a Prolog program by the slight change between the '|' (commitment) operator and the '!' (cut) operator.

There are two possible views of this transformation technique. One is to regard this as compilation from a Horn-clause program to a guarded-Horn-clause program. By compiling OR-parallelism into AND-parallelism, we eliminate a multiple environment mechanism which is in general necessary for parallel search since each path of a search tree would create its own binding environment. The other view is to regard it as transformation of a Prolog program. This transformation serves as simplification in the sense that the predicate '**bagof**' and the unbinding mechanism can be eliminated. Moreover, this transformation may remarkably improve the efficiency of a search program, as we will see in Chapter 7.

Our technique has another important meaning. By making search performed in a single environment, it becomes possible to introduce a mechanism for 'controlling' the search. That is, our technique may provide a starting point for more intelligent search.

A transformed program, viewed as a GHC program, emulates the OR-parallel and AND-sequential execution of the original program. The original OR-parallelism is compiled into AND-parallelism as stated above, and the sequential execution of conjunctive goals is realized by passing a continuation around. The AND-parallelism of GHC we use is a simple one, since two conjunctive goals solving different paths of a search tree have no interaction except when solutions are collected.

A continuation is a data structure which represents remaining tasks to be done before we get a solution. The notion of a continuation was effectively used also in Concurrent Prolog and GHC compilers on top of Prolog (Ueda and Chikayama [1985]) to implement a goal queue. The difference is that here we use a stack instead of a queue.

3. Previous Research

Implementation technique of exhaustive search in parallel logic programming languages can be found in (Hirakawa, Chikayama and Furukawa [1984]) and (Clark and Gregory [1984b]). Their approach is to describe an interpreter of Horn-clause programs in Concurrent Prolog (Shapiro [1983]) or PARLOG (Clark and Gregory [1984a]), but the following problems could be addressed:

(1) The interpreter approach loses efficiency.

(2) The multiple environment mechanism is implemented as a run-time creation of new variants of terms.

Here, a variant is a term created by systematically replacing all the occurrences of the variables in an original term by fresh variables.

Problem (1) will not be serious, since it could be resolved by a partial evaluation technique. Alternatively, we could directly write a compiler which corresponds to the original interpreter without much difficulty, as we did in (Ueda and Chikayama [1985]). On the other hand, Problem (2) seems serious.

The reason why we need multiple environments is that different unifiers can be generated when we rewrite a goal in two or more ways by using different program clauses at the same time. Therefore, when we interpret an exhaustive search program, we make a necessary number of variants of the current set of goals and the partially determined solution prior to the simultaneous derivation. The above interpreters made some optimization to reduce the amount of variants to be created, but they did not completely avoid run-time creation of them.

However, run-time creation of variants is a time-sensitive operation. The semantics of GHC is designed so that it is not affected by *anti-substitution* (Ueda [1986]) which replaces an occurrence of some term T in the guard/body of a clause by a fresh variable X and adds the goal $X{=}T$ in that guard/body. Anti-substitutability serves as an acid test for new features among other implications of it. Applying anti-substitution to a goal for creating a variant, say '`copy(`T_1`,`T_2`)`', we get a conjunction '$T_1{=}T_3$`, copy(`T_3`,`T_2`)`'. This rewriting clarifies that the value of the first argument of '`copy`' may be instantiated with potential delay. Thus the predicate '`copy`' is incompatible with anti-substitutability, and GHC cannot give any reasonable semantics to it. In sequential Prolog also, the predicate '`copy`' should be considered extralogical, because it cannot be defined without the extralogical predicate '`var`' which checks if its argument is currently an uninstantiated variable. The use of extralogical predicates should be discouraged, since it introduces semantical complexity and it hinders description of programming systems and support from them.

Carlsson [1984] presented implementation of exhaustive search in functional programming. His and our approaches are alike in that both use continuations; however, the differences seem more important than the similarities. Firstly, our technique takes parallel execution into account. Secondly, our approach compiles away the problem of environment management while his approach requires creation of variants when collecting solutions. Thirdly, our technique generates logic programs, and so can be used as a transformation tool within logic programming.

4. A Simple Example

To illustrate the difference between the previous method and ours, let us consider the example of decomposing a list using the '`append`' predicate:

```
:- append(U,     V,[1,2,3]).                     (4 - 1)
   append([],    Z,Z       ).                    (4 - 2)
   append([A|X],Y,[A|Z]    ) :- append(X,Y,Z).   (4 - 3)
```

From the head of Clause (4−3), we get a partial solution U=[1|X]. Then we get three instances for X, namely [], [2], and [2,3], by recursive calls. However, these three solutions cannot share the common prefix '[1|' as long as the value of a variable is represented by a reference pointer rather than by an association list, and this is why we have to make variants of the partial solution [1|X].

Our method, on the other hand, first rewrites Clause (4 − 3) as follows:

```
append(X2,    Y,[A|Z]  ) :- append(X,Y,Z), X2=[A|X].                    (4-4)
```

The predicate '=' unifies its two arguments. It can be defined by a single unit clause

```
X = X.
```

We assume that body goals are executed from left to right, following head unification. Then, while Clause (4 − 3) generates answer substitutions in a top-down manner, Clause (4 − 4) generates them in a bottom-up manner by combining ground terms. The first output argument X2 remains uninstantiated until the first recursive goal, which may fork because of the two candidate clauses, succeeds. Therefore, we need not make variants of the partial solution upon the recursive call. Clause (4 − 4) is not tail-recursive, so we must instead push the remaining task of consing A and X to obtain X2 onto the stack representing a continuation. However, since the variable A has a ground value, the information to be stacked can be represented as a ground term and hence the continuation need not be copied when the goal append(X,Y,Z) forks.

Now we are prepared for the elimination of nondeterminism. Figure 1 shows a GHC program which returns the result equivalent (up to the permutation of solutions) to the following DEC-10 Prolog goal:

```
:- ..., bagof((X,Y), append(X,Y,Z), S), ... .                           (4-5)
```

```
Calling form:      :- ..., ap(Z,'L0',S,[]), ...

ap(Z,Cont,S0,S2) :- true | ap1(Z,Cont,S0,S1), ap2(Z,Cont,S1,S2).

ap1(Z,Cont,S0,S1) :- true | cont(Cont,[],Z,S0,S1).

ap2([A|Z],Cont,S0,S1) :- true | ap(Z,'L1'(A,Cont),S0,S1).
ap2(Z,     _,  S0,S1) :- otherwise | S0=S1.

cont('L1'(A,Cont),X,Y,S0,S1) :- true | cont(Cont,[A|X],Y,S0,S1).
cont('L0',        X,Y,S0,S1) :- true | S0=[(X,Y)|S1].
```

Fig. 1. List Decomposition Program

Search corresponding to the two clauses of 'append' is performed by the conjunctive goals 'ap1' and 'ap2'. Their arguments are as follows:

(i) the input (i.e., the third) argument of the original program,

(ii) the continuation,

(iii) the head of the difference list of solutions, and

(iv) its tail.

Since Clause $(4-2)$ is a unit clause, the corresponding predicate '**ap1**' activates the 'remaining tasks' by calling the predicate '**cont**' for continuation processing. At that time, two output results, **[]** and the input argument itself, are passed to the continuation processing goal. The predicate '**ap2**' checks if the input argument has the form **[A|Z]**, and if so, activates the first goal in the original clause with the information used by the second goal attached to the continuation. If the input argument is not of the form **[A|Z]**, the unification of the input argument fails and the empty difference list is returned immediately.

The predicate '**cont**' does continuation processing. If the continuation has the form **'L1'(A,Cont)**, it pushes **A** in front of the output **X** and calls '**cont**' to process the rest of the continuation, **Cont**. If the continuation has the form **'L0'**, it inserts the two outputs it received into the difference list. The function symbols constructing the continuation can be regarded as indicating the locations of the original program: **'L0'** indicates the end of Clause $(4-1)$ and **'L1'** indicates the end of the recursive call of Clause $(4-4)$. Interestingly, the predicate '**cont**' is very similar to an efficient (non-naive) list reversal program: The continuation in this example is essentially a list which represents the first part of each solution (which is a pair of lists) in a reversed form. Different solutions to be collected are created by different calls of '**cont**' which reverse different substructures of the shared continuation.

The program in Figure 1 collects the solutions from '**ap1**' and '**ap2**' by the concatenation of difference lists, but this is not a fair way of collection. If the first clause of some predicate produced infinite number of solutions, we could not see any solutions from the second clause. When we need a fair collection, we must collect solutions by using a '**merge**' predicate implemented fair.

We can interpret Figure 1 also as a Prolog program, provided that the '**|**' operator is replaced by the '**!**' operator, that the '**otherwise**' goal in the second clause of '**ap2**' is deleted, and that the second clause of '**ap2**' is guaranteed to be the last clause of '**ap2**'.

5. General Transformation Procedure

This chapter first presents the class of Horn-clause programs to which the technique as illustrated in Chapter 4 can be easily and mechanically applied, and then briefly shows the transformation procedure. We use the permutation program (Figure 2) as an example.

```
perm([],     []).
perm([H|T], [A|P]) :- del([H|T], A, L), perm(L, P).

del([H|T], H, T).
del([H|T], L, [H|T2]) :- del(T, L, T2).
```

Fig. 2. Permutation Program

First of all, we show the class of Horn-clause programs to which our transformation technique is applicable:

• *A Transformable Program*

A program is transformable if it enjoys the following property when the body goals in each clause are executed from left to right, following head unification:

— The arguments of every goal appearing in the program can be classified into input arguments and output arguments. When some goal is called, its input arguments must have been instantiated to ground terms, and then the goal must instantiate its output arguments to ground terms when it succeeds.

Although the above property may look restrictive at a glance, most programs which do not use the notion of 'multiple writers' (see Chapter 6) or the notion of a difference list (which can be an incomplete data structure) will enjoy this property. Programs which use multiple writers require pre-transformation as described in Chapter 6. On the other hand, programs which make use of difference lists could be handled by extending the above notion of input and output, as long as they allow static dataflow analysis. This conjecture is based on the observation that when we write a Prolog program which handles difference lists, we usually fully recognize how uninstantiated variables appear in the data structures.

One way to give input/output modes to a program would be to make the programmer declare them for every goal arguments appearing in the program. However, a more realistic way will be to make the programmer declare the mode of (the arguments of) the top-level goals only and to 'infer' the modes of other goals according to the following rules:

• *Moding Policy for a Single Goal*

(a) Arguments which have been instantiated to ground terms upon call are regarded as input (though they could be classified otherwise).
(b) All the other arguments are regarded as output.

The mode inference and the check whether the program is transformable can be done in a simple static analysis. We must perform the following analysis for each clause and for each mode in which the predicate containing that clause may be called:

• *Mode Analysis of a Single Program Clause*

(1) Mark all the variables appearing in the input head arguments as *ground*.
(2) While there is a body goal yet to be analyzed, do the following repeatedly:
  (i) Determine the mode of the next body goal according to the above moding policy for a single goal. Here, those terms which are composed only of variables marked as *ground* and function symbols, and only those, are regarded as ground terms.
  (ii) Then mark all the variables appearing in the output arguments of that goal as *ground*.
(3) Check if the variables appearing in the output head arguments are all marked as *ground*. If the check succeeds, terminate the analysis of this clause with success; otherwise report failure.

Given Declaration: perm(+, -). ('+': input, '-': output)

```
         +        -
perm( [],       []).
         +         -                  +        -    -          +  -
perm([H|T], [A|P]) :- del([H|T], A, L), perm(L, P).

         +     -    -
del([H|T], H,    T).
         +     -        -                  +   -   -
del([H|T], L, [H|T2]) :- del(T, L, T2).
```

Fig. 3. Mode Analysis of the Permutation Program

Initially, only the modes of top-level goals are known; possible modes of other goals are incrementally obtained during the above analysis. Therefore, the whole algorithm of the mode analysis should be as follows. In the following, S denotes a set of 'moded' predicates. A moded predicate is a predicate with a mode in which it is called; different modes of a predicate correspond to different moded predicates.

- *Mode Analysis of an Entire Program*

(A) Let S be a set of the moded predicates whose calls appear in the (declared) top-level goal clause. Mark those predicates as *unanalyzed.*

(B) Repeatedly do the following until no *unanalyzed* predicate remains in S. That is, take an *unanalyzed* predicate from S, unmark it, and analyze all its clauses using the above algorithm, adding to S with the mark *unanalyzed* all moded predicates whose calls are newly found during the execution of Step (2) .

Figure 3 shows the analyzed permutation program.

It is easy to prove, by induction on the number of steps of resolution, that a successfully analyzed program instantiates the output arguments of each goal to ground terms upon successful termination, provided ground terms are given to the input arguments.

A successfully analyzed program is then transformed according to the following steps:

(1) If there is any predicate to be called in two or more different modes, give a unique predicate name for each mode.

(2) Rewrite each clause into the normal form as follows:

(2a) For each clause other than unit clauses, replace output head arguments $T_1, \ldots,$ T_n by distinct fresh variables $V_1, \ldots, V_n$, and place the goals $V_1{=}T_1, \ldots, V_n{=}T_n$ at the end of the clause.

(2b) For each goal G in the body of each clause, replace its output arguments $T_1, \ldots,$ T_n by distinct fresh variables $V_1, \ldots, V_n$ and place the goals $V_1{=}T_1, \ldots,$ $V_n{=}T_n$ immediately after G unless $T_1, \ldots, T_n$ are distinct variables not appearing in the previous goals or the clause head.

(3) Transform each predicate in the program.

Step (1) removes multi-mode predicates. This transformation attaches the concept of a mode to each *predicate* as well as to each predicate *call.*

```
perm([],    []).
perm([H|T],X) :- del([H|T],A,L), /*L1*/ perm(L,P), /*L2*/ X=[A|P].

del([H|T],H,T).
del([H|T],X,Y) :- del(T,L,T2), /*L3*/ X=L, Y=[H|T2].
```

Fig. 4. Normal Form of the Permutation Program

```
<1> p([],    Cont,S0,S1) :- true | contp(Cont,[],S0,S1).
<2> p([H|T],Cont,S0,S1) :- true | d([H|T],'L1'(Cont),S0,S1).
<3> p(L,     _,    S0,S1) :- otherwise | S0=S1.

<4> d(L,Cont,S0,S2) :- true | d1(L,Cont,S0,S1), d2(L,Cont,S1,S2).

<5> d1([H|T],Cont,S0,S1) :- true | contd(Cont,H,T,S0,S1).
<6> d1(L,     _,   S0,S1) :- otherwise | S0=S1.

<7> d2([H|T],Cont,S0,S1) :- true | d(T,'L3'(H,Cont),S0,S1).
<8> d2(L,     _,   S0,S1) :- otherwise | S0=S1.

<9> contp('L2'(A,Cont),P,S0,S1) :- true | contp(Cont,[A|P],S0,S1).
<10> contp('L0',          P,S0,S1) :- true | S0=[P|S1].

<11> contd('L3'(H,Cont),L,T2,S0,S1) :- true |
          contd(Cont,L,[H|T2],S0,S1).
<12> contd('L1'(Cont),  A, L,S0,S1) :- true |
          p(L,'L2'(A,Cont),S0,S1).
```

Fig. 5. Transformed Permutation Program

The purpose of Step (2b) is to simplify output arguments in a goal. It is clear that a program which has passed the mode analysis and then has been rewritten according to Steps (1) and (2) is still in the transformable class. Figure 4 shows the normal form of the permutation program.

Now we will show the outline of Step (3), the main part of our transformation method. Figure 5 shows the result applied to the permutation program of Figure 4. In the following, we indicate in braces what in the example of the permutation program are mentioned by each term appearing in the explanation.

(a) The arguments of a transformed predicate are made up of
  - the input arguments of the original predicate,
  - the continuation, and
  - the head and the tail of the difference list for returning solutions.

  Each transformed predicate is responsible for doing the task of the original predicate, followed by the task represented by the continuation.

(b) For a predicate {'perm'} of which at most one clause can be used for reducing each goal, the transformed predicate consists of the transformed clauses {<1>, <2>} of the original ones (See (i)). For a predicate {'del'} of which more than one clause may be applicable for reduction, we give a separate subpredicate name {'d1', 'd2'} to each transformed clause {<5>, <7>}, and let the transformed predicate {'d'} call all these subpredicates and collect solutions.

(c) The body of a clause {<1>, <5>} transformed from a unit clause calls a goal for continuation processing {'contp', 'contd'}. This goal is given as arguments the output values {[], (H,T)} returned by the original unit clause.

(d) The body of a clause {<2>, <7>} transformed from a non-unit clause calls the predicate {'d'} corresponding to the first body goal {'del'} of the original clause (See (e) and (j)).

(e) When calling a (transformed) predicate {e.g., 'd' in <7>} corresponding to the i-th body goal G_i {the recursive call of 'del'} of some clause, we push the label {'L3'} indicating the next goal G_{i+1} together with the input data {H} used by the subsequent goals $G_{i+1}, \ldots, G_n$ {X=L, Y=[H|T2]}. When calling a predicate {'p'} corresponding to the top-level goal {say 'perm(L,X)' where L is some ground term}, we give as the initial value of the continuation the label {'L0'} indicating the termination of refutation together with the data {*none*} necessary for constructing a term to be collected {X}.

(f) Predicates for continuation processing are composed of clauses {<9>, <10>, <11>, <12>} each corresponding to the label pushed in Step (e). These clauses are classified according to the predicates immediately before those labels and are given separate predicate names {'contp', 'contd'}.

(g) Each clause {e.g., <12>} of a predicate for continuation processing makes input data {L} for the next goal {perm(L,P)} indicated by the received label {'L1'}, by using the information {*none*} stacked with the label and the output {A, L} of the last goal. Then it calls a predicate {'p'} corresponding to the next goal (See (e) and (j)).

(h) The clause {<10>} for processing the label {'L0'} indicating termination generates a term to be collected {P} from the output {P} of the top-level goal and the information {*none*} stacked with the label, and returns a difference list having that term as a sole element.

(i) For those transformed predicates {'p', 'd1', 'd2'} which may fail in the unification of the input arguments, backup clauses {<3>, <6>, <8>} are generated which return empty difference lists when the unification fails.

(j) In spite of the above rules, no transformed predicates are generated for '=' and other system predicates; they are processed immediately 'on the spot', followed by the next task {<9>, <11>}.

It is worth noting that in spite of our restriction, a transformed program can handle some non-ground data structure correctly. That is, the portions of an input data structure which are only passed around and never examined by unification need not be ground terms. For example, when we execute the following goal,

```
:- p([A,B,C], 'L0', S, []).
```

S will be correctly instantiated to a list of six permutations:

```
[[A,B,C],[A,C,B],[B,A,C],[B,C,A],[C,A,B],[C,B,A]].
```

6. On the Class of Transformable Programs

For the technique described above to be useful from a practical point of view, the transformable class of Horn-clause programs defined in Chapter 5 must be large enough to express our problems naturally. The problem in this regard is that we often make use of the notion of 'multiple writers'. By 'multiple writers' we mean two or more goals sharing some data structure and trying to instantiate it cooperatively and/or competitively. In Prolog programming, such a data structure is usually represented directly by a Prolog term and it is operated by the direct use of Prolog unification; a typical example is the construction of the output data of a parser program.

However, this programming technique has problems from the viewpoint of the applicability of our transformation:

(1) It is generally impossible to analyze statically which part of the shared data structure is instantiated by which goal.

(2) The shared data structure may not be instantiated fully to a ground term.

Problem (2) is considered a problem also from a semantical point of view. When extracting some information from the shared data structure generated by a search program, we have to use the extralogical predicate 'var' to see whether some portion of the data structure is left undetermined. One may argue that we need not use the predicate 'var' if we analyze the data structure after making it ground, that is, after instantiating its undetermined portions to some ground terms such as new constant symbols. He may further argue that making a term ground never calls for the predicate 'var' since we can accomplish this by trying to unify every subterm of it with a new constant. However, then, the search program which generates a non-ground result and the program to make it ground will be in the relationship of multiple writers, and the latter program should never start before the former program has finished because the latter must have a lower priority with respect to instantiation of the shared data structure. This means we have to use the concept of sequentiality or priority between conjunctive goals, both of which are concepts outside Horn-clause logic.

Let us consider Problem (2) in terms of the declarative semantics of logic programs (Lloyd [1984]). Collection of solutions makes it possible to count the number of solutions, as Warren [1982] says. Then what must be regarded as the number of solutions if they can contain variables? The number of maximally general answer substitutions? The number of elements of the minimal Herbrand model that are instances of the original goal? Both seem unsatisfactory. It seems that the number of solutions can be reasonably defined only by disallowing non-ground solutions, as long as we do not have a notion of types.

Anyway, we must make some pre-transformation to such a Horn-clause program in order to apply our transformation technique. That is, we must change the representation of the shared data structure to a ground-term representation—a list of binding information

Table 1. Performance of Exhaustive Search Programs (in msec.)

Program	*Original* ('**bagof**')	*Original* (*search only*)	*Transformed*	*Number Of Solutions*
List Decomposition (50 elements)	836	4	27	51
Permutation Generation (5 elements)	354	34	57	120
5-Queens	45	20	28	10
6-Queens	90	75	106	4
7-Queens	441	325	446	40
8-Queens	1796	1484	1964	92

generated by each writer. Each writer must receive the current list of binding information and return a new one as a separate argument. When a writer is to add some binding information, it must check the consistency of the current and the new information to be added. This checking could be done by trying to construct the original representation from scratch each time, but it could be done more efficiently by adopting an appropriate data structure (possibly other than a list of bindings) for the binding information.

Comparing the original and the proposed implementation schemes of multiple writers from a practical point of view, the proposed scheme is apparently disadvantageous in the ease of programming. However, the difference does not lie in the specification of the abstract data but only in the ease of its implementation, which should not be so essential a problem since accumulation of programming techniques and program libraries should alleviate the difficulty.

Efficiency is another point on which comparison should be made. Although the original representation is suitable for the execution using backtracking, it requires a multiple environment mechanism for OR-parallel execution, which may cause additional complexity and overhead (Ciepielewski and Haridi [1983]). The proposed pre-transformation may make the consistency checking somewhat expensive, but will make parallel execution much easier because no multiple environment mechanism is necessary.

Sometimes Problem (2) could be resolved more easily. Consider a parser of English sentences which checks the agreement of number. Neither a noun phrase nor a verb phrase may determine whether the subject is singular or plural, in which case a variable indicating the number may be left uninstantiated. In this case, however, it is easy to rewrite the program so that the analyzer of the noun phrase returns two possible values for that variable in OR-parallel instead of leaving it uninstantiated.

7. Performance Evaluation

Table 1 compares the performance of original and transformed programs.

The programs measured are those described above, and an *N-queens* program with N being 5, 6, 7 and 8. The *N-queens* program we used was in the transformable class defined in Chapter 5.

All programs were measured using DEC-10 Prolog on DEC2065. For each original program, the execution time of exhaustive search (by forced backtracking) *without* collection of solutions was measured as well as the execution time by the '**bagof**' primitive. The '**setof**' primitive was not considered because the sorting of solutions was inessential for us. Each program was measured after possible simplification which took advantage of the fact that Prolog checks candidate clauses sequentially.

As Table 1 shows, the proposed program transformation improved the efficiency of exhaustive search by 6 times for the permutation program and by more than 30 times for the list decomposition program '**append**'. This remarkable speedup was brought about by specializing the task of collecting solutions to fit within the framework of Horn-clause logic, while the '**bagof**' primitive uses a extralogical feature similar to '**assert**' which an optimizing compiler cannot help. A program such as *N-queens*, which has a small number of solutions compared with its search space, cannot therefore expect remarkable speedup; the transformed *N-queens* program got slightly slower except for *5-queens*. After manual optimization, however, the transformed *8-queens* program surpassed the original '**bagof**' version.

Another important point to note is that in the case of *8-queens*, the transformed program was only by 25% slower than the original program which does *not* collect solutions and which makes use of the dedicated mechanism for search problems, namely automatic backtracking. This suggests that the transformed program could not be improved very much without changing the search algorithm.

8. Summary and Future Works

We have described a method of compiling a Horn-clause program for exhaustive search into a GHC program or a deterministic Prolog program. Although not stated above, the method using the concept of a continuation can be applied also to the case where only one solution is required. Our method also provides the possibility of introducing control into search, since all activities are made to be performed in a single environment.

We restricted the class of Horn-clause programs to which our method is applicable. However, this class is never trivial and it is expected that we should not have so much difficulty in writing a program within this class or its natural extension. Rather, we believe that it is important from a practical point of view to show the class of Horn-clause programs which can be transformed without loss of efficiency and without resort to extralogical predicates. Programs to which our method is essentially inapplicable seem to require semantical considerations before trying to extend our method.

The loss of performance by not using such dedicated mechanisms as automatic backtracking was small. Conversely, we found that our technique may greatly improve the efficiency of exhaustive search that has been done by using the '**bagof**' primitive.

The proposed transformation eases parallel search in that it eliminates the need of multiple environments, but it never eliminates other problems on resource management.

Resource management is still an important problem for realizing parallel search. Therefore, our results need not and should not be interpreted as reducing the significance of OR-parallel Prolog machines: Specialized hardware can always perform better for a special class of programs. While our purpose was primarily to examine the possibility of efficient search on a general-purpose parallel machine, we expect also that our technique will be utilized for improving the efficiency of OR-parallel Prolog machines. Comparison of these two approaches should be an interesting research in the near future.

References

Bowen, D. L. (ed.), Byrd, L., Pereira, F. C. N., Pereira, L. M. and Warren, D. H. D. [1983] *DECsystem-10 Prolog User's Manual.* Dept. of Artificial Intelligence, Univ. of Edinburgh.

Carlsson, M. [1984] On Implementing Prolog in Functional Programming. In *Proc. 1984 Int. Symp. on Logic Programming,* IEEE Computer Society, pp. 154-159.

Ciepielewski, A. and Haridi, S. [1983] A Formal Model for OR-Parallel Execution of Logic Programs. In *Proc. IFIP '83,* Mason, R. E. A. (ed.), Elsevier Science Publishers B. V., Amsterdam, pp. 299-305.

Clark, K. L. and Gregory, S. [1984a] *PARLOG: Parallel Programming in Logic.* Research Report DOC 84/4, Dept. of Computing, Imperial College of Science and Technology, London.

Clark, K. L. and Gregory, S. [1984b] *Notes on the Implementation of PARLOG.* Research Report DOC 84/16, Dept. of Computing, Imperial College of Science and Technology, London, 1984. Also in *J. of Logic Programming,* Vol. 2, No. 1 (1985), pp. 17-42.

Hirakawa, H., Chikayama, T. and Furukawa, K. [1984] Eager and Lazy Enumerations in Concurrent Prolog. In *Proc. Second Int. Logic Programming Conf.,* Uppsala Univ., Sweden, pp. 89-100.

Lloyd, J. W. [1984] *Foundations of Logic Programming.* Springer-Verlag, Berlin Heidelberg New York Tokyo.

Naish, L. [1985] All Solutions Predicates in Prolog. In *Proc. 1985 Symp. on Logic Programming,* IEEE Computer Society, pp. 73-77.

Shapiro, E. Y. [1983] *A Subset of Concurrent Prolog and Its Interpreter.* Tech. Report TR-003, Institute for New Generation Computer Technology, Tokyo.

Ueda, K. [1985] *Guarded Horn Clauses.* ICOT Tech. Report TR-103, Institute for New Generation Computer Technology. Also to appear in *Lecture Notes in Computer Science,* Springer-Verlag, Berlin Heidelberg (1986).

Ueda, K. [1986] *Guarded Horn Clauses.* Doctoral Thesis, Information Engineering Course, Faculty of Engineering, Univ. of Tokyo.

Ueda, K. and Chikayama, T. [1985] Concurrent Prolog Compiler on Top of Prolog. In *Proc. 1985 Symp. on Logic Programming,* IEEE Computer Society, pp. 119-126.

Warren, D. H. D. [1982] Higher-order extensions to PROLOG: are they needed? In *Machine Intelligence 10,* Hayes, J. E., Mitchie, D. and Pao, Y. -H. (ed.), Ellis Horwood, Chichester, England, pp. 441-454.

Compiling OR-parallelism into AND-parallelism

Michael Codish and Ehud Shapiro

Department of Computer Science
The Weizmann Institute of Science
Rehovot 76100, Israel

Abstract

This paper suggests a general method for compiling OR-parallelism into AND-parallelism. An interpreter for an AND/OR-parallel language written in the AND-parallel subset of the language induces a source-to-source transformation from the full language into the AND-parallel subset. This transformation can be identified and implemented as a special purpose compiler or applied using a general purpose partial evaluator.

The method is demonstrated to compile a variant of Concurrent Prolog into an AND-parallel subset of the language called Flat Concurrent Prolog (FCP). It is also shown applicable to the compilation of OR-parallel Prolog to FCP. The transformation identified is simple and efficient. The performance of the method is discussed in the context of programming examples. These compare well with conventionally compiled Prolog programs.

1. Introduction

Concurrent Prolog [16], Parlog [2], Guarded Horn Clauses (GHC) [21] and Flat Concurrent Prolog (FCP) [10] are examples of concurrent logic programming languages. The common aspects of these languages are that they support parallel and commited choice non-deterministic semantics. In addition they use a single assignment convention, communication via shared variables and simple data flow synchronization. The computational model of these languages allows two forms of parallelism to be exploited: AND-parallelism and OR-parallelism. These correspond to the two forms of non-determinism in the model: process selection and clause selection.

A number of difficult implementation problems must be solved in order to support OR-parallelism in a language. These involve management of multiple environments and communication between environments as well as the management of hierarchical process structures. Experience has shown that the AND-parallel subset of a language is sufficient for most applications; it is easier to implement and more efficient as well. The problem with implementing only the AND-parallel subset of a language is that the expressiveness of the language is restricted.

This paper suggests a general method to compile OR-parallelism into AND-parallelism. An interpreter for an AND/OR-parallel language written in the AND-parallel subset of the language induces a source-to-source transformation from the full language into the AND-parallel subset.

The method is demonstrated using an interpreter for an AND/OR-parallel variant of Concurrent Prolog called Safe Concurrent Prolog [3] (SCP) written in FCP. This interpreter simulates OR-parallelism using AND-parallel processes and a mechanism for mutual exclusion. It is shown to induce a simple and efficient transformation from SCP into FCP. The transformation produces a speed up of two orders of magnitude over interpreted programs. An optimized transformation is achieved by the combination of the interpreter and a partial evaluator developed by Safra [13].

Several compilation examples are presented. An OR-parallel Prolog interpreter due to Kahn is used to provide for the compilation of various Prolog programs into FCP. The results compare well with similar programs written in GHC [9] and Prolog [12].

2. Language Description

Concurrent Prolog was originally described in [16]. A Concurrent Prolog program is a set of guarded horn clauses of the form:

$$H :- G \mid B$$

where H is the head, G (Guard) and B (body) are sets of procedure calls. Procedure calls may be solved in any order and thus may be viewed as a system of parallel processes. A program may be viewed as a set of rewrite rules to be applied non-deterministically on the processes. A process may be rewritten to a clause body if it unifies with the head of the clause and the clause guard can be solved. Processes are synchronized using data flow synchronization via read-only annotations on variables (i.e. $X?$). A procedure is a set of clauses each of which has the same head predicate.

The flexibility and expressiveness of the language have been demonstrated on a wide range of applications [17]. An initial implementation was sufficient to explore the new formalism but was slow, inadequate for large applications and did not correctly implement OR-parallelism [15,22]. A full implementation of Concurrent Prolog proved to be a nontrivial task.

Flat Concurrent Prolog (FCP) is the AND-parallel subset of Concurrent Prolog in which the guards are simple system defined test predicates. The practicality of the language has been demonstrated on a number of sizable applications which includes a compiler, programming environment and sections of an operating system [10]. Most of the applications written in Concurrent Prolog were found to be either already in the flat subset or easily converted to it by hand [1]. An efficient compiler for Flat Concurrent Prolog and a programming environment written in the language have been implemented [18] on a uniprocessor.

Safe Concurrent Prolog (SCP) is a variant of Concurrent Prolog which supports both AND-parallelism and OR-parallelism. The language avoids the semantic and implementation problems identified in the context of Concurrent Prolog [15,22]. The main design choice of SCP was to add an annotation to the syntax of Concurrent Prolog and to apply a safety restriction [5,3] to the executions of a program. The added annotation declares for each variable a *mode* while the safety restriction states that an execution of a program will confirm to the syntactic mode declaration.

The new annotation is termed *write-enable* and denoted by '↑'. It distinguishes between *input* and *output* variables in a clause. Output variables are those which occur annotated in the clause head; all other variables in the clause are input variables. This specification is similar to the mode declarations of Parlog [2] but more flexible since it applies to variables rather than arguments.

The write-enable annotations provide a static definition of which variables a guard may instantiate. They also determine which variables in the global environment are accessible from a guard system. Input variables appearing in a guard are defined to be accessible during the computation of that guard; output variables are defined to be inaccessible. The safety restriction states that the guard of a procedure is not allowed to write on an input variable. Safe Concurrent Prolog is the set of ↑-annotated Concurrent Prolog programs whose executions confirm to this specification.

The general problem of verifying that the executions of a program will confirm to the syntactic specification of its write-enable annotations is undecidable [3]. This is true not only of SCP but of Parlog as well. Both SCP and Parlog contain syntactically recognizable subsets. Programs in these subsets are termed *syntactically safe* programs. The syntactic conditions which determine these subsets imply that an execution of a program will not violate the safety restriction.

The computation of an SCP program creates multiple environments but an implementation of the language does not require complex mechanisms to manage them. This is due to the static definition of communication between environments and the safety restriction. In addition, an implementation may be optimized to allocate local copies of variables during compilation.

An operational semantics for Safe Concurrent Prolog is presented in [3] and forms the basis for the implementation described in the next section.

3. A Safe Concurrent Prolog Interpreter

A working implementation for Safe Concurrent Prolog has been written in FCP. It is a two stage process consisting of three components: a syntactic safety checker, a precompiler and an interpreter. The first stage involves a syntactic safety check and the precompilation of a program. The second stage involves the interpretation of the precompiled program.

The precompiler provides facilities for the implementation of the commit operator and allocates local copies of global output variables. It sets up the communication between global and local environments that will be needed at run-time. Each clause *Head :- Guard | Body* of an annotated program is precompiled to a *clause triplet* consisting of:

- a unique identifier to support mutual exclusion at commitment.
- a modified copy of the clause, *NewHead :- Guard | Body*, in which annotated terms of *Head* are replaced by new variables.
- a copy of the original head.

A procedure *number_of_clauses/2* which defines the number of clauses in each procedure of the program is added to the precompiled program.

3.1 The Interpreter

The interpreter is a direct implementation of the operational model described in [3]. It contains three procedures: ***solve_and*** for solving conjunctions (spawning AND-parallelism), ***solve_or*** for applying the clauses of a program to a goal (spawning OR-parallelism) and ***commit*** for simulating commit. The operational model allows concurrent execution of these procedures but requires the commit operation to be atomic.

To solve a unit goal, each of the precompilied clauses for that goal are applied to it. This involves unifying the head of the modified clause with the goal and spawning subgoals for the guards of each modified clause. If the computation of a guard terminates successfully then the corresponding clause may commit. At most one clause may commit for a given goal. The other components of a clause triplet, the unique identifier and the original copy of the clause head are used to simulate the commit operation. The former is used for mutual exclusion, the latter for unification of local and global environments at commit time. The correct implementation of the commit operation is conceptually difficult but can be expressed as a concise and elegant three line FCP program

Guard systems instantiate only output variables and have direct access to input variables in the global environment. This is due to annotated terms in the original clause heads being copied to new variables in the modified clauses and to the safety restriction.

The computation of a (conjunctive) goal G is initialized by spawning solve_and processes for the subgoals of G. If all the subgoals reduce to ***true*** then the computation succeeds. The ***short circuit technique*** due to Takeuchi [19] is used to detect successful termination of a computation. The processes of a computation are chained in a circuit, each process acting as an open switch. A process which terminates closes the switch. When all of the processes have terminated the entire circuit is shortened and successful termination can be detected.

Logical variables are used to represent links connecting processes in a circuit. A process is invoked with two variables ***Left*** and ***Right*** connecting it to the neighbour left and right processes in the circuit. Two processes that are connected share a common link variable. Each process that terminates unifies its ***Left*** and ***Right*** variables. When all the processes have terminated the entire chain becomes one variable. The leftmost and rightmost processes contain the circuit ***ends***. One of the circuit ends is instantiated to a constant. When the circuit is short the other circuit end becomes instantiated to this constant.

```
solve(Goal, Result) :-
    solve_and(Goal, true, Result).

solve_and(true, Link, Link).
solve_and((A, B), Left, Right) :-
    solve_and(A, Left, Middle),
    solve_and(B, Middle, Right).
solve_and(A, Left, Right) :-
    otherwise |
    number_of_clauses(A, N),
    solve_or(A, N?, ME, Left, Right).
```

Figure 3.1a: Spawning AND-parallelism

Figure 3.1a implements the solve_and process. A solve_and process is invoked with two variables ***Left*** and ***Right*** connecting it to the neighbor left and right processes in the circuit. Each process that reduces to ***true*** unifies its ***Left*** and ***Right*** variables. One of the circuit ends is instantiated to the constant *true* and the other to the result variable of the computation. When the circuit is short the result variable becomes instantiated to *true.* A process *solve_and(A, L, R)* for a unit goal A spawns solve_or processes corresponding to each of the clauses for goal A. Note that the *otherwise* predicate in the guard of the third clause is an FCP kernel predicate which succeeds if all the other guards in the procedure fail [10]. An otherwise kernel may be replaced with the negation of the other guards of the procedure.

Each solve_or process, *solve_or(A, N, ME, L, R)*, attempts to solve the guard of a clause for A and to commit the computation to the body of this clause. Two processes are spawned; a solve_and process to solve the guard and an associated commit process. All of the solve_or processes for a given goal operate concurrently and may attempt to commit if the computation of their guard reduces to *true.* At most one solve_or process may succeed to commit.

Figure 3.1b implements the solve_or process. Each process receives a variable representing the goal A, a unique identifier N from the clause triplet, an occurrence of a mutual exclusion variable ME and occurrences of the left and right links of its parent solve_and process.

```
solve_or(_,0,_,_,_).
solve_or(A,N,ME,Left,Right) :-
    N > 0 |
    clause(N,(A :- G | B),A1),
    solve(G?,Result),
    commit(Result?,N,ME,A1,A,B,Left,Right),
    N1 := N - 1,
    solve_or(A,N1?,ME,Left,Right).
```

Figure 3.1b: Spawning OR-parallelism

A commit process succeeds if the associated guard computation has reduced to *true*, no other commit process for the same goal has committed and the respective global and local environments unify. It *suspends* until there is sufficient information to succeed and if any of the above conditions do not hold it terminates having *failed to commit.*

A commit process that succeeds commits the computation to the body of the corresponding clause. A system of solve_and processes corresponding to the body is inserted to the circuit between the left and right links of the reducing solve_and process.

```
commit(true,N,N,Head,Head,Body,L,R) :-
    solve_and(Body,L,R).
commit(_,_,_,_,_,_,_,_) :- otherwise | true.
```

Figure 3.1c: Commit Processes

Figure 3.1c implements the commit process. A commit process *commit(Result?, N, ME, Local, Global, Body, Left, Right)* contains: a result variable for the associated guard computation, an identifier from the clause triplet, a mutual exclusion variable, a copy of the local environment from the clause triplet, a copy of the global environment, the body of the modified clause and the left and right links of the parent solve_and process.

The result variable *Result* of the guard computation will become instantiated to *true* if this guard computation is successful. The unique identifier N of a committing clause is unified with the mutual exclusion variable ME preventing other clauses from committing.

Properties of The Commit Operator

The atomicity of the commit operator relies upon the atomicity of unification and commitment in FCP. A commit goal succeeds if it unifies with the head of the first clause in the commit procedure. This unification is an atomic action which does four things. It verifies that the associated guard computation reduced to *true* and that no other clause has committed. It unifies the global and local environments and prevents other clauses from committing by instantiating the mutual exclusion variable. Reduction to the body of the committing clause need not be part of this atomic action.

Two main strategies are generally used to detect the failure of a clause to commit; *early detection* and *late detection* [11]. The first strategy requires that the inability of a clause to commit be detected as early as possible. This can be difficult to implement as complex mechanisms are required to repeatedly check the consistency of environments. For this reason late detection, which delays the consistency checks until termination of the associated guard computation, is generally implemented.

In the above implementation a process may fail to commit either because another process instantiates the mutual exclusion variable or because the local and global environments become inconsistent. In extended versions of the interpreter which differentiate between suspension and failure a process may fail to commit also in the case that its associated guard computation fails. The implementation relies on the order independence of unification in FCP to achieve an elegant solution for early detection. This allows immediate failure if either the environments become inconsistent or the mutual exclusion variable becomes instantiated.

In a distributed implementation the processes associated with a computation may reside on different processors. The algorithms for distributed unification and distributed commit are relatively simple in FCP [14] thus the above program also specifies a distributed commit operator for Safe Concurrent Prolog.

4. Compiling SCP to FCP

The convenience of implementing an AND/OR language using the flat subset has been demonstrated above. A simple interpreter for SCP has been implemented in FCP. There remains the problem of efficiency; a level of meta-interpretation normally may cost a factor of 4 - 20 in execution time [17]. In the case of an interpreter which simulates OR-parallelism one could expect this factor to be much larger. The results below indicate an overhead of two orders of magnitude over compilation.

An interpreter $I_{L_1}^{L_2}$ written in a language L_1 for a language L_2 induces a transformation T: $L_2 \rightarrow L_1$. For a given interpreter this source-to-source transformation can be identified and applied to programs in L_2 to produce programs in L_1. Such transformations can be identified and implemented automatically using a technique called *partial evaluation* [4,6,20].

4.1 The Source-to-Source Transformation

The SCP interpreter written in FCP induces the simple source-to-source transformation shown in figure 4.1. A Safe Concurrent Prolog procedure:

$$\{\text{Clause}_i\}_{i=1}^{n}$$

is transformed into a Flat Concurrent Prolog program:

$$\{\text{Procedure}_i\}_{i=0}^{n}$$
$$\{\text{Commit}_i\}_{i=1}^{n}.$$

A procedure is invoked by calling *Procedure*$_n$. Each *Procedure*$_i$ process tries to solve the guard of *Clause*$_i$, to commit the computation to the body of that clause and invokes *Procedure*$_{i-1}$.

$Clause_i$: $Head(Global)$:- $Guard(Global) \mid Body(Global)$.

$Procedure_i$: $Head_i(Global, ME, Res)$:-
$\quad Guard_i(Local, ME1, Res1)$,
$\quad Commit_i(Res1?, ME, Global, Local, Res)$,
$\quad Head_{i-1}(Global, ME, Res)$.
$Head_i(Global, ME, Res)$:- $otherwise \mid Head_{i-1}(Global, ME, Res)$.

$Procedure_0$: $Head_0(\_,\_,\_)$:- $true \mid true$.

$Commit_i$: $Commit_i(true, \underline{i}, Head, Head, Res)$:- $Body_i(ME, Res)$.
$Commit_i(\_,\_,\_,\_,\_)$:- $otherwise \mid true$.

Figure 4.1: The transformation to FCP induced by the SCP interpreter

4.2 Partial Evaluation

Partial evaluation is an important program transformation technique which has recently received increased attention. It involves a specialization of a general function with respect to a partial description of its input to derive a residual function in the remaining variables. This technique can be applied to generate compilers from interpreters [4,6,7]. An Interpreter corresponds to the general function; a given program to a partial description of its input. A specialization of the interpreter to the given program corresponds to a residual function. Given an interpreter $I_{L_1}^{L_2}$ and a partial evaluator PE for L_1 then the transformation T induced by the interpreter $I_{L_1}^{L_2}$ can be applied automatically using the partial evaluator.

$$\text{T: L2} \rightarrow \text{L1}$$
$$\text{T}(\text{P}_{L_2}) = \text{PE}(\text{I}_{L_1}^{L_2}, \text{P}_{L_2})$$

The combination of an FCP partial evaluator developed by Safra [13] with the interpreter presented above has been applied to compile SCP to FCP. This is shown to provide an optimization of the transformation in Figure 4.1 which was identified manually.

Another application of partial evaluation involves a refinement of the syntactic safety check. A general program P which is not syntactically safe can be specialized with respect to a specific goal G (using the techniques of partial evaluation). Often the specialized program is syntactically safe. In this case we say that the program P is *syntactically safe with respect to goal G.* The OR-parallel Prolog interpreter presented in Program 4.4 is an example of a program which is syntactically safe with respect to some goals (i.e. some Prolog programs).

4.3 Example 1

Program 4.2 is a Safe Concurrent Prolog program which determines if two binary trees are isomorphic. Two trees are isomorphic if their corresponding subtrees are isomorphic in either order. Leaves are isomorphic if they are identical. The isotree program is an example of a program whose execution depends on OR-parallelism. It is not immediately expressed as a *flat* program (i.e. a program with simple guards). Program 4.2 is a restriction of a the more general Concurrent Prolog program which could also output an isomorphic tree for a given input tree.

```
isotree(leaf(X),leaf(X)).
isotree(tree(A,B),tree(C,D)) :-
    isotree(A,C) | isotree(B,D).
isotree(tree(A,B),tree(C,D)) :-
    isotree(A,D) | isotree(B,C).
```

Program 4.2: SCP isotree

The isotree program was compiled to FCP using the transformation in Figure 4.1 and using Safra's partial evaluator. The optimized transformation produced by the later is shown in program 4.3.

In Program 4.3 the first clause for *isotree3* calls *isotree2*. The structures in the head of *isotree3* are eliminated and only the variables are conveyed to *isotree2*. The information regarding the removed structures is implicitly conveyed. It is for this reason that *isotree2* contains only one clause; any goal is sure to unify with the head of this clause. It is also for this reason that the second clause for *isotree3* calls *isotree1* instead of *isotree2*; a goal that did not unify with the head of *isotree3* will not unify with the head of *isotree2*.

Another optimization performed by the partial evaluator involves the simplification of the *commit* procedures. In this example it is known at compile time that the local and global environments are consistent as they are identical. The *commit* procedures have been generalized to a single *commit* procedure with an additional argument.

```
isotree3(tree(A,B),tree(C,D),MEV,Res) :-
    isotree3(A,D,MEV1,Res1),
    commit(Res1?,3,MEV,B,C,Res),
    isotree2(A,B,C,D,MEV,Res).
isotree3(T1,T2,MEV,Res) :- otherwise |
    isotree1(T1,T2,MEV,Res).

isotree2(A,B,C,D,MEV,Res) :-
    isotree3(A,C,MEV1,Res1),
    commit(Res1?,2,MEV,B,D,Res).

isotree1(leaf(A),leaf(A),1,true).
isotree1(_,_,_,_) :- otherwise | true.

commit(true,N,N,T1,T2,Res) :-
    isotree3(T1,T2,MEV,Res).
commit(_,_,_,_,_,_) :- otherwise | true.
```

Program 4.3: FCP isotree from partial evaluation

The Flat Concurrent Prolog isotree program shown in Program 4.3 will return a result *true* in the case that the original SCP program succeeds. It returns no result in the case that the original Program were to fail or suspend.

The derived FCP isotree program was run for several example goals and compared with similar programs in other languages (see Table 7.1). In general the FCP program derived by the transformation in Figure 3.1 introduced an improvement of two orders of magnitude over interpretation for these examples. Other optimization introduced by the partial evaluator provided an additional speed-up of 25%.

4.4 Example 2

Program 3.4 contains an OR-parallel Prolog interpreter written in Concurrent Prolog which is due to Ken Kahn. To simplify the interpreter, it is assumed that each Prolog clause A :- $B_1, \ldots, B_n$ is represented as A :- $[B_1, B_2, \ldots, B_n \mid Bs]\backslash Bs$, i.e. the body of the clause is a difference-list. A predicate *clauses(A,Cs)* is assumed, which returns in *Cs* the list of clauses which are potentially unifiable with *A*.

The interpreter maintains a continuation of goals *As* to be solved. It attempts, in OR-parallel, to unify its first goal with the heads of the clauses in the program (clause 2). If successful, it concatenates the goals in the body of the clause in front of the continuation, and recurses with the new continuation (clause 3). The interpreter terminates when the continuation is empty (clause 1), and commits.

```
solve([ ]).                                              %1
solve([A | As]) :-                                       %2
    clauses(A?, Cs), resolve(A?, Cs?, As?).
resolve(A, [(A : -Bs\As) | Cs], As) :-                   %3
    solve(Bs?) | true.
resolve(A, [C | Cs], As) :-                              %4
    resolve(A, Cs?, As) | true.
```

Program 4.4: OR-parallel Prolog interpreter

Program 4.4 is an incomplete program as it calls an unspecified predicate *clauses/2*. It is completed by adding to it the *clause* form of a Prolog program. Unfortunately, any completion of Program 3.4 is not syntactically safe. Therefore the correctness of the transformation to FCP depends on prior verification that it is being applied to an SCP program. The completion of the OR-parallel Prolog interpreter with respect to a Prolog program which only tests variables is in particular always an SCP program.

Program 4.5 is an FCP isotree program derived by applying partial evaluation to the completion of the OR-parallel Prolog interpreter with respect to a Prolog isotree program. Notice that the implicit append call has been partially evaluated away and that similar optimizations to that in Program 4.3 have been introduced.

Program 4.5, like the OR-parallel Prolog interpreter maintains a continuation of goals which are yet to be solved. Each *isotree* goal contains a current goal to be reduced and a continuation of other goals to be reduced. A successful reduction of *isotree3* or *isotree2* reduces the current goal to two subgoals. One of these is the new current goal and the other is added to the continuation. A successful reduction of *isotree1* removes a goal from the continuation. A computation is successful if the current goal reduces to *true* and the continuation is empty. If a goal from the continuation fails the entire continuation is discarded. This provides an optimization which prunes the search tree.

```
isotree3(tree(A,B),tree(C,D),As,ME,Res) :-
    isotree3(A,D,[isotree(B,C) | As],ME1,Res1),
    commit(Res1?,3,ME,Res),
    isotree2(A,B,C,D,As?,ME,Res).
isotree3(T1,T2,As,ME,Res) :-
    otherwise |
    isotree1(T1,T2,As?,ME,Res).

isotree2(A,B,C,D,As,ME,Res) :-
    isotree3(A,C,[isotree(B,D) | As],ME1,Res1),
    commit(Res1?,2,ME,Res).
isotree1(leaf(X),leaf(X),[isotree(T1,T2) | As],ME,Res) :-
    isotree3(T1,T2,As?,ME1,Res1),
    commit(Res1?,1,ME,Res).
isotree1(leaf(X),leaf(X),[ ],1,true).
isotree1(_,_,_,_,_):- otherwise | true.

commit(true,N,N,true).
commit(_,_,_,_) :- otherwise | true.
```

Program 4.5: FCP OR-parallel isotree

5. Optimizations and Extensions

The above SCP interpreter is a basic implementation of the computational model for Safe Concurrent Prolog. It models correctly the semantics but does not consider efficiency. Also, there is no distinction in the model between failing and suspending computations. A series of extensions and optimizations of the model and its interpreter have been implemented. These include an interpreter which reports failure, extensions for interpretation of kernel predicates and several optimizations to the basic model. A detailed description of the extended and optimized interpreters can be found in [3] as well as several examples of applying their induced transformations.

5.1 An interpreter which reports failure

This interpreter represents a slight extension to the computation model. A goal is said to *fail* if none of the clauses in the program can be used to reduce it. In terms of the basic interpreter this means that all of the commit processes spawned for the goal terminated having failed to commit the computation.

An extended interpreter is defined such that the *Result* variable is instantiated to *true* or *false* if the goal succeeds or fails respectively. The interpreter will *suspend* if the corresponding computation suspends.

Determining the failure of a goal is implemented using the same technique used to determine the success of a computation. A goal process is defined to fail if all of the corresponding commit processes failed to commit the computation. All of the commit processes corresponding to a goal are connected in a circuit. One end of the circuit is instantiated to the constant *false*. The other end of the circuit is instantiated to the result variable of the computation. Each commit process that fails to commit the computation closes a switch. If all of the commit processes fail to commit the computation the result variable becomes instantiated to *false* signifying that the corresponding goal fails. The result variable may be instantiated to either *true* or to *false*, dependent on which circuit closes. Figure 5.1 contains an SCP interpreter which reports failure and Figure 5.2 the result of partial evaluation of this interpreter with respect to the isotree program.

```
solve_and(true, Link, Link, Res).
solve_and((A, B), Left, Right, Res) :-
    solve_and(A, Left, Middle, Res),
    solve_and(B, Middle, Right, Res).
solve_and(A, Left, Right, Res) :-
    otherwise |
    number_of_clauses(A, N),
    solve_or(A, N?, ME, Left, Right, Res, false, Res).
solve_or(_, 0, _, L, R, Link, Link, _).
solve_or(A, N, ME, Left, Right, OrL, OrR, Res) :-
    N > 0 | clause(N, (A :-  G | B), Local),
    solve(G?, GR),
    commit(GR?, N, ME, Local, A, B, Left, Right, OrL, OrM, Res),
    N1 := N - 1,
    solve_or(A, N1?, ME, Left, Right, OrM, OrR, Res).
commit(true, N, N, Head, Head, Body, L, R, OrL, OrR, Res) :-
    solve_and(Body, L, R, Res).
commit(_, _, _, _, _, Link, Link, _) :- otherwise | true.
```

Figure 5.1: Extended SCP Interpreter

```
isotree(T1, T2, Res) :- isotree3(T1, T2, ME, Res).
isotree3(t(A, B), t(C, D), ME, Res) :-
    isotree3(A, D, ME1, Res1),
    commit3(Res1?, ME, B, C, Res, OrL),
    isotree2(A, B, C, D, ME, Res, OrL).
isotree3(T1, T2, ME, Res) :- otherwise | isotree1(T1, T2, ME, Res).
commit3(true, 3, B, C, Res, _) :-
    isotree3(B, C, ME1, Res).
commit3(_, _, _, _, G, G) :- otherwise | true.
isotree2(A, B, C, D, ME, Res, OrL) :-
    isotree3(A, C, ME1, Res1),
    commit2(Res1?, ME, B, D, Res, OrL).
commit2(true, 2, B, D, Res, _) :-
    isotree3(B, D, ME1, Res).
commit2(_, _, _, _, _, false) :- otherwise | true.
isotree1(leaf(A), leaf(A), 1, true).
isotree1(_, _, _, false) :- otherwise | true.
```

Program 5.2: Extended FCP isotree program from partial evaluation

5.2 Optimizing the SCP interpreter

During the execution of the SCP interpreter various processes may become irrelevant to the rest of the computation but continue to execute. There are several general cases in which groups of processes whose abortion would not affect the continuation of the computation can be identified and discarded.

A trivial example concerns the set of all processes which have not terminated when the interpreter has finished solving the initial goal. Clearly any such processes are irrelevant and can be aborted. There are two additional cases in which processes may be aborted. These are termed AND-abort and OR-abort.

A conjunction of goals is defined to fail if any one of its conjuncts fails. In this case all of the other goals in the conjunction may be aborted. A conjunction of processes is implemented as a circuit of solve_and processes. Since failure of any single solve_and process instantiates the result variable of the circuit to a constant *false*, AND-abort can be implemented as a generalization of the previous optimization. Each OR-parallel subcomputation is provided with a local variable to trigger an abort of the local subcomputation. Local abort variables are necessary to prevent the failure of one OR-parallel computation from affecting other environments. The local abort variables must be linked to their global counterparts so that abortion of a global computation can be propagated.

A disjunction of solve_or processes is defined to succeed if any one solve_or process succeeds. In this case all other processes in the disjunction may be aborted. A disjunction of processes is implemented as a circuit which includes a mutual exclusion variable common to all processes. The implementation of OR-abort uses this variable which becomes instantiated when any one solve_or process has succeeded to commit. A trigger is used to instantiate the local halting variable whenever the associated mutual exclusion variable becomes instantiated.

6. Performance Results

The basic program transformation identified in figure 5.1 provides a speed up of two orders of magnitude over interpretation for nontrivial examples. Partial evaluation optimizes this transformation and provides an additional speed up of 25%. The basic interpreter can be extended to differentiate between failure and suspension inducing an extended transformation. The loss of speed is 10%. An interpreter which aborts insignificant computation may often provide additional optimization. The FCP programs were executed on the Logix [18] FCP system. For comparison, Prolog programs were run on Quintus Prolog and a result from [9] is used to compare with GHC. The comparison is made on the cpu run time, the number of logical reductions and the number of process creations. All programs were run on a Sun workstation.

Tables 7.1 presents performance results of the *isotree* example. The generic example used to compare the different programs is *isotree(T, T)*, where T is a balanced tree with 128 distinct leaves. The FCP isotree examples (interpreted and compiled) traverse the entire search space in parallel. The Prolog program used for comparison searches the space using a depth first strategy with backtracking. The results quoted for this program measure the time and number of reductions it took to traverse the entire search space, including backtracking.

The following are compared:

Basic Int The SCP interpreter executing the SCP isotree program.

Basic Tra The FCP isotree program produced by the basic transformation. (one call in the guards)

Basic Pev The partially evaluated FCP program, derived from the isotree program.

FCP OPP The program derived by partial evaluation of FCP OR-parallel Prolog interpreter and the Prolog isotree program.

Ext Int An extended SCP interpreter which reports failure executing the isotree program.

Ext Pev An extended FCP isotree program which reports failure derived by partial evaluation of the isotree program.

GHC A GHC isotree program run on Levi's GHC abstract machine [9]

Qprolog A Prolog isotree program run on Quintus Prolog (results include backtracking).

	CPU (secs)	Process reductions	Process creations
Basic Int	470.00	300,000	40,000
Basic Tra	3.00	3,280	1,800
Basic Pev	**2.35**	2,300	1,300
FCP OPP	2.80	2,350	1,500
Ext Int	670.00	300,000	40,000
Ext Pev	2.70	3,000	1,300
GHC	**3.80**	3,700	2,000
Qprolog	1.00	1,025	

Table 7.1: Results For *isotree* Programs

Additional examples and performance results can be found in [3]. These include examples for the optimized and extended interpreters and the transformations induced by them. These examples were compiled using the FCP partial evaluator.

7. Related Work

A method to eliminate OR-parallelism from Parlog programs is suggested in [5]. This method involves calling a conjunction of meta-calls for the guards of a procedure. Each meta-call contains additional *result* and *abort* variables. The first *meta-guard* to succeed causes the computation to reduce to the appropriate clause's body and triggers the abortion of the other *meta-guards.* This provides a transformation conceptually similar to the one suggested in this paper but is less efficient, less general, and requires the definition and implementation of a complex system predicate.

Ueda's Guarded Horn Clauses [21] also supports a restricted form of OR-parallelism. The main decision choice of GHC was to eliminate multiple OR-parallel environments from Concurrent Prolog. The language involves a runtime-check which replaces Parlog's compile-time safety check to prevent guards from writing on global variables. This also provides a synchronization mechanism; a guard that attempts to write on a global variable is suspended until the variable is sufficiently instantiated. Nevertheless, GHC seems to be no more expressive than SCP. Programs which are excluded from Parlog or SCP appear to have no useful meaning in GHC. The method of compilation presented in this paper is in particular applicable to GHC.

8. Conclusions

A general method to compile OR-parallelism to AND-parallelism has been demonstrated. An interpreter written in the AND-parallel subset of a language can be defined to interpret OR-parallelism. The method is demonstrated for the case of SCP, an AND/OR-parallel variant of Concurrent Prolog. A simple interpreter for SCP written in FCP is described. This interpreter induces a transformation from SCP to FCP, which is shown to be simple and efficient. A FCP partial evaluator is shown to optimize this transformation further.

The compilation method suggested in this paper is applicable, in particular, both to Parlog and to GHC. The OR-parallelism supported by these languages is restricted from creating multiple environments. Thus it can always be eliminated using the techniques presented in this paper. The results presented suggest that a good way to implement Parlog and GHC is to first implement their AND-parallel subsets. The full languages may then be compiled into these subsets.

Acknowledgements

Many thanks are due to Steve Taylor and Shmuel Safra for enumerous helpful discussions and suggestions.

References

[1] C. Bloch, "Source-to-Source Transformations of Logic Programs", Weizmann Institute Technical Report CS84-22, 1984.

[2] K.L. Clark and S. Gregory, "PARLOG: Parallel programming in logic", Research Report DOC 84/4, April, 1984.

[3] M. Codish, "Compiling OR-Parallelism To AND-Parallelism", Weizmann Institute of Science, Masters Thesis.

[4] Y. Futamura, "Partial evaluation of computation process – an approach to a compiler-compiler", *Systems, Computers, Controls*, Vol. 2, No. 5, 1971, pp. 721–728.

[5] S. Gregory, "Design, Application and Implementation of a Parallel Logic Programming Language", Phd. Thesis, Imperial College of Science and Technology, 1985.

[6] N.D. Jones, P. Sestoft, H. Sondergaard, "An Experiment in Partial Evaluation: The Generation of a Compiler Generator", Institute of Datalogy, University of Copenhagen, Denmark, 1985.

[7] K. Kahn,"The Compilation of Prolog Programs Without the use of a Prolog Compiler", UPMAIL, The Dept. of Computing Science, Uppsala University, 1984.

[9] J. Levi, "A GHC Abstract Machine and Instruction Set", 1985, Proceedings of 3rd ICLP, 1986.

[10 C. Mierowsky, S. Taylor, E. Shapiro, J. Levy and M. Safra, "The design and implementation of Flat Concurrent Prolog", Weizmann Institute Technical Report CS85-09, 1985.

[11] T. Miyazaki, A. Takeuchi and T. Chikayama, "A sequential implementation of Concurrent Prolog based on the shallow binding scheme", *1985 Symposium on Logic Programming*, IEEE Computer Society, 1985, pp. 110–118.

[12] *Quintus Prolog Reference Manual*, Quintus Computer Systems Inc., 1985.

[13] S. Safra, " Partial Evaluation of Concurrent Prolog", 1986, to appear as a Weizmann Institute Tech. Report.

[14] S. Safra, S. Taylor, E. Shapiro, "Distributed Execution of Flat Concurrent Prolog", Unpublished note, 1985.

[15] V.A. Saraswat, "Problems with Concurrent Prolog", Unpublished note.

[16] E. Shapiro, "A subset of Concurrent Prolog and its interpreter", ICOT Technical Report TR-003, February, 1983.

[17] E. Shapiro, "Concurrent Prolog: A Progress Report", 1985, preliminary version.

[18] W. Silverman, A. Houri and M. Hirsch, "Logix user manual, release 1.1", Weizmann Institute of Science, 1985.

[19] A. Takeuchi, "How to solve it in Concurrent Prolog", Unpublished note, 1983.

[20] A. Takeuchi and K. Furukawa, "Partial evaluation of Prolog programs and its application to meta programming", ICOT Technical Report TR-126, 1985.

[21] K. Ueda, "Guarded Horn Clauses", ICOT Technical Report TR-103, 1985.

[22] K. Ueda, "Concurrent Prolog re-examined", to appear as ICOT Technical Report.

Shared Memory Execution of Committed-choice Languages

Jacob Levy

Department of Computer Science
Weizmann Institute of Science
Rehovot 76100, Israel

Abstract

We presents a framework for execution of Committed-choice Logic Programming languages on shared memory multiprocessors. Synchronization of exclusive access issues are explored.

1. Introduction

Recently several shared memory multiprocessors have become commercially available. Such computers feature two to thirty processors operating on a shared memory area [1].

Many Committed-choice Logic Programming languages and dialects have been recently proposed. Among these are Concurrent Prolog [2], PARLOG [3] and Guarded Horn Clauses [4]. Implementations of these languages for uniprocessors are available today [3,5,6].

This paper develops a framework for **parallel** execution of Committed-choice Logic Programming languages. The model is targeted for execution on shared memory architectures. Both the data structures and an execution algorithm are presented. The framework is suitable for execution of GHC and PARLOG and it can be adapted for Concurrent Prolog also.

Initially, synchronization issues resulting from parallel execution are disregarded. A later section of the paper examines these problems and extends the basic framework to solve them. Some of the solutions proposed for the synchronization problems are correct only for shared memory architectures. These architecture-specific decisions are discussed in a later section.

The motivation for this work is twofold. Firstly, shared memory architecures are available today at competitive prices and therefore it is attractive to use them for Committed-choice Logic Programming languages. Secondly, although non-shared memory architectures may also become widely available, in the future each node of such a machine may contain several processing elements operating on a shared memory area. Therefore, the problem of executing Committed-choice Logic Programming languages on these architecures may have to be addressed then.

The next section discusses the design and presents the data structures and an execution scheme in the form of a finite state machine. Section 3 discusses features of shared memory architectures that are needed to correctly implement this scheme. Section 4 enhances the framework to deal with synchronization issues. Section 5 discusses the architecture-dependent decisions specific to shared memory systems.

2. Basic Framework

The design presented here for parallel execution of Committed-choice Logic Programming languages such as Concurrent Prolog, PARLOG and Guarded Horn Clauses is common to the execution of all of these languages. The details of each language will not be reviewed.

2.1 Overview

The traditional view of the computation tree of Committed-choice languages presents alternating levels of disjunctions (Or-nodes or **goals**) and conjunctions (And-nodes or **guards**). The tree is rooted in an initial goal, and attempts to satisfy it with all applicable clauses generate disjoint Or-branches. Each clause generates a guard system or And-branch. To solve a guard system, the conjunction of guard goals has to be satisfied.

In the current model, instead of concentrating on goals and clauses, the computation necessarry to satisfy a goal with its applicable clauses is viewed as a unit. A unit encompasses unification of the goal with the head of all applicable clauses and subsequent commitment of one of these clauses. The computation tree is viewed as a interconnected tree of computation units, as in Figure 1. Goals are represented by circles and clauses by square boxes. For example, to solve goal **G6**, clauses **C9** through **C12** have to be tried.

The computations to advance the state of a computation unit are encoded by a finite-state machine. The state of a computation unit is constructed from the computations of individual potentially applicable clauses, the states of the computations of individual potentially applicable clauses and the goal to be solved.

Several records are used to represent the computations of a computation unit. Goals to be solved are represented by **goal records**. Computations of potentially applicable clauses are represented by **guard tuples**. These data structures are discussed in a following subsection.

The computation represented by the computation tree is advanced by a set of processes, each executing a copy of the finite-state machine. The goals which currently remain to be solved are divided into two groups - the goals whose computation cannot currently be advanced, or **suspended** goals, and the goals whose computation can currently progress, or **ready** goals.

The computation of a process proceeds by repeatedly selecting a goal from the pool and advancing its state, until the goal is solved. The solution of a goal is a **reduction**. The stages of a reduction are explained in the next subsection. As a result of a reduction, new goals may be added to the pool of ready goals, to be solved by later reductions.

Many processes can concurrently attempt to reduce a single goal with potentially applicable clauses. The synchronization issues evolving from this design are dealt with in a later section. For now, it is sufficient to note that actions must always take into account the latest information about the state of the computation and that this state must be checked frequently. Thus, when a computation becomes redundant, the process should notice this and avoid unneeded work.

2.2 Stages of a Reduction

The stages of a reduction are depicted in Figure 2. Their meaning is –

- In parallel, the unification of the goal with the heads of each clause in the set of potentially applicable clauses is attempted. This is the **unification** step.
- For the clauses for which the first step ended successfully, the goals in the guard are created. This is the **guard spawning** step.
- When one of the guards is solved successfully, the goal commits with this clause. The computations of other potentially applicable clauses are aborted. This is the **commitment** step.
- The goal is replaced in its guard system by the body goals of the committing clause. This is the **body spawning** step.

Unification of the goal with the head of a clause may result in **success**, **failure** or **suspension**. If a unification suspends, the goal is associated with the variable causing the suspension. When that variable is instantiated, the goal is added to the ready goals pool, and the reduction is repeated.

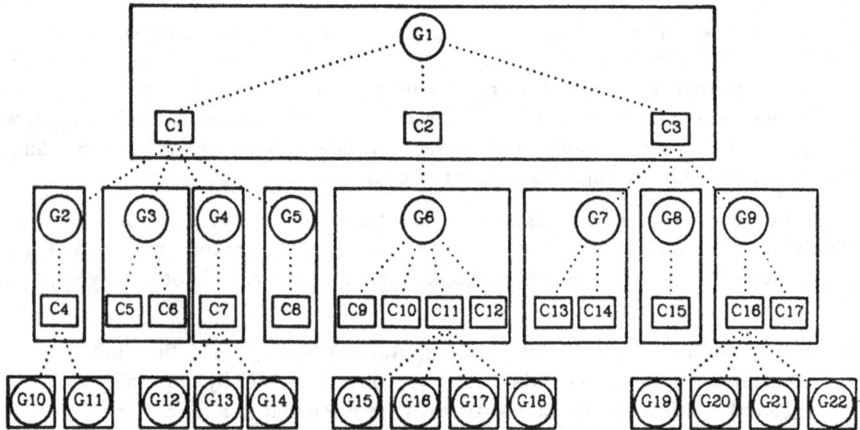

Figure 1. A Computation Tree Partitioned into Computation Units

2.3 Data Structures

A goal is represented by a **goal record**. The fields are –

- **Procedure** – a reference to a list of potentially applicable clauses for this goal.
- **Arguments** – a reference to the arguments of the goal.
- **Guard Tuple** – a reference to the guard tuple representing the guard in which this goal is computing. Guard tuples are described below.
- **Status Vector** – a vector of memory locations, one for each potentially applicable clause. Status vectors are described below.
- **Env Vector** – a reference to a vector of environments, one for each potentially applicable clause. Environments are explained below.
- **Ready** – set to NULL when the goal record is not in the ready goals pool. It is set to

some non-NULL value if it is currently in the ready goals pool.

- **Link** – used for management of the ready goals pool.

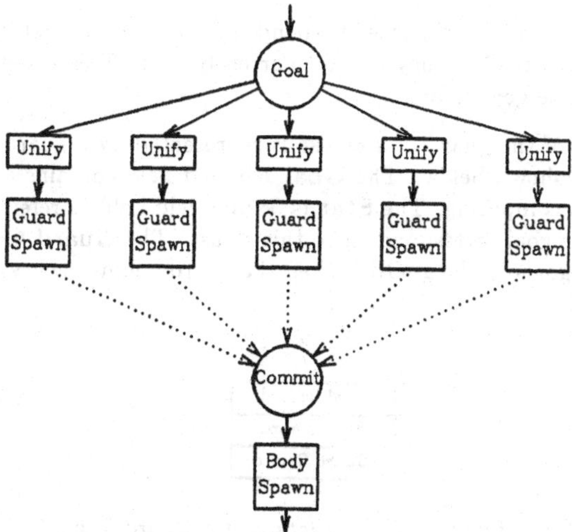

Figure 2. The Stages of a Reduction

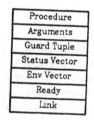

Procedure
Arguments
Guard Tuple
Status Vector
Env Vector
Ready
Link

Figure 3. The Structure of a Goal Record

The status vector is a vector of memory locations, one for each potentially applicable clause. The value of a location is one of seven manifest constants, as follows -

- **UNIFY** - This clause is ready to start its **unify** step.
- **UNIFYING** - This clause is now executing its **unify** step.
- **SPAWN** - This clause is ready to start the **guard spawning** stage.
- **SPAWNED** - This clause is now executing its **guard spawning** step.
- **COMMIT** - This clause is ready to start its **commitment** step.
- **COMMITTED** - This clause has passed the **commitment** step and is now executing its **body spawning** step.
- **FAIL** - The **unify** step or the computation of the guard of this clause have failed.

The environment vector is a vector of memory locations, one for each potentially applicable clause. A location in the vector is either NULL, or a reference to a vector of value cells. The value cell vector has the number of locations needed to represent the environment of the corresponding clause.

When a variable which has associated suspended goals becomes instantiated these goals are added to the ready goals pool, if they are not currently in it. This is determined with the aid of the **Ready** field of the goal record.

The computation of the guard of a clause is represented by a guard tuple. The structure of a **Guard Tuple** is shown below. The **Goal Record** field contains a reference to the goal for which this guard is computing. The **Status Word** field holds a reference to the location in the status vector of the goal corresponding to this clause. The **Guard Count** field records the number of computing goals in the guard. When the guard count reaches 1, this clause is ready to commit for its goal.

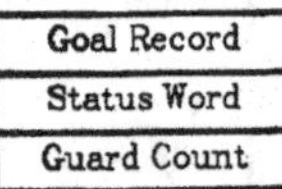

Figure 4. The Structure of a Guard Tuple

2.4 Execution Scheme

This subsection describes an abstract encoding of the computations associated with a computation unit. The data structures of the previous subsection are used in this discussion. The discussion is divided into two subsections. The first presents a generalized outline of the program, and the second subsection develops a detailed, commented description. The program presented in the first subsection performs the computation associated with the solution of a computation unit. In figure 2, the paths and stages of such a computation were depicted. Many processes can advance the computation of a unit, with the restriction that only one process may be working on any specific path. Thus, the path from the goal through the **unify** state to the **guard spawn** state for a clause can be advanced at any time by only one process.

The program specified in the following subsections causes a process to advance the computation of a computation unit on one of the paths. When the computation on this path cannot be advanced further, the process finds another path to work on. Paths are selected from left to right, which corresponds to the textual order of appearance of clauses in the program.

2.4.1 Abstract Encoding.

Each process is executing a copy of the following program.

START:
retrieve a goal from the ready pool.
UNIFY:
if there are no more clauses to try, go to SUSPEND.
try to unify **current goal** with head of **current clause.**
if successful, go to GUARD-SPAWN.

if unification failed or suspended
go to UNIFY to try the next clause.
GUARD-SPAWN:
if guard system of **current clause** is empty go to COMMIT.
spawn the guard system of **current clause.**
go to UNIFY to try the next clause.
COMMIT:
if some other clause already committed for this goal go to START.
do 'language specific' actions at commitment.
if these actions failed or suspended,
go to UNIFY to try next clause.
if the 'language specific' actions caused a variable
which has associated suspended goals to be instantiated,
insert the suspended goals in the ready pool.
set **committing clause** to **current clause.**
set **current goal** to father of **current goal.**
set **current clause** to clause whose guard system contains
current goal.
go to BODY-SPAWN.
BODY-SPAWN:
if the body system of **committing clause** is empty
if **current goal** is last goal in its guard system go to UNIFY
else go to START.
spawn the body system of **committing clause.**
go to START.
SUSPEND:
if some clause committed already for this goal go to START.
if any unifications resulted in suspension
do the suspensions, go to START.
if some clauses have a non-empty guard system go to START.
propagate failure of **current goal.**
if failure did not propagate to root of computation tree
go to START.

The next section shows these stages in terms of the described data structures.

2.4.2 Detailed Description of the Design.

A reduction starts at the **START** label. The **START-UNIFY** label is used when a recursive commitment occurs. Here, the state of the computation of the current reduction is initialized.

START:
retrieve a goal from pool of ready goals.
set **current goal** to goal retrieved.
set Ready field of **current goal** to NULL.
START-UNIFY:
set **guard tuple** to guard tuple referenced by **current goal.**
set **current clause** to first potentially applicable clause.

The **UNIFY** label is reached when the unification of the goal with the head of some clause is attempted. If this clause already committed control transfers to the **START** state. If the unification of this clause has previously failed or has already succeeded once or is currently being attempted by another process, or if the guard has already been created, the next clause is tried. If this clause is ready to commit, control transfers to the **COMMIT** label. Otherwise the state of the current clause is set to **UNIFYING** to indicate that this process is currently attempting this unification. The unification of the goal with the head of the clause is attempted. If this is successfull, if the state is still **UNIFYING**, the computation of this clause proceeds to the **guard spawning** step. If a failure occurs, the next clause is tried. If a suspension occurs, the state of this clause is reset to **UNIFY** and the next clause is tried.

```
UNIFY:
     if current clause is NULL (* no more clauses *)
          go to SUSPEND.
     if status word for current clause is COMMITTED go to START.
     if status word is FAIL or SPAWN or SPAWNED or UNIFYING
          set current clause to next potentially applicable clause,
          go to UNIFY.
     if status word is COMMIT go to COMMIT.
     if status word is UNIFY
          set status word for current clause to UNIFYING.
          attempt the unification.
          if the result is success
               if the status word for current clause is not UNIFYING
                    set current clause to next potentially applicable clause,
                    go to UNIFY.
               set the status word for current clause to SPAWN,
               go to GUARD-SPAWN.
          if the result is failure
               set status word for current clause to FAIL,
               set current clause to next potentially applicable clause,
               go to UNIFY.
          if the result is suspension
               if the status word is UNIFYING
                    set status word for current clause to UNIFY.
               set current clause to next potentially applicable clause,
               go to UNIFY.
```

The **GUARD-SPAWN** label is reached when this clause is ready to start the creation of its guard system. First, if the status is not **SPAWN** the next clause is tried. Otherwise the status is set to **SPAWNED**, to indicate that the guard has already been created, and the goals are spawned. Before each goal is created, if the status is not **SPAWNED**, the rest of the goals are not created and the next clause is tried.

```
GUARD-SPAWN:
     if status word for current clause is not SPAWN
          set current clause to next potentially applicable clause,
          go to UNIFY.
     set status word for current clause to SPAWNED.
     if the guard system is empty
          if status word for current clause is not SPAWNED
```

```
            set current clause to next potentially applicable clause,
            go to UNIFY.
        set status word for current clause to COMMIT,
        go to COMMIT.
    create and initialize a guard tuple for this guard system.
    for each goal in guard system
        if status word for current clause is not SPAWNED
            set current clause to next potentially applicable clause,
            go to UNIFY.
        spawn this goal, set its Ready field to TRUE, and
        increment the guard count of the guard tuple.
    set current clause to next potentially applicable clause.
    go to UNIFY.
```

The **COMMIT** label is reached when an empty guard system is found in the **UNIFY** state, or when some guard is solved. The code at the **DO-WAKEUP** label reactivates goals when variables they were suspended on are instantiated and transfers to the **CONTINUE-COMMIT** label. If the status for the current clause is not **COMMIT** the next clause is tried. Otherwise, any language-specific actions at commitment time are performed. If the result of these actions is failure, the status for this clause is set to **FAIL** and the next clause is tried. If the result is a suspension, the next clause is tried. Otherwise the status for this clause is set to **COMMITTED**, the status for all other clauses is set to **FAIL**, and the computation proceeds at the **body spawning** step.

```
COMMIT:
    if status word for current clause is not COMMIT
        setcurrent clause to next potentially applicable clause,
        go to UNIFY.
    do 'language-specific' commitment actions.
    if the result of commitment actions is failure
        set status word for current clause to FAIL,
        set current clause to next potentially applicable clause,
        go to UNIFY.
    if the result is suspension
        set current clause to next potentially applicable clause,
        go to UNIFY.
    set status word for current clause to COMMITTED.
    set status words for all other potentially applicable clauses to FAIL.
    if the language-specific actions instantiated variables having
    associated suspended goals,
        go to DO-WAKEUP. (* will return to CONTINUE-COMMIT *)
CONTINUE-COMMIT:
    set committing clause to current clause.
    set current goal to father of current goal.
    set current clause to clause whose guard system contains current goal.
    go to BODY-SPAWN.
```

The **BODY-SPAWN** label is reached after one clause has committed for a goal. If the body system of the committing clause is empty, and the guard count is 1, the current clause can commit for the current goal. The status word for the current clause is set to **COMMIT** and control is transferred to the **START-UNIFY** label. If the guard count is not 1, it is decremented and another goal is retrieved for reduction. If the body system of the committing clause contains goals, these are created. Before each goal is created, if the status word for the current clause is not **SPAWNED**, the rest are not created, and control is transferred to the **START** label.

```
BODY-SPAWN:
    if body system of committing clause is empty
        if guard count is 1
            if status word for current clause is not SPAWNED
                go to START.
            set status word for current clause to COMMIT.
            go to START-UNIFY.
        decrement guard count by 1.
        go to START.
    for each goal in body system
        if status word for current clause is not SPAWNED
            go to START.
        spawn this goal and increment the guard count of the guard tuple.
    decrement guard count in guard tuple.
    go to START.
```

The **SUSPEND** label is reached when the set of potentially applicable clauses is exhausted and no clause has committed in this process. If some status word is **COMMITTED**, a clause has already committed in another process. If there are suspensions, control transfers to the DO-SUSPEND state. If there are clauses which have an active or a solved guard, or if another process is currently attempting the reduction of this goal through some clause, another goal is retrieved for reduction. Otherwise, if all status words are **FAIL**, the failure of the current goal is propagated.

```
SUSPEND:
    if one of the status words is COMMITTED go to START.
    if some of the unifications resulted in suspension go to DO-SUSPEND.
    if at least one of the status words is SPAWN or SPAWNED
    or COMMIT or UNIFYING
        go to START.
    if all status words are FAIL go to DO-FAILURE.
        (* if we got here -> implementation error *)
```

The code sections at the **DO-WAKEUP**, **DO-SUSPEND** and **DO-FAILURE** labels are not part of the primary computation cycle of the program and are not shown here. The full code is given in [9].

3. Features of Shared Memory

Before describing the issues of synchronization, it is appropriate now to discuss what hardware features are required in order to implement the solutions to these problems. This section will list the assumptions made about the underlying shared memory architecture.

Shared memory architectures generally allow to declare specified memory areas as shared among processes. Other memory areas are not shared among processes. This feature must be supported by the architecure so that exclusive access to process-private memory is enforced by the operating system. Some shared memory architectures also support dynamic creation of shared memory areas. This feature is not required.

Shared memory architectures allow concurrent reading and writing of a memory location by many processes. This yields either the old value or the new value of the location. This feature is required and is used throughout the following discussion. When many processes attempt to write to the same memory location concurrently, their actions are synchronized through synchronization primitives. Primitives should be provided to allow implementation of a locking protocol. A special memory area on which atomic **test-and-set** or **test-and-increment** operations can be safely performed must be available. Mapping of locks to actual memory locations and exclusive access to memory locations through the use of these operations should be enforced by software.

An important assumption in all the following code is that executing an atomic operation on a memory location span approximately the same duration regardless of its address. It is also implicitly assumed that the atomic operations are fast. These are valid assumptions for shared memory architectures, but not in a non-shared memory architecture.

4. Extended Framework

here the framework is extended to deal with synchronization problems. These problems can be divided into two classes - problems due to the presence of shared memory, and problems caused by the requirement for atomicity of certain operations on a goal. The current discussion will be concerned only with the second class of synchronization problems.

4.1 Overview

The scheme presented in section 2 did not take into account synchronization problems, caused by allowing many processes to advance the computation of a goal concurrently. The target languages allow only one clause to commit for a goal. Thus, the implementation must ensure that the computation of only one clause for a given goal is allowed to reach the **SPAWN-BODY** state. Also, the work involved in spawning the goals of the guard of a clause should be performed only once.

A process must attempt to minimize the amount of unneeded work done. If the computation of a process becomes unneeded because of actions of another process, this should be noticed as soon as possible. Therefore, before each major computation step, the state of the current clause is checked and compared to a **required** state. If the current state is not equal to the required state, the computation of this clause by this process has become unecessary.

These requirements are correctly implemented by the following protocol -

- When a process is ready to advance the state of the computation of one clause to the next state, it must obtain exclusive access to the current goal record.
- When the process obtains exclusive access to the current goal record, the state of the current clause is examined. If it is still the same as the required state, the state of the current clause is advanced to the new value. Otherwise the computation of the current clause is abandoned.

- The process releases exclusive access to the current goal record.

All clause state transitions require exclusive access to the goal record.

4.2 Exclusive Access Management

Exclusive access is managed by associating a lock with each goal record. When a process requires exclusive access to a goal record, it attempts to lock the lock. This operation fails while another process holds the lock, so the first process must busy-wait for the lock. When the lock is released, if there are several processes which are attempting to lock this lock, one of them succeeds. The other processes continue to busy-wait for the lock.

A lock must be associated with every guard tuple. This is needed to ensure exclusive access while the guard count field is updated. A lock is also associated with each variable. When a process instantiates a non-local variable, it attempts to lock the variable's associated lock. Until the lock is held by this process, the computation cannot proceed.

4.3 Execution Algorithm

The execution scheme presented below is an extension of the algorithm presented in section 2.4.2. The new code is shown in bold print. As in section 2.4.2, the code is interspersed with comments. These comments discuss only synchronization problems and their solution. For a description of the underlying algorithm, see 2.4.2.

START:
    lock queue.
    lock goal record at queue head.
    dequeue the goal at queue head.
    set current goal to goal dequeued.
    set Ready field of current goal to NULL.
    unlock queue.
    unlock current goal.
START-UNIFY:
    set guard tuple to guard tuple referenced by current goal.
    set current clause to first potentially applicable clause.

Dequeueing a goal and setting the **Ready** field of the goal record to NULL constitute a critical section. If this code section is not protected, the **ready** field may be set to NULL even though the goal is in the ready pool.

No synchronization is necessary in order to read the status word for the current clause. However, when it is to be modified, the process must obtain exclusive access to the current goal record.

UNIFY:
    if current clause is NULL (* no more clauses *)
        go to SUSPEND.
    lock current goal record.
    if status word for current clause is COMMITTED

```
        unlock current goal record, go to START.
    if status word is FAIL or SPAWN or SPAWNED or UNIFYING
        unlock current goal record,
        set current clause to next potentially applicable clause,
        go to UNIFY.
    if status word is COMMIT
        unlock current goal record,
        go to COMMIT.
    if status word is UNIFY
        set status word to UNIFYING.
        unlock current goal record.
        attempt the unification.
        if the result is success
            lock current goal record,
            if status word of current clause is not UNIFY
                unlock current goal record,
                set current clause to next potentially applicable clause,
                go to UNIFY.
            set status word for the current clause to SPAWN,
            unlock current goal record,
            go to GUARD-SPAWN.
        if the result is failure
            lock current goal record,
            set status word for current clause to FAIL,
            unlock current goal record,
            set current clause to next potentially applicable clause,
            go to UNIFY.
        if the result is suspension
            lock current goal record,
            if status word for current clause is UNIFYING
                set status word to UNIFY,
            unlock current goal record,
            set current clause to next potentially applicable clause,
            go to UNIFY.
```

Instead of releasing each new goal to the ready goals pool as it is created, the goals are saved in a special area called the **pending goals pool**. When all goals have been created, they are released all at once to the ready goals pool. If this were not done the guard could become empty because goals added to it are solved faster than they are created. Saving the goals in a temporary area and releasing them all for computation at once solves this problem.

```
GUARD-SPAWN:
    set pool of pending goals to empty.
    lock current goal record.
    if status word is not SPAWN
        unlock current goal record,
        set current clause to next potentially applicable clause,
        go to UNIFY.
    set status word for current clause to SPAWNED.
    unlock current goal record.
    if the guard system is empty
```

```
        lock current goal record.
        if status word of current clause is not SPAWNED
            unlock current goal record,
            set current clause to next potentially applicable clause,
            go to UNIFY.
        set status word for current clause to COMMIT,
        unlock current goal record,
        go to COMMIT.
    create and initialize a guard tuple for this guard system.
    for each goal in guard system
        if status word of current clause is not SPAWNED
            set current clause to next potentially applicable clause,
            go to UNIFY.
        create this goal and add it to pool of pending goals.
        set Ready field in created goal to TRUE.
    set guard count to number of goals in pending goals pool.
    lock queue.
    insert all goals in pending goals pool into ready goals queue.
    unlock queue.
    set current clause to next potentially applicable clause.
    go to UNIFY.
```

The code below guarantees that only one clause can reach the **COMMITTED** state. The lock on the current goal record is held for a period whose length depends on the time taken by the 'language-specific commitment actions'. In PARLOG, there is no additional work to be done at commitment. In Concurrent Prolog the time consumed by commitment actions may be considerable.

```
COMMIT:
    lock current goal record.
    if status word of current clause is not COMMIT
        unlock current goal record.
        set current clause to next potentially applicable clause,
        go to UNIFY.
    do 'language-specific' commitment actions.
    if the result of commitment actions is failure
        set status word for current clause to FAIL,
        unlock current goal record,
        set current clause to next potentially applicable clause,
        go to UNIFY.
    if the result is suspension
        unlock current goal record,
        set current clause to next potentially applicable clause,
        go to UNIFY.
    set status word for current clause to COMMITTED.
    set status words for all other potentially applicable clauses
    to FAIL.
    unlock current goal record.
    if the language-specific actions instantiated variables having
    associated suspended goals,
        go to DO-WAKEUP. (* will return to CONTINUE-COMMIT *)
CONTINUE-COMMIT:
```

```
set committing clause to current clause.
set current goal to father of current goal.
set current clause to clause whose guard system contains current goal.
go to BODY-SPAWN.
```

The code at the **BODY-SPAWN** label is similar to the code at **GUARD-SPAWN**. It is not shown here, but only in [9].

The goal record is locked while reading the status words for all clauses, to ensure consistency while reading the values. Inconsistencies could arise if one process is reading the status vector while another is modifying some of its slots.

```
SUSPEND:
    lock current goal record.
    if one of the status words is COMMITTED
        unlock current goal record,
        go to START.
    if some of the unifications resulted in suspension
        unlock current goal record,
        go to DO-SUSPEND.
    if at least one of the status words is SPAWN or SPAWNED
    or COMMIT or UNIFYING
        unlock current goal record,
        go to START.
    if all status words are FAIL
        unlock current goal record,
        go to DO-FAILURE.
    (* if we got here -> implementation error *)
```

5. Architecture-specific Design Decisions

The design presented above depends on the presence of shared memory in several ways. The construction of the program allows a process to proceed when a lock is requested only after the lock is actually granted. Until then, the process busy-waits for the lock to become available. This is acceptable in a shared memory architecture, for the following reasons.

Firstly, locking operations are fast, and require approximately the same computation time regardless of the address of the location to be locked. Secondly, the code sections where a lock is held are of minimal duration. Thirdly, the program is designed so that a process requires a lock on at most two objects at the same time. When locks on two objects are needed, a strict ordering on the locking operations is enforced, so that deadlock is avoided. Lastly, locking is not necessary if a process only reads a memory location. This is guaranteed by the assumption that a consistent value will be read even if a write to the same location is in progress.

In a non-shared memory architecture, making a process busy-wait until a lock is granted is wasteful. The time needed to obtain the lock varies from request to request according to the address of the requested lock relative to the placement of the requesting process. When locking operations are not guaranteed to be fast, it is expensive to minimize the length of sections where locks are held. For example, it is possible for a process to hold the lock to the current goal record from the **unify** stage through the **guard spawning** stage without releasing it. The design presented here breaks this code up into several small sections where holding the lock is actually critical, interspersed with code where the lock is unneeded.

If locking operations are relatively expensive, it is more desirable for a process to hold many locks at once. At several places in the code of the previous section, locks are released in order to avoid situations where deadlock could occur, only to be acquired again later.

In a non-shared memory architecture, it is necessary to obtain locks also to read a remote memory location [7]. This increases the expense of locking operations even further.

All these considerations lead to a totally different approach when a planning for non-shared memory architectures. Such a design, for execution of Flat Concurrent Prolog [8], is currently being developed [7]. The main differences with the current design are as follows – Only one process (or processor) can advance the computation of a unit at any time. When a locking operation is needed as part of the computation of a clause, the computation of this clause is abandoned and the next clause is tried. The request for the lock is added to a table kept for this purpose. Only when all clauses have been tried and none have committed, the lock requests are actually issued. The computation unit is suspended until one of the locks is granted. When one of the locks is granted, the computation of this goal is restarted, in a similar manner to reactivation after suspension on a variable.

6. Summary

A scheme for parallel execution of Committed-choice Logic Programming languages on shared memory architectures was presented. The assumptions about the underlying architecture were discussed. The issues evolving from the need to synchronize access to shared resources were explored, and a refined version of the framework taking these issues into account was presented.

References

[1] J. Dongarra, A Comparative Study of Commercial MultiProcessors, to appear as ANL-MCS Technical Report, 1985.

[2] E. Shapiro, A Subset of Concurrent Prolog and Its Interpreter, Technical Report TR-003, ICOT, Tokio, February 1983.

[3] K.L.Clark and S. Gregory, PARLOG: a Parallel Logic Programming Language, Research Report DOC 84/15, Dept. of Computing, Imperial College, London, June 1984.

[4] K. Ueda, Guarded Horn Clauses, Technical Report TR-103, ICOT, Tokio, June 1985.

[5] J. Levy, N. Friedmann and E. Shapiro, Concurrent Prolog - Two New Implementation Schemes, to appear as Weizmann Institute Technical Report, 1985.

[6] J. Levy, A GHC Abstract Machine and Instruction Set, Weizmann Institute Technical Report CS85-11, August 1985.

[7] S. Taylor, M. Safra, E. Shapiro, L. Hellerstein and U. Bar-on, A Distributed Unification Scheme for Flat Concurrent Prolog, to appear as Weizmann Technical Report, 1985.

[8] C. Mierowski, Design and Implementation of Flat Concurrent Prolog, Weizmann Institute Technical Report CS84-21, 1984.

[9] J. Levy, Shared-memory Execution of Committed-choice Languages, To appear as Weizmann Institute Technical Report.

Logic Program Semantics for Programming with Equations

Joxan Jaffar and Peter J. Stuckey

Department of Computer Science
Monash University
Victoria 3168
Australia

Abstract

We consider logic programming-like systems which are based on solving equations in a given structure as opposed to obtaining unifiers. While such systems are elegant from an operational point of view, a logical interpretation of the programs is not always apparent. In this paper, we restrict ourselves to the class of structures $\Re$ satisfying the *eliminable variable property*: we can construct an explicit definition, in the form of one system of equations, of the set of solutions to any $\Re$-solvable system of equations. Correspondingly, we consider only the class of equality theories E such that every E-unifiable system of equations has an E-mgu. We then state three properties which provide basic relationships between E and $\Re$. We prove that their satisfaction establishes an equivalence between a program considered as an equation solving engine (with respect to a structure) and the program considered as a logic program (with respect to a corresponding equality theory). A logical basis for these programs is thus given.

1. Introduction

There are important logic programming-like systems which are based primarily on determining the solvability of equations over a structure as opposed to obtaining unifiers. A very notable example is PROLOG-II [Colmerauer 82] whose central mechanism is the solving of equations over the structure of infinite trees. These equation-solving based systems have the particular advantage of having very intuitive operational semantics. This is because the basic operational step is performed with respect to a *specific* domain of discourse or structure. Consequently there is a wider scope for efficient implementation.

Unification-based systems, on the other hand, have the fundamental advantage of having logical semantics. These systems deal with a specific structure implicitly. For example, in PROLOG we have the empty theory and the intended structure is the Herbrand universe. In the literature, many semantic results identify the theory at hand and its "least" model [Jaffar et al. 85]. In general, however, it may be difficult to find a theory whose least model corresponds to the intended structure.

In this paper, we address the problem of logical semantics for equation solving systems over a class of structures. The structures under consideration are those which have the *eliminable variable property*: similar to [Colmerauer 84], we define that $\mathfrak{R}$ has such a property iff an explicit definition of the solutions of any $\mathfrak{R}$-solvable equation can be constructed and is of the form of one system of equations.

Our main results are as follows. We first identify some elementary properties on an equality theory E with respect to a structure $\mathfrak{R}$. These properties fall far short of requiring that $\mathfrak{R}$ is the least model of E. We show that if E satisfies these elementary properties, then there is an equivalence between a program considered as a equation solving engine (with respect to $\mathfrak{R}$) and the program considered as a logic program (with respect to E). A logical basis for these programs is thus given.

We use three example systems throughout this paper. The first is (pure) PROLOG; here we are dealing with solving equations over the Herbrand universe. The second is (pure) PROLOG-II, and here we are dealing with solving equations over rational trees. Finally, we consider a logic programming system for the structure of linear arithmetic in rational numbers. Calling this system PROLOG-Q, we deal here with solving linear arithmetic equations.

2. Preliminaries

We use the symbols Σ, Π and V to denote our denumerable collections of functors, predicate symbols and variables respectively. $\tau(\Sigma)$ and $\tau(\Sigma \cup V)$ denote, respectively, the ground terms and the terms possibly containing variables. An *atom* is of the form $p(t_1, \ldots, t_m)$ where p is an m-ary symbol in Π and $t_i \in \tau(\Sigma \cup V)$, $1 \leq i \leq m$. *Equations* are of the form $s = t$, where s and t are terms. A *system* is then defined to be a finite set of equations. A *Horn equality theory* E is a (finite or infinite) collection of *Horn equality clauses*, this last being of the form

$$e \leftarrow e_1, e_2, \ldots, e_n, \text{ or}$$
$$\leftarrow e_1, e_2, \ldots, e_n$$

where $n \geq 0$ and e and e_i, $1 \leq i \leq n$, are equations. When E is consistent, it gives a finest congruence on $\tau(\Sigma)$ and we call the collection of E-classes the *E-universe*; notationally, we use $\tau(\Sigma)/E$. Similarly we have the *E-base*:

$$\{p(d_1, \ldots, d_n) : p \in \Pi \text{ is n-ary and } d_i \in \tau(\Sigma)/E,\ 1 \leq i \leq n\}$$

A *structure* $\mathfrak{R}$ for an alphabet Σ consists of a domain $D_{\mathfrak{R}}$ and an assignment, to each n-ary $f \in \Sigma$, a function $D_{\mathfrak{R}}^n \rightarrow D_{\mathfrak{R}}$.

A *program* is a finite collection of *clauses* of the form

$$A \leftarrow B_1, B_2, \ldots, B_n$$

where $n \geq 0$ and A and B_i, $1 \leq i \leq n$, are atoms.

The following notational conventions are adopted for notational convenience and ease of proofs. We use symbols i, j, k, n and m to denote numbers. We use possibly subscripted symbols w, x, y and z to denote variables. We use possibly subscripted symbols A, B and C to denote atoms. We use possibly subscripted symbols p and q to denote predicate symbols. We use possibly subscripted symbols f and g to denote functors. We use the symbol ~ to denote finite sequences of objects such as terms, atoms, clauses, etc. Thus, e.g., $\tilde{s} = \tilde{t}$ may denote the finite system of equations $\{s_1 = t_1, \dots, s_m = t_m\}$, and $\tilde{\exists}$ is used for existential closure.

An E-substitution θ is a finite set $\{x_1/t_1, \dots, x_n/t_n\}$ where the x_i's are distinct variables and the t_i's are terms, not containing occurrences of x_i's. The natural extensions of this function to map terms to terms, atoms to atoms, formulas to formulas etc. are again denoted by θ. *Composition* of substitutions is defined in the usual manner, and an E-substitution α is *more general than* β (denoted $\alpha \leq_E \beta$) if there is an E-substitution γ such that $\beta = \alpha\gamma$. An E-substitution θ is an *E-unifier* of e iff $E \models e\theta$. An E-unifier which is more general than every E-unifier is called a *most general E-unifier.* We associate a substitution $\theta = \{x_1/t_1, \dots, x_n/t_n\}$ with a system of equations, denoted $\hat{\theta}$, as follows: $\hat{\theta} = \{x_1 = t_1, \dots, x_n = t_n\}$.

A *goal* is a sequence of zero or more atoms. A *(P, E)-derivation sequence* for a goal G_0 is a (finite or infinite) sequence of goals G_i, $i \geq 0$, such that where G_i is a goal of the form

$$A_1, A_2, \dots, A_m,$$

(a) if there is a collection of m variants of clauses in P

$$B_1 \leftarrow \tilde{C}_1$$
$$B_2 \leftarrow \tilde{C}_2$$
$$\dots$$
$$B_m \leftarrow \tilde{C}_m$$

(b) such that there exists an E-unifier θ_i of the system

$$A_1 = B_1, \dots, A_m = B_m,$$

then (c) G_{i+1} is

$$\tilde{C}_1\theta_i, \tilde{C}_2\theta_i, \dots, \tilde{C}_m\theta_i.$$

A (P, E)-derivation sequence is *successful* if some G_i is empty. As usual, the *answer substitution* of such a sequence is $\theta_1\theta_2\dots\theta_i$. A (P, E)-derivation sequence is *finitely failed* with length i if θ_i cannot be formed. Note that a (P, E)-derivation sequence is either successful, finitely failed or infinite.

Similarly we can define a *(P, $\mathfrak{R}$)-derivation sequence* for $(\tilde{e}_0 \mid G_0)$ as a (finite or infinite) sequence of *goals* $(\tilde{e}_i \mid G_i)$, $i \geq 0$, such that where G_i consists of a sequence of zero or more atoms

$$A_1, A_2, \dots, A_m,$$

and $\tilde{e}_i$ is an $\mathfrak{R}$-solvable system of equations,

(a) if there is a collection of m variants of clauses in P

$$B_1 \leftarrow \tilde{C}_1$$
$$B_2 \leftarrow \tilde{C}_2$$
$$\dots$$
$$B_m \leftarrow \tilde{C}_m$$

such that (b)

$$\tilde{e}_i \cup \{ A_1 = B_1, \dots, A_m = B_m \}$$

is $\mathfrak{R}$-solvable, then (c) G_{i+1} is

$$\tilde{C}_1, \tilde{C}_2, \dots, \tilde{C}_m.$$

and $\tilde{e}_{i+1}$ is

$$\tilde{e}_i \cup \{ A_1 = B_1, \dots, A_m = B_m \}$$

A (P, $\mathfrak{R}$)-derivation sequence is *successful* if some G_i is empty. A (P, $\mathfrak{R}$)-derivation sequence is *finitely failed* with length i if no $\mathfrak{R}$-solvable system (b) can be formed. Note that a (P, $\mathfrak{R}$)-derivation sequence is also either successful, finitely failed or infinite.

Where A denotes a ground atom over Π and Σ, we define

SS(P, E) = {A: there exists a successful (P, E)-derivation sequence for A}

FF(P, E) = {A: all (P, E)-derivation sequences for A are finitely failed with length $\leq$ n for some n}

Corresponding notions also occur for (P, $\mathfrak{R}$)-derivation sequences; let A denote a goal of the form $(\tilde{e} \mid p(\tilde{t}))$ where all the variables in $\tilde{t}$ appear in $\tilde{e}$ and $\tilde{e}$ has precisely one $\mathfrak{R}$-solution. Intuitively, $\tilde{e}$ "grounds" $p(\tilde{t})$. Then,

SS(P, $\mathfrak{R}$) = {A: there exists a successful (P, $\mathfrak{R}$)-derivation sequence for A}

FF(P, $\mathfrak{R}$) = {A: all (P, $\mathfrak{R}$)-derivation sequences for A are finitely failed}

We finally deal with *complete logic programs* P* corresponding to programs P and *unification complete equality theories* E* corresponding to Horn equality theories E. Essentially, P* contains formulas of the form

$$p(\tilde{x}) \leftrightarrow \left\{ \begin{array}{l} \exists\tilde{y}_1(\tilde{x} = \tilde{t}_1 \ \wedge \ \tilde{A}_1) \\ \exists\tilde{y}_2(\tilde{x} = \tilde{t}_2 \ \wedge \ \tilde{A}_2) \\ \quad\cdots \\ \exists\tilde{y}_n(\tilde{x} = \tilde{t}_n \ \wedge \ \tilde{A}_n) \end{array} \right\}$$

corresponding to the collection of all clauses in P with p in the heads:

$$p(\tilde{t}_1) \leftarrow \tilde{A}_1$$
$$p(\tilde{t}_2) \leftarrow \tilde{A}_2$$
$$\cdots$$
$$p(\tilde{t}_n) \leftarrow \tilde{A}_n$$

where $\tilde{y}_i$ denotes the variables in the ith clause not appearing in $\tilde{x}$. The formal definition may be obtained from [Jaffar et al. 84]. In this paper, a unification complete equality theory E* *corresponding to* E is such that for every system of equations $\tilde{e}$,

$$E^* \models (\tilde{e} \leftrightarrow \hat{\theta})$$

where θ is a most general E-unifier for $\tilde{e}$. Note that we interpret this condition to mean that $E^* \models \neg\exists\tilde{e}$ if $\tilde{e}$ is not E-unifiable.

We conclude this section with two results of [Jaffar et al 85].

Theorem A. Let A be a ground atom over Π and Σ. Then A has a successful (P, E)-derivation sequence iff $(P, E) \models A$.

Theorem B. Let E* be a unification complete equality theory corresponding to E. Let A be a ground atom over Π and Σ. Then A has only finitely failed (P, E)-derivation sequences iff $(P^*, E^*) \models \neg A$.

3. $\mathcal{E}$-theories and $\mathcal{E}$-structures

Here we define the class of theories and structures considered in this paper. We say that a Horn equality theory E is an *$\mathcal{E}$-theory* if for every system of equations $\tilde{e}$, there is an algorithm which constructs an E-mgu for $\tilde{e}$ in the case where $\tilde{e}$ is E-unifiable. Using similar notation, we say that a structure $\mathfrak{R}$ is an *$\mathcal{E}$-structure* if the following two conditions hold over all systems $\tilde{e}$:

(1) There exists a reduction algorithm which operates on systems. The algorithm proceeds by applying zero or more *$\mathfrak{R}$-reduction steps*, and we use the notation

$$\tilde{e} \overset{\mathfrak{R}}{\Rightarrow} \tilde{e}_1 \overset{\mathfrak{R}}{\Rightarrow} \tilde{e}_2 \overset{\mathfrak{R}}{\Rightarrow} \cdots \overset{\mathfrak{R}}{\Rightarrow} \tilde{e}_n$$

to denote n $\mathfrak{R}$-reduction steps. If $\tilde{e}$ is $\mathfrak{R}$-solvable, then $\tilde{e}_n$ is in *reduced form*, i.e. of the form

$$x_1 = t_1(\tilde{y})$$
$$x_2 = t_2(\tilde{y})$$
$$\dots$$
$$x_m = t_m(\tilde{y})$$

where the $\tilde{x}$ and $\tilde{y}$ are disjoint and $\tilde{x}$ contains only distinct variables. If, on the other hand, $\tilde{e}$ is not $\mathfrak{R}$-solvable, then $\tilde{e}_n$ is in *contradictory form*, a form whose precise definition is not required here.

(2) For every two systems $\tilde{e}_i$ and $\tilde{e}_j$ such that $\tilde{e}_i \overset{\mathfrak{R}}{\Rightarrow} \tilde{e}_j$, $\mathfrak{R} \models (\tilde{e}_i \leftrightarrow \tilde{e}_j)$.

The following property establishes the main relationship we require between an $\mathcal{E}$-theory and an associated $\mathcal{E}$-structure. We say that a Horn equality theory E and a structure $\mathfrak{R}$, both having the alphabet Σ, *correspond to one another* if for every ground equation system $\tilde{e}$,

Property 0: $E \models \tilde{e}$ iff $\mathfrak{R} \models \tilde{e}$.

We conclude this section with three example logic programming systems. Firstly,

3.1 PROLOG

The equality theory E here is the empty one, and it is well known that E is an $\mathcal{E}$-theory. The structure $\mathfrak{R}$ is simply the Herbrand Universe, and clearly E and $\mathfrak{R}$ correspond. We use a variant of the naive unification algorithm to present the following system transformation steps and thus we show that $\mathfrak{R}$ is an $\mathcal{E}$-structure. As usual, $\tilde{e}$ denotes the system at hand:

(1) Delete from $\tilde{e}$ an equation of the form $x = x$.

(2) Replace an equation in $\tilde{e}$ of the form $f(\tilde{t}) = f(\tilde{u})$ by the equations $\tilde{t} = \tilde{u}$.

(3) Replace an equation in $\tilde{e}$ of the form $t = x$, where t is not a variable, by $x = t$.

(4) If an equation $x = t$ where t does not contain an occurrence of x, appears in $\tilde{e}$, then replace all other occurrences of x in $\tilde{e}$ by t.

Thus the contradictory form here can be defined as a system containing an equation of one of the forms: (a) $f(\tilde{t}) = g(\tilde{u})$, where f and g are distinct functors, or (b) $x = f(\tilde{t})$ where $\tilde{t}$ contains an occurrence of x.

3.2 PROLOG-II

The intended domain of discourse here is the set of rational trees over some alphabet, say Σ_0. Let us denote the set of these trees by $RT(\Sigma_0)$. The equality theory contains all formulas of the form

$$\left\{\begin{array}{r} x_1 = t_1(\tilde{x}, \tilde{y}) \\ \& \; x_2 = t_2(\tilde{x}, \tilde{y}) \\ \cdots \\ \& \; x_k = t_k(\tilde{x}, \tilde{y}) \end{array}\right\} \leftrightarrow \left\{\begin{array}{r} x_1 = c_1(\tilde{y}) \\ \& \; x_2 = c_2(\tilde{y}) \\ \cdots \\ \& \; x_k = c_k(\tilde{y}) \end{array}\right\} \qquad (3.2)$$

where the Skolem functors c_i are not in Σ_0. Intuitively, these functors serve as a finite representation of possibly infinite rational trees. See [Jaffar et al. 84] for a more detailed discussion on this theory. Also therein is a proof that E is an $\mathcal{E}$-theory, and that E and $RT(\Sigma_0)$ correspond.

The structure $\mathfrak{R}$ we define here has the rational trees $RT(\Sigma_0)$ as its domain. The functional assignment is defined in two parts: (a) for functors $f \in \Sigma_0$, $\mathfrak{R}(f(\tilde{t}))$ is the tree with root label f and whose sons are given by $\mathfrak{R}(\tilde{t})$. (b) for other functors c_i, consider the (only) axiom in which c_i appears, say

$$\left\{\begin{array}{r} x_1 = t_1(\tilde{x}, \tilde{y}) \\ \& \; x_2 = t_2(\tilde{x}, \tilde{y}) \\ \cdots \\ \& \; x_k = t_k(\tilde{x}, \tilde{y}) \end{array}\right\} \leftrightarrow \left\{\begin{array}{r} x_1 = c_1(\tilde{y}) \\ \& \; x_2 = c_2(\tilde{y}) \\ \cdots \\ \& \; x_k = c_k(\tilde{y}) \end{array}\right\}$$

It is well known that the set of equations on the left hand side of this is such that there is a canonical way of representing all the $RT(\Sigma_0)$-solutions. Namely, this is by an explicit definition of x_i, $1 \leq i \leq n$, as a *rational term*, say $t(\tilde{y})$. Such a rational term is a function in the sense that that it maps each sequence of rational trees $\tilde{y}$ in $RT(\Sigma_0)$ into a rational tree in $RT(\Sigma_0)$. We define that $\mathfrak{R}$ assigns this function to c_i.

The first five reduction steps for systems are as in [Colmerauer 82]; the sixth one is introduced for technical reasons.

(1) Delete from $\tilde{e}$ an equation of the form x = x.

(2) If the equation x = y appears in $\tilde{e}$, where x and y are different, and x appears elsewhere in $\tilde{e}$, then replace all other occurrences of x in $\tilde{e}$ by y.

(3) Replace an equation in $\tilde{e}$ of the form t = x by x = t where t is not a variable.

(4) Replace two equations in $\tilde{e}$ of the form x = t and x = u by the equations x = t and t = u where t is the smaller (in terms of symbols) of the two terms t and u.

(5) Replace an equation in $\tilde{e}$ of the form $f(\tilde{t}) = f(\tilde{u})$ by the equations $\tilde{t} = \tilde{u}$.

(6) If $\tilde{e}$ is of the form of the left hand side of (3.2), then replace $\tilde{e}$ by the right hand side of (3.2).

Thus the contradictory form here can be defined as a system containing an equation of the form $f(\tilde{t}) = g(\tilde{u})$, where f and g are distinct functors in Σ_0.

3.3 PROLOG-Q

The intended structure here is linear arithmetic over the rational numbers. Therefore $\Sigma = \{+, .\} \cup Q$ where Q contains all the constants representing the rational numbers. We choose E to contain the usual field axioms. The reduction steps for our structure $\Re$, which corresponds to E, are based on the naive Gaussian elimination method for solving linear systems. Hence we present only a sketch below. Let the system $\tilde{e}$ contain n variables $x_1, x_2, \dots, x_n$.

(1) [Triangularise] Replace an equation in such a way that the coefficient of one variable becomes zero.

(2) [Back-substitution] If (1) is no longer applicable, obtain, if possible, solutions in the form

$$x_i = a_{i,1}.t_1 + a_{i,2}.t_2 + \dots + a_{i,k}.t_k + a_i$$

Thus t_i, $0 \leq i \leq k$, are new variables introduced by this algorithm in case $\tilde{e}$ is $\Re$-solvable. Clearly we should define that a system is in contradictory form if it contains an equation of the form 0 = c where the constant symbol c denotes a rational number different from 0.

4. Main Results

In the previous section we stated Property 0 which ensures the equivalence of the theory and structure at hand for ground equations. In this section, we state two more properties whose purpose is to ensure each reduction step in the equation solving process is compatible with the theory. We then show that satisfaction of Properties 0, 1 and 2 gives rise to a formal logical foundation to the programming system at hand.

For all systems $\tilde{e}_i$, $\tilde{e}_j$ and $\tilde{e}_k$ such that $\tilde{e}_i \overset{\Re}{\Rightarrow} \tilde{e}_j$, and $\tilde{e}_k$ is in contradictory form:

Property 1: $E \models (\tilde{e}_j \rightarrow \tilde{e}_i)$

Property 2:
(a) $E^* \models (\tilde{e}_i \rightarrow \tilde{e}_j)$
(b) $E^* \models \neg\tilde{e}_k$

In what follows E and R will denote an $\mathcal{E}$-theory and $\mathcal{E}$-structure respectively. Our first result establishs a relationship between a system, its E-mgu and its reduced form:

Proposition 1. Let E and $\Re$ satisfy Properties 0 and 1. Then,

(1) An equation system $\tilde{e}$ has an E-mgu θ implies that $\tilde{e}$ has a reduced form $\tilde{e}_n$ and $\tilde{e}_n$ has E-mgu θ.

(2) An equation system $\tilde{e}$ has a reduced form $\tilde{e}_n$ implies that $\tilde{e}$ has an mgu θ where $\hat{\theta} = e_n$.

Proof. (1) It is easy to see that $\tilde{e}$ has a reduced form $\tilde{e}_n$. Now $E \models \tilde{e}\theta\gamma$, for γ grounding $\tilde{e}\theta$, and hence, by correspondence, $\Re \models \tilde{e}\theta\gamma$. Thus $\tilde{e}$ is $\Re$-solvable, and since $\Re$ is an $\mathcal{E}$-structure, $\tilde{e}_n$ cannot be in contradictory form. For the rest of the proof, consider the chain of reasoning: By hypothesis

(a) $E \models \tilde{e}\theta\gamma$ for all substitutions γ grounding $\tilde{e}\theta$.

Furthermore, for all β grounding $\tilde{e}$, $E \models \tilde{e}\beta$ iff $\beta \leq_E \theta$. Since E corresponds to $\Re$, (a) is equivalent to

(b) $\Re \models \tilde{e}\theta\gamma$ for all substitutions γ grounding $\tilde{e}\theta$.

Since $\Re$ is an $\mathcal{E}$-structure, (b) is equivalent to

(c) $\Re \models \tilde{e}_n\theta\gamma\delta$ for all substitutions δ grounding $\tilde{e}_n\theta\gamma$.

Since E corresponds to $\Re$, (c) is equivalent to

(d) $E \models \tilde{e}_n\theta\gamma\delta$ for all substitutions δ grounding $\tilde{e}_n\theta\gamma$.

Suppose there exists another ground E-unifier for $\tilde{e}_n$ β, then backtracking from (d) to (a) we see that $E \models \tilde{e}\beta$ and hence β is an instance of θ. Hence θ is an mgu for $\tilde{e}_n$.

(2) Since $\tilde{e}_n$ is in reduced form, $\tilde{e}_n$ can be denoted by $\hat{\theta}$. Clearly $\Re \models \tilde{e}_n\theta\gamma$ for all substitutions γ grounding $\tilde{e}_n\theta$. Furthermore, for all β grounding $\tilde{e}_n$, $\Re \models \tilde{e}_n\beta$ iff $\beta \leq_E \theta$. Since $\Re$ is an $\mathcal{E}$-

structure, $\mathfrak{R} \models \tilde{e}\theta\gamma$ for all substitutions γ grounding $\tilde{e}\theta$. This is equivalent to, since E corresponds to $\mathfrak{R}$, E $\models \tilde{e}\theta\gamma$ for all substitutions γ grounding $\tilde{e}\theta$. Suppose there exists a ground E-unifier β for $\tilde{e}$. Then we see that $\mathfrak{R} \models \tilde{e}_n\beta\delta$, where $\beta\delta$ grounds $\tilde{e}_n$, and hence β is an instance of θ. ◊

Corollary. Let E and $\mathfrak{R}$ satisfy Properties 0 and 1. Then, an equation system $\tilde{e}$ has an E-mgu iff it is $\mathfrak{R}$-solvable. ◊

We come now to a central lemma which establishes a close correspondence between (P, E)-derivations and (P, $\mathfrak{R}$)-derivations. We first need two preliminary results:

Proposition 2. Let E and $\mathfrak{R}$ satisfy Properties 0 and 1. If $\tilde{e} \cup \tilde{e}'$ is $\mathfrak{R}$-solvable and α is an E-mgu of $\tilde{e}$, then $\tilde{e}'\alpha$ is E-unifiable. ◊

Proposition 3. If α is an E-mgu of $\tilde{e}$ and β is an E-mgu of $\tilde{e}'\alpha$, then $\alpha\beta$ is an E-mgu for $\tilde{e} \cup \tilde{e}'$. ◊

Now let

$$(\tilde{e}_0 \mid \tilde{B}_0), (\tilde{e}_1 \mid \tilde{B}_1), \dots , (\tilde{e}_i \mid \tilde{B}_i), \dots$$

be a finite or infinite (P, $\mathfrak{R}$)-derivation sequence and let

$$\tilde{B}_0\alpha_0, \tilde{B}_1\alpha_1, \dots , \tilde{B}_i\alpha_i, \dots$$

be a finite or infinite (P, E)-derivation sequence. We say these two sequences *correspond* to each other if $\alpha_0 \alpha_1 \dots \alpha_i$ is an E-mgu of $\tilde{e}_i$ for every i.

Corresponding Derivations Lemma: Let $\tilde{e}$ be an equation system with E-mgu α.
(a) Every (P, $\mathfrak{R}$)-derivation sequence on $(\tilde{e} \mid A)$ has a corresponding (P, E)-derivation sequence on $A\alpha$.
(b) Every (P, E)-derivation sequence on $A\alpha$ has a corresponding (P, $\mathfrak{R}$)-derivation sequence on $(\tilde{e} \mid A)$.

Proof. (a) We proceed by induction on the length of the (P, $\mathfrak{R}$)-derivation sequence. The base case clearly holds. For the induction step let $(\tilde{e}_i \mid \tilde{B}_i)$, i = 0, 1, ... , k, denote the first k+1 goals in the (P, $\mathfrak{R}$)-derivation sequence. By the induction hypothesis there is a (P, E)-derivation sequence $\tilde{B}_i\alpha_i$, i = 0, 1, ... , k−1, corresponding to the first k goals in the above (P, $\mathfrak{R}$)-derivation sequence. Let $\tilde{C}$ denote the heads of the input clauses used to obtain the k+1'th goal in the (P, $\mathfrak{R}$)-derivation sequence. Thus $\tilde{e}_k = \tilde{e}_{k-1} \cup \{\tilde{B}_{k-1} = \tilde{C}\}$ and $\tilde{B}_k$ is given by the bodies of these input clauses. By Proposition 4 and the induction hypothesis that $\alpha_0 \alpha_1 \dots \alpha_{k-1}$ is an E-mgu of $\tilde{e}_{k-1}$, the equations $\{\tilde{B}_{k-1} = \tilde{C}\} \alpha_0 \alpha_1 \dots \alpha_{k-1}$ are E-unifiable. By using the standard variable renaming convention, we can have that none of $\alpha_0, \alpha_1, \dots , \alpha_{k-1}$ substitute variables in $\tilde{C}$ and none of $\alpha_0, \alpha_1, \dots , \alpha_{k-2}$ substitute variables in $\tilde{B}_{k-1}$. Thus the E-unifiable system $\{\tilde{B}_{k-1} = \tilde{C}\} \alpha_0 \alpha_1 \dots \alpha_{k-1}$ is the same as $\{\tilde{B}_{k-1}\, \alpha_{k-1} =$

$\tilde{C}$}. Letting α_k be the mgu of this system it follows that $\tilde{B}_k \alpha_k$ can be the next goal in the (P, E)-derivation sequence. We finish off by showing that the induction hypothesis continues to hold. Since $\alpha_0 \alpha_1 \dots \alpha_{k-1}$ is an E-mgu of $\tilde{e}_{k-1}$ and α_k is an E-mgu of $\{\tilde{B}_{k-1} = \tilde{C}\} \alpha_0 \alpha_1 \dots \alpha_{k-1}$, we have, by using Proposition 5, that $\alpha_0 \alpha_1 \dots \alpha_{k-1} \alpha_k$ is an mgu for $\tilde{e}_k$.

(b) We proceed by induction on the length of the (P, E)-derivation sequence. Once again, the base case is straightforward. For the induction step, let $\tilde{B}_i\alpha_i$, $0 \leq i \leq k$, denote the first k+1 goals in the derivation and there is a (P, $\mathfrak{R}$)-derivation sequence $(e_i \mid \tilde{B}_i)$, $0 \leq i < k$ corresponding to the first goals in the (P, E)-derivation. Let $\tilde{C}$ denote the heads of the input clauses used to obtain the k+1'th goal in the (P, E)-derivation sequence. Thus α_k is an E-mgu of $\tilde{B}_{k-1}$ and $\tilde{C}$, and $\tilde{B}_k$ is given by the bodies of these input clauses. It suffices to show that $\tilde{e}_k = \tilde{e}_{k-1} \cup \{\tilde{B}_{k-1} = \tilde{C}\}$ has a reduced form.

As in part (a) above, $\{\tilde{B}_{k-1} \alpha_{k-1} = \tilde{C}\}$ is the same as $\{\tilde{B}_{k-1} = \tilde{C}\} \alpha_0 \alpha_1 \dots \alpha_{k-1}$. Thus the latter system also has an E-mgu α_k. Using the induction hypothesis and Proposition 5, $\tilde{e}_k$ has an E-mgu $\alpha_0 \alpha_1 \dots \alpha_{k-1} \alpha_k$. The Proposition 3 can now be used to show that this system has a reduced form. ◊

The above lemma shows a one-one association between (P, $\mathfrak{R}$)-derivation sequences and (P, E)-derivation sequences. We thus have the following intimate connection between successful (P, $\mathfrak{R}$)-derivation sequences and (P, E)-derivation sequences, and similarly for finitely failed sequences.

Corollary: Let $\tilde{e}$ be an equation system with E-mgu α. Then

(a) $(\tilde{e} \mid A)$ has a successful (P, $\mathfrak{R}$)-derivation with terminal goal $(\tilde{e}' \mid \{\})$ iff $A\alpha$ has a successful (P, E)-derivation with answer substitution β where β is an E-mgu of $\tilde{e}'$.

(b) $(\tilde{e} \mid A)$ has only finitely failed (P, $\mathfrak{R}$)-derivations iff $A\alpha$ has only finitely failed (P, E)-derivations. ◊

We now present one main result of this section which characterises the goals which have successful (P, $\mathfrak{R}$)-derivation sequences in terms of logical consequence of P and our theory E. The general result of Theorem A establishes an equivalence between successful (P, E)-derivations and logical consequence under P and E. Augmenting these results with the corollary above, we have our theorem on the soundness and completeness of successful (P, $\mathfrak{R}$)-derivation sequences:

Theorem on Successful (P, $\mathfrak{R}$)-derivations. Let $\tilde{e}$ be an $\mathfrak{R}$-solvable equation system. Then $(\tilde{e} \mid A)$ has a successful (P, $\mathfrak{R}$)-derivation sequence iff (P, E) & $\tilde{e} \models \tilde{\exists} A$. ◊

We now focus our attention to finitely failed derivations. To get the second main result of this section, all we require is to show:

Unification Completeness Lemma: Let E and $\mathfrak{R}$ be a corresponding $\mathcal{E}$-theory and $\mathcal{E}$-structure satisfying Properties 0, 1 and 2. Then, E is unification complete.

Proof. Let $\tilde{e}$ be any equation system and let $\tilde{e} = \tilde{e}_0 \overset{\Re}{\Rightarrow} \tilde{e}_1 \overset{\Re}{\Rightarrow} \dots \overset{\Re}{\Rightarrow} \tilde{e}_k$ so that $\tilde{e}_k$ is either a reduced or contradictory form. Now we have $E \models (\tilde{e}_i \leftrightarrow \tilde{e}_{i+1})$ by virtue of Properties 1 and 2.

Suppose firstly that $\tilde{e}$ has no reduced form, i.e. $\tilde{e}_k$ is in contradictory form. Then we use Property 2(b) to have that $E \models \neg\tilde{e}_k$. Since $E \models (\tilde{e}_i \leftrightarrow \tilde{e}_{i+1})$, for $0 \le i < k$, $E \models \neg\tilde{e}$ as desired. If, on the other hand, $\tilde{e}$ has a reduced form $\tilde{e}_k$, e.g.

$$\begin{aligned} x_1 &= t_1(\tilde{y}) \\ \& \ x_2 &= t_2(\tilde{y}) \\ &\dots \\ \& \ x_m &= t_m(\tilde{y}) \end{aligned}$$

then let θ denote the substitution

$$\begin{aligned} x_1 &/ t_1(\tilde{y}) \\ \& \ x_2 &/ t_2(\tilde{y}) \\ &\dots \\ \& \ x_m &/ t_m(\tilde{y}) \end{aligned}$$

By Proposition 3 and its corollary, $E \models (\tilde{e}_k \leftrightarrow \hat{\theta})$. Since $E \models (\tilde{e}_i \leftrightarrow \tilde{e}_{i+1})$, for $0 \le i < k$, we have $E \models (\tilde{e} \leftrightarrow \hat{\theta})$ as desired. ◊

We can now establish the soundness and completeness of finitely failed (P, $\Re$)-derivations in terms of logical consequence from the complete program P* and a unification complete theory E corresponding to $\Re$. By the above lemma and Theorem B,

Theorem on Finitely Failed (P, $\Re$)-Derivations. Let E and $\Re$ satisfy Properties 0, 1 and 2. Let $\tilde{e}$ be a $\Re$-solvable system. Then, $(\tilde{e} \mid A)$ has only finitely failed (P, $\Re$)-derivation sequences iff $(P^*, E) \,\&\, \tilde{e} \models \neg A$. ◊

We conclude here with the unification-complete equality theories E* corresponding to each of our three examples:

4.1 PROLOG

We choose E* to be given, as in [Clark 78], contain all axioms of the form:

$f(\tilde{t}) \neq g(\tilde{u})$
$x \neq t(x)$
$f(\tilde{t}) = f(\tilde{u}) \rightarrow \tilde{t} = \tilde{u}$

where f and g are distinct functors and t(x) is a term containing an occurrence of the variable x. Is easy to verify, for each of the three steps in 3.1, that Property 1 holds. That Property 2(a) holds follows just as easily, whilst the proof that Property 2(b) holds follows from the definition of contradictory form. That is, if a system $\tilde{e}$ has an equation of the form $f(\tilde{t}) = g(\tilde{u})$, then the appropriate instance of the first axiom scheme above shows that $E^* \models \neg\tilde{e}$; if, on the other hand, $\tilde{e}$ contains an equation of the form $x = f(\tilde{t})$ where $\tilde{t}$ contains an occurrence of the variable x, then the appropriate instance of the second axiom scheme above shows that $E^* \models \neg\tilde{e}$; Thus E*, by the Unification Completeness Lemma, is unification complete.

4.2 PROLOG-II

The theory E* we use here is obtained by augmenting E, as given in 3.2, with all axioms of the form:

$f(\tilde{t}) \neq g(\tilde{u})$,
$f(\tilde{t}) = f(\tilde{u}) \rightarrow \tilde{t} = \tilde{u}$

where f and g are distinct functors. Once again, Properties 1 and 2(a) are easily established: the proof in the case of all but step (5) in 3.2 is trivial; for step (5), we use the appropriate instance of the second axiom scheme above. To see that Property 2(b) holds, observe that if $\tilde{e}$ is in contradictory form, then the first axiom schema gives $E^* \models \neg\tilde{e}$. Thus E* is unification complete.

4.3 PROLOG-Q

The theory we use here is obtained by augmenting the theory mentioned in 3.3 with all axioms of the form:

$0 \neq c$

where the constant c denotes rational numbers different from 0. That Properties 1 and 2(a) hold for E* follows from that fact that the field axioms imply that the various steps in Gaussian elimination give equivalent systems of linear arithmetic equations. As above, to see that Property 2(b) holds, observe that if $\tilde{e}$ is in contradictory form, then the above axiom schema gives $E^* \models \neg\tilde{e}$. Thus E* is unification complete.

5. Conclusion

We have considered logic programming-like systems based on solving equations over a given kind of structure as opposed to obtaining unifiers with respect to a given equality theory. We then showed that if the theory and structure at hand satisfy certain basic properties, then the equation solving programs may be interpreted as being *logic* programs in this theory. These properties simply require the theory and structure are equivalent for ground equations, and that each single step of the reduction mechanism for simplifying and solving equations is compatible with the equality theory corresponding to the structure. Thus the well known semantics for logic programs with equality are applicable to the programs based on the equation solving operational model.

6. References

[Clark 78] K.L. Clark, "Negation as Failure", in *Logic and Databases*, H. Gallaire and J. Minker (Eds.), Plenum Press, New York, pp 293-322, 1978.

[Colmerauer 82]
A. Colmerauer, "PROLOG II - Reference Manual and Theoretical Model", Internal Report, Groupe Intelligence Artificielle, Universite Aix-Marseille II, October 1982.

[Colmerauer 84]
A. Colmerauer, "Equations and Inequations on Finite and Infinite Trees", *Proc. 2nd. Int. Conf. on Fifth Generation Computer Systems*, Tokyo, pp 85-99, November 1984.

[Jaffar et al 84]
J. Jaffar, J-L. Lassez and M.J. Maher, "A Logical Foundation for PROLOG II", Technical Report 44, Dept. of Computer Science, Monash University, December 1984. [Revised November 1985]

[Jaffar et al. 85]
J. Jaffar, J-L. Lassez and M.J. Maher, "A Logic Programming Language Scheme", in *Logic Programming: Relations, Functions and Equations*, D. DeGroot and G. Lindstrom (Eds), Prentice-Hall, 1985.

ON THE SEMANTICS OF LOGIC PROGRAMMING LANGUAGES

Alberto Martelli and Gianfranco Rossi

Dipartimento di Informatica
Universita' di Torino
Via Valperga Caluso, 37 - 10125 TORINO

Introduction

A distinctive feature of logic programming is to have a very simple syntax and a clear semantics based on the intepretation of programs as Horn clauses in first order logic [1]. However programming languages based on logic, such as Prolog, have many additional features (ordering among clauses, cut, call, evaluable expressions) which cannot be accounted for by the above mentioned semantics, but which are necessary to make the language usable in practice. Several attempts were made to give the semantics of real logic programming languages by means of different operational or denotational techniques [2] [3] [4] [5]. Furthermore several papers have dealt with the implementation of Prolog interpreters or compilers, by describing the techniques and data strucutres suitable for efficient implementations [6] [7] [8].

According to many of the above approaches, logic programming languages seem to have a quite peculiar semantics and to require implementation methods completely different from those of conventional programming languages. In this paper we take the opposite approach of stressing the similarities between the two kinds of languages. Starting from a simple interpreter giving the operational semantics of a Prolog-like language (with infinite rational trees), several versions are derived from it where the main features of the language are described by means of the standard concepts of the semantics of programming languages such as environment, store, continuations, closures. As a consequence it will be possible to borrow implementation techniques from traditional languages.

This approach gives a sound framework for extending logic programming languages along the lines of existing programming languages in order to make them a useful tool. An example is given in Section 5, where clauses are extended to allow definitions of local clauses. We believe that the approach of defining a language together with its semantics is the best one to get a simple and powerful language, and experiences have shown many times how dangerous can be to design a language without a clear understanding of its semantics.

1. Non-deterministic interpreter

As the first step, a non-deterministic interpreter is defined, based on the operational semantics proposed by Colmerauer [9] which allows to account both for the standard case of finite terms and for the case of infinite (rational) trees. This semantics defines a computation of a program P as a sequence of state transitions:

$$(G_0,S_0) \Rightarrow (G_1,S_1) \Rightarrow \ldots \Rightarrow (\emptyset,S_n)$$

where for each i (i=1,n), G_i is the sequence of goals to be proved and S_i is a <u>system of equations in solved form</u>. Such a system is defined as a set of equations of the form

$$\{x_1 = t_1 \\ x_2 = t_2 \\ \ldots \\ x_n = t_n\}$$

where the x_i's are distinct variables and the t_i's are terms (variable or not). Using systems of equations it is possible to properly deal with infinite (rational) terms, whereas semantics using explicit substitutions like that based on SLD-resolutions [10], fails on this task. The same computation model is also used in [11], in conjunction with a different unification algorithm, where the notion of equation is replaced with that of multiequation.

An abstract implementation is shown in Figure 1 to specify this semantics in the form of a logic program (the usual DEC-10 Prolog syntax is used for convenience, but features of logic programming languages such as nondeterministic selection of clauses are assumed).

```
prove([], DB, FSys, FSys).
prove([Goal|GList], DB, Sys, RSys):-
    getclause(DB, SClause),
    rename(SClause, Sys, clause(Head,Body), NSys),
    unify(Head, Goal, NSys, NewSys),
    append(Body, GList, NewGList),
    prove(NewGList, DB, NewSys, RSys).
```

Figure 1 - Non-deterministic interpreter.

Predicate "getclause' selects one of the clauses in the program database DB. Predicate "rename" renames variables in the selected clause with new names not used in Sys yet, and modifies accordingly the system, i.e. by adding an equation xi='unbound' for each new variable.[1] The new clause is represented in its abstract syntax as the term clause(Head,Body), where the Head is a term and the Body a list of terms. Predicate "unify" unifies its first two arguments by suitably changing the system. In the case of failure of the unification process, "unify" fails and another untried clause in DB is selected. The final system (FSys) is the result (RSys) of the computation.

This semantics requires that the list of all the goals to be solved is passed from one computation state to the next one. Following Van Emden [2], we can say that the sequence of computation states generated by the above interpreter is structured as a <u>search tree</u>. It is quite easy to transform the above interpreter into an equivalent one in which, at each step of the computation, the selected goal is completely solved before passing to the next state. In this case the computation will be structured as a <u>proof tree</u> [2]. The new interpreter is shown in Figure 2.

```
prove([], DB, FSys, FSys).
prove([Goal|GList], DB, Sys, RSys):-
    clauses(Goal, DB, SClauses),
    try(Goal, SClauses, DB, Sys, NewSys),
    prove(GList, DB, NewSys, RSys).

try(Goal, [Clause|CList], DB, Sys, RSys):-
    rename(Clause, Sys, clause(Head,Body), NSys),
    unify(Head, Goal, NSys, NewSys),
    prove(Body, DB, NewSys, RSys).
try(Goal, [Clause|CList], DB, Sys, RSys):-
    try(Goal, CList, DB, Sys, RSys).
```

- Figure 2 -

[1] It is convenient to modify the above definition of system in solved form allowing a variable to be bound either to a term or to the costant 'unbound' so that each distinct variable can be explicitly associated to an equation in the system (unbound variables are naturally represented in [5] as multiequations of the form $\{x_i\}=\emptyset$).

Predicate "clauses" is used for reducing the number of attempts to call "unify". It gives in SClauses all clauses of the database DB whose predicate name is the same as that of the Goal (or, more generally, which match somehow the Goal).

This interpreter uses two procedures "prove" and "try" which recursively call each other, in a similar way to the program for traversing AND/OR trees given in [4]. "prove" has the task to demonstrate the conjunction of goals in GList; "try" tries to match a given goal with one of the clauses in DB, calling "prove" again to solve the conjunction of goals in the right hand side of the selected clause.

In both interpreters only OR-alternatives (i.e. unifying clauses) are selected non-deterministically, while AND-alternatives (i.e. goals to be proved) are not, since the first goal of the GList is always selected first. In the first interpreter OR-non-determinism is assumed to be implemented within the predicate "getclause", while in the second interpreter it is made explicit in the definition of the "try" procedure.

2. Logic as a programming language

In this section we will stress similarities between logic and conventional programming languages, based on the well known paradigm of considering clauses as procedure definitions and goals as procedure calls.

Usually in programming languages a distinction is made between code and data. Here clauses are the code whereas data are contained in the system of equations. It is thus convenient to distinguish between two different kinds of terms: those contained in a clause (the source terms) and those contained in the system (the constructed terms) [8].

From this viewpoint the renaming operation can be considered as the operation of transforming a source term into the corresponding constructed term. This operation can be carried out by referring to an environment where variable identifiers of a source term are associated with the new variable names. By introducing the environment explicitly into the interpreter, it is possible to perform the renaming of a goal only when it has to be solved, thus avoiding to rename the whole clause as soon as it is extracted from the database. Now the renaming operation becomes very close to the operation of evaluating the actual parameters in a procedure call of a conventional language. The new interpreter is shown in Figure 3.

```
prove([], DB, Env, FSys, FSys).
prove([Goal|GList], DB, Env, Sys, RSys):-
    clauses(Goal, DB, SClauses),
    copy(Goal, Env, CGoal),
    try(CGoal, SClauses, DB, Sys, NewSys),
    prove(GList, DB, Env, NewSys, RSys).

try(Goal, [clause(V,Head,Body)|_], DB, Sys, RSys):-
    mkenv(V, Sys, NSys, NewEnv),
    copy(Head, NewEnv, CHead),
    unify(Goal, CHead, NSys, NewSys),
    prove(Body, DB, NewEnv, NewSys, RSys).
try(Goal, [_|CList], DB, Sys, RSys):-
    try(Goal, CList, DB, Sys, RSys).
```

Figure 3 - Interpreter with environment

The abstract syntax of a clause has now a further argument V consisting of the list of variable identifiers of a clause. "mkenv" builds a new environment by associating a new variable name to each variable identifier of the list V and modifies the system by adding the new unbound variables. Predicate "copy" renames its first argument according to the bindings in the environment. Note that the environment contains only local variables because the language has no scope rules.

This interpreter has many similarities with an interpreter of a conventional imperative language. In particular the semantics of a logic program depends on an environment and a system of equations, in a similar way to the semantics of an imperative language depends on an environment and a store. Like the store, a system is a global modifiable object; on the contrary, environments are non-modifiable objects local to each clause. A system can be modified during unification as the store is modified with assignments, although many differences exist on the bindings which can be created in the two cases.

In practice, a system of equations can be easily implemented with an imperative language as a (possibly) cyclic data structure, where each variable name is interpreted as the address of a memory cell containing the variable binding. For instance, the following system of equations and environment

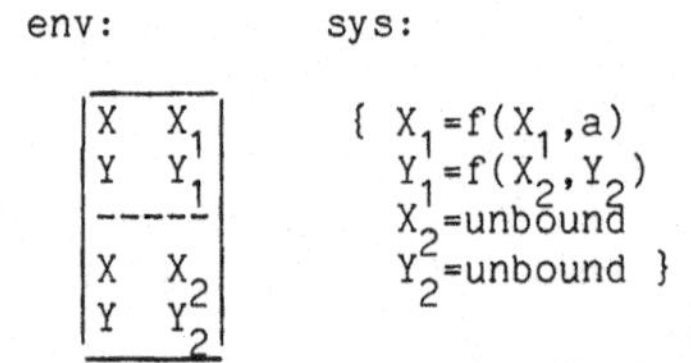

can be implemented with the data structures (note that X_1 is bound to a cyclic structure)

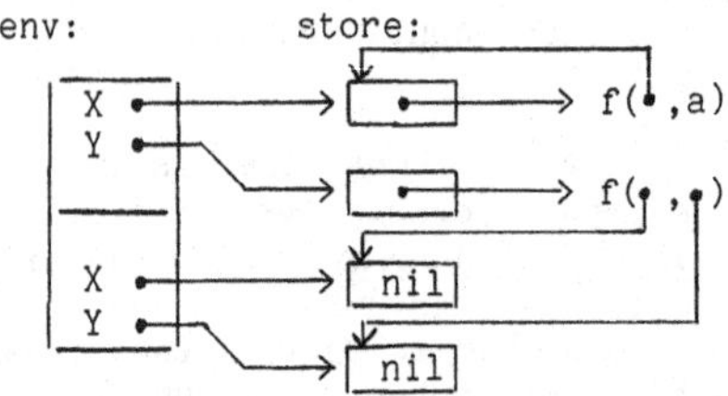

If X_1 and Y_1 have to be unified later, then the store is modified as follows

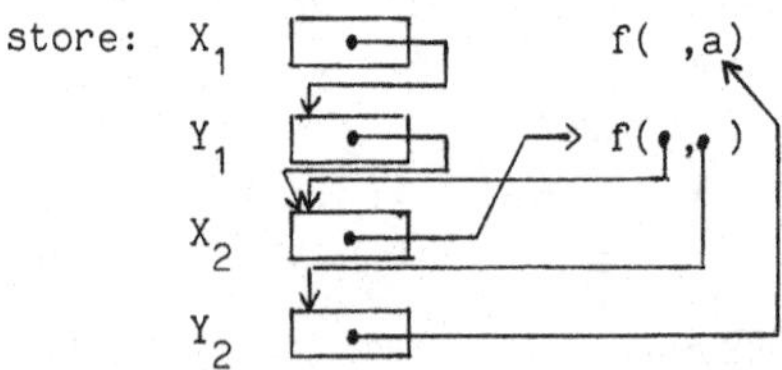

where the binding for X_1 have been modified by "unify" to allow the unification process to terminate.

Note that we have not yet defined exactly the structure of a goal. In logic programming a goal should be a predicate name applied to a list of terms. However some authors (and some Prolog implementations) do not consider predicate names as distinct from functors, and define a goal or the head of a clause simply as a term. In this case, a goal can also be a variable, and its meaning is to evaluate the term bound to it as if it were a predicate call. This is exacly what Prolog provides with the "call" primitive. Although this feature can be quite useful in practice, it is not very sound from a semantical point of view because the term bound to the variable is dealt with, in the same program, in two different ways, namely as a structure and as a predicate call, depending on the position of the variable in the program.

3. Structure copying and structure sharing

The interpreter of section 2 could be optimized in several ways for reducing the amount of copied data.

A substantial improvement can be achieved by combining the "copy" and "unify" predicates. In this way, two source terms can be compared during unification without copying them, and a term will be copied only when it is bound to a variable, because in this case it has to be inserted into the system. The new version of the procedure "unify" will thus have as arguments to be unified, instead of two terms, two pairs consisting each of a term and an environment, which we will call closure, by analogy with the technique used to implement functions or procedures or parameter passing in conventional languages. Most of the descriptions of the so called structure copying technique given in the literature [6] [7] are actually based on this optimization.

The use of closures can be extended by allowing also constructed terms to be represented in this form. This technique is the well known structure sharing technique, used in many Prolog implementations and derived from similar techniques used by Boyer and Moore in theorem proving. An advantage of this solution is that terms are never copied, and a drawback is that the environment is referred from the store, thus preventing collection of the environment during backtracking (to solve this problem solutions such as distinguishing between local and global variables have been proposed). Furthermore, in some cases the structure sharing technique cannot be adopted because the unification algorithm requires the construction of new terms, such as the common part of two terms in Martelli and Montanari algorithm [12].

Advantages and disadvantages of the two techniques with respect to space and time efficiency of interpreters and compilers have been thoroughly investigated in the literature [7] [8] [5].

4. Iterative interpreter

A tail recursive (iterative) deterministic interpreter could be obtained from the above version by applying the transformations for AND and OR elimination described by Fuchi [4]. The new interpreter has two more arguments which are respectively an AND-continuation and an OR-continuation. The AND-continuation, like a continuation of the conventional denotational semantics, is a function describing the rest of the computation from a certain state to the end [5]. Since we are using a first order formalism, this function will be represented as usual as a stack of activation records. On the other hand the OR-continuation is a stack of elements each consisting of the state of a computation which could be resumed by a backtracking operation, and is used to implement non-determinism.

The interpreter is given in Figure 4. AR is the stack of activation records and BT is the backtracking stack. If used in the standard way, i.e. with all parameters but the last one bound to ground terms, this interpreter is deterministic and fails if there is no solution. Procedure "unify" never fails: in case of unsuccessful unification it returns "err" as the value of the resulting system. Correct systems have the form sys(S) in order to distinguish them by pattern matching from erroneous systems.

```
prove(GList, DB, Env, err, AR, [bt(OGoal,OCList,OSys,OAR)|BT], RSys):-
    try(OGoal, OCList, DB, OSys, OAR, BT, RSys).
prove([], DB, Env, sys(FSys), [], BT, sys(FSys)).
prove([], DB, Env, sys(Sys), [ar(GList,NEnv)|AR],BT,RSys):-
    prove(GList, DB, NEnv, sys(Sys), AR, BT, RSys).
prove([Goal|GList], DB, Env, sys(Sys), AR, BT, RSys):-
    clauses(Goal, DB, SClauses),
    copy(Goal, Env, CGoal),
    try(CGoal, SClauses, DB, sys(Sys), [ar(GList,Env)|AR], BT, RSys).
```

```
try(Goal, [], DB, Sys, AR, [bt(OGoal,OCList,OSys,OAR)|BT], RSys):-
    try(OGoal, OCList, DB, OSys, OAR, BT, RSys).
try(Goal, [clause(V,Head,Body)|CList], DB, Sys, AR, BT, RSys):-
    mkenv(V, Sys, NSys, NewEnv),
    copy(Head, NewEnv, CHead),
    unify(Goal, CHead, NSys, NewSys),
    prove(Body, DB, NewEnv, NewSys, AR, [bt(Goal,CList,Sys,AR)|BT], RSys).
```

Figure 4 - Deterministic interpreter

This interpreter is in a form suitable for translation in a conventional imperative language, and it is quite easy to account in it for optimizations such as tail recursion.

Since this interpreter introduces an ordering in the selection of clauses, it is possible to have in the language the "cut" of Prolog. To describe this feature, activation records must be modified by adding to them the backtrack stack. Then, when a cut is encountered, it is sufficient to pass as OR-continuation the backtrack stack taken from the activation record instead of the current one [3].

5. Local and global environments

To show the usefulness of our approach, in this section we propose to add the standard programming languages concept of block to logic programming languages.

The database of the previous interpreters can be considered as a global clause environment, whereas environments of variables are only local. We might extend logic programming languages to allow also local declarations of clauses, that is by allowing to add to the body of a clause the definition of clauses which should only be visible from within the body itself (like local procedures declarations in block structured programming languages). Of course this new feature immediately raises the issue of scope rules, which require explicit quantification of the local variables of a clause, in order to distinguish between local and non-local variables.

For instance in Figure 5 we rewrite the interpreter of Figure 2 by defining "try" locally to "prove" (we make use of an easily intuitive syntax for the new language). Note that the number of arguments of "try" is substantially reduced.

```
prove([], DB, FSys, FSys).
prove([Goal|GList], DB, Sys, RSys):-
   LOCALVARS: SClauses, IntSys
   LOCALCLAUSES:
        try([Clause|_]):-
            LOCALVARS: Head, Body, NSys, NewSys
            rename(Clause, Sys, clause(Head,Body), NSys),
            unify(Head, Goal, NSys, NewSys),
            prove(Body, DB, NewSys, IntSys).
        try([_|CList]):-
            try(CList).
    clauses(Goal, DB, SClauses),
    try(SClauses),
    prove(GList, DB, IntSys, RSys).
```

- Figure 5 -

Introduction of blocks in logic programming languages allows to achieve the quite useful feature of dynamically changing the program database without having to resort to operations with side effects like "assert" and "retract". In fact, local clauses are added to the database whenever the enclosing body is executed, and removed at its end. A further step would be to have the database as an object of the language with explicit insert or remove operations, as suggested for instance in [13], and similar to the concept of module.

The operational semantics of the new language can be given by extending the interpreter of Figure 3 as it is shown in Figure 6. The new interpreter uses two environments, both consisting of a stack of local environments, one for data bases of clauses (DBEnv) and the other one for variable bindings (VarEnv). Each element of the database environment will be a closure consisting of a source clause together with the two environments where it is defined:

```
closure(Clause, DBEnv, VarEnv).
```

An abstract syntax for clauses might be the following

```
clause(LocalVars, Head, LocalClauses, Body).
```

```
prove([], DBEnv, VarEnv, FSys, FSys).
prove([Goal|GList], DBEnv, VarEnv, Sys, RSys):-
    clauses(Goal, DBEnv, SClauses),
    copy(Goal, VarEnv, CGoal),
    try(CGoal, SClauses, Sys, NewSys),
    prove(GList, DBEnv, VarEnv, NewSys, RSys).

try(Goal, [closure(clause(V,H,LC,B),DBEnv,VarEnv)|_], Sys, RSys):-
    mkenv(V, Sys, NSys, NVarEnv),
    copy(H, [NVarEnv|VarEnv], CHead),
    unify(Goal, CHead, NSys, NewSys),
    mkLDBEnv(LC, NDBEnv, [NVarEnv|VarEnv], LDBEnv),
    mkDBEnv(LDBEnv, DBEnv, NDBEnv),
    prove(B, NDBEnv, [NVarEnv|VarEnv], NewSys, RSys).
try(Goal, [_|CList], Sys, RSys):-
    try(Goal, CList, Sys, RSys).
```

Figure 6 - Interpreter with local environments.

Predicate "copy" will now refer to the whole variable environment, and "clauses" extracts from the database environment a list of closures. Predicate "mkLDBEnv" builds a local database environment (LDBEnv) containing the closures of all local clauses, and "mkDBEnv" builds a global environment (NDBEnv) by adding the local database environment LDBEnv to DBEnv. Because local clauses can be defined recursively, the database environment in the closure of a clause is the environment containing the closure itself, i.e. the database environment is a cyclic structure. Such a structure cannot be defined directly as a term, in standard logic. On the other hand this would be possible, and very easy, by using as a metalanguage a logic language with infinite terms such as the one proposed by Colmerauer and mentioned in Section 1.

Note that, whereas the scope rules for the variable environment can be the usual ones of block structured languages, it is not obvious how to define the meaning of predicate "clauses", since in some cases we would like local clauses to hide more global ones, and sometimes to be added to them.

6. References

[1] van Emden M.H. and Kowalski R.A., The Semantics of Predicate Logic as a Programming Language, Journal of the ACM 23(4),1976.

[2] van Emden, M.H., An Interpreting Algorithm for Prolog Programs, in Proc. 1st Int. Logic Programming Conf., Marseille, 1982.

[3] Jones N.D. and Mycroft A., Stepwise Development of Operational and Denotational Semantics for Prolog, in Proc. 1984 Int. Symp. on Logic Programming, Atlantic City, N.J., 1984.

[4] Fuchi K., Logical Derivation of a Prolog Interpreter, in _Proc.of the Int. Conf. on 5th. Generation Computer Systems 1984_, Tokyo, Japan, Nov. 6-9, 1984.

[5] Carlsson, M. On Implementing Prolog in Functional Programming, in _Proc. 1984 Int. Symp. on Logic Programming_, Atlantic City, N.J., 1984.

[6] Bruynooghe, M. The memory management of PROLOG implementations; in _Logic Programming_ (K.L. Clark and S-A. Tarnlund eds.), Academic Press, 1982, 83-98.

[7] Mellish, C.S. An Alternative to Structure Sharing in the Implementation of a Prolog Interpreter; in _Logic Programming_ (K.L. Clark S-A. Tarnlund eds.), Academic Press, 1982, 99-106.

[8] Warren, D.H.D., Implementing Prolog - compiling predicate logic programs, DAI research report 39-40, Dept. of A.I., Edinburgh Univ., 1977.

[9] Colmerauer, A. Prolog and Infinite Trees; _Logic Programming_ (K.L. Clark and S-A. Tarnlund eds.), Academic Press, 1982.

[10] Apt,K.R. and van Emden, M.H. Contributions to the theory of logic programming, _Journal of the ACM 29(3), 1982_.

[11] Martelli, A. and Rossi, G., Efficient Unification with Infinite Terms in logic Programming, in _Proc.of the Int. Conf. on 5th. Generation Computer Systems 1984_, Tokyo, Japan, Nov. 6-9, 1984.

[12] Martelli, A. and Montanari, U., An Efficient Unification Algorithm, _ACM TOPLAS_, _4_, 2 (April 1982).

[13] Bowen, K.A., Meta-Level Programming and Knowledge Representation, _New Generation Computing_, 3 (1985), pp. 359-383.

Towards a Formal Semantics for Concurrent Logic Programming Languages

Lennart Beckman
Upmail, Uppsala University
P.O. Box 2059, S-750 02 Uppsala, Sweden

Abstract

A method for giving a formal semantics of concurrent logic programming languages is proposed. It is shown how the semantics can be defined in terms of a concurrent execution model, based on Milner's CCS (Calculus of Communicating Systems). The method is illustrated by describing the main features of Relational Language, Concurrent Prolog and Guarded Horn Clauses.

1. Introduction

A number of concurrent logic programming languages have been proposed, e.g. *Relational Language*, [ClGr, 81], *Parlog, Concurrent Prolog*, [Sh, 83], and *Guarded Horn Clauses* [Ue, 85].

The languages are fairly well established, and implementations have been proposed and are being made. There does not exist, however, a formal definition of their semantics. The languages are informally defined by a natural language description of their operational semantics. Different approaches to the problem of giving a formal semantics are being made, e.g. [Sa, 85].

A formal definition is needed as a basis for correct implementations, as basis for comparison between different strategies in the languages, and for analyses of the languages.

In order to give a formal semantics, we need a formal description of a system of concurrent actions. A natural way to do this is to use one of the existing formal description techniques developed for describing concurrent processes. Among the possible alternatives are *Petri Nets*, (see i.e. [Pe, 81], *CSP* Communicating Sequential Processes, [Ho, 78], *CCS*, Calculus of Communicating Systems, [Mi, 80], [Mi, 82].

Milner's CCS provides us with a primitive for describing synchronization of processes and valuepassing between them, i.e. an *action* in the terminology of CCS. An expression in CCS can be interpreted as a tree of possible behaviors. We can describe a resolution step as an action in the CCS-system, and can interpret a CCS expression as a (maximal) resolution-tree.

Concurrent logic programming languages restrict the number of allowed resolution step (e.g. by consumer/producer variables). In CCS, this characteristic can be accomplished by introducing corresponding restrictions in the definition of the transition-relations defining CCS actions. The corresponding interpretation of CCS-expressions will be a subtree of the former.

In this paper, we shall briefly review the essential properties of CCS together with some modifications that are made in order to get a model for logic programs. This is discussed in detail in [BeGuWæ, 86], together with proofs of the soundness and completeness of the model.

We shall continue in this paper to apply this conception to a few concurrent logic programming languages in order to show how a formal semantics can be developed. A final comment on the limitations of the present approach will be given.

2. CCS

In Milner's CCS, processes, *agents*, are described by behavior expressions. A family of transition-relations is defined over agents, indicating possible actions of the these. An agent performing an action transforms into a new agent. The relation is given in terms of an axiom schema defining the actions possible for simple expressions, and inference rules defining possible actions for more complex algebraic expressions. (See Appendix A for details).

Milner defines equivalence relations over agents in terms of behaviors. These equivalences relate agents that in some sense can perform the same actions. Given the equivalence relations, it is possible to infer calculation rules, which makes it possible to rewrite an agent in another form, generating the same behavior.

The composition operator, $|$, is used to model the concurrent actions of two agents. The plus operator, $+$, is used to model non-deterministic choice. A calculation rule, the Expansion Theorem in [Mi, 80], (see also appendix A), states that a composition expression can be rewritten into a sum. Thus concurrency is modeled as a choice of interleavings. We will use this rule to expand the composition of concurrent processes into a form that can easily be interpreted as a resolution-tree.

2.1 Modifications to CCS

CCS does not provide a suitable system directly. We need to introduce a few modifications. First we need to remove the distinction between input and output actions in standard CCS. Secondly, we need to define internal communication between two agents to be allowed when the terms in question are unifiable. The details of this are explored in [BeGuWæ, 86], and are given in Appendix B.

3. A model of logic programs

Let us for the moment define the CCS representation of logic program executions by means of an example. The formal definitions are given in [BeGuWæ, 86] and in Appendix C .

Consider the following logic program, P.

$$
\begin{aligned}
&p(y) \leftarrow q(x), r(x,y)\\
&q(2) \leftarrow\\
&r(1,1) \leftarrow\\
&r(z,z) \leftarrow
\end{aligned}
\tag{1}
$$

Each clause is mapped into a CCS agent. The head is mapped into an overlined action, and the body-predicates into not-overlined actions. This means that the head can communicate with the body of other agents. The first agent can informally be defined as follows *"first, do the $\overline{p}(y)$ action, then the $q(x)$ and $r(x,y)$ actions in any order, and possibly start the agent all over again.*

$$
\begin{aligned}
A &\equiv \overline{p}(y).\,(q(x) \mid r(x,y) \mid A)\\
B &\equiv \overline{q}(2).\,B\\
C &\equiv \overline{r}(1,1).\,C\\
D &\equiv \overline{r}(z,z).\,D
\end{aligned}
\tag{2}
$$

The program as such is modeled into a composition of the agents A, B, C and D. Formally, this transformation is defined as a mapping R : *logic programs* $\mapsto$ *agents*. Let $E = R(P) \stackrel{\text{def}}{=} (A \mid B \mid C \mid D)$. This system is able to communicate internally, and is also able to perform external actions. The expansion theorem (Appendix A), states that this composition expression can be rewritten into an expression of sums, which is easier to interpret.

If we apply the expansion theorem once, we find that E is equal to (i.e. can perform the same actions as) a sum of (i.e. choice between) a $\overline{p}$-action, a $\overline{q}$-action and $\overline{r}$-actions. After the $\overline{p}(y)$ action, follows the composition of the rest of agent A and the others. After the other agents follow the expression E itself, due to the recursive definition of the agents.

$$E \sim \overline{p}(y).\underbrace{((q(x) \mid r(x,y) \mid A) \mid B \mid C \mid D)}_{E'} +$$

$$\overline{q}(2).(A \mid B \mid C \mid D) +$$
$$\overline{r}(1,1).(A \mid B \mid C \mid D) +$$
$$\overline{r}(z,z).(A \mid B \mid C \mid D) \tag{3}$$

Consider next E'. Let us exclude all not overlined actions (by a *restriction* in CCS). We find that the agent can perform three internal actions, τ, by communication between the first agent, and the $\overline{q}(2)$, $\overline{r}(1,1)$ and $\overline{r}(z,z)$ actions of the other agents. The expansion theorem states that this can be written as the following sum.

$$E' \sim \tau_q.\underbrace{((r(x,y) \mid A) \mid B \mid C \mid D)\{2/x\}}_{E''} +$$

$$\tau_r.\underbrace{((q(x) \mid A) \mid B \mid C \mid D)\{1/x, 1/y\}}_{E'''} +$$

$$\tau_r.\underbrace{((q(x) \mid A) \mid B \mid C \mid D)\{z/x, z/y\}}_{E''''} +$$

$$\text{a repetition of } \overline{q}(2) \text{ etc.} \tag{4}$$

We continue to apply the expansion theorem to (4), and the result is:

$$E'' \sim \tau_r.\underbrace{(A \mid B \mid C \mid D)}_{E}\{2/y\} \tag{5}$$

The E''' expression cannot continue with any actions, since the value of x in $q(x)$ has been bound to 1. The agent with no possible action is called NIL in the CCS system.

$$E''' \sim NIL \tag{6}$$

On the other hand E'''' is more successful:

$$E'''' \sim \tau_q.\underbrace{(A \mid B \mid C \mid D)}_{E}\{2/z\} \tag{7}$$

A model for CCS-expressions can be given in terms of behavior trees. We interpret a sum as a division into different branches, and "." as a sequence. The expression above can be interpreted as the following tree.

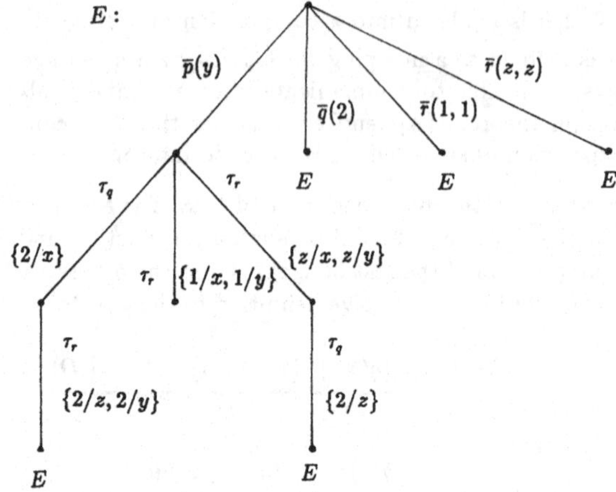

We can also give the expression an interpretation in terms of a subset of the Herbrand base for the program. The details of this is given in Appendix D and in [BeGuWæ, 86]. We find that those branches of the tree that end in E itself represent successful execution sequences. The ground instances of the p, q and r predicates that are consistent with the substitutions constitute the *process semantics* for E. In this case it will be $\{p(2), q(2), r(1,1), r(2,2)\}$.

4. Formal Semantics of Concurrent Languages

Let us now use the process representation of logic programs to illustrate the execution of concurrent logic programming languages. What we want to do is to give a precise definition of those aspects of the languages that concern synchronization, valuepassing and concurrent execution. We find that some properties of existing languages are possible to define formally with this representation, whereas other more or less well-defined properties will rise some difficulties.

We begin by noting that the CCS model of a logic program execution defines *all* possible concurrent executions. Actual concurrent languages prohibit some of these. A corresponding restriction can be put on the CCS model by introducing restrictions on the definitions of the transition-relations. This will yield new transition-relations that are subsets of the original.

These restricted transition relations will in turn yield different equivalence relations, which will give modified calculation rules. In particular, the modified Expansion Theorem will equate a composition expression with a sum that has fewer terms than originally. The tree interpretation of the expression will contain fewer branches than the original tree. Thus, the omitted branches correspond to prohibited executions.

Operational semantics of these languages are thus given in terms of the transition relation in the CCS formalism.

The examples below show how this can be done for a few languages. Relational language is chosen as an example of concurrent logic programming languages since many other languages assume some of its major features. Concurrent Prolog and Guarded Horn Clauses are chosen since they contain interesting variations of these ideas. Since the objective of the definitions of the formal semantics of these languages is to illustrate the method, some simplifications have been made.

5. Applications of the Method

5.1 Relational Language

In the *Relational Language* of Clark and Gregory [ClGr, 81] several ideas common to later parallel logic programming languages are presented. Relational Language contains AND-parallel execution of conjunctive goals, a method for communicating between the corresponding processes by means of shared variables, and a reduction of OR-parallelism to the choice of one alternative.

In sequential PROLOG the possibility to attempt to solve a goal in more than one way, if several clauses can be chosen for unification, is given by the ability to backtrack, and create new bindings to variables. In a parallel logic programming system, parallel attempts to solve a goal can be made, each having its own context of variable bindings.

For efficiency reason, Relational Language has chosen only to attempt to find *one* of the possible solutions. Thus, it does not need backtracking or local contexts of variable bindings.

The choice of which solution to pursue is non-deterministic in the sense that it is a function of the possibly non-deterministic evaluation of other parts of the program.

In Relational Language an extension to Horn clauses is made. The antecedents of a clause are divided into *guard* and *body*. This is written as

$$P \leftarrow G_1, \ldots, G_k || B_1, \ldots, B_n, \quad n, k \geq 0$$

where ||, which we can call the *commit*-operator, separates the guard from the body.

The declarative semantics of the clause is the same as it would be if the || was replaced by a ",", i.e. the right hand side of the clause is treated as a conjunction.

5.1.1 Synchronization

In Relational Language, the AND-parallel solution of goals in a conjunction is attempted by parallel calls to concurrent processes. The shared variables by which these processes communicate are called *channel variables.* The synchronization between AND-parallel processes is done by defining the instances of these variables as either producer or consumers. Only one producer instance is allowed for each channel variable.

In our model, this correspond directly to the introduction of a restriction in the possible substitutions that are the result of an action. We can introduce the restriction in the definition of the actions possible for a $\alpha(\tilde{t}).\, E$ expression, (Appendix B).

Definition 1. *Let the transition relation between a* $\alpha(\tilde{t}).\, E$*-expression and another expression be defined by*

$$\alpha(\tilde{t}).\, E \xrightarrow{\alpha(\tilde{t})} E\theta$$

where

i)

$$\text{if } \alpha \in \textit{bodygoals}$$
$$\theta = \{v/x : x \in var(\tilde{t})\} \setminus \theta'$$
$$\theta' = \{v/x : x \in consumer(\tilde{t}) \text{ and } v \text{ is not a variable}\}$$

ii)

$$\text{if } \alpha \in \textit{guardgoals}$$
$$\theta = \{v/x : x \in var(\tilde{t})\} \setminus \theta''$$
$$\theta'' = \{v/x : v \text{ is not a variable}\}$$

where $consumer(\tilde{t})$ *is the set of consumer variables in* $\tilde{t}$ *and* $var(\tilde{t})$ *is the set of variables in* $\tilde{t}$.

This modification to the transition-relation permits only actions that are synchronized correctly.

5.1.2 Example

Let us modify the program in our example in the following way:

$$p(y) \leftarrow q(x_{prod}), r(x_{cons}, y)$$
$$q(2) \leftarrow$$
$$r(1,1) \leftarrow$$
$$r(z,z) \leftarrow$$

In the expansion of the CCS-expression E several terms will be missing. Equation (4), i.e. the expansion of E', will only contain one term.

$$E' \sim \tau_q . \underbrace{((r(x,y) \mid A) \mid B \mid C \mid D)\{2/x\}}_{E''} \tag{8}$$

E'' will remain unchanged, and the corresponding tree is as follows:

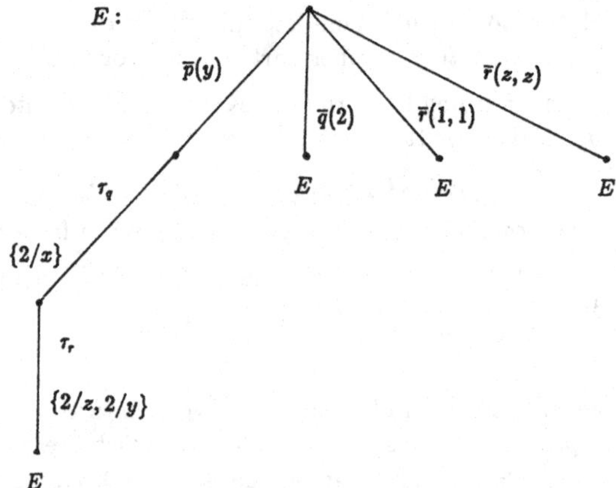

5.1.3 Commit

The informal operational semantics state that the guards of a clause have to be solved before the goals in the body. Furthermore, only one clause of several OR-parallel candidates is allowed to proceed. The first clause that has solved its guards is chosen.

Let us first state the restriction in the CCS model corresponding to the first of these properties. We need to prohibit the actions that correspond to bodygoals not only until the guard actions have been made, but until all actions invoked by these have been made. The explicit definition of this in the CCS model will be complex, if at all possible. Consider instead the following implicit definition.

Definition 2. *Assume that actions can have the attributes body or guard. Let the definition of internal communication also obey the restriction:*
"If the α-action is a body-action, then all corresponding guard-actions and all actions of expression these have communicated with must have been executed first".

Let us turn to the choice of one alternative in an OR-parallel execution, which is another consequence of the operational semantics of the commit-operator. The choice of alternatives is represented in the CCS model as terms in sum, together with other choices in the model (e.g. interleavings, successful and non-successful branches).

The introduction of commit-operator in the language makes it possible for an execution to fail, that otherwise would have been successful. The system might have committed to an unsuccessful clause, and killed other potentially successful candidates. We can describe this in the CCS formalism in the following manner.

An interpretation of a CCS representation of a logic program can be given in terms of Herbrand interpretations. This is formally given in Appendix D as a function $\mathcal{F}$ from CCS expressions to subsets of the Herbrand base for the language in question. We make a modification to this definition, so it excludes those atoms that we are not sure to be able to reach.

Assume that the commit-operator of a logic program is mapped into a commit-action, $||_{commit}$, in the CCS representation, in the same way as other goals. Let these be able to communicate with a commit-agent, generating a τ_{commit}-action.

We are interested in execution sequences that starts out like a successful sequence but ends in NIL, i.e. a failure, instead of the original expression. Such sequences correspond to executions that come to a dead-end. If such an expression contains a τ_{commit}-action, this means that we might have committed the system to this sequence, in spite of the impending failure. The corresponding instances of the atom in question, that are members of the *process semantics* of the program, will thus be unsafe, in the sense that an attempt to prove them *might* fail due to an unlucky commit.

We can characterize this set in the CCS-notation in the following way. Consider first the set of atoms which fail after an unsafe commit. (Compare this definition with the formal definition of the semantics of the CCS representation of a program, in Appendix D).

Definition 3 (Commit and fail).
For any logic program P, with the associated Herbrand base B_P, and for which $E = R(P)$, let the partial function
$\mathcal{D}$: *Agents* $\mapsto 2^{B_P}$ *be defined by*

$$\mathcal{D}(E) = \{\delta(\tilde{t})\theta \in B_P : E \stackrel{\bar{\delta}(\tilde{t})\tau^{*}\tau_{commit}}{\Longrightarrow} E'\theta,$$
$$E' \stackrel{\tau^{*}}{\Longrightarrow} NIL,$$
$$\textit{where } \tau_{commit} \textit{ is unsafe}\}$$

A commit action is informally defined as unsafe if it occurs after all preceding guard communications are followed by their commit-actions, i.e. the commit occurs while trying to prove a body-goal.

Consider now that part of $\mathcal{F}(E)$ that are not part of the set of potential failures. We can call this set the *Minimal semantics* of the program. It is the set of those atoms, that are sure to have successful executions, regardless of the introduction of the non-deterministic commit.

Definition 4 (Minimal Semantics). *For any logic program P, with the associated Herbrand base B_P, and for which $E = R(P)$, let the partial function*
$\mathcal{M}$: *Agents* $\mapsto 2^{B_P}$ *be defined by*

$$\mathcal{M}(E) = \mathcal{F}(E) \setminus \mathcal{D}(E)$$

We can hence define a program as *safe* iff $\mathcal{M}(R(P)) = \mathcal{F}(R(P))$.

5.1.4 Example

Let us modify the program in our example as follows:

$$p(y) \leftarrow q(x_{prod}), r(x_{cons}, y)$$
$$q(2) \leftarrow$$
$$r(v, v) \leftarrow true||s(v)$$
$$r(z, z) \leftarrow$$
$$s(1) \leftarrow$$

The tree interpretation of the corresponding CCS-expression will be as follows:

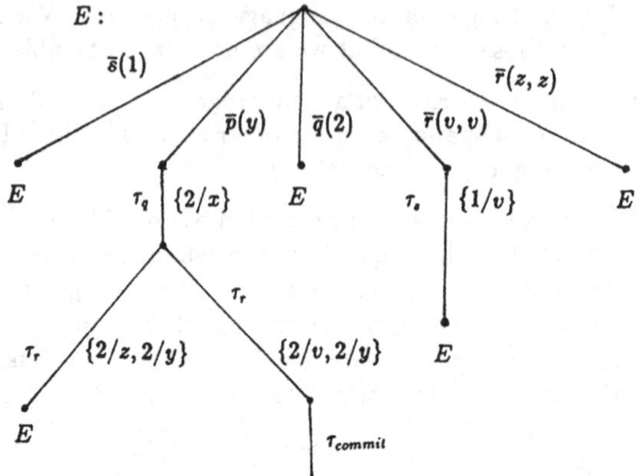

The process semantics, $\mathcal{F}(R(P))$, will be the same as before, except for the addition of $s(1)$ of course, but the minimal semantics will not contain $p(2)$.

5.2 Concurrent Prolog

In *Concurrent Prolog* by Shapiro [Sh, 83] we find many of the properties of Relational Language. One difference is the introduction of read-only variables as the means of synchronization instead of the producer/consumer notion. Furthermore, the restriction from Relational Language that guards cannot bind variables is omitted.

Commit is treated in a similar manner to Relational Language, and the discussion above is relevant to Concurrent Prolog.

5.2.1 Read-only variables

In Concurrent Prolog clauses, an occurrence of a variable can be read-only annotated. The meaning of this annotation is that a read-only annotated occurrence of a variable shall not be instantiated by any unification.

The informal operational semantics of the read-only annotation, is that the unification of a read-only term X? with a term Y is defined by the following: *If Y is a non-variable then the unification succeeds only if X is non-variable, and X and Y are recursively unifiable. If Y is a variable the the unification of X? and Y succeeds, and the result is a read-only variable.* [Sh, 83].

This could be described in the same way as producer/consumer instances of variables discussed earlier. However, since read-only annotation only prohibits a communication in our model as long the variable has not been given a value, the condition in the restriction of the transition-relation is not well-defined. If the action contains both read-only and other instances of the same variable, the manner in which this action is done influences the result. Ueda [Ue, 85] discusses this problem in some detail.

In the present CCS-model, unification is described as an atomic action. Since the possibly concurrent behavior of unification affects the result in Concurrent Prolog, a discussion of Concurrent Prolog could be made if unification is described in more detail as concurrent agents in CCS.

5.2.2 Local Contexts

In our model, the scope of variables is such that all variables are available for all later actions in the same sequence. On the other hand, different sequences, i.e. different terms in a sum, have nothing to do with each others variables. This corresponds to the local contexts of OR-parallel processes in the execution of guards in Concurrent Prolog.

In these contexts, variables can become inconsistent with values given by other AND-parallel processes. In our model, all variables are common to all such processes, and we model thus the immediate detection of inconsistency. Ueda, in [Ue, 85], points out that the early detection of inconsistency is an expensive strategy. An implementation could choose to postpone consistency check until commit-time, or even after commit-time (late-detection, in Ueda's terminology).

The postponement of consistency check of variables corresponds to the introduction of new variables at every communication action, e.g. a substitution into indexed variables. To model commit-time detection of inconsistency, we can model the commit-operator as a substitution back into the original variables, if possible. This will give us more terms in our sums of alternatives, some of which will end in the NIL-agent. These terms corresponds to an attempt which cannot be pursued but which is tried until we find that it is impossible, corresponding to the postponed detection of an inconsistency.

5.3 Guarded Horn Clauses

As an alternative to Concurrent Prolog, Ueda has proposed *Guarded Horn Clauses*, [Ue, 85:2]. It uses the same syntax, with a head, guards, a commit operator, and body goals. In Guarded Horn Clauses, no annotation of variables is given by the user. The desired synchronization and sequencing is obtained by distinguishing between variables in the head, guards and the body, and in different ways restricting their possibilities to be substituted by unification.

We can model this as restrictions in the transition relation in the following way. First of all, variables are given attributes, depending on where in the clause they occur.

- All occurrences of variables that also occur in the head of a clause are given the attribute *"headvariable in $Agent_i$"*.
- Occurrences of variables doesn't occur in the head but in the guard are given the attribute *"guardvariable in $Agent_i$*.
- Occurrences in the body of variables that also occur in the guard but not in the head, are given the attribute *"guardvariable-in-body in $Agent_i$"*.

Furthermore, we define that a commit-action in $Agent_i$ deletes all attributes of type $Agent_i$.

We introduce also an addition to the definition of *internal communication* stating that when an internal communication takes place, attributes are spread to the variables involved in both directions.

We will then find that we can describe the possible executions in terms of these attributes to the variables. We introduce the following restrictions in the definition of the transition-relation, in the definition of not-overlined actions.

Definition 5. *Let the action relation between a $\alpha(\tilde{t})$. E-expression and other expression be defined by*

$$\alpha(\tilde{t}).\,E \xrightarrow{\alpha(\tilde{t})} E\theta$$

where

$\theta = \{v/x : x \in var(\tilde{t})$

if x has the attribute

- *headvariable: v must be a variable*
- *guardvariable; v can be any term*
- *guardvariable-in-body variable:*
  v must be a variable
- *otherwise v can be any term}*

An interesting difference between Guarded Horn Clauses and the preceding languages, is that we do not need to introduce the rather complex sequencing condition that we introduced in the description of them. The desired sequencing is taken care of by the restrictions on variable substitutions. This permits also the start of execution of goals in the body before committing, if these do not bind variables erroneously.

5.3.1 Example

In GHC, the consumer/producer relationship between instances of variables in our example, is achieved in the following way:

$$p(y) \leftarrow q(x) \| r(x, y)$$

$$q(2) \leftarrow$$

$$r(1,1) \leftarrow$$

$$r(z,z) \leftarrow$$

The restricted expansion of the corresponding CCS-expression, will not be exactly the same as was the case of Relational Language. The E' expression in our example will in this case contain two terms, the second corresponding to the communication between r actions, which does not bind any guard-variable.

$$E' \sim \tau_q . \underbrace{((r(x,y) \mid A) \mid B \mid C \mid D)\{2/x\}}_{E''} +$$

$$\tau_r . \underbrace{((q(x) \mid A) \mid B \mid C \mid D)\{z/x, z/y\}}_{E''''} +$$

a repetition of $\overline{q}(x)$ etc.

The continuation of these sequences are the same as in the original example, which gives us the following tree interpretation of the execution.

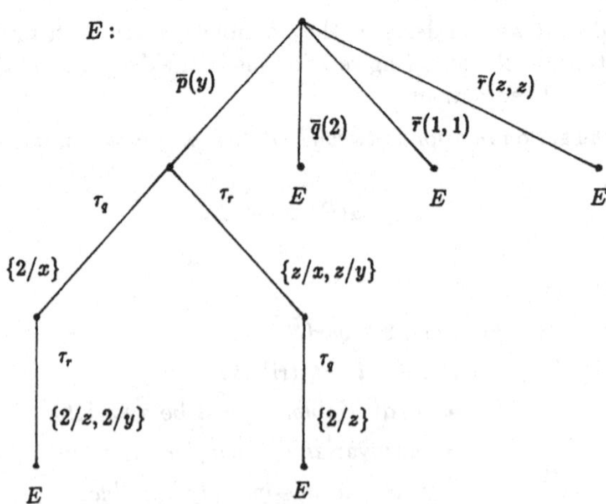

6. Concluding remarks

From the applications of this method to the description of existing concurrent logic programming languages we can draw some interesting conclusions. We find that not all properties of these languages are trivial to describe.

One example is the use of the commit-operator for stating the temporal order of guards and body in Relational Language. This property does not seem too complicated to describe informally, but gives us difficulties when trying to state in this model. This gives us reason to question whether the model is optimal, and if a different strategy can give a simpler model.

We can on the other hand note that we found it much easier to describe Guarded Horn Clauses. The important properties of GHC could be described in terms of the definition of the transition relation in CCS.

What we can establish is that it is possible to discuss concurrent logic programming languages in terms of CCS representations, and that it is possible that this is an interesting alternative to give an operational semantics to these languages. One interesting continuation of this work is to describe one language, e.g. Guarded Horn Clauses, in detail. Another way to proceed is to study how the method as such can be improved.

7. Acknowledgments

The original idea of modeling logic program clauses as CCS agents is due to Dr Rune Gustavsson. The description of Guarded Horn Clauses is made in close cooperation with Mattias Waldau at Upmail. Other members of the Upmail research group, and especially Annika Wærn, have contributed to the development by helpful discussions. An open-hearted discussion with Dr Ehud Shapiro contributed to the completeness of the model, and also to my own understanding of the problems.

8. References

[Be, 85] Beckman, L: Semantics for a Computational Model for Parallel Execution of Logic Programs,Upmail Technical Report 31

[BeGuWæ, 86] Beckman L, Gustavsson R, Wærn A: An Algebraic Model of Parallel Execution of Logic Programs,In *Proceedings of the Symposium of Logics in Computer Science*, Cambridge, June 1986

[ClGr, 81] Clark K L, Gregory S: A Relational Language for Parallel Programming,In *Proceedings of the ACM conference on Functional Programming Languages and Computer Architecture*, Oct 1981

[Ho, 78] Hoare C A R: Communicating Sequential Processes,*C ACM, vol 28, No 8*

[Ll, 84] Lloyd, J W: *Foundations of Logic Programming*,Springer Verlag

[Mi, 80] Milner R: *A Calculus of Communicating Systems*,LNCS Vol 92, Springer Verlag, 1980

[Pe, 81] Peterson, J L: *Petri Net Theory and the Modeling of Systems*,Prentice-Hall

[Sa, 85] Saraswat, V: An operational semantics for CP[↓, |, &, ;],Report, DCS Carnegie-Mellon University, 1985

[Ue, 85] Ueda, K: Concurrent Prolog Re-Examined,ICOT Technical Report TR-102

[Ue, 85:2] Ueda, K: Guarded Horn Clauses,ICOT Technical Report TR-103

[Sh, 83] Shapiro, E: A Subset of Concurrent Prolog and its Interpreter,ICOT Technical Report, TR-003

[Wæ, 85] Wærn, A: A Computational Model for Parallel Execution of Horn Clause Programs,To appear as a Upmail Student Report

Appendix A. CCS

In CCS, we have a set $\mathcal{A}$ of *agents*, and a set *Act* of atomic *actions*. For each action $\alpha \in Act$ its inverse is defined, and belongs to *Act*.

For each action $\alpha \in Act$ and each tuple of terms $\tilde{v}$, a binary relation $\xrightarrow{\alpha(\tilde{v})}$ is defined. The intended meaning of $(E, E') \in \xrightarrow{\alpha(\tilde{v})}$, or $E \xrightarrow{\alpha(\tilde{v})} E'$, is that E may perform the action α with the value-tuple $\tilde{v}$ and become E'.

The relations are defined in terms of an axiom schema for the sequence-operator, ".", and inference rules defining other expressions.

Definition 6(Transition relation).
A family of relations $\longrightarrow$: $Expr \times Expr$ *is defined as following:*

Inaction:

$$NIL \text{ has no actions}$$

Action:

$$\alpha(x_1 \dots x_n).\,E \xrightarrow{\alpha(v_1 \dots v_n)} E\{v_1/x_1 \dots v_n/x_n\}$$

$$\overline{\alpha}(v_1 \dots v_n).\,E \xrightarrow{\overline{\alpha}(v_1 \dots v_n)} E$$

$$\tau.\,E \xrightarrow{\tau} E$$

Composition:

$$\frac{E_1 \xrightarrow{\alpha(\tilde{v})} E_1'}{E_1 \mid E_2 \xrightarrow{\alpha(\tilde{v})} E_1' \mid E_2}$$

$$\frac{E_2 \xrightarrow{\alpha(\tilde{v})} E_2'}{E_1 \mid E_2 \xrightarrow{\alpha(\tilde{v})} E_1' \mid E_2}$$

$$\frac{E_1 \xrightarrow{\alpha(\tilde{x})} E_1' \quad E_2 \xrightarrow{\overline{\alpha}(\tilde{v})} E_2'}{E_1 \mid E_2 \xrightarrow{\tau} E_1' \mid E_2'}$$

Summation:

$$\frac{E_1 \xrightarrow{\alpha(\tilde{v})} E_1'}{E_1 + E_2 \xrightarrow{\alpha(\tilde{v})} E_1'}$$

$$\frac{E_2 \xrightarrow{\alpha(\tilde{v})} E_2'}{E_1 + E_2 \xrightarrow{\alpha(\tilde{v})} E_2'}$$

Restriction:
Suppose $\alpha \notin L$. Then the following hold:

$$\frac{E_1 \xrightarrow{\alpha(\tilde{v})} E_1'}{E_1 \backslash L \xrightarrow{\alpha(\tilde{v})} E_1' \backslash L}$$

Expression variables:

$$\frac{E\{fix(X, E)/X\} \xrightarrow{\alpha(\tilde{v})} E'}{fix(X, E) \xrightarrow{\alpha(\tilde{v})} E'}$$

A shortform for fix-expression is useful. Define that $X \equiv E$ shall mean $fix(X, E)$.

An important calculation rule in Milner's algebra, is the rule stating the relationship between composition-expressions and summation-expressions. The rule holds under Milner's *strong* and *observation* equivalence-relations.

Proposition 1. *If*

$$B = (B_1 \mid \ldots \mid B_m) \setminus A$$

where each B_i is a sum of guards. Then:

$$B \sim \sum(\delta.((B_1 \mid \ldots \mid B_i' \mid \ldots \mid B_m) \setminus A) +$$

where $\delta . B_i'$ is a summand of B_i, and $\delta \notin A$

$$+\sum(\tau.((B_1 \mid \ldots \mid B_i' \mid$$
$$\mid \ldots \mid B_j' \mid \ldots \mid B_m) \setminus A)$$

where $\delta . B_i'$ is a summand of B_i and $\bar{\delta} . B_j'$ is a summand of B_j.

Appendix B. Modifications to CCS

In Milner's CCS, a communication action with valuepassing is defined as passing a value from an output port to an input port, (see [Mi, 80, page 70] and Appendix A). We want to make a modification to this, since we want to model communication as a negotiation between two agents, resulting in variable substitutions in both. We do not want to introduce any direction of the data flow in the representation of Horn clauses, which would introduce unwanted control over the executions.

Definition 7. *For the binary relation* action with valuepassing, $\xrightarrow{\alpha(\tilde{t})}$, *over expressions of agents , the following axiom holds*

$$\alpha(\tilde{t}).\, E \xrightarrow{\alpha(\tilde{t})} E\theta$$

$$\bar{\alpha}(\tilde{t}).\, E \xrightarrow{\bar{\alpha}(\tilde{t})} E\theta$$

where $\theta = \{v/x : x \in var(\tilde{t})\}$,
$\tilde{t}$ is any term, $var(\tilde{t})$ is the set of variables in $\tilde{t}$.

We need also to modify the definition of *composition*, $|$, which intends to model the joint behavior of two concurrent processes.

We want to state that an internal communication, τ, can take place when the terms involved are unifiable. Furthermore, we want the subsequent variable substitution to apply to a system of agents, not only to the pair involved in the actual communication. Thus we no longer describe a system of autonomous processes, interacting only by communication, but a system of related processes, interacting both by communication and sharing variables.

Definition 8 (Composition).
Let the $\xrightarrow{\alpha(\tilde{t})}$ relation obey the inference rule
i)

$$\frac{E \xrightarrow{\alpha(\tilde{t})} E'\theta}{(A_1 \mid \ldots \mid E \mid \ldots \mid A_n) \xrightarrow{\alpha(\tilde{t})} (A_1 \mid \ldots \mid E' \mid \ldots \mid A_n)\theta}$$

ii)

$$\frac{\begin{array}{l}(A_1 \mid \ldots \mid E \mid \ldots \mid F \mid \ldots \mid A_n) \xrightarrow{\alpha(\tilde{t}_1)} \\ \quad (A_1 \mid \ldots \mid E' \mid \ldots \mid F \mid \ldots \mid A_n)\theta_1, \\ \qquad (A_1 \mid \ldots \mid E \mid \ldots \mid F \mid \ldots \mid A_n) \xrightarrow{\bar{\alpha}(\tilde{t}_2)} \\ \qquad\quad (A_1 \mid \ldots \mid E \mid \ldots \mid F' \mid \ldots \mid A_n)\theta_2\end{array}}{\begin{array}{l}(A_1 \mid \ldots \mid E \mid \ldots \mid F \mid \ldots \mid A_n) \xrightarrow{\tau} \\ \qquad (A_1 \mid \ldots \mid E' \mid \ldots \mid F' \mid \ldots \mid A_n)\theta\end{array}}$$

iff

$$\tilde{t}_1\theta = \tilde{t}_2\theta$$

where

$$\theta = \theta_1\theta_2$$

and if $\theta = \{v_i/x_i : i = 1, \ldots n\}$, *then no* x_i *occurs in* $\{v_i : i = 1, \ldots n\}$.

Furthermore, to ensure that we do not get problems with collisions of variable, we state that variables are uniquely defined by an expression.

A shortform for fix-expression is useful. Define that $X \equiv E$ shall mean $fix(X, E)$.

Appendix C. Logic programs as CCS expression

In order to define formally the CCS representation of a set of Horn clauses, we begin by defining a function, R, from sets of Horn clauses to CCS expressions. The value of the function is the composition of the CCS representation of each individual clause, which are given by the function r.

Definition 9.
Let a function $R : \{sets\ of\ Horn\ clauses\} \mapsto Agents$ *be defined by*

$$R(\{C_1 \cdots C_n\}) =$$

$$= r(C_1) \mid \cdots \mid r(C_n)$$

The CCS agent representing one Horn clause can perform actions corresponding to the predicates in the clause. Since communication in CCS can be performed between an action and its inverse, actions corresponding to head-predicates, head-actions, are represented as inverse to those representing body-predicates, body-actions.

We use the fix-operator to define the agents recursively, since a clause may be used arbitrarily many times in an execution. Furthermore, we want to model top-down resolution, which we obtain by placing the sequence operator, ".", between the head-action, and the rest of the clause, thus defining the temporal order of these. The body actions may be performed in any order, which is represented by the composition operator.

Definition 10.
Let a function $r : \{Hornclauses\} \mapsto Agents$ be defined by:

i)
$$r(p \leftarrow q_1, \ldots q_n) =$$
$$= fix(X \quad \overline{p}.(q_1 \mid \cdots \mid q_n \mid X))$$

where $n = 1, \ldots$

ii)
$$r(p \leftarrow) =$$
$$= fix(X \quad \overline{p}.X)$$

iii)
$$r(\leftarrow q_1, \ldots q_n) =$$
$$= fix(X \quad (q_1 \mid \cdots \mid q_n))$$

iv)
$$r(\Box) = fix(X \quad \tau.X)$$

Appendix D. Herbrand interpretations of CCS expressions

The CCS representation $R(P)$ of a program P models the possible calculations of the program. We can give a semantic meaning to the CCS model as the set of positive results of these computations, $\mathcal{F}(R(P))$. This can be given as a subset of the Herbrand base , B_P, for the program. We can then compare the semantic meaning of the process model of a program, the *process semantics*, with the declarative semantics of the program, its least Herbrand Model, M_P (see e.g. [Ll, 84]).

This enables us to state a soundness and completeness result for the CCS model. It can be shown that for every program, the process semantics is equal to the declarative semantics, $\forall P : \mathcal{F}(R(P)) = M_P$. This is explored in more detail in [Be, 85], [Wæ, 85] and [BeGuWæ, 86].

If, for an agent E, there exists a composition of the transition-relation of the form $\xrightarrow{\overline{\delta(\tilde{t})}} \cdot \xrightarrow{\tau} \cdots \xrightarrow{\tau}$, (which we will denote by $\stackrel{\overline{\delta(\tilde{t})}\tau^*}{\Longrightarrow}$), that is such that $E \stackrel{\overline{\delta(\tilde{t})}\tau^*}{\Longrightarrow} E\theta$, this agent has a successful execution sequence. The condition that the transitions shall eventually return to a new occurrence of the agent itself is due to the recursive definition of the agents corresponding to clauses. This corresponds to the solution of all subgoals, when proving $\delta(\tilde{t})$.

The $\overline{\delta}(\tilde{t})$-action in the beginning of the sequence indicates that the agent is ready to communicate with an agent corresponding to the goal $\delta(\tilde{t})$ and then perform a successful execution. The set of ground instances of $\delta(\tilde{t})$, with the restriction put on them by the substitutions θ, will thus be the success set of the executions of the process representation of the logic program.

Definition 11 (Herbrand Interpretations of Agents).
For any logic program P, with the associated Herbrand base B_P, and for which $E = R(P)$, let the partial function
$\mathcal{F} : Agents \mapsto 2^{B_P}$ be defined by

$$\mathcal{F}(E) = \{\delta(\tilde{t})\theta \in B_P : E \stackrel{\overline{\delta(\tilde{t})}\tau^*}{\Longrightarrow} E\theta\}$$

Design of a Prolog-Based Machine Translation System

Michael C. McCord
IBM Thomas J. Watson Research Center
P. O. Box 218
Yorktown Heights, NY 10598

1. Introduction

Machine translation bears a special relationship to Prolog, because (1) machine translation is one of the most practicable natural language processing applications, and (2) natural language processing is one of the most successful and natural applications of logic programming.

There is a more specific historical connection. The application of Prolog to natural language was a major motivation for Alain Colmerauer in his work on the development of Prolog. Furthermore, prior to this, in the period 1967-70, Colmerauer worked on a machine translation project, the TAUM project (Traduction Automatique Université de Montréal). In connection with this project, Colmerauer developed a grammar language, *Q-systems* (Colmerauer, 1971), which had some of the features of logic grammars and Prolog. The TAUM-METEO system (Colmerauer et al., 1971, Kittredge et al., 1973, Kittredge, Bourbeau and Isabelle, 1976), which translates weather forecasts, is entirely written in Q-systems. TAUM-METEO produces high-quality output (with rejection of approximately 20% of the input), and is in production use (8.5 million words per year) by the Canadian Environment Department (see Isabelle and Bourbeau, 1985).

There is resurgent interest in machine translation today as a practicable natural language processing application, with the emergence of some large, production-quality systems. Two recent special issues of *Computational Linguistics* (Vol. 11, Nos. 1-3) are devoted to machine translation. The survey article by Slocum (1985) and other papers in these special issues present evidence of the practicality of MT.

Interesting recent work on MT using Prolog has been done by Huang (1984a, 1984b, 1985) on an English-Chinese translator, using definite clause grammars and a semantic case system.

The purpose of the present paper is to describe an experimental English-German translation system, **LMT** (Logic-based Machine Translation), which has evolved out of previous work by the author on logic grammars. The next section gives an overview of the system and an outline of the rest of the paper.

2. Overview of LMT and issues of design

The implementation of **LMT** in Prolog is consequential for its design. The high-level features provided by Prolog are especially appropriate for natural language processing, promoting clarity and efficiency (see, *e.g.*, Pereira and Warren, 1980). It is worth noting that **LMT**, although fairly large by now, is written *entirely* in Prolog (except for a few lines of trivial system code). No need has been seen for other methods, even for quick access to large dictionary disk files. The version of Prolog used is VM/Prolog (written by Marc Gillet), running on an IBM 3081.

The translation system is organized in a modular way. The grammar for analysis of the source language (English) is written completely independently of the task of translation. In fact, this grammar produces logical forms that have been used in an experimental database query system (McCord, 1982, 1986), and in the experimental knowledge base systems of (Teeple and Yee, 1985) and (Teeple, 1985). The components of **LMT** dealing specifically with translation do not index into the grammar rules, as, for example, in the LRC system (Bennett and Slocum, 1985).

An interesting sort of modularity exists in the English grammar itself, whereby syntax, lexicon, and semantic interpretation closely interact, yet manage to be clearly separated. The lexicon exerts control over syntactic analysis through the use of slot-frames in lexical entries and slot-filling methods in syntax, as well as through type matching with semantic types taken from lexical entries. Yet the syntax rules look completely syntactic. And the syntactic analysis trees look like surface structure trees, with annotations showing grammatical relations (including remote relations due to extraposition). But the terminal nodes of these trees are *semantic items* (explained below), which contain word-sense predications and can be used in building logical forms as semantic representations of sentences. These logical forms are built by a separate semantic interpretation component which deals with problems of scoping of quantifiers and other modifiers.

One important design issue for natural language analysis is the choice of parsing algorithm. An advantage of logic grammars is that they (like context-free grammars, which are a special case) are generally amenable to experimentation with different parsing algorithms (sometimes amounting to different proof procedures), since they can be understood declaratively. When logic grammars are translated directly into Prolog, the parsing algorithm will be top-down (recursive-descent), but interesting work has been done with alternative methods. See, *e.g.*, (Warren, 1975), (Kowalski, 1979), (Pereira and Warren, 1983), (Matsumoto, Tanaka and Kiyono, 1986), and (Uehara, Ochitani, Kakusho and Toyoda, 1984). The variant of logic grammar (*Modular Logic Grammar, MLG*) used in **LMT** is compiled directly into Prolog, so that parsing is top-down. This is done mainly to take advantage of direct Prolog execution, although there are some inherent advantages to top-down analysis, such as better handling of left extraposition. Bottom-up analysis allows easier handling of sentence fragments. General left-recursive grammar rules are not allowed with top-down depth-first parsing, and this is often a motivation for use of bottom-up methods (especially for languages like Japanese which have lots of left-recursive constructions). However, the MLG formalism includes a reasonably convenient device (the *shift operator*) for building left-recursive analysis structures while using right-recursive rules. A more detailed description of the MLG formalism and the English grammar will be given in the following section.

Given that the English grammar can produce both syntactic structures and logical forms, what should be used in the translation system as the point of transfer to German? Initially, my intent was to use the logical forms. The main argument for this was that (1) the logical form analyses express the complete meaning of the source text, and (2) there is no doubt that for perfect translations, one must in general have a complete semantic analysis of the source text (and employ world knowledge to get it). The logical form analyses are expressions in a logical form language **LFL** (McCord, 1985a, 1986). Although the *formalism* for **LFL** is intended to be language-universal, there is actually a different version of **LFL** for every natural language, because most of the predicates are word senses in the natural language being analyzed. The original scheme, then, for **LMT** was to analyze English text into English **LFL** forms, then transfer these to German **LFL** forms, then generate German text.

This is neat, and may be investigated again later; but, for the sake of practicality, the compromise has been to use the syntactic analyses produced by the grammar as the point of transfer. Useful MT systems must generally work with rather large domains, and the trouble with the use of logical forms is that too many decisions must be made and too much world knowledge is needed to produce correct analyses for a large domain. For example, **LFL** forms for degree adjectives like *good* are focalizers (McCord, 1985a, 1986), where the base argument shows the base of comparison for the adjective. In general, it may be difficult to determine such arguments. In the syntactic structure, arguments of focalizers are not yet determined; *but* for the purposes of translation, such scoping problems can often (though not always) be ignored. They can often be sidestepped because the same ambiguity exists in the target language. For example, *That is good* can easily translate into *Das ist gut* without deciding "good with respect to what?".

Another point is that in the case of languages as close as English and German, it is simply more direct to transfer syntactic structure to syntactic structure. For more discussion of the practicality of a syntactic transfer method, see (Bennett and Slocum, 1985).

It should be emphasized that the syntactic analysis trees produced by the grammar do contain some of the ingredients of semantic interpretation. The terminal nodes contain word sense predications, and semantic type matching has been used in constraining parses. Although the arguments of focalizers are not yet filled in, the arguments of verb and noun senses (corresponding to complements), are filled in (inasmuch as they can be determined by the syntax of the sentence, plus a few heuristics). Furthermore, type matching and certain preference heuristics (described in Section 3 below) are used in attaching adjunct modifiers (like adjunct prepositional phrases).

The transfer component of **LMT** converts an English syntax tree into the *German transfer tree*. This is a syntax tree which (normally) has the same shape as the English tree, but has different node labels: feature structures appropriate for German syntax and morphology. Its terminal nodes are (normally) citation forms of German words, together with feature structures which determine the inflections of the words in German surface structure.

The transfer algorithm works in a simple way, in one pass which works top-down and left-to-right, yet manages to get a lot done, making German word choices and essentially producing all required German feature structures (like case markers). This is facilitated by use of logical variables and unification. The entries of the transfer lexicon are largely Prolog unit clauses, used in transfer for simultaneous determination of German translations of words and associated inflectional markings for complements of these translations. Details of the transfer phase and the transfer lexicon will be given in Section 4.

After transfer, the main things lacking are the production of German word order and the application of German inflectional morphology.

German word order, realized in a German surface structure tree, is obtained by applying a battery of tree transformations to the transfer tree. The pattern matching used in determining the applicability of these transformations is mainly Prolog unification; but there is an augmentation used in matching sublists, which is written in Prolog and compiled into Prolog. Transformations actually do a bit more than change word order, but the general idea is to get as much right as possible during transfer aside from word order. Application of these transformations is called *restructuring*, and this phase will be described in more detail in Section 5.

The inflection phase is the last. The citation word forms, together with their feature structures, are given to a German morphological rule system to produce inflected forms, and these are put out in a linear string representing the German sentence. The morphological rule system consists partly of tables (given of course as Prolog unit clauses) and partly of Prolog conditional clauses. Some of the tables constitute what is normally thought of as a German monolingual lexicon. Some details of the inflection phase are given below in Section 6.

Most of information needed for inflection is actually produced by transfer, but inflection is not done *during* transfer, partly because some of the feature structures produced by transfer do not become fully instantiated until transfer is complete, and partly because restructuring does produce some words that need to be inflected.

To summarize the organization of **LMT**, then, the phases are (1) English analysis (handled by a Modular Logic Grammar), (2) transfer, (3) restructuring, and (4) inflection.

Section 7 briefly describes the status of the system as of March, 1986.

3. The English analysis grammar, ModL

The term *grammar* is being used in this paper in the broad sense of a system that associates semantic representations with sentences (and may also associate syntactic analyses). A *Modular Logic Grammar (MLG)* (McCord, 1985a) has a *syntactic component* (with rules written in a certain formalism), and a separate *semantic interpretation component* (using a certain methodology). The English MLG used in **LMT** is called **ModL**, and has evolved since 1979. Most of the ingredients have been described previously in (McCord 1981, 1982, 1985a), so only a brief description will be given here, in the following subsections, with emphasis on new ingredients.

3.1. The MLG formalism

Metamorphosis Grammars (MG's) (Colmerauer, 1975, 1978) are like type-0 phrase structure grammars, but with logic terms for grammar symbols, and with unification used for rewriting instead of simple replacement. In an MG in *normal form*, the left-hand side of each rule is required to start with a non-terminal, followed possibly by terminals. Definite Clause Grammars (DCG's) (Pereira and Warren, 1980), are the special case of normal form MG's corresponding to context-free phrase structure grammars; *i.e.*, the left-hand side of each rule consists of a non-terminal only. In MG's (and DCG's), any of the grammar symbols can have arguments, and these can be used to constrain the grammar as well as to build analysis structures. MG's (in normal form) can be compiled directly into Horn clauses (Colmerauer, 1978) (hence run in Prolog for parsing and generation), by adding extra arguments to non-terminals representing difference lists of word strings being analyzed. In MG's, the right-hand side of a rule can also contain ordinary Horn clause goals, which translate into themselves in the compilation to Horn clauses.

The syntactic component of an MLG is like a DCG, but with three extra ingredients: (1) There is a declaration of *strong non-terminals* (preceding the listing of syntax rules). And the right-hand sides of syntax rules can contain (2) *logical terminals*, and (3) *shifted non-terminals*. These will be explained below.

The syntax rule compiler of an MLG compiles the syntactic component into Prolog (as with MG's), but takes care of analysis structure building, so that the grammar writer does not have to bother with the bookkeeping of adding non-terminal arguments to accomplish this (as in MG's). Also, since systematic structure-building is in the hands of the rule compiler, it is easier to write metagrammatical rules.

The MLG rule compiler has two options for structure building. The compiled grammar can operate in a *one-pass mode*, in which **LFL** representations are built directly during parsing, through interleaved calls to the semantic interpreter, and no syntactic structures are built. Or it can operate in a *two-pass mode*, in which syntactic structures are built during parsing, and these are passed to the semantic interpreter in a second pass. The two-pass mode is used for **LMT**.

In both modes, the *same* semantic interpreter is used, in spite of getting called in an interleaved way in the one-pass mode. It has a clear separation from the syntax rules and deals with problems of scoping.

In the two-pass mode, the automatically built syntactic analysis tree is like a derivation tree, but with two differences. One of these involves *strong non-terminals*. A non-terminal not declared strong is called *weak*. A syntax rule whose left-hand side is a strong (weak) non-terminal is called a *strong (weak)* rule. In the analysis tree, nodes get built corresponding to the application of strong rules, but not weak rules. Intuitively, strong non-terminals should be considered as major categories, weak non-terminals as auxiliary categories. The reduced analysis tree has nodes that are actually relevant for semantic interpretation -- and for machine translation. The other way in which the analysis tree differs from a derivation tree has to do with *shifted non-terminals*, and will be explained below.

For the one-pass mode, the significance of strong non-terminals is that the calls to the semantic interpreter are compiled in at the end of strong rules, but not weak rules.

The *logical terminals* that can appear on the right-hand sides of rules are the building blocks for analysis structures, just as ordinary terminals are building blocks for the word strings being analyzed. In the two-pass mode, the terminal nodes of syntactic analysis trees are logical terminals. The terminal node daughters of a node corresponding to a strong non-terminal NT are just the logical terminals encountered while expanding NT (possibly through other, weak non-terminals). In the one-pass mode, the logical terminals encountered while expanding a strong rule are passed into the call to semantics compiled in at the end of the rule, where they are "combined" to form an interpretation of the phrase analyzed by the rule.

Logical terminals are special cases of *semantic items*, which are, more generally, terms that get built up by semantic interpretation. These are terms of the form Op-LF. Here LF is a logical form (an **LFL** expression), and in the special case of a logical terminal, LF is usually a word-sense predication, like `see(X,Y)`. The term Op, called an *operator*, determines how the semantic item will combine with other semantic items during semantic interpretation. For example, if the semantic item `l-man(X)` (here the operator `l` stands for *l*eft-conjoin) modifies the item `l-see(X,Y)`, then the result is: `l - man(X)&see(X,Y)`.

The semantic interpreter does more than simply combine semantic items. Before combining them, it moves them about in the process of *reshaping*, in order to get them into a position that reflects their intended scopes. Thus, the interpreter deals with natural language scoping problems by giving semantic items a "life of their own". After reshaping and modification through all levels of the tree (working from the bottom up), one arrives at a semantic item for the whole sentence. Its logical form component is the **LFL** analysis for the sentence.

Although the semantic interpreter is not used in **LMT**, the **LFL** predications appearing in the syntactic analyses are used; and, in general, the fact that **ModL** is used to produce **LFL** analyses has shaped the syntactic component to some extent. For details of semantic interpretation and **LFL**, see (McCord, 1981, 1982, 1985a).

The purpose of the *shift operator* (denoted by %) is to produce left-recursive structures while using right-recursive rules. Left-recursive structures occur in English noun phrases like *my oldest brother's wife's father's car.*

A noun phrase grammar fragment with shift that handles this is as follows:

```
np  ==> determiner: np1.
np1 ==> premodifiers: noun: np2.
np2 ==> apostrophe_s: np%np1.
np2 ==> postmodifiers.
```

where `np` is declared a strong non-terminal and all others are weak. (The colon operator on the right-hand side of MLG rules denotes the usual sequencing.) The occurrence of an apostrophe-s triggers a *shift* back to the state np1 where we are looking at the premodifiers (say, adjectives) of a noun phrase. In making the transition, though, the provisional syntactic structure being built (in the two-pass mode) for the noun phrase is changed: All daughters constructed so far are made the daughters of a new node, with label np (the left operand of the shift operator), and this new node is made the initial daughter in the new provisional syntactic structure.

In general, the rigft-hand side of an MLG syntax rule can contain a *shifted non-terminal*, which is of the form Label%NT, where Label is a term (to be used as a node label), and NT is a weak non-terminal. The idea, in rather procedural terms, is: (1) Take the list of daughters built so far for the active tree node (corresponding to the most recently activated strong rule), and make it the complete daughter list of a new node Mod with label Label; and then (2) proceed with NT, using Mod as the initial daughter of the active tree node.

The above description applies to the two-pass mode. The difference for the one-pass mode is that instead of building a new special syntax tree node, a special call to semantic interpretation is compiled in.

The explicit methods used by the rule compiler are described in more detail in (McCord, 1985a).

3.2. Metagrammatical rules

There are two grammatical constructions that are so pervasive and cut across ordinary grammatical categories to such an extent, that they invite treatment by metagrammatical rules: *coordination* and *bracketing*. *Coordination* is construction with *and, or, but,* etc. *Bracketing* consists of the enclosure of sentence substrings in paired symbols like parentheses, other types of brackets, dashes, and quotes. Also, in text formatting languages, there are paired symbols used for font change and other formatting control. **LMT** is being written to process the source text for the IBM SCRIPT/GML formatting language (as well as ordinary text), so it is important to handle such formatting control symbols. [Note that "bracketing" symbols can be nested (as in this sentence).] Use of metarules allows one to make coordination and bracketing more "invisible" to the parser and translator.

Coordination has been treated metagrammatically in several systems. In the logic programming framework, treatments include those in Dahl and McCord (1983), Sedogbo (1984), and Hirschman (1986). The first of these implemented coordination metarules in an *interpreter* for the logic grammar, whereas the last two implement them in a syntax rule compiler. Bracketing with ordinary parentheses is treated in the LRC system (Bennett and Slocum, 1985) by reliance on LISP's handling of parentheses.

There is a limited treatment of coordination and bracketing through metarules in the MLG rule compiler. Specifically, the implementation is for coordination and bracketing of complete *phrases*, where a phrase is a word string analyzed by a strong non-terminal. Any phrase (type) can be coordinated, any number of times, using the usual coordinating conjunctions, commas, and semicolons, as well as the *both-and, either-or* constructions. Bracketing of a phrase (with nesting to any level) is allowed in contexts where the phrase could occur grammatically anyway (as in this sentence). There is another kind of bracketing which is more like apposition or coordination, where a phrase type is repeated. This is not currently implemented, but would not be difficult.

The current restriction to coordination of *complete* phrases (without identifying gaps) is not quite as severe as it might seem, because (1) there are quite a few phrase types (including verb phrases, verb groups, and noun groups), and for these, all appropriate associations of variables are made, and (2) examples with real gaps often do at least get parsed because of optional constituents.

In order to accommodate bracketing, the Prolog representation of a syntax tree (node) is now a term syn(Lab,B,Mods), where Lab is the node label, Mods is the list of daughters, and B is the list of brackets enclosing the phrase represented by the node. (Each member of B is actually a symbol for a *pair* of brackets.)

This "factored out" representation of brackets allows the translation component of **LMT** to handle brackets in a way that is transparent to most of the rules. The result is that if a phrase is bracketed in a certain way in the English source, then "the corresponding phrase" will automatically be bracketed in the same way in the German translation.

Coordination and bracketing are handled in an integrated way by the rule compiler. For each strong non-terminal, the following is done. Let us say the non-terminal has name p, to be concrete, and suppose it has one argument (before compilation), for the sake of simplicity. (Additional arguments are just carried along, but the first argument of a non-terminal is treated specially in MLG's -- see (McCord, 1985a).) The existing syntax rules for p are compiled essentially as in (McCord, 1985a), but the name given to the head predicate is changed to pbase, representing the *simple* (non-coordinated, non-bracketed) form of the phrase. In addition, the metarules create four additional Prolog rules -- for the original p, not for pbase.

The first additional rule is:

```
p(F,syn(Lab,B1,Mods),U,Z) <-
  copyfeas(p,F,F0) &
  bbrackets(B,U,V) &
  preconj(PC,Mods,Mods1,V,W) &
  pbase(F0,B,Syn0,W,X) &
  pconj(F0,F,PC,Syn0,syn(Lab,B1,Mods1),X,Y) &
  ebrackets(B1,Y,Z).
```

In each of these predications besides copyfeas, the last two arguments represent difference lists for word strings. The purpose of copyfeas is to make a (possible) copy of part of the feature argument F, to allow for differences in parts of the feature structures of the coordinated phrases. The procedure bbrackets ("begin-brackets") reads the list B (possibly empty) of brackets from the word list (represented by difference list (U,V).) A possible "preconjunction" (like *both*) is gotten by preconj. Then the simple non-terminal pbase is called. Then pconj gets the remainder of the coordinated phrase, and ebrackets closes off the brackets.

There are three rules for the "continuation" pconj. The first of these gets most types of conjunctions, makes another call to pbase, and finally calls pconj recursively. The second allows termination. The third is like the first, but gets other types of conjunctions. Thus, with termination in the middle of these three rules, a *preference* is created for certain types of coordination at the given phrase level. The details of this preference coding will not be given here.

The first rule for pconj is:

```
pconj(F0,F,PC,syn(p:F0,nil,Mods0),Syn,X,W) <-
  optionalcommma(X,T.U) &
  coord(T,PC,a,p,Op,LF) &
  copyfeas(p,F,F1) &
  pbase(F1,nil,syn(p:F1,nil,Mods1),U,V) &
  coordcomb(p,T,F0,F1,F2) &
  pconj(F2,F,nil,
        syn(p:F2,*,syn(p:F0,nil,Mods0):
                   Op-LF:
                   syn(p:F1,nil,Mods1):nil),
        Syn,V,W).
```

Here coord tests that the terminal T is a coordinating conjunction, allowing preconjunction PC, being of type (a,p) (the type required for the *first* pconj rule as opposed to the third), and having associated logical terminal Op-LF. The procedure coordcomb combines features of conjuncts (this includes the treatment of number for coordinated noun phrases).

The second rule for `pconj` (termination) is trivial, and will not be given. The third is essentially like the first, but requires a different conjunction type in the call to `coord`.

Note that some category-specific information for coordination does have to be written, mainly in the rules for `copyfeas` and `coordcomb`. However, default rules exist for these in **ModL**, so that one does not have to write special rules for all categories. On the whole, the amount of rule writing is greatly reduced by the metarules.

3.3. Syntactic techniques in ModL

The syntactic component of **ModL** is basically an extension of that in (McCord, 1982), which was written as a DCG. In particular, slot-filling techniques are used in **ModL** for handling complements of verbs, nouns, and adjectives. However, there are some improvements of the basic techniques, which will be described in this section.

As in the earlier grammar, the analysis of the complements of a verb (or noun or adjective) is directly controlled by a slot frame which appears in the lexical entry of the verb. There is a general non-terminal `postmods` which receives the slot frame of the verb, chooses slots (non-deterministically, and not necessarily in the order in which they appear in the slot frame), and tries to fill the slots by *slot-filling rules* indexed to specific slot names. The procedure `postmods` also finds adjunct postmodifiers. Slot-fillers (complements) correspond to arguments of the verb-sense predication, and adjuncts correspond to outer modifiers of it in logical form.

By itself, the free choice of slots and adjuncts for postmodification allows for free ordering of these postmodifiers; but of course the ordering should not be completely free, so some constraints are needed. An improved method of expressing such constraints has been implemented in **ModL**.

To see how this works, let us look at the **ModL** rule (slightly simplified) for the non-terminal `predicate` which gets the verb and its postmodifiers:

```
predicate(Infl,E,X,C) ==>
   vc(Infl:E,Y,Slots):
   voice(Infl,X,Y,Slots,Slots1):
   $theme(X,Slots,Z):
   postmods(vp,nil,Slots1,E,Z,C).
```

(The `$` sign signals that its operand is a Prolog goal.) Here `Infl` is the inflectional feature structure of the verb, `E` is the semantic type of the verb, `X` is the *marker* for the grammatical subject of the verb (a variable typed by semantic and syntactic features of the subject), and `C` is the *modifier context* for `predicate` (to be explained below).

The non-terminal `vc` (*verb compound*), which is the only strong non-terminal in this rule, gets the head of the predicate. (This normally consists of a single word, but could be a compound like *time share*. It does not include auxiliary verbs as premodifiers; these are treated as separate, higher verbs.) The call to `vc` determines the marker `Y` for the *logical* subject of the verb, and the slot list `Slots` of the verb.

The procedure `voice` handles the passive transformation as a *slot list transformation*, and `theme` computes the marker `Z` for implicit subjects in complements like "John wants *to leave*", and "John wants Bill *to leave*". For these, see the discussion in (McCord, 1982).

The first rule for `postmods`, which gets slot fillers (as opposed to adjuncts), is as follows, slightly simplified (we leave off the treatment of the modifier context argument for now).

```
postmods(Cat,State,Slots,E,Z) ==>
   $selectslot(Slot,State,Slots,Slots1):
   filler(Slot,Z):
   postmods(Cat,Slot.State,Slots1,E,Z).
```

What is of interest here (compared with McCord, 1982) is the use of the `State` argument, whose purpose is to constrain the free ordering of postmodifiers. In the earlier grammar, states were a linearly ordered set of symbols isomorphic to the natural numbers, and the idea was that postmodification by a given slot (or adjunct type) can *advance* the state to a certain level, or leave it the same, but can never go backwards. The trouble with this (as implemented) was that `postmods` could try filling a "late state" slot when an *obligatory* "early state" slot has not been filled yet. (This doesn't cause any wrong parses, but it is inefficient.)

The cure involves looking not only at the postmodifiers that have already been found, but also at the obligatory slots that are still pending. The *state* is now just the list of slots and adjunct types that have already been used. (Building up of this list can be seen in the above rule for `postmods`.)

The procedure `selectslot` selects a `Slot` from the current list `Slots`, with `Slots1` as the remainder. In so doing, it looks at the current state as well as the remaining slots to exercise the constraints.

The specific constraints themselves are expressed in the most straightforward way possible -- as ordering relationships `S1<<S2`, where `S1` and `S2` are slots or adjunct types. *Slots* are represented as terms `slot(S,Ob,Re,X)`, where (1) `S` is the slot name (like `obj` or `iobj`), (2) `Ob` indicates whether the slot is obligatory or optional, (3) `Re` indicates whether the slot has a *real* filler, or a *virtual* filler (because of left extraposition), and (4) `X` is the marker (a typed variable) for the slot filler. *Adjunct types* are simple symbols (like `avcl` for *adverbial clause*) which divide adjuncts into broad types. Specific ordering constraints are:

```
slot(iobj,*,r,*) << slot(obj,*,r,*).
slot(obj,*,r,*) << slot(S,*,r,*)  <-  S=/iobj.
slot(*,*,r,*) << avcl.
```

The idea of `selectslot` is then simple. It selects a slot `S` non-deterministically from the current slot list `Slots`, leaving remainder `Slots1`; but it checks that (1) there is no member `S1` of `State` such that `S<<S1`, and (2) there is no obligatory slot `S2` in `Slots1` such that `S2<<S`.

The basic idea of "factoring out" the control of constituent ordering into simple ordering relationships has been used in other systems, for example in the systemic grammar system of (Hudson, 1971) and the follow-up of (McCord, 1975), and more recently in the ID/LP formalism (Gazdar and Pullum, 1982).

A second improvement in **ModL** concerns *preference attachment* of postmodifiers in the sense of (Wilks, Huang and Fass, 1985), (Huang, 1984a, 1984b). The problem is simply stated: When we have parsed part of a sentence, as in *John saw the way to send a file...*, and we see a further phrase *to Bill*, then does this attach to *file, send, way,* or *saw*? *I.e.*, which final phrase of the partial sentence does it modify? If the initial segment were instead *John described the way to create a file...*, then the answer would be different.

The method of handling this in **ModL** is basically similar to that in the work of Huang, Wilks, and Fass cited above, but seems slightly simpler and more general, because of the systematic use of `postmods` in **ModL**. The implementation involves the modifier context argument (the last argument) of `postmods`.

It should be mentioned first that the modifier context is used not only for handling preference attachment, but also for left extraposition. The modifier context contains a pair of *topic* terms `(T,T1)` used as in (McCord, 1982) to represent a left-extraposed item `T`, with `T1` equal to `nil` or `T` according as `T` is or is not used as a virtual filler (or adjunct) by `postmods`.

A *modifier context* is a term of the form `c(T,T1,Pend)`, where `(T,T1)` is a topic pair and `Pend` is a *pending* stack. The latter is a list whose members are *pending frames*, which are terms of the form `Cat.E.Slots`, giving a phrase category (verb or noun), the semantic type of the head, and the current slot list of the head (some slots may already be used). A pending frame describes what is possible for further modifiers of a given head word (adjunct modification depends on the category Cat and the semantic type E).

Using modifier contexts, an essentially complete version of the slot-filling rule for postmods is:

```
postmods(Cat,State,Slots,E,Z,c(T,T2,Pend)) ==>
  $selectslot(Slot,State,Slots,Slots1):
  filler(Slot,Z,c(T,T1,(Cat.E.Slots1).Pend)):
  postmods(Cat,Slot.State,Slots1,E,Z,c(T1,T2,Pend)).
```

Thus, in the call to filler, the current pending frame is stacked onto the pending stack. A rule for filling, say, an object slot with a noun phrase would pass this larger modifier context argument into the noun phrase, where the higher context is then available.

On a given level for postmods, the most pressing question is how to attach prepositional phrases. Slot-filling is always preferred over adjunct modification on a given level. So if the given head word has a prepositional object slot pobj(Prep) matching the given preposition, then only this will be tried.

To decide whether a pp can attach as an adjunct modifier, the pp rule looks at the pending stack to see if there are pending prepositional case slots that could take the given preposition, and, if so, it will not be tried. The semantic type of the head word is also used to block adjunct attachment of a pp (if the type required by the preposition sense doesn't match). Currently the grammar does not try to *compare* semantic types for preferences, but this could be done since the pending stack, with all the higher types, is in place.

The last improvement to be mentioned (briefly) in this section is in the treatment of noun compounds. Noun compounds were treated in a limited way in (McCord, 1982), by allowing noun premodifiers of the head noun to fill slots in the head noun, as in *mathematics student*. In the syntactic structure, these noun premodifiers were all shown on the same level, as daughters of the noun phrase, although the slot-filling attachment to the head corresponds logically to a right-branching structure. But of course noun compounds in English can exhibit any pattern of attachment, with the patterns corresponding to the ways one can bracket *n* symbols. This is important to capture.

The shift operator allows one to produce all patterns of attachment, left-branching, right-branching, and all combinations in between, while using right-recursive rules. The following small grammar produces all possible bracketings:

```
np  ==> +N.
np  ==> +N: np%np1.
np1 ==> np.
np1 ==> np: np%np1.
```

Here np is a strong non-terminal and np1 is weak, and +N signals that N is a terminal.

In **ModL**, a somewhat more complicated form of this fragment is used in the noun compound rules. Each subcompound gets a slot list and a marker variable associated with it, and there is a procedure attach (an extension of that in (McCord, 1982)), which allows one subcompound to attach to another. Adjectives are included in the pot, but the rules for attaching them are of course different. The potential to get any pattern of attachment exists in the rules, but again *preferences* are implemented. Roughly, the idea is this: As a new noun (or adjective) N is read, if (1) the structure N0 already built has a head that is a noun and (2) N *can* attach to N0, then one requires this immediate attachment, building a left-branching structure. Otherwise, one continues with right-branching and attaches the larger compound to N0.

This scheme prefers left-branching for a sequence of nouns, *if* attach allows it, but prefers a right-branching structure for a sequence of adjectives followed by a noun.

Currently, attach does not deal with "creative" attachments, where the relationship between the two subcompounds is not mere slot-filling or apposition, but where the combination involves some extraneous relationship, as in *music box* and *work clothes*. But an extended version of `attach` which handles such combinations would still be used in the existing algorithm.

3.4. Treatment of the lexicon in ModL

One feature of the lexicon is that the storage format of lexical entries is not the same as the format seen by the syntactic component. Both formats are Prolog clauses (mainly unit clauses), but there is *compiling*, or *preprocessing* of lexical entries. There are two main reasons for this. One reason is that lexical compiling allows for abbreviated forms in the storage format, with a system of defaults for the compiled forms. The compiled forms are convenient for efficient parsing, but take up more storage space. The second reason is that the compiler can create different formats for different applications of **ModL**. This will be illustrated below.

The **ModL** lexicon is divided into two parts, the *open-class lexicon*, and the *special lexicon*. The open-class lexicon contains entries for verbs, nouns, and adjectives, mainly the citation forms of such words. This part of the lexicon is organized in such a way that it can be stored in large disk files, and entries can be looked up efficiently (by Prolog routines). Morphological analysis (in Prolog) is done in combination with look-up in this lexicon, in order to recognize derived forms of open-class words. Open-class words are looked up, and their entries are compiled, only when they specifically occur in input text. This avoids overloading the Prolog rule space.

The special lexicon consists of entries for closed-class words (like determiners and prepositions), as well as a few of the most commonly used verbs and nouns (like *be*). These entries are compiled when **ModL** is initialized and they are all stored in the Prolog rule space.

The entries in the open-class lexicon are of the form:

```
Word < Description1 < Description2 < ... .
```

An example (using some defaults), is:

```
attempt < v(infcmp) < n(ninfcmp).
```

This says that `attempt` is a verb with complement slot `infcmp` and a noun with complement slot `ninfcmp`. In general, each *description* is a lexical description of the word as a verb, noun, or adjective. Normally, these descriptions are of a citation form, but for irregularly inflected words, inflection forms can be included, as in

```
become < v(predcmp) < ven(become).
```

where it is shown that `become` is the past participle of itself.

A given open-class word `W` should occur in only one clause of the form `W < Descriptions`; *i.e.*, all of the descriptions for a given word should be included in the same entry. This is necessary for efficient look-up in disk files and use of the morphology procedures.

The general, complete format (without use of defaults) for a verb citation description is `v(Sense,E,X,Slots)`, where `Sense` is a name for a sense of the verb, `E` is the semantic type of the verb (as a whole), `X` is the semantic type of the subject, and `Slots` is the slot list, each slot having a possible semantic type associated with it (as a semantic type for the filler). An example for the verb *give* might be:

```
v(give1,action,human,(obj:concrete).(iobj:animate)).
```

An abbreviation convention allows one to omit any initial sequence of these arguments. If the sense name is omitted, it will be taken to be the same as the citation form. Omitting types is equivalent to having no typing requirements. For an intransitive verb with no typing and only one sense, the description could be simply `v`, with no arguments.

The lexical compiler translates a `v` description into a unit clause for the predicate `verb` and adds it to the rule space. This has arguments corresponding to the full form of the `v` entry, but the verb sense is made into a predication, and the slots in the slot list are converted into the fuller form `slot(S,Ob,Re,X)` described in the preceding section. (There can be optional and obligatory forms of the same slot.) The marker variable `X` is actually of the form `V:SemT:SynT`, where `V` is a pure variable, `SemT` is the semantic type associated with the slot, and `SynT` is a variable which gets associated with a syntactic feature structure for the slot-filler, during parsing. The subject type is converted into a similar marker variable for the subject.

The verb sense predication created by the compiler has arguments corresponding to these marker variables (for the subject and the slots, in the order given), but there is an option in the compiler: When **ModL** is being used to create **LFL** forms, these arguments will just be the pure (untyped) variables associated with the marker variables. But when **ModL** is used in **LMT**, the arguments will be the complete (typed) marker variables. This ready access to the typing (semantic and syntactic) of complements, by direct storage in the word sense predication, is very useful for transfer in **LMT** (for choosing word transfers), and will be illustrated in the next section.

Lexical compiling also operates on the semantic types appearing in the abbreviated entries. The whole semantic type system is specified in a network specified by rules like

```
animate <=> male | female.
animate <=> human | nonhuman.
human => intelligent.
```

allowing cross-classification. In the abbreviated lexical entries, one just specifies leaf nodes in this network, and the compiler converts such a feature bundle into a single Prolog term (a tree) used in unification type matching. Use of such trees is a generalization of a method used by Dahl (1977).

Prolog routines have been written that do fairly efficient look-up of open-class entries in large disk files. The technique is to use binary index trees, stored in the Prolog rule space, to narrow down the range of search, then to use binary search with disk reads that specify record numbers.

In addition to this main **ModL** lexicon, there is an auxiliary interface to the UDICT lexicon (Byrd, 1983, 1984). This contains around 65,000 citation forms, with a morphological rule system to get derived forms of these words. The **ModL** rule compiler also can convert the descriptions of this system to the format that the syntactic component likes to see.

4. The transfer component of LMT

The transfer component takes an English syntactic analysis tree `syn(Cat,B,Mods)` and converts it to a German tree `syn(GCat,B,GMods)` which normally has the same shape. Before discussing the transfer method in general, let us look at an example. The English sentence is *The woman gives a book to the man*. The syntactic analysis tree produced by **ModL** is:

```
s:fin(pers3,sg,pres,ind)
   np:X:a(h):*
      detp:X:a(h):*
         the(P,Q))
      woman(X:a(h):*)
   verbph:fin(pers3,sg,pres,ind):e(ha,nil)
      give(X:a(h):*, Y:c:*, Z:a(h):*)
      np:Y:c:*
         detp:Y:c:*
            a(P1,Q1)
         book(Y:c:*)
      ppnp:to:Z:a(h):*
         np:Z:a(h):*
            detp:Z:a(h):*
               the(P2,Q2)
            man(Z:a(h):*)
```

Each non-terminal node label in the tree is of the form NT:F, where NT is the principal functor of the strong non-terminal responsible for the node, and F is the first argument (the *feature* argument) of NT. The feature arguments for the np nodes are just the marker variables for these nodes. For the sake of simplicity in the display of this tree, the third components (the syntactic feature structures) of np markers are just shown as stars. The terminals in the syntactic analysis tree are actually logical terminals, but we do not display the operator components, since these are not relevant for **LMT**. Also, we do not display the node labels for noun compounds (nc) and verb compounds (vc) unless these compounds have more than one element.

The most relevant thing to notice in the above tree is that the node for the verb give contains variables X, Y, Z associated with the three complements of the verb. Transfer of this verb form simultaneously chooses the German verb and marks features on its (German) complements by binding X, Y, Z to the proper German cases. The entry for the verb *give* in the transfer lexicon is the following unit clause:

```
gverb(give(nom:*,acc:*,dat:*),geb).
```

In transfer, the first argument of this is matched against the give form in the tree, and we get bindings X=nom, Y=acc, and Z=dat, which determine the cases of the complements. The transfer tree is as follows:

```
vp(ind(s),fin(pers3,sg,pres,ind):l,nil)
   np(n(cn),nom,sg:sg,f,A1)
      det(nom,sg,f,A1)
         d + det(nom,sg,f,A1)
      frau + nc(n(cn),nom,sg,f,A1)
   vp(ind(vp),fin(pers3,sg,pres,ind):l,nil)
      geb + vc(ind(vp),fin(d(def),sg,pres,ind):l,nil)
      np(n(cn),acc,sg:sg,nt,A2)
         det(acc,sg,nt,A2)
            ein + det(acc,sg,nt,A2)
         buch + nc(n(cn),acc,sg,nt,A2)
      ppnp(vp(ind(vp),fin(pers3,sg,pres,ind):l,nil),dat)
         np(n(cn),dat,sg:sg,m,A3)
            det(dat,sg,m,A3)
               d + det(dat,sg,m,A3)
            mann + nc(n(cn),dat,sg,m,A3)
```

The three noun phrases in this tree have the correct case markings as a result of the above verb transfer, so that we will eventually get *die Frau*, *ein Buch*, and *dem Mann*. A transformation (to be discussed below) moves the dative noun phrase, and the eventual translation (after inflection) is *Die Frau gibt dem Mann ein Buch.*

The top-level procedure, `transfer`, of the transfer component works in a simple, recursive way, and is called in the form

```
transfer(Syn,MCat,GSyn)
```

where `MCat` is the German node label on the mother of the node `Syn` being transferred. (In the top-level call, `MCat` is equal to the symbol `top`.)

The definition of `transfer`, slightly simplified, is:

```
transfer(syn(ECat,B,EMods),MCat,syn(GCat,B,GMods)) <-
   trancat(ECat,MCat,GCat) &
   tranlist(EMods,GCat,GMods).
transfer(Op-Pred,MCat,GWord+GCat) <-
   tranword(MCat,Pred,GWord,GCat).

tranlist(EMod:EMods,MCat,GMod:GMods) <-
   transfer(EMod,MCat,GMod) &
   tranlist(EMods,MCat,GMods).
tranlist(nil,*,nil).
```

Thus, `transfer` translates a `syn` structure (a non-terminal node of a tree) by translating the node label (by a call to `trancat`) and then recursively translating the daughter nodes. Terminal nodes (words) are translated by a call to `tranword`.

Note that `transfer` does the transfer in a simple top-down, left-to-right way. The German feature structures (showing case markings, for instance) that get assigned to nodes in the left-to-right processing are often *partially instantiated*, and do not get fully instantiated until controlling words are encountered further to the right. For example, the German feature structure assigned to the subject noun phrase in the above example does not get the case field assigned until the verb is processed.

The clauses for `trancat` (which transfers node labels) are mainly unit clauses. The basic problem is to transfer an English feature structure to a German feature structure, allowing for differences in a suitable way. For example, the number of an English noun phrase often determines the number of the corresponding German noun phrase, but not always. The main `trancat` clause that transfers a noun phrase label is:

```
trancat(np:Case:SemT:np(NType,Number,*,*), MCat,
        np(NType,Case,Number,Gender,AdjDecl)).
```

The first component, `NType`, of the German (and the English) `np` feature structure is the *noun type*, which encodes categorization of the head noun. Noun subcategories include common nouns, pronouns, proper nouns, and adjectives. Adjectives are further subcategorized as verbal (verb participles) and non-verbal, and the *comparison feature (positive, comparative, superlative)* for adjectives is also shown in `NType`.

The second component, `Case`, in the German `np` structure is unified with the first component of the English marker variable. As indicated above, this gets unified with an actual case by application of a verb transfer rule.

The third component, `Number`, of the German `np` structure is taken directly from the English structure, but is of such a form that the actual number of the German noun phrase can come out different from that of the English, as will be explained below.

The fourth component, `Gender`, is not determined by `trancat`, although `trancat` is responsible for unifying gender features of various constituents of the noun phrase. The actual gender (`m`, `f`, `nt`) is determined by `tranword`.

The last component has to do with adjective declensions (strong vs. weak), and will be discussed in Section 6.

The German feature structure for a noun compound (`nc`) (including a simple head noun) has a similar form to an `np` structure.

How is the `Number` field used? This is actually a compound term of the form `Num:CNum`, where `Num` is the actual number (`sg` or `pl`) of the English noun phrase (which may be a coordinated noun phrase), and `CNum` is a term that reflects the coordination structure. For example, for the noun phrase *the man and the woman*, the number structure is `pl:(N1&N2)`, where the subphrase *the man* has number structure `sg:N1`, and *the woman* has number structure `sg:N2`.

During transfer, the second components of the number structures of *simple* noun phrases are just variables, and these get bound by `tranword` to the numbers of the German translations. The *default* is to unify the German number with the English number (for a simple noun phrase), but the transfer lexicon can override this, as in the case of *scissors/Schere*. Given this determination of the German numbers of the simple `np` components of a coordinated `np`, the German number of the whole can be determined from the second component of the number field. In the case of coordination with *and/und*, the result will simply be plural in German (as in English). For coordination with *or/oder*, though, German is different from English. In English, the number of the disjunction is the same as that of its last component, whereas in German the disjunction is plural if and only if at least one of its components is plural.

So, for the noun phrase *the men or the woman*, the English number structure is `sg:(N1|N2)`, where the number of *the men* is `pl:N1`, and the number of *the woman* is `sg:N2`. After transfer, this number structure for the translation *die Männer oder die Frau* becomes `sg:(pl|sg)`. The second component of this, `pl|sg`, determines a final number of `pl` for the translation. On the other hand, *the knife or the scissors* is plural, but the translation, *das Messer oder die Schere*, has number structure `pl:(sg|sg)` and so is singular.

In the sample transfer tree above, one can see other examples of the transfer of feature structures, for which `trancat` is responsible. In the `vp` feature structures, the second component is of the form `Infl:Infl1`, where `Infl` is the English inflection and `Infl1` is to be the final German inflection. The default is for `Infl1` to become equal to `Infl`, but this doesn't always happen. The English inflection might be overridden by a transformation. For example, **LMT** translates *The man wants the woman to buy a car* to *Der Mann will, daß die Frau einen Wagen kauft.* The infinitive clause complement of *wants* becomes a finite clause complement of *will.*

The procedure

```
tranword(MCat,EWord,GWord,GCat)
```

is the interface to the transfer lexicon. It takes the (German) category `MCat` of the node dominating a terminal with English `EWord` (represented as a word-sense predication), and associates with these the German translation `GWord` and its associated feature structure `GCat`. (Often `GCat` will be taken to be the same as `MCat`.) The procedure `trancat`, in looking at the category `MCat`, can call various more specific transfer procedures, like `gverb` and `gnoun`, associated with various parts of speech. The clauses for these constitute the transfer lexicon. We have already seen a sample clause for `gverb`.

One allowance that has to be made is that the subject of the English verb may not correspond to the subject of the German verb. This occurs with the translation of *like* into *gefallen*, where we can translate *I like the car* into *Mir gefällt der Wagen*. The transfer entry for the verb *like* is

```
gverb(like(dat:*,nom:X),ge+fall,*:X).
```

The extra argument of `gverb` is the marker of the German subject. In such cases, `tranword` must make sure that the German verb (if finite) agrees with the actual German subject.

The case markers that can appear in transfer entries include not only the standard four cases (`nom`, `acc`, `dat`, and `gen`), but also prepositional case markers (for `pp` complements of German verbs), which are of the form `pc(Prep,Case)`. This form signifies that the specific preposition `Prep` appears, followed by a noun phrase with case `Case`. For example, the transfer entry for *search (something) for (something)* is

```
gverb(search(nom:*,acc:*,pc(nach):*),durch+such).
```

Since the arguments of the English predications given to `gverb` (and other transfer procedures) are complete marker variables, the semantic and syntactic types appearing in these can be used in determining the proper translations. For instance, the verb *eat* translates into *essen* or *fressen* according as the subject is human or non-human. The corresponding `gverb` entries are:

```
gverb(eat(nom:a(h):*,acc:*),ess).
gverb(eat(nom:a(nh):*,acc:*),fress).
```

Care is taken in the `tranword` rules involving `gverb` to handle auxiliary verbs correctly. One problem is to get the right case marking on the German subject and the right inflection on the highest auxiliary, even though the English subject may not correspond to the German subject of the "main" verb.

In particular, care with case marking must be taken in the translation of passives. In a German passive, the grammatical subject may correspond to a direct object in the active form, but it may not correspond to an indirect object (as it may in English). Thus, **LMT** translates *The car was given to the man* into *Der Wagen wurde dem Mann gegeben*, but translates *The man was given a car* into *Dem Mann wurde ein Wagen gegeben* (where *ein Wagen* is the grammatical subject). Currently, **LMT** translates the English passive only by the use of *werden*. The use of *sein* and active forms will be tackled eventually.

In the translation of the perfect *have*, the *haben/sein* distinction is made by feature markings on the English verb complement of *have*. It could be argued that this is an exception to the principle that the English grammar is written independently of the task of translation, but the distinction made by the required features is largely semantic.

The transfer rules for nouns and adjectives involve many of the same issues as those for verbs, since these words have similar complementation to that of verbs.

It should be mentioned that the English morphological system sees to it that *ly*-adverbs are associated with the corresponding adjectives, so that there needn't be special transfer entries for most adverbs. The transfer procedure `gadv` for adverbs just calls the transfer procedure `gadj` for adjectives (with the very same English predication form). However, `gadv` checks exceptional adverb transfers before using the adjective default.

How does **LMT** treat situations in which there is not a word-for-word correspondence in translations? Of course transformations can add, delete, or rearrange words, and examples of these will be discussed in the next section. But, in keeping with the principle of getting as much right as possible during transfer, various methods are used in transfer, too.

One method is that the "result" arguments of transfer lexicon entries can contain compound terms that represent word sequences. The most general form is `W1#W2`, which represents `W1` followed by `W2` (with a separating blank). This form is used, for example, in cases where the verb translation is a reflexive verb. The verb *refer to* translates to *sich beziehen auf*, and the transfer entry is:

```
gverb(refer(nom:F,pc(auf,acc):*),refl(*:F)#be+zieh).
```

The term `refl(X)` representing the reflexive contains the feature structure of the German subject, so that it may be realized as the correct form of the reflexive pronoun by the inflection component.

A special compound form shows up in the representation of separable-prefix verbs, which are of the form `Prefix:Verb`. (As exhibited above, *in*separable-prefix verbs are given in the form

Prefix+Verb.) A separable prefix can become a separate word through a transformation that recognizes the special form and moves the prefix appropriately.

One could say that the translation of noun compounds involves a many-to-one correspondence, since these are given as a group of words in English, but often as a single word in German. The procedure trancat is responsible for marking the nc feature structures of the components of a noun compound prior to the head word. The *case* component of this structure is marked by a special case symbol comb (*combining form*), which signals that the noun is part of a noun compound and will be given a special form by the inflection component. More details are given below in Section 6. The notion that German nouns have idiosyncratic combining forms comes from Wolff (1983).

Finally, there is a general facility for handling idiomatic multiword translations. The first clause for transfer given earlier in this section actually is more general than indicated. Instead of calling tranlist, it calls a more general procedure tranphrase. This can call not only tranlist, but also the phrasal transfer procedure gphrase, with entries like:

```
gphrase(pp,for(*,*).purpose(*,gen:*),'zum Zweck').
```

This is responsible for making translations like *for purposes of this discussion* --> *zum Zweck dieser Diskussion*.

5. The restructuring component

The top-level restructuring procedure

```
restructure(Syn,Syn1)
```

applies transformations to a syn tree Syn, producing another syn tree Syn1. This works recursively on the tree. At each level, the daughter nodes are first recursively restructured, and then transformations for the given level are applied (their order matters) until no more can apply. Thus, the definition can be given as:

```
restructure(syn(Cat,B,Mods),syn(Cat2,B2,Mods2)) <- /&
  restructlist(Mods,Mods1) &
  alltransforms(syn(Cat,B,Mods1),syn(Cat2,B2,Mods2)).
restructure(Mod,Mod).

restructlist(Mod:Mods,Mod1:Mods1) <-
  restructure(Mod,Mod1) &
  restructlist(Mods,Mods1).
restructlist(nil,nil).

alltransforms(Syn,Syn2) <-
  transform(Trans,Syn,Syn1) &/&
  alltransforms(Syn1,Syn2).
alltransforms(Syn,Syn).
```

Note that in this scheme, transformations on a given level are applied *after* the recursive restructuring of daughter nodes. The alternative schemes of applying them all *before* recursive restructuring, or applying some designated transformations before and others after recursive restructuring, were tried. But these other schemes led to problems with a workable ordering of the list of transformations.

Specific transformations are given by rules for transform. Its first argument is just a label for the transformation, like verbfinal, which is used in tracing (in a fuller definition of restructure).

One could write rules for `transform` directly, but in **LMT** transformational rules are written in a slightly more convenient notation and then compiled into rules for `transform`.

The main purpose of the alternative format is to provide an augmentation of the pattern matching of Prolog in which specially marked terms can match *sublists* of lists. Specifically, when a term of the form `%X` is written syntactically as a member of a list, then `X` matches (unifies with) any sublist in that position. This can be used both in analyzing and constructing lists. As an example, the expression `a:b:%X:c:d:nil` would match the list `a:b:u:v:w:c:d:nil` and unify `X` with `u:v:w:nil`. (Similar conventions have been used in many pattern matchers dealing with lists.) In this implementation, such extended list expressions can be embedded arbitrarily in Prolog terms.

The form for a transformation given to the rule compiler is:

```
Label --
    A ===> B
    <- Condition.
```

Here `A` and `B` are arbitrary Prolog terms, containing possible extended list expressions. The `Condition` is a Prolog goal, and it can be omitted if desired. This rule is compiled into a `transform` rule of the form:

```
transform(Label,A1,B1) <-
    ASplit & Condition & BSplit.
```

Here the original pseudo-term `A` involving `%` elements has been re-expressed as an ordinary term `A1` and a conjunction `ASplit` of calls to `conc`, which concatenates lists. Similarly, `B` is re-expressed as `B1` and `BSplit`.

As an example, a simplified version of the German `dative` transformation is

```
dative --
    syn(vp, B, %LMods:Obj:IObj:RMods)
    ===>
    syn(vp, B, %LMods:IObj:Obj:RMods)
      <- case(Obj,acc) & case(IObj,dat).
```

This is compiled into the `transform` rule:

```
transform(dative, syn(vp,B,Mods), syn(vp,B,Mods1)) <-
   conc(LMods, Obj:IObj:RMods, Mods) &
   case(Obj,acc) & case(IObj,dat) &
   conc(LMods, IObj:Obj:RMods, Mods1).
```

For efficiency, the `Condition` is inserted between `ASplit` and `BSplit`, because `Condition` normally contains constraints whose arguments become known immediately after execution of `ASplit`.

Currently there are twenty-two transformations in **LMT**. It should be emphasized that the **LMT** design does not require as many transformations as some natural language system designs using transformations, because (1) the English analyses are fairly rich, and (2) there is an effort to get as much right as possible during transfer. We will look at some of the transformations now.

The transformation `relclause` is defined as follows:

```
relclause --
    syn(vp(dep(rel(Case,Type,Num,Gen)),I,M), B, Mods)
    ===>
    syn(vp(dep(rel),I,M), B, (',' +punc):
                             (drel+pro(Case,Num,Gen)):
                             %Mods:
                             (','+punc):nil).
```

This is responsible for adding a relative pronoun and surrounding commas to the relative clause. In the English analysis tree, no relative pronoun is explicitly shown. (In certain cases it can even be omitted in the English sentence.) Thus, *The man I saw is my brother* translates into *Der Mann, den ich sah, ist mein Bruder*. There are variants of this relative clause transformation dealing with cases like *The book to which I referred is old*, which translates to *Das Buch, auf das ich mich bezog, ist alt*. **LMT** gives exactly this same translation for each of the English sentences: *The book which I referred to is old*, *The book that I referred to is old*, and *The book I referred to is old*.

There is a similar transformation `compclause`, which adds the word *daß* and commas to a finite complement clause. Thus, *Hans knows Peter is my brother* translates into *Hans weiß, daß Peter mein Bruder ist*.

The last example illustrates the need to move the verb to the end of a dependent clause. This is done by the transformation `verbfinal`, defined as follows:

```
verbfinal --
    syn(vp(dep(T),I,M), B, %Mods1:VC:Mod:Mods2)
    ===>
    syn(vp(dep(T),I,M), B, %Mods1:Mod:VC:Mods2)
      <- syncat(VC,vc(*,*,*)) &
         ¬clausal(Mod) & ¬allpunc(Mod:Mods2).
```

The idea is simply that the verb `VC` hops over the modifier `Mod` to its right, provided that `Mod` is not *clausal* (to be explained) and provided that the remaining modifiers (including `Mod`) do not consist solely of punctuation. For example, in the translation of the noun phrase *the man that gave the woman the book*, the verb *gab* moves all the way to the end of the relative clause, producing: *der Mann, der der Frau das Buch gab*. Note that `verbfinal` may apply several times, until the verb has moved as far as it can go. (It is possible to be a bit more efficient by writing an auxiliary procedure to perform the movement.)

The point in not hopping over *clausal* elements in `verbfinal` is illustrated with the translation of the noun phrase *the man that told me that Hans bought a car*, which is *der Mann, der mir sagte, daß Hans einen Wagen kaufte*. Here *sagte* hops over *mir*, but not over the *daß* clause. Roughly, *clausal* elements are phrases whose heads are verbs.

But an interesting situation for `verbfinal` arises when there is a clausal element which is on the right end of the tree, but which is not a sister of the verb being moved. This occurs in the translation of the noun phrase *the man that gave the woman the book I referred to*. Here *gab* should not move past the final relative clause, and the result should be: *der Mann, der der Frau das Buch gab, auf das ich mich bezog*. The final clausal element could actually be embedded several levels. To handle this, there is a transformation `clauseraise`, ordered before `verbfinal`, which raises such final clauses. Its definition is simply:

```
clauseraise --
    syn(Cat, B, %Mods:syn(Cat1,B1,%Mods1:Syn:nil):nil)
    ===>
    syn(Cat, B, %Mods:syn(Cat1,B1,Mods1):Syn:nil)
       <- clausal(Syn).
```

This may operate through several levels before the result of the raising is pertinent to `verbfinal`.

The transformation `verbfinal` also handles (without extra effort) the word ordering in auxiliary verb constructions, because of the treatment of auxiliary verbs as higher verbs. Thus, the sentence *Hans will have bought the car* is structured as *Hans [will [have [bought the car]]]*. Before transformations, the translation will be structured as *Hans [wird [haben [gekauft den Wagen]]]*. The verb phrases headed by *haben* and *gekauft* are dependent, so `verbfinal` operates on them to give: *Hans [wird [[den Wagen gekauft] haben]]*. (The phrases hopped over are not cases of *clausal* elements.)

Right movement of separable verb prefixes in independent clauses is similar to right movement of the verb in dependent clauses. This is handled by two transformations, one to separate the prefix, the other to move it. In this case, too, the moved item does not hop over clausal elements. An example for the separable-prefix verb *aufbereiten (edit)* is in the **LMT** translation of the sentence

Hans edited the file that he had created, which is *Hans bereitete die Datei auf, die er erstellt hatte*. In dependent clauses, the separable prefix stays with the verb, although inflection has to treat it specially for past participles and *zu* infinitive forms.

Ordering of transformations is important in that `clauseraise` must be ordered before `verbfinal` and the separable prefix transformations. In turn, it is important to order the `dative` transformation before all of these. If the dative noun phrase to be moved contains a final clausal element, then this element should *not* be a barrier to rightward movement of a verb or separable prefix. If `dative` operates first, the final clausal element will go with the whole dative noun phrase, and will not have a chance to be raised by `clauseraise`, which only sees clausal elements on the extreme right of the clause in which it operates. Thus, for the sentence *Hans knew that Peter had given a book to the woman he saw*, the translation is *Hans wußte, daß Peter der Frau, die er sah, ein Buch gegeben hatte*.

Another example of a transformation is `verbsecond`, which operates in independent clauses:

```
verbsecond --
    syn(vp(ind(s),I,M), B, Mod:%Mods1:
          syn(vp(ind(vp),I1,M1),B1,%Mods2:Verb:Mods3):Mods4)
    ===>
    syn(vp(ind(s),I,M), B, Mod:Verb:%Mods1:
          syn(vp(ind(vp),I1,M1),B1,%Mods2:Mods3):Mods4)
       <- Mods1=/nil & glex(Verb,V,vc(*,*,*)).
```

As the name indicates, this moves the verb so that it is the second modifier of the independent clause. As a result, the sentence *Probably the file was created by Hans* translates into *Wahrscheinlich wurde die Datei von Hans erstellt*, where *wurde* is moved into second position by `verbsecond`.

A final example of a transformation is `possessive`, which deals with left-branching possessive noun phrase constructions, as in *my oldest brother's wife's father's car*. The `possessive` transformation is responsible for converting such structures into a sort of right-branching mirror image, where extra definite articles are added: *der Wagen des Vaters der Frau meines ältesten Bruders*. The definition of `possessive`, without its condition, is as follows:

```
possessive --
    syn(NPCat, B, PossNP:NC:Mods)
    ===>
    syn(NPCat, B, Det:NC:PossNP:Mods).
```

The condition tests that the components of the pattern are what their names suggest, assigns the genitive case to the possessive noun phrase `PossNP`, and creates a definite article `Det` that agrees with the whole noun phrase.

6. The inflection component

The inflection component takes the output tree from the restructuring component and produces the character string representing the final German translation.

The first main step in this process is to create a simple list from the tree. This list consists mainly of the terminal nodes of the tree, taken in their left-to-right order, but pairs of bracketing symbols are added at the two ends of bracketed phrases. (Recall that bracketing of a phrase, possibly by more than one bracket pair, is marked on the phrase as a whole in the second component of the `syn` structure for the phrase.) Final punctuation for sentences is also added.

The second step of the inflection component calls an auxiliary procedure `infl` on each of the elements of the list. This is what one normally means by inflection, and is the main topic of this section.

The last step is to convert the list of inflected elements into a simple character string. This includes handling blanks, punctuation, and capitalization appropriately. For example, several commas may appear in a row, because transformations like `relclause` simply add commas at both ends, and several may pile up. Nouns are represented in lowercase in the lexicons, so they get capitalized at this point. Also the conglomeration of noun compounds is done in this step, although currently this is done simply with hyphens.

So, the substantial part is the procedure

```
infl(Word,Cat,WordForm)
```

which takes a `Word` and its associated category `Cat`, and produces the inflected `WordForm`. The main idea of `infl` is to dispatch the task to auxiliary procedures dealing with particular parts of speech, depending on `Cat`. But there is recursion in `infl`, because `Word` may actually be a compound element (such as a reflexive verb, or an adjective-noun combination), as indicated above in the section on transfer. Also, the categorial information (in the second argument of `infl`) must be tidied up before dispatching it. For example, it is here that the actual number of coordinated noun phrases is computed from the forms described in the section on transfer. This number is needed for finite verb inflections (for subject/verb agreement).

The specific inflectional procedures called by `infl` have names like `gverbf` and `gnounf`. They take the citation form of a word, plus inflectional features, and produce the inflected form of the word. The rules for these procedures and their ancillary procedures constitute the German morphological rule system and the German monolingual lexicon. The lexicon consists of unit clauses containing morphological information about words that cannot be derived by general rules.

The idea of course is to do as much as possible by general morphological rules so as to keep the lexicon as small as possible. It turns out then that the monolingual lexicon consists mainly of entries for strong verbs and common nouns. Also, there is some idiosyncrasy in the comparative and superlative forms of adjectives, although only the exceptions need be listed.

Strong verb entries are just unit clauses giving the principal parts, like the following for the verb *geben (give)*:

```
vst(geb,gib,gab,geb,gäb).
```

Verb inflection uses the usual conjugation paradigms, stored mainly as unit clauses, plus the `vst` entries in the case of strong verbs, as well as conditional rules that look at the spelling of the citation form as an aid in applying the paradigms. Details will not be given here, although a bit will be said below about a tool used in looking at the spelling.

Currently, the transfer lexicon helps out the inflection component a bit. For example, as indicated in Section 4, verb transfers show separable-prefix verbs in the form `Pre:Verb` and inseparable-prefix verbs in the form `Pre+Verb`.

Also, for some noun transfers that are compound forms, the structure is shown in the transfer entry, as in *schlüssel+wort* for *keyword*. In such cases, the inflectional features can be found from those of the last component. However, noun features are obtained by examining the noun's spelling for certain common endings like *keit* and *chen*. Additionally, certain common prefixes (like *vor*) are stripped off of the spelling, and the inflectional features of the remainder are used. All in all, since there is so much compositionality in German nouns, the noun lexicon of base forms needn't be nearly as extensive as the transfer lexicon for nouns.

The monolingual noun entries are of the form:

```
gn(Noun,Gender,Class,PluralForm,CombiningForm).
```

The Class is the declension class. Currently there are six declension classes, some of them with subclasses. The argument for the plural form can be omitted in those entries in which the plural form is computable from the citation form and the class. The CombiningForm is a symbol that determines the form taken by the noun when it appears in a noun compound (before the head noun). The idea that this form is listed idiosyncratically comes from Wolff (1983).

The declension of adjectives is very regular, although one must be concerned with the choice between the strong adjective declension and the weak declension (which is determined by the determiner of the noun phrase). The logical variable (call it AdjDecl) appearing in last position in the feature structure symbols in noun phrase constituents (see Section 4) is used to control the adjective declension. (By unification, the same variable appears in all the constituents.) The significance of AdjDecl is that it will be bound either to st, in which case all the adjectives in the noun phrase will be strong, or to wk, in which case they will all be weak. AdjDecl does not actually get bound until inflection time. If there is a determiner, then the determiner type (*der* or *ein* type), plus the particular position in the declension paradigm for this determiner class, will bind AdjDecl appropriately to st or wk. If there is no determiner, then AdjDecl will be bound by default to st by inflection of the first adjective.

The inflectional system handles the comparison of adjectives and adverbs, but details will not be given here.

In doing morphology for both German and English, **LMT** uses two convenient procedures, based on pattern matching, for breaking apart words. The procedure

```
end(Pattern,Word,InitialPart)
```

matches Pattern to a final segment of Word and binds InitialPart to the part of Word resulting from stripping off this suffix. The Pattern can be (1) a known atom, (2) a variable, or (3) of the form Pat1.Pat2 where Pat1 and Pat2 are patterns. Variables match single characters, and Pat1.Pat2 matches in turn what Pat1 matches followed by what Pat2 matches. There is a symmetric procedure for looking at the beginning of a word:

```
beg(Pattern,Word,RestWord)
```

Most morphological rules can be written by use of these two analyzing/testing procedures, together with concatenation of atoms.

7. Status of the system

LMT handles all of the examples and constructions given above, in addition to several other types of constructions (like interrogative forms) not illustrated for lack of space. Testing and vocabulary development are being done with the IBM CMS Editor (XEDIT) manuals (which we have online), as well as with a collection of made-up sentences that illustrate key grammatical constructions. Every effort is being made to keep the rules of the system general. As with most MT systems, it is assumed that there will be some postediting of the output. At this point, **LMT** is doing a fairly reasonable translation of the first section of the XEDIT Reference Manual. The first few sentences and their **LMT** translation are as follows:

> *XEDIT subcommands and macros follow the same rules and conventions. For purposes of this discussion, "subcommand" refers to both XEDIT subcommands and XEDIT macros. The general format of XEDIT subcommands is: (fig.) At least one blank must separate the subcommand name and the operands, unless the operand is a number or a special character. For example, NEXT8 and NEXT 8 are equivalent. At least one blank must be used to separate each*

operand in the command line unless otherwise indicated. The maximum length of an XEDIT subcommand issued from an EXEC procedure or from an XEDIT macro is 256 characters.

XEDIT Unterbefehle und Makros folgen den gleichen Regeln und Konventionen. Zum Zweck dieser Diskussion bezieht sich "Unterbefehl" sowohl auf XEDIT Unterbefehle als auch auf XEDIT Makros. Das allgemeine Format von XEDIT Unterbefehlen ist: (fig.) Mindestens ein Leerzeichen muß den Unterbefehls-Namen und die Operanden abtrennen, es sei denn der Operand ist eine Zahl oder ein spezielles Zeichen. Zum Beispiel sind NEXT8 and NEXT 8 äquivalent. Mindestens ein Leerzeichen muß verwendet werden, jeden Operanden in der Befehls-Zeile abzutrennen, es sei denn anderweitig angezeigt. Die maximale Länge eines XEDIT Unterbefehls, die von einer EXEC Prozedur oder von einem XEDIT Makro herausgegeben wird, ist 256 Zeichen.

The average processing time per sentence in this example (including English analysis time) was 160 milliseconds. The average time per sentence for English syntactic analysis was 105 milliseconds. As indicated in Section 2, the Prolog system being used is VM/Prolog on an IBM 3081. VM/Prolog is an interpreter, written in assembler language. There are some compiler-like facilities, although they are not used in **LMT**.

As for the size of **LMT**, there are now about 1,950 Prolog clauses, not including the lexicons. In the lexicons there are an additional 1,750 clauses, approximately. The transfer lexicon (which need only deal with citation forms) now has about 550 entries. The XEDIT Reference Manual uses a vocabulary involving approximately 1,500 citation forms.

Although work on the English grammar **ModL**, in various stages and forms, has been done off and on since 1979, work on the translation system began in January, 1985, and has involved about eleven months of the author's time. A report (McCord, 1985b) was given at the Colgate MT conference. In November, 1985, Susanne Wolff, who has a linguistics Ph.D. and is a native speaker of German, began part-time work. She has been adding to and improving the lexicon and morphological system, as well as providing checks and advice on German syntactic constructions.

References

Bennett, W. S. and Slocum, J. (1985) "The LRC machine translation system," *Computational Linguistics*, vol. 11, pp. 111-121.

Byrd, R. J. (1983) "Word formation in natural language processing systems," *Proc. 8th International Joint Conference on Artificial Intelligence*, pp. 704-706, Karlsruhe.

Byrd, R. J. (1984) "The Ultimate Dictionary Users' Guide," IBM Research Internal Report.

Colmerauer, A. (1971) "Les systèmes-Q: un formalisme pour analyser et synthétiser des phrases sur ordinateur," Groupe TAUM, Université de Montréal.

Colmerauer, A. et al. (1971) "TAUM-71," Groupe TAUM, Université de Montréal.

Colmerauer, A. (1975) "Les grammaires de métamorphose," Internal Report, Groupe d'Intelligence Artificielle, Univ. d'Aix-Marseille.

Colmerauer, A. (1978) "Metamorphosis grammars," in L. Bolc (Ed.), *Natural Language Communication with Computers*, Springer-Verlag.

Dahl, V. (1977) "Un système déductif d'interrogation de banques de données en espagnol," Doctoral Thesis, Univ. Aix-Marseille.

Dahl, V., and McCord, M. C. (1983) "Treating coordination in logic grammars," *American Journal of Computational Linguistics*, vol. 9, pp. 69-91.

Gazdar, G., and Pullum, G. K. (1982) "Generalized phrase structure grammar: a theoretical synopsis," Indiana University Linguistics Club.

Hirschman, L. (1986) "Conjunction in meta-restriction grammar," to appear in the *Journal of Logic Programming*.

Huang, X-M. (1984a) "The generation of Chinese sentences from the semantic representations of English sentences," *Proc. International Conference on Machine Translation*, Cranfield, England.

Huang, X-M. (1984b) "Dealing with conjunctions in a machine translation environment," *Proc. of Joint ACL and COLING Meeting, 1984*, pp. 243-246, Stanford, California.

Huang, X-M (1985) "Machine translation in SDCG formalism," in (Nirenburg, 1985, these references), pp. 135-144.

Hudson, R. A. (1971) *English Complex Sentences*, North-Holland.

Isabelle, P. and Bourbeau, L. (1985) "TAUM-AVIATION: Its technical features and some experimental results," *Computational Linguistics*, vol. 11, pp. 18-27.

Kittredge, R. et al. (1973) "TAUM-73," Groupe TAUM, Université de Montréal.

Kittredge, R., Bourbeau, L., and Isabelle, P. (1973) "Design and implementation of a French transfer grammar," COLING-76, Ottawa.

Kowalski, R. (1979) *Logic for Problem Solving*, North-Holland.

Matsumoto, Y., Tanaka, H., and Kiyono, M., (1986) "BUP: A bottom-up parsing system for natural languages," in *Logic Programming and its Applications*, M. van Caneghem and D. H. D. Warren, Eds., pp. 262-275, Ablex.

McCord, M. C. (1975) "On the form of a systemic grammar," *Journal of Linguistics*, vol. 11, pp. 195-212.

McCord, M. C. (1982) "Using slots and modifiers in logic grammars for natural language," *Artificial Intelligence*, vol 18, pp. 327-367. (Appeared first as 1980 Technical Report, University of Kentucky.)

McCord, M. C. (1981) "Focalizers, the scoping problem, and semantic interpretation rules in logic grammars," Technical Report, University of Kentucky. Appeared in *Logic Programming and its Applications*, M. van Caneghem and D. H. D. Warren, Eds., Ablex, 1986.

McCord, M. C. (1984) "Semantic interpretation for the EPISTLE system," *Proc. Second International Logic Programming Conference*, pp. 65-76, Uppsala.

McCord, M. C. (1985a) "Modular logic grammars," *Proc. 23rd Annual Meeting of the Association for Computational Linguistics*, pp. 104-117, Chicago.

McCord, M. C. (1985b) "LMT: A Prolog-Based Machine Translation System" (extended abstract), in (Nirenburg, 1985, these references), pp. 179-182.

McCord, M. C. (1986) "Notes on natural langauge processing in Prolog," IBM Internal Report.

Nirenburg, S. (1985), Editor, *Proc. of the Conference on Theoretical and Methodological Issues in Machine Translation of Natural Languages*, Colgate University, Hamilton, NY, August 14-16, 1985.

Pereira, F. and Warren, D. H. D. (1980) "Definite clause grammars for language analysis - a survey of the formalism and a comparison with transition networks," *Artificial Intelligence*, vol. 13, pp. 231-278.

Pereira, F. and Warren, D. H. D. (1983) "Parsing as deduction," *Proc. 21st Annual Meeting of the Association for Computational Linguistics*, pp. 137-144, Cambridge, Mass.

Sedogbo, C. (1984) "A meta grammar for handling coordination in logic grammars," *Proc. Conference on natural language understanding and logic programming*, pp. 137-149, Rennes, France.

Slocum, J. (1985) "A survey of machine translation: its history, current status, and future prospects," *Computational Linguistics*, vol. 11, pp. 1-17.

Teeple, D (1985) "Reasoning in Embedded Contexts," IBM Research Report RC11539, IBM TJ Watson Research, Yorktown Heights.

Teeple, D and Yee, M. (1985) "KNOWMAN: A Natural Language Knowledge Manager," Internal IBM Report.

Uehara, K., Ochitani, R., Kakusho, O., and Toyoda, J. (1984) "A bottom-up parser based on predicate logic: a survey of the formalism and its implementation technique," *Proc. 1984 International Symposium on Logic Programming, IEEE*, pp. 220-227, Atlantic City, NJ.

Warren, D. H. D. (1975) "Earley deduction," Technical Note, Department of Artificial Intelligence, Univ. Edinburgh.

Wilks, Y., Huang, X-M., and Fass, D. (1985) "Syntax, preference and right-attachment," *Proc. 9th International Joint Conference on Artificial Intelligence*, Los Angeles.

Wolff, Susanne (1983) *Lexical Entries and Word-Formation*, Ph.D. dissertation, New York University. Distributed by Indiana University Linguistics Club.

Parallel Logic Programming for Numeric Applications

Ralph Butler, Ewing Lusk, William McCune, and Ross Overbeek

Mathematics and Computer Science Division
Argonne National Laboratory
Argonne, Illinois 60439

ABSTRACT

In this paper we report on a series of experiments involving the use of various dialects of parallel logic programming to express and control parallelism. The central goal of these experiments was to explore the possibility of writing numeric code for multiprocessors while expressing the synchronization requirements using logic programming. We considered three dialects of parallel logic programming: Parlog, Delta-Prolog, and Flat Concurrent Prolog. The experiments involved the formulation of a well-known, highly-parallel algorithm in each of the three languages. In one case (Parlog, semi-manually compiled code for an implementation of an extended Warren Abstract Machine), we were also able to compare the performance of the resulting program with that of the same problem expressed in C, with monitors as the added parallelism construct. We present speedups obtained for the C and Parlog versions. The experiments illustrate the effect of granularity size on attainable degrees of parallelism. Based on the limited evidence from these experiments, we offer some conclusions on the suitability of logic programming languages for programming multiprocessors.

1. Introduction

1.1. Background

Recent years have seen the availability of parallel processors increase dramatically. These range from the fastest machines, typically with a small number of processors (Cray X-MP, Cray-2) to machines with larger numbers of slower processors (Encore Multimax, Sequent Balance 8000). In the case of machines that do not support global memory (e.g., Intel, IPSC, NCube), even larger numbers of processors can be coordinated. These are only partially even representative; many other parallel machines with widely varying architectures are either commercially available, coming on the market soon, or nearing usability in experimental facilities.

Techniques for programming these machines are only now beginning to develop. The success of vectorizing compilers in utilizing the specialized hardware of vector machines with little or no guidance from the programmer has not been repeated in the case of parallel machines (at least so far). While it is true that there is interest in automatically finding ways to "parallelize" existing code, it is also true that programmers are conceiving new algorithms that are intrinsically parallel, and need ways of expressing these algorithms that lend themselves to efficient implementation on a wide class of machines.

The earliest commercially available multiprocessors have so far been targeted at large-scale numeric computations. This has meant that the primary programming language has been FORTRAN, with various extensions for specifying and controlling the parallelism. Increasingly, as UNIX becomes the standard operating system for such machines, C has become available as well. A number of efforts have been aimed at easing the difficulties in programming multiprocessors using procedural languages. In our estimation, the central problem has not been solved; writing codes that perform numeric computations and successfully exploit multiple processors is still a difficult, error-prone activity.

* This work was supported by the Applied Mathematical Sciences subprogram of the Office of Energy Research, U.S. Department of Energy, under contract nr. W-31-109-Eng-38.

A great deal of work has been done in the area of expressing multiprocessing algorithms in dialects of logic programming[1, 11, 14]. Most of this work has centered on the ability to express algorithms as elegantly as possible. We hope to be able to utilize the insights expressed in these works, while maintaining the performance required in numeric applications. Many highly parallel algorithms of importance in the scientific community can be expressed in two parts: a collection of computationally-intensive units of work that are each to be executed by a single process, and a set of synchronization and communication requirements by which the parallel execution of the units of work will be coordinated. In many cases a logic programming language like Prolog may be inappropriate for the individual units of work (a language like C or FORTRAN may have efficiency advantages because it allows destructive assignment) but logic programming may be a useful approach for expressing the parallelism. This would give rise to bilingual programs in which each component of the algorithm is expressed in a language at as high a level as is appropriate. The size of the individual units of work relative to the amount of synchronization is called the *granularity* of the parallel algorithm.

1.2. Goals

It is the primary goal of this paper to examine the practicality of this approach. In particular, we explore the hypothesis that logic programming can be used to express the synchronization requirements of parallel algorithms, and that if the computationally intense parts of the algorithm are expressed in a language appropriate for the problem, such bilingual programs can be as efficient and exhibit as much parallelism as if they were written entirely in a lower level language with extensions for parallelism. We also study the effect of varying granularity within a given algorithm.

Rather than invent our own parallel logic programming language, we chose three such languages that have been described in the literature and are supported by serious implementation efforts. By encoding the same algorithm in each of Parlog, Flat Concurrent Prolog, and Delta-Prolog, we were able to compare the ease of formulating our algorithm in each of the languages. We will comment on their relative ease of use, but emphasize that the work was carried out on only one algorithm chosen without any regard to how will it "fit" any of the dialects.

In each case, we went as far as we could in actually running the resulting programs. In the case of Parlog, this involved running it, with the computational part written in C, on a commercially available multiprocessor (the Sequent Balance 8000). We obtained executable code for the Parlog by utilizing a compiler from Prolog to abstract machine code and making a few minimal modifications manually. Then we executed the (parallelized) object code on the parallel WAM system developed at Argonne National Laboratory. In the case of Flat Concurrent Prolog, we ran the synchronization part of the algorithm on the Logix simulator. For Delta-Prolog, we executed the synchronization part of the algorithm on the Delta-Prolog system.

1.3. The Problem

The algorithm chosen for this test is an example we have used extensively in experimenting with multiprocessors. Versions in C, FORTRAN, or both have been run on the Denelcor HEP, the Sequent Balance 8000, and the Encore Multimax. A Pascal version has been run on an Argonne-built 8-processor machine called the Lemur. In every case it has been possible to effectively utilize the multiprocessor hardware; that is, to keep all processors busy. In other words, the algorithm is highly parallelizable.

The example represents a prototypical grid problem. The essential characteristics of this class of grid problems are as follows:

1. The computation involves a *cellular space*. That is, a grid exists that divides the space into cells.
2. Each cell has a *state* characterized by one or more numeric values.
3. A *neighborhood function* exists that defines the set of neighbors for a given cell.
4. Time is thought of as a discrete sequence $t_0, t_1, t_2, \ldots$. There exists a *transition function* that defines the state of a cell at time t_{i+1} in terms of the state of the cell and its neighbors at time t_i.

In our example, we have chosen a particularly simple case. We have a two-dimensional space in which the state of each cell (x,y) is represented by a single floating-point value $\phi(x,y)$. We assume that ϕ is given on the boundary cells and arbitrarily assign 0 to the interior cells. The neighbors of a cell are just the four cells that share the bounding faces of the cell. The transition function is defined as follows:

Cells on the boundary have constant states. For each nonboundary cell, the state at time t_{i+1} is just the average of the states of the neighboring cells at time t_i.

This example, while simple, does have some physical significance. As time progresses, the values in the cells converge to a solution of LaPlace's equation $\nabla^2\phi = 0$, with the original values of ϕ on the boundary. (The problem of solving LaPlace's equation with fixed boundary conditions is called the *Dirichlet problem*.) This computation occurs in electromagnetic theory, among other places. In our example, we ran the problem for a fixed number of iterations, rather than applying some convergence criterion. This allows us to vary the total size of the run easily.

A grid problem of the type we are considering here obviously has a great deal of exploitable parallelism. We use two grids in memory, where the states of cells are updated from one grid to the other and then back again. This doubles the memory requirement for the problem, but greatly simplifies the synchronization logic and allows for more parallelism than if the grid were updated in place. The synchronization requirements are only that neighbors of a cell have completed the same number of iterations as the cell itself before it is updated using their values. By varying the number of cells updated in a single dispatchable "unit of work", the granularity of the parallelism can be easily varied for experimental purposes. The problem will be described in greater detail below.

1.4. Results

The experiments demonstrate that logic programming can be an effective approach to the specification of synchronization. The degree to which it is convenient to use is at least partially illustrated by the program listings included below. Investigation of the efficiency of at least one implementation suggests that the granularity of the parallelism may need to be increased in order to obtain the same efficiency as that obtained by a more usual approach based on monitors or semaphores). The implications of this result for parallel logic programming are discussed in the final section of this paper.

2. The Solutions

2.1. Overview

The computational and synchronization portions of the grid problem have been firmly separated in each of the solutions presented below. The computational portion is coded in C, and remains fixed for all solutions. It is well understood and is described elsewhere [9]. The synchronization portion of the problem is of most interest here. It is coded in C for the first solution, and coded in various parallel logic programming dialects for the remaining solutions. The purpose of this exercise is to demonstrate the utility of logic programming for synchronization of concurrent processes and to compare it to the widely-used synchronization mechanism, *monitors*, employed in the C solution.

2.2. Monitors and the C Solution

The C solution is an implementation using monitors. The monitors were developed as a set of macros by Lusk and Overbeek [9,7] to support portability of multiprocessing software. Because monitors play such an important role in this solution, they are described here.

A *monitor* is an abstract concept consisting of three parts:

1. a shared resource, or a data structure representing the resource,
2. the code to initialize the shared structures, and
3. the code which performs the critical section operations on the resource.

The operations of a monitor may be called by any process at any time. It is necessary, however that only one process be permitted to enter the monitor at one time. In other words, from a process's point of view, the monitor is a serially reusable resource. This does not imply that the invoking processes are completely serialized; they are merely serialized through their critical sections in which they access a shared resource through the monitor. Permission to enter the monitor is typically gained through the use of some locking mechanism, e.g. a test-and-set primitive. This portion of code is usually machine dependent and best hidden in macros.

It is convenient to think of a monitor as an enclosure protecting some item or group of items. The items must be protected because they are shared among processes, and only one process at a time should be allowed to use them. In applications such as the grid problem, the items being protected are the data structures representing a group of subproblems to be solved. This pool of problems changes dynamically as problems are dispatched to processes which may in turn put more problems in the pool.

A monitor typically represents an efficient synchronization mechanism. A process merely enters the monitor, claims a problem to solve, and then leaves. The overhead for entering and leaving the monitor can be quite small if the hardware supports a locking mechanism. The overhead for claiming a problem can also be quite small, if handled correctly. For example, consider the grid problem, where a subproblem may be a column that is to have new values computed. (Using individual cells instead of columns would be an example of extremely small grain size; we will use columns instead.) In such a case, it should be sufficient to allow each process to claim a single integer value containing the index of the column to be computed, rather than having to waste the time passing each process an entire column of floating point values. The claiming of a single integer value requires very little overhead.

In the C solution, multiple processes may be spawned to solve a single grid problem. If only one process is created, then that process solves the entire problem alone. The basic loop in each process is:

```
while (there are more columns to compute)
        {
        ASKFOR the index of a column to compute
        if (an index was obtained)
              {
              compute the new column values
              POST this subproblem as done
              }
        }
```

The ASKFOR is a macro invocation which generates the code to enter the monitor, obtain the next subproblem (column), and exit the monitor.

Within the ASKFOR is code defining what it means to get the next subproblem. Here, the next subproblem is not simply the next column in the grid, but the next column, say at iteration i, whose nearest neighbors have completed iteration $i-1$. At the start of a grid computation, all columns are marked as ready to be computed. Some delays may be encountered later however, as one column's computations may terminate before its neighbors' computations. The POST operation determines, by checking the number of iterations completed by its nearby neighbors, whether the completion of this problem allows others to be placed in the pool of problems. The ASKFOR and POST operations are general-purpose operations for multiprocessing, but their exact behavior depends on the data structures representing the problem pool.

2.3. The Logic Programming Solutions

.3.1. Communication Via Shared Variables

Shared variables are a common method for communication among concurrent processes in the logic pro-ramming community. For completeness we discuss this communication mechanism separately before going into ıe details of each logic programming solution.

In Listing 1, the `send` and `receive` procedures have been established to support the necessary communi-ation paths. These procedures are intended to define an abstract data type which we call a *stream*. The idea is to onstruct a stream from one process to another and to send information through the stream to a receiving process. his mechanism of establishing communication channels via shared variables (which get instantiated to the list of ommunicated values) is common to several of the languages for concurrent logic programming. Each dialect ffers some mechanism for insuring that the `receive` operations do not occur before the corresponding `send` perations take place, thus allowing producer and consumer processes to execute in parallel. That is, if the consu-ıer process were invoked with an uninstantiated variable as the message, it would suspend until the producer had nstantiated the variable. If Listing 1 were executed by a sequential Prolog system, the producer `roduce_msgs` would build a list of (all of the) messages and then pass it on to the consumer `onsume_msgs`.

The `communicate_n_times` procedure is invoked as a query to Prolog with an integer indicating the umber of messages to send to the receiver, and a variable representing the stream to use for the communication.

```
communicate_n_times(N,Stream) :-
     produce_msgs(N,Stream),
     consume_msgs(N,Stream).

produce_msgs(0,_).
produce_msgs(N,Stream) :-
     N > 0,
     send(N,Stream,Tail_stream),
     M is (N - 1),
     produce_msgs(M,Tail_stream).

consume_msgs(0,_).
consume_msgs(N,Stream) :-
     N > 0,
     receive(N,Stream,Tail_stream),
     M is (N - 1),
     consume_msgs(M,Tail_stream).

send(Msg,Stream,Tail_stream) :-
     Stream = [Msg|Tail_stream].

receive(Msg,Stream,Tail_stream) :-
     Stream = [Msg|Tail_stream].
```

Listing 1. Communication Via Streams

To create the illusion of a continuous stream of messages, the `send` procedure instantiates a stream to a list onsisting not only of the message to be sent, but also containing an uninstantiated variable which represents the emainder of the stream. For example, when the first integer is to be sent by `produce_msgs`, it invokes `send` vith the parameters `N`, `Stream`, and `Tail_stream`. `N` is the message to be sent, `Stream` is the stream to se for the communication, and `Tail_stream` is instantiated to the "continuation" of the stream. The `send` rocedure instantiates `Stream` to the list `[N|Tail_stream]`. The `consume_msgs` procedure then receives the message from the stream by invoking `receive` to extract the message from the stream. In a parallel environment, `receive` must suspend until the unification can occur without instantiating `Stream`.

The `send` and `receive` operations have been coded as separate procedures in this example to make the concept clear. They each consist of only one instruction however, and thus, would typically not be coded as separate procedures in a program. Instead, each procedure invocation would be replaced by the single instruction in the procedure body. These optimizations have been made in the solutions presented below.

2.3.1.1. The Parlog Solution

Listing 2 shows our Parlog[2] code to solve the grid problem. It has been tested on a Parlog simulator for accuracy of the representation, but no timings were obtained from the simulator run. The timings reported in Section 3, Table 2, were obtained by compiling a similar program with a sequential Prolog compiler, then manually inserting the appropriate parallelism instructions in to the assembler code, and finally assembling and running the resulting program on the WAM system at Argonne.

```
mode grid(?,?,?).                              /* Parlog.  "&" is sequential AND, */
grid([X,Y],Iter,Numcol) :-                     /* "," is parallel AND,            */
    init_grid([X,Y],G) &                       /* ":" is commit,                  */
    grid_run(G,[X,Y],Iter,Numcol) &            /* "<=" is one-way unification.    */
    print_grid(G,Iter) &                       /* init_grid, grid_trans,          */
    del_grid(G).                               /* print_grid, and del_grid are    */
                                               /* foreign subroutines.            */
mode grid_run(?,?,?,?).
grid_run(G,[X,Y],Iter,Numcol) :-
    grid_start(G,[X,Y],Iter,Numcol,1,[go|TLI],TLI).

mode grid_start(?,?,?,?,?,?,^).
grid_start(G,[X,Y],Iter,Numcol,Col,[go|TLI],TLI) :-
    I is (X - 1), Col >= I.
grid_start(G,[X,Y],Iter,Numcol,Col,LI,LO) :-
    I is (X - 1), Col < I :
    C is Col + Numcol &
      /* The following pair of calls is made in parallel. */
  ( grid_col(G,Iter,Numcol,Col,0,LI,LO,[go|TRI],TRO) ,
    grid_start(G,[X,Y],Iter,Numcol,C,[go|TRO],TRI) ).

mode grid_col(?,?,?,?,?,?,^,?,^).
grid_col(G,Iter,Numcol,Col,Iter,LI,LO,RI,RO).
grid_col(G,Iter,Numcol,Col,Done,[go|TLI],LO,[go|TRI],RO) :-
      /* Suspend until "go" appears on both input streams.   */
    Done < Iter :
    grid_trans(G,Col,Done,Numcol) &
    LO <= [go|TLO] &        /* Send "go" onto both output streams to     */
    RO <= [go|TRO] &        /* signal that grid_trans has completed.     */
    I is Done + 1 &
    grid_col(G,Iter,Numcol,Col,I,TLI,TLO,TRI,TRO).
```

Listing 2. The Parlog Solution

Two notes about the Parlog implementation should be made. The first note is that each procedure is preceded by a mode declaration indicating whether each argument to the procedure is an input (?) or output (^

gument. The mode declarations express unification constraints. A non-variable input argument in the head of a ause can only be used for input matching. That is, if a goal can unify with a head only by further instantiating n input argument of the goal, then the call suspends until the input argument becomes bound (by some other pro- ess). A term in an output position of a goal must be an unbound variable at the time of the call; otherwise an rror occurs. For example, if the `send` and `receive` procedures were coded in Parlog, the mode declarations ould be `send(?,^,?)` and `receive(^,?,^)`.

Parlog uses "," as the parallel-and operator, and "&" as the sequential-and operator. It is not uncommon to ee Parlog code which makes almost exclusive use of the parallel-and. These programs typically achieve serializa- on through the suspension of processes which are waiting for input variables to be instantiated. Our view, as escribed in detail in the Section 3, is that large granularity parallelism is of the most benefit in many applica- ons. For this reason, we tend to code Parlog much the same as sequential Prolog, using the parallel-and only in iose instances where large problems may be executed in parallel. Gregory[4] offers a more complete and flexi- le position, proposing that granularity be established during compilation. In the long run, this will undoubtedly epresent the most tenable position. The use of and-parallelism in the grid problem is described below.

In Listing 2, the first procedure, `grid`, is the interface to the outside world. It is queried by the user to egin a grid computation. For example, the query

grid([202,202],500,1).

equests that the grid computation be performed for a 200 by 200 grid (the two extra columns are for the fixed oundaries). The number of iterations specified for each column is 500, and the number of columns to be pro- essed as a single unit of work (which determines the granularity) is 1.

The grid procedure invokes several procedures to assist it in its work. Note that only one of those pro- edures is listed, since we are presenting only the synchronization portion of the code. The remainder of the code s "hidden" as foreign subroutines written in C.

The `grid_run` procedure invokes the first copy of `grid_start`. `Grid_start` is a recursive pro- edure which, on each invocation, selects a new section of the grid, `Numcol` columns wide, and invokes a copy f `grid_col` to process that section. A single iteration of computation on one section of the grid may be egarded as a unit of work to be performed by some process. A copy of `grid_col` may be viewed as equivalent a process. But, it is important to note that a given execution of the program may have a fixed number of sys- em processes devoted to it, and that number may be smaller than the number of copies of `grid_col`. Thus, ach copy of `grid_col` is actually a schedulable task that may be handled by any free system process.

Recall that the $(i+1)$-st iteration of computation on a given section of the grid can proceed only after itera- ion i on it and on each of its nearest neighbors has been completed. Each copy of `grid_col` expects a "go" on s left and right input streams before it proceeds with a computation. Therefore, these streams must be initialized vith "go" before the first iterations can begin.

`Grid_start` puts a "go" on both the right and left inputs of a copy of `grid_col` and then recursively nvokes itself to start the next `grid_col`. `Grid_start` also creates the communication channels between the opies of `grid_col` by establishing the right output stream of `grid_col` n as the left input of `grid_col` +1. The left output of `grid_col` $n+1$ becomes the right input of `grid_col` n. The boundaries are special ases. The left output of the leftmost `grid_col` invocation is connected to its own left input. The right output f the rightmost `grid_col` is connected to its right input.

The copies of `grid_col` communicate via these streams to decide when it is time to perform the next ransformation on a section of the grid. When a copy of `grid_col` completes a single iteration on its section of he grid, it sends a "go" to its nearest column neighbors, because an iteration on a given column of the grid cannot roceed until that of its nearest neighbors is completed. Once a copy of `grid_col` has received a "go" on both s left and right inputs, it invokes the foreign subroutine `grid_trans` to perform the computations.

One of the major points of interest in this program is the parallel-and (",") in the `grid_start` procedure. One copy of `grid_col` is started concurrently with a new copy of `grid_start` which of course starts another grid_col. Thus, multiple copies of grid_col are initiated and run concurrently. These multiple copies of grid_col represent relatively large granularity parallelism. It is quite easy to adjust the granularity by altering the value of Numcol, so that a single copy of grid_col processes several columns of the grid in one iteration.

Making only limited use of the parallel-and operator as described above, we found the Parlog implementation of the grid problem to be very straightforward. Parlog lends itself quite readily to the idea of programming in sequential "Prolog" with minor adjustments to exploit large-granularity parallelism.

2.3.1.2. The Flat Concurrent Prolog Solution

Flat Concurrent Prolog (FCP) is a derivative of Concurrent Prolog [10, 14] with the restriction that it supports only system-defined predicates in the guard. We coded a solution to the grid problem in FCP and tested the synchronization on a simulator[13]. The code is in Listing 3.

```
grid([X,Y],Iter,Numcol) :-   /* Flat Concurrent Prolog.              */
                             /* "|" is commit,   "," is parallel AND, */
                             /* "?" is read-only annotation.          */
    init_grid([X,Y],G),
    grid_run(G,[X,Y],Iter,Numcol,sigs(done,S1)),
    /* When grid_run has completed, S1 is instantiated to "done" */
    print_grid(G,S1?,S2),
    del_grid(G,S2?).

grid_run(G,[X,Y],Iter,Numcol,sigs(L,R)) :-
    wait(G) |
    grid_start(G,[X,Y],Iter,Numcol,1,[go|TLI?],TLI,sigs(L,R)).

grid_start(G,[X,Y],Iter,Numcol,Col,[go|TLI],T,sigs(L,L)) :-
    I := X - 1, Col >= I | T = TLI.
grid_start(G,[X,Y],Iter,Numcol,Col,LI,LO,sigs(L,R)) :-
    I := X - 1, Col < I, C := Col + Numcol |
    grid_col(G,Iter,Numcol,Col,0,LI?,LO,[go|TRI?],TRO,sigs(L,M)),
    grid_start(G,[X,Y],Iter,Numcol,C,[go|TRO?],TRI,sigs(M,R)).

grid_col(G,Iter,Numcol,Col,Done,_,_,_,_,sigs(L,L)) :-
    Done =:= Iter | true.
grid_col(G,Iter,Numcol,Col,Done,[go|TLI],LO,[go|TRI],RO,sigs(L,R)) :-
    /* Suspend until "go" appears on both input streams. */
    Done < Iter, I := Done + 1 |
    grid_trans(G,Col,Done,Numcol,S1),
    /* When S1 is instantiated, send "go" on both output streams. */
    setup_out(LO,TLO,RO,TRO,S1?),
    grid_col(G,Iter,Numcol,Col,I,TLI?,TLO,TRI?,TRO,sigs(L,R)).

setup_out([go|TLO],TLO,[go|TRO],TRO,S) :- wait(S) | true.
```

Listing 3. The Flat Concurrent Prolog Solution

From the point of view of the grid problem, there are two major differences between FCP and Parlog. The first is the way in which unification constraints are expressed, and the second is that FCP has no sequential AND operator.

In FCP, unification constraints are given for a particular invocation of a procedure, rather than for the rocedure in general, as in Parlog. In FCP, to express that a variable in a call is an input variable, a read-only nnotation ("?") is appended to the variable in the call. The behavior of the streams in the FCP solution is the ame as in the Parlog solution. For example, see the last `grid_col` call in Listing 3. The read-only annotations n the input streams cause the call to suspend until the streams become instantiated.

The lack of a sequential AND operator in FCP requires extra arguments which serve as synchronization ags (control tokens), and the use of the `wait` primitive. (`wait(X)` causes the clause to suspend until `X` ecomes instantiated by some other process). The procedures `init_grid`, `grid_run`, `print_grid`, and `el_grid` are invoked concurrently, but they must be executed sequentially. `grid_run` must suspend until `G` ecomes instantiated, `print_grid` must suspend until all iterations an all columns have completed, and `el_grid` must suspend until `S2` becomes instantiated by `print_grid`. In addition, in procedure `rid_col`, `setup_out`, which instantiates the output streams, must suspend until `grid_trans` has com- leted.

.3.2. Communication Via Events

Some dialects of parallel logic programming permit processes to communicate through a mechanism known s an *event*. When two processes wish to communicate, they establish complementary sides of an event goal. 'his is similar to the rendezvous mechanism in Ada, in which both communicating processes must synchronize, ather than just the one sending a message. The notion of event also has origins in the language CSP[5].

.3.2.1. The Delta-Prolog Solution

In Delta-Prolog[11] the sending process typically designates its event goal by "!" (this has a different mean- ng than the cut symbol), and the receiving process designates its event goal by "?". When one process reaches its vent goal, it suspends until another process reaches the complementary goal. At that point they may both roceed if certain conditions are met. For example, consider the case in which process 1 has the goal

t(x) ! e

vhere the t(x) is some term and the "e" is the name of the event. Process 2 may have the complementary goal

t(a) ? e

After the two processes both reach their event goals, they may proceed because the associated terms unify. n exchange of information takes place because the variable x in process 1 becomes instantiated to "a". Thus, ommunication has occurred, as well as synchronization.

In Listing 4 we see that all of the communication via streams has been eliminated. Instead, two event goals re present in each copy of the `grid_col` procedure. These event goals communicate with the two nearest eighbors through two events named `Left` and `Right`, where `Left` and `Right` are variables containing values hat uniquely identify copies of `grid_col`. (Note: we have taken the liberty of using numerical values for vent names, although this is not allowed in Delta-Prolog. In the version that was actually run, nonnumeric ames wer constructed dynamically.)

```
grid([X,Y],Iter,Numcol) :-              /* Delta-Prolog.                 */
    init_grid([X,Y],G),                 /* "//" is parallel AND,         */
    grid_run(G,[X,Y],Iter,Numcol),      /* ","  is sequential AND.       */
    print_grid(G,Iter),                 /* t!e and t?e are complementary */
    del_grid(G).                        /* event goals.                  */

grid_run(G,[X,Y],Iter,Numcol) :-
    grid_start(G,[X,Y],Iter,Numcol,1).

grid_start(G,[X,Y],Iter,Numcol,Col) :-
    I is (X - 1), Col >= I, !.
grid_start(G,[X,Y],Iter,Numcol,Col) :-
    C is Col + Numcol,
  ( grid_col(G,[X,Y],Iter,Numcol,Col,0) //   /* in parallel */
    grid_start(G,[X,Y],Iter,Numcol,C) ).

grid_col(G,[X,Y],Iter,Numcol,Col,Iter) :- !.
grid_col(G,[X,Y],Iter,Numcol,Col,Done) :-
    grid_trans(G,Col,Done,Numcol),
    I is Done + 1,
    Left = Col,
    Right is Col + Numcol,
    /* For each of Left and Right, if not at boundary then wait for event. */
  ( Left  > Numcol   ->  go ? Left  ; true ),
  ( Right < (X - 1)  ->  go ! Right ; true ),
    grid_col(G,[X,Y],Iter,Numcol,Col,I).
```

Listing 4. The Delta-Prolog Solution

In this solution, no data transfer takes place between the processes; only synchronization occurs, indicating that adjacent neighbors have completed their current iterations. As a left neighbor, a copy of `grid_col` invokes the event goal `go ! Right`. As a right neighbor, it invokes the event goal `go ? Left`. The neighbors, of course, invoke the complementary goals. When two neighbors reach their complementary event goals, the "go" terms are unified to complete the communication, and the two processes proceed.

Note that this implementation handles the boundary columns somewhat differently from the previous solutions. Here, `grid_col` checks to see if there is a left neighbor, and only if there is does it issue the "?" to wait for a go message. Also, it only issues the "!" goal if there is a right neighbor.

2.3.3. Implementing Events Via Back Communication in Streams

The logical variable enables a stream to be used for two-way communication[15, 14, 4]. A producer can send a message containing an unbound variable to a consumer. The consumer can then instantiate the variable, which in effect, sends a message (the instantiation) back to the producer. Listing 5 is the relevant part of a Parlog program that uses this approach for the grid problem. After `grid_trans` completes, if we are not at the left boundary, then we should wait for the message `go(Y)` to appear on the input stream (left side); when it appears, we instantiate `Y`; this concludes the left synchronization event. If we are not at the right boundary, then we send the message `go(X)` on the output stream (right side) and wait for `X` to become instantiated; when it does, the right synchronization event has occurred. The result is similar to the Delta-Prolog events in Listing 4. One difference is that the streams in Parlog must be arguments to the procedure, whereas the event names in Delta-Prolog are global, as in CSP.

```
mode grid_col(?,?,?,?,?,?,?,^).
grid_col(G,[X,Y],Iter,Numcol,Col,Done,LI,RO) :-
    Done < Iter
    :
    grid_trans(G,Col,Done,Numcol) &
    Left is Col - Numcol &
    Right is Col + Numcol &
       /* For each of left and right, if not at boundary,  */
       /* then synchronize.   "<=" is one-way unification. */
    ( Left > 0          -> [go(Y)|TLI] <= LI & Y <= ok ; true ) &
    ( Right < (X - 1)   -> RO <= [go(X)|TRO] & ok <= X ; true ) &
    I is Done + 1 &
    grid_col(G,[X,Y],Iter,Numcol,Col,I,TLI,TRO).
```

Listing 5. Events in Parlog

. Results

Our goal in performing these experiments was to explore the practicality of bilingual programming for arallel numerical algorithms. We chose to actually implement a common grid computation, using Parlog to xpress the synchronization and C for the computationally-intensive components. Since we do not currently have Parlog compiler for our abstract machine (a derivative of David H. D. Warren's "abstract Prolog machine"[16]), /e used a Prolog compiler and manually modified the generated Warren assembler code. The mechanism for upporting "foreign subroutines" in the abstract machine allowed us to conveniently install the C routines as ntrinsics invokable from Parlog. We do not have, at this point, a complete environment for supporting bilingual rogramming on multiprocessors, but we do have enough of the environment completed to evaluate the practical-ty of such techniques.

To prove useful, bilingual programming of the type described in this paper must satisfy two criteria: it must nake the expression of synchronization more convenient, and it must result in programs that execute with accept-ble performance. In our view, these are the two main points that must be studied in detail. While it is true that esearchers writing code to run on large multiprocessors (e.g., the CRAY-XMP, CRAY-2, or CRAY-3) do not eriously consider using anything but FORTRAN, it is also true that they are experiencing some difficulty in actu-lly exploiting the capabilities of such machines. The proper expression of the synchronization requirements in rocedural languages like FORTRAN or C can be quite difficult. While it is clear that a problem exists, it is not lear that a suitable alternative has been established. Shapiro has eloquently advocated the use of logic program-ning for the expression of algorithms commonly viewed as numeric (most notably [12]), but we know of no work hat has yet reached the point of being a practical tool for use in parallel numeric computations.

.1. Convenience in Programming

The act of performing these experiments clarified a number of issues for us. They may be summarized as ollows:

1. The formulation of the synchronization required for the grid computation in almost any dialect of logic programming is clearer than the corresponding version expressed with monitors in a procedural language.
2. On the other hand, it may be substantially more complex than specialized tools available within procedural languages (e.g., see [3]). These specialized techniques offer substantial simplifications, but are only applicable to a restricted class of algorithms.
3. The notion of event in Delta-Prolog offered a simpler form of communication than the duplex communication via two channels used in both the Parlog and FCP versions. It was possible to implement

something quite similar to events in both Parlog and FCP, but it did not seem as natural, and the requirement that the name of the event be established via a shared variable was inconvenient (on the other hand, the global nature of event names in Delta-Prolog is subject to all of the naming convention questions that have arisen in the context of teleprocessing networks).

4. The sequential AND operator (in Parlog and Delta-Prolog) was convenient. Synchronization via a control token (see [6]) was viewed as a serious inconvenience. Similarly, we found the expression of sequencing via mode constraints (in Parlog) substantially more comprehensible than the corresponding approach via read-only annotation (in FCP).

3.2. Performance and Granularity

The issue of performance is always present, and always difficult to assess in any objective fashion. It is common for two competent researchers to examine the same set of timings and come to widely varying conclusions, due frequently to hidden, unstated assumptions. In any discussion of performance on multiprocessors, the concept of granularity plays a central role. When it is not brought out explicitly, the results can be quite surprising.

The granularity of a problem refers to the execution time between synchronization and communication operations. In non-numeric problems, the whole notion can become blurred (due to the widely varying time to perform operations requiring no synchronization), but in numeric problems that have a regular structure granularity is an important concept. In a problem like the grid computation, the granularity is typically measured in terms of floating point operations (which tend to dominate the execution time). For example, on an n by n grid in which processing the elements in a single column represents a "computational task", the granularity might be given as "about $4n$ additions + n divisions = $5n$ floating-point operations."

The essential question becomes "How large must the granularity be to effectively exploit bilingual programming on common multiprocessors?" Obviously, the results produced by our implementation are subject to numerous qualifications. However, the timings produced by our system (running on a Sequent Balance 8000 with 12 processors) do offer a starting point for examining such a question. They are shown in Tables 1 and 2.

Results with Monitors in C

Size	Iterations	Processes	Time
20	10	1	84
20	10	2	67
20	10	4	75
100	10	1	1870
100	10	2	970
100	10	5	476
200	10	1	7400
200	10	2	3755
200	10	5	1615
200	10	10	1079

Table 1.

The two tables give the results for three distinct grid sizes–20 by 20, 100 by 100, and 200 by 200. Table 1 gives the results of a C program using monitors for synchronization[8, 9]. In this case, a computational task amounts to computing new values for a single column in the grid. Table 2 gives the results using a bilingual program. In this case, a computational task amounts to computing new values for a sequence of contiguous columns. The number of columns included in a computational task is specified by the extra column of entries in Table 2.

Results Using Logic Programming				
Size	Iterations	Processes	Columns	Time
20	10	1	1	343
20	10	1	5	131
20	10	2	1	190
20	10	2	5	77
20	10	4	1	144
20	10	4	5	89
100	10	1	1	3249
100	10	1	10	1961
100	10	1	20	1890
100	10	2	1	1763
100	10	2	10	996
100	10	2	20	1061
100	10	5	1	1113
100	10	5	10	450
100	10	5	20	728
200	10	1	1	10514
200	10	1	10	7548
200	10	1	20	7421
200	10	2	1	4530
200	10	2	10	3853
200	10	2	20	3798
200	10	5	1	3060
200	10	5	10	1719
200	10	5	20	1668
200	10	10	1	2148
200	10	10	10	933
200	10	10	20	1127

Table 2.

While the values in the table are peculiar to the machine (a Sequent Balance 8000 with 12 processors), a compiler, and our implementation of an abstract machine to support logic programming, several general points are worth noting:

1. At very low granularity (see the 20 by 20 grid), even the C program experiences significant degradation due to synchronization. The bilingual program attains roughly comparable performance only when the granularity is increased (for just the bilingual program) by 5. At the same granularity, the bilingual program performs very poorly.

2. At larger granularities, the overhead introduced by message passing is quite tolerable. Note that on the 200 by 200 grid, the best time was actually attained by the bilingual program (on the other hand, the C version would undoubtedly perform as well, if it were modified to exploit the same granularity).

3. Note the effects of making the granularity too high. The most desirable situation is attained when the units of work are large enough to make synchronization overhead negligible, but the pool of work is large enough to hide any effects due to termination or nonhomogeneous execution rates for the processes.

While it is the case that grid computations performed using large granularity on a sizable grid can effectively be performed by a bilingual program, we are concerned about the need for fairly large granularity. Indeed, almost any synchronization mechanism will function well, given a suitably large granularity. In particular, we believe that serious performance issues are raised for those proposing logic programming dialects as a "systems programming" language. There is a real need to improve the efficiency of the communication and synchronization mechanisms in parallel logic programming languages.

Acknowledgements

We would like to thank Jaakov Levy, Jose Cunha, and Steve Gregory for their comments and help.

References

1. Keith Clark and Steve Gregory, "PARLOG: Parallel Programming in Logic," Research Report DOC 84/4, Department of Computing, Imperial College of Science and Technology (April 1984, revised June, 1985).
2. Keith Clark and Steve Gregory, "PARLOG: Parallel Programming in Logic," *ACM Transactions on Programming Languages and Systems* **8**(1) (January, 1986).
3. Barney Glickfeld and Ross Overbeek, "Quasi-automatic parallelization: a simplied approach to multiprocessing," Technical Report ANL-855-70, Argonne National Laboratory (October 1985).
4. Steven Gregory, *Design, application and implementation of a parallel logic programming language*, Doctoral Thesis, Imperial College of Science and Technology, London, September 1985.
5. C. A. R. Hoare, "Communicating Sequential Processes," *Communications of the ACM* **21**(8), pp. 666-677 (August 1978).
6. A. J. Kusalik, "Serialization of process reduction in Concurrent Prolog," *New Generation Computing* **2**(3), pp. 835-843 (1984).
7. Ewing L. Lusk and Ross A. Overbeek, "Implementing Multiprocessing Algorithms Now," pp. 5-10 in *New Directions in Software for Advanced Computer Architectures, ANL/MCS-TM-32*, MCS, Argonne National Laboratory (August 1984).
8. E. L. Lusk and R. A. Overbeek, "Use of Monitors in FORTRAN: a Tutorial on the Barrier, Self-Scheduling Do-Loop, and Askfor Monitors," in *Parallel MIMD Computation: The HEP Supercomputer and its Applications*, ed. J. S. Kowalik, The MIT Press (1985).
9. E. L. Lusk, R. L. Stevens, and R. A. Overbeek, "A tutorial on the use of monitors in C: writing portable code for multiprocessors," ANL-85-2, Argonne National Laboratory (January 1985).
10. Colin Mierowsky, "Design and implementation of Flat Concurrent Prolog," CS84-21, Weizmann Institute of Science (December 1984).
11. Luis Moniz Pereira and Roger Nasr, "Delta-Prolog: a distributed logic programming language," in *Proceedings of FGCS*, Tokyo (November 1984).
12. Ehud Shapiro, "Systolic programming: a paradigm of parallel processing," Technical Report CS84-16, Weizmann Institute of Science (January 1985).
13. Ehud Shapiro, William Silverman, Avshalom Houri, and Michael Hirsch, *Logix User Manual for Release 1.1*, August, 1985.
14. Ehud Y. Shapiro, *A Subset of Concurrent Prolog and Its Interpreter*, (preprint, Weizmann Institute of Science, January 1983).
15. D. H. D. Warren, "Logic programming and compiler writing," *Software - Practice and Experience* **10**, pp. 97-125 (1980).
16. D. H. D. Warren, "An Abstract Prolog Instruction Set," SRI Technical Note 309, SRI International (October 1983).

Sequential and Concurrent

Deterministic Logic Grammars

Harvey Abramson

Department of Computer Science
University of British Columbia
Vancouver, B.C.
Canada

1. Introduction.

The logic grammars which have been introduced over the past few years have so far been compiled into non-deterministic sequential logic programs (see [Abramson,1984a], [Abramson,1984b], [Colmerauer,1978], [Dahl,1984], [Dahl&Abramson,1984], and [Pereira&Warren,1980]). In running the compiled programs under a Prolog interpreter, the non-determinism is simulated by a depth-first backtracking control strategy. Recently, there have been attempts to define logic programming languages which directly exploit the possibilities of concurrency inherent - theoretically - in logic programming. The most successful such languages, Parlog [Clark&Gregory,1984] and Concurrent Prolog [Shapiro,1983], however, make use of committed nondeterminism as a control strategy rather than full and/or parallelism. The form of a clause in these languages is roughly:

r(t1,...,tk) :- <guards> : <body>.

Both the guards and the body are a conjunction of goals. In attempting to evaluate a goal r(p1,...,pk), all clauses for the relation r are attempted in parallel. Here, attempted means matching the head of the clause and successful evaluation of the guards. From those clauses which are successfully attempted, one is selected, and the others are discarded. This is "don't care" or "committed" nondeterminism: the discarded calls are not cared about, or, one is committed to a particular choice once made. In practice, the first attempt to succeed is chosen. In the two languages mentioned there are also synchronization mechanisms for delaying calls to make sure that certain arguments are instantiated. In Concurrent Prolog this is done by annotating arguments as read-only; in Parlog, mode declarations specify which arguments are input or output arguments. During the attempt to evaluate a goal, any arguments, say in a guard, which are not instantiated when they should be, result in a suspension until the variable in question, shared by some other process, is more fully instantiated.

There is an obvious problem in parsing in a committed nondeterministic setting. From the productions which may be successfully attempted, the processor will select one, commit to it, and ignore all the others. This will obviously allow the derivation to continue one more step, but it may not allow the derivation to continue to a successful conclusion. For example, suppose we had the following productions for a nonterminal "x" and we were parsing in a setting of committed nondeterminism:

```
x ::= [].
x ::= a, b, c.
```

Suppose at some point in the parse, both productions were successfully attempted (assume empty guards) but that the processor had chosen the empty production to commit to. Even though the input may be parsed as an "a" followed by a "b" and a "c", the wrong production (always applicable because of the empty right hand side) will have been chosen and a parse will not be found.

Clearly, if there is to be any class of logic grammars for which there is a simple direct translation of grammar rules to concurrent logic program clauses in a setting of committed nondeterminism, then that production (clause) must always be selected which will allow a derivation to continue to a successful conclusion (if one exists). This will happen if at any time at most one production can be used to continue a derivation. Fortunately, there is a subclass of context free grammars, the LL(k) grammars, which provides a model for such a class of logic grammars. The class of LL(k) grammars consists of those unambigous context free grammars in which input is parsed top down from left to right with k-symbol lookahead. The lookahead enables one to uniquely determine which production is to be used in continuing a parse. If no production is applicable, then the input string is not in the language generated by the grammar. This class is deterministic in the sense that it can be accepted by a deterministic pushdown automaton.

We shall use the following LL(1) grammar, taken from [Aho&Ullman,1977], first to show how deterministic grammars may be compiled as sequential logic programs and then, generalizing, compiled to concurrent logic programs with "don't care" nondeterminism (note the paradox: deterministic grammars compile easily into don't care nondeterministic logic programs!).

1.1. Sample grammar.

```
e ::= t,e_prime.

e_prime ::= "+",t,e_prime.
e_prime ::= [].

t ::= f,t_prime.

t_prime ::= "*",f,t_prime.
t_prime ::= [].

f ::= "a".
f ::= "(",e,")".
```

1.2. The one character lookahead relation.

The following unit clauses define the one character lookahead relation for the sample grammar. The first argument to the predicate "lookahead" is a production, and the second is a list of characters which permit use of that production in a derivation. For example, the production "e::=t,e_prime" may be used if searching for an "e" and if the first unused character in the input string, the lookahead character, is either an "a" or a "(".

```
lookahead((e::=t,e_prime),"a(").
lookahead((e_prime::="+",t,e_prime),"+").
lookahead((e_prime::=[]),")?").
lookahead((t::=f,t_prime),"a(").
lookahead((t_prime::="*",f,t_prime),"*").
lookahead((t_prime::=[]),"+)?").
lookahead((f::="a"),"a").
lookahead((f::="(",e,")"),"(").
```

The "?" is used to mark the end of the input string. The "lookahead" predicate may be calculated following an algorithm given in [Aho&Ullman,1977] and is easily specified in Prolog (although some version of "setof" must be used). The hand-coding of LL(k) grammars into Prolog clauses was very briefly mentioned in [Stabler,1983].

2. Compilation to sequential logic programs.

Although our principal motivation is to find a class of concurrent logic grammars, we begin with the compilation of deterministic grammars to sequential logic program clauses: the sequential case is itself interesting and gives the foundation of the method to be developed for the concurrent case.

In compiling LL(k) grammars to sequential logic programs we would like to take advantage of the determinacy of production use in a derivation. We shall do so by treating the lookahead examination as a guard on use of a clause compiled from a production. The logic program clauses generated from the above grammar will each have as their first goal a call to a predicate called "ll_guard". This is a predicate of arity 4: the first argument is the original production used to index into the lookahead predicate; the second argument is treated as a node in the tree representation of the derivation and is a function symbol of the form guard(X), recording the lookahead string X (see [Abramson,1984a] for a description of Definite Clause Translation Grammars and the automatic formation of a derivation tree); the last two arguments represent the input string as a difference list. For the LL(1) case, the "ll_guard" predicate is specified as:

```
ll_guard(LookAhead,guard(X),[X|Xs]) :-
  lookahead(LookAhead,List),
  member(X,List),!.
```

This does not use up any characters in the input string but merely examines them. The cut, once the lookahead "List" has been accessed, and the first character of the input string has been shown to be a member of that list, is used to ensure that there will be no backup in trying to use any other productions. (A clever compiler might avoid generating choice points which would not be used.)

Here follows the set of clauses generated for the above sample grammar. The call to "ll_guard" is automatically inserted by the grammar compiler. The third argument to the function symbol "node" represents an empty set of semantic rules. See [Abramson,1984a] regarding the semantic component of grammar rules.

```
e(node(e,[Guard,T,E_prime],[]),S1,S3) :-
  ll_guard((e::=t,e_prime),Guard,S1),
  t(T,S1,S2),
  e_prime(E_prime,S2,S3).

e_prime(node(e_prime,[Guard,[+],T,E_prime],[]),S1,S4) :-
  ll_guard((e_prime::=[+],t,e_prime),Guard,S1),
  c(S1,+,S2),
  t(T,S2,S3),
  e_prime(E_prime,S3,S4).

e_prime(node(e_prime,[Guard,[]],[]),S1,S2) :-
  ll_guard((e_prime::=[]),Guard,S1),
  S1=S2.

t(node(t,[Guard,F,T_prime],[]),S1,S3) :-
  ll_guard((t::=f,t_prime),Guard,S1),
  f(F,S1,S2),
  t_prime(T_prime,S2,S3).

t_prime(node(t_prime,[Guard,[*],F,T_prime],[]),S1,S4) :-
  ll_guard((t_prime::=[*],f,t_prime),Guard,S1),
  c(S1,*,S2),
  f(F,S2,S3),
  t_prime(T_prime,S3,S4).

t_prime(node(t_prime,[Guard,[]],[]),S1,S2) :-
  ll_guard((t_prime::=[]),Guard,S1),
  S1=S2.

f(node(f,[Guard,[a]],[]),S1,S2) :-
  ll_guard((f::=[a]),Guard,S1),
  c(S1,a,S2).

f(node(f,[Guard,['('],E,[')']],[]),S1,S4) :-
  ll_guard((f::=['('],e,[')']),Guard,S1),
  c(S1,'(',S2),
  e(E,S2,S3),
  c(S3,')',S4).
```

The predicate "c" is used to absorb a single terminal symbol:

```
c([X|Y],X,Y).
```

The controlling predicate "e" appends the endmarker, in this case, "?", calls the starting nonterminal of the grammar, and pretty prints the result:

```
e(Source) :-
  append(Source,[?],EndMarked),
  e(Guard,EndMarked,[?]),
  pretty(Guard).
```

For example, a call of "e("a*a")" yields:

```
e
  guard(a)
  t
    guard(a)
    f
      guard(a)
      [a]
    t_prime
      guard(*)
      [*]
      f
        guard(a)
        [a]
      t_prime
        guard(?)
        []
  e_prime
    guard(?)
    []
```

3. Compilation to concurrent logic program clauses.

We shall illustrate the compilation of a deterministic grammar to a (don't care) concurrent logic program using the language Concurrent Prolog as a target; compilation to Parlog is similar, and we shall indicate how it is to be done below. The basic idea is to turn the predicate "ll_guard" into a true guard on the generated clause and each nonterminal into a concurrent process. An attempt is made to reduce the generated clause only if the guard succeeds. The processes corresponding to nonterminals must be synchronized so that there is, in the LL(1) case, a character in the input string against which a guard may succeed or fail. The synchronization is accomplished by annotating the first of the two hidden arguments with a "?", the read-only annotation. If the input string is not yet sufficiently instantiated, the process delays until an input character has appeared. Here are the generated Concurrent Prolog clauses for our sample grammar. The commit operator is indicated by a ";".

```
e(node(e,[Guard,T,E_prime],[]),S1,S3) :-
  ll_Guard((e::=t,e_prime),Guard,S1);
  t(T,S1?,S2),
  e_prime(E_prime,S2?,S3).

e_prime(node(e_prime,[Guard,[]],[]),S1,S2) :-
  ll_Guard((e_prime::=[]),Guard,S1);
  S1? = S2.

e_prime(node(e_prime,[Guard,[+],T,E_prime],[]),S1,S4) :-
  ll_Guard((e_prime::=[+],t,e_prime),Guard,S1);
  c(S1?,+,S2),
  t(T,S2?,S3),
  e_prime(E_prime,S3?,S4).

t(node(t,[Guard,F,T_prime],[]),S1,S3) :-
  ll_Guard((t::=f,t_prime),Guard,S1);
  f(F,S1?,S2),
  t_prime(T_prime,S2?,S3).

t_prime(node(t_prime,[Guard,[]],[]),S1,S2) :-
  ll_Guard((t_prime::=[]),Guard,S1);
  S1? = S2.
```

```
t_prime(node(t_prime,[Guard,[*],F,T_prime],[]),S1,S4) :-
  ll_Guard((t_prime::=[*],f,t_prime),Guard,S1);
  c(S1?,*,S2),
  f(F,S2?,S3),
  t_prime(T_prime,S3?,S4).

f(node(f,[Guard,['('],E,[')']],[]),S1,S4) :-
  ll_Guard((f::=['('],e,[')']),Guard,S1);
  c(S1?,'(',S2),
  e(E,S2?,S3),
  c(S3?,')',S4).

f(node(f,[Guard,[a]],[]),S1,S2) :-
  ll_Guard((f::=[a]),Guard,S1);
  c(S1?,a,S2).
```

Ve use the following definition of "member" in the Concurrent Prolog setting:

```
member(X,[Y|_]) :-
  X = Y ; true.

member(X,[Y|Z]) :-
  dif(X , Y);
  member(X,Z).
```

'he definition of the "ll_guard" predicate must be changed slightly since it examines the input string: it delays ntil there is a character in the input stream and the lookahead "List" has been supplied:

```
ll_guard(LookAhead,guard(X),[X|Xs]) :-
  lookahead(LookAhead,List),
  member(X?,List?).
```

'he controlling predicate now calls on the Concurrent Prolog interpreter to solve the goal "e", with the endıarked input string, yielding if succesful, the derivation tree "T":

```
e(Source) :-
  append(Source,"?",EndMarked),
  solve(e(T,EndMarked,"?")),pretty(T).
```

ı the case of Parlog, the compiler from grammars to Parlog clauses would have to annotate the processes orresponding to nonterminals with mode declarations which would insure that the last but one argument is an nput variable. The predicate "ll_guard" would act as a guard to the generated Parlog clauses.

. Generalized deterministic grammars.

We have so far shown how LL(k) grammars could be compiled directly into either sequential or don't care ondeterministic logic programming languages. The class of LL(k) languages is in some respects a restrictive one: does not include all context free grammars, for example. Thus, one could not take an arbitrary context free rammar and transform it into an LL(k) grammar and then generate an efficient logic program (efficient in the ense of not requiring backtracking). In practice, however, many languages (probably most programming nguages) can be formulated using LL(k) grammars. It is fairly likely that any language (presumably, for conenience to the user, a fairly restricted subset of natural lanaguage) which might be used as a command language) a logic operating system could be specified by an LL(k) grammar for some small value of k. One would then be ble to use the hardware of a concurrent logic machine to handle the necessary grammatical processing directly ather than relying on an attached sequential grammar processor for this task.

There are, however, some obvious generalizations of the techniques displayed above which get out of the resrictive LL(k) class.

Firstly, the guards may be generalized to do more than look at a certain number of characters of the input tream. Grammar productions could be written in the form:

nonterminal ::= <guards>: <right-hand side>

where the nonterminal "expands" to the right-hand side only if the guards are succesfully evaluated. It would be up to the grammar writer to provide specifications of the guards so that the wrong production is not selected in the committed nondeterministic setting.

Secondly, the nonterminal symbols may be allowed, as in the case of Definite Clause Grammars or Definite Clause Translation Grammars, to have more arguments than just those automatically added by the compiler from grammar rules to logic programming clauses. This certainly takes the grammar rules out of the very restrictive LL(k) class, and even, as is well known from the DCG and DCTG experience, out of the class of context free grammars.

Thirdly, the right-hand side of extended grammar rules may also include communication with concurrent processes other than ones corresponding to nonterminal symbols. As in the case of DCGs and DCTGs, one might use the notation in the right-hand part of a grammar rule:

{ concurrent_process(A,...,Z) }

to specify that some concurrent process with shared variables "A" to "Z" must be successfully reduced for parsing to succeed.

One should also note that in the concurrent setting derivations may be of infinite length. The guards above are used to determine whether a derivation may be continued or not: they do not enforce any restrictions on the length of input. Thus, one may think of the generalized grammar rules as allowing one to do grammatical processing on streams rather than on finite strings. In this view, the grammar rules provide a notation for operating on what might be termed a "hidden stream": it is a mechanical task to generate the concurrent logic program clauses which make that stream explicit as above in the simple LL(1) case.

5. Future investigations.

One area of investigation which may be of great interest in the application of deterministic concurrent logic grammars is natural language parsing. Marcus has reported considerable success with a deterministic bottom up parser which is essentially an LR(3) parser. It is tempting to speculate that a top down analogue of his parser can be as succesful. Of further interest are the opportunities of exploiting concurrency in grammatical processing.

On a less speculative level, one would like to have the grammatical processes in the concurrent setting as efficient and as inexpensive as possible. For much of the time the process corresponding to a nonterminal may be inactive, coming alive only when some input had arrived on its input stream. These processes could presumably be efficiently implemented by having them do a busy wait or be blocked until activated.

Acknowledgment

This research was supported with the aid of an SUR grant from IBM Canada.

References.

[Abramson,1984a]

Abramson, H., *Definite Clause Translation Grammars,* Proceedings 1984 International Symposium on Logic Programming, Feb. 6-9, 1984, Atlantic City, New Jersey, pp. 233-241.

[Abramson,1984b]

Abramson, H. *Definite Clause Translation Grammars and the Logical Specification of Data Types as Unambiguous Context Free Grammars,* Proceedings of the International Conference on Fifth Generation Computer Systems, Tokyo, Nov. 6-9, 1984.

[Clark&Gregory,1984]

Clark, K. & Gregory, S., *Parlog: Parallel Programming in Logic,* Imperial College, Research Report DOC 94/4, London, 1984.

[Colmerauer,1978]

Colmerauer, A., *Metamorphosis Grammars,* in Natural Language Communication with Computers, Lecture Notes in Computer Science 63, Springer, 1978.

[Dahl,1984]

Dahl, V. *More on Gapping Grammars,* Proceedings of the International Fifth Generation Computer Systems Conference, Tokyo, 1984.

[Dahl&Abramson,1984]

Dahl, V. & Abramson, H. *Gapping Grammars,* Proceedings - Second International Logic Programming Conference, Uppsala, Sweden, 1984.

[Pereira&Warren,1980]

Pereira, F.C.N. & Warren, D.H.D, *Definite Clause Grammars for Language Analysis,* Artificial Intelligence, vol. 13, pp. 231-278, 1980.

[Shapiro,1983]

Shapiro, E.Y., *A subset of Concurrent Prolog and its interpreter,* Technical Report TR-003, ICOT, Tokyo, 1983.

[Stabler,1983]

Stabler, E., *Deterministic and bottom-up parsing in Prolog,* Proceedings, AAAI, pp. 383-386, 1983.

A Parallel Parsing System for Natural Language Analysis

Yuji Matsumoto
ICOT Research Center
Institute for New Generation Computer Technology
1-4-28, Mita, Minato-ku, Tokyo 108 Japan

1. Introduction

Recent trends in computational linguistics focus attention on context-free grammars for natural language grammar formalism. Although it is arguable whether natural languages can be adequately described by context-free grammars, the view is certainly supported by recent important work in linguistics [Pullum 82],[Gazdar 85],[Kaplan 82].

DCG (Definite Clause Grammar) formalism, proposed by Pereira and Warren [Pereira 80], is based on Horn clause logic and can be seen as a context-free grammar formalism reinforced by unification between arguments in nonterminal symbols and attached Prolog procedures. It is powerful enough to cope with most of the grammar theories employing context-free grammar forms for description of the syntactic structure.

In this paper we assume DCG formalism as the user language for specifying grammars, and present an efficient and general parsing system which operates in parallel logic programming languages such as Parlog [Clark 84] and GHC (Guarded Horn Clauses) [Ueda 85]. This system was tested in the Parlog interpreter [Gregory 84] and the same program incidentally runs in Prolog as well with little modification.

We stay with the nondeterministic parsing method throughout in this paper, though there is another trend in parsing natural languages concerning deterministic methods, eg. [Marcus 80]. The reason for this is that we adopted the DCG formalism for expressing grammars and we wanted to make the description of grammar rules as independent as possible of each other and of the procedural semantics of the parsing system. However, there could be some restrictions on the forms of grammar rules or on the way of expressing extra conditions because we employ the bottom-up strategy for our parsing algorithm and make use of parallel logic programming languages.

The algorithm of our system is based on the conccurent process model of parallel logic programming languages originating from Relational Language [Clark 81]. As will be seen in a later section, what our parsing method does is virtually equivalent to what most of the efficient parsing algorithms, so-called tableau methods, do. The most important feature of our method is that the grammar rules and the dictionary are completely compiled into the logic programming language and the system does not need any program to interpret the grammar and the dictionary. Furthermore, the tableau itself is also compiled in the program. More precisely, an item that is normally kept in a tableau is represented as either a process or an item in a stream and no item in the streams is duplicated.

The next section describes the basic algorithm forming the basis of our system. A naive way is shown for transforming grammar rules and dictionary into a Prolog program which clearly illustrates our approach. The subsequent two sections consider how to make the system more efficient and extend it to work in parallel logic programming languages. In Section 5 we compare our system with other parsing algorithms for context-free grammars in order to estimate the computational complexity. We consider Chart parsing [Kay 80] and point out the similarity between them. Lastly we discuss how to incorporate context-dependent information in the system. Extra conditions included in DCG rules are not difficult to incorporate in the system if Prolog is accessible to the parallel logic language or all the extra conditions are written in the parallel language itself. However, we need a special consideration on the arguments in nonterminal symbols. This problem is discussed briefly.

2. Basic Algorithm

In this and the following sections we will deal not with DCG rules, but with bare context-free grammar rules. This simplification helps to convey the essential idea more easily. We also exclude grammars containing empty production rules and cyclic sets of rules. The first restriction comes from the fact that our algorithm is basically a bottom-up parser. The latter is designed to make sure that no process runs into an infinite loop. Though a cyclic set of rules is a special case of a set of left recursive rules, which can cause infinite loops in the case of some top-down parsing algorithms, our system can contain them.

Our basic algorithm is the left-corner parser [Aho 72], in which phrases are constructed from bottom to top and from left to right. Whenever a phrase of a certain nonterminal symbol is obtained, the algorithm checks whether that phrase can be used to make up a larger and more complete structure extending the previously constructed partial structures or to make it as the left-most element of a new tree structure. These processes proceed until every possibility is tried. We have given this procedural semantics to DCGs by transforming each DCG rule into a certain form of a Prolog clause. This system is called the BUP system [Matsumoto 83,84].

In this section we show another way of achieving the same effect on a grammar written in the DCG formalism. To keep the history of the parsing processes of left-corner parsing, it is necessary to remember not only the sequence of rules used so far but also the internal positions in these rules reached by the parsing process. This is easily done if each position in the right-hand side of every grammar rule has an identifier to distinguish itself from others. Suppose each nonterminal or terminal symbol is defined as a predicate of Prolog and has two arguments, one for the data coming from its left in the sentence and the other for the data to pass to the right. The data that move around between the grammar symbols are sequences of identifiers giving the history of parsing process. This consideration leads to the following transformation of the context-free grammar rule (1) into Prolog clauses (2). In the right-hand side of the grammar rule, the symbol 'id' followed by a figure stands for an identifier and is not a grammatical symbol.

```
(1)  a --> b,  id1  c, id2  d.

(2)  b(X,[id1|X]).
     c([id1|X],[id2|X]).
     d([id2|X],Y) :- a(X,Y).
```

Lists are used to represent the history of the parsing process and each nonterminal symbol of the grammar is defined as a Prolog predicate. If a nonterminal symbol receives 'id1' as the top element of the list, this means that nonterminal symbol 'b' has already been found and the corresponding part in rule (1) has been used in the parsing process. The sequence of identifiers can be expressed by defining identifiers as functors, that is, (2) is alternatively written (2)'. We use this notation rather than lists because it is easier to read.

```
(2)' b(X,id1(X)).
     c(id1(X),id2(X)).
     d(id2(X),Y) :- a(X,Y).
```

A simple rule like (3) is transformed into the Prolog clause (4).

```
(3)  vp --> verb.

(4)  verb(X,Y) :- vp(X,Y).
```

This shows that nonterminal symbol 'verb' can be immediately reduced to the nonterminal 'vp'. Note that nonterminal and terminal symbols need not be treated differently.

The following grammar (5) written in DCG formalism is transformed into the Prolog program (6). Again, the figures preceded by the symbol 'id' are identifiers for particular positions in the grammar rules.

```
(5)  s --> np,  id1  vp.
     np --> det,  id2  noun.
     np --> det,  id3  noun,  id4  relc.
     relc --> [that],  id5  s.
     vp --> verb.
     vp --> verb,  id6  np.
     det --> [the].
     noun --> [man].
     noun --> [woman].
     verb --> [loves].
     verb --> [walks].
(6)  np(X,id1(X)).
     vp(id1(X),Y) :- s(X,Y).
     det(X,id2(X)).
     noun(id2(X),Y) :- np(X,Y).
     det(X,id3(X)).
     noun(id3(X),id4(X)).
     relc(id4(X),Y) :- np(X,Y).
     that(X,id5(X)).
     s(id5(X),Y) :- relc(X,Y).
     verb(X,Y) :- vp(X,Y).
     verb(X,id6(X)).
     np(id6(X),Y) :- vp(X,Y).
     the(X,Y) :- det(X,Y).
     man(X,Y) :- noun(X,Y).
     woman(X,Y) :- noun(X,Y).
     loves(X,Y) :- verb(X,Y).
     walks(X,Y) :- verb(X,Y).
```

Now the Prolog clauses in (6) give a left-corner backtracking parsing program for the context-free grammar (5). In order to parse an input sentence, for example, "the man walks", all we have to do is simply to call the following Prolog goals.

(7) `the(begin,X),man(X,Y),walks(Y,end).`

The terms '**begin**' and '**end**' in these goals are constants identifying the beginning and terminal positions in the sentence. Note that one variable is shared by each consecutive pair of goals, which is used to pass the history of the parsing process from left to right. Another Prolog clause (8) is required to complete the parsing program. This checks if a sentence structure is constructed by using up the whole words in the sentence.

(8) `s(X,Y) :- X==begin,Y==end.`

Figure 1 shows the parsing process starting from the Prolog goals (7). A single arrow shows that a goal is reduced to another goal(s) through the matching process with the head of a clause. A double arrow indicates the assignment of values to the arguments of the goal by unification. This Prolog program goes through every possible analysis for the given sequence of words utilizing the backtracking mechanism of Prolog.

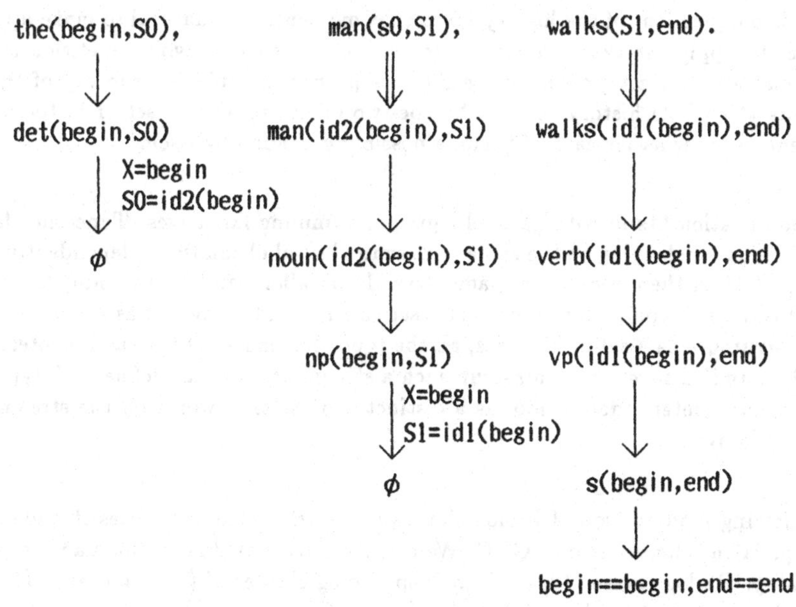

Figure 1. Sample Parsing

3. Parallel Parsing

The parsing program shown in the preceding section is now examined to make it more efficient and suitable for parallel execution. A close look at the Prolog program reveals that there are two kinds of clauses in it. We refer to them as type-one clauses and type-two clauses. Structurally a clause of type-one has a variable for its first argument in the head while a clause of type-two has structured data for its first argument in the head. During the execution of the program, type-one clauses start to construct a new tree structure taking themselves as left-corner constituents of a tree structure. The first clause in (6) is an example of this type. It puts an identifier '**id1**' on the top of the sequence it receives. A type-two clause matches the first element of the received sequence against the element in its first argument. If they are equal it makes either a new Prolog call or a new data structure. The second clause in (6) makes a new call corresponding to a nonterminal '**s**' if the first element of the sequence is '**id1**'. This identifier is removed from the sequence on calling the new Prolog call, since it is no longer necessary to keep this particular fragment of the history. The sixth clause in (6) works in a different way. If the first element in the received sequence is '**id3**', it puts another identifier '**id4**' on top of the sequence after removing the previous identifier. This corresponds to the process of extending the partially constructed tree structure. In either case, each type-two clause works on a particular identifier.

This algorithm is actually not so efficient. Its time complexity is exponential with respect to the length of the sentence since many repetitive computations occur in the parsing process. These are caused by the definition of type-one clauses in that they put an identifier on the received data of the history without regard to its content. Therefore, subsequent computation is independent of the history up to that moment. It is natural to make up a set of all histories to apply the type-one clauses to this set in order to avoid repetition caused by type-one clauses. So, a type-one clause puts its proper identifier on the top of the set that represents the whole history so far. A type-two clause receives a set of histories and examines them to see whether each of them is possibly extended by itself.

This modification fits in with parallel logic programming languages. Type-one clauses and type-two clauses belonging to the same nonterminal symbol can run independently, that is, in parallel. Both of them receive the same data. In parallel logic programming languages like Parlog or GHC it is common to represent a set as a list and to treat it as a stream. If we assume a list structure as a set of histories, all the type-one clauses of the same nonterminal symbol can be bundled together to make up such a stream and we can define each type-two clause of the same nonterminal symbol as a distinct process that works on the stream and modifies it accordingly.

The following modification of Prolog clauses into Parlog clauses realizes this idea. We can define equivalent clauses also in GHC. We employ Parlog syntax in this paper because of its readability. Parlog clause (10) is given from Prolog clauses of (9). Clauses of (12) are Parlog definitions of type-two clauses shown in (11).

```
(9)  det(X,id2(X)).
     det(X,id3(X)).

(10) mode det1(?,^).
     det1(X,[id2(X),id3(X)]).

(11) noun(id2(X),Y) :- np(X,Y).
     noun(id3(X),id4(X)).
```

```
(12) mode noun2(?,^).
     noun2([],[]).
     noun2([id2(X)|T],Y) :- |
          np(X,Y2),
          noun2(T,Y1),
          merge(Y1,Y2,Y).
     noun2([id3(X)|T],[id4(X)|Y]) :- |
          noun2(T,Y);
     noun2([_|X],Y) :- |
          noun2(X,Y).
```

Clauses defined in Parlog assume that the received data, i.e., the data given to its first argument, is a list (or a stream) of histories, though the first argument is expressed by the same variable name as in Prolog clauses. As can be seen in the program, the stream is a list of streams each of which is headed by an identifier. Generally speaking, type-one clauses collect all possible left-corner branches starting at their own position. There is a special case for type-one clauses where some of the original type-one clauses have a variable for their second argument. Such a clause is to be derived from a grammar rule the right-hand side of which consists of only one symbol. For example, type-one clauses in Prolog like (13) are transformed into a Parlog clause (14).

```
(13) verb(X,Y) :- vp(X,Y).
     verb(X,id6(X)).
```

```
(14) mode verb1(?,^).
     verb1(X,[id6(X)|Y]) :- |
          vp(X,Y).
```

When there is more than one such clause, their outputs are merged together.

Type-two clauses of the same nonterminal are defined as a set of or-processes, each of which specializes in a distinct identifier that can extend partially completed tree structures in the stream. The first clause in (12) is for the case when the stream is empty. The second clause accepts the identifier 'id2'. This means the completion of a noun phrase and it produces a goal for 'np' along with another call for 'noun2' for the remaining data in the stream. The third clause deals with the case where the noun is used to modify a partially completed tree generating a larger but still incomplete tree structure. The last definition in (12) is referred to only when all other processes have failed to utilize the first element in the stream. Note that this clause is separated from the preceding clauses by a colon not by a full stop. This is a Parlog convention which indicates that this clause should be executed only when all the preceding clauses fail. This clause throws away the first element in the stream and calls itself with the remaining data.

Each nonterminal symbol is now defined by a pair of a type-one process and a type-two process as follows.

```
(15) mode noun(?,^).
     noun(X,Y) :- |
          noun1(X,Y1),
          noun2(X,Y2),
          merge(Y1,Y2,Y).
```

Although the use of merge processes guarantees higher parallelism, merging is not a cheap operation and it can be avoided by using a data structure called difference lists. A difference list consists of a pair of lists and represents a list as the difference of these two lists. The programs shown in this section also run in Prolog with a simple modification. Using difference lists in Prolog makes the program more efficient since we can do away with merge operations. The following definitions from (16) to (19) written in Prolog are equivalent to the definitions (10), (12), (14) and (15). This modification is also available in the Parlog program but restricts the order of execution. Hereafter, difference lists are used in the Prolog definition. Note that the operational semantics of Prolog guarantees that the streams are completely constructed when they are passed to the next processes. In the following, the first argument in a definition of a nonterminal symbol works as an input stream and the second and third arguments represent a difference list that functions as the output stream.

```
(16) det1(X,[id2(X),id3(X)|Yt],Yt).
(17) noun2([],Y,Y)  :- !.
     noun2([id2(X)|T],Y,Yt)  :- !,
          np(X,Y,Y1),
          noun2(T,Y1,Yt).
     noun2([id3(X)|T],[id4(X)|Y],Yt)  :- !,
          noun2(T,Y,Yt).
     noun2([_|T],Y,Yt)  :- !,
          noun2(T,Y,Yt).
(18) verb1(X,[id6(X)|Y],Yt)  :- !,
          vp(X,Y,Yt).
(19) noun(X,Y,Yt)  :- !,
          noun1(X,Y,Y1),
          noun2(X,Y1,Yt).
```

If we bring in some syntax sugar, we can get rid of all the nuisance difference lists. As a matter of fact, DCG syntax can be used to express the program more simply and clearly. The clauses from (16)' to (19)' represent exactly the same clauses from (16) to (19).

```
(16)' det1(X)  --> !,
          [id2(X),id3(X)].
(17)' noun2([])  --> !.
      noun2([id2(X)|T])  :- !,
          np(X),
          noun2(T).
      noun2([id3(X)|T])  --> !,
          [id4(X)],
          noun2(T).
      noun2([_|T])  --> !,
          noun2(T).
(18)  verb1(X)  --> !,
          [id6(X)],
          vp(X).
(19)  noun(X)  --> !,
          noun1(X),
          noun2(X).
```

The modifications of the program in this section necessitates some alterations to the definition of nonterminal symbol '**s**'. One way of doing it is to change the initial goals for (20) and add the clause shown in (21) or (22) to the definition of '**s2**' (type-two clauses for nonterminal symbol '**s**'). The former is to be added to the Parlog program and the latter to the program with difference lists.

```
(20) the([begin],X),man(X,Y),walks(Y,Z),fin(Z).

(21) s2([begin],[end]).

(22) s2([begin]) --> !,
         [end].
```

The definition for '**s2**' given here produces the term '**end**' that indicates the completion of a sentence structure. The process '**fin**' is a user- defined predicate and is positioned at the end of the initial goals, which receives the stream produced by the last word in the sentence and checks if the stream contains the term '**end**'. The application and the definition of this process depend on the user's intention for this parsing system.

4. Top-down Prediction

A straightforward improvement in efficiency is achieved by employing a condition referred to as 'oracle' in LINGOL [Pratt 75] or as 'reachability' in Chart Parsing [Kay 80]. We call this 'top-down prediction' here according to the way it is used in coupling with the bottom-up strategy.

The second grammar rule of the grammar shown in (5) means that a determiner followed by a noun is a possible structure of a noun phrase. Suppose a determiner is found in the parsing process. Making use of this rule corresponds to sending the identifier associated with this rule. There are two things to be noted here. The first is that using this rule gives rise to an expectation of a noun at the position just after the determiner. This gives a positive reason for building up a noun structure at that position. In this case a noun is referred to as a top-down prediction at that position in the sentence. Top-down predictions are obtained dynamically during the parsing process. The second point is that usage of a particular grammar rule should be guaranteed by at least one top-down prediction. The left-hand side of the grammar rule mentioned above is a noun phrase. In order to to guarantee that this grammar ruleis a part of a larger constituent, at least one of the top-down predictions at that position must be a noun phrase or must be something which can have a noun phrase as its left-most descendant. If there is no such top-down prediction, there is no place for the noun phrase which will eventually be constructed by this grammar rule. Top-down prediction is very useful in avoiding bottom-up searches which have no place to go. Whether a nonterminal symbol can be a left-most descendant of another nonterminal symbol is precomputable from the grammar rules. The left-most element on the right-hand side of a grammar rule is possibly a left-most descendant of the nonterminal symbol on the left-hand side of the rule. The relation we are talking about is defined as the transitive and reflexive closure of the set of such pairs. We refer to this relation as the link relation and say that a nonterminal symbol links to another if they satisfy this relation.

There are several ways to incorporate this idea in our parsing program. We introduce one idea which we are employing currently. A stream given to nonterminal symbols is a stream of streams each of which is headed by an identifier. An identifier is a unique symbol for a particular position in a grammar rule, and uniquely specifies a nonterminal symbol that follows the identifier in the grammar rule. This nonterminal symbol is exactly what is expected as the top-down prediction at the corresponding position in the sentence. The mapping from identifiers to nonterminal symbols is of course obtainable when context-free grammar rules are translated into the parsing program. The special identifiers '**begin**' and '**end**' predict '**s**' and nothing, respectively. The top-down prediction is easily made use of by modifying type-one clauses. In the original program shown in Section 2, a type-one clause corresponds to the left-most element on the right-hand side of a grammar rule and produces an identifier. The production of this identifier should be blocked if the nonterminal symbol on the left-hand side of the original grammar rule is not predicted by the identifier it received. In the parallel definition of a type-one clause, an identifier is blocked only when the corresponding nonterminal symbol is not predicted by any head identifiers in the input stream. In other words, a type-one clause passes its own identifier to the output stream if at least one head identifier in the input stream is known to predict the nonterminal symbol on the left-hand side of the original grammar rule.

In our current implementation, the process of the top-down prediction is realized by a process of filtering. This process receives the input stream to a type-one clause and throws all the unusable elements away producing a new input stream for the type-one caluse. The definition of type-one clause (10) now becomes (23).

```
(23) det1(X,Y) :-
        tp_check(X,np,New_X),
        tp_output(New_X,[id2(New_X),id3(New_X)],Y).
```

In this definition, '**tp_check**' is the filtering process which allows passing only the elements in '**X**' whose head identifier predicts a noun phrase. '**New_X**' is the output of this filter. The process '**tp_output**' returns the data at the second argument to the third argument if '**New_X**' produces at least one element. Otherwise, it returns empty to the third argument. Note that these two processes run in parallel, that is, two identifiers '**id2**' and '**id3**' are passed to the next process even when the stream in their argument is still incomplete. Also note that the filtering process is shared by two output identifiers since both of the corresponding grammar rules have '**np**' on their left-hand side. When there is more than one filtering process, ie, more than one '**tp_output**', their outputs are merged.

5. Comparison with Chart Parsing

In order to estimate the time and space complexity of our parsing method, we compare it with Chart Parsing [Kay 80].

Chart Parsing consists of processes constructing a data structure called a chart, which is equivalent to so-called well-formed substring table and is conceptually depicted as a directed graph. Each element in a chart is a term representing a partially or perfectly constructed tree structure. A partially constructed tree is expressed by a term with some empty slots, and a perfectly constructed tree is expressed by a term that represents a tree structure with no empty slot. They are referred to as an active edge and an inactive edge when they are represented by a directed graph. Chart Parsing is actually not a parsing algorithm but an algorithm schema, as its author says. The process of constructing terms in a chart (or edges in a directed graph) varies according to the control given to the schema. We will point out the similarity between our parsing method and Chart Parsing with bottom-up control.

Vhen a bottom-up strategy is given to Chart Parsing, it operates with two rules. One rule s to start building up new tree structures from a perfectly constructed tree (ie, an inactive dge). When an inactive edge is obtained, this means that a complete nonterminal symbol s constructed. Referring to the grammar rules, this rule produces all the partially complete erms (ie, active edges) that have the current nonterminal symbol as the left-most element n the right-hand side. The second rule is for filling an empty slot in a partially complete erm with a complete term.

There is a very close one-to-one correspondence between bottom-up Chart Parsing and ur parsing algorithm. In our parsing algorithm the first and second rules of Chart Parsing orrespond to processes performed by type-one clauses and type-two clauses, respectively. nactive edges are represented by calls of nonterminal symbols in the program and active dges are represented by elements in streams being passed to nonterminal symbols.

#	Locus	Length	Term
1	0	1	[failing]a
2	0	1	[failing]prp
3	1	1	[students]n
4	2	1	[looked]v
5	3	1	[hard]a
6	3	1	[hard]av
7	0	1	[[failing]a [?]n]np
8	0	1	[[failing]prp [?]]np
9	0	2	[[failing]a [students]n]np
10	0	2	[[failing]prp [students]n]np
11	0	2	[[[failing]a [students]n]np [?]vp]s
12	0	2	[[[failing]prp [students]n]np [?]vp]s
13	2	1	[[looked]v [?]a]vp
14	2	1	[[looked]v [?]av]vp
15	2	2	[[looked]v [hard]a]vp
16	2	2	[[looked]v [hard]av]vp
17	0	4	[[[failing]a [students]n]np [[looked]v [hard]a]vp]s
18	0	4	[[[failing]prp [students]n]np [[looked]v [hard]a]vp]s
19	0	4	[[[failing]a [students]n]np [[looked]v [hard]av]vp]s
20	0	4	[[[failing]prp [students]n]np [[looked]v [hard]av]vp]s

Figure 2. The Chart

The important differences between these two methods are that our algorithm is comiled into a Parlog or Prolog program and that partial results need not be kept in something ike a well-formed substring table. In Chart Parsing, adjacency of two edges is checked by he location and the length associated with terms. A chart keeps them together with coresponding terms. Our algorithm, however, does not require them since the original words n a given sentence are connected by shared variables and the data representing active edges re passed through these variables, each of which indicates a specific position in the original entence. The definition of clauses ensures that a tree structure is never created repeatedly unless some grammar rules are duplicated. Figure 2 shows the chart created by bottom-up Chart Parsing using the grammar rules (24) [Kay 80]. In this table, a term represents a tree, locus shows the position of the term in the sentence and length is the number of words in the term. Question marks in a term indicate undefined parts in the term.

(24)
```
s --> np, vp.
np --> a, n.
np --> prp, n.
vp --> v, a.
vp --> v, av.
a --> [failing].
a --> [hard].
n --> [students].
v --> [looked].
av --> [hard].
```

The main parts of the Parlog program obtained from these grammar rules are shown in (25). (25) consists only of the essential clauses. Some more clauses should be added to complete the program. Top-down predictions are omitted in this program.

(25)
```
np1(X,[id1(X)]).
a1(X,[id2(X)]).
prp1(X,[id3(X)]).
v1(X,[id4(X),id5(X)]).

vp2([id1(X)|T],Y) :-
    s(X,Y1),
    vp2(T,Y2), merge(Y1,Y2,Y).
n2([id2(X)|T],Y) :-
    np(X,Y1),
    n2(T,Y2), merge(Y1,Y2,Y).
n2([id3(X)|T],Y) :-
    np(X,Y1),
    n2(T,Y2), merge(Y1,Y2,Y).
a2([id4(X)|X1],Y) :-
    vp(X,Y1),
    a2(T,Y2), merge(Y1,Y2,Y).
av2([id5(X)|T],Y) :-
    vp(X,Y1),
    av2(T,Y2), merge(Y1,Y2,Y).

failing(X,Y) :-
    a(X,Y1), prp(X,Y2), merge(Y1,Y2,Y).
hard(X,Y) :-
    a(X,Y1), av(X,Y2), merge(Y1,Y2,Y).
students(X,Y) :-
    n(X,Y).
looked(X,Y) :-
    v(X,Y).
```

(26) is the initial calls of Parlog program for parsing the same sentence. Figure 3 shows the execution of this program.

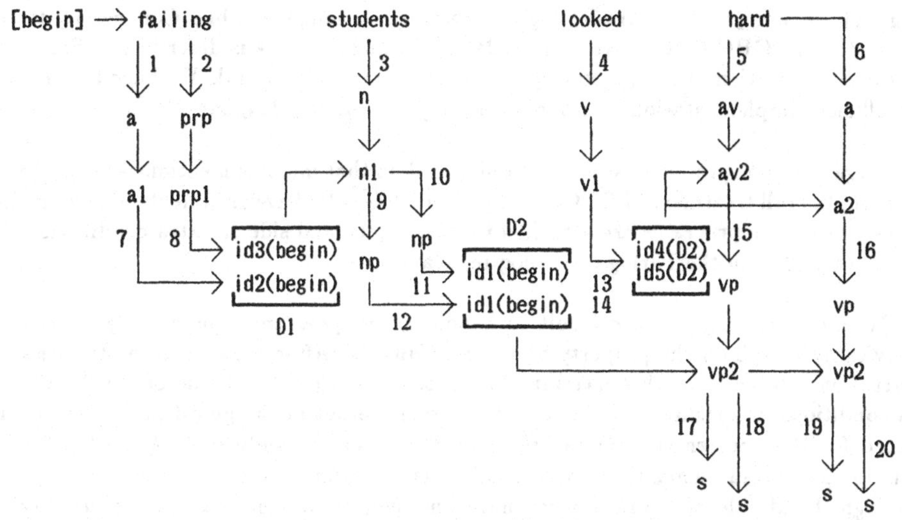

Figure 3. A Sample Execution of Parallel Parsing

```
26) failing([begin],D1),students(D1,D2),looked(D2,D3),hard(D3,D4),fin(D4).
```

In the figure, arrows indicate calls of new processes or creation of data. Double arrows are the flow of the data structure. Numbers are associated with arrows to show the correspondence between processes in Chart Parsing and in our algorithm. Arrows that do not have a number correspond to the creation of type-one or type-two literals from nonterminal symbols. Note that the analysis starting from each word in the sentence does not depend on the analysis of other places. It is affected by other processes only when it refers to the data passed from these processes. For example, the analysis starting from 'looked' can proceed even if 'D2' is not instantiated. The analysis starting from 'hard' is suspended on calling 'av2' or 'a2' if 'D3' is still an uninstantiated variable. In Figure 3, the vertical direction more or less shows the time axis. Processes on the same level can operate in parallel. From this figure, we can see that the time complexity of our algorithm is to be proportional to the height of the analysis tree, which is in the worst case equivalent to the length of the given sentence.

The space complexity of our algorithm is no worse than that of Chart Parsing since no data structure is duplicated. Furthermore, if variables in our program are shared as in Prolog, it requires less space than the chart. Subterms must be copied to register a newly constructed term in the chart whereas they need not be copied in our algorithm because of the shared variables. In the case of parallel execution, the time complexity largely depends on the treatment of logical variables in parallel logic programming languages.

5. Conclusions

This paper briefly described the idea of our parallel parsing system based on parallel logic programming languages. Our specification of the parsing program runs not only on

Parlog but on many other parallel logic programming languages like Concurrent Prolog [Shapiro 83] and GHC that derive from Relational Language. As is described in Section 3, Prolog implementation of our parsing system is also practically useful. We have to wait now for an efficient implementation of a parallel logic programming language.

There are some problems with our parsing system that must be mentioned here. We did not explain the full treatment of DCG rules. When DCG rules have arguments in nonterminal symbols and Prolog programs are attached in their right-hand side as extra conditions, they must be coupled with the Parlog or Prolog program.

Extra conditions are not difficult to handle in our program though some restrictions are inevitably placed on the property of extra conditions. After the transformation there is in general one clause for each nonterminal symbol in the right-hand side of any DCG rule. Extra conditions in a right-hand side of a DCG rule are put in the guard part of the clause produced for the nonterminal symbol preceding these extra conditions. According to our bottom-up procedural semantics, extra conditions preceding the first nonterminal symbol in the right-hand side of a rule do not have any significant meaning. Users are advised not to write extra conditions there, or they are put at the guard part of the clause for the first nonterminal symbol of the rule even when a user writes some extra conditions at the beginning of the rule. In the programs shown in preceding sections, type-one clauses with the same nonterminal symbol are bundled up into one clause. However, type-one clauses having different extra conditions cannot be bundled up simply. Such clauses should be defined separately and their outputs are merged later. Another restriction is that the operational semantics of the derived program prohibits extra conditions from having nondeterminacy. This is because extra conditions are treated as guards.

Another problem arises when nonterminal symbols have arguments and they contain uninstantiated variables. Variables in an argument may be passed to more than one place in the stream data. The data structures moving through a shared variable are something like tree structures. We have to note that substructures in different branches in a data structure are in different environments. Although they can share the value of a variable, an instantiation to one variable must not affect the value of the same variable in different environments. The easiest way to avoid this difficulty is to copy the value of a variable any time the variable is passed to more than one environment. However, such a simple treatment may cause a space explosion. A more moderate and safe way is to copy the value of a variable which is included in the output of a type-two clause any time the guard part of the clause finishes successfully. The treatment of this problem is crucial for our system to be practical. Development of a parsing system in Prolog based on this idea is now under way.

Acknowledgments

This work was mainly done while the author was working with the Logic Programming Group at Imperial College of Science and Technology. The author wishes to express his thanks to Professor Kowalski for giving him the opportunity to work in his group. Discussions with the members of his group and of the Natural Language Group were very valuable. Thanks are also due to the British Council, which supported the author's stay at the College.

References

[Aho 72] Aho, A.V. and J.D.Ullman, 'The Theory of Parsing, Translation, and Compiling,

Volume 1: Parsing,' Prentice-Hall, 1972.

[Clark 81] Clark, K.L. and S.Gregory, "A Relational Language for Parallel Programming," Imperial College Research Report DOC 81/16, July 1981.

[Clark 84] Clark, K.L. and S.Gregory, "PARLOG: Parallel Programming in Logic," Research Report DOC 84/4, Imperial College, April 1984.

[Gazdar 85] Gazdar, G., E.Klein, G.K.Pullum and I.A.Sag, 'Generalized Phrase Structure Grammar,' Basil Blackwell Publisher Ltd, 1985.

[Gregory 84] Gregory, S., "How to Use Parlog (C-Prolog Version)," Department of Computing, Imperial College, Oct. 1984.

[Kaplan 82] Kaplan, R.M. and J.Bresnan, "Lexical-Functional Grammar: A Formal System for Grammatical Representation," Chap.4 of 'The Mental Representation of Grammatical Relations' J. Bresnan (ed.), MIT Press, pp.173-281, 1982.

[Kay 80] Kay, M., "Algorithm Schemata and Data Structures in Syntactic Processing," XEROX Palo Alto Research Center, CSL-80-12, Oct. 1980.

[Marcus 80] Marcus, M.P., 'A Theory of Syntactic Recognition for Natural Language,' The MIT Press, 1980.

[Matsumoto 83] Matsumoto, Y., et al., "BUP: A Bottom-Up Parser Embedded in Prolog," New Generation Computing, vol.1, no.2, pp.145-158, 1983.

[Matsumoto 84] Matsumoto, Y., M.Kiyono and H.Tanaka, "Facilities of the BUP Parsing System," Proceedings of Natural Language Understanding and Logic Programming, Rennes, 1984.

[Pereira 80] Pereira, F.C.N. and D.H.D.Warren, "Definite Clause Grammars for Language Analysis – A Survey of the Formalism and a Comparison with Augmented Transition Networks," Artificial Intelligence, 13, pp.231-278, 1980.

[Pratt 75] Pratt, V.R., "LINGOL – A Progress Report," Proc. the 4th IJCAI, pp.422-428, 1975.

[Pullum 82] Pullum, G.K. and G.Gazdar, "Natural Languages and Context-free Languages," Linguistic and Philosophy 4, pp.471-504, 1982.

[Shapiro 83] Shapiro, E.Y., "A Subset of Concurrent Prolog and Its Interpreter," ICOT Technical Report, TR-003, Feb. 1983.

[Ueda 85] Ueda, K., "Guarded Horn Clauses," Proc. The Logic Programming Conference, ICOT, 1985.

Equivalences of Logic Programs

(Extended Abstract)

M. J. Maher
Dept. of Computer Science
University of Melbourne[1]

1. Introduction

One of the most important relationships between programs in any programming language is the equivalence of such programs. This relationship is at the basis of most, if not all, programming methodologies. Each method of giving a semantics to programs induces a, possibly different, equivalence relation on programs. Thus it is essential to investigate how these equivalences are related, especially for logic programming where there are many methods of giving semantics to programs.

So far, there has not been any systematic treatment of ideas of equivalence of logic programs. This has led to programs being described in the literature as "equivalent", but it is left to the reader to infer from the context the type of equivalence which is meant. For example, the programs P_1 and P_2 in Figure 1 might easily be said to be equivalent, yet in many senses they are not equivalent (for instance, P_1 and P_2 are not logically equivalent).

P_1:	Even(0)	P_2:	Even(0)
	Even(S^2(x)) ← Even(x)		Even(S(x)) ← Odd(x)
	Odd(S(0))		Odd(S(x)) ← Even(x)
	Odd(x) ← Even(S(x))		

Figure 1

This paper provides a systematic comparison of the relative strengths of various formulations of equivalence. These formulations arise naturally from several well-known formal semantics for logic programs. Different formulations which define identical equivalences offer the possibility of different frameworks in which to reason about programs, and hence of greater flexibility. We can also

1 Author's current address: IBM T.J. Watson Research Center, Yorktown Heights, NY 10598, USA.

use stronger equivalences to reason about programs and then be assured that the programs are also equivalent in an intended weaker sense, which might not be as suitable for reasoning.

We begin, in Section 2, by briefly summarising some formal semantics of logic programs. We then introduce, in Section 3, two syntactic notions of equivalence. One is shown to correspond to the equality of functions T_P of programs. We use this to study two continuity properties of T_P by characterizing syntactically the programs with these properties. In Section 4 we formulate different notions of equivalence based upon different semantics of logic programs. We examine these equivalences and those of Section 3 and determine their relative strength (i.e. whether equivalence of two programs in one sense implies their equivalence in another sense). In particular, we show that logical equivalence of programs ($P_1 \leftrightarrow P_2$) is identical to equality of the functional semantics of [Lassez and Maher 83, 84] ($[\![P_1]\!] = [\![P_2]\!]$). Section 5 extends the work of Section 4 to the important case where two programs employ different function or predicate symbols. As an example, we determine which equivalences are preserved by a program transformation. This transformation is of independent interest since it answers two open problems of [Sebelik and Stepanek 80].

2. *Preliminaries*

A *language* consists of three disjoint sets: the variables V, the function symbols Σ and the predicate symbols Π. We take the approach that a language is fixed and that programs and queries can use only the variables of V, function symbols of Σ etc. We assume that the language contains "enough" variables, function symbols of a given arity etc. to write a program and query it effectively. The Herbrand universe HU and the Herbrand base HB are defined for a given language.

The proofs of some later results assume the existence of a potentially unbounded number of constant symbols in Σ which do not appear in the relevant program (called *new* constants). The same effect could be obtained with one new function symbol (of arity > 0). This assumption has a close analogue in the use of logic interpreters such as PROLOG: queries are permitted to use function symbols which are not employed in the program. In this setting, the assumption is more appropriate than the assumption, employed by many, that queries use only those function symbols which appear in the program.

The existence of new constants allows the application of the following simple result of logic [Shoenfield 67]:

Theorem on Constants

Let L' be a language obtained from L by the addition of new constants and let T be a theory axiomatized in L. Then for every formula A in L and every substitution θ of the form

$$\{ x_1 \leftarrow c_1, \dots , x_p \leftarrow c_p \}$$

where the x_i's are free variables of A and the c_i's are distinct new constants we have

$$(L)\, T \models A \text{ iff } (L')\, T \models A\theta$$

We use an over tilde ~ to denote a list or sequence of objects. For example, $\tilde{x}$ may denote a list of variables and $\tilde{t}$ a list of terms.

In this paper we consider only definite clause logic programs.

The function T_P, introduced by [van Emden and Kowalski 76], is by now well-known. Application of T_P corresponds to one-step deductions, using P, of ground atoms from ground atoms. The function corresponding to deductions of any number of steps is denoted by $[\![P]\!]$ [Lassez and Maher 83, 84], and can be defined by $[\![P]\!](X) = \bigcup_{i=0}^{\infty}(T_P + Id)^i(X)$ where Id is the identity function and $(f + g)(X) = f(X) \cup g(X)$. This was the intended semantics of programs in [O'Keefe 85]. There is a partial order on functions defined in the following manner: $f \leq g$ iff $\forall X\, f(X) \subseteq g(X)$.

The operational model we will use is fair SLD-resolution [Lassez and Maher 84]. We consider the two sets of ground atoms which can have terminating computations: the success set SS(P) = { A : A has a successful SLD-derivation for P } and the finite failure set FF(P) = { A : A has a finite failed SLD tree for P }. Fair SLD-resolution guarantees that A is in FF(P) exactly when a query $\leftarrow$ A terminates with failure, independent of the specific computation rule.

There are two well-known logical semantics for a logic program. One straightforwardly considers the program to be a conjunction of the universal closure of the clauses. The second takes the program P to be shorthand for a *complete logic program* (or completion of P) [Clark 78], consisting of an equality theory E* (dependent only on Σ) and a collection of predicate definitions P*. For example, Figure 2 gives the completions of the programs of Figure 1 (omitting E*).

There are a number of significant relationships between the different things we have defined. We can express, in many ways, the set of successful ground atoms, $T_P\uparrow\omega = lfp(T_P) = [\![P]\!](\phi) = SS(P) = \{A: P \models A\} = \{A: P^*, E^* \models A\}$, and the set of failed ground atoms, $FF(P) = \overline{T_P\downarrow\omega} = \overline{\bigcap_{i=0}^{\infty} T_P^i(HB)} = \{A: P^*, E^* \models \neg A\}$. Furthermore, it is easy to show that the fixedpoints of T_P are the Herbrand models of P* and the fixedpoints of $[\![P]\!]$ are the Herbrand models of P (where we use the standard set representation of Herbrand models).

Definitions lacking from this paper and the proofs of the above relationships can be found in [Lloyd 84] or [Maher 85]. Although, for reasons of space, proofs have been omitted from this paper, they can be found in [Maher 85].

P_1^* Even(x) $\leftrightarrow$ $x=0 \lor \exists y\ x=S^2(y) \land Even(y)$
Odd(x) $\leftrightarrow$ Even(S(x))

P_2^* Even(x) $\leftrightarrow$ $x=0 \lor \exists y\ x=S(y) \land Odd(y)$
Odd(x) $\leftrightarrow$ $\exists y\ x=S(y) \land Even(y)$

Figure 2

3. *Subsumption-Equivalence*

We introduce two forms of equivalence based only on the syntactic form of definite clauses. We use the notion of subsumption, which is well-known in automatic theorem proving. Let C_1 and C_2 be the definite clauses $A \leftarrow B_1, \ldots, B_n$ and $G \leftarrow D_1, \ldots, D_m$ respectively. C_1 is *subsumed* by C_2 if there is a substitution θ such that $A = G\theta$ and $\{D_1\theta, \ldots, D_m\theta\} \subseteq \{B_1, \ldots, B_n\}$. A subsumed clause is, in a sense, already encapsulated in the subsuming clause. Some subsumption algorithms (for general clauses) and an analysis of their complexity can be found in [Gottlob and Leitsch 85]. The following proposition gives a well-known link between subsumption and logical implication.

Proposition 1
Let $\tilde{x}$ be all the variables in clause C_1 and $\tilde{y}$ be all the variables in clause C_2.
If C_2 subsumes C_1 then $\forall\tilde{y}\ C_2 \rightarrow \forall\tilde{x}\ C_1$

We say that two clauses are *subsumption-equal* if each subsumes the other. By the proposition above, such clauses are logically equivalent. A *redundancy* in a clause occurs when there are two identical atoms in the body of the clause or a non-renaming instance of the clause subsumes the original clause. A clause without redundancy is said to be *reduced*. The definition of reduced clause here is different, although equivalent, to that of [Plotkin 70].

Part (a) of the following proposition shows that the reduced clauses are canonical representatives of the equivalences classes formed by subsumption-equality. Part (b) suggests a method to find the reduced form of a clause C: if C is not reduced, obtain a factor C' as in the proposition and apply this process to C' until a reduced clause is found. If two atoms in the body of a clause C unify with most general unifier θ then the clause obtained from $C\theta$ by retaining only one occurrence of duplicated atoms is called the *factor* of C. Since the body of a factor of C must contain fewer atoms than the body of C, the method suggested by (b) must terminate. This algorithm is essentially that of Plotkin.

Proposition 2

(a) Every clause is subsumption-equal to a unique (up to variable renaming) reduced clause.

(b) A clause C is not reduced iff C has a factor C′ which subsumes C.

Any set of clauses P can be reduced to a more compact but logically equivalent set of clauses by partitioning the clauses of P according to subsumption-equality, choosing the reduced clause from each class, and then deleting those clauses which are subsumed by some other clause. The resulting set is called the *canonical set of clauses* or *canonical form* for P. Two programs are *subsumption-equivalent* if they have the same canonical form. It follows from the construction of the canonical form that P_1 is subsumption-equivalent to P_2 iff every clause of P_1 is subsumed by some clause of P_2 and vice versa.

The canonical set of clauses may still contain tautologies. A *tautology* is a logic formula which always (i.e. under every interpretation and valuation) evaluates to True. A definite clause is a tautology only when an exact copy of the head appears in the body. By deleting all the tautologies from a canonical set of clauses we obtain the *weakly canonical set of clauses*, which gives rise to *weak subsumption-equivalence* between two programs which have the same weak canonical form. P_1 is weakly subsumption-equivalent to P_2 iff every clause of P_1 is logically implied by some clause of P_2 and vice versa.

There is a strong link between the $\leq$ ordering on functions T_P derived from sets of clauses, and subsumption.

Proposition 3

Every clause of P_2 is subsumed by some clause in P_1 iff $T_{P_1} \geq T_{P_2}$.

It follows immediately that the syntactic notion of subsumption-equivalence of sets of clauses and the semantic notion that sets of clauses P which define the same function T_P are "equal", are identical.

Theorem 4

P_1 is subsumption-equivalent to P_2 iff $T_{P_1} = T_{P_2}$

A consequence of these results is that, for finite sets of clauses P_1 and P_2, we can now determine whether or not $T_{P_1} = T_{P_2}$, $T_{P_1} \leq T_{P_2}$, etc. without dealing directly with the functions.

The weak canonical form of a program can be regarded as the natural form of a program since a set of clauses which is not weak canonical may result in extra, useless computation or non-terminating behaviour which would otherwise not occur. We can give a characterization of weakly subsumption-equivalent programs in terms of the function T_P.

Proposition 5

P_1 is weakly subsumption-equivalent to P_2 iff $T_{P_1} + Id = T_{P_2} + Id$

For some properties of the function T_P we are able to characterize syntactically those sets of clauses P such that the property holds. These results, when taken with the obvious algorithm for computing the canonical form of a set of clauses, will mean that the presence or absence of such properties can be determined simply and without the need to deal directly with the functions.

T_P is *distributive* if $T_P(\bigcup_{i \in I} X_i) = \bigcup_{i \in I} T_P(X_i)$ for every collection $\{ X_i : i \in I \}$ of subsets of HB. But, since T_P is continuous, this condition is equivalent to $T_P(X \cup Y) = T_P(X) \cup T_P(Y)$ $\forall X,Y \subseteq HB$. Distributive programs correspond to Nilsson's ideas on decomposition of data bases of facts [Nilsson 82].

A program is *binary* if the body of each clause in P contains at most one atom. [Tarnlund 77] has shown that every computable function is computable by a binary program. Binary programs have been further investigated by [Sebelik and Stepanek 80].

Theorem 6

T_P is distributive iff P is subsumption-equivalent to a binary set of clauses

T_P is *down-continuous* if, for every decreasing chain $\{I_j\}$, $\bigcap_{j \in J} T_P(I_j) = T_P(\bigcap_{j \in J} I_j)$ Interest in down-continuous functions stems from an interest in when the greatest fixedpoint of T_P, gfp(T_P), is equal to $T_P{\downarrow}\omega$. If T_P is down-continuous then gfp(T_P) = $T_P{\downarrow}\omega$. This property has important implications for inferring falsehood from failure (in a finite time) to succeed (i.e. the negation-as-failure rule). In particular it implies that it is only necessary to consider Herbrand models when determining whether ground literals are logical consequences of the corresponding complete program. However the cases where T_P is down-continuous do not constitute all cases where gfp(T_P) = $T_P{\downarrow}\omega$.

A variable in a clause is said to be *local* if it appears only in the body of that clause.

Theorem 7

Suppose $|HU| = \infty$. T_P is down-continuous iff P is subsumption-equivalent to a set of clauses such that no clause has local variables.

If $|HU|$ is finite then T_P is always down-continuous, since any infinite descending chain must stabilize for some finite k (i.e. $\exists k$ such that $\forall j \geq k$ $I_j = I_k$).

[Fitting 85] defines a class of general logic programs (i.e. allowing negated atoms in clause bodies) which he claims are the only acceptable programs. In particular, the only definite clause programs P he considers acceptable are those for which T_P is down-continuous. From the above theorem it would seem that this class is too restrictive since, for example, transitivity cannot be expressed naturally, and possibly cannot be expressed at all.

Subsumption-equivalence has also proved useful in characterizing syntactically some (but not all) programs P which can be decomposed into subprograms P_1 and P_2 such that $[\![P]\!] = [\![P_1]\!] + [\![P_2]\!]$ or $[\![P]\!] = [\![P_1]\!] \circ [\![P_2]\!]$ [Maher 85, Lassez and Maher 83, 84].

4. Equivalences of Logic Programs with a Common Language

We assume in this section that programs are all written with the same language L. We will consider a number of formulations of equivalence based upon either the logical semantics, the operational semantics or the functional semantics. The last named provides three forms of equivalence: programs having the same T_P function, programs having the same $(T_P + Id)$ function and programs having the same $[\![P]\!]$. The operational semantics provides two: programs having the same success set and those with the same finite failure set. Logical semantics also contributes two: logical equivalence and programs having logically equivalent completions with respect to E*. Additionally, we have two notions of equivalence based on the syntax: subsumption-equivalence and weak subsumption-equivalence. (Note that there are other notions of equivalence which have not been included.)

We already know that some of these equivalences are the same in the sense that they give the same equivalence classes of programs and we also know that there are other different formulations for some of the equivalences. For example, the equalities $SS(P) = [\![P]\!](\phi) = lfp(T_P) = \{A \in HB: P \models A\}$ give rise to four different formulations of the same equivalence relation.

The following theorem shows that equality of the closure operators $[\![P]\!]$ and logical equivalence of programs are identical relationships between logic programs. Thus two programs have the same logical consequences exactly when they always produce the same generated set from the same starting axioms. This result is somewhat surprising, since $[\![P]\!]$ deals only with ground atoms whereas logical consequence concerns all logic formulas. There are two main contributing factors to this result: first, the special nature of definite clause theories which is such that the set of logical consequences of a theory is determined by the set of *atomic* logical consequences, and second, the existence of new constants which makes it possible to "lift", using the Theorem on Constants, from ground logical expressions to expressions with variables.

Theorem 8

(a) If $P_1 \rightarrow P_2$ then $[\![P_1]\!] \geq [\![P_2]\!]$

(b) If $[\![P_1]\!] \geq [\![P_2]\!]$ then $P_1 \rightarrow P_2$

(c) $[\![P_1]\!] = [\![P_2]\!]$ iff $P_1 \leftrightarrow P_2$

An important relationship between two equivalences is their relative strength. We say $\sim_1$ is *(strictly) stronger* than $\sim_2$ if whenever $P \sim_1 Q$ then $P \sim_2 Q$ for all programs P and Q (and $\sim_2$ is not stronger than $\sim_1$). Thus the stronger the equivalence, the finer the partition induced. Two equivalences which are stronger than each other are the same in the sense that they define the same equivalence classes.

Clearly equivalence wrt T_P is stronger than equivalence wrt $(T_P + Id)$, which, by the definition of $[\![P]\!]$, must be stronger than equivalence wrt $[\![P]\!]$. Clearly also, equivalence wrt $[\![P]\!]$ is stronger than equality of success sets since $SS(P) = [\![P]\!](\phi)$. These relations can easily be seen to be strict. We know from the previous section that equivalence wrt T_P is the same as subsumption-equivalence and equivalence wrt $(T_P + Id)$ is the same as weak subsumption-equivalence.

Logical equivalence of the completions of programs P_1 and P_2 implies that P_1* and P_2* have the same models. We can word the operational equivalences in terms of models of P* since SS(P) is the set of ground atoms which are true in all models of P*, and FF(P) is the set of ground atoms which are false in all models of P*. Thus logical equivalence of completions is stronger than each of the operational equivalences.

In fact equivalence of completions is strictly stronger than the combination of these two equivalences (and so also of the equivalences individually). Consider the complete programs { $A \leftrightarrow B$, $B \leftrightarrow B$, $D \leftrightarrow D$ } and { $A \leftrightarrow D$, $B \leftrightarrow B$, $D \leftrightarrow D$ }. For both programs $SS = FF = \phi$ and yet the interpretation which makes A and B true and D false is a model for the first complete program but not the second. Moreover, the set of atoms for which all fair ground derivations are finitely failed (called GGF in (Jaffar et. al. 86)) is the same for both programs. Thus it seems that some kind of trace information is necessary to distinguish between logically unequivalent complete programs by their operational behaviour.

We can show that subsumption-equivalence is the most fundamental of the equivalences we consider here, if we can show that it is stronger than equivalence of completed programs. Suppose C_1 subsumes C_2. Then, using Proposition 1, $E^* \models D_1 \rightarrow D_2$ where D_i is the disjunct in P* corresponding to C_i. So we can omit D_2 from P* and retain a logically equivalent complete program. It follows that subsumption-equivalent sets of clauses give rise to logically equivalent complete logic programs.

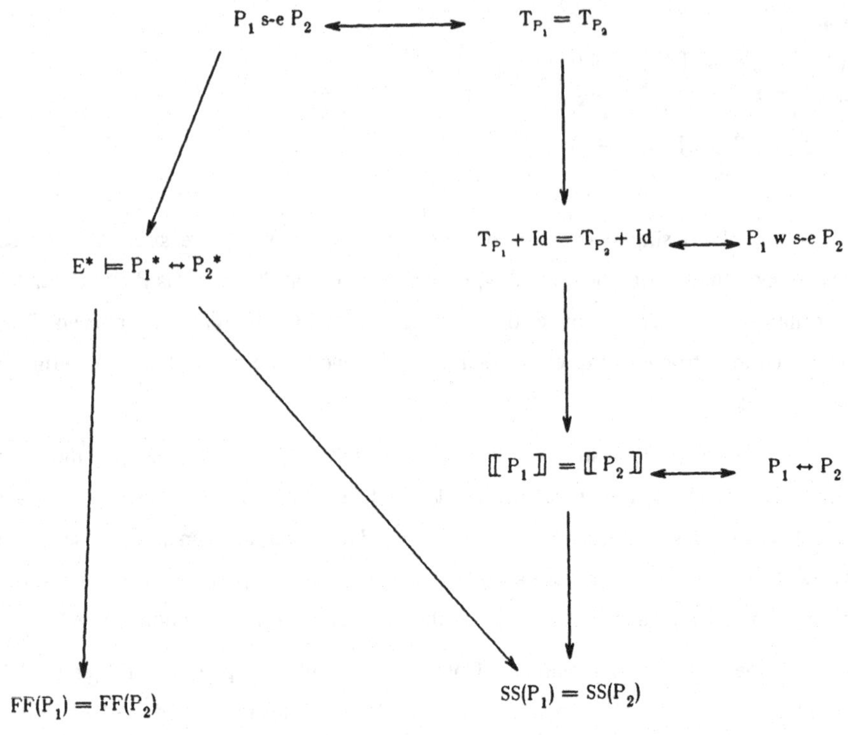

Figure 3. Relationships between Equivalences

In Figure 3, an arrow from $\sim_1$ to $\sim_2$ denotes that $\sim_1$ is stronger than $\sim_2$. The results of this section are summarized by

Theorem 9

Figure 3 exhibits the relative strengths of the formulations of equivalence we have considered.

[Maher 85] has counter-examples to show that Figure 3 has not omitted any arrows. One counter-example of interest comes from the example of Figures 1 and 2. This shows that, although $P^* \rightarrow P$, logical equivalence of completions does not imply that the original programs were logically equivalent. This is seen by noting that, although $E^* \models P_1^* \leftrightarrow P_2^*$ in that example, Even(S(0)) $\in [\![P_2]\!](\{Odd(0)\}) - [\![P_1]\!](\{Odd(0)\})$ i.e. $P_2 \models$ Odd(0) $\rightarrow$ Even(S(0)) but $P_1 \models$ Odd(0) $\rightarrow$ Even(S(0)) does not hold. This example also demonstrates one advantage of Theorem 9. It is a simple matter to prove that $E^* \models P_1^* \leftrightarrow P_2^*$. We can conclude, by Theorem 9, that P_1 and

P_2 have the same success and finite failure sets. This result would otherwise have required an induction argument.

On the other hand, neither is logical equivalence of programs stronger than equivalence of completions: { A ← B } and { A ← B; A ← A } are logically equivalent but their completions are not.

5. *Equivalences of Logic Programs in Different Languages*

Often we wish to regard two programs as equivalent although they may use different predicate or function symbols. Some transformation systems find it useful to introduce auxiliary predicates [Tamaki and Sato 84], while others introduce new data structures, that is, new function symbols [Hansson and Tarnlund 82].

One of the simplest ways to define equivalence on programs written within different languages is to use the standard definitions of equivalence, but to restrict the "input" and "output" to a common sublanguage of the two languages. This method of definition creates some anomalies since any two programs written in disjoint languages would be equivalent. However this method *is* appropriate where the difference in language of two programs arises from different definitions of the same predicates. For example, if P_1 is

Sorted(x, y) ← Slowsorted(x, y)

plus the definition of Slowsorted, and P_2 is

Sorted(x, y) ← Quicksorted(x, y)

plus the definition of Quicksorted, then this method would make the two equivalent if they agreed on Sorted. The derivation of a more efficient, "equivalent" program P_2 from a perhaps naive, but easy-to-prove-correct P_1, is a standard programming methodology. [Hogger 80] has applied this methodology to logic programming.

Let L_1 and L_2 be two languages and let L denote their greatest common sublanguage. We assume that L has the properties required from a language at the beginning of this paper, that is, enough variables, constants etc. We redefine the equivalences used previously to allow for the fact that the programs may use languages larger than L. However these definitions will reduce to those used earlier when $L_1 = L_2 = L$.

Subsumption-Equivalence in L: The canonical forms of P_1 and P_2 are in L and are equal.

Weak Subsumption-Equivalence in L: The weak canonical forms of P_1 and P_2 are in L and are equal.

Equivalence wrt T_P *in L:* $T_{P_1}(X) \cap HB(L) = T_{P_2}(X) \cap HB(L)$ for every $X \subseteq HB(L)$

Equivalence wrt T_P+*Id in L:* $(T_{P_1} + Id)(X) \cap HB(L) = (T_{P_2} + Id)(X) \cap HB(L)$ for every $X \subseteq HB(L)$

Equivalence wrt $[\![P]\!]$ *in L:* $[\![P_1]\!](X) \cap HB(L) = [\![P_2]\!].(X) \cap HB(L)$ for every $X \subseteq HB(L)$

Equality of Success Sets in L: $SS(P_1) \cap HB(L) = SS(P_2) \cap HB(L)$

Equality of Finite Failure Sets in L: $FF(P_1) \cap HB(L) = FF(P_2) \cap HB(L)$

Logical Equivalence in L of Completions: For every logic formula A expressible in L, P_1^*, $E^* \models A$ iff P_2^*, $E^* \models A$

Logical Equivalence in L: For every logic formula A expressible in L, $P_1 \models A$ iff $P_2 \models A$

Many, though not all, of the relationships depicted in Figure 3 still hold for the more general case and Figure 4 reflects this. The proofs are essentially the same as the simpler case and, of course, the counter-examples remain valid.

Theorem 10

Figure 4 exhibits the relative strengths of the formulations of equivalence listed above.

However logical equivalence is now strictly stronger than equivalence wrt $[\![P]\!]$. Strictness comes from considering the programs $P_1 = \phi$ and $P_2 = \{ P(a) \}$ where a is not in L. We have $[\![P_1]\!](X) \cap HB(L) = [\![P_2]\!](X) \cap HB(L) = X$ for every $X \subseteq HB(L)$ and $P_2 \models \exists x\, P(x)$ but $P_1 \models \exists x\, P(x)$ does not hold.

If P_1 and P_2 are (weakly) subsumption-equivalent in L then the corresponding results of the previous section show directly that the programs are equivalent wrt T_P (T_P+Id) in L. The programs ϕ and $\{ A \leftarrow B \}$, where A is in L and B is not, give a counter-example to the converses.

Example

Consider the following transformation which will transform any logic program into a program which is binary and stratifiable. A set of clauses P is *stratifiable* [Sebelik and Stepanek 80] if there is a function $s : \Pi \rightarrow N$ (the natural numbers) and a predicate symbol Q (the *principal* predicate symbol) such that:

(a) $s(Q) = 0$

(b) if the clause $A(\tilde{x}) \leftarrow B_1(\tilde{y}), \ldots, B_n(\tilde{z})$ is in P then $s(B_i) = s(A) + 1$ for i=2,3,...,n

(c) for i=1 either $B_1 = A$ or $s(B_1) = s(A) + 1$.

We assume that for each distinct n-ary predicate symbol A we can choose a distinct n-ary function symbol a (we represent it by the lower case of the predicate symbol) which does not appear in the language L_1 of the original program P. We also need a new binary predicate symbol Q, a binary function symbol . which we write in infix form, and a constant symbol NIL. These are added to L_1 to form L_2. Thus in this case L_1 is the greatest common sublanguage.

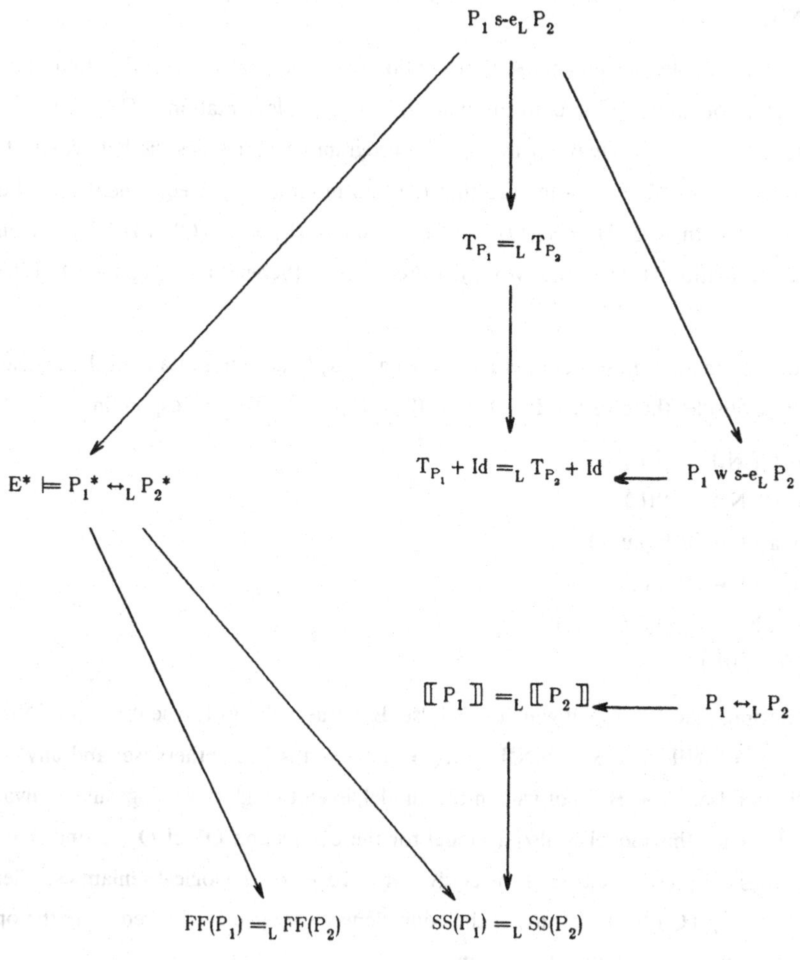

Figure 4. Relationships between Equivalences with Common Language L

The clauses that are in the new program Q are determined as follows:

For every predicate symbol A in P include the clause

(1) $A(\tilde{x}) \leftarrow Q(\text{ NIL}, a(\tilde{x}).\text{NIL})$

For every clause $A(\tilde{s}) \leftarrow B_1(\tilde{t}_1), \ldots, B_n(\tilde{t}_n)$ in P with n>0, include the clause

(2a) $Q(u, a(\tilde{s}).v) \leftarrow Q(\; b_1(\tilde{t}_1). \ldots .b_n(\tilde{t}_n).u, v)$

If n=0 then the new clause is

(2b) $Q(u, a(\tilde{s}).v) \leftarrow Q(u, v)$

Also add the following two clauses

(3) $Q(x.y, \text{NIL}) \leftarrow Q(\text{NIL}, x.y)$

(4) Q(NIL, NIL)

The new program essentially implements SLD-resolution with two goal stacks rather than the one stack which is (conceptually) used in conventional PROLOG implementations. Clearly there is a fair SLD-resolution selection strategy for the original program which mimics the behaviour of the new program for queries in L_1. This implies that the two programs have equivalent operational behaviour in the sense that $SS(P) = SS(Q) \cap HB(L_1)$ and $FF(P) = FF(Q) \cap HB(L_1)$. Consequently the transformation answers the two open problems in [Sebelik and Stepanek 80] in the affirmative.

Although the transformation preserves operational behaviour, Q does not retain all the logical relationships of P. Consider the program P = { A ← B, B; B ← B }. The corresponding Q is

A ← Q(NIL, a.NIL)

B ← Q(NIL, b.NIL)

Q(u, a.v) ← Q(b.b.u, v)

Q(u, b.v) ← Q(b.u, v)

Q(x.y, NIL) ← Q(NIL, x.y)

Q(NIL, NIL)

Consider the Herbrand model of Q in which A is false, B is true, Q(x, y) is true if x = y = NIL or if x = NIL and y = b.NIL or if x = b.NIL and y = NIL and is false otherwise, and any other predicate is always false. A ← B is not true in this model, even though this is logically equivalent to a clause of P. Since this model is also a model for the completion Q* of Q we find that the transformation does not preserve either of the equivalences based on the logical semantics. Clearly $A \in [\![P]\!](\{B\})$ but $A \notin [\![Q]\!](\{B\})$. Thus, of the equivalences we have considered, only the operational ones are preserved by the transformation.

6. Discussion

A different approach to equivalence from that of Sections 4 and 5 for programs with (possibly) different languages could be based on a mapping of one language into the other which preserved arity. We could use this mapping to translate one program into the same language as the other. This would provide us with a form of equivalence in which two programs which simply use different predicate names could be described as equivalent. This approach can easily be combined with the equivalences considered in this paper.

The results presented in this paper have been proved for untyped definite clause logic programs. They can easily be extended to definite clauses typed in the manner of [Mycroft and O'Keefe 84], ut only provided the type system does not insist that, for example, an object of type list(α) must e of the form NIL or x.y. In this case the Theorem on Constants cannot be applied. Similarly, he use of inequalities and negation in the program invalidates the use of this Theorem. The exension of our results to these cases is currently under investigation.

Iowever when a "semantic unification" (i.e. a unification based on an equality theory) is used, the emantics are somewhat similar to those for standard unification [Jaffar et. al. 84, 86], and many f our results continue to hold [Maher 85].

7. *Conclusion*

For applications such as deductive databases employing the Open World Assumption, failed derivations have a lesser importance. In this case, use of the identical equivalences based upon the unctional semantics $[\![P]\!]$ and the logical consequences of P allows the application of two different nd powerful tools to reason about programs. In particular, these equivalences seem ideal for disussing the deductive structure of such deductive databases, independent of any particular state f the database of facts.

Vhen negation-as-failure is used in evaluating queries, the equivalence of completed programs is nore appropriate. This equivalence is only slightly stronger than (high level) operational equivlence and the well-developed formalism of logic is available to facilitate reasoning about programs.

Acknowledgements: I thank Joxan Jaffar and Jean-Louis Lassez for their comments on a previous ersion of this paper, which helped improve the presentation. This research was supported by the Australian Computer Research Board and the Australian Department of Science. This paper was rinted using IBM facilities.

References

K.L. Clark, Negation as Failure, in: Logic and Databases, H. Gallaire, J. Minker (eds.), Plenum Press, 1978.

M.H. Van Emden and R.A. Kowalski, The Semantics of Predicate Logic as a Programming Language, Journal of the ACM 23, 4 (1976), 733-742.

G. Gottlob and A. Leitsch, On the Efficiency of Subsumption Algorithms, Journal of the ACM 32, (1985), 280-295.

M. Fitting, A Kripke-Kleene Semantics for Logic Programs, Journal of Logic Programming 2, 4 1985), 295-312.

A. Hansson and S.A. Tarnlund, Program Transformation by a Function that Maps Simple Lists into D-Lists, Proc. Workshop on Logic Programming, S.A. Tarnlund (ed.), Debrecen, Hungary, July 1980.

C. J. Hogger, Derivation of Logic Programs, Journal of the ACM 28, 2 (1981), 372-392.

J. Jaffar, J-L. Lassez and M.J. Maher, A Theory of Complete Logic Programs With Equality, Proc. Conference on Fifth Generation Computer Systems, Tokyo, November 1984, 175-184.

J. Jaffar, J-L. Lassez and M.J. Maher, A Logic Programming Language Scheme, in: Logic Programming: Relations, Functions and Equations, D. DeGroot, G. Lindstrom (eds.), Prentice Hall, 1986. Also TR84/12 Dept. of Computer Science, University of Melbourne, 1984.

J-L. Lassez and M.J. Maher, The Denotational Semantics of Horn Clauses as a Production System, Proc. AAAI-83, Washington D.C., August 1983, 229-231.

J-L. Lassez and M.J. Maher, Closures and Fairness in the Semantics of Programming Logic, Theoretical Computer Science 29, (1984), 167-184.

J.W. Lloyd, Foundations of Logic Programming, Springer-Verlag, 1984.

M.J. Maher, Semantics of Logic Programs, Ph.D. dissertation, University of Melbourne, 1985.

A. Mycroft and R.A. O'Keefe, A Polymorphic Type System for Prolog, Artificial Intelligence 23, 3 (1984), 295-307.

N.J. Nilsson, Principles of Artificial Intelligence, Springer-Verlag, 1982.

R.A. O'Keefe, Towards an Algebra for Constructing Logic Programs, Proc. Symposium on Logic Programming, Boston, 1985.

G.D. Plotkin, A Note on Inductive Generalization, in: Machine Intelligence 5, B. Meltzer, D. Michie (eds.), Edinburgh University Press, 1969, 153-165.

J. Sebelik and P. Stepanek, Horn Clause Programs Suggested by Recursive Function, Proc. Workshop on Logic Programming, S.A. Tarnlund (ed.), Debrecen, Hungary, July 1980.

J.R. Shoenfield, Mathematical Logic, Addison-Wesley, Reading, Mass., 1967.

H. Tamaki and T. Sato, Unfold/Fold Transformation of Logic Programs, Proc. 2nd. Logic Programming Conference, Sweden, July 1984, 127-138.

S.A. Tarnlund, Horn Clause Computability, BIT 17, 2 (1977), 215-226.

Qualified Answers And Their Application To Transformation

Phil Vasey

Dept. of Computing , Imperial College

LONDON

1. Introduction

Recent papers have investigated the partial evaluation of logic programs for differing purposes. Takeuchi & Furukawa [6] used the technique to specialise interpreters, whereas Venken [8] used partial evaluation for in-line code replacement (macro expansion) for both PROLOG programs and queries to deductive databases. The common link between these two applications is a meta-level interpreter which can terminate for non-empty collections of goals.

In this paper we describe an abstract interpreter for generating qualified answers which can be used both at compile-time and run-time. Its compile-time use corresponds to the technique of partial evaluation, and can be used for program specialisation, macro expansion, query optimisation and transformation. The boundaries dividing these areas are characterised by the manner in which the abstract interpreter is used. Its main application at run-time is in advisory-style expert systems. Such systems would not generate exact advice, but hypothetical advice according to the given evidence.

The abstract interpreter will be exemplified for the task of program transformation. This will be followed by further small examples illustrating the other application areas.

Notation

Constants of the object language such as <u>aspirin</u> will be underlined. Object-level relations, functions and variables are denoted by lower-case identifiers and are distinguished by their context. For example, in the instance of append :-

    append(front , [] , [head <u>second</u> | tail])

<u>second</u> is a constant, the identifiers front, head and tail denote variables, [] represents the empty list and non-empty lists are constructed by the infix functor |.

The logical connectives we use are -> (implication), if (reverse implication), iff (equivalence), and (conjunction), or (disjunction) and not (negation). The quantifiers are V (universal) and E (existential).

What do we mean by qualified answers ?

Given a program P and query Q an exact answer is a substitution Ø for free variables such that the instance Q•Ø follows from the program. A qualified answer imposes hypotheses H such that the theorem [Q•Ø if H•Ø] follows from the program. Consider asking whether the brackets (<u>open</u> and <u>close</u>) of the list [x y <u>close</u> z] are perfectly nested. An exact answer would be of the form :-

    x=<u>open</u>   y=<u>open</u>   z=<u>close</u>

whereas two qualified answers are :-

    y=<u>open</u>   if   bracket-pair(x,z)
    x=<u>open</u>   if   not a-bracket y   and   not a-bracket z

What do we mean by transformation ?

Transformation is the logical reconstruction of one collection of formal statements (the source) in terms of another (the target). Examples of such collections are specifications, programs, data, queries etc.. The purpose of a transformation is to generate target statements which are more amenable to computation. Hence the rules of computation of the target language influence the transformation process. An illustration of transformation [3] is the derivation of sorting algorithms (quick-sort, merge-sort etc.) from formal statements which only specify the concept of sorting.

2. Qualified Answers

In this section an abstract interpreter will be developed for generating qualified answers. Like most specialised interpreters its roots lie in Kowalski's [4] DEMO relation for demonstrating the solvability of queries about programs. The abstract algorithm for DEMO was of the form :-

DEMO(program , query) D1
    if SELECT(query , next-goal , rem-query)
    and REDUCE(program , rem-query , next-goal , Ø , sub-query)
    and JOIN(sub-query , rem-query , new-query)
    and APPLY(Ø , new-query , new-query')
    and DEMO(program , new-query')
DEMO(program , query) D2
    if EMPTY(query)

Clause D2 states that an empty query follows from any program. For non-empty queries (clause D1) the strategy is to reduce a selected goal to some sub-query, join the sub-query to the remaining queries and then demonstrate the result. All of the work concerning resolution and substitutions is hidden inside the REDUCE relation.

Our specialised interpreter, QDEMO, has two additional arguments. First of all the substitution parameter is made explicit, acting as an environment for resolution steps rather than being applied to the queries in a piece-wise manner. The second addition is an argument for representing qualifications. It is such that queries do not necessarily follow from a program alone, but from the amalgamation of program and qualifications.

[program and qualifications•Ø] |- query•Ø

A re-formulation of this sentence shows how QDEMO can generate theorems. The revised specification states that "[qualifications•Ø -> query•Ø]" is a theorem about the "program".

program |- [qualifications•Ø -> query•Ø]

Note that in both instances the substitution Ø is applied to the qualifications as well as the query. Variables will be shared during evaluation so that the qualifications are relevant to the original query. The abstract program for QDEMO is based entirely upon the abstract program for DEMO. Clause D3 is a replica of clause D1 except that substitutions need no longer be applied. Let substitutions be represented by entry ($Ø_{in}$) and exit ($Ø_{out}$) points.

QDEMO(program , query , $< Ø_{in}\ Ø_{out} >$, qualifications) D3
    if SELECT(query , next-goal , rem-query)
    and REDUCE(program , next-goal , $<Ø_{in}\ Ø_{new} >$, sub-query)
    and JOIN(sub-query , rem-query , new-query)
    and QDEMO(program , query , $< Ø_{new}\ Ø_{out} >$, qualifications)
QDEMO(program , query , $< Ø\ Ø >$, query) D4

Continued application of clause D3 will, like clause D1 for DEMO, reduce a query to a collection of sub-goals. However, whereas DEMO only terminates for empty collections (clause D2), QDEMO terminates for any collection (clause D4). That is, the qualifications can be any node (conjunction of goals) in the AND/OR search tree.

3. Example

The unary relation "balanced" holds when the brackets in a list of tokens are prefectly nested. That is, for each opening bracket there is a corresponding closing bracket seperated by a balanced sub-list.

```
balanced []                                                        B1
balanced [ head | tail ]                                           B2
    if  not a-bracket head
    and balanced tail
balanced [ open | tail ]                                           B3
    if  bracket-pair( open , close )
    and append( between , [ close | after ] , tail )
    and balanced between
    and balanced after
```

Clause B1 asserts that the empty list [] is balanced. Clause B2 deals with non-empty lists where the head is not a bracket. Such a list is balanced if the tail is balanced. Finally clause B3 concerns non-empty lists which begin with an opening bracket. In this case the list is balanced if the tail can be partitioned about some closing bracket such that the sub-list between and the remaining list after are themselves both balanced.

Note that the append relation is used for the partitioning in contrast to its normal mode when joining lists together. The order in which candidate closing brackets are selected as the focal point of the partition is fixed by the underlying interpreter. Because of this strict ordering the choice is often wrong. Indeed, for a PROLOG interpreter with left-to-right scheduling of goals and clauses the worst case is :-

[[[......... [ ] ....]]]

and the algorithm is of order 2^N where N is the number of nested bracket pairs. The target of our transformation is a linear algorithm for determining balancedness even in the worst case.

Difference Lists

Before presenting the transformation, first consider the following programs for reversing the elements of a list. The notation m-n represents the difference between lists m and n such that the relation append(l,n,m) holds for some list l.

```
reverse( [] , [] )
reverse( [ head | tail ] , revlist )
    if  reverse( tail , revtail )
    and append( revtail , [ head ] , revlist )

dreverse( [] , m-m )
dreverse( [ head | tail ] , m-n )
    if  dreverse( tail , m - [ head | n ] )
```

The first program is the well-known naive reverse and the latter is an iterative reverse program. There is a direct relationship between the two since the clauses of dreverse follow from the clauses of reverse by exploiting the associativity of append. The specification is :-

```
dreverse( l , m-n )  iff  (E r) [ append(r,n,m)  and  reverse(l,r) ]
```

It is our experience that whenever append occurs in a program, changing the data structure from lists to difference lists is often a fruitful transformation. Since our original problem is one such instance we define a new relation for testing the balancedness of difference lists :-

dbalanced m-n iff (E l) [append(l,n,m) and balanced l] B4

4. Lemmas

Clauses D3 and D4 for QDEMO employ resolution to reduce a query to any sub-query. This gives us the capability of macro expanding programs and rules by evaluating their definiens. However, transformation often involves the technique of "folding" as developed by Burstall & Darlington [1] and applied to logic programs by Tamaki & Sato [7]. We therefore propose a further clause for QDEMO which uses lemmas to transform queries. Suppose that in addition to the source program there are also lemmas of the form [lhs -> rhs]. From such lemmas we have :-

[[program and qualifications•Ø] |- [goals and rhs] • Ø]

if [[program and qualifications•Ø] |- [goals and lhs] • Ø]

which states that any query containg "rhs" can be strengthened to a similar query containing "lhs".

QDEMO(program , query , < $Ø_{in}$ $Ø_{out}$ > , qualifications)
  if APPLY-A-LEMMA(query , < $Ø_{in}$ $Ø_{new}$ > , new-query)
  and QDEMO(program , new-query , < $Ø_{new}$ $Ø_{out}$ > , qualifications)

Two such lemmas are the only-if part of the definition of dbalanced and the associativity of append (or rather its functional counterpart).

dbalanced m-n -> (E l) [append(l,n,m) and balanced l] L1

[append(b,c,b+c) and append(a,b+c,l)] -> [append(a,b,a+b) and append(a+b,c,l)] L2

Before applying a lemma two important checks need to be made concerning quantification.

i) Existential variables in the right-hand side of the lemma can only be matched with distinct variables of the query. If it were otherwise then the meaning attached to such existential variables would be altered.

ii) A variable of the query bound to an existential variable of the lemma must not occur elsewhere in the query.

For the lemma corresponding to the only-if part of the definition of dbalanced (L1) the following two expressions are instances of queries which violate the rules above :-

i) append(b1,a,t) and balanced b2 and ......

ii) append(b,a,t) and balanced b and person b and ......

Figure 1 is the AND/OR search tree for the query "dbalanced m-n" which incorporates the application of lemmas L1 and L2. The tips of the trees represent the qualifications generated, and from which the following three theorems can be deduced :-

dbalanced m-m T1
dbalanced [head | m] - n T2
  if not a-bracket head
  and dbalanced m-n

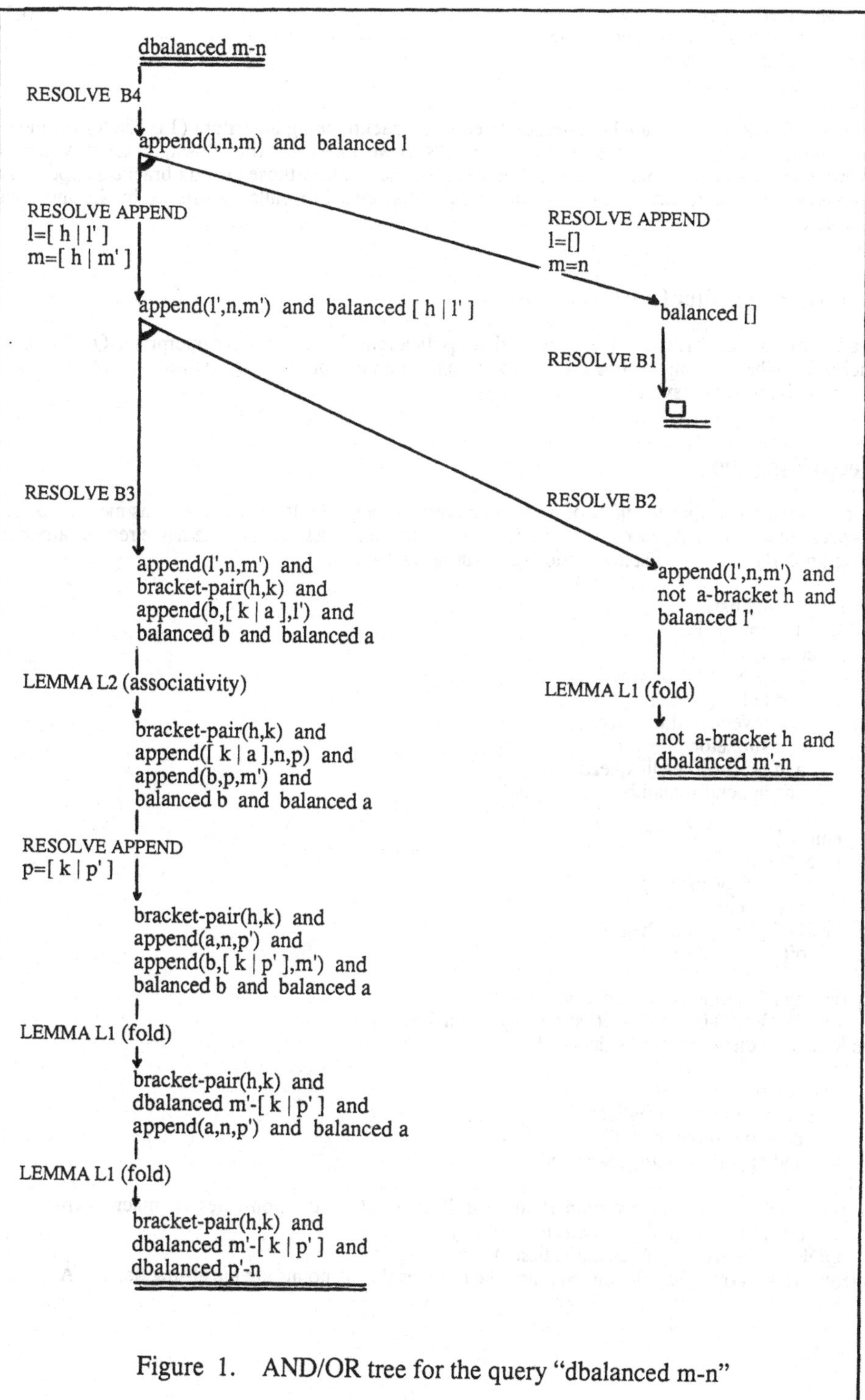

Figure 1. AND/OR tree for the query “dbalanced m-n”

```
dbalanced [ open | m ] - n                                   T3
    if  bracket-pair( open , close )
    and dbalanced m - [ close | p ]
    and dbalanced p-n
```

Theorem T3 forms the crucial clause in a linear, non-backtracking algorithm (T1-T3) for testing the balancedness of lists represented as difference lists. It works by stacking closing brackets whenever opening brackets are encountered, and then popping the stack as those closing brackets appear. The stack is not an explicit structure but the implicit stack of procedure calls constructed by the underlying interpreter.

5. Other Applications

In addition to transformation there are further applications for the abstract interpreter QDEMO. We briefly describe its compile-time use for macro expansion and program specialisation and its run-time use in advisory expert systems.

Macro Expansion

Macro expansion is the technique of in-line code replacement. For logic programs this means replacing a procedure call by that procedure's definiens. For example, consider again the naive reverse algorithm (program NR) and some list abstraction rules (program LA).

```
reverse(list,list)
    if  empty list
reverse(list,revlist)
    if  head-of(list,head)
    and tail-of(list,tail)
    and reverse(tail,revtail)
    and singleton headlist
    and head-of(headlist,head)
    and append(revtail,headlist,revlist)

empty []
singleton list
    if  tail-of(list,tail)
    and empty tail
head-of([ head | tail ],head)
tail-of([ head | tail ],tail)
```

By finding all solutions to the query :-
QDEMO(NR+LA,"reverse(list,revlist)",Ø,qualifications)
the following theorems can be deduced :-

```
reverse([],[])
reverse([ head | tail ],revlist)
    if  reverse(tail,revtail)
    and append(revtail,[head],revlist)
```

In general, for an object program P and a collection of abstraction rules A, macro expansion is characterised by finding all solutions to the query :-
QDEMO(P+A , R , Ø , qualifications) ?
where R ranges over the relations of P and the only resolution points are the abstractions of A.

Program Specialisation

Program specialisation usually concerns the tailoring of meta-level interpreters for specific object-level programs. For example, consider an interpreter for inexact reasoning (program IR) and a specific object program for prescribing drugs (program DP).

```
SHOWALL( query , p1#p2 )
    if   SELECT( query , agoal , rem-query )
    and SHOW( agoal , p1 )
    and SHOWALL( rem-query , p2 )
SHOWALL( query , truth )
    if   EMPTY query

SHOW( agoal , p1+p2 )
    if   REDUCE( agoal , sub-query , p1 )
    and SHOWALL( sub-query , p2 )

prescribe(person,drug)
    if   complains-of(person,sympton)
    and suppresses(drug,sympton)
        with-certainty 80

suppresses(aspirin,pain)
        with-certainty 60

suppresses(lomotil,diarrhoea)
        with-certainty 45
```

By finding all solutions to the query :-
QDEMO(IR+DP , "SHOW(should-take(person,drug) , probability)" , Ø , qualifications)
the following two theorems can be deduced :-

```
SHOW( "should-take(person,aspirin)" , 80 + ( p1 # ( ( 60 + truth ) # truth ) ) )
    if   SHOW( "complains-of(person,pain)" , p1 )

SHOW( "should-take(person,lomotil)" , 80 + ( p1 # ( ( 45 + truth ) # truth ) ) )
    if   SHOW( "complains-of(person,diarrhoea)" , p1 )
```

In general, for a meta-level interpreter IDEMO defined by program I, specialisation of IDEMO for some object-level program P is characterised by finding all solutions to the query :-
QDEMO(I+P , "IDEMO(R)" , Ø , qualifications) ?
where R ranges over the relations of P and the only resolution points are the relations of I.

Brother of "Query the User"

The applications presented so far (transformation, macro expansion and specialisation) have all been compile-time uses of qualified answers. Perhaps one of its most exciting uses, though, is at run-time. "Query the User" as presented by Sergot [5] allowed some relations (defined as interactive) to belong to an external world or data base. As the title suggests this external world is usually considered to be a user, although this need not necessarily be the case. We propose the run-time generation of qualified answers as a brother of "Query the User". Consider once more the program for testing balancedness (B1-B3) together with some rules about brackets (B5-B8).

```
a-bracket open                                  B5
    if   bracket-pair(open,close)
a-bracket close                                 B6
    if   bracket-pair(open,close)
bracket-pair( begin , end )                     B7
bracket-pair( start , stop )                    B8
```

If we posed the question "Are the brackets of list [x y end z] perfectly nested ?" to a PROLOG interpreter and also to the QDEMO relation, some solutions might be :-

PROLOG	x=begin	y=begin	z=end
	x=start	y=begin	z=stop

QDEMO	y=begin	if bracket-pair(x,z)
	y=begin	if not a-bracket x
		and not a-bracket z
	x=begin	if not a-bracket y
		and not a-bracket z

Not only do the qualified answers characterise the solution space more succinctly (simply bracket-pair(x,z) rather than the specific PROLOG substitutions of x and z), they include two additional answers which would not be generated using negation-as-failure [2]. In the context of advisory expert systems these are two very important attributes.

References

[1] Burstall, R. and Darlington, J.
"Transformation for developing recursive programs"
J. ACM, Volume 24, No. 1, pp 44-67, 1975

[2] Clark, K.
"Negation as failure"
Logic and Data Bases (Eds. Gallaire, H. and Minker, J.), Plenum Press, pp 293-322, 1978

[3] Clark, K. and Darlington, J.
"Algorithm classification through synthesis"
Computer Journal, pp 61-65, 1980

[4] Kowalski, R.
"Logic for problem solving"
North Holland Press, pp 227-228, 1979.

[5] Sergot, M.
"A query-the-user facility for logic programming"
Integrated Interactive Computer Systems (Eds. Degano, P. and Sandwell, E.),
North Holland Press, pp 27-41, 1983.

[6] Takeuchi, A. and Furukawa, K.
"Partial evaluation of PROLOG programs and its application to meta programming"
Res. Rep., ICOT Research Centre, Tokyo, Japan, 1985.

[7] Tamaki, H. and Sato, T.
"Unfold/fold transformation of logic programs"
Proceedings of ICLP, pp 127-138, 1984.

[8] Venken, R.
"A PROLOG meta-interpreter for partial evaluation and its application to source-to-source transformation and query optimisation"
Proceedings of ECAI, 1984.

PROCEDURES IN HORN-CLAUSE PROGRAMMING

M.A. Nait Abdallah
Department of Computer Science
University of Western Ontario
London, Ontario, Canada

Abstract

In this paper we show the relevance of the notion of procedure to logic programming. We explain how this feature can be obtained by extending first-order logic programs to programs written in a fragment of second-order logic, and outline a combinatory theory of such logic programs. We show how various algebraic structures and abstract data types can be expressed in this framework. We explain how to construct derivations in this setting.

. **Introduction**

Logic is the archetype language for expressing formalized mathematics, and because programming uses well-defined and formalized languages, logic presents an obvious interest for computer scientists.

Indeed, there are numerous approaches for using logic as a programming language. Quoting just a few, we list here some logics and their computer science approximative counterparts:

λ-calculus	LISP, Scheme LISP Automath Functional programming
Combinatory logic	Backus FP-systems
First-order logic (Horn clauses)	PROLOG

Of course the correspondence between the two columns is far from perfect. As an example, LISP uses dynamic binding whereas lambda-calculus uses static binding; and PROLOG (if we exclude newer versions such as PROLOG II [4]) uses in a peculiar way a restricted subset of first-order logic. The programming version of first-order logic has gained wider popularity over the past ten years, and has become to be known as "Logic programming", even though this may seem an over-generalization. In any case, first-order predicate logic programming has a clear advantage, which is the following : a wide range of information, from numerical computations using natural numbers to predicative information such as handled by data bases and expert systems can be easily expressed. The best-known current implemented version of first-order logic programming is the programming language PROLOG.

Besides its well-known advantages, the PROLOG kind of logic programming has also some shortcomings. As an example, the restriction to *first-order* logic implies that no predicate variables are allowed, even though in some cases, such variables seem to be relevant. Sometimes, such cases have been handled by introducing "meta-level programming"[1], a feature outside of the logic itself. Although the notion of "language and metalanguage amalgamation" bears fuller investigation from a theoretical point of view, quite a few of its applications to logic programming can be obtained more easily in the much simpler higher order logic setting which we outline in this paper, or by using *ions* as in [10]. Some examples will be presented later in the discussion.

Another problem arises when we need a procedure definition/procedure call mechanism. Indeed, two basic programming tools are missing in classical first–order logic programming, namely *types* and *procedures*. Kowalski's [8] interpretation of each definite clause (or set of definite clauses for a given predicate) as being a procedure by itself (the lefthand side being the heading of the procedure, and the righthand side being the body of the procedure) is not always as helpful as one would like it to be: how do we handle and structure 10,000 one–line different procedures that together define an operating system ? This absence of procedures is a major problem if we are to handle very large programs in logic programming.

On the other hand, the notion of procedure constitutes the backbone of *λ–calculus*, which is a logic of order ω. Representing information inside the λ–calculus, however, is not an easy task. Of course, a formalization of mathematics inside λ–calculus is possible [2], but it is not used in practice.

We suggest in this paper a new notion of procedure for Horn–clause programming, inspired from λ–calculus and algebraic semantics. We believe this notion is more in line with other programming languages than Kowalski's. Kowalski [8] regards the empty clause □ as "*a nameless procedure with an empty body*". Outside of logic programming, where the meaning of such a "procedure" is *intuitively* obvious (although it carries no epistemological value), there is no place in programming languages semantics where such a notion of "nameless procedure with an empty body" makes sense. In the same paragraph however, Kowalski also interprets the empty clause as a halt *statement*. This second interpretation is closer to our view; it yields an object similar to a *statement* or an *expression* in other programming languages, where the dichotomy 'statements/expressions' versus 'procedure/function definitions' is clearly recognized. Indeed, looked at from the computed answer substitution point of view, the empty clause works like the *identity* combinator λx.x applied to the environment. In our view, logic programming procedures (as defined in our paper) are the counterpart of the usual notion of procedure (or function) in other languages. *Resolution of goals* resembles *evaluation of expressions* in that the resolution of a given goal is reduced to the resolution of the next goal (similarly the evaluation of a given expression is reduced to the evaluation of the next expression). *Resolution of goals* also resembles *execution of statements* because it has side–effects on substitutions. Thus the *resolution of goals* corresponds to the *execution of imperative instructions* (or *evaluation of expressions* with side–effects), and *substitutions* correspond to *environments*. Indeed, the execution of imperative statements acts upon the current environment in the same way as the resolution of goals acts upon the current computed answer substitution. In the actual framework we are describing in this paper, resolution steps for a goal behave very much like evaluation steps for an arithmetical expression. Notice that when seen in this way, non–determinism in logic programs resembles much non–determinism in other programming languages as provided by explicit *choice* primitives.

In this paper we show how to tie up the first–order predicate logic approach and the λ–calculus approach together by using Church type theory [3] in order to define procedures in logic programming. The natural character of such procedures is made explicit through various examples. We show how to express a large spectrum of algebraic structures and abstract data types by using these procedures. We also explain, through several examples, how to effectively compute with logic programs using such procedures. Our main goal in this construction is to introduce the notions of *hierarchization* and *modularization* into the usual framework of logic programming.

We now discuss a case where procedures and variables are relevant. Let us consider the following logic program:

= { 1. $\leq(0, s(x)) \leftarrow$

2. $\leq(s(x), s(y)) \leftarrow \leq(x, y)$

3. ordered([x]) $\leftarrow$

4. ordered([x y | z]) $\leftarrow \leq(x,y)$ & ordered([y | z]) }

The first two definite clauses define an ordering on elements (here codings of natural numbers), and clauses 3. and 4. use this ordering for defining ordered lists of such elements. Notice that the latter clauses use only "results" from the former clauses. Thus, if we decide to change our ordering on elements, we only need to change clauses 1. and 2., and the rest of the program will remain unchanged if we keep the same name for the ordering on elements. This means that we have here an *implicit* procedure call mechanism: "$\leq$" in clauses 3. and 4. may be seen as a predicate *variable*, whose "value" is *imported* from clauses 1. and 2. A possible alternative for the ordering $\leq$ might be:

{ 1. $\leq(x, y) \leftarrow$ divides(x,y)

2. divides(x,y) $\leftarrow$ ... }

where divides(x,y) means that x divides y; in this ordering x is smaller than y iff x divides y. Furthermore, since the "value" of predicate ordered depends on the "value" of predicate $\leq$, ordered is also itself a predicate variable. Using shorter names for these variables:

$$\varphi = \text{ordering on elements}, \ \chi = \text{ordering on lists}$$

we sugest the following syntax for the definition of the procedure "ordering on elements" used in our logic program:

= $\exists\ \varphi$.

{ 1. $\varphi(0, s(x)) \leftarrow$

2. $\varphi(s(x), s(y)) \leftarrow \varphi(x,y)$ }

This procedure *exports* an ordering predicate (whose formal name here is φ). Similarly, we have the following procedure for the notion of ordered lists:

= $\forall\ \varphi.\ \exists\ \chi$.

{ 1. $\chi([x]) \leftarrow$

2. $\chi([\ x\ y \mid z\ ]) \leftarrow \varphi(x,y)$ & $\chi([\ y \mid z])$ }

Thus, from a logical point of view, procedure ζ is simply a *second order logic* formula. But it has a meaning from the programming point of view as well. This procedure *imports the ordering predicate* φ (ordering on elements), and *exports* the ordering predicate χ (ordering on lists).

As a *general* rule, the *imported* variables will be *universally quantified*, and the *exported* variables will be *existentially quantified*; furthermore the procedure headings will have the form: $\forall$ <list of imported variables> $\exists$ <list of exported variables>. The above second–order formula defining ζ will be read by using the following *substitutional interpretation* of quantification : *For any actual parameter list* (α ; β) *corresponding to the formal parameter list* (φ ; χ), *for any given set of rules for solving* α, *a subset of rules for solving* β *is given by the substituted logic program* $[\alpha/\varphi\ \beta/\chi]Q$, *where* Q *designates the body (matrix) of the formula:*

$\{$ 1. $\chi([x]) \leftarrow$
  2. $\chi([\ x\ y \mid z\ ]) \leftarrow \varphi(x,y)\ \&\ \chi([\ y \mid z])$ $\}$

In procedure calls, the list of exported predicates and the list of imported predicates are separated by semi-colons. Thus if ($\leq$; ordered) is the actual parameter corresponding to (ρ ; χ), a call to procedure ζ with these parameters will be written ζ($\leq$; ordered). Thus a logic program with procedure calls corresponding to the original program will be:

$\{$ 1. $\xi(\ ;\ \leq) \leftarrow$
  2. $\zeta(\ \leq\ ;$ ordered $) \leftarrow$ $\}$

The first call corresponds to the first two clauses of our original program, and the second call corresponds to the last two clauses of the original program. The first call is executed by substituting the body of ξ (with actual parameter substituted to formal parameter) to the call itself. And similarly for the second call. These two calls are not sufficient for defining the meaning of the logic program P they constitute. We need in addition the two equations defining procedures ξ and ζ.

Notice that procedure ζ may be called more than once in the same program with ***different*** orderings on elements, thus yielding ***different*** orderings on lists. For example we may take the ordering on elements given by:

$\kappa = \exists\ \varphi.$
$\{$ 1. $\varphi(x,\ y) \leftarrow$ divides(x,y)
  2. divides(x,y) $\leftarrow$ ... $\}$

The following logic program uses both orderings and defines two kinds of ordered lists:

$\{$ 1. $\xi(\ ;\ \leq) \leftarrow$
  2. $\zeta(\ \leq\ ;$ ordered $) \leftarrow$
  3. $\kappa(\ ;\ <^*) \leftarrow$
  4. $\zeta(\ <^*\ ;$ div–ordered$) \leftarrow$ $\}$

The above ordering algorithm is by no means an exception. Using the procedural notation sketched so far, we can express for example the following abstract data types.

natural–number = $\exists$ is–number 0 is–zero s sum eq .
{ is–number(0) ←
  is–number(s(x)) ← is–number(x)
  is–number(z) ← sum(x,y,z)
  is–zero(0) ←
  sum(0,y,y) ← is–number(y)
  sum(s(x),y,s(z)) ← sum(x,y,z)
  eq(x,0) ← is–zero(x)
  eq(s(x),s(y)) ← eq(x,y)
}

array = $\forall$ is–value is–index eq . $\exists$ is–array e retrieve store.
{ is–array(e) ←

```
is-array(store(X,i,x)) ← is-array(X) & is-index(i) & is-value(x)
retrieve(store(X,i,x),i,x) ← is-array(X) & is-index(i) &
                                 is-value(x)
retrieve(store(X,j,x),i,z) ← diff(i,j) & retrieve(X,i,z)
diff(i,j) ← ~(eq(i,j))
}
```

Further examples on how to express various algebraic structures using logic programming procedures are given later on in the Appendix to this paper.

I. Computing with logic programming procedures

A clue on how the above procedures can be used for computing is given by recursive program schemes. We first consider the recursive definition of factorial:

f(n) <= if n = 0 then 1 else n*f(n−1) fi

and compute f(2). We then obtain the following derivation, where $\rightarrow^r$ denotes a rewriting step, and $\rightarrow^s$ denotes a simplification step. A rewriting step consists in replacing a function name by its definition, and a simplification step consists in computing values of the base functions used in the definition. Thus:

f(2) $\rightarrow^r$ if 2 = 0 then 1 else 2*f(2−1) $\rightarrow^s$
$\rightarrow^s$ 2*f(1) $\rightarrow^r$ 2*(if 1 = 0 then 1 else 1*f(1−1) $\rightarrow^s$
$\rightarrow^s$ 2*1*f(0)
$\rightarrow^r$ 2*1*(if 0 = 0 then 1 else 1*f(0−1)) $\rightarrow^s$
$\rightarrow^s$ 2*1*1 $\rightarrow^s$ 2

Thus the two basic steps in recursive program schemes are ***simplification*** and ***rewriting***.

Similarly, let us consider now a goal g, and a logic program Q possibly containing procedure calls. The problem is to solve g in Q. The analogy with the above example i.e., between (Q,g) and f(2) is given by the correspondance:

$$f \longleftrightarrow Q, \quad 2 \longleftrightarrow g$$

The terms upon which we must now perform derivations are couples of the form (Q,g), where g is a goal and Q is a logic program. Such terms (Q,g) we call ***ions***. An ***empty ion*** is an ion whose goal part is empty i.e., such an ion has the form (Q,) for some logic program Q. Each derivation step starting from an ion will be of one of the two kinds: either a simplification step or a rewriting step.

A ***simplification step*** (or ***resolution step***) is defined by: (Q,g) → (Q,g') if and only if g → g' is a derivation step in the usual sense. Namely, there exists a triple $\langle\lambda,r,\vartheta\rangle$ where λ is an occurrence of an atom in g, r is a rule variant A ← B_1 & ... & B_m from Q with no variable in common with g, and ϑ is a most general unifier for A and the atom of occurrence λ in g. Goal g' is then obtained from goal g by simply replacing the atom of occurrence λ in g by $B_1\vartheta$ & ... & $B_m\vartheta$, and applying substitution ϑ to all the other atoms of g.

A *rewriting step* may be of several kinds. The first kind is the *procedure call rule* step and is defined by : (Q,g) → (Q',g) iff Q → Q' is a rewriting of Q into Q' obtained by replacing some procedure call in Q by the body of the procedure where the formal parameters have been substituted by the actual parameters. Indeed, the procedure call has to be syntactically correct.

These two kinds of derivation steps may be reformulated as follows:

SLD rule :

g → g' is an SLD derivation step using a clause from logic program P

$$\frac{g \rightarrow g' \text{ is an SLD derivation step using a clause from logic program P}}{(P,g) \rightarrow (P,g').}$$

Procedure call rule:

$$\frac{\xi(\vec{\alpha}\ ;\ \vec{\varepsilon}) \rightarrow^{\Sigma} [\vec{\alpha}/\vec{\varphi},\ \vec{\varepsilon}/\vec{\chi}]Q}{(P \cup \{\xi(\vec{\alpha}\ ;\ \vec{\varepsilon}) \leftarrow\},\ g) \rightarrow (P \cup [\vec{\alpha}/\vec{\varphi},\ \vec{\varepsilon}/\vec{\chi}]Q,\ g)}$$

(i.e.,if $\xi = \forall \vec{\varphi}.\ \exists \vec{\chi}.$ Q is a procedure declaration, and $\xi(\vec{\alpha}\ ;\ \vec{\varepsilon})$ is a correct call to ξ, then we may apply the Algol 60 copy rule.)

Another kind of rewriting step will be discussed later on in this paper.
A *successful derivation* is one which ends with an empty ion.

Example :
Consider the following logic procedures definitions:

$\xi_1 = \forall\ \rho.\ \exists$ rel.
{ 1. rel([x]) ←
2. rel([x y | z]) ← ρ(x,y) & rel([y | z]) }

$\xi_2 = \exists\ \pi.$
{ 1. $\pi(\alpha,\ \beta)$ ←
2. $\pi(\beta,\ \gamma)$ ← }

together with the logic program P defined by:

P = { 1. ξ_1(≤ ; ordered) ←
2. ξ_2(; ≤) ← }

and consider the query ← (P, ordered([$\alpha\ \beta\ \gamma$]). Then we obtain the following derivation:

1. ← (P, ordered([$\alpha\ \beta\ \gamma$]))
2. ← (P_1, ordered([$\alpha\ \beta\ \gamma$])) — 1, call rule for predicate ordered
3. ← (P_1, ≤(α, β) & ordered([$\beta\ \gamma$])) — 2,P_1(1.2) MT
4. ← (P_2, ≤(α, β) & ordered([$\beta\ \gamma$])) — 3,call rule

. ← (P_2, ordered([β γ])) 4,P_2(2.1) MT

. ← (P_2, $\leq(\beta, \gamma)$ & ordered([γ])) 5,P_2(1.2) MT

. ← (P_2, ordered([γ])) 6,P_2(2.2) MT

. ← (P_2,) 7,P_2(1.1) MT

where the values of logic programs P_i are:

P_1 =

{ 1.1 ordered([x]) ←
1.2. ordered([x y | z]) ← $\leq$(x,y) & ordered([y | z]) }
2. ξ_2(; $\leq$) ← }

P_1 =

{ 1.1 ordered([x]) ←
1.2. ordered([x y | z]) ← $\leq$(x,y) & ordered([y | z])
2.1. $\leq(\alpha, \beta)$ ←
2.2. $\leq(\beta, \gamma)$ ← }

Thus the derivation is a successful derivation.

II. Algebraic structures as conditional logic procedures with parameters

In this section we show how some higher-order operations on data structures (in the functional programming sense), and some algebraic structure definitions require a more sophisticated kind of logic procedures. We examine the additional rewriting rules these new procedures require, and give two examples. The first example is a rather classical one, as it simply expresses the APL-like operation of reducing an array by some arithmetical operation. The second example is more complicated, as it gives an example of how to solve a higher-order question (procedural question) in this setting.

Definition :

A conditional logic procedure is a logic procedure of the form:

$$\xi = \forall \vec{\varphi}.\ \exists \vec{\chi}.\ \{\ B_1\ \&\ \ldots\ \&\ B_m \rightarrow Q\ \}$$

where Q is a logic program and the B_i's are either procedure calls or atoms.

Some examples of conditional procedures are as follows.

II.1 HIGHER ORDER PROCEDURES AS CONDITIONAL PROCEDURES :

Using also the same notation as in the previous section, we can also express more "computational" procedures. The following example shows how to reduce an array using some APL-like operation (examples are : sum of an array, product of the elements of an array, etc.)

reduction-of-array = ∀ is-index is-value op is-array e . ∃ Red .
{

```
array(is-value, is-index, eq; is-array, e, retr, sto) →
        {
          Red(sto(e,i,a),a) ← is-index(i) & is-value(a)
          Red(sto(X,i,a),y) ← Red(X,x) & op(a,x,y) &
                        is-array(X) & is-value(a) & is-index(i)
        }
}
```

Other examples could be given as well.

III.2 ALGEBRAIC STRUCTURES AS CONDITIONAL PROCEDURES :

transitive closure T of a binary relation (2-relation) R on a set A:

This procedure imports two predicates A and R, and exports one predicate T, so it is intuitively of type (A,R) → T.

```
trans-clos-2-rel = ∀ A R . ∃ T .
        { 2-relation(;R, A, A) →
                { T(a,b) ← R(a,b) & A(a) & A(b)
                  T(a,c) ← T(a,b) & T(b,c)
                }
        }
```

equivalence relation E generated by a binary relation R on a set A:

This procedure imports two predicates A and R, and exports one predicate E, so it is intuitively of type (A,R) → E. It defines the smallest equivalence relation containing a given binary relation.

```
equiv-rel = ∀ A R . ∃ E .
        { 2-relation(;R,A,A) →
                { trans-clos-2-rel(A,R ; E) ←
                  E(a,b) ← R(a,b)
                  E(a,c) ← E(a,b) & E(b,c)
                  E(a,a) ← A(a)
                  E(a,b) ← E(b,a)
                }
        }
```

Further examples are given in the Appendix.

III.3 COMPUTING WITH CONDITIONAL PROCEDURES:

Conditional procedures require, in order to be used in a derivation, an additional derivation rule, which is as follows:

Modus ponens rule :

$(P \cup \{B_1 \leftarrow; \ldots ; B_m \leftarrow\} \cup \{ B_1 \ \& \ \ldots \ \& \ B_m \rightarrow P'\} \ , g) \rightarrow$

$\rightarrow (P \cup \{B_1 \leftarrow; \ldots ; B_m \leftarrow\} \cup P' , g)$.

xample :

Let $Q = Q_0$ be the following logic program :

. index(α) ←
. index(β) ←
. index(γ) ←
. *natural-number*(; v, 0, is-zero, s, sum, eq) ←
. mult(s(0),x,x) ← v(x)
. mult(s(x),y,z) ← mult(x,y,u) & sum(y,u,z)
. *array*(v,index,eq ; is-arr,e,ρ,σ) ←
. *reduction-of-array*(index,v,mult,is-arr,e ; prod) ←

The procedure definitions we use in Q are those given so far in the aper.

Let ← g be the following (first-order) goal clause:

. ← prod($\sigma(\sigma(\sigma(e,\alpha,s(0)),\beta,s^2(0)),\gamma,s^3(0))$, x)

sking for the product of the elements of a 3-element array (1,2,3) indexed by he set of keys { α, β, γ }.

Then solving goal g in Q_0 yields a successful derivation, with $x = s^6(0)$ as the nswer substitution. The details of this derivation are given in Part 3 of the Appendix to his paper.

V. Conclusion

The above discussion has raised the issue of leaving *first-order* predicate logic, nd programming in *higher-order* logic. The occurrence of predicate variables in the tudy of search strategies is not an epiphenomenon. In fact, a significant part of (pure) irst-order logic is not much used by mathematicians, as they do not take advantage of a ossibly unbounded number of quantifiers in their statements. They rather define *tructures* which are objects of higher-order type, and go into *higher-order logic.* nalogously, in programming, although the number of formal parameters a procedure may ave is only bounded by implementation considerations, this is a quite uninteresting fact *er se.* The real power of a programming language comes from its procedures and its data tructures (again *higher-order* objects).

Higher-order logic programs are also interesting on their own, when higher-order gic is not simply used as here as a mechanism for providing procedures for first-order gic programs. For example, using such a program allows us to solve the problem of the xistence of the inverse image of an element under a function f. More precisely let I be he "inverse image" operator. Then we want to show:

$$\exists I \; \forall f \; \forall y \; \forall x \quad f(x) = y \;\Rightarrow\; f(I(y,f)) = y$$

solution is given by the following higher-order logic program adapted from [7] :

1. $=(f(x),y) \leftarrow$
2. $\in(C(y),y) \leftarrow \in(x,y)$
3. $\in(x,\sigma(P)) \leftarrow P(x)$
4. $P(x) \leftarrow \in(x,\sigma(P))$

together with the goal clause:

5. $\leftarrow =(f(I(y,f)),y)$

which both yield the derivation:

6. $\leftarrow \in(I(y,f),\ \sigma(\lambda u.=(f(u),y)))$	$P = \lambda u.=(f(u),y)$ 4,5 MT
7. $\leftarrow \in(z,\ \sigma(\lambda u.=(f(u),y)))$	2,6; $I = \lambda yf.C(\sigma(\lambda u.=(f(u),y)))$
8. $\leftarrow [\lambda u.=(f(u),y)](z)$	4,7
9. $\leftarrow =(f(z),y)$	8, β–reduction
10. $\Box$	1,9 MT $z = x$

Whence the answer substitution $I = \lambda yf.C(\sigma(\lambda u.=(f(u),y)))$.

Many features of first–order logic programming *a la* PROLOG easily extend to higher–order programming in typed λ–calculus. The main problem, however, with this kind of logic programming inside the full typed λ–calculus [3] has to do with *unification* and *reduction*. Huet [6] and Lucchesi [9] have shown that the existence of unifiers for third order languages is undecidable. Goldfarb [5] has shown that the unification problem for second order languages is also undecidable. Also, β–equality (or βη–equality) has to be dealt with in the unification algorithm, because typed λ–terms are usually not in normal form. This fact has led us to adopt a *bottom–up* approach to the extension problem of logic programming, starting from a "small" superset of first–order logic programming, rather than a *top–down* approach starting from the full typed λ–calculus.

To summarize and conclude the above discussion, it seems that current Prolog should be considered as the assembly language of a genuine logic programming system yet to be constructed. Indeed it lacks, as we have seen, what constitutes the main core of mathematics and most high–level programming languages: it lacks structures. Our notion of procedure is intended to contribute to fill in this gap. The main intuition behind this notion is that any predicate logic formula of the form $\forall$ x $\exists$ y. P can be seen as a program with two ports, with x as the input port, y as the output port, and P as the body of the program.

Acknowledgements: The author is indebted to E.A. Ashcroft, M.H. van Emden and I. Guessarian for many helpful comments.

Bibliography

[1]. Bowen K.A. and Kowalski R.A. : Amalgamating language and metalanguage, in Logic Programming, K.L. Clark and T.–S. Taernlund ed, Academic Press (1982), pp 153–172

[2]. de Bruijn N.G. : A survey of the project Automath, in To H.B. Curry Essays on Combinatory Logic, Lambda–Calculus and Formalism, J.R. Hindley and J.P. Seldin eds, Academic Press (1980), pp.597–607

[3]. Church A. : A formulation of the simple theory of types, JSL Vol 5 (1940), pp 56–68

[4]. Colmerauer A. : Prolog and infinite trees, in Logic Programming, K.L. Clark and S.–A. Taernlund ed, Academic Press (1982),pp. 153–172

[5]. Goldfarb W.G. : The undecidability of the second–order unification problem, TCS 13 (1981), pp. 225–230

[6]. Huet G. : The undecidability of unification in third order logic, Information and Control 22, 3 (1973) pp. 257–267

[7]. Jensen D.C. and Pietrzykowski T.: Mechanizing ω–order type theory through unification, TCS 3, (1976), pp. 123–171

[8]. Kowalski R.A. : Predicate logic as programming language, IFIP 1974, North Holland (1974), pp. 569–574

[9]. Lucchesi C.L. : The undecidability of the unification problem for third order languages, report CSRR–2059, Dep. of Appl. Anal. and CS, University of Waterloo (1972)

[10] Nait Abdallah M.–A. : Ions and local definitions in logic programming, in Theoretical Aspects of Computer Science, B. Monien and G. Vidal–Naquet eds, Springer LNCS 210, (1986), pp. 60–72

APPENDIX

This appendix is divided in three parts. The first part lists some examples of algebraic structures defined as logic procedures. The second part of the appendix gives an example of conditional procedure. The last part gives an example of a derivation using conditional procedures.

1. Algebraic structures as logic procedures with parameters

In this section we show how various algebraic structures definitions can be easily expressed as procedures in logic programming. Similar examples could be given for abstract data types.

ALGEBRAIC STRUCTURES AS TYPE THEORY PROCEDURES :

2–relation = ∀ R. ∃ A B.
{ is–set(A) ←
is–set(B) ←
A(x) ← R(x,y)
B(y) ← R(x,y) }

3–relation = ∀ R.∃ X_1 X_2 B.
{ is–set(X_1) ←
is–set(X_2) ←
is–set(B) ←
$X_1(x_1)$ ← R(x_1, x_2, y)
$X_2(x_2)$ ← R(x_1, x_2, y)
B(y) ← R(x_1, x_2, y) }

1-function = ∀ f. ∃ A B.
{ *2-relation*(f; A, B) ←
eq(x,y) ← f(a,x) & f(a,y)
eq(x,x) ← }

2-function = ∀ F.∃ X_1 X_2 B.
{ *3-relation*(F ;X_1, X_2, B) ←
eq(u,v) ← F(x_1, x_2, u) & F(x_1, x_2, v)
eq(x,x) ← }

semigroup = ∃ G F.
{ *2-function*(F ;G, G, G) ←
G(z) ← F(x, y, z) & G(x) & G(y)
eq(u,v) ← F(x, y, r) & F(r, z, u) & F(y, z, s) & F(x, s, v)}

monoid = ∃ G F e.
{ *semi-group*(;G, F) ←
G(e) ←
F(x, e, x) ←
F(e, x, x) ← }

II. Algebraic structures as conditional procedures

semi-group homomorphism:

hom-sg = ∀ G F G' F'. ∃ f.
{ *semi-group*(;G, F) & *semi-group*(;G', F') →
{*1-function*(f ;G, G') ←
eq(u,v) ← F(a, b, x) & f(x,a) & f(a,a') & f(b,b') & F'(a', b, v)}
}

III. Examples of a derivation using conditional logic procedures with parameters

Let Q = Q_0 be the following logic program :

1. index(α) ←
2. index(β) ←
3. index(γ) ←
4. *natural-number*(; v, 0, is-zero, s, sum, eq) ←
5. mult(s(0),x,x) ← v(x)
6. mult(s(x),y,z) ← mult(x,y,u) & sum(y,u,z)
7. *array*(v,index,eq ; is-arr,e,ρ,σ) ←
8. *reduction-of-array*(index,v,mult,is-arr,e ; prod) ←

The procedure definitions we use in Q are those given so far in the paper.

Let $\leftarrow$ g be the following (first-order) goal clause:

0. $\leftarrow \mathrm{prod}(\sigma(\sigma(\sigma(e,\alpha,s(0)),\beta,s^2(0)),\gamma,s^3(0)),\ x)$

asking for the product of the elements of a 3-element array (1,2,3) indexed by the set of keys $\{\ \alpha,\ \beta,\ \gamma\ \}$.

Then solving goal g in Q_0 leads to the following sequence of derivation steps starting from ion $(Q_0,\ g)$. (Clearly, other sequences are possible). Definite clauses used in resolution steps (i.e. SLD-steps) are referred to by using their number in the corresponding logic program Q_i. The items selected for simplification are underlined.

1. $\leftarrow (Q_0,\ \underline{\mathrm{prod}}(\sigma(\sigma(\sigma(e,\alpha,s(0)),\ \beta,\ s^2(0)),\ \gamma,\ s^3(0)),\ x))$
2. $\leftarrow (Q_1,\ \underline{\mathrm{prod}(\sigma(\sigma(\sigma(e,\alpha,s(0)),\beta,s^2(0)),\gamma,s^3(0)),x)})$
   procedure call rule for predicate *prod*, $Q_0(8)$
3. $\leftarrow (Q_2,\ \underline{\mathrm{prod}(\sigma(\sigma(\sigma(e,\alpha,s(0)),\beta,s^2(0)),\gamma,s^3(0)),x)})$ 2, Modus Ponens, $Q_2(7)$, $Q_0(8)$
4. $\leftarrow (Q_2,\ \mathrm{prod}(\sigma(\sigma(e,\alpha,s(0)),\beta,s^2(0)),x') \ \&\ \mathrm{mult}(s^3(0),x',x)\ \&$
   $\&\ \mathrm{is\text{-}arr}(\sigma(\sigma(e,\alpha,s(0)),\beta,s^2(0))\ \&\ v(s^3(0))\ \&\ \underline{\mathrm{index}(\gamma)}$ 3,Q_2(8.2) MT
5. $\leftarrow (Q_2,\ \mathrm{prod}(\sigma(\sigma(e,\alpha,s(0)),\beta,s^2(0)),x') \ \&\ \mathrm{mult}(s^3(0),x',x)\ \&$
   $\underline{\mathrm{is\text{-}arr}}(\sigma(\sigma(e,\alpha,s(0)),\beta,s^2(0))\ \&\ v(s^3(0))$ 4,Q_2(3) MT
6. $\leftarrow (Q_3,\ \mathrm{prod}(\sigma(\sigma(e,\alpha,s(0)),\beta,s^2(0)),x') \ \&\ \mathrm{mult}(s^3(0),x',x)\ \&$
   $\underline{\mathrm{is\text{-}arr}(\sigma(\sigma(e,\alpha,s(0)),\beta,s^2(0))}\ \&\ v(s^3(0))$
   5, procedure call rule for predicate $\underline{\mathrm{is\text{-}arr}}$
7. $\leftarrow (Q_3,\ \mathrm{prod}(\sigma(\sigma(e,\alpha,s(0)),\beta,s^2(0)),x') \ \&\ \mathrm{mult}(s^3(0),x',x)\ \&\ \underline{\mathrm{is\text{-}arr}(\sigma(e,\alpha,s(0))}\ \&$
   $\mathrm{index}(\beta)\ \&\ v(s^2(0))\ \&\ v(s^3(0))$ 6,Q_3(7.2) MT
8. $\leftarrow (Q_3,\ \mathrm{prod}(\sigma(\sigma(e,\alpha,s(0)),\beta,s^2(0)),x') \ \&\ \mathrm{mult}(s^3(0),x',x)\ \&\ \underline{\mathrm{is\text{-}arr}(e)}\ \&\ \mathrm{index}(\alpha)\ \&$
   $v(s(0))\ \&\ \mathrm{index}(\beta)\ \&\ v(s^2(0))\ \&\ v(s^3(0))$ 7,Q_3(7.2) MT
9. $\leftarrow (Q_3,\ \mathrm{prod}(\sigma(\sigma(e,\alpha,s(0)),\beta,s^2(0)),x') \ \&\ \mathrm{mult}(s^3(0),x',x)\ \&\ \underline{\mathrm{index}(\alpha)}\ \&\ v(s(0))\ \&$
   $\mathrm{index}(\beta)\ \&\ v(s^2(0))\ \&\ v(s^3(0))$ 8,Q_3(7.1) MT
10. $\leftarrow (Q_3,\ \mathrm{prod}(\sigma(\sigma(e,\alpha,s(0)),\beta,s^2(0)),x') \ \&\ \mathrm{mult}(s^3(0),x',x)\ \&\ v(s(0))\ \&\ \underline{\mathrm{index}(\beta)}\ \&$
    $v(s^2(0))\ \&\ v(s^3(0))$ 9,Q_3(1) MT
11. $\leftarrow (Q_3,\ \mathrm{prod}(\sigma(\sigma(e,\alpha,s(0)),\beta,s^2(0)),x') \ \&\ \mathrm{mult}(s^3(0),x',x)\ \&\ \underline{v}(s(0))\ \&\ \underline{v}(s^2(0))\ \&$
    $\underline{v}(s^3(0))$ 10,Q_3(2) MT
12. $\leftarrow (Q_4,\ \mathrm{prod}(\sigma(\sigma(e,\alpha,s(0)),\beta,s^2(0)),x') \ \&\ \mathrm{mult}(s^3(0),x',x)\ \&\ \underline{v(s(0))}\ \&\ v(s^2(0))\ \&$
    $v(s^3(0))$
    11, procedure call rule for predicate v, $Q_3(4)$
13. $\leftarrow (Q_4,\ \mathrm{prod}(\sigma(\sigma(e,\alpha,s(0)),\beta,s^2(0)),x') \ \&\ \mathrm{mult}(s^3(0),x',x)\ \&\ \underline{v(0)}\ \&\ v(s^2(0))\ \&$
    $\&\ v(s^3(0))$ 12, Q_4(4.2) MT
14. $\leftarrow (Q_4,\ \mathrm{prod}(\sigma(\sigma(e,\alpha,s(0)),\beta,s^2(0)),x') \ \&\ \mathrm{mult}(s^3(0),x',x)\ \&\ \underline{v(s^2(0))}\ \&\ v(s^3(0))$
    13, Q_4(4.1) MT
15. $\leftarrow (Q_4,\ \mathrm{prod}(\sigma(\sigma(e,\alpha,s(0)),\beta,s^2(0)),x') \ \&\ \mathrm{mult}(s^3(0),x',x)\ \&\ \underline{v(s(0))}\ \&\ v(s^3(0))$
    14, Q_4(4.2) MT
16. etc...
17. $\leftarrow (Q_4,\ \underline{\mathrm{prod}(\sigma(\sigma(e,\alpha,s(0)),\beta,s^2(0)),x')}\ \&\ \mathrm{mult}(s^3(0),x',x))$
18. $\leftarrow (Q_4,\ \mathrm{prod}(\sigma(e,\alpha,s(0)),x'')\ \&\ \mathrm{mult}(s^2(0),x'',x')\ \&\ \mathrm{mult}(s^3(0),x',x))$

.....

19. ← (Q_4, mult($s^2(0)$,x",x') & mult($s^8(0)$,x',x)) x" = s(0)

...

20. ← (Q_4,) x = $s^6(0)$

where the logic programs Q_i used are as follows:

```
Q0 =
    {
1. index(α) ←
2. index(β) ←
3. index(γ) ←
4. natural-number( ; v, 0, is-zero, s, sum, eq) ←
5. mult(s(0),x,x) ← v(x)
6. mult(s(x),y,z) ← mult(x,y,u) & sum(y,u,z)
7. array(v,index,eq ; is-arr,e,ρ,σ) ←
8. reduction-of-array(index,v,mult,is-arr,e ; prod) ←
    }

Q1 =
    {
1. index(α) ←
2. index(β) ←
3. index(γ) ←
4. natural-number( ; v, 0, is-zero, s, sum, eq) ←
5. mult(s(0),x,x) ← v(x)
6. mult(s(x),y,z) ← mult(x,y,u) & sum(y,u,z)
7. array(v, index, eq ; is-arr,e,ρ,σ) ←
8. array(v, index, eq ; is-arr, e, retr, sto) →
                              {
                                prod(sto(e,i,a),a) ← index(i) & v(a)
                                prod(sto(X,i,a),y) ← prod(X,x) & mult(a,x,y) &
                                          is-arr(X) & v(a) & index(i)
                              }
    }

Q2 =
    {
1. index(α) ←
2. index(β) ←
3. index(γ) ←
4. natural-number( ; v, 0, is-zero, s, sum, eq) ←
5. mult(s(0),x,x) ← v(x)
6. mult(s(x),y,z) ← mult(x,y,u) & sum(y,u,z)
7. array(v,index,eq  ; is-arr,e,ρ,σ) ←
8.1  prod(σ(e,j,a),a) ← index(j) & v(a)
```

```
8.2 prod(σ(X,j,a),y) ← prod(X,x) & mult(x,a,y) & is−arr(X) & v(a) & index(j)
    }

Q3 =
    {
1. index(α) ←
2. index(β) ←
3. index(γ) ←
4. natural−number( ; v, 0, is−zero, s, sum, eq) ←
5. mult(s(0),x,x) ← v(x)
6. mult(s(x),y,z) ← mult(x,y,u) & sum(y,u,z)
7.1 is−arr(e) ←
7.2 is−arr(σ(X,j,x)) ← is−arr(X) & index(j) & v(x)
7.3 ρ(σ(X,j,x),j,x) ← is−arr(X) & index(j) & v(x)
7.4 ρ(σ(X,j,x),k,z) ← diff(k,j) & ρ(X,k,z)
7.5 diff(k,j) ← ~(eq(k,j))
8.1 prod(σ(e,j,a),a) ← index(j) & v(a)
8.2 prod(σ(X,j,a),y) ← prod(X,x) & mult(x,a,y) & is−arr(X) & v(a) & index(j)
    }

Q4 =
    {
1. index(α) ←
2. index(β) ←
3. index(γ) ←
4.1 v(0) ←
4.2 v(s(x)) ← v(x)
4.3 v(z) ← sum(x,y,z)
4.4 is−zero(0) ←
4.5 sum(0,y,y) ← v(y)
4.6 sum(s(x),y,s(z)) ← sum(x,y,z)
4.7 eq(x,0) ← is−zero(x)
4.8 eq(s(x),s(y)) ← eq(x,y)
5. mult(s(0),x,x) ← v(x)
6. mult(s(x),y,z) ← mult(x,y,u) & sum(y,u,z)
7.1 is−arr(e) ←
7.2 is−arr(σ(X,j,x)) ← is−arr(X) & index(j) & v(x)
7.3 ρ(σ(X,j,x),j,x) ← is−arr(X) & index(j) & v(x)
7.4 ρ(σ(X,j,x),k,z) ← diff(k,j) & ρ(X,k,z)
7.5 diff(k,j) ← ~(eq(k,j))
8.1 prod(σ(e,j,a),a) ← index(j) & v(a)
8.2 prod(σ(X,j,a),y) ← prod(X,x) & mult(x,a,y) & is−arr(X) & v(a) & index(j)
    }
```

HIGHER-ORDER LOGIC PROGRAMMING

Dale A. Miller and Gopalan Nadathur
Computer and Information Science
University of Pennsylvania
Philadelphia PA 19104–6389 USA

Abstract: In this paper we consider the problem of extending Prolog to include predicate and function variables and typed λ-terms. For this purpose, we use a higher-order logic to describe a generalization to first-order Horn clauses. We show that this extension possesses certain desirable computational properties. Specifically, we show that the familiar operational and least fixpoint semantics can be given to these clauses. A language, λProlog that is based on this generalization is then presented, and several examples of its use are provided. We also discuss an interpreter for this language in which new sources of branching and backtracking must be accommodated. An experimental interpreter has been constructed for the language, and all the examples in this paper have been tested using it.

Section 1: Introduction

The introduction of higher-order objects has been a major consideration in the realm of functional programming, and indeed these have proved to be very valuable in languages such as Lisp, Scheme, and ML. It is of interest therefore to consider the possibility of introducing such objects into a logic programming language. We examine this issue in this paper.

It is our belief that any attempt at providing a logic programming language like Prolog with the ability to deal with higher-order objects must be based on an extension to the underlying logic. Consider for example the facility Lisp provides for constructing lambda expressions which can be passed as parameters and can, later, be used as programs. In the setting of logic programming this corresponds to permitting predicate variables which may be instantiated by lambda expressions and allowing goals to be expressions that need to be lambda normalized before they are invoked. Given its logical basis, this feature is not directly available in Prolog. However, an argument may be made (eg. [D. H. Warren, 1982]) that no extension to Prolog or to the underlying logic is necessary by demonstrating how certain uses of this feature can be encoded in the first-order language. In our opinion, such an argument is inappropriate. First of all, it is desirable to provide for higher-order features such as the ones above in a natural and theoretically well understood fashion and from this perspective the ability to encode certain uses of predicate variables in the existing language is clearly not sufficient. Furthermore, the nature of objects in the paradigm of logic programming is somewhat different from that in the paradigm of functional programming. The question of what it means to have genuine higher-order objects in a logic programming language, therefore, is itself open to examination, and it seems that a study of this question should rely on an underlying logic.

In this paper we present a logic programming language that permits functions and predicates as objects. This language is based on a logic that uses the mechanism of the typed λ-calculus for

This work has been supported by NSF grants MCS8219196-CER, MCS-82-07294, AI Center grants NSF-MCS-83-05221, US Army Research office grant ARO-DAA29-84-9-0027, and DARPA N000-14-85-K-0018.

constructing predicate and function terms and permits a quantification over such constructions. Using this logic we find that we are able to describe a higher-order generalization of the first-order Horn clauses which shares many computational properties with its first-order counterpart. These clauses can be used to define a programming language that allows function and predicate variables and whose term structure is now that of λ-terms. One consequence of this is the provision of Lisp-like features. However, extending the notion of terms also gives the language a much richer set of data structures, and the operations of λ-conversion and unification on these provides a computational paradigm not found earlier in either logic or functional programming paradigms. It must be pointed out that the features that are provided are higher-order in a strictly logical sense. They do not include features popularized by, for example, the `setof` and `bagof` constructs [D. H. Warren, 1982]; these extensions are perhaps better classified as meta or control level extensions since they involve endowing a logic programming language with an understanding of its own ability to prove. We do not focus on these meta level aspects in this paper, but we note that they may be added to our language in a manner analogous to their addition to Prolog.

The structure of this paper is as follows. In Section 2 we describe the higher-order logic that we use as the basis of our language. Following this, in Section 3, we present our generalization to Horn clauses and discuss their formal properties. We have designed a programming language which includes not only these higher-order characteristics but also features like parametric polymorphic types and modules, that have already been found useful in other contexts (eg. ML and [Mycroft and O'Keefe, 1985]). This language, called λProlog, is described in Section 4, where several examples of its use are also presented. Finally, Section 5 discusses theorem-proving in the context of our clauses, and then uses this to describe an interpreter for λProlog. An experimental interpreter has been built along these lines, and all the examples in Section 4 and [Miller and Nadathur, 1985] have been tested on it.

Section 2: A Higher-Order Logic

The term "higher-order logic," as it is often understood, pertains to a logic whose language admits function and predicate variables, and in which such variables are interpreted as ranging over arbitrary functions and relations on any given domain. By virtue of Gödel's incompleteness theorems, it is known that a logic of this kind is not recursively axiomatizable and that its set of valid sentences is not effectively enumerable. Such a logic is not very interesting from our viewpoint, since our purpose is to use theorem-proving as the method of computation. Fortunately there is a higher-order logic that involves a weaker notion of quantification that can be recursively axiomatized. The Simple Theory of Types, presented by Church in [Church, 1940], is a typed λ-calculus formulation of this logic. The higher-order logic, called $\mathcal{T}$, that we use as the basis of our programming language is derived from the Simple Theory of Types. In this section we present a brief exposition of $\mathcal{T}$. A detailed account of the logic and its proof-theoretic properties are beyond the scope of this paper, and the interested reader is referred to [Church, 1940] and [Miller, 1983].

The language of $\mathcal{T}$ is a *typed* language in the sense that each well formed formula of the system has associated with it a type symbol. We assume that we are given a set $\mathcal{S}$ of *sorts* or *primitive types*, a set $\mathcal{V}$ of *type variables*, and a set $\mathcal{C}$ of *type constructors* where each type constructor has a unique positive arity. The types of $\mathcal{T}$ are then defined inductively by the following rules:

(1) Each sort and each type variable is a type.
(2) If c is an n-ary type constructor and $t_1, \ldots, t_n$ are types, then $(c\ t_1 \ldots t_n)$ is a type.
(3) If t_1 and t_2 are types, then $t_1 \rightarrow t_2$ is a type.

The set S must contain the sorts o and i; o is intended to be the type of propositions and i is the type of individuals. These are the only sorts that are necessary in the logic, but we shall assume here that S also contains the sort *int* for integer. $\mathcal{V}$ must be a denumerable set and we assume that α and β are included amongst its members. We also assume that C contains the type constructor *list* of arity 1. A type in which type variables occur is intended to correspond to the set of all its type instances that do not contain any type variables; a type t' is said to be a *type instance* of another type t just in case it is obtained from t by replacing simultaneously some of the variables in t with types. The type $t_1 \rightarrow t_2$ is also called a *function* type. We adopt the convention that $\rightarrow$ is right associative, *i.e.* we read $t_1 \rightarrow t_2 \rightarrow t_3$ as $t_1 \rightarrow (t_2 \rightarrow t_3)$. A type $t_1 \rightarrow t_2$ in which no type variables occur is intended to be the type of functions whose domain is of type t_1 and whose codomain is of type t_2.

We now turn to the well formed formulas of $\mathcal{T}$. Here we assume that we are given a set of constants and a denumerable set of variables, and that each element of these sets is specified with a particular type. The set of constants contains at least the following symbols that are referred to as the *logical constants* of $\mathcal{T}$:

Constant	Type
$\wedge$	$o \rightarrow o \rightarrow o$
$\vee$	$o \rightarrow o \rightarrow o$
$\supset$	$o \rightarrow o \rightarrow o$
$\sim$	$o \rightarrow o$
true	o
Π	$(\alpha \rightarrow o) \rightarrow o$
Σ	$(\alpha \rightarrow o) \rightarrow o$

The remaining constants are called the *nonlogical constants*. The following is a familiar set of such constants that we shall find occasion to use in this paper:

Constant	Type
cons	$\alpha \rightarrow (list\ \alpha) \rightarrow (list\ \alpha)$
nil	$(list\ \alpha)$
+	$int \rightarrow int \rightarrow int$
−	$int \rightarrow int \rightarrow int$
*	$int \rightarrow int \rightarrow int$

The formulas of $\mathcal{T}$, with their respective types, are defined inductively by the following rules:

(1) A variable of type t is a formula of type t.
(2) A constant whose specified type is t is a formula of type t', for any t' which is a type instance of t. Thus *cons* is a formula of type $int \rightarrow (list\ int) \rightarrow (list\ int)$ as well as of type $(list\ \beta) \rightarrow (list\ (list\ \beta)) \rightarrow (list\ (list\ \beta))$.
(3) If f_1 is a formula of type $t_1 \rightarrow t_2$ and f_2 is a formula of type t_1, then the *application* of f_1 to f_2, written $(f_1\ f_2)$ is a formula of type t_2. We assume that application is left

associative, *i.e.* we read $(f_1\ f_2\ f_3)$ as $((f_1\ f_2)\ f_3)$. Functions of many arguments are represented here in a curried form.

(4) If x is a variable of type t_1 and f is a formula of type t_2 then the *abstraction* of f by x, written $(\lambda x\ f)$, is a formula of type $t_1 \to t_2$; the abstraction is said to *bind* x and its *scope* is said to be f.

A formula in which no variables occur free is said to be a *closed* formula; an occurrence of a variable, x, in a formula is a *free* occurrence if it is not in the scope of an abstraction that binds x. A type symbol is considered to occur in a formula if it occurs in the type of some variable or constant of the formula. If a formula is the result of substituting types for some of the type variables in another formula, then the former is said to be a type instance of the latter. A formula in which type variables occur is to be interpreted as a scheme - it represents the set of all its type instances in which no type variables occur. Type variables thus provide a form of quantification over types. However, no explicit quantification is provided for, and the implicit universal quantification of a type variable that occurs in a formula is obviously over the whole formula. A stronger type system and a better formalization of the formulas that we have presented here is perhaps obtained through the use of explicit type quantification as in the second-order lambda calculus ([Reynolds, 1985], [Fortune, Leivant and O'Donnell, 1983]), but we do not pursue this aspect in this paper. The use that we make of type variables does not add anything to the logic, but it does provide a valuable form of polymorphism in the programming language that we shall define. In that context type constructors conspire with type variables to provide a form of *parametric polymorphism*. For instance, *cons* may be used to construct many different kinds of lists, the elements of each such list being homogenous.

λ-conversion plays an important role in $\mathcal{T}$. Let x be a variable and let t and A be terms. If there is no abstraction in A in whose scope x appears free and which also binds a free variable of t then we say that t is *free for x in A*. We write $A[t/x]$ to represent the result of replacing all free occurrences of x in A by t; obviously this is a meaningful operation only if t and x have the same type and t is free for x in A. The following three operations now comprise λ-conversion.
α-conversion: Replacing $(\lambda x\ A)$ with $(\lambda y\ A[y/x])$ provide y is free for x in A.
β-conversion: Replacing $(\lambda x\ A)t$ with $A[t/x]$ and vice versa provided t is free for x in A.
η-conversion: Replacing A with $\lambda z(Az)$ and vice versa if A has type $\alpha \to \beta$ and z has type α, provided z is not free in A.

A formula A is said to be convertible to another formula B if B can be obtained from A by a sequence of λ-conversions. Two formulas are considered equal if they are each convertible to the other; further distinctions can be made between formulas in this sense by omitting the rule for η-conversion, but we feel that these are not important in our context. We shall say here that a formula is a *λ-normal formula* if it has the form

$$\lambda x_1 \ldots \lambda x_n\ (h\ t_1\ \ldots\ t_m) \qquad \text{where } n, m \geq 0,$$

where h is a constant or variable, $(h\ t_1\ \ldots\ t_m)$ does not have a function type, and, for $1 \leq i \leq m$, t_i also has the same form. We call the list of variables $x_1, \ldots, x_n$ the *binder*, h the *head* and the formulas $t_1, \ldots, t_m$ the arguments of such a formula. It is known that every formula, A, can be converted to a λ-normal formula that is unique upto α-conversions. We call such a formula a λ-normal form of A and we use $\lambda norm(A)$ to denote any of these alphabetic variants.

The type o plays a special role in $\mathcal{T}$. A formula with a function type of the form $t_1 \rightarrow \ldots \rightarrow t_n \rightarrow o$ is also classified as a *predicate* of n arguments whose i^{th} argument must be of type t_i. Predicates are use to denote sets and relations. For example, predicates of type $int \rightarrow o$ represent sets of integers, predicates of type $(int \rightarrow o) \rightarrow o$ represent sets of sets of integers, and predicates of the type $\alpha \rightarrow (list\ \alpha) \rightarrow o$ represent binary relations between objects of any type a in which no type variables occur and the corresponding type $(list\ a)$. Formulas of type o are called *propositions*; notice that these formulas must have an empty binder. The logical constants $\wedge$, $\vee$, and $\supset$ correspond to the familiar propositional connectives, and we shall adopt the customary infix notation for these. The symbols Π and Σ are used in conjunction with the abstraction operation to represent universal and existential quantification over propositions: $\forall x\ f$ is an abbreviation for $\Pi(\lambda x\ f)$ and $\exists x\ f$ is an abbreviation for $\Sigma(\lambda x\ f)$. Derivability in $\mathcal{T}$, denoted by $\vdash_{\mathcal{T}}$, is a notion that pertains to propositions and is an extension of the notion for first-order logic. The axioms of $\mathcal{T}$ are the substitution instances of the propositional tautologies, the formula $\forall x\ Bx \supset Bt$, and the formula $\forall x\ (Px \wedge Q) \supset \forall x\ Px \wedge Q$. The rules of inference of the system are *Modus Ponens*, *Universal Generalization*, *Substitution*, and *λ-conversion*. λ-conversion is essentially the only rule in $\mathcal{T}$ that is not in first-order logic, but combined with the richer syntax of formulas in $\mathcal{T}$ it makes more complex inferences possible. $\mathcal{T}$, unlike the Simple Theory of Types, is a logic that is not *extensional*; *i.e.* given two 1-ary predicates P and Q it may be possible to prove $\forall x\ (Px \equiv Qx)$ in $\mathcal{T}$ without being able to prove that P and Q are equal.

We are interested in $\mathcal{T}$ because it possesses several properties that make it a suitable basis for the kind of programming language that we desire. It provides a mechanism for constructing function and predicate terms and for permitting variables to range over such constructions, and this was our main reason for looking for a higher-order logic. Further the proof-theory for $\mathcal{T}$ bears a close resemblance to that of first-order logic; for instance there is a generalization to Herbrand's Theorem [Miller, 1983] that holds for $\mathcal{T}$. This property shall be of importance when we consider the task of designing an interpreter for our language. Finally there is a sublogic of $\mathcal{T}$ that generalizes the definite clauses of first-order logic while preserving several of their computational properties. It is this sublogic that we examine in the next section, and that we use later to define our programming language.

Section 3: Higher-Order Definite Clauses and their Properties

We shall henceforth assume that we have a fixed set $\mathcal{K}$ of nonlogical constants. The *positive Herbrand Universe* is identified in this context to be the set of all the λ-normal formulas that can be constructed using the nonlogical constants in $\mathcal{K}$ and no logical constants other than *true*, $\wedge$, $\vee$ and Σ. We use the symbol $\mathcal{H}^+$ to denote this set. Propositions in this set are of special interest to us. We shall use, perhaps with subscripts, the symbol G to denote an arbitrary such proposition throughout this paper. Notice that the head of such a formula is either a predicate constant or variable or one of the constants *true*, $\wedge$, $\vee$, and Σ. Of these formulas we single out those that have nonlogical constants as their heads. We shall call such formulas *atoms*, and we use the symbol A uniformly to denote an atom.

A *(higher-order) definite clause* is defined to be the universal closure of a formula of the form $G \supset A$, *i.e.* the formula $\forall \bar{x}\ (G \supset A)$ where $\bar{x}$ is an arbitrary listing of all the free variables in G and A. These clauses are our generalization of the Horn clauses of first-order logic. There are certain relationships between these that should be pointed out. First-order Horn clauses are contained n our definite clauses under an implicit encoding. This encoding essentially assigns types to he first-order terms and predicates: variables and constants (*i.e.* 0-ary function symbols) are ssigned the type i, function symbols of arity $n > 0$ are assigned the type $i \rightarrow \ldots \rightarrow i \rightarrow i$, with $+ 1$ occurrences of i, and n-ary predicate symbols are assigned the type $i \rightarrow \ldots \rightarrow i \rightarrow o$, with occurrences of i. Looked at differently, our definite clauses contain within them a polymorphic nany-sorted version of first-order Horn clauses. The formula on the left of the $\supset$ in a higher-order lefinite clause may contain nested disjunctions and existential connectives. This generalization nay be dispensed with in the first-order case because of the existence of appropriate normal orms. For the higher-order case, it is more natural to retain the embedded disjunctions and xistential quantifications since substitutions have the potential for reintroducing them. Finally -terms may occur in the higher-order clauses and the quantifications in these clauses may involve unction and predicate variables. This is a genuine extension provided by our clauses, and is the ery reason why we study them.

Parallel to the first-order case, we wish to accord a computational interpretation to our lefinite clauses. Let $\mathcal{P}$ be a set of definite clauses, and let G have no type variables in it. We want o think of $\mathcal{P}$ as a program and of G as *query* or a *goal*. The computation involved is then to be hat of answering the query. The sense in which the query is to be answered may be made precise s follows. Let us define a substitution to be a finite sequence of pairs, $\varphi = \langle\langle x_1, t_1\rangle, \ldots, \langle x_n, t_n\rangle\rangle$, here the x_i's are distinct variables, and, for each i, t_i is a formula of the same type as x_i; φ is said o be a substitution for $x_1, \ldots, x_n$ and its *range* is the set $\{t_1, \ldots, t_n\}$. The application of φ to a ormula B, written as φB, is defined to be $\lambda norm([\lambda x_1 \ldots \lambda x_n\ B]t_1 \ldots t_n)$. Let $\bar{y}$ be an arbitrary isting of all the variables free in G. Now, we want the query G to be answered affirmatively if $\vdash_{\mathcal{T}} \exists \bar{y}\ G$ and we also want an affirmative answer to be accompanied by a substitution for $\bar{y}$ uch that $\mathcal{P} \vdash_{\mathcal{T}} \varphi G$.

The latter may not always be possible if $\mathcal{P}$ is any arbitrary set of formulas. However, the ollowing theorem assures us that it is indeed possible for a collection of definite clauses. Here nd in the rest of the paper we reserve the terms *positive* substitution for one whose range is a ubset of $\mathcal{H}^+$, and *closed* substitution for one whose range consists of closed formulas. We also se the symbol $\mathcal{P}$ uniformly to denote a (possibly empty) set of definite clauses, and we write $[\mathcal{P}]$ o denote the set of formulas of the form $\varphi(G \supset A)$ where $\forall \bar{x}\ (G \supset A)$ is a type instance of a ormula of $\mathcal{P}$ which contains no free type variables, and φ is a positive, closed substitution for $\bar{x}$.

Theorem 1: Let $G \in \mathcal{H}^+$ be a closed proposition that has no type variables in it. Then the ollowing are true:

(1) If G is $G_1 \wedge G_2$ then $\mathcal{P} \vdash_{\mathcal{T}} G$ if and only if $\mathcal{P} \vdash_{\mathcal{T}} G_1$ and $\mathcal{P} \vdash_{\mathcal{T}} G_2$.

(2) If G is $G_1 \vee G_2$ then $\mathcal{P} \vdash_{\mathcal{T}} G$ if and only if $\mathcal{P} \vdash_{\mathcal{T}} G_1$ or $\mathcal{P} \vdash_{\mathcal{T}} G_2$.

(3) If G is $\Sigma\ B$ then $\mathcal{P} \vdash_{\mathcal{T}} G$ if and only if there is a closed formula $t \in \mathcal{H}^+$ such that $\mathcal{P} \vdash_{\mathcal{T}} \lambda norm(Bt)$.

(4) If G is an atom then $\mathcal{P} \vdash_{\mathcal{T}} G$ if and only if there is a formula $G_1 \supset G \in [\mathcal{P}]$ such that $\mathcal{P} \vdash_{\mathcal{T}} G_1$.

The proof of this and the other theorems in this paper may be obtained from the results in Miller and Nadathur, 1986]. As a consequence of this theorem we may attribute a procedural nterpretation to a clause. Consider the definite clause $\forall \bar{x}(G \supset A)$. G may either be *true* or compound formula containing conjunctions, disjunctions, and existential quantifiers. If G is *rue*, then the clause is logically equivalent to $\forall \bar{x} A$, and is to be interpreted as a fact. Otherwise we interpret it as a procedure declaration, where the non-logical head of A is the name of the procedure being defined, and G is the procedure body which is to be used to compute it. Note that by virtue of this theorem we need only consider positive substitutions in order to establish a goal from a set of definite clauses. This fact, in conjunction with the observation that a positive substitution when applied to an element in $\mathcal{H}^+$ produces another element in $\mathcal{H}^+$, enables us to define, even in the presence of predicate variables, a theorem-prover for this sublogic that is based on this procedural interpretation of clauses. We shall consider such a theorem-prover shortly.

It is possible to explicate the meaning of a set of definite clauses in a more direct manner by associating with it a set of atoms. The idea is similar to that used in the first-order case (see [Apt and van Emden, 1982] and [van Emden and Kowalski, 1976]) and may be made precise in the following manner. Let us define an *interpretation* to be any set of closed atoms in which no type variables occur. Relative to an interpretation I we may define a *derivation sequence* to be a finite sequence $G_0, G_1, \ldots, G_n$ of closed propositions in $\mathcal{H}^+$ in which no type variables occur and for each $i \leq n$,

(1) G_i is *true*, or
(2) G_i is an atom and G_i λ-converts to some member of I, or
(3) G_i is $G_i^1 \vee G_i^2$ and there is a $j < i$ such that G_j is G_i^1 or G_j is G_i^2, or
(4) G_i is $G_i^1 \wedge G_i^2$ and there are $j, k < i$ such that G_j is G_i^1 and G_k is G_i^2, or
(5) G_i is ΣG and there is a closed formula $t \in \mathcal{H}^+$ and a $j < i$ such that G_j is $\lambda norm(Gt)$.

If G is the last element of such a sequence, we say that I *satisfies* G and we denote this relation by $I \models G$.

Given a set of definite clauses $\mathcal{P}$, we associate with it a mapping $T_\mathcal{P}$ from interpretations to interpretations which is such that $A \in T_\mathcal{P}(I)$ if and only if there is a formula $G \supset A \in [\mathcal{P}]$ such that $I \models G$. It is not difficult to see that $T_\mathcal{P}$ is monotone and continuous on the set of all interpretations. $T_\mathcal{P}$ therefore has a least fixed point which is given by $T_\mathcal{P}^\infty(\emptyset) = \bigcup_{n=0}^{\infty} T_\mathcal{P}^n(\emptyset)$. It is this subset of $\mathcal{H}^+$ that we think of as being determined by $\mathcal{P}$, and we call it the *denotation* of $\mathcal{P}$. The computation that is involved in answering a query G may be viewed as that of determining whether there is a closed substitution instance of G that is satisfied in the denotation of $\mathcal{P}$. The consistency of this view with the earlier operational view is the content of the following theorem:

Theorem 2: Let G be a closed formula with no type variables. Then $T_\mathcal{P}^\infty(\emptyset) \models G$ if and only if $\mathcal{P} \vdash_T G$.

Section 4: The λProlog language

Our programming language, λProlog, is based on higher-order definite clauses. Since their underlying logics are similar, we find it convenient to adopt several features of the syntax of Prolog in λProlog. Symbols that begin with capital letters, both in clause definitions and in type definitions, are treated as variables. All other symbols represent constants. The symbols `,`, `;`, and `:-` are used for $\wedge$, $\vee$ and $\supset$ respectively, and clauses are written backwards. Variables occuring in clauses are assumed to be implicitly universally quantified.

There are, however, a few differences. We need to represent λ-terms and the symbol \ is reserved for this purpose: $\lambda X\, A$ is written in λProlog as `X \ A`. The constant `sigma` is reserved for Σ. A curried notation is adopted since it is especially convenient in our context, and application is represented by juxtaposition. Types must be associated with every (term) constant and variable and this is achieved via a type declaration that has the format `type token logical_type`.

We have found it useful to organise declarations into modules and have introduced this notion as a structuring concept in λProlog. Modules are, in our context, named environments within which operator and type declarations may be associated with tokens, and defining clauses may be presented for predicate constants. The following is an illustration of this structure:

```
module tiny.
op 255 xfx :-.
op  40 xfx =.
type :- o -> o -> o.
type =  A -> A -> o.
onep X :- X = 1.
identity_fun F :- (X\ X) = F.
```

Operator declarations override the default prefix application precedence, and are similar to those in Prolog: `op 225 xfx :-` corresponds to op(225,xfx,:-) in Dec10 Prolog syntax. Type and operator declarations are considered attributes of a module and are not side effects. In general, very little type information needs to be given, since most of it can be inferred from the context. The rules for inferring types are essentially those used in ML [Milner, 1978]. In performing such an inference, we assume that all occurrences of a bound variable within the scope of its abstraction and all occurrences of a constant in a module have the same type. As an instance of such a type determination, the types of the constants onep and `identity_fun` can be inferred to be `int -> o` and `(A -> A) -> o`, respectively. Our module parser is able to perform such a type determination, and in this case it assumes that these are also part of the type declarations in the module. The module `tiny` also associates defining clauses with the predicates onep and `identity_fun`. This module, thus, defines eight associations: two operator specifications, four type declarations (two explicit, two inferred), and two predicates with their definite clauses.

A module may also import several other modules. The effect of this operation is to make available the operator and type declarations and the definite clauses of the imported modules in the module being defined. The precise logical characterization of this operation with regard to the clauses depends on an assimilation of implication into the body of definite clauses, and an attempt in this direction may be found in [Miller, 1986].

We assume, in the rest of this section, that the module `basics` contains all type and operator declarations for many standard Prolog logical constructions. The following module, which imports `basics`, then provides an illustration in λProlog of some standard list manipulation programs.

```
module lists.
import basics.
type cons A -> (list A) -> (list A).
type nil (list A).
append nil K K.
append (cons X L) K (cons X M) :- append L K M.
memb X (cons X L).
memb X (cons Y L) :- memb X L.
member X (cons X L) :- !.
member X (cons Y L) :- member X L.
```

Here, cut (!) is intended to have the same operational meaning as it does in Prolog, *i.e.* it removes all backtracking points. The following type information is inferred and is also assumed to be a part of this module's definition.

```
type append (list A) -> (list A) -> (list A) -> o.
type memb (list A) -> (list A) -> o.
type member (list A) -> (list A) -> o.
```

One of the novelties of λProlog is the provision of predicate variables. The following module offers an illustration of this facet:

```
module age.
import basics lists.
type age i -> int -> o.
type have_property (A -> o) -> (list A) -> (list A) -> o.
have_property P (cons X L) (cons X K) :- P X, have_property P L K.
have_property P (cons X L) K :- have_property P L K.
have_property P nil nil.
mappred P (cons X L) (cons Y K) :- P X Y, mappred P L K.
mappred P nil nil.
have_age L K :- have_property (Z\(sigma X\(age Z X))) L K.
same_age L K :- have_property (Z\(age Z A)) L K.
age sue  24.
age bob  23.
```

This module defines the predicate `have_property` whose first argument must be a predicate and is such that `(have_property P L K)` is true if K is some sublist of L and all the members in K satisfy the property expressed by the predicate P. Using `have_property` the predicate `have_age` is defined such that `(have_age L K)` is true if K is a sublist of the objects in L which have an age. Notice that there is an explicit quantifier imbedded in the predicate used to define `have_age`. The predicate `(Z\(sigma X\(age Z X)))`, which may be written in logic as $\lambda z \exists x \; age(z,x)$, is true of an individual if that individual has an age. The predicate `same_age` whose definition is obtained by dropping that quantifier defines a slightly different property; `(same_age L K)` is true only when the objects in K have, in addition, the same age.

In the cases considered above, predicate variables that appeared as the heads of goals were fully instantiated before the goal was invoked. This kind of use of predicate variables is similar to the use of apply and lambda terms in Lisp; the λ-contraction followed by the goal invocation essentially simulates the apply operation. However, the variable head of a goal need not always be fully instantiated, and in such cases there is a question concerning what substitution should be returned. Consider for example the query `(P bob 23)`. One value that may be returned for P is `X\Y\(age X Y)`. But there are many more substitutions which also satisfy this goal; `X\Y\(X = bob, Y = 23)`, `X\Y\(Y = 23)`, `X\Y\(age sue 24)`, etc. are all terms that could also be picked.

Clearly there are too many such substitutions to pick from and then backtrack over. Our decision is to use only the substitution that corresponds to the largest "extension" in such cases; in the above case, for example, the term `X\Y\true` would be picked. It is possible to make such a choice without adding to the incompleteness of an interpreter, and we comment on this issue in Section 5. For the moment we note that this decision does not trivialize the use of predicate variables. Assume for instance that a predicate `concept` of type `(i -> o) -> o` has been defined. Then the query `concept P, P t` would still be a meaningful one. This query would entail looking for a predicate term which is a concept, and then asking if `t` is in its extension.

As we noted, the addition of predicate variables is a little like adding Lisp's notions of apply and lambda expressions to Prolog. The additions of function variables and higher-order unification, however, are in an entirely new direction. Consider adding the following definite clauses at the the end of the module `lists`.

```
mapfun F (cons X L) (cons (F X) K) :- mapfun F L K.
mapfun F nil nil.
```

The type for `mapfun` would be inferred to be `(A -> B) -> (list A) -> (list B) -> o`. Given the goal `(mapfun (X\(g X X)) (cons a (cons b nil)) L)`, our interpreter would return the list `(cons (g a a) (cons (g b b) nil))` as the answer substitution for `L`. In other words, if the first two arguments are instantiated then the list that results from applying the first argument to each element of the second would be returned as the value of the third argument. Notice that mapping a function over a list is quite different from mapping a predicate over a list as in the mappred procedure defined earlier. In the latter case the idea of applying a predicate, say `P`, to an argument, say `X`, entails creating a new goal – the λ-normal form of `(P X Y)` for some variable `Y`. The value placed in the list is an instance of `Y` that enables this goal to be derived. In mapping a function over a list, no new goals are constructed. The function is simply applied to the argument and the resulting λ-normal form is the value entered into the list. Since mapping a function is weaker than mapping a predicate, the problem of discovering functions which successfully map a list into another list is better defined and does not always permit trivial solutions. For example, consider the goal,

```
(mapfun F (cons a (cons b nil)) (cons (g a a) (cons (g a b) nil))).
```

Here there is exactly one substitution for `F` which satisfies this goal, namely `F` gets `X\(g a X)`. Notice that backtracking may occur on unifying substitutions as well. In searching for an answer substitution a depth-first interpreter would first consider unifying `(F a)` with `(g a a)`. There are four possible substitutions for `F` that are unifiers:

```
X\(g X X)     X\(g a X)     X\(g X a)     X\(g a a).
```

If any of these other than the second is picked, the interpreter would fail in matching `(F b)` with `(g a b)`, and would therefore have to backtrack.

λ-terms obviously provide much richer data structures than those afforded by simple first-order terms, and there are situations in which this richness in λProlog can be exploited. Examples of its use in the realms of knowledge representation and natural language semantics may be found in [Miller and Nadathur, 1985] and [D. S. Warren, 1983]. Another realm in which it is useful is that of program transformations. [Huet and Lang, 1978] indicates how program transformation algorithms may be written rather directly by encoding program structures using λ-terms, and then using higher-order unification. The following module presents a program that may be used to do the *unfolding* transformation.

```
type if (env -> bool) -> A -> A -> A.
type while (env -> bool) -> (env -> env) -> (env -> env).
type unfold (A -> (env -> env)) -> (A -> (env -> env)) -> o.
unfold (X\(while (Cond X) (Prog X)))
       (X\(if (Cond X)
              (E\(while (Cond X) (Prog X) (Prog X E)))
              (F\F))).
```

The predicate `unfold` can be used to expand a `while`-loop into an `if` construction. Consider the goal,

`unfold (W\(while (lessthan W 10) (advance W 1))) Q.`

The unique solution to this goal returns the following substitution for `Q` that is computed entirely within the unification process.

`W\(if (lessthan W 10) E\(while (lessthan W 10) (advance W 1) (advance W 1 E)) F\F)`

The clause defining `unfold` is used with the variables `Cond` and `Prog` bound to `W\(lessthan W 10)` and `U\(advance U 1)` respectively in this computation.

The provision of polymorphic types *and* function types adds an interesting complexity to the language. Consider the following module.

```
module interpreter.
import basics lists.
interp H true.
interp H (G1, G2) :- interp H G1, interp H G2.
interp H (G1; G2) :- interp H G1; interp H G2.
interp H (sigma G) :- interp H (G X).
interp H A :- memb Clause H, instan Clause (A :- G), interp H G.
instan (pi B) C :- instan (B X) C.
instan C C.
```

Here, `interp` is a two place predicate. If `Cs` is a list of closed definite clauses and `G` is a goal then `(interp Cs G)` succeeds if and only if there is a proof of an instance of `G` from the clauses in `Cs`. This program constitutes an interpreter for that subset of λProlog in which type variables are not permitted in definite clauses. In the first clause of `instan`, the variable `B` has type `A -> o` for some type variable `A`. When this clause is invoked, this type variable must be instantiated. A value for that type variable may only be obtained by examining the term with which it is getting unified. In other words, this is a case where a function type needs to be determined dynamically. When `instan` is called from `interp` there is a fully instantiated term in its second argument, so this does not constitute a problem. It may, however, be the case that when a type variable needs to be determined at runtime the term that needs to be examined is not instantiated in such a way as to provide an actual type. This would happen, for example, if `instan` is invoked with only its second argument instantiated. Such a situation may cause a problem for the interpreter, and we discuss it further in the next section.

Section 5: An Abstract Interpreter for Definite Clauses

We now desire a mechanism for finding proofs in $\mathcal{T}$ for a goal of the form $\exists \bar{x} G$ from a set of definite clauses $\mathcal{P}$. In its abstract description we expect such a mechanism to be complete, i.e. it should return a positive answer whenever a derivation does exist. Furthermore, whenever it provides a positive answer, it should also provide a substitution φ for $\bar{x}$ such that $\mathcal{P} \vdash_{\mathcal{T}} \varphi G$. The structure of such a mechanism is easily obtained from Theorem 1 in Section 3. However we desire to describe it at a sufficient level of detail so that it may form the basis of an interpreter for λProlog. In order to do so we need to consider briefly the problem of unifying typed λ-terms.

Let us call a pair of terms of the same type a *disagreement pair*. A *disagreement set* is a finite set $\{\langle t_1, s_1\rangle, \ldots, \langle t_n, s_n\rangle\}$ of disagreement pairs, and a *unifier* for this disagreement set is a substitution θ such that, for each $i \leq n$, θt_i is λ-convertible to θs_i. The *higher-order unification problem* is the problem of determining whether a disagreement set can be unified and, when it can be, of providing a unifier for it. We note that in the general case the question of existence of unifiers is only undecidable [Goldfarb, 1981]. Also, when unifiers do exist, there may not be a most general unifier. Nevertheless, a systematic search can be made for unifiers which succeeds in discovering them whenever they exist. We outline, with a small modification, the procedure in [Huet, 1975] which conducts such a search.

Certain disagreement sets, called *solved sets* here, have trivial unifiers (although computing all their unifiers can be quite hard). Certain other disagreement sets, called *failed sets* here, are easily seen to have no unifiers. The search for a unifier proceeds by attempting to reduce a given disagreement set to either a solved set or a failed set. Central to this process are the operations SIMPL, TRIV and MATCH. SIMPL attempts to simplify a disagreement set by looking at pairs of terms whose heads cannot be changed by substitutions. It either decides that the terms of at least one such pair cannot be unified, or reduces the question of unification of the terms of each such pair to that of the unification of their arguments. In the first-order case, this corresponds to descending through the pair of terms simultaneously so long as no variables are encountered and the term structures are identical at the top. Given a disagreement set $\mathcal{D}$, SIMPL returns the marker $\mathcal{F}$ if it has determined that $\mathcal{D}$ has no unifiers, or it produces a *simplified* disagreement set $\mathcal{D}'$ that has the same set of unifiers as $\mathcal{D}$. If $\mathcal{D}'$ is not a solved set then substitutions are necessary to continue the reduction process. TRIV examines a simplified disagreement set and returns the set of pairs in it of the form $\langle x, t\rangle$ where x is a variable and t is a term in which x does not appear free. (An implementation of TRIV may, of course, drop this "occur-check" condition, trading soundness with efficiency.) If there are such pairs, then any one of them may be used as a substitution to simplify the disagreement set further. SIMPL and TRIV are used repeatedly till either the set has been successfully reduced to a solved or failed set, or no further simplifications are possible. In the latter case strictly higher-order considerations are needed to carry the search process forward. This is the domain of the MATCH procedure. When MATCH is applied to a simplified disagreement set, it first picks a pair in the set and then produces a finite set of substitutions that help in unifying that disagreement pair. MATCH is therefore a non-deterministic function, since the value it returns depends of the choice of disagreement pair. We do not describe the structure of MATCH here due to a lack of space.

We may now define a notion of derivation relative to a set of definite clauses $\mathcal{P}$. Let us use, perhaps with subscripts, the symbols $\mathcal{G}$ to denote a finite subset of $\mathcal{H}^+$, $\mathcal{D}$ to denote a disagreement set and θ to denote a substitution. Then the triple $\langle \mathcal{G}_2, \mathcal{D}_2, \theta_2\rangle$ is said to be $\mathcal{P}$*-derived* from the triple $\langle \mathcal{G}_1, \mathcal{D}_1, \theta_1\rangle$ if the former is obtained from the latter by one of the following steps; in this definition, we say that a variable is *new* if it is does not occur free in any of the formulas that appear in $\langle \mathcal{G}_1, \mathcal{D}_1, \theta_1\rangle$.

(1) *Goal reduction and backchaining steps:* Let G be some member of $\mathcal{G}$ and let $\mathcal{G}'$ be the result of removing that occurrence of G from $\mathcal{G}$. In the first four cases below, set $\mathcal{D}_2 := \mathcal{D}_1$ and $\theta_2 := \emptyset$. We refer to the first five cases as *goal reduction* steps and the last one as the *backchaining* step.

   (a) If G is *true*, then $\mathcal{G}_2 := \mathcal{G}'$.

   (b) If G is $G_1 \wedge G_2$ then $\mathcal{G}_2 := \{G_1, G_2\} \cup \mathcal{G}'$.

   (c) If G is $G_1 \vee G_2$, then $\mathcal{G}_2 := \{G_1\} \cup \mathcal{G}'$ or $\mathcal{G}_2 := \{G_2\} \cup \mathcal{G}'$.

   (d) If G is ΣB, then $\mathcal{G}_2 := \{\lambda norm(By)\} \cup \mathcal{G}'$ for some new variable y.

   (e) If G has a variable, y of type $\alpha_1 \to \ldots \to \alpha_n \to o$, as its head, then set $\theta_2 := \{\langle y, \lambda x_1 \ldots \lambda x_n true\rangle\}$, $\mathcal{G}_2 := \theta_2\mathcal{G}'$, and $\mathcal{D}_2 :=$ SIMPL$(\theta_2\mathcal{D}_1)$. Here, the type of x_i is α_i, for $i = 1\ldots, n$.

   (f) Otherwise, G has a nonlogical constant as its head. Let $\forall\bar{x}\ (G' \supset A)$ be a type variable free, type-instance of a clause in $\mathcal{P}$. Set $\theta_2 := \emptyset$, $\mathcal{G}_2 := \{G'\} \cup \mathcal{G}'$, and $\mathcal{D}_2 := \mathcal{D}_1 \cup$ SIMPL$(\{\langle G, A\rangle\})$. Here we assume that the variables $\bar{x}$ are new.

(2) *Unification step:* If $\mathcal{D}_1$ is neither $\mathcal{F}$ nor a solved set, then we either apply TRIV or MATCH.

   (a) If TRIV$(\mathcal{D}_1) \neq \emptyset$ then for any $\sigma \in$ TRIV$(\mathcal{D}_1)$ set $\theta_2 := \sigma$, $\mathcal{G}_2 := \sigma\mathcal{G}_1$ and $\mathcal{D}_2 :=$ SIMPL$(\sigma\mathcal{D}_1)$.

   (b) Let Θ be some value returned for $MATCH(\mathcal{D}_1)$. If Θ is empty, then $\mathcal{D}_1$ is recognized as a failed set. In this case, set $\mathcal{G}_2 := \mathcal{G}_1$, $\mathcal{D}_2 := \mathcal{F}$, and $\theta := \emptyset$. Otherwise, pick $\sigma \in \Theta$, and set $\theta_2 := \sigma$, $\mathcal{G}_2 := \sigma\mathcal{G}_1$ and $\mathcal{D}_2 :=$ SIMPL$(\sigma\mathcal{D}_1)$.

A sequence $\langle \mathcal{G}_i, \mathcal{D}_i, \theta_i\rangle_{i\leq n}$ in which, for each $i < n$, $\langle \mathcal{G}_{i+1}, \mathcal{D}_{i+1}, \theta_{i+1}\rangle$ is $\mathcal{P}$-derived from $\langle \mathcal{G}_i, \mathcal{D}_i, \theta_i\rangle$, is called a *$\mathcal{P}$-derivation* sequence. In addition, if $\mathcal{D}_0 = \emptyset$, $\theta_0 = \emptyset$ and $\mathcal{G}_0 = \{G\}$ then the sequence is said to be a $\mathcal{P}$-derivation sequence for G. Notice that sequences for which $\mathcal{G}_n = \emptyset$ and $\mathcal{D}_n$ is either a solved set or $\mathcal{F}$, cannot be extended. If $\mathcal{G}_n = \emptyset$ and $\mathcal{D}_n$ is a solved set, we say that that $\mathcal{P}$-derivation of G is a *proof of G from $\mathcal{P}$*, and that the substitution $\theta_n \circ \cdots \circ \theta_1$ is its *answer substitution.* The following theorem establishes the soundness and completeness for this notion of proof.

Theorem 3: Let $\exists\bar{x}G$ be a closed goal formula which contains no type variables. $\mathcal{P} \vdash_{\mathcal{T}} \exists\bar{x}G$ if and only if there is a $\mathcal{P}$-derivation sequence which is a proof of G from $\mathcal{P}$. In the latter case, if θ is the answer substitution for the sequence and σ is a unifier for the final solved set, then $\mathcal{P} \vdash_{\mathcal{T}} G'$ for every ground instance G' of $\sigma \circ \theta\ G$.

Notice that if $\mathcal{P}$ and G are essentially first-order, the final solved set of a proof of G from $\mathcal{P}$ is always empty, so σ can be taken to be the empty substitution. In this case, the notion of an answer substitution coincides with the usual (first-order) definition.

The mechanism that we desired at the beginning of this section may be described as one that starts with the triple $\langle\{G\}, \emptyset, \emptyset\rangle$ and performs an exhaustive search for a proof of G from $\mathcal{P}$. There are several choices in extending a derivation sequence, but most of these are inconsequential. A complete procedure may for instance choose to do any one of the unification steps or a backchaining step or one of the goal reduction steps 1(a)-1(d). Within the unification step 2(b), however, the choice of substitution may be critical. A similar observation applies to the choice of clause in 1(f).

In constructing an interpreter for λProlog, it appears inappropriate to perform a breadth-first search even where necessary, and trade-offs need to be made between completeness and practicality. We have designed an interpreter that performs a depth-first search with backtracking that s similar to the one standard Prolog interpreters perform: It always chooses to do a unification step, applying TRIV, whenever possible. When a choice of goal has to be made it picks the first n the list. In determining a clause to use (1(f)), it picks the first appropriate one in a predetermined ordering. However there are a few points peculiar to our language that bear mentioning: (1) Before using 1(e) to solve a goal with a variable, y, as its head it is necessary for completeness o check that y does not appear free in an argument of any of the other goals or in the associated disagreement set. Our interpreter does not perform such a check, preferring instead not to reorder goals in the goal list. (2) Even after a clause has been chosen in 1(f), it is still necessary to choose a type instance of it. Our solution to this problem is to permit type variables in goals and to delay their determination until term unification. SIMPL and TRIV can be easily modified to deal with such variables, but there are problems in adapting MATCH to deal with type variables that need to be instantiated to function types. When it encounters such a case, our interpreter gives up and indicates a run-time error. A better analysis of this problem is clearly necessary, and must be based on a stronger formalization of type quantification. (3) Choices may have to be made in the unification step, and backtracking points need to be maintained for these as well. Our interpreter saves such points and can backtrack over them. We have implemented no control primitives for the unification search process. Although such controls will most certainly be necessary for various kinds of programs, we have been successful at running many λProlog programs which make non-trivial uses of higher-order unification without such controls.

There are several other issues pertaining to the interpreter that need to be discussed, but we omit these here due to a limitation on space.

Section 6: Conclusions

In this paper we have investigated the issue of introducing higher-order objects into a logic programming language. Toward this end we have used a higher-order logic to generalize the first-order Horn clauses. Our theoretical results show that this generalisation preserves certain important computational properties. We have described a programming language that is based on these results, and we have also outlined an interpreter for this language. Our current implementation of an interpreter was not designed with efficiency in mind. We are now investigating the design of an abstract machine to support a more efficient implementation.

The language that we have presented here gives first-class logical status to typed λ-terms of all types, and this constitutes a considerable enrichment to the data structures of Prolog. This enrichment brings with it a cost, viz a branching in unification, that at first sight may appear prohibitive. However, there are certain points to be noted. First of all, branching occurs only in cases that involve genuinely higher-order unification, and in these cases the cost may not be unacceptable. Moreover there are several uses of λ-terms where the unification involves no branching at all. Examples in this category include all the uses of Lisp-like features described in [D. H. Warren, 1982] and situations where the λ-terms are used solely for the purpose of performing computations through reductions. In cases like these the language described here provides a clear and theoretically well-understood implementation. Finally, our preliminary investigations indicate that an interpreter for λProlog may be written in such a way that it performs very efficiently for the first-order fragment without jeopardizing its ability to deal with higher-order terms. If this is indeed true, then the new additions to the language would be achieved in a manner that is strictly conservative.

Section 7: References

[Apt and van Emden, 1982] Krzysztof R. Apt and M. H. van Emden, "Contributions to the Theory of Logic Programming" *JACM*, Vol 29 (1982), 841 – 862.

[Church, 1940] Alonzo Church, "A Formulation of the Simple Theory of Types," Journal of Symbolic Logic **5** (1940), 56 – 68.

[Fortune, Leivant and O'Donnell, 1983] Steven Fortune, Daniel Leivant, and Michael O'Donnell, "The Expressiveness of Simple and Second-Order Type Structures", J.ACM Vol. 30(1), January 1983, pp. 151-185.

[Goldfarb, 1981] Warren D. Goldfarb, "The Undecidability of the Second-Order Unification Problem," *Theoretical Computer Science* **13** (1981), 225 – 230.

[Huet, 1975] Gérard P. Huet, "A Unification Algorithm for Typed λ-calculus," Theoretical Computer Science **1** (1975), 27 – 57.

[Huet and Lang, 1978] Gérard P. Huet, Bernard Lang, "Proving and Applying Program Transformations Expressed with Second-Order Patterns" *Acta Informatica* **11** (1978), 31 – 55.

[Miller, 1983] Dale A. Miller, "Proofs in Higher-order Logic," Ph. D. Dissertation, Carnegie-Mellon University, August 1983.

[Miller, 1986] Dale A. Miller, "A Theory of Modules for Logic Programming," University of Pennsylvania Techincal Report, 1986.

[Miller and Nadathur, 1985] Dale A. Miller, Gopalan Nadathur, "A Computational Logic Approach to Syntax and Semantics," 10th Annual Symposium of the Mathematical Foundations of Computer Science, IBM Japan, May 1985.

[Miller and Nadathur, 1986] Dale A. Miller, Gopalan Nadathur, "An Abstract Interpreter for a Higher Order Extension of Prolog," forthcoming UPenn technical report, December 1985.

[Milner, 1978] Robin Milner, "A Theory of Type Polymorphism in Programming," *Journal of Computer and System Sciences* **17**, 348 – 375, 1978.

[Mycroft and O'Keefe, 1985] A. Mycroft and R. A. O'Keefe, "A Polymorphic Type System for Prolog," *Artificial Intelligence*, Vol. 23(3), August 1984.

[Reynolds, 1985] J. C. Reynolds, "Three Approaches to Type Structure", Proceedings of the International Joint Conference on Theory and Practice of Software Development, March 1985.

[van Emden and Kowalski, 1976] M. H. van Emden, R. A. Kowalski, "The semantics of predicate logic as a programming language," J.ACM 23, 4 (Oct. 1976), 733 – 742.

[D. H. Warren, 1982] D. H. D. Warren, "Higher-order extension to PROLOG: are they needed?", *Machine Intelligence* 10, 1982, pp. 441 – 454.

[D. S. Warren, 1983] David Scott Warren, "Using λ-Calculus to Represent Meaning in Logic Grammars" in the Proceedings of the 21st Annual Meeting of the Association for Computational Linguistics, June 1983, 51 – 56.

ABSTRACT INTERPRETATION OF PROLOG PROGRAMS

C. S. Mellish
Cognitive Studies Programme
University of Sussex

1. Introduction

This paper represents part of a formalisation of previous practical work on proving properties of Prolog programs [Mellish 81, Mellish 85], which has been able to derive automatically the following information:

(1) Mode declarations (information about the instantiation modes in which predicates are used)

(2) Determinacy information (information about the number of solutions that predicates can produce)

(3) Information about shared structures (this can be used, for instance, to indicate places where "occur checks" might be desirable)

We would like to formalise our work on Prolog programs in terms of <u>abstract interpretations</u>. The notion of using abstract interpretations to prove properties of programs has been used successfully with other languages (eg. [Cousot and Cousot 77], [Mycroft 80], [Sintzoff 72]). The basic idea is to start with a precise description of the meaning of Prolog programs in terms of the normal execution strategy. This description can then be given the <u>standard interpretation</u>, which characterises exactly what and how the program computes but may not allow interesting properties to be proved in a computationally feasible way. Alternatively, it can be given consistent <u>abstract interpretations</u>, in which the program is thought of as computing in an abstract domain where less information about the data objects is taken account of. Results of computations in this abstract domain then reflect properties of the program operating in the standard way.

The formalisation of abstract interpretation of Prolog developed here differs from that being produced by [Jones 85] in that our main goal is to close the gap (with the minimum mathematical machinery) between the theory and the actual algorithms already used by us. This probably means some sacrifice in generality.

2. Canonical Terms

In order to talk about what a Prolog program computes, we need to have a way of talking about logical terms that allows us to ignore the problem of variants (terms that are identical apart from the choice of variable names). Thus, we would like to say that the two Prolog clauses:

```
foo(X,X).
```

and

```
foo(Y,Y).
```

have the same meaning, even though different names are used for the variables in the two cases. Our method of ignoring variance is to introduce the notion of a <u>canonical term</u>. A canonical term can be thought of as the equivalence class (under variance) of a logical term. We can write it in the same way as a term, but with special tokens replacing the variables in a way that preserves "sharing". For instance, one could use a scheme that "numbers" the variables according to a left-right traversal of the term (as does the DEC-10 Prolog 'numbervars' predicate).

If T is the set of logical terms and CT the set of canonical terms, we require there to be two functions:

```
gen:  T  -> CT   ("generalise")
inst: CT -> T    ("instance")
```

The function 'gen' takes an ordinary term to its equivalence class, eg.

```
gen("foo(X,X,W)") = gen("foo(Y,Y,X)") = "foo(@1,@1,@2)"
```

The function 'inst' produces, for a canonical term, an example term that is in the equivalence class. Of course, there may be infinitely many such terms. The idea is that, every time 'inst' is used, the variables introduced are randomly chosen distinct variables that have never been used before (an alternative and better formulation would probably involve providing 'inst' with an argument specifying a set of variables not to be used). This is a way of ensuring that variable name clashes do not occur when, for instance, a term from one clause is manipulated at the same time as a term from another. Put another way, "inst o gen" is a "safe" variable renaming function for terms. Since the result of 'inst' involves some randomness, one should check that in any use of it the results computed do not depend on the precise variable names chosen.

3. Program Traces

Our description of the meaning of Prolog programs is formulated in terms of traces. A given Prolog program defines a set of traces, which reflect the possible intermediate states in the satisfaction of initial queries. A trace of a Prolog query is a 4-tuple:

<IN,OUT,NUM,SUBTRACES>

where IN and OUT are a record of the query itself and of the instantiation of the query at the end of successful execution (both elements of CT). In some circumstances (see below), OUT may be the special value INCOMPLETE, which is not an element of CT. NUM is the number of the clause being used to satisfy the query. Finally there is a (possibly empty) sequence of traces SUBTRACES for all the subgoals introduced by the given clause being used to satisfy the given initial query.

The 'trace' relation relates a query to a possible (maybe partial) trace of the execution of that query. The following equations for 'trace' represent a formal description of Prolog execution (with the restrictions noted below):

q trace $\langle q, \text{INCOMPLETE}, 1, \langle\rangle\rangle$

q trace $\langle q, q', i, \langle t_1 \ldots t_n\rangle\rangle$ if

clause i is: $H \text{ :- } B_1, \ldots B_k.$

s_0 = unify(q,H) is not FAIL

for $j = 1 \ldots n$, $(n \le k)$

gen($s_{j-1}(B_j)$) trace t_j

if $j < n$ then $t_j(2)$ is not INCOMPLETE

if $t_j(2)$ is not INCOMPLETE then
s_j = compose(unify($t_j(2)$,B_j), s_{j-1})

if $t_n(2)$ = INCOMPLETE then q' = INCOMPLETE
otherwise q' = gen($s_n(H)$)

(see Appendix A for an explanation of some of my notation). In this definition, 'unify' is a version of unification which takes a canonical term and an ordinary term as arguments:

unify(x,y) = mgu(inst(x),y)

here 'mgu' is ordinary unification. In addition, 'compose' is normal unifying com-osition of substitutions [Sickel 76]. Intuitively, s_j is the substitution that has een applied to the clause after the successful satisfaction of the jth subgoal B_j. he notion of trace allowed here includes incomplete executions. This is important, ecause one generally wants to consider the work done by the Prolog system pursuing oals that do not succeed, as well as those that do. If the second component of a race is INCOMPLETE, this represents the fact that the satisfaction of the query is ot complete. Note that a subtrace of a trace can only be marked INCOMPLETE if it is he last subtrace and the main trace is itself INCOMPLETE.

In fact, the definition of 'trace' does not take account of Prolog's incomplete epth-first search strategy and disregards the effect of "cuts". Thus we assume a ersion of Prolog that, given a goal, will eventually consider all clauses that ight enable that goal to be satisfied. Such a system will obviously compute a uperset of the answers that a standard Prolog computes.

The use of traces in our formulation of Prolog enables us to describe formally section 6 below) the minimum that a program is expected to do in order to handle a iven set of input queries. This thus provides an alternative to the minimal func-ion graph notion of [Jones and Mycroft 86]. We seem to be able to get by with some-hat less machinery this way.

. Further Concepts Involving Traces

It is convenient to define the notion of <u>subtrace</u>. If t is a trace, then t' is subtrace of t if either:

t' is t

r

t' is a subtrace of t_j for some t_j in t(4)

inally, it is useful to introduce a "time ordering" as a way of traversing traces. trace contains two canonical terms and zero or more subtraces. Each of these tself contains two canonical terms and other traces, and so on. We impose a "time rdering" on the positions in a trace where these canonical terms appear. If t is a race, we can refer to the two positions in t as follows:

IN(t) - the position of the "input" canonical term (the first component)

OUT(t) - the position of the "output" canonical term (the second component)

hen if t is a trace and

$t = \langle q, q', i, \langle t_1 \ldots t_k \rangle \rangle$

hen

$IN(t) < IN(t_j) < OUT(t_j) < OUT(t) \qquad j = 1 \ldots k$

$OUT(t_j) < IN(t_{j+1}) \qquad j = 1 \ldots k-1$

ntuitively, this is the order in which the terms are generated in a Prolog execu-ion. Thus, when a goal is invoked the Prolog interpreter firstly deals with that oal in its initial instantiation state. It then deals with all the subgoals. inally, the final (successful) instantiation state of the goal is available.

. Input and Output of a program

Having described Prolog execution by means of traces, we now develop an alter-ative formulation, which is more appropriate for the applications we have in mind, and show that it is consistent with the original. Given a program and a (possibly infinite) set of desired queries DQ, one is interested in the ways in which predicates may be called during the satisfaction of those queries, and the ways in which subgoals may be successfully satisfied. The two sets 'input' and 'output' are defined accordingly. Once again, we characterise queries, etc. in terms of canonical terms, ie.

DQ, input, output are subsets of CT

Here is a recursive definition of the 'input' and 'output' of a given program P and given desired queries DQ. We are interested in possible values of 'input' and 'output' which satisfy these equations. This definition is "conservative", ie. characterises supersets of the desired sets. This does not matter for most "collecting" applications ie. applications where we are interested in finding out what sorts of situations _might_ arise.

input = DQ U

$\bigcup_{H \text{ :- } B_1..B_i..B_k \text{ in } P}$ {summarise(s,B_i) |
exists j in input
unify(j,H) = s_0 is not FAIL
s is in bo(s_0,$\langle B_1..B_{i-1}\rangle$) }

output =

$\bigcup_{H \text{ :- } B_1...B_k \text{ in } P}$ {summarise(s,H) |
exists j in input
unify(j,H) = s_0 is not FAIL
s in bo(s_0,$\langle B_1...B_k\rangle$) }

bo(s_0,$\langle B_1...B_k\rangle$) = S_k where

S_0 = {s_0}

S_i = {compose(s',s'') | s'' is in S_{i-1}
exists j in output
unify(j,B_i) = s' is not FAIL}

Here 'summarise' is defined by:

summarise(s,t) = gen(s(t))

Note that 'bo' returns sets of substitutions. In particular, it will return many possible variants of any given substitution. This does not matter, as the contribution to 'input' and 'output' always goes through an application of 'gen'.

6. Completeness of 'input' and 'output'

For a "collecting" application, we require that any 'input' and 'output' calculated according to the above equations, do indeed contain all the possibilities. Put more formally, we require that if:

(1) q is in DQ

(2) q trace t

(3) t' is subtrace of t and

(4) input and output are solutions to the above equations

then

(1) the canonical term at IN(t') is in input

(2) the canonical term at OUT(t') is in output (unless it is INCOMPLETE)

For simplicity, we will during the proof refer to any solutions to the above quations simply as 'input' and 'output', deferring the discussion of existence and niqueness of solutions until later. We prove the result by induction, using the time ordering" on positions in the trace introduced earlier.

.1. <u>The Base Case</u>

The CT in the trace which comes earliest in the time ordering is the original oal at IN(t). This is q. Thus we need to show that q is in 'input'. From the defin- tion, 'input' contains DQ. Since q is in DQ, it is therefore in 'input'.

.2. <u>Induction step</u>

Assume that the result is true for all canonical terms appearing "earlier" in he trace than some position P (P not being IN(t)) and let the canonical term at P e Q. There are two cases to consider:

1) P is IN(t') for some subtrace. In this case, we wish to show that Q is in 'input'.

2) P is OUT(t') for some subtrace. In this case, we wish to show that Q is in 'output'.

ase 1. Since P is not IN(t), it must be a position in a subtrace which appears mbedded within another trace. Assume P is in one of the immediate proper subtraces f

$T = <q',q'',i,<t_1...t_n>>$

et B_j, s_j, H be defined as in the definition of 'trace' and let

$P = IN(t_m)$, ie. $Q = t_m(1)$ $(1 <= m <= n)$

ow, because clause number i is "H :- $B_1..B_m..B_k$", 'input' contains:

{summarise(s,B_m) | exists j in input
unify(j,H) = s_0 is not FAIL
s in bo(s_0,$<B_1..B_{m-1}>$) }

hich contains (by the induction hypothesis applied to IN(T), a position in the race "before" P):

{summarise(s,B_m) | unify(q',H) = s_0 is not FAIL
s in bo(s_0,$<B_1..B_{m-1}>$)}

y the lemma (see Appendix B), bo(s_0,$<B_1..B_{m-1}>$) contains s_{m-1}. Thus the above set ontains the element:

summarise(s_{m-1},B_m))

hich is $t_m(1)$, ie. Q, since gen($s_{m-1}(B_m)$) trace t_m.

ase 2. Assume that Q appears in the subtrace $<q',Q,i,<t_1...t_k>>$, and that H, B_j, s_j re defined as usual. We need to show that Q is in 'output'. Since clause i is "H - $B_1...B_k$", 'output' contains:

{summarise(s,H) | exists j in input
unify(j,H) = s_0 is not FAIL
s in bo(s_0,$<B_1...B_k>$) }

y the lemma, bo(s_0,$<B_1...B_k>$) contains s_k. Hence 'output' contains:

gen(s_k(H))

hich is Q.

7. Existence and uniqueness of solutions

For any given program, there may be many (or no) solutions to the above equations for 'input' and 'output'. If there is more than one solution, then, since each solution contains the canonical terms we are interested in, we require to find the least solution. This will be the one that contains the least "noise". If we are not interested in all details of 'input' and 'output', but are content with some abstract characterisation of these sets, we may be able to guarantee that, when the equations are interpreted in an appropriate abstract domain, a least fixed point exists and can be computed finitely. In particular, this will be the case when the abstract domain corresponding to CT is finite. In this case, a least fixed point is guaranteed to exist, since the equations are monotonic on <input,output>. A certain amount of noise is introduced, first by the step from traces to the equations for 'input' and 'output' and secondly by the choice of a given abstract interpretation from the standard interpretation of these equations. Whether this noise is too much to allow the least fixed point to yield any useful information seems to be a matter for empirical investigation.

8. Abstract Interpretations of 'input' and 'output'

We now consider in more detail how we can obtain abstract interpretations of 'input' and 'output'. First of all, here is a summary of the sets and basic functions assumed by the standard interpretation of the equations:

```
T     - the set of logical terms
CT    - the set of canonical terms

Subst - the set of substitutions (partial functions: Vars -> T)

unify:       CT x T -> Subst U {FAIL}
 (almost standard unification)
summarise:   Subst x T -> CT
 (substitution application + generalisation)
compose:     Subst x Subst -> Subst
 (unifying substitution composition)
```

We will obtain abstract interpretations of the equations by interpreting some of these functions as operations in other, more abstract, domains. In fact, we will consider interpretations where the sets and functions are as follows:

```
D      - the set of "descriptions" of terms
CD     - the set of "canonical descriptions"
DSubst - the set of "descriptive substitutions"
(partial functions: Vars -> D)

unify:     CD x T           -> DSubst U {FAIL}
summarise: DSubst x T       -> CD
compose:   DSubst x DSubst -> DSubst
```

Here D is a set of "descriptions" that can be associated with terms (for instance, indicating which variables they might contain or what their instantiation state is). During standard Prolog execution, elements of Subst are computed, associating values (elements of T) with the variables in clauses. In this more general context, we consider variables being associated, via elements of DSubst, with descriptions (elements of D). The set CD is used here only with complete literals from the program. It bears the same relation to D that CT bears to T, in that it holds descriptions that are independent of variable naming. Elements of CD may also be more condensed descriptions than the corresponding elements of D. In general, the sets D and CD may have partial orderings (denoted "<="), where $d_1 <= d_2$ means that d_2 is more general than d_1 (ie. describes a larger set of terms). The partial ordering on D induces a natural partial ordering on DSubst.

In this more general framework, the standard interpretation involves choosing

```
D = T
CD = CT
```

hat we would like to do now is to establish sufficient conditions for an interpre- ation of the above kind to be "correct". In order for us to judge whether an nterpretation is consistent with the standard interpretation, we need to know what he desired description of any term and canonical term is. This must be given by bstraction functions:

```
 alpha: T  -> D
Calpha: CT -> CD
```

further abstraction function:

```
Salpha: Subst -> DSubst
```

s induced naturally by 'alpha'. Now in order for an interpretation to be con- istent, we need to have the following result:

```
for all x in CT,
    if x is in output then
        there is a y in output' such that
            Calpha(x) <= y
```

here output' is any solution to the above equations for 'output', with the various ets and functions interpreted in the abstract domain. A similar result is required or 'input'. Thus computing in the abstract domains gives us the information we need plus possibly some noise) about what might occur during the running of the Prolog rogram.

Unpacking these requirements into requirements to be satisfied by the abstract nterpretations of the functions 'unify', 'compose' and 'summarise' we can derive he following set of sufficient conditions for correctness. Note that in this sec- ion of the paper, but no other, we need to refer simultaneously to the standard and o the abstract interpretations of the symbols 'unify', 'compose' and 'summarise'. e will refer to the standard interpretations by the symbols themselves and the bstract interpretations by 'UNIFY', 'COMPOSE' and 'SUMMARISE'.

```
Calpha(summarise(s,t)) <= SUMMARISE(Salpha(s),t)
Salpha(compose(s1,s2)) <= COMPOSE(Salpha(s1),Salpha(s2))
Salpha(unify(ct,t))    <= UNIFY(Calpha(ct),t)

SUMMARISE is monotonic on its first argument
COMPOSE is monotonic on each argument independently
```

. <u>Example Applications</u>

Here we will briefly describe two applications of the above ideas, indicating ow they fit into the framework established.

First of all, in the <u>mode declarations</u> application we seek to derive informa- ion about the instantiation states of goals that arise during the execution of a esired query. For this application, we use

```
D = P({II, IM, IU, UU})
```

here

```
II - totally ground
IU - instantiated to a term with totally uninstantiated components
IM - instantiated to a term which is not II or IU
U  - totally uninstantiated
```

hat is, we describe a variable by a set of instantiation states that it might have. n a canonical description of a literal, we are only interested in the predicate and he possible instantiation states of the arguments. Thus:

```
CD = Pred x D*
```

The mapping 'summarise' from DSubst x T to CD is fairly straightforwardly defined. It involves summarising the instantiation state of each argument of the term, giving the information about variable values provided in the descriptive substitution. For instance:

summarise({X/{II} Y/{UU}}, foo(g(X),adam,Y)) = <foo,<{II},{II},{UU}>>

The function 'unify' is used to make a descriptive substitution from the comparison of a canonical description and a term. For instance,

unify(<foo,<{II},{IU}>>), foo(g(X),Y)) = {X/{II} Y/{IU}}

Note that unification cannot fail, as long as the elements of CD and T have the same predicate. The function 'compose' is used to combine two descriptive substitutions, associating with each variable the "most instantiated" description given by one of the substitutions. For instance:

compose({X/{IU} Y/{UU,II}}, {Y/{IU} Z/{II}}) = {X/{IU} Y/{IU,II} Z/{II}}

In fact, [Debray 85] has shown that this abstract interpretation is only consistent with the standard interpretation if extra assumptions are made about the clauses. This is because the condition on COMPOSE is not satisfied in general (where "aliasing" may occur between variables). There are alternative (more conservative) definitions of COMPOSE which do not have this problem. Alternatively, if we only allow the descriptions {II} and {II,IM,IU,UU}, the system is valid.

In the *shared structures* application, we are interested in what structures (complex terms or variables) may be shared between predicate arguments. Here,

D = P(Vars)

That is, we keep a record, for each variable, of what other variables' values its value may share structure with. In canonical descriptions, we wish to be independent of variable naming. Thus we keep track of the predicate of a literal, together with the set of argument number pairs where sharing may take place:

CD = Pred x P(N^2)

To produce a canonical description from a descriptive substitution and a term, 'summarise' looks for repetitions of variables between argument positions. These variables may occur explicitly as constituents of the terms, or they may appear inside the descriptions of other variables. For instance:

summarise({X/{} Y/{Z}}, foo(X,f(adam,Y),g(X),Z)) = <foo,{<1,3>,<2,4>}>

The function 'unify' takes the information about sharing argument positions from a canonical description and produces a substitution to force this sharing on the variables in a term. For instance:

unify(<foo,{<1,3>}>, foo(X,X,Y)) = {X/{Y}}

The function 'compose' combines together two descriptive substitutions, computing the "worst case" of which variables may share. For instance:

compose({X/{Y}}, {Y/{Z W}}) = {X/{Y Z W} ...}

We believe that our general conditions are satisfied by this abstract interpretation (which obviously needs further definition than is given here), although this is not the abstract interpretation that will give the "tightest" results. Useful theoretical work on the detection of shared structures has been done by [Plaisted 84] and [Sondergaard 85].

10. Computing 'input' and 'output'

In this section, we will assume that the clauses for 'input' and 'output' are always being interpreted in some abstract domain. If we have a particular program nd wish to evaluate 'input' and 'output', we need to find a fixed point to the quations. If there is more than one fixed point, the least one (ie the one which as the smallest sets) will give us the most information, because (by sections 6 and) any existing solution characterises all the things that can possibly occur during program execution, together with some extra noise. If the set CD is finite (as is he case in both of our examples) we can compute the least fixed point of the equaions for 'input' and 'output' by a standard iterative process. That is, we start by ssociating the value {} with both 'input' and 'output'. We then apply the equations s rewrite rules to obtain new values for both (calculated by using the previous set f values). This process is repeated until a fixed point of the equations is eached. This must eventually happen, as P(CD) is finite and the equations represent monotonic function on the pair of values. This section outlines a general straegy for evaluating 'input' and 'output', rather than necessarily being the most fficient method for any given application.

In practice, it is useful to start by partially evaluating the equations, takng account of the given program and desired queries. This can be thought of as takng place in a sequence of stages. First, we unfold the equations for each clause. ach clause in fact makes a number of contributions to the unfolded set of equaions. First, it is used once for each subgoal in its body to derive part of input'. Secondly, it is used in one place only to derive part of 'output'. If the lause has k goals in the body, the first set of contributions make use of o(s_0,<B_1,...B_r>) for r from 1 to k-1, and the final contribution makes use of o(s_0,<B_1,...B_k>). So, for instance, if we had the clause:

```
foo(X,Y) :- baz(X), zang(X,Y).
```

n the program, the equations for 'input' and 'output' would be something like:

```
input = ... U {summarise(s,"baz(X)")|
                exists j in input,
                unify(j,"foo(X,Y)") = s0 is not FAIL,
                s is in bo(s0,<>)}
            U {summarise(s,"zang(X,Y)")|
                exists j in input,
                unify(j,"foo(X,Y)") = s0 is not FAIL,
                s is in bo(s0,<"baz(X)">)}

output = ... U {summarise(s,"foo(X,Y)")|
                 exists j in input,
                 unify(j,"foo(X,Y)") = s0 is not FAIL,
                 s is in bo(s0,<"baz(X)","zang(X,Y)">}
```

ssuming that functions like 'summarise' preserve the main predicate of a literal, e can then organise the cases by predicate, giving a set of equations for the input' and 'output' of particular predicates p (which we denote by "input/p" and output/p" respectively). In general, 'unify' will only succeed if its two arguments re associated with the same predicate. The "right hand sides" of the equations can hus also be specialised to deal with "input/p" and "output/p" for specific prediates p. This would yield for the above example:

```
input/baz = ...  U {summarise(s,"baz(X)")|
                     exists j in input/foo,
                     unify(j,"foo(X,Y)") = s0 is not FAIL,
                     s is in bo(s0,<>)}
input/zang = ... U {summarise(s,"zang(X,Y)")|
                     exists j in input/foo,
                     unify(j,"foo(X,Y)") = s0 is not FAIL,
                     s is in bo(s0,<"baz(X)">)}

output/foo = ... U {summarise(s,"foo(X,Y)")|
                     exists j in input/foo,
                     unify(j,"foo(X,Y)") = s0 is not FAIL,
                     s is in bo(s0,<"baz(X)","zang(X,Y)">}
```

e can now further unfold the 'bo' terms and move all existential quantifiers to the left, giving:

```
    input/baz = ...
        U                  {summarise(s,"baz(X)")|
     j in input/foo         s = unify(j,"foo(X,Y)") is not FAIL}

    input/zang = ...
        U                  {summarise(compose(s',s),"zang(X,Y)")|
     j in input/foo         s = unify(j,"foo(X,Y)") is not FAIL,
     k in output/baz        s' = unify(k,"baz(X)") is not FAIL}

    output/foo = ...
        U                {summarise(compose(s'',compose(s',s)),
     j in input/foo       s = unify(j,"foo(X,Y)")  is not FAIL,
     k in output/baz      s' = unify(k,"baz(X)") is not FAIL,
     l in output/zang     s'' = unify(l,"zang(X,Y)") is not FAIL}
```

It can be seen from the definition that, given fixed values in the 'input' and 'output' sets required, $bo(s_0,<B_1,...B_{r+1}>)$ is easily computed from $bo(s_0,<B_1,...B_r>)$. This is reflected by the duplications in the above equations. Moreover, all the substitutions are only computed in order that they can be applied in sequence to terms in the clause. So in fact we can obtain these equations (with the subterms possibly further unfolded for symbolic values of j, k, l) by a single pass through each clause "H :- B_1, ... B_n", as follows:

(1) Producing an expression for:

s0 = unify(j,H)

(2) For i = 1, ..n, (where the predicate of B_i is p_i):

a) recording the contribution summarise(s_{i-1},B_i) to input/p_i,
b) producing an expression for

si = compose(unify(x,B_i),s_{i-1})
where x is the appropriate symbolic quantity for an element of output/p_i,

(3) Recording the contribution of summarise(s_n,H) to output/p

In our previous paper [Mellish 81], we have called stages 1 and 2b <u>history updating</u> and stages 2a and 3 <u>position updating</u> (for the mode declarations application).

The result of this partial evaluation is a set of equations for contributions to the "input/p" and "output/p" quantities. For instance, in the mode declarations application the above program fragment would result in equations as follows:

```
    input/baz = ...
        U                  {baz(j(1))}
     j in input/foo

    input/zang = ...
        U                  {zang(j(1) ^^ k(1),j(2))}
     j in input/foo
     k in output/baz

    output/foo = ...
        U                  {foo(j(1) ^^ k(1) ^^ l(1),j(2) ^^ l(2))}
     j in input/foo
     k in output/baz
     l in output/zang
```

for some operation "^^". We can maintain a single hashed datastructure containing n entry for each quantity to be computed (ie. "input/p" and "output/p" for each redicate "p"). This entry contains a current value and the equations contributing o the quantity. In the equations, other quantities (indicated here by the symbols j', 'k', 'l') are represented by pointers to their entries in the central datas-ructure. It is therefore very easy, given a particular quantity, to evaluate its quation (using the current values of other quantities) and see whether the result s the same as the current value.

Having put the equations in a suitable form, the computation now involves terating through the quantities, for each one replacing the current value with the esult of evaluating its equation, until no more changes occur. Each current value tarts off as the the bottom element of a finite lattice (the empty set), and each quation can be viewed as a monotonic function on tuples of values in this lattice. his is therefore the standard way of calculating a least fixed point, and is uaranteed to converge.

At one point, we investigated keeping track, for each quantity, of the quanti-ies that depended on it, so that if the value of one quantity changed the other uantities that might be affected could be immediately reconsidered. This technique romised a saving, since in this way we could avoid having to recompute values that ould not possibly have changed. In fact, the extra overhead of keeping a global ist of quantities to be reconsidered (and checking for duplications in this list) as not worth the effort, and our current programs simply iterate through the com-lete set of quantities until no more changes occur. It seems to be rare for more han about 6 complete iterations to be required anyway. The tradeoffs between these wo approaches might be different if we were using a language with assignment (we ere using Prolog).

1. Acknowledgements

Thanks are due to the Alvey Directorate and Chris Hankin and Richard Sykes of mperial College for organising the Workshop on Abstract Interpretation at the niversity of Kent, 1985. The occasion of this workshop was the necessary spur to urther investigate the theoretical basis of my previous practical work.

Thanks are also due to the Science and Engineering Research Council, whose pro-ision of an Advanced Fellowship has given me the time to pursue this research.

2. References

ousot, P. and Cousot, R., "Abstract Interpretation: a Unified Lattice Model for Static Analysis of Programs by Construction or Approximation of Fixpoints", Principles of Programming Languages, 1977.

ebray, S. K., "Automatic Mode Inference for Prolog programs", Technical Report #85/019, State University of New York at Stony Brook, 1985.

ones, N. D., "Concerning the Abstract Interpretation of Prolog", draft paper, DIKU, Copenhagen, 1985.

ones, N. D. and Mycroft, A., "Data Flow Analysis of Applicative Programs using Minimal Function Graphs", Principles of Programming Languages, Florida, USA, 1986.

ellish, C. S., "The Automatic Generation of Mode Declarations for Prolog Programs", Paper presented at the Workshop on Logic Programming for Intelligent Systems, Los Angeles, 1981 (also DAI Research Paper 163, Dept of Artificial Intelligence, University of Edinburgh).

ellish, C. S., "Some Global Optimisations for a Prolog Compiler", Journal of Logic Programming, Vol 2, No 1, 1985.

ycroft, A., "The Theory and Practice of Transforming Call-by-need into Call-by-value", in Springer Lecture Notes in Computer Science, No 83, Springer Verlag, 1980.

Plaisted, D., "The Occur-Check problem in Prolog", Procs of the International Symposium on Logic Programming, Atlantic City, USA, 1984.

Sickel, S., "A Search Technique for Clause Interconnectivity Graphs" IEEE Trans. on Computers, C-25(8), 1976.

Sintzoff, M., "Calculating Properties of Programs by Valuations on Specific Models", in Sigplan Notices Vol 7, No 1, 1972.

Sondergaard, H., "An Application of Abstract Interpretation of Logic Programs: Occur Check Reduction", DIKU, Copenhagen, 1985.

Appendix A: Notation

As my character set is rather restricted, my notation may be opaque at times. Here is an explanation of the main conventions.

P(....)	Powerset
{ ... }	Set brackets
< ... >	Tuple brackets
t(n)	Accessing a component of a tuple or a logical term
^	Exponentiation (eg. N^2 is N x N)

Appendix B: Lemma

Lemma: Let q_0 trace T and $t' = <q,q',i,<t_1 \ldots t_n>>$ be a subtrace of T, with B_j, s_j and H defined as usual. Moreover, let s_0 be unify(j,H) for some j in 'input' and the main result hold for all positions in the trace up to OUT(t_m) in T (or IN(t') if m=0) ($0 <= m <= n$). Then s_m is in bo(s_0,$<B_1 \ldots B_m>$).

Proof by induction on m.

m = 0. bo(s_0,<>) = {s_0}, which contains s_0.

Assume that the result is true for m-1.

$$\text{bo}(s_0,<B_1 \ldots B_m>) = \{\text{compose}(s',s_{m-1}') \mid s_{m-1}' \text{ in bo}(s_0,<B_1 \ldots B_{m-1}>) \text{ exists i in output unify}(i,B_m) = s' \text{ is not FAIL}\}$$

which contains by the inductive hypothesis

$$\{\text{compose}(s',s_{m-1}) \mid \text{exists i in output unify}(i,B_m) = s' \text{ is not FAIL}\}$$

By the main induction hypothesis, gen(s_m(B_m)) (ie. t_m(2)) is in 'output'. So the set contains the element:

$$\text{compose}(\text{unify}(t_m(2),B_m))),\ s_{m-1})$$

which is s_m by definition.

Verification of Prolog Programs Using An Extension of Execution

Tadashi KANAMORI

Mitsubishi Electric Corporation
Central Research Laboratory
Tsukaguchi-Honmachi 8-1-1
Amagasaki,Hyogo,JAPAN 661

Hirohisa SEKI

ICOT Research Center
Institute for New Generation Computer Technology
Mita 1-4-28,Minato-ku
Tokyo,JAPAN 108

Abstract

An approach to proving properties of Prolog programs exploiting characteristics of Prolog is described. The most important feature of this approach is the use of an extension of execution, which is a generalization of the conventional Prolog interpreter. We use the extended execution to show that a property S in a class of first order formulas, called S-formulas, is a logical consequence of the completion of a program P. This approach is (1) simple because we need only an extention of the Prolog interpreter, (2) understandable because properties are processed keeping their original forms as far as possible and (3) without waste because we carry it out without unnecessary explicit strengthening of P. We show how the extended execution works for the same example in the Boyer and Moore Theorem Prover (BMTP).

Keywords : Program Verification, Prolog, Natural Deduction, Theorm Proving.

Contents

1. Introduction

Logic programming attracts attention because of its clear semantics. This would seem to make verification (and other meta-processing and manipulation) of programs simpler and easier. But only a few studies have investigated verification effectively [5],[9],[22].

In this paper we describe an approach to proving properties of Prolog programs exploiting characteristics of Prolog. The most important feature of this approach is the use of an extension of execution, which is a generalization of the conventional Prolog interpreter. We use extended execution to show that a property S in a class of first order formulas,called S-formulas, is a logical consequence of the completion of a program P. This approach is (1) simple because we need only an extention of the Prolog interpreter, (2) understandable because properties are processed keeping their original form as far as possible and (3) without waste because we carry it out without unnecessary explicit strengthening of P. We show how the extended execution works for the same example in the Boyer and Moore Theorem Prover (BMTP). One very interesting result is that two different heuristics of BMTP, "generalization" and "cross-fertilization", are performed in a unified way by one of our inference rules,"simplification".

After summarizing preliminary materials in Section 2, we present a framework of verification of Prolog programs in Section 3. Though the word "verification" in general might lead to misunderstanding, we mean this framework when we use the word. In Section 4,we describe a class of deductions, which is a generalization of the behavior of Prolog interpreter. In Section 5, we show that extended execution can play the role of first order inference and be integrated into provers with induction like the Boyer-Moore Theorem Prover (BMTP) by very simple examples. Then we present the example used in Boyer and Moore [4] for comparison. Lastly,in Section 6, we discuss other works and our actual verification system.

2. Preliminaries

In the following, we assume familiarity with the basic terminology of first order logic such as term, atom(atomic formula), positive and negative literals, formula, substitution, most general unifier (m.g.u.) and so on. We also assume knowledge of the semantics of Prolog such as completion, minimum Herbrand model and transformation T of Herbrand interpretations (see [1],[6],[7],[8],[11]). We follow the syntax of DEC-10 Prolog [17]. Variables appearing in the head of a definite clause are called *head variables*. Other variables are called *internal variables*. As syntactic variables, we use X, Y, Z for variables, s, t for terms, A, B for atoms and $\mathcal{F}, \mathcal{G}, \mathcal{H}$ for formulas possibly with primes and subscripts. In addition we use σ, τ for substitutions, $\mathcal{F}_{\mathcal{G}}(\mathcal{H})$ for replacement of *all* occurrences of a formula $\mathcal{G}$ in a formula $\mathcal{F}$ with $\mathcal{H}$ and $\mathcal{F}_{\mathcal{G}}[\mathcal{H}]$ for replacement of an occurrence of a formula $\mathcal{G}$ in a formula $\mathcal{F}$ with $\mathcal{H}$.

2.1. Polarity of Subformulas

We generalize the distinctions of positive and negative goals. The *positive* and *negative subformulas* of a formula $\mathcal{F}$ are defined as follows (see [18],[16],[15]).

(a) $\mathcal{F}$ is a positive subformula of $\mathcal{F}$.

(b) When $\neg\mathcal{G}$ is a positive (negative) subformula of $\mathcal{F}$, then $\mathcal{G}$ is a negative (positive) subformula of $\mathcal{F}$.

(c) When $\mathcal{G}\wedge\mathcal{H}$ or $\mathcal{G}\vee\mathcal{H}$ is a positive (negative) subformula of $\mathcal{F}$, then $\mathcal{G}$ and $\mathcal{H}$ are positive (negative) subformulas of $\mathcal{F}$.

d) When $\mathcal{G} \supset \mathcal{H}$ is a positive (negative) subformula of $\mathcal{F}$, then $\mathcal{G}$ is a negative (positive) subformula of $\mathcal{F}$ and $\mathcal{H}$ is a positive (negative) subformula of $\mathcal{F}$.

e) When $\forall X \mathcal{G}, \exists X \mathcal{G}$ are positive (negative) subformulas of $\mathcal{F}$, then $\mathcal{G}_X(t)$ is a positive (negative) subformula of $\mathcal{F}$.

Example 2.1. Let $\mathcal{F}$ be

∀ X,W (label(W) ∧ordered(X) ⊃∃Y insert(X,W,Y)).

Then $\exists Y insert(X, W, Y)$ is a positive subformula of $\mathcal{F}$.

2.2. S-formulas and Goal Formulas

Let $\mathcal{F}$ be a closed first order formula. When $\forall X \mathcal{G}$ is a positive subformula or $\exists X \mathcal{G}$ is a negative subformula of $\mathcal{F}$, X is called a *free variable* of $\mathcal{F}$. When $\forall Y \mathcal{H}$ is a negative subformula or $\exists Y \mathcal{H}$ is a positive subformula of $\mathcal{F}$, Y is called an *undecided variable* of $\mathcal{F}$. In other words, free variables are variables quantified universally, and undecided variables are those quantified existentially when $\mathcal{F}$ is converted to its prenex normal form.

Example 2.2.1. Let $\mathcal{F}$ be

∀ A (list(A)⊃∀B ∃C append(A,B,C)).

Then A and B are both free variables, while C is an undecided variable.

A closed first order formula S is called a *specification formula* (or *S-formula* for short) when

a) no free variable in S is quantified in the scope of quantification of an undecided variable in S and

b) no undecided variable appears in negative atoms of S.

In other words, S-formulas are formulas convertible to prenex normal form $\forall X_1, X_2, \ldots, X_n \exists Y_1, Y_2, \ldots, Y_m \mathcal{F}$ and no $Y_1, Y_2, \ldots, Y_m$ appear among the negative atoms of $\mathcal{F}$. Note that S-formulas include both universal formulas $\forall X_1, X_2, \ldots, X_n \mathcal{F}$ and usual execution goals $\exists Y_1, Y_2, \ldots, Y_m\ (A_1 \wedge A_2 \wedge \cdots \wedge A_k)$.

Example 2.2.2. Let S be

∀ A (list(A)⊃∀B ∃C append(A,B,C)).

Then S is an S-formula, because free variables A and B are quantified outside $\exists C$, and C appears only in the positive atom $append(A, B, C)$. A universal formula $\forall A, B(reverse(A, B) \supset reverse(B, A))$ and an execution goal $\exists C append([1, 2], [3], C)$ are also S-formulas.

A formula G obtained from an S-formula S by leaving free variable X as it is, replacing undecided variable Y with $?Y$ and deleting all quantifications is called a *goal formula* of S. Note that S can be uniquely restorable from G. In the following, we use goal formulas in stead of original S-formulas. Goal formulas are denoted by F, G, H.

Example 2.2.3. An S-formula

∀ A (list(A)⊃∀B ∃C append(A,B,C))

is represented by a goal formula

list(A)⊃append(A,B,?C).

A universal formula $\forall A, B(reverse(A, B) \supset reverse(B, A))$ and an execution goal $\exists C\ append([1, 2], [3], C)$ are represented by $reverse(A, B) \supset reverse(B, A)$ and $append([1, 2], [3], ?C)$ respectively.

Remark. This representation corresponds to the backward application of ∀-introduction and ∃-introduction to positive $\forall X\mathcal{G}$ and $\exists X\mathcal{G}$ and the forward application of ∀-elimination and ∃-elimination to negative $\forall X\mathcal{G}$ and $\exists X\mathcal{G}$ in natural deduction.

2.3. Manipulation of Goal Formulas

Lastly we introduce two manipulations of goal formulas.

One is an application of a class of substitutions. A substitution σ for G is called a *deciding substitution* when σ instantiates no free variable in G.

Example 2.3.1. Let S be

∀ A,B,U ((list(A) ⊃∃C append(A,B,C)) ⊃(list(A) ⊃∃C append([U|A],B,C)))

Then the goal formula of S is

(list(A) ⊃append(A,B,C)) ⊃(list(A) ⊃append([U|A],B,?C))

The most general common instance of $append([U|A], B, ?C)$ and the head of the second definite clause for *append* is obtained by a deciding substitution $\sigma = <?C \Leftarrow [U|?C']>$. $\sigma(G)$ represents an S-formula

∀ A,B,U ((list(A) ⊃∃C append(A,B,C)) ⊃(list(A) ⊃∃C′ append([U|A],B,[U|C′])))

Another manipulation is a *reduction* of goal formulas with the logical constants *true* and *false*. The *reduced form* of a goal formula G,denoted by $G\downarrow$, is the normal form in the reduction system defined as follows :

$\neg true \rightarrow false,$	$\neg false \rightarrow true,$
$true \wedge G \rightarrow G,$	$false \wedge G \rightarrow false,$
$G \wedge true \rightarrow G,$	$G \wedge false \rightarrow false,$
$true \vee G \rightarrow true,$	$false \vee G \rightarrow G,$
$G \vee true \rightarrow true,$	$G \vee false \rightarrow G,$
$true \supset G \rightarrow G,$	$false \supset G \rightarrow true,$
$G \supset true \rightarrow true,$	$G \supset false \rightarrow \neg G.$

Example 2.3.2. Let G_1 and G_2 be

(true ⊃reverse(C,A)) ⊃(true ∧append(C,[U],B) ⊃reverse(B,[U|A]))

(false ⊃reverse(C,A)) ⊃(false ∧append(C,[U],B) ⊃reverse(B,[U|A])).

Then $G_1\downarrow$ is $reverse(C, A) \supset (append(C, [U], B) \supset reverse(B, [U|A]))$ and $G_2\downarrow$ is *true*.

3. Framework of Verification of Prolog Programs

3.1. Programming Language

Our programming language is an extension of Prolog. We introduce **type** constructs into Prolog to separate definite clauses defining data structures from others defining procedures,e.g.,

```
type.
   list([ ]).
   list([X|L]) :- list(L).
end.
```

'he body of **type** is a set of definite clauses whose head is an atom with a unary predicate defining a ata structure. (**type** in our verification system corresponds to *shell* in BMTP.) Procedures are defined ›llowing the syntax of DEC-10 Prolog [17],e.g.,

```
append([ ],K,K).
append([X|L],M,[X|N]) :- append(L,M,N).
reverse([ ],[ ]).
reverse([X|L],M) :- reverse(L,N),append(N,[X],M).
```

Throughout this paper, we study pure Prolog consisting of definite clauses "B :- $B_1, B_2, \ldots, B_m$" $m \geq 0$) and regard a finite set of definite clauses P as their conjunction. We assume that variables in ach definite clause are renamed at each use so that there occurs no conflict of variable names.

.2. Specification Language

The main construct of our specification language is "**theorem**" to state a theorem to be proved,e.g.,

theorem(halting-theorem-for-append).
  ∀ A:list,B ∃ C append(A,B,C).
end.

he body of **theorem** must be a closed S-formula. Any variable X in quantifications may be followed y a type qualifier : p (e.g.,:list above). $\forall X : p\mathcal{F}$ and $\exists X : p\mathcal{F}$ are abbreviations of $\forall X(p(X) \supset \mathcal{F})$ and $X(\mathcal{F} \wedge p(X))$, respectively.

.3. Formulation of Verification

Let S be a specification in an S-formula, M_0 be the minimum Herbrand model of P and P^* be the ›mpletion of P. We adopt a formulation as follows : Model-theoretically speaking, verification of S ith respect to P is to show $M_0 \models S$. Proof-theoretically speaking, it is to prove S from P^* using first rder inference and some induction. (Of course, the proof-theoretical formulation is weaker than the odel-theoretical formulation. See Section 5 for induction.)

The most important difference between our verification system and BMTP is that specifications in MTP are quantifier-free (i.e., universal) formulas while ours are S-formulas. Though we prove quantifier-ee specifications of the form $\forall X_1, X_2, \ldots, X_n(A_1 \wedge A_2 \wedge \cdots \wedge A_m \supset A_0)$ in most cases, the consideration of kistential quantifiers is inevitable because of the effects of internal variables in Prolog. For example, ippose we prove $\forall X, Y(condition(X, Y) \supset p(X, Y))$ with respect to a program $p(X, Y)$:- $q(X, Z), r(Z, Y)$. hen we must prove $\forall X, Y(condition(X, Y) \supset \exists Z(q(X, Z) \wedge r(Z, Y)))$ substantially.

. An Extension of Execution

If we follow the previous formulation of verification, it is necessary to generalize the Prolog execution ›mehow so that we can perform first order inference on S-formulas. Our logic system needs to treat uantifiers carefully, i.e., it requires a distinction of free variables and undecided variables (cf.[2]). Ioreover it needs to process logical connectives other than ∧ appropriately, because S has a more ›mplicated form than usual execution goals (cf.[16] and Schütte [19]). Our logic system consists of the following seven inference rules. (See the following explanation for their notations.) Each rule says that the subgoals in S-formulas above the line are generated from the goal in S-formulas below the line. We assume variables in specification S are renamed appropriately so that there occurs no conflict of variable names.

∧-deletion
$$\frac{G_H[H_1] \qquad G_H[H_2] \qquad \cdots \qquad G_H[H_k]}{G_+[H_1 \wedge H_2 \wedge \cdots \wedge H_k]}$$

∨-deletion
$$\frac{G_H[H_1] \qquad G_H[H_2] \qquad \cdots \qquad G_H[H_k]}{G_-[H_1 \vee H_2 \vee \cdots \vee H_k]}$$

⊃-deletion
$$\frac{G_H[\neg H_1] \qquad\qquad G_H[H_2]}{G_-[H_1 \supset H_2]}$$

DCI
$$\frac{\sigma_1(G_A[\wedge_{i=1}^{m_1} B_{1i}]) \downarrow}{G_+[A]} \quad \frac{\sigma_2(G_A[\wedge_{i=1}^{m_2} B_{2i}]) \downarrow}{G_+[A]} \quad \cdots \quad \frac{\sigma_k(G_A[\wedge_{i=1}^{m_k} B_{ki}]) \downarrow}{G_+[A]}$$

NFI
$$\frac{G_A[false] \downarrow \quad \sigma_1(G_A[\wedge_{i=1}^{m_1} B_{1i}]) \downarrow \quad \cdots \quad \sigma_k(G_A[\wedge_{i=1}^{m_k} B_{ki}]) \downarrow}{G_-[A]}$$

simplification
$$\frac{\sigma(G)_A(true) \downarrow \qquad\qquad \sigma(G)_A(false) \downarrow}{G}$$

oracle decision
$$\frac{\sigma(G)}{G}$$

4.1. Case Splitting

∧ may appear in more complicated ways in goal formulas.

∧-Deletion

Let G be a goal formula. When H is a positive subformula of the form $H_1 \wedge H_2 \wedge \cdots \wedge H_k$ ($k > 1$) and each undecided variable $?X$ appearing in H_i appears only in H_i ($1 \leq i \leq k$), we generate k new AND-goals $G_H[H_1], G_H[H_2], \ldots, G_H[H_k]$, where undecided variables in G and not in H are renamed and not shared between $G_H[H_i]$ and $G_H[H_j]$ ($i \neq j$).

Example 4.1.1. Let S be

∀ A,B,C (append(A,B,C)∧list(C) ⊃∃D reverse(A,D)∧∃E reverse(B,E)).

Then the goal formula of S is

append(A,B,C)∧list(C) ⊃reverse(A,?D)∧reverse(B,?E).

By applying ∧-deletion, we have 2 AND-goals

append(A,B,C)∧list(C) ⊃reverse(A,?D).

append(A,B,C)∧list(C) ⊃reverse(B,?E).

Remark. ∧-deletion corresponds to backward application of ∧-introduction in natural deduction.

∨ is one of the new logical connectives in goal formulas not appearing in usual execution goals.

∨-Deletion

Let G be a goal formula. When H is a negative subformula of the form $H_1 \vee H_2 \vee \cdots \vee H_k$ ($k > 1$) and each undecided variable $?X$ appearing in H_i appears only in H_i ($1 \leq i \leq k$), we generate k new AND-goals $G_H[H_1], G_H[H_2], \ldots, G_H[H_k]$, where undecided variables in G and not in H are renamed and not shared between $G_H[H_i]$ and $G_H[H_j]$ ($i \neq j$).

Example 4.1.2. Let S be of the form

$\forall$ S,T ((S=T $\vee$S<T $\vee$T<S) $\supset(\cdots)$).

Then the goal formula of S is

(S=T $\vee$S<T $\vee$T<S) $\supset(\cdots)$.

By applying $\vee$-deletion, we have 3 AND-goals

S=T $\supset(\cdots)$.

S<T $\supset(\cdots)$.

T<S $\supset(\cdots)$.

Remark. $\vee$-deletion corresponds to forward application of $\vee$-elimination in natural deduction.

Another important logical connective is $\supset$.

$\supset$-Deletion

Let G be a goal formula. When H is a negative subformula of the form $H_1 \supset H_2$ and each undecided variable $?X$ appearing in H_i appears only in H_i ($1 \leq i \leq 2$), we generate two new AND-goals $G_H[\neg H_1]$ and $G_H[H_2]$, where undecided variables in G and not in H are renamed and not shared between $G_H[H_i]$ and $G_H[H_j]$ ($i \neq j$).

Example 4.1.3. Let S be

$\forall$ U,B,C,D_1,D_2 ((append(B,C,D_2) $\supset D_1 = D_2$) $\supset$(append(B,C,D_2) $\supset$[U|D_1]=[U|D_2])).

Then the goal formula of S is

(append(B,C,D_2) $\supset D_1 = D_2$) $\supset$(append(B,C,D_2) $\supset$[U|D_1]=[U|D_2]).

By applying $\supset$-deletion, we have AND-goals

$\neg$ append(B,C,D_2) $\supset$(append(B,C,D_2) $\supset$[U|D_1]=[U|D_2]).

$D_1 = D_2$ $\supset$(append(B,C,D_2) $\supset$[U|D_1]=[U|D_2]).

Remark. $\supset$-deletion corresponds to forward application of $\supset$-elimination with $\bot_C$ in natural deduction.

4.2. Definite Clause Inference

We generalize the execution of positive goals using polarity.

Definite Clause Inference(DCI)

Let A be a positive atom in a goal formula G and "B :- $B_1, B_2, \ldots, B_m$" be any definite clause in P. When A is unifiable with B by a deciding m.g.u. σ, we generate a new OR-goal $\sigma(G_A[B_1 \wedge B_2 \wedge \cdots \wedge B_m]) \downarrow$ ($B_1 \wedge B_2 \wedge \cdots \wedge B_m$ is *true* when $m = 0$.) All new variables introduced are treated as fresh undecided variables.

Example 4.2.1. Let S be

$\forall$ A,B,U ((reverse(A,B)$\supset$reverse(B,A))$\supset$(reverse(A,[U|B])$\supset$reverse([U|B],A))).

Then the goal formula of S is

(reverse(A,B) $\supset$reverse(B,A)) $\supset$(reverse(A,[U|B]) $\supset$reverse([U|B],A))

We can apply DCI to *reverse*$([U|B], A)$ and it is replaced with *reverse*$(A, ?C) \wedge$ *append*$(?C, [U], B)$. Note that the internal variable is treated as an undecided variable $?C$.

Example 4.2.2. When S is an existential formula of the form $\exists Y_1 Y_2 \cdots Y_m (A_1 \wedge A_2 \wedge \cdots \wedge A_k)$, i.e., of the form of usual execution goals, the goal formula of S is $?\text{-}A_1, A_2, \ldots, A_k$. (The juxtaposition delimited by "," denotes conjunction and $?\text{-}G$ denotes the goal formula obtained by replacing every variable Y in G with $?Y$.) Then usual execution is applied to $?\text{-}A_1, A_2, \ldots, A_k$.

Remark. DCI correspond to using the "if" part of formulas in P^* as assumptions in natural deduction. The soundness of DCI is guaranteed most easily by replacing equivalence with equivalence using P^* first and then constructing a proof of G from proofs of $\sigma(G_A[B_1 \wedge B_2 \wedge \cdots \wedge B_m])$ using $\vee$-introduction.

4.3. "Negation as Failure" Inference

We also generalize the execution of negative goals using polarity.

"Negation as Failure" Inference(NFI)

Let A be a negative atom in a goal formula G. We generate new AND-goals $G_A[false] \downarrow$ and $\sigma(G_A[B_1 \wedge B_2 \wedge \cdots \wedge B_m]) \downarrow$ for every definite clause "B :- $B_1, B_2, \ldots, B_m$" in P, whose head B is unifiable with A ($B_1 \wedge B_2 \wedge \cdots \wedge B_m$ is *true* when $m = 0$.). All new variables introduced are treated as fresh free variables. (Note that A always includes only free variables and σ may be any m.g.u. without restriction.)

Example 4.3.1. Let S be

$\forall$ A,B,U ((reverse(A,B)$\supset$reverse(B,A))$\supset$(reverse([U|A],B)$\supset$reverse(B,[U|A]))).

Then the goal formula of S is

(reverse(A,B) $\supset$reverse(B,A)) $\supset$(reverse([U|A],B) $\supset$reverse(B,[U|A]))

We can apply NFI to *reverse*$([U|A], B)$. The first goal obtained by replacing the atom with *false* is trivially *true*. In the second goal,the atom is replaced with *reverse*$(A, C) \wedge$*append*$(C, [U], B)$. Note that the internal variable is treated as a free variable C.

Example 4.3.2. Let S be a specification of the form $\neg A$ where A is a ground atom. Suppose there exist k definite clauses whose heads are unifiable with A by m.g.u.s $\sigma_1, \sigma_2, \ldots, \sigma_k$. When NFI is applied to A, we have $k + 1$ AND-goals $(\neg false) \downarrow$, $(\neg(\sigma_1(B_{11} \wedge B_{12} \wedge \cdots \wedge B_{1m_1}))) \downarrow$, $(\neg(\sigma_2(B_{21} \wedge B_{12} \wedge \cdots \wedge B_{1m_1}))) \downarrow$, $\ldots$, $(\neg(\sigma_k(B_{11} \wedge B_{12} \wedge \cdots \wedge B_{1m_1}))) \downarrow$. The first goal formula is trivially *true*. Other goal formulas are of the form $\forall X_1, X_2, \ldots, X_n \neg(A_1 \wedge A_2 \wedge \cdots \wedge A_m)$, because internal variables introduced from the bodies of the definite clauses are free variables in the generated goal formulas. We can continue applying NFI by selecting atoms in each body of the goal formula. When a selected atom has no unifiable head, the only goal formula generated is the first one, which is always *true*. When all goal formulas are reduced to *true*, $\neg A$ is proved. This is exactly the "Negation as Failure" rule in the usual sense (see [Clark 79]).

Remark. NFI correspond to using the "only if" part of formulas in P^* as assumptions in natural deduction. The soundness of NFI is guaranteed most easily by replacing equivalence with equivalence using P^* first and then constructing a proof of G from proofs of $\sigma(G_A[B_1 \wedge B_2 \wedge \cdots \wedge B_m])$ using $\vee$-elimination.

4.4. Simplification

We sometimes simplify goal formulas by assuming that some atom is *true* or *false* (cf.[16]).

Simplification

Let G be a goal formula. When $A_1, A_2, \ldots, A_m$ are positive atoms and $A_{m+1}, A_{m+2}, \ldots, A_n$ are negative atoms unifiable to A by a deciding m.g.u. σ ($0 \leq m \leq n$), we generate new AND-goals $\sigma(G)_A(true) \downarrow$ and $\sigma(G)_A(false) \downarrow$.

In the following examples, σ are both $<>$ and undecided variables are not instantiated. For more general simplifications with instantiation of undecided variables, see 5.3.

Example 4.4.1. Let G be a goal formula

(add(X,Y,Z) ⊃add(Y,X,Z)) ⊃(add(X,Y,Z) ⊃add(Y,s(X),s(Z)))

of an S-formula

∀ X,Y,Z ((add(X,Y,Z) ⊃add(Y,X,Z)) ⊃(add(X,Y,Z) ⊃add(Y,s(X),s(Z)))).

Because $\sigma = <>$ is a deciding substitution and unifies the positive atom $add(X,Y,Z)$ and the negative atom $add(X,Y,Z)$, we generate new AND-goals

(true ⊃add(Y,X,Z)) ⊃(true ⊃add(Y,s(X),s(Z))) ↓,

(false ⊃add(Y,X,Z)) ⊃(false ⊃add(Y,s(X),s(Z))) ↓,

i.e., $add(Y,X,Z) \supset add(Y,s(X),s(Z))$ and *true*. This inference corresponds to generating

(Y+X)+1=Y+(X+1)

from

X+Y=Y+X ⊃(X+Y)+1=Y+(X+1)

in functional programs, i.e., using the equation $X+Y=Y+X$ in the premise and throwing it away. This is called *cross-fertilization* in BMTP [4].

Example 4.4.2. Let G be a goal formula

(reverse(A,C) ⊃reverse(B,A)) ⊃(reverse(A,C) ∧append(C,[U],B) ⊃reverse(B,[U|A]))

of an S-formula

∀ A,B,C,U ((reverse(A,C) ⊃reverse(C,A)) ⊃((reverse(A,C)∧append(C,[U],B))⊃reverse(B,[U|A]))).

Because $\sigma = <>$ is a deciding substitution and unifies the positive atom $reverse(A,C)$ and the negative atom $reverse(A,C)$, we generate new AND-goals

(true ⊃reverse(C,A)) ⊃(true ∧append(C,[U],B) ⊃reverse(B,[U|A])) ↓,

(false ⊃reverse(C,A)) ⊃(false ∧append(C,[U],B) ⊃reverse(B,[U|A])) ↓,

i.e., $reverse(C,A) \supset (append(C,[U],B) \supset reverse(B,[U|A]))$ and *true*. This inference corresponds to generating

reverse(C)=A ⊃reverse(append(C,[U]))=[U|A]

from

reverse(reverse(A))=A ⊃reverse(append(reverse(A),[U]))=[U|A]

in functional programs, i.e., replacement of the special term $reverse(A)$ with a variable C. This is called *generalization* in BMTP [4].

Remark. Simplification performs the role of inference rules in natural deduction not mentioned so far. It corresponds to discharging of assumptions at ⊃-introduction. It also corresponds to application of $\bot_C$, because the use of $\bot_C$ is equivalent to additional axioms of all formulas of the form $\mathcal{F} \vee \neg \mathcal{F}$ (which is more similar to Gentzen's original system).

4.5. Oracle Decision

The last inference rule is never applied automatically in our verification system.

Oracle Decision

When ?X is an undecided variable in a goal formula G and when $\sigma = <?X \Leftarrow t>$ is a deciding substitution, we generate a new goal $\sigma(G)$. All new variables introduced are treated as fresh undecided variables.

Remark. Oracle decision corresponds to resolving the ambiguity in the forward application of ∀-elimination and the backward application of ∃-introduction in natural deduction.

5. Examples of Verification

In this section, we show how extended execution is used in verification of Prolog programs.

5.1. First Order Inference by Extended Execution

First we show the simplest first order inference performed by extended execution. Let us prove the following *th*1 (cf. Kowalski [14],p.223).

theorem(th1).
  ∀ U ¬ append([ ],[U],[ ]).
end.

Extended execution proceeds as follows.

¬ append([ ],[U],[ ])
  ⇓ NFI for append([ ],[U],[ ]) (there is no unifiable head and $\neg false\downarrow$ is *true*)
true

This concludes "$P^* \vdash th1$".

5.2. Inductive Proof with Extended Execution

Now we show the use of extended execution with induction. Let us prove the following *th*2 (cf.Kowalski [14] pp.221-222).

theorem(th2).
  ∀ A:list append(A,[ ],A).
end.

Before describing the verification process, we explain computational induction following Clark [7] p.75-76. The *list* relation is the smallest set of terms that includes [ ] and that, for any term s, includes $[s|t]$ whenever it includes t. Hence, suppose $Q(A)$ is a formula with a free variable A. For any Herbrand interpretation, $Q(A)$ will denote some set of terms. If this set includes [ ], i.e.,

Q([ ])

is true,and if it includes $[s|t]$ whenever it includes t, i.e.,

∀ A,U (Q(A)⊃Q([U|A]))

is true, then the set $Q(A)$ includes all terms in the *list* relation. In other words,

$\forall$ A (list(A)$\supset$Q(A))

is true of the *list* relation and such $Q(A)$. Hence we get the following computational induction scheme :

$$\frac{Q([\,]) \qquad \forall A,U\ (Q(A) \supset Q([U|A]))}{\forall A\ (list(A) \supset Q(A))}$$

Let $Q(A)$ be *append*$(A, [\,], A)$.

Base Case

The subgoal $Q([\,])$ is represented by a goal formula *append*$([\,],[\,],[\,])$.

append([ ],[ ],[ ])
⇓ DCI for append([ ],[ ],[ ])
true

Induction Step

The subgoal $Q(A)\supset Q([U|A])$ is represented by goal formula *append*$(A, [], A) \supset$ *append*$([U|A], [], [U|A])$.

append(A,[ ],A)$\supset$append([U|A],[ ],[U|A]))
⇓ DCI for append([U|A],[ ],[U|A])
append(A,[ ],A) $\supset$append(A,[ ],A)
⇓ simplification w.r.t. append(A,[ ],A) and append(A,[ ],A)
true

This concludes "$P^* \vdash th2$".

5.3. An Example for Comparison

A well-known property of "*reverse*" is described as follows (Boyer and Moore [4]).

theorem(reverse-reverse).
$\forall$ A,B (reverse(A,B) $\supset$reverse(B,A)).
end.

Let us prove *reverse-reverse* using extended execution and computational induction. The same discussion for *reverse* relation holds as for the *list* relation above. We have a computational induction scheme as follows.

$$\frac{Q([\,],[\,]) \qquad \forall A,B,C,U\ (Q(A,C) \wedge append(C,[U],B) \supset Q([U|A],B))}{\forall A,B\ (reverse(A,B) \supset Q(A,B))}$$

Now let $Q(A, B)$ be *reverse*(B, A). (We omit the details of how Q is found. See [12].)

Base Case (Level 1)

The subgoal $Q([\,],[\,])$ is represented by goal formula *reverse*$([\,],[\,])$. The extended execution of *reverse*$([\,],[\,])$ proceeds as follows.

<u>reverse([ ],[ ])</u>

⇓ DCI for reverse([ ],[ ])

true

Induction Step (Level 1)

The subgoal $\forall U, A, B, C(Q(A,C) \wedge append(C,[U],B) \supset Q([U|A],B))$ is represented by goal formula $reverse(C,A) \wedge append(C,[U],B) \supset reverse(B,[U|A])$. Now let $new\text{-}p(L,M,N,X)$ be a procedure defined by

new-p(L,M,N,X) :- reverse(N,L),append(N,[X],M).

Then the *new-p* relation is also computed by the following program. (This is justified by Tamaki-Sato's transformation [21]. For lack of space we omit the details. See [12]).

new-p([ ],[X],[ ],X).

new-p(L,[Y|M],[Y|N],X) :- new-p(L_1,M,N,X),append(L_1,[Y],L).

The theorem to be proved is now

∀ A,B,C,U (new-p(A,B,C,U)⊃reverse(B,[U|A])).

and the computational induction scheme is

$$\frac{\forall U\ Q([\ ],[U],[\ ],U) \quad \forall A,B,C,U,A_1,V\ (Q(A_1,B,C,U) \wedge append(A_1,[V],A) \supset Q(A,[V|B],[V|C],U))}{\forall A,B,C,U\ (reverse(C,A) \wedge append(C,[U],B) \supset Q(A,B,C,U))}$$

Now let $Q(A,B,C,U)$ be $reverse(B,[U|A])$. By applying computaional induction,we have two goals.

Base Case (Level 2)

The subgoal $\forall U Q([\ ],[U],[\ ],U)$ is represented by goal formula $reverse([U],[U])$.

<u>reverse([U],[U])</u>

⇓ DCI for reverse([U],[U])

<u>reverse([ ],?C)</u> ∧append(?C,[U],[U])

⇓ DCI for reverse([ ],?C)

<u>append([ ],[U],[U])</u>

⇓ DCI for append([ ],[U],[U])

true

Induction Step (Level 2)

The subgoal $\forall A,B,C,U,A_1,V(Q(A_1,B,C,U) \wedge append(A_1,[V],A) \supset Q(A,[V|B],[V|C],U))$ is represented by goal formula $reverse(B,[U|A_1]) \wedge append(A_1,[V],A) \supset reverse([V|B],[U|A])$.

reverse(B,[U|A_1])∧append(A_1,[V],A)⊃<u>reverse([V|B],[U|A])</u>

⇓ DCI for reverse([V|B],[U|A])

reverse(B,[U|A_1])∧append(A_1,[V],A) ⊃reverse(B,?A_2)∧<u>append(?A_2,[V],[U|A])</u>

⇓ DCI for append(?A_2,[V],[U|A])

<u>reverse(B,[U|A_1])</u>∧append(A_1,[V],A) ⊃<u>reverse(B,[U|?A_1])</u> ∧append(?A_1,[V],A)

⇓ simplification w.r.t. reverse(B,[U|A_1]) and and reverse(B,[U|?A_1])

<u>append(A_1,[V],A)</u> ⊃<u>append(A_1,[V],A)</u>

⇓ simplification w.r.t. append(A_1,[V],A) and append(A_1,[V],A)
true

his concludes "$P^* \vdash$*reverse-reverse*".

. Discussion

Our approach is similar to that adopted by Tärnlund, Haridi et al [9],[10],[22] using natural deduction irectly, and accomodating various manipulations of programs into a monolithic logical framework. Theirs human-oriented and keeps the intuitive information each formula has so that the quality of the human iterface of interactive systems is not degraded. It also has the advantage of providing opportunities to tilize results on normal proof constructions. But it is different from ours in the following five respects.

.) Our inferences are sound for more restricted formulas with less cost.

Their proof construction handles quantification relations by additional processing (see [10] pp.568-69) in order to guarantee that the inferences are sound. It needs to get the relations of quantifiers by ollowing proof trees, whenever a variable (undecided variable in this paper) is bound to a term which icludes a star variable (free variable in this paper). Because their system considers general formulas, their iferences are not complete. For lack of space, we have omitted the formal discussion of the soundness f our extended execution. But our inferences are sound and need less additional processing, because e restrict attention to S-formulas. Moreover,we conjecture its completeness, that is, any S-formula S is rovable by extended execution if and only if S is a logical consequence of P^*.

2) Our approach is more strongly based on unification.

Their approach is closer to the original natural deduction. Our approach is based on it, but its avor is much closer to usual execution in Prolog, because the main inferences are based on unification. Simplification is not used in their approach.) This makes equational inferences completely implicit except when = is used in P) and performs several steps of equational inference in one step.

3) Our proof construction is in linear format.

Their proof tree construction is faithfull to normal proof construction in natural deduction. Corresponding charging and discharging of assumptions, their proof construction changes its mode between "forward" nd "backward" (see [10]). In our approach, instead of explicit charging and discharging of separated ssumptions, we keep assumptions and conclusions in a single formula of the form $\mathcal{F} \supset \mathcal{G}$. (In this point, ur approach is closer to sequent calculus, cf.[2].) This makes it possible to construct the corresponding roof trees (in natural deduction) bi-directionally and to proceed in a linear format.

4) Our system is verification-dedicated and controlled by many heuristics.

Their system is regarded as an extension of execution with respect to general formula programs. urs is an extension with respect to definite clause programs. We take full advantage of the fact that the ompletion P^* of a definite clause program P consists of formulas of a special form, though we do not trengthen P explicitly to P^*. It disturbs the quantification relations in the generated subgoals so little hat the inferences for verification can be kept rather simple. Actual applications of extended execution are controlled by many BMTP-like heuristics in our verification system [4],[13]. This can be considered a kind of meta-inference ([20],Bowen and Kowalski [3]).

(5) Our inferences are integrated into a proof system with induction.

For lack of space we omitted the details of how induction formulas are generated automatically. When there is no more forwards in verification, we apply inductions and generate new induction goals [12] as BMTP resorts to well-founded induction. In many cases we can apply de Bakker and Scott's computational induction, which skips several steps of inferences and generates more processed goals than naive structural inductions. For example, in the proof of *reverse-reverse*, the subgoal in **Induction Step** generated by naive structural induction is

$\forall$ A,U ($\forall$C (reverse(A,C)$\supset$reverse(C,A)) $\supset\forall$B (reverse([U|A],B)$\supset$reverse(B,[U|A])))

and we need to apply NFI and simplification before applying the deeper level induction. In addition,we do not need to guarantee termination of predicates in theorems to be proved because we employ semantics based on the minimum Herbrand model, the least fixpoint of the transformation T of Herbrand interpretations (see Clark [7] pp.75-76).

7. Conclusions

We have shown how the interpreter of Prolog can be extended to execute more general formulas and how it can be utilized to verify specifications of Prolog programs.

This extended execution is an element of our verification system Argos/V for proving properties of Prolog programs, the first version of which was developed from April 1984 to March 1985. It consists of about 7000 lines in DEC-10 Prolog and takes about 9.5 seconds (CPU time of DEC2060 with 384 kw main memory) to prove *reverse-reverse* automatically. More than 50 theorems have already been proved automatically and the number is increasing.

Acknowledgements

Our verification system Argos/V is a subproject of Fifth Generation Computer System(FGCS) "Intelligent Programming System". The authors would like to thank Dr.K.Fuchi (Director of ICOT) for the opportunity of doing this research and Dr.K.Furukawa(Chief of ICOT 1st Laboratory) and Dr.T.Yokoi(Chief of ICOT 2nd Laboratory) for their advice and encouragement.

References

[1] Apt,K.R. and M.H.van Emden, "Contribution to the Theory of Logic Programming", J. ACM, Vol.29, No. 3, pp. 841-862,1982.

[2] Bowen,K.A., "Programming with Full First-Order Logic", Machine Intelligence 10 (J.E.Hayes, D.Michie and Y-H.Pao Eds), pp.421-440,1982.

[3] Bowen,K.A. and R.A.Kowalski, "Amalgamating Language and Metalanguage in Logic Programming", in Logic Programming (K.L.Clark and S-Å.Tärnlund Eds), Academic Press,1980.

[4] Boyer,R.S. and J.S.Moore, "Computational Logic", Academic Press, 1979.

[5] Clark,K.L. and S-Å.Tärnlund, "A First Order Theory of Data and Programs", in Information Processing 77 (B.Gilchrist Ed), pp.939-944,1977.

[6] Clark,K.L., "Negation as Failure", in Logic and Database (H.Gallaire and J.Minker Eds), pp. 293-302,

1978.

[7] Clark,K.L., "Predicate Logic as a Computational Formalism", Chap.4, Research Monograph : 79/59, TOC, Imperial College, 1979.

[8] van Emden,M.H. and R.A.Kowalski, "The Semantics of Predicate Logic as a Programing Language", J. ACM, Vol. 23, No. 4, pp. 733-742, 1976.

[9] Hansson,A. and S-Å.Tärnlund, "A Natural Programming Calculus", Proc.6th International Joint Conference on Artificial Intelligence, pp.348-355, 1979.

[10] Haridi,S. and D.Sahlin, "Evaluation of Logic Programs Based on Natural Deduction", Proc. 2nd Workshop on Logic Programming, 1983.

[11] Jaffar,J.,J-L.Lassez and J.Lloyd, "Completeness of the Negation as Failure Rule", Proc. IJCAI83, Vol.1, pp.500-506, 1983.

[12] Kanamori,T.and H.Fujita, "Formulation of Induction Formulas in Verification of Prolog Programs", ICOT Technical Report, TR-094, 1984.

[13] Kanamori,T.and K.Horiuchi, "Type Inference in Prolog and Its Applications", ICOT Technical Report, TR-095, 1984.

[14] Kowalski,R.A., "Logic for Problem Solving", Chap. 10-12, North Holland, 1980.

[15] Manna,Z.and R.Waldinger, "A Deductive Approach to Program Synthesis", ACM TOPLAS, Vol. 2, No. 1, pp. 90-121,1980.

[16] Murray,N.V., "Completely Non-Clausal Theorem Proving", Artificial Intelligence, Vol. 18, pp. 67-85, 1982.

[17] Pereira,L.M.,F.C.N.Pereira and D.H.D.Warren, "User's Guide to DECsystem-10 Prolog", Occasional Paper 15, Dept. of Artificial Intelligence, Edinburgh, 1979.

[18] Prawitz,D., "Natural Deduction,A Proof Theoretical Study", Almqvist & Wiksell, Stockholm, 1965.

[19] Schütte,K., "Proof Theory", (translated by J.N.Crossley), Springer Verlag, 1977.

[20] Stering,L. and A.Bundy, "Meta-Level Inference and Program Verification", in 6th Automated Deduction (W.Bibel Ed), Lecture Notes in Computer Science 138, pp. 144-150, 1982.

[21] Tamaki,H. and T.Sato, "Unfold/Fold Transformation of Logic Programs", Proc. 2nd International Logic Programming Conference, pp. 127-138, 1984.

[22] Tärnlund,S-Å., "Logic Programming Language Based on A Natural Deduction System", UPMAIL Technical Report, No. 6, 1981.

Detection and Optimization of Functional Computations in Prolog

Saumya K. Debray *David S. Warren*

Department of Computer Science
State University of New York at Stony Brook
Stony Brook, NY 11794

Abstract: While the ability to simulate nondeterminism and return multiple outputs for a single input is a powerful and attractive feature of Prolog, it is expensive both in time and space. Since Prolog programs are very often functional, i.e. do not produce more than one distinct output for a single input, this overhead is especially undesirable. This paper describes how a program may be analyzed statically to determine which literals and predicates are functional, and how the program may then be optimized using this information. Our notion of "functionality" subsumes the notion of "determinacy" that has been considered by various researchers. Our algorithms are less reliant on features such as *cut*, and thus extend more easily to parallel execution strategies than others that have been proposed.

1. Introduction

The ability to simulate nondeterminism is a powerful feature of Prolog. It permits the succinct and readily understandable expression of logical alternatives that would require complex constructs in many programming languages. However, the additional runtime support needed to remember previous states, and backtrack to them on failure, can incur significant overheads. This overhead is especially undesirable since Prolog predicates are very often functional, and do not need this generalized backtracking ability. Knowledge about the functionality of predicates can be used to make significant improvements in the space and time requirements of a program. Knowing that a predicate is functional may make it possible, for example, to avoid having to record a system state to backtrack to, to effect early reclamation of space on the runtime stack, and to avoid unnecessary search.

Traditionally, the means of controlling Prolog's search has been through *cuts* inserted by the programmer. This, however, makes programs harder to understand declaratively (see, for example, [11]). An alternative is to treat the cut as a low-level primitive that should be used infrequently by the programmer, if at all, but which may be generated by the compiler in the course of generating optimized code for execution in a sequential environment. In this view the cut is not seen as a language feature intrinsic to Prolog, but as an implementation feature of sequential Prolog. (It is not obvious whether cuts are very useful in parallel execution schemes.) To emphasize the distinction between user-supplied cuts and those generated by the compiler, we will refer to the latter as "*savecp/cutto pairs*" (the reason for these names is discussed in Section 5.1). It then becomes the responsibility of the compiler to determine which parts of the program involve redundant search, which can be eliminated by inserting

---

This work was supported in part by the National Science Foundation under grant number DCR-8407688.

savecp/cutto pairs. In this paper we explore ways of doing this by inferring the functionality of predicates and literals. A special case of functionality, that of determinacy, has been investigated by Mellish [9] and Sawamura and Takeshima [12], while a notion similar to that of functionality has been considered by Mendelzon in the restricted setting of databases (i.e. assuming the absense of function symbols, and that some predicates are wholly defined by ground clauses) [10]. Our approach is both more general and less operational. It does not rely exclusively on user-supplied cuts to infer functionality, thereby promoting what we believe is a better programming style. It also enables us to optimize certain cases where a particular call of a predicate may be functional even though the predicate itself is not.

We assume the reader is acquainted with the basic concepts of logic programming, in particular Prolog. The rest of the paper is organized as follows: Section 2 introduces various concepts that are used later in the paper. Section 3 defines and discusses functionality and sufficient conditions for functionality. Section 4 describes an algorithm for the static inference of functionality. Section 5 discusses some compile-time optimizations that are possible with knowledge of functionality. Section 6 concludes with a summary.

2. Preliminaries

2.1. The Language

A Prolog program consists of a set of predicate definitions. A predicate definition consists of a sequence of clauses. Each clause is a sequence of literals, which are either atomic goals or negations of atomic goals. Prolog clauses are generally constrained to be definite Horn, i.e. have exactly one positive literal. The positive literal is called the *head* of the clause, and the remaining literals, if any, constitute the *body* of the clause; a clause with only negative literals is referred to as a *goal*. The meaning of each clause is the disjunction of its literals, that of the program being the conjunction of the clauses. We will adhere to the syntax of DEC-10 Prolog and write clauses in the form

$$p :- q_1, \ldots, q_n.$$

which can be read as "p *if* q_1 *and* . . . *and* q_n".

A literal is a static component of a clause. In an execution of the program, the corresponding dynamic entity is a call, which is a substitution instance of an alphabetic variant of the literal. A call to an n-ary predicate p can therefore be considered to be a pair $\langle p/n, \overline{T} \rangle$ where $\overline{T}$ is an n-tuple of terms which are arguments to the call. When the predicate being referred to in a call is clear from the context, we will omit the predicate name and refer to the call by its tuple of arguments. We refer to calls corresponding to a literal as *arising from* that literal. If the predicate symbol of a literal L is p, then L will be said to *refer to* the predicate p.

Operationally, a predicate, a clause for a predicate or a literal in the body of a clause can be thought of as denoting a relation over pairs of tuples of terms. Thus, if D is the set of terms (possibly containing variables) in a program, then an n-ary predicate (clause, literal, call) denotes a subset of $D^n \times D^n$. The first element of the pair represents the "input", or calling, values of its arguments, and the second, the "output", or returned values. We will refer to such relations as *input-output relations.* If a pair $\langle t_1, t_2 \rangle$ is in the input-output relation of a predicate p, and θ is the most general unifier of t_1 and t_2, then we will say that a call t_1 to p can *succeed* with the substitution θ. Notice that for any pair $\langle t_1, t_2 \rangle$ in an input-output relation, t_2 must be a substitution instance of t_1.

We will sometimes wish to ignore values returned for "void" or "anonymous" variables, i.e. variables that occur only once in a clause. Given an n-tuple T and a set of argument positions $A = \{m_1, \ldots, m_k\}$, $1 \leq m_1 < \ldots < m_k \leq n$, let the *projection* of T on A denote the k-tuple obtained by considering only the values of the argument positions $m_1 \ldots m_k$ of T. Then, the projection of an input-output relation on a set of argument positions can be defined as follows:

Definition: Given an input-output relation R and a set of argument positions A, the *projection of R on A*, written $\pi_A(R)$, is the set of pairs $\langle S_I, S_O \rangle$ such that for some pair $\langle T_I, T_O \rangle$ in R S_I is the projection of T_I on A, and S_O is the projection of T_O on A.

This is analogous to the projection operation of relational databases. Notice that the projection of an input-output relation of a predicate p on a set of argument positions A is precisely the input-output relation obtained for a new predicate defined by p, but with the arguments in the head restricted to those in A. Thus, for $A = \{1, \ldots, k\}$ and R the input-output relation for an n-ary predicate p, $\pi_A(R)$ is precisely the input-output relation of a predicate p', which is defined by the single clause

$$p'(X_1, \ldots, X_k) :- p(X_1, \ldots, X_n).$$

Additionally, we will sometimes wish to restrict our attention to a horizontal slice of the input-output relation of a predicate. To this end, we define the notion of input restriction:

Definition: Let R be the input-output relation for an n-ary predicate (clause, literal) in a program, and let T be a set of n-tuples of terms. The *input restriction* of R to T, written $\sigma_T(R)$, is the set of pairs $\langle S_I, S_O \rangle$ in R such that S_I is in T.

Most Prolog implementations execute clauses according to their textual top-to-bottom order in the search for a proof, and resolve literals within a clause according to their textual left-to-right order. These orderings induce data and control dependencies which are crucial to the analysis of program properties such as functionality. Throughout this paper, we assume this evaluation ordering on clauses and literals. We also assume that we are dealing with static programs, i.e. programs which do not change at runtime because clauses are *asserted* or *retracted*.

2.2. Negative Goals

It is possible to have negative literals in the body of a clause. The semantics of negated goals is given in terms of unprovability by finite failure; it coincides with logical negation (with respect to the "completed" predicate) under certain conditions – the set of program clauses must have a minimal model and all negated goals to be proved must be ground [4]. It turns out that if a variable occurs within a negated goal, then *as long as this variable does not appear anywhere outside the negation,* it behaves logically as a universally quantified variable. This is evident if we consider the clauses

```
p(X) :- not( q1 ), r(X).
q1 :- q(Z).
```

where the negation has the expected semantics. Unfolding the negated literal in the clause for q after appropriately renaming variables gives

```
p(X) :- not( q(Y) ), r(X).
```

where the variable renaming guarantees that variables in the negated goal do not appear elsewhere in the clause outside the negation. The negated goal here can be thought of as representing the statement "for no instance of Y is $q(Y)$ provable". Such negated goals play an important role in our analysis of functionality.

2.3. Modes and Functional Dependencies

In general, Prolog programs are undirected, i.e. can be run either "forwards" or "backwards", and do not distinguish between "input" and "output" parameters for a predicate. However, in most programs, individual predicates tend to be used with some arguments as input arguments and others as output arguments. Knowledge of such directionality, expressed using *modes* [1, 14], enables various compile-time optimizations to be made. Mode information can either be supplied by the user, in the form of mode declarations, or be inferred from a global analysis of the program [6, 8]. Mode information also plays an important role in the inference of functionality.

It is convenient to think of the mode for an n-ary predicate as representing a set of n-tuples of terms. The modes we consider are quite simple: **c** represents the set of ground terms, **f** the set of variables and **d** the set of all terms. Thus, if a predicate $p/3$ has mode $\langle \mathbf{c},\mathbf{f},\mathbf{d} \rangle$ in a program, then it will always be called with its first argument ground and its second argument uninstantiated in that program; however, nothing definite can be said about the instantiation of its third argument. In general, a mode for an n-ary predicate will be an n-tuple over $\{\mathbf{c},\mathbf{d},\mathbf{f}\}$. A call to a predicate with arguments $\overline{X}$ is *consistent* with the mode of that predicate if $\overline{X}$ is in the set of tuples of terms represented by that mode.

If we assume an "input" mode for a predicate or clause for a predicate, it is possible to propagate it (from left to right, if we assume the usual evaluation order) to literals in the body and obtain modes for these literals [6]. The modes so inferred will be said to be *induced* by the input mode. Thus, given the clause

```
p(X,Y) :- q(X,Z), r(Z,Y).
```

and the mode $\langle \mathbf{c},\mathbf{f} \rangle$ for $p/2$, the induced mode for the literal $q(X,Z)$ is $\langle \mathbf{c},\mathbf{f} \rangle$. If we also know that $q/2$ always binds its arguments to closed terms on success, then we can assume that if execution succeeds through $q(X,Z)$ then Z will be bound to a closed term, so that the induced mode for $r(Z,Y)$ is $\langle \mathbf{c},\mathbf{f} \rangle$.

The notion of *functional dependencies* is well known in relational database theory. Given a predicate $p(\overline{X})$, if there exist subsets of its arguments $\overline{U}$, $\overline{V} \subseteq \overline{X}$ such that a ground instantiation of the arguments $\overline{U}$ uniquely determines the instantiation of the arguments $\overline{V}$, then $\overline{U}$ is said to *functionally determine* $\overline{V}$ in p (written '$\overline{U} \rightarrow \overline{V}$'), and $\overline{V}$ is said to *depend functionally* on $\overline{U}$. We will anticipate what follows by mentioning that knowledge of functional dependencies, together with mode information, can be used to determine when a call can return at most one solution.

3. Functionality

The notion of "determinacy" has usually been identified with "having no alternatives" (e.g. see [14]). Thus, Sawamura et al. define determinacy as, essentially, "succeeding at most once" [12]. Mellish defines a goal as determinate if it "will never be able to backtrack to find alternative solutions" [9]. Unfortunately, such definitions are inherently operational in nature and procedures to infer determinacy tend to rely heavily on the presence of cuts in the user's program. This has two drawbacks: (*i*) it encourages bad programming style, and (*ii*) it does not extend gracefully to parallel execution schemes even though such schemes would benefit from knowledge of determinacy.

We consider a more general property of predicates, *functionality*, where all alternatives produce the same result, which therefore need not be computed repeatedly. The difference between the determinacy and functionality is illustrated by the following example:

Example 1: The predicate

p(a).

p(X) :- p(X).

is functional, since the set of solutions it produces is the singleton {p(a)}. However, since it can produce this solution infinitely many times, it is not determinate in the traditional sense. •

Functionality subsumes determinacy: clearly, determinacy implies functionality; however, as the example above shows, the converse is not true.

Functionality can be considered at the level of literals, clauses and predicates. We define these notions as follows:

Definition: Let C be the set of calls that can arise from a literal L in a program Π; let R be the input-output relation of L, and A its non-void argument positions. Then, L is functional in Π iff $\pi_A(\sigma_C(R))$ is a function.

A literal is *functional relative to a mode M* iff it is functional relative to every set of calls consistent with M.

In other words, a literal is functional if any call that can arise from it is functional on its non-void arguments.

Definition: Let C be a set of calls to a predicate (clause) with input-output relation R. The predicate (clause) is functional relative to C iff $\sigma_C(R)$ is a function.

A predicate (clause) is functional relative to a mode iff it is functional relative to every set of calls consistent with that mode.

If a literal (clause, predicate) is not functional, it will be said to be *relational*. Not surprisingly the functionality of a predicate is in general undecidable ([12] proves the recursive unsolvability of deciding the special case where a call can succeed at most once). However, sufficient conditions can be given for functionality:

Proposition 1: A literal $p(\overline{X})$ is functional relative to mode M if either (*i*) the predicate p is functional relative to mode M, or (*ii*) if there are subsets $\overline{U}$, $\overline{V} \subseteq \overline{X}$ such that (a) $\overline{U} \cup \overline{V} = \overline{X}$; (b) $\overline{U}$ functionally determines $\overline{V}$ in p; and (c) in any call consistent with mode M, each argument in $\overline{U}$ is ground.

unctional dependencies are especially relevant here because Prolog, as has been pointed out y many researchers, is very well suited as a query language for relational databases, and ecause the detection of functionality is important if futile searches through large relations are o be avoided. For the purposes of this paper, we will assume that the relevant functional ependencies have been supplied to the functionality analyzer.

It is possible to generalize Proposition 1 to take void variables into consideration. Conder a literal $p(\overline{X})$, with $\overline{U}$, $\overline{V}$, $\overline{W} \subseteq \overline{X}$ such that $\overline{U} \cup \overline{V} \cup \overline{W} = \overline{X}$, where $\overline{U} \rightarrow \overline{V}$ and $\overline{V}$ consists only of void variables. Then, $p(\overline{X})$ can be rewritten as a literal $q(\overline{Y})$, where $\overline{Y} =$ $\cup \overline{V}$ and q is a new predicate, defined by the clause

q($\overline{Y}$) :- p($\overline{X}$).

rom Proposition 1, the literal $q(\overline{Y})$ is functional relative to a mode M if for any call constent with M, each argument in $\overline{U}$ is ground. But this argument extends in a straightforward ay to the original literal, $p(\overline{X})$. This allows us to state the following proposition:

roposition 2: A literal $p(\overline{X})$ is functional relative to a mode M if there are subsets $\overline{U}$, $\overline{V}$, $\overline{V} \subseteq \overline{X}$ such that (a) $\overline{U} \cup \overline{V} \cup \overline{W} = \overline{X}$; (b) $\overline{U}$ functionally determines $\overline{V}$ in p; (c) in any all consistent with M, each term in $\overline{U}$ is ground; and (d) $\overline{W}$ consists only of void variables.

xample 2: Consider a predicate *emp(Id, Name, Dept, Sal, PhoneNo)*, which is an employee elation whose arguments are the employee's identification number, name, the department he orks for, his salary and phone number. Assume that the predicate has the functional dependencies *Id* → *Name* ("an employee can have only one name") and *Id* → *Sal* ("an employee can ave only one salary"). Then, the literal

. . ., emp(12345, EmpName, _, Sal, _), . . .

functional. Here, the arguments {Id, Name, Dept, Sal, PhoneNo} can be partitioned into the ets {*Id*}, {*Name,Sal*} and {*Dept, PhoneNo*} where *Id* → *Name* and *Id* → *Sal*, *Id* is a ground erm in the literal and {*Dept, PhoneNo*} correspond to anonymous variables. However, the teral

. . ., emp(12345, EmpName, _, Sal, PhoneNum), . . .

nay not be functional, since an employee can have more than one phone number. •

roposition 3: A clause is functional relative to a mode M if there is a cut to the right of any teral in the body of the clause which is not functional relative to its mode induced by M.

sufficient condition for the functionality of a predicate in a program is that each clause of he predicate be functional, and further that at most one clause succeed for any call to that redicate in that program. This is expressed using the notion of *mutual exclusion* of clauses:

efinition: Two clauses *C1*, *C2* for a predicate, with input-output relations R_{C1}, R_{C2} respectively, are mutually exclusive relative to a set of calls C iff for every $c \in C$, either $\sigma_{\{c\}}(R_{C1}) =$ or $\sigma_{\{c\}}(R_{C2}) = \emptyset$.

Two clauses for a predicate are mutually exclusive relative to a mode M iff they are mutully exclusive relative to every set of calls consistent with M.

In other words, if two clauses of a predicate are mutually exclusive relative to a set of calls, then it is not possible for any call in this set to succeed through both clauses. Clauses which are mutually exclusive relative to the set of all calls to the corresponding predicate in that program will be referred to simply as *mutually exclusive*. The following propositions establish sufficient conditions for the static determination of mutual exclusion among clauses.

Proposition 4: Two clauses are mutually exclusive relative to any mode if there is a cut in the body of the textually antecedent clause.

Proposition 5: Two clauses are mutually exclusive relative to a mode M if there is a subset $\overline{U}$ of the argument positions in their heads whose values are not unifiable, and each term in $\overline{U}$ is ground in any call to the corresponding predicate that is consistent with M.

Example 3: The clauses

p(a, f(X), Y) :- q1(X, Y).
p(b, f(g(Y)), Z) :- q2(Y, Z).

are mutually exclusive given the mode $\langle$**c,d,d**$\rangle$; however, they may not be mutually exclusive given the modes $\langle$**d,c,d**$\rangle$ or $\langle$**d,d,c**$\rangle$. •

It is possible to weaken this condition somewhat, so that the relevant terms in the calls are not required to be ground, as long as they are "sufficiently instantiated" to discriminate between the clauses. We do not pursue this further here.

Proposition 6: Two clauses for a predicate p of the form

$p(\overline{X})$:- p_1, $q(\overline{Y}_0)$, $r(\overline{Y})$.
$p(\overline{X})$:- p_2, not($q(\overline{Y}_1)$), $s(\overline{Z})$.

are mutually exclusive relative to a mode M if $q(\overline{Y}_1)$ subsumes $q(\overline{Y}_0)$, and either (*i*) p_1 and p_2 are identical literals which are functional relative to their mode induced by M; or (*ii*) no call arising from p_2 instantiates any variables.

Proof: Assume $q(\overline{Y}_1)$ subsumes $q(\overline{Y}_0)$, i.e. there is a substitution θ such that $\overline{Y}_1\theta = \overline{Y}_0$. If (*i*) p_1 and p_2 are identical functional literals, then any call to them will succeed with the same substitution σ_0, and $\overline{Y}_1\sigma_0$ subsumes $\overline{Y}_0\sigma_0$. If (*ii*) calls arising from p_2 do not instantiate any variables (e.g. if p_2 is a negated literal or a test), then if the substitution after unification with the head is σ_0 and the substitution after succeeding through the goal p_1 is σ_1, then $\overline{Y}_1\sigma_0$ subsumes $\overline{Y}_0\sigma_0\sigma_1$.

Under these conditions, therefore, $\overline{Y}_1$ always subsumes $\overline{Y}_0$ at runtime. Thus, at runtime if the goal $q(\overline{Y}_0)$ is called with substitution σ and succeeds, then the goal $q(\overline{Y}_1\sigma)$ will also succeed. Therefore, the goal not($q(\overline{Y}_1\sigma)$) will fail. Conversely, the goal not($q(\overline{Y}_1)$) can succeed only if no instance of $q(\overline{Y}_1)$ succeeds, which means that $q(\overline{Y}_0)$ must fail. Thus, the two clauses can never both succeed for any given call, i.e. they are mutually exclusive. □

Proposition 6 gives a weaker condition for the mutual exclusion of clauses than requiring cuts in their bodies, since the clauses

$p(\overline{X})$:- $q(\overline{Y}_0)$, $r(\overline{Y})$.
$p(\overline{X})$:- not($q(\overline{Y}_1)$), $s(\overline{Z})$.

here $q(\overline{Y}_1)$ subsumes $q(\overline{Y}_0)$ is not equivalent to the clauses

$p(\overline{X})$:- $q(\overline{Y}_0)$, !, $r(\overline{Y})$.
$p(\overline{X})$:- $s(\overline{Z})$.

$q(\overline{Y}_0)$ is not functional. These conditions are applicable even in parallel evaluation contexts, hile conditions involving cuts do not extend naturally to execution strategies that are not equential.

From the point of view of inference, we will distinguish between two kinds of mutual xclusion: that which can be inferred without any knowledge of the functionality of any user-efined predicate or literal, and that which requires knowledge of the functionality of user-efined predicates. We will refer to the former as *simple mutual exclusion*, and the latter as *erived mutual exclusion.* Notice that in Proposition 6, in the case where p_1 and p_2 refer to uilt-in predicates whose functionality is known, this proposition gives a condition for simple utual exclusion.

roposition 7: A predicate is functional relative to a mode *M* if its clauses are pairwise mutu-lly exclusive relative to mode *M*, and each clause is functional relative to mode *M*.

roof: Since the clauses are pairwise mutually exclusive relative to mode *M*, at most one clause an succeed for any call to the predicate consistent with *M*. Since each clause is functional elative to *M*, any invocation of it can succeed in at most one way. Hence any call to the redicate consistent with *M* can succeed in at most one way, i.e. the input restriction of its nput-output relation to these calls is a function. □

. Inferring Functionality

The basic idea in the inference of functionality is to solve a set of simultaneous, possibly ecursive, equations over a set of propositional variables. This is similar to the technique for he inference of determinacy used by Mellish [9]. As an example, consider a predicate *p* whose efinition is of the form

(cl_1) p :- $p_{11}, p_{12}, \ldots, p_{1n_1}$.

(cl_2) p :- $p_{21}, p_{22}, \ldots, p_{2n_2}$.

. . .

(cl_m) p :- $p_{m1}, p_{m2}, \ldots, p_{mn_m}$.

y Proposition 7, *p* is functional if each of its clauses $cl_1, \ldots, cl_m$ is functional, and they are airwise mutually exclusive. If we strengthen this condition to *if and only if* for the inference rocedure,[1] we can set up a set of equations of the form

$$\text{func\_p} = \text{MutEx}_p \wedge \text{func\_cl}_1 \wedge \ldots \wedge \text{func\_cl}_m$$

here each of the variables is propositional, func_p being true only if *p* is functional, func_cl$_1$ if lause cl_1 is functional, and so on. MutEx$_p$ is true if the clauses for *p* are pairwise mutually xclusive, false otherwise. The functionality of each clause depends, from Proposition 3, on the

[1] Note that this strengthening is conservative, i.e. it may lead to a loss of precision but not of soundness.

functionality of the literals in its body. This enables us to add the equations

$$\text{func\_cl}_1 = \text{func\_p}_{11} \wedge \text{func\_p}_{12} \wedge \ldots \wedge \text{func\_p}_{1n_1}.$$

$$\ldots$$

$$\text{func\_cl}_m = \text{func\_p}_{m1} \wedge \text{func\_p}_{m2} \wedge \ldots \wedge \text{func\_p}_{mn_m}.$$

Each of the variables func_p, func_p_{11}, func_cl_1 etc., are referred to as *functionality status flags.* We also set up equations for the propositional variable $MutEx_p$ if necessary.

We first present an algorithm which takes only simple mutual exclusion of clauses into account. The algorithm is proved sound. The fact that only simple mutual exclusion is considered does not affect soundness, but results in some functional predicates being inferred to be relational. In a later section, we consider derived mutual exclusion and show how it can be converted to the case of simple mutual exclusion, so that the algorithm and its soundness proof go through as before.

4.1. Functionality with Simple Mutual Exclusion of Clauses

4.1.1. The Algorithm

The algorithm for functionality analysis takes as input a set of clauses comprising the program, a set (possibly empty) of modes for predicates in the program, and a set (possibly empty) of functional dependencies that hold for predicates in the program. Associated with each literal, clause and predicate is its *functionality status*, which is a variable ranging over {**T**, **F**, ⊥}. These values represent, respectively, functionality, relationality and lack of knowledge regarding functionality. Each predicate p also has an associated flag, MutEx_p, also ranging over {**T**, **F**, ⊥}, with a value of **T** indicating that the clauses of the predicate are pairwise simple mutually exclusive, **F** indicating that the clauses are not pairwise simple mutually exclusive and ⊥ indicating lack of knowledge. Initially, the functionality status of every literal, clause and predicate, and the MutEx flag of every predicate, is ⊥.

The analysis proceeds in three stages, as described below:

Stage I:

(*i*) Each literal that can be inferred to be functional from Propositions 1 and 2 using mode and functional dependency information has its functionality status set to **T**. The mode for each literal is assumed to be the same as the mode for the predicate it refers to.[2]

(*ii*) Each negated literal has its functionality status set to **T**.

(*iii*) Each literal referring to a built-in predicate known to be functional has its functionality status set to **T**.

(*iv*) For each predicate, if its clauses can be determined to be pairwise simple mutually exclusive from Propositions 4, 5 and 6, then its MutEx flag set to **T**, else it is set to **F**. If a predicate is defined by a single clause, then its clauses are trivially pairwise mutually exclusive, so its MutEx flag is set to **T**.

Stage II: The algorithm iterates through the following steps until there is no change in an iteration:

[2] It may be possible to do better than this if modes are inferred from the program rather than declared by the user.

) Each literal whose functionality status is $\perp$ has the value of its functionality status set to that of the predicate it refers to.

i) Each clause whose functionality status is $\perp$ has the value of its functionality status determined as follows: if any literal (to the right of the rightmost *cut* in the clause, if the clause contains cuts) in the clause has a functionality status **F** then that of the clause is **F**; else if any literal (to the right of the rightmost *cut* in the clause, if the clause contains cuts) has functionality status $\perp$ then that of the clause is $\perp$; else the functionality status of the clause is **T**.

ii) Each predicate whose functionality status is $\perp$ has its functionality status computed as follows: if its MutEx flag is **F** then its functionality status is **F**. Otherwise, if the functionality status of any of its clauses is **F** then that of the predicate is **F**; else if the functionality status of any clause is $\perp$ then that of the predicate is $\perp$, else the functionality status of the predicate is **T**.

tage III: Once the iteration stops, all functionality status flags that still have the value $\perp$ are hanged to **T**.

.1.2. Correctness

To show the soundness of the algorithm, we will show that any predicate inferred to be unctional is in fact functional. To this end, it suffices to show that any predicate that is relaonal has its functionality status flag set to **F** when the algorithm terminates. The full proofs re omitted for reasons of length; the reader is referred to [5] for details.

emma 1: If the clauses for a predicate p are not pairwise mutually exclusive, then MutEx_p is et to **F** in Stage I of the algorithm.

ach literal in a program can give rise to a number of calls during execution, each call defining search tree. The algorithm can be thought of as computing over an abstraction of these ees, which can be characterized by defining the notion of *relational depth*:

efinition: Consider a call C in a program, and let T_C be the corresponding search tree. For ach pair of succesful leaf nodes $\langle i,j \rangle$ in T_C giving distinct sets of substitutions for the non-void ariables in C, let $\delta_{i,j}$ be the depth of the least common ancestor of the pair in T_C. The relaonal depth of the call C, $\rho(C)$ is defined to be the least depth $\delta_{i,j}$ of all such pairs $\langle i,j \rangle$, if the all is relational, and ∞ otherwise.

efinition: Let C be the set of calls to a relational predicate p in a program. The *relational epth* of the predicate p is defined to be $\min_{c \in C} \rho(c)$.

emma 2: The relational depth of a relational call (predicate) is finite, and fixed for a given rogram.

heorem (Soundness): If a predicate is relational in a program, then its functionality status is nferred to be **F** by the algorithm.

roof: By induction on the relational depth N of the predicate. □

4.2. Functionality Inference for Derived Mutual Exclusion

We have considered an algorithm for functionality inference which considered only simple mutual exclusion of clauses. It is possible to expand the set of predicates inferred to be functional if derived mutual exclusion is also taken into account. It turns out that the problem of functionality inference in the presence of derived mutual exclusion of clauses can be transformed to the simple mutual exclusion case in a fairly straightforward way, so that the results of the previous section remain directly applicable.

Recall that two clauses of the form

$p(\overline{X})$:- p_1, $q(\overline{Y}_0)$, $r(\overline{Y})$.

$p(\overline{X})$:- p_2, not($q(\overline{Y}_1)$), $s(\overline{Z})$.

are derived mutually exclusive relative to a mode *M* if $q(\overline{Y}_1)$ subsumes $q(\overline{Y}_0)$ and p_1 and p_2 are identical literals referring to a user-defined predicate that is functional relative to its mode induced by *M*. In this case, the mutual exclusion cannot be detected in Stage I of the algorithm. Notice, however, that there are two components to inferring derived mutual exclusion (*i*) the subsumption of one literal by another, which can be detected by inspection in Stage I and (*ii*) the functionality of a user-defined predicate, which has to be inferred in Stage II of the algorithm. Once the subsumption of literals has been detected, derived mutual exclusion depends only on the functionality of user-defined predicates. It is now straightforward to transform the propositional equations governing the functionality of predicates, replacing each mention of derived mutual exclusion by the functionality of the appropriate predicate. This gives a set of equations where the functionality of each predicate depends only on those of other predicates. These equations can be solved as described earlier.

5. Functional Optimizations

In this section we briefly consider some of the optimizations that can be made with knowledge about the functionality of predicates.

5.1. Controlling Backtracking: savecp and cutto

One of the functional optimizations we will discuss is the insertion of cuts. For this, we briefly describe the primitives used in our system to implement *cut*. In any implementation of cut, it is necessary to know how far to cut back to in the stack of choice points. One way of doing this is to note the current choice point at an appropriate point in execution, and cut back to this point when a cut is encountered. In our system, this is done via two primitives *savecp/1* and *cutto/1*. These are internal primitives that are introduced by the compiler, and unavailable to the user (unlike the otherwise similar *mark(Label)* and *!(Label)* of [13]). The call *savecp*(X) saves the current choice point in the variable X, while the call *cutto*(X) sets the current choice point to that saved in the variable X. Thus, a predicate with a cut in it,

$p(\overline{X})$:- $q(\overline{Y})$, !, $r(\overline{Z})$.

$p(\overline{X})$:- $s(\overline{U})$.

is transformed by the compiler to

$p(\overline{X})$:- savecp(W), p1($\overline{X}$,W).

p1($\overline{X}$,W) :- q($\overline{Y}$), cutto(W), r($\overline{Z}$).
p1($\overline{X}$,_) :- s($\overline{U}$).

here *W* is a new variable not occurring in the original definition of *p*, and *p1* is a new predi-ate not appearing in the original program. In general, *savecp* and *cutto* can be used to racket the calls whose choice points are to be cut.

.2. Functionality and the Insertion of Cuts

If a call is functional, it can succeed with at most one answer. Therefore, once this answer as been obtained, further search for other solutions for that call cannot produce any new solu-ions, and so a *savecp/cutto* pair may be inserted by the compiler around the corresponding teral without (in most cases) affecting the semantics of the program. (There are certain non-ogical contexts in which cuts so introduced can affect program semantics: this is discussed ater.)

It will usually be profitable to insert *savecp/cutto* pairs around functional literals referring o nonfunctional predicates, as in Example 2 above. If a predicate is itself functional, then it vill generally be preferable to insert cuts in the clauses defining it (except possibly the last lause) rather than around literals referring to it.

xample 4: Consider the predicate

big_shot(Id,EmpName) :- emp(Id, EmpName, _, Salary, _), Salary > 50000.

iven the mode ⟨**c,d**⟩ for *big_shot/2* and the functional dependencies *Id* → *Name, Id* → *Salary* or the predicate *emp(Id, Name, Dept, Salary, PhoneNo)*, it can be inferred that the literal eferring to *emp* in the clause above is functional. Since the predicate *emp* is not itself func-ional, this is transformed to

big_shot(EmpName,Id) :-
savecp(X), emp(EmpName, Id, _, Salary, _), cutto(X), Salary > 50000.

Further optimization is possible if we consider sequences of functional literals. Define a *ail_back_to* relation over pairs of literals, with the following semantics: *fail_back_to(p1,p2)* is rue if execution should backtrack to the goal corresponding to literal *p2* if the goal orresponding to literal *p1* fails (this relation is fairly trivial given Prolog's naive backtracking trategy, but nontrivial *fail_back_to* relations can be given for more sophisticated backtracking trategies [2, 3]). For functional calls, the *fail_back_to* relation is transitive. In other words, iven a sequence of literals

. . . p1, . . ., p2, . . ., p3, . . .

vhere *p1, p2* and *p3* are functional literals and the *fail_back_to* relation has the tuples ⟨*p3,p2*⟩ nd ⟨*p2,p1*⟩, then execution can can fail back directly to *p1* on failure of the goal *p3*, i.e. ⟨*p3,p1*⟩ s in the *fail_back_to* relation. This property can be used to produce more efficient code for ontiguous functional calls, as the example shows:

Example 5: Consider the clause

p(X,Y) :- q(X,Z,_), r(Z,Y,_), s(X,Y).

Assume that both *q/3* and *r/3* have the mode $\langle$**c,f,f**$\rangle$, and that both *q/3* and *r/3* have the first argument functionally determine the second. The calls to *q/3* and *r/3* in the clause above are functional, and the clause can therefore be transformed to the following in a straightforward way:

```
p(X,Y) :- savecp(U), q(X,Z,_), cutto(U), savecp(V), r(Z,Y,_), cutto(V), s(X,Y).
```

However, since the two functional calls were contiguous in the original clause, the transitivity of the *fail_back_to* relation can be used to obtain the following clause, which is more efficient in both space and time:

```
p(X,Y) :- savecp(U), q(X,Z,_), cutto(U), r(Z,Y,_), cutto(U), s(X,Y).
```

•

5.3. Avoiding Cuts in Functional Predicates

The obvious way to improve functional predicates and literals is to cut out useless backtrack points, as illustrated in the preceding examples. However, this still involves creating the backtrack points, which is not inexpensive. Under certain circumstances, more efficient code can be generated for functional predicates if cuts are not generated. This section considers two such situations.

5.3.1. Clause Indexing

It is often possible to avoid laying down a choice point altogether for a call to a functional predicate, by proper clause indexing. In such cases, adding cuts to the clauses of the predicate is effectively a pessimization. A better strategy is to have the compiler either build sophisticated indices, or transform the program, based on mode information and analysis of mutual exclusion of clauses, so that Prolog's usual indexing scheme will suffice to avoid laying down choice points (typically, Prolog systems, e.g. [14, 15], index on the principal functor of the first argument of each clause). The additional effort involved at compile time may very well be offset by the space and time savings accruing from not having to put down a choice point at each call. In such cases, since no choice point is being laid down, cuts in the bodies of clauses are no-ops if they serve only to cut the clause selection alternatives, and constitute unproductive overhead.

Example 6: Consider the predicate

```
process([],[]).
process([','(X,Y) | Rest], [T | TRest]) :- process_comma(X,Y,T), process(Rest,TRest).
process([';'(X,Y) | Rest], [T | TRest]) :- process_semicolon(X,Y,T), process(Rest,TRest).
process([not(X) | Rest], [T | TRest]) :- process_not(X,T), process(Rest,TRest).
```

The clauses for *process/2* are mutually exclusive if it is always called with its first argument a closed term. However, in order to avoid laying down a choice point for it, it is necessary to look beyond the principal functor of its first argument, which is the same for three of its four clauses. This can be done either by building a more sophisticated index for this predicate, or by transforming it to the following at compile time:

```
process([],[]).
process([H | L], [TH | TL]) :- process1(H,TH), process(L,TL).
```

```
process1(','(X,Y), T) :- process_comma(X,Y,T).
process1(';'(X,Y), T) :- process_semicolon(X,Y,T).
process1(not(X), T) :- process_not(X,T).
```

ere, *process1/2* is a new predicate not appearing elsewhere in the program. It is evident that the transformed program, the usual indexing mechanism of Prolog suffices to avoid laying own choice points for calls to *process/2* or *process1/2*. •

.3.2. Functional Optimizations in Parallel Execution Strategies

Functionality and mutual exclusion can also be exploited in parallel evaluation strategies. or example, in OR-parallel strategies such as [7, 16], if two clauses are known to be mutually xclusive, then the processes for one of them can be killed off (or ignored) as soon as the other ne succeeds. The amount of information that needs to be maintained associated with a goal an also be reduced if it is known a priori that it will not produce more than one set of bindgs. However, since the cut is a control mechanism best suited for sequential execution straegies, it forces sequentialization of execution under parallel evaluation strategies in order to ive the expected behaviour. It may be therefore be preferable not to have cuts in the original rogram, but instead let the compiler infer mutual exclusion and functionality and generate ode appropriate to the execution environment.

.4. Functionality and Cut Insertion : Some Caveats

The previous section discussed the bracketing of deterministic calls with *savecp/cutto* airs to avoid useless backtracking. There are situations, however, where such transformations an alter the semantics of the program. The example below illustrates this:

xample 7: Consider a predicate to count the number of occurrences of an element in a list:

```
numocc(Elt, L, N) :- bagof(Elt, member(Elt,L), EltL), length(EltL, N).
```

here *member/2* and *length/2* are defined in the usual way. If numocc is always called with e first two arguments ground, then the call to *member/2* is functional. However, bracketing is call to *member/2* with a *savecp/cutto* pair would give incorrect answers. •

he problem arises because in this case number of successes is what is important, not just the nswer. One could argue that *numocc/3* is better written as a recursive predicate free of nongical constructs such as *bagof*: the point of the example is to illustrate the fact that cuts hould not be inserted blithely without taking the context into account. Other such examples an be constructed, involving side effects such as *read* or *write* operations, where altering the umber of successes can affect the semantics of the program. For this reason, caution should e exercised in inserting cuts. For example, cuts should be inserted at a point only if it can be uaranteed that the search tree below that point is free of side effects. Fortunately, in welltructured programs, most of the situations where it is permissible to insert cuts can be etected statically without great difficulty.

. Summary

The paper considers the question of inferring the functionality of Prolog predicates. The otion of functionality subsumes that of determinacy. Not being an inherently operational otion, it tends to rely on features such as the "cut" to a much lesser extent, and thereby

…ourages a better style of programming and extends gracefully to parallel evaluation strategies. Sufficient conditions for functionality are given, and an algorithm described for the automatic inference of functionality of predicates. Some functional optimizations are described, and conditions under which some of these optimizations can affect program semantics, and hence be inapplicable, are described.

7. References

1. M. Bruynooghe, "Adding Redundancy to Obtain More Reliable and More Readable Prolog Programs", in *Proc. 1st. Int. Logic Programming Conference*, Marseille, France, 1982.
2. M. Bruynooghe and L. M. Pereira, "Deduction revision by intelligent backtracking", in *Implementations of Prolog*, J. A. Campbell, (ed.), Ellis Horwood Ltd., Chichester, 1984.
3. J. Chang and A. M. Despain, "Semi-Intelligent Backtracking of Prolog Based on Static Data Dependency Analysis", in *Proc. 1985 Symposium on Logic Programming*, Boston, July 1985, 10-21.
4. K. L. Clark, "Negation as Failure", in *Logic and Data Bases*, H. Gallaire and J. Minker, (eds.), Plenum Press, New York, 1978.
5. S. K. Debray, "Detection and Optimization of Functional Computations in Prolog", Technical Report #85/020, Dept. of Computer Science, SUNY at Stony Brook, Stony Brook, NY, Aug 1985.
6. S. K. Debray, "Automatic Mode Inference for Prolog Programs", Technical Report #85/01?, Department of Computer Science, SUNY at Stony Brook, Stony Brook, NY, June 1985.
7. S. Haridi and A. Ciepielewski, "An Or-Parallel Token Machine", TRITA-CS-8303, Dept. of Telecommunication Systems - Computer Systems, Royal Institute of Technology, Stockholm, May 1983.
8. C. S. Mellish, "The Automatic Generation of Mode Declarations for Prolog Programs", DAI Research Paper 163, Dept. of Artificial Intelligence, University of Edinburgh, Aug. 1981.
9. C. S. Mellish, "Some Global Optimizations for a Prolog Compiler", *J. Logic Programming*, **2**, (Apr. 1985), 43-66.
10. A. O. Mendelzon, "Functional Dependencies in Logic Programs", in *Proc. 11th. ACM Int. Conf. on Very Large Data Bases*, Stockholm, Sweden, Aug. 1985.
11. R. A. O'Keefe, "On the Treatment of Cuts in Prolog Source-Level Tools", in *Proc. 1985 Symposium on Logic Programming*, Boston, July 1985, 73-77.
12. H. Sawamura and T. Takeshima, "Recursive Unsolvability of Determinacy, Solvable Cases of Determinacy and Their Applications to Prolog Optimization", in *Proc. 1985 Symposium on Logic Programming*, Boston, July 1985, 200-207.
13. R. Venken, "A Prolog Meta-Interpreter for Partial Evaluation and its Application to Source-to-Source Transformation and Query Optimization", in *Proc. ECAI 84*.
14. D. H. D. Warren, "Implementing Prolog - Compiling Predicate Logic Programs", Research Reports 39 and 40, Dept. of Artificial Intelligence, University of Edinburgh, 1977.
15. D. H. D. Warren, "An Abstract Prolog Instruction Set", Technical Note 309, SRI International, Menlo Park, CA, Oct. 1983.
16. D. S. Warren, M. Ahamad, S. K. Debray and L. V. Kale, "Executing Distributed Prolog Programs on a Broadcast Network", *Proc. 1984 Int. Symp. on Logic Programming*, Atlantic City, New Jersey, Feb. 1984.

CONTROL OF LOGIC PROGRAM EXECUTION BASED ON THE FUNCTIONAL RELATION

Katsuhiko Nakamura

School of Science and Engineering
Tokyo Denki University
Hatoyama-machi, Saitama-ken, 350-03 Japan.

Abstract This paper is concerned with the use of the information about the functional relations in logic programs to eliminate unnecessary recomputation. The method can be applied to control the execution of logic programs by specifying the functional relations so that no undesirable solution is generated. Some fundamental properties of the functionality in logic programs is discussed and a condition for the applicability of a specified functional relation to a goal is shown.

1. Introduction

Although logic programs generally define relations, the relations are frequently functional. Many practical Prolog programs are written to compute the functions such that the output of a program is a function of the input. The functionality in the logic or Prolog programs is closely related to determinacy in the execution of the programs.

The objective of this paper is to discuss the functionality in logic programs for the purpose of realizing a new logic programming system not using the cut and other procedural mechanisms. We investigate the following problems:

(1) Use of the knowledge of the functionality to eliminate unnecessary recomputation and to make the program execution deterministic.

(2) Control of the execution by specifying functional relations so that no undesirable solution is generated.

The functionality in logic programs has been discussed in several papers. In (Clark 1979), a method is shown to prove that an argument of a predicate is a function of other arguments. A kind of the functional specification has been implemented in IC-Prolog as control annotations (Clark et al 1982). Hassen et al (1982) presented a logic programming language in which functions as well as relations are defined as programs.

Our problems are also related to optimizations in Prolog compilers by mode declaration (Warren 1977) and automatic detection of determinacy and the mode (Mellish 1985). An advantage of our approach is that it depends on the functionality which is not a procedural notion nor dependent to any particular search strategy. The purpose of this work is common to those of declarative determinism (Nilson 1984) and Heuristic Prolog (Nakamura 1985).

2. Preliminaries

A substitution is a mapping from a set of variables into a set of terms. For a term (or a clause) T and a substitution s, the instance denoted by [T]s is the term (the clause) obtained by replacing each X of the variables in T defined in s by its value s(X). A variant of a clause C is an instance [C]s such that the substitution s is a one-to-one correspondence of variables defined for all the variables in C.

A (logic) program is a sequence of clauses. Each goal in a query is computed by applicating clauses in the program. By application of a clause to a goal, we mean the process consisting of:

(1) unification for the goal and the head of the clause, and

(2) subsequent computation of the subgoals in the clause in the case of a non-unit clause.

If the computation terminates successfully, an answer substitution is obtained. We call the instance of the goal by the answer substitution the solution.

For a program P, a (logical) consequence of P is a unit clause defined recursively by:

(1) An instance of a unit clause in P is a consequence of P.

(2) If a clause A :- $B_1,\ldots,B_n$. is in P and all $[B_i]$s are consequences of P for a substitution s and all $1 \leq i \leq n$, then an instance of [A]s is a consequence of P.

Note that a consequence is not necessarily ground, i.e. the consequence may contain variable(s), in our definition. The computation for any goal G and any program P is supposed to have the following soundness and completeness properties.

(1) Every solution of the computation for G and P is a consequence of P.

(2) If an instance G' of G is a consequence of P, then there is a solution such that G' is an instance of the solution.

In the example programs, we follow the syntax of the Edinburgh version of Prolog (Clocksin and Mellish 1981).

. Functional Relations in Logic Programs

irst we define the notion of functional relation in a predicate with wo arguments. Let P be a program defining a predicate p(X,Y). We ay that the second argument Y is the function of the first argument , if there does not exist a triple of ground terms s, t, and u with t u such that both unit clauses p(s,t) and p(s,u) are consequences of '. We denote this functional relation by

p(i,o).

'he first argument X is called the input argument, and the second rgument Y the output argument with respect to this functional 'elation.

This definition can be easily extended to predicates with rbitrary numbers of arguments and with input and output arguments in rbitrary positions. Note that the definition includes the functional elations with no input argument and no output argument, e.g. p(o,o) nd p(i,i), respectively.

Example 1 Consider the predicate r defined by the program:

```
r(a,b,c).
r(d,b,c).
r(b,b,d).
r(c,d,d).
```

'e have the functional relations r(i,o,o), r(i,i,o), r(i,o,i), and (i,i,i).

Example 2 The predicate append is defined by the program:

```
append([],Y,Y).
append([A|X],Y,[A|Z]) :- append(X,Y,Z).
```

general logical consequence of this program is

```
append([A1,A2,...,An],Y,[A1,A2,...,An|Y]).
```

'herefore, it is not difficult to show that

append(i,i,o), append(i,o,i), append(o,i,i),

nd append(i,i,i).

n the other hand, we do not have the relation append(o,o,i), because oth

append([],[A|Y],[A|Y])

nd append([A],Y,[A|Y])

re consequences of the append program.

The following two propositions are direct consequences of the efinition.

Proposition 1 Any predicate p defined by a logic program has he functional relation p(i,i,⋯,i).

Proposition 2 Suppose that a predicate p defined by a program has a functional relation $p(u_1,u_2,\cdots,u_n)$. Then, p also has the functional relation $p(v_1,v_2,\cdots,v_n)$ with $v_i > u_i$ or $v_i = u_i$ for all $1 \le i \le n$, where the order > is defined by i > o.

For a predicate p with two arguments we have the following implication relation.

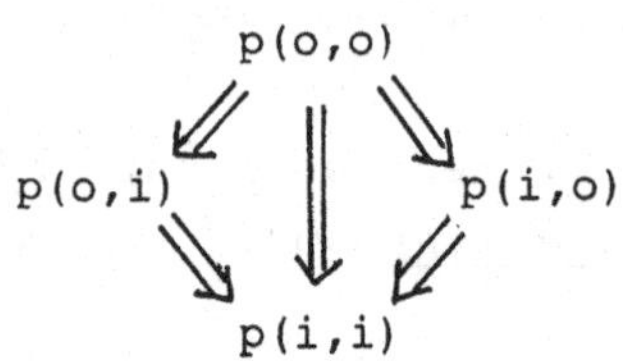

4. Detecting Functional Relations in Programs

On the detection of functional relations in logic programs, we have the following fundamental proposition.

Proposition 3 The following decision problem is recusively unsolvable: For any logic program defining a predicate p and a functional relation R, determine whether p has R.

Proof Consider the program for the predicate p:

```
p(a,b).
p(a,X) :- q(X).
```

This program has the functional relation p(i,o) if and only if the goal q(X) has the unique solution q(b). It is known that there exists no algorism that, for each program and each goal, determines whether a specific solution will be generated. (q.e.d.)

In many cases, we can test the functionality of a program by computing some simple query and the program. For the functional relation p(i,o), the query

```
?- p(X,Y),p(X,Z),Y \= Z.
```

generates "counter-examples" of the functional relation. It has no solution if the program has p(i,o). The computation, however, may fall into an infinite loop in ordinary Prolog systems. Therefore we require some special interpreter for this computation that detects repetition of a goal and its variants and discontinues their computation. Another simple method for the computation is to restrict the maximum depth in the search tree to a finite value.

5. Functionality and Determinacy

We say that a goal is logically deterministic, if it has a unique solution. In many Prolog systems, a logically deterministic goal is not necessarily operationally deterministic. For example, consider the append program and the logically deterministic goal

```
append([a,b,c],[d,e],Z)
```

After the first solution Z = [a,b,c,d,e] is obtained, most Prolog interpreter tries to find another solution in the backtracking, because the second clause in the program is remained to be applied. In Prolog, the cut is used to make this goal deterministic as in the following program.

```
append ([],Y,Y) :- !.
append([A|X],Y,[A|Z]) :- append(X,Y,Z).
```

However, every append goal is operationally deterministic for this program. For example, the query

```
?-append(X,Y,[a,b,c]).
```

has only one solution: X = [] and Y = [a,b,c]. We can represent the determinacy of this program by the functional relation append(o,o,o).

The knowledge of functional relations in a program can be used to eliminate unnecessary recomputation for a logically deterministic goal without affecting the computation of goals with other input-output relations.

It is important for implementing our method to determine whether a functional relation is applicable to the computation of a goal. Obviously, if all the input arguments are ground terms with respect to a functional relation, this relation is applicable to the goal. On the other hand, an input argument can be a variable, for example, in the case the program consists of only one unit clause p(X,f(X)) and the goal is p(Y,Z). The following proposition suggests a condition for the applicability of a functional relation.

Proposition 4 Suppose that a program P defines a predicate p with a functional relation R and that, for a goal G and P, there are two or more solutions. If all the terms in the input arguments (with respect to R) of one of the solutions are identical with, or variants of, the corresponding terms of the goal G, then the other solution(s) are instance(s) of this solution.

<u>Proof</u> We prove this proposition for the case that R = p(i,o). It can be easily extended to general cases. Suppose that two solutions p(u',w) and p(x,y) are obtained from a goal p(u,v), where u, v, w, x, and y are terms and u' is a variant of u. By the soundness of the computation, the solutions are consequences of the program. Furthermore, for any substitution s with [u']s = x, the instance [p(u',w)]s is also a consequence of the program. Because of the

relation p(i,o), the instance [p(u',w)]s should be a variant of p(x,y). Hence, p(x,y) is an instance of p(u',w). (q.e.d.)

In most cases, a general solution is more important than its instance, and it is rare that a special-case solution is obtained after a general solution in a practical computation. Therefore, we can consider a goal to be deterministic, whenever we obtain a solution such that all the terms in the input argument(s) are identical with, or variants of, the terms in the solution.

6. Control of Execution by Specifying Functional Relations

Our method can be also used to control the execution of logic programs without using the cut: By specifying the functional relations we can eliminate the recomputation in the backtracking that may generate another undesirable solution(s). An advantage of this method is that the specification of the functional relations does not affect the computation of other input-output relations. On the other hand, Prolog programs with the cut generally work only for particular input-output relation.

We can compare this method with declarative determinism (Nilson 1984) and the PROVE-ONCE operator in LM-Prolog (Carlsson and Kahn 1982). In (Nilson 1984), it is shown that any Prolog program can be translated to an equivalent logic program without cut by using declarative determinism. Since the declarative determinism for a predicate p is equivalent to the specification of p(o,o,···,o), the cut can be also eliminated by our method.

This method can be applied for the definition of the predicate not. In Prolog, the not is defined by the program:

```
not(P) :- call(P),!,fail.
not(P).
```

We specify the relation not(o), and define the not by the program without the cut using the special predicate fail1:

```
not(P) :- call(P),fail1.
not(P).
```

The built-in predicate fail1 does not cause backtracking and simply makes the parent goal not(P) failure when the application of the clause is deterministic. The execution does not work correctly if we use the fail in this program, because even if the goal P succeeds the fail causes backtracking and the parent goal succeeds by the application of the second clause.

The applicability of a functional relation to a goal is closely related to the check of validness for negation-as-failure rule. If the above goal call(P) succeeds and the functional relation not(i) is applied to the computation of the goal not(P), it is ensured that no variable in P is instantiated in the computation of the goal P and that the computation of not(P) is valid.

7. Implementation

A method for specifying a functional relation is to assert a unit clause called a functional declaration in the database of a Prolog system as the mode declaration in DEC-10 Prolog (Warren 1977). A functional declaration for a predicate p with p(i,o) is

function(p(i,o)).

It is essential for the implementation of our method that the system can efficiently decide the applicability of functional relations to an computation of a goal. From Propositon 4, the system requires for this decision to know whether a variable in a input argument is instantiated in the computation of the goal. Unfortunately, it is not straightforward to incorporate this method efficiently with the current Prolog systems employing either structure sharing (Warren 1977) or non structure sharing (Mellish 1980), because the system must trace all substitutions to variables including those located in "deep" positions of the goal in the computation of the goal.

The detection of functional relations in programs and the elimination of unnecessary recomputation can be implemented as optimizations in the compiler.

8. Concluding Remarks

We have shown some fundamental properties of the functional relations in logic programs and presented a new method for controling logic program execution based on the functionalty. For implementing our method efficiently, further investigations are necessary on the efficient determination of the applicability of functional relations to a goal and on the automatic detection of functional relations from programs. The information of functional relations in Prolog programs would be also useful for debugging and consistency check of the programs and databases.

References

Carlsson, M. and Kahn, K.M. (1983), LM-Prolog User Manual, Technical Report No. 24, UPMAIL, Computing Science Department, Uppsala

University, Sweden.

Clark, K. L. (1979), Predicate logic as a computational formalism, Research Monograph 79/59 TOC, Department of Computing, Imperial College, London.

Clark,K. L., McCabe, F.G., and Gregory, S. (1982), IC-Prolog language features, in (Clark, K. L. and Tärnlund, S-Å. eds.) Logic Programming, Academic Press, London, pp.253-266.

Clocksin, W.F. and Mellish, C.S. (1981), Programming in Prolog, Springer-Verlag, Berlin.

Hansson, Å, Harridi, S., and Tärnlund, S-Å. (1982), Properties of a logic programming language, in (Clark, K. L. and Tärnlund, S-Å. eds.) Logic Programming, Academic Press, London, pp.267-280.

Mellish, C. S. (1980), An alternative to structure sharing in the implementation of a PROLOG interpreter, Research Paper 150, Department of Artificial Intelligence, University of Edinburgh.

Mellish, C. S. (1985), Some global optimizations for a PROLOG compiler, Jour. of Logic Programming Vol. 2, No. 1, pp.43-66.

Nakamura, K. (1985), Heuristic Prolog: logic program execution by heuristic search, in Proc. of Logic Programming Conference, ICOT, also to appear in Lecture Notes in Computer Science, Springer-Verlag.

Nilson, M. (1984), Declarative determinism in Prolog implementations, UPMAIL, Computing Science Department, Uppsala University, Sweden.

Warren, D. H. D. (1977), Implementing PROLOG-compiling predicate logic programs, Research Report Nos.39 and 40, Dept. of Artificial Intelligence, University of Edinburgh.

Declarative Graphics

Richard Helm
Kim Marriott
Department of Computer Science, University of Melbourne
Parkville, Victoria 3052, Australia

Abstract

A standard approach to describe pictures is the use of formal grammars. This, and the strong link between definite clause grammars and logic programming, motivates the design of the declarative picture specification language presented here. The language is relational and rule based. A specification is akin to a definite clause grammar and may be executed bottom-up for picture recognition or top-down for generation. Picture execution provides features of constraint based graphic programming. A picture specification may be viewed as a data structure allowing programs to reason about a picture's structure and to manipulate it for dynamic and interactive applications.

Keywords and Categories: I.2.3-Logic Programming, I.3.4-Picture Description Languages

. Introduction

'here is a significant difference between the way in which people think of pictures and the way in which hey are forced to describe pictures to computers in conventional programming languages.

ı conventional programming languages a picture description is a precise sequence of instructions for rawing that picture [NeS79][FoD82]. Each instruction implicitly depends on previous instructions, thus xcluding even a single instruction can result in havoc on the display. Moreover, the same procedural escription cannot easily be used to recognise the pictures it can draw.

lowever, people naturally think of pictures in terms of graphic primitives, such as lines or circles; roperties of these primitives, such as colour; and relations between sub-pictures, such as above or arker. They naturally decompose complex pictures into simpler sub-pictures. People can non-eterministically use a picture's description in a bottom-up manner for recognition and in a top-down ıanner for generation. Consequently logic programming is well suited for computer graphics.

.lready there exist a number of varying approaches to providing graphic extensions to the logic rogramming language Prolog: Kowalski[Kow82] discusses the use of Prolog to teach computational eometry to children; Pereira's[Per83] uses Prolog to represent pictures as relations and reason about ıeir structure; Julien's[Jul82] extension to micro-Prolog represents pictures as lists; and MProlog's Eagle raphics[Dom84] implements a 3D generalisation of LOGO's turtle graphics.

standard approach to describe pictures is the use of formal grammars[Gip75][Sti75][Fu82]. This, and ıe strong link between definite clause grammars and logic programming[Col78][PeW80], motivates our esign of the declarative picture specification language presented here.

ı the first section we describe the relational and rule based picture specification language. In this nguage a specification is akin to a definite clause grammar and may be used for both a picture's ecognition and generation. Pictures are defined as graphical primitives, transformed pictures or combinations of other pictures. Picture combinations are described by two types of rules which distinguish between combinations of independent and dependent pictures. The dependencies between pictures are defined by relations appearing in the rules.

A specification may be directly executed bottom-up for picture recognition or top-down for generation. In section 2 we present a non-deterministic interpreter to do this. It takes into account graphic transformations and we discuss the effect graphic compositing operators have on the order in which pictures may be generated. We indicate the relationship between the declarative semantics of definite clause logic programs and picture specifications.

In section 3, we show how the non-deterministic execution of picture specifications provides features of the constraint based graphic programming language THINGLAB[Bor81].

A picture specification may also be viewed as a hierarchical graphic data structure. In section 4 we show how this permits user programs to both reason about a picture's structure and to manipulate it for dynamic and interactive applications. Combinations of independent picture allow particularly efficient picture modification and display updating. We briefly describe how these features are used in the implementation of a simple picture editor and a window manager.

In section 5 we describe how unique features of MU-Prolog[Nai85] have allowed a particularly simple implementation of this language. These provide the non-deterministic evaluation of relations as constraints and also co-routining. Co-routining gives an elegant way to interface user programs with graphics. This is exemplified in the implementation of a program which animates the execution of logic programs. Also in this section, we describe a technique used in our implementation that uses unification to access pictures by approximate location.

The paper concludes with an appraisal of related work and suggestions for future research, where we note that much of a picture's generation could occur in parallel, suggesting the possibility of a highly parallel graphic processor.

2. A Declarative Picture Specification

This section describes the picture specification language. In this language, pictures are graphical primitives, picture transformations or combinations of other pictures. A picture may have associated *attributes*, such as colour, pattern or location, which act as parameters to the picture. As this language is declarative, a picture's appearance is fully determined by its attribute values; there is no notion of global attributes. Also, because the language is declarative, it does not define how a picture is to be generated or recognised, rather it only defines a picture's structure and the relationships between the parts of that picture.

Graphic Primitives & Transformations

Ultimately, every picture can be decomposed into graphic primitives, such as polygons, lines or text. The definition of a primitive must include all attributes which affect its appearance. Unbound attributes are denoted by variables which are identifiers having an initial capital letter. A primitive is denoted by a term of the form

$$primitive(Attribute_1, \cdots, Attribute_n)$$

For example, a blue polygon could be described by

polygon([(100,200),(200,200), $\cdots$,(70,250)],*blue*, $\cdots$)

here this polygon's edge is represented by the list of points [(100,200),(200,200),...,(70,250)].

graphic transformation is an operation that maps pictures into other pictures. There are different ypes of transformations: geometric transformations, such as dilate, translate and rotate which map oints to points; restriction transformations, such as clip, which remove selected parts of a picture by estricting its domain; those transformations which alter the effect an attribute has on a picture's ppearance, such as the stained glass window transformation which, for example, makes all red parts of a icture appear blue, or the shade transformation which, given the position of the light source(s), shades a icture; and lastly, those transformations which alter the appearance of certain sub-pictures in a picture, ich as by changing all circles to squares.

he transformation t with attributes $A_1, \cdots ,A_n$ applied to picture P is denoted by

$$t(P,A_1, \cdots ,A_n)$$

xamples of geometric and restriction transformations are

rotate(Picture, 90°)
translate(Picture,(X,Y))
clip(Picture, Region)

here is a trade off between the power of transformations and that of primitives. The use of simple rimitives can be compensated for by the use of more powerful transformations and vice versa. However, allow concise picture descriptions the language should provide a suitably expressive set of primitives nd transformations.

ombining Pictures

ecause people naturally decompose complex pictures into simpler sub-pictures, we allow pictures to be escribed as hierarchical combinations of sub-pictures.

ften, the structure of a real-world object is reflected in the structure of its corresponding picture as ter-dependencies between sub-pictures. For example, in a picture of a VLSI circuit the location of each ib-circuit's picture depends upon the location of its neighbouring sub-circuits.

owever, in some pictures, the relationship between sub-pictures does not correspond to any physical ependency; the sub-pictures are independent. For example, the pictures of individual people in a crowd ene.

oting the distinction between inter-dependent and independent pictures, we allow pictures to be ombined in two ways; as either compositions or collections.

combination of inter-dependent pictures is denoted by a rule of the form

$$P \leftarrow R_1, \cdots ,R_m,P_1 \& \cdots \& P_n$$

icture P is said to be a ***composition*** of sub-pictures $P_1, \cdots ,P_n$. The inter-dependencies between the ib-pictures are defined by shared attributes and the relations $R_1, \cdots ,R_m$, which are defined by definite ause logic programs [Kow83]. These determine the relationships and constraints that must hold etween the sub-pictures' attributes. For example, the rule

```
square((BotLeftx,BotLefty),EdgeLength) ←
        plus(BotLeftx,EdgeLength,TopRghtx),
        plus(BotLefty,EdgeLength,TopRghty),
        line([(BotLeftx,BotLefty),(TopRghtx,BotLefty)],red,solid) &
        line([(TopRghtx,BotLefty),(TopRghtx,TopRghty)],red,solid) &
        line([(TopRghtx,TopRghty),(BotLeftx,TopRghty)],red,solid) &
        line([(BotLeftx,TopRghty),(BotLeftx,BotLefty)],red,solid)
```

states that a square, defined in terms of its bottom left corner and a side length, consists of four solid red lines.

In this example, squares might be more conveniently described in terms of opposite corners, or polar co-ordinates might be more convenient than cartesian co-ordinates. Relations appearing in the body of a rule may be used to convert attributes from one representation to another, allowing pictures to be described in the way most convenient for the application.

A combination of independent pictures is denoted by a rule of the form

$$P \leftarrow \{P_1 \& \cdots \& P_n\}$$

Picture P is said to be a *collection* of pictures $P_1, \cdots, P_n$. Collections allow independent pictures to be grouped together and treated as one. For example, the collection of faces forming a crowd may be described by

```
crowd ← {
        face(brown,brown,(10,20)) &
        face(auburn,green,(15,22)) &
        face(platinum-blonde,blue,(10,21)) &
              .
              .
              .
        }
face(HairColour, EyeColour, Location) ←
        nose( Location) &
        eyes( EyeColour,Location) &
        hair( HairColour,Location) &
              .
              .
              .
```

Because a collection contains unrelated pictures, attributes are not shared between the head and body of the rule or between pictures in the body.

Distinguishing between collections and compositions allows the implementation to take advantage of picture independence. As we shall see, this is particularly useful for picture manipulation and display.

The graphical compositing operator, &, determines how pictures are overlaid when they are combined. Possible operators include *plus*, *ontop* and *behind*. Other operators for compositing digital images can be found in [PoD84].

Because the image appearing on a physical device may be considered to be a picture composed of the sub-pictures actually appearing on that device, this image may be described by a declarative picture specification. Such an image appearing on a graphics screen could, for example, be composed of a screen background and a collection of sub-pictures.

screen ← *background &*
foreground

foreground ← {
$picture_1$ *&*
.
.
.
$picture_n$
}

5. Generating and Recognising Pictures

An actual displayable or recognisable picture is created from a picture specification by giving a *picture instance*. A picture instance is denoted by $P<G,R>$, where P is a term and G and R are, respectively, geometric and restriction transformations. The restriction transformation is applied before the geometric transformation. These could be represented by a homogeneous transformation matrix and a clipping region. Usually, the geometric transformation associated with a picture instance is the identity transformation and the picture instance is not restricted to any region.

A picture instance defines a tree-like *picture hierarchy*. For example, the picture instance, *clip*(*square*((5,5),10),R')$<G,R>$ has the picture hierarchy

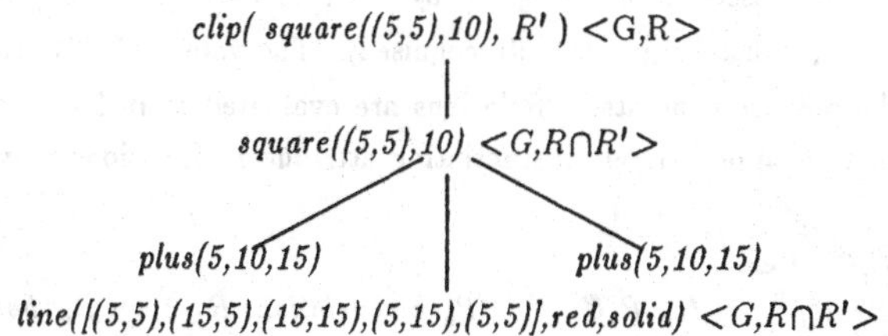

The root node of this hierarchy is the picture instance, the internal nodes are either combinations or transformations of pictures, and the leaf nodes are graphic primitives or relations instances.

Each picture node of the hierarchy has associated geometric and restriction transformations which are determined by the transformations that have been applied to the picture associated with that node. The graphic primitives of the hierarchy constitute the *picture image*, which corresponds to an actual displayable or recognisable picture. For example, the previous hierarchy has picture image *line*([(5,5),(15,5),(15,15),(5,15),(5,5)],*red*,*solid*)$<G,R\cap R'>$.

If the picture image is ground it represents a single picture. If, however, the picture image contains variable attributes, the hierarchy represents a set of pictures. For example, the picture instance, *clip*(*square*((X,Y),10),R')$<G,R>$ represents a set of clipped squares.

A picture hierarchy may be considered as a data-structure representing a picture. We now give a non-deterministic, recursive algorithm that traverses a picture hierarchy, calculating all necessary geometric and restriction transformations at each node. This algorithm can be used for both picture recognition and generation. To recognise a picture, the hierarchy is traversed in a bottom-up manner. To generate a picture, the hierarchy is traversed top-down.

This algorithm is an interpreter for picture specifications. Generating a picture, is considered as executing its specification.

Graphic Primitives & Transformations

Generating(recognising) a graphic primitive results in the primitive's display(recognition)

traverse(P,<G,R>) $\Leftarrow$
P is a primitive
generate(recognise) Prim<G,R>

To generate(recognise) a transformed picture $t(P,A)$, the untransformed picture P is generated(recognised) with the appropriately modified geometric and restriction transformation. The following is for restriction and invertible geometric transformations.

$$
\begin{aligned}
& traverse(\ \mathcal{G}(P,A),<G,R>) \Leftarrow \\
& \quad G' = \mathcal{G}_A \circ G \\
& \quad R' = \mathcal{G}_A^{-1} R \\
& \quad traverse(P,\ <G',\ R'>)
\end{aligned}
$$

$$
\begin{aligned}
& traverse(\ \mathcal{R}(P,Region),<G,R>) \Leftarrow \\
& \quad R' = R \cap Region \\
& \quad traverse(P,\ <G,R'>)
\end{aligned}
$$

Where $\mathcal{G}(P,A)$ denotes the picture P geometrically transformed by $\mathcal{G}_A$ and $\mathcal{R}(P,Region)$ denotes the picture P restricted to region *Region*.

Combined Pictures

To generate(recognise) a composed picture P given by the rule $P \leftarrow R_1, \cdots, R_m, P_1 \& \cdots \& P_n$ each of the sub-pictures $P_1, \cdots, P_n$ must be generated(recognised). The values of P's attributes are passed to its sub-pictures and relations are evaluated. Relations are evaluated as in logic programming and may act as test or be satisfied by appropriately instantiating attributes. Relations may be evaluated in any order.

$$
\begin{aligned}
& traverse(P,<G,R>) \Leftarrow \\
& \quad \exists\ rule\ P \leftarrow R_1, \cdots, R_m, P_1 \& \cdots \& P_n\ and\ relations\ R_1, \cdots, R_m\ hold \\
& \quad \forall P_i\ traverse(\ P_i,\ <G,R>)
\end{aligned}
$$

To generate(recognise) a collection P given by the rule $P \leftarrow P_1 \& \cdots \& P_n$ each of the sub-pictures $P_1, \cdots, P_n$ must be generated(recognised).

$$
\begin{aligned}
& traverse(P,<G,R>) \Leftarrow \\
& \quad \exists\ rule\ P \leftarrow \{P_1 \& \cdots \& P_n\} \\
& \quad \forall P_i\ traverse(\ P_i,\ <G,R>)
\end{aligned}
$$

When generating combinations the order in which sub-pictures are allowed to be generated depends upon the graphic compositing operator. Associative and commutative operators, such as &, allow the sub-pictures to be generated in any order, even in parallel. However, for non-associative or non-commutative operators, such as *behind* or *ontop* the order of the sub-pictures is important. If the sub-pictures are generated in the wrong order an incorrect image may result.

This algorithm is independent of internal picture representations, such as bitmaps or display lists, and is independent of the physical display device. By modifying *traverse* so that the execution of a graphic primitive produces the appropriate display commands, *traverse* may be used to generate images on an output device or to return some internal representation of the picture.

The declarative semantics of picture specifications are closely related to those of definite clause logic programs. For logic programming the declarative semantics of a definite clause program are provided by its least model. The function T is used to show the equivalence between these semantics and its operational semantics, providing soundness and completeness results for SLD resolution [Llo84].

A more involved but similar approach leads to analogous results for picture specifications. The image set gives declarative semantics. A generalisation of the function T constructs the set of ground recognizable images. This can be shown to be equivalent to the image set. It can then be shown that picture generation computes this ground recognizable image set. Thus all images generated from a picture instance are recognisable and all recognisable images can be generated. A formal treatment of these results may be found in [HeM86].

4. Constraint Based Graphic Programming

A rule composing pictures can define relationships between its attributes. Thus, when executing a composed picture, attribute values may be inherited, that is passed from picture to sub-picture, or synthesised, that is passed from sub-pictures to picture.

The successful evaluation of relations may be viewed as constraint satisfaction. Thus the language provides some capabilities of the constraint based graphic programming language THINGLAB[Bor81]. The following definition of a quadrilateral, based on an example from THINGLAB illustrates this.

```
quadrilateral( Pt1, Pt2, Pt3, Pt4, MPt1, MPt2, MPt3, MPt4) ←
        lineWithMidPoint(Pt1,Pt2,MPt1) &
        lineWithMidPoint(Pt2,Pt3,MPt2) &
        lineWithMidPoint(Pt3,Pt4,MPt3) &
        lineWithMidPoint(Pt4,Pt1,MPt4) &
        parallelogram(MPt1, MPt2, MPt3, MPt4)

lineWithMidPoint(P1,P2,M) ←
        P1 − M = M − P2,
        line([P1,P2],solid,blue)

parallelogram(Pt1, Pt2, Pt3, Pt4) ←
        Pt1 − Pt2 = Pt4 − Pt3,
        Pt1 − Pt4 = Pt2 − Pt3,
        line([Pt1,Pt2,Pt3,Pt4,Pt1],dashed,red)
```

The corresponding pictures give a visual proof of the geometry theorem that the mid-points of any quadrilateral form a parallelogram.

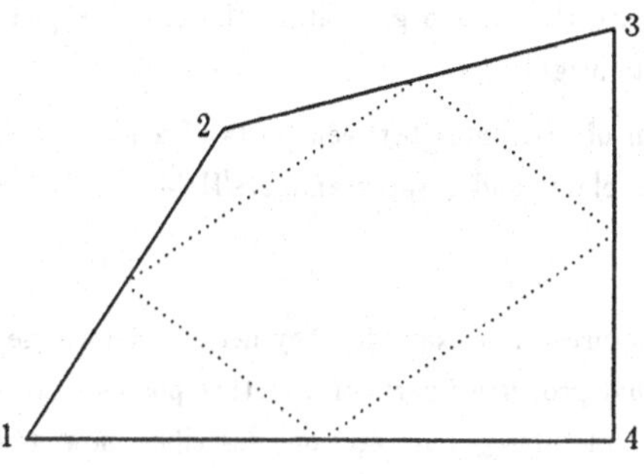

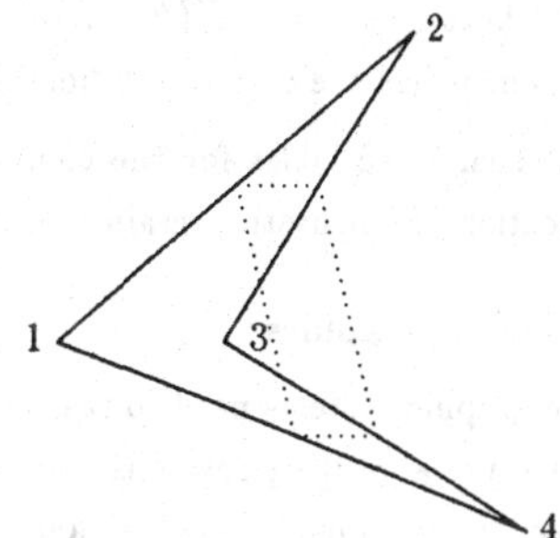

Given any combination of 4 independent points or mid-points of the quadrilateral, the remaining points may be calculated from the constraints. Constraint based graphic programming requires a truly relational language because, when executing a picture, the relationships between dependent pictures must be maintained, regardless of which attributes are bound. This could be achieved by appropriately ordering the relations' evaluation using MU-Prolog with its wait declarations. It cannot be easily achieved using Prologs having strict left to right goal evaluation.

Attributes shared between pictures act as constraints, which might, for example, define points that pictures have in common. For instance, the VLSI picture specification

```
inverter( Input, Output, Gnd, Vdd) ←
        passTransistor( Input, Gnd, Middle) &
        pullupTransistor( Middle, Vdd, Output)

cascadeOfInverters( Input, Output, Gnd, Vdd ) ←
        inverter( Input, Middle, Gnd1, Vdd1) &
        inverter( Middle, Middle1, Gnd2, Vdd2) &
        inverter( Middle1, Output, Gnd3, Vdd3) &
        metalWire( [Gnd,Gnd1,Gnd2,Gnd3]) &
        metalWire( [Vdd,Vdd1,Vdd2,Vdd3])
```

may be used to generate a cascade of 3 inverters

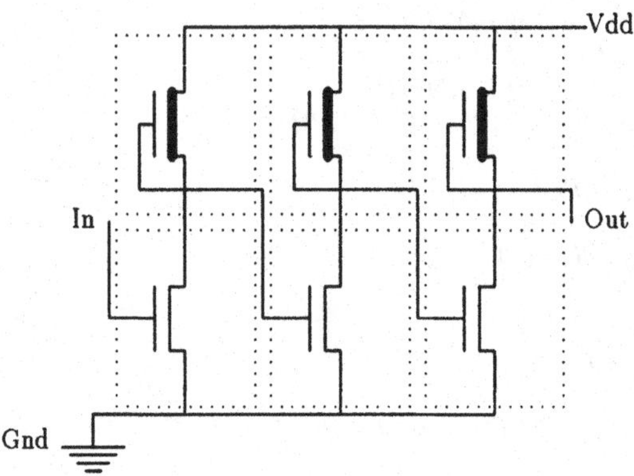

Shared attributes, such as *Middle* in *inverter*, ensure that, when generating the circuit's picture, each VLSI component has the correct relationship with its neighbours.

The use of shared variables for the communication of attributes between parts of a picture also allows the specification of stochastic terrain models, graftal plants and graph grammars[HeM86].

5. Interactive Graphics

Interactive graphic systems need to reason about pictures. For example, they need to determine at which part of a picture a locating device is pointing, or what properties parts of a picture possess. Also, it must be possible to continually modify and redisplay pictures. This section describes how the picture specification language may be used for interactive graphics.

Because a picture specification explicitly represents a picture's structure, it is possible, given a picture instance, to access a picture's underlying structure. This allows a picture to be viewed as a hierarchical raphical database of its sub-pictures.

Every picture's sub-picture has a name; a list of its ancestor pictures. This provides a symbolic reference o that sub-picture. For example, consider the specification

$$P \leftarrow \{P_1 \& P_2\}$$
$$P_1 \leftarrow R_1, P_{11} \& P_{12}$$

vith hierarchy

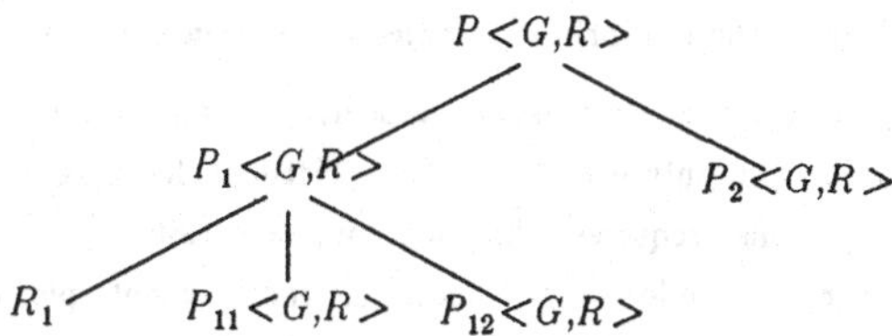

P's sub-pictures have names $P.P_1.[]$, $P.P_1.P_{11}.[]$, $P.P_1.P_{12}.[]$, $P.P_2.[]$.

The following recursive, non-deterministic algorithm finds the names of all sub-pictures of a given oicture.

sub_picture(P.[])
sub_picture(P.P$_i$.Rest) $\Leftarrow$
 $\exists rule P \leftarrow P_1 \& \cdots \& P_n$ *or* $P \leftarrow \{P_1 \& \cdots \& P_n\}$
 $\exists P_i$ *s.t. sub_picture(P$_i$.Rest)*
sub_picture(transformation(P,A$_1$, $\cdots$ *,A$_n$).P.Rest)* $\Leftarrow$
 sub_picture(P.Rest)

The relation *sub_picture(P.SubP)* returns all sub-picture of picture *P*. So, if we have an "album" of photographs

album $\leftarrow$ {
 photo$_1$
 .
 .
 .
 photo$_n$
 }

ome of which contain people's faces, the relation

sub_picture(album.photo. $\cdots$ *.face(HairColour,EyeColour,Location).[])*

eturns all photographs in the album containing faces,

Access to the picture structure means it is straightforward to write a similar algorithm to *sub_picture* which, together with each atom in a picture's name, returns the associated transformations <G,R>. This algorithm may be used to determine at which pictures a locator device is pointing, or which sub-pictures are currently visible on a display device.

A sub-picture's name is very similar to the object path used in THINGLAB [Bor81]. However, they differ n as much as, sub-parts of an object always have unique paths whereas two sibling sub-pictures that are he same picture instance have the same name.

n an interactive graphic system it is desirable to be able to ascertain the properties of a picture. These properties often fall into one of two categories, existential or universal. A property is existential if a picture holds that property when any of its sub-pictures do. For example the properties "a picture has a ed subpart" and "a picture intersects a particular region" are existential. A property is universal if a picture holds that property when all of its sub-pictures do. For example the properties "a picture is entirely red" and "a picture is contained in a particular region" are universal. Once again, because a picture's structure is explicitly represented in its specification, determining such properties is easy.

Access to the picture structure solves the "Structure of Drawings" problem, first described in [Sut66]. Essentially this problem arises when a program does not have access to the underlying picture structure and it requires the selection of a non-primitive picture. A locator can only return the graphical primitive that has been selected, while the program, without access to the picture structure, cannot determine from the graphical primitive which of the non-primitive objects has been selected.

Interactive computer graphics requires that images appearing on an output device be repeatedly changed. Because a picture specification can only describe a static picture, changing a picture requires changing its specification. Conceptually, this requires the deletion, addition or replacement of rules in the specification. However, because collections consist of independent pictures, a collection may be conveniently modified by selectively adding and deleting individual pictures from it. The following two commands add or delete the picture, *Picture*, to or from the collection, *Collection*.

assertCollection(Collection, Picture)
retractCollection(Collection, Picture)

These commands, in effect, treat collections as relational graphical databases, allowing pictures in a collection to be accessed by their attributes. Thus, all auburn haired people in the *crowd* picture can have their hair dyed blonde.

$\forall$ *face(auburn,EyeColour,Location)* $\in$ *crowd.*
retractCollection(crowd, face(auburn,EyeColour,Location)),
assertCollection(crowd, face(blonde,EyeColour,Location))

When a sub-picture from a composition is changed those parts of the picture depending upon it must be regenerated as other parts of the picture may depend upon it. In the worst case regeneration of the entire picture is required. However, when a collection is changed, complete regeneration is not required, as its sub-pictures are independent of the rest of the picture.

Most graphic systems represent pictures by using either executable procedures, or a graphic data-structure, such as a display list. Although procedures provide clear, directly executable picture descriptions, they are difficult to modify or manipulate and so, in general, are not suitable for interactive systems. Conversely, data-structure based representations are flexible and easy to manipulate, but are difficult to understand and must usually be maintained by the graphic system as a compiled form of some other picture representation [FoD82].

However, picture specifications may be treated as both procedures and data-structures. Hence, they combine the advantages of both representations: they are easily understood; directly executable; and simple to modify and manipulate. Thus, picture specifications are suitable for both static and interactive computer graphics.

6. Sample Applications

We have found the use of collections, non-determinism, access to picture structure and co-routining to be particularly useful in a number of applications.

A Window Manager

Multiple overlapping windows can dramatically increase the amount of information displayed on a computer terminal and are a common feature of many current graphic interfaces.

In the window manager, all windows are split into rectangular areas called window panes. Visible window panes, which correspond to the visible portions of a window, are kept in a collection called *screen*. Obscured panes, which correspond to those portions of a window obscured by other windows, are kept in a collection *offscreen*. Since any picture in *screen* appears on the physical display, windows can be made to appear on the screen by asserting their visible panes into *screen*.

Splitting windows into obscured and visible panes and keeping these in their respective collections means that the operations of deleting or moving a window forward only require swapping window panes between *screen* and *offscreen*. Swapping panes is simple and efficient as unification may be used to access panes in collections by either their location or by the name of the window pane.

The use of collections and unification to access panes has meant that only very simple programs were required to implement the window manager. In contrast, window managers written in conventional programming languages, such as Pike's[Pik83], require complex data structures and algorithms.

Interactive Picture Editor

Another application is the window based and menu driven interactive graphics editor for producing PIC [Ker82] diagrams. Pictures are either PIC primitives, with all their attributes specified, or complex pictures, which are dilated and translated collections of other pictures.

A picture instance is created by first selecting an existing picture as the prototype. An Aid [FuB78] for that picture type then interactively determines the value of attributes with infinitely many possible values, such as location or associated text of the new picture. Attributes with a finite number of possible values, such as line style or thickness, are the same as the prototype's.

Modification of an existing picture's finite valued attributes is similar to picture creation. The existing instance is the prototype for the replacement picture. The user selects the replacement picture from a menu containing all pictures differing in one finite attribute value from the prototype. The replacement picture's infinite valued attributes are just those of the prototype.

Pictures are easily deleted, the selected instance is simply removed from the appropriate collection.

Almost all interaction is via a mouse. Given a location on the screen, the editor uses the picture's specification to determine which object has been selected. If, when selecting a picture, more than one object is admissible, the editor chooses one, backtracking until the user is happy.

The editor is simple, short and quite powerful. Its simplicity arises from the ease of collection manipulation, access to picture structure and non-determinism.

Program Animation

It has been shown that the animation of a conventional computer program's execution is extremely beneficial for teaching, debugging and as an aid to analysis of such programs [BrS84]. We suggest, the potential benefits of program animation may prove to be greater for declarative programming languages such as pure logic programming in which how the program executes is not specified.

An example is the animation of the 8-queens problem, in which individual queens are placed on a displayed chessboard as a solution is constructed. When a partial solution is rejected and the program backtracks, attacking queens are selectively erased from the chessboard and placed elsewhere. This continues until a solution is found.

A second example is an execution tracer which animates Prolog programs by dynamically displaying the evolving proof tree. As a variable is bound the display of all goals containing that variable is dynamically updated. During execution, as the logic program backtracks, failed branches of the proof tree may be either erased completely or redrawn in a different colour. The latter is very useful, as, by observing a program's failed branches, its efficiency may be determined.

Such animations vividly illustrate the effect of different control strategies, such as wait declarations, have upon the efficiency of a program's execution

Both these examples use co-routining, where one routine incrementally draws an object as another incrementally constructs it. This appears to be a generally useful technique for this type of application.

Other applications include: a graphic front-end to CHAT-80[WaP82], a deductive database which allows natural language queries; a user interface for WindCode[TDM85], an expert system in building regulations concerned with wind loading; and the recognition and display of context-free and context-sensitive picture grammars including those for fractal mountains and graftal plants[HeM86].

7. Implementation

It is a straightforward task to implement an interpreter for picture specifications using MU-Prolog. Essentially, the procedure *traverse* is such a Prolog interpreter. MU-Prolog allows runtime re-ordering of query evaluation depending on variable bindings, allowing the execution of graphic primitives and relations to be delayed until their attributes are suitably instantiated. This is not possible in Prologs which use strict left to right goal evaluation.

Collections of pictures were not implemented using rules. Rather, each picture in a collection is stored as a fact. This allows built in database predicates to be used to manipulate pictures in a collection. Each picture in a collection is stored with its approximate bounding region. Thus, the picture

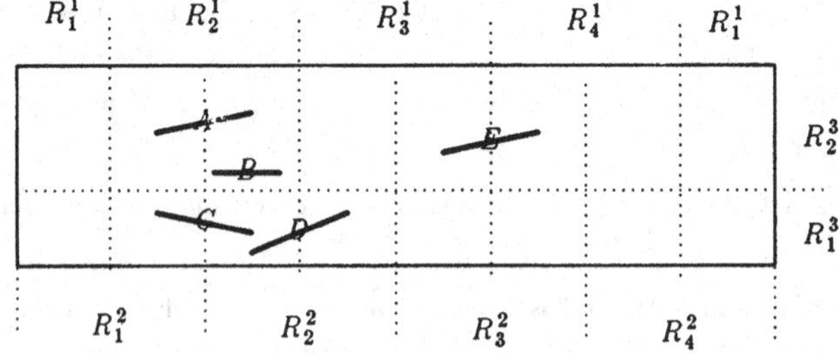

described by the collection *p←a&b&c&d&e* is represented by the facts

p(a, [region(2,_),region(_,_),region(2,_)])
p(b, [region(2,_),region(2,_),region(2,_)])
p(c, [region(2,_),region(_,_),region(1,_)])
p(d, [region(_,_),region(2,_),region(1,_)])
p(e, [region(_,_),region(3,_),region(2,_)])

The list representing a picture's approximate bounding region is such that two picture's approximate regions intersect if and only if their corresponding terms unify. Thus to display all pictures which fall inside the intersection of regions R_2^1, R_2^2 and R_2^3 only those pictures whose approximate regions unify with *[region(2,_),region(2,_),region(2,_)]*

need be displayed, that is pictures *a* and *b*. This useful technique is described more fully in [HeM86].

Rather than building an interpreter for the language, picture specifications could have been compiled into Prolog clauses, much as is done for definite clause grammars [PeW80].

The interface to actual graphic devices was provided by defining the graphic primitives in terms of device dependent graphical system predicates. Currently, the system is implemented for a Vectrix VX384 and for the Hewlett-Packard AGP and DGL graphic libraries.

8. Comparison with other work

Picture Description Languages

Mallgren and Shaw [MaS78] introduce a formalism for describing a single, static picture instance using composition, transformations and primitives. They give a Pascal algorithm to traverse this description for generation. Our language extends theirs by providing descriptions for classes of pictures and considering non-static pictures. Mallgren and Shaw did not regard their formalism as an implementable graphics programming language, rather, they used it to guide their development of graphic facilities in conventional programming languages [Mal82]. In contrast, our language is an actual graphics programming language.

Logic Programming Based Graphics

Graphic extensions to Prolog, such as [GWA84] and MProlog's Eagle Graphics[Dom84] are procedural, relying implicitly on Prolog's computation rule to produce the precise sequence of instructions to display a picture. Hence, these approaches suffer some limitations of conventional graphic languages.

Pereira[Per83] describes a system in which a picture's structure is represented by relations in the Prolog database. This representation may be used both to generate an image and to determine which objects have been interactively selected. Because pictures are represented using only relations and not rules, it is not possible to define general dependencies between pictures.

Other extensions treat pictures as terms such as GLOG[EgC83], [Kow82] or Julien's graphic extension to Micro-Prolog [Jul82] which represents pictures as lists. These systems treat pictures as data-structures and do not consider them as executable descriptions. In Julien's system, for example, primitives are without attributes and may be points, lines or labels. Pictures are combined by appending the lists representing the pictures. Transformations are predicates that take a picture as one argument and produce the transformed picture as another. A picture is displayed by recursively traversing the list and sending commands for the primitives to the graphics device.

9. Future Research

An interesting topic for future research is the development of a dedicated graphics processor for executing picture specifications. Much of the picture generation can occur in parallel.

Sub-pictures can be generated in parallel if they are independent of each other. This always true for sub-pictures in a collection. In general, sub-pictures in a composition are not independent. However, we believe that at run-time attributes of such sub-pictures are often fully instantiated. Thus, they are independent and so, can be generated in parallel.

Another topic for future research concerns optimal picture regeneration. Because pictures in a composition may be inter-dependent, modifying a member of a composition can require the regeneration of the entire picture. However, by using dependency analysis, like that performed for intelligent backtracking [CLP84], only those parts of the picture dependent upon the modified picture would need to be regenerated.

Acknowledgements

The authors wish to thank their supervisor Jean-Louis Lassez and colleagues Graeme Port and Rajeev Gore. We also wish to thank Lee Naish and Isaac Balbin for the use of his online logic programming bibliography.

The authors also acknowledge, CSIRO Division of Building Research, Pyramid Technology Corp., and IBM for their partial support of this research.

References

[Bor81] A. Borning, The Programming Language Aspects of ThingLab, a Constraint-Oriented Simulation Laboratory, *ACM Trans. Prog. Lang. and Systems* Vol. 3, (4), Oct. 1981, 343-387.

[BrS84] M.H. Brown & R. Sedgwick, A System for Algorithm Animation, *Computer Graphics SIGGRAPH 84* ACM, Vol. 18, (3) July 1984, 177-186.

[CLP84] T.Y. Chen, J. Lassez & G.S. Port, Maximal Unifiable Subsets and Minimal Non-Unifiable Subsets, Tech. Rep. 84/16, Dept. of Computer Science, University of Melbourne, 1984.

[Col78] A. Colmerauer, Metapmorphosis Grammars, *Natural Language Communication with Computer*, (L. Bolc,Ed), Springer Verlag, 1978, 133-189.

[Dom84] A. Doman, Graphic Procedures for Prolog. SzKI, Hungary, June 1984.

[EgC83] P. Eggert & K. Chow, Logic Programming Graphics and Infinite Terms. TR-83-02, Dept. of Computer Science, UCSB, June 1983.

[FoD82] J.D. Foley & A.V. Dam, Fundamentals of Interactive Computer Graphics, The Systems Programming Series, Addison-Wesley, 1982.

[Fu82] K.S. Fu, Syntactic Pattern Recognition and Applications, Prentice-Hall, 1982.

[FuB78] R.P. Futrelle & G. Barta, Towards the Design of an Intrinsically Graphical Language, *Computer Graphics SIGGRAPH 78*, Vol. 12 (3), Aug. 1978, 28-32.

[Gip75] J. Gips, Shape Grammars and their Uses, Birkhauser-Verlag, Basel 1975

[GWA84] J.C. Gonzalez, M.H. Williams & I.E. Aitchison, Evaluation of the Effectiveness of Prolog for a CAD Application, *Computer Graphics and Applications*, IEEE, Mar. 1984, 67-75.

[HeM86] A.R. Helm & K. Marriott, Declarative Graphics, Melbourne University, Forthcoming.

[Jul82] S.M.P. Julien, Graphics in Micro-PROLOG, DOC 82/17, Imperial College, London, Sept. 1982.

[Ker82] B.W. Kernighan, PIC - A Language for Typesetting Graphics, *Software Practice & Experience*, Vol. 12 (1), Jan. 1982, 1-21.

[Kow82] R.A. Kowalski, Logic as a Computer Language for Children, *ECAI-82*, 1982.

[Kow83] R.A. Kowalski, Logic Programming, *IFIP*, 1983, 133-145.

[Llo84] J.W. Lloyd, Foundations of Logic Programming, Springer-Verlag, 1984.

[MaS78] W.R. Mallgren & A.C. Shaw, Graphical Transformations and Hierarchic Picture Structures, *Computer Graphics and Image Processing*, Academic Press, Vol. 8, 1978, 237-258.

[Mal82] W.R. Mallgren, Formal Specification of Graphic Data Types, *Transactions on Programming Languages*, ACM, Vol. 4, (4), 1982, 687-710.

[Nai85] L. Naish, Negation and Control in Prolog, Ph.D. thesis, Dept. Computer Science, Melbourne University, 1985

[NeS79] W.M. Newman ,R.F. Sproull , Principles of Interactive Computer Graphics, McGraw Hill Ltd. 1979

[Per83] F. Pereira, Can Drawing be Liberated from the Von Neumann Style? Tech. Note 282, AI Center, SRI International. June 1983

[PeW80] F.C.N. Pereira, D.H.D. Warren, Definite Clause Grammars for Language Analysis - A Survey of the Formalism and a Comparison with Augmented Transition Networks, *Artificial Intelligence* North Holland Vol. 13 1980 231-278

[Pik83] R. Pike, Graphics in Overlapping Bitmap Layers, *Transactions on Graphics* ACM New York Vol. 2 (2) 1983 135-160

[PoD84] T. Porter ,T. Duff, Compositing Digital Images, *Computer Graphics SIGGRAPH 84* ACM Vol. 18 (3) July 1984 253-259

[Sti75] G. Stiny, Pictorial and Formal Aspects of Shape and Shape Grammars, Birkhauser-Verlag, Basel 1975

[Sut66] I.E. Sutherland, Computer Graphics: 10 Unsolved Problems, *Datamation* 22-27 May 1966

[TDM85] J.Y.L. Texier ,A. Doman ,B.S. Marksjo ,R. Sharpe, Use of Prolog with Graphics including CAD, *Ausgraph 85* Brisbane August 1985 81-85

[WaP82] D.H.D Warren, F. Pereira. An Efficient, Easily Adaptable System for Interpreting Natural Language Queries, *Am. J. Computational Linguistics.* 8(3-4),110-119. 1982

Test-pattern Generation for VLSI circuits in a Prolog Environment

Rajiv Gupta
Department of Computer Science
SUNY at Stony Brook
NY 11794 USA
Net-Address: raju@sbcs.csnet

Subject Index: Testing, Automatic test-pattern generation, Logic programming, Simulation

Abstract

This paper presents a way of specifying, simulating and testing complex VLSI circuits in a logic programming environment. Prolog has been shown to be suitable for the above purpose in many earlier works ([7], [8], [9], [10], [11]). However, it is noted that the prolog implementations of the above tasks are slower than the corresponding implementations in procedural languages. We show that various optimizations are possible to enhance the execution speed and this, coupled with the uniformity offered by Prolog, can make it the language of choice. The suitability of Prolog for high-level fault injection and concurrent fault simulation is also investigated in this paper. A wide variety of circuits can be specified in a convenient and readable way, using Prolog, while providing a good compromise between functional simulation and formal verification of VLSI circuits. The following results are shown:

1. Prolog eminently supports hierarchical development and mixing of descriptions at various hierarchical levels. This fact can be used in test-pattern generation by mixing the functional and implementation specifications of various modules. Only the modules that are faulty need to be expanded to their implementations and a functional description of all the other modules can be used, resulting in considerable gain in efficiency.

2. High-level fault injection can be easily implemented in Prolog by a hierarchical naming convention described in the paper.

3. Concurrent fault simulation can be viewed as an optimization of the Prolog control strategy and by saving some select (non-masking) results from previous computations, the wasteful recomputations can be avoided.

This research was supported by the National Science Foundation, under grant DCR-8401624 and by an external research grant from Digital Equipment Corporation.

1 Introduction

The ever decreasing feature size and the resulting increase in the complexity of very large integrated circuits have posed a serious problem of circuit testing. While an ad-hoc approach is preposterous for any circuit with more than a few hundred devices, semiautomatic/automatic test pattern generation techniques suffer from the following problems which limit their applicability:

- Most CAD tools restrict fault modeling to either the logic gate or the switch level. This forces the test generator to flatten the hierarchical structure of a design down to the level at which faults are modeled. The resulting loss in execution speed is tremendous. Thatte and Abraham [6] used register transfer level for modeling faults and reported very good fault coverage. Our approach is more general. We model faults at every hierarchical level used in the description of a circuit and not limit them to any one particular level in the design.

- The test-pattern generators are very inefficient in terms of time because of the large number of circuits that need to be simulated and the large number of test patterns involved. Large savings can be accrued by concurrent simulation [1] coupled with functional testing ([4], [3]). We show that both of these can be combined in a Prolog environment.

- Most of the existing fault simulators have a very low level fault injection facility. Also, they do not take advantage of replicated components. We introduce a way of naming hierarchically organized components. To introduce a fault in the circuit the, designer provides a *fault injection vector*, which describes the path in the component tree from the root to the faulty component. This vector is passed down the component hierarchy to the target component, and at that point the functional description of the component is replaced by its malfunction specification.

In this paper we argue that Prolog can be effectively used for specification, simulation, high-level fault injection and test-pattern generation for VLSI circuits. The next Section describes the three types of specifications we will be using for test-pattern generation. These specifications capture the behavior, the implementation and the malfunction aspects of a design. Section 3 gives details of high-level fault injection in a hierarchical description of a circuit. In Section 4 we list various optimizations in Prolog control strategy that speed up the test-pattern generation process. The concluding remarks are presented in the last section.

2 Hardware Specification using Prolog

The pattern matching and automatic backtracking mechanisms of Prolog have been used by various researchers to specify the functionality and the implementation details of digital circuits ([7], [8], [9], [10], [11]). A specification in Prolog consists of (a) a set of ground clauses that describe the basic elements in the design (b) clauses formed by grouping together the basic clauses, reflecting the interconnections in the circuit. Since the Prolog interpreter does not have any knowledge of what level of abstraction a clause represents, a circuit component, once defined, can be used at any level of the design. The following is a specification of a four bit full-binary adder (Texas Instrument SN74LS83), shown in Fig. 1.

```
carry(ispec,A,B,Ci,Co) :-
    and2(Ci,A,X),and2(Ci,B,Y),and2(A,B,Z),nor3(X,Y,Z,Co).
sum(ispec,A,B,Ci,Co,S) :-
    and2(Co,Ci,X), and2(Co,A,Y), and2(Co,B,Z),
    and3(A,B,Ci,W), nor4(X,Y,Z,W,S).
single_stage(ispec,A,B,Ci,S,Co) :-
    carry(ispec,A,B,Ci,Co), sum(ispec,A,B,Ci,Co,S).
adder(ispec,[[],[],Ci],[[],Ci]).
adder(ispec,[[A1|R1],[B2|R2],Ci],[[S1|R3],Co]) :-
    single_stage(ispec,A1,B2,Ci,S1,C1),
    adder(ispec,[R1,R2,C1],[R3,Co]).
adder4(ispec,[[A1,A2,A3,A4],[B1,B2,B3,B4],Ci],[[S1,S2,S3,S4],Co])
    :-  not(A2,A2bar),not(B2,B2bar),not(A4,A4bar),not(B4,B4bar),
        adder(ispec,[[A1,A2bar,A3,A4bar],[B1,B2bar,B3,B4bar],Ci],
        [[S1bar,S2,S3bar,S4],Co]), not(S1bar,S1),not(S3bar,S3).
```

In the above description, for the sake of brevity, we have left out the clauses for and2, and3, nor3 and nor4. The specification, (supplemented with the definition of and2 etc.), can be directly used for simulation. We call the above specification an implementation specification. The following advantages can be immediately noted:

- Prolog's backtracking and unification mechanisms provide the circuit simulator and thus no separate simulator is needed.
- The definition of adder4 is actually a specific case of an adder. In fact what we have is a "component schema" and a circuit can have many invocations of it. Thus one can construct a 32 bit adder with no extra effort. This shows how a Prolog specification can be very efficient in terms of space.

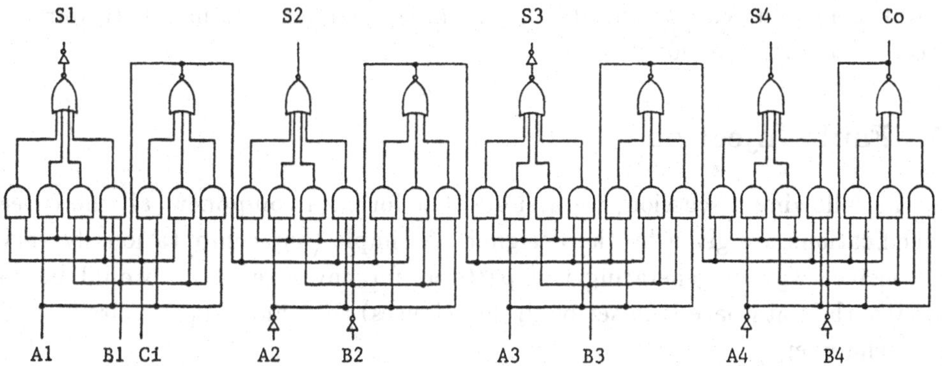

Figure 1: Four-bit full binary adder (from Texas Instruments catalog SN74LS83)

We want to use Prolog specifications for generating test-patterns. Conventionally, the process of test-pattern generation has been time consuming because of lengthy calculations (propagating logic values) on a very large graph (the VLSI circuit). We hope to remedy the situation by encapsulating the complexity of all the components in high level abstractions.

We call these abstractions the functional specifications of the components. The functional specification (fspec for short) can replace the implementation details as long as the component is not faulty. For components that are faulty, or have a faulty sub-component, two more specifications are needed viz. the implementation specification (ispec) and the malfunction specification (mspec). We have already give the implementation specification of a four-bit adder. The fspec for the same adder is:

```
adder4(fspec,[I1,I2,Ci],[O,Co]) :-
   bin2int(I1,X),bin2int(I2,Y),Z is X+Y+Ci,int2bin(Z,O,Co).
```

This simply states that O is the sum of I1, I2 and Ci, and the resulting carry is Co. This specification avoids the particular logic used to implement the adder. In general such an abstract definition would be much faster to simulate than the detailed, implementation bound definition.

A malfunction specification tries to capture the possible anomalies in the component behavior. The following clause models the logical fault in the adder resulting from an 'anding' short circuit between the two lowest order bits.

```
adder4(mspec,[I1,I2,Ci],[O,Co]):-
    adder4(fspec,[I1,I2,Ci],[[O1,O2,O3,O4],Co]),
    and3(O1,O2,Ox), O = [Ox,Ox,O3,O4].
```

Additional faults can be specified in a similar manner. We now turn our attention to fault injection.

3 Fault Injection

In the following discussion, we assume that for each component all the three specifications are given by the designer. A simple (but computationally very expensive) way of generating test-patterns for any given fault would be to modify the data-base (the set of Prolog clauses) to define a faulty circuit and pose the query:

```
?:- circuit(ispec,I,O), faulty_circuit(ispec,I,Of), not(O,Of).
```

where 'not' has been appropriately defined. In this query, we are looking for the input vector I which produces different outputs for the faulty and the normal circuit. As we shall see in Section 4, this computation can be optimized in several ways.

One difficulty, which is immediately apparent, is that one has to manually construct the definition of the faulty circuit. Also, for the sake of efficiency, we would like to use the functional specifications of sub-circuits, whenever possible. A way to do this is to pass a fault injection vector (FIV) down the component hierarchy. An FIV is a list of components which specifies the path from the root to a faulty component in the component tree. For example, to simulate malfunctions in `adder4` in `d_unit5`, which is in `alu16` of the `circuit`, the FIV will be `[circuit, alu16, d_unit5, adder4]`. This is passed as an argument to each clause. Each node strips off the first entry in the FIV, and tries to match it against its own name. If the name matches, it is one of the components on the path to the faulty component. In that case it switches to its implementation specification and passes the remaining FIV to each one of its sub-components. All other components, not on the path to any faulty component use their functional specification. Lastly, when a node gets the terminal value in FIV and its name matches it, the node switches to its malfunction specification. Notice that in the above example the faults are being simulated at the component level and not at the switch or gate level.

It is not difficult to see how the process outlined above can be automated. The prolog interpreter can easily be modified to rewrite all the clauses and incorporate a goal in each clause that manipulates the FIV and checks if the component is affected or not. The scheme has the advantage that test patterns are deduced automatically from the description of the components and the faults they can have. It also increases the speed, as majority of the sub-circuits are simulated at the functional level. We now turn our attention to various optimizations that can be done through simple modifications to the prolog interpreter.

4 Concurrent Fault Simulation and Optimized Test Pattern Generation

At the root of the problem of test-pattern generation is the problem of searching enormous search spaces inherent in the large VLSI circuits. The problem has been shown to be NP-complete. Our proposed use of the functional specification of the components is a partial remedy to this problem. Other types of optimizations are possible in Prolog. The following is the list of proposed optimizations:

- It is possible to detect, statically, the clauses that are deterministic; if the clauses are reordered so that the deterministic ones are computed first a lot of unnecessary backtracking can be avoided.

- An attempt to unify the normal and the faulty circuit (stored as a structure) will fail. However, such an attempt (with slight modification in the unification algorithm), would bring out the places where the normal and the faulty circuit differ. Since the same input will be applied to both the circuits, one can assert clauses stating:

  1. the output of the components which are non-faulty and are not on the path to the faulty component should be the same and should be *non-masking* (observability criterion).
  2. the output of the faulty component and all the components on the path to the faulty component in the faulty circuit, should *not* be equal the output of the same components in the normal circuit (detectability criterion).

  This will prune the search space significantly.

- The circuit unification mentioned in (2) can be extended to the simultaneous simulation of a many faulty circuits (concurrent fault simulation). The Prolog interpreter can be modified to store in a table, some select variable bindings returned by the clauses. Instead of recomputing these clauses, there results can be directly recalled from the table and the resulting gain in speed will be substantial.

5 Concluding Remarks

Various changes to the prolog interpreter were suggested for efficient test-pattern generation. These changes include (a) incorporation of high-level fault injection, (b) reordering clauses to avoid wasteful backtracking, (c) asserting new clauses so that faults are not masked, and (d) storing partial results to avoid recomputation. We have successfully specified, simulated and generated test patterns for many large examples, using prolog. Since a large portion of the circuit is simulated at the functional level, the gain in speed is substantial. Our initial experimentation in the use of prolog for designing VLSI circuits indicates that a designer can specify, simulate and test his circuits in a uniform manner, without resorting to a different tool for each of the above activities.

Acknowledgements: I want to thank David S. Warren for his helpful comments and discussions.

References

[1] E. Ulrich, T. Baker, *The Concurrent Fault Simulation of Nearly Identical Digital Networks* , (Jun 1973), Design Automation Workshop Proc., pp 145-160, IEEE Computer, pp 39-44, (Apr 1974).

[2] M. R. Barbacci, G. E. Barnes, R. G. Cattell, D. P. Siewiorek, *Symbolic Manipulation of Computer Descriptions: The ISPS Computer Description Language* , Technical Report CMU-CS-79-137, Carnegie-Mellon University, Computer Science Department, (Aug 1979).

[3] M. R. Barbacci, W. B. Dietz, L. Szewerenko, *Specification, Evaluation, and Validation of Computer Architecture Using Instruction Set Precessor Description*, Technical Report CMU-CS-79-118, Carnegie-Mellon University, Computer Science Department, (1979).

[4] Kwok-Woon Lai, *Functional Testing of Digital Systems* , CMU-CS-81-148, Dept. of Computer Science, Carnegie-Mellon University, Pittsburgh, (Dec 1981).

[5] S. B. Akers, *Functional Testing with Binary Decision Diagrams*, Proceedings of 8th International Conference on Fault

Tolerant Computing(FTCS-8), pp 75-82, IEEE Comp. Society, June 1978.

[6] S. M. Thatte, J. A. Abraham, *Test generation for Microprocessors* IEEE Trans. Comput., V C-29, (Jun 1980).

[7] P. W. Horstmann, *Design for Testability using Logic Programming*, IEEE International Conference, Cherry Hill, NJ, (Oct 1983).

[8] P. W. Horstmann, *Functional Simulation using Logic Programming*, TR-83-17, Syracuse University, Syracuse, NY, (Aug 1983).

[9] P. W. Horstmann, *Expert Systems and Logic Programming for CAD* , pp 37-46, VLSI Design, (Nov 1983).

[10] Norihisa Suzuki, *Concurrent Prolog as an Efficient VLSI Design Language*, pp 33-40, Computer, (Feb 1985).

[11] Fumihiro Maruyama, Masahiro Fujita, *Hardware Verification*, Computer, pp 22-32, (Feb 1985).

[12] W. F. Clocksin, C. S. Mellish, *Programming in Prolog*, Springer-Verlag, New York, NY, (1981).

[13] M. A. Breuer, A. D. Friedman, *Diagnosis and Reliable Design of Digital Systems*, Computer Society Press, Inc. 1976.

Using Prolog to Represent and Reason about Protein Structure

C.J. Rawlings[+], W.R. Taylor[*], J. Nyakairu[+*], J. Fox[+], M.J.E. Sternberg[*]

[+]Biomedical Computing Unit, Imperial Cancer Research Fund, London WC2A 3PX and [*]Laboratory of Molecular Biology, Dept. of Crystallography, Birkbeck College, London WC1E 7HX

SUMMARY

Logic programming methods have been used to represent and reason about protein structural topology. A description of the relative positions (the topology) of protein structural features enabled declarative representations of super-secondary structures to be used to search for structural motifs. An important feature of this approach is the ability to reason symbolically about complex topological structures in terms of a small set of simple spatial relationships.

INTRODUCTION

Proteins are linear polymers (polypeptides) of amino acids that execute the structural, procedural and control information held in the genetic material of the cell (DNA). Protein structure is determined by the order of amino acids in the polypeptide chain specified by its gene (DNA) sequence. The 3D structures of more than 150 proteins have been determined by X-ray crystallography and in most proteins, there are regular secondary structures; β-strands (which hydrogen bond to form a β-sheet) and/or α-helices. The relative positions of the secondary structures is called the protein topology. Over the last ten years many topological motifs have been observed in proteins. For example, in proteins with β-sheets, 4 β-strands can be arranged so as to form a pattern known as a Greek key because of its resemblance to decorations on Greek vases [1].

An understanding of protein topology is central to some studies of protein structure since topological motifs impose constraints on allowed conformations which can be exploited in algorithms to predict protein structure from their amino acid sequence [2,3]. Furthermore, the presence of some topological motifs is best explained in terms of the pathway of protein folding and thus the identification of motifs provides clues to the nature of some folding pathways. Topological motifs may also be important structural units that could be exploited in the design and engineering of synthetic proteins.

Most analyses of topological features have been performed by visual inspection of diagrams of structures by experts [1,2]. However, the number of known structures is increasing and it is becoming harder to maintain a comprehensive list of topological motifs. Automated methods for the representation and study of protein topology are therefore required to assist the analysis and prediction of protein structure. This paper reports the use of the logic programming language PROLOG to represent and reason about the topology of β-sheet proteins. A previous account of this work [4] recommended such methods as the basis for intelligent front ends to molecular graphics facilities.

REPRESENTATIONS OF PROTEIN STRUCTURE

In order to clarify discussions of protein structure and reveal possible principles of protein folding, molecular biologists have developed a hierarchy of simplified representations of the precise path of the polypeptide chain. One form (Figure 1(a)) represents each β-strand as an arrow, α-helices as a spiral and a thin wire for the connecting regions. The protein prealbumin is represented in this form and Figure 1 shows the stacking of one β-sheet formed from strands 'f,e,b,c' on the second formed from strands 'h,g,a,d' together with a short α-helical region just after strand 'e'. The next level of abstraction (Figure 1(b)) has each β-strand denoted by a triangle with the apex indicating strand direction. α-helices are denoted by circles [5]. In protein domains such as prealbumin in which there is a stacked pair of β-sheets, the structure can be abstracted into a β-barrel. For example, edge strand 'f', which is adjacent to strand 'e' is abstracted as being adjacent to both strand 'h' and strand 'e'. Similarly strand 'c' can be considered adjacent to strands 'b' and 'd'. From such an abstraction, the relative positions of all the strands can be denoted in a planar form [1] (Figure 1(c)).

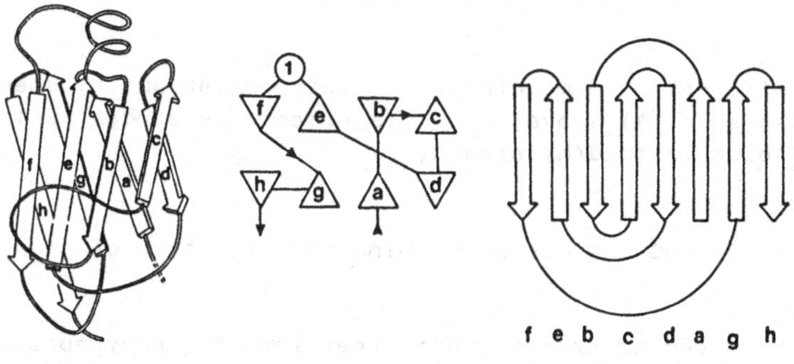

(a) (b) (c)

Figure 1. Abstract representations of protein structure

PROLOG REPRESENTATION

A FORTRAN program has been written to convert data in the Brookhaven data files [6] into PROLOG ground clauses that describe the relative positions and orientations of β-strands in a β-sheet. The principal aims in the choice of representation were to use a binary relational model of the data in order to keep the query semantics simple [7] and to make all inferences about protein structure using PROLOG. The FORTRAN program was restricted to data conversion.

The PROLOG clauses automatically derived from the Brookhaven databank are illustrated in Figure 2(a), where part of the output from a conversion of the prealbumin entry (2PAB) is shown. This study was restricted to topological motifs formed from β-strands. The relationships described in the PROLOG database include the β-structural organisation hierarchy. The layers represented explicitly by *is_part_of(STRUCTURE,SUPER_STRUCTURE)* are β-strand, sheet and domain. The path taken by the polypeptide strand is described by *follows(S2,S1)*, the relative orientation of strands by *is_parallel_to(strand(A),strand(B))* or alternatively *is_antiparallel_to(strand(A),strand(B))* and the neighbour relationship between strands in each sheet is defined by *is_databank_neighbour_of(strand(A),strand(B))*.

```
(a)
protein_name(p2pab,'PREALBUMIN (HUMAN PLASMA)').

is_part_of(strand(f),sheet(B))    is_part_of(strand(e),sheet(B))

follows(helix(1),strand(e))       follows(strand(f),helix(1))

is_antiparallel_to(strand(e),strand(b))
is_antiparallel_to(strand(f),strand(e))

is_databank_neighbour_of(strand(f),strand(e))

(b)
is_part_of(sheet(A),domain(a))    is_leftmost(strand(f),sheet(A))
is_located(sheet(A),above)        is_oriented(strand(a),up)
is_parallel_to(strand(h),strand(f))
```

Figure 2. PROLOG clauses describing the structure of prealbumin

In addition to secondary structural features, the polypeptide sequence data, the positions in the sequence and the cartesian coordinates of the α-carbon backbone of each structural element are also converted to PROLOG format. The PROLOG clauses at this stage partially describe a structure equivalent to the abstract circle and triangle diagram drawn manually to illustrate features at the level of protein superecondary structure [5] (Figure 1(b)). In order to complete the ROLOG representation to reflect the published protein structure, dditional clauses were added manually to compensate for information ot given in the Brookhaven database. In a structure such as realbumin which consists of a stacked pair of β-sheets, neither the elative position of the β-sheets nor the absolute orientation of any trand is specified in the Brookhaven databank. PROLOG clauses escribing the topology of the following representative proteins were onstructed from the Brookhaven data bank: prealbumin (2PAB), carbonic nhydrase C (1CAC), α-chymotrypsin (tosyl) (2CHA), concanavalin A 2CNA), immunoglobulin Fab V_H and C_{H1} domains (3FAB), Staphylococcal uclease (2SNS), superoxide dismutase (2SOD) and tomato bushy stunt irus protein (2TBV).

EPRESENTATION OF TOPOLOGICAL MOTIFS

he representation of protein super-secondary β-structural motifs was ntended to be easy to construct and understand for a non-PROLOG user, e a declarative description of the structure and reflect the omplexity hierarchy of β-structures suggestive of a possible folding heory [8]. Figure 3 illustrates predicates that describe the β-airpin, the 3 stranded β-meander, the 4 and 5 stranded Greek keys and he 6 stranded jelly roll motifs. The functor name is the name of the otif, the first argument is the motif type where each list element is n integer that specifies the the number of strands crossed in moving rom the current strand to the next sequential strand of the motif 1]. This argument has been excluded in the simpler motifs to implify presentation. The second argument is a term that contains a ist of the strands in the motif.

reek keys and jelly rolls can spiral in either a right or left-handed ense. Accordingly, rules for determining handedness are used (Figure). A general definition of a Greek key is used and then the andedness rules determine the handedness of the structure found. The ame handedness rules are used for all Greek keys. This is both conomical and more importantly, knowledge about how the handedness of reek keys is determined is kept independent of the motif definition.

OPOLOGICAL REASONING

uper-secondary structural motifs are often distributed over more than ne β-sheet and also occur in β-barrels. In previous studies where uper-secondary structure have been identified by eye [1,5,8], the opological transformation from the structural cartoon (Figure 1(a)) o a 2-dimensional representation (Figure 1(c)) has been achieved anually, sometimes using an intermediate representation (Figure (b)). In order for the PROLOG system to find all potential tructures, rules were incorporated that represent the reasoning equired to make the same topological transformations.

```
hairpin([1], strands([A,B]) ) :-
        succeeds(B,A),
        adjacent(A,B),
        are_antiparallel(A,B).
```

```
meander([1,1], strands([A,B,C]) ) :-
        hairpin([1], strands([A,B])),
        hairpin([1], strands([B,C])).
```

```
greek_key([3,1,1], strands([A,B,C,D])) :-
        succeeds(B,A),
        adjacent(A,D),
        are_antiparallel(A,D),
        meander([1,1], strands([B,C,D])).
```

```
greek_key([3,1,1,3], strands([A,B,C,D,E])) :-
        greek_key([3,1,1], strands([A,B,C,D])),
        greek_key([1,1,3], strands([B,C,D,E])).
```

```
jelly_roll( [5,3,1,1,3], strands([A,B,C,D,E,F])) :-
        succeeds(B,A),
        adjacent(A,F),
        are_antiparallel(A,F),
        greek_key([3,1,1,3],strands([B,C,D,E,F])).
```

Figure 3. Topological motifs described as PROLOG predicates

The essential inferences in the topological reasoning involve the recognition of circular β-barrels and single and pairs of stacked linear β-sheets. If a stacked pair are found, such as in prealbumin (Figure 1) the strands on the edges of the structure are treated as adjacent. The actual or apparent circular structures may then be simply opened at arbitrary point(s) in order to generate a linear structure (Figure 1(c)). Since the absolute position and orientation of strands in the β-sheet must be determined from many transitive relations and one terminating clause, much of the intermediate reasoning consists of transitive closure. This of course poses a

```
greek_key(Handed,Type,Strands) :-
        greek_key(Type,Strands),
        is_handed(Handed,greek_key,Strands).
```

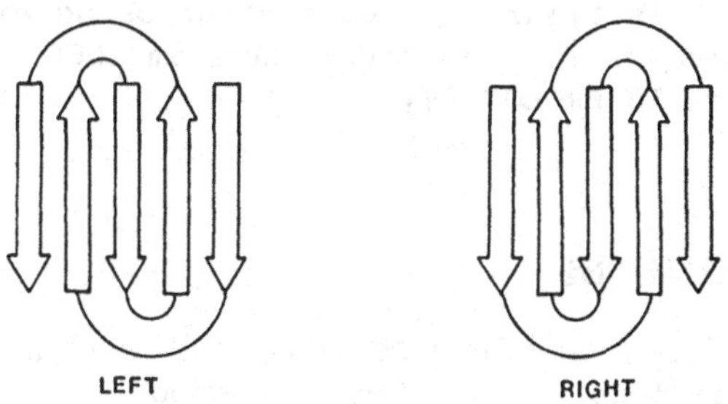

Figure 4. Left and right handed Greek keys

ignificant problem when reentrant (e.g. circular) structures are epresented as transitive relations unless checks are made to prevent nfinitely recursive procedures.

ESULTS

PROLOG definition of a structural motif can be used as a query to he intensional database resulting from the combination of the opological reasoning and the extensional database. Satisfaction of uch a query unifies the STRANDS argument of the rule with a list of trands that constitute the motif. From the indentity of the strands an be found the amino acid sequence or the cartesian coordinates of he α-carbon backbone of the motif. The results can be then used or further analysis or as input to a graphics system capable of isplaying or highlighting the motif. The system has been used in his way to confirm postulated constraints on secondary structures mposed by their positions in a motif. Furthermore, since each motif efinition is also a theorem describing the structure of a protein old, hypothetical folding pathways can be described and by automatic eduction the hypothesis proven true or false. Such techniques rovide a basis for powerful and flexible tools to help molecular iologists explore their understanding of protein structure.

nquiries of both kinds were successfully performed on proteins elected as representing examples of all the β-structural motifs. ach enquiry requires PROLOG to search its current database for a mall number of successful solutions from a very large search space. n order to achieve maximum efficiency, subgoals were ordered so that he simplest goals were executed first. Variables in the body of the ule are thus unified as soon as possible to reduce the number of esatisfactions (backtracking) by more complex (costly) goals. ecause the reasoning system is a logic program, the order of subgoals can be changed to demonstrate the benefits of static optimisation of subgoal ordering without affecting the outcome. An approximately 6 fold improvement was observed in the execution time for the best subgoal order in a definition of a 4 stranded Greek key compared to a reverse ordering. This figure was consistent using either interpreted or compiled programs on an unloaded DECsystem 2060 running Edinburgh University DECsystem-10 PROLOG [9].

DISCUSSION AND CONCLUSIONS

This study demonstrates that PROLOG can provide a method of capturing abstract representations of protein topology. PROLOG provides a mechanism for expressing queries that can not only extract information from the database directly, but more importantly, can infer structural relationships not represented explicitly, using topological reasoning based on a hierarchical description of structural motifs that reflect the organisation of protein structure.

Developing from a small number of simple definitions to complex rules defining topological motifs was found to be simple in PROLOG because the rules were comprehensible. Furthermore, the flexibility of logic programming methods meant that subordinate rules could be used in a to extend the query language [10]. These features also contributed to the economy of program code. The topological reasoning occupied 143 lines of executable PROLOG (49 rules, 21 procedures). The definitions of motifs occupied 49 lines (12 rules, 6 procedures).

We have now developed a representation of protein topology that preserves the relative positions of the secondary structural features in 3D space (Figure 1(a)) and have extended the reasoning to accomodate the increase in detail. The move to a 3D representation was required in order to infer automatically those clauses that until now were added manually (Figure 2(b)) and to reason about topological motifs in 3D space such as those containing α-helices, whose structure prevented straightforward planar abstractions. Motifs in this class include 4 fold helical bundles, mononucleotide binding folds, and βαβ subunits.

The extra reasoning required to support the semantic representation of 3D topology increase the response time beyond what is acceptable for interactive use. However, we are now in a position to investigate the sources of the combinatorial expansions of search space and identify to performance bottlenecks. We intend to use this knowledge to pursue the development of specialized meta-level inference methods that preserve the declarative semantics of the program, but improve performance. An example might be a special method to perform transitive closure on circular structures. It will be valuable to see if the meta-level inference methods required for this domain are similar to to those used for solving physics problems [11].

CKNOWLEDGEMENTS AND GRANTS

he authors wish to acknowledge support from the Royal Society (MJES), he Science and Engineering Research Council (WRT, JN) and the mperial Cancer Research Fund (CJR and JF).

EFERENCES

1. Richardson, J. (1977) *β-Sheet Topology and the Relatedness of proteins* Nature, 268, 495-500
2. Cohen, F.E., Sternberg, M.J.E., Taylor, W.R. (1982) *Analysis and Prediction of the Packing of α-Helices against a β-Sheet in the Tertiary Structure of Globular Proteins* Journal of Molecular Biology, 156, 821-862
3. Taylor, W.R., Thornton, J.M. (1983) *Prediction of Super-Secondary Structure in Proteins* Nature, 301, 540-542
4. Rawlings, C.J., Taylor, W.R., Nyakairu, J., Fox, J., Sternberg, M.J.E. (1985) *Reasoning About Protein Topology Using the Logic Programming Language Prolog* J. Mol. Graphics, 3, 151-157
5. Sternberg, M.J.E., Thornton, J.M. (1977) *On the Conformation of Proteins: The Handedness of the Connection between Parallel β-Strands* Journal of Molecular Biology, 110, 269-283
6. Bernstein, F.C., Koetzle, T., William, G.J.B., Meyer,E. Jr., Brice, M.D., Rodgers, J.R., Kennard, O., Shimanouchi, T., Tasumi, M. (1977) *The Protein Data Bank: A Computer-based Archival File for Macromolecular Structures* Journal of Molecular Biology, 112, 535-542
7. Kowalski, R (1979) *Logic for Problem Solving* In: Artificial Intelligence Series, 7, North Holland Press, Amsterdam
8. Ptitsyn, O.B., Finkelstein, A.V. (1980) *Similarities of Protein Topologies: Evolutionary Divergence - Functional Convergence or Principles of Folding?* Annual Reviews of Biophysics, 13, 339-386
9. Bowen, D.L., Byrd, L., Pereira, F.C.N., Pereira, L.M., Warren, D.H.D. (1982) *DECsystem-10 PROLOG USER'S MANUAL* University of Edinburgh, Dept of Artificial Intelligence
10. Futo, I., Darvas, F., Szeredi, P. (1978) *The application of Prolog to the development of QA and DBM systems* In: Logic and Databases, Eds: Gallaire, H., Minker, J., Plenum Press
11. Bundy, A., Byrd,L., Mellish, C. (1982) *Special Purpose but Domain Independent Inference Mechanisms* Proceedings, European Conference AI,1982, 67-74

A New Approach for Introducing Prolog to Naive Users

Oded Maler, Zahava Scherz and Ehud Shapiro

Weizmann Institute of Science
Rehovot 76100, Israel

Abstract

Most Prolog textbooks are based on gradual presentation of Prolog's concepts, as well as some concepts from logic. We think that this order of presentation used in most books is inadequate for readers with little prior experience with logic, mathematics or programming. In this paper we introduce a new approach for teaching Prolog to these "naive" users. Within our framework, the order of concept introduction is based upon the order used in teaching logic: from propositions to predicates. We believe that this approach will ease the difficulties encountered by newcomers to Prolog, and will provide a good basis for better understanding of logic, programming, data-base theory, and perhaps also other relevant disciplines.

The choice of Prolog as a first programming language is also discussed, and we argue that it is a better choice than conventional languages in the same sense that those languages are considered better than machine languages. This claim however should be empirically verified.

1. Problems with currently used approaches.

Prolog textbooks (e.g. [2, 3, 4, 7]) usually begin with the introduction of the basic Prolog concepts: terms, facts, queries, conjunctive queries and rules. The concept of logical variables is usually inserted in the sections discussing queries and expanded during the discussion of rules. This order of presentation may be appropriate for teaching Prolog to individuals that have been previously exposed to mathematical logic or other branches of mathematics (e.g. computer science students). However we feel that there are many other potential users of Prolog who need a different treatment. Those "naive" users face too many problems simultaneously at the beginning of a Prolog course. Some of these problems are listed below:

1) The newcomer to Prolog might as well be a newcomer to computers and programming (and also to typing). The rigid and unsophisticated (compared with human-to-human communication) form of human-machine dialogues in their current state can constitute a very high barrier for these first time users, a fact usually ignored by computer hackers.

2) Most people are unfamiliar, or at least unexperienced with formal mathematical notation such as functions, arguments, brackets, and variables. This is the cause for many syntax errors and bugs in beginners' programs, and the effect of these errors on learning motivation is magnified by the previously mentioned general unfamiliarity with computers. This problem may prevent the learning of more advanced programming techniques involving compound terms.

3) The linkage between the syntactic and semantic distinctions among atoms and variables

are not intuitive, and usually cause additional confusion. This problem, as well as problem 2, has been tackled by interfaces like Micro-Prolog's SIMPLE and MITSI ([1, 2]) by assigning to variables only names like X and Y or names starting with a prefix such as 'some' or 'any'. The advantages and disadvantages of these and other features of the 'friendly syntax' approach are discussed in [5], which is an extended version of this paper.

4) The technical details of entering clauses into the data-base ('loading', 'consulting'), removing them, and asking queries are poorly treated in some books, or appear in inappropriate places, i.e. places one usually reaches only after having written and loaded some programs, which is like hiding the key inside the box it should open. This problem is also addressed by the Micro-Prolog book and environment that use an opposite approach by mixing technical information with teaching material.

2. The proposed approach.

The following sub-sections describe briefly the outline of the teaching material for a Prolog course designed by the authors for children in secondary school. An experimental course using such an approach is currently being taught in a class of 16 years old students. Conclusions from this experiment will be reported in the future. We feel that the teaching material can be used for teaching much younger students.

2.1 Propositional Prolog.

In order to override some of the above-mentioned difficulties, we start our discussion with a propositional subset of Prolog. This allows us to explain concepts like facts, queries, conjunctions and rules, without dealing with predicates, arguments or variables. The insight for this reordering of concepts has two origins:

1) It has been found useful to exemplify Prolog's computational behavior using simple rules like a:-b,c.

2) This same order of presentation is used in most books for teaching logic.

Furthermore, the understanding of the propositional version and the awareness to its practical expressive limitations naturally motivates the student to accent the use of predicates and variables later on.

A box and its manager.

The course starts with the description of a box, into which one can insert objects or remove them from it. Initially the box and the objects are graphically represented, but soon we move to symbolic representation using words. The computer (or the Prolog interpreter) is introduced as quite a dumb manager we hire for mediating between us and the box. This manager is implemented by a standard Edinburgh-style interpreter (Wisdom Prolog [6]) augmented with a very simple menu-driven shell that enables the users to switch easily between 'consult' and 'query' modes, to get a listing of the box's contents, etc.

The dumbness of the manager, expressed by its inability to recognize spelling mistakes, is a first example of the rigidity of human-computer dialogues. The fact that the manager cannot tell meaningful objects from meaningless ones treating both as strings of letters, is another good example of the nature of logic and of computers.

Another important principle is that one cannot remove from a box an object that has not been inserted into that box before. This "empty box assumption" is analogous to the "closed world assumption" used in data-base theory, and it seems to be very intuitive when we speak about boxes and objects. A query like **?- apple.** is regarded as representing the sentence "Is there an apple in the box?". The experience with objects during this "pre-logical" stage eases later the understanding of negation in logic and in Prolog. This stage may be skipped if the students are mature enough.

The propositional box.

After the student has practiced the manipulation of objects using the computerized box manager, we suggest a new idea: suppose our head is a similar box, and our knowledge is a collection of information items residing in our brain. These information items can stand for beliefs, facts, hypotheses, opinions, etc. and can be manipulated in our personal box through processes such as learning, forgetting and answering questions. So why wouldn't we try to transfer our knowledge into the computerized box by inserting propositions we believe to be true?

The manager "agrees" to manipulate propositions too, but with some syntactic restrictions: no spaces are allowed between single words in a sentence. The words should be either appended into one large "word" or connected to each other using underscores, e.g. **socrates_is_greek.**. The yes/no answers for queries about such propositions are still regarded as questions about the existence of "objects" in the box, but from this point, the notions of truth, provability and knowledge start proliferating implicitly and explicitly through the teaching material as explained below.

The dumb manager keeps on demonstrating the limitations of computers compared to humans; he cannot tell true sentences from false ones and he is ready to insert both into the box. He is ready to accept contradicting facts as well. He will not answer affirmatively questions about true propositions that has not been entered before, and will ignore semantical identities among syntactically different sentences.

Conjunctive queries.

Conjunction is initially demonstrated in natural language sentences using the word 'and'. We show the student that using the current notation, the manager cannot see the relationship between a conjunction and its conjuncts, e.g. the conjunction **the_tree_is_green_and_the_tree_is_tall** and its components **the_tree_is_green** and **the_tree_is_tall**. Inserting the first into the box does not guarantee positive answers to the second and third, and vice versa. The manager needs a special symbol in order to distinguish the conjunction symbol from other strings. This need for a conjunctive connective is satisfied according to an "agreement" with the manager: we insert atomic facts separately, but we are allowed to ask conjunctive queries using commas between the conjuncts, e.g.

?- the_tree_is_green , the_tree_is_tall.

The semantics of conjunctive queries is straightforward within the box paradigm. We just sk using one query whether two or more objects are inside the box. The same syntactic rinciples that had led to the introduction of the conjunction connective, are used later for the ntroduction of the disjunction and implication connectives.

Rules or virtual propositions.

The implication concept is also introduced using natural language. We informally show the tudent how deduction using Modus Ponens works. As expected, the manager cannot do the ame if the implication sentences are given in a human-like 'if-then' format. As in conjunction, special connective is needed.

The semantics of these 'rules' is less intuitive using the box model. It can be regarded as way to shorten the writing of conjunctive queries (a "macro"), or by borrowing the data-ase theory notion of 'virtual relation' (or 'logical record'). Our box contains now two kinds of bjects: those that are "really" there, and those that look "as if" they are in the box depending n the existence of other objects. From this point on the concept of provability is in the air, vaiting to take the place of the decaying concept of being inside the box.

Rule chaining.

Reasoning chains are quite intuitive, and are very simply explained in propositional Prolog, vithout the burden associated with explaining full Prolog proof mechanism, including unifica-ion, substitution and instantiation.

Disjunction and alternative rules.

Teaching disjunction raises a typical conflict: is the teaching of logic our main goal, or re we setting the foundation for potential software engineers. Pure Prolog does not contain lisjunction, but all versions use straightforward hacks to implement it. The questions concerned vith Prolog programming style has not been definitively answered yet, but one legitimate trend s to use the minimal set of operators needed for writing programs, and in our case that means voiding the use of 'or' in the body of a rule, limiting oneself to the use of alternative rules and acktracking. On the other hand, disjunction is no less intuitive concept than conjunction, and t is by no means 'inferior' to the latter from a logical point of view.

Within our framework disjunction is introduced in a similar way to conjunction, but with ess enthusiasm (which means a shorter discussion), and soon afterwards, the option for writ-ng alternative rules with identical heads is introduced, showing the equivalence among both nethods.

.2 Unary Prolog and logical variables.

Having completed the introduction of propositional Prolog, we make one small but impor-ant step towards full Prolog. This is done by using one-place predicate symbols as a more ystematic way to represent properties of objects. This single argument enables the introduc-ion of variables, and of existential quantification. Universal quantification is demonstrated only after the introduction of binary predicates, even though it could be introduced within the unary framework.

Unary predicates for describing object properties.

The limited intelligence of the box and its manager is attributed to the way propositions are referred to — as a single string of characters. The manager's inability to find similarities among similar (from our point of view) statements, is a major barrier for a more intelligent behavior. After some examples of natural language sentences having the same pattern, the student is told how to translate them into a concise formal notation using a predicate symbol, an argument and parentheses, e.g. **green(tree)**.. This translation includes removal of words such as 'is' and other "cosmetic" features of human language. At a first glance this notation does not contribute much to the expressive power of the language beside decreasing the number of possible ways to represent a statement. The main advantage of this notations lies in the use of variables.

Variables in unary existential queries.

The concept of existentially quantified variables is demonstrated through natural language words that denote unspecified objects: 'who' , 'something', 'a person', 'one' etc. When such words are used in sentences, they refer to entities that their identity is unknown at that moment. After showing these words, we pose a problem to the student: suppose we want to find out who is Greek, i.e. for which individual a fact about his Greekness is contained in the box. After showing the impractical solution of asking queries which are virtually propositional about each potential individual, we express our wish for queries of the form: **?- greek(who)**. But how can we tell the unspecified individual 'who' from the possibly distinct individual 'who'? As always, a syntactic agreement with the manager is achieved, yielding the standard Edinburgh Prolog naming conventions: words starting with a capital letter or an underscore are treated as variables, while other words or numbers are regarded as constants. Such variables are implicitly existentially quantified when they appear in queries.

The manger's response to such existential queries is explained using a very informal description of unification ("matching") and substitution. This discussion is concluded by a repeated note on the meaning of negative answers in Prolog, as a result of possibly missing or misspelled information, and by an explanation how to acquire multiple solutions to such queries.

Variables in conjunctive queries.

Conjunctive queries without shared variables act as two separate queries as in propositional Prolog. Shared variables add to the expressive power of the language, and is the basis of almost any useful Prolog program. This concept is quite easy to explain using unary predicates.

2.3 Full pure Prolog.

At this point we lift any restriction about the number of arguments in a predicate, and by this concluding the introduction of Prolog.

3inary and n-ary predicates for describing relations among objects.

Unary predicates have been found useful for describing propositions about properties of bjects, but they are not sufficient for representing other classes of propositions. These yet ncovered propositions describe certain relationships among two or more entities. We teach the udent how to express such sentences by letting the predicate symbol stand for the relation, nd letting the argument represent the related objects. After some examples we emphasize the on-uniqueness of the selected relational schematta (choice of predicate symbol and arguments, rder of arguments) and the consistency that should be maintained by the programmer while eferring to various instances of the same relation.

Queries in full Prolog are not different in principle from unary queries, but they start demon-rating the real power of Prolog in using one fact as a basis for answering different queries ('Who Abraham's son?', 'Who is Isaac's father?' and so on). Note that binary relations are the start-ig point in most books, and are the core of texts for beginners ([1, 4]), whereas in our approach hey are introduced fairly late.

Variables in facts and rules.

Universal quantification is informally introduced using words like 'everybody' or 'all'. Our greement with the manager conducts him to refer to variables appearing in facts as such. These nable the insertion of facts like 'everybody likes beans' into the box, yielding a positive answer r every similar queries about individuals that like beans.

The use of universal quantification of variables appearing in heads of rules is a bit more tuitive, and the introduction of Prolog is concluded by comprehensive examples of facts, rules nd queries, stated in natural language, Prolog, and an intermediate logical-natural language.

At this point we can abandon the box and its manager, and talk more explicitly about data-ases, syntax rules and interpreters, as we, along with some of the students advance to more phisticated applications of Prolog.

3. Why Prolog?

This section addresses three related questions:

1) Is logic programming a good programming paradigm to start with?
2) Is Prolog a good language for teaching logic programming and logic?
3) Is the dialect of Prolog that we use suitable for educational purposes?

As expected, our answers to these questions are positive, yet we think that the answers to ie second and third questions depend on the goals of teaching.

.1 Logic programming vs. conventional programming.

One argument against using Prolog as a first language is that it is more difficult to understand ian conventional procedural languages like Pascal or Basic. We think that this false impression caused by two factors. First, most of this criticism comes from people who have already crossed ie (quite large) barrier of mastering a conventional programming language. Such persons no more remember the early frustrating struggle with the new esoteric principles of conventional programming, principles that look intuitive after some period of experience. Secondly, the tasks assigned to students in Prolog programming courses are usually more difficult than the tasks assigned to Pascal beginners.

Another potential claim against logic programming is its deviation from the machine behavior. We think that this additional layer of transparency between the language and the machine is a good property of the language. One can learn Pascal without knowing of machine language nor registers, machine language can be taught without knowledge of logic design nor microcode and logic design is well understood even if the student does not know of electrons or alternating current. Starting with the upper more abstract layer does not prevent the discovery of the lower ones later. As conventional high-level language programmers may enjoy the discovery of assembly language principles, some logic programmers may later, according to personal interest or professional needs, get involved in (relatively) lower level languages.

We believe that logic programming is closer to the way naive users see computers. Popular phrases such as "tell the computer I paid my bill", "ask the computer about this problem" or "does the computer know this and that" are all based on a metaphor seeing the computer as someone who is fed with knowledge and information, and who supplies answers according to what he "knows". Prolog and other knowledge-based systems fit nicely within this mental image, and they are more intuitive then the constructs of procedural languages. (The reader is asked to remember his or her first encounter with statements like X:=X+1 in Algol or Pascal not to mention the X=X+1 of Fortran and Basic).

Additional arguments for using a logic programming language as a first language are derived from the assumption that this kind of knowledge-based programming will become the dominant style of programming in the future. As most of the naive users are young, it is no use working hard to teach them skills that might later become useless. School students of today are more likely to become AI programmers or knowledge engineers (or, of course, "just" users) than Cobol or Fortran (or C, Pascal, Basic or PL/1) programmers. We think our course gives them a good basis for acquiring the skills needed for the performance of these tasks.

3.2 Prolog as subset of logic and of logic programming.

Prolog, as a materialization of abstract concepts, contains some restrictive features that are not inherent in logic or in logical thinking. Among these features are the use of Horn clauses instead of full predicate calculus, the use of top-down resolution as the only proof procedure, and most notably, the details of the proof procedure employed by Prolog: depth-first left-to-right search with backtracking. Even though we do not mention this control feature explicitly in the introductory chapters of our teaching material, the student might encounter some non-intuitive consequences of it during program development (e.g. non-termination of query computation due to indirect recursion).

We think however that Prolog is a sufficiently good approximation of the ideas behind logic programming for most purposes, and that it can supply a good informal introduction to mathematical logic and knowledge-based programming. Other expressiveness-related extensions or control features can be easily implemented by meta-interpreters written in Prolog itself. The widespread use of Prolog, and the lack of any alternative standard in logic programming virtually prevents the current use of other variants.

.3 Why this dialect of Prolog?

We use Edinburgh Prolog for various reasons. We think that for "real" programs, its syntax onventions are better than those of SIMPLE Micro-Prolog. The emphasis on aspects related to uture evolution of programming and mathematical-logical skills is a characteristic property of ur project, as opposed to the priorities of the corresponding Imperial College project described n [4]. In both projects the students are meant to grasp the principles and apply them to their ubject matter in other non-programming disciplines, but we also want to give them a head-start n the way to become Prolog programmers or logicians.

The choice of Edinburgh syntax does not say that in our opinion symbols like :- or , are uperior to other notations such as ←, if, & or and. Our framework is not sensitive to such hoices, as all choices are regarded as agreements between the manager and us.

4. Future extensions.

Some of the problems that are to be addressed by future work are:

1) How should nested and recursive terms be introduced?

2) What is a better way to teach recursion? How should the teaching of recursion be paired with the concept of recursive data structures?

3) Can (and should) lists be taught without an explicit discussion of recursive data structures in basic syntax?

4) When and how should control issues be explained?

5) In what ways should graphical representation of terms, rules and proof procedure be incorporated in the teaching material?

6) How and when should essential evaluable predicates (such as arithmetic evaluation or input/output) be taught?

References.

[1] J. Briggs, *Micro-Prolog Rules!*, Logic Programming Associates, London, 1984.

[2] K. Clark and F. McCabe, *Micro-Prolog — Programming in Logic*, Prentice-Hall, Englewood, 1984.

[3] W. Clocksin and C. Mellish,*Programming in Prolog*, Springer-Verlag, Berlin, 1981.

[4] R. Ennals, *Beginning Micro-Prolog*, Ellis Horwood, Chichester, 1984.

[5] O. Maler, Z. Scherz and E. Shapiro, A New Approach for Introducing Prolog to Naive Users, Technical Report CS86-3, The Weizmann Institute, 1986.

[6] S. Safra, Wisdom Prolog Interpreter, Unpublished, 1984.

[7] L. Sterling and E. Shapiro, *The Art of Prolog*, MIT Press, (to be published).

Prolog Programming Environments: Architecture and Implementation

Takashi Chikayama
Institute for New Generation Computer Technology
4–28, Mita 1–chome, Minato-ku, Tokyo Japan

1. What are Required

It is widely recognized that programming environments affect the productivity of programmers in a quite significant way. Sometimes, even the system designers' productivity in the *qualitative* aspects might be greatly influenced by the availability of reasonable programming environments. This is not only true when programs are developed in conventional procedural languages, but also true when logic programming languages are used.

Above everything, the performance of the language processing system is of great importance. If a language processor fails to process programs with more than 1,000 lines, no practical applications can be written on the system. If a language processor is a hundred times slower compared with, say, a Fortran program doing the same job, non-experimental users may not take the existence of the language processor into their account at the first place. The processing speed is required not only in the final software product, but also during the system development phase. Slow response time of the development system damages the developers' concentration seriously.

Needless to say, quality of tools common with conventional procedural languages, such as editors, file systems, etc. are very important. However, a commonly observed difficulty here is that such tools available on conventional machines are designed based on the concepts of procedural languages, and the interface with the logic programming language systems apt to be quite awkward. Usually, not all the facilities provided by the operating system can be utilized directly from the programs written in logic programming languages, because, for example, certain facilities may require table-like structures which do not agree with the memory management scheme of the logic programming language implementation.

Tools specific to the logic programming languages are of course important. Especially, tools for finding bugs cannot but be specific to the language. There are two different schemes for debugging logic programs. One is by traditional program tracers customized for logic programming languages. The other is by (possibly interactive) program analyzers relying on the *logical* characteristics of the language. For both, availability of good man-machine interface tools (such as multiple window systems) makes great advantage.

Programs that are executed in *parallel* are very hard to debug. Unfortu-ately, parallel logic programming languages cannot be complete exceptions. Iowever, their clean semantics compared with conventional parallel languages ives various possibilities in constructing powerful debugging tools. Essentially, rogram analysis methods for sequential logic programs can also be applied to arallel programs. Tracers can have clearer models compared with procedural anguages, which may enable easy-to-understand tracing of the execution.

Problems are also with the languages themselves. It is almost impossible o develop programs larger than 10,000 lines with simple Prolog without any rogram structures but predicates. Some sort of modular structures are in-lispensable. The tools for the language should utilize such structures of the anguage for debugging ease.

. PSI and SIMPOS

Recognizing the above requirements, ICOT initiated its development ef-ort of the Personal Sequential Inference machine PSI and its operating system IMPOS (Sequential Inference Machine Programming and Operating Systems), lmost immediately after its foundation in 1982. The first version of the hard-vare and SIMPOS version 2.0 are now being used for development of various pplication software.

The machine language of PSI, called KL0, is a logic programming language vith all the essential features of Prolog and various extensions which enabled the lescription of the whole operating system. The description language of SIMPOS, SP, is a still higher level language with object-oriented features suitable for vriting large-scaled programs such as SIMPOS. ESP is used also for application rograms on PSI.

SIMPOS provides various features for ease of debugging ESP programs, s well as those features also available on conventional *work stations* such as he multiple windows system. As SIMPOS is written completely in ESP and nables any access (including *inheritance*) from the application programs, there s no such awkwardness as seen in Prolog systems on conventional machines.

DESIGN OVERVIEW OF THE NAIL! SYSTEM†

Katherine Morris
Jeffrey D. Ullman
Allen Van Gelder
Stanford University
Stanford, CA 94305, USA

ABSTRACT: We describe the design decisions made for the NAIL! (not another implementation of logic!) system, an advanced form of DBMS where queries may involve a large collection of Prolog-like rules used for query interpretation. A discussion of the ways NAIL! semantics differs from Prolog is followed by an exposition of the principal ideas in the system design. These points include the partition of predicates into strongly connected components to represent the structure of recursions and the "capture rule" organization for selecting query processing strategies. Other ideas include the way distinctions between bound and free arguments are capitalized upon and the persistence of previously discovered facts about the way to handle certain queries. We also survey the recent work on the processing of recursively defined queries conducted by the NAIL! group and others with similar computational models.

I. NAIL! SOURCE LANGUAGE

NAIL! is an implementation of Prolog-like rules with two major departures fror Prolog:

1. Where Prolog systems have a built-in notion of how logical rules are to b treated as programs, NAIL! assumes that the system has both the ability an obligation to find a near-optimal way of handling a query and its attendan set of rules.
2. While Prolog systems tend to assume that the database is small, NAII assumes it is large. Further, NAIL! assumes that the response to a query i the one normally expected of DBMS's: the set of all tuples that match th query. Thus, while Prolog systems normally explore the database a tupl at a time, NAIL! tends to work with whole relations, e.g., when computin joins.

The NAIL! source language is essentially pure Prolog, with two additions: *nc* and *findall*, to be discussed shortly. It is designed to handle ordinary databas

† Work supported by NSF grant IST–84–12791 and a grant of IBM Corp.

perations, (often called "Datalog") where there are no function symbols, as well s more traditional forms of rules, where there are function symbols in the rules.

xample 1: A typical Datalog program might be used to define views of data, or nforce security constraints. In the following example, *empdata*(*Emp*, *Sal*, *Dept*) nd *deptdata*(*Dept*, *Mgr*) are database relations with the obvious meaning; view *ecure* is designed to enforce security by zeroing all salaries above 100000, while *iew* is a view designed to relate employees and their managers through depart- ents, i.e.,

$$view = \pi_{Emp,Sal,Mgr}(empdata \bowtie deptdata)$$

he NAIL! rules are:

$secure(E, S, D)$:- $empdata(E, S, D)$ & $S \leq 100000$.
$secure(E, 0, D)$:- $empdata(E, S, D)$ & $S > 100000$.
$view(E, S, M)$:- $secure(E, S, D)$ & $deptdata(D, M)$.

ote we use & for "and" rather than the typical Prolog comma, but otherwise, AIL! conforms to DEC-20 Prolog syntax. In particular, $[a, b, c \mid R]$ denotes a st whose first three elements are a, b, and c, and whose remaining elements are he list R; also, [] denotes the empty list. □

xample 2: The following program is not typical of database operations, yet e intend that NAIL! should handle it. The program defines a list to be "good" all its elements are good.

goodlist([]).
goodlist([$X \mid Y$]) :- *good*(X) & *goodlist*(Y).

In NAIL!, the intended meaning of a query *goodlist*(X) is to give all the lists satisfying *goodlist*. As this set will be infinite, unless the set *good* is empty, e normally expect that the response of NAIL! will be to state that the query annot be answered. We do not want it to give only one solution for X, nor do e want it to go into an infinite loop.

In general, it is undecidable whether a program will loop or whether the set f solutions is infinite, yet we can handle many simple cases, such as this one, orrectly.

We also expect that in response to the query *goodlist*([a, b, c]), NAIL! will eturn either the empty relation (effectively, "false"), if a, b, and c are not all good lements, and the relation containing only the empty tuple (effectively, "true"), f they are. □

Queries in NAIL! are predicates with arguments either bound or free. The nswer to the query is the set of tuples consisting of values for the variables that nake the predicate true. For example, the answer to query *view*($E, S, jones$) n the database of Example 1 is the set of employee-salary pairs such that the employee works in a department of which Jones is a manager, and the salary i that earned by the employee, or zero if his salary is above 100000.

II. NAIL! SEMANTICS

The important departure from Prolog is in the semantics. NAIL! associates wit each predicate symbol a relation, computed by taking the least fixed point of th rules (see [14, 16, 17]). As long as we stay within pure Prolog (no negations, cut or assumptions about the order in which rules or subgoals are explored), thi interpretation is well understood [5, 20]. In fact, a principal difference betwee NAIL! and Prolog is that NAIL! has a fully declarative semantics that in all case is independent of the order of rules in the program and the order of subgoal within a rule. NAIL! has no separate operational semantics.

In order to extend Horn clauses with the "nonlogical" features *not* an *findall*, it is necessary to clarify the quanitification of variables. In NAIL! a quantification is implicit and is governed by two simple, uniform rules:

1. A variable appearing in the head of the rule is universally quantified at th scope of the entire rule.
2. A variable not appearing in the head of the rule is existentially quantified a the lowest scope that includes all occurrences of that variable; in particular, variable only appearing within the scope of a *not* or a *findall* is existentiall quantified within that operator.

These quantification rules are illustrated in the following examples.

Example 3: For the next several examples we shall assume the database relatior are:

married(mary, tom)	*male(frank)*	*age(frank,* 20)
married(tom, mary)	*male(john)*	*age(john,* 25)
	male(tom)	*age(mary,* 30)
		age(tom, 30)

In the following NAIL! rule, we intend *bachelorAge* to contain the ages of u married males.

$$bachelorAge(Z) \text{ :- not } married(X,Y) \ \&\ male(X) \ \&\ age(X,Z).$$

In NAIL! this rule is treated as though it were the first order sentence:

$$\forall Z\,(\exists X\,(\neg\exists Y\, married(X,Y) \wedge male(X) \wedge age(X,Z)) \rightarrow bachelorAge(Z))$$

Observe the difference in the way X and Y are quantified. Thus, in the semanti of NAIL!, the *bachelorAge* relation contains the expected two tuples:

bachelorAge(20)
bachelorAge(25)

It is worth contrasting this result with the interpretations of two other popul ersions of Prolog.

First, consider DEC-20 Prolog with the corresponding rule, which employs + as the negation-by-failure operator:

$$bachelorAge(Z) \text{ :- } \backslash + \; married(X,Y),\; male(X),\; age(X,Z).$$

ince both X and Y are variables when the goal *married*(X,Y) is called, this ositive goal succeeds and its negation fails. In effect, DEC-20 Prolog treats both ariables X and Y as though existentially quantified *below* the negation. As a esult, no *bachelorAge* solutions are found.

Second, consider MU-Prolog [11], which tries to avoid the problem that DEC-0 Prolog encountered by providing a "sound negation" operator, "$\sim$." The $\sim$ perator postpones negative subgoals until their variables are bound to ground erms. In effect, MU-Prolog treats both variables X and Y as though existentially uantified *above* the negation. Unfortunately, Y never becomes bound, so MU-'rolog also finds no *bachelorAge* solutions.

We believe that the NAIL! approach to the *not* operator offers the most atural interpretation, with simple syntax and semantics. □

The *findall* operator works very much the same as in Cprolog. Variables hat occur in the context surrounding the *findall* as well as within it function as group by" parameters, as illustrated in the next example.

xample 4: Consider the two rules

$$p(L) \text{ :- } findall(X,\; (age(X,Y)\; \&\; Y > 20),\; L).$$
$$q(Y,L) \text{ :- } findall(X,\; (age(X,Y)\; \&\; Y > 20),\; L).$$

ogether with the database relations of Example 3. The *findall* can be read in vords approximately as "Unify L with a list of terms X such that X has age Y nd Y is greater than 20." In the rule for p the variable Y is local to the *findall*, o is not treated as a "group by" parameter. The relation for p has the single uple $p([john, mary, tom])$. In contrast, in the rule for q the variable Y occurs utside the *findall*, so *is* treated as a "group by" parameter. The relation for q as two tuples, $q(25,\ [john])$ and $q(30,\ [mary, tom])$. □

One of the first things the NAIL! compiler does is partition the predicates nto strongly connected components (SCC's), in a graph where predicate p has redicate q as a successor if there is a rule with p at the head (left side) and q n the body (right side). This graph is called the *dependency graph* of the logic rogram. Thus, mutually recursive predicates are grouped into one SCC, while ll nonrecursive predicates, including database relations, are in SCC's by them-elves. We may visualize a second graph, called the *reduced graph*, whose nodes re SCC's of the dependency graph. In the reduced graph the SCC containing redicate p has another SCC containing q as a successor if there is a rule for p hat contains a subgoal with predicate symbol q in the body. In other words, the reduced graph inherits arcs from the dependency graph in the natural way.

We may work bottom-up in the reduced graph, which must of course b acyclic, defining the relations associated with the predicates of one SCC by th least fixed point of an operator that treats predicate symbols of predecessor SCC' as given (possibly infinite) database relations. This approach corresponds t defining the semantics as a sequence of least fixed point expressions, one for eac SCC, as described in [5], and so we call this the *iterated fixed point semantics*. A long as we deal with pure Prolog, the iterated fixed point semantics is equivalen to the least fixed point semantics of [2, 20].

However, in order that the iterated fixed point semantics make sense, w require that, in a given rule, no predicate appearing within a *not* or *findall* ma be in the same SCC as the head of that rule. In the terminology of [19], a logi program that satisfies this condition with respect to *not* is called *free of recursiv negation*. It is shown there that for a wide class of such programs, the iterate fixed point semantics is equivalent to the *tight tree semantics*, whose definitio is beyond the scope of this paper. A desirable feature of the tight tree semantic within this class of logic programs is that every atom is either true or false.

In summary, NAIL! semantics is based on the idea that we provide fixe point semantics for each SCC only. If the SCC for predicate p has a successo SCC with q, then the relation for q is determined prior to the relation for p.

III. SYSTEM OVERVIEW

The NAIL! system is sketched in Fig. 1. As mentioned, the source program rul are processed by a front end, whose primary function is to break the predicat into strong components and set up data structures that make manipulation o these components easy. Occurrences of *not* and *findall* are broken out so tha these operators do not occur except in rules with a single atom on the righ side. Certain Prolog shorthands, for "or" and "implies," are also broken out an replaced by several equivalent rules.

Capture Rules

A query is interpreted through a framework called "capture rules." The ide behind capture rules were described in [16], and we shall give some of the detai of the actual strategy used shortly. In brief, a capture rule is a pair of algorithm

1. An algorithm, the *capture rule* itself, that looks at a SCC and decides wheth a particular algorithm for evaluating relations (the "substantiation," define below) can be applied to the SCC.
2. A *substantiation algorithm* that computes the relations corresponding t the predicates of the SCC; the substantiation must be correct whenever th capture rule says it applies.

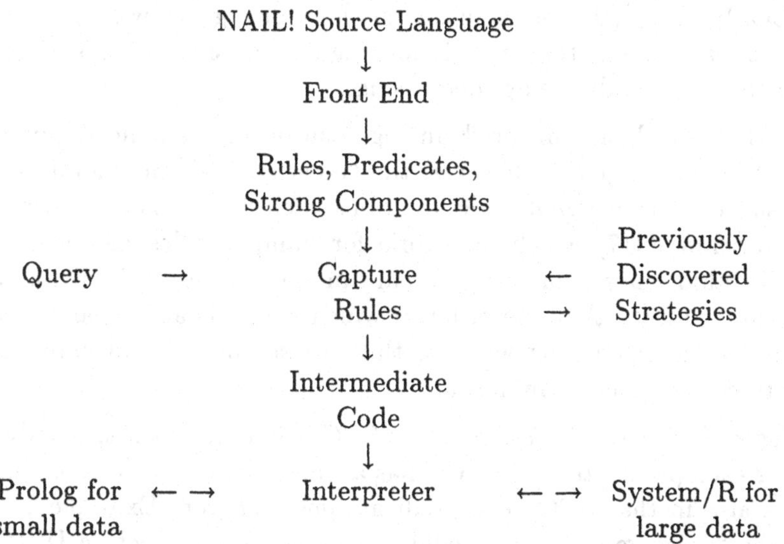

Fig. 1. Sketch of NAIL!.

:esearch on Capture Rules

/hile one could contemplate any sort of capture rule, in practice it is essential ıat the two algorithms involved in a capture rule both be efficient. The reason that we do not want to spend forever either in the query optimization or in the uery execution phases. Thus, we are limited in what we can choose as a capture ıle, and a large portion of the research in logical database systems concerns ıe discovery of what substantiation algorithms are appropriate for what classes f rules. Some of this work has been conducted in the context of capture rules y members of the NAIL! research group at Stanford, and there has also been a ariety of papers on the general subject of strategies for processing logic programs ıat can be adapted to the capture rule framework in a straightforward way.

The following is a brief synopsis of what we regard as promising directions, lassified by the type of query-processing strategy discussed. The reader should lso consult [4] for a survey of Datalog query-processing algorithms.

1. *Top-Down Capture Rules.* Strategies in this group tend to mimic Prolog, constructing a tree of subgoals whose solutions collectively yield all tuples that match the query; the tree is built top-down and evaluated bottom-up. One of the most important issues to be faced when designing a test for applicability of a top-down capture rule is determining whether a Prolog program converges, given information about which arguments are bound and which are free in recursive calls to subgoals. Naish [11] gives an algorithm for proving convergence, although his algorithm is exponential in the size of

an SCC. In [1, 14], a more efficient test for convergence was given, but, like [11], the test requires that we tell, looking only at single SCC's, that certain arguments of a predicate are decreasing.

In [17], an algorithm for deducing relationships among argument sizes across SCC's was given. However, the "most general" polynomial-time test for a subset of convergent logic programs is elusive. It is unknown whether the algorithm of [17], which only works for "unique" rules, can be generalized without taking more than polynomial time for the test. Finally, all of these algorithms assume that the order in which subgoals are expanded is given; the complexity of testing whether there *exists* an order of expansion that leads to convergence is unknown.

2. *Strategies for Linear Rules.* A *linear* SCC is one in which the body of each rule for each predicate in the SCC has at most one occurrence of a predicate that is also in that SCC. The predicate *goodlist* from Example 2 is linear, as is the "same generation" predicate *sg* discussed in Section IV (Example 5). The linear recursions appear to account for the vast majority of all recursive rules. The logic-processing algorithm of [6], although presented as a general Datalog algorithm, is probably best suited for linear rules only. A number of other algorithms for processing linear Datalog are known [3], and interestingly, it does not appear that any of the strategies mentioned in that paper dominate the others.

3. *Recursion Elimination.* In some simple cases, an apparently recursive program, e.g.,

$$p(X,Y) :- p_0(X,Y).$$
$$p(X,Y) :- p(X,Z) \ \& \ q(Y).$$

where q and p_0 are database relations, or predicates outside the SCC of p, can be replaced by an equivalent nonrecursive program, in this case:

$$p(X,Y) :- p_0(X,Y).$$
$$p(X,Y) :- q(Y).$$

The question of whether a Datalog program can have recursion removed in this sense was considered by [7, 12], and together, these papers yield a necessary and sufficient condition for a large family of programs consisting of a single basis rule and a single, linear recursive rule. However, it has recently been shown by Gaifman and Vardi that the general problem is undecidable, even for programs with a single, linear recursive rule.

While recursions that are not really recursions are unlikely to be encountered frequently in practice, the same techniques are used in [13] to eliminate some of the nonrecursive subgoals from recursive rules. A good example of the distinction drawn in [13] is between the rules

$buys(X,Y)$:- $cheap(Y)$ & $likes(X,Y)$
$buys(X,Y)$:- $cheap(Y)$ & $knows(X,Z)$ & $buys(Z,Y)$

where $cheap(Y)$ can be eliminated from the second rule, and

$buys(X,Y)$:- $rich(X)$ & $likes(X,Y)$
$buys(X,Y)$:- $rich(X)$ & $knows(X,Z)$ & $buys(Z,Y)$

where $rich(X)$ cannot be eliminated.

4. *Dynamic Strategies.* When all else fails, at least for SCC's that are Datalog programs (no function symbols), one can find the set of all "different" subgoals, and compute their relations simultaneously. A number of algorithms of this type have been proposed, and they differ primarily in when they regard subgoals as "different." For example, [10] treats two subgoals separately unless their arguments are isomorphic, up to renaming of variables. The approach of [8, 9] is to merge all subgoals with the same predicate, at the same time attempting to limit examination of tuples to "relevant" values. Van Gelder [18] developed a similar algorithm that distinguishes subgoals by the bound/free pattern of arguments, a technique that sometimes provides significant leverage in restricting search to "relevant" values. Also explored in this paper is the application of "acyclic hypergraph" techniques (see [15]) to the question of term ordering and binding of variables in an order that minimizes work.

ersistence of Strategy Facts

y an algorithm to be discussed in Section V, the NAIL! system searches for the apture rule with the most efficient substantiation with which to capture each CC required to answer the query. As we shall briefly mention in Section IV, the apture rules are applied not directly to SCC's, but rather to "rule/goal graphs," hich include information on bound and free arguments and variables. Thus, iere may in fact be many different capture rules that are, for some bound/free rgument pattern, the best capture rule to use for a given SCC. When such a election of a capture rule is made for an SCC and bound/free pattern, it is emembered permanently, and can be used by subsequent queries or even within ie processing of a single query.

ntermediate Code

here is a simple intermediate code (ICODE) in which the substantiation algothms (which actually compute the relation for a subgoal, using operations such s those of relational algebra) are expressed. We shall not got into much detail ere. Suffice it to say that the data model in which the ICODE operates allows atoms to take relations or integers as values. A single atom, say a, can also rep resent a list of relations, and these "versions" of a can be indexed, with the term $index(a, i)$ representing the version i of a. The maximum-indexed version ma also be regarded as the top of a stack, and the list of versions may be pushed o popped.

A representative ICODE operation is $eqjoin(r(...),\ s(...),\ t(...))$, where th ...'s represent any list of terms, as in Prolog, e.g.,

$$eqjoin(r([X \mid Y], Z),\ s(X, W),\ t(f(X, Y), g(Z, W)))$$

The meaning of this operation is to set the relation t equal to all the values c the head ever produced by repeating the Prolog program

$$t(f(X, Y), g(Z, W)) :\!-\ r([X \mid Y], Z),\ s(X, W).$$

However, the algorithm used is not one where the above clause is simulated, whicl would take time $O(n^2)$ if both relations had n tuples. Rather we sort the tuple for r and s and take a natural join, which algorithm takes time $O(n \log n)$ plu the number of tuples produced.

Present System Status

At the time of this writing, we have written in Prolog a front end that convert NAIL! source into the appropriate data structure representing strong component and their rules. We also have an implementation of ICODE and some rudimentar capture rules that produce ICODE.

We are in the process of bringing the system over to the IBM RT PC, wher the ICODE will be interpreted in such a way that operations on small amount of data will be executed by Prolog, and operations on large relations will b implemented by SQL, a database system running under the AIX operating syster on the RT.

IV. CAPTURE RULES AND RULE/GOAL GRAPHS

As we mentioned in the previous section, the preferred rule processing strateg often depends on which arguments to a predicate are bound and which are fre When applying a capture rule to a SCC, it is often essential that we expand th SCC into a *rule/goal graph* by showing the rules for each predicate in the SC explicitly, and by adding *adornments*, which distinguish between bound and fre arguments of predicates and variables of rules. For example, p^{bf} is a rule/go graph node corresponding to predicate p with first argument bound and secon argument free. If r is a rule with variables X, Y, and Z, we can use r^{fbf} t represent an occurrence of rule r with a constant substituted for Y (in genera we use lexicographic order for variables in adornments of rule nodes).

xample 5: The following rules define the *sg* predicate to mean "cousins at the me generation." We assume *par* is a database relation, and $par(C, P)$ means at P is C's parent.

r_1: $sg(X, X)$.
r_2: $sg(X, Y)$:- $par(X, Xpar)$ & $par(Y, Ypar)$ & $sg(Xpar, Ypar)$.

ppose also we are interested in a goal sg^{bf}, i.e., a query like sg('Joe', W), where e first argument is bound and the second free. Predicate *sg* forms a SCC by self, one that is dependent on the SCC for the *par* relation. We may convert e *sg* SCC into the rule/goal graph of Fig. 2.† The variables of rule r_2 are taken be X, Y, $Xpar$, and $Ypar$, in that order, and the adornment of r_2 indicates eir bound/free status in the same order. □

$$
\begin{array}{ccc}
r_1^b & \leftarrow & sg^{bf} \\
 & & \uparrow \downarrow \\
par^{bf} & \leftarrow & r_2^{bfff} \\
 & & \downarrow \\
 & & par^{fb}
\end{array}
$$

Fig. 2. Rule/goal graph for same generation predicate.

The *sg* rule/goal graph makes sense only if we realize that when there are veral terms on the right of a rule, like r_2, we can choose any order for their valuation. Algorithms like that of [11] in MU-Prolog use heuristics for ordering, ut we expect that typical SCC's will be small enough that we can consider l possibilities in general, with an eye towards finding an order that allows the cursion to maintain the same adornment (pattern of bound and free variables). general, expansion of a SCC into a rule/goal graph will result in several copies each predicate, with different adornments.

We can take advantage of the fact that one term has been evaluated to ovide a set of bindings for a variable. Thus, par^{bf} corresponds to the first rm, $par(X, Xpar)$. Presumably, with a bound value for the first argument, we n solve par^{bf} to obtain a set of values for the second argument. These values n be passed one-at-a-time to an sg^{bf} solver, which provides bindings for $Ypar$. hose values are passed one-at-a-time to a par^{fb} solver, to obtain values of Y that orrespond to the given bound value of X. This process of *sideways information*

† **In the NAIL! implementation, arcs of the rule/goal graph run from a subgoal to its rules, and from a rule to the subgoals of its body; this direction is opposite to that used in [16].**

passing is part of most capture rules, since ordering of literals in a clause body i often crucial to the efficiency of the query evaluation.

V. QUERY PROCESSING STRATEGY

In developing the query processing strategy, our aim is to find efficiently a captur rule with the cheapest substantiation algorithm for the given adorned goal. T avoid repeating searches, we store all the discoveries we make about capturin adorned goals, such as "*capture rule C can be used to capture the adorned pre icate* p^{bf}." These `capturable` facts may be used several times in processing query, and are preserved across queries. In addition, we record the negative di coveries we make, such as "*capture rule C cannot be used to capture the adorne predicate* p^{ff}."

To help us find the cheapest substantiation algorithm, we order the captu rules by the ease of substantiation, and secondly by ease of testing the captu rule. For purposes of illustration here and in the following Example 6, assum we have these three capture rules:

c$_1$: If p is a database predicate with an index on its second argument, we ca capture p^{fb} by database lookup using the index.

c$_2$: If p is a database predicate, we can capture p^{ff} by database lookup.

c$_3$: If q is a non-recursive NAIL! rule, then we can capture q if we can captu all its subgoals, changing their order if necessary.

Clearly, capture rule **c**$_1$ is to be preferred over the rule **c**$_2$.

One assumption we make is that bound adornments are never harder tha free adornments. For example, **c**$_2$ may also be used to capture p^{fb}, if necessar We write "$A \preceq B$" to mean that adornment A is no harder than the adornme B. For example, $bf \preceq ff$. This relationship does not define a total order, sinc for example, $bf \not\preceq fb$ and $fb \not\preceq bf$. There is a natural extension to adorned goa if p^A and p^B are adorned goals, we say $p^A \preceq p^B$ if $A \preceq B$.

There may be a better way to capture a specific goal than the way we u to capture a goal with a more general adornment. For this reason, we start b testing the easiest capture rules before deciding to use the more expensive rule In our example, it means we only use **c**$_2$ to capture p^{fb} if the easier **c**$_1$ cannot b used.

So far, we've written about capturing individual adorned goals. In fact, th capture rules operate on an entire SCC at a time (the SCC of the adorned goa We only store the fact that we captured the given adorned goal; we do not sto facts for each adorned goal in its SCC since in most cases, there is only one ent point to a SCC from outside it. If there are multiple entry points, we do mo work. The capture rule may call the strategy-finding algorithm recursively capture other SCC's that are successors to the SCC in the adorned rule/go graph generated by the adorned goal. The algorithm we use is given in Fig. 3.

```
capture(Goal, A, ValidMethods, Method)
    :-
    member(Method, ValidMethods) &
    canCapture(Goal, A, Method, ValidMethods).
canCapture(Goal, A, Method, ValidMethods)
    :-
    (capturable(Goal, A', Method) & A ≼ A')
    ->                              /* Using stored capturable fact.   */
        true
    else
    (uncapturable(Goal, A', Method) & A ≽ A')
    ->                          /* Found a stored uncapturable fact.   */
        fail
    else
    /* Otherwise, check whether the Method capture rule applies, */
    /* and "remember" the results.   */
    checkApply(Method, Goal, A, ValidMethods)
    ->
        assert(capturable(Goal, A, Method))
    else
        (assert(uncapturable(Goal, A, Method)) &
        fail).
```

Fig. 3. Applying capture rules. Read "`p -> q else r`" as "if `p` then `q` else `r`".

In the evaluation algorithm, `capture`, we use the `member` predicate to generate methods from the list of `ValidMethods` given initially. The `canCapture` rule then tests whether the adorned goal can be captured using `Method` on it and using only methods in the list `ValidMethods` on its successors. There are three branches within the rule:

1. We can capture the adorned goal if we've already captured the same goal with the same or a more general adornment, using the capture rule `Method`.
2. We can't capture the goal with this capture rule if we've already found that we can't capture it with the same adornment or a less general one, using the capture rule `Method`.
3. Otherwise, check whether the capture rule can be applied: the `checkApply` predicate checks whether the capture rule `Method` can be used to capture the adorned goal, using the capture rules in the list `ValidMethods` on the *successors* of that goal. Rules for `checkApply` (see Example 6, below) find the adorned goals (if any) that are successors of the SCC of `Goal` and call

capture recursively on them. If Method applies to the current SCC and al the successors can be captured, then checkApply succeeds and Goal (wit adornment A) is asserted to be capturable; otherwise Goal (with adornmen A) is asserted to be uncapturable.

Once a capture rule for the query is found, the substantiation algorithms fo the methods found applicable to each SCC are used to generate ICODE for th query. This stage uses information† saved while applying the capture rules.

Example 6: The following is a simple rule, where r and s are database predicate with indices on their second arguments:

$$p(X,Y) :\!-\ r(X,Z)\ \&\ s(Z,Y).$$

Suppose we start with the query $p(X,a)$ and the list of capture rule methoc available is

ValidMethods = $[\mathbf{c}_1, \mathbf{c}_2, \mathbf{c}_3]$

as described above. We call capture on p^{fb}. Referring to Fig. 3, canCaptur fails with Method instantiated to $\mathbf{c}_1$ and $\mathbf{c}_2$, as p^{fb} is not a database predicat Upon further backtracking, it tries $\mathbf{c}_3$. The checkApply rule for $\mathbf{c}_3$ is given i Fig. 4.

```
checkApply(c3, Goal, A, Methods)
    :-
    nonRecursive(Goal) &
    sublist(M, Methods) &
    ruleGoalGraph(Goal, A, SCC, Successors) &
    captureList(Successors, M).
```

Fig. 4. Testing applicability of the capture rule $\mathbf{c}_3$.

The sublist predicate is used to generate successively longer prefixes of th Methods list. Predicate ruleGoalGraph produces the rule/goal graph of the SC based at the adorned goal p^{fb}. Since the goal in this case is not recursive, th SCC is trivial. Successors is the list of adorned goals that are successors p^{fb}. On backtracking, ruleGoalGraph produces all possible rule/goal graphs, b reordering subgoals.‡ captureList simply calls capture on each of the adorne goals in the list, passing its second argument M as the ValidMethods list f capture.

---

† In the actual implementation, this is stored as part of the capturable facts, but t details have been omitted here.

‡ We assume that each subgoal binds all the variables appearing in it, and these bindin are passed on to other subgoals; this is known as *sideways information passing* [16].

Now we illustrate how using prefixes of the `ValidMethods` leads to discovery f the most efficient capture method. In its first attempt,

```
checkApply(c3, ...)
```

alls `capture` recursively, through `captureList`, trying to capture the two suboals r^{ff} and s^{bb}. These are the adornments that result from computing r first nd using its Z values, together with the Y bindings from p, to compute s. At his point, the `ValidMethods` list just contains $\mathbf{c}_1$. Since we cannot capture r^{ff} sing $\mathbf{c}_1$, the call to `capture` fails. Now `checkApply(c3, ...)` backtracks and `uleGoalGraph` permutes the order of r and s, putting s first. The second arument of s is bound by the Y of the goal p. By computing s first, we get Z indings for the second argument of r. This leads to the new adornments, s^{fb} nd r^{fb}. Now we try to capture s^{fb} and r^{fb} using $\mathbf{c}_1$.

This attempt succeeds, so we assert the facts that we can capture r^{fb} and ^{fb} using $\mathbf{c}_1$, and p^{fb} using $\mathbf{c}_3$. We store enough information about the successful apture rules so that we can generate the intermediate code for the query $p(X,a)$.

If there is a later query $p(X,b)$, we can use the stored discoveries to capture ne query immediately, using the first `canCapture` rule. □

.CKNOWLEDGEMENTS

Iike Bender contributed to the design of the intermediate code. Moshe Vardi nade a number of contributions to the design of the overall system. The design rofited from open discussions in which many people, such as Andy Freeman, Jeff 'aughton, and Marianne Winslett participated.

REFERENCES

[1] F. Afrati, C. Papadimitriou, G. Papageorgiou, A. R. Roussou, Y. Sagiv, and J. D. Ullman, "Convergence of Sideways Query Evaluation," *Proc. Fifth ACM Symposium on Principles of Database Systems*, pp. 24–30, 1986.

[2] K. R. Apt and M. H. Van Emden, "Contributions to the theory of logic programming," *J. ACM* **29**:3, pp. 841–862, 1982.

[3] F. Bancilhon, D. Maier, Y. Sagiv, and J. Ullman, "Magic sets and other strange ways to implement logic programs," *Proc. Fifth ACM Symposium on Principles of Database Systems*, pp. 1–15, 1986.

[4] F. Bancilhon and R. Ramakrishnan, "An amateur's introduction to recursive query processing strategies," to appear in the proceedings of the 1986 SIGMOD Conf. on Management of Data, May, 1986.

[5] A. K. Chandra and D. Harel, "Horn clauses and the fixpoint hierarchy," *Proc. Second ACM Symposium on Principles of Database Systems*, pp. 158–163, 1982.

[6] L. J. Henschen and S. A. Naqvi, "On compiling queries in recursive firstorde databases," *J. ACM* **31**:1, pp. 47–85, 1984.

[7] Y. E. Ioannidis, "Bounded recursion in deductive databases," UCB/ERI M85/6, Dept. of EECS, UC Berkeley, Feb., 1985.

[8] M. Kifer and E. L. Lozinskii, "Query optimization in logical databases," unpublished memorandum, Dept. of CS, SUNY, Stony Brook, NY, 1985.

[9] E. L. Lozinskii, "Inference by generating and structuring deductive databases," *Proc. Ninth Intl. Joint Conf. on AI*, pp. 173–177, 1985.

[10] D. McKay and S. Shapiro, "Using active connection graphs for reasoning with recursive rules," *Proc. Seventh Intl. Joint Conf. on AI*, pp. 368–374 1981.

[11] L. Naish, "Negation and control in Prolog," Ph. D. thesis, Univ. of Melbourne, 1985.

[12] J. F. Naughton, "Data independent recursion in deductive databases," *Proc Fifth ACM Symposium on Principles of Database Systems*, pp. 267–279 1986.

[13] J. F. Naughton, "Optimizing function-free recursive inference rules," Dept of CS, Stanford Univ., to appear.

[14] Y. Sagiv and J. D. Ullman, "Complexity of a top-down capture rule," STAN-CS–84–1009, Stanford Univ., 1984.

[15] J. D. Ullman, *Principles of Database Systems*, Computer Science Press Rockville, Md., 1982.

[16] J. D. Ullman, "Implementation of logical query languages for databases," *ACM Trans. on database Systems* **10**:3, pp. 289–321, 1985

[17] J. D. Ullman and A. Van Gelder, "Testing applicability of top-down captur rules," STAN–CS–1046, Stanford Univ., 1985.

[18] A. Van Gelder, "A message passing framework for logical query evaluation," to appear in the proceedings of the 1986 SIGMOD Conf. on Management c Data, May, 1986.

[19] A. Van Gelder, "Negation as failure using tight derivations for general logi programs," unpublished memorandum, Stanford Univ., 1986.

[20] M. H. Van Emden and R. A. Kowalski, "The semantics of predicate logic a a programming language," *J. ACM* **23**:4, pp. 733–742, 1976.

A Superimposed Codeword Indexing Scheme for Very Large Prolog Databases

Kotagiri Ramamohanarao and *John Shepherd*
Department of Computer Science, University of Melbourne
Parkville, Victoria 3052, Australia

Abstract

This paper describes a database indexing scheme, based on the method of superimposed codewords, which is suitable for dealing with very large databases of Prolog clauses. Superimposed codeword schemes provide a very efficient method of retrieving records from large databases in only a small number of disk accesses. The scheme described in this paper extends the standard techniques of superimposed coding to handle general Prolog terms, including functors and variables, thus making it simple to store Prolog rules in the database.

Keywords: Partial-match retrieval, Prolog, hashing, descriptors, optimisation

. Introduction

.s logic programming is applied to more and more diverse areas, there will be an increasing need for ›gic programming systems to manipulate and reason about very large bodies of knowledge. It is not ifficult to imagine a large expert system which reasons in a complex problem domain requiring 100,000 ıles to capture all of the relationships associated with the domain. Deductive database systems, in nifying concepts from logic programming and relational database systems, also bring logic programming ystems into contact with large knowledge bases.

Vhile the mechanisms for controlling the execution of logic programs have become more and more efined, knowledge retrieval mechanisms for large-scale logic programming systems have not yet been xtensively studied. This paper describes a database indexing scheme, based on the method of uperimposed codewords, which is suitable for dealing with very large databases of Prolog clauses. uperimposed codeword schemes provide a very efficient method of retrieving records from large atabases in only a small number of disk accesses. Classical superimposed codeword schemes [6] have onsidered database records whose fields have no structure, whereas the "fields" in Prolog clauses can be ructured and can contain variables. This system extends the standard superimposed codeword schemes pecifically, it extends the scheme described in [7]) to support the storage and retrieval of general Prolog rms which contain functors and variables. As a consequence, Prolog rules can be stored quite naturally the database.

'he remainder of this section introduces the notion of partial match retrieval and describes a "standard" nplementation of a superimposed codeword indexing scheme [7] to provide some background and otation for the second section. The second section concentrates on the extensions which have made ossible the handling of variables and functors. The scheme described in section two has been nplemented in C under UNIX and the third section presents some performance figures for a database ontaining one million facts. The fourth section compares our scheme with other recent approaches.

This work was performed as part of the Machine Intelligence Project at the University of Melbourne. It was ıpported by the Commonwealth Department of Science and Pyramid Technology, Australia.

1.1. Partial Match Retrieval

We consider a database relation to be a set of *records*, where each record consists of a number of *attribute* values. A *query* specifies a set of "interesting" values for some or all of the attributes of a particular relation. Executing a query on a database is intended to select a set of records from the database which have these values for the corresponding attributes. The problem is referred to as the *partial match retrieval* problem.

For example, the query `employee(_,secretary,_,_)` would match records such as:

```
employee(john,secretary,admin,22000)
employee(jane,secretary,research,24000)
employee(judy,secretary,sales,25000)
```

or any employee record with `secretary` as the second attribute. Note that in the above example, the "_" is used to denote an attribute whose value is not specified.

The process of matching a Prolog goal with clause-heads or facts in a database (either internal or external to the Prolog system) corresponds naturally to a partial match retrieval problem. The ground terms in the goal represent the values of the known attributes, while the variables represent the unspecified attributes. In our database system we treat a request to match a Prolog goal with an external database as a partial match query on the database, and provide the solutions (matches) one at a time via backtracking.

1.2. Superimposed Coding

In a superimposed coding scheme (for example, [6,7]), each record in the database is associated with a *descriptor* (bit-string). This descriptor is formed by superimposing (bitwise OR-ing) the *codewords* for the individual attributes in a record. The codewords, in turn, are formed by using the attribute *value* to generate a series of bit positions to be set to 1; one possible implementation of codeword generation is to use the attribute value as a seed for a random number generator which generates the bit positions.

In order to determine which records satisfy a partial match query, the record descriptors, rather than the records themselves, are searched. Matching is performed by AND-ing the descriptor for the query with the descriptor for each record in the database. Since the bits in the query descriptor will be a subset of the bits in the descriptor of any matching record, the AND operation must result in the the same bit string as the query descriptor for a matching record. Thus a search of the record descriptors alone suffices to indicate all of the records which satisfy the query.

Because the superimposing process ORs together full-length codewords to form the record and query descriptors, it is possible for records which do not match the query to have descriptors whose bits are a superset of the query descriptor bits. This leads to records which match the query at the descriptor level but which do not actually match the query. Such records are termed *false matches*. A search of the record descriptors, as described above, may indicate a number of these non-matching records as potential matches in addition to all of the correctly matching records. By choosing a large codeword size for a given database, however, one can make the probability of false matches occurring very small.

In the scheme described above, the query descriptor is compared (AND-ed) with *every* record descriptor in order to answer a query and so the whole descriptor file must be retrieved from secondary storage. However, in general, only a small number of bits are set in the query descriptor and therefore only a few bits of each record descriptor actually need to be examined. Therefore, following [6], we arrange the record descriptors in bit-sliced fashion so that we only need to examine those few bit slices that are relevant. Instead of viewing the descriptor file as N bit-strings, each containing b bits, we view it as a it-strings (*slices*) each containing N bits. The ith slice is a list of the ith bits of all descriptors. If the th bit in the ith slice is set, then this indicates that the kth record has the ith bit set in its descriptor. he result of AND-ing the slices specified by the query descriptor is a slice which represents a list of all otentially matching records. When the jth bit in the resultant slice is set, then we know that the jth ecord is a potential match.

ven if we use the bit-sliced representation, the total number of *bits* which must be examined is still rge (the length of the slices is equal to the maximum number of records in the database). The efficiency f superimposed coding can be further improved using a scheme described in [7,8]. In this scheme, the atabase is partitioned into segments. A descriptor is then associated with each segment which is formed a similar manner to the record descriptors. However, the segment descriptor is constructed using the ttribute values from every record in the segment. Clearly, descriptors for segments need to be very uch larger than record descriptors if there are not to be a large number of false matches. To answer a uery on such a database, we first examine the segment descriptors to determine which segments contain otential matches. We then examine only these segments for record matches.

hoosing optimal values for database parameters such as the record and segment codeword lengths is an nportant problem, and can dramatically affect the performance of the database. If the codeword is too nall, then we cannot represent relations with many attributes without incurring an increase in the false atch probability. Similarly, if we set more than a small fraction of the bits in the codeword, then the uperimposing leads to a potential increase in false matches. However, if we set insufficient bits in the odeword, we cannot "discriminate" as well between different attribute values. Methods for deriving ptimal parameters are discussed in detail in [5,7].

. Extending Superimposed Coding for Prolog

o far, we have considered only databases where all the records stored in the database have all attributes pecified. In addition, we have implicitly considered attribute values to be atomic, that is, without any elevant) internal structure. When we come to consider databases of Prolog terms, both of these ssumptions are no longer valid. Any indexing scheme which is to be used to store and retrieve Prolog rms must address two issues: the representation of variables and the representation of structures.

Ve begin with the observation that a record like:

```
employee(fred,clerk,admin,10000)
```

orresponds to a Prolog fact. We can consider the relation name, `employee`, to be a functor (or redicate), and the attributes to be the arguments of that functor. In the above example, each of the rguments (attributes, keys) is specified, corresponding to a ground Prolog term. We would also like to ore Prolog rules containing variables and structures (such as `name(fred,smith)`) in the database.

.1. Representing Variables

order to represent variables in records, we append a number of bits (which we will call *mask bits*) to e end of each descriptor to indicate whether the attributes are ground. Each bit in this *mask* is ssociated with a particular attribute in the record; when the mask bit is set to 1, this indicates that the orresponding attribute has not been specified, that is, it corresponds to a Prolog variable. When a mask it is set to 0, this indicates that the corresponding attribute is specified.

he process of determining matches now becomes slightly more complicated, with the query now nsidered to be a set of query codewords, one for each of the specified attributes. A potential match curs with a record when each of these codewords satisfies a matching property with respect to the record descriptor. A query codeword has this matching property when either its bit-string is a subset of the record descriptor bit-string or the corresponding mask bit is set in the record descriptor. We AND the bit-slices related to a particular attribute value and, as well, we OR the bit-slice for the mask corresponding to that attribute. This process is repeated for each attribute value and the results are AND-ed together to give us the potential records which match the query.

2.1.1. Example

Consider the following codewords, where each attribute generates two bit positions in a codeword of length 15 bits:

```
john     00010 00000 10000
clerk    01001 00000 00000
admin    00010 00100 00000
```

Consider now the following *record* containing variables (note that we are using the Prolog convention that names beginning with upper-case letters refer to variables):

```
employee(Name,clerk,admin,Salary)
```

If we wish to store this record in the database, the record descriptor will be identical to the descriptor we would have generated by considering this as a query. However, we now need to append four mask bits to the descriptor to indicate the specified and unspecified attributes, yielding the record descriptor:

```
01011 00100 00000 1001
```

Consider now a *query* such as `employee(john,clerk,Dept,Salary)`. In this case, slices 3 and 10 are AND-ed for the attribute value `john` and then OR-ed with its mask slice (slice 15), yielding a result which we will denote R_1. Similarly, slices 1 and 4 are AND-ed for the attribute value `clerk` and then OR-ed with its mask slice (slice #16), resulting in R_2. R_1 and R_2 are then AND-ed to give the set of all potential record matches, R. This computation is depicted in figure 1.

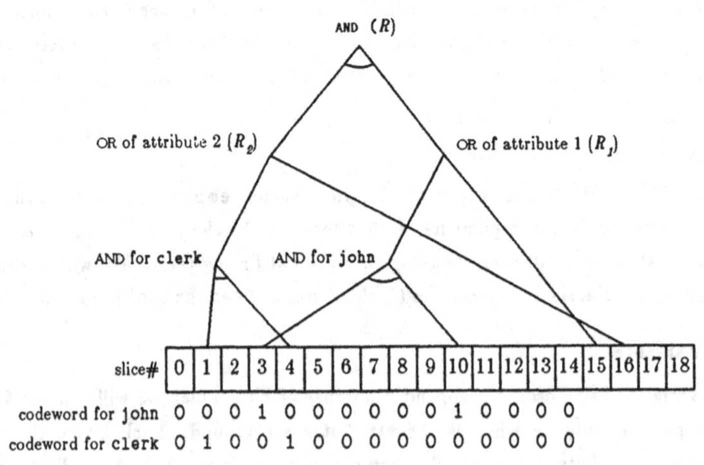

Figure 1

.2. Representing Structures

ɔ represent structures, we consider a structure first as a single attribute to determine the total number ˈ bits which need to be set in its codeword. We then divide the "available" bits among the components ˈ the structure according to a weighting scheme. The codeword for the entire structure is generated by ıperimposing the codewords for each of the components, generated with the appropriate number of bits. ˈote that, unlike previous schemes which partitioned the codeword (for example [9]), each component of structure still has the full width of the codeword available in which to set the allocated number of bits. his method provides better discrimination of codewords and hence lower *false matches*.

ɔr variables within structures, we require a specification of the maximum complexity of the structure. iiven such a specification, we simply allocate one mask bit for each component in the structure to ıdicate whether it is variable or not. Therefore, the number of mask bits required is equal to the umber of components in the maximum structure specification. If a structure is less complex than the ɔecification indicates, we simply ignore the mask bits which were allocated for the "unused" ɔmponents. If a structure is more complex than the specification, we prune it and any components hich are outside the specification of the structure are ignored for indexing purposes. For example, a ıaximum structure specification such as `X(Y(F))` implies that terms such as `f(g(c))`, `f(h(a))` and `(b)` can be fully represented. A term such as `f(g(h(d)))` is pruned to `f(g(h))` in the indexing ɛpresentation, while `f(a,b)` is truncated to `f(a)`. Due to this pruning, neither `d` nor `b` contributes ı the codeword generation (but they are still stored in the database). Note that terms such as `f(a,b)` ɒd `f(a)` appear to be identical after the truncation of `f(a,b)`. However, the indexing scheme uses ıe arity as well as the functor in generating the codeword and therefore generates distinct codewords.

.2.1. Examples

Ve wish to obtain descriptors for the following facts:

`p(f(a,X),d)`   `p(X,d)`   `p(f(a,b),X)`   `p(g(c,b),X)`

ˈhe codewords for the individual attributes, the complete database with descriptors (including mask bits) ɒd the bit-slices are shown in figure 2. The *'s indicate that the values of the corresponding mask bits ɾe ignored in the matching process. This is because we never allow the functor component of a ɾucture to be unspecified.

Key:	Codeword:
f	00010 00000 10000
a	01001 00000 00000
b	00000 01010 00000
c	10000 00000 00010
d	00010 00100 00000
g	00000 00001 00001

Rec#	Record:	Descriptor:
0	p(f(a,X),d)	01011 00100 10000 0010
1	p(X,d)	00010 00100 00000 1**0
2	p(f(a,b),X)	01011 01010 10000 0001
3	p(g(c,b),X)	10000 01011 00011 0001

Rec#	Descriptor:															Bit mask:			
0	0	1	0	1	1	0	0	1	0	0	1	0	0	0	0	0	0	1	0
1	0	0	0	1	0	0	0	1	0	0	0	0	0	0	0	1	*	*	0
2	0	1	0	1	1	0	1	0	1	0	1	0	0	0	0	0	0	0	1
3	1	0	0	0	0	0	1	0	1	1	0	0	0	1	1	0	0	0	1
Slice#	0	1	2	3	4	5	6	7	8	9	10	11	12	13	14	m0	m1	m2	m3

Figure 2

For a query `p(f(a,X),Y)` we have the query codewords:

```
f    00010 00000 10000
a    01001 00000 00000
```

We need to examine only slices 1,3,4,10, and the mask slices. f sets bits 3 and 10, while a sets bits 1 and 4. The query process can be expressed as:

```
(((1 AND 4) OR m1) AND (3 AND 10)) OR m0
```

where AND and OR represent bit-wise AND-ing and OR-ing of bit-slices.

The diagram in figure 3 shows the complete process.

2.3. Representing Prolog Rules

A Prolog rule, displayed in prefix functional notation, such as `:-(p(X,Y), (q(X,Z), r(F,Y)))`, may be stored directly in an external database. We need indexing information only for the first argument to match with the "head" of the rule, and no index bits are generated for the "body" part.

Note that this representation stores all rules in one relation (the ":-" relation). Prolog programs contain large numbers of rules with considerable variation in the arity and complexity of arguments in the head. It is thus necessary to either define a very general structure for the head, most of which will usually be wasted, or to suffer from pruning inaccuracy when indexing on rules with large heads. For better performance, all rules related to one procedure should be stored in a single relation. In this scheme, the above rule could be represented as:

```
p(X, Y, (q(X,Z), r(F,Y)))
```

3. Performance of an Example Database

The scheme described above has been implemented in C under UNIX. The optimisations described in section 2 (bit-slice representation and two-level descriptors) have been used, as well as a clustering

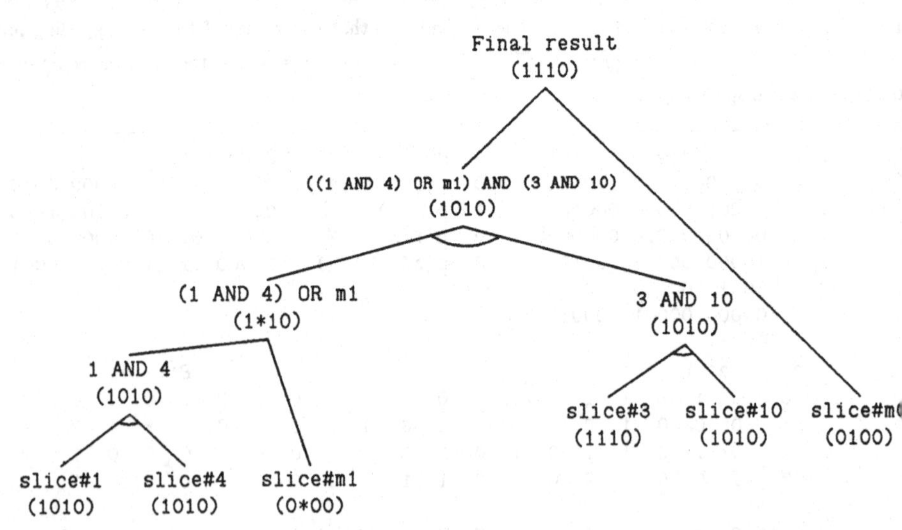

Figure 3

heme (described in [3]) which attempts to keep "similar" records in a small subset of the available gments. The implementation also uses caching of segment memory buffers and file descriptors to rther improve the performance in the UNIX environment.

o evaluate the performance of this scheme, we built a database containing one millions records which escribed paths between machines in the UUCP network:

```
path(Source,Destination,Cost,[Node,Node,...])
```

sing a false match probability of 1 in one million at segment level and of 1 in 2000 at record level, we btained the following performance figures for the system implemented in C on a Pyramid 90x with one Eagle" disk drive (details of the database parameters used in this experiment may be found in [5]):

Insertion rate:	6 records per CPU second
Retrieval rate:	(query dependent) 1000 records per CPU second (maximum) 350 records per CPU second (average)

or queries of the form `path(source,dest,_,_)` (which have a unique answer):

Average segment matches:	2.0
Average record matches:	1.1

. Comparison with other Schemes

here have been several schemes published to accomplish the representation of Prolog clauses [1,9], but l are different in some respect to this scheme.

/ise and Powers [9] consider two methods of encoding Prolog clauses, one involving pure superimposed odewords as in [6] and the other utilising disjoint codewords as described in [3,4] (where the descriptor partitioned into fields and the codeword for each attribute is generated so as to fit exactly into a ecified field). They suggest that "if superimposed coding is to be meaningfully used, then the database ust be variable-free", and use their superimposed codeword scheme only for storing ground Prolog auses. In their disjoint codeword scheme (which they call "field encoded words"), they represent ariables by setting every bit in the field for any unspecified attribute and represent structures by artitioning the fields in the same way as the entire descriptor was partitioned. Their schemes are itially intended to be used for clause indexing in the internal database, but they also refer to [8] and ggest that multi-level descriptors can be used to obtain acceptable performance for indexing clauses in condary storage.

uto et al. [1] use the idea of a "bit mask" to represent variables, but appear to use a disjoint codeword heme to form descriptors. The "bit mask", which is strictly redundant in a disjoint codeword scheme, us serves the purpose of speeding up the matching process by allowing them to omit comparisons of the elds which correspond to the variables. They are concerned primarily with indexing unit clauses to iminate unnecessary unifications during resolution, and do not make clear how their scheme handles ructures. However, it is relatively easy to see how it could be extended by recursively partitioning the elds and by adding more bits to the mask.

ur scheme uses superimposed coding even for arbitrary Prolog terms, including variables. uperimposed coding is superior to the disjoint coding scheme because each attribute provides a full idth codeword rather than a small part of it, and thus yields less false matches for a given descriptor ze.

All of these methods, including the one presented in this paper, have one property which is sometimes undesirable in Prolog programs: they allow no control over the order in which clauses are fetched from the database. In particular, a user cannot guarantee that clauses will be retrieved in the same order as they were asserted. This could be handled by using an extra attribute to indicate the order rank of the clause with a slight increase in the processing of queries. Alternatively, ordering of clauses could be achieved by "switching off" clustering, and inserting records into the database in order. However, this would only be feasible when the average number of records retrieved per query is small.

5. Conclusions

Using an extension of the two-level superimposed coding scheme in [7], it is possible to store and retrieve general Prolog terms efficiently from an external (to Prolog) database. With the addition of optimisations such as clustering and caching on segment buffers, an extremely efficient retrieval system can be developed.

We have implemented our two-level superimposed coding scheme with clustering and caching in C on a Pyramid 90x, Vax 11/780, and Perkin-Elmer 3240 (all running UNIX 4.2BSD) and on an Elxsi 6400 (running UNIX System V). The indexing scheme has been interfaced to the MU-Prolog system [2].

Acknowledgements

We would like thank Bill Ross and James Thom for their careful reading of earlier drafts of this paper.

References

1. I. Futo, F. Darvas and P. Szeredi, "The application of Prolog to the development of QA and DBM systems", in *Logic and Data Bases*, H. Gallaire and J. Minker (editor), Plenum Press, New York, 1978, 347-376.
2. L. Naish, "MU-Prolog 3.2 Reference Manual", Technical Report 85/11, Department of Computer Science, University of Melbourne, November 1985.
3. K. Ramamohanarao, J. W. Lloyd and J. A. Thom, "Partial-match Retrieval using Hashing and Descriptors", Technical Report 82/1, Department of Computer Science, University of Melbourne February 1982.
4. K. Ramamohanarao, J. W. Lloyd and J. A. Thom, "Partial-match Retrieval using Hashing and Descriptors", *ACM Transactions on Database Systems 8*, 4 (December 1983), 552-576.
5. K. Ramamohanarao and J. Shepherd, "A superimposed codeword indexing scheme for very large Prolog databases", Technical Report 85/17, Department of Computer Science, University of Melbourne, November 1985.
6. C. S. Roberts, "Partial match retreival via the method of superimposed codes", *Proceedings of the IEEE 67*, 2 (1979), 522-528.
7. R. Sacks-Davis and K. Ramamohanarao, "A two level superimposed coding scheme for partial match retrieval", *Information Systems 8*, 4 (1983), 273-280. Originally appeared as Technical Report 82/2, Department of Computer Science, University of Melbourne, 1982.
8. J. Samanek, "Partial-match retrieval using multi-level superimposed codes", M.Sc. Thesis University of New South Wales, April 1982.
9. M. J. Wise and D. M. W. Powers, "Indexing Prolog clauses via superimposed codewords and field encoded words", *Proceedings of the IEEE Conference on Logic Programming*, Atlantic City, NJ January 1984, 203-210.

Interfacing Prolog to a Persistent Data Store

D.S. Moffat & P.M.D. Gray

Dept. of Computing Science
University of Aberdeen
Aberdeen, Scotland

ABSTRACT

A method is described for implementing a general database supporting objects, which is tightly coupled to Prolog. This provides the Prolog interpreter with database storage for its clauses. It also allows one to create and access from Prolog objects of arbitrary type such as frames with attached procedures. The interface from Prolog allows the full use of the computational and database facilities of the PS-Algol implementation language, within the framework of an Abstract Data Type scheme, which is based on an implementation of modules in Prolog. The paper describes how evaluable predicates can be written in PS-Algol and made to backtrack, thus providing a neat symbiosis between the two languages.

. INTRODUCTION

any people have suggested representing unit clauses in Prolog by relations tored in a relational database. Gallaire (1983) discusses various alternative ays of connecting Expert Systems with databases. In his terminology, we have mplemented a PROLOG+ system with a generalised object database handling the storage f Prolog clauses. In the terminology of Jarke and Vassiliou (1984) we have made a tight coupling" between the database and Prolog.

he language PS-Algol (Atkinson et al. 1983) and its object management system play a arge part in our system. PS-Algol is a language with a rich variety of data types hich can be used to construct objects which will persist on secondary storage. uch objects may be connected by pointers to form semantic nets or whole databases. e have already modified Prolog so that it allows us to save compiled programs as bject databases which, when used at a later date, can be incrementally loaded. We ave also implemented an interface between Prolog and PS-Algol which allows arameterised calls to be made between the two languages. This is similar to work one in POPLOG (Mellish & Hardy 1983) where Prolog is interfaced to POP-11 and to a esser extent LOGLISP (Robinson & Sibert 1982) which implements a logic language in isp. Our aim is to use PS-Algol as a database systems programming language in hich to experiment with different storage and indexing strategies for Prolog lauses. For example, PS-Algol has already been used with great success to implement a Daplex database (Atkinson & Kulkarni 1984), which stores a variety of entity ypes in a network structure. Procedures written in our Prolog can be used to earch such a network (Gray 1985). This paper considers the complementary strengths f Prolog and PS-Algol, and how best to exploit this by the design of a suitable nterface.

n the next section we say why Prolog requires an object store rather than a relaional store and show how PS-Algol is suited. We next present the system architecure and then concentrate on aspects of the Prolog / PS-Algol interface. In secion 4 we show how PS-Algol procedures can be made backtrackable by treating backracking as stream generation. In 5 and 6 we look at modularity and how private erms can be used to implement abstract data types. Section 7 shows how specialised lause storage can be hidden by treating clauses as an abstract data type. Performance figures are given in section 8 and finally in section 9 we draw some concluions.

2. GENERALISED OBJECT STORAGE for PROLOG

Several systems have used a specialised database system to store/acces Prolog clauses on/from secondary store. For example MU-Prolog (Lloyd 81) allows a collection of unit clauses with the same name and arity, which is Prolog's version of a relation, to be stored in a file with indices to support partial match retrieval. The system can be tuned through use of choice vectors and provides an efficient management of relational data. In Prolog-in-C (Bruynooghe 81) relations can be stored in a multi-level B-tree. Queries with partially defined keys can be answered substantially quicker than they can be from a sequential search. However, many Prolog applications deal with objects that do not fit easily into the Relational Model - consider the following.

i) Semantic nets show meta-relationships between relations rather than simple values. Also the links between nodes may be implemented by pointers (Database references in CProlog).

ii) If Prolog is being used to implement an object oriented paradigm we may have Prolog rules as attached procedures.

iii) List structures are common objects and should be stored with pointers connecting individual cells rather than as binary relations.

A general survey of databases and reasons for using PS-Algol is given in Gray, Moffat & du Boulay (1985). Briefly we use PS-Algol because it provides an object store, transparency, compacting of memory, concurrency of database access and a commitment recovery mechanism. In many ways the system is similar to the disk storage used with ABSYS (Elcock et al. 1971).

3. SYSTEM ARCHITECTURE

We have integrated a Prolog interpreter with the Persistent Object Management System (POMS) of PS-Algol. This gives all Prolog objects the right to persist in a PS-Algol database. By interfacing Prolog with PS-Algol we can have more efficent access to the disk through auxiliary data structures and can also operate on extended data types not normally found in Prolog. The architecture is as follows -

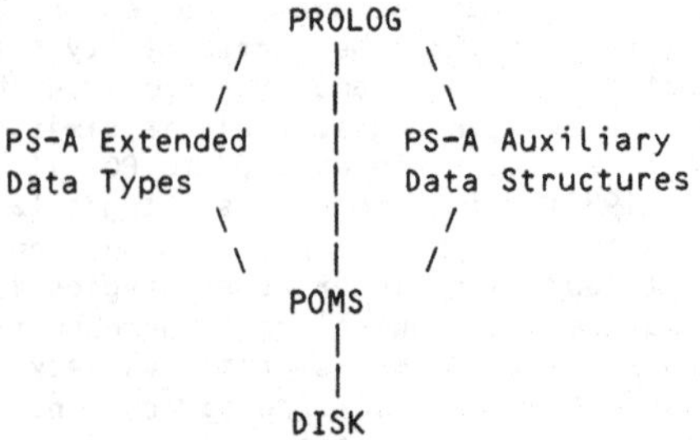

We will explain the interface between POMS and disk which manages the transfer of all data between primary memory and backing store. The object store on disk is partitioned into "databases" which act as write-lockable units. Objects in one database may reference objects in another, and following an inter-database reference will cause the distant database to be opened (provided it is not write locked). A database is either write locked by one user or else it can be opened by multiple users to read and share information concurrently.

A newly created database consists of an empty table, the root, into which name:reference pairs may be entered. On "committing" a database all new or updated bjects reachable from the root are copied to disk with their pointers being eplaced by Persistent Identifiers (PIDs), effectively disk pointers. Thus to send network of objects to disk we ensure that it is referenced from an object already n the database and "commit" that database. On opening an existing database one gets he top-level table from which all lower objects may be reached. Any attempts to ereference a PID are trapped and the appropriate object is read into memory. We ill now look more closely at the three routes through which Prolog can get data rom secondary store.

.1. Prolog to POMS

e partition Prolog's program space by having modules and we have a builtin proedure "commit" which commits individual modules to PS-Algol databases. It is mplemented by simply connecting the module name table, from which all of a module's lauses can be reached, to the root of a database. Modules are restored from these atabases by reading in just the module name table. The actual clauses are read nto memory as and when someone tries to dereference their PIDs. The "commit" proedure supercedes the original "save". Further, having the saved state as a database rather than as a file means that it can be safely shared between users.

.2. Prolog via PS-A with auxiliary data structures to POMS

e can have auxiliary data structures, such as hash tables and btrees, which give us ast access to Prolog clauses. These data structures are maintained by PS-Algol outines since the PS-Algol language provides a much higher level of abstraction of he persistent store than does the POMS system. Prolog uses these structures by aking parameterised callouts to PS-Algol.

.3. Prolog via PS-A extended data types to POMS

S-Algol has a much greater richness of types than does Prolog and we make these vailable to Prolog as "tokens" which can be passed about within Prolog but which an only be operated on by making callouts to PS-Algol routines. Gray (1985) escribes how such tokens can be used from Prolog to provide efficent access to a aplex database stored in Persistent storage. In section six we show how access to okens can be controlled by using abstract data types.

. INTERFACING PROLOG AND PS-ALGOL

ne of the main issues in interfacing Prolog and PS-Algol is their different control tategies. In Prolog, calls to predicates can be retried, through backtracking, to enerate alternatives: in PS-Algol each call to a procedure uses a new invocation. ne method of resolving this disparity is to remove the backtracking element by colecting all alternative solutions and to return them together as a set. This is the pproach taken by LOGLISP. A problem with this is that often we only want a single esult at a time which we can inspect and then decide if we require more. More eriously there is a problem if there are an infinite number of solutions.

he other method of resolving the difference in control is to make the 'one-shot' rocedures backtrackable. POPLOG takes this approach in interfacing Prolog and OP-11. Both POP-11 and Prolog are compiled to a common form (POP-11 virtual achine code) and backtracking is achieved by procedures passing "continuations," hich are explicit return addresses (Mellish and Hardy 1983). In our system where oth languages maintain their separate identities this is not possible so we use enerators which produce results by lazy evaluation, as a method of simulating backracking.

.1. Backtracking and Stream Generation

allouts to PS-Algol procedures are made via the evaluable predicate ps_apply:

    ps_apply(Proc_Name, Input, Output)   where

Proc_Name is the name of a PS-Algol procedure, Input is a list of arguments for th procedure and Output is a list of arguments which is unified with the resul returned from the procedure. On backtracking, ps_apply will resucceed if ProcNam can produce a new binding for Output. Here is a definition in Prolog of ho ps_apply is implemented -

```
ps_apply(Proc, In, Out) :- getgen(Proc, In, Gen),
                           callgen(Gen, Out).

callgen(Gen, Out)       :- Gen ->> Out,
                           (Out == nil, !, fail ; true).

callgen(Gen, Out)       :- callgen(Gen, Out).
```

evaluable predicates:

    getgen(P, I, G)   given the name of a PS-Algol procedure, P,
                      and input argument I return a generator G.

    G ->> X   get the next value from the generator, G,
                      and unify it with X.

The generator returned by getgen will produce a new value every time it is calle via the ->> operator until there are no more values, when it will return nil an cause callgen to fail. The second clause for callgen causes the generator to b recalled on backtracking. The generator must contain sufficent state information s that it can produce the next value when it is asked. The first class status of pro cedures in PS-Algol makes them ideal for implementing generators since procedure can be passed as arguments and returned as results. Here is a simple example of PS-Algol implementation of a generator of positive integers in the range [1..100] -

```
structure anint(int result)

let genint = proc( ->proc( ->pntr))
begin
    let i := 0
    proc( ->pntr)
    begin
        i := i + 1;
        if i>100 then nil else anint(i)
    end
end
```

Genint is a procedure which takes no arguments and returns a procedure which itsel takes no arguments and returns a pointer to a structure. In PS-Algol the valu returned from a procedure is the last expression in that procedure. Thus callin genint will return a procedure which, whenever it is called, will return the nex postive integer, wrapped up in a structure. The variable 'i' is declared in a outer scope from that of the procedure returned from genint and hence exists betwee calls. Note also that 'i' is local to genint and hence multiple uses of the genera tor will each use a different instance of 'i'. In Prolog 'getgen(genint, [], Gen) returns in Gen the procedural result of calling genint, and thus every call of Gen >>X unifies X with the next integer in the stream.

The state information required for generating a stream of numbers is simply the las number generated, and needs only one integer location. More complex states can b implemented by having several outer scope variables. State variables can be ini tialised by passing a list of parameters through the second argument of getgen an ps-apply, as in the examples of section 8.

. MODULES AND VISIBILITY OF NAMES

ny Prolog systems provide modules as a means of partitioning the program space. this end procedures in modules have private names which cannot be seen from outide. In our scheme modules also serve as the runtime representation of an opened tabase (path 3.1). We may also use a module as a unit in which to hide the calouts to ps_apply when implementing a specialised interface or accessing extended ta types - paths 3.2 and 3.3.

ike most systems we have public procedures which can be seen from outside of their fining or home module, and private procedures which are strictly local to a proedure. Unlike all except MProlog (Szeredi 1982) we also allow terms to be both blic and private. Public terms allow data to be free of any module association d to move freely between modules. Private terms are used to represent abstract ta types. A private term is internally tagged with the name of its module and ification of terms is extended to incorporate the tag. Thus private terms can ly unify with free variables or other terms from the same module. We redefine univ" etc. to only succeed on private terms if being used in that term's home dule. Consider this simple example -

```
module m1                              module m2
        public p,q.                            r(t(_)).
        private t.                     endmodule.

        p(t(_)).
        q(t(_)):-...
endmodule.
```

ile 'in' module m2 we try the following queries

```
?- p(X), q(X).  yes, assuming q succeeds.
?- p(X), r(X).  no - illegal access to private term
?- p(X), X=..L. no - illegal access to private term
```

ffat (1986) describes more fully our implementation of modules and in particular fines a language for resolving multiply defined procedures and for binding proedures which have been passed as public terms. This provides facilities for ploratory programming.

. USING PRIVATE TERMS TO PROVIDE ADTs

ur case for having private terms is that it allows a convenient implementation of stract data types (ADT). ADTs allow data representations and the operations over em to be hidden. Terms in Prolog provide us with record types and we can use them implement an ADT by

representing it by a term declared to be private and by

) ensuring that all the procedures that are to manipulate it (its methods) are defined in the same module as publics.

or example

```
mod m1
    public newobj, method1, method2.
    private t.

    newobj(t(...)).
    method1(t(....),A,B) :- .....
    method2(t(....),t(....)) :- ....
endmod
```

From outside of m1 we can call 'newobj' with an unbound argument, Ob say, and it becomes instaniated to the private term 't'. Ob will not unify with terms from other modules and we cannot open it with 'univ' etc.. The variable Ob is a reference to an object whose internal representation is unknown. The only way to manipulate it is to call upon the method procedures defined in its home module. Of course someone could call "newobj" with a bound argument and use it as a test, or call the "method"s with free arguments and use them as generators. Such calls may fail but they will not reveal an ADT's representation.

In our system, where we propose to have types from PS-Algol existing in Prolog, such an ADT mechanism will be very valuable. In the example Ob may be a PS-A picture or vector say, and the bodies of the methods would make callouts to PS-A via the ps_apply procedure. Two other systems which provide ADTs are Furukawa et al. (1983) and Mycroft & O'Keefe (1983). Both of these systems require type declarations for all of the ADT procedures. Our system is type free and uses the unification of Prolog to control access to ADTs. It is more suitable when we want to hide a representation but do not want the extra discipline of typing our program. It could be considered as a primitive which could be used to implement a Furukawa type scheme at a later date if desired.

We are experimenting with the use of procedures expressed in Prolog which search for a pattern match with a collection of linked nodes in a network database. This makes use of the tight coupling between Prolog and the database through predicates defined in one module, using ps-apply. Backtracking in the Prolog interpreter controls the search, with Prolog variables bound to terms like Ob which hide pointers that move through the network. This makes good use of the ability of the persistent heap to maintain pointer structures, combined with the ability of Prolog to express a recursive search. This use of Prolog for navigation is suggested by Zaniolo (1984) and by Gray (1985). It will be interesting to compare it with a search of an equivalent relational database.

7. PROLOG CLAUSES as an ABSTRACT DATA TYPE

Our system uses PS-Algol programs and auxiliary data structures to speed access to certain Prolog predicates. New predicates can only be added to such auxiliary data structures by going through special update programs. We would like the special knowledge of how such predicates are actually stored to be localised within a module so that external users could treat them as ordinary predicates. We propose that predicates can be considered as an ADT, with the metapredicates like assert and retract as the operations that can be applied to them. If a predicate is to be stored in a special way then we provide a specialised assert and retract together with a rule which has the predicate as its head and a body that accesses the auxiliary data structure. For example, consider a module in which student clauses are actually stored in a PS-Algol maintained btree.

```
module stud
public student.
    assert(student(Name, Add)) :-
        ps_apply(btree_enter,[studentdb,key(Name),Add],[]).
    retract(student(Name, Add)) :-
        ps_apply(btree_delete,[studentdb,key(Name),Add],[]).
    student(Name, Add) :- nonvar(Name),!,
        ps_apply(btree_lookup,[studentdb,Name],[Add]).
    student(Name, Add) :-
        ps_apply(btree_scan,[studentdb,Add],[Name]).
endmodule.
```

will also have two-place versions of assert and retract, where the extra argument the module name in which the assert/retract will take place. The single argument rsions will operate in the current module. Thus "assert(Term, Module)" will use e definition for assert found in Module otherwise it will assert Term into Module ing the default definition.

PERFORMANCE

order to give an idea of the system's performance we have measured its speed lative to the original interpreter on which it is based (CProlog 1984). Firstly, en used on a range of benchmarks (Wilk 1983) which take no account of its database cilities the new system is 20% slower than the original. This is because the rategy of heap allocation is different and the interpreter can no longer make art address-based assumptions about types.

a guide to the performance of the direct Prolog to POMS link we compared it with e analogous save and restore. Committing a new program, containing ordinary Pro-g clauses, to a database takes ten times longer than a save of the same program d its restoration now takes three times longer. However, the new restore works crementally on a demand basis, and, on committing, the system only copies new or dated objects to the database, whereas the old restore and save were total. Hence e new system performs better when we only access or change small parts of a large ogram. The POMS interface is also much more powerful, in that it allows non-olog objects to be saved in a database.

e utility of calling out to PS-Algol for fast access to clauses was measured by mparing the time to access unit clauses which had been stored in a PS-Algol table dexed under one of their arguments, with the time for sequential access by Prolog. e time taken via the PS-Algol table was constant for between 1 and 2000 clauses d was of order(n) for the sequential access. The times were equal for an 'n' of 0. In some systems clause indexing on a single key can be done very efficiently the interpreter itself but the strength of using PS-Algol is that we can use it a vehicle for experimenting with different and more complex indexing techniques.

CONCLUSION

is paper describes an implementation of a general database supporting objects, ich is tightly coupled to Prolog. Instead of just modifying the Prolog inter-eter by providing a transparent facility for storing unit clauses, we have chosen rich interface to the implementation language PS-Algol, which allows the Prolog ogrammer to define his own evaluable predicates both for computation and for data-se access. We have described how such predicates can be made apparently to back-ack, which allows us for example, to explore a large database without storing and terialising large intermediate sets. We have also shown how to use module naming cilities to implement abstract data types, representing objects, whose "methods" y be implemented either in PS-Algol or in Prolog. Finally, we have shown how to ore different types of unit clauses via different database storage techniques, by sociating special methods of assert and retract.

The aim is to achieve a symbiosis of Prolog and PS-Algol which makes use of the stong points of each language. We do not wish to see Prolog degenerating into a universal language like PL/1, but we do wish to use its powerful planning and pattern matching facilities in conjunction with the computation and database facilites needed for applications. The system, as described, provides just these facilities.

10. ACKNOWLEDGEMENTS

We would like to thank Ben du Boulay and also the referees for many useful suggestions. This work is supported by a grant from the U.K. Science and Engineering Research Council.

11. REFERENCES

[Atkinson 83] Atkinson,M.P. et al. (1983), "An Approach to Persistent Programming", Computer Journal (26), 360-366.

[Atkinson 84] Atkinson,M.P. & Kulkarni,K.G. (1984), "Experimenting with the Functional Data Model" ,in "Database: Role and Structure", Stocker, Gray & Atkinson (eds.), Cambridge Univ. Press, pp 311-338.

[Bruynooghe 81] Bruynooghe,M. "Prolog in C implementation", University of Louvain, 1981. [CProlog 84] 15 Pereira,F., Damas,L., Byrd,L. & O'Keefe,R.A.. Dept. of Architecture, University of Edinburgh, 1984.

[Elcock 71] Elcock,E.W., Foster,J.M., Gray,P.M.D., McGregor,J.J. & Murray,A.M. (1971) "ABSET: A programming language based on sets: Motivation and examples", in "Machine Intelligence 6", B.Meltzer & D.Michie (eds.).

[Furukawa 83] Furukawa, Nakajima & Yonezawa (1983), "Modularization and Abstraction in Logic Programming", ICOT report TR-022, Tokyo.

[Gallaire 83] Gallaire,H. (1983), "Logic Data Bases vs Deductive Data Bases", Proc Logic Programming Workshop 1983, Algarve, Ed. L.M.Pereira.

[Gray 85] Gray,P.M.D. (1985), "Efficient Prolog Access to Codasyl and FDM Databases", Proc. ACM SIGMOD 1985 Conf., ed. S. Navathe, pp 437-443.

[Gray et al85] Gray,P.M.D. & Moffat,D.S. & du Boulay,J.B.H.. Persistent Prolog: Secondary Storage Manager for Prolog. Proc. Appin Workshop on "Data Types and Persistence", ed. M.P.Atkinson, P.Buneman & R.Morrison, Springer Verlag (to be published).

[Jarke 84] Jarke,M. & Vassiliou,Y. (1984), "Coupling expert systems and database management systems" in "Artificial Intelligence Applications for Business", ed. W.Reitman, Ablex, Norwood, NJ.

[LLoyd 81] Lloyd,J.W.. "Implementing Clause Indexing in Deductive Database Systems", Report 81/4, Computer Science Dept., Univ. Melbourne.

[Mellish 83] Mellish,C.S. & Hardy,S. (1983), "Integrating Prolog into the Poplog Environment", Proc. IJCAI-83, Karlsruhe, ed. A.Bundy.

[Moffat 86] Moffat,D.S.. (1986), "Modules in Persistent Prolog", Dept. of Computing Science, University of Aberdeen.

[Mycroft 83] Mycroft,A. & O'Keefe,R. (1983), "A Polymorphic Type System for Prolog", in Proc. Logic Programming Workshop, Algarve.

[Robinson 82] Robinson, J.A. & Sibert, E.E.. "LOGLISP: An Alternative to Prolog" in Machine Intelligence 10, Ellis Horwood, 1982.

[Szeredi 82] Szeredi,P. (1982), "Module Concepts for Prolog", in Proc. Prolog Programming Environments Workshop, Linkoping, Sweden.

[Wilk 83] Wilk, P.F.. (1983), "The Production and Evaluation of a Set of Prolog Benchmarks", D.A.I., University of Edinburgh.

[Zaniolo 84] Zaniolo, C. (1984), "Prolog; a Database Query Language for All Seasons", Proc. 1st Expert Database Systems Workshop, ed. L.Kerschberg Univ. S.Carolina.

A GENERAL MODEL TO IMPLEMENT DIF AND FREEZE

P. Boizumault

I.M.A.
3, place A. Leroy
49000 Angers

L.I.T.P.
CNRS LA 248
75251 Paris Cedex 05

This paper draws a general pattern to add the two famous rolog-II's predicates dif and freeze [COLM82,83], [KANO82], VnCAN82,84], to any classical Prolog interpreter, whether using tructure-sharing or whether using copying. This model allows us to enefit directly from the initial space saving techniques in addition o backtrack already developped for the local stack [WARR77,83], BRUY80], [MELL80], [McCAB81], [BOWE83], [CLOC85].

First, we describe our general model expressing it by a set of rimitives. Then, we implement them for a structure-sharing epresentation of terms and for a copying one. Finally we show that ll classical mechanisms used for optimally recovering space can be irectly applied, without any modifications.

THE GENERAL MODEL :

As shown in M. Van Caneghem's thesis [VnCAN84], dif can be xpressed in terms of freeze. So, we only describe the implementation f freeze.

We introduce a fourth stack specially to manage frozen goals, in rder to benefit directly from the classical space saving techniques n addition to backtrack already developped for the local stack reclaiming activation records as soon as determinism can be detected WARR77], [BRUY80], [MELL80], optimizing tail end calls [WARR80,83], McCAB81], [CLOC85], [BOIZ83,85]).

First, we describe the main idea which guided our study, and the esultant architecture of the working area. Then, we adapt the lassical binding algorithm to this new situation. Finally, we mplement the predicate freeze.

.1 The main idea :

The realising of a frozen goal is associated with the binding of free variable [VnCAN84], [GREU85]. In this attempt, the memory ocation representing such a variable is temporary used to store the utting aside. This introduces two sorts of free variables : the truly" free ones (associated to undef) and the frozen ones.

But a same variable may be bound to more than one frozen goal. We represent this association by a list stored in a special area : the frozen goals stack. This choice [BOIZ86], contrary to Prolog-II, will allow direct application of the space saving techniques already developped in classical interpreters.

1.2 A new working area architecture :

We add a fourth stack specially to manage the frozen goals :

- . A local stack.
- . A global stack.
- . A stack of frozen goals.
- . A trail.

Each activation record allocated on the local stack owns a control part and an environment part. We add to every choice point a further control field indicating the top of the frozen goals stack before its building. On bactracking, this extra field is used to restore the initial state of the frozen goals stack.

The second stack is used to represent complex terms. Its allocation can be static by structure-sharing [WARR77], or made at run-time by copying [MELL80], [BRUY76,80], [McCAB81].

The frozen goals stack stores the associations between frozen variables and waiting goals. It is a push-down list allocated by the binding algorithm, and reclaimed on backtracking.

The trail always resets to their old values, variables which are bound to delays. But each record has henceforward two fields : the first one always indicates the address of the variable´s cell, and the other one describes its initial value. This takes into account the specific requirements due to the double notion of free variable.

1.3 The unification algorithm :

The unification algorithm is exactly the same as the classical one (a frozen variable is always seen as an unbound one). But, we must adapt the binding algorithm to manage the putting aside of frozen goals.

1.3.1 Two new primitives :

Let bind(x,t) the procedure which links classically the variable x to the term t. With frozen variables, we must distinguish adding a new goal to an existent list (bindf0), from joining two lists of frozen goals (bindf1).

Procedure bindf0(x,b,l) associates the variable x to the waiting list of frozen goals "b.l", while procedure bindf1(x,l1,l2), where l1 and l2 are two existent frozen goals lists, binds the variable x to "l1.l2". Both these procedures allocate a new record at the top of the frozen goals stack.

.3.2 The new binding algorithm:

Without any frozen variable, its behaviour is exactly the same as he initial one using the procedure bind. Let now x be a frozen ariable, l1 its waiting goal list, an t the term we want to bind x :

```
        Begin
         Let y the dereferenced value of t :
          If y is an atom or a structure
             Then bind(x,y);
                  l1 is setting off
             Else                     (* y is a free variable *)
               If y is a "true" free variable
                  Then bind(y,x)
                  Else              (* y is a frozen variable *)
                    let l2 the waiting goals list of y;
                     bindf1(x,l2,l1);
                     bind(y,x);
        End
```

So, unifying two frozen variables consists in taking the new list ack to only one, and binding the other to the previous one.

.4 The evaluable predicate freeze :

The evaluable predicate freeze(x,b) postpones the execution of he goal b until x takes a non variable value :

```
    Begin
        Let t the dereferenced value of x :
          If t is an atom or a structure
             Then b is activated
             Else                          (* t is a free variable *)
                If t is a "true" free variable
                  Then bindf0(t,b,nil)
                  Else            (* t is a frozen variable *)
                    Let l the waiting goals list of t;
                    bindf0(t,b,l)
    End
```

As in the binding algorithm, we distinguish t truly free, from t rozen variable. In the first case, we create a new waiting goals ist for b, in the other one, we insert b at the head of the existent ist l.

REPRESENTING TERMS BY STRUCTURE SHARING :

We implement our model for a term representation using tructure-sharing. First we extend Warren's definition of a global ariable. Then we implement the two primitives bindf0 and bindf1. inally we give an example.

.1 A new global variable definition :

We extend Warren's definition of a global variable [WARR77] in rder that each variable appearing as first argument of a predicate reeze will be global.

The aim of this extension [BOIZ86] is both to avoid references from the local stack to the frozen goals stack (a frozen variable will be always a global one), and to make strictly global the execution environment of a frozen goal (all variables appearing in a frozen goal are global).

2.2 Primitives expression :

The procedure bindf0(x,b,l) creates a new record at the top of the frozen goals stack :

. A pointer to the waiting goal b.
. A pointer to the execution environment of b.
. A pointer to the waiting list l.

Then the procedure links x (which is compulsorily global), by creating in the second part of the cell representing x, a pointer to this new record (the first part is always associated to undef like another free variable).

The procedure bindf1(x,l1,l2) also allocates a new record at the top of the frozen goals stack :

. A pointer to the waiting list l1.
. unused (l1 is already a frozen goals record).
. A pointer to the waiting list l2.

Then x is linked to this new record as in the previous procedure.

So, the first field of a frozen goals stack record references the code area (bindf0) or the frozen goals stack (bindf1). The second one is a pointer to the global stack. Finally, the third is always a pointer to the frozen goals stack. So, the frozen goals stack never references the local stack.

2.3 Example :

```
test -> p(x) q(x);
p(x1) -> h(x1) freeze(x1,s(x1)) freeze(x1,t(x1));
q(alpha) ->;
h(y) ->;
t(alpha) ->;
s(alpha) ->;
```

Let see the binding state before execution of the first predicate freeze : (x and y are local variables, while x1 is a global one)

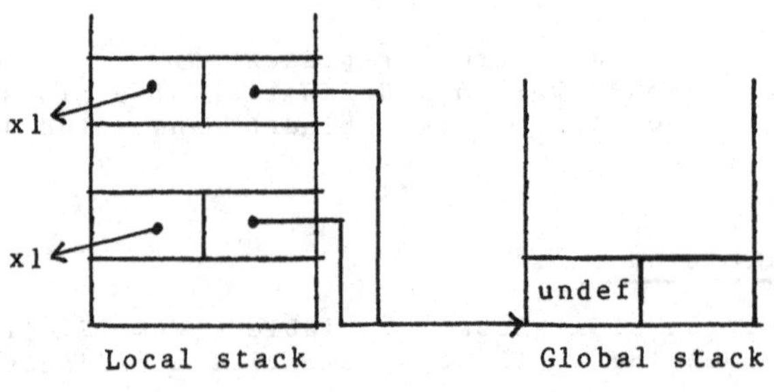

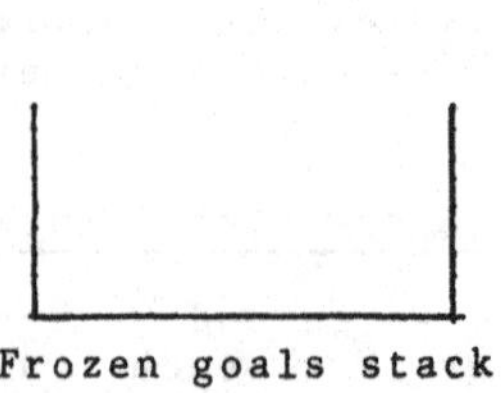

When freeze(x1,s(x1)) is activated, bindf0 allocates a first ecord on the frozen goals stack (goal, execution environment of this oal, nil). Then x1 is linked to this record while the first part of ts global cell is always undef.

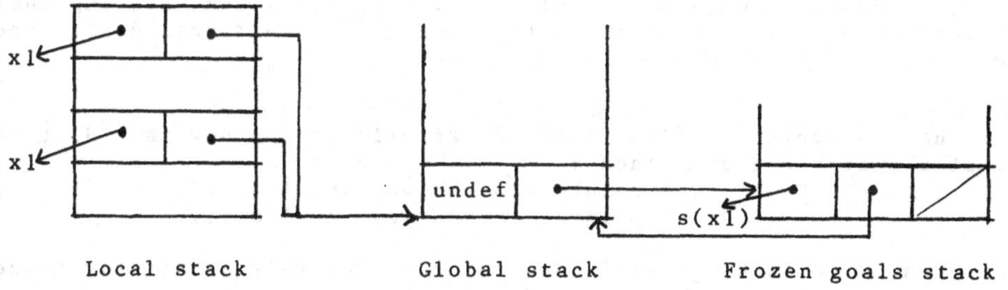

Then, freeze(x1,t(x1)) is activated. A new record (goal, its xecution environment, already existent list) is created at the top of he frozen goals stack. Then x is linked to this value.

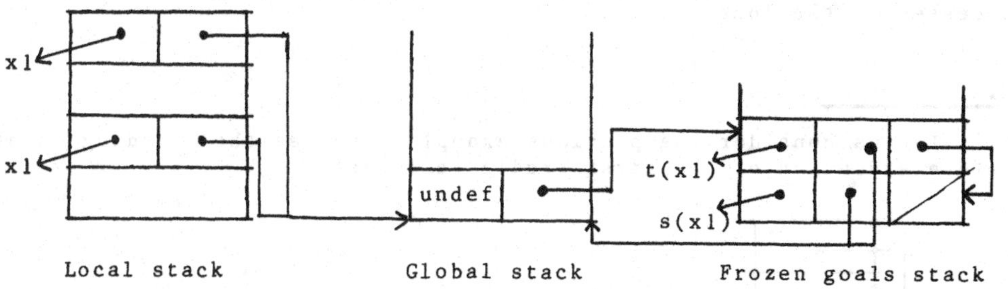

Then, q(x) is proved. So x1 gets the atomic value alpha, and the aiting goals list is activated. So litterals t(x1) and s(x1,x2) uccessively succeed.

REPRESENTING TERMS BY COPYING :

Our model can also be applied for a copying representation of erms [BRUY76,80], [MELL80], [McCAB81], [WARR83], [CLOC85]. First we escribe the implementation of the two procedures bindf0 and bindf1, nd then, we give an example.

.1 Primitives expression :

Procedures bindf0 and bindf1 both allocate two fields records at he top of the frozen goals stack.

The procedure bindf0(x,b,l) first copies [BRUY80], [MELL80], the oal b in the global stack. Then, it allocates a new record at the op of the frozen goals stack :

- . A pointer to the copy of b.
- . A pointer to the waiting list l.

Finally x is bound to this new record by allocating a pointer in he cell representing it.

As in the structure-sharing implementation, we want to preserv the initial properties of the local stack (it never references th frozen goals stack). So we must avoid a final pitfall : in spite o the copy of the goal b, the location representing x is always on th local stack (by example, x is truly free and does not appear in b) In such a case, we make a copy of x in the global stack, linking thes two locations. Then we bind x (copy cell) to the frozen goals stac record.

The procedure bindf1(x,l1,l2) first allocates a new record at th top of the frozen goals stack :

. A pointer to the waiting list l1.
. A pointer to the waiting list l2.

Then, x is linked to this new record. How x is an already froze variable, the memory location used is on the copy stack.

So, the first field of a frozen goals stack record references th copy stack (bindf0), or the frozen goals stack (bindf1). So, like i the structure-sharing representation, the frozen goals stack neve accesses to the local stack.

3.2 Example :

Let us consider the previous example, and see the binding stat before execution of the first predicate freeze :

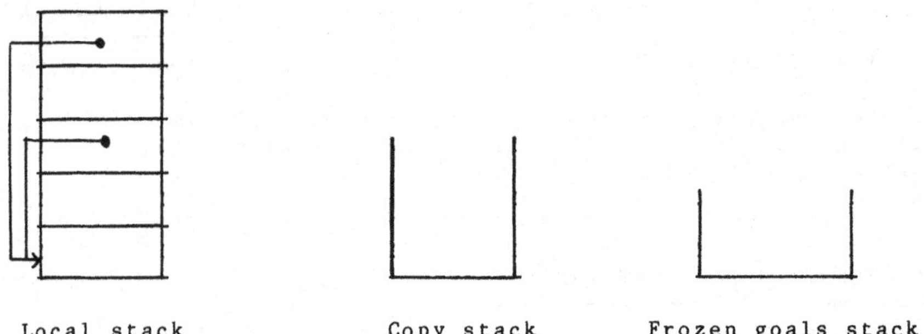

Local stack Copy stack Frozen goals stack

When freeze(x1,s(x1)) is activated, bindf0 copies the goal on th global stack, allocates a record on the frozen goals stack, and link x1.

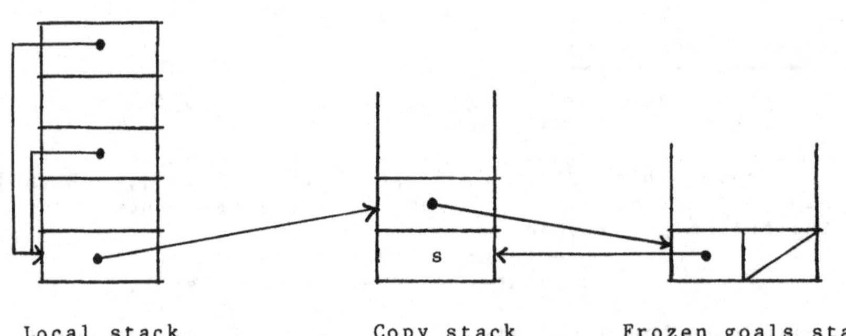

Local stack Copy stack Frozen goals stack

Then, freeze(x1,t(x1)) is activated. A copy of the goal is made, nd x1 is bound to the new list of waiting goals.

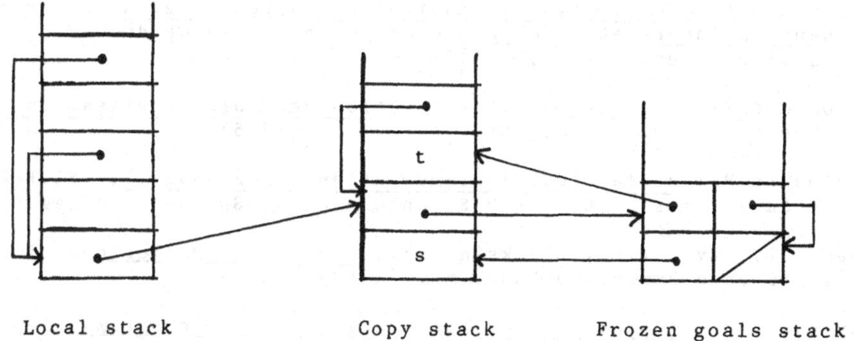

Then, q(x) is proved. So x1 gets a non variable value (alpha), nd the waiting goals list is activated. Then the litterals t(x1) and (x1) successively succeed.

SPACE SAVING TECHNIQUES CAN BE DIRECTLY APPLIED :

All the mechanisms allowing an optimal memory management of the ocal stack (reclaiming activation records as soon as determinism can e detected, optimizing tail end calls) can be directly applied, ecause the local stack behaviour is exactly the same as a classical ne.

First, the initial three stacks architecture prevents from angling references on the local stack, and from access in the sense lobal-local [WARR77], [MELL80], [BRUY76,80]. Then, either using tructure-sharing or copying, records on the frozen goals stack never ccesses a local stack information. Finally, the local stack never eferences the frozen goals stack. (in structure-sharing, a frozen ariable is always global; by copying, it is always the copy cell hich is linked to the waiting goals list).

So space recovery in addition to backtrack is from now allowed on he local stack, as in a classical architecture. More, all these echanisms can be directly applied without any modification, as the ocal stack keeps an identical behaviour ("it never sees the frozen oals").

Our model reconciles the already developped techniques for nplementing a Prolog interpreter with the particular needs of dif and reeze, thereby regaining an optimal memory management. Dif and reeze can henceforward be added to any Prolog interpreter whether sing stucture-sharing or whether using copying.

Acknowledgements : we are grateful to J.F. Perrot for having nspired and commented this work.

References :

Boizumault P., Sur la transformation de l'appel terminal en iteration dans un interprete Prolog, 2ndes journees Prolog du CNET, M. Dincbas editeur, (1983).

Boizumault P., Etude de l'interpretation de Prolog Realisation en Lisp These de 3ieme cycle, Univ. Paris VI, (1985).

Boizumault P., A classical implementation for Prolog-II, ESOP 86, Lecture Notes in Computer Science n° 213, Springer-Verlag (1986).

Bowen D.L., Byrd L.M., Clocksin W.F., A portable Prolog compiler, Logic Programming Workshop'83, (1983).

Bruynooghe M., An interpreter for predicate logic programs, Report CW10, Katholieke Universiteit Leuven, (1976).

Bruynooghe M., The memory management of Prolog implementations, Proc. Logic Programming Workshop, Debrecen, (1980).

Clocksin W.F., Design and simulation of a Prolog sequential machine, New Generation Computing, vol 3, n°1, (1985).

Colmerauer A., Prolog-II: Manuel de reference et modele theorique, G.I.A., Univ. Aix-Marseille, (1982).

Colmerauer A., Kanoui H., Van Caneghem M., Prolog bases theoriques et developpements actuels, TSI vol 2 n°4, (1983).

Greussay P., X-Prolog-II : un Prolog-II experimental, Doc on line, Vax Litp, (1985).

Kanoui H., Manuel d'exemples de Prolog-II, G.I.A, Univ. Aix-Marseille (1982).

Mac Cabe F.G., Micro-Prolog programmer's reference manual, Logic Programming Associates Ltd, (1981).

Mellish C.S., An alternative to structure-sharing in the implementation of a prolog interpreter, Proc. Logic Programming Workshop, (1980).

Van Caneghem M., Manuel d'utilisation de Prolog-II, G.I.A., Universite Aix-Marseille, (1982).

Van Caneghem M., L'anatomie de Prolog-II, These, Univ. Aix-Marseille, (1984).

Warren D.H.D., Implementing Prolog, D.A.I. research reports 39/40, Univ. Edinburgh, (1977).

Warren D.H.D., An improved Prolog implementation which optimizes tail recursion, Proc. Logic Programming Workshop, Debrecen, (1980).

Warren D.H.D., An abstract Prolog instruction set, Technical note 309, S.R.I. International, (1983).

Cyclic Tree Traversal

Martin Nilsson and Hidehiko Tanaka
The Tanaka Laboratory, Graduate School of Information Engineering,
Department of Electrical Engineering, The University of Tokyo,
Hongo 7-3-1, Bunkyo-ku, Tokyo 113

bstract: Programs which process tree ructures usually cannot handle cyclic trees. is paper describes some new, very simple, and ficient algorithms for detecting and traversing clic trees. Traversed structures do not have to modified. Tail recursion optimisation can be sed, which reduces stack requirements greatly. e overhead for non-cyclic structures is very nall.

nification is discussed as an application.

Introduction

ne procedure in fig. 1-1 is a simple procedure r traversing binary tree structures.

```
traverse(x)
{  if leaf(x) then process(x)
   else {
      traverse(left(x));
      traverse(right(x));
   }
}
```

Fig. 1-1 Non-cyclic tree traversal

A serious problem with this procedure is that if t is applied to a "cyclic tree" such as the one in ig. 1-2, i.e. a tree where a node points back to ne of its ancestors, it will never terminate. In a eal implementation, the program will either oop for ever, or stop when the program stack or ome other memory area overflows.

afe algorithms for cyclic trees are important nd have received much attention, especially oncerning Prolog unification (Col 81), (Fag 83), Fil 84), (HS 84), (Knu 81), (Muk 83), (YKTM 84). he problem of traversing trees with cycles is a ore general problem than the problem of nding cycles in sequences studied in e.g. (Knu 1) and (SeSz 79). This paper presents methods r traversing cyclic trees. Our methods are

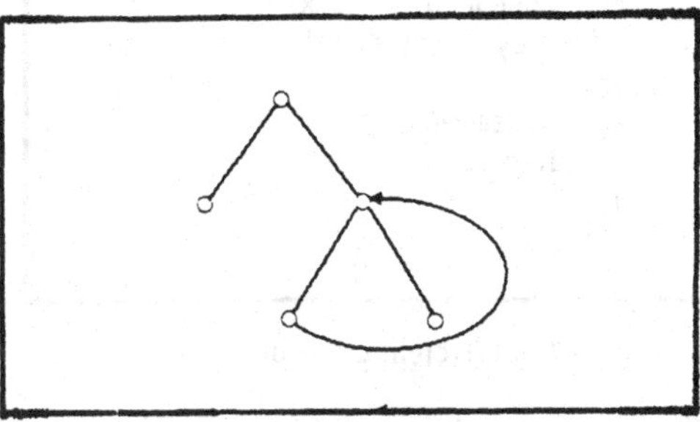

Fig. 1-2 Cyclic tree

based on cycle detecting algorithms for lists (Knu 81), which we generalise to detect and traverse cyclic trees. The main idea is the following:

> Suppose we traverse trees in left-to-right, depth-first order. If we are walking down a path from the root of the tree, and encounter a node <u>already seen before on this path</u>, we have found a cycle. Thus we can use a list detection algorithm on this path. Termination follows from the termination of the list algorithm.

We will introduce the general case of traversing cyclic trees by first studying detection of cyclic trees (NTM 86).

In our examples, we only use binary trees. Generalisation from binary trees to general trees is straightforward. We will use three primitive functions operating on a tree x: the Boolean *leaf(x)*, which says if x is a leaf, and *right(x)*, and *left(x)*, which extract the left and right subtrees.

For lists, cycles can be detected by saving all past nodes in a table, and compare every new node with the old ones. If equal, a cycle has been found.

For trees, we should only save <u>all elements seen on the current path</u> from the root. The recursive procedure traverse in fig. 1-3 implements this algorithm for trees. Note that during the execution, all the past nodes on the current path will be available in the internal procedure argument stack during the execution.

```
traverse(x)
{  if leaf(x) then process(x)
   else if search_stack(x)
     then cycle_detected;
   else {
      traverse(left(x));
      traverse(right(x));
   }
}
```

Fig. 1-3 Inefficient cycle detector

The section in boldface is the addition for cycle detection. The procedure *search_stack(x)* compares *x* with previous arguments to *traverse* saved on the stack.

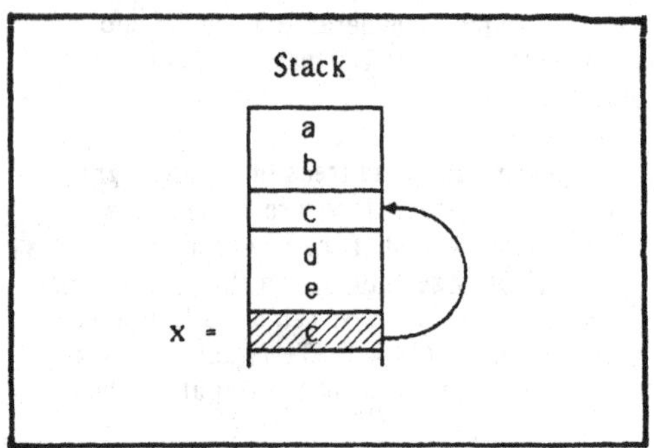

Fig. 1-4 *search_stack* finds past occurrences

As trees become deep, this algorithm becomes very inefficient. The search time increases in proportion to the depth, so the total time for a path of depth N will be $O(N^2)$. There are several more clever algorithms for finding cycles in lists (Knu 81), which can be generalised to handle trees: *Floyd's algorithm* keeps two pointers into the list. They are initially the same, but on every recursion, one of them moves one step forward, while the other pointer moves two steps forward. If the pointers become equal, a cycle has been found. A cycle will be found on the first repetition of an element.
Brent's algorithm remembers the latest 2^k:th element in the list. The subsequent elements are compared with this. Equality means that a cycle has been found. A disadvantage with this algorithm is that it takes longer before cycles are found. If the sequence repeats after N steps, Brent's algorithm stops within 3N steps.

Termination of Floyd's and Brent's algorithms is easy to show, and is given as an exercise in (Knu 81).

In section 2, we will generalise Floyd's and Brent's algorithms to detect and traverse cyclic trees. The idea is that trees can be traversed by trimming the stack when a cycle is detected, and continuing from there. Floyd's algorithm finds cycles after fewer steps, while Brent's algorithm is easier to use with tail recursion optimisation (TRO), shown in section 3. Some variants, including a heuristic detector, are described in section 4. Unification is discussed as an application in section 5. The relation to other work, discussion and conclusions are in sections 6 and 7.

2. Traversing cyclic trees

We will generalise Floyd's and Brent's algorithms to cyclic tree traversal, in depth-first, left-to-right order.

Floyd's and Brent's algorithms, as described in section 1, become directly applicable for detection of cyclic trees, if we replace the word "list" by "current path from the root of the tree."

Let us assume that the procedure argument stack can be referred to as an array, *stack*, with the stack pointer represented by a variable, *top*. This stack starts from position one, when *traverse* is first called. We also assume that data other than arguments (return addresses, frame pointers, etc) are made "invisible" by some method, e.g. address calculation.

Instead of letting Floyd's slow pointer step one step, and the fast pointer two steps on every iteration, we let them step a half, and one step, respectively. Then, the fast pointer will be the current argument to traverse. The slow pointer will be just in the middle of the argument stack. Floyd's algorithm for cyclic trees is shown in fig. 2-1.

(When *top* is odd, the result of the division is not so important. When following Brent's algorithm strictly, the comparison is only performed for even values of *top*.)

```
traverse(x)
{  if leaf(x) then process(x)
   else if x = stack[top/2]
     then cycle_detected;
   else {
      traverse(left(x));
      traverse(right(x));
   }
}
```

Fig. 2-1 Floyd cycle detector

‹t L(n) be the least power of two ≤ n. We get ‹ent's algorithm by replacing *stack[top/2]* in ‹g. 2-1 by *stack[L(top)]*. We will look up very ‹w stack elements for comparison. If we put ‹ese stack elements in a separate small stack (of ‹ze at most $\log_2$ of the maximal depth), we can ‹oid looking into the internal stack. This makes ‹possible to optimise tail recursion for Brent's ‹gorithm (see section 3).

‹g. 2-2 shows such a Brent algorithm for cyclic ‹ee detection. The latest 2^k:th (i.e., the ‹top):th) node in the current path is saved in a ‹riable, *check*. The previous value of *check* is ‹ved in the small stack by *pushsmall*. *check* ‹ould be initialised to a value which avoids ‹cidental match with *x*.

```
traverse(x)
{  if leaf(x) then process(x)
   else if x = check
     then cycle_detected
   else if power_of_2(top) then {
     pushsmall(check);
     check := x;
     traverse(left(x));
     traverse(right(x));
     check := popsmall;
   } else {
      traverse(left(x));
      traverse(right(x));
   }
}
```

Fig. 2-2 Brent cycle detector

‹e test *power_of_2(top)* can be computed very ‹sily: It is equivalent to *top & (top-1) = 0*, ‹here *&* denotes bitwise AND.

The overhead in this program is almost only the comparison of *x* with *check*, and the computation and test of *top & (top - 1)*. This can be done in about four machine instructions per iteration. The very little data required for this overhead may be contained in fast memory, like registers or micro store.

We shall now see how we can extend the detection algorithms to traverse cyclic trees, i.e. continue after a cycle has been detected.

If we walk down a path from the root of a tree, and if we encounter a node already seen before on this path, we have found a cycle. Then, if we back up the path to just before the reoccurrence of any node, and go down the next branch in depth-first order, we will be able to continue traversing the rest of the tree without getting stuck in this cycle.

This is the central idea behind the traversal algorithms. The key point is the procedure *cycle_detected*. For mere detection, it is enough if this procedure simply calls an error handling routine, etc. For traversal, however, the procedure should trim the stack down to just <u>before the first repetition of a node on the current path</u>.

Such a procedure can in fact be implemented efficiently: Suppose a cycle is detected. That means that the stack top element *x* has already appeared in this path, and has been saved earlier in the stack. The distance between the <u>first</u> and the <u>second</u> occurences of x in the stack will be the cycle's period, and the first repetition of a

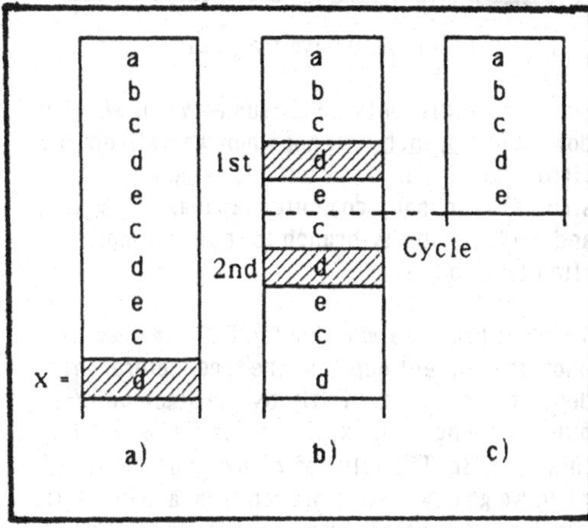

Fig. 2-3 The *cycle_detected* procedure

node in the path (i.e. the start of the cycle) must be between those occurences of x. In this way, we can easily find the beginning of the cycle, trim the stack back to that point, and continue with the next branch after the cycle. This method works identically for both Floyd and Brent type algoritms.

In fig. 2-3, a) shows the state of the stack when the cycle is first detected. In b), the first two occurrences of the stack top element are found, and in c) the stack has been trimmed to before the cycle.

3. Tail recursion optimisation

Since Brent's algorithm does not refer to the internal stack, we can easily implement TRO, as shown in this section.

Treé traversal programs are usually implemented in a more efficient way than *traverse* in fig. 1-1: The last call to *traverse* in the body can be replaced by a jump to the beginning, so we can write a non-cycle detecting version of *traverse* as in fig. 3-1.

```
traverse(x)
{LOOP:
   if leaf(x) then process(x)
   else {
      traverse(left(x));
      x := right(x);
      goto LOOP;
   }
}
```

Fig. 3-1 Tail recursive traversal

Stack space will only be consumed when we walk down a left branch, but not when we walk down a right branch. This is practical, since tree structures in many computer languages (e.g. Lisp and Prolog) usually branch to the right more often than to the left.

To adapt Brent's algorithm for TRO, we need to know the current depth in the tree. Before, the depth was given implicitly by the stack pointer, but now we need an explicit variable, *depth* for this purpose. The value of *depth* must be saved when we go down a left branch from a node, so the depth can be restored when it is time to go down the right branch.

When we return to a node after traversing its left subtree, the small stack must be trimmed back to the appropriate level. For this purpose, we keep the depth when the stack was last updated in a variable, *update_depth*.

From outside *traverse*, it is called with the depth argument = 1, and the variable *check* initially set to something which will not accidentally match x.

```
traverse(x, depth)
{LOOP:
   if leaf(x) then process(x)
   else if x = check then cycle_detected
   else {
      depth := depth + 1;
      if power_of_2(depth) then {
         update_depth := depth;
         pushsmall(check);
         check := x;
      }
      traverse(left(x), depth);
      while depth < update_depth do {
         check := popsmall;
         update_depth := update_depth/2;
      }
      x := right(x);
      goto LOOP;
   }
}
```

Fig. 3-2 TRO Cyclic tree traversal

Note that the procedure *cycle_detected* now also must remember to adjust the small stack to its appropriate size.

We will refer to this as our basic algorithm. The memory used will be linear in the maximum number of left branches in a path, and logarithmic in the maximum number of right branches.

4. Variations of the basic algorithm

We will describe some methods for increasing the efficiency, particularly for non-cyclic structures. Also, we describe a cycle detecting heuristic version of the basic algorithm.

The algorithm in fig. 3-1 can be reduced further: There is only one recursive call to *traverse* in its body. We know that when *traverse* exits, and the stack is not empty, execution must ntinue at the point just after this recursive ll. If the stack becomes empty, execution is nished. The algorithm can be implemented rectly as a loop, without any procedure calls, we explicitly use primitives *push* and *pop* for ving and fetching past nodes on the stack:

```
LOOP:
    if leaf(x) then {
       process(x);
       x := pop;
       if not stack_empty then {
          x := right(x);
          goto LOOP;
       }
    } else {
       push(x);
       x := left(x);
       goto LOOP;
    }
```

Fig. 4-1 Open loop traversal

nce most trees will probably be rather shallow, e way to increase the efficiency for non-cyclic ructures may be to delay detection tests until a rtain depth is reached. In our basic algorithm is can be done by calling *traverse(x,depth)* th *depth* > 1.

nother method to lower the overhead is to use a st procedure with a simplified heuristic tection algorithm. It cannot handle cycles, but en it detects something which could be a cle, a cycle handling, slower procedure takes er. Our basic algorithm can be changed into ch an algorithm by saving nodes, not according depth in the tree, but according to the order in ich they are seen during traversal. This means at we will not need so much stack handling in e program. We will surely find any cycle, though the algorithm sometimes "finds" cases ich are not cycles, i.e. when a non-terminal btree is shared by two subtrees.

version of the basic algorithm which combines th these methods to detect cycles is shown in . 4-2.

N = 1. It follows from Brent's algorithm that s algorithm stops within 3n iterations, where s the number of nodes in the tree (shared btrees are counted as separate).

```
  d := N;
LOOP:
  if leaf(x) then {
     process(x);
     x := pop;
     if not stack_empty then {
        x := right(x);
        goto LOOP;
     }
  } else if x = check then
     slow_traverse_instead
  else {
     d := d + 1;
     if power_of_2(d) then check := x;
     push(x);
     x := left(x);
     goto LOOP;
  }
}
```

Fig. 4-2 Heuristic cycle detector

5. Application: Unification

Unification with occur check should fail as soon as a cycle is found in any argument. After successful unification, the result should be traversed to check that it doesn't contain any cycle. For unification without occur check, we need to find a repetition of a pair of arguments, *(x,y)*, to consider it a cycle.

The described methods for cycle traversal are easily adapted for both kinds of unification. Without cycle detection, a *unify* procedure consumes at least 2 units of stack memory for descending a left branch. With cycle traversal similar to that in fig. 3-2, *unify* will consume 3 units.

An attractive alternative may be to combine a fast heuristic detector with a slower, cycle-handling unifier.

The unification procedure in fig. 5-1 shows a Brent type unification procedure. The two arguments to *unify* are the two structures to match. The procedures *dereference*, *bind*, *variable*, and *constant* are subroutines which: looks up a variable binding; binds a variable; tests if its argument is a pointer; and tests if its argument is a constant, respectively. (Here, it is assumed that the second argument is stored in the stack position above the first argument.)

```
unify(x,y)
{  x := dereference(x);
   y := dereference(y);
   if variable(x) then {
      bind(x,y); return(true);
   } else if variable(y) then {
      bind(y,x); return(true);
   } else if constant(x) or constant(y) then {
      return(x = y);
   } else if x = stack[top/2] and
           y = stack[top/2 + 1] then {
      cycle_detected;
   } else {
      return(unify(left(x),left(y)) and
             unify(right(x),right(y)));
   }
}
```

Fig. 5-1 Brent type unification

6. Related work and Discussion

Several algorithms for detection of cyclic structures have been published. They generally fall into three different categories:

- Pointers are (temporarily) replaced in the structures.
- Pointers are marked by tag bits.
- Some past nodes are saved and compared to new nodes.

Pointer replacements require undoing after execution. If restore information is saved on the stack, TRO becomes less practical. The memory complexity becomes O(L+R), where L and R are the maximum number of left and right branches in paths in the tree. Main memory references are needed for pointer replacements, which penalises non-cyclic structures. Since structures have to be changed, these methods are hard to use with read-only memory, or for shared structures in a parallel processing environment. An advantage is that these algorithms detect cycles after very few steps.

Tag marking also needs O(L+R) memory units. Unless the tags are in a separate table, the properties of these methods become similar to pointer replacement schemes. A separate tag bit table is uncomfortable because of its size and time for initialization.

The presented cyclic tree handling algorithms are the only ones we know of the third kind. The TRO cyclic tree traversal uses O(L + log(L+R)) memory units for non-cyclic structures. If there is a cycle on depth d, it will be discovered within depth 3d on the same path. The disadvantage is that these algorithms will be slow if there are many cycles in the structure.

For a real implementation, a good idea may be to combine fast heuristic detectors in hardware with slower, cycle handling algorithms in software.

7. Conclusions

The methods in this paper perform very well, regarding memory space and locality, low overhead for non-cyclic structures, and ability to handle read-only or shared structures. When cycles are very frequent, our methods could be combined with algorithms which have low overhead for cycles.

8. Acknowledgements

We are grateful for comments by Keiji Hirata and Hanpei Koike. The ideas reported were partly studied in Sweden at UPMAIL, under sponsorship by the Swedish National Board for Technical Development. This research was possible thanks to a generous scholarship given by the Japanese Ministry of Education.

In particular, we are deeply grateful to the late professor Tohru Moto-oka. By the outside world, he may perhaps be mostly remembered for his central role in the Fifth Generation Computer Project and countless other projects, but among his students and many other friends, he will always be remembered for his great generosity and kind heart.

9. References

(Col 81) Colmerauer, A.: "Prolog and Infinite Trees". In Clark, K. and Tärnlund, S.-Å.: (eds.): "Logic Programming." Academic Press, 1982.

(Fag 83) Fages, F.: "Note sur l'unification des termes de premier ordre finis et infinis." In conf. proc. Dincbas, M. (ed.): "Programmation en logique," Perros-Guirrec, France, March 22-23, 1983.

(Fil 84) Filgueiras, M.: "A Prolog interpreter

ɔrking with infinite terms". In Campbell, J.A. d.): "Implementations of Prolog." Ellis ɔrwood, Chichester, 1985.

IS 84) Haridi, S., Sahlin, D.: "Efficient nplementation of unification of cyclic ructures." In Campbell, J.A. (ed.): mplementations of Prolog." Ellis Horwood, hichester, 1985.

(nu 81) Knuth, D.E.: "The Art of Computer rogramming," vol. 2, Seminumerical Algorithms, nd ed., problems 3.1.6-7, p. 7, 517-518. ddison-Wesley, 1981.

Auk 83) Mukai, K.: "A Unification algorithm for finite Trees." In Bundy, A. (ed.): Proc. of the t. Joint Conf. on Artificial Intelligence, August 983.

JTM 83) Nilsson, M., Tanaka, H., Moto-oka, T.: Detection of Cyclic Tree Structures:" In The panese Information Processing Society: Proc. 2nd Nat. Japanese Conf. Information Processing, C-6.1986.

eSz 79) Sedgewick, R. and Szymanski, S.G.: "The mplexity of Finding Periods." In Proc. ACM mp. Th. Comp. 11, p. 74-80, 1979.

KTM 84) Yuhara, M., Koike, H., Tanaka, H., oto-oka, T.: "A Unify Processor Pilot Machine r PIE." In Proc. of the Japanese Logic ogramming Conference '84, Tokyo, March 1984.

Completeness of the SLDNF-resolution for a class of logic programs.

R. Barbuti

Dipartimento di Informatica
Universita' di Pisa
Corso Italia, 40 - 56100 Pisa
Italy

M. Martelli

CNUCE
C.N.R.
Via S. Maria 36
56100 Pisa
ITALY

and

CASE Center
Syracuse University
120 Hinds Hall
Syracuse N.Y. 13210
U.S.A.

Abstract: The paper gives a completeness result of SLDNF-resolution for a large class of logic programs. The characteristics of this class (structured programs) are mostly related to the possibility to decide always if a ground atom is or not a logical consequence of a program (i.e. they are related with total functions). Another characteristic of structured programs is that they allow to compute only ground substitutions. Most of the known completeness results (for example those for hierarchical programs) are special cases of this result. The class of structured programs is large enough to allow to write general programs with recursive definitions.

Work partially supported by Esprit Project 530 (Epsilon)

Introduction

ıe problem of the completeness of the SLDNF-resolution has been considered a very important one by any authors [10]. In general the SLDNF-resolution is not complete, but it is possible to restrict the kind programs considered and in this case to prove the completeness. Many papers characterize some asses of logic programs with this property.

lark [8], and then Shepherdson [15,16] and Lloyd and Topor [12], proved that programs without cursion and hierarchically defined have such a property. This result is relevant to the area of logic data ıses where, generally, recursion is not used. These systems generalize the standard relational data bases: l the relations are defined on finite domains. In this framework, the completeness is guaranteed by the ct that every query results in a finite set of solutions.

ecently, there have been many proposals to extend the class of deductive data bases to cope with infinite omains (see for example [11]). In these systems, it is not reasonable to require the same kind of onditions to obtain completeness. However, a less strong (but still important) completeness result can be onsidered the one that requires the termination of the evaluation for ground queries (containing also egative atoms).

et us note here that in the literature, what is known as *Query Evaluation Process* (QEP) [5,12] is actually e SLDNF-resolution with a safe computation rule [8,10].

ı a previous paper [2] we characterize a class of programs on infinite domains, including recursive efinitions, for which the Query Evaluation Process for ground formulas is finite. For this class of ograms the Negation as Failure rule is equivalent to the Closed World Assumption. This result can be seful not only in the data base area, but also in many other applications of logic programming, such as pert systems, etc.

hese results are able to capture some characteristics of logic programs, but the problem of the ompleteness of the SLDNF-resolution is still open and, as Lloyd says in [10], it is an urgent priority to lve it.

ı [6] we define a class of programs, called *structured* , for which the completeness of the LDNF-resolution holds. The conditions required to be a structured program are not so strong as the erarchical constraint [8] and it seems reasonable that many useful general programs (not necessarily atabase oriented) fall in this category.

ı Section 2. and Section 3. some previous results, and particularly those presented in [2,6], are summarized. In Section 4., starting from these results, we present, as an example, a general program (containing recursive definitions) for which the SLDNF-resolution is complete.

2. A characterization of categorical theories

In the following we assume the reader to be familiar with the terminology and notations used in [10], the Closed World Assumption rule (CWA) [14], the Negation as Failure rule (NF) and the concept of a completed program comp(P) [8].

The relations between the CWA and the NF rule are well described by the following diagram [10]:

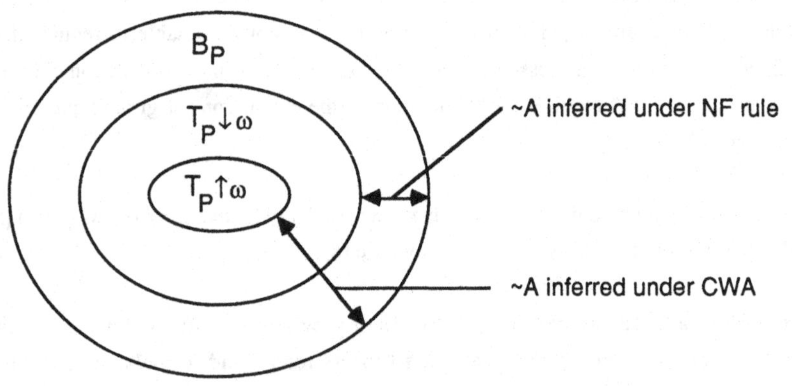

where

B_P is the Herbrand Base

$\{A \in B_P : \sim A$ can be inferred under the NF rule$\} = B_P \setminus T_P\downarrow\omega$

$\{A \in B_P : \sim A$ can be inferred under the CWA$\} = B_P \setminus T_P\uparrow\omega$

and where

T_P is the mapping from interpretations to interpretations associated with the program P.

$T_P\uparrow\omega$ is the limit of the chain obtained by iteratively applying T_P to the empty set (that is $T_P\uparrow\omega$ is the least fixpoint of T_P) and it is equal to the success set of P.

$T_P\downarrow\omega$ is the limit of the chain obtained by iteratively applying T_P to B_P (note that $T_P\downarrow\omega$ is i general greater than the greatest fixpoint of T_P).

he completeness result for the NF rule [9] states that if P is a program and $A \in B_P$ then if $\sim A$ is a gical consequence of comp(P) then A is in $F_P = B_P \setminus T_P\downarrow\omega$. F_P , the finite failure set of P is the set f all atoms $A \in B_P$ such that the goal $\leftarrow A$, using a fair SLD-resolution , finitely fails.

part from this interesting result, it can be important to find under which conditions the *query evaluation rocess* (QEP) is complete.

lark and Shepherdson [8,15] prove that the QEP is complete for those programs which satisfy the *ierarchical constraint* and the *covering axiom.*

n important result is obtained by Shepherdson [15,16]: if the program is hierarchical and satisfies the overing axiom then the QEP is complete for all allowed queries under all selection rules. Allowed queries re those in which each variable occurring in a negative literal occurs also in a positive one.

n [12], Lloyd and Topor rivisit the work of Clark and Shepherdson and give the following definitions nd results that will be useful in the following.

hey call ***admissible*** a general program clause if every variable of it occurs either in the head or in a ositive literal of the body.

hey call it *allowed* if every variable of the clause occurs in a positive literal of the body; a goal G is *llowed* if every variable of it occurs in a positive literal; finally, given a general program P and a eneral goal G, $P \cup \{G\}$ is *allowed* if:

) every clause in P is admissible;
) every clause in the definition of a predicate occurring in a positive literal in G or in the body of a clause in P is allowed;
) G is allowed.

hen they define when the evaluation of a goal *flounders* :

iven a general program P, a general goal G and a safe computation rule R, the evaluation of $P \cup \{G\}$ ia R flounders if at some point in the evaluation a goal is reached which contains only non-ground egative literals.

t this point they can state the following result (Proposition 1 in [12]):

Given a general program P, a general goal G such that $P \cup \{G\}$ is allowed and a safe computation rule R, this implies that:

a) the evaluation of $P \cup \{G\}$ via R never flounders;

b) every R-computed answer substitution for $P \cup \{G\}$ is a ground substitution for all the variables in G.

Let us recall that the CWA for Horn clause programs is categorical, i.e. any ground atom is either true or false. Unfortunately, this does not mean that it is always possible to decide the falsity of a ground atom in fact the QEP can result in an infinite computation . The only ground facts that can be proved false (with respect to a program P) are those atoms which are the logical consequence of comp(P), i.e. those provable with the NF rule.

From a termination point of view, this means that, in general, the QEP for a program P and a goal $\leftarrow A$ with A as a ground literal is not complete.

It is easy to see that a condition for a program P that implies this completeness property is that the program has a unique fixpoint $T_P\uparrow\omega$. which is equal to $T_P\downarrow\omega$. In this case the CWA is equivalent to the NF rule. This means that, if a ground atom A does not belong to $T_P\uparrow\omega$, then $\sim A$ is a logical consequence of comp(P). This is equivalent to saying that the QEP is complete for ground queries.

Definition 1: A program P is *ground-categorical* if the QEP for the program P and a goal $\leftarrow A$ with A a ground literal is complete. ♦

Note that if $T_P\uparrow\omega = T_P\downarrow\omega$, then the program P is ground-categorical.

The only class of programs which have been proved to be ground-categorical are those which satisfy the hierarchical constraint (as it results from Theorem 8 in [15]). See also [12] for an interesting discussion of the application of these concepts to the world of deductive data bases.

In some cases, the hierarchical constraint can be relaxed allowing also recursive programs. In [2] we characterize a class of programs which are ground-categorical. To describe this class let us give some definitions.

efinition 2: A mapping $A: I \rightarrow O$ is a *non deterministic total function* iff it is either a total nction or it is the relation obtained by the union of a finite number of non deterministic total functions om I to O. ♦

efinition 3: (*projection*) Let us consider a n-ary relation R on the domain $= I_1 \times ... \times I_n$. It is possible to permute the order of the domains I_i by a permutation π thus obtaining e new domain $D_\pi = I_{1\pi} \times ... \times I_{n\pi}$, such that $(<i_1, ..., i_n>)\pi = <i_{1\pi}, ..., i_{n\pi}>$ with $_1, ..., i_n> \in D$ and $<i_{1\pi}, ..., i_{n\pi}> \in D_\pi$.

$_\pi$ can be partitioned in two domains $D_{1\pi} = I_{1\pi} \times ... \times I_{k\pi}$ and $D_{2\pi} = I_{(k+1)\pi} \times ... \times I_{n\pi}$. *projection* R' of R is an application from I to O such that

$I = D_{1\pi}$ $(0 < k < n)$, $O = D_{2\pi}$ and

$R'(<i_1, ..., i_k>) = <o_1, ..., o_{n-k}>$ iff $R(<i_1, ..., i_k, o_1, ..., o_{n-k}>\pi^{-1})$ is true,

$(<i_1, ..., i_k> \in I, \quad <o_1, ..., o_{n-k}> \in O)$,

(k = n) $I = D$, O = {true, false} and

$R'(<i_1, ..., i_n>)$ = true iff $R(<i_1, ..., i_n>)$ is true,

and

$R'(<i_1, ..., i_n>)$ = false iff $R(<i_1, ..., i_n>)$ is false $(<i_1, ..., i_n> \in I)$. ♦

ne following proposition is proved in [6].

roposition 1: Given a relation R, if there exists a projection R' which is a non deterministic total nction such that not all its arguments (k<n) are taken as input, then there exists another projection R'' hich is also a non deterministic total function and has all the arguments as input. ♦

et us now consider a Horn clause program P.

efinition 4: A program P is *generally functional* iff every n-ary relation R (defined in P) is such at:

there exists a projection $R': I \rightarrow O$ of R such that R' is a non deterministic total function, and for any n-tuple $s = <i_1, ..., i_k, o_1, ..., o_{n-k}>\pi^{-1}$ (where π is the permutation associated to R') such that all the i_i 's are ground terms, the goal

$\leftarrow R\ (s)$

has a finite evaluation tree, no matter which fair selection rule is used (effectiveness of the definition). ♦

Note that all of the above definitions (when applied to Horn clause programs) deal with total functions where the considered domain is the whole Herbrand Universe (or cartesian products of it). It can be useful in many cases to consider total functions on a subset of the Herbrand Universe. This can easily be achieved with a typed language (in which the Herbrand Universe is partitioned) [3, 13]. The above definitions and the following results can be easily extended to cope with types.

The following theorem (proved in [2]) characterizes the class of ground-categorical (non-general) programs.

Theorem 1: Given a program P : P is ground-categorical iff P is generally functional. ♦

The proof shows that if P is generally functional then $T_P\uparrow\omega = T_P\downarrow\omega$ and then it is always decidable if a ground atom A is or not a logical consequence of P. The *only if* part is obvious because the success set is a recursive set and its characteristic function can be choosen as the projection.

Note that for Proposition 1 it would be always possible to consider the projection which has all the arguments as input. Nevertheless, in many cases, it is much easier to reason using a different projection. The relevance of the theorem comes from the fact that any of these projections can be used (and not only the trivial one).

Note that for generally functional programs the CWA is equivalent to the NF rule since the complement of the success set (with respect to the Herbrand base) is exactly the SLD finite failure set.

For these programs Theorem 16.3 of [9] becomes

Theorem 2: Let P be a generally functional program and $A \in B_P$; the following formulas are equivalent:

a) $A \in F_P$.

b) $A \notin T_P\downarrow\omega$.

c) $A \notin T_P\uparrow\omega$.

d) A is in the SLD finite failure set.

e) A is not in the success set.

For every fair computation rule R, the corresponding SLD-tree for $P \cup \{\leftarrow A\}$ via R is finitely failed.

) $\sim A$ is a logical consequence of comp(P).

he following formulas are also equivalent:

') $A \notin F_P$.

') $A \in T_P\uparrow\omega$.

') $A \in T_P\downarrow\omega$.

') A is not in the SLD finite failure set.

') A is in the success set. ♦

bviously, the class of generally functional programs is not decidable (it can easily be proved isomorphic the class of total functions). Therefore it is not possible to give a general algorithm to decide if a rogram P is generally functional.

ı [2] we give a decision algorithm for a subclass of generally functional programs: program which have primitive recursive projection. The decision is based on the syntactic structure of the definition thus llowing also to prove the effectiveness of the relation definitions.

. Completeness of the SLDNF-resolution

this Section we summarize the results of [6] about the completeness of SLDNF-resolution for general rograms.

et us start by considering that SLDNF-resolution for a program P and a goal G not general preserves e usual correctness and completeness results.

heorem 3: Let P be a program, G a goal and R a (fair) computation rule. Then for every correct swer substitution θ for comp(P) $\cup \{ G \}$, there exist a R-computed answer substitution σ for $\cup \{ G \}$ and a substitution γ such that $\theta = \sigma\gamma$. ♦

he proof is a trivial combination of Theorem 9.5 and Proposition 14.5 of [10]. The NF rule is never applied and the SLD-resolution coincides with the SLDNF-resolution.

Now let us take a program P that is generally functional but not general and a general goal G. Moreover let $P \cup \{ G \}$ be *allowed* [12].

Theorem 4: Let P be a generally functional program, G a general goal, R a fair and safe computation rule and $P \cup \{ G \}$ allowed. For every ground correct answer substitution θ for comp(P) $\cup \{ G \}$, θ is an R-computed answer substitution for $P \cup \{ G \}$. ♦

The proof (given in [6]) is based on the ground-categoricity property of P, and on Proposition 1 of [12 which says that in this case the evaluation of $P \cup \{ G \}$ does not flounder and that every R-computed answer substitution is a ground substitution.

Note that a stronger version of Theorem 4 (the proof is analogous) can be given imposing that only thos predicates in G that are used in negated literals must be generally functional in P. But for the characterization of the class of programs that will be given later, Theorem 4 seems more adequate.

Let us now build a hierarchy of programs.

Definition 5: A program P is *structured* if it is in $\mathbf{P_i}$, where:

P is in $\mathbf{P_0}$ iff P is a generally functional program (not general).

P is in $\mathbf{P_{i+1}}$ iff $P = P' \cup P''$ is a general program such that:

- the bodies of the relations in P' can contain as positive literals the relations defined in both P' and P'', but as negated literals, only relations defined in P'';
- P'' is in $\mathbf{P_i}$;
- P without the negated literals in the clause bodies is generally functional. ♦

Note: all the clauses that define a relation are in $\mathbf{P_i}$ iff at least one of them is in $\mathbf{P_i}$; all the clauses of a definition are always at the same level of the hierarchy.

A goal G is said in $\mathbf{P_i}$ if the set of relations used for computing it are in $\mathbf{P_i}$.

A concept similar to the structured program can be found in [4] (integrity constraints that do not *depend on* the relations they are constraining), in [7] (the language **C** where programs can be partially ordered nto subprograms P_i such that $P_i \leq P_j$ iff P_j contains an occurrence of $\sim P_i$) and in a similar concept, *ratified* programs, defined in [1] (structured programs are also stratified).

et us recall now some Lemmas proved in [6].

emma 1: If P is structured and allowed then P is ground-categorical. ♦

The proof is carried out by induction on the structure of P.

emma 2: If P is structured and allowed then comp(P) is consistent. ♦

The proof comes from Lemma 1 and Theorem 3 of [15].

emma 3: Let P be a structured program and $P^\wedge$ be P without the negated atoms and $= \forall\, (A_1 \wedge ... \wedge A_n)$ where $A_1 ,..., A_n$ are atoms. If F is a logical consequence of comp(P) then it is logical consequence of $P^\wedge$: (comp(P) $\models$ F) $\Rightarrow$ ($P^\wedge \models$ F). ♦

The proof comes from Proposition 14.4 of [10] and from the structure of P.

y using these Lemmas, we can prove [6] the following Theorem:

heorem 5: *(completeness of SLDNF-resolution for structured programs)*

et P be a structured program, G a general goal, R a fair and safe computation rule and $P \cup \{ G \}$ llowed. Every ground correct answer substitution θ for comp(P) $\cup \{ G \}$ is also a R-computed answer ıbstitution for $P \cup \{ G \}$. ♦

. An example of a structured program.

ı this Section we present a simple structured program P.

/e discuss its structureness by showing that the positive part $P^\wedge$ (P without negated atoms) is generally ınctional and by checking that negative atoms do not introduce additional recursion.

o show that the positive part $P^\wedge$ is generally functional we must check the following condition (see also] for a more detailed discussion):

- Each base relation R (that is defined only in terms of itself) must be proved to have a projection R' which is a non deterministic total function.
- Each clause right part $(R_1,...,R_n)$ in the definition of a non base relation must express functional composition among the non deterministic total function projections $R_1',...,R_n'$ of $R_1,...,R_n$.
- Each non base relation must be proved to have a non deterministic total function projection.

Recall that a non deterministic total function is a total function or the union of a finite number of non deterministic total functions (Definition 2).

Recall also that, if a relation R has a non deterministic total function projection such that not all its arguments are considered as input, then R has a non deterministic total function projection in which all the arguments are input (Proposition 1).

Note that, in the following, the checking of non deterministic total functionality is carried out in a non-formal way, and the program is considered defined on a typed domain (containing natural numbers and lists of naturals).

The program P is:

P1 *less-or-equal* (0,X) ←
P2 *less-or-equal* (*succ*(X), *succ*(Y)) ← *less-or-equal* (X,Y)

P3 *sorted*(*nil*) ←
P4 *sorted*(*cons*(X,*nil*)) ←
P5 *sorted*(*cons*(X,*cons*(Y,Z)) ← *less-or-equal* (X,Y), *sorted*(*cons*(Y,Z))

P6 *append*(*nil*,Y,Y) ←
P7 *append*(*cons*(X,Y),Z,*cons*(X,W)) ← *append*(Y,Z,W)

P8 *perm*(*nil*,*nil*) ←
P9 *perm*(X,*cons*(Y,Z)) ← *append*(X1,*cons*(Y,X2),X), *append*(X1,X2,X3), *perm*(X3,Z)

P10 *generate*(*0*, *cons*(*0*,*nil*)) ←
P11 *generate*(*succ*(N),*cons*(*succ*(N),Z)) ← *generate*(N,Z)

P12 *rand*(N,Y) ← *generate*(N,X), *perm*(X,Y), ~*sorted*(Y)

The program define a relation *rand* which generates non-sorted lists (second argument) containing all the natural numbers in the interval [*0*, N]. *Rand* is a naive random generator.

To obtain sequence permutations the program defines the relation *perm* whose realization is based on the ifference list method.

et us now check the non deterministic total functionality by analysing relation by relation.

ss_or_equal This relation has the obvious non deterministic total function projection in which all the arguments are input and the output is a truth value. This projection is a total function.

orted Analogous to *less_or_equal*. Note that in the body of clause P5, functional composition among projections is obtained by the *and* operator. This is possible because the results of projections of *less_or_equal* and *sorted* are boolean values.

ppend This relation has the obvious total function projection in which the first two arguments are input and the third is output. Recall that, in this case, also the projection in which all the arguments are input is a non deterministic total function. Finally, let us note that the projection in which the third argument is input and the first two are output is a non deterministic total function too. In fact, this projection can be considered as the union of a finite number of total functions (this number depends on the length of the third argument, but it is always finite). Each total function partitionates (in a specific way) the input list in two sublists. The relevance of this late projection is given by its use in showing the non deterministic total functionality of *perm*.

erm The most sophisticated relation in *P*; to show its non deterministic total functionality we must use two different projections of *append*. The first

$$append'(X_1,X_2) = X_3$$

which is the standard one; and the second

$$append''(X_3) = \langle X_1,X_2 \rangle$$

which results in a pair of sublists. Note that, in the following, to select the components of a pair we use the operators ↓1 and ↓2.

Perm has a non deterministic total function projection by considering the second argument as input and the first one as output. In this way we can translate clauses P8 and P9 into the non deterministic total function definition:

$$perm(nil) = nil$$

$$perm(cons(Y,Z)) = append'(\downarrow 1(append''(perm(Z))), \quad cons(Y, \downarrow 2(append''(perm(Z)))))$$

Let us furtherly remark that the relevance of non deterministic total functions is that their evaluations always terminate with a finite number of solutions.

enerate This relation has the obvious non deterministic total functional projection with the first argument as input and the second one as output.

rand It is easy to see that the positive part of *rand* (clause P12 without the literal ~*sorted*(Y)) has the non deterministic total function projection with all the arguments as input. To express functional composition in the body, we must consider the projection of *perm* with all arguments as input and boolean output.

From this analysis we can derive that the program P without negative atoms is generally functional.

Furtherly, P is structured. In fact P12 is allowed, and the negative literal does not introduce additional recursion. Then SLDNF-resolution for goals G, such that $P \cup \{ G \}$ is allowed, is complete.

4. Conclusions

In this paper we describe a class of programs for which the SLDNF-resolution is proved complete. This class is characterized by:

- being structured;
- being allowed;
- the use of a safe computation rule.

An obvious stronger result is to combine a program of this class with other programs that do not use negation and having goals that, with the whole program, are still allowed. The use of Theorem 2 and Theorem 5 will also ensure completeness.

As a final remark, let us note that hierarchical programs are in this class and the examples in [10] that caused problems are not.

Hierarchical programs are not recursive and then are easily organized in a structured program. Moreover a hierarchical program without the negated atoms is generally functional because of being easily provable to be decidable (the lowest level in the hierarchy contains only unit clauses and the other levels are defined in terms of the previous ones).

The examples in [10] that are not solved by forcing the programs to be allowed are mostly like the following program:

R(a) <-- P(a)

R(a) <-- ~P(a)

P(X) <-- P(f(X))

his program is not structured because the relation *P* is not generarally functional (see Definition 4).

eferences

. Apt, K.R., Blair, H. and Walker, A. Towards a Theory of Declarative Knowledge. IBM Internal Report, Yorktown Heights, (1985).

. Aquilano, C., Barbuti, R., Bocchetti, P. and Martelli M. Negation as Failure: Completeness of the Query Evaluation Process for Horn Clause Programs with Recursive Definitions. To appear in the *Journal of Automated Reasoning*.

. Asirelli, P., Barbuti, R. and Levi, G. Types and Declarative Static Type Checking in Logic Programming. Proc. Programming '84, Primorsko, Bulgary, (1984).

. Asirelli, P., De Santis, M. and Martelli M. Integrity Constraints in Logic Databases.*Journal of Logic Programming* 2, 3 (1985) 221-232.

. Barbuti,R. and Martelli,M. Programming in a Generally Functional Style to Design Logic Data Bases. Internal Report of CASE Center, Syracuse University, (1986).

. Barbuti,R. and Martelli,M. Completeness of SLDNF-resolution for Structured Programs. (1985), Submitted for publicaton.

. Chandra, A.K. and Harel D. Horn Clause Queries and Generalizations. *Journal of Logic Programming* 2, 1 (1985) 1-15.

. Clark, K.L. Negation as Failure. in *Logic and Data Bases* , (Gallaire, H. and Minker, J. Eds), Plenum, New York, (1978) 293-322

. Jaffar, J., Lassez, J-L. and Lloyd, J.W. Completeness of the Negation-as-Failure Rule. Proc. 8th IJCAI, Karlsruhe, (1983) 500-506.

0. Lloyd, J.W. *Foundations of Logic Programming* . Springer-Verlag, Symbolic Computation Series, (1984).

1. Lloyd, J.W. and Topor, R.W. A Basis for Deductive Data Base Systems.*Journal of Logic Programming* 2, 2, (1985) 93-109.

2. Lloyd, J.W. and Topor, R.W. A Basis for Deductive Data Base Systems II. Techn. Rep. 85/6, Dept. of Comp. Science, Univ. of Melbourne, (1985).

3. Mycroft, A. and O'Keefe, R. A Polymorphic Type System for PROLOG. Proc. Logic Programming Workshop, Portugal, (1983) 107-122.

4. Reiter, R. On Closed World Data Bases. in *Logic and Data Bases* , (Gallaire, H. and Minker, J. Eds), Plenum, New York, (1978) 55-76.

15. Shepherdson, J.C. Negation as Failure: A Comparison of Clark's Completed Data Base and Reiter's Closed World Assumption. *Journal of Logic Programming 1* , 1, (1984) 51-79.

16. Shepherdson, J.C. Negation as Failure II *Journal of Logic Programming* 2, 3, (1985) 185-202.

Choices in, and Limitations of, Logic Programming.

Paul J. Voda

Department of Computer Science, The University of British Columbia,
Vancouver, B.C. Canada V6T 1W5.

. Introduction.

he current trend in logic programming based on PROLOG [see for instance 5] is to enhance the positive compu- tion of Horn clauses with negations. Negations in a wider sense admit arbitrary predicate applications to be egated. In a narrower sense only negations of identities are admitted. The latter research is inspired by PRO- OG2 of Colmerauer [6]. The current approach to arbitrary negated predicate aplications is based on Clark's egation as failure [3]. The basic philosophy is to delay all negations until all arguments are ground [see 12,4,10]. he incompleteness of negation as failure in the classical sense poses a natural question. Under what circumstances nd at what cost can we have a better, possibly classical, negation?

'e argue in this paper that although classical negation is certainly attainable by full theorem proving, the price volves a full resolution among the positive and negative predicates in the goal. This amounts to the use of the w of excluded middle implementable only at a high cost. Moreover, the gain of the excluded middle is negligible nless we are prepared to employ induction in the framework of logic computations. We shall therefore argue in e favor of logic computations without the excluded middle somewhat in the spirit of intuitionism.

'e propose to deal with identities and inequalities directly and not to delay negated predicates. Negated predi- ates are evaluated *dually* to the computation method employed with positive predicate calls. Although we do not ropose a concrete method here, we nevertheless fully characterize the logic computations without the excluded iddle. This is achieved by a formal system called CTP. We then define logic computations to be synonymous ith provability within CTP. We have proposed to treat computations proof-theoretically earlier [17]. We have one it by setting up a formal theory characterizing the operational semantics of a programming language. This operational in that it directly mimics actual computations. CTP is in this sense a pure logic formulation of what an be expected to be logically computable.

'oting that the logic programming in the style of PROLOG seems to deal exclusively with recursively enumerable redicates, we propose a simplification of CTP-like computations in a form of what we call non-deterministic Pas- al. From this simple model we can see that logic programming, instead of being full theorem proving, just xtends the traditional programming in two respects. It introduces non-determinism and abolishes the distinction etween the input/output specification of formal parameters.

. Syntax of Logic Programs and the Universe of Discourse

'egations in PROLOG programs [see for instance 5] have two important consequences for the syntax of logic pro- rams. Firstly, we are leaving the domain of Horn clauses. This is because

$$A \leftarrow \neg B \,\&\, C \;\; \textit{is the same as} \;\; A \vee B \leftarrow C.$$

econdly, in order to compute negated predicate calls, we need both *if only* and *if* implications. We need the *osure* of a predicate [3,10] which is just another way of saying that each predicate is defined by a biconditional. he biconditionals force upon us explicit connectives and quantifiers. For instance, when computing without nega- on we need only the positive form of *Append*:

$$Append(x, y, z) \leftarrow x = 0 \,\&\, z = y \vee x = [h, t] \,\&\, z = [h, t'] \,\&\, Append(t, y, t').$$

f course, this will be given in PROLOG by two clauses. If we want to compute also negated *Appends* we mediately need explicit disjunction and existential quantifiers:

$$Append(x, y, z) \leftrightarrow x = 0 \,\&\, z = y \vee \exists h, t, t' \,(x = [h, t] \,\&\, z = [h, t'] \,\&\, Append(t, y, t')).$$

Existential quantifiers turn into universal ones under negation. Thus we are better off if we abandon the restrictiv syntax of Horn Clauses and use the full formalism of predicate calculus instead.

The next question we have to settle is the question of the domain of the discourse. What are the objects denote by our terms? The standard position in programming with PROLOG is that the domain is composed entirely fror the syntactic material as given by the constants and function symbols used in the program, i.e. by the so calle Herbrand Universe [13,15]. The standard procedure in the presence of negation is to close off the domain by th so called *closure axioms* [3,10] stipulating that there is nothing else in the domain and that the domain is freel generated by the function symbols. This last means that the identity is syntactic.

The closure of domains gives a different model for each program. We have argued in [16,17] that we are better o if we start with a fixed domain and with a fixed theory axiomatizing it. We then treat logic programs as exten sions of the fixed theory by a controlled addition of new predicates by so called *definitional extensions* [see fo instance 13]. Definitional extensions are a subset of *conservative extensions* and they guarantee the consistency c extended theories. With a fixed domain and theory we have a simple form of induction axioms. Induction is nc directly used for logic computations but it is needed for reasoning about programs. With a closed Herbran universe we need an inductive clause for each function symbol. We shall henceforth adopt a fixed domain an theory as the basis for logic programming. Our choice of a fixed domain is, however, not critical to the followin discussion; the argument can be still rephrased to deal with Herbrand domains.

Our domain will be basically the S-Expressions of LISP. For theoretical reasons it is sufficient to start with on atom only. From a practical point of view it is better to admit numbers, strings and identifiers as atoms and clos the domain off by pairing. This domain has been shown sufficient by the success of programming in LISP. W call the domain *Pairs*.

We shall use $[\mathbf{a}, \mathbf{b}]$ as the binary operation of *pairing*. Prolog systems usually use the notation **a.b** for the sam operation. We shall in this paper use only one atom 0 corresponding to *nil* of LISP. Pairing associates to th right, so $[\mathbf{a}, \mathbf{b}, \mathbf{c}]$ stands for $[\mathbf{a}, [\mathbf{b}, \mathbf{c}]]$. Note that we do not introduce a special list notation and write the lis $(\mathbf{a}\ \mathbf{b}\ \mathbf{c})$ simply as $[\mathbf{a}, \mathbf{b}, \mathbf{c}, 0]$.

We have axiomatized this domain by the theory TP (Theory of Pairs). It has 0 and pairing as the only functio symbols. TP starts with two atomic predicate symbols: identity $=$ and list membership $\in$. Both are techn cally binary symbols but because of pairing all predicate symbols can be taken as unary. We can write $\mathbf{P}(\mathbf{a}, \mathbf{b})$ a an abbreviation for $\mathbf{P}([\mathbf{a}, \mathbf{b}])$. We shall write $\mathbf{a} = \mathbf{b}$ and $\mathbf{a} \in \mathbf{b}$ as abbreviations for $=(\mathbf{a}, \mathbf{b})$ and $\in(\mathbf{a}, \mathbf{b}$ respectively. Formulas are composed of atomic formulas using the standard connectives and quantifiers. The basi TP can be extended by the addition of new predicate symbols via conservative extensions.

We have axiomatized TP by the standard logical axioms and axioms of identity plus the following non-logic ones.

$$[x, y] = [v, w] \rightarrow x = v \;\&\; y = w$$
$$\neg\, x \in 0$$
$$x \in [y, z] \leftrightarrow x = y \vee x \in z$$
$$\mathbf{A}(0) \;\&\; \forall \mathbf{x}, \mathbf{y}\ (\mathbf{A}(\mathbf{x}) \;\&\; \mathbf{A}(\mathbf{y}) \rightarrow \mathbf{A}(\mathbf{x}, \mathbf{y})) \rightarrow \forall \mathbf{x} \mathbf{A}(\mathbf{x})$$

The first axiom expresses the uniqueness of pairing (the converse is an axiom of identity), the second and thir describe list membership. The fourth one is a schema of induction axioms.

Without loss of generality we can assume that all definitions of predicates and formulas to be computed ar expressed in *positive* notation. Positive notation uses only conjunctions, disjunctions, and negations as connectives Negations can occur only on the level of atomic formulas $\mathbf{a} \neq \mathbf{b}$, $\mathbf{a} \notin \mathbf{b}$, and $\neg\, \mathbf{P}(\mathbf{a})$. Every formula can b transformed into an equivalent positive formula by moving negations towards atomic formulas by De-Morga laws.

Among the formulas of the possibly extended TP there is a subclass of formulas composed only of identities, con nectives, and quantifiers without any other predicate symbols (neither $\in$ nor the introduced predicates **P**). W call such formulas *decidable* formulas, or d-formulas. D-formulas will play a special role in our logic computations There is an algorithm which given a closed d-formula decides whether the formula is true or false.

The algorithm can be obtained indirectly by interpreting TP into the second order theory of two successors whic is decidable [1]. We have to use a second order theory because TP is effectively a theory of infinitely many succes sors. We are preparing a paper which gives a direct and efficiently implementable decision procedure for d rmulas of TP. This paper will be an extension of [18]. For the purposes of this paper the exact form of the algo-hm is not important. We shall rely only on its existence.

ROLOG programs use function symbols as data constructors. Data constructors can be interpreted into TP in e straighforward way [see 16,17]. Briefly, we need to designate a different pair for each function symbol used. r instance, in PROLOG we can use two function symbols $leaf(\mathbf{a})$ and $tree(\mathbf{a}, \mathbf{b})$ to describe binary trees. We n interpret these functions by explicit definitions into TP as

$$leaf(x) = [0, x] \text{ and } tree(x, y) = [[0, 0], x, y].$$

is interpretation satisfies the closure requirements in that the properties

$$leaf(x) \neq tree(y, z)$$
$$leaf(x) = leaf(y) \rightarrow x = y$$
$$tree(x, y) = tree(v, w) \rightarrow x = v \,\&\, y = w$$

ld.

Logic Computations

e shall use in this paper the terms *logic programming* and *logic computations* as synonyms. The original idea of gic programming was to equate it with (possibly user guided) *theorem proving* in classical predicate calculus. re PROLOG without negation can achieve the equivalence only if disjunctions (alternatives) are computed in rallel. PROLOGs with soundly implemented negations [4,12] compute much less than what can be classically oved. We shall argue in this section that the completeness can be achieved only at a high price in terms of iciency and the gain will be only marginal in terms of added computing power. We take the stand that full eorem proving, important as it is, should be used only for program transformation and verification. Logic com-tations should use more efficient algorithms.

the logic computations with negations based on the model of PROLOG we use two kinds of predicates. These e explicitly defined and recursive predicates. PROLOG predicates

$$P(a)$$
$$P(b)$$
$$R(x) \leftarrow \neg\, P(x) \,\&\, S(x)$$

ve the following explicit definition by biconditionals

$$P(x) \leftrightarrow x = a \lor x = b \tag{1}$$
$$R(x) \leftrightarrow \neg\, P(x) \,\&\, S(x). \tag{2}$$

example of a recursive predicate is the predicate *Append* given in section (2). Explicitly defined predicates can always admitted into TP by definitional extension. Recursively defined predicates can be admitted as conserva-e extensions under certain restrictions on the form of recursion. In both cases we have a guarantee that in the ndard model the predicates have interpretations.

logic program can be then understood as a suitable conservative extension of TP by both explicit and recursive edicates. A *computation* of a formula $\mathbf{A}(x_1, x_2, \ldots, x_n)$ using only previously introduced predicates can be fined as an attempt to find one or more sets of terms $\mathbf{a}_1, \mathbf{a}_2, \ldots, \mathbf{a}_n$ such that $\mathbf{A}(\mathbf{a}_1, \mathbf{a}_2, \ldots, \mathbf{a}_n)$ is valid in all dels of TP (both standard and non-standard) satisfying the axioms of TP and the defining axioms for all expli-or recursive predicates used in **A**. A similar definition is given for the computation of Horn Clause based logic grams [10]. A computation strategy is called *complete* if the terms $\mathbf{a}_i$ are found whenever they exist for all erpretations of predicates satisfying their definitions and for all formulas **A**.

hough this formulation amounts to more than the mere demonstration of validity because the terms $\mathbf{a}_i$ have to found, one can extend the methods explained for instance in Kleene's Mathematical Logic [9] to obtain a com-te algorithm. The method of Kleene admits the demonstration of validity in the presence of possibly infinitely ny axioms. In our case we have to extend the method so we can search for the terms $\mathbf{a}_i$ as well. So we shall be e to find such terms if there are any, otherwise we can go on searching forever. From the theoretical point of w we thus know that there is a complete algorithm for computability. Obviously, this algorithm is not directly ble in practical computations.

Without trying to implement the above suggestion for an algorithm we can first ask the question whether it i feasible to strive for the classical completeness of logic computations. Horn Clause based systems do not allov infinitely many axioms which may be required in TP. We have here on mind the axioms of induction. Althoug heuristics have been employed in practical theorem provers to select appropriate induction axioms [see for instanc 2], the choice of the induction axioms eventually boils down to enumerating all axioms and trying them one afte another.

In the presence of infinitely many axioms we have to deal with three kinds of choices out of infinite domains du ing the logic computations: the choice of the terms $\mathbf{a}_i$, the choice of the instantiations of existential quantifiers (fo the $\exists$-introduction right), and the choice of axioms used. With resolution based techniques only the last tw choices are necessary, the terms $\mathbf{a}_i$ are found automatically. The existential instantiations are obtained by th choice of candidates for the resolution. In order to justify the term *logic programming* at all, we cannot afford t abandon the potentially infinite search involved in the existential instantiation but most of us would agree that w do not want to search for the axioms as well. As a consequence, logic programming will not be complete in T with induction. How about dropping the axioms of induction and insisting on complete computability within T without induction? We have to realize first of all that almost all interesting properties of recursive predicates ca be derived only with the help of induction. Without axioms of induction we cannot even prove the simple theorem

$$Append(x, 0, x).$$

Without induction we would have to restrict ourselves to the derivation of simple properties like

$$R(x) \rightarrow S(x) \qquad (3$$

for the predicate R defined by (2). The formula(3), after the substitution for $R(x)$, yields

$$P(x) \vee \neg S(x) \vee S(x). \qquad (4$$

We use now the law of excluded middle. To rephrase the same argument in terms of resolution, we add to th clauses obtained from the axioms (1) and (2) two new goal clauses $R(k)$ and $\neg S(k)$ where k is a Skolem constan We then resolve the first goal clause against the clause $\neg R(x) \vee S(x)$ obtained from (2). This yields $S(k)$ whic is resolved against the second clause of the goal $\neg S(k)$. Such an intra-goal resolution goes beyond the Ho Clause based resolutions. In the latter we always have a single clause goal and the only possible resolutions a repeated resolutions against the clauses obtained from the axioms.

This very simple minded example suggests that if we want to use classical negation in the PROLOG-like settin we have to employ excluded middle, or alternatively we have to accept *true* resolution matching a positive pred cate application against a negative one in all goals. Proposed extensions of PROLOG to handle negations do n include excluded middle or intra-goal resolution. This can be demonstrated with one proposal [11] where in ord to prove (3) we add a new axiom

$$F \leftarrow R(x) \,\&\, \neg S(x)$$

and try to prove the goal

$$\leftarrow \neg F.$$

The computation will not go anywhere if the predicate S is both satisfied and falsified by infinitely many values.

The current trends in the accomodation of negation into the PROLOG-like setting remind us of the intuitionist approach. By the elimination of excluded middle we can intuitionistically prove $\mathbf{A} \vee \mathbf{B}$ only by demonstratin either $\mathbf{A}$ or $\mathbf{B}$. Similarly, $\exists x \mathbf{A}(x)$ is proved by finding one term $\mathbf{a}$ such that $\mathbf{A}(\mathbf{a})$ is provable. This suggests th we might hope that logic computation is synonymous with the intuitionistic derivability. Unfortunately this is n the case with the proof of (3). The formula (3) can be proved intuitionistically although its classical (but n intuitionistic) equivalent $\forall x\, (\neg R(x) \vee S(x))$ cannot. This is because $\mathbf{A} \,\&\, \mathbf{B} \rightarrow \mathbf{A}$ is derivable intuitionistically.

We have demonstrated that there is no hope for classical negation in the logic computations unless we are willin to employ the excluded middle or, equivalently intra-goal resolution. Suppose we opt for the excluded middl What do we stand to gain? Not very much, indeed. We shall be able to demonstrate simple minded theorems lik (3). The bulk of the interesting theorems are provable only with induction which we have ruled out. What do w stand to lose? Quite a lot, indeed. We have the additional burden of exploring all possible resolutions within th goal clauses. The situation will get worse when deep recursion is involved. The goal clauses will explode and will the number of potential candidates for resolution.

he use of deep recursion actually demostrates the barrier between logic computations and classically complete eorem proving. During theorem proving most of the variables are uninstatiated and calls to recursive predicates e expanded only occassionaly for a case analysis. Such expansion is very flat as opposed to the deep recursion pansion in logic computations where most of the variables are instantiated and allow the recursion to proceed.

'e think that without induction, the gain of classicaly complete logic computations is practically negligible while e price in terms of efficiency is quite steep. We suggest that the requirement of classically complete logic computions be replaced by the requirement that the computations are complete in a certain form of intutionistic callus.

. Proposed Framework for Logic Computations

the last section we have argued against the law of excluded middle in logic computations. The use of excluded iddle boils down to the use of axioms of the form $P(\mathbf{a}) \vee \neg P(\mathbf{a})$ for a predicate P and a term $\mathbf{a}$. In this section e develop a logical calculus CTP (for *Computational* TP) as a subtheory of TP. CTP does not generally admit e excluded middle. The notion of logic computation can be then redefined as an attempt to find for a given forula $\mathbf{A}(z_1, z_2, \ldots, z_n)$ of an extension of TP one, or more, sets of terms $\mathbf{a}_1, \mathbf{a}_2, \ldots, \mathbf{a}_n$ such that $(\mathbf{a}_1, \mathbf{a}_2, \ldots, \mathbf{a}_n)$ is CTP provable.

he theory CTP is a subtheory of TP and it has the same language. It will be axiomatized in the style of entzen [see for instance 8,14]. For that purpose we interpret a slight extension of sequents directly as formulas TP. We shall write

$$\mathbf{N}_1, \mathbf{N}_2, \ldots, \mathbf{N}_n \rightarrow \mathbf{P}_1, \mathbf{P}_2, \ldots, \mathbf{P}_p \mid \mathbf{D}_1, \mathbf{D}_2, \ldots, \mathbf{D}_d \tag{1}$$

here d, n, $p \geq 0$ and the formulas $\mathbf{D}_i$ are d-formulas as an abbreviation for the formula

$$0 = 0 \;\&\; \mathbf{N}_1 \;\&\; \mathbf{N}_2 \;\&\; \cdots \;\&\; \mathbf{N}_n \rightarrow 0 \neq 0 \vee \mathbf{P}_1 \vee \mathbf{P}_2 \vee \cdots \vee \mathbf{P}_p \vee 0 \neq 0 \vee \mathbf{D}_1 \vee \mathbf{D}_2 \vee \cdots \vee \mathbf{D}_d.$$

he use of $0 = 0$ permits any of the lists N_i, P_i, and D_i to be empty. We shall abbreviate possibly empty finite sts of formulas by capital Greek letters Γ, Δ, Π, etc.

ll axioms of CTP have the form

$$\Gamma \rightarrow \Pi \mid \Delta$$

here the formulas in Γ and Π are arbitrary positive formulas, the formulas of Δ are d-formulas, and the univerl closure of the sequent

$$\rightarrow \;\mid \Delta$$

true. Note that the existence of the decision algorithm for the d-formulas of TP guarantees that we can always cognize an axiom of CTP.

or improved readability we shall use a dot notation. For instance the rule of inference

$$\frac{\Gamma_1, \mathbf{A}, \Gamma_2 \rightarrow \Pi \mid \Delta}{\Gamma_1, \mathbf{B}, \Gamma_2 \rightarrow \Pi \mid \Delta}$$

ill be abbreviated as follows.

$$\frac{\cdots \mathbf{A} \cdots \rightarrow \cdots \mid \cdots}{\cdots \mathbf{B} \cdots \rightarrow \cdots \mid \cdots}$$

r the five operators of positive formulas there are five inference rules for the introduction of quantifiers and conctives on the left and five rules for the introduction on the right. They are the standard rules of Gentzen's callus.

$$(\neg \mathbf{L})\ \frac{\cdots \rightarrow \cdots \mathbf{A} \cdots \mid \cdots}{\neg \mathbf{A} \cdots \rightarrow \cdots \cdots \mid \cdots} \qquad (\neg \mathbf{R})\ \frac{\cdots \mathbf{A} \cdots \rightarrow \cdots \mid \cdots}{\cdots \cdots \rightarrow \cdots \neg \mathbf{A} \mid \cdots}$$

$$(\&\,\mathbf{L})\ \frac{\cdots \mathbf{A}, \mathbf{B} \cdots \rightarrow \cdots \mid \cdots}{\cdots \mathbf{A} \,\&\, \mathbf{B} \cdots \rightarrow \cdots \mid \cdots} \qquad (\vee \mathbf{R})\ \frac{\cdots \rightarrow \cdots \mathbf{A}, \mathbf{B} \cdots \mid \cdots}{\cdots \rightarrow \cdots \mathbf{A} \vee \mathbf{B} \cdots \mid \cdots}$$

$$(\&\,\mathbf{R})\ \frac{\cdots \rightarrow \cdots \mathbf{A} \cdots \mid \cdots, \quad \cdots \rightarrow \cdots \mathbf{B} \cdots \mid \cdots}{\cdots \rightarrow \cdots \mathbf{A} \,\&\, \mathbf{B} \cdots \mid \cdots}$$

$$(\vee L)\ \frac{\cdots A \cdots \to \cdots \mid \cdots, \quad \cdots B \cdots \to \cdots \mid \cdots}{\cdots A \vee B \cdots \to \cdots \mid \cdots}$$

$$(\exists L)\ \frac{\cdots A(x) \cdots \to \cdots \mid \cdots}{\cdots \exists x A(x) \cdots \to \cdots \mid \cdots} \qquad (\exists R)\ \frac{\cdots \to \cdots A(a) \cdots \mid \cdots}{\cdots \to \cdots \exists x A(x) \cdots \mid \cdots}$$

$$(\forall L)\ \frac{\cdots A(a) \cdots \to \cdots \mid \cdots}{\cdots \forall x A(x) \cdots \to \cdots \mid \cdots} \qquad (\forall R)\ \frac{\cdots \to \cdots A(x) \cdots \mid \cdots}{\cdots \to \cdots \forall x A(x) \cdots \mid \cdots}$$

In the rules (∃L) and (∀R) the variable **x** does not occur freely in the bottom sequents. In the rules (∃R) ar (∀L) **a** is an arbitrary term.

The next two rules introduce a d-formula left and right.

$$(dL)\ \frac{\cdots \cdots \to \cdots \mid \cdots, \neg A}{\cdots A \cdots \to \cdots \mid \cdots} \qquad (dR)\ \frac{\cdots \to \cdots \cdots \mid \cdots A}{\cdots \to \cdots A \cdots \mid \cdots}$$

The formula **A** does not contain defined predicates.

For each predicate **P** extending TP we add two inference rules introducing a call to **P** left and right respectively If the predicate **P** extends TP with the new axiom

$$P(x) \leftrightarrow A(x) \tag{1}$$

where **A** is a positive formula containing at most the variable **x** free then CTP contains two rules

$$(PL)\ \frac{\cdots A(a) \cdots \to \cdots \mid \cdots}{\cdots P(a) \cdots \to \cdots \mid \cdots} \qquad (PR)\ \frac{\cdots \to \cdots A(a) \cdots \mid \cdots}{\cdots \to \cdots P(a) \cdots \mid \cdots}$$

A positive formula $A(x_1, x_2, \ldots, x_n)$ can be logically computed if we can find terms $a_1, a_2, \ldots\ a_n$ such that th sequent

$$\to A(a_1, a_2, \ldots, a_n) \mid$$

is CTP provable. The computation will obviously proceed by the substitution of bodies **A(a)** for the predicat calls **P(a)**. The bodies are then evaluated by a dual set of rules depending whether the predicate call was positiv **P(a)** or negative ¬ **P(a)**. Parts of the computed formulas which do not contain predicate calls are adjoined t the decidable parts of sequents. A computation can stop only when a CTP axiom is reached, i.e. the universal clo sure of the decidable part of the sequent is true. This arrangment does not allow the excluded middle for formula which are not d-formulas.

The computation of a negated predicate by the dual left rules without a delay demonstrates that the customar delay of negated predicates in PROLOG is weaker in terms of computatibility. This can be demonstrated by very simple example of $P(x) \leftrightarrow x \neq 0$. The PROLOG goal $\neg P(x)$ will be infinitely delayed whereas the left rule allow to find the solution $x = 0$ by proving $\neg P(0)$.

By the induction on length of CTP proofs one can demonstrate that all CTP provable sequents

$$\to A(a_1, a_2, \ldots, a_n) \mid$$

are valid (they are actually theorems of TP). If we make sure that TP is extended conservatively by the nev axioms of the form (1) then the subtheory CTP must be consistent.

The relation between CTP and intuitionistic TP must be investigated by further research. One is, however, not subset of the other. For instance the sequent

$$\to \forall x(x = 0 \vee x \neq 0) \mid$$

is CTP provable by the employment of (**dR**). The same formula is not intutionistically provable because it relie on the excluded middle where neither of the disjuncts is provable. On the other hand, consider the formula (3 from section 3 expressed in the sequent form as

$$\to \neg R(x) \vee S(x) \mid .$$

After the application of rules (∨ **R**), (¬ **L**), (**RL**), and (& **L**) the formula reduces to

$$\neg P(x), S(x) \to S(x) \mid \tag{2}$$

which is intutionistically provable. The formula (2) is generally not CTP provable. It can be proved only if P holds for all x, which is not the case, or one can completely remove all defined predicates from both calls to $S(x$

repeated application of rules for S. This point can be demonstrated by the CTP proof of the sequent

$$\rightarrow \neg R(x) \vee \neg P(x) \mid \tag{3}$$

ing the definitions of predicates from section (2). After a similar sequence of rules as above, we reduce the proof (3) to the proof of

$$S(x), P(x) \rightarrow P(x) \mid . \tag{4}$$

pplications of (**PL**), (**dL**), (**PR**), and (**dR**) turn (4) to the CTP axiom

$$S(x) \rightarrow \ \mid \neg (x = a \vee x = b), x = a \vee x = b.$$

deed a good PROLOG should do the proof of (3).

all predicates ever called in a formula contain only explicitly defined predicates without any recursion then the rmula can be computed because the predicates can be eliminated by a repeated substitution of bodies. This eans that all queries about practical data bases should be fully answered.

y giving a formal system CTP we have characterized the notion of logic computation *syntactically*. Computaons of PROLOG are typically characterized semantically in terms of logical consequence [10]. The semantic aracterization must give an interpretation to the formulas of CTP in such a way that the axiom system is comete, i.e. a formula is provable iff it is valid in all interpretations. We note here that the presence of recursive edicates makes TP incomplete in the sense of Gödel, i.e. there are unprovable formulas true in the standard iiverse of pairs. Thus the interpretation of CTP will have to permit both standard and non-standard models of P. Classical interpretations are not applicable to either CTP or intuitionistic calculus because of the restricted w of excluded middle. Intuitionistic predicate calculus can be interpreted with the help of Kripke's models. For e interpretation and the proof of completeness see for instance [14]. We believe that similar models can be conructed for CTP. But we think that the gain of such a semantic characterization will be only marginal. This is cause the models of intuitionistic calculus just mimic the proof rules.

TP is a good vehicle for the syntactic characterization of logic computations but it does not directly provide for implementable algorithm. This is because one has to guess both the satisfying terms $\mathbf{a}_i$ and the terms for (**∃R**) d (**∀L**). The terms $\mathbf{a}_i$ and the terms for **∃R** can be guessed either by unification in the style of PROLOG or by lutions of systems of equations in the style of PROLOG2 [6]. The latter does not provide directly for quantifiers it they can be handled by the method explained in our paper [18] where the solution of equations is extended to clude connectives and existential quantifiers. The treatment of universal quantifiers on the right and existential antifiers on the left will have to be investigated. The author knows of no implementation of a logic language hich computes universal quantifiers without full resolution. The next section proposes a simple schema for iiversal quantifiers.

A Non-Deterministic Pascal Model

om the experience with logic programming we are willing to claim that all predicates used in programs are cursively enumerable over pairs (obviously, the notion of recursive functions is defined only for natural numbers it it can be naturally defined also for the domain of pairs [16]). If a recursively enumerable relation can be tisfied for a certain argument, it can be found in finite time, otherwise the computation may fail to terminate. here is a simple visualization of recursively enumerable predicates in terms of what we call the non-deterministic ascal model. Each predicate corresponds to a Pascal procedure. All arguments are input/output. A nonterministic Pascal procedure can fail when a condition is not met or it calls a failing procedure. When a produre satisfies all predicates and tests then it succeeds. Output values of arguments and values of local variables riables are generated as the result of tests within the body. The separator ";" corresponds to the conjunction. rking of processes corresponds to disjunctions. Procedure calls and equality tests can be negated. Local variles correspond to existential quantifiers. Loops express the universal quantifiers, a terminating loop corresponds a bounded quantifier.

The predicate *Append* has the following procedural form.

```
procedure Append(x, y, z);
  var h, t, t';
  fork
    x = 0; z = y |
    x = [h, t]; z = [h, t']; Append(t, y, t');
  end
```

The predicate $Sublist(x, y) \leftrightarrow \forall z\ (z \in x \rightarrow z \in y)$ has the following Pascal-like form.

```
procedure Subset(x, y);
  for z while z ∈ x do z ∈ y
```

When a predicate is called negatively, its complement is invoked. The complement of *Append* is

```
procedure NotAppend(x, y, z);
begin
  fork x ≠ 0 | z ≠ y end;
  for h, t, t' while x = [h, t]; z = [h, t'] do
    NotAppend(t, y, t');
end.
```

We are not suggesting any algorithm for computing non-deterministic Pascal beyond observing that just as identi ties have a combined role of tests and assignments also the inequalities must act in this dual role. For instance th identity $x = 0$ tests the value of x if it is instantiated or assigns to it 0 if not. Similarly, $x \neq 0$ must test the vari able x if instantiated and assign a generic non-zero value to it if uninstantiated. This corresponds to a delaying c negations in some Prolog interpretations. Negated procedures are computed by computing complements, rathe than by delaying. The paper [18] deals with identities of TP, the PROLOG2 paper [6] also includes inequalities but does not allow negated predicate calls and quantifiers. We are preparing a paper on the full decision procedur for the d-formulas of TP.

6. Conclusions

A formula **A** is CTP provable if one can find a d-formula **D** such that both **D** → **A** and **D** hold. We ca strengthen our computations by strengthening the class of formulas we decide. In the domain of pairs with atom including integers and strings we should include among the d-formulas the relation **a**<**b** ordering integers an strings. This is because the theory of ordering is decidable both in integers and strings. The ordering can b extended to pairs to express the relation of being a sub-pair. In terms of the Pascal model this means that, i addition to the identities and negated identities, we should be prepared to take over the inequalities into th environment during computations. This corresponds to the delaying of these atomic relations. Note that we do nc delay defined predicates but compute them negatively by employing dual set of rules as suggested by the rules c left introductions of CTP.

The incorporation of decidable predicates into the environment (into the class of d-formulas) can be achieved onl at the cost of a certain overhead associated with the maintainance of the set of partially instantiated atomi predicates. In the paper [18] we have proposed a one-variable formulation of TP which significantly simplifies th overhead associated with the management of system of equations and inequalities. As we have mentioned befor we are preparing a paper presenting a decision algorithm for identities and inequalities within this framework This algorithm can be efficiently implemented on a computer. At the same time we are testing these ideas in practical implementation of our logic programming language R-Maple. R-Maple is designed as a data-base syste where the explicitly defined predicates of the form

$$R(x) \leftrightarrow x = \mathbf{a}_1 \vee \cdots \vee x = \mathbf{a}_n$$

are stored as files. Since the terms $\mathbf{a}_i$ are generally n-tuples composed by pairing we can enumerate all n-tupl satisfying a relational data-base in this form. The implementation of R-Maple will include also types and t above explicit data bases among the class of decidable formulas. As a consequence all queries within this fram work can be fully answered.

s a final remark we note here that the incorporation of various decidable predicates into the environment rresponds to computation with constraints. Constraints are another intensively studied topic.

Barwise J. (ed.), Handbook of Mathematical Logic; North-Holland 1977.

Boyer R., Moore J., A Computational Logic; Academic Press, 1979.

Clark K., Negation as Failure. Logic and Data Bases (H. Gallaire ed.); Plenum Press 1978.

Clark K., Ennals J., McCabe F., A Micro-Prolog Primer. Logic Programming Associates Ltd, London 1981.

Clocksin W., Mellish C., Programming in Prolog, Springer Berlin 1981.

Colmerauer A., Kanoui H., Van Caneghem M., Prolog, Theoretical Principles and Current Trends; Technology and Science of Informatics, vol. 2, North Oxford Academic, 1983.

] Hinman P., Recursion-Theoretic Hierarchies, Springer 1978.

Kleene S., Introduction to Meta-Mathematics; North Holland 1952.

Kleene S., Mathematical Logic; North Holland 1963.

0] LLoyd J., Foundations of Logic Programming; Springer Berlin 1984.

1] LLoyd J., Topor R., Making Prolog More Expressive; Journal of Logic Programming 1984 no. 3.

2] Naish L., An Introduction to MU-Prolog, Tech. Report Dept. of Comp. Science University of Melbourne, 1982.

3] Shoenfield J., Mathematical Logic, Addison-Wesley, 1967.

4] Takeuti G., Proof Theory; North Holland 1975.

5] Van Emden M., Kowalski R., The Semantics of Predicate Logic as a Programming Language; Journal of ACM, vol 23. 1976.

6] Voda P., Theory of Pairs, Part I: Provably Recursive Functions; Technical Report of Dept. Comp. Science UBC, Vancouver December 1984.

7] Voda P., A View of Programming Languages as Symbiosis of Meaning and Computations; New Generation Computing, Tokyo, February 1985.

8] Voda P.J., Computation of Full Logic Programs Using One-Variable Environments; New Generation Computing, vol.4 no. 2, May 1986.

NEGATION AND QUANTIFIERS IN NU-PROLOG

Lee Naish

Machine Intelligence Project
Department of Computer Science
University of Melbourne
Parkville 3052
Australia

ABSTRACT

We briefly discuss the shortcomings of negation in conventional Prolog systems. The design and implementation of the negation constructs in NU-Prolog† are then presented. The major difference is the presence of explicit quantifiers. However, several other innovations are used to extract the maximum flexibility from current implementation techniques. These result in improved treatment of "if", existential quantifiers, inequality and non-logical primitives. We also discuss how the negation primitives of NU-Prolog can be added to conventional systems and how they can improve the implementation of higher level constructs.

1. INTRODUCTION

The negation facilities of conventional Prolog systems leave much to be desired. Firstly the fact that the main primitives for negation, `\+` `\=` and `->` [Bowen 82], are implemented unsoundly has received much attention. To avoid incorrect answers, programmers must take care that the negation primitives are only called when sufficiently instantiated. This restricts the style of programming, but would not be so bad if there were tools available to help verify that all calls to negation primitives are safe. If such tools were simply incorporated into current systems, however, many spurious error reports would be made, because of the non-logical use of the primitives and the need for quantifiers.

Another major failing of Prolog is that the semantics of most programs using negation is not at all clear. There are three main reasons for this. The first is the use of cut for negation

† NU-Prolog is the successor of MU-Prolog.

he straightforward declarative meaning of many Prolog clauses is simply wrong, due to nplicit negations introduced by previous clauses. This is exemplified well in the **max** program elow. We also include an appalling way of expressing a conjunction of inequalities, actually sed by some people.

```
max(A, B, A) :- A >= B, !.
max(A, B, B).          % implicit A < B

p(X) :-
        X = a, !, fail;
        X = b, !, fail;
        .....
```

Unfortunately, the uses of cut for negation cannot easily be distinguished from the uses r extra-logical applications, avoiding redundant solutions, removing redundant backtrack oints etc. Many Prolog programmers add a generous sprinkling of totally useless cuts to their rograms too.

A second reason for the unclear semantics of Prolog programs is due to the abuse of nsound negation for non-logical purposes. Some examples, such as using double negation to rove a goal without binding any variables, are fairly blatant. In general, though, it is very ifficult to tell if the use of negation primitives is intended to be logical. The third reason for nclear semantics is the lack of expressive power of negation in Prolog. What is lacking is a ay to clearly distinguish between existentially and universally quantified variables. Goals of e form ∀Y **not p(X,Y)** can be implemented in Prolog, but the goal will not be ground when alled, so it cannot easily be distinguished from a non-logical use of negation.

To clean up negation in Prolog, three things are necessary:

1) The negation primitives must be designed so that the logical uses of negation primitives can be clearly distinguished from the non-logical uses. Non-logical use should also be reduced. This implies that the logical primitives must be sufficiently expressive.

2) The negation primitives must be implemented soundly. The most flexible way to achieve this is for calls to the primitives to delay until they are sufficiently instantiated. For systems which no not support coroutines, there should be versions of the primitives available which report errors if the calls are insufficiently instantiated.

3) The use of cut must be kept to a minimum, and preferably eliminated entirely. If cut is to be retained in the language, this implies that reasonable uses of cut can be expressed by the negation primitives, and the primitives should be implemented efficiently.

In the rest of this paper, we describe the negation facilities of NU-Prolog, and how they n improve other Prolog systems. We first argue in favour of explicit quantifiers for negation d describe how they are expressed in NU-Prolog. Section 3 discusses the declarative and erational semantics of the constructs using quantifiers. This extends the basic set of negation imitives available in other languages. The next section discusses implementation by using a t of low level primitives. In section 5, we show how explicit quantifiers can be used for non-logical applications more flexibly than the standard primitives. Section 6 discusses how the implementation of Extended Prolog [Lloyd 84] can be made more efficient by utilising NU-Prolog's more flexible set of negation primitives. Next, we argue that the negation constructs of NU-Prolog would considerably improve conventional Prolog systems, even though the implementation would be less flexible. Section 8 contains our conclusions.

2. EXPLICIT QUANTIFIERS

In pure Prolog, the quantification of variables is very simple. Head variables are universally quantified for the whole clause and variables local to the body are existentially quantified. Implicit quantification is therefore not too confusing. When negation is introduced it is still possible to retain this simple quantification, but it reduces the expressive power. It is quite common to want universally quantified local variables within negations (we give examples later). Rather than having three different categories of implicitly quantified variables (and more with nested negations), our contention is that the quantifiers for negation should be explicit. In Meta Prolog [Bowen 85] all variables are explicitly quantified. Working out the exact logic of a problem involving negation and quantifiers is quite complex and error prone. By making quantifiers explicit, programmers are forced to think the problem through and people reading a program can extract the semantics very easily. We give other advantages of explicit quantifiers later. NU-Prolog uses the following syntax for quantifiers.

```
all V Goal
some V Goal
```

These are read as for all **V Goal** and for some **V Goal**, respectively. **V** is a list of variables (actually any term) local to **Goal**, a Prolog goal. Our current implementation uses a DEC-10 Prolog parser written in Prolog, with modifications to allow prefix binary operators. Internally, **all V G** is the term **all(V,G)**.

3. BASIC CONSTRUCTS

It is not possible to use all quantifiers on all goals in NU-Prolog. Rather, there are a small number of constructs, with optional quantifiers, that are recognised and compiled. We believe this is the key set of negation primitives for Prolog.

3.1. Not

Quantifiers for **not** are often needed, especially for database programming and queries. There are two equivalent constructs for this in NU-Prolog.

```
all V not Goal
not some V Goal
```

The semantics is that of ∀V ¬**Goal**. Below is an example of a predicate for finding people who take no computer science courses.

```
no_cs(P) :-
        all Unit not takes(P, cs, Unit).
```

Without quantifiers for **not**, an extra predicate is needed to express these semantics:

```
no_cs(P) :- not some_cs(P).

some_cs(P) :- takes(P, cs, Unit).
```

›r simple negations especially, this can reduce readability and is rather tedious for ogrammers. Where sound implementations of negation are available but lack quantifiers, ch as in MU-Prolog† [Naish 85a], there is a temptation to revert back to the unsound gation. Quantifiers give the programmer a choice.

Operationally, **not** delays until all the global (that is, unquantified) variables are ground, en proceeds with the normal negation as failure implementation, failing if and only if the gated goal succeeds. If the quantified variables are local to the call then they must be bound at the time of the call, ensuring correct behaviour.

2. If–Then–Else

One of the most common uses of cut is to implement the semantics of **if-then-else**.)'Keefe 85] argues that an if-then-else construct can replace nearly all occurrences of cut. The ntax in NU-Prolog is as follows.

```
        if some V C then A else B
```

he semantics is that of $\exists V(C \wedge A) \vee (\neg\exists V\ C \wedge B)$. The **else** portion is optional, giving the mantics of $\exists V(C \wedge A) \vee (\neg\exists V\ C)$. Like **not**, this construct delays until the global variables e ground. In fact, **if-then-else** subsumes **not**. **C** is called first, and if it succeeds **A** is lled; otherwise **B** is called. The implementation is simplified if we only allow the quantified riables to appear in **C**. Then only the first solution to **C** need be considered. However, it is ten useful to have the quantified variables in **A** also. Consider the procedure below, which arches for values of a key in an association list and, if the key is not present, adds it to the t.

```
lookup(Key, Val, AL, NewAL) :-
        if some V member(Key-V, AL) then
                Val = V,                % V is quantified
                NewAL = AL
        else
                NewAL = (Key-Val).AL.
```

When **A** shares quantified variables with **C**, all solutions to **C** must be considered. therwise, some solutions to $\exists V(C \wedge A)$ may be lost. This could occur in the example above, if contained multiple elements with the same key. LM-Prolog's **if** construct [Carlsson 83] also turns all solutions to the condition, but does not wait until global variables are ground, so it is sound.

† MU-Prolog has a library predicate for negation which allows quantifiers by explicitly stating all obal variables. There is no corresponding predicate for if–then–else, to date.

3.3. Inequality

Inequality is a very important negation primitive in Prolog, especially for implementing advanced forms of negation by transforming programs [Schultz 84]. In NU-Prolog, it is expressed as follows.

```
all V T1 ~= T2
```

The semantics is that of $\forall$V T1 $\neq$ T2. Allowing universal quantifiers for inequality is very useful. A reasonably common application, checking that a variable is not bound to a cons cell is hard to express without it. The following program, for "flattening" lists of lists, illustrates the need for this.

```
flatten([], []).
flatten([].A, B) :- flatten(A,B).
flatten((A.B).C, D) :- flatten(A.B.C, D).
flatten(A.B, A.C) :- A ~= [], all X.Y A ~= X.Y, flatten(B, C).
```

MU-Prolog has an inequality predicate which allows universal quantifiers also. However it is less expressive, since the quantifiers are implicit and multiple occurrences of a quantified variable are not possible. Operationally, ~= delays until sufficiently instantiated, though not necessarily ground. If the two terms don't unify, the call succeeds. If the two terms can be unified without binding any global variables, the call fails. Otherwise, the call delays.

3.4. All Solutions

The specification and sound implementation of an all solutions predicate with clear declarative semantics is discussed in [Naish 85b]. The only change we suggest is that **some** be used to identify local (existentially quantified) variables, instead of **^**.

```
solutions(Term, some V Goal, Set)
```

Formally, the semantics is that of

$$\forall X(\exists\, L_1,\ldots,L_n(\texttt{Goal} \wedge X{=}\texttt{Term}) \leftrightarrow \texttt{member(X, Set)}) \wedge \texttt{sorted(Set)}$$

where $L_1,\ldots,L_n$ are the variables in **Term** and **V**, **member** is the standard list membership predicate and **sorted(Set)** is true if **Set** is a sorted list with no duplicated elements. Briefly **Set** is the set of all instances of **Term**, for which **Goal** is true.

3.5. Existential Quantifiers

One reasonable use of cut which has received little attention is the elimination of duplicate solutions. DEC-10 Prolog's **once** construct is a more structured form of this. Consider the following predicate, for testing if two nodes in a graph are connected.

```
connected(A, B) :- path(A, B, Path), !.
```

If **A** and **B** are ground at the time of the call, only one path need be found. Extra solutions to **path** result in redundant identical solutions to **connected**. Logically, **Path** is existentially quantified, and only one value is needed. In NU-Prolog, this can be expressed as follows:

```
connected(A, B) :- some Path path(A, B, Path).
```

Although the quantifier is redundant logically, it can be used to signify that only one olution should be sought if the global variables are ground. If the global variables are not round, **some** has no effect. **connected** can still be used to generate pairs of connected nodes, lbeit with some repetitions. This contrasts with the version using cut (or **once**,) which would nly ever return one answer.

. IMPLEMENTATION

The implementation we suggest initially transforms the high level constructs, outlined bove, into low level primitives. The transformation can be done by a preprocessor (like our urrent implementation), an early pass of the compiler or a general-purpose macro processor. 'he advantage of compile time transformation is that less work is needed at run time. The ain saving is in explicitly stating global variables, instead of local variables. It is the global ariables that we wait for, test and save in **not**, **if**, **some** and **solutions**. In the following iscussion, we will use V to denote quantified variables and G to denote the global variables, of ie various constructs. The global variables are those which do not appear in the first rgument of **all**, **some** or **solutions**.

if and **not** can be transformed into the same low level primitive:

```
if some V C then A else B  ----->  $if(G, C, A, B)
if some V C then A         ----->  $if(G, C, A, true)

all V not Goal     ----->  $if(G, Goal, fail, true)
not some V Goal    ----->  $if(G, Goal, fail, true)
```

```
$if(G, C, A, B) :-
        when_ground(G, (C, !, A ; B)).
```

hen_ground delays until its first argument is ground, then calls its second argument. We use iis just as a specification of the behaviour of **$if**. In practice, it is best to partially open code nd compile it (being careful about the scope of the cut). If **C** and **A** share quantified variables, e must use "soft cut", which does not destroy choice points in **C**. Otherwise, it is best to use ie normal "hard" cut. Since the computation of the condition cannot bind any global ariables, the implementation of cut can be optimized. Normally, a segment of the trail must e scanned for global variable references, and compacted. In the case of safe negation, this is ot necessary. When the condition is a simple test, such as **<**, it is possible to do even better. /e can emit code to do a test and branch, rather than create a choice point and almost nmediately destroy it.

some can be implemented as follows.

```
some V Goal  ----->  $some(G, Goal)
```

```
$some(G, Goal) :-
     ground(G), !, call(G), !.
$some(G, Goal) :-
     call(G).
```

round(G) succeeds if **G** is ground. As with **$if**, this should be open coded and the implementation of (both) cuts can be optimized.

The implementation of **solutions**, in Prolog, is outlined in [Naish 85b], and we will not go into details here. It relies on the sound implementation of inequality with universal quantifiers (we discuss this application later). The implementation is simplified if the global variables are made explicit, so we apply a transformation similar to the others.

```
solutions(T, some V Goal , S) -----> $solutions(G, T, Goal, S)
```

Implementation of inequality is the most difficult. It is best done with a specialised kernel predicate. The most straightforward method is with a predicate such as **$not_eq/3**. However considerably more flexibility is obtained if we have the power to test for equality and return a result, rather than just succeed or fail. In our implementation, based on [Warren 83], it is best to keep the local variables explicit:

```
all V T1 ~= T2  ----->  $is_eq(V, T1, T2, fail)
```

The semantics of **$is_eq(V, T1, T2, R)** is that of

(∃V T1=T2 ∧ R=true) ∨ (∀V T1≠T2 ∧ R=fail)

Operationally, if **T1** and **T2** unify without binding any global variables, **R** is unified with **true**. If **T1** and **T2** don't unify, **R** is unified with **fail**. Otherwise, **$is_eq** delays, and is retried when it is further instantiated. The retrying can be optimized so identical parts of the two terms are not unified several times. It is sufficient to attempt to unify the frontiers of terms which causes global variables to be bound in the previous attempt. This can sometimes improve the order of efficiency (see [Naish 85c]).

The ability to return a result is very useful for implementing extra control facilities, meta interpreters and other languages, such as Guarded Horn Clauses [Ueda 85]. Of particular importance is the ability to implement equality within **if** well. Consider the following program, which implements a logical term comparison predicate using **compare**†.

```
term_compare(C, T1, T2) :-
     if T1=T2 then
          C = (=)
     else
          compare(C, T1, T2).
```

With the implementation of **if** we outlined, this would unfortunately delay until both terms were ground. Using disjunction and inequality instead can cause nondeterminism and unnecessary computation. With **$is_eq**, we can transform **if**, so it proceeds as soon as the terms are sufficiently instantiated.

```
if some V T1=T2 then A else B ----->
     $is_eq(V, T1, T2, R), if R=true then A else B
```

This transformation is very useful if **$is_eq** is implemented as a kernel predicate. **$is_eq**

† The semantics of term_compare can be defined by an infinite number of facts. This is not true of compare, which is sensitive to the order of execution.

ɔuld also be implemented in terms of a specialised version of **if**, though this seems more ifficult.

. NON-LOGICAL USES

If only local variables are quantified, the implementations we have described are sound. If lobal variables are quantified, they may be instantiated at the time of the call, resulting in nsoundness. In fact all, the standard unsound negation primitives can be implemented in this ay. We give **\+** as an example. Here, **G** is quantified but appears outside the scope of **all**.

```
\+ G :- all G not G.
```

his would be a major drawback of explicit quantifiers were it not for the fact that it can be etected at compile time. The compiler could reject such constructs and force programmers to se the standard unsound primitives for non-logical applications. Should this be done? onsider the following two examples.

```
pick([], _, []).
pick(Term-Glob.Sets, Glob, Term.Set) :-
            pick(Sets, Glob, Set).
pick(Term-Glob1.Sets, Glob, Set) :-
            all Glob1 Glob1 ~= Glob, % Glob1 is global
            pick(Sets, Glob, Set).
```

This is taken from [Naish 85b], and is the part of the implementation of **solutions** which eeds inequality with universal quantifiers (the details of what it does are not important here). iewing **pick** in isolation, it is indeed non-logical. However, from the global view of olutions, variables in **Glob1** in the inequality should indeed be universally quantified. This is uite logical. These semantics cannot be implemented soundly with **\=**, and cannot even be xpressed with implicit quantifiers.

```
sort(In, Out) :- some Out slowsort(In, Out).
```

slowsort is an example of a predicate which, when called with the first argument ground, as only one solution, even though its execution creates many choice points (generating ermutations and testing them). Thus, the use of **some** here is sound and, when **In** is ground, ill save half the execution time on average.

Having gone to so much trouble implementing sound negation primitives, it does seem a ame to prevent their use in examples such as these. The syntax is also useful for expressing mantics more clearly in many meta level applications. We conclude that quantified global ariables should be allowed. However, in keeping with the principle that non-logical code ould be clearly distinguished from logical code, we use a different syntax for the quantifiers. NU-Prolog, the quantifiers **all** and **some** do not allow global variables, but **g_all** and **some** (with the same meaning) do. Our current implementation is the same, except that some the optimizations (such as that for cut) are not possible. With **if**, **not**, **some** and **~=**, **all** and **g_some** give more power than the logical plus standard non-logical primitives.

Given that we have all the power of the standard unsound primitives (and more), it i natural to ask if we need them. Unfortunately, portability dictates than they should b available. However, their use should be actively discouraged, to eliminate the ba programming habits which have been acquired. One way to do this is provide less debuggin support. The same argument applies to cut. The techniques [O'Keefe 85] gives for eliminatin cuts can be applied to NU-Prolog.

Two research problems associated with **g_all** and **g_some** are still being investigated Firstly, we hope to integrate them into **solutions** more, so that answers containing copies o local variables may be returned (this is non-logical). Secondly, there is a potential ambiguity i the operational semantics. At run time, a quantified variable and an unquantified variable ma be bound to (a term containing) the same variable. Such variables are currently treated a quantified in `~=` and unquantified in other constructs. This is due to the difference in wha variables are explicit in the low level primitives. The alternative treatment may sometimes b useful, though the implementation is less efficient.

6. EXTENDED PROLOG

Extended Prolog [Lloyd 84] allows quantifiers and extra connectives, such as implication It is currently implemented on top of MU-Prolog, using a library predicate to implement soun negation with quantifiers. We agree with this approach, and NU-Prolog is an ideal targe language. The ideas in this paper are not intended to be a substitute for Extended Prolog Instead, we have attempted to extract the fundamental constructs which should b implemented at the lower level, where the programmer has complete control over th operational semantics. The only one of these that Extended Prolog currently uses is **not**. B utilising NU-Prolog's richer set of primitives more fully, the implementation can be considerabl improved. It must also be made more complex, of course, and some control decisions must b made.

Firstly `~=` should be used where appropriate, rather than using `=` and **not**, which delay until ground. Secondly, **some** should be used. Currently, Extended Prolog discards suc existential quantifiers. As we have shown, this can result in extra computation and repeate solutions. Automatic insertion of existential quantifiers is not trivial, since it depends on th order of subgoals, which is a control decision. Finally, Extended Prolog does not currently us **if**. It could be used to implement existential quantifiers and some disjunctions. For example, i is generally better to implement `(A -> B)` as `(if A then B)`, where possible, rather tha `(not A ; B)`. These are also control decisions.

7. CONVENTIONAL PROLOG IMPLEMENTATIONS

Without the ability to delay calls, the style of programming with negation is necessaril restricted. Despite this, conventional Prolog systems would benefit considerably by adoptin the negation constructs of NU-Prolog. With just a simple unsound implementation, th language additions encourage a more logical style of programming and make semantics muc clearer. Providing soundly implemented primitives is even better. Instead of delaying whe sufficiently instantiated, the primitives could just print an error message and possibly abort. his is sufficient to stop misuse of the logical primitives, and can be used for debugging normal se. The DEC-10 Prolog library predicate **not** is implemented like this. A dual system could e used to avoid any loss of speed. For testing and debugging, sound negation primitives should e used, but for final compilation, the fastest (probably unsound) primitives could be used stead.

To encourage the use of the NU-Prolog negation constructs, we have implemented such a stem for the DEC-10 family of Prologs. It takes the form of two preprocessors and some brary predicates for the sound negation primitives. Many systems should be able to use hooks ke **expand_term** to transform the constructs, rather than separate preprocessors. Sound ersions of **$some**, **$if** and **$is_eq** (or **$not_eq**) are quite easy to implement, though without ft cut, **if** must sometimes be implemented by calling the condition twice. The unsound nplementation uses **once**, \+, ->, \= and **setof**, which are all open-coded.

. CONCLUSIONS

Very few Prolog implementations have sound implementations of negation built in. This, e lack of quantifiers and poor programming style result in unclear semantics for most Prolog rograms. The design of the negation primitives in NU-Prolog enables and encourages mantics to be expressed clearly, by using explicit quantifiers and sound primitives. Non-gical applications can also be implemented in this framework. These constructs can be used improve the treatment of negation in all Prolog systems. The specific implementation in U-Prolog allows far greater flexibility than any previous Prolog system:

1) Soundness is achieved by delaying calls to primitives when they are insufficiently instantiated.

2) The explicit quantifiers on **not**, **if** and ~= give greater expressive power than in other systems.

3) **some**, a logical analogue of **once**, has been implemented for the first time.

4) A sound and efficient all solutions predicate is available.

5) Quantified variables in **if** can be used in the **then** clause.

6) **$is_eq** gives more flexibility than inequality, in a variety of applications.

7) Having a single set of negation constructs but allowing **g_all** and **g_some**, gives more power than the logical and standard non-logical constructs together.

Our implementation is based on various forms of **$if**, **$some** and **$is_eq**. This small set primitives can be implemented efficiently using current techniques, and forms an excellent sis for the many higher-level constructs.

9. REFERENCES

[Bowen 82]

D. L. Bowen, L. Byrd, F. C. N. Pereira, L. M. Pereira and D. H. D. Warren, Decsystem-10 Prolog User's Manual, Occasional Paper 27, DAI, University of Edinburgh, 1982.

[Bowen 85]

K. A. Bowen and T. Weinberg, A Meta-Level Extension of Prolog, *Proceedings of the 2nd IEEE International Symposium on Logic Programming*, Boston, July, 1985.

[Carlsson 83]

M. Carlsson and K. M. Kahn, LM-Prolog User Manual, UPMAIL Technical Report 24, Computer Science Department, Uppsala University, Sweden, 1983.

[Lloyd 84]

J. W. Lloyd and R. W. Topor, Making Prolog More Expressive, *Journal of Logic Programming 4*, (1984).

[Naish 85a]

L. Naish, The MU-Prolog 3.2 Reference Manual, Technical Report 85/11, Department of Computer Science, University of Melbourne, November 1985.

[Naish 85b]

L. Naish, All Solutions Predicates in Prolog, *Proceedings of IEEE Symposium on Logic Programming*, Boston, July, 1985.

[Naish 85c]

L. Naish, Negation and Control in PROLOG, Technical Report 85/12, Ph.D. Thesis Department of Computer Science, University of Melbourne, 1985.

[O'Keefe 85]

R. A. O'Keefe, On the Treatment of Cuts in Prolog Source-Level Tools, *Proceedings of the 2nd IEEE International Symposium on Logic Programming*, Boston, July, 1985.

[Schultz 84]

J. W. Schultz, The Use Of First-order Predicate Calculus As A Logic Programming System, M.Sc Thesis, Department Of Computer Science, University Of Melbourne, 1984.

[Ueda 85]

K. Ueda, Guarded Horn Clauses, Technical Report TR-103, ICOT, 1985.

[Warren 83]

D. H. D. Warren, An Abstract Prolog Instruction Set, Technical Report 309, Artificial Intelligence Center, SRI International, 1983.

Gracefully adding negation and disjunction to Prolog

David L Poole
Randy Goebel

Logic Programming and Artificial Intelligence Group
Department of Computer Science
University of Waterloo
Waterloo, Ontario, Canada N2L 3G1

Abstract

We show how one can add negation and disjunction to Prolog, with the property that there is no overhead in run time if we do not use the negation, and we only pay for the negation when we actually use it. The extension is based on Loveland's MESON proof procedure, which requires that a negative ancestor search and availability of contrapostive forms of formulae be added to Prolog. We identify a property of literals that can be statically determined, in order to avoid using the full generality of the full clausal proof procedure when not required.

1. Introduction

There are two reasons for wanting to add negation to Prolog. The first is a desire to express incomplete knowledge of some domain. For example we may know that someone's professor is either David or Robin, but we don't know which. The second is that we may want our system to have predictive power [Poole86]. That is, we desire a system that maintains a consistent refutable theory which should have predictive power. This requires an ability to demonstrate inconsistency, or to derive a contradiction.

In Poole et al. [Poole86] we exploit a general method of adding negation and disjunction to Prolog. This is the known technique of using the contrapositives of all formulae and searching back up the relevant "and" branches of the resolution proof tree for the complement of each newly generated subgoal [Umrigar85, Loveland78].

There is a folklore that Horn clauses can be made efficient, but if we add negation, then we get to a full resolution system [Robinson65] which are inherently inefficient. When constructing a system for diagnosing faults (based on DART [Genesereth85]) in electrical circuits, we found that much of the knowledge could be specified as Prolog assertions, and didn't require the ancestor search or all contrapositive forms. It then occured to us that there were classes of formulae which could be detected before search time, which could be expressed as Prolog assertions, and so gain the corresponding efficiency. Here we attempt to characterise such classes. It is intended that one would be able to add clauses to a collection of assertions and let the system automatically detect where Horn-clause-like (although the class is larger then just Horn clauses) implementation strategies can be used. Note that we need not restrict ourselve to clausal systems, as one of us has previously shown how to transform clausal theorem-provers into non-clausal theorem-provers [Poole84].

The goal here is to determine when the general procedure is unnecessary, so that the overhead of using the contrapositive formulae and searching back up the proof tree is, when possible, avoided. We do this by defining a syntactic classification of atomic symbols in a general clause which allows us to statically determine subgoals for which the use of contrapositives or the ancestor search is unnecessary. This class is larger than that of definite clauses. Of course a corollary is that if a subsystem is definite, then it can be implemented as Prolog. We thus pay for the extra cost for using true negation only when necessary and only in the cases where it will make a difference.

Notice that adding negation to Prolog is equivalent to adding disjunction, as $a \vee b$ is equivalent to $a \leftarrow \neg b$.

2. Syntax

Here we present a syntax that will incorporate normal clause form and Prolog's definite clauses as special cases. We first define an atomic symbol to be as in Prolog. A **literal** is an atom or the negation of an atom. The negation of a is written $\neg a$. A **clause** has the form

$$L_1 \vee \cdots \vee L_k \leftarrow L_{k+1} \wedge \cdots \wedge L_n ;$$

where L_i is a literal. If $k=1$ and all of the literals are atoms then this is a definite clause, as in Prolog. If $k=n$ then we have the normal definition of a clause [Chang73, Robinson79].

We assume the commutativity and associativity of conjunction and disjunction. Semantically, the order of the literals in the left and right parts of a clause is irrelevant. Note that in a particular proof procedure the order may affect the efficiency or the completeness, and so it may be appropriate to modify the search strategy for the particular problem.

As in Prolog we have the notion of a query. The query

$$?L_1 \wedge \cdots \wedge L_n ;$$

is defined to mean, add to the current set of clauses C the clause

$$? \leftarrow L_1 \wedge \cdots \wedge L_n ;$$

where "*?*" is a new atom, then ask the question, "is *?* a logical consequence of the given clauses."

3. Semantics

The interpretation of the set of clauses C is the normal model-theoretic semantics, viz.

P	*true*	*false*	*true*	*false*
Q	*true*	*true*	*false*	*false*
$\neg P$	*false*	*true*	*false*	*true*
$P \wedge Q$	*true*	*false*	*false*	*false*
$P \vee Q$	*true*	*true*	*true*	*false*
$P \leftarrow Q$	*true*	*false*	*true*	*true*

An answer *yes* means that *?* is a logical consequence of the clause set C. That is, *?* is true in every model of C.

In summary, a clause is false in some interpretation if and only if all of the $L_1, \cdots, L_k$ are false, and $L_{k+1}, \cdots, L_n$ are all true in that interpretation. The following lemma trivially follows from the semantics:

Lemma 1. We can swap a literal from one side of the "$\leftarrow$" to the other if we negate it.

For any clause c, a **contrapositive** of c is the clause with exactly one literal on the left hand side of the "$\leftarrow$," that results from applying lemma 1 to c. Note that if there are n literals in a clause, there are n contrapositive forms of that clause.

The **normal form** of a clause c is an equivalent clause without any negation symbols (i.e., any literal with a not sign, is moved to the other side of the arrow). Note that any clause has a unique normal form (up to associativity and commutativity of conjunction and disjunction). For example the clause $a \vee b \leftarrow c \wedge \neg d$ has the contrapositive forms

$a \leftarrow \neg b \wedge c \wedge \neg d$
$b \leftarrow \neg a \wedge c \wedge \neg d$
$\neg c \leftarrow \neg a \wedge \neg b \wedge \neg d$
$d \leftarrow \neg a \wedge \neg b \wedge c$

nd the normal form $a \vee b \vee d \leftarrow c$.

. The proof procedure

The Prolog proof procedure is augmented to have accessible (1) the contrapositive of ach clause in the clause set C, and (2) to search up the relevant proof tree branch for the egation of the current subgoal. The second modification corresponds to "reductio ad bsurdum" or "proof by contradiction." (See Umrigar and Pitchumani [Umrigar85] for an xample implementation in Prolog.)

We define the negative ancestor rule as "If g is a subgoal which unifies with the negaion of an ancestor, then we can mark g proven."

The proof procedure becomes: a goal g is proven if (1) there is a contrapositive form f an input clause that unifies with g, such that all of the literals on the right hand side of he contrapositive form are proven, or (2) g unifies with an ancestor literal $\neg g$ such that ll substitutions are consistent.

```
% prove (G ,A ) is true if and only if Clauses ⊨A ⊃G
prove (G ,A )←
        member (G ,A );
prove (G ,A )←
        clause (G ,B )
        neg (G ,GN )
        proveall (B ,[GN |A ]);

% proveall (L ,A ) is true iff Clauses ⊨A ⊃Lᵢ for each Lᵢ∈L
proveall ([],A );
proveall ([G |R ],A )←
        prove (G ,A )
        proveall (R ,A );

% neg (X ,Y ) is true if X is the negative of Y , both in their simplest form
neg (not (X ),X )←
        ne (X ,not (Y ));
neg (X ,not (X ))←
        ne (X ,not (Y ));

% clause (H ,B ) is true if there is the contrapositive form of an input clause
%     such that H is the head, and B is the body.
%     in particular, we know Clauses ⊨B ⊃H
```

Figure 1 Full clausal theorem prover in Prolog

We can express this procedure in terms of a Prolog provable relation (cf. [Bowen82, Bowen85]) as in fig. 1. The following theorem holds for the proof procedure of fig. 1:

Theorem 1. The proof procedure is correct with respect to the above semantics, and is complete in the sense that if *?* is logically entailed by a consistent set of clauses, then there is a proof for *?*.

Proof. (1) Correctness. To prove the correctness, we need to show that each of the rules above is true with respect to the intended interpretation. The first clause of the definition of *prove* is correct as it says, "If $G \in A$ then $L \supset A$," which is trivially correct. The second clause for *prove* says "If $Clauses \models B \supset G$ and $Clauses \models A \cup \{\neg G\} \supset B$ then $Clauses \models A \supset G$", which is true by transitivity of implication, and by noticing that "if $Clauses \models A \cup \{\neg G\} \supset G$ then $Clauses \models A \supset G$."

(2) Completeness follows directly from the completeness of MESON proof procedure [Loveland78].

5. Prolog compatible subsystems

Now arises the question that, if we have a set C of general clauses, must we always have available all contrapositives and search up the tree, or can we statically determine conditions under which we do not need to do these things? If so, a portion of our processing can be as efficient as Prolog. In particular, we would like to pay the extra cost only in proportion to our use of the extra-Prolog features. Of course, if all of the clauses are indeed definite then we do not require the modifications. However, we would also like to see if there is some larger class of clauses for which we do not need to use the contrapositives and search up the tree; i.e., to determine, if possible, some non-trivial subset of the clause set C for which the modifications can be ignored.

To do so, first define a literal L to be **relevant** within a set of clauses if L is provable within the context of its ancestors. That is L can be proven under the assumption of $\neg M$ for ancestors M of L. In other words, we can generate a set A such that *prove* (L, A) can be derived.

Now consider the cases where we actually need to search up the tree from a goal g to find an ancestor unifying with $\neg g$. All of the three following conditions below must hold for the ancestor search to be useful:

1. $\neg g$ is relevant;
2. $\neg g$ is askable (i.e., can be generated as a subgoal) and
3. within a subproof of $\neg g$ we can generate a subgoal of g.

If one of the above conditions cannot occur, then we do not need to consider searching for a negated ancestor of g.

The second concern is with conditions under which we need to form the contrapositive of a rule so that L is on the left hand side. This is required when:

1. L is askable and
2. L is relevant

If one of the conditions 1 or 2 cannot be the case, then we do not need the contrapositive forms. Of course the first case is uninteresting as if L is never asked the contrapositive will never be used.

Now the idea is to describe a way to statically determine, for some set of literals, that the contrapositive or the searching for a negated ancestor is unnecessary.

.1. Statically determined classes of predicates

We define weaker notions of relevant and askable which can be computed at compile ime, namely **potentially relevant** and **potentially askable**. If some goal is neither potenially relevant nor potentially askable, we do not need contrapositive forms where that iteral is on the left hand side. We need only do an ancesor search if both it and it's negaion are potentially relevant and potentially askable.

Potentially askable is a relation on signed predicate symbols and sets of signed predicate symbols. If L is a literal, the signed predicate symbol **corresponding** to L has the same sign as L and the predicate symbol of the atom composing L. Intuitively, the signed predicate symbol of L is obtained by stripping the arguments from the atom in L. Potenially relevant is a property of signed predicate symbols.

Potentially askable is defined as:

1) $?$, exported symbols or signed predicate symbols are potentially askable relative to {} (see discussion of section 5 for explanation of exported symbols);

2) if p is potentially askable relative to S, and L is a literal corresponding to p, and $L \leftarrow L_1 \wedge \cdots \wedge L_k$ is the contrapositive of a clause, then each p_i corresponding to L_i such that $p_i \notin S$ is potentially askable relative to $\{p\} \cup S$.

Potentially relevant is defined as:

1) if p is potentially askable relative to S and $\neg p \in S$ then p is potentially relevant;

2) if $L \leftarrow L_1 \wedge \cdots \wedge L_k$ is the contrapositive of a clause such that L corresponds to p, and if the p_i corresponding to the L_i are potentially relevant, then so is p.

Theorem: if L is relevant and askable, then its corresponding signed literal is potentially relevant and potentially askable.

Proof: assume L is relevant and askable. Consider the proof tree containing L. Transform this into a tree containing the signed predicated corresponding to the literals in the proof tree. Remove all paths in the tree which form cycles (i.e., if there is a p as an ancestor of p, then remove that branch and all associated subtrees). This tree then shows that p is potentially askable and potentially relevant.

Corollary: Only if a literal is potentially relevant and potentially askable do we need consider contrapositives of rules with it on the left hand side.

Corrolary: We need only search ancestors for negated literals if both the literal and its negation are both potentially askable and potentially relevant.

Proposition: Given a set of definite clauses, the determination of potentially relevant and potentialy askable is adequate to show that we need only consider the normal Prolog search tree (i.e. we need never consider other contrapositive forms, or need to do an ancestor search).

Proof: the negative of a predicate symbol is never potentially askable. This is because given a subgoal which is a negative atom, we always produce one more subgoal which is a negative atom. All ancestors are negative so the negative ancestor rule never works, and we never have one potentially provable. The procedure terminates as there are only a finite number of signed predicates to consider.

6. Implementation

The properties potentially relevant and potentially provable are decidable and can be computed at input time. We need only consider is what elements are potentially askable relative to {}. There are three possibilities, depending on how much we know about potential queries:

1. If we know what forms a query may take, then we only need make the corresponding signed predictes potentially askable relative to {}, and deriving all other potentially askable things from this.

2. If we have a module system with restricted exports, we can make the syntactic restrictions for each module and make the classes local to each module. By restricting the exports from each module, we can then make the elements of the export list initially askable relative to {}. As all calls inside the module are assumed to be local, we need not worry about negative calls outside the module.
3. The other possibility is to consider each possible call that can be given the system. That is make every signed predicate symbol potentially askable relative to {}. This is not as bad as it may seem, as if some signed predicate has been considered askable relative to anything then we have no need to reconsider it as askable relative to the empty set. We can also stop attemtps to prove potential askability if we have found a subgoal which has already been proven to be potentially relevant.

7. Compiling Into Prolog

The way we have used this is to compile the clauses into Horn clauses. This is done as follows:

If some atom, L, and its negation are both potentially askable and potentially relevant, then we replace it with $pr(L,A)$ and its negation with $pr(n(L),A)$, and make the first rule in the definition of L and $n(L)$,

$$pr(L,A) \leftarrow member(n(L),A);$$
$$pr(n(L),A) \leftarrow member(L,A);$$

We then create contrapositives of all rules such that only potentially askable and provable predicates appear on the left hand side of the rule. Those rules with a pr on the left hand side and the right hand side must add the head element to the ancestor list on the right hand side. For example the clause $h \leftarrow t$, where h, $\neg h$, t and $\neg t$ are potentially askable and provable becomes

$$pr(h,A) \leftarrow pr(t,[h|A]);$$
$$pr(n(t),A) \leftarrow pr(n(h),[n(t)|A]);$$

8. Example

Consider the following set of clauses (with all arguments removed); note there is a recursive call between c, $\neg e$ and g.

$a \leftarrow b \wedge c;$
$a \vee b \leftarrow d;$
$c \vee e \leftarrow f;$
$\neg g \leftarrow e;$
$g \leftarrow c;$
$g;$
$f \leftarrow h;$
$h;$
$d;$

The following are both potentially askable and potentially relevant: a, $\neg a$, b, $\neg b$, c, d $\neg e$, f, g, h. Therefore we need only check the contrapositive and ancestors of a and b Note that all but the first two clauses can be implemented as Prolog clauses, even though they are not.

9. Conclusion

We have shown a general method for adding true negation and disjunction to a Horn Clause language. We have given a method for statically determining cases for which we do not need to use the extra machinery and can compute answers with the same machinery as for Horn Clause logic.

This technique is currently being implemented in the Theorist system [Poole86], which requires negation to prove that theories are inconsistent.

Acknowledgements

This research was supported by National Sciences and Engineering Research Council of Canada grant A0894.

References

[Bowen82] K. Bowen and R.A. Kowalski (1982), Amalgamating language and metalanguage in logic programming, *Logic Programming*, A.P.I.C. Studies in Data Processing 16, K.L. Clark and S.-A. Tarnlund (eds.), Academic Press, New York, 153-172.

[Bowen85] K.A Bowen and T. Weinberg (1985), A meta-level extension of Prolog, *IEEE 1985 Symposium on Logic Programming*, July 15-18, Boston, Massachusetts, 48-53.

[Chang73] C.L. Chang and R.C.T. Lee (1973), *Symbolic Logic and Mechanical Theorem Proving*, Academic Press, New York.

[Genesereth85] M.R. Genesereth (1985), The use of design descriptions in automated diagnosis, *Qualitative Reasoning about Physical Systems*, D.G. Bobrow (eds.), MIT Press, Cambridge, Massachusetts, 411-436.

[Loveland78] D.W. Loveland (1978), *Automated theorem proving: a logical basis*, North-Holland, Amsterdam, The Netherlands.

[Poole84] D. Poole (1984), Making "clausal" theorem provers "non-clausal", *Proceedings of the Fifth Biennal Conference of the Canadian Society for the Computational Studies of Intelligence*, May 15-17, University of Western Ontario, London, Ontario, 124-126.

[Poole86] D.L. Poole, R.G. Goebel, and R. Aleliunas (1986), Theorist: a logical reasoning system for defaults and diagnosis, *Knowledge Representation*, N.J. Cercone and G. McCalla (eds.), Springer-Verlag, New York [invited chapter, submitted September 10, 1985].

[Robinson65] J.A. Robinson (1965), A machine-oriented logic based on the resolution principle, *ACM Journal* **12**(1), 23-41.

[Robinson79] J.A. Robinson (1979), *Logic: Form and Function*, Artificial Intelligence Series 6, Elsevier North Holland, New York.

[Umrigar85] Z.D. Umrigar and V. Pitchumani (1985), An experiment in programming with full first-order logic, *IEEE 1985 Symposium on Logic Programming*, July 15-18, Boston, Massachusetts, 40-47.

Memory Performance of Lisp and Prolog Programs[1]

Evan Tick
Computer Systems Laboratory
Stanford University

Abstract

A comparison between a Lisp and Prolog architecture based on memory performance i presented. Four Lisp programs were translated into Common Lisp and Prolog abstrac machine instruction sets. The translated programs were emulated and memory referenc counts collected. Memory usage statistics indicate how the two languages d fundamental computations in different ways with varying efficiency. Additiona measurements of commercial systems running on a conventional host are presented.

Introduction

A comparison between program languages is a perilous undertaking. With sentimen often running high[1, 2], comparing Lisp and Prolog is fraught with danger. This pape compares the memory performance of a subset of the Gabriel benchmarks[3] formulated i Common Lisp and Prolog. The programs were compiled into abstract machin architectures that were emulated and memory reference statistics collected. Ra measurements are biased by the compilers, architectures and methods of emulation. Fo example, the Common Lisp compiler does a poor job of translating two dimension arrays (primarily due to the complexity of the Common Lisp specification) and y Prolog doesn't even have arrays. The Prolog architecture sports a complex instruction s compared to the Common Lisp architecture, which has a more reduced instruction set.

The Common Lisp statistics were generated by instrumenting an experiment Common Lisp compiler written at Hewlett Packard. In order to maintain portabilit among several different architectures, this Common Lisp compiler generates code for a abstract register-based Lisp machine, similar to that used by Portable Standard Lisp The abstract Lisp machine code is then translated to code for the target machine, in thi case an HP9000 Series 237. Measurements given in this paper were made by modifyin the abstract machine code generated for each benchmark to include instructions fo incrementing counters to reflect the dynamic referencing activity.

---

[1]The work described herein was supported by an IBM Graduate Fellowship and by NASA-Am under consortium NCA2-1R745-406

The Warren abstract machine (WAM) architecture[5] was used to collect Prolog atistics. The Prolog system measured is described in Tick[6] with the exception of the ompiler. The compiler has been extended to include generation of efficient code for ithmetic expressions, lifting of simple first goals to the head, and introduction of onditional branches allowing peephole removal of choice point instructions.

Differences Between Lisp and Prolog

In this discussion, "Lisp" and "Prolog" are used synonomously with the Lisp and rolog dialects, architectures and compilers used in this study. Certainly there is no ındamental limitation preventing either language from emulating features of the other; owever, the languages were initially designed to support different programming aradigms. Thus Prolog, for example, avoids implementing destructive array operations ıd gotos. The Lisp design philosophy has become muddled through the years. If one onsiders Common Lisp a standard, this implies a bias towards a large, general purpose nguage. In this respect, one may consider Prolog's logical framework a hinderance to ktensibility.

Both compilers are constrained by a design criteria of portability and therefore mplicity. For instance, the Lisp compiler does not optimize across `cond` clauses, sallowing an optimization wherein stack frame creation is avoided before a trivial ause. For Prolog, this optimization is explicitly incorporated into the architecture with parate `call` and `allocate` instructions.

Both architectures are based on a register set through which procedure arguments are ıssed and a stack in which procedure frames hold local variables. The number of gument registers used in the measured programs are approximately equal for the two chitectures. Not suprisingly, the Lisp architecture has fewer state registers than Prolog. his is primarily because of two operations built into the Prolog architecture: unification ıd backtracking. Prolog's ability to backtrack requires at least three state registers (`B`, `B`, `TR`). Prolog unification uses at least two temporary registers.

The Lisp linkage convention is simpler than the Prolog linkage. The Lisp caller kecutes a `link` instruction, which pushes a return address on the exec stack (estack). he callee executes an `exit` instruction which pops the return address. The Lisp ocedure stack is a pure stack, and the compiler knows the size of each frame, so that ıkage between frames and/or frame sizes are not needed. Prolog linkage can be either mpler or more complex than Lisp, i.e., a frame is not necessarily created. The Prolog ıller does not push a return address, but rather loads the continuation pointer, `CP`, with e program counter, `P`. A trivial callee, i.e. a unit clause or a clause with trivial goals, turns by resuming control at `CP`. A callee with non-trivial goals pushes `CP` onto the ocedure stack. A callee with local variables (permanent variables) must also push a pointer to the previous frame because the Prolog procedure stack is not a pure stack, i.e the currently active frame need not be on the top of stack. Two other words of optiona information are included in the frame for this implementation. Both Lisp and Prolo architectures implement tail recursion (last call) optimization.

Both architectures pass arguments through registers. A Lisp function, by conventio returns a result through register one. Prolog passes both input arguments and (possibl zero or multiple) output arguments though registers with no convention for allocatio The Lisp compiler does not optimize register usage to allow directly using values fro the argument registers. All code in the body of a function accesses arguments from th stack frame. The Prolog compiler does optimize this type of register usage. Argumen registers are used whenever possible, and only saved into a frame when unsafe condition prevail (subsequent predicates must be called).

Measurements

The programs chosen from the Gabriel benchmarks - Tak, Deriv, Puzzle and Boyer were selected because others purposely used destructive operations which could not b expressed in Prolog without algorithmic transformation. Thus the selection may b viewed as favoring Prolog *by default*, i.e. programs problematic to Prolog ar conspicuously absent. Nevertheless, these programs, as a group and I assum individually, are supposedly representative of Lisp usage.

Note that garbage is not collected in these tests. The programs were coded in Prolo using the same algorithms and input data as the Lisp programs, with data structure natural to Prolog (source listings and raw measurements are presented in Tick[7]). Deriv i an exception, where the natural Prolog definition, based on a binary expression tre requires an algorithm different from that of Lisp, based on the use of `mapcar`. Note th Deriv takes the derivative of `3*x*x+a*x*x+b*x+5` just once, c.f., Gabriel[3]. Th answers produced, simplified differently, include 17 operators for Lisp and 20 operato for Prolog.

Calls to Common Lisp functions were recorded either as invocations of "builtin primitive functions (e.g. `cons` or `symbol-function`) or, when the functions were n considered primitive (e.g. `member` or `equal`), the references were recorded fo instrumented versions of the system functions. Prolog considered builtin predicates suc as `arg/3` and `functor/3` primitives, and counted only data references (and on instruction reference) for these. Prolog counted trials in Puzzle using special purpos primitives to avoid the overheads of `assert/1` and `retract/1`.

Dynamic reference statistics are shown in Table 1. The raw data counts precede simpl statistics. The instructions per procedure call are the least accurate, specifically fo

	Tak			Boyer		
	Lisp	Prolog	L/P	Lisp	Prolog	L/P
proc calls	63609	63608		890666	319978	
instr exec	683792	811008		9093949	4108606	
data ref	667891	508865	1.31	8200807	6909376	1.19
instr ref	747401	938226	0.80	12078345	4784395	2.52
instr/proc	10.75	12.75		10.21	12.84	
data ref/instr	0.97	0.63		0.90	1.68	
instr ref/instr	1.09	1.16		1.33	1.16	

	Deriv			Puzzle		
	Lisp	Prolog	L/P	Lisp	Prolog	L/P
proc calls	38	18		21350	19831	
instr exec	598	269		12172280	499477	
data ref	515	520	1.01	3711662	827041	4.49
instr ref	708	361	1.96	15759345	609068	25.9
instr/proc	15.63	14.94		570.10	25.19	
data ref/instr	0.87	1.93		0.30	1.65	
instr ref/instr	1.19	1.34		1.29	1.22	

Table 1: Dynamic Reference Characteristics of Benchmarks

olog because entry into redo ports is not counted. For the majority of the programs, the sp architecture displays the simple nature of its instruction set, producing a lower mber of memory references per instruction than Prolog. In contrast, Prolog displays e complex nature of its instruction set, producing a lower number of instructions ecuted. The Lisp instruction formats are more precisely defined than the Prolog rmats. Counts of Prolog instruction words fetched are conservative to facilitate nulator implementation. For these reasons, instructions executed are not an accurate atistic in this study. It does, however, give a gross indication of how well the mapping om source language to the host architecture is for these particular programs.

ref/instr	weight	Lisp	Prolog	Prolog + shadow regs
data	by program	0.76	1.47	0.99
	by reference	0.73	1.52	1.02
instr	by program	1.23	1.22	1.22
	by reference	1.30	1.17	1.17

Table 2: Mean References Per Instruction

The reference statistics are summarized in Table 2. Prolog shadow registers are a cond bank of state registers used to buffer choice points, eliminating the need to ference memory during shallow backtracking[6]. Tak is not affected by shadow registers cause no backtracking occurs. The other programs have their total data references duced by 36% on average - all savings coming from a reduction in choice point ferences. Table 3 summarizes the percentage of references made to each memory area.

A high variance exists due to the anomalies, Tak and Puzzle. For both languages reference types, ordered by required bandwidth, are code, stack and heap. Shadov registers is an example of hardware that exploits locality in Prolog backtracking. Othe Prolog memory organizations, optimizing other types of references, are described an measured in Tick[6]. Similar Lisp memory organizations have also been analyzed, fo instance RISC I register windows studied by Ponder[8].

lisp	Tak	Boyer	Deriv	Puzzle
frame	40.4%	23.2	23.7	5.1
estack	6.7	5.5	6.0	0.2
fluid	0.0	1.3	1.3	4.9
heap	0.0	10.4	11.1	8.8
code	52.8	59.6	57.9	80.9

prolog	Tak	Boyer	Deriv	Puzzle
cp	0.0	23.9	25.3	25.9
env	35.2	18.8	15.3	2.3
heap	0.0	11.0	16.5	23.9
trail	0.0	1.5	1.9	5.4
pdl	0.0	4.0	0.0	0.0
code	64.8	40.9	41.0	42.4

Table 3: Relative Memory Area Referencing Statistics

Tak is meant to solely exercise tight, tail recursive procedure calls. The Prolo compiler optimizes Tak data references somewhat better than Lisp at the cost of a increased number of instruction references. A previous, less efficient Prolog compile produced significantly worse code (which included a choice point) making 56% mo data references than the current Prolog compiler. For the other benchmarks, neith Prolog compiler optimizes to any advantage. Puzzle is highly variant because the patter matching portion of the algorithm maps significantly more efficiently onto Prolog tha Lisp.

Deriv and Boyer data references are similar in number for Lisp and Prolog. Th complete set of measurements for Boyer, a mock theorem prover and the most "realistic of the programs, are given in Table 4. Prolog makes an equal percentage of da references to the stack (cp + env = 72%) as Lisp (frame + estack = 71%). With shado registers, however, Prolog stack references are reduced to 57%. One cost of th reduction is an increase in the relative percentage of heap references, an area displayin less locality. In general, Prolog displays a lower ratio of reads to writes as compared wi Lisp and procedural languages. In the stack, this is attributed to the Prolog emulato which writes four bookkeeping words per environment - Lisp writes one word. In Boye although Prolog makes fewer heap references than Lisp, it makes almost twice th number of Lisp heap writes. This is caused by extensive structure copying in the Prolc architecture. A structure sharing Prolog architecture would certainly do better here.

isp

rea	read	%	write	%	total	%	%
ame	2985383	63.3	1720907	36.6	4706290	23.2	57.4
uid	134593	53.8	126343	46.2	260936	1.3	3.2
eap	1656306	78.8	452894	21.2	2109200	10.4	25.7
stack	562191	50.0	562190	50.0	1124381	5.5	13.7
ode	12078345	100.0	0	0.0	12078345	59.6	
otal	17416818	85.9	2862334	14.1	20279152		

rolog

rea	read	%	write	%	total	%	%
p	1079577	38.7	1710154	61.3	2789731	23.9	40.4
nv	1233111	56.0	967551	44.0	2200662	18.8	31.9
eap	435842	34.0	846213	66.0	1282055	11.0	18.6
ail	38348	22.3	133680	77.7	172028	1.5	2.5
dl	231480	49.8	233420	50.2	464900	4.0	6.7
ode	4784395	100.0	0	0.0	4784395	40.9	
otal	7802753	66.7	3891018	33.3	11693771		

rolog with shadow registers

rea	read	%	write	%	total	%	%
p	235852	74.6	80145	25.4	315997	3.4	7.1
nv	1233111	56.0	967551	44.0	2200662	23.9	49.6
eap	435842	34.0	846213	66.0	1282055	13.9	28.9
ail	38348	22.3	133680	77.7	172028	1.9	3.9
dl	230616	49.8	232556	50.2	463172	5.0	10.4
ode	4784395	100.0	0	0.0	4784395	51.9	
otal	6958164	75.5	2260145	24.5	9218309		

Table 4: Boyer Measurements

Sun-3 Comparisons

Table 5 presents execution times of the programs running on a 16MHz Sun-3[9]. Sun ommon Lisp compiles into native code and Quintus Prolog compiles into abstract achine code (different than WAM) which is emulated, therefore care should be taken omparing these measurements among themselves and to previous measurements. Boyer nd Deriv illustrate that the Lisp is well-mapped onto the Sun, whereas the Prolog is artially-mapped. I believe the fluctuation between Puzzle and Tak (in Table 5) is rimarily due to the compilers.

Warren reports that Prolog Deriv is 1.1 to 2.6 times faster than Lisp Deriv[10]; however, e was measuring different systems (DEC10 Prolog and Stanford Lisp), a different Lisp nction and different input data. DEC10 Prolog *is* compiled into native code, possibly aking his comparison more fair than the one presented here.

program	Sun Common Lisp	Quintus Prolog	Lisp:Prolog
Boyer	15.08 sec	25.50 sec	0.59
Deriv	4.24 sec	6.30 sec	0.67
Puzzle	8.44 sec	2.43 sec	3.47
Tak	0.47 sec	4.59 sec	0.10

Table 5: Lisp - Prolog Comparison on a Sun-3

The SUN-3 statistics are given, despite the numerous caveats, to complement th abstract machine measurements. Certain programs favor Lisp whereas previously Prolo was favored. This difference emphasizes that the Prolog abstract machine mode assumes available all necessary state registers and state transfers.

Conclusions

Evidence was given that Prolog has greater *semantic content* than Lisp. Two resul were given based on the assumption that memory bandwidth is the fundament performance bottleneck.

The first result was that Lisp is better mapped onto current machines than Prolog. Th was tenuously supported by comparisons between commercially available Lisp an Prolog systems. Although "apples vs. oranges", comparing these implementations serve to indicate that Lisp runs faster than Prolog on hardware with a limited number of sta registers. Whether Prolog can approach Lisp performance on conventional machines primarily dependent on how much of the Prolog state can be contained in available sta registers and if advanced Prolog compilers can be built.

The second result was that Prolog has a greater potential to exploit the additional sta and state transfers advanced hardware can offer. The high semantic content or *potency* a language is indicated, for a given program, by a high mean number of memor references per instruction executed and a low total number of instructions execute From the statistics presented in this paper, Prolog displayed greater potency than Lis because the functionality of backtracking and unification are integrated into Prolog an its architecture. Shadow registers were given as an example of advanced hardwa reducing the bandwidth requirement of this increased potency. Note that although Lis can also take advantage of advanced hardware, e.g., register windows, Lisp's low semantic content implies a greater number of instructions executed and therefore low overall memory performance.

In summary, to execute a given application fast, one wishes to both

- reduce the semantic gap between the architecture and the language.
- increase the semantic content of the language, increasing its performance potential.

As shown, available hardware and compiler technology constrains these criteria, urrently favoring Lisp. Future technology may well favor Prolog.

Acknowledgments

I thank Bob Shaw (Stanford) for his generous help supplying and analyzing the Lisp atistics, Rich Warren (MCC) for supplying the Sun-3 Prolog statistics and Richard 'Keefe for helping translate Boyer.

References

1. C. Gutierrez, ''Prolog Compared With Lisp'', *Symposium on LISP and Functional Programming*, ACM, 1982.
2. R. A. O'Keefe, ''Prolog Compared With Lisp?'', Research Paper 181, Dept. of Artificial Intelligence, University of Edinburgh, 1982.
3. R. P. Gabriel, ''Performance and Evaluation of Lisp Systems'', Research Paper 111, Computer Science, Stanford University, 1984.
4. M. L. Griss and A. C. Hearn, ''A Portable LISP Compiler'', *Software - Practice and Experience*, Vol. 11, No. 6, June, 1981.
5. D. H. D. Warren, ''An Abstract Prolog Instruction Set'', Tech. report 309, Artificial Intelligence Center, SRI International, 1983.
6. E. Tick, ''Prolog Memory-Referencing Behavior'', Technical Report 85-281, Computer Systems Laboratory, Stanford University, 1985.
7. E. Tick, ''Lisp and Prolog Memory Performance'', Technical Report 86-291, Computer Systems Laboratory, Stanford University, 1985.
8. C. Ponder, ''"...but will RISC run LISP??" (a feasibility study)'', Research Paper 83/122, Dept. of EECS, University of California at Berkeley, 1983.
9. B. Joy and S. Gadol, ''Sun Common Lisp Benchmarks: Some Early Results'', Sun Microsystems Inc., Mountain View, 1985.
10. D. H. D. Warren and L. M. Pereira, ''Prolog - The Language and its Implementation Compared with Lisp'', *Symposium on AI and Programming Languages*, ACM, August 1977.

The Design and Implementation of a High-Speed Incremental Portable Prolog Compiler

Kenneth A. Bowen, Kevin A. Buettner, Ilyas Cicekli, Andrew K. Turk

Logic Programming Research Group
School of Computer & Information Science
Syracuse University
Syracuse, NY, 13210 USA

Abstract

The design and implementation of a relatively portable Prolog compiler achieving 12K LIPS on the standard benchmark is described. The compiler is incremental and uses decompilation to implement retract, clause, and listing, as well as support the needs of its four-port debugger. The system supports modules, garbage collection, database pointers, and a full range of built-ins.

1. Introduction

In the course of exploring implementation techniques for metalevel extensions of Prolog (cf. Bowen and Kowalski [1982], Bowen and Weinberg [1985], Bowen [1985]), it became apparent that a fast flexible Prolog system would be a useful tool to serve as a starting point for developing experimental implementations of the extended Prolog systems. In late 1984, we planned to base the system on the designs of Warren [1983], implementing a byte-code interpreter for the abstract machine in C, while implementing the compiler itself in Prolog.

We were fortunate to join forces with the group working at Argonne National Laboratory (Tim Lindholm, Rusty Lusk, and Ross Overbeek) which was interested in the implementation of Prolog on multiprocessor machines. They had already written a portable byte-code interpreter in C on a VAX 780. Unfortunately, the performance of the Argonne WAM was disappointing. The naive reverse benchmark (nrev) ran at only about 4K LIPS. We concluded that the relatively slow speed was due to a combination of the portability requirements and the data structures necessary for multi-processor implementation.

The disappointing performance of the Argonne WAM, coupled with an interest in implementing a Prolog system on 68000-based machines, led Turk to begin exploring a new implementation of a byte-code interpreter written in C, while as a group we continued work on the compiler.

In late February of 1985 we had a first version of the compiler itself operational in C-Prolog. Unfortunately, we found ourselves hampered by C-Prolog's restricted memory size and apparent lack of significant tail recursion optimization and garbage collection. The compiler itself had grown fairly large, reflecting our explorations of various optimization techniques. When we began to boot the compiler on itself, we were frustrated to discover that our compiler immediately overran the maximum allowable local and global stack spaces.

This work supported in part by US Air Force grant AFOSR-82-0292 and by US Air Force contract F30602-81-C-0169. The authors are very grateful to the following people for numerous valuable conversations on the topics of this paper: Hamid Bacha, Aida Batarekh, Keith Hughes, Jim Kajiya, Kevin Larue, Jacob Levy, Tim Lindholm, Rusty Lusk, Jon Mills, Hidey Nakashima, Ross Overbeek, Karl Puder, and Toby Weinberg.

At this time, Buettner, in a one month burst of enthusiasm, roughed out a new byte-code interpreter for the abstract machine coupled with an implementation of a moderately sophisticated compiler, all written in C. We now found ourselves in the (perhaps enviable) position of possessing three distinct implementations of the abstract machine (all written in C) and two compilers, one written in C and the other in Prolog.

While there were some differences in structure between the compilers, they both operated on basically the same principles. On the other hand, our two home-grown implementations of the abstract machine appeared to use significantly different techniques, and of course differed markedly from the Argonne implementation. Since both of our local WAMs executed nrev at better than 6K LIPS and both authors asserted that not all opportunities for optimization had been exploited, we decided to pursue development of both machines and compilers in parallel.

In the course of the summer of 1985, both machines evolved towards a common structure, and began achieving speeds in nearing 10K LIPS on nrev. We also had the interesting experience of booting the Prolog-based version of the compiler using the C-based Prolog compiler. Both of the Syracuse abstract machines were evolving towards a common structure, so we chose Buettner's system as the basis for the rest of our work.

We completed the Prolog-based version of the compiler and delivered a copy to the Argonne group in late August '85. It is expected that this will be made publicly available along with the Argonne WAM sometime in the near future. The rest of this paper will describe the design, structure, and facilities of the C-based system. We will assume familiarity with Byrd, Pereira and Warren [1980], Pereira, Pereira, and Warren [1978], and Warren [1983].

2. Organization of the System

To the user, our system has the appearance of a standard Edinburgh-style interactive interpreter. However, it is really an incremental compiler. Thus we have no need to support a separate interpreter with all the difficulties of consistency between a compiler and an interpreter. Briefly, the major services provided by the system are as follows:

- The compiler is resident in the system, incrementally compiling original and added program clauses (including those added by assert) as well as goals.

- Programs may be organized into modules which are independent of file structure in that multiple modules may be included in a single file (a single module can also be spread over several files). Visibility of procedures is controlled by use of import/export declarations. Clauses not appearing within a module declaration are stored in a default global module. Constants and functors are globally visible.

- Garbage compaction of the global stack (heap) and trail is provided using a pointer-reversal algorithm of Morris[1978]. No garbage collection is provided for the code space.

- Run-time use of retract, clause, and listing is accomplished via a general decompilation technology (described in detail in Buettner [1985]). This technology is also used to support the debugging subsystem.

- A full four-port debugging model (cf. Byrd[1980]) is provided. It relies on the decompilation technology mentioned above and accomplishes its task by constructing linked lists representing the local stack frame entry and exit on the global stack (heap). It is largely complete, though some standard commands remain to be implemented.

• Database pointers are supported. These exist as Prolog terms which can occur in other terms and predicates.

The system supports the full range of built-ins standard in Edinburgh-style Prolog systems. Some are implemented in C, with the rest being written in Prolog and compiled by the system.

The code for the system occupies approximately 135K bytes of virtual memory (76K bytes of physical memory) when loaded. The machine will run nrev at 12K LIPS on a list of length 100. Nrev reverses a 1000 element list at 10.5K LIPS. The lower speed reflects the time spent in garbage collection.

3. Compilation

The Prolog-based compiler includes a lexical analyzer and DCG parser to read in Prolog source code. This is necessary because systems like the Argonne WAM do not have a built-in reader. The parser performs its variable analysis on the fly, and produces a term which represents a clause. Another pass translates the clause representation into a sequence of abstract machine instructions. Uninstantiated logical variables are used to represent code addresses inside the compiler.

During the second pass, the intermediate code for the individual clauses constituting a procedure is connected by indexing instructions. Our method of indexing, which differs from Warren [1983], will be described later. The output of the second pass is a complex Prolog term representing the procedure. Assembly amounts to a traversal of this term, calculating symbolic addresses as necessary, and linearizing the entire structure. Loading is then straight-forward.

The C-based version of the compiler utilizes a standard Prolog reader to read the clauses as terms. It makes one pass through the term, performing its variable analysis and building appropriate tables. On a second pass through the term, it generates and loads the instructions for the clause, linking them into the naive try-me-else indexing chain for the procedure. Full indexing for the procedure is generated when the module containing the procedure is sealed.

Both compilers optimize argument register usage and can re-order certain operations to streamline the resulting code. In addition, a small amount of "clause lookahead" is used so that variables will end up in the correct registers for the first subgoal. Argument registers are reused whenever possible.

4. Indexing

The indexing code for a procedure has two tasks to accomplish. When the indexing argument (normally A0) references an unbound variable, the machine must attempt each clause of the procedure in the correct order. If the indexing argument dereferences to a non-variable, the indexing code should select only those clauses which could possibly match while excluding the majority of the useless clauses which would fail.

We have not modified the indexing instructions of Warren [1983], but we do employ them in a different manner. Focusing on the first argument of a procedure, a *block* of clauses is a maximal subset of the clauses for the procedure, contiguous in the given clause ordering, all of whose first head arguments are of the same type, either constant, compound term (other han list), variable, or list. The compiler uses indexing instructions at the lowest level to ontrol access to each block, with second-level indexing instructions to control transfers etween blocks.

Try chains and *try_me chains* define linked lists of code patches that the machine will raverse at runtime. These code patches can either be individual clauses, blocks of clauses overned by switch instructions, or nested *try chains.* A *try chain* consisting of try, retry nd trust instructions is used to link clauses together when the indexing code itself must be hysically seperate from the clause code. A *try_me chain* interleaves the clause code and he indexing code by using the try_me_else, retry_me_else and trust_me instructions.

)ur indexing method creates one *try_me chain* that links all the clauses of a procedure to- ;ether in the right order. This chain is used when the indexing argument references an un- ound variable. *Try_me chains* are simple to compile and easy to change after an assert or etract.

Vhen the indexing argument contains a non-variable, the machine will use a *try chain* to ac- ess clauses. Access to clauses in this chain will be controlled by switch instructions to elim- nate useless clauses. Since all *try chains* are physically seperate from the clauses they ;overn, the system can rewrite the non-variable indexing for a procedure without recompil- ng the clauses in the procedure.

Vhile using two seperate indexing chains uses more instructions than the method presented n Warren [1983], the same number of choicepoints are created at runtime. The extra flexi- ility afforded by seperate indexing chains is worth a few more instructions in the code pace. Figures 4.1 and 4.2 schematically indicate the structure of our scheme.

5. Cut

'or the most part, we have implemented the instruction set of Warren [1983] with only ninor modifications. The most significant extension to date is the addition of a new nachine register, called *cutpt,* and new instructions to manipulate it. These instructions nd their effects are listed below. The last instruction is only necessary in the compilation f soft cuts.

Instruction	Action
set_B_from_cutpt	B := cutpt
set_B_from Yn	B := Yn
save_cutpt_in Yn	Yn := cutpt
save_B_in Yn	Yn := B

Figure 5.1. Instructions Necessary for Cut.

The problem with cut is that the compiler cannot always know how many choice points will e created for a procedure containing a cut. Consider the following trivial program, whose ource consists of the two facts f(a) and f(b):

```
f/1:    switch_on_term       C1a,L1,fail,fail
L1:     switch_on_constant   2,[a:C1, b:C2]
C1a:    try_me_else          C2a                 % f(
C1:     get_constant         a,A0                %   a)
        proceed                                  %   .
C2a:    trust_me_else        fail                % f(
C2:     get_constant         b,A0                %   b)
```

```
    proceed                                    % .
```

When the first clause C1 is executed, there can be either zero or one choice points for the procedure f/1. The compiler cannot detect which is the case because it depends on the incoming value in the first argument register A0. If the incoming value in A0 is the constant *a*, there will be no choice point created for the procedure f/1, but if the incoming value in A0 is an unbound variable, there will be one choice point created for the procedure f/1. Therefore, cutting a procedure is not as simple as removing the topmost choicepoint.

The new register *cutpt* is treated in the abstract machine as follows. The value of the B register is automatically stored in the cutpt register by a *call* or an *execute* instruction. This records the address of the last choice point before the next procedure is invoked. The current value of the cutpt register is saved in each choice point along with the other machine registers. The cutpt register is reset from the value stored in the last choice point when backtracking occurs.

The cutpt register contains the address of the last choicepoint created before entering a procedure. By simply moving this value into the B register, the machine can remove all the choicepoints created by the current procedure, no matter how many there were. Since cutpt is modified by every subgoal, the compiler must store the cutpt in a permanent variable to preserve it across a call.

The following examples illustrate how the compiler uses these instructions to compile cuts.

Example 1: p :- q1, !, q2.

```
    allocate          1
    save_cutpt_in     Y0
    call              q1/0,1
    set_B_from        Y0
    deallocate
    execute           q2/0
```

Example 2: p :- !.

```
    set_B_from_cutpt
    proceed
```

Example 3: p :- q1, q2, !.

```
    allocate          1
    save_cutpt_in     Y0
    call              q1/0,1
    call              q2/0,1
    set_B_from        Y0
    deallocate
    proceed
```

This approach can be optimized.

6. Conclusions

The abstract machine design of Warren [1983] together with the compilation technique uggested by his examples are a sound piece of software engineering. We have filled in some aps such as the implementation of cut which were omitted in his discussion, and have ntroduced modifications in the pursuit of refining and optimizing performance. The present ystem provides an excellent basis for our primary goal, the pursuit of implementations of neta-level Prolog systems. Our approach will be to introduce modifications to the abstract nachine providing the required functionality, the primary one being a change in the treatnent of the code space. This will be coupled with appropriate changes in the compilers. Ve expect this to lead to efficient implementations of the experimental systems.

'. References

Bowen, K.A., and Kowalski, R.A., Amalgamating language and metalanguage in logic programming, in *Logic Programming*, ed. K. Clark and S.-A. Tarnlund, 1982, pp 153-72.

Bowen, K.A., and Weinberg, T., A meta-level extension of Prolog, *1985 Symposium on Logic Programming*, Boston, IEEE, 1985, pp. 48-53.

Bowen, K.A., Meta-Level programming and knowledge representation, *New Generation Computing*, 3, 1985, pp. 359-383.

Buettner, K.A., Decompilation of compiler Prolog clauses, submitted.

Byrd, L., Prolog debugging facilities, in Byrd, Pereira, and Warren, 1980.

Byrd, L., Pereira, F., and Warren, D., *A Guide to Version 3 of DEC-10 PROLOG*, Dept. of Artificial Intelligence, Univ. of Edinburgh, 1980.

Morris, F.L., A time- and space-efficient garbage collection algorithm, *Communications of the ACM*, 21, (1978), pp. 662-665.

Pereira, L.M., Pereira, F.C., and Warren, D.H.D., *User's Guide to DECsystem-10 PROLOG*, Dept. of Artificial Intelligence, Univ. of Edinburgh, 1978.

Warren, D.H.D., An abstract Prolog instruction set, SRI Technical Report, 1983.

switch_on_term •, •, FS, LS

try
retry
trust

CB1: switch_on_constant

constant block

FS: try
trust

FB: switch_on_functor

functor block

try
retry
...
trust

variable block

CB2: switch_on_constant

constant block

LS: try
trust

try
retry
...
trust

list block

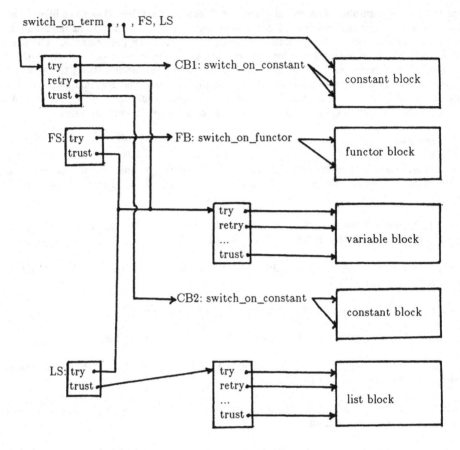

Figure 4.1. Overall indexing structure.

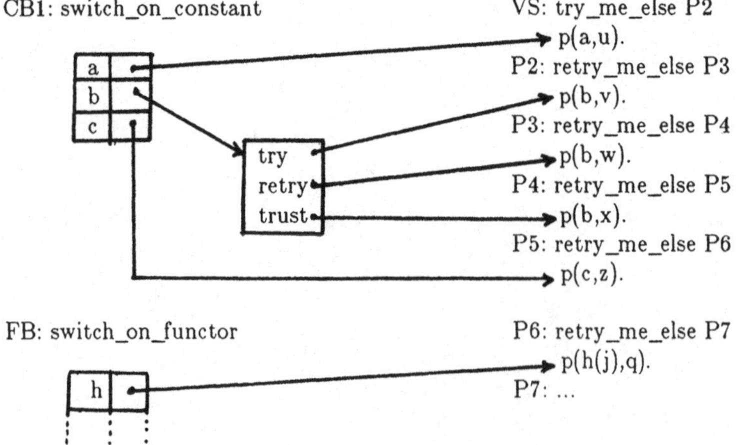

Figure 4.2. Detail of indexing structure.

Compiler Optimizations for the WAM

Andrew K. Turk

Logic Programming Research Group
School of Computer & Information Science
Syracuse University
Syracuse, NY, 13210 USA

Abstract

series of Warren Abstract Machine (WAM) implementation techniques are presented. hese techniques and compilation strategies are designed for use in a highly optimized naive code Prolog compiler. A thorough knowledge of the WAM and Prolog compilation is ssumed.

. Motivations

n conventional hardware, it is necessary to compile Prolog to native machine code for opimal performance. Ideally, a native code compiler can work along side one of the many yte-code compilers which already exist. This paper outlines a series of optimizations which an be used by an intelligent compiler to translate WAM byte-codes into the native machine anguage of a conventional machine. Most of these strategies need not be applied to every lause and procedure; the compiler is relatively free to decide which method is best, or at east take advice from the programmer. It is assumed that the optimizations will only be pplied to static code.

. An Overview of Native Code

VAM byte-codes can be naively translated into native code in a straightforward fashion. ach of the steps and conditionals which must be performed by the byte-code interpreter nust also be executed by native code. When these steps are directly translated into a naive code stream, the overhead inherent in the interpreter is eliminated. However, much nore can be done than the simple elimination of the interpreter.

3. The Read/Write Mode Bit

Varren's original design incorporates a mode bit which tells the machine whether it's in ead mode or write mode. Many hardware and software interpreters actually use a mode it. However, mode bits are expensive and difficult to manage in a native code system. ortunately, there is a straightforward method which eliminates the bit and retains its funcionality.

The mode bit is set by *get* instructions and must be maintained through the execution of he following *unify* instructions. Instructions which change the mode (either *get*s or *put*s) annot occur between a *get* and its *unify*s. The simplest way to eliminate the mode bit is to ompile each *unify* sequence twice, once for write mode and again for read mode. First, the ode to dereference the register in question is emitted. Following that is a conditional ranch to the read mode sequence (which directly follows the write mode sequence). Right

---

his work supported in part by US Air Force contract number F30602-81-C-0169.

after the conditional is the first instruction of the write mode sequence. A branch around the read mode code is placed after the last write mode instruction.

No "continuation branch" is needed after the read mode code because the next instruction corresponds to rest of the clause. *Put* instructions force the machine into write mode. This is done only so that the *unify* instructions will work properly. Since the mode is always write after a *put*, there is no need to compile a separate sequence for read mode. Some software implementations achieve the same effect with a set of *unify* instructions that always work in write mode. The compiler should emit the write mode sequence first in order to make write mode propagation more effective.

4. Write Mode propagation

Compiled constants and variables do not change the mode. However, when an unbound variable is passed into a clause at runtime, a *getStruct* or *getList* will force the machine into write mode. Not only will that particular *getStruct* or *getList* invoke write mode, but any substructure corresponding to that instruction must also run in write mode. This is because all of the *unifyVar* instructions in the original *unify* sequence run in write mode, and therefore create fresh unbound variables on the heap.

When write mode is propagated to a *getStruct F, An* or a *getList An*, the machine can infer that An contains a reference to an unbound variable on the heap. Because of this, the runtime dereference and tag check for undef can be skipped. This can amount to a significant savings for programs which spend a lot of time in head matching.

Unfortunately, there is no way to propagate read mode. Furthermore, without undue overhead, the write mode of an instruction can only be propagated to its "leftmost" subtree. This is due to the fact that there is no way to distinguish between a propagated write mode and a non-propagated write mode.

In order to implement this technique, the compiler takes advantage of the fact that the *unify* sequences are compiled once for write mode and once for read mode, with a branch in between. If the compiler detects that the mode can be propagated from some parent *get* instruction to a child *get*, the "continuation branch" in the parent's code will jump PAST the dereference and check for undef, directly into the write mode *unify* sequence of the child. If the mode for the child can be propagated, then its continuation branch will skip the dereference and check for undef of the next *get*, and so on.

Whenever the mode cannot be propagated, the parent's "continuation branch" will enter the child's *get* at the beginning. In order to capitalize on this optimization, the byte-code should match head structure in long left-descending chains so that the mode can be propagated as far as possible.

5. Shallow Backtracking on the WAM

Other Prolog implementations distinguish between two different types of backtracking: deep backtracking and shallow backtracking. Shallow backtracking occurs when the current choicepoint is the topmost object on the local stack; everything else is deep backtracking. However, we will restrict the definition of shallow backtracking to cases where some clause has failed in head matching and another clause remains to be tried in the same procedure.

Most WAM implementations have a single global subroutine or label which resets the machine and argument registers after a failure. This routine is used in the compilation of a *set* instructions when an incoming argument doesn't match. However, in order to optimize for shallow backtracking, the native code compiler should compile these actions in-line along with every *retry* and *trust* instruction.

Seen in this light, each *retry* resets the argument registers, resets the machine registers, updates a field in the choicepoint, unwinds the trail and finally jumps to the next clause. Each part of the *retry* has an entry point, and if no argument registers were changed by the previous clause, the machine can simply jump past that part of the *retry*, just as if the mode were being propagated.

Suppose that a procedure contains two clauses, numbered 0 and 1. Failure in the head of clause 0 will always cause shallow backtracking. Each instruction in the head of clause 0 which might cause failure must have some way of causing the machine to fail (i.e., branching to a failure label). Furthermore, the compiler will know how many registers might have been modified in clause 0 prior to each instruction.

Thus, the *trust* separating clause 0 from clause 1 will be arranged so that the first register modified in clause 0 is the last one reset in the *trust*. The second register modified will be the second to last reset, and so on.

By doing this, the compiler can have the first possibly failing instruction in clause 0 jump past almost all of the compiled *trust* because only a few registers have been changed. The last possibly failing instruction in clause 0 will fail into the beginning of the *trust* in order to reset all the changed registers.

Since the compiler calculates where to jump during shallow backtracking, the nextClause field in the choicepoint record is only used for deep backtracking. Clause 1 is the last clause in the example procedure, and it can only cause deep backtracking. The compiler cannot calculate the failure label in this case, and must emit code to jump to the failure label stored in the choicepoint. Failure labels in choicepoints always point at the first instruction of a compiled *retry* or *trust* in order to reset all the machine registers.

3. Improved Choicepoints

Many procedures are compiled with a type of indexing which uses two *try* instructions. These procedures are composed of a series of blocks of clauses with a *try* for each block. In addition, there is a *try* which laces all the blocks together. Under certain circumstances the machine can detect at run-time that only one clause in a particular clause can possibly match. In this case, the inner *try* instruction is not executed and the second choicepoint is not created.

Since the creation of a choicepoint is a very expensive operation in terms of both space and time, the compiler should strive to avoid unnecessary choicepoints. A closer examination of the second choicepoint occasionally used in the indexing scheme shows that all its fields except for B and the address of the next clause are duplicated from the first choicepoint. In fact, the only interesting part is the address of the next clause because the B field simply points to the first choicepoint.

Two choicepoints can be collapsed into one if the next clause field of the hypothetical second choicepoint is included in the first. In particular, the two fields are allocated together in the first choicepoint and function like a small stack. A *try* instruction pushes an address on the stack, a *retry* changes the topmost entry and a *trust* pops the stack by one.

Since present compilation technology never requires more than two choicepoints per procedure, this sub-stack can be manipulated directly as an array. A *try* simply copies the first field into the second and a *trust* copies the second into the first. Sophisticated indexing techniques which require more than two choices may become available.

In this case, it will be advantageous to have another register which points to the topmost stack entry in the most recent choicepoint.

The only restriction is that the compiler must be able to know which *try* instruction will be executed first and which *trust* will be executed last. This is because the first *try* needs to allocate the choicepoint, while the last *trust* will deallocate it.

This technique avoids a great deal of space and time overhead by collapsing multiple choicepoints into a slightly larger initial choicepoint. More importantly, it means that the compiler can calculate exactly how much local stack space will be needed by the procedure at compile time. This allows it to allocate other objects below a procedure's choicepoint, such as an environment, and to share these objects between clauses.

7. Avoiding Environment Allocation

An environment is required for any clause that has more than one subgoal. The environment must be allocated before the any use of a permanent variable and before the call to the first subgoal. Since most implementations do not have a top of stack (TOS) register, the TOS must be calculated dynamically. This involves a conditional test and possibly an indirect load and an addition. Many byte-code compilers emit code so that the allocate instructions occur as late as possible in the hopes that the clause will not match and the environment need not be allocated.

However, procedures that use at least one *try* in their indexing always calculate the TOS in order to put a choicepoint on the stack. Thus, after a choicepoint has been laid down, the B register contains the TOS. The compiler can recognize this and compile references to permanent variables as offsets from B instead of E. Once the head of the clause has successfully matched, CP and E are copied into the local stack and E is updated to reflect the new environment.

This technique cannot be applied to procedures which optionally use zero or one choicepoint. Obviously, if no choicepoint was pushed on the stack, then B does not contain the TOS. In this case, there is a good chance that the procedure will be determinate anyway, and the compiler should not be overly concerned about optimizing for failure.

8. Improved Argument Registers

There are two drawbacks in the way argument registers are reset after failure in the WAM. First, many registers will be reloaded even though they were never modified in the first place. One solution to this problem to make use of shallow backtracking. However, many registers are still reloaded from the choicepoint even though they will never be referenced due to early failure in the head. Fortunately, this problem can also be minimized by a careful compiler.

This technique involves reloading argument registers from the choicepoint of a nondeterminate procedure only when absolutely necessary. Normally, the effective address of an argument register is either a host machine register or an offset into the argument array. However, the compiler can change the effective address of the first top-level occurrence of an rgument register in the code to be an offset into the current choicepoint.

Thus, the compiled *retry* instructions will not include code to restore certain argument registers. The first effective address of such a top-level argument register corresponds to the stored value of that register. The machine should not change the contents of the choicepoint, but it is free to read whatever is necessary. This amounts to treating the choicepoint as a read-only cache of saved argument registers.

Two potential difficulties arise. Some of the instructions which are optimized away in bytecode (e.g., *getVar X1, A1*) cannot be eliminated with this scheme. Since the failure code will not reload certain argument registers, the compiler must explicitly restore all such registers that appear in the clause code.

Furthermore, *trust* instructions delete the topmost choicepoint and in the process remove the initial copies of the argument registers. To eliminate this problem, the compiler must emit code which only deletes a choicepoint after the head of a clause has matched or only after the head has failed. In the latter case, the machine would delete the topmost choicepoint and then jump to the deep backtrack label of the previous choice.

A careful combination of this method and shallow backtracking should be more effective than either method alone. Register usage between clauses and the "determinateness" of the procedure will influence how the compiler emits code to reset the state after shallow backtracking.

9. Backtrackable Assignment

This next technique is not an optimization, nor is it unique to native code prolog implementations, but it was developed along with the other methods in this paper.

Backtrackable assignment appears to be a useful device for a number of different applications. It requires that extra information be stored on the trail for certain entries: those that were assigned to. The extra information is a copy of the particular cell before it was destructively assigned.

Naive implementations of backtrackable assignment either place a tag bit on each trail entry, or store a reset value with each reset address. The former requires that the tag bit be checked on each trail entry during failure and the latter doubles the size of the trail. Fortunately, a simple method exists which pays no overhead for normal trail entries.

The idea is to interleave two separate stacks, one for normal trail entries and one for reset-to-value entries. Each stack will have a pointer to the topmost element. TR points at the topmost normal trail entry, while TR' points at the topmost reset-to-value pair. This is similar to the way choicepoints and environments are interleaved on the local stack.

Each time a normal unification is trailed, an address is pushed onto the trail and TR is incremented. During a destructive assignment, a pointer to the cell, the contents of the cell, and the previous TR' are pushed on the trail with TR being incremented by. TR' is updated to reflect the new entry.

When backtracking requires cells to be reset, the machine compares the copy of TR in the backtrack frame with TR'; the higher of these two is copied into a temporary location Temp. The part of the trail between Temp and the current contents of TR represents a contiguous block of normal trail entries. The machine can loop though these, decrementing

Temp and resetting variables to undef without checking any tags or worrying about strange objects in its path. If Temp is higher than the copy of TR in the backtrack frame, then Temp points at a reset-to-value entry which resets the variable and decrements Temp accordingly. Otherwise, no reset-to-value entries occur in the current trail segment.

This process continues by repeatedly untrailing a block of normal trail entries (possibly an empty block), and then untrailing a reset-to-value entry. When all the appropriate trail entries have been removed, TR will point at the top of the trail and TR' will point at the most recent reset-to-value entry.

10. Conclusions

A number of optimized compilation techniques have been presented. An advanced compiler should be able to make use of them when it has determined that a particular procedure can be made more efficient. The optimizations are relatively independent so the compiler is not forced into a few rigid compilation models.

11. References

E. Tick
Prolog Memory-Referencing Behavior,
Research Paper 85-281, Computer Systems Laboratory,
Stanford University, 1985.

D.H.D. Warren
An Abstract Prolog Instruction Set
Technical Note 309, Artificial Intelligence Center, Computer Science
and Technology Division, SRI International, 1983.

Fast Decompilation of Compiled Prolog Clauses

Kevin A. Buettner

Logic Programming Research Group
School of Computer & Information Science
Syracuse University

ABSTRACT

Serious Prolog implementations in recent years have been primarily compiler-based, nearly all of which are founded on the abstract instruction set of Warren [1983]. The performance achieved by such implementations greatly outstrips that attainable in interpreter-based systems. Unfortunately, the sophistication of these compiler-based environments is often inferior to environments of interpreter-based systems to the extent that a "compatible" interpreter is often required for serious software development. Among the deficiencies of these environments, database operations such as assert, retract, and clause seem to be particularly afflicted. In addition, the ability to debug compiled code has been either non-existent or at best, very constrained.

Unlike compiler technology of many traditional languages, there is little reason for this to be the case in Prolog. An efficient implementation of retract, listing, and clause by decompilation of compiled clause code is the subject of this paper. Techniques used in the implementation of the decompilation process have also proven useful in the implementation of the standard four port debugger found in many Prolog systems.

Introduction

The programming language *Prolog* has a number of builtin predicates for operating on the global database. Among these operations, the predicates *assert*, *retract*, and *clause* are found in most Prolog systems. Due to their non-logical nature, these predicates have gained a certain notoriety in the logic programming community. In spite of the bad press that these operations have gotten, many practical and useful programs are written which need and require these operations although in theory it is possible to dispense with them.† The view of the author is that these operations are important and should be provided in modern Prolog systems. Even languages which claim a sounder logical foundation with respect to the database operations‡ have implementation problems similar to those found in ordinary Prolog.

The first Prolog environments were interpreter based. The database operations are relatively easy to implement in these environments due to the similarity between the run-time data structures and the code structures. At the present, the trend seems to be towards compiler-based Prolog environments. Most current compiler-based implementations have

This work supported in part by U.S. Air Force contract number F30602-81-C-0169.

† It is often possible to reorganize programs so that assert and retract are not used, but at the expense of efficiency and quite often clarity of expression.

‡ e.g, metaProlog (cf. Bowen and Weinberg [1985]) provides the operations addTo and dropFrom which are used to create new theories from old ones.

their roots in the abstract machine of David Warren [1983]. With the advent of this compiler-based technology, implementation of the database operations has become more challenging due to the fact that the run-time data structures are quite a bit different from the code structures. The run-time data structures are much the same as they were under interpreter-based implementations, but the code structures are different; they are now sequences of instructions to execute. Implementation of the *assert* operation with this new technology isn't too difficult. All one needs to do is invoke the compiler on the clause to assert, obtain the sequence of instructions and link these into the indexing scheme.

It is the implementation of either retract or clause that is more interesting. These operations are similar in that we must be able to take fairly arbitrary patterns and find a clause in the database which matches these patterns. Again for interpreter-based systems, this isn't usually very hard due to the similarity between the run-time structures and the code structures. But matching clauses in a compiler-based system is more difficult. As observed by Clocksin [1985] in his discussion of the implementation of Prolog-X, there are basically three ways to organize the database so that this matching may be performed:

1) Save a copy of the source clause in addtion to the compiled clause. Clocksin points out that many compiler-based LISP systems use this technique. But for a number of reasons, this technique is unsatisfactory for Prolog.
2) Keep only the compiled clause code in the database and decompile it when matching needs to be performed. Performing the decompilation efficiently is the subject of this paper.
3) Compile and insert into the database a unit clause which relates the source structure with the database reference of the real clause code. This is the method that Prolog-X uses. Clocksin notes that it enjoys the advantage that clause searching and matching are done by the usual mechanisms of the abstract machine. It has the disadvantage that compilation takes approximately twice as long since each clause is compiled twice and approximately twice as much space is required in the database.

This paper describes a way of running certain of the abstract machine instructions in a different "mode" causing a clause to decompile itself. Very few limitations exist on the types of compiler optimizations that may be performed. Even for extremely optimized code, however, there are ways to augment the output of the compiler so that the methods described will still work. In the ensuing discussion of the decompilation technique, familiarity with the abstract machine described by Warren [1983] is assumed.

Decompilation

Suppose we have a source clause of the following form:

$$H \text{ :- } G_1,\ldots,G_m .$$

This translates (schematically) to:

match args of H
set up args of G_1
call $g_1/n_1,ES_1$
set up args of G_2
call $g_2/n_1,ES_2$
.
.
.
set up args of G_m
execute g_m

In the above, **call** and **execute** are actual instructions. *match* represents the sequence of get and unify instructions that perform the head matching. *set up* refers to a sequence of put and unify instructions that install arguments for the call or execute instructions. In practice, the initial *match* and *set up* instructions are often merged as an optimization. This assumption will not affect the process which we are about to describe.

Before discussing the nitty gritty details, it should be noted that a fair amount of structure is created by the object code in normal execution. For example, if the clause is run with all uninstantiated arguments, by the time of the first call the original variables will be instantiated to structure representing the arguments in the head of the clause. Similarly, just before a call or execute, the A registers contain the arguments of the goal about to be called. To get back the structure of the entire clause entails taking these pieces and wrapping them up with the appropriate functors that represent the head, goals, commas between the goals, and the ":-" between the head and the goals. The decompilation technique will be discussed in two stages. The first stage is to look at an object code transformation that when run by the underlying Prolog engine will give back the original clause structure. The second stage is rather easy; ways to avoid *doing* the actual transformation are considered.

A transformation that will take object code representing a clause (in the above form) and produce object code which can be run with a single argument (which may have varying levels of instantiation) and return the structure (or pieces of the structure as the level of instantiation requires) will now be described. The idea is to tack on a prologue to the beginning of the code which will create the uninstantiated variables for the head and set up the clause predicate name. The prologue will create something of the form

$$h(Arg_1, Arg_2, \ldots, Arg_{n_0}) \text{ :- } G$$

The A registers will have pointers to the variables $Arg_1 \ldots Arg_{n_0}$ respectively. Because the A registers contain pointers to variables, the get instructions in the *match* section of the clause code will be forced into write mode and will create structure. We don't want the call and execute instructions to run, so we replace them with code which will unload the argument registers and produce the appropriate goal structures.

Schematically, the transformation looks like this:

Original Code	Transformed Code	Comments
	get_structure :-/2, A1	Prologue
	unify_variable As	
	unify_variable At	
	get_structure h/n_0,As	
	unify_variable A1	
	.	
	.	
	.	
	unify_variable An_0	
match args of H	*match* args of H	
set up args of G_1	*set up* args of G_1	
call g_1/n_1,ES_1	get_structure ','/2, At	Call Transformation
	unify_variable As	
	unify_variable At	
	get_structure g_1/n_1,As	
	unify_local_value A1	
	.	
	.	
	.	
	unify_local_value An_1	

.		
.		
.		
set up args of G_m	*set up* args of G_m	
execute g_m	get_structure g_m /n_m ,At unify_local_value A1 . . unify_local_value An_m proceed	Execute Transformation

Notes:

- The As and At in the above transformation refer to unused temporary (argument) registers.
- unify_local_value instructions are used to insure that pointers in structure built on the heap also point to objects on the heap. This is necessary due to the fact that an argument register may have a pointer to a variable on the local stack. If a unify_value instruction is used in this situation, a pointer from the heap to the local stack is installed causing a dangling reference when the environment is deallocated.

The above transformation scheme will work for clauses with at least one goal where both the head and each of the goals has at least one argument. As it stands, it will not work for unit clauses or for clauses which have nullary goals. These cases, however, are not difficult to handle. For unit clauses, the prologue changes slightly. When it is necessary to work with a nullary goal, a get_constant instruction is used instead of a get_structure instruction. For example, the prologue for a unit clause whose head has no arguments is:

```
get_constant  h,A1
```

The prologue for a unit clause with one or more arguments is

```
get_structure   h/n0,A1
unify_variable  A1
.
.
.
unify_variable  An0
```

An execute instruction with no arguments translates to

```
get_constant   gm /nm ,At
proceed
```

It is left as an exercise for the reader to fill in the other variations. It is possible to define the translations so that there are no variations between unit clauses and rules, but in practice these variations cause little difficulty. The translation procedure given here has the added advantage that in attempting to match (unmatchable) partially instantiated clauses failure can occur quite early. To make the translation procedure more uniform, it would be necessary to delay building the structure for the :- until the execute instruction. It would also be necessary to translate proceed instructions, which are currently untouched.

As an example, consider the clauses that make up part of a popular benchmark:

```
nrev([],[]).
nrev([H|T],L) :- nrev(T,RT), conc(RT,[H],L).
```

his compiles to the following object code:

```
nrev/2:
            switch_on_term      L434,
                                L440,
                                L464,
                                fail
L434:       try_me_else         L458,2 %
L440:       get_nil             A1            % nrev([],
            get_nil             A2            %      [])
            proceed                           % .

L458:       trust_me_else       fail,2        %
L464:       allocate                          %
            get_list            A1            % nrev([
            unify_variable      Y1            %       H |
            unify_variable      A1            %        T],
            get_variable        Y2, A2        %       L) :-
            put_variable        Y3, A2        % nrev(T,RT)
            call                nrev/2,3      % ,
            put_unsafe_value    Y3, A1        % conc(RT,
            put_list            A2            %      [
            unify_value         Y1            %       H |
            unify_nil                         %       []],
            put_value           Y2, A3        %      L)
            deallocate                        %
            execute             conc/3        % .
```

erforming the transformation on the first clause gives:

```
            get_structure       nrev/2,A1
            unify_variable      A1
            unify_variable      A2
            get_nil             A1            % nrev([],
            get_nil             A2            %      [])
            proceed                           % .
```

he instructions of the code new to the clause are italicized. The switch and try_me_else structions were not included because they form part of the *procedure* nrev/2 rather than e first clause of nrev/2. The second clause for the nrev procedure transforms to:

```
            get_structure       ':-'/2,A1
            unify_variable      A4
            unify_variable      A5
            get_structure       nrev/2,A4
            unify_variable      A1
            unify_variable      A2
            allocate                          %
            get_list            A1            % nrev([
            unify_variable      Y1            %       H |
            unify_variable      A1            %        T],
            get_variable        Y2, A2        %       L) :-
            put_variable        Y3, A2        % nrev(T,RT)
            get_structure       ','/2,A5
            unify_variable      A4
            unify_variable      A5
```

```
get_structure          nrev/2,A4
unify_local_value      A1
unify_local_value      A2
put_unsafe_value       Y3, A1            % conc(RT,
put_list               A2                %     [
unify_value            Y1                %       H |
unify_nil                                %       []],
put_value              Y2, A3            %     L)
deallocate                               %
get_structure          conc/3,A5
unify_local_value      A1
unify_local_value      A2
unify_local_value      A3
proceed
```

The reader should think of each of these transformations above as a unary unit clause. A1 should point to the structure to be matched or a variable. In the latter case, when the proceed instruction is reached, the variable will be instantiated to the clause structure. Of course, the original variable names will be missing; these may be filled in if desired by a number of different methods†.

In a real implementation, it will be undesirable to perform the actual translation. What should be done instead is to run the code for the prologue elsewhere, jump to the start of the clause code and interpret the call and execute instructions in a different manner. This interpretation of the call and execute instructions can be realized in at least two ways.

The first way of reinterpreting the call and execute instructions is to add another mode bit to the machine. This may in fact be worthwhile since *clause* and *retract* are, in some programs, quite heavily used. In one mode, the call and execute instructions behave normally; in the other mode, the sequence of *get* and *unify* instructions is performed. To set the mode bit, it may be desirable to create a new instruction which will also perform code for the prologue and branch to the start of the clause.

The second method involves setting breakpoints on the call and execute instructions. The break routine is responsible for performing the sequence of *get* and *unify* instructions corresponding to the call or execute instruction and for setting the next breakpoint if any. The very first breakpoint is set by the code that does the prologue. This second method is quite appropriate for a software implementation of the Prolog engine; implementing mode bits is quite expensive in software. On the other hand the first method, described in the preceding paragraph, may be more suitable for a hardware implementation of the Prolog engine.

In the C-based Prolog system written at Syracuse University, the second technique is used. The prologue is actually implemented as part of a builtin which returns the clause structure of a given clause.‡ This builtin also sets a breakpoint on the first call (or execute)

---

† If it is important to fill in the original variable names, another clause vname(DBRef,VNameList) may be asserted. DBRef is a reference to the clause in the database. VNameList is a list of the variables (as atoms) that occur in the clause from left to right with no duplications. To reinstall the variable names, the clause structure obtained from the decompilation process should be traversed from left to right. Every time a *hole* (variable) is found in the structure, it is filled in with the first element in the variable name list. After filling a hole, the first element of the list is discarded and the rest of the list is used for the remainder of the traversal.

‡ The builtin is called as clause_structure(ProcName,Arity,DBRef,Struct) where ProcName and Arity are the predicate name and arity of the clause referenced by DBRef. Struct is usually an output argument and represents the source structure of the clause. An additional builtin is provided for obtaining an initial data base reference to the first

nstruction, if any, and sets the P register (program counter) to the start of the clause to ecompile. When the clause is done "executing", it has decompiled itself.

imitations

The limitations of this method have to do with the implementations of =/2, var/1, onvar/1, and similar builtins.

Some compilers emit the following code for =/2:

```
put argument one, A1
put argument two, A2
get_value   A1,A2
```

rovided that the get_value instruction doesn't fail, the above method described will work ine; the problem is that the resulting structure won't always be the same as the original tructure. The meaning of the two clauses will be the same, but syntactically, they won't e. The reason for this is that the transformation fails to take into account the fact that et_value is used in place of a call to the equality predicate. If the get_value instruction is eplaced by a call to =/2 or perhaps an instruction that performs the same function as *et_value A1,A2* then the decompilation method will work.

Even worse, some compilers transform clauses with =/2 in them. For example,

```
p(X,f(g(X),Y)) :- X=h(Y).
```

nay be transformed to

```
p(h(Y),f(g(h(Y)),Y)).
```

gain, the decompilation procedure will work, but probably not as expected.

Another problem results in the way that var/1 is implemented in some compilers.

```
p(c,X) :- var(X).
```

nay be implemented as.

```
        get_constant       c,A1
        put_value          A2,A1
        switch_on_term     L1,fail,fail,fail
L1:     proceed
```

gain, the problem is that a transformation isn't defined for the switch_on_term instruction. t would be possible to define a transformation, but unwise since this same instruction may e used to implement nonvar also. A better approach is to create instructions which implement the var and nonvar operations and define the obvious transformations on them for the lecompilation process.

Similar problems exist (in some compilers) for other operations. Either by making xplicit calls or by defining new machine instructions, these problems can usually be voided. If either making an explicit call or defining a new machine instruction is unsatisfactory or it is difficult to distinguish one abstract machine instruction from another (as in ompilation to native code), a small amount of additional information may be retained in he clause header for decompilation purposes. This information is simply a vector of breakpoint offsets into the clause code. Along with the breakpoint offset may be stored the

lause of a procedure given the module, predicate name, and arity. Another builtin is sed to find the next clause in the indexing scheme, failing when it finds no more. With hese builtins, it is possible to implement clause/2, clause/3, and listing/1. Additional uiltins designed for removing references and inserting new ones are provided for implementing retract and assert.

predicate name and arity of the call if this information is unavailable by examining the object code. It is the author's opinion that the design of the compiler and decompiler should be coupled. Correct decisions about what the compiler produces will make the process of locating calls, executes, and special code for builtins relatively painless.

Conclusions

The methods described in this paper have applications beyond implementation of clause, retract, and listing. The method of setting breakpoints may be used to implement debuggers (in particular, the standard four-port debugger). In a nutshell: breakpoints are set on the next call, execute or proceed instruction and the next failure address (obtained from the top choice point). When the breakpoint is executed, the appropriate call, redo, fail, or exit message is printed. Redo and fail messages are printed when the failure breakpoint was reached. One or more exit messages are printed when a breakpoint corresponding to a proceed instruction is executed. Call messages are printed on call and execute instructions. Because of the generalized tail recursion optimizations in the Warren architecture, it is necessary to maintain debug frames. These frames contain such information as the previous debug frame, the parent debug frame, the call structure and whether the instruction that caused this frame to be created was an execute or a call. These frames may be safely kept on the heap; in fact keeping the frames on the heap permits a clever implementation of deciding how many redo messages to print when a failure occurs.

Both the decompilation and debugging methods have been implemented in a system constructed at Syracuse University. The underlying compiler is very fast, incremental, and has an interactive interface. All of the flexibility of an interpreted system is achieved in this compiler-based system. Moreover there are no interface or portability problems as are often found in systems which require both an interpreter and a compiler.

References

Bowen, K. A. and Weinberg, T. A Meta-level Extension of Prolog. *1985 Symposium on Logic Programming*. pp. Boston, IEEE, pp. 48-53, 1985.

Clocksin, W. F. Implementation Techniques for Prolog Databases. *Software—Practice and Experience,* 15(7). pp. 669-75, 1985.

Warren D. H. D., An Abstract Prolog Instruction Set. Technical Note 309. Artificial Intelligence Center, SRI International, 1983.

Logic Continuations[1]

Christopher T. Haynes

Computer Science Department
Indiana University
Lindley Hall 101
Bloomington, Indiana 47405 USA

bstract

Ve develop a 'complete' embedding of logic programming into Scheme—a lexically scoped Lisp ialect with first-class continuations. Logic variables are bound in the Scheme environment and he success and failure continuations are represented as Scheme continuations. To account for the emantics of logic variables and failure continuations, the state-space model of control is modified a novel way that generalizes the trail mechanism. This assures that logic variable bindings are roperly restored when continuations are invoked to perform 'lateral' control transfers that are ot possible in a traditional logic programming context. It is thereby possible to obtain greater ontrol over logic program behavior by using continuations as first-class objects.

. Introduction

Iuch of the attraction of logic programming systems is that the programmer is relieved of responbility for specifying control behavior. The system automatically performs resolution theorem roving according to a built-in search strategy, such as the depth-first search of Prolog [6]. Howver, difficulties arise when the built-in strategy does not suit the programmer's needs. Facilities ay be provided to modify the default strategy, such as Prolog's cut, but there are still cases in hich these facilities are awkward or inefficient.

Of particular interest in artificial intelligence applications is the control paradigm of *nonlind backtracking*. For example, a process that starts in control state A may pass a choice point and proceed to some state C (Figure 1 [a]). It is then decided that the choice made at B was robably not a good one, for it has taken much time to get to C and little progress has been made oward the goal. Therefore control backtracks to B and another choice is taken which leads to a ate D (Figure 1 [b]). It may be that from D the second choice looks even worse than the first, nd it is desired to perform a 'lateral' control transfer back to C (dotted line).

Such transfers of control are not possible in most systems because control information is located on a single stack that must be popped when backtracking from C to B. Such backtracking *blind*, because it is impossible to return to the previous state. If it is possible to record the ontrol state at C and return to it sometime after backtracking to B, then the backtracking is *on-blind*. Control information must be heap allocated to allow an arbitrary number of non-blind acktracking choice points, for control can then form a tree structure with an arbitrary number branches. Applications of non-blind backtracking include variations on breadth-first search.

1 This work was supported by the National Science Foundation under grant number DCR 85-01277.

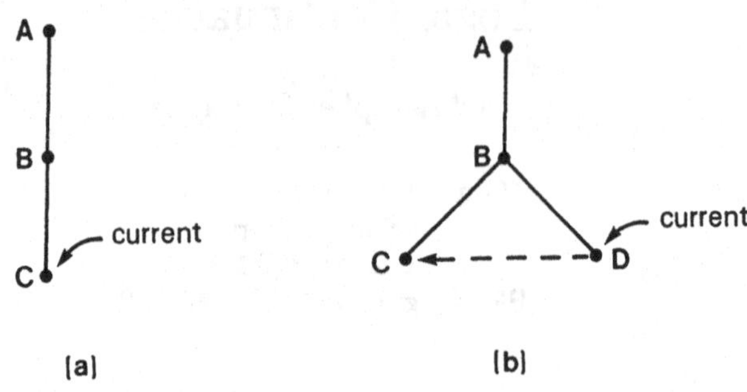

Figure 1. Non-blind backtracking.

The control state of a computation is known as its *continuation,* because it controls how the computation will continue in the absence of explicit control transfers. In particular, every application has a *current* continuation, which may be viewed as a function of one argument. This continuation expects to receive the value returned by the application, with which it will continue the computation. If continuations are made available as functional objects, they provide an abstraction of control that may be used to implement a variety of non-standard control behaviors. For maximum generality, continuations must be *first-class* objects that can be passed to and returned from functions, stored in data structures, and invoked any number of times from any point in a computation. It is possible to 'mark' the current position in the control tree if its continuations may be saved. Control may then be transferred to the marked point by simply invoking its continuation.

The thesis of this paper is that greatest control flexibility is provided by 'completely embedding' logic programming facilities in a procedural language that provides first-class continuations. In particular, this allows unrestricted use of non-blind backtracking and lateral control transfers. It is necessary, however, to assure that logic variable bindings are properly maintained when continuations are invoked. This may be accomplished automatically using a mechanism developed in this paper.

The embedding developed here is presented in Scheme, because Scheme provides the programmer with access to continuations. Scheme is a dialect of Lisp that is applicative order, lexically scoped, and properly tail-recursive [5,7,21]. Most importantly, Scheme treats functions and continuations as first-class objects. Scheme's **rec**, **letrec** and **for-each** are similar to Lisp's **label**, **labels** and **mapc**, respectively. It is hoped that other naming differences are self-evident. The function **call-with-current-continuation**, abbreviated **call/cc**, must be passed a function of one argument. This argument is in turn passed the current continuation, which is the control context of the **call/cc** application represented as a functional object of one argument.[2] Informally, this continuation represents the remainder of the computation from the **call/cc** application point. At any future time this continuation may be invoked with any value, which is

[2] Using **call/cc** we can define **catch**, a version of Landin's J operator [16,18,21]:
(catch *id exp***)** ≡ **(call/cc (lambda (***id***)** *exp***))**.

ıen taken as the value of the **call/cc** application [9,10]. Since continuations never return con- ·ol to their invocation point, the control context of a continuation application may be garbage ɔllected (unless it has been saved with another **call/cc**).

Though Scheme is our chosen means of expression, it must be emphasized that the principle ·chnique developed in this paper is applicable to any language with first-class continuations.

In the next section we present an embedding taxonomy, which is followed by an embedding f logic programming into Scheme. We are then prepared to present a variant of the state-space ıodel that allows the full power of continuations to be used in the context of logic programming. 'inally, we address some efficiency issues and discuss the value of complete embeddings in the eneral context of non-procedural languages.

. A taxonomy for embeddings

number of logic programming embeddings, of widely differing character, have been reported in ıe literature. The following taxonomy of embeddings attempts to clarify the varying degrees of nbedding found in these systems. It may also be of use in classifying other embeddings.

In general, the term *embedding* refers to an implementation in which the embedded language enefits from the programming environment of the embedding, or implementation, language. hese benefits may simply be such facilities as structure editors and memory management [19]. *unctional embeddings* also allow functions in the embedded and embedding language to call one nother conveniently, as in QLOG [15] and POPLOG [17].

Further embedding is achieved when the embedded and embedding languages share a common ıvironment, so that identifier references in the embedded language refer directly to identifier ındings in the embedding language. Such an *environment embedding* may be obtained only when ıe embedded language is compiled into the embedding language, and the embedding language ıpports first-class functions (or *closures*).[3] It may be advantageous to implement some segments f a large program in the embedded language and others in the embedding language, so that the ıcilities of each language may be used where most appropriate. An environment embedding rovides convenient and efficient transfer of information between these segments. Of course care ıust be used to assure that each segment respects the semantics of the other; in particular, ssignment to logic variables would risk violation of logic programming semantics.

Finally, a *complete embedding* is obtained with an environment embedding in which the ɔntrol context may be obtained at any stage in the computation, and then invoked at any future me in order to return to that context. This is possible with an embedding language, such as cheme, that supports first-class continuations. However, special care is required to assure that hen a continuation is invoked the values of logic variables are properly restored to their values at ıe time the continuation was created. A complete embedding provides a semantically consonant nion of both the environment and control contexts of the embedding and embedded languages.

[3] Environments contained in closures must be heap allocated to allow indefinite extent of environment bindings. omorowski states that Prolog's variable binding and control mechanisms require stack structures distinct from ose of the embedding language [15]. This is true only when the embedding language lacks first-class functions ıd continuations.

	⟨pred⟩ ::= **(**⟨relation⟩ ⟨term⟩***)**	predication form
	⟨clause⟩ ::= **(logic-lambda (**⟨id⟩***) (**⟨term⟩***)** ⟨pred⟩***)**	clause form
	⟨term⟩ ::= *Scheme expressions with value in T*	term form
	⟨relation⟩ ::= *Scheme expressions with value in R*	relation form
	D = *Scheme values (except references)*	denotable values
lvar ∈	$V = ref(\text{unbound}) \mid ref(D) \mid ref(V)$	logic variables
term ∈	$T = D \mid V \mid T \times T$	terms
fk ∈	$K_f = cont()$	failure continuations
sk ∈	$K_s = cont(K_f)$	success continuations
rel ∈	$R = T^* \rightarrow P$	relations
pred ∈	$P = [K_f] \rightarrow K_f$	predications
clause ∈	$C = [T, K_f] \rightarrow K_f$	clauses
	alt : $C^* \rightarrow R$	alternation function
	seq : $P^* \rightarrow P$	sequencing function

Figure 2. Syntax, types and functionality of a logic embedding.

The environment embeddings of logic programming into Scheme by Felleisen [8] and Srivastava, Oxley and Srivastava [20] fail to be complete embeddings. Though first class continuation are shared by the embedded and embedding language, they do not restore logic variable binding when invoked. Thus there are meaningful continuation invocations which, if performed in thes embeddings, will violate the semantics of logic programming.

The problem of restoring logic variable values is related to the problem of restoring th values of dynamic (or fluid) bindings. The *state-space* model of control was originally develope to solve the dynamic binding problem and to implement a generalization of unwind-protect in th presence of first-class continuations [2,9,11]. The central result of the present paper is a new form of state-space model for the maintenance of logic variable bindings in the event of any meaningfu continuation invocation.[4]

3. An environment embedding of logic programming

In this section we develop an environment embedding of logic programming in Scheme. Thoug the embedded and embedding languages share a common control environment, this fails to b a complete embedding because no attempt is made to restore logic variable bindings upon continuation invocation. The primary purpose of this embedding is to provide a framework withi which to present a complete embedding that avoids this restriction; however, it is hoped that th simple structure of this embedding will be of some interest in its own right.

We use non-structure sharing [12,13,17]: a logic variable is represented as a referenc (pointer), which may refer either to a value, to another logic variable with which it has bee unified, or to a unique value denoting 'unbound'. See Figure 2 for a logic variable domain equation, as well as syntax and type definitions for other elements of this embedding. (The symbol on the left indicate the standard identifiers names that will be used for objects of their typ

[4] We shall see that certain continuation invocations are not meaningful, for they are inconsistent with logi programming semantics.

```
(define unify
  (lambda (term1 term2 fk)
    (letrec
      ([bind (lambda (var term subst)
               (cond [(bound-lvar? var) (unify1 (lval var) term subst)]
                     [else (extend-subst subst var term)]))]
       [unify1 (lambda (term1 term2 subst)
                 (cond [(eq? term1 term2) subst]
                       [(lvar? term1) (bind term1 term2 subst)]
                       [(lvar? term2) (bind term2 term1 subst)]
                       [(and (pair? term1) (pair? term2))
                        (unify1 (car term1) (car term2)
                          (unify1 (cdr term1) (cdr term2) subst))]
                       [else (unbind! subst) (fk)]))])
      (unify1 term1 term2 '()))))
```

Figure 3. Unification procedure.

the program segments that follow.) For efficiency, invisible pointers may be used instead of eferences [12,20]. We name the logic variable constructor, selector, binder, type predicate and ound predicate functions **lvar**, **lval**, **bind-lvar!**, **lvar?** and **bound-lvar?**, respectively.

We take a *substitution* to be simply a set of logic variables. **Extend-subst** is passed a ubstitution, an unbound logic variable and a value. It binds the logic variable to the value, and eturns a substitution extended with this variable. **Unbind!** takes a substitution and unbinds ach of its logic variables (by assigning their reference the unbound value).

A ⟨term⟩ may be any Scheme expression; however its value is interpreted as a structure built f pairs, logic variables and literals. The function **unify** (Figure 3) unifies two terms. If unification ucceeds, a substitution of all logic variable bindings created by the unification is returned. If it ails, any bindings created up to the point of failure are undone, and then the failure continuation assed to **unify** is invoked. (The occurs check has been omitted for simplicity.)

Failure continuations are represented as functions of no arguments, since no information need e passed when failing. They may be obtained with the function **call-with-current-failure-ontinuation**, abbreviated **call/cfc**:

```
(define call/cfc
  (lambda (f)
    (call/cc
      (lambda (k)
        (f (lambda () (k any)))))))
```

ny indicates an irrelevant value that will be ignored; failure continuations are essentially com-nand continuations. Initially, we represent success continuations simply as continuations provided y the primitive **call/cc** function.

The convention for the use of success and failure continuations is critical to the structure of logic programming embedding. We opt for 'upward failure continuations' [12], in the manner of

```
(define alt
   (lambda clause-values-list
      (lambda term
         (lambda (fk)
            (call/cc
               (lambda (sk)
                  (do ([cvl clause-values-list (cdr cvl)])
                      [(null? cvl) (fk)]
                      (call/cfc
                         (lambda (fk)
                            (sk ((car cvl) term fk))))))))))

(define seq
   (lambda preds
      (lambda (fk)
         (do ([preds preds (cdr preds)]
              [pred-fk fk ((car preds) pred-fk)])
             [(null? preds) pred-fk]))))
```

Figure 4. Alternation and sequencing functions.

Felleisen [8]: in the event of success, a failure continuation is passed upward by either returning it from a function or invoking a success continuation with it. Subsequent invocation of this failure continuation causes backtracking to the point of success. Other alternatives include passing success continuations to the theorem prover and returning in the event of failure [4,17], passing a continuation which is always invoked with true or false, indicating success or failure [20], passing separate success and failure continuations [14,23], and representing the failure continuation as a stream of frames [1,4]. Continuations may be represented either as data structures [4,1], closures [17,23], or encapsulations of the system control state [8,14,20], as we do here.

Predications (or *atoms*) are represented as Scheme applications in which the function position evaluates to a *relation* and the arguments evaluate to terms. When the relation is applied to the terms, a function is returned that takes a failure continuation. If the terms fail to satisfy the relation, this failure continuation is invoked. Otherwise, the predication returns a new failure continuation that, when invoked, attempts to satisfy the relation in a new way (and invokes the original failure continuation if there are no more ways).

For example, we express the Prolog predication **member(A,[1,B])** as **(member A (list 1 B))**. Assume the value of identifier **A** is an unbound logic variable and the value of **B** is a logic variable bound to 2. (By convention, Scheme identifiers that are bound to logic variables begin with capital letters. Also, when no ambiguity results we refer to logic variables by the name of the associated Scheme identifier; for example, "**A** is unbound".) Upon receiving the **A** and **(list 1 B)** terms, the member relation returns a predication which is passed a failure continuation κ_{f1}. A new failure continuation, κ_{f2}, is then returned with **A** bound to **1**. When κ_{f2} is invoked the application will return (to its original continuation) a third failure continuation κ_{f3}, leaving **A** bound to (the logic variable) **B**. Invoking κ_{f3} results in **A** being unbound and κ_{f1} being invoked

A relation is formed by passing *clause values* to the **alt** function (Figure 4).[5] A new failure ontinuation is obtained for each clause invocation using **call/cfc**. The clause either returns failure continuation (which is passed to the success continuation, **sk**, of the predication that ivoked the relation) or it invokes the failure continuation. The failure continuation of the last ause is the failure continuation of the predication.[6]

Because clauses may introduce new logic variables whose scope local to the clause, the op- ration for creating clauses must be a special form (it cannot be a function). By analogy with ambda, the standard special form that evaluates to a function, we call the form for creating lauses **logic-lambda**. It is implemented as a syntactic extension (macro) that transforms an xpression of the form

```
(logic-lambda (id1 ... idk) (term1 ... termm) pred1 ... predn)
```

ito an expression of the form

```
(lambda (term fk)
   (let ([id1 (lvar unbound)] ... [idk (lvar unbound)])
      (let ([subst (unify term (list term1 ... termm) fk)])
         (logic-bind (seq pred1 ... predn) subst fk))))
```

his expression evaluates to a clause that takes a term and a failure continuation. The *term* nd *pred* expressions are evaluated in an extended environment which associates $id_1, \ldots, idkl$ ith new logic variables that are initially unbound. A list of the clause terms is unified with e argument term, returning a new substitution if successful. The predications of the clause are en called sequentially under control of the **seq** function (Figure 4). Each predication receives a ilure continuation. If successful, it returns a new failure continuation. This failure continuation then passed to the next predication or, in the case of the last predication, returned as the sult of the clause. When a failure continuation returned as the result of the clause is invoked, is necessary to unbind the logic variables introduced by a clause. This is managed by the **ogic-bind** function:

```
(define logic-bind
   (lambda (pred subst fk)
      (pred (lambda () (unbind! subst) (fk)))))
```

his unbinding could be performed more efficiently using a trail [3,13]. However, in the next ction we extend logic-bind to manage the *rebinding* of logic variables in the event control is ansferred back into clauses via *success* continuation invocation. The trail mechanism is not fficient in this more general context.

---

5 A mechanism for maintaining a data base of relations has been added to this embedding, but in this paper e are not concerned with such issues.

6 Alt may be refined somewhat by replacing the do termination clause with `[(null? (cdr clauses)) ((car auses) term fk)]`. This is similar to evlis tail recursion [22].

The Prolog relation

```
append([],Y,Y).
append([HT],Y,[HZ]) :- append(T,Y,Z).
```

is expressed in this embedding as

```
(define append
   (relation
      [('() Y Y)]
      [((cons H T) Y (cons H Z)) (append T Y Z)]))
```

where **relation** is a simple syntactic extension that, in the above case, expands into

```
(define append
   (alt (logic-lambda (Y) ('() Y Y))
        (logic-lambda (H T Y Z) ((cons H T) Y (cons H Z)) (append T Y Z)))))
```

Each rule is expanded into a **logic-lambda** expression that contains a list of the logic identifier used in the rule, the pattern list, and finally the predications of the rule.

We define the traditional Prolog *fail* and *is* operations as simple examples. *Fail* is simply predication that always fails. This is accomplished by immediately invoking the failure contin uation passed to the predication. Thus we define **fail** to be the function **(lambda (pred-fk** **(pred-fk))**.

Is predications are of the form **(is** *var function argument* ...**)**, where *var* evaluates to logic variable, and *function* is a Scheme function that is to be passed the given arguments. First any logic variables in the arguments are replaced by their values. If any of these logic variable are unbound, then the **is** predication fails. Otherwise, the function is applied to the arguments obtaining some answer *ans*. Now if *var* is an unbound logic variable, then it is bound to *ans* an the predication succeeds; otherwise, if *var*'s value is the same as *ans*, the predication succeeds In all other cases, it fails. This is accomplished by the Scheme function

```
(define is
   (lambda (var function . args)
      (lambda (fk)
         (let ([args (lval* args)])
            (for-each (lambda (arg) (cond [(lvar! arg) (fk)])) args)
            (let ([ans (apply function args)])
               (cond
                  [(not (bound-lvar? var)) (bind-lvar! var ans) fk]
                  [(equal? (lval* var) ans) fk]
                  [else (fk)]))))))
```

where **lval*** recursively copies a list structure replacing logic variables by their values.

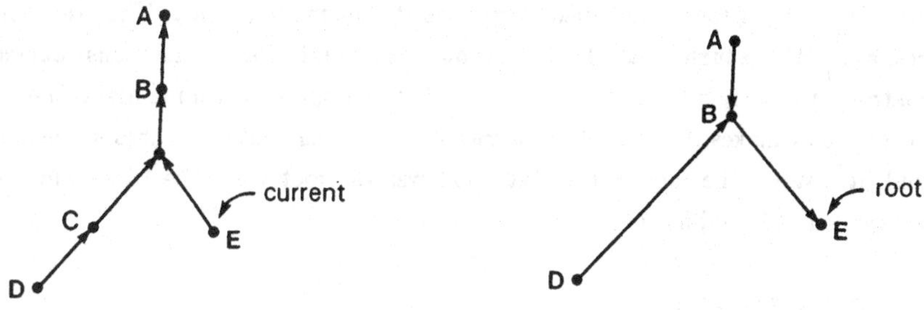

Figure 5. Control tree (left) and corresponding state-space (right).

Prolog's *cut* may be incorporated into this embedding by extending **alt** so that it dynamically ›r fluidly) binds **fk**. Cut may then be defined as **(lambda (pred-fk) (fluid fk))**, where **fluid** ›turns the fluid binding associated with its argument. Relations might be defined with different ersions of **alt**, where each version binds **fk** to a distinct fluid identifier. This would allow a redication in one relation to 'cut' another relation. The state-space model presented in the next ection can be extended in a straightforward way to adjust fluid bindings when continuations are ıvoked [9,11].

. A state-space model for logic continuations

ı this section we deal with the special difficulty presented by first-class continuations in the ›ntext of logic programming: when invoking a continuation it may be necessary to modify the indings of logic variables. Of course when a failure continuation is invoked it may be necessary › unbind certain logic variables. But upon invoking a 'lateral' success continuation, as when ımping from one leaf to another of the control tree, it is also necessary to restore the values of ›gic variables accessible at the destination point to the values they had at the time that point as marked. To manage this unbinding and rebinding of logic variables we modify the state-space ıodel of control.

A *state-space* is a tree with one node (or *state*) for each logic-bind. It is distinct from the ›ntrol tree discussed earlier, though they are related: the undirected image of the control tree ıay be coalesced (removing nodes not associated with logic-binds) to obtain the undirected image ' the state-space. Though the state-space has fewer nodes, the critical difference is in the position ' the root, and therefore the direction of the edges (which point towards the root in both cases). ı the control tree the root is the original control state, while in the state-space the root is the ırrent state. It follows that the ancestors of a given frame in a control tree are the control ames that could be reached by a series of returns (without continuation invocation). In the ›rresponding state-space the ancestors of a state are those states corresponding to frames that ould be reached by an (undirected) traversal of the control tree from the frame corresponding › the given state to the current frame. See Figure 5. We say a state *s* is *active* if the root of the ate-space corresponds to a descendent of *s* in the control tree, or if the root is *s* itself.

We represent the state-space of a computation by a globally bound object that responds to messages. The current root is returned in response to the message **root**. The other four possible messages, **extend!**, **return!**, **fail!** and **reroot!**, cause state-space transitions. **Extend!** is used when control enters a logic-bind; it adds a new state to the space, which maintains the substitution being bound, and makes it the root. **Return!** is used when control returns successfully from a logic-bind; it restores the root to the state that was the root when the logic-bind was entered. The new version of logic-bind is

```
(define logic-bind
   (lambda (pred subst fk)
      (let ([state (state-space 'root)])
         ((state-space 'extend!) (make-state subst))
         (let ([ans (pred (lambda () (unbind! subst) (fk)))])
            ((state-space 'return!) state)
            ans))))
```

The **fail!** and **reroot!** state-space messages are used when failure or success continuations, respectively, are invoked; they make the destination continuation the root and may adjust some logic variable values, as will be described presently. The new versions of **call/cc** and **call/cfc** are

```
(define call/cc
   (lambda (f)
      (prim-call/cc
         (lambda (k)
            (let ([state (state-space 'root)])
               (f (lambda (v)
                     ((state-space 'reroot!) state)
                     (k v))))))))

(define call/cfc
   (lambda (f)
      (prim-call/cc
         (lambda (k)
            (let ([state (state-space 'root)])
               (f (lambda ()
                     ((state-space 'fail!) state)
                     (k any))))))))
```

where **prim-call/cc** is the original **call/cc** function. These are the only operations on the state-space; the user may not manipulate it directly.[7]

States are represented internally as cons cells. (See Figure 6.) The car of a state cell is an object that responds to the state transition messages, while the cdr is a link that points to the nearest state in the direction of the root, or nil if the state is the root. Hence each state cell may be viewed as a list, the last element of which is the root. With each of the state transition

[7] For convenience we define the state-space globally in this paper, but in a production system its scope should be restricted to the **call/cc**, **call/cfc** and **logic-bind** functions.

```
(define state-space
   (let ([root (list (lambda (msg) do-nothing))])
      (lambda (msg)
         (case msg
            [(root) root]
            [(extend! return! fail! reroot!)
             (lambda (new-state)
                (case msg
                   [(extend!) (set-cdr! root new-state)]
                   [(return! fail! reroot!)
                    (reverse! new-state)
                    (for-each (lambda (x) (x msg)) root)])
                (set! root new-state))]))))
```

Figure 6. Initial logic state-space.

essages a new state must be passed, which becomes the root. In the **return!**, **fail!** and **reroot!** cases, the state links are adjusted to point to the new root by simply reversing the links the list headed by the new state. Think of picking up the tree by the new state and giving it a ood shake so that all paths lead to the new root. Each of the objects associated with states on e reversed list (which now begins with the old root) is then passed the state-space transition essage and will modify its local state as required.

Each state has an associated substitution and status. Substitutions are provided with the lditional operations **save!** and **restore!**, which save and restore the substitution's logic variable alues using storage local to the substitution. The status is either *in*, *out* or *returned*: *in* indicates at the state is active (in the sense defined earlier); *returned* indicates the state is inactive because ontrol returned via a successful resolution; and *out* indicates the state is inactive because control assed out of the descendent subtree by invoking a continuation. Since new states are immediately itered, their status is initially *in*. (See Figure 7.)

When a state object receives a transition message, response will depend on both its current atus and the type of message. There are three statuses and three types of messages, so there e nine possibilities to consider.

Return! is used only by logic-bind to restore the state-space root to the state s_1 in which e logic-bind was entered. Thus the **return!** message is received by only two states: s_1 and the ate s_2 created by the logic-bind. The status of both s_1 and s_2 will be *in*, and the only effect of e **return!** is to change the status of s_2 to *returned*. (At the time the **return!** message is sent, is already the root. s_1 detects this by noticing its cdr link is nil, and thereby avoids changing s status.)

The status of an active state is always *in*, for control can only leave the subtree via a logic-nd return (which sets the status to *returned*) or via invocation of a success continuation. In the tter case, the **reroot!** message is sent to the state and its status becomes *out*. (Note that the **reroot!** message is also sent to the new root, which does nothing when it notices its cdr link is l.) Control can only reenter the subtree via invocation of a success or failure continuation. In

```
(define make-state
   (lambda (subst)
      (let ([status 'in])
         (rec local-state
            (list
               (lambda (msg)
                  (case msg
                     [(return!)
                      (cond [(not (null? (cdr local-state)))
                             (set! status 'returned)])]
                     [(fail!)
                      (case status
                         [(returned) (set! status 'in)]
                         [(in) do-nothing]
                         [(out) (error "can't fail when out")])]
                     [(reroot!)
                      (case status
                         [(returned) (error "can't reroot when returned")]
                         [(in) (cond [(not (null? (cdr local-state)))
                                      (set! status 'out)
                                      (save! subst)])]
                         [(out) (set! status 'in)
                                (restore! subst)])])))))))
```

Figure 7. **Make-state** for a logic state-space.

the former case, a **reroot!** message will again be received, which will return the status to *in* i the state was left via a success continuation. A state with status *returned* can only be reentere via a failure continuation.

When control leaves a state via a success continuation, the values of the state's substitutio variables are saved in the substitution. They are subsequently restored whenever the state i reentered via another success continuation. The state-space mechanism exists solely to implemen this operation and to assure that its integrity is maintained. This integrity would be violated if failure continuation were used to reenter a state with status *out*, or if a state with status *returne* were reentered via a success continuation.

5. Efficiency considerations

The code presented here was designed for clarity, not speed, and many efficiency improvement are possible. For example, the **alt**, **seq** and **unify** function applications could be compiled in-lin [8], the state-space could be built up of data structures instead of procedures, and the **(case ms** ...) dispatches of the **state-space** and **make-state** functions could be avoided by in-line codin of the state-space operations in **logic-bind**, **call/cc** and **call/cfc**. Other standard maneuvers such as tail recursion optimization, should also be applicable in many cases.

Our main efficiency concern is the price paid for the state-space mechanism in an optimize implementation. Though a definitive answer awaits the development of such an implementation few observations are appropriate at this time. The logic state-space may be viewed as a gen-alization of the trail mechanism: the state-space is capable of rebinding as well as unbinding gic variables, and may take on a tree structure, rather than being strictly linear. This requires lditional run time tag checking and heap, rather than stack, allocation. However, these ad-tional costs may be avoided much of the time by an implementation that can 'cheat without tting caught'. For example, if it can be proved that no **call/cc** or **call/cfc** operations will be rformed during a particular phase of execution, then the system is free to revert to the tradi-onal stack allocated trail. It even seems possible for a system to routinely use a trail, and only nvert the trail information into an extension of the state-space when a continuation is actually tained. The state-space overhead is then incurred only when the user requires its generality. related 'pay as you go' approach is used by some Scheme compilers that stack allocate control formation until **call/cc** is invoked, at which time the stack is copied to the heap.

In many cases when the generality of a logic state-space would be used, the alternatives e also expensive and likely to be less efficient than employing a well implemented logic state-ace. For example, to achieve non-blind backtracking the alternatives are repeating part of a mputation, or explicitly saving and restoring necessary information. (This is analogous to the plicit stack management required to simulate recursion in a non-recursive language.) Other proaches to increasing control flexibility, such as LOGLISP's breadth-first search parameters 9], also introduce overhead and are less general.

Conclusion

principle advantage of non-procedural programming languages, such as Prolog, is that they oid the necessity of repeatedly specifying commonly occurring patterns of control. This is done providing a complex default control mechanism, such as Prolog's depth-first search. Problems ise when variations on the default control mechanism are required. Some variations may be commodated by auxiliary control mechanisms, such as Prolog's cut, but other variations may difficult or impossible to achieve with such specialized mechanisms.

We have shown that the power of non-procedural program specification may be provided ong with the ability to obtain non-standard control behavior on occasion. This is accomplished embedding the non-procedural mechanism in a traditional procedural language whose control echanism (principally procedure call) is simple and well understood. Greatest flexibility is tained when the embedding language makes continuations available as first-class objects of mputation.

Special precautions must be taken in contexts, such as logic programming, in which changes ay be made to the environment of a control context that must be accounted for when control returned to the control context (via a continuation invocation). We have shown how the state-ace model of control may be extended to account for changes in the bindings of logic variables. ntinuations may then be used to obtain greater control flexibility in logic programs.

knowledgements: We thank Matthias Felleisen, Dan Friedman and Peter Williams for their tailed comments on this paper.

References

[1] Abelson, H., and Sussman, G.J., with Sussman, J., *Structure and Interpretation of Compute Programs*, MIT Press, 1985.

[2] Baker, H.G., Jr., Shallow Binding in Lisp 1.5, *C. ACM*, **21**:565–569 (1978).

[3] Bruynooghe, M., The memory management of PROLOG implementations, in: K.L. Clark an S.-A. Tärnlund (eds.), *Logic Programming*, Academic Press, New York, pp. 83–98 (1982).

[4] Carlsson, M., On implementing Prolog in Functional Programming, *New Generation Com puting*, **2**:347–359 (1984).

[5] Clinger, W.C., Ed., The Revised Revised Report on Scheme, Computer Science Departmen Technical Report No. 174, Indiana University, Bloomington, Indiana, 1985, and Artificia Intelligence Memo No. 848, MIT, Cambridge, Massachusetts, 1985.

[6] Clocksin, W.F. and Mellish, C.S., *Programming in Prolog, Second Edition*, Springer-Verlag New York, 1984.

[7] Dybvig, R.K., and Smith B., *The Scheme Programming Language*, Prentice-Hall, 1986.

[8] Felleisen, M., Transliterating Prolog into Scheme, Computer Science Department Technica Report No. 182, Indiana University, Bloomington, Indiana, 1985.

[9] Friedman, D.P., and Haynes, C.T., Constraining control, *Conf. Record of the Twelfth Annu ACM Symposium on Principles of Programming Languages*, pp. 245–254 (1985), revised i Computer Science Department Technical Report No. 183, Indiana University, Bloomingto Indiana, 1985.

[10] Friedman, D.P., Haynes, C.T. and Kohlbecker, E., Programming with continuations, i P. Pepper (ed.), *Program Transformation and Programming Environments*, Springer-Verlag New York, pages 263–274 (1984).

[11] Hanson, C., and Lamping, J., Dynamic Binding in Scheme, unpublished manuscript, 1984.

[12] Kahn, K.M., and Carlsson, M., How to implement Prolog on a LISP Machine, in: J.A. Camp bell (ed.), *Implementations of PROLOG*, Halstead Press, New York, pp. 117–134 (1984).

[13] Kluźniak, F., and Szpakowicz, S., *Prolog for Programmers*, Academic Press, 1985.

[14] Kohlbecker, E., eu-Prolog, Computer Science Department Technical Report No. 155, Indian University, Bloomington, Indiana, 1984.

[15] Komorowski, H.J., QLOG—the programming environment for Prolog, in: K.L. Clark an S.-A. Tärnlund (eds.), *Logic Programming*, Academic Press, New York, pp. 315–324 (1982

[16] Landin, P. A correspondence between ALGOL 60 and Church's lambda notation, *C. ACM* **8**:89–101 and 158–165 (1965).

[17] Mellish, C., and Hardy, S., Integrating Prolog in the POPLOG environment, in: J.A. Camp bell (ed.), *Implementations of PROLOG*, Halstead Press, New York, pp. 147–162 (1984).

[18] Reynolds, J.C., Definitional interpreters for higher-order programming languages, *Proceeding of the 25th ACM National Conference*, pp. 717–740 (1972).

[19] Robinson, J.A., and Sibert, E.E., LOGLISP: motivation, design and implementation, i K.L. Clark and S.-A. Tärnlund (eds.), *Logic Programming*, Academic Press, New York, p 299–314 (1982).

[20] Srivastava, A., Oxley, D., and Srivastava, D., An(other) integration of logic and function programming, *Proceedings of The IEEE Symposium on Logic Programming*, pp. 254–26 (1985).

[21] Sussman, G.J., and Steele, G.L., Jr., Scheme: an interpreter for extended lambda calculus", Artificial Intelligence Memo No. 349, MIT, Cambridge, Massachusetts, 1975.

[22] Wand, M., Continuation-based program transformation strategies, *J. ACM,* **27**:164–180 (1980).

[23] Wand, M., A semantic algebra for logic programming, Computer Science Department Technical Report No. 134, Indiana University, Bloomington, Indiana, 1983.

CUT & PASTE - defining the impure Primitives of Prolog

CHRIS MOSS
Imperial College, London

Abstract

Prolog consists of the Horn Clause subset of predicate logic interpreted by a fixed (left to right, depth first) evaluation strategy and a number of non-logical primitive predicates. The most fundamental of these are 'cut' for control of execution, 'assert' and 'retract' for changing the database, and input-output. Whatever the desirability of these features for the logic programming languages of the future there is general agreement as to the need of these for Prolog as a practical programming language for today.

Despite their apparently simple definition there is considerable diversity in the details of the implementation of these primitives and some experiments to demonstrate this diversity are reported. We then suggest definitions that could be agreed and implemented by everyone.

Control - The Cut Primitive

The cut is an efficiency hack which allows considerable control over the 'non-deterministic' nature of Prolog. Its behaviour can be best illustrated by the following program:

```
a(X) <- b(X)& ! & c(X).
a(X) <- d(X).
b(e).  b(f).
c(X).
d(g).
```

Without the cut, "!", the query ?-a(Z) would have three solutions: Z=e,f,g. With the cut the query has only a single solution, Z = e. In other words, further solutions of any subgoals appearing before cut in the clause are inhibited, and any other clauses for the same predicate are also ignored. In the example, the call to c always succeeds; in general, of course, it will not.

If we wish to give a declarative, rather than operational, meaning to the cut, we can only do so in terms of rewriting the clauses. The above definition of 'a' may be rewritten:

```
a(x) <- first(b(X)) & c(X).
a(x) <- not(b(X)) & d (X).
```

where 'first' and 'not' are meta-level predicates which are somewhat closer to logical concepts. 'first' finds a single solution to the goal which is its argument and corresponds to the logical notion "there exists a solution" with the additional constraint that it is the first such solution. (This is called 'once' in C-Prolog.) 'not' corresponds to logical negation. Neither of these correspondences to standard logic are exact, but, with the addition of extra constraints, they are usable in, for instance, a program transformation system that needs to preserve meaning.

Both the cut and the declarative rewriting can be simply extended to situations where more than one cut appears, either in the same or different clauses.

Thus **with cut** **equivalent**

```
a(x) <- b(x)&!&c(x)     |    a(x)<- first(b(x)) & c(x)
a(x) <- d(x)&!&e(x)     |    a(x) <- not(b(x)) & first (d(x)) & e(x)
a(x) <- f(x).           |    a(x) <- not(b(x)), not(d(x)) & f(x).
```

here pattern matching is used in the head of the clause the rewriting becomes a ittle more complicated though it may lead to a simpler set of rewritten clauses.

his analysis suggests at least two other sets of primitives. One, which is emantically simpler, is to provide a cut which does not prevent backtracking within he clause, together with a "first solution" or functional call. Such a pair has een explored by Smolka (1984) and does not appear to be much more complicated to mplement in a Prolog enviroment. The other is a "non-directional" cut suggested by arren (1986) in which the negations would apply to previous as well as subsequent lauses. This is more applicable in parallel evaluation enviroments.

omplications arise from two sources: other "logical" operators in clauses, such as isjunction; and the meta call facility. These variations have been explored by a est program, contained in appendix 1, which has been run on a total of 24 Prolog mplementations yielding 11 different sets of behaviour.

Cuts within a disjunction

he occurrence of 'or' in a clause has two possible interpretations. It may be onsidered as a simple rewriting rule, or as a predicate defined by Prolog clauses. hus the original program is rewritten (using | as the disjunction symbol):

```
a(x) <- b(x)& ! & c(x) | d(x).
```

here are two established interpretations for this:

1) treat "or" as a standard Prolog clause and use a straightforward interpretation f metacall such that the cut operates in the clause in which it appears.

```
X|Y <- X.
X|Y <- Y.
```

2) Handle 'or' specially such that it is transparent to cut, together with the ther logical operators such as 'and'. This was established by the Edinburgh DEC-10 ompiler and was later copied by Waterloo Prolog and many other systems, though not ithout problems (see below).

he problem with the first interpretation arises when we consider the use of cut in ny realistic situation including the program above. In addition to the 'meta-nterpretation' of cut, we also have the meta-interpretation of 'and':

```
X & Y <- X & Y.
```

seemingly meaningless clause which only makes sense when you consider the iffering role of '&' on each side (indeed many Prologs will force some syntactic istinction such as use of brackets or prefix form in declaring this).

e parsing of the example above which makes use of 'or' is

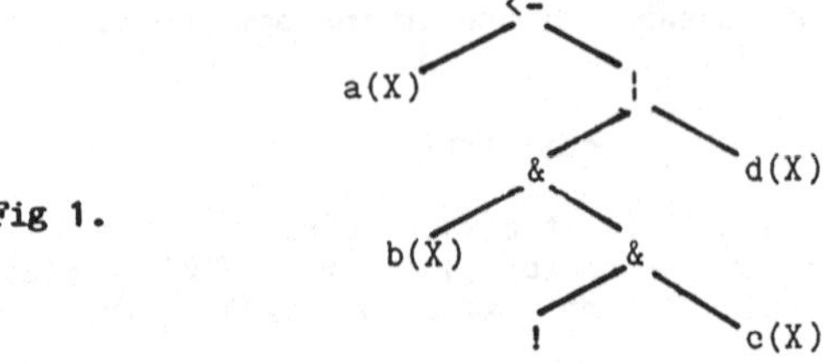

Fig 1.

This demonstrates that the scope of the cut is in this case only the 'and' clause in which it occurs - and it is to all intents and purposes useless. It also demonstrates the relative inefficiency of this code, especially in a compiled context: the evaluation includes a total of 4 metacalls, which are relatively expensive operations involving some type of linkup with the predicate definition - an operation usually done at compile-time.

It is thus obvious why the majority of implementations have opted for the second interpretation. The major exception to this is the 'microProlog' family of list-based implementations, and it is instructive to see why they have not.

In microProlog a clause is represented by a list of which the first element is the head of the clause, and the rest of the list is the body. The body as a list is then an implicit conjunction. It uses the identifier 'OR' for disjunction which is defined as follows

```
((OR X Y) ¦ X)
((OR X Y) ¦ Y)
```

using its 'Core' LISP like syntax, where a predicate name occurs **after** the brackets and a cons pair is written (X¦Y).

OR takes as arguments two lists of subgoals, and the tail of the list representing the clause for OR is thus replaced by one or other of these lists. This has the effect of "raising" any conjunctions within the disjunction so that only one metacall is required, instead of four in the implementation above. It also means that a cut behaves the same inside a conjunction as it does when it appears alone.

The original clause is written in this syntax (with / for cut) as

```
((a X) (OR ((b X) / (c X)) ((d X)) ))
```

so that the instantiated form of the clauses for OR is

```
((OR ((b X) / (c X)) ((d X))) (b X) / (c X))
((OR ((b X) / (c X)) ((d X))) (d X))
```

The cut therefore appears at the top level and so both systems give the same results. However, if we were to introduce another clause into the example, there would be a difference (here we revert to standard syntax):

```
a(X) <- b(X) & ! & c(X) ¦ d(X)
a(X) <- e(X).
b(b). b(c). c(b). d(d). e(e).
```

In this example micro would give two answers - X=b and X=e, whereas the Edinburgh approach only gives a single answer, X=b.

One therefore reaches the curious condition in micro Prolog in which the introduction of a single "or" does not change the semantics, but having a mixture of "or" and alternative clauses does change the meaning. For micro the decision to use

R is all or nothing.

```
.e.  a <- b                 is equivalent to     a <- b|c|d.
     a <- c
     a <- d             but not equivalent to    a <- b|c.
                                                 a <- d.
```

or any conjunction of conditions b, c and d including cut. We conclude therefore hat microProlog's treatment is not satisfactory.

Cut and Metacall

second semantic problem of cut is its relation to the metacall. The effect of a etacall is generally to evaluate a new query which is constructed as a term uring the evaluation of a query. In most cases this forms an entirely self ontained query which does not affect the normal evaluation procedure of the system. ut is an exception to this. If passed to a procedure it is like a packaged time omb waiting to step in and wreck the established semantics of the clause. It also omplicates the compilation of clauses.

Consider the sentence

```
a(X) <- X & b.
a(X) <- c.
```

he second clause is always reachable **unless** X happens to contain a cut. Thus nything that is to be stated about this clause must allow this as a possibility. A ore extreme case of the same is the clasue

```
a(X) <- b(Y) & Y.
```

n this case the cut may be returned by the procedure b and therefore affect the valuation of the clause itself by cutting out backtracking possibilities at a igher level. Much of the effect of "ancestor cut" found in Waterloo Prolog among thers may thus be obtained, albeit only with the co-operation of the calling rocedures.

his leaves the very real question "do we need the cut within the metacall?". It as been asserted by some that this facility gives an ability that cannot be rovided without it. An example quoted is the task of writing a metalevel Prolog nterpreter for clauses which may themselves include cuts.

t is easy to demonstrate the falsity of this claim by giving a construction which s equivalent to passing cut as a parameter, but does not involve it. Suppose we ave a metacall in the midst of the body of a call,

```
... & X & ...
```

hich we wish to instantiate to either a cut or some other goal. Then we may write he subgoal

```
... & (X=! & ! | X) & ...
```

hen in the first case the cut will be executed anyway, cutting out any backtracking n the clause. In the second case it will not be executed but the disjunction will ucceed or fail depending on what X is.

e therefore conclude that cut should not be allowed to act through a metacall. his is easily enforced by replacing any metacall X by an equivalent statement call(X), as in C-Prolog, for instance. Then even if the cut has an effect, as it may in the case call(a(X)&!b(X)), its effect will be strictly local and will not afect the semantics of the calling clause.

Assert and Retract

One of the features that distinguishes Prolog from pure Horn Clauses is the ability of a Prolog program to change its own set of axioms. This is typically done by two predicates, assert and retract, which occur in many variations which we do not examine. Between them, they extend in practice the power of Horn Clauses. For instance, it is possible to write a procedure to find all solutions to a problem using only negation but it is an order n^2 algorithm in the number of solutions, whereas with assert and retract it can be done in order n.

Like cut, assert is defined simply to provide a practical programming system. It is not logically consistent: any variables in the term which is asserted which happen to be unbound at the time are effectively universally quantified, and on backtracking the added clause is not removed. In addition the old and new database are not named in any way. Nonetheless assert appears in this form in virtually every Prolog.

There are many differences in practice however which are demonstrated by a series of tests which have been applied to 12 systems giving 9 different answers (see appendix 2).

(1) It cannot always be used. For instance, in several systems if a predicate is compiled then assert will succeed but have no apparent effect. This points to a need for declarations: a predicate should at least be able to take the characteristics 'static' and 'dynamic', and if it is 'static' then the assert should fail.

(2) The added clause may not be found if execution of the predicate concerned has already commenced. The precise effect of this varies from system to system and relates to the precise data structure used to implement the clause structure. (see fig. 2) Typically, when a backtracking pointer is established on entry to a clause it points to the next possible clause that can match.

If there are no other clauses, many systems will not bother to build a backtrack frame. Thus if the clause being executed is the last, then on the failure of that clause, no back-tracking will be done. However, if there is an intervening clause, the system may well 'find' the extra clause.

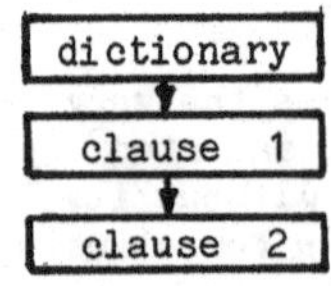

Fig 2.

This does not have to be directly self-modifying code, nor does the assert need to be a subgoal of the clause; it only has to be invoked chronologically after the activation of the clause and before it is finally failed. Hence any use of assert to maintain 'flags' or' global variables' is susceptible to this variation. The variability can usually be removed by insisting on a functional (once only) call.

A similar situation is encountered with retract. One might expect that there would be some symmetry in the tests (as tests 3 and 4 correspond to 7 and 8 respectively in appendix 2). But this is too much to ask. There are several seemingly random variations reflecting implementation decisions.

(3) Retract, in most Edinburgh-like systems, is reinvoked on backtracking, and will attempt to delete the next matching clause. This behaviour is out of character with most of the other built-in predicates in Prolog systems and can be vicious: an incorrectly coded program can easily lead to an entire relation being

eleted by accident.

t is almost certainly due to the common use and encouragement of another predicate repeat' for coding repetitive tasks. Apart from encouraging 'non-logical' rogramming, the repeat construct cannot be used to convert a retract primitive hich does not backtrack into one which does. The reason is that when it has etracted all possible clauses, retract will fail and the clause above will go into n infinite repeat-fail loop. Thus a non-logical set of programming techniques has hanged the definition of another predicate in a way that is arguably dangerous. more sensible approach would be to use a version of repeat that converts a non-acktracking primitive into a backtracking one. An example of such a efinition is given in appendix 3.

4) Assert and retract, when used together, can have a number of unpredictable ffects. The most dramatic is to crash the system, which arises from ignoring the dvice of David Warren et al (1977) to ensure that the Prolog system can never ead to an undefined result. This can arise after a clause is retracted if the arbage space can be reclaimed immediately and overwritten by some other data tructure. Then an 'orphaned' backtrack pointer which points to this clause can asily cause havoc. This behaviour has been observed in several systems though the recise sequence of actions to precipitate it varies from system to system.

his leads to a constraint on releasing the clause space until after the termination f a program which does indeed prove a restriction for some systems which mplement their own environment written in Prolog, particularly if memory is imited. The solution suggested below overcomes this problem.

How important are variations in assert?

e must ask whether the variations assert and retract that we have discussed are mportant, or whether they are marginal and could be left as 'undefined' in a tandardisation of Prolog.

o answer this question one needs to catalogue the main uses of assert and retract. ithout any pretense of completeness we may list the following:

1) Storing of partial results, or lemmas as in the implementations of the setof' predicate.
2) Editing of databases and programs. This generally requires more precise ontrol than assert and retract, though these are formally adequate. For instance ne may wish to assert or retract a clause at any specified position.
3) Maintenance of 'global variables'. These might be used to control execution f a program (such as tracing), though one does not encourage their use as a ubstitute for a parameter, which is a throwback to a Fortran style of programming.
4) Completion of the database by knowledge added by input-output.

ost of applications (1) and (2) treat the creation and deletion of relations as a hole so that the issues above are not relevant. But (3) and (4) interleave ssertion and use in a way that would be affected by differences. These examples an also be classified as 'self-modifying' programs because in Prolog there is no istinction between a 'database access' and the execution of a program. Any rogram which both tests a predicate and adds to it is in a real sense self-odifying.

f one has started to evaluate a predicate, should any changes to that predicate ffect the solution? As we have seen, if the answer to this question is in any way yes', it is difficult to give a consistent operational semantics, let alone a eclarative semantics.

he situation is similar to the classic 'readers-writers' problem on files and there is a similar solution: namely, any reader who has started reading should continue tc see the same file. Any changes made by a writer should only be seen by a reader whc starts reading afterwards.

This does not define the protocol between different writers; one solution is tc 'lock' the file but this makes little sense in a Prolog context. Instead we take writing as an atomic act and depend on the evaluation strategy of Prolog to define the order in which updates take place.

The implementation of this strategy is not as difficult as it may appear. It simply consists of constructing a separate list each element of which points to the appropriate clause, and which is constructed as a "difference-list" in Prolog; i.e. the last element of the list is indicated explicitly in the dictionary entry.

clause 1
clause 2
clause 3

The common operations - adding or withdrawing from the head or tail of the list - are then relatively cheap actions which do not involve recopying the whole list. To add an item at the end we simply change the last pointer and the end pointer. Tc add or delete an item near the top involves changing only a small part. Whe reading the list we take a copy of the last element pointer and stop reading when we reach that and not when the pointer indicates a null. An outdated list is never deleted explicitly, but only garbage collected. Thus it will be delete automatically when the last 'reader' has finished.

The semantics of this treatment, though not given here, are much simpler than the alternatives. This is because when a clause is invoked one can inspect the databas and decide exactly which clauses are relevant and never change this decision.

Note that the change can only be considered an atomic act if retracts are non resatisfiable. If they were resatisfiable a pointer would be left somewhere in th middle of the set of clauses. In the resatifiable implementation suggested i appendix 3, each retract is a separable operation which starts from the head of th clause. If efficiency is an important consideration, then the 'retractall procedure is probably what is required.

Conclusions

As in the early days of any programming language, most large Prolog program hav been developed and used on a single implementation. Increasingly people are wantin to be able to transfer programs between different implementations. While it i relatively easy to translate different syntaxes, the subtle differences betwee evaluable predicates are more dangerous as the differences may not show up unde casual testing.

Cut and paste (assert) are the most fundamental evaluable predicates in Prolog an different implementations show many subtle differences which are exactly the typ which might cause such problems.

We have suggested theoretical reasons for adopting one specific implementation c cut and this paper may clarify the reasons for this. In the case of assert, ou solution solves a number of problems at the cost of some redesign to the basic dat structures.

I would like to thank the many Prolog users and implementers on the network who toc the time to run the programs mentioned in the appendix and send me the results.

This work was performed under an Esprit grant on logic programming enviroments.

References

. Smolke: Making Control and Data Flow in Logic Programs Explicit. 1984 ACM unctional Programming Conferences. p311-322.

.H.D. Warren, L.M. Pereira, F.C.N. Pereira: PROLOG - The language and its mplementation compared with Lisp. Proc. Symposium on Artificial Intelligence and rogramming Languages, 1977. SIGPLAN Vol. 12 (8).

.H.D. Warren: Sequential and Parallel Implementations of Prolog. Seminar at mperial College 1986.

Appendix 1

```
* Tests to distinguish various implementations of cut */

est1 :- do('Testing that cut is implemented). ', t1).
est2 :- do('Test if cut acts within disjunction', t2).
est3 :- do('Test if it cuts previous choices within disjunction', t3).
est4 :- do('Test if cut acts when passed as metacall', t4).
est5 :- do('Test if & cut acts within metacall', t5 ).
est6 :- do('Test if cut acts through not', t6).

o(Message,Test) :- w(Message), Test, !.
o(Message,Test) :- w('Does act').
(X) :- write(X), nl.
 :- w('Does not act').

1  :- (true
 ;w('Did not cut alternatives correctly'), fail),
 !, w('Succeeds going forwards'), fail.
1  :- w('Failed to cut goal').
2  :- (!
 ;w('Fails to cut disjoint alternatives')), fail.
2  :- t.
3  :- t3a(X),(!,fail
          ;w('Fails to cut disjunction')).
3  :- t.

t3a(!).
t3a(X) :-
 w('Did not cut alternatives'),
 fail.
t4  :- t3a(X), X,
 w('Ok going forwards'),fail.
t4  :- t.
t5  :- t5a(X), X, fail.
t5  :- t.
t5a((true,!)).
t6  :- not(not(!)), fail.
t6  :- t.
```

esults Implementation	Test 1	2	3	4	5	6
EC-10 (Comp)	Y	Y	Y	Y	Y	Y
aterloo, MUprolog, Quintus(Int), NH(1.3), Salford, Criss, Prolog-1, BIM, York	Y	Y	Y	Y	Y	N
uintus (Int)	Y	Y	Y	Y	Y	I
Prolog(1.5)	Y	Y	Y	Y	N	N
rolog-2 (Int, Comp)	Y	Y	Y	N	N	Y
EC-10 (Int), C-Prolog, Prolog-X	Y	Y	Y	N	N	N
OPLOG, LM-Prolog	Y	Y	Y	I	I	I
uintus (Comp)	Y	Y	I	N	N	N
icro, sigma	Y	N	N	Y	Y	N
NSW	Y	N	N	Y	N	N
CL	Y	N	N	N	N	N

here Y means did cut, N means did not cut and I means that it was trapped as an llegal use and failed.

Appendix 2

```
   /* Tests to distinguish various implementations of assert */
main :- test1, test2, test3, test4, test5, test6, test7, test8, test9.

test1 :- do('1. Test assert on existing predicate',t1).
test2 :- do('2. Test assert on new predicate',t2).
test3 :- do('3. Does it find added 3rd clause on backtracking', t3).
test4 :- do('4. Does it find added next (last) clause on backtracking', t4).
test5 :- do('5. Test retract on single element clause',t5).
test6 :- do('6. Does retract backtrack? ', t6).
test7 :- do('7. Does retract work on invoked clause',t7).
test8 :- do('8. Does retract work on next (last) invoked clause',t8).
test9 :- do('9. Test retracts and asserts on invoked clause', t9).

do(Message,Test) :- w(Message), Test, !.
do(Message,Test) :- w('No Clause found').
w(X) :- write(X), nl.
t :- w('Added clause').
tr :- w('Failed to retract clause').

t1  :- assert((t1a :- t)), t1a.
t1a :- w('Clause 1'),fail.
t2  :- assert((t2a :- t)), t2a.
t3  :- assert((t3:-t)),fail.
t3  :- fail.
t4  :- assert((t4:-t)),fail.
t5  :- retract((t5a :- tr)), t5a.
t5a :- tr.
```

```
t6  :- retract((t6a:-X)),fail.
t6  :- t6a.
t6a :- tr.
t6a :- w('Does not backtrack').
t7  :- t7a, fail.
t7  :- fail.
t7  :- tr.
t7a :- retract((t7:-tr)),!.
t8  :- t8a, fail.
t8  :- tr.
t8a :- retract((t8:-tr)),!.
t9  :- retract((t9:-w('Second'))),
       assert((t9:-t)),fail.
t9  :- w('Second').
```

Results	1	2	3	4	5	6	7	8	9
Dec-10, interpreted	CA	A	A	A	N	F	N	N	A
muprolog, Prolog-1	CA	A	A	A	N	N	N	N	A
micro prolog (CP/M-80)	CA	A	A	N	E	D	F	N	A
sigmaprolog (unix)	CA	A	A	N	E	D	N	F	A
sigmaprolog (Dec front)	CA	A	A	N	N	F	N	F	A
poplog	CA	A	N	N	N	N	F	F	S
NIP, Prolog-86, UNSW	CA	A	A	N	N	N	N	F	S
cprolog	CA	A	A	N	N	N	N	N	A
Dec-10 compiled	CN	N	N	N	N	F	F	F	S

where letters stand for the first letter of the message printed out by the test, an E stands for a "no such predicate" error message. Note that in the latter case yo may have to split up the "main" procedure into several parts.

Appendix 3

back(Act) takes as parameter a call to built-in predicate Act which does no backtrack, and turns it into a one that does backtrack sensibly.

e.g. retractb(C) <- repeat(retract(C)).
defines a version of retract which attempts to resatisfy the clause o backtracking.

Definition in Prolog:

```
back(Act)  <- back1 (Act, Result) &
              (Res = true
              | Res = fail & ! & fail).
back(Act) <- back(Act).
back1(Act, true) <- Act & !.
back1(Act, fail).
```

Tokio: Logic Programming Language Based on Temporal Logic and Its Compilation to Prolog

M.Fujita*, S. Kono**, H.Tanaka**, T.Moto-oka**

* FUJITSU LABORATORIES LTD.
** Department of Electronic Engineering, University of Tokyo

ABSTRACT

Tokio is a temporal logic programming language. It is a sophisticated extension of Prolog intended for specification of concurrent programs. Its basic execution is a resolution of Linear Time Temporal Logic [1]. Tokio also has an extension that can execute Interval Temporal Logic [2]. The resolution consists of three parts. These are: unification of temporal variables, reduction including temporal operators, and controlling intervals. We developed a Tokio compiler in Prolog.

Temporal logic from the point of view of logic programming

We have been studying hardware specification in a logic programming language [3]. Logic programming has many attractive points.

Program validity is directly related to logical consequence.

Unification serves as a powerful connection between procedures.

It is easy to extract parallelism from a program.

wever, logic programming is rather idealistic. In general, declarave meaning, which is the meaning of a logical formula, is somewhat dependent of procedural meaning. Algorithm implementations are not scribed in detail in Prolog. For example, consider the difference tween a loop and a recursion. Both repetitions have self-reference inters for execution. The difference is that a recursion creates new vironments in each cycle time, while a loop does not. In traditional nguages, stack and frame are used explicitly.

For example, the loop is the one form of repetition available in rtran. On the other hand, there is no loop in Prolog. This is cause Prolog variables have no state, i.e. single assignment in ture. In order to make a loop meaningful, new variables must be eated at each repetition. For this reason, loops cannot be directly pressed in Prolog. Needless to say, repeat-fail-loops destroy the lationship between declarative meanings and procedural meanings.

In logic programming, the order of execution is not strictly ecified. Although this freedom is suitable for getting high conrrency from original program, detailed descriptions with full specifation of complex timing are difficult.

Temporal logic is a promising tool for the design and descriptio of hardware. A loop is represented using the state of a variable, and both parallelism and sequentiality are easily described using temporal operators. There are many kinds of temporal logic. Here we use two of them: Linear Time Temporal Logic (LTTL) [1] and Interval Temporal Logic (ITL) [2]. We have been used LTTL for hardware description [3]. Many researchers use propositional logic, because it has a decision procedure [4]. However, the compact descriptions of first order temporal logic make it desirable. Moszkowski developed a language called Tempura based on ITL, and implemented in lisp [5]. We here present a temporal logic programming language called Tokio based on a resolution of LTTL. Tokio Logic is an extension of LTTL containing some temporal operators of ITL. Tokio can be considered a logic programming version of Tempura.

Tokio is used primarily for hardware specification and simulation Tokio is expressive and executable enough for hardware description Execution of Tokio is not efficient in itself. Tokio consumes a lot o memory in backtracking and a lot of time in unification of tempora logic variables. Like other languages, fast, efficient execution is o primary importance. However, a much more important issue is to establish a method of translating Tokio to a real implementation (i.e. silicon compiler). We anticipate the output of the compiler to be Registe Transfer Level hardware description language, or some other practica concurrent languages such as GHC [7]. Tokio supports simulation o early-time-specification, which is an important hierarchal design tool Our final goal is logic circuit synthesis using Tokio.

In the rest of this chapter, we briefly introduce LTTL and ITL In chapter 2, we discuss the basic execution mechanism of Tokio. Th execution of Tokio consists of three parts: unification of tempora variable, reduction including temporal operators and an extension wit ITL's operators. In chapter 3, we presents a sample hardware descrip tion. The example is a hardware sorter for a database machine [6] The technique of compiling Tokio to Prolog is described in chapter 4 In the last chapter, we discuss the relation among GHC [7], Tempura T-Prolog [15] and Tokio.

1.1. Linear Time Temporal Logic

Tokio is based on Linear Time Temporal Logic (LTTL). LTTL i based on discrete time concepts, i.e. it has a minimum unit of time Variable and predicate meanings are determined for each state, i.e instants in time. Therefore, variables may have many values dependin on the time at which they are evaluated. There are three major ter poral operators in LTTL: next or @, always and until.

First we discuss the @ operator. @P means P is true at the next stat i.e. next clock period.

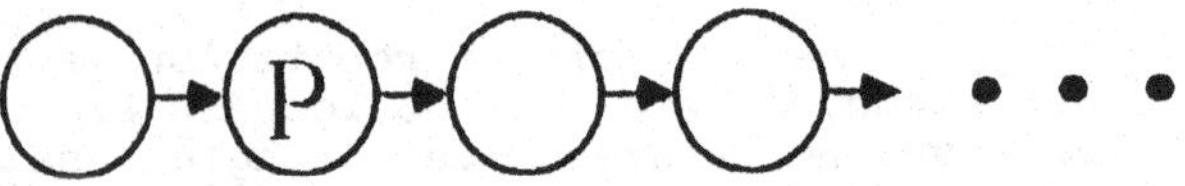

Fig. 1 @P next operator

There are two kinds of equality in Tokio. The first kind of equali is an identity. This type of equality means two values are equal all states. This is also called temporal equality. The other kind equality is single state equality, that is, the two variables' valu are equal only at the present instant and not necessarily equal future states (Fig. 2).

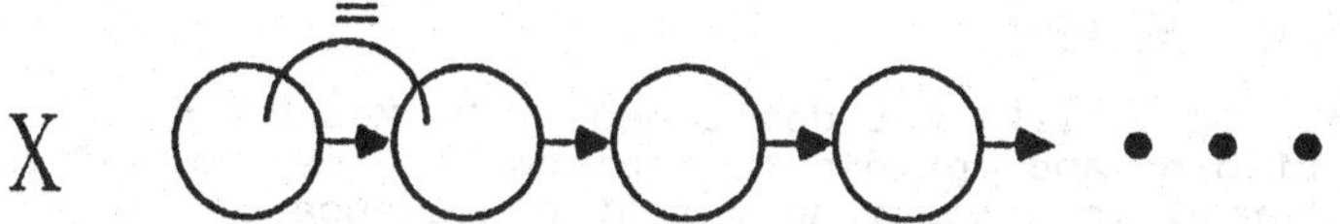

Fig. 2 Reference to Next Time Value

.e syntax of Tokio is very similar to that of DEC-10 Prolog [8]. ›rds beginning with a capital letter are variables. In (1), = symbol- .es single state equality. The two X's denote the same variable. .ese two X's are equal in all states. The value of X at present is ;ual to the value of X in the next state.

```
@X = X                          (1)
```

The next major operator is the <u>always</u> operator. <u>Always</u> describes predicate that is true in all states (Fig.3).

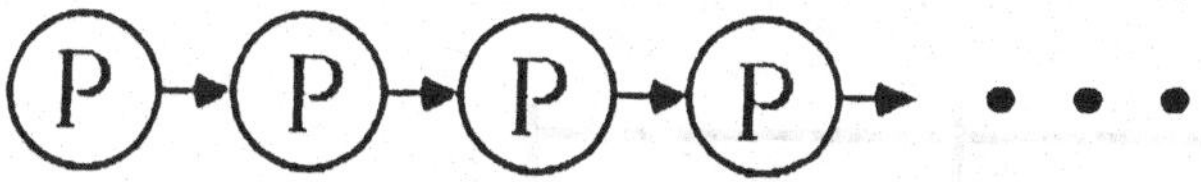

Fig. 3 #P Always Operator

stead of the square notation used in [1], we symbolize <u>always</u> with #. is defined recursively using the <u>next</u> operator. This operator is a ttle different from the @ operator. However as far as LTTL concerned, ›o operators are same.

```
#P :- P,next(#P).               (2)
```

-', ',' and '.' indicate implication, conjunction, and termination, ›spectively. In Tokio, a clause is an axiom, i.e. it is true for all :ates.

.nally we introduce the <u>until</u> operator.

```
p until q                       (3)
```

ıis means that p is true for all states until the state in which q ›comes true (Fig.4).

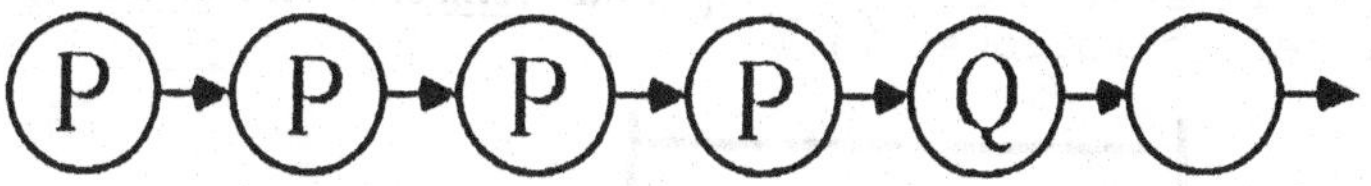

Fig. 4 P until Q

<u>ıtil</u> can also be defined using the @ operator.

```
P until Q :- Q,!.               (4)
P until Q :- P,@(P until Q).
```

›te that the cut operator of first clause indicates negation of Q in a ›cond clause. In order to satisfy the close world assumption, Q must ›t have temporal operator and undefined variables when this operator › evaluated. Tokio can be extented to handle Interval Temporal Logic. ı the following section, we briefly review ITL.

1.2. Interval temporal logic

Interval temporal logic (ITL) was developed by B. Moszkowski [2]. I this logic, variable and predicate meanings are determined for eac interval. An interval is a continuous finite sequence of states. I this section, five operators are introduced: chop, length, halt, fi and keep.

The chop operator is a binary operator. This operator splits a interval into two parts. '&&' symbolizes the chop operator. '; expresses the chop operator used in [2], however, since ';' denotes th or operator in Prolog, we use '&&' to avoid confusion.

P && Q (5)

The meaning of (5) is related to three intervals. Consider an interva I, diveded into two consecutive parts: Ip represents the former por tion, and Iq, the later. If P is true during Ip, and Q is true durin Iq, then (5) is true during I (Fig.5).

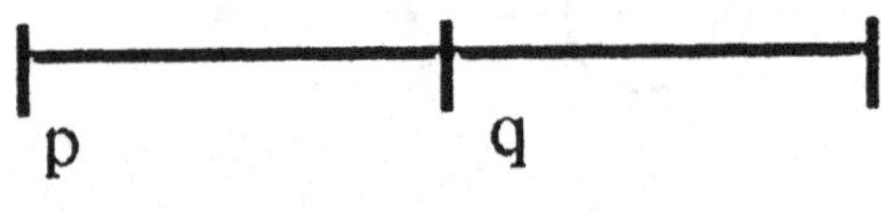

Fig. 5 p && q

The length operator specifies the length of an interval (Fig.6).

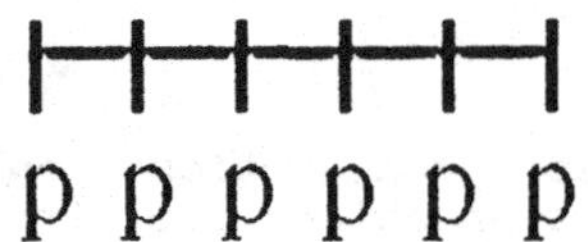

Fig. 6 length 5

The length of an interval is the number of states contained in th interval minus one.

p :- length(5). (6)

In (6), p is true on the interval which has 6 states. Length must be nonnegative integer. Using chop and length, the next operator in IT can be defined as follows (7).

Fig. 7 @ operator in ITL

@P <-> length(1) && P (7)

This type of next is called strong in [5], because if the interv length is 0 then @P is false. In the other word, this operator exten an interval. An interval whose length is 0 is called empty. In t case of the LTTL next operator, it is succeeded even in an empty inte vals. The next operator is independent of the interval.

```
next(P) <-> length(1) && P      (8)
or next(P) <-> empty
```

ıis kind of next is called weak. The conditional statement which is ·lated to empty requires special treatment in Tokio. The following ıree statements are important.

```
halt(P) <-> #(P->empty, not(P)->not(empty)).
fin(P)  <-> #(empty->P).           (9)
keep(P) <-> #(not(empty)->P).
```

ıe halt(P) statement means that the interval length is determined by ıe formula P. Keep(P) means P is true for all states except the one : the end of the interval. Fin(P) means P is true only in the final :ate of the interval.

3. Tokio combines LTTL and ITL

LTTL can easily describe concurrency using conjunctions; however, ·quentiality is not so easily described. ITL's chop operator is supe- .or to LTTL's until operator for the description of sequentiality. p : q simply means that q will be executed after the termination of p. ı the other hand, p until q means that p is true until q holds. This :atement does not specify the termination of p.

The key concepts describing the relationship between ITL and LTTL :e local and interval variables [10]. Local means ITL expressions ıat do not depend on when an interval ends. In another words, mean- ıgs of local variables or predicates are decided in the first time state) of the interval. LTTL concepts are all translated into local ›ncepts in ITL. In order to introduce the chop operator to Tokio, we se interval variables corresponding to each Tokio clause. These vari-)les are all LTTL variables and they are generated by existential ıantifiers. Tokio Variables have different meaning from ITL vari-)les, because interval variables are only associated with clauses. ıis means that all the variables in Tokio are local.

```
p :- q && r.        ....    Ip
q.                  ....    Iq      (10)
r.                  ....    Ir
```

›, Iq and Ir are all interval variables. Each variable represents its ›rresponding interval. The Chop operator generates the intervals Iq ıd Ir from Ip using an existential quantifier. This corresponds to ›litting an interval into two parts.

.4. An extension of Horn clause for temporal logic

The Horn clause is a restricted form of logic formula. It consists f two parts: head and body.

```
head :- body.                       (11)
```

ıis means that the head is implied by the body. Variables in a head ·e all universally quantified and variables in a body are all existen- ially quantified. A head must be an atomic predicate. Roughly speak- ıg, a Tokio Horn clause is a Horn clause including temporal operator ı its body.

In Tokio, there are some restrictions. To avoid a circularly tructured temporal variable, the @ function is only allowed in the xpression =. The primitive temporal operators such as next or chop perator are not allowed in the head of Horn clause.

2. Resolution of Tokio

The execution of Tokio is a kind of resolution of LTTL. Unification and reduction generate a model incrementally. In LTTL, the mode is generated for each state. It is also necessary to unify tempora variables.

* Reduction on multi-state model

* Unification on temporal variable

Our Tokio also has an ITL extension. Generation of interval variabl is the third execution unit.

* Generation of interval variables

There are the three main execution units of Tokio.

2.1. Reduction to the future

If there are no temporal operators, the reduction of Tokio i identical to that of Prolog. A predicate including the next operato defines another state. These predicates are enqueued with the environment corresponding to the next state, and will be reduced later. Queuing is necessary to execute Tokio formula in the proper temporal order We call this property a healthy execution. On the other hand, the execution order of a predicate referring to the same state need not b specified. In order to execute system predicates or numeric calculations, the execution order must be determined by the data dependency.

Tokio executes the predicates corresponding to a given state i the same way as Prolog does. This is only a practical solution. I this manner Tokio includes Prolog in itself. In Tokio there are tw kind of reduction: Prolog-wise reduction and time-wise reduction (Fig 8).

write(0) write(2) write(3)

write(1)

Fig. 8 Two way reduction

```
?-@ @write(3),@write(2),write(0),write(1).     (12)
0123
yes
```

'?-' means a goal in Tokio. Notice that the next statement is execute after the current state.

2.2. Unifier for temporal logic variable

A Tokio variable assumes many different values. These values a generated incrementally as time advances. Unification is a bas operation for accessing these values. Unification consists of tw primitives.

1) to select current state value and successive state values.

This is very much like car and cdr.

to unify all the values of successive states.

he former type of unification is performed by an = and @. The later ype of unification is executed in a head of clause. Consider a simple ounter in Tokio.

```
counter(X) :- #(@X=X+1).                        (13)
?- X=0,counter(X),#write(X),length(3).
0123
yes
```

ounter increments the value of X in each state. The variable X in the oal is unified in all states with variable X in the counter clause. On e other hand, in the definition of counter = predicates unifies the ext state of variable X and the incremented value of variable X in the rrent state.

3. Interval generator using interval variable

The interval variables in Tokio consists of two parts in our nplementation. These are the ending time of the interval, and the flag interval completion. This flag is generated in each time clock. ome ITL operators use this flag directly; for example, the fin and eep operators are not executed until this flag is determined. Tokio as a waiting queue for the fin and keep operators.

The interval variable is generated only by a chop operator. The onsistency of the interval length is checked in every state. The ength of an inner interval must be less or equal than the length of an ıter interval.

One feature of Tokio is automatic interval length tuning. Tokio se a simple strategy for interval determination: the shortest possible ıterval is selected. Tokio tries to cut off the interval which does ot have length specification. Controlling the interval length is perormed by backtracking. This mechanism is known to useful in goal riented simulation [15]. If there is a maximum interval length, Tokio an generate all the necessary length combination of the intervals. his is very useful when it is necessary to join processes.

```
qs(X) :- split(X,H,L) && qs(H),qs(L).           (14)
```

14) is a part of quick sort. First qs splits a list X into two parts: and L, and then performs qs for each part. Because length of parts ay be different, two qs may use different lengths of time. In the redicate split, using a temporal operator such as temporal assignment hich is not dependent on the length of interval, qs can be written in form which is not depended on interval length. In such a case, the ength of qs is automatically tuned and each qs has the same interval ength.

. Hardware description in Tokio

In this section, a sample description of a pipeline merge sorter s presented. The pipeline merge sorter is a component of the relaional database machine GRACE [6]. A sorter prototype was already vailable. The pipelining details are described in Tokio.

.1. Pipeline merge sorter in Tokio

Fig.10 is a sample description of a pipelineed merge sort.

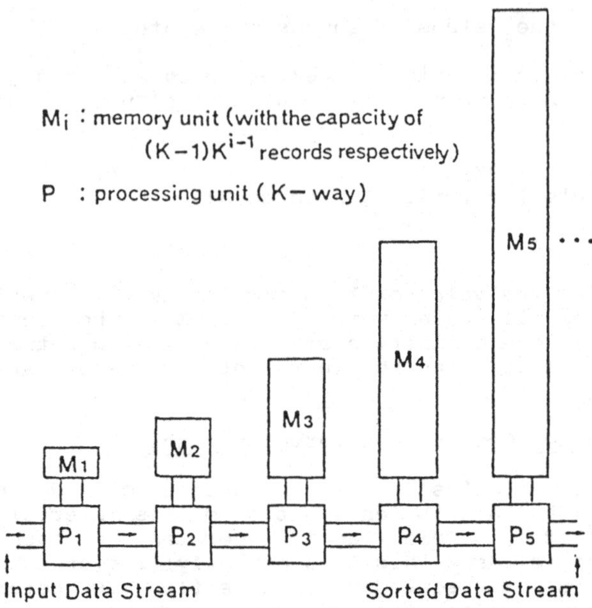

Fig. 9 Organization of Pipeline Merge Sorter

It has enough information to specify timing of the pipeline. This is three-stage-pipeline. There are three sorters. proc describes sorter. The first and second variables in proc are input and output o each pipeline sorter. X, Y, and Z are used as three different inpu buffers. T represents count of input data. P and PP are constants o each processor. It has three major parts. At first, if there is n data then proc is in a waiting state. In an active state, there are tw parts: load and merge. Load and merge work concurrently in this pro gram.

Load also has two phases. In the first phase, input data is stored int the input buffer: Z. In the second phase, input data is stored into th merge buffer: Y. These two phases are selected by the count of inpu data. The size of input data is always the power of 2, and fixed t each processor. The variable T is used to count up the input data.

In the merge process, the third buffer: X and the merge buffer: Y ar merged into output. If either buffer is empty, according to the stat of loading phase, input buffer: Z is changed to X.

Whole processes are combined using conjunctions, and work concurrently In the program test, there are 4 processes: a data generator and three stage pipeline merge sorter. The execution sample is shown i Fig.11. Cpu time is measured on VAX11/730.

```
| ?- tokio test.
[][][][][][][][][][][1][2][3][5][6][10][20][100][]
18 clock and 18.0834 sec.
```

Fig. 11 Sample Execution

4. Compilation to Prolog

The compilation to Prolog is the easiest and fastest way to imple ment the language. So long as objects in Prolog codes do not hav

```
est :- Strdata = [10,20,5,100,1,6,2,3],
    datagen(Strdata, Data),
    pipe(Data, Out),
    length(18),
    #write(Out).

         % Data Generator

atagen([],[]).
atagen([H|T],Out) :-
    Out = [H],
    @T = T, @datagen(T,Out).

         % Pipeline Merge Sorter

ipe(I0,Out) :-
    I1 = [], I2 = [], Out = [],
    proc_start(I0,I1, 2,1),
    proc_start(I1,I2, 4,2),
    proc_start(I2,Out,8,4).

    % Processor Unit

roc_start(I,O,P,PP) :-
    X = [], Y = [], Z = [], T = 1,
    #proc(I,O,X,Y,Z,T,P,PP).

roc(I,O,X,Y,Z,T,P,PP) :- X=[],Y=[],I=[],!,
    @X=X, @Y=Y, @Z=Z, @O=[], @T=1.
roc(I,O,X,Y,Z,T,P,PP) :-
     load(I,O,X,Y,Yn,Z,Zn,T,P,PP),
    merge(I,O,X,Y,Yn,Z,Zn,T,P,PP).

oad(I,O,X,Y,Yn,Z,Zn,T,P,PP) :- T=<PP, !,
    append(Z,I,Zn), @Z=Zn, Yn=Y,
    @T=T+1.
oad(I,O,X,Y,Yn,Z,Zn,T,P,PP) :-
    append(Y,I,Yn), @Z=[],
    if T<P then @T=T+1 else @T=1.

erge(I,O,X,Y,Yn,Z,Zn,T,P,PP) :-X=[],Yn=[],!,
    @O=[], @Y=Yn,
    if T=PP then @X=Zn else @X=X.
erge(I,O,X,Y,Yn,Z,Zn,T,P,PP) :- X=[A|L],Yn=[],!,
    @O=[A], @Y=Yn,
    if T=PP then @X=Zn else @X=L.
erge(I,O,X,Y,Yn,Z,Zn,T,P,PP) :-X=[],Yn=[B|N],!,
    @O=[B], @Y=N,
    if T=PP then @X=Zn else @X=X.
erge(I,O,X,Y,Yn,Z,Zn,T,P,PP) :-X=[A|L],Yn=[B|N],!,
    if A<B then
        @O=[A], @X=L, @Y=Yn
    else
        @O=[B], @Y=N, @X=X.

ppend(Nil,L,L1) :- Nil=[],L=L1.
ppend(X,L,Y) :-[H|T]=X,[H1|M]=Y,
     H=H1,append(T,L,M).
```

Fig. 10 Pipeline Merge Sort

assert or retract, they can be compiled efficiently by a Prolog compiler. The basic compilation method of Tokio is the same as that o GHC compiler to Prolog [7]. These use the queue structure for scheduling and in-line development of unifications. Our compiler also has macro facility for the development of second order predicates such as meta-call. The main features of Tokio are listed below.

1) Multi-time queue structure for reduction

2) In-line development of unification and generating local unifier

3) Macro facility, which enables control abstractions

In the following section, details relating to these points are discussed.

4.1. Multi-time queue

Three main queues are used in Tokio. In this compiler the queue is generated incrementally, corresponding to one state. All these queues are D-list and make a list structure in state order.

```
[$t(N, F, K, C),           ...   1st state
 $t(N1,F1,K1,C1),          ...   2nd state
 $t(N2,F2,K2,C2)|          ...   3rd state
 Q]                        ...   rest of states
```

Fig. 12 Tokio queue structure

The queue N is for next queue, F is for fin queue, K is for keep queue The fourth element: C keeps the interval variables and current time Interval variables indicating ending time of the interval and end fla correspond to each clause in this way. Fig.13 shows simple compil examples.

```
% cprolog
C-Prolog version 1.5
Tokio consulted 57168 bytes 66.6166 sec.
| ?- com([tm,user],user).                    % start compile
|: p :- q, r.                                % input clause
p(_0,_1):-q(_0,_2),r(_2,_1).                 % compile output
|: p :- next(q), r.
p([$t((q(_0,_1),_2),_3,_4,_5)|_0],_6):-
   r([$t(_2,_3,_4,_5)|_1],_6).
|: p :- next(next(next(r))).
p(
    [_0,_1,$t((r(_2,_3),_4),_5,_6,_7)|_2],
    [_0,_1,$t(_4,_5,_6,_7)|_3]).
|: p(X,Y) :- X=Y.
p(_0,_1,_2,_2):-
    unifyNow(_0,_3),unifyNow(_1,_3).
|: eq(X,X).
eq(_0,_1,_2,_2):-unifyAll(_0,_1).
|: p(X,Y) :- @X=Y.
p(_0,_1,_2,_2):-
    unifyNext(_0,_3),unifyNow(_3,_4),
    unifyNow(_1,_4).
```

Fig. 13 Sample Compile

In our interpreter [9], one state queue structures is used. Th multi-time queue has the following advantages:

Nested next operator is compiled into single enqueue.

Compilation algorithm becomes more symmetric to current state and next state.

2. Unifier generation

In order to express multi-state variables, the stream representa- on is used. These states are created incrementally, and there must be incomplete part at its tail, which contains the rest of states. kio uses node: $t for this list (Fig. 14).

```
| ?- Tokio length(5),X=1,
counter(X),#write(X).
123456
X = $t(1,$t(2,$t(3,
    $t(4,$t(5,$t(6,_))))))
```

Fig. 14 Temporal Variable Representation

ere are two types of constant in Tokio. The first one is a constant a single state. The second one is a constant in all states. The ject of Tokio is a mixture of these two constants. The unification Tokio must be applied to these structures.

There are two kinds of unification in Tokio.

Unification on head of clause: Unification is performed for all successive states.

Unification in the = predicate: Unification is performed for the current state.

e Tokio variable is a list of logical variables. The second type of ification selects the value of a variable in the current state. This ification is very much like car in a list structure. The part rresponding to the cdr selector is also available in Tokio. This is ne by next operator.

Unification in the next predicate: Unification is performed for next successive states.

the Tokio compiler these primitives are compiled into the following edicates.

```
unifyAll(X,Y)  ...  unifies all state values of X and Y
unifyNow(X,Y)  ...  Y is a current state value of X
unifyNext(X,Y) ...  Y contains all successive state of X
```

mporal variable structure is analyzed using these predicates. The ifyAll statement includes a double loop: a loop for structures and a op for time structure. If both unifyNow and unifyNext are necessary a single clause, the combined clause unifyNowNxt is used.

Because of the double loop of unifyAll, structure in a head slows wn operation of Tokio considerably. Like a GHC to Prolog compiler, -line development of head unification is effective. In GHC, only a st structure is expanded, because the most important structure in GHC a stream which is a list. In Tokio, structure in the head is used a type of variable, and list has no special meaning. So Tokio pands all head unifications in-line.

4.3. Control abstraction in temporal logic

In Prolog, there is no while-do statement. Prolog cannot abstrac control structures containing loops, because it is difficult to expres how to create new variables in recursion. On the other hand, Tokio car express while-loops very easily.

```
while P do Q :- P,!,(Q && while P do Q).             (15)
while P do Q :- empty.
```

4.4. Compiler Statistics

Fig.15 details the statistics of this compiler.

program	clause size (byte size) source	object	execution time (sec) on Vax11/730 (0.2 Mips) Interpreter	Compiler	Prolog
append (30list) (all state)	3 (49)	3 (177)	10.6	0.8	0.13
append (single state)	3 (92)	3 (224)	27.9	2.0	0.13
pipeline merge sorter	15 (1380)	27 (5726)	154.4	18.0	----

Fig. 15 Tokio compiler

C-Prolog [13] is used as a basic Prolog. This Tokio compiler is times faster than the Tokio interpreter in Prolog, and 7 times slowe than original Prolog if Tokio is used as a Prolog.

5. Comparison with related languages

In this chapter, Tokio is compared with Tempura, GHC and T-Prolog

5.1. Comparison with Tempura

Tokio is a logic programming version of Tempura. Useful ITL operators come from Tempura. According to logic programming concepts, ther are several features in Tokio.

1) Backtracking to the past: Tokio has a backtracking mechanism a just like that of Prolog. These backtracking mechanisms enabl automatic interval length tuning. Actually Tokio is a kind c branching time temporal logic.

2) Unification over the temporal logic variables: Tokio is actually pseudo concurrent programming language. The execution order in or state is uncertain. The bidirectional assignment of unificatic makes the concurrent programming easy.

3) The program is the extension of a Horn clause.

Tempura does not have backtracking and unification. Actually Tok: can execute a somewhat wider range of temporal logic formula than Te pura. On the other hand, the execution of Tempura is faster, and co sumes less memory than that of Tokio. Tempura use some lambda expre sion for its representation. It needs temporal logic type expressi such as stbtype (stable type). In Tokio, such a type is expressed as structure in head.

Tempura has two kinds of variables: stable and non-stable. The orresponding element in Tokio is a static variable which is implemented with a record statement, that is, assert. These variables are eeded for the description of circuit containing many registers. These ariables are not good elements as far as formal verification is conerned. Notice that in the description of the pipeline merge sorter, nly list structures are used.

Finally, Tokio is based on LTTL. Verification of the synchronization part of Tokio will be possible using the LTTL verification method. TL operators in Tokio is translated into LTTL operators using interval ariables.

.2. Comparison with GHC

Guarded Horn Clause [7] is a stream parallel logic programming anguage. Tokio is used for specification, while GHC is used for ctual representation of parallel programming.

The main difference between GHC and Tokio is a guard. Guard is a election point of disjunction. In Tokio, selection is performed by acktracking as in Prolog. On the other hand, GHC's guard selects the lause whose execution of guard parts is completed fastest. It cuts ff other selections, so GHC has no backtracking. Backtracking is a owerful verification tool.

Another difference is the concept of time. Tokio has a minimum nit of time. GHC has no such minimum unit. In a clocked circuit or n a systolic programming, Tokio is superior to GHC. For example, consider a simple producer-consumer.

okio

```
    ?-X=1, #produce(X), #consume(X).
    produce(X) :- @X=X+1.                         (17)
    consume(X) :- write(X).
```

HC

```
    ?-produce(1,X), consume(X).
    produce(X,T)    :- X1 := X+1 |
              T=[X|T1], produce(X1,T1).          (18)
    consume([X|T]) :- write(X)  |
              consume(T).
```

n GHC, synchronize of two processes is difficult; for example, synhronization requires structure in head for the suspension of 'consume' nd guard. On the other hand, Tokio has built-in synchronized clock. t is very easy to write synchronized programs. The previous pipeline erge sorter is one example.

.3. Comparison with T-Prolog

T-Prolog [15] is a Simula like simulation system on Prolog. All he process in T-Prolog is represented by a Prolog-like description hich has predicates relating to time concept such as <u>during</u>, or <u>after</u>. sing these operators T-Prolog can express useful temporal relations hips among parallel process. In the following example [15], Dick irst waits decision of which safe should be open, then sends tools for is friends.

-Prolog

```
    DICK_GETS_THE_MONEY(*BANK,*SAFE):
         WAIT(IDENTIFIER(*SAFE)),          (19)
         HAS(TOOLS,*SAFE), SEND(TOOLS).
```

```
Tokio
     dick_gets_the_money(Bank, Safe, Tools):-
          keep(Safe=undef) &&                (20)
          has(Safe, Tools).
```

A process is executed in serial way. However T-Prolog uses complicated primitives to describe communications, for example, SEND and WAIT. Assignment of a variable in T-Prolog can be used as a synchronization tool in the same way of GHC. In Tokio, all the communications are represented by a formula including temporal variables. T-Prolog cannot express communications by its variables, because its variables have no state. Only a truth value of predicate has states in T-Prolog. On the other hand, Tokio variables have states. It is suitable for the hardware description, because the state of connection lines are changed in each time. The synchronization mechanism is separated from variables in Tokio. The basic mechanism of synchronization is a chop operator.

T-Prolog has a backtracking in time. This is a good tool for the goal oriented simulation. The backtracking mechanism of Tokio can work like T-Prolog. However our backtracking is based on each clock period, not on each event.

The current implementation of Tokio is not suitable for actual parallel execution. In a real situation, the problem is healthy execution, i.e. relationship between actual time and Tokio time. Once Tokio is running under some parallel machine, it is difficult to execute Tokio in a healthy way, i.e. execution in the correct time order. To execute Tokio program in a healthy way, it is better to translate it to other hardware or parallel programming language, because the description of Tokio is an abstract one and it includes the difficult task of temporal variable unification.

6. Conclusion

Tokio is temporal logic language suitable for specification of concurrent algorithms and simulation. The compilation to Prolog is a efficient implementation of Tokio. We have written Tokio interpreter and compiler in C-Prolog [13]. There are many hardware description examples which include the unify-processor of a Parallel inference engine: PIE [14] and systolic array matrix multiplication. We plan to develop a Tokio verifier. This is based on an LTTL verifier using Prolog [11].

Many thanks to those people. Mr. Okano wrote a pipeline merge sorter. Vince help us with his English. Dr. Tsang give us many useful discussion.

References

[1] Z. Manna and A. Pnueli, "Verification of Concurrent Programs, Part 1: The Temporal Framework", Dept. of Computer Science, Stanford Univ. Report STAN-CS-81-836, June 1981.

[2] B.C. Moszkowski, "Reasoning about Digital Circuit", Rep No.STAN-CS-83-970 Dept. of Computer Science, Stanford Univ. July 1983.

[3] M. Fujita, H. Tanaka and T. Moto-oka, "Logic Design Assistance with Temporal Logic", IFIP 7th Computer Hardware Description Languages and their Applications, August 1985.

[4] P. Wolper, "Temporal logic Can Be More Expressive", 22nd Annual Symposium on Foundation of Computer Science, October 1981.

[5] B.C. Moszkowski, "Executing Temporal Logic Programs", Rep. No.55 Computer Laboratory, Univ. of Cambridge, 1984.

[6] M. Kituregawa, H. Tanaka and T. Moto-oka, "Relational Algebra Machine GRACE", Lecture Notes in computer Science 147, Springer-Verlag, March, 1983.

[7] K. Ueda, "Guarded Horn Clauses", TR-103, ICOT, 1985.

[8] W.F Clockskin and C.S Melish, "Programming in Prolog", Springer-Verlag, New York, 1981.

[9] S. Kono T. Aoyagi, M. Fujita, H. Tanaka, "Implementation of temporal logic programming language Tokio", to be appeared as "Proceedings of LPC'85", Lecture Notes in Computer Science Springer-Verlag.

[10] M. Fujita, S. Kono, H. Tanaka and T. Moto-oka, "Assistance in Hierarchical and Structured Logic Design Using Temporal Logic and Prolog", to be appeared in IEE proceedings-E COMPUTER AND DIGITAL TECHNIQUES.

[11] M. Fujita, H. Tanaka and T. Moto-oka, "Specifying Hardware in Temporal Logic & Efficient Synthesis of State-Diagrams Using Prolog", Proc. of FGCS '84, Tokyo Japan, November 1984.

[12] M. Fujita, "Logic Design Assistance with Temporal Logic", Doctoral Dissertation, Information Engineering, University of Tokyo, 1984.

[13] F. Pereira, "C-Prolog Users Manual Version 1.5",EdCAD, Edingburh Univ. 1984.

[14] T. Moto-oka, H. Tanaka, H. Aida, K. Hirata and T. Maruyama, "The Architecture of a Parallel Inference Engine -PIE-", Proc. of FGCS '84, Tokyo, Japan, November 1984.

[15] I. Futo, J. Szeredi, "T-PROLOG A VERY HIGH LEVEL SIMULATION SYSTEM GENERAL INFORMATION MANUAL", 1011 Budapest I. Iskcla utca, April 1981.

THE OR-FOREST DESCRIPTION FOR THE EXECUTION OF LOGIC PROGRAMS

Sun Chengzheng and Tzu Yungui
Department of Computer Science
Changsha Institute of Technology
Changsha, China

ABSTRACT

This paper presents a new method for describing the execution of logic programs -- the OR-forest description.

The OR-forest description can explicitly describe both AND- and OR parallel execution of logic programs and avoid a class of redundancies in describing OR-parallel execution, overcoming the two major drawback of the traditional OR-tree discription.

1. Introduction

Our research goal is to design a computer architecture supporting both AND- and OR-parallel execution of logic programs expressed in the Horn clause subset of the predicate logic. We start from abstract levels and move step by step towards concrete implementation details. The description for the execution of logic programs, which is the topi of this paper, is one of the steps in our top-down approach.

Traditionally, the execution of logic programs is described as an OR-tree (i.e. a search tree in [1]). Each node in an OR-tree is labeled by a goal and each branch of a node represents a way of solvin the goal associated with the node (Section 2.1). The multiple branche of the OR-tree for a program can be viewed as the multiple computation units of the program. The computation units defined in this way are logically independent, a very important property in achieving highly parallel processing of logic programs. Many parallel execution models based on the OR-tree description have been proposed, such as the OR-parallel model by Dr.Ciepielewski [2], and the Goal-Rewriting model by Dr.Goto[3].

The ability and the manner to describe the parallel execution of logic programs are very important qualities of a describing method. The OR-tree description can explicitly describe the OR-parallel execution of a program by multiple branches of the tree corresponding to the program and has the advantage of high independence of each OR-parallel computation unit. However, the OR-tree description has two major drawbacks: one is the lack of the ability to describe AND-parallel execution, the other is the redundancies in describing OR-parallel execution (Section 2.2). In order to provide a proper framework for developing execution models which could efficiently exploit both AND- and OR-parallelisms in logic programs, it is necessary to investigate a new describing method which can not only retain the merits of the traditional OR-tree description, but also overcome the two drawbacks mentioned above.

In this paper, we first analyse the traditional OR-tree description. Then, the OR-forest description is proposed and discussed.

2. The OR-tree Description

.1. Basic Concepts

Some concepts relevant to the following sections are introduced elow:

1) Sequencial One-step Execution Rule (SOER)

Given a goal G = A1,...,Ai-1, Ai, Ai+1,...,Am m>=1
If
1. Ai is the subgoal selected from G,
2. in the program, there exists a clause
   B0 ← B1,B2,...,Bn n>=0
   such that
   Ai θ = B0 θ
   is satisfied (θ is the most general unification substitution between Ai and B0).

then, the following new goal G' can be derived from G:
G' = (A1,...,Ai-1,B1,B2,...,Bn,Ai+1,...,Am) θ

Because this execution rule executes the subgoals of a goal in a equential manner, and the derivation of G' from G requires the nification substitution between Ai and B0, which can be obtained in ne execution step, we call it Sequential One-step Execution Rule, or OER.

If there exist K clauses which have heads that can be unified with e selected subgoal, K new goals can be derived by SOER.

2) OR-tree

Given a logic program, an initial goal IG, and a selection rule, e execution of the logic program can be uniquely described as an R-tree. Nodes of the OR-tree are labeled by goals and created in the ollowing way:

1. The root node is labeled by IG.
2. For any node labeled by goal G, if G is a null goal, the node is a leaf node. Otherwise, the selection rule is used to select one subgoal from G and K clauses with heads that are unifiable with the selected subgoal are picked out from the program.

   (1). If K = 0, the node labeled by G becomes a leaf node.
   (2). If K > 0, the node labeled by G has K successors labeled by G'1,G'2,...,G'K, respectively, which are the new goals derived from G by SOER (Fig.1).

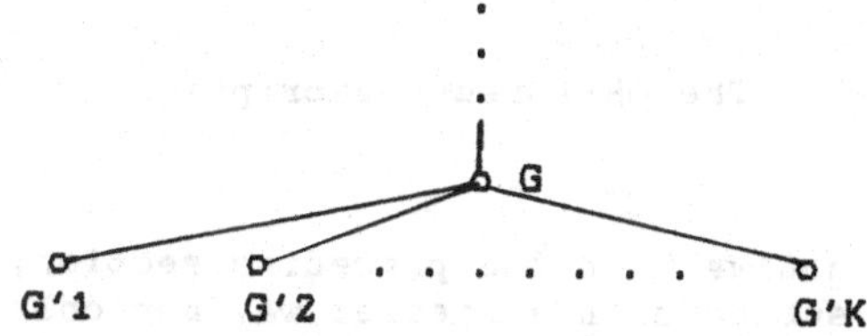

Fig.1. A node and its successors in an OR-tree

(3) OR-parallel Execution and AND-parallel Execution

By OR-parallel execution, we mean simultaneous search of more than one way of solving a goal.

By AND-parallel execution, we mean simultaneous execution of more than one subgoal of a goal. There are several methods for AND-parallel execution [4,5]. Our method for AND-parallel execution is that more than one subgoal is executed in parallel only if they share no variables at the time of execution . In the remainder of this paper, subgoals sharing no variables at the time of execution are called independent subgoals, and the meaning of the term of AND-parallel execution is limited to simultaneous execution of independent subgoals.

2.2. Analysis of the OR-tree Description

As we have known, the OR-tree description is sufficient for developing sequential execution models (sequential search of the tree combined with a backtracking mechanism) and OR-parallel execution models (parallel search of the tree). However, the OR-tree has some drawbacks. As an example, consider a goal ←A,B,C. Suppose that A and B are mutually independent, C is interdependent of both A and B, and there are m ways of solving A and n ways of solving B. The OR-tree description for the execution of this goal is shown in Fig.2. By analysing Fig.2, we can draw the following two conclusions:

1. The OR-tree is unable to express the AND-parallel execution of a goal (e.g. the executions of A and B are described sequentially in Fig.2).
2. The OR-tree is able to describe the OR-parallel execution of a goal by multiple branches of the node labeled by the goal. However, when a goal labeling a node contains multiple independent subgoals (e.g. A and B in Fig.2) and there are multiple ways of solving each subgoal, some of the subgoals (e.g. B in Fig.2) will repetitiously occur in all the successors of the node labeled by that goal, which could cause redundant executions (the same subgoal is executed in more than one goal) when the tree is searched in parallel.

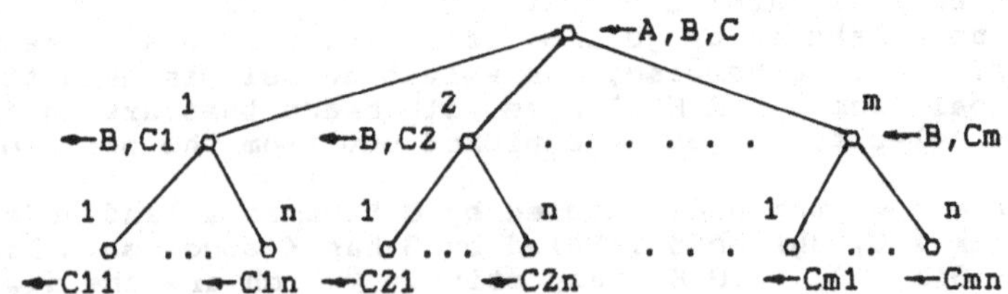

Fig.2 The OR-tree description for the execution of ←A,B,C

3. The OR-forest Description

3.1. Basic Ideas

According to the analysis in the preceding section, it is necessary to treat independent subgoals in a special way not only for describing AND-parallel execution but for avoiding redundancies in describing OR-parallel execution as well.

Consider a goal G labeling a node of an OR-tree. If the subgoals n G are interdependent (sharing some variables) with each other, we reat them in the same way as in the traditional OR-tree description. therwise, the subgoals in G are partitioned into groups:

g0, g1, g2, ..., gn   n > 1

hich satisfy the following two conditions:

1. For 1 =< i < j =< n, any subgoal in gi must be independent of every subgoal in gj.
2. For 1 =< i =< n, any subgoal in g0 should be interdependent of at least one subgoal in gi (g0 can be an empty group without subgoal).

hen, we describe the execution of G in the following way:

1. N independent son trees are derived, with the root nodes of the son trees labeled by g1,g2,...,gn, respectively.
2. The creation of the successors of the node(called seed node) labeled by G will depend on the combination of the solutions to those subgoals. If gi has Ki solutions (1=<i=<n), the number of the successor nodes is K = K1 x K2 x ... x Kn.

According to the new ideas introduced above, a tree may derive some on trees and a son tree in turn may derive some new son trees, so a ollection of OR-trees can be created in describing the execution of a rogram. We call this collection of OR-trees an OR-forest.

Because of the introduction of independent son trees, we can not nly describe the OR-parallel execution of a goal by multiple branches f a node labeled by the goal, but also describe the AND-parallel xecution of a goal by multiple son trees derived from a seed node abeled by the goal. Moreover, since the execution of an independent roup of subgoals is described by only one independent son tree, edundancies caused by the repetitious occurances of some independent ubgoals are eliminated from description.

.2. An Example

To illustrate the new ideas introduced in Section 3.1, consider the ollowing logic program:

Initial goal: ← A(x),B(y),C(z),D(y,z),E(x,y,z)

Clauses:

1.	A(x) ← A1(x)	6.	C(5) ←
2.	A1(1) ←	7.	C(6) ←
3.	A1(2) ←	8.	D(3,5) ←
4.	B(3) ←	9.	D(3,6) ←
5.	B(4) ←	10.	E(1,3,5) ←

First, the subgoals in the initial goal should be partitioned into

g0 = E(x,y,z)   g1 = A(x)   g2 = B(y),C(z),D(y,z)

ased on this partition, two son trees are derived with g1 and g2 abeling the two root nodes (Fig.3-(b),(c)). Then, the subgoals in g2 ill be partitioned into:

g0' = D(y,z)   g1' = B(y)   g2' = C(z)

and another two son trees are derived with g1' and g2' labeling the tw root nodes (Fig.3-(d),(e))

Since the tree for g1' has 2 null goals corresponding to 2 solutions

$$\theta b1 = \{ 3/y \} \qquad \theta b2 = \{ 4/y \}$$

and the tree for g2' has 2 null goals corresponding to 2 solutions

$$\theta c1 = \{ 5/z \} \qquad \theta c1 = \{ 6/z \} ,$$

the seed node in the tree for g2 has 2 x 2 = 4 successors labeled by the following goals

$$(D(y,z))\theta b1 \circ \theta c1 = D(3,5) \qquad (D(y,z))\theta b1 \circ \theta c2 = D(3,6)$$
$$(D(y,z))\theta b2 \circ \theta c1 = D(4,5) \qquad (D(y,z))\theta b2 \circ \theta c2 = D(4,6) .$$

Since the tree for g1 has 2 null goals corresponding to 2 solution

$$\theta a1 = \{ 1/x \} \qquad \theta a2 = \{ 2/x \}$$

and the tree for g2 has 2 null goals corresponding to 2 solutions

$$\theta 1 = \{ 3/y, 5/z \} \quad \theta 2 = \{ 3/y, 6/z \}$$

the seed node in the tree for the initial goal (Fig.3-(a)) has 4 successors labeled by the following goals

$$(E(x,y,z))\theta a1 \circ \theta 1 = E(1,3,5) \qquad (E(x,y,z))\theta a1 \circ \theta 2 = E(1,3,6)$$
$$(E(x,y,z))\theta a2 \circ \theta 1 = E(2,3,5) \qquad (E(x,y,z))\theta a2 \circ \theta 2 = E(2,3,6).$$

The OR-forest for the above program consists of 5 OR-trees, as shown in Fig.3 (seed nodes are denoted by *).

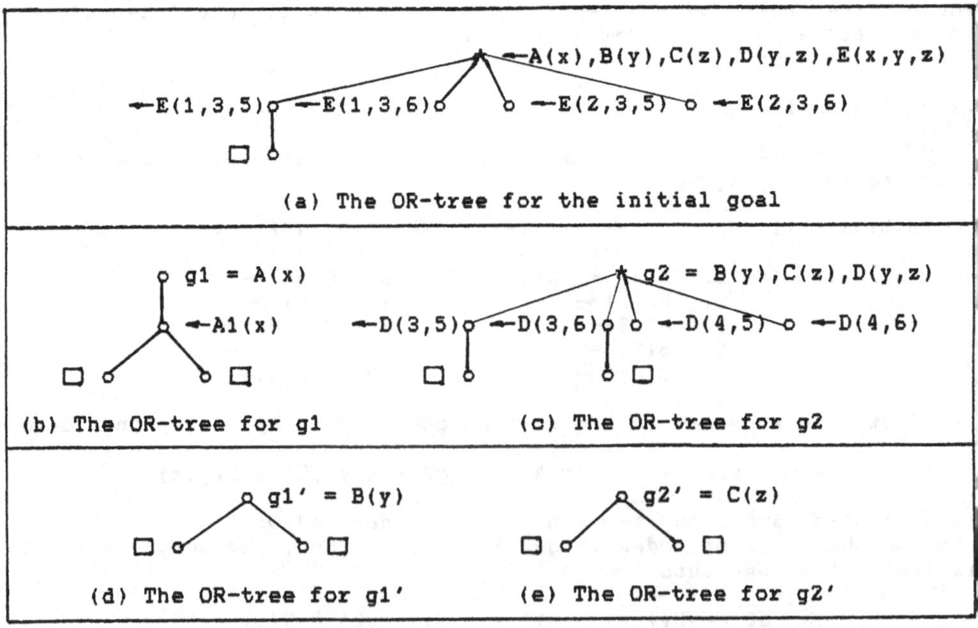

(a) The OR-tree for the initial goal

(b) The OR-tree for g1 (c) The OR-tree for g2

(d) The OR-tree for g1' (e) The OR-tree for g2'

Fig.3 The OR-forest description for a logic program

.3. Definitions

Some of the concepts introduced in Section 3.1 are defined more recisely below.

1) Parallel Multiple-step Execution Rule (PMER)

Given a goal G
If 1. G contains n mutually independent groups of subgoals: $g1, g2, \ldots, gn$, $1 < n$.
2. gi has a solution θi, $1 \le i \le n$.
then, the following new goal G' can be derived from G:

$$G' = (G - \{ g1, g2, \ldots, gn \}) \theta 1 \circ \theta 2 \circ \ldots \circ \theta n$$

Because this execution rule executes n mutually independent groups f subgoals in a parallel manner, and the derivation of G' from G equires a solution to each group of subgoals which can be obtained in ossiblely multiple execution steps, we call it Parallel Multiple-step xecution Rule, or PMER for short.

Theorem For a goal G containing n mutually independent groups of ubgoals $g1, g2, \ldots, gn$ ($1 < n$), if gi has Ki solutions, $1 \le i \le n$, $\le$ Ki, then the number of new goals which can be derived from G by MER is $K1 \times K2 \times \ldots \times Kn$.

Proof: Let
1. Si be the set of solutions to gi:
$Si = \{ \theta i1, \theta i2, \ldots, \theta iKi \}$ $1 \le i \le n$
2. S be the Cartesian product of the n solution sets:
$S = S1 \times S2 \times \ldots \times Sn$

According to the definition of PMER, one element in S can be used o derive one new goal from G, thus our result comes from

$$|S| = |S1| \times |S2| \times \ldots \times |Sn| = K1 \times K2 \times \ldots \times Kn$$

Q.E.D.

2) OR-forest

Given a logic program, an initial goal IG, an identification rule nd a selection rule, the execution of the logic program can be niquely described as an OR-forest. An OR-forest is a collection of ndependent OR-trees. Nodes of the OR-trees are labeled by goals and reated in the following way:

1. One of the root nodes of the trees is labeled by IG.
2. For any node labeled by goal G, if G is a null goal , the node is a leaf node. Otherwise, the identification rule is used to detect if G contains mutually independent groups of subgoals.
   (1) If no mutually independent groups of subgoals are discovered, the selection rule is used to select one subgoal from G and K clauses with heads that are unifiable with the selected subgoal are picked out from the program.
      (a) If K = 0, the node labeled by G becomes a leaf node.
      (b) If K > 0, the node labeled by G has K successors labeled by G'1,G'2,...,G'K, respectively, which are new goals derived from G by SOER.
   (2) If n mutually independent groups of subgoals g1, g2, ..., gn (n > 1) are identified, the node labeled by G becomes a seed node and n son trees are derived with root nodes labeled

by g1,g2,...,gn, respectively. Assume the son tree for gi contains Ki leaf nodes labeled by null goals (corresponding to Ki solutions to gi),1 =<i=< n. Let K = K1 x K2 x ...x Kn

(a) If K = 0, the node labeled by G becomes a leaf node.
(b) If K > 0, the node labeled by G has K successors labeled by G'1,G'2,...,G'K,respectively, which are new goals derived from G by PMER.

In the definition of an OR-forest, the derivation of son trees depends on the given identification rule which is used to discover and partition independent subgoals. If the given identification rule is an empty rule which is unable to discover and partition independent subgoals, the OR-forest for the program will contain only one OR-tree which is the same as a traditional OR-tree. Hence, we can regard the traditional OR-tree description as a special case of the OR-forest description with an empty identification rule, and a traditional OR-tree as a special OR-forest consisting of only one tree.

4. The Process Model Based on the OR-forest Description

The description of the execution of logic programs is actually a framework of execution models. We have developed a process model -- PSOF (Parallel Search of Or-Forests) based on the OR-forest description. A detailed discussion of PSOF is beyond the scope of this paper, so only an outline of PSOF is given below.

In PSOF, the parallel search of an OR-forest is carried out by search prcesses.
During the search of the forest for a program, a search process is created for each node of a tree in the forest.
The first search process is created by the execution system.
If a search process reaches an ordinary node of a tree, it creates successor processes for the successor nodes of the node.
If a search process reaches a seed node of a tree, it first create slave processes for the root nodes of the corresponding son trees. After receiving and combining the solutions from its slave processes, the process creates successor processes for the successor nodes of the seed node.
A search process terminates when all its successor processes have been created.

The main features of PSOF include:

1. OR-parallel execution of a goal is carried out by successor processes simutaneously searching multiple branches. All the processes searching the same tree are logically independent and do not need to communicate. Backtracking is not necessary in execution, making the various execution strategies, such as depth-first, breadth-first or their amalgamation, possible through scheduling the search processes.
2. AND-parallel execution of a goal is conducted by slave processes simultaneously searching multiple son trees. A slave process sends a messeage to its master process only when it reaches a leaf node, so the frequency of communication is low and the independence of search processes is high.

More information about PSOF, including the creation, abortion, and termination of search processes, can be found in another paper [6] by the authors.

5. Conclusion

An explicit description of both AND- and OR-parallel execution is rucial to developing models which could efficiently exploit both AND- nd OR-parallelisms in logic programs. The traditional OR-tree escription is able to explicitly describe the OR-parallel execution of program by multiple branches of the tree for the program, but unable o describe the AND-parallel execution of a program. Thus, parallel xecution models based on the OR-tree description usually can exploit nly OR-parallelism in logic programs. In contrast, the OR-forest escription, presented in this paper, can explicitly describe both AND- nd OR-parallel execution of a programs by means of multiple trees and ultiple branches of a tree. Therefore, execution models based on the R-forest description, such as PSOF outlined in Section 4, can aturally exploit both AND- and OR-parallelisms in logic programs by arallel search of an OR-forest.

In a traditional OR-tree, if a goal contains multiple independent ubgoals and there are multiple ways of solving each independent ubgoals, some of the subgoals will be executed repetitiously when the ree is searched in parallel. This kind of redundant execution can be voided in two possible ways. One is to keep the OR-tree description nchanged but incorporate a redundancy check mechanism in the execution ystem to dynamically identify and eliminate those redundancies. The ajor drawback of this approach is the considerable overhead involved n the redundancy checks. The other approach is to change the manner f description to eliminate such kind of redundancy from the tree, nsuring that this kind of redundant execution will not happen in xecuting programs. The OR-forest description presented in this paper s an example of the second approach which avoids this kind of edundant executions without any cost of redundancy checks.

Compared to models based on the traditional OR-tree description, odels based on the OR-forest description not only have the advantage f exploiting AND-parallelism when the son trees are searched imultaneously, but also have another advantage of avoiding a class of edundant executions even when the son trees are searched sequentially or lack of processing elements.

REFERENCES

1] Kowalski, R. A. "Logic for Problem Solving," Elsevier- North Holland, New York, 1979.

2] Ciepielewski, A. "Towards a Computer Architecture for OR-parallel Execution of Logic Programs," Ph.D. Thesis, Dept. of Computer Systems, Royal Institute of Technology, TRITA-CS-8401, May 1984.

3] Goto, A., Tanaka, H. and Moto-oka, T. "Highly Parallel Inference Engine PIE -- Goal Rewriting Modle and Machine Architecture," New Generation Computing, Vol.2., No. 1, pp.37 - 58, OHMSHA, 1984.

4] G.H.Pollard, "Parallel Execution of Horn Clause Programs," Ph.D. Thesis, Imperial College of Science and Technology, University of London, 1981.

5] Conery, J.S. "The AND/OR Process Model for Parallel Interpretation of Logic Programs," Ph.D. Thesis, Dept. of Information and Computer Science, UC Irvine, 1983.

6] Sun Chengzheng and Tzu Yungui,"PSOF: A Process Model Based on the OR-forest Description," TR-85-6032, Dept. of Computer Science, Changsha Institute of Technology, China, 1985.

Author Index

192: Automata on Infinite Words. Proceedings, 1984. Edited by ivat and D. Perrin. V, 216 pages. 1985.

193: Logics of Programs. Proceedings, 1985. Edited by R. Parikh. 424 pages. 1985.

194: Automata, Languages and Programming. Proceedings, 5. Edited by W. Brauer. IX, 520 pages. 1985.

195: H. J. Stüttgen, A Hierarchical Associative Processing tem. XII, 273 pages. 1985.

196: Advances in Cryptology. Proceedings of CRYPTO '84. ed by G. R. Blakley and D. Chaum. IX, 491 pages. 1985.

197: Seminar on Concurrency. Proceedings, 1984. Edited by). Brookes, A. W. Roscoe and G. Winskel. X, 523 pages. 1985.

198: A. Businger, PORTAL Language Description. VIII, pages. 1985.

199: Fundamentals of Computation Theory. Proceedings, 1985. ted by L. Budach. XII, 533 pages. 1985.

200: J. L. A. van de Snepscheut, Trace Theory and VLSI Design. 0–140 pages. 1985.

201: Functional Programming Languages and Computer Architure. Proceedings, 1985. Edited by J.-P. Jouannaud. VI, 413 pages. 5.

202: Rewriting Techniques and Applications. Edited by . Jouannaud. VI, 441 pages. 1985.

203: EUROCAL '85. Proceedings Vol. 1, 1985. Edited by Buchberger. V, 233 pages. 1985.

204: EUROCAL '85. Proceedings Vol. 2, 1985. Edited by F. Caviness. XVI, 650 pages. 1985.

205: P. Klint, A Study in String Processing Languages. VIII, 165 es. 1985.

206: Foundations of Software Technology and Theoretical Comer Science. Proceedings, 1985. Edited by S. N. Maheshwari. IX, pages. 1985.

207: The Analysis of Concurrent Systems. Proceedings, 1983. ted by B. T. Denvir, W. T. Harwood, M. I. Jackson and M. J. Wray. 398 pages. 1985.

208: Computation Theory. Proceedings, 1984. Edited by A. wron. VII, 397 pages. 1985.

209: Advances in Cryptology. Proceedings of EUROCRYPT '84. ted by T. Beth, N. Cot and I. Ingemarsson. VII, 491 pages. 1985.

210: STACS 86. Proceedings, 1986. Edited by B. Monien and G. al-Naquet. IX, 368 pages. 1986.

211: U. Schöning, Complexity and Structure. V, 99 pages. 1986.

212: Interval Mathematics 1985. Proceedings, 1985. Edited by K. kel. VI, 227 pages. 1986.

213: ESOP 86. Proceedings, 1986. Edited by B. Robinet and Wilhelm. VI, 374 pages. 1986.

214: CAAP '86. 11th Colloquium on Trees in Algebra and gramming. Proceedings, 1986. Edited by P. Franchi-Zannettacci. 306 pages. 1986.

215: Mathematical Methods of Specification and Synthesis of ftware Systems '85. Proceedings, 1985. Edited by W. Bibel and P. Jantke. 245 pages. 1986.

216: Ch. Fernstrom, I. Kruzela, B. Svensson, LUCAS Associative ay Processor: Design, Programming and Application Studies. XII, 3 pages. 1986.

217: Programs as Data Objects. Proceedings, 1985. Edited by H. nzinger and N. D. Jones. X, 324 pages. 1986.

218: Advances in Cryptology – CRYPTO '85. Proceedings, 85. Edited by H. C. Williams. X, 548 pages. 1986.

219: Advances in Cryptology – EUROCRYPT '85. Proceedings, 85. Edited by F. Pichler. IX, 281 pages. 1986.

Vol. 220: RIMS Symposia on Software Science and Engineering II. Proceedings, 1983 and 1984. Edited by E. Goto, K. Araki and T. Yuasa. XI, 323 pages. 1986.

Vol. 221: Logic Programming '85. Proceedings, 1985. Edited by E. Wada. IX, 311 pages. 1986.

Vol. 222: Advances in Petri Nets 1985. Edited by G. Rozenberg. VI, 498 pages. 1986.

Vol. 223: Structure in Complexity Theory. Proceedings, 1986. Edited by A. L. Selman. VI, 401 pages. 1986.

Vol. 224: Current Trends in Concurrency Overviews and Tutorials. Edited by J. W. de Bakker, W.-P. de Roever and G. Rozenberg. XII, 716 pages. 1986.

Vol. 225: Third International Conference on Logic Programming. Proceedings, 1986. Edited by E. Shapiro. IX, 720 pages. 1986.